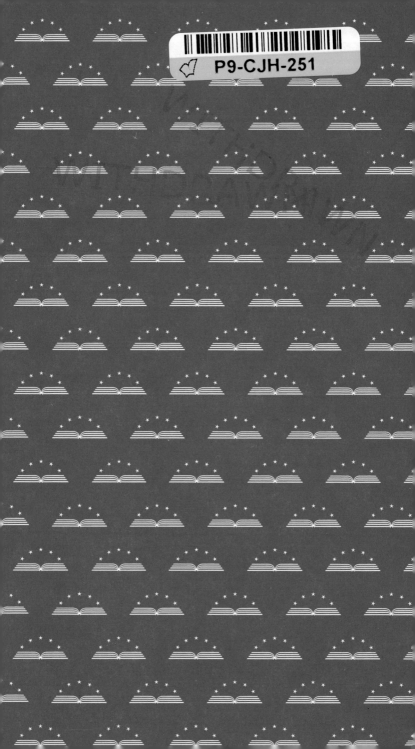

WITHDRAWN

Library of America, a nonprofit organization,
champions our nation's cultural heritage
by publishing America's greatest writing in
authoritative new editions and providing resources
for readers to explore this rich, living legacy.

VIRGIL THOMSON

VIRGIL THOMSON
THE STATE OF MUSIC
& OTHER WRITINGS

The State of Music
Virgil Thomson
American Music Since 1910
Music with Words
Other Writings

Tim Page, *editor*

THE LIBRARY OF AMERICA

Visit our website at www.loa.org.

Texts by Virgil Thomson copyright © 2016
by Virgil Thomson Foundation, Ltd.

Frontispiece p. 176 used by permission of the William Gedney
Collection, Duke University David M. Rubenstein Rare Book &
Manuscript Library. PEANUTS comic strip p. 519 copyright © 1954
by Peanuts Worldwide LLC. Distributed by Universal Uclick.
Reprinted with permission. All rights reserved.

This paper meets the requirements of
ANSI/NISO Z39.48–1992 (Permanence of Paper).

Distributed to the trade in the United States
by Penguin Random House Inc.
and in Canada by Penguin Random House Canada Ltd.

Library of Congress Control Number: 2015935696
ISBN 978–1–59853–467–2

First Printing
The Library of America—277

Manufactured in the United States of America

Virgil Thomson:
The State of Music & Other Writings
is published with support from the

VIRGIL THOMSON FOUNDATION, LTD.

Contents

Book Reviews

THE STATE OF MUSIC

Contents

A 1961 Preface

THIS BOOK was written in 1939. By November of that year, when it was issued, Europe was in armed conflict. The two decades that have passed since then have witnessed a world war, the deliberate murder of millions, the substitution for the customary class warfare of an international economic war called "cold," a stabilization of trade-union privilege at the highest level ever known, the partition of Germany, the isolation of China. The last decade has encountered too a revolt of the colonial peoples, and undergone in Europe and America a prosperity boom.

Music during this time, save for a certain broadening of its distribution, has changed little. That is why it has been possible to envisage reprinting now a book depicting its state twenty years back. For music as an art evolves ever so slowly; and even its business is conservative, resistant to change.

Mostly what has changed in twenty years is the economic and political background. These changes, however, are so tremendous that almost everybody under thirty-five is dazzled by them, unable to see through them or around them, tends in consequence to view today's world of art as also full of novelty.

It is not necessary, of course, that young people have a great knowledge of history. A belief in their own time is far more useful. But when we see them, as we do today in music, painting, and poetry, mistaking for deep originality and for invention diluted versions of our century's earlier masters (who really *were* radical), then one does feel moved to remind them that we too, when young, had an intellectual life and that an inflated market is merely an inflated market.

This book is completely out of date as regards fees, art prices, and the cost of living. It describes, on the contrary, a world that had suffered for ten years from monetary depression. During those years, especially after Germany had sacrificed both personal and religious freedom to a controlled economy, the West went liberal. At least the Popular Front in France and the New Deal in America represented an effort to redefine wealth so as to include working power and to give this power a protection comparable to that constitutionally accorded to real property.

The book is constantly preoccupied, in consequence, as indeed we all were in those days, with establishing a practical basis for demanding and obtaining, as musicians, a voice in the directing of music's affairs. We no longer believed in the disinterestedness of the amateurs and the businessmen who were still trying to administer our properties when they couldn't even handle their own.

That aspect of the book is not out of date at all. Indeed the recall of such reflections can be useful against the time when some other crisis, economic or political, may force the workers in art—today's young or tomorrow's—to rise from their beds of ease. The outer world is moving fast, but art is a permanent value. And if the makers of art do not claim as a permanent right their intellectual privileges and just emoluments, nobody will do it for them. Quite the contrary, unless they watch out very carefully, some church, some state, some business combine will be running their lives. And it should not be so. I do not myself believe today will last; but whether it lasts or not, all should be ready for change and for taking advantage of it.

It is because I find the esthetic and the economico-political aspects of the book so largely valid still that I do not feel impelled to write another version of it, a 1960 version. Its quality and its nature are of 1939. The young people—and I do hope they will read it—may be shocked at how much we cared, and surprised at our thinking we could change anything. But that is exactly the point; we could and did. Before World War II individual people actually could change things or get them changed. Since that time private and small-group actions have become more hazardous. This is the secret canker at the heart of today's young. And nothing can be done about it. But life was better, even without money, when fear was not there.

Among the artistic professions discussed in this book, the one least altered in twenty years is that of poetry. England and France, I should say, are suffering, though perhaps only temporarily, a diminution of its flow. The United States goes right on producing the chief contributions to English-language poetry, just as South America does for Spanish. Germany, though inactive now, has seen fulfilled in life and closed by death the career of Bertolt Brecht, a rare one for our century in that Brecht was both a dramatic poet and a political poet of the left, in a time when few poets have been gifted for the stage and when most of the finer ones have traveled with the right in politics.

With respect to their income sources, poets have not changed at all. They teach, lecture, read, sell manuscripts, and marry. In France they live off the practices of diplomacy and art criticism (being paid for the latter in pictures they can sell later, and do). In New York they write art criticism, but do not get paid in pictures, or very much in money either. They may, after ten years, be rewarded with a mission by a modern museum.

Now poets' publicity is the shield and buckler of modern art, has been so since early in the century. Picasso's name has been made, sustained, and kept before the public by poets—by Max Jacob, Gertrude Stein, Guillaume Apollinaire, Jean Cocteau, André Breton, and Paul Eluard. These authors, plus Louis Aragon, also furnished Picasso with the intellectual nourishment he needed for keeping his output contemporary, saved him the trouble of going places and reading books. They earned their pay; I've no reproach to make them. But I do reproach American poets, who are contributing little of value just now to any painter's culture and surely nothing at all to the public's understanding of art, with jeopardizing what is left of their colleagues' intellectual position by writing on a subject outside their experience. With their professional integrity about all they have left in life, they should be more careful of it. Book reviewing pays better and is less demeaning.

Painters themselves are benefiting vastly from the new prosperity. As my dealer friends tell me, everything sells. They also tell me that an American school of painting now exists, that it is visible everywhere as today's dominant school, and that this school leads the market. Esthetic controversy too runs higher in America than elsewhere—that bitter war between "abstract" painting and the "figurative." The outlying regions, from Paraguay to Vietnam, are producing pictures, just as they erect buildings, that are imitated as closely as possible from the modernistic work exposed in New York. It is only at the market centers of painting, New York and Paris, that the classical techniques and the planned image are being defended. One has only to walk through the biennial world shows of São Paulo and Venice to realize the facile one-worldness with which all God's chillun got modern art. And I mean slapdash modern art, wildly ostentatious and superficial but unquestionably paying allegiance to the "abstract" masters.

These masters, from the Dutch and Russian pioneers of 1910 through the mature work of Mondrian—by way of the Cubists, the Futurists, the Dada toy-makers, and the Surrealists—were already history when this book was written. And the accidental and "action" techniques had been practiced for nearly two decades. Indeed, to my knowledge, no such new techniques have been discovered since. What has changed is their distribution, now vast, for they are even taught in kindergartens. Also the coming into fame of an American school that practices artistic freewheeling exactly as it drives cars—with refinement and with gusto.

My chapter on the painters, therefore, I find to be out of date chiefly with regard to their general prosperity, though that has always in our century run higher than the prosperity of poets or of composers. The esthetics of art are exactly as before 1940, and the painters behave both in the studio and out exactly as they have always done. Wealth is becoming to them; they remain bohemian and good fellows. And wholly inept at organization, even the Americans.

Music, on the other hand, though its esthetics remain also much the same, has undergone a considerable reorganization of its distribution, its patronage, and its pedagogy. European radio, state-owned and tax-supported, has become a major agent for commissioning and disseminating contemporary work. America, for tax reasons, has developed foundational support for music. And even our government, under the Eisenhower administration, has sent music, ballet, and theater troupes round the world and enlarged its cultural offices abroad, its libraries, and its art shows, to a point where all these now count as items of cultural export. And our music schools are, at least for the present, the best. We are the only country, moreover, besides France, that has first-class composers of all ages and all schools. Every other nation, compared to these two, seems provincial, sectarian, or in some other way limited.

Back in the 1930's, as this book explains, the W.P.A., or Works Progress Administration, played a vigorous rôle in American music both for executants and for composers. Being basically a program for alleviating poverty, it died when war ended the depression. ASCAP, on the other hand, the American Society of Composers, Authors and Publishers, was playing no significant rôle at all in serious music at the time. And BMI, a rival society owned by broadcasters, had not come into being. The battle between these two leviathans, started in 1940, is still being fought. I shall not go into its nature or progress save to point out that both sides have found they need the intellectual support, the prestige, of the serious composer and have now come round to collecting and distributing in quite impressive amounts performance fees for serious music.

As a result, and also as a result of enlarged foundational patronage, today's young composers get commissioned, paid, played, and even published. They are not yet living on their take; only five standard composers in America can do that. The rest still teach, mostly in universities. But they are better off than their European confreres, who are paid less for their teaching. And the whole composing tribe today, especially in America, has more outlet for its product than formerly.

This prosperity, like that of the painters, has changed nothing in the musician's way of working, though it will need to be considered by the reader when this book gets now and then over-tearful about the composer's sad lot. The absence of easy money during the 1930's will also seem to many a sufficient explanation for the book's constant preoccupation with reorganization and reform. Financial crisis, of course, can easily provoke such thoughts. But a stimulus, while explaining perhaps the existence of its reaction, does not necessarily explain it away. Thought once taken must be judged as thought. I believe, moreover, that today's crisis in musical style—for music has a style crisis just as painting has—may be better resolved by economic descriptions, sociological studies of the market, and reflections about political theory than by esthetic reasoning. That part of the book, however unconvincing my conclusions may seem, remains its fundamental message and one far less outdated than an unreflecting boom generation might tend to consider it. Outdated by what, I ask?

Music's stylistic crisis is discussed a good deal in the book. The history of our musical language from early Christian psalmody through today's arithmetical abstractions is a continued story. The late eighteenth century witnessed for the literature

of music its highest point of organization, flexibility, spacious-
ness, and expressive variety. The evolution of our idiom's tonal
possibilities and the codification of its grammar were complete
by 1914. Since that time expressive variety has still been possible,
because every age uses its language to describe its own gamut of
feelings. But there has been no further structural growth, only
constriction. Now to abandon the formal language and to replace it by arithmetical structures is a perfectly legitimate effort
on the part of our electronic and otherwise advance-minded
composers. It is also a normal effort to an age brought up on
the mystical idea that progress is a continuum rather than on
the scientific studies of evolution and growth that demonstrate
such processes to possess usually a beginning, a middle, and
an end.

Today's fixation on musical experiment comes from both
impulses. One is to assume that innovation is the only historic
value. The other is to believe that innovation is always available.
These two propositions define the ideals of today's musical left
wing. And both are unacceptable to the right and center. The
right and center, in fact, tend to consider the left as not advanced at all, merely mistaken. And the bitterness with which
the dispute is conducted is further aggravated by rivalries involving commissions, performances, publication, and jobs.

In so far as it is a war between generations, the younger one
will win, of course, by mere survival. But the "advanced" position, as a position, is weaker today than last year. Its supply of
ideas for innovation, its inspiration, is failing visibly. Its leaders
are carefully, and not always under cover, moving to the right.
Its next year's job-defenses will certainly follow another line.
The whole quarrel, I must say, is futile and tiresome; but there
it is. Prose literature in general, that of the young certainly, has
never been more naturalistic than now; poetry, painting, and
music, by workmen of any age, have rarely been more mannered. This is today's stalemated situation at ten years past the
middle of a century that has formerly known huge activity in
the arts.

With the worlds of transport and politics in rapid movement,
with consumer production (and population) rocketing, with
revolution on the march in every continent, and with matter
itself turned active and unimaginably destructive, the arts, save

possibly history and reporting, the arts today seem relatively static, certainly timid, sectarian, and prissy. It might be the time to write another *State of Music*, but I do not think so. What music needs right now is the sociological treatment, a documented study of its place in business, in policy, and in culture. I am not prepared by training for such a work. Nor need I report much more on just music itself. I did that in the New York *Herald Tribune* from 1940 through 1954, and the results have been published in three books. The best I can do right now is to annotate this one and send it forth again.

It is a period piece certainly, but also a historic one, since no similar sum-up has been attempted since. The chapters about painters and poets are a bit frivolous, always were. The straight musical parts are better. Even the chapter on the economic conditioning of musical style, admittedly a scherzo, has in it far more than just a nubbin of truth. The account of music's business life has had to be put in accord with today's business facts. The political and organizational analysis of music reads to me still for the most part as correct, though it may seem to many, in a time that finds all political thought suspect and any proposal terrifying that might make any organization more efficient, bad taste to bring such matters up at all.

Save for a few corrections of phrase, most of my additions have been placed in brackets and printed along with the text to permit cursive reading. Once in a while I have omitted a page or paragraph that merely itemized some former status. In view of the sometimes extensive additions, it may turn out I have rewritten *The State of Music* after all. I hope not. I liked the book as it was, still have for it some esteem. Enough, in fact, that I have only tried bringing it up to date at all in order to avoid being judged a period piece myself.

What I have not tried to do, could not possibly do, is to compensate for the fact that while the world has been changing a lot, and music a little, I have aged by twenty years. From a smart aleck just turned forty I have become an elder statesman. I may not be any wiser now, but more people believe what I say. Consequently, I am more careful about my language. Translating my thoughts of yesteryear, however, into my language of today would not benefit them. They are better in the words of their time, belong there, mean more. Anybody who can use them in the living that he is doing will surely be able to use also a bit of the truculent temper with which they are expressed. That is part of their urgency. And if the ideas themselves lack urgency now, there is no point in reprinting this book.

I may write another book one day. If I do, it will be about other ideas and another time. But both that time and my view of it will have grown out of those described here. "Music Between the First Two World Wars," the present theme, is surely but the first act of a drama. At least it is the first one in which I played an adult rôle. Everything in music before 1914 belongs to history anyway, and not because a big war started then but because a long evolution ended then. My adult musical life happens to be contiguous with the time of music's beginning to be not any more a part of a clear historical development. Like English literature after Shakespeare or French after Racine, music seems to be more a matter of change, constant change in subject and sound, than of growth.

This constant change, as in the literary products of mature languages, takes place more and more against a backdrop of the art's own history. Music in our time may be only the banal story of its mishaps and adventures since 1914. Nevertheless the play is not over. And since 1939 there have been changes of scenery and of tempo. A second act is surely going on. But one cannot foresee now its curtain-line.

It has been some pleasure, going over this book, to resee a past time through an eyewitness then twenty years younger. It is for readers twenty and more years younger now that I have made changes. My generation may well have preferred it as it was. But they don't need it. Today's young people may, just may, find in it some tiny spark or taper for helping them to explore the larger labyrinth that music has become since World War II.

V. T.

I

Our Island Home

OR

What it feels like to be a musician

EVERY PROFESSION is a secret society. The musical profession is more secret than most, on account of the nature of music itself. No other field of human activity is quite so hermetic, so isolated. Literature is made out of words, which are ethnic values and which everybody in a given ethnic group understands. Painting and sculpture deal with recognizable images that all who have eyes can see. Architecture makes perfectly good sense to anybody who has ever built a chicken coop or lived in a house. Scholarship, science, and philosophy, which are verbalizations of general ideas, are practiced humbly by all, the highest achievements of these being for the most part verifiable objectively by anyone with access to facts. As for politics, religion, government, and sexuality, every loafer in a pub or club has his opinions, his passions, his inalienable orientation about them. Even the classical ballet is not very different from any other stylized muscular spectacle, be that diving or tennis or bull-fighting or horse-racing or simply a military parade.

Among the great techniques, music is all by itself, an auditory thing, the only purely auditory thing there is. It is comprehensible only to persons who can remember sounds. Trained or untrained in the practice of the art, these persons are correctly called "musical." And their common faculty gives them access to a secret civilization completely impenetrable by outsiders.

The professional caste that administers this civilization is proud, dogmatic, insular. It divides up the rest of the world into possible customers and non-customers, or rather into two kinds of customers, the music-employers and the music-consumers, beyond whom lies a no man's land wherein dwells everyone else. In no man's land takes place one's private life with friends and lovers, relatives, neighbors. Here live your childhood playmates, your enemies of the classroom, the soldiers of your regiment, your chums, girl-friends, wives, throw-aways, and the horrid little family next door.

13

Private human life is anything but dull. On the contrary, it is far too interesting. The troublesome thing about it is that it has no real conventions, makes no inner sense. Anything can happen. It is mysterious, unpredictable, unrehearsable. Professional life is not mysterious at all. The whole music world understands music. Any musician can give to another a comprehensible rendition of practically any piece. If there is anything either of them doesn't understand, there are always plenty of people they can consult about it.

The profession rules are extremely simple. In the unwritten popular vein, or folk-style, anything goes. If a piece is written out and signed, then all the musician has to do is to execute the written notes clearly, accurately, and unhesitatingly at such a speed and with such variations of force as are demanded by the composer's indications, good common sense, and the limitations of the instrument. Inability to do this satisfactorily can be corrected by instruction and practice. The aim of instruction and practice is to enable the musician to play fast and slow and loud and soft in any known rhythm, whether of the pulsating or of the measured kind, without any non-deliberate obscurity, and without any involuntary violation of the conventions of tonal "beauty" current in his particular branch of the art. The musician so prepared is master of his trade; and there are few emergencies in professional life that he cannot handle, if he still likes music.

Private life, on the other hand, is beset by a thousand insoluble crises, from unrequited love to colds in the head. Nobody, literally nobody, knows how to avoid any of them. The Christian religion itself can only counsel patience and long-suffering. It is like a nightmare of being forced to execute at sight a score much too difficult for one's training on an instrument nobody knows how to tune and before a public that isn't listening anyway.

Yet plain private life has to be lived every day. Year after year we stalk an uncharted jungle with our colleagues and our co-citizens. We fight with them for food and love and power, defending ourselves as we can, attacking when we must. The description of all that is the story-teller's job. I would not and could not compete. From the musical enclosure or stockade, all that really counts is the easy game near by, the habitual music-consumer.

Sometimes a consumer is musically literate to the point of executing string quartets in the home. Sometimes he can't read a note. He is still a consumer if he likes music. And he likes music if he has visceral reactions to auditory stimuli.

Muscular reactions to such stimuli do not make a music-lover. Almost anybody can learn to waltz, or to march to a drum. My father and his mother before him were what used to be called "tone-deaf." They never sang or whistled or paid any attention to musical noises. The four to six hours a day piano practice that I did for some years in my father's house never fazed either of them. They would read or sleep while it was going on as easily as I read or sleep on a railway train. Their rhythmic sense, however, was intact and quite well-developed. They could even recognize a common ditty or hymn-tune, provided they knew the words, by the prosodic patterns of its longs and shorts. I do not doubt that intensive drilling could have developed their musical prowess to more elaborate achievements. Knowing their lives as I do, I doubt if either of them would have had a better life for having wasted time on an enterprise for which he had no real gift.

The music-consumer is a different animal, and commerce with him is profitable. We provide him with music; he responds with applause, criticism, and money. All are useful. When Miss Gertrude Stein remarked that "artists don't need criticism; all they need is praise," she was most certainly thinking about the solitary arts, to which she was especially sensitive, namely, easel-painting and printed poetry. The collaborative arts cannot exist without criticism. Trial and error is their *modus operandi*, whether the thing designed for execution is a railway-station, a library, a "symphonic poem," a dictionary, an airplane for transatlantic flights, or a tragedy for public performance.

Consumer-criticism and consumer-applause of music, as of architecture, are often more perspicacious than professional criticism and applause. What one must never forget about them is that the consumer is not a professional. He is an amateur. He makes up in enthusiasm what he lacks of professional authority. His comprehension is intuitive, perfidious, female, stubborn, seldom to be trusted, never to be despised. He has violent loves and rather less violent hatreds. He is too unsure for hatred, leaves that mostly to the professionals. But he does get pretty upset sometimes by music he doesn't understand.

On the whole he is a nice man. He is the waves around our island. And if any musician likes to think of himself as a granite rock against which the sea of public acclaim dashes itself in vain, let him do so. That is a common fantasy. It is a false image of the truth, nevertheless, to group all the people who like listening to music into a composite character, a hydra-headed monster, known as The Public. The Public doesn't exist save as a statistical concept. A given hall- or theater- ful of people has its personality, of course, and its own bodily temperature, as every performer knows; but such an audience is just like any other friend to whom one plays a piece. A performance is a flirtation, its aim seduction. The granite-rock pose is a flirting device, nothing more. The artist who is really indifferent to an audience loses that audience.

While I was growing up in Kansas City, the consumers I came in contact with were very much as I describe them here. Later, when I went to college, I encountered a special variety, the intellectual music-fancier. This is a species of customer who talks about esthetics all the time, mostly the esthetics of visual art. He views modern music as a tail to the kite of modern painting, and modern painting as a manifestation of the Modern Spirit. This is all very mystical, as you can see. Also quite false. There is no Modern Spirit. There are only some modern techniques. If it were otherwise, the market prices of music and painting and poetry would not be so disparate as they are.

The intellectual music-fancier is useful as an advertising medium, because he circulates among advance-guard consumers. He is psychologically dangerous to musicians, however, because he insists on lecturing them about taste. He assumes to himself, from no technical vantage point, a knowledge of musical right and wrong; and he is pretty sacerdotal about dispensing that knowledge. He is not even a professional critic, responsible to some publication with a known intellectual or advertising policy. He is likely to have some connection with the buying or selling of pictures. He is a snob in so far as he is trying to get something without paying for it, climbing at our expense. And his climb is very much at our expense if we allow him to practice his psychological black magic on us, his deadly-upas-tree rôle, in the form either of positive criticism or of a too-impressive negation. On the whole, he is not as nice a man as the less intellectual consumer; and he must be handled very firmly indeed.

In dealing with employers, professional solidarity, lots of good will, and no small amount of straight human forbearance are necessary. Musicians back-stage quarrel a good deal among themselves. They practically always present a united front to the management. It isn't that one dislikes the management especially, or disapproves of his existence. He is simply a foreigner. On the job to be done, he just doesn't speak our language.

Verbal communication about music is impossible except among musicians. Even among them there is no proper language. There is only technical jargon plus gesture. The layman knows neither convention. He cannot gesture about another man's trade, because a trade's sign language is even more esoteric than its jargon. If he knows a little of either, communication merely becomes more difficult, because both jargon and sign language have one meaning for the outside world, a dictionary meaning if you like, and five hundred meanings for the insider, hardly one of which is ever the supposed meaning. The musician and his employer are like an Englishman and an American, or like a Spaniard and an Argentine. They think they are differing over principles and disliking each other intensely, when they are really not communicating at all. For what they speak, instead of being one language with different accents, as is commonly supposed, is really two languages with the same vocabulary. The grammar is the same grammar and the words are the same words, but the meanings are not the same meanings. The plain literal meanings of words like pie, lamb, and raspberry are different enough between America and the British Isles. For an inhabitant of either country even to suspect what the other fellow means by general words like gratitude, love, loyalty, revenge, and politeness requires years of foreign residence.

So it is between us and our non-musical collaborators. Preachers and theatrical directors, for instance, will practically always ask you to play faster when they mean louder; and they get into frightful tempers at what they think is a too-loud background for a prayer or soliloquy. Nine times out of ten the musician is playing just this side of inaudibility and is killing the effect not by playing noisily but by playing *espressivo*. He thinks an expressive scene needs an expressive accompaniment. It rarely occurs to him, unless told, to play *senza espressione*. He doesn't mind playing so when told, because the *senza espressione* is a legitimate, though rarish, musical effect. It just doesn't occur to him usually.

It is impossible, however, for a layman to ask a musician to play without expression. He can demand a little less agony when the player gets clean out of hand, but that is as far as he can think technically. Even if he knows the term *senza espressione*, he imagines it to mean "in a brutal or mechanical manner," which it doesn't. To musicians it means "without varying noticeably the established rhythm or the dynamic level." It is far from a brutal or mechanical effect. It is a very refined effect, particularly useful for throwing into relief the expressive nature of whatever it accompanies.

Film-directors are particularly upsetting to the musician, because, dealing with photography as they do, they live in constant fear lest music, the stronger medium, should take over the show. At the same time, they want it to sustain the show whenever the show shows signs of falling apart. They expect you, wherever the story is unconvincing or the continuity frankly bad, to deceive the audience by turning on a lot of insincere hullabaloo. Now insincerity on the part of actors and interpreters is more or less all right, but insincere authorship leads to no good end. Theater people and musicians all know this. Film people do not seem to. For all the skill and passion that have gone into the making of movies, the films are still a second-rate art form, like mural painting, because they try to convince us of characters and motivations that their own authors do not believe in, and because they refuse a loyal co-operation with music, their chief aid, choosing naively to use the more powerful medium as whitewash to cover up the structural defects of the weaker. It takes lots of tact and persistence to pull off a creditable job in such an industry.

The most successful users of music are the concert organizers. They confine themselves to saying yes and no. The workman never has much trouble with an employer who knows what he doesn't want. On the contrary, negation simplifies everything;

and one can then proceed by elimination. What gives a musician the jitters is positive criticism, being told in advance what the result should sound like. Such talk sterilizes him by bringing in emotive considerations (the layman's language lending more moral-value connotation to technical words than the workman's language does) at a moment when successful solution of the problem in hand, that of speaking to an audience expressively (though not necessarily *con espressione*), demands that he keep all moral values and taste-connotations out of his mind.

I am trying to tell in this roundabout way what it feels like to be a musician. Mostly it is a feeling of being different from everybody but other musicians and of inhabiting with these a closed world. This world functions interiorly like a republic of letters. Exteriorly it is a secret society, and its members practice a mystery. The mystery is no mystery to us, of course; and any outsider is free to participate if he can. Only he never can. Because music-listening and music-using are oriented toward different goals from music-making, and hence nobody really knows anything about music-making except music-makers. Everybody else is just neighbors or customers, and the music world is a tight little island entirely surrounded by them all.

2

The Neighbors

OR

Chiefly about painters and painting

IT IS NOT HEALTHY for musicians to live too close to the confraternity. The white light of music is too blinding, and professional jealousies are a fatigue. One needs friends of another mind. A great deal of my own life seems to have been passed among painters. My sister, who was ten years older than I, was a china-painter. She earned a good living at it and paid for my music lessons, bought me my first piano. The house was full always of her colleagues and customers and the blessed odor of turpentine. To this day that resinous acridity seems to me the normal atmosphere for music to breathe and grow in.

Perhaps that is why Paris, where one is surrounded by painters, has always reminded me of Kansas City; and no doubt that is why I feel at home there. Because Paris contains, or did some years ago, by census, sixty thousand artist-painters earning their living at their trade. Believe it or not, sixty thousand professional easel-painters. Naturally one is surrounded by them. And a pleasant lot they are too, cheerful and healthy and leading regular lives.

Not orderly lives, by any means, because disorder, both material and moral, is of the essence in a painter's life. Their incomes and their love-lives are as jumpy as a fever chart. Their houses are as messy as their palettes. They view life as a multiplicity of visible objects, all completely different. A dirty towel in the middle of the floor, wine-spots on the piano keys, a hairbrush in the butter plate are for them just so many light-reflecting surfaces. Their function is to look at life, not to rearrange it. All of which, if it makes for messiness in the home, also makes for ease in social intercourse. This plus the fact that they all have perfectly clear consciences after four o'clock, or at whatever hour the daylight starts giving out.

The painter's whole morality consists of keeping his brushes clean and getting up in the morning. He wakes up with the light, tosses till the sun is overhead, then gets up and starts moving around. He works moving around. Drawing, engraving, and water-color sketching can be done seated. But oil painting must be done on foot, walking back and forth. It entails no inconsiderable amount of physical exercise and that among turpentine fumes, which keep the lungs open. Hence your painter is on the whole a healthy and a cheerful man. His besetting maladies are digestive, due to poverty, undernourishment, and irregular meals. He requires lots of food. In middle and later life he sometimes has rheumatism. But he is seldom too ill to paint.

As soon as the light goes bad his painting day is over. He thereupon refreshes his mind by making love to his model or by quarreling with his wife, and goes out. From four till midnight he is gay and companionable. After midnight he is disagreeable, because he knows he should be in bed. It is chiefly after midnight that he takes to alcohol, when he takes to it at all. He is a man of moderate habits, abundant physical energy, and a lively though not scholarly mind. (He doesn't like to tire his eyes by sustained reading.) He has social charm, generosity (except about other painters), and a friendly indifference to music that is a constant refreshment for musicians. Unseduced by the mere charm of sounds, unimpressed by the ingenuities of musical workmanship and the triumphs of voluntary stylization, he goes straight to the heart of the matter when he goes in for music at all. He will sometimes tell you in five words what a piece is all about, a thing no musician ever knows and no music lover ever even tries to know.

He is usually non-political, though his ways are democratic. He resides among the poor, visits in châteaux, and walks unscathed through the intrigues of the literary cenacles. He makes love to princesses as if they were housemaids and to housemaids as if they were princesses, accepting service and presents from both. He has no class hatred because he has no class. He combines the ferocious independence of the solitary intellectual with the dignity of the skilled manual worker.

He bands together for esthetic purposes much more frequently than for economic. Unlike the musician, who is a union man and a petty bourgeois with an organized orientation in class-struggle tactics and consequently a tendency toward political affiliations (he is usually either a Third-International

Communist or an extreme-right reactionary*); unlike the poet, who has an over-elaborate education and no economic place in society at all and who tends hence to shoot the works politically by attaching his unrequited social passions to some desperate and recondite cause like Catalan autonomy, Anglo-Catholicism, or the justification of Leon Trotsky;† unlike the sculptors and the architects, who in order to function at all must pass their lives in submission among politicos and plutocrats; unlike the doctors, the scholars, and the men of science, who are a whole social class to themselves, and who function as a united political party for the maintenance of that strangle-hold on the educational system which they acquired during the nineteenth century; unlike the manufacturers and the merchants, who know their cops and their aldermen and who always vote (to say the least); unlike actors and theater people, who, whether poor or prosperous, are vagabonds, but who do have a trade-union of sorts and an enormous class solidarity; the painter is a man of no fixed economic orientation, no class feeling, and very little professional organization of any kind.

Since the abolition of the guilds by the French Revolution, no painters' union or academy has even been seriously effective. (Similarly, no dealers' consortium or trust has ever put the economic squeeze on painters as a group.) The British Royal Academy is little more than a Kiwanis club or a Fifth Avenue Merchants' Association. American Artists' Equity is notoriously ineffective at defending the painter's rights in the sale of his reproductions and at collecting what is owed him by clients and dealers. The painters don't even run an educational institution of any very dependable kind. They refuse to systematize. There is some virtue in this refusal. Alone among all the higher skills, painting is still learned rather than taught. In the state-endowed academies, in the private ateliers, in art students' leagues, in life classes at provincial museums, oil painting and its allied techniques are considered by students and instructors alike to be progressively acquired skills rather than a corpus of esoteric knowledge progressively administered. Even the Dynamic

*Still true in South America.
†In 1960, read Algerian autonomy, Zen Buddhism, or beatnik Bohemia.

Symmetry racket, which is an attempt to subject easel-painting, so recently free from their domination, to the ancient rules of decorative design, must eventually be submissive to the judgment of the Seeing Eye.

The Seeing Eye has no opinions. A still-life, a nude, a landscape (no matter what sentimental tie-up may be involved in the painter's choice of subject), is exactly what the painter puts down and what any beholder sees when he looks at it. Very little more is involved. The painter's technique, however complete, however analytic, can only describe particular objects. It is incapable of stating a general idea or of depicting the emotional, the utilitarian value of anything. Hence the great moral freedom of painters as a race. They keep a cleaner separation than any other kind of man I know between their lives and their works, even, in their work, between vision and execution. Their vision is personal and subjective, their rendering of it precise, objective, non-emotional. All the emotional things like sexuality, politics, elegance, family life, and religion are kept strictly in the background of their lives as private games, subjects for talk, indulgences for the darker hours of the day.

They can accept without mental trickery the dictates of fashion and of politics about what fashion and politics think is appropriate subject-matter for painting, especially if large commissions are involved. What do they care whether their model is supposed to represent Jesus Christ or Lucifer or Love in Idleness or Mr. John Rockefeller or The Conquest of Tahiti or The Workingman Triumphant or Agriculture Shaking Hands with the Machine-Age? He is just a model to them. And the drapery is just so many varied textures, each reflecting light in its own way to the Seeing Eye. An apple, a banknote, a pair of buttocks, all is one to them, because all is infinite multiplicity.

[In 1960, masses of them have followed the fashion (a strictly upper-class one) for concealing the subject-matter. This is accomplished through stylistic devices variously known as action painting, abstract expressionism, and (to use my word for it) crypto-Impressionism. Such concealment works less well for union halls, churches, post offices, or travel posters than for restaurants, night clubs, hotels, international administrations, and university premises. It does not work at all for portraiture.

But painting, in a time of easy money, follows the taste of those spending that money. And the taste of today's ruling group in the West favors a minimum of imagery.]

Mark you, my portrait of The Painter is of the ideal, or rather the average painter, the easel-painter as he exists among his sixty thousand brethren in Paris or New York. The painter in isolation is another man. If you take him out of his water and put him on an island somewhere, out of the reach of other painters and with no access to a picture merchant, or if you send him to teach in some provincial agglomeration where there is no rivalry and no market, he goes very bad indeed. All alone he must cover the social gamut. He must drink and make merry and change wives and raise children; he must go to cock-fights and gamble and collect folklore and spend money; he must patronize the local whore-house and picket the local pants factory and waste his eyes reading books. It is too big a job. If the booze doesn't get him, the bourgeoisie must. A sad man indeed is the painter exiled from his kind.

An embittered man is the painter who over-indulges in applied art. Patterns, posters, costumes, theater, the painter does better than the specialists. Because where the specialists have only a bag of tricks, the painter has some hard-earned general knowledge about color, light, proportion, and arrangement for high visibility. He enjoys making applications of this knowledge, playing new tricks on old trades, giving everything style, getting paid for it. The indulgence is a pleasant one indeed. The effects of over-indulgence are emptiness, staleness, sterility, and bad temper.

Even the much-admired virtuoso-skills allied to oil painting should not be indulged in any more than is necessary to prove that one can do them if one has to. The etching, the dry-point, the silver-point, the water-color are too pretty to be much good. It is easy to do them with charm, well-nigh impossible to give them any force. Preoccupation with such minor matters is the mark of a painter who is trying to go commercial respectably or professorial with impunity.

Commissioned portrait painting is also a deviation. Because the problems of painting are three and only three: animate objects, inanimate objects, and scenery. The sum-up of them all is the licentious picnic (the landscape with draped figures, undraped figures, and food). The portrait that isn't ordered is perfectly legitimate. It is just a draped figure, and resemblance doesn't matter. But facial resemblance, which is what people pay for in paid portraits, is outside the canon of painting. It is a trick, a gift. It cannot be learned or taught. The painter who can pull it off steadily seldom pays much attention to the serious problems of painting. Doesn't have to, because resembling portraiture is well paid. He is ashamed, though, because he is held in low esteem by his kind. Moreover, that psychic intimacy with the sitter that is necessary for the execution of good portraiture is upsetting to the nervous system and undermines character; also the continuous frequenting of politicians and of the rich that is necessary both to get portrait-commissions and to execute them is in itself a full-time occupation and not a very noble one.

As for mural painting, only second-raters ever do it a second time. The only special technique involved is the getting of jobs. Excellent painting can perfectly well be done on a wall, of course, or on a ceiling. It can be done on a bar-mirror in epsom salts, on a candy-box, on the back of a hairbrush, or around the legs of a piano. It must always be an image, it must depict something, however abstractly. It must create an illusion. If it sacrifices representation to anything else it is decorative design; and that is another man's trade. The real trouble about large-scale mural painting in our epoch is that unless it is executed in a precious material, in which case it is not free-hand painting but something else, it must inevitably compete with other large-scale paid-advertising in color, that is to say, electric signs and billboards. In consequence, it tends towards blatancy and over-simplification and thus fails to profit by those fuller resources of the painter's technique the deployment of which would be his only legitimate excuse for being engaged in paid-advertising at all.

[In 1960, the current scheme is to employ in business rooms and executive offices not wall paintings but framed oil pictures chosen for their lack of easily read imagery and the known high price of their painters' signatures. Such pictures have a resale value, of course, that murals do not; and any of them will go into any office as well as any other. Abstract or non-figurative painting has come thus to serve business as a symbol of disinterested effort while actually, in a time of rising art prices, making money for the firm. The painter, moreover, in this happy deal has been spared the indignity of practicing applied art.]

There is no way around it. The painter who doesn't paint pictures is a routine man and a bore. The painter who is predominantly an easel-painter is a noble animal and a charming neighbor. He is the type-practitioner in our age of the arts both beautiful and liberal. This has not always been so. The seventeenth century had its priests and preachers whom it counted on for inspiration, as well as for the work of the world; these directed the religious wars and the colonial expansions, the exploration of three continents and the taming of wild folk. The eighteenth had its philosophers and journalists, its generalizing men of letters, counted on them for social guidance and for prophecy. The nineteenth century sucked its vitality for industrial and business expansion out of poets, musicians, and scientists. Big business today lives on the calculators and the mathematical physicists, while the arts of music and literature, completely divorced from the realities of supra-national cooperation, fecundate in a vacuum, drawing their moral support in this depressing enterprise from the only really classless man there is, the painter, and leaving to him in turn the center of the world's artistic stage, as well as the privilege of collecting most of the receipts.

The depiction of the visible world might well have been left to him too, did not journalism and photography cover the ground more thoroughly. As a matter of fact, painting and photography work very well side by side, just as poetry and journalism go hand in hand and often hand in glove. The boom in oil painting that has lasted from 1860 on, from the Pre-Raphaelites and the Impressionists through the Cubists, Surrealists, Neo-Romantics, and neo-abstractionists is exactly contemporary with the rise of commercial photography. Photography has taken over from painting nearly that whole mass of boring and fastidious work that is represented by illustration, documentation, and personal portraiture. Both arts have prospered in consequence.

But with all the photography that goes on in the world (there is even "abstract," or non-representational photography), one might expect the photographers themselves to be more in evidence than they are. I must say they are fairly noticeable in

Germany, which is the ancestral home of The Toy, her modern form of toy-consciousness being a passion for optical instruments and for playing with them in public. Elsewhere, although everybody knows a photographer or two, one is rarely surrounded by them as one is surrounded by painters in Paris, by men of letters in London, by musicians in Vienna, by schoolteachers in Boston, and by publicists in New York.

They are strange little men, photographers, always a bit goofy and incommunicable. They live on idiosyncratic observation, on fancy. Practicing the most objective technique known to art, they cherish a violent life of the imagination. They are sad, pensive, and introverted, lead their lives in rain-coats. They have bad complexions and are riddled with chronic diseases, usually of nervous origin. [Their women's-wear wing, on the other hand, wears dudish clothes, drives foreign cars, frequents the glamour world, and collects art. They still have allergies.]

Journalists are plentiful everywhere and entertaining too, full of jokes and stories. Only their jokes are not very funny and their stories not quite true. Their information is always incomplete, because nobody tells them the truth about anything. Though they think themselves pundits all, their philosophy of life and their techniques of expression are incurably, dogmatically superficial. Their private lives are full of banal domesticity and melodrama. They are, to a man, either dyspeptic or alcoholic or both. They must be avoided in bands, because they bring out the worst in one another. Singly they are warm and companionable, make devoted friends.

As for the sculptors and the architects, they are a pretty negligible company. The former are personally vain and professionally pretentious. They are troublesome when they turn up; but they turn up rarely nowadays, their art being in decline. The latter exist in abundance but are tame and lacking in savor. They frequent the rich and are impressed. They marry above them and send their children to schools they can't afford. They are good enough neighbors; they will always lend you a cup of oil. But there is no real sustenance in them.

Theatrical people are better. They are ostentatious and repetitive, but they have a playfulness and a complete lack of grown-up morality that are refreshing. They are superb in times of depression. In the long run, of course, they are unfrequentable on account of their late working-hours, just as vocalists are unfrequentable because they are always having to go to bed. The latter are companionable and good cooks (I count them among the non-musical neighbors because, as everybody knows, they are mostly not very musical), but they are neurotic. They can't drink or smoke or stay up after ten o'clock without worrying about themselves. And they are completely fee-minded. Dancers are auto-erotic and have no conversation.

No, seriously, it is the painters who by their numbers, by their charm and healthiness, and by their unique social freedom, have imposed upon the twentieth century their own type as the model of what an artist should be like. If all art in Walter Pater's day could be said to "aspire to the condition of music," all artists, certainly all artists today, aspire to the condition of the painter, envying him his regular life, his cheerfulness, his fecundity, his vigorous energies, his complete lack of emotional complexity, and (among the higher-flight ones) certainly, yes, very certainly, his income.

3
Survivals of an Earlier Civilization
OR
Shades of poets dead and gone

Poetry is the oldest of the arts and the most respected. The musical tradition we practice has scarcely a thousand years. Architecture, sculpture, and decorative design have passed since ancient times through so many esthetic revolutions that very little is left in them of any authoritative tradition. Improvisational one-man easel-painting in oil (painting as we know it) dates barely from the seventeenth century.

Poetry, as we know it, goes straight back to the Greeks and to the Hebrew children. There has been no interruption for twenty-five hundred years in the transmission of its technical procedures, no hiatus in the continuity of its comprehension by the literate classes of Europe. It has survived changes in religion, political revolutions, the birth and death of languages. Its classic masters enjoy a prestige scarcely exceeded by that of the Holy Evangelists. By populace and scholars alike they are admired above confessors and martyrs, priests, prophets, historians, psychologists, romancers, and ethical guides, and far above statesmen or soldiers, orators or newshawks. For they and their heirs are the recognized masters of the most puissant of all instruments, the word.

The poetic prestige remains, but the poetic function has contracted. As champions of the arts of love, poets made war for centuries on the Christian Church and won. As analysts of its motivations and as experts of amorous device, they were the undisputed masters of that subject till Sigmund Freud, a nerve doctor, beat them at it in our own day. (Karl Marx, a nineteenth-century economist, had already beaten them at social analysis and at political prophecy.) With love now the specialty (in every aspect) of the medical profession, with government (both past and future) better understood by sectarian political groups and better explained by journalists, with dramaturgy better practiced in Hollywood and Joinville, and story-telling done more convincingly by the writers of police-fiction, what is there left

29

for the poet to do that might even partially justify his hereditary prestige?

He could retreat into "pure" poetry, of course; and he often tries to. Much good may it do him. Because the sorry truth is there is no such refuge. In recent years the poets have talked a good deal about "purity." I am not sure what they mean by "pure" poetry, unless they mean poetry without a subject-matter; and that means exactly nothing.

Music and painting can exist perfectly well without a subject-matter, at least without any obvious or stated subject-matter. Painting of this kind is called "abstract." Musicians used to distinguish between "program" music and "absolute" music. The latter term meant music without a literary text or any specific illustrative intention, that is to say, instrumental music of an introspective nature. Neither "abstract" painting nor "absolute" music is any "purer" than any other kind of painting or music, and no painter or musician ever pretends it is. It is merely more obscure. When painters speak of "purity of line," they mean a complete lack of obscurity. When they speak of a "pure" color, they mean a shade that is unequivocal. Say an artist's intentions are "pure," if you must. That means he is not commercial-minded. The word *pure* cannot possibly have any meaning when applied to the content or structure of literature. Poetry could be pure only if it could be devoid of meaning, which it can't. You can make nonsense poetry, certainly; you can dissociate and reassociate words. But you cannot take the meanings out of words; you simply can't. You can only readjust their order. And nobody can or ever does write poetry without a subject.*

What subjects, then, are available to the poet today? Practically none. Money, political events, heroism, science, mathematical logic, crime, the libido, the sexual variations, the limits of personality, the theory of revolution: the incidents of all these are more graphically recited by journalists, the principles better explained by specialists. There really isn't much left for the heirs of Homer and Shakespeare to do but to add their case-histories

---

* "Purity," as applied to poetry, was chiefly used by the French and referred, I think, to the philosophical non-involvement and near-to-hermetic verbiage of Mallarmé, Rimbaud, Valéry, and their later derivatives.

to the documentation of introspective psychology by the practice of automatic writing. Highly trained in linguistics (though
the philologists are not bad at that either) and wearing the
mantle of the Great Tradition, admired unreasonably and feared
not unreasonably (for they are desperate men), they still have,
as poets, no civil status, no social function, no serious job to
do, and no income.

They haven't even any audience to speak of. For some time
now they have been depending mainly on one another for applause. Hence the pretentiousness and the high intellectual tone
of all they write. I mean that for fifty years poetry has mostly
been read by other poets, and that for a good thirty years now it
has mostly been written to be read by other poets. [Add twenty
years to these figures.]

The impasse is complete. Contemporary civilization has no
place for the poet save one of mere honor. Science, learning,
journalism, fiction, religion, magic, and politics, all his ancient
bailiwicks, are closed to him formally and completely. He is
allowed to render small services to these now and then as a dis-
seminator of existing knowledge. He is always regarded, however, by the specialists as a possible betrayer; and consequently
at no time is he allowed to speak on such subjects with any but
a temporarily delegated authority.

His lot is a tragic one. Nothing is left him of his art but an
epigone's skill and some hereditary prestige. This last is still
large enough to give him face in front of his co-citizens and to
keep up the recruiting. It doesn't pay anything at all, of course.
It won't buy a beer, a bus-fare, or a contraceptive. Nor does it
prevent the darkest despair from seizing him when he is alone.
[Nowadays a bit of a market has developed for lectures, readings, personal appearances, and the sale of manuscripts.]

The prestige of classic poetry is enough to explain the market
among cultured women for poets as lovers. I use the word *market* deliberately, because in these love affairs a certain amount of
money nearly always changes hands. The poet with no job and
no private resources is a liability to his intimates. If he has a job,
he is usually too busy working at it to take on seriously a love
affair with a woman of leisure. If he has money from home, he
always keeps somebody else or spends it on riotous living. Any
independent woman who gets involved with a poet had better

figure that he is going to cost her something sooner or later, if only for bailing him out of hospitals.

For poets live high. When one is as poor as they, budgets make no sense and economies make no sense. Nothing makes any sense but basic luxury—eating well, drinking well, and making love. Independent and well-to-do women whose sex-mechanisms are excited by intellectual conversation are very useful indeed to poetry, provided they don't go motherly. (Poets don't care much for maternal types and they have a horror of fatherhood.) They serve the poet as muse, audience, and patroness all in one as long as they last. This isn't long usually. They get scared off by the violence of it all, as well as by the expense, and take up with a musician.

Everything the poet does is desperate and excessive. He eats like a pig; he starves like a professional beauty; he tramps; he bums; he gets arrested; he steals; he absconds; he blackmails; he dopes; he acquires every known vice and incurable disease, not the least common of which is solitary dipsomania.

All this after twenty-five, to be sure. Up to that age he is learning his art. There is available a certain amount of disinterested subsidy for expansive lyrical poetry, the poetry of adolescence and early manhood. But nobody can make a grown-up career out of a facility for lyrical expansiveness. That kind of effusion is too intense, too intermittent. The mature nervous system won't stand it. At about twenty-six, the poets start looking around for some subject-matter outside themselves, something that will justify sustained execution while deploying to advantage all their linguistic virtuosity.

There is no such subject-matter available. Their training has unfitted them for the rendering of either those religious-political-and-epic or those humane-philosophical-and-dramatic subjects that were formerly the special domain of poetry. They are like certain scions of ancient families who have been brought up to look and act like aristocrats but who don't know beans about government. They even write more like heirs of the great dead than like creators of living literature. Their minds are full of noble-sounding words and a complete incomprehension of everything that takes place beyond the rise and fall of their own libidos. They cannot observe; they cannot even use words and syntax objectively. They are incurably egocentric.

This explains the high mortality, both literary and physiologi-
cal, that takes place among poets around the age of thirty. Faced
with a cultural as well as an economic impasse, some hang on
just long enough to finish a few extended but essentially lyrical works conceived in the mid-twenties and then die of drink,
dope, tuberculosis, or even plain suicide. Others, especially in
England, become journalistic correspondents at twenty-six. The
French tend toward the civil and consular services. Americans
become pedagogues or reporters. A few marry rich widows.
This last solution need not be counted as a literary mortality.
On the contrary, it gets the poet over some difficult years of
transition without forcing him into drugs or invalidism; so that
when the lady sees financial ruin approaching, the poet can and
most frequently does start a new literary life, this time as a prose
author with an objective method and a recognizable integration
to his time and society.

For the poet who insists on remaining a poet, there is a compromise formula. He must manage to get through his youth
either with a small patrimony or with enough health left to
allow him to work at a regular job of some kind, preferably
not connected with literature. [Grants and fellowships help.]
In this case he usually settles down in the thirties to steady
domesticity with a woman approaching (though never topping) his own social class and disappears into the landscape of
ordinary life, carefully budgeting his leisure, his income, and his
alcoholic intake. He keeps up his poetic correspondence (one
of the strange things about poets is the way they keep warm
by writing to one another all over the world) and occasionally
takes part in esthetic controversy, all the while laying regularly
but slowly his poetic eggs and publishing them in book form
at three-to-five-year intervals. These eggs are called "poems
of some length," and they essay to treat of historical or sociological subject-matter in the epic style. The manner is always
essentially lyrical, however; and since lyricism without youth,
without expansiveness, and without heat is a pretty sad affair,
the best that can be said of these estimable efforts is that they
are "the work of a mature talent," that they are "masterly,"
that they show a "profound feeling" for something or other.
The fact remains that they are fairly ineffectual and are less
read, on the whole, than his youthful works. An edition of five

hundred to two thousand copies is disposed of, with luck, to libraries and bibliophiles, both of these last being collectors of poetry for its prestige-value. Sometimes the edition doesn't sell at all, in which case the publisher puts down his loss to prestige-advertising. Most publishers do a few such volumes a year, because they think it a good idea to have some poetry in the catalogue. You never know.

These middle-aged poets are just as charming as ever and much easier for peaceable persons to go about with than the young ones, because their habits are not such a strain on one's vitality. They are busy men with always time for a chat. They love to do you favors. They are good fathers, faithful husbands, and fine hosts. Once in a while they go out on an all-night binge; and their wives don't really mind, because a binge makes hubby feel like a dangerous fellow again. It builds him up to himself. And at no risk. Because he never does anything on these nights-out but sit with a crony and talk.

Poets at any age make sound friends. They are always helping you out of jams. They give you money. They respect your working hours but don't scold you when you don't work. They practice conversation as an art and friendship as a religion. I like too their violence, their fist-fights with cops, their Parisian literary wars. [My publisher says they are more peaceful now. Does he know, I wonder, all the tougher beatniks of the San Francisco dock school? And as I write, Cocteau and Breton are still at it, with hammer and tongs, in the Paris press.] The displays of pure bitterness that one observes among them in England I find less invigorating, because the intensity of these seems to be due not so much to professional disagreement as to that exercise of social hatred within one's own class that seems to be the characteristic and special quality of British life just now. [Poets seem to have almost completely disappeared from the English literary scene.]

I like their human warmth, their copious hospitality (however poor they may be), their tolerance about morals and their intolerance about ideas, their dignified resignation at all times. I even like their wives and their animals (for they mostly have wives and they all have cats or dogs or horses). Mostly I like their incredible loyalties. They are the last of honor and chivalry. They may be sordid sots or peaceful papas or gigolos on a leash.

They imagine themselves to be knights-errant jousting before the Courts of Love. And they act accordingly, observing incomprehensibly delicate scruples, maintaining till death principles and refinements of principles that reason, common sense, and social convention have long since discarded as absurd. I knew a poet once who refused to salt his food when dining at a certain house, because, intending later to make love to the hostess, he would have considered it a breach of his obligation as a guest to attempt any violation of his host's home-life after having "eaten his salt." He was remembering, no doubt, some Arabic or medieval saw. He was not remembering that the "salt" of the precept could only have nowadays a symbolic meaning and that the food he partook of had already been salted in cooking anyway.

I like also their preoccupation with religion, the black arts, and psychoanalysis, and their inability to practice any of these consistently, even in an amateur way. They could, of course, if they were not, at the same time, so egocentric and so responsible to a tradition. Anybody can be clairvoyant or perform a miracle here and there who really wants to and who isn't afraid of the techniques. Unfortunately the techniques are all extremely dangerous to handle. That these techniques occasionally work there is, I think, no question. Illnesses, accidents, cures, and suicides, the favorable or unfavorable outcome of amorous projects and business deals, even the finding of lost objects, can be and every day are effected from a distance by interested outsiders. Prophecy is extensively carried on today through the techniques of numerology and of astrological calculation. A more active interference in other people's affairs is operated by the employment of three different kinds of technique. The hocus-pocus of medieval black art is far from uncommon, as are also the rituals of voodoo and fetich. Prayer, incantation, and trance are even commoner. Wilful exploitations of animal magnetism, of psychological domination, and of euphoric states are the bases of organized religions practicing openly. These last means are employed quite frankly in every domain of modern life, even (and by both sides) in class warfare. Organized salesmanship depends on little else, as do equally the morales of citizen armies and of militant political parties.

The poets seldom succumb to the temptation of tampering

with any of these techniques, though they are not infrequently the victims of such practice by members of their own households. They don't do it themselves because the practice of poetry is exactly contrary in method to the exertion of secret or of psychological influences. Poetry is practiced today and, so far as I know, is only practiced in the manner that used to be called the tradition of Humane Letters, which is to say that it is written by one man to be read by all men and that it makes to him who reads it exactly whatever sense it would make to any other disinterested reader. Its vocabulary consists of neutral dictionary words. Magic practices, on the other hand, require the use of an emotional and hermetic vocabulary comprehensible in its full meaning only to initiates and hence effective psychologically far beyond the dictionary meanings of the words used or the normal significance of the gestures that accompany them. For all his egocentricity, the poet is not anti-social. The practice of magic is thoroughly anti-social, because all the techniques of it depend for their working on the breakdown of somebody's personality.

Now the barriers of personality are the highest product of culture and of biological evolution. Their erection is the *modus operandi*, and the interplay of persons and groups around them is the unique end of what almost anybody means by civilization. Naturally their destruction is anti-social and anti-cultural. And just as naturally, the poets, being the direct heirs of the oldest tradition of thought in civilization, are more aware than most men of the existence of anti-cultural practices and of the danger to all concerned of any self-indulgence in that direction.

Organized religions and organized devotion to revolutionary political ideals are rarely in the long run anti-social, though I would not say so much for high-powered salesmanship. The poet's objection to organized religions (and most poets are, if not anti-religious, at least anti-clerical) is that all religions are opposed to the intellectual tradition; they are the enemies of poetry and humane letters. And so are all enterprises that keep large groups of people united by the exploitation of animal magnetism (read "sex-appeal"), mental domination, and euphoric states. Such enterprises are, by definition, not anti-social if large numbers of people are involved. They are simply anti-cultural. They may be aimed at an admirable end, and they are very tempting indeed if they seem to be about to effect political changes of a collectivist nature. But no matter how eager your poet may be to aid in the achievement of the desired end, he views with alarm any means of doing so that might render those left alive after the achieving of it mentally unfit to enjoy the thing achieved. His greatest value in revolutionary movements, for instance, is his annoyance-value, his incessant and tiresome insistence on the maintenance at all times of the full intellectual paraphernalia.

Laymen are likely to think the poets are just being fanciful when they talk about magic and sorcery. This is not so. They are talking very good sense indeed, though the terminology may be antiquated. As a matter of fact, they are the only group of men in the world that has any profound prescience about the unchaining of the dark forces that has taken place in our century. Their chief utility to us all is that they help us to fight those dark forces by the only effective means there is or ever has been. I mean the light of reason, the repetition of sage precept, and the continual application to all the dilemmas of human life of the ancient and unalterable principles of disinterested thought.

It seemed a few years ago as if psychiatry might be about to provide a bulwark against obscurantism. The number of psychiatrists and psychoanalysts who have themselves fallen for the delights of mental domination, who, by inducting their patients into a state of euphoria through which no reality can pierce, have covered up their failure to produce in these an integrated and realistic attitude toward society, the number, I say, of such physicians is too large. As venal a branch of science as that cannot be counted a bulwark of civilization. No doubt the material handled is dangerous. For the subconscious can only be plumbed by breaking down all personal barriers; there cannot be left even the curtained impersonality of the confessional. The slightest misstep in the handling of this doctor-patient intimacy produces a permanent enslavement of the patient and another scar on the already hard-boiled crust of the doctor's sensitivity. Let us charitably call such physicians "martyrs to science," like those laboratory-men who lose hands finger by finger working with radium. The intimacy of psychoanalysis is very much like radium, in fact, and like black magic too. It works, of course. But many a body and many a soul gets burned to a crisp in the process.

Poets are always getting burned; but mostly it is only their bodies that suffer, as anybody's body does who fans his youth into a flame. They rarely get burned by poetry. For the material of poetry is words, and words by themselves can only give off light. They never give off heat unless arranged in formulas. Poets hate formulas.

This is what Parisian literary wars are mostly about. They are attacks on formulas that have become powerful within the profession. The clearest statement of principle goes bad if it is repeated too often. It ceases to be a statement and becomes a slogan. It loses its clear meaning and takes on power. The literary mind considers (and rightly) that any statement which carries more power than meaning is evil. War is therefore declared on the author of the statement in point, by another author, usually on some pretext of personal prestige. As the war goes on from wisecrack to manifesto to calumny, authors get involved who don't even know the original belligerents or the incidents of provocation. Everybody calls everybody else horrid names and a great deal of wit is unleashed. Then it all dies down and everybody makes up. But the formula, having now been subjected both to the light of reason and to all the thirty-two positions of ridicule, is no longer any good to anybody. Analysis and laughter have broken its back. The Demon is foiled. Demagogy is frustrated. Poetry is thereupon vigorous again and abundant till the next time a formula starts to rear its Sacred Head.

When I speak of statements that have more power than meaning, I am not referring to hermetic poetry, obscure poetry, or ordinary nonsense. These are not meaningless matters. On the contrary, they are over-full of meaning. Some poets wish to mean so many things at once that they can only write at all by the technique of multiple meaning, the most ancient of all poetic techniques, by the way, and newly come again to favor through the prestige of the physical sciences, which have made spectacular advance in our century by means of the dissociationist discipline. There is non-Aristotelian poetry just as there is non-Euclidian geometry. You cannot subject poetry to the conventions of common sense. Not, at least, if you want it to mean anything more than journalism does. There is that kind of verse, of course, too; and it sells extremely well; but it is journalistic verse for vulgar usage, fake folklore. I might cite Kipling, Edgar Guest, R. W. Service, and E. A. Robinson as successful practitioners of it. It bears the same relation to poetry that *Mighty Lak' a Rose* does to music. Nobody in the profession takes it any more seriously than that. William Blake, Mallarmé, Gertrude Stein, and Lewis Carroll, on the other hand, however hermetic, however obscure or nonsensical, are taken very seriously indeed by the profession. They are taken as a bitter pill by many, but they are taken seriously by everybody, however little any given poet may enjoy their competition. Even the plain public knows them for original masters.

There is no way out of the poet's plight. The best he can do for the present is to write poetry as if nobody were listening (a supposition not far from the truth) and to occupy the rest of the day as best he can. Earning money by writing poetry is out of the question, unless he can adapt himself to the theater, which is not easy for him to do. The real difficulty about writing poetry is filling up the other twenty-three and a half hours a day. For, compared with the laboriousness of music writing and oil painting, there is very little real work involved in poetical composition. Lengthy reflection is involved and mental discipline and the nervous intensity of occasional concentration. But none of these takes time out of a man's life. The mind prepares itself in secret, underneath life's surface occupations. Putting down the result on paper is no job at all compared to the stroke-by-stroke improvisation of an oil-painting or the note-by-note inditing of a musical score.

If the poet works at a regular job, he hasn't got enough time to shake around and keep his ideas in solution. He crystallizes. If he doesn't work at a regular job, he has too much leisure to spend and no money. He gets into debt and bad health, eats on his own soul. It is very much too bad that his working-life includes so little of sedative routine.

I have mentioned the theater as a possible outlet for poetry and as a source of financial intake for the poet. For fifty years the poets and theater people have been flirting with one another. In the great times of poetry they did more than that, of course; but even still some poet every now and then writes a playable play in verse. In our own day E. E. Cummings, T. S. Eliot, W. H. Auden, and Bertolt Brecht have held the attention of theater audiences that did not consist merely of other poets. On the whole, however, your modern poet conceives his art as a solo performance. He despises interpreters and relinquishes with great reluctance the splendid isolation of print. Also, theater people themselves, although less devoted than poets imagine to the naturalistic style, are nevertheless a bit suspicious of the modern poet's hermetism. The poet, of course, is suspicious of everything that has to do with money-making. (Poor child, he has rarely made any since Tennyson.) Also, his confirmed egocentricity makes it difficult for him to render character objectively, which it is necessary for him to do if the poetic theater is to be anything more than a morality-play or a cerebral revue.

The musical theater, the opera, he approaches with more good will than he does the spoken theater, though he is not too happy even there about sharing honors with a composer. I realize that the composer usually steals the show, sometimes deliberately; but still it is not certain that a loyal collaboration with composers and singers would always leave the poet in second place. It most certainly would not if the art of intoned heroic declamation ever got revived. Such a revival would be necessary if tragedy were to become popular again in our ultra-musical age. And the rebirth of a popular taste for tragedy is not at all inconceivable in a world where moral elegance, economic determinism, and personal defeat are about the only aspects under which the interplay between character and social forces can be described convincingly.

Let me sum up by repeating. That music is an island, like Ceylon or Tahiti, or perhaps even more like England, which Bossuet called "the most famous island in the world." That the waters around it are teeming with digestible fish that travel in schools and are known as painters. That swimming around among these at high speed and spouting as they go are prehistoric monsters called poets, who terrify all living things, fish and islanders alike. That these monsters are quite tame, however, in spite of their furious airs, and that since they have no industrial value just now, and since their presence offers no real danger to musical life or to the fishing industry (for they attack only one another), they are allowed to survive and are occasionally given food. Indeed, their evolutions offer a spectacle that is considered by the islanders to be not only picturesque but salutary, instructive, and grand.

4

Life among the Natives

OR

Musical habits and customs

M USICAL SOCIETY consists of musicians who compose and musicians who do not. Those who do not are called "musical artists," "interpreters," executants, or merely "musicians." Those who do compose have all been executants at one time or another. One only learns to create performable works of music by first learning to perform. The longevity of musical works, however, is dependent on their being performable by executants other than the composer. This particular relation between design and execution is peculiar to music.

There is no such thing today as a serious painter who doesn't execute his own canvases. In the great days of Italian painting there was a tradition of workmanship that envisaged and even required the use of apprentice help. Veronese, for example, was a factory of which the large-scale execution and quantity production were only made possible, at that level of excellence, by the existence of such a tradition. The movie studios today produce as they do by means of a not dissimilar organization. Such formulas of collaboration are indispensable whenever a laborious art has to meet a heavy public demand. Even still the "mural" painters use assistants. But without an apprentice system of education, it is not possible to train assistants in a brush technique similar to the master's, or to depend on them for quick comprehension of his wishes. Hence the co-operation is not very efficient, and little important work can be delegated. Art-painting is really a one-man job today.

Poetry too is nowadays a one-man job. It neither derives from declamatory execution nor contemplates its necessity. Poets don't begin life as actors or elocutionists, and certainly actors and elocutionists do not commonly or normally take up poetic composition. Poetry, like prose writing, is not even recited at all for the most part. It is merely printed. Such reading of it as still goes on takes place privately, silently, in the breast; and although many efforts have been made to reinvigorate the art by bringing it out of the library and back to the stage and to the barrel-house (there is also a certain market for *viva voce* "readings" at women's clubs and on the radio and for recordings of the poet's voice), on the whole your enlightened poetry-fancier still prefers his poetry in a book. There are advantages and disadvantages in the situation, but discussion of them would be academic. The facts are the facts. And one of the cardinal facts about the poetic art today is that declamation is not essential to it.

Music is different from both poetry and painting in this respect. A musical manuscript is not music in the way that a written poem is poetry. It is merely a project for execution. It can correctly be said to consist of "notes" and to require "interpretation." It has about the same relation to real music that an architect's plan has to a real building. It is not a finished product. Auditive execution is the only possible test of its value.

Architects seem to get on perfectly well without having to pass their youth in the building trades. The successful composers of the past (and of the present) have all been musical artists, frequently virtuosos. The celebrated exceptions of Berlioz and Wagner are not exceptions at all. Because Berlioz was master of the difficult Spanish guitar, and Wagner was a thoroughly trained conductor. (He could also play the piano well enough to compose quite difficult music at it, though not well enough to perform that music effectively after it was written.) Conducting, as we know it, was at least half his invention (Mendelssohn was partly responsible too), and he wrote the first treatise on the subject. He was one of the most competent executants of his century, unbeatable in an opera-pit.

A further special fact about music writing is that it is not only a matter of planning for execution but also of planning for execution by another, practically any other, musician. It may not be better so, but it is so. Interesting and authoritative as the composer's "interpretation" of his own work always is, necessary as it is frequently for the composer, in order to avoid misreading of his intentions, to perform or conduct his own piece the first time or two it is played in public, still a work has no real life of its own till it has been conducted or performed by persons other than the composer. Only in that collaborative form is it ripe, and ready to be assimilated by the whole body of music-consumers. A musical page must be translated into sound and, yes, interpreted, before it is much good to anybody.

At this point criticism enters. It used to amuse me in Spain that it should take three children to play bullfight. One plays bull and another plays torero, while the third stands on the sidelines and cries "olé!" Music is like that. It takes three people to make music properly, one man to write it, another to play it, and a third to criticize it. Anything else is just a rehearsal.

The third man, if he plays his rôle adequately, must analyze the audition into its two main components. He must separate in his own mind the personal charm or brilliance of the executant from the composer's material and construction. This separation is a critical act, and it is necessary to the comprehension of any collaborative art-work.

Criticism of the solitary arts is possible but never necessary. In the collaborative arts it is part of the assimilation-process. It is not surprising, therefore, that the criticism of music and of the theater should be vigorously practiced in the daily press, and widely read, and that architectural criticism, which occupies whole magazines to itself, should be exercised by reputable scholars as well as by the most celebrated architects of our time, whereas the daily reporting of painting shows turns out to be almost nothing but merchants' blurbs and museum advertising. Poetry-reviewing, on account of poetry's small public, is pretty well limited to the advance-guard literary magazines. When verse is covered by the daily and weekly press, the reviewing of it is done by definitely minor poets, who fill up their columns with log-rolling.

The separateness of design and execution in the collaborative arts is not necessarily to the esthetic disadvantage of these, as the poets like to pretend. It is, on the whole, rather an advantage, I think; but we shall speak of that another time. Music's particular version of that duality, in any case, is what makes composers the kind of men they are. The necessity of being a good executant in order to compose effectively makes their education long and expensive. Of all the professional trainings, music is the most demanding. Even medicine, law, and scholarship, though they often delay a man's entry into married life, do not interfere with his childhood or adolescence.

Music does. No musician ever passes an average or normal

infancy, with all that that means of abundant physical exercise and a certain mental passivity. He must work very hard indeed to learn his musical matters and to train his hand, all in addition to his school-work and his play-life. I do not think he is necessarily overworked. I think rather that he is just more elaborately educated than his neighbors. But he does have a different life from theirs, an extra life; and he grows up, as I mentioned some time back, to feel different from them on account of it. Sending music students to special public schools like New York's High School of Music and Art or the European municipal conservatories, where musical training is complemented by general studies, does not diminish the amount of real work to be got through. It merely trains the musician a little more harmoniously and keeps him from feeling inferior to his little friends because of his musical interests. In any case, musical training is long, elaborate, difficult, and intense. Nobody who has had it ever regrets it or forgets it. And it builds up in the heart of every musician a conviction that those who have had it are not only different from everybody else but definitely superior to most and that all musicians together somehow form an idealistic society in the midst of a tawdry world.

For all this idealism and feeling of superiority, there is nevertheless a rift in the society. The executant and the composer are mutually jealous.

The executant musician is a straight craftsman. His life consists of keeping his hand in, and caring for his tools. His relation to the composer is that of any skilled workman in industry to the engineer whose designs he executes. He often makes more money than the composer, and he refuses to be treated as a servant. He is a hard-working man who practices, performs, gives lessons, and travels. He not infrequently possesses literary cultivation. He is impressed by composers but handles them firmly and tries to understand their work. His secret ambition is to achieve enough leisure to indulge in musical composition himself. Failing that, to become an orchestral conductor. He doesn't mind teaching but on the whole prefers to play. He doesn't become a confirmed pedagogue except under economic pressure, when he can't earn a living by execution. He enjoys excellent health, can't afford to waste time being ill, in fact, and often lives to an advanced age. He pretends to a certain bohemianism, is really a petty bourgeois. His professional solidarity is complete. His trade-unions are terrifyingly powerful and not unenlightened. Economically, humanly, and politically the workman he most resembles is the printer.

The composer is a transmuted executant. He practices execution as little as possible, but he hasn't forgotten a thing. It is his business to know everything there is to know about executants, because he is dependent on them for the execution of his work. Executants, being embarrassed by the composer's broader knowledge, try to avoid the composer. Composers, on the other hand, fearing to be cut off from communication with the executant world, are always running after executants and paying them compliments and begging to be allowed to play chamber-music with them, in the hope of picking up some practical hints about instrumental technique. On the whole, composers and their interpreters get on politely but not too well. Composers find executants mean, vain, and petty. Executants find composers vain, petty, and mean. I suspect the executant's potential income level, which is much higher than the composer's, is at the bottom of all this jealousy and high-hatting.

Composers by themselves don't get on too badly either, but they don't like one another really. They are jovial, witty, back-biting. When young they keep up a courteous familiarity with one another's works. After thirty they preserve an equally courteous ignorance of one another's works. Their professional solidarity is nil. Even in the well-organized and very effective European societies for the collection of performing-rights fees, they are likely to let a few semi-racketeers do the work. They grumble no end about how they are robbed by managers, by performers, and by their own protective associations; but they don't do anything to change matters. Politely gregarious but really very little interested in one another, they are without any of that huddling tendency that poets have, without the simple camaraderie of the painters, and with none of that solid fraternalism that is so impressive among the musical executants. [Enormous advances in composer solidarity, noted elsewhere in this book, have taken place since 1940.]

The island of music is laid out in four concentric circles:

¶1. The outer one defines the requirements of Minimum Musicianship. These are musical literacy and an ability to play some instrument otherwise than by ear. Singing doesn't count in the literacy test. The basic instrumental skill usually turns out to be piano-playing. There are some exceptions; but roughly speaking, our musical state can be said to consist of fourth-grade pianists.

¶2. The next circle includes everybody who can play any instrument properly. Call this the region of Special Skills. It is divided into pie-shaped sections, each representing an instrument. The pianoforte has its section here just as the other instruments do, and there is a small terrain allotted to singers. The singers who have a right to inhabit the region of Special Skills are more often than not those who have had operatic experience. Although the pie-shaped sections are pretty well walled off one from another, they are open at both ends. There is free access to them from the surrounding suburbs of Minimum Musicianship, and through any of them it is possible to pass into the higher circles.

¶3. The third region is Orchestral Conducting. Its altitude and climate are salubrious; the good things of life, including high public honor, abound. The superiority of conducting as a professional status over mere instrumental virtuosity is due to the fact that its practice requires a broader understanding of both technique and style than playing an instrument does. Its practitioners have a happy life, not only on account of the attendant honors and general prosperity, but also because it is technically the easiest specialty in all music. Residence in this region is usually limited, however, to persons who have migrated into it from the region of Special Skills. There is no other access normally.

¶4. The inner circle and summit of our mountain-city is Musical Composition. One does not have to go through Orchestral Conducting to get there; one can jump right over from Special Skills. It is a little difficult to get there directly from Minimum Musicianship. It is the summit of music because extended composition requires some understanding of all musical problems. Composers are the superior class in a musical society for the simple reason that they know more than anybody else does about music. This superiority is not necessarily reflected in their income-level.

The opera singer is a special form of singer and a special form of musician. He is the only kind of singer, for instance, who has to know something about music, though he doesn't have to know much. He bears the prestige of a great art-form and dresses handsomely for the rôle. His glamour in the nineteenth century was equal to that of conductors and movie-stars today, and he is still not badly paid when he has work.

The way he lives is the way all other executants would like to live; his house is the type-habitation of the Musical Artist. Not plain slummy like the poet's narrow hole, or barn-like and messy like the painter's, the musical artist's house or flat can best be described, I think, as comfortable but crowded. No doubt the model is, unconsciously, a star's dressing-room. It is full of professional souvenirs and objects of daily utility all mixed up together. It resembles at once a junk-shop, a photographer's vestibule, a one-man museum, and a German kitchen. There is always food around. The furniture is luxurious-looking but nondescript. No matter how spacious the rooms, the inhabitants are always too big for them.

Any musician has a tendency to fill up whatever room he is in, but the opera singer is especially permeating. He just naturally acts at all times as if he were singing a solo on a two-hundred-foot stage. His gestures are large and simple; and he moves about a great deal, never looking at anybody else and never addressing a word to anybody privately, but always speaking to the whole room. He has a way of remaining quiet, motionless almost, when not speaking, but alert, like a soloist between cues. He is hard-working, handsome, healthy (though somewhat hypochondriac). When hope is gone he drinks. Till then he cares for his health and is cheerful. He knows entertaining anecdotes and loves to do imitations of his colleagues. He lives embedded among scores and photographs and seldom moves his residence.

Composers, on the other hand, are always moving. A painter I know calls them "neat little men who live in hotel-rooms."

They are frequently unmarried; but unmarried or not, they are super-old-maids about order. [Bachelor composers, to mention only the dead, include Handel, Beethoven, Schubert, Liszt, Chopin, Brahms, Moussorgsky, Rossini, and Ravel.] The papers on their desks are arranged in exact and equidistant piles. Their clothes are hung up in closets on hangers. Their shirts and ties are out of sight, and their towels are neatly folded. There is no food around. There isn't even much music around. It is all put away on shelves or in trunks. Ink and pencil are in evidence and some very efficient rulers. It looks as if everything were ready for work, but that work hadn't quite yet begun.

Living in hotels and temporary lodgings, and frequently being unmarried, your composer is a great diner-out. Of all the artist-workers, he is the most consistently social. Those painters who live in touch with the world of decorating and fashion are not infrequently snobs, for all their camaraderie and democratic ways. The composer is not a snob at all. He is simply a man of the world who dresses well, converses with some brilliance, and has charming manners. He is gracious in any house, however humble or grand; and he rarely makes love to the hostess. He eats and drinks everything but is a bit careful about alcohol, as sedentary workers have to be.

He has small illnesses often and gets over them. His diseases of a chronic nature are likely to be seated in the digestive organs. He rarely lives to a great age unless he keeps up his career as an executant. After all, the child who practices an instrument properly usually learns to live on what muscular exercise is involved in musical practice and in the ordinary errands of education. If he continues throughout his adult life some regular instrumental activity, he keeps well and lives to be old. If he gives up that minimum of muscular movement and alternates heavy eating with the introspective and sedentary practice of musical composition, he is likely to crack up in the fifties, no matter how strong his digestive system or his inherited organic constitution.

If he can survive the crack-up, he is good for another twenty years, frequently his finest and most productive. Your aged poet is rarely as vigorous a poet as your young poet. Your aged painter is tired, and his work is repetitive. The grandest monuments of musical art are not seldom the work of senescence. *Parsifal* was written at seventy, *Falstaff* after eighty. Brahms published his first symphony at forty. Rameau's whole operatic career took place after fifty. Beethoven's last quartets, Bach's *Art of the Fugue*, César Franck's entire remembered repertory, were all composed by men long past their physical prime.

The composer does not have a turbulent life, even in youth, as artists are commonly supposed to. He is too busy working at his trade. He leads, I should say, the quietest of all the art-lives. Because music study takes time, music writing is laborious, and manuscript-work cannot often be delegated to a secretary. In middle life your composer takes rather elaborate care of his health.

His professional prestige and social charm, moreover, can bring him opportunities for wealthy marriage. His behavior in such a marriage will be described in another chapter.

5
Life in the Big City
OR
The civil status of musicians

THE MUSICAL EXECUTANT is an artisan wage-worker. He executes other men's patterns and is paid by the hour. At least, that is his minimum wage. He has no choice about what pieces he executes unless he is a soloist. A solo artist can choose among various works acceptable to the management those for which he has a special preparation. Even he cannot go far against the management's wishes, because management has full veto power at all times. Formerly only orchestral musicians belonged to a union. There is now in the United States a soloists' union also, called the American Guild of Musical Artists, an affiliate, like the American Federation of Musicians, of the American Federation of Labor. Both unions are well-organized and powerful. Both wear the same workman's uniform, which is the formal afternoon or evening dress of the upper classes. This is recognized by some tax-administrations, notably the French, as a workman's uniform, the price of one or two such outfits being deductible from any executant's annual gross income.

The organizing of musical performances is a business like fruit-vending, even though it may, as in the case of subsidized opera houses and symphonic ensembles, run a business deficit and count itself hence a philanthropy. The impresario business has begun recently, both in Europe and in America, to follow the big-business pattern of interlocking directorates and mergers. Music publishing cannot fail to follow this pattern. [Broadcast Music, Inc., or BMI, formed in 1940, constitutes a pooling of radio and recording rights for a hundred or more publishers, both "popular" and "standard."]

The composing of music, on the other hand, is a profession like engineering or literary authorship. The individual composer has usually, in consequence, a dual or even a triple status in society. As an executant he is a workman. As a publisher's employee, a concert organizer, or a salaried instructor in a school, he is either a business man or a white-collar proletarian. Teaching, as I shall explain later, is not in itself a profession.

Composition is a profession, however, just like law and medicine. To be more exact, it is a profession like literature, scholarship, science, and invention, if I may be allowed to group the professions according to their ways of collecting money for professional services. Law, medicine, architecture, and engineering operate on either the salary or the fee-system. Members of the previously named professions, however, derive their emoluments from the commercial exploitation by outsiders of patents, copyrights, and other property rights recognized by law as inherent in original work. Painters and sculptors operate on both systems. A commissioned portrait or decoration is comparable to a surgical operation, to a lawsuit, to the designing of a house or bridge. It is paid for at some price agreed upon in advance. A picture or statue executed privately and sold to the customer in its finished state occasionally gets paid for several times. Most commonly its first sale-price is all the artist ever gets out of it. But there is in France a legal provision by which the creator (and his estate for fifty years after the creator's death) receives a percentage of the profit every time a work of his is resold at an advanced price. Since most French picture-dealers keep no books, this royalty fee is really collectible only after a work has been sold twice at public auction. I mention it to show that in France, at least, the creator of plastic art has not only his right of original sale but also a legal right to share in whatever profits are derived by anybody from subsequent commercial exploitation of his work.

Such a right is granted in our western societies only to authors and original designers, rarely to executants, though the more celebrated musical interpreters and performing groups have always been paid on a royalty basis for the sale of their recordings. [In America the recording industry now pays, under union pressure, several million dollars a year into a fund that is disinterestedly administered (by a lawyer) to create work for union musicians. This is done to compensate for the non-payment of royalties to all those who have recorded anonymously for minimum fees.]

Literary workers collect royalties too on signed translations, these being considered by the Authors' League of America and by the *Société Française des Gens de Lettres* as a form of creative effort. The translator of any work that is no longer copyrighted in its original language occasionally collects a full author's-royalty (the minimum is ten per cent of the retail price). The translator of a copyrighted work merely receives either a flat sum, or a part (usually one-fourth) of the author's ten per cent. The same conditions apply to musical "arrangements," though music publishers prefer, whenever possible, to pay a fixed fee for these. ASCAP distributes performing rights for an "arranged" piece of one-tenth to one-fourth its time value as an original work.

I mention these apparent exceptions in order to make it perfectly clear that even in border-line cases our western societies consider original design as something just a little bit more important than execution. Either it is paid a special fee, or it is granted a share in the profits of exploitation, or both. And although in some cases the designer is allowed, and in others obliged, to execute his own designs, his civil status as a creator is different from and superior to that of the ordinary executant workman. The workman may earn more money. The exploiter may be a millionaire. The creator, the designer, however, has special economic rights not only in capitalist society but also in the U.S.S.R. and in the people's republics of central Europe. Persons enjoying such rights belong to what are called the Professional Classes, just as much as priests and lawyers and doctors do.

They also enjoy certain intellectual rights, commonly spoken of as their Professional Integrity. All professions bear the following marks of their integrity:

¶I. Members of the profession are the final judges on any question involving technique. This is not true in the crafts, where the worker, although he may have a better idea about execution than his director, must nevertheless follow the pattern and employ the material prescribed for him by somebody else. No executant musician, for instance, has the right to perform publicly an altered or reorchestrated version of a piece of music without the composer's consent; and he can be pursued in the courts if he does so. If a surgeon, however, prefers to cut out appendices with a sterilized can-opener, no power in western society can prevent him from doing so, excepting the individual patient's refusal to be operated on at all. The nurse, who is a craftsman, is subject to the doctor in every technical matter.

Told to administer treatment in one way, she can be denied the right to practice again in any first-class hospital if she insists on giving it in some other way. And although her expulsion from organized nursing will be voted on by her peers, her misconduct nevertheless consists in having disobeyed a formal command of the medical man on the case, that is to say, of her professional superior. Armies function in this same way, and so do police-forces. That is why soldiering is not a profession. It is a craft, because in a pinch everybody can be forced to take orders, even about technique, from some political authority. No professional man takes technical orders from anybody.

¶2. The professional groups operate their own educational machinery and are the only persons legally competent to attest its results. Nobody but a group of lawyers or doctors can certify to any state the fitness of a candidate to practice law or medicine. Nobody but the painters' section of the *Académie des Beaux Arts* can appoint other painters to judge the competitions for the *Prix de Rome* in painting. Nobody else can even set the problem. Nobody but composers can attest a student's mastery of the classical techniques of musical composition or admit him to membership in any performing-rights society. There are in America, I admit, a certain number of prize competitions still judged by orchestral conductors and concert managers, though fewer than formerly. I realize also that even trade-unions set their own standards of skill for membership. But these standards have nothing to do with real competence. They go up or down in difficulty according to the ability of the union to provide labor to the market. Some unions, that of the painters, plasterers, and paperhangers, for example, have been known to close their doors to all new membership for a period of time. This is a radical move, purely economic in motivation, that is practically never imitated by the professional bodies, receptivity toward talent being always their official policy.

¶3. Their professional solidarity is unique and indissoluble. Merchants fight one another into bankruptcy. Workmen can be turned against one another on nationalistic, religious, racial, politico-philosophical, all sorts of partisan grounds. Not so the professional men. They fight their battles in private, present a united front to the state and to the customers. They even advertise their professional differences a bit, in order to show how busy they are at keeping the tradition pure. Rarely do they allow controversy to diminish their authority or their receipts. The medical profession, ever pugnacious toward the practitioners of novel therapeutic systems (like osteopathy and chiropractic) will ostracize these if they can. If not, they invite them to join up. Every profession administers a body of knowledge that is indispensable to society, and it administers that knowledge as a monopoly. Even divinity, the most quarrelsome of the professions, has its solidarity, as witness the constant collaboration, on all sorts of public matters, of the Cardinal Archbishop of New York with the Protestant Episcopal Bishop and the leader of the Reformed Jews. In every American city the Ministerial Alliance constitutes, in fact, a sort of pooling of religious interests for the prestige of all the clergy and for advantages to religion in general.

For pedagogical purposes the professions are usually divided into the liberal, the technical, and the artistic. The first includes medicine, law, science, scholarship, and divinity. The second includes the various branches of engineering. The third is made up of literature, painting, sculpture, and musical composition. Architecture has a tendency in America to get classed with the technical group on account of its association in modern building with the engineering sciences. In Europe it is still considered, however, as one of the Beautiful Arts and is taught in the same academies as painting, sculpture, and engraving. This grouping of the liberal and technical professions versus the Beautiful Arts is embedded in our whole educational system, to the rather considerable neglect of artistic instruction. The distinction is purely a pedagogical one. In practice the professions group themselves otherwise.

Economically considered, they fall into three other groups. Law, medicine, architecture, and divinity constitute the rich group. There are impoverished persons in this group, of course, especially among the clergy. But divinity can and frequently does get very well paid, at least in perquisites; and time was when religious foundations were rich like states. Some still are. Persons exercising a profession of the rich group live chiefly on the fee, or hold-up, system. They charge what the traffic will bear.

Literature, scholarship, science, and musical composition make up the poor group. Their practitioners are small proprietors who live by leasing to commercial concerns the property rights in their work.

Painting, sculpture, and engineering are a rich-and-poor group. Their members live sometimes on fees, sometimes on royalties, sometimes, as in the case of engineers, by bartering their future patent rights against a salary. There are enormous differences of financial standing among them at any given level of competence.

Professions of this third group are loosely organized and full of dissension. Politically, their members lean to the extreme right or to the extreme left, according to the size of their income and their feeling of security in it.

Professions of the second group are moderately well-organized, and their members are for the most part politically liberal. The poets are an exception in the latter respect, because they have no incomes. They are politically radical, in consequence; at least they like to express radical opinions, of either a tory or a revolutionary nature.

Professions in the first group are highly and very competently organized. Their memberships are quick to assimilate technical advance. Politically they are conservative. And they have a complete strangle-hold on the educational system.

They seized this after the French Revolution. Rather it was offered them by a triumphant bourgeoisie, which wanted to break the power of the clergy over legal studies and of the guilds over craft-training. The latter power was particularly annoying, because the high guild-standards of workmanship and the durability of artisan products were preventing a flooding of the market with industrial stuff. So the guilds were abolished (on grounds of liberty, equality, and fraternity). Craft-training has never since been as efficient. Everybody is sent to the same public schools now and instructed in the Liberal Arts. The entire population is subjected to an enforced elementary education and a certain amount of enforced secondary education, most of which is calculated to prepare a very small number of students for entrance into the professional schools. The "professions" envisaged are three—law, medicine, and white-collar engineering, plus the pseudo-craft of pedagogy. The real crafts, including musical execution, are not much provided for; and the Beautiful Arts are considered from the consumer's and the distributor's rather than from the maker's point of view.

Professional preparation for music, painting, and sculpture were long excluded from our universities on the ground that they were not Liberal Arts. All that this meant was that they cannot be taught by mere pedagogues. They must be taught, like medicine, by practitioners. [Nowadays every college in the land offers practical instruction, with credit, in music and painting. Europe still segregates its young artists and painters in strictly professional conservatories.]

The medieval schools did not recognize the Beautiful Arts as we define them. They classed all transmissible knowledge as belonging either to the liberal arts or to the crafts. Complete instruction in both was provided for, however, in medieval society. Painting, sculpture, and architecture were considered to be crafts. Music (its grammar and composition) was listed among the liberal arts.

Today all these are certainly professions. I do not think it is possible to consider them otherwise or to describe their designers (in so far as these live by their work as designers) as belonging to any social group other than that part of the bourgeoisie known as the Professional Classes. Economically the composer acts just like a literary author. Intellectually he behaves rather like a surgeon. Morally, if I may be allowed that antiquated term to describe the way people think about themselves, he is likely to compare himself to the priest. In any case, he is a professional man. The only difference between him and the lawyer, for example, is the fact that the profession he belongs to is one that happens just now to be less generously compensated for its services to society.

6

How Composers Eat

OR

Who does what to whom and who gets paid

IT IS NOT NECESSARY here to go into the incomes of musical executants. They have engagements or they don't. If they don't, they take pupils. If they can't get pupils they starve. If they get tired of starving they can go on relief. Unemployed musicians of high ability and experience are shockingly numerous in America. The development of sound-films and the radio has thrown thousands of them into technological unemployment. The musicians' union has a very large relief budget, however, and the W.P.A. formerly gave musical work to many. Eventually their situation is that of all artisan wage-workers in crowded crafts. Their large numbers and their powerful union organization have made it advisable to handle the problem of large-scale indigence among them by means of a definite social policy. This policy is operated in part directly by the union itself (plus some free-lance philanthropic organizations like the Musicians' Emergency Relief Committee) and partly by the state and federal governments through unemployment insurance and Social Security.

Composers, being professional men and none too well organized either, have not yet found themselves the object of public concern. They do have, however, their little financial problems, I assure you, not the least of which is bare existence.

The poet of thirty works, whenever possible, at something not connected with literature. The composer practically always works at music, unless he can manage to get himself kept. He plays in cafés and concerts. He conducts. He writes criticism. He sings in church choirs. He reads manuscripts for music publishers. He acts as music librarian to institutions. He becomes a professor. He writes books. He lectures on the Appreciation of Music. Only occasionally does he hold down a job that is not connected with music.

A surprisingly large number of composers are men of private fortune. Some of these have it from papa, but the number of those who have married their money is not small. The

composer, in fact, is rather in demand as a husband. Boston
and New England generally are noted for the high position
there allotted to musicians in the social hierarchy and for the
number of gifted composers who have in consequence married
into flowery beds of ease. I don't know why so many composers marry well, but they do. It is a fact. I don't suppose their
sexuality is any more impressive than anybody else's, though
certainly, as intellectuals go, the musician yields to none in that
domain. After all, if a lady of means really wants an artistic husband, a composer is about the best bet, I imagine. Painters are
notoriously unfaithful, and they don't age gracefully. They dry
up and sour. Sculptors are of an incredible stupidity. Poets are
either too violent or too tame, and terrifyingly expensive. Also,
due to the exhausting nature of their early lives, they are likely
to be impotent after forty. Pianists and singers are megaloma-
niacs; conductors worse. Besides, executants don't stay home
enough. The composer, of all art-workers in the vineyard, has
the prettiest manners and ripens the most satisfactorily. His intellectual and his amorous powers seldom give completely out
before death. His musical powers not uncommonly increase.
Anyway, lots of composers marry money, and a few have it
already. Private fortune is a not unusual source of income for
musicians. It is not as difficult for a rich man to write music as
it is for him to write poetry. The class censorship is not so strict.
The only trouble about wealth is that spending it takes time.
The musician who runs all over town giving lessons and playing
accompaniments has often just as much leisure to write music
as does the ornamental husband of a well-to-do lady living in
five elegant houses.

Many composers are able to live for years on gifts and doles.
Include among these all prizes and private commissions. I don't
suppose anybody believes nowadays that money one has earned
is any more ennobling than money one hasn't. Money is money,
and its lack of odor has often been remarked. Gifts sometimes
have strings, of course; but so has any job its inconveniences.
Equally punctured, I take it, is the superstition formerly current
that struggle and poverty are good for the artist, who is a lazy
man and who only works when destitute. Quite the contrary, I
assure you. Composers work better and faster when they have a
bit of comfort. Too much money, with its attendant obligations,

is a nuisance to any busy man. But poverty, illness, hunger, and cold never did any good to anybody. And don't let anyone tell you differently.

The number of composers who live on the receipts from their compositions is very small, even in Europe, though on both of the northwestern continents that number is larger in the field of light music than it is in the domain of massive instrumentation and extended form. We owe it indeed to the composers of light music that we get paid at all for our performing rights, since it is they who have always organized the societies for exacting such payment and furnished the funds for fighting infringers in the courts.

Royalties and performing-rights fees are to any composer a sweetly solemn thought. They are comparatively rare, however, in America, since composers, even composers of popular music, are nothing like as powerfully organized there for collecting them as the electrical and banking interests (whose shadow darkens our prospects of profit in all musical usages) are for preventing their being collected. So that when every now and then some composer actually makes enough money off his music to sleep and eat for a while, that is a gala day for the musical art. He feels like a birthday-child, of course, and fancies himself no end. Let him. His distinction carries no security. And he had better keep his hand in at performing and teaching and writing and at all the other little ways he knows of turning a not too dishonest extra penny. He had better seize on the first flush of fame too to "guest-conduct" his own works. This brings in two fees at once, one for his conducting and one for his performing rights. Invariably the composer who has enough composer-income to live on can pick up quite decent supplementary sums, as well as keep his contacts fresh, by not giving up entirely traffic in the by-products of his musical education. [Since this was written both ASCAP and BMI have developed vastly as collectors and distributors of performance-rights in "serious" music. And the foundations are commissioning composers.]

I have been running on in this wandering fashion because I wanted to show how flexible is the composer's economic life and how many strings he has to his bow. Briefly, the composer's possible income-sources are:

¶1. Non-Musical Jobs, or Earned Income from Non-Musical
Sources.

¶2. Unearned Income from All Sources.
   [a.] Money from home
     (x.) His own
     (y.) His wife's
   [b.] Other people's money
     (x.) Personal patronage
       i. Impersonal subsidy
       ii. Commissions
     (y.) Prizes
     (z.) Doles

¶3. Other Men's Music, or Selling the By-Products of His
Musical Education.
   [a.] Execution
   [b.] Organizing musical performances
   [c.] Publishing and editing
   [d.] Pedagogy
   [e.] Lecturing
   [f.] Criticism and musical journalism
   [g.] The Appreciation-racket

¶4. The Just Rewards of His Labor.
   [a.] Royalties
     (x.) From music published
     (y.) From gramophone-recordings
   [b.] Performing-rights fees.

Every composer receives the money he lives on from one of
these sources. Most have received money from several. I have
lived on nearly all of them at one time or another.

Between the extremes of being too rich for comfort and
being really poor, the amount of money composers have doesn't
seem to affect them very much. Photogenic poverty and ostentatious spending are equally repugnant to their habits. The
source of their money has, however, a certain effect on their
work. We have noted that the composer, being a member of the
Professional Classes, enjoys all the rights and is subject to the

obligations of what is known as Professional Integrity. This does not mean that he enjoys complete intellectual freedom. He has that only with regard to the formal, or structural, aspects of his art. His musical material and style would seem to be a function, at any given moment, of his chief income-source.

7

Why Composers Write How

OR

The economic determinism of musical style

B EFORE I GO ON to explain how a composer's chief income-
source affects his musical style, I think I had better say
what is ordinarily meant by style in music. It is not the same
thing as style in literature, for instance, which is mostly considered nowadays to be personal. The word style is employed in
four ways with regard to music.

Its most precise usage is a technical one. The phrases "fugal
style," "canonic style," "modal style," and the like are all descriptions of syntactic devices. They are methods of achieving
coherence. More recent devices of similar nature are the "chromatic" style, the "atonal" style, the "dissonant tonal" style, even
the "jazz" or "swing" style. These last two refer, of course, to
rhythmic texture within a given tonal syntax; but the rhythmic
texture of jazz is just as much a technical device for achieving
coherence as the twelve-tone-row system of atonality is.

The ensemble of technical procedures plus personal mannerisms that marks the work of any given composer or period
of composition is also referred to as the style of that composer
or period. One can say that a piece is written in the style of
Schumann or in the style of Handel or in the style of Debussy.
Writing "in the style of" is taught at some music schools. It is
used in musical practice chiefly for the "faking" (improvisation
from a figured bass) of harpsichord accompaniments to pre-
nineteenth-century music and for the composition of Roman
Catholic masses, the "style of Palestrina" having been firmly
recommended to modern composers by Pope Pius X's encyclical of 1903 known as *De Motu Proprio*.

Pianistic, violinistic, vocal, and similar adjectives, when they
qualify the word "style," indicate a manner of writing that is
convenient to the instruments so referred to, that is "grateful"
to execute upon them, or that suggests their characteristics.

The word is used sometimes also in a qualitative sense. An
artist is said to perform with "good" or "bad" style. A piece may

not be said to be written in good or bad style, but if it is well written it may be said to have "style."

For the present discussion I shall try to limit the word to its first associations, to the divers syntactic devices that are available to any composer. This is the commonest usage of the word as applicable to musical composition. A composer's choice among these devices I shall call his stylistic orientation. It will not be necessary, I think, to employ the executional and qualitative meanings at all. It will be necessary, however, to distinguish between style and subject-matter.

The subject-matter of vocal music is its verbal text. The subject-matter of theater-music is whatever the stage-directions say it is. The subject-matter of an instrumental concert piece is not necessarily what the composer says it is. If he calls it *The Rustle of Spring* or *Also Sprach Zarathustra*, we can take him at his word. But if he calls it *Fifth Nocturne* or *Symphony in F*, we can never be sure. Sometimes it is an objective piece that was written to illustrate some program that he isn't telling us, and sometimes it is a depiction of non-verbalized visceral feelings. In the latter case, the subject-matter is pretty hard to describe verbally. "Absolute" was the nineteenth-century term the Germans used for such music. That meant that no matter how the composer wrote it or what he was thinking about, the piece could be satisfactorily enjoyed without verbal aids. The term "absolute" being now superannuated, I propose to substitute "introspective"; and I think we can apply it as "absolute" was applied, to all music that has no verbal text, no specific usage, and no evocative title.

Let us now return to the four sources of income and examine their relation to the composer's work in general and to his stylistic orientation in particular.

¶I. *Non-Musical Jobs, or Earned Income from Non-Musical Sources.*

The composer who lives by non-musical work is rare; but still there are some. The chief mark of his work is its absence of professionalism. It is essentially naïve. It breaks through professional categories, despises professional conventions. The familiarity with instrumental limitations and current interpretative traditions that composers have who are constantly working with the executant world is of great practical advantage in most re-spects. Your naïve composer has no such mastery of well-known methods, no such traditional esthetic. The professional makes esthetic advance slowly, if at all, progressing step by step, in touch at all times with the music world. The naïf makes up his music out of whole cloth at home. He invents his own esthetic. When his work turns out to be not unplayable technically, it often gives a useful kick in the pants to the professional tradi-tion. The music of Modest Moussorgsky, of Erik Satie, and of Charles Ives did that very vigorously indeed.

The naïfs show no common tendency in stylistic orientation. Their repertory of syntactical device is limited to what they can imitate plus what they make up for themselves. They are like children playing alone. Their subject-matter is likely to be the great literary classics, their comprehension of these atavistic and profoundly racial. They put Dante to music, and Shakespeare, Dialogues of Plato, the Book of Revelation. They interpret these in terms of familiar folklore, remembered classics, and street-noises. They derive their melodic material from hymns and canticles, from jazz-ways and darn-fool ditties. They quote when they feel like it. They misquote if they prefer. They have none of the professional's prejudices about "noble" material or about stylistic unity. They make music the way they like it, for fun. The naïfs are rare whose technique is ample enough to enable them to compete at all with Big Time. They mostly flower unknown and unheard. Those whom we do encoun-ter are angels of refreshment and light, and their music is no small scandal. Its clarity is a shock to the professional mind. It doesn't hesitate about being lengthy or about being brief, and it neglects completely to calculate audience-psychology. It is not made for audiences. As Tristan Tzara said of Dada, it is a "private bell for inexplicable needs." It is beyond mode and fashion. It is completely personal and gratuitous.

¶2. *Unearned Income from All Sources.*

[a.] *Money from home*

(x.) *His own*

The composer whose chief revenue comes from invested capital shows the following marks of his economic class:

His subject-matter reflects the preoccupations of his kind. In the present age it reflects that avoidance of serious remarks that is practiced in capitalist circles today. He tends to write playful music, to seek charm at the expense of emphasis. He abounds in witty ingenuities. He is not given much just now to writing introspective music. Before World War I, when refined Europeans with incomes gave up most of their time to introspection, both sentimental and analytic, the financially independent composer wrote a great many symphonies and reveries. Ernest Chausson and Albéric Magnard should serve to fix the pre-war type for us. Francis Poulenc will do for the European post-war capitalists. In America there is John Alden Carpenter.

The stylistic orientation of the rich composer is toward the French salon-school. He goes in for imagistic evocation, witty juxtapositions, imprecise melodic contours, delicacy of harmonic texture and of instrumentation, meditative sensuality, tenderness about children, evanescence, the light touch, discontinuity, elegance. Debussy is his ideal and model, though Debussy himself was not financially independent till after his second marriage.

(y.) *His wife's*

The composers who have married their incomes are not so likely to be Debussyans as they were in 1920. If they marry too young they don't get much time to write music anyway. They are put through the paces of upper-class life pretty much all day long. [Or else forced into films and TV and teaching, to prove to the family that they *can* earn money.] If they marry in middle life, their working habits are already formed. Also their stylistic orientation. Sometimes nothing changes at all, especially if there isn't too much wealth around. If there is a lot of it, class pressure is pretty strong. The composer subjected to this is likely to turn toward capitalistic proletarianism. There are two common forms of this. One is the exploitation of ornamental folklore (somebody else's folklore). The other is a cult of urban populistic theatrical jazz (jazz by evocation) and of pseudo-Viennese waltzes.

The relation of music-writing to unearned income is about like this. Unquestionably children get the best preparation for professional life in families that are well enough off to have access to good instruction. In families where there is big money around, the children are always kept so busy learning how to live like rich people that serious musical instruction is usually out of the question. The families of professional men, of school teachers, of civil service employees, and of shopkeepers continue to supply the bulk of talent to the artistic professions. [Skilled union labor is rising now as a favorable background for urbane leisure and educational access.] The musician rarely inherits from such a family enough to live on once he is grown and educated. In richer families he seldom learns much music. When he does, or when, having mastered his art in less disturbing circumstances, he insures his future income by marriage, there is nothing to prevent his achieving the highest distinction as a composer. He does, however, tend to write the kind of music I describe.

The sources of contributory income are without effect on the gentleman composer (or on any other for that matter), unless they provide what would be enough money to live on if he were not independent, and unless, of course, the professional experience entailed may give him a bias toward the pianoforte or the violin or some other instrument. He has class bias about both subject-matter and style, but he does not have any of the occupational conditionings of the musical journalist, of the pedagogue, or of the executant concert artist.

[b.] *Other people's money*

Let us take for granted that every professional composer has had access by one means and another to adequate instruction. It is necessary to assume this, because if he hasn't by the age of twenty-five come into contact with all the chief techniques, he must count as a naïve composer. The naïfs, like the composers of popular music, can achieve high distinction; but their music is never influenced by the source of the money they live on. If it were, they would not be naïve. Naïfs exist in all classes of society. Professional musicians are mostly bourgeois, indeed mostly petty bourgeois.

It is not certain that this is the necessary class situation of the composer, as we have just seen. It is simply that the rich are mostly too busy and the poor too poor to get educated in musical technique. Musical instruction is so expensive, even in slum music schools, that only the bourgeoisie has complete access to it; and only those families who live in the more modest economic levels of the bourgeoisie have sufficient leisure to oversee a proper musical upbringing. This is why, although there is some ruling-class art-music, there is no proletarian art-music at all except what is written at the proletariat from somewhere above. The poor farmer and the mountaineer, the slum child and the segregated Negro, have open to them only the simple popular ways, the folk-ways. They make beautiful music, very beautiful music indeed. Jazz, swing, ho-downs, chanties, hymn-lore from the Southern uplands, work-songs, dance-ditties, cowboy laments, fiddle-jigs, torch songs, blues, ballads from the barrack-room and barrel-house, children's games, prison wails, collegiate comics, sentimental love-songs, country waltzes, mambos, sambas, Lindy hops, and the syncopated Scotch-African spirituals—nine-tenths of all these are made up and brought to their definitive shape by poor people. It isn't musical vigor or inspiration that the poor lack. They have everything for making music but access to the written tradition. Massive instrumentation and the structural devices that make possible the writing of long pieces are the property of the trained musician, and he comes mostly from the lower levels of the bourgeoisie.

(x.) *Personal patronage*

Let us now tell how a composer (we have already got him educated) gets hold of money to live on when he hasn't a rich papa or wife. It is extraordinary the amounts of money, just plain gift money, that a composer with some social charm (and they all have that) can put his fingers on, especially in early manhood. Some go on getting it till they die.

There seem to be two formulas for giving money to composers. One is direct subsidy. The other is the commissioning of works. The latter is really a kind of subsidy, because the ordering of musical works is practically never an expression of a patron's or of a foundation's musical needs. Half the time they don't even have the work performed once it is delivered. In cases where they do, there is always an air of philanthropy around, and a careful disclaiming of any responsibility on the patron's part for the nature and content of the piece. The piece is usually an orchestral or chamber-work called *Symphony* or *Sonata* or something equally non-committal on the composer's part.

i. *Impersonal subsidy*

Composers living on subsidies personal or impersonal tend to write introspective music of strained harmonic texture and emphatic instrumental style. They occasionally write very long pieces. They are not much bothered about charm, elegance, sentiment, or comprehensibility, though they are seldom deliberately hermetic. They go in for high-flown lyricism and dynamic punch, less for contrapuntal texture, unless that seems to heighten lyrical expansiveness. They are revolters against convention. At least, that is their pose. Beethoven is their ideal; and they think of themselves as prophets in a wilderness, as martyrs unappreciated, as persecuted men. Appearing to be persecuted is, of course, their way of earning their living. The minute they lose the air of being brave men downed by circumstances, they cease to get free money. Because people with money to give away don't like giving it to serene or successful characters, no matter how poor the latter may be. When a composer who has been living for some years on patronage and gifts starts earning money, there is always a noticeable change in his music. His subject-matter becomes less egocentric. His musical style becomes less emphatic and a good deal easier to follow. He eventually stops over-writing the brass in his orchestral scores.

ii. *Commissions*

Composers are rare who can pull down commissions all their lives. But my theories about economic determinism do not demand that the composer live from any given source for a long time before his music begins to reflect that source. On the contrary, I maintain that composers vary their manner from piece to piece in direct conformity with their income-source of the moment, the subject-matter and the stylistic orientation of any musical work being largely determined by the source of the money the composer is living on while writing that piece.

Privately commissioned works, therefore, should show some kind of uniformity. Which they do. Less Beethovenesque than the works of the steadily subsidized, less violent, and less animated by personal dynamism, they lean toward an abstract style. I am not even certain that the international neo-classic style was not invented as a sort of *lingua franca* that could be addressed to any possible patron or patroness anywhere in the Western world. [The 1960 international style is similarly functional, but it is chromatic and twelve-tonish instead of diatonic.] During the 1920's there were just about enough available patronesses in America, France, Belgium, Germany, England, Switzerland, and Hungary, all put together, to enable a clever composer to get hold of with luck about one of these commissions a year. This gave him a basic income of from one to two thousand dollars.

What was the international style for commissioned works? It was a dissonant contrapuntal manner welded out of the following heterogeneous elements, all chosen for their prestige value:

A. The animated contrapuntalism of J. S. Bach,
B. The unresolved dissonances of Debussy and Richard Strauss, and
C. The Berlioz tradition of instrumentation.

   This is the instrumentation of Berlioz, Bizet, Saint-Saëns, Rimsky-Korsakov, Chabrier, Debussy, Ravel, and Stravinsky. It is differential instrumentation. Clarity and brilliance are achieved by keeping the different instruments at all times recognizably separate. A thin and reed-like fiddle-tone is presupposed.

   The rival tradition is that of Meyerbeer, Wagner, Brahms, Tchaikovsky, Mahler, Strauss, and Puccini. This is absorptive instrumentation. Emotional power and tonal weight are achieved by lots of doubling at the unison, which is to say by the building up of composite instrumental timbres, all sounding somewhat alike but differing greatly in weight and carrying power. It presupposes a husky and vibrant fiddle tone. The German tradition is a perfectly good one, as you can see from the big names connected with it. It has not enjoyed the same international prestige, however, since World War I, as the Franco-Russian.

D. To these elements were added frequently a fourth, the reconstructed or modern French sonata-form—a device practiced originally by the pupils of César Franck and expounded at Vincent d'Indy's Schola Cantorum.

The sonata-form was invented in Berlin by K. P. E. Bach; and it flowered in Vienna as the favored continuity device of Haydn, Mozart, Beethoven, Schubert, Schumann, Brahms, and Mahler.

It was introduced into France by Reyer in 1845, practiced and fought for by Camille Saint-Saëns, and finally domesticated by César Franck. Since the death of Johannes Brahms it has been very little practiced in Vienna. What is practiced today in Paris (and internationally) is not the Viennese sonata-form at all. It is a French reconstruction for pedagogical purposes. D'Indy is largely its inventor. It is based on certain practices of Haydn and Beethoven. It has not yet been successfully introduced into Vienna. It enjoys world-wide prestige, however, a prestige borrowed from that of the Viennese masters and based on the extreme simplicity of the reconstruction, all of which makes it just fine for the Appreciation books. The Viennese form, when it was alive, was never very teachable, because no two examples of it were ever near enough alike to make standardization possible. The good ones all seem to be exceptions to some rule of which nobody has ever seen a typical case in point. [Neither Haydn, Mozart, nor Beethoven ever spoke of sonata-form. The first reference to it in print occurs, according to Paul Henry Lang, in 1828.]

The French orchestral palette presents no especial difficulties. Any good student can handle it. And the writing of animated counterpoint in the dissonant style is easy as falling off a log. The real difficulty about any contrapuntal style is length and always has been. Now the modern-music fan likes his pieces fairly long. Nothing under twenty minutes will impress him very much. And twenty minutes of wiggly counterpoint are too much (because too vague) for anybody. [This applies equally to today's pulverized (or one-note-at-a-time) counterpoint.] Bach had the same problem to face. Fugal construction helped him over many a bad moment. But modern audiences won't listen to fugues very long or very often. They lack punch. Sonata-form, even in its rather static reconstructed version, is about the only dependable device (outside of literary texts and verbal programs) that will enable a composer to give continuity to a long and varied movement. [Today's involvement with canonic textures and rhythmic permutations, though inevitable to an atonal style, makes for even less variety.]

It offers free play to sustained lyricism, to stormy drama, and to emphatic orchestration. But there are two musical styles it cannot digest very well, the animated contrapuntal and the strictly dissonant. The first is inimical to it because that kind of counterpoint, whether practiced in a Brandenburg concerto or in an improvised jazz session, being a cerebral manifestation, is viscerally static. And sonata-form is only good for dramatizing visceral states, which are never static, which, quite to the contrary, are constantly varying in intensity, constantly moving about over the pleasure-pain and the tranquillity-anxiety scales. Systematic dissonance is inimical to the essential virtues of sonata-form for a similar reason, those virtues being all of a dramatic nature. The sonata is abstract musical theater, a dramatization of non-verbalized emotions. There is no sonata without drama, struggle, the interplay of tensions. Systematic dissonance, like systematic consonance, is the contrary of any such interplay. It too is viscerally static.

For the bright young composers of the world, who knew all this long ago, to have gone in as thoroughly as they did, between the years of 1920 and 1935, for such an indigestible mixture, such a cocktail of culture as the international neo-classic style, leaves us no out but to ascribe to them a strong non-musical motivation. The sharing of the available private commissions of the Western world among a smallish but well-united group of these composers I maintain to have been the motivation. That and the corollary activities of winning prizes and foundational awards and eventually, when all the prizes and all the possible commissions have been had, of grabbing off one of the fancier institutional teaching jobs. [The adoption after World War II of another international style (this one chromatic) and its triumph in all the European modernistic festivals, as well as over the German publishers' cartel and over the commissioning of music by European radio establishments, make it fairly clear that I was right about the earlier one.]

In any case, all international styles are God's gift to pedagogy. That we shall go into in another place, perhaps. Here just let me mention the slight but interesting differences possible within the internationalist conception.

For commissions and festivals, a long piece is indicated in dissonant contrapuntal style, neutral in emotional content and hermetic in expression. It should be a bit difficult to listen to and very difficult to comprehend, yet withal skillful enough in instrumentation that nobody could call the work incompetent. A maximum of impressiveness and a minimum of direct significance are the desiderata.

(y.) *Prizes*

For prize-competitions the above strict formula needs a little alleviation. Sometimes the injection of a lush tune here and there will satisfy the judges of the candidate's fitness for eventually pleasing a large public. More respectable, however, is the substitution of folklore for original melodic material. Folklore, as you can easily see, adds popular charm without the loss of cultural prestige. [Today folklore is out, Indian or Japanese influence very much in.] A high dosage of dissonance proves the candidate's modernism. A bit of counterpoint will show his good will toward pedagogy. And brilliant orchestration guarantees musicianship. Prize committees, mark you, never judge musical mastery on anything but orchestration. They can't. Because counterpoint is too easy to write; anyone can do it; everything sounds well enough; no judgment of its merits is possible. And harmony is difficult to judge; the gulf is of but a hairsbreadth between superb and lousy. Melodic material, tunes, can only be judged by the way they stand up under usage. Formalized construction is not one of the essential elements of music, but that too can only be judged from usage. Instrumentation is the one element of musical composition that is capable of being judged objectively today, because it is the one element that is taught, learned, and practiced according to a tradition that has been unbroken for a hundred years, and that is accepted intact, especially the French version of it, by all educated musicians.

The international-style music world used to be a well-organized going concern, with its own magazines, its "contemporary music" societies, its subsidies, its conspiracies, and its festivals. Of late years business has not been so good. Private commissions are scarce, institutional funds diminished, the societies defunct or moribund, the public fed-up. The high-pressure salesmanship that forced into the big orchestral concerts (by pretending that an international movement should be supported on nationalistic grounds) music that was never intended for anything but prize-winning and the impressing of other musicians, has given a black eye to all music written since 1918. The general music public and the trustee class have both revolted. The conductors have seized the occasion to pull all the cover over to their side of the bed, thus leaving quite out in the cold the problem of contemporary composition in large form (which presupposes as an essential factor in the equation the presence of a large general public). I know there still appear new pieces periodically on the orchestral programs, though less frequently than before 1932, the year in which the trustees of the Philadelphia Symphony Society formally warned Leopold Stokowski to lay off modern music. Everywhere the preceding decade's chief offender (the international style) is taboo. Boston is an exception in this, because one of the movement's chief survivors, Walter Piston, is head of the Department of Music at Harvard; and his works must of course be performed. The new pieces most orchestras play nowadays are in the vein of pre-war post-Romanticism. They are chiefly by school-teachers and children just out of the conservatories. They are often tuneful and pleasing. They seldom get a second performance, however, even when the first goes over big, as it does not infrequently. I don't think the conductors quite want any composer to have a very steady public success. They consider success their domain. And their success depends on keeping orchestral performance a luxury product, a miraculously smooth, fabulously expensive, and quite unnecessary frame for sure-fire classics.

[This paragraph describes the end of the Depression decade. In 1960, at the end of a boom decade, an internationally subsidized contemporary-music combine is prospering again, with trustees and general public again resisting it.]

(z.) *Doles*

A special category of patronage is the government dole. When home-relief is a composer's chief source of income, he isn't likely to write music at all. Life is too difficult, too desolate. When, as in Europe, it is less than minimum sustenance, he tends to become proletarian class-conscious, to tie up with a Marxian party (usually the Communist), and to produce angry music of exaggerated simplicity and a certain deliberate vulgarity.

The W.P.A., America's work-relief organization, never had a Composers' Project. A number of composers were engaged, however, to write music for theatrical productions; and quite a few more were placed on the regular Music Project as executants. The W.P.A. theater people did quite well by music. They showed as good taste in their choice of composers as they did in their choice of plays and directors. The Federal Theater was for the years 1935 and 1936 the most vigorous new art movement in the whole West. The music written for its productions varied greatly in style and subject-matter, as all music must that is ordered with a specific art purpose in view. The composers who wrote music for the Federal Theater are not classifiable as dole-subjects or charity-cases. They were earning their living by musical composition, and their music bears all the marks of music that has paid its way.

[Today, in 1960, there is no work-relief, only temporary unemployment insurance. Commissions designed, however, for a specific sort of performance (and paying for that performance), such as The Ford Foundation orchestra and opera commissions, are not dissimilar to work-relief, though they are aimed less at helping composers than at creating repertory.]

¶3. *Other Men's Music, or Selling the By-Products of His Musical Education.*

[a.] *Execution*
People who earn their bread by playing the piano or playing the organ or playing the violin or conducting, by musical interpretation in short, are the most timid of all when they start writing music. They have only one idea in their heads and that is to write "gratefully" for the instrument in question. They often succeed in doing so. Their subject-matter is likely to be pale, wan, and derivative.

This was not always so. Exploring the musical possibilities of any new instrument or medium is a job for persons who play that instrument. The history of violin-composition in the seventeenth century, of writing for the harpsichord and for the organ clear up to the death of J. S. Bach, of piano music in the nineteenth century, of jazz music in our own, is the history of performing virtuosos who composed. From the time of Corelli and Domenico Scarlatti to Chopin and Franz Liszt, all the solo instruments were the springboards of musical art; and many of the greatest masters of musical composition earned their living by instrumental virtuosity, even by the interpretation of other men's work. Richard Wagner was about the last of the great interpreter-composers in the non-popular tradition. [Strauss and Mahler were also conductor-composers. Today we have Manuel Rosenthal, Leonard Bernstein, Juan José Castro, and Carlos Chavez.]

Today all composers can play an instrument still, and most can conduct if they have to, but they avoid doing either steadily. Instrumental virtuosity and the interpretation of "classical" music have both reached the point of diminishing artistic returns to the composer. The expansion of techniques has so slowed down that regular practice is no longer a source of constant revelation to him. Rather it stupefies his imagination and limits his musical horizon.

This is not true in the jazz-world, where technique is still expanding. Duke Ellington has been a number-one jazz-pianist and a number-one jazz-composer. But the music of Ignaz Paderewski, of Ferruccio Busoni, of Charles-Marie Widor, and of Fritz Kreisler (even including his clever fakings of early violin-writers) cannot possibly be considered to be anything like so high-class as their respective instrumental performances were.

A bit of concert work is good for composers in their youth. The organ and the kettledrums seem to be especially useful for amplifying the musical conceptions of people brought up on the pianoforte or the violin. The first introduces them to quantitative meter. The second sharpens their sense of pitch. Both are invaluable trainings in rhythmic exactitude and in notation.

[b. and c.] *Organizing, publishing, and editing*

The organizing of concerts and the publishing business are both bad for composition. They are businesses, not crafts. They contribute nothing to a composer's musical experience. The composers who get involved with them write music less and less. Arranging and editing are all right. The trouble with them is that they don't pay enough. It is rare that a composer can exist on their proceeds for any length of time. They are best done by performers and conductors as a side-line.

[d.] *Pedagogy*

I sometimes think the worst mischief a composer can get into is teaching. I mean as a main source of income. As a supplementary source a little of it doesn't hurt, is rather good, in fact, for clarifying and refreshing the mind. A little criticism or musical journalism is good too. A lot of either is not so good, because they both get you worried about other men's music. Whenever the by-products of his musical education become for any length of time the main source of a composer's income, occupational diseases and deformities set in.

As everybody knows, school-teachers tend to be bossy, pompous, vain, opinionated, and hard-boiled. This is merely their front, their advertising. Inside they are timid and over-scrupulous. Their music, in consequence, comes out looking obscure and complex. Its subject-matter, on the other hand, and its musical material are likely to be over-subtle and dilute. When we say nowadays that a work is "academic" we mean all this and more. We mean that the means employed are elaborate out of all proportion to the end achieved.

When I speak of pedagogues I mean teachers who live by their teaching, whether they teach privately or in institutions. All teachers who live by teaching are alike. The holders of si-necure posts are an exception. The director of any French con-servatory, for instance, is always an elderly composer of distinc-tion. He is not expected to do anything but an overseer's job, to protect, from the vantage point of his years and experience, the preservation intact, with all necessary renewals, of whatever tradition of musical instruction that institution represents. He is not expected to bother with administrative detail or to drum up trade for his institution or to have anything whatsoever to do with trustees. He may dine occasionally with the Minister of Public Instruction and the Secretary for the Fine Arts. An hour a day will cover all his duties. His job lasts till he dies, short of public moral turpitude on his part. A smaller sinecure sometimes available to young composers is the librarianship of a conservatory. The rarity of sinecures in the United States is one-half the trouble with music-teaching. Save for the oc-casional composer-in-residence who teaches part-time, almost any young person's college job ends by taking about fifty hours a week to accomplish and to keep. The other half is what is the matter with music-teaching anywhere, with living off any of what I have called the by-products of a musical education. It is the constant association with dead men's music that they entail. Only in vacation time, if there is any money left to take a vacation, does the school-teacher get a chance to forget all that, to put the classics out of reach at the bottom of his mind, well out of the way of the creative act. Daily dealing with the music of the past is probably all right after fifty. It never fails to produce in a younger man a derivative manner of writing that no amount of surface-complexity can conceal.

Teachers tend to form opinions about music, and these are always getting in the way of creation. The teacher, like the parent, must always have an answer for everything. If he doesn't he loses prestige. He must make up a story about music and stick to it. Nothing is more sterilizing. Because no one can make any statement three times without starting to believe it himself. One ends by being full of definite ideas about music; and one's mind, which for creative purposes should remain as vague and unprejudiced as possible, is corseted with opinions and *partis pris*. Not the least dangerous of these *partis pris* is the assumption that since the finest examples of musical skill and stylization from the past (the so-called "classics") are the best models to expose before the young, they are necessarily the best models for a mature composer to follow in his work. This is very nearly the opposite of the real truth. As Juan Gris used to say about painting, "the way to become a classic is by not resembling the classics in any way."

When I speak of teaching, I mean teaching for money; and I deplore it, for composers, as a habit-forming vice. I would not wish, however, that the young composer be denied access to professional advice. He is, in fact, not denied it. Professional composers are only too delighted to read over the works of the young and to give practical advice where needed. They enjoy the homage implied; they like the chance to steal a good trick; they like seeing their own tricks stolen and advertised. All this can take place without any exchange of money. It is free graduate-instruction. Elementary instruction (which is a bore to give) must always be paid for, and usually the student gets his best money's worth from regular pedagogues who are not composers.

Allow me, please, at this point to digress a little further on the subject of how people learn to write music. You never learn anything technical except from somebody who possesses technique. You can only learn singing from someone who has sung, piano-playing from a reasonably competent pianist, conducting from a conductor; and you can only acquire so much of these techniques as the instructor himself has mastered. There are, however, elementary subjects which are so conventional that their mastery requires no personalized skill and implies no higher achievement. It is not necessary, for example, or even very desirable to try to learn grammar from a poet. Any school-teacher is better, can show you better how to parse, decline, and diagram according to accepted convention. So with solfeggio, counterpoint, fugue. They are stylized drills, not living skills. Harmony is the difficult branch to learn, because it is neither really stylized nor really free. I doubt if anybody can teach it satisfactorily; but even still a routine pedagogue is usually quicker and more effective about it than a composer is. Orchestration is different. It can only be learned from a composer or from a professional orchestrator. The subject is a completely practical one and requires a practical man. All the text-books are by practical men like Berlioz and Strauss and Rimsky-Korsakov and Widor. Musical form is also a practical matter. It is scarcely a subject at all and can only be advised about after the fact. There is no text-book on the subject, no formal instruction available.

How then can musical education be organized so that the instructor's as well as the student's interest may be respected? Singing and playing must be taught, as they are now, by singers and players or by ex-singers and ex-players. The elements of musical theory (that is to say harmony, counterpoint, fugue, and musical analysis) should be taught, as they are not always now, by trained seals, which is to say by persons especially prepared for that drill-work, by pure pedagogues. Instrumentation must be taught by composers; there is no way around it. But since the composer is not much benefited musically by teaching, some arrangement must be reached that will serve his interests as well as the student's. One of the best is to use as professors of instrumentation only men over fifty. These can teach an hour a day something they know without getting vicious about it. Also, the whole system of musical instruction must be co-ordinated and watched over by a composer, an elderly one preferably, and one for whom the job is either a sinecure or else a quite negligible source of income. It should never be full-time work.

As for the actual composition of music in the early stages of a student's career, he had better keep that as separate as possible from his life as a student. Let him show his efforts to other composers, to friends, to anybody but to his professors. Unless the teacher in question is or has been a successful composer, the student will only get confusion and discouragement out of him.

[e. and f.] *Lecturing, criticism, and musical journalism*
Turning an odd penny here and there by lecturing doesn't count. Earning one's bread by lecturing does. But lecturing is not a trade in itself; it is always something else. Either it is teaching, or it is criticism, or it is the Appreciation-racket, or it is musical interpretation. Sometimes it is all four. I mention it separately, merely because it is a common way of earning money.

Criticism and musical journalism are also frequent sources of contributive income to composers. They seldom provide a full living. The only kind of written musical criticism that really feeds its writer is a permanent post on a metropolitan daily. Musical composition seems to be quite impossible to combine with such a full-time job. [I managed it, all the same, as music critic of the New York *Herald Tribune* from 1940 to 1954.] In any case, these "major" critics never seem to write much music, not the way dramatic critics write plays. Writing occasional articles, however, is an inveterate habit of composers. The profession is incurably literate. Such writing is interesting to the musical public, because it is both authoritative and passionately prejudiced. It is interesting to the composer because he can use it to logroll for his friends and to pay off old scores against his enemies, as well as to clarify for himself periodically his own aesthetic prejudices. Also, the forced attendance at concerts that writing criticism entails keeps him informed of current trends in musical production. Left to himself, he has rather a tendency to avoid hearing music, to insulate himself against all currents and to fecundate in a vacuum. Now a vacuum is not a very good place to fecundate in; at least it is not a good place to cook up collaborative art. Daily intercourse with other men's music deforms any composer's work in the direction of a rather timid traditionalism. Such is the music of the school-teachers, the choir-masters, the touring virtuosos, and the conductors. But a complete ignorance of what is going on in the world of music is even more deforming. One doesn't so much need to know what the other composers are up to as one needs to know what the interpreters are up to. One needs to keep in touch with what happens when scores get made audible.

Painters can fecundate in a vacuum if they really have to; the naïve painters are numerous. Poetry too can flourish far from the madding crowd and often does, going off periodically into hermit-like retirement being quite a habit of poets. Think too of all the excellent lyrical verse that gets written year after year by private persons. Music, even naïve music, has always been written in or near the great centers of musical activity. The isolated composer, like the isolated surgeon or architect, is a rare animal.

As I said before, contributive sources of income seldom influence a composer's stylistic orientation. Only a full support can do that. Their chief influence is technical. Just as a little teaching is good for any musical executant, and a little musical execution for any composer, a little criticism is a valuable experience too for any musician. It teaches him about audiences. Nobody who has ever tried to explain in writing why some piece got a cold reception that he thought merited better, or why some musical marshmallow wowed them all, has ever failed to rise from his desk a wiser man. And the composer who has written criticism with some regularity—who has faced frequently the deplorable reality that a desired audience-effect cannot be produced by wishful thinking—inevitably, unconsciously, in spite of his most disdainful intentions, cannot help learning a good deal that is practical to know about clarity, coherence, and emphasis.

Composers' criticism is useful to the layman also. As I have said before, the function of criticism is to aid the public in digesting musical works. Not for nothing is it so often compared to bile. The first process in that digestion is the breaking-up of any musical performance into its constituent elements, design and execution. In this analytic process, the composer is of the highest utility. All musicians can judge the skill of a musical execution, because all musicians are executants. (The practice of publishing musical criticism written by musical illiterates is disappearing from even the provincial press.) But if the critic is only an executant and has never practiced musical creation, his interest is held far more by the refinements of execution than by the nature of the music itself. Inevitably he tends to glorify the executant (with whom he identifies himself) and to neglect or to take for granted the piece played. Because of the fact that performers advertise and composers don't, the criticism of composition in the musical trade-weeklies is a complimentary gesture only and is extremely limited in space. Even the daily press, for all its official good will toward novelty, cannot get around the fact that the work of prosperous persons like conductors, opera-singers, and touring virtuosos has more "news-value" than the work of composers, most of whom don't even make a living from their work. So that inevitably most musical criticism is written from the performer's point of view.

The composer-critic identifies himself imaginatively with the author of any work he hears. He knows exactly (or has a pretty good idea) when the composer and the interpreter are in the groove and when they are getting in each other's hair. He is likely to be a shade indifferent about execution, unless the latter is quite out of keeping with the style of the work executed. Nevertheless, he does know about execution, in addition to knowing about design; and he can explain to others wherein their pleasure or displeasure is due to the design and wherein to execution and where to a marriage of the two.

The criticism of poetry is written nowadays almost exclusively by poets for other poets to read. It is highly technical and bitterly controversial. The layman scarcely ever sees it. It has nothing to do with any absorptive process among the reading public, because there isn't any reading public for poetry. The criticism of painting is written by collectors, museum-directors, and dealers' hired men. Since a painting is a piece of property and hence always belongs to somebody, any criticism written by the person it belongs to or by anybody connected with him or by anybody who has a rival picture or kind of picture to sell or who makes his living by showing pictures or by advising buyers, is about as interesting as musical criticism would be if it were written by the manager of the New York Philharmonic. Painters writing about one another, when they don't go over-fulsome, can be pretty nasty; they often lack even that commercial courtesy that dealers' representatives preserve toward one another. Prefaces to the catalogues of dealers' shows and many of their reviews are blurbs by unemployed poets; they are not even openly paid advertising. The writing of art-history (which is criticism too, of course) is more reliable. At least it is when it is written by scholars with a steady job and no dealer- or museum-connections. On the whole, there just is no criticism of contemporary painting and not very much of poetry. There is only blurb and bitterness.

Music, theater, and architecture have a copious literature of contemporary criticism, because they have, to begin with, a public, and because that public is essentially disinterested. It doesn't own works of music or plays; and works of architecture, though they are real property, are not often owned by the persons who use them. The dominating rôle in this copious literature of criticism is played by the composers, the dramatic authors, and the architects themselves. Dancing and the movies have also a good public, and lots of criticism of them gets published. Most of it, unfortunately, is either trivial or venal, because choreographers and cinema-directors, the only people who know anything about design in their respective arts, have so far mostly kept out of it.

No art in its first expansive period needs criticism anyway. There isn't time to bother with anything but creation and distribution. With further expansion of the movie-trades momentarily arrested by international trade-wars, by financial crises, and by the menace of television, a certain amount of soul-searching does go on in the movie-world; and a few historical books have been written. It is quite certain that if the movies continue to function as an entertainment-form we shall see an increasing amount of critical writing about them from persons experienced in their making. [Ditto for television.]

[g.] *The Appreciation-racket*

Every composer is approached from time to time by representatives of the Appreciation-racket and offered money to lecture or to write books about the so-called Appreciation of Music. Unless he is already tied up with the pedagogical world, he usually refuses. If he makes his living as a teacher, refusal is difficult. I've seen many a private teacher forced out of business for refusing to "co-operate" with the publishers of Appreciation-books. Refusal of public-school credits for private music-study is the usual method of foreclosure. The composer who teaches in any educational institution except a straight conservatory is usually obliged to "co-operate." The racket muscles in on him. His name will be useful; his professional prestige will give a coloration of respectability to the shady business. He is offered a raise and some security in his job. He usually accepts.

Every branch of knowledge furnishes periodically to the layman digests of useful information about that branch of knowledge and elementary hand-books of its technique. Simplified explanations of the copyright laws, of general medicine for use in the home, of the mathematics of relativity, of how to build a canoe, a radio-set, or a glider, of home dressmaking, of garden-lore, of how to acquaint yourself with classical archaeology in ten volumes, and of how to see Paris in ten days—this literature is in every way legitimate. Some of the most advanced practitioners in every branch of knowledge have at one time or another paused to write down in non-technical language what was going on in those branches. The artistic professions have a large literature of this sort, the present book being an example. Biographies of celebrated musicians, histories of the symphony orchestra with descriptions of the commoner instruments, synopses of opera plots, memoirs of singers and their managers, even of musical hostesses, all go to swell the general knowledge about music and how it lives. Works of a scholarly or pedagogical nature, like treatises on harmony, on acoustics, on instrumentation, or bibliographies of historical documents, need no justification at all. They are instruments for the direct transmission of professional knowledge.

What needs some explaining is the Appreciation-literature, which transmits no firm knowledge and describes no real practice. The thing nearest like it is the physical culture advertisement that proposes to augment the muscular and virile forces of any customer who will buy the book and do what it says for five minutes a day. Obviously, five minutes a day of gymnastics, any kind of gymnastics, with or without a book, will inside a week produce a temporary enlargement of the muscles exercised. Equally, the deliberate listening to music, any kind of music, five minutes a day for a week will sharpen momentarily the musical listening-ability. If the Appreciation-racket were no more than a pretext for habituating listeners to musical sounds, it would be a legitimate advertising device, destined, with luck, to swell the number of possible concert-customers.

What distinguishes it from the physical culture schemes is

the large number of reputable musicians, philanthropic foundations, and institutions of learning connected with it and the large amounts of finance-capital behind it. So much money and so much respectability behind a business that hasn't very much intrinsically to recommend it is, to say the least, suspect.

When I say the books of Music-Appreciation transmit no firm knowledge and describe no real practice, you will either believe me or you won't. I have no intention of exposing in detail here the operating methods of that sinister conspiracy or of attacking by name the distinguished musicians who have signed its instruments of propaganda. If you are a musician, all I need say is, just take a look at the books. If you are not, avoid them as you would the appearance of evil.

It is as difficult for the layman to avoid contact with Music-Appreciation as it is for the musician. Children in elementary schools get it handed out to them along with their sight-singing. So far as it is just a substitution of European folklore for American folklore and made-up exercises, not much real harm is done. At least, not as long as the center of attention remains instruction in sight-singing rather than the tastefulness of the pieces sung. It is in the secondary schools, with the introduction into education of mere listening, that is to say, of a passive musical experience, to replace performance, which is an active experience, that Appreciation begins to rear its ugly head. In secondary schools, especially in those where instruction is accomplished according to the pedagogic devices known as Progressive Education, passivity seems to be the chief result sought. A proper, that is to say, an enthusiastic, receptivity to canned musical performance is highly prized by "progressive" educators.

In colleges the Appreciation of Music is a snap course, and as such it fills a need for many a busy (or lazy) student. As anything else it is hard to defend. For professional music-students it is confusing, because the explanations are esthetic rather than technical; and esthetics are a dangerous waste of time for young practical musicians. What they need is musical analysis and lots of execution according to the best living traditions of execution. For non-professional students also it is a waste of time that might be spent on musical practice. The layman's courses for adults in ordinary civil life are an abbreviated version of the collegiate Appreciation-courses. They offer nothing more (technically) than could be learned in one music lesson from any good private teacher. The rest is a lot of useless and highly inaccurate talk about fugues and sonata-form, sales-talk for canned music really.

The basic sales-trick in all these manifestations is the use of the religious technique. Music is neither taught nor defined. It is preached. A certain limited repertory of pieces, ninety per cent of them a hundred years old, is assumed to contain most that the world has to offer of musical beauty and authority. I shall explain in a moment how this repertory is chosen by persons unknown, some of them having no musical authority whatsoever. It is further assumed (on Platonic authority) that continued auditive subjection to this repertory harmonizes the mind and sweetens the character, and that the conscious paying of attention during the auditive process intensifies the favorable reaction. Every one of these assumptions is false, or at least highly disputable, including the Platonic one. The religious technique consists in a refusal to allow any questioning of any of them. Every psychological device is used to make the customer feel that musical non-consumption is sinful. As penance for his sins he must:

A. Buy a book.
B. Buy a gramophone.
C. Buy records for it.
D. Buy a radio.
E. Subscribe to the local orchestra, if there is one.

As you can see, not one of these actions is a musical action. They are at best therapeutic actions destined to correct the customer's musical defects without putting him through the labors of musical exercise. As you can see also, they entail spending a good deal more money than a moderate amount of musical exercise would entail. Persons whose viscera are not audito-sensitive need very little musical exercise anyway. To make them feel inferior for not needing it and then to supply them with musical massage as a substitute for what they don't need is, although a common enough commercial practice, professionally unethical.

If you will look at almost any of the Appreciation-books you will notice:

A. That the music discussed is nearly all symphonic. Chamber-music (except string-quartets) and the opera are equally neglected.
B. That the examples quoted are virtually the same in all the books.
C. That they are quoted from a small number of musical authors.
D. That 90% of them were written between 1775 and 1875 and are called Symphony Number Something-or-Other.

All this means that by tacit agreement Music is defined as the instrumental music of the Romantic era, predominantly symphonic and predominantly introspective. At least that that repertory contains a larger amount of the "best" music than any other. This last assumption would be hard to defend on any grounds other than the popularity of the symphony orchestras (plus their gramophone recordings and radio transmissions) performing this repertory.

A strange thing this symphonic repertory. From Tokyo to Lisbon, from Tel-Aviv to Seattle, ninety per cent of it is the same fifty pieces. The other ten is usually devoted to good-will performances of works by local celebrities. All the rest is standardized. So are the conductors, the players, the soloists. All the units of the system are interchangeable. The number of first-class symphony orchestras in the world is well over a thousand. Europe, exclusive of the Soviet Union, counts more than two hundred. Japan alone is supposed to have forty. They all receive state, municipal, or private subsidy; and the top fifty have gramophone- and radio-contracts. All musical posts connected with them are highly honorific. Salaries, especially for conductors and management, are the largest paid anywhere today in music. The symphony orchestras are the king-pin of the international music-industry. Their limited repertory is a part of their standardization. The Appreciation-racket is a cog in their publicity machine.

It is not my intention here to go into the virtues and defects of the system beyond pointing out that the standardization of repertory, however advantageous commercially, is not a result of mere supply and demand. It has been reached by collusion between conductors and managers and is maintained mostly by the managers, as everybody knows who has ever had anything to do with the inside of orchestral concerts. To take that practical little schematization of Romanticism for the "best" in music is as naïve as taking chain-store groceries for what a gourmet's merchant should provide. For a composer to lend the prestige of his name and knowledge to any business so unethical as that is to accept the decisions of his professional inferiors on a matter gravely regarding his profession. I do not know whether it would be possible to publish a book or offer a course of instruction in music-appreciation that would question the main assumptions of the present highly organized racket and attempt to build up a listener's esthetic on other assumptions. I doubt if it would, and the experience of various well-intentioned persons in this regard tends to support my doubts. Their attempts to disseminate musical knowledge among musically illiterate adults seem to have led them eventually to substitute for instruction in listening some exercise in musical execution, such as choral singing or the practice of some simple instrument like the recorder. It would seem that such execution, which, however elementary, is a positive musical act, gives not only its own pleasure of personal achievement but also not inconsiderable insight into the substance of all music.

Do not confuse the Appreciation-racket with the practice of musical analysis or with the exposition of musical history. These are legitimate matters for both students and teachers to be occupied with. I am talking about a real racket that any American can recognize when I describe it. It is a fake-ecstatic, holier-than-thou thing. Every school and college, even the most aristocratically anti-musical, is flooded with it. Book-counters overflow with it. Mealy-mouthed men on the air serve it in little chunks between the numbers of every symphony-orchestra concert broadcast. It is dispensed in high academic places by embittered ex-composers who don't believe a word of it. It is uncritical, in its acceptance of imposed repertory as a criterion of musical excellence. It is formalist, in its insistence on preaching principles of sonata-form that every musician knows to be either non-existent or extremely inaccurate. It is obscurantist, because it pretends that a small section of music is either all of music or at least the heart of it, which is not true. It is dogmatic, because it pontificates about musical "taste." Whose taste? All I see is a repertory chosen for standardization purposes by conductors (who are musicians of the second category) and managers (who are not even musicians), and expounded by unsuccessful pianists, disappointed composers, and all the well-meaning but irresponsible little school-teachers who never had enough musical ability to learn to play any instrument correctly.

The musical ignorance of the army of teachers that is employed to disseminate Appreciation should be enough to warn any musician off it. Most composers are wary at first. Then it becomes tempting, because the money looks easy; and they think they at least will not be disseminating ignorance. Also in academic posts there is considerable straight pressure brought to bear. Nine times out of ten the young composer who is trying to make a modest living out of teaching harmony or piano-playing is ordered to get up a course in Appreciation (the tonier institutions are now calling it Listening) whether he wants to or not. He can make his own decision, of course; but I am telling him right now what will happen if he gets caught in those toils. He will cease to compose.

It always happens that way. No professional man can give himself to an activity so uncritical, so obscurantist, so dogmatic, so essentially venal, unless he does it to conceal his fundamental sterility, or unless he does it with his tongue in his cheek. In the latter case he gets out of it pretty quick. In the former case he gets out of composition instead. He gets out with some regret, because his professional status is lowered. But there is nothing to be done about that. Appreciation-teaching is not even a Special Skill of any kind. It is on the level of Minimum Musicality, as everybody in music knows.

So your composer who sticks at it becomes an ex-composer and an embittered man. Always beware of ex-composers. Their one aim in life is to discourage the writing of music.

[These paragraphs on Music Appreciation have been preserved in the present edition because I enjoy their fine fury. Also because they brandish for the first time two fighting terms that have since been widely used in musical polemics. These are Appreciation-racket and the Fifty Pieces. Both are still capable of inflicting insult because both still bear a high percentage of truth. Within two years, indeed, after this book's appearance, documented studies of both subjects had become available—of music as it was being explained to laymen over the radio by the late Walter Damrosch, and of the standard orchestral repertory as programed by sixteen subscription societies since 1812. The Appreciation studies appeared in a quarterly published by the Institute of Social Research, *Studies in Philosophy and Social Science*, later in book form. The orchestral repertory was analyzed in a 1941 pamphlet from the University of Indiana by Dr. John H. Mueller and his wife Kate Hevner, these studies being later amplified and published in book form by Dr. Mueller.

Both books are now standard texts in musical sociology. And they are far more devastating than my remarks. The researches that went into these studies, though in progress when I wrote this book, had not yet appeared in print. Nor was I aware of them. But the disquiet that musicians felt about Appreciation and about the standardized repertory had already so far penetrated the universities that sociologists had picked these subjects out as matters meriting investigation.

As of 1960, the radio offers little of either Music Appreciation or orchestral repertory. The explaining of music to laymen in our colleges is pretty firmly in the hands of musical technicians. (Even musicologists are not generally allowed to teach the course.) And orchestral performances are disseminated for the most part (in America) by public concerts and by recordings. The recording companies still restrict their orchestral output to fairly familiar stuff, indeed very much so right now, the vogue for stereophonic or binaural reproduction having given them another excuse for recording the standard works all over again. They have usually found some such technological pretext about every ten years since recording began, and they will go on doing so, I am sure, until philanthropic (or government) subsidy shall have taken the responsibility for recording symphonic, chamber, and operatic music out of commercial hands, as it did long ago their performance.]

¶4. *The Just Rewards of His Labor.*

This brings me to the last kind of composers' income, namely, receipts from his own musical works as published, performed, or recorded. It is sad that these should come last. If they were not so rare they would naturally have come first. Well, the facts are the facts. Performing-rights fees and royalties on copies sold are about the last thing any composer need ever expect to live on. His children sometimes come in for a bit of gravy. (The heirs of Ethelbert Nevin are doing quite well, thank you.)

I had better explain here something about royalties and performing-rights fees. Printed music brings to its composer (theoretically) a fee of ten per cent of the marked retail price for every copy sold. I say theoretically, because many European publishers don't pay anything to the author. They think they are doing enough for him when they publish his work at all. If he pays the expenses of publication, he is usually allowed his ten per cent. Gramophone recordings also bring to the composer a royalty of so much per record sold. This fee is generally paid. The performing-rights fees of published music, like the recording fees, are currently shared between the publisher and the composer. If a piece has words, the author of the words gets a part of the composer's share.

There exist in all Western countries mutual protective societies of composers, authors, and publishers, whose purpose in life is to enforce the payment of performing-rights fees by producing organizations. In Europe these societies cover all the public usages of music, whether there is an admission-charge or not, by cinemas, theaters, broadcasting stations, opera houses, concert halls, churches, cafés, night-clubs, and municipalities. Even musical mendicants are not exempt from payment. In the United States the American Society of Composers, Authors, and Publishers, commonly known as ASCAP, functions similarly, but really covers not much except the usages of dance music and popular songs. [More now, especially from radio.] Theatrical music is covered, by courtesy, through the Dramatists' Guild of the Authors' League of America. No performing-rights fees are collected in America at all, except by individual contract (which means there is no minimum payment), from symphony orchestras, traveling concert-artists, the major opera houses, the churches, schools, colleges, and clubs. [The last four are still exempt.] In many cases of unpublished works in large form played by chamber or symphonic organizations, no fee is paid to the composer at all, not even a rental fee for the use of score and parts. This situation will not long continue, but for the present it is the case. It is the unique and sole reason for the existence in Europe of a much larger number of art-composers who live off their just share in the profits of the commercial exploitation of their work than exists in the United States. [Still true.] Such composers are almost non-existent in America. Let us call them, for the sake of brevity, successful composers (successful being understood here to mean earning a living by writing music).

Of all the composing musicians, this group presents in its music the greatest variety both of subject-matter and of stylistic orientation, the only limit to such variety being what the various musical publics at any given moment will take. Even the individual members of the group show variety in their work from piece to piece. This variety is due in part to their voluntary effort to keep their public interested and to enlarge their market. (Stylistic "evolution" is good publicity nowadays.) A good part of it is due also to the variety of usages that are coverable by commercially ordered music. Theater, concert, opera, church, and war demand a variety of solutions for individual esthetic cases according to the time, the place, the subject, the number and skill of the available executants, the social class, degree of musical cultivation, and size of the putative public. Music made for no particular circumstance or public is invariably egocentric. Music made for immediate usage, especially if that usage is proposed to the composer by somebody who has an interest in the usage, is more objective and more varied.

Successful composers are often accused of repeating themselves. In real truth they repeat themselves less often than the unsuccessful ones do. The latter keep writing the same piece over and over in the hope they can make it clearer next time, make people understand somehow. Successful men are often accused of "compromising," too, of compromising with public taste (which is assumed to be bad taste and profitable to cater to). I assure you that first-string composers have reputations to keep up, and that anyone who has a paying public (however small) is less tempted to "write down" to that public than the prize-and-commission-supported are to "write up" to musical snobs. I also assure you that public taste is not necessarily bad taste, any more than private taste is necessarily good taste, and that the quickest way for a successful composer to stop being a success is for him to vulgarize his work. Success is like travel; it broadens a man, makes him at once more objective and more passionate about the things that matter to him. There must be inconveniences about living off the just rewards of one's labor, but I don't know what they are. I have never known an artist of any kind who didn't do better work when he got properly paid for it.

The composer who lives on music-writing invariably tends toward the theater. Handel and Verdi and Gershwin are classic examples. I do not know, in the last two or three hundred years, of any composer who has lived for very long off the commercial profits of symphonic and chamber music. The song-writers don't do too badly, and certainly Richard Strauss receives, now that he is old, a respectable income from his non-operatic music. [Igor Stravinsky too, since Strauss's death.] But by and large, the theater is where the money is and where most of the composers are who have once had a taste of that money. Movies, opera, incidental music, ballet, these are the musical forms that feed their man. Composers who get fed by them have plenty of time to write a more disinterested music if they wish. Many do. All I am saying is that the commercially successful professional composer (and by commercially successful I mean he eats) is likely to be a theater man. That is his occupational deformity, if any.

¶ *To sum up and conclude*:

Every composer's music reflects in its subject-matter and in its style the source of the money the composer is living on while writing that music. This applies to introspective as well as to objective music.

The quality of any piece of music is not a function of its author's income-source. One has only to remember history to know otherwise. J. S. Bach and César Franck were church organists. Handel and Verdi and Gluck and Rameau were theater men. Beethoven skimped along on patronage and publishers' fees. Wagner (after his exile) and Tchaikovsky lived on gifts. Chopin and Liszt were concert-pianists and also gave lessons. Mendelssohn was a gentleman of means. Haydn received a salary for writing music and for organizing musical entertainments at the country house of one Count Esterházy. Schumann was a

musical journalist. A great many modern composers are pedagogues. One might mention Hindemith, Schoenberg, d'Indy,
and practically all the Americans. Bernstein and Chavez are
conductors. Satie was a post-office employee, Moussorgsky a
customs official, Cui a chemist. Mozart did everything in music
at one time or another except journalism. Palestrina and Debussy lived on their musical receipts till they got tired of starving and married rich widows. One could go on, but I think this
should be enough to show that excellent music can be written
on almost any kind of money.

Anyone who wishes to follow this matter through musical
history in more detail is warned not to consider contributive
income as very important. It amplifies a composer's practical
experience, when it has to do with music; but it does not determine either his style or his subject-matter. Nothing does that
but what he is actually living on. Nothing impresses a man very
deeply except what pays him a living wage.

8

Composers' Politics

OR

Professional bodies versus the secular state

LET US DO a little more summing-up before we go on.

The composer is a neat little man who lives in a small flat or hotel-room and has charming manners. His neatness, like that of the engineers, is due to the fact that exactitude, in his profession, pays receipts. His charming manners are a result of his multiple civil status. As an executant musician or as a teacher, he is a laboring man, a time-worker, a union-member, a white-collar proletarian, skilled in class warfare and trained to conceal his class feelings. As a composer he belongs to the bourgeois Professional Classes, with all that means of pride and intellectual authority. As the author of published or frequently played works, he is a small proprietor who leases out his property-rights for exploitation by commercial interests. In these last two capacities, he enjoys the greatest access to culture and the greatest freedom of thought that our century has to offer, that of the petty bourgeoisie. As son or husband, he is not infrequently a private capitalist, a man of means, with all the freedom of action that only an unearned income can give. Is it any wonder that his ways are gracious and that his tongue is smooth? Is it any wonder that the manner of his work should change from year to year and even from month to month as the play of these class forces gives first one and then another the dominant financial rôle in his life.

The nature of these variations we have just described. How a non-musical job produces non-traditional music. How an inherited income that is big enough to live on produces music that reflects the censorships and preoccupations of the investing classes, music that is delicate, frivolous, introspective, or vulgar, as delicacy, frivolity, introspection, or vulgarity are being done at any given time in those circles. How a married income is likely to interrupt the function of composition altogether, or else to act on the composer in the same way as any other direct subvention or patronage. These last would seem to produce

revolt-music, excepting in the case of special awards and commissions, which, to the contrary, produce a quite rigid sort of international conformism. Pedagogy makes for complication, musical execution for brilliance, criticism for the wow-technique.
Traffic with the Appreciation-racket produces sterility. Living
on the rewards of one's labors as a composer would seem to be
the preferable situation, even though that entails almost inevitably doing a certain amount of theatrical work, held by many
musicians (incorrectly, I think) to be lowering. Unfortunately
and very curiously, considering the enormous quantities of art-
music consumed every year all over the world, the composer
who lives by composing is a rare animal.

Let me remind you once more that when I speak of a source
of income I mean a source that produces enough income to live
on. Let me remind you also that with the exception of being
able to live on the receipts from the exploitation of one's music,
which seems really to improve the quality of a composer's work,
and of trafficking with the Appreciation-racket, which is death,
no money is any better or any worse than any other money. The
source of the money, however, what the composer has to do to
get it or to keep it, produces a certain occupational deformity,
a stylistic conditioning. That is all. Perfectly good music, music
of the highest excellence, always has been written, and still is,
under any of these conditionings.

So far we have considered the composer's individual behavior. Let us now look at his group movements. What are his
politics, for instance; and what does he do about them?

Let me make clear right at the start what I mean by political words. I shall try to use them all in the way they are most
commonly understood, I think, by English-speaking people,
avoiding, where possible, usages that are still confined to sectarian groups. A political policy is a program of government, an
impersonal thing. Politics is the wangle about who executes it,
a personal thing. To put it more briefly, policy is what you do
and politics is who does it. Political principles are impersonal.
They are ideas, something people think and talk about. Political
action is personal. It is what any man really does to change economic or social conditions. It is not necessarily in accord with
what he thinks are his political principles. In order that political action be effective on the part of private citizens, it must of

necessity be group action. Group action always entails joining something. Time-workers and piece-workers join trade-unions. Craft-workers in the arts call their unions guilds or alliances. Small proprietors and professional men call theirs associations. Capitalists call theirs Institutes or Leagues.

Policy, which is a line of conduct, what is actually being done, or is capable of being done, in any given society or class of same, is a mysterious quantity. Sometimes it is discussed in advance, sometimes not. Sometimes it is the result of reflection on the part of a small group of persons. Sometimes it is the expression of unanimous public desire and is not reflected about at all, because the thing to be done seems to everybody an obvious and proper thing to do. But whether a certain line of policy is taken spontaneously or is imposed by a small and self-conscious group, it has no necessary relation whatever to the persons governing or holding office during the time that policy is in effect. This dichotomy is particularly noticeable in societies which have a visible parliamentary procedure and some popular voting. In nineteenth-century England, for example, the formula of social reform was that the Liberals proposed changes and agitated for them, but that the opponents of such changes, the Conservatives, actually voted most of them into law and administered the new mechanisms.

I realize that I am venturing here quite unprotected on the disputed ground of how history gets made. I realize also that I am not giving much consideration to the purely personal weight of certain men in power at certain times. It seems to me that the cases of a Julius Cæsar, a Charlemagne, a Louis XIV, a Napoleon, a Lenin, a Hitler, are more spectacular than frequent. Crystallizations of events take place around them, perhaps even within them. The sluggish stream of history rolls on for the most part quite independent of who is riding any visible raft at any given moment.

Politics is the business of raft-riding. In the so-called democratic countries it is operated on a two-party system. These two parties, variously named in different countries and frequently subdivided, are always only two, the ins and the outs. There is collusion between them, as we all know. The only serious points of difference have to do with patronage (who gets what job) and responsibility (who gets the buck passed to him when a particularly unpleasant bit of work is about to be done). The procedure is the same under the so-called autocratic governments, only the ins and the outs don't call themselves two parties. In modern autocracies, any form of organization among the outs is discouraged; and the word party is used only by the ins.

All this explanation may seem a bit unnecessary and obvious. Certainly it is not original with me. It is, I think, the philosophy of history and government most commonly accepted today among persons who have any philosophy of history and government at all.

The workings of practical politics, that is to say, of office-holding, touch the composer's life very little today in England and the United States, because there are virtually no jobs open there to musicians on state or federal pay-rolls. The W.P.A. [defunct by 1943] offers some; and the procedure for getting them is not unlike that for getting government art-jobs in Mexico and on the European Continent, where the state subsidizing of music and music-education brings an enormous number of posts connected with these into the pattern of bureaucratic administration. It might be interesting to examine the effect of government job-holding on musical style. I do not have any very firm ideas on the subject. I have never been able to put my finger on a case where I could note any influence at all. There is a little, perhaps, on the choice of objective literary subject-matter. But the sources of style (and of introspective subject-matter too) are what you do to earn money, not who signs the pay-check. A harmony-teacher is a harmony-teacher and a conductor a conductor, whether he works for a government bureau or for a private foundation. He is only different when he works for a students' or an executants' co-operative. There is probably a trifle more of intellectual and esthetic freedom for everybody under a bureaucratic set-up than there is under the privately financed musical set-up of England and the United States. [Also, as in Europe's state radio establishments, many more jobs for composers.] Certainly all tendencies toward dogmatic conservatism on the part of state-supported musicians seem to produce by reaction all sorts of vigorous corrective tendencies among those who do not have state jobs. The only difference between the democratic and the autocratic countries in this matter is that in the more authoritarian cultures, the corrective tendencies flourish under cover (or in exile). A great deal of the more advanced German music is now written in the United States, for instance; and we hear that in Vienna American swing music, which has the civil status of prohibition alcohol, is consumed passionately in musical speakeasies.

All this is preliminary to the question of what are the composer's politics. The composer's political action, like his musical style, is determined by his chief income-source. By political action I mean what he does in a group to conserve or to improve his economic privileges. State job-holding has to do with party politics; and although it is quite as legitimate as any other form of job-holding, it is not a form of political action. Joining a union of state job-holders is a political action. Neither is voting a political action. It is too private, for one thing. For another, it has nothing, except rarely, to do with governmental policy. It has only to do with the choice of political executants. As political action it is cart-before-horse.

We hear about musicians voting for this and that candidate or party ticket. A great many of them, I assure you, don't vote at all. We hear also a great variety of opinions expressed in the music world about foreign policy and about many other matters that citizens are not allowed to vote on. Of direct political action one sees a good deal too, but often it is in no way related to the musician's voting or to his political talking, which are just camouflage and vary mostly according to the neighborhood the musician lives in.

Let us take up the income-sources in order again:

The naïf, the non-professional composer, takes his political action with whatever group he gets his living from or among.

The composer who lives on inherited capital is solidly with the investors always. He may join the Musicians' Union for protective reasons. He is not a union-minded man. In any dispute between the union and the management he sides with the management.

The composer who lives on married money, like the composer who lives on personal subsidies, is of a divided mind. A poor man himself, he is anti-rich. But as a tolerated member of the wealthy classes, though he is granted lots of pleasant perquisites, he is not allowed to do anything opposed to their interests. The resulting tension comes out in his music as the revolt-tendency I mentioned before. In his conversation he pretends a great sympathy for the underdog. In union matters he sides with capital. But take his income away; and his stored-up hatred of the rich, plus his intimate knowledge of their ways, makes him a leader in class warfare.

The subsidized composer acts politically just like the one who marries his income. They are both kept-men. The subsidy must, however, be enough to keep him. One hundred dollars a month of well-assured income is about the minimum. [Two hundred are needed now.] If the subsidy goes lower than that, or if it seems likely to terminate at any moment, his mentality is not that of the kept-man any more, but of the chronically unemployed; and his political action at such moments follows that of the unemployed masses. The Home Relief dole, for instance, is an insufficient subsidy. [Work Relief (the W.P.A.), which paid $93.86 a month, was just sufficient to count as subsidy; and it did so count for the easel-painters. The only reason why it didn't for composers is that there was no provision in the Federal Music Project for free musical composition. All the composers in the W.P.A. were doing a specified musical work of some kind. They were earning the salary they were living on and hence felt no need for personal revolt.]

[It is also significant that none of the music for which Soviet composers have been disciplined by their government contains any expression of personal revolt. It merely shows faults of taste, as taste is judged by the Central Committee of the Communist Party. The famous love scene behind a curtain in Shostakovich's *Lady Macbeth of Mzensk*, for example, was termed "vulgar" and his Ninth Symphony "light-minded" and "frivolous." And Prokofiev was always suspected, sometimes accused, of a Western and bourgeois tendency toward stylistic "advance" that was out of step with the "democratic realism," or populist tone, that the government, as the employer and protector of these composers, felt entitled to require of them. Nor may we suppose that Soviet composers do not accept this requirement. I am acquainted with no musical work produced by any of them that would seem in any way to express personal unhappiness.]

Western conductors and concert artists make a show of political conservatism. They are impressed by money and hanker for

the sumptuous life. They express horror at the musical ignorance of the masses, imagine themselves as Haydn *bei* Esterházy
or as Leonardo at the Court of Francis I. They think they own
Musical Taste, should be allowed to administer this as a Vested
Right, and be handsomely paid for doing so. They even vote
with the rich. But underneath all this ornamental glub-glub
they are solidly anti-capital. In union disputes they almost never
take the producer's side. They either take the proletarian side
or shut up, because they are completely dependent for their
livelihood on the good will of union musicians.

The critics are conversationally either Marxian or Machiavel-
lian. In action they are all very much alike. They have no craft
union and no professional body with teeth in it. A few belong
to the Newspaper Guild. Those of them who really earn their
living by criticism are tied up, heart, voice, and hand, with the
symphony-orchestra interests, which means the radio and gramophone interests, which means in turn the electrical-patents-
and-banking combine.

The teachers are trade-unionists. School-teachers love joining
unions, and they run their unions with a minimum of venal-
ity. The French school-teachers' union is the hard-headedest,
the most independent, and the most determined group in the
General Labor Confederation. The teachers' unions in America,
although quite radical in their principles and often firm in action, are devoured by a desire to have everybody understand
that their members are not just ordinary laboring men. They are
doomed to disappointment. They are white-collar proletarians
and nothing else. That a good deal of teaching, especially advanced teaching, should be done by master workmen is necessary and inevitable. That a teacher has any knowledge or training which raises him above the position that is his on account
of what he actually knows about some subject, I deny. I mean
that pedagogy is not a profession like musical composition, nor
even a trade like piano-playing. It has no traditions, no body of
esoteric knowledge, no special skill, and no authority. All any
teacher knows over and above such real knowledge as he may
have of his subject is a half-dozen rules of thumb that anybody
can learn in fifteen minutes. I don't mean to say one teacher isn't
a more skillful pedagogue than another. Quite the contrary. I
mean no system of pedagogy is any better than any other. The

fact that there are so many systems on the market (they are as numerous in America as religions) means that there is no tradition. If the teacher knows his subject and keeps his temper, the student can usually be depended on to get everything out of him that he can digest.

There is no way around it. The school-teachers, much as they would like to be considered an intellectual caste, are really white-collar proletarians; and politically they act as such. They vote with their intellectual neighborhood, as everybody else does, their particular neighborhood being principally left-liberal. Their organized activities are aimed at getting some kind of authority over school curricula and at defending their salaries and their tenure of office from the depredations of trustees and schoolboards, who represent in such disputes the profit motive and the authoritarian methods of finance-capital.

Getting mixed up with the Appreciation-racket, which is practically a political action in itself, is as suicidal to the composers' group as it is to the individual musical author.

The composer who lives by his composition shows little difference between his political opinions and his political actions. His small but real independence renders camouflage unnecessary. Like most small proprietors, he is a liberal. He defends himself through professional guild-associations against the depredations of finance-capital, which is always attacking his professional integrity or his income. He joins up with music publishers (also, at present, mostly small proprietors) to enforce the payment of performing-rights fees by producing organizations. He acts with his publisher against the time-workers whenever his profit is in jeopardy. He pays his secretary and his copyists as little as he can, which is to say that, like any other manufacturer, he pays his helpers exactly what it would cost him to replace them.

So far we have been talking about direct political action. Indirect political action, such as membership in general political parties, the self-supporting composer tends rather to avoid. It lowers his standing in the profession and tends to lower the prestige of the profession itself. Fighting openly as a group for economic amelioration does not lower the prestige of the profession. On the contrary, every material advantage so gained serves to raise it in public esteem.

The political actions that professional men engage in outside the professional body always create dissension within the body and thus tend to fail of their purpose. I maintain that the only legitimate purpose of any political action is a group purpose, and that the members of all the professions belong more inalienably to their profession than they do to any other social group. This is unquestionably true of those professional men who live by the practice of their profession. After 1929 (it began rather earlier in Germany), there was a good deal of ostentatious joining by composers in England, France, and America, of Communist Parties adhering to the Third International. In the next decade a large part of the public activity of those parties had to do with foreign policy, a matter that concerns the musical profession only indirectly. This open recourse of composers to indirect political action began to produce in the mid-1930's (by the immutable laws of reaction) a similar activity by other composers in the opposite direction. An approximately equal number of them got openly mixed up with social reactionaries, and all of a sudden the profession was split asunder on matters not directly concerning it. Instead of presenting a united front to their respective governments for the purpose of pressing their just demands, they went around taking "stands" on foreign policy, the unionization of heavy industry, and soil-conservation. This happened in all the Western countries except Italy and Russia. Germany put a rather melodramatic stop to it in 1933. In England, France, and the United States it lasted till the war came. The upshot of all such activities everywhere was the same. Not a single economic advantage was gained by the composer for his profession or by the profession for him in any country during the years (now over, alas) when any economic group could have practically anything it asked for out of any government.

Having missed the train when it was going, there is now a tendency to huddle together and say how sad is the lot of the composer. If I may be allowed to pronounce a little sermon on that text, I should like to point out, from the model of the medical profession, just how professional solidarity really works when it works.

The professions derive their power in society from their intellectual autonomy. They are self-perpetuating bodies. They reproduce their kind without aid or interference and present themselves to the state through their professional organizations. These organizations determine all matters regarding the technique of professional education and professional practice. Their internal functioning is democratic. The term "republic of letters" is the description of an analogous ideal.

The business of any professional body is to administer the corpus of that profession's knowledge. An intellectual republic demands of its members a minimum standard of professional skill, a high degree of collaborative effort, and the acceptance of collaborative responsibility. It demands, therefore, of any political authority under which it lives complete intellectual autonomy. In return, it grants to the political authority (grants grudgingly, however, and hands over only under pressure) the right to control the social usages of professional knowledge. On the question, for instance, of whether there is or is not to be health insurance, music instruction in the slums, state theater, or a new bridge, the professional bodies who will be involved in the execution of those projects can only recommend. The political authority decides yes or no. When the political authority says yes, the professionals execute the project; and they execute it in their own way. When the political authority says no, the project is not executed. The state's bailiwick is (if we must) subject-matter; the profession's is technique.

Professions deal with the political authority as one state deals with another, which is to say diplomatically, economic warfare and passive resistance being, of course, diplomatic moves like any other. The defining of public health, safety, and expediency, at any given moment, is the privilege, the duty of the state. The defining of truth, beauty, falsehood, and correct syntax is at all times the duty of the intellectual republic. The political state may be organized after any known theory of political economy or any imaginable symbolism. The intellectual state is always organized as a classless society that owns all its means of production and reproduction and administers these by the procedures commonly known as internal democracy, which means open discussion of everything and the voting on policies as well as persons.

By the firm practice of such intellectual autonomy, any profession can obtain from any political state public honor and economic privilege. By neglecting to run its own house and messing around with things that are unquestionably Cæsar's, it never fails to end in a state of economic *and intellectual* slavery.

The medical men and the engineers have done well by themselves on such a program. Even the Hitler government handled them with gloves. The lawyers everywhere, having tampered too much with party politics, have lost practically all their intellectual prestige. They still make money; and they still have their dominant rôle in legislation in a few countries, though this cannot last very much longer if they continue to derive their chief income from political perquisites and from aiding the maneuvers of industrial banking. The poets enjoy no economic consideration in any Western society, because they have failed to make clear to the literary profession itself just what rôle they can play in literary life that other writers can't. They are pretty vague, as a matter of fact, about their rôle in both life and letters. Their intellectual integrity is still intact, however. They do nobody's intellectual dirty-work, as the journalists and the screen-writers do. The painters, the least organized of the artists, are economically subject to picture merchants and to the pseudo-philanthropic museum racket. (The museums seem to be responsible economically to everybody but the painters they expose.)

The music world has more solidarity than any of the other art worlds. A further organization is necessary at this time, however, if composers, the only possible governing group in any complete and authoritative organization of music, are to assume that responsibility. The executant musicians are allied with the American Federation of Labor, as is proper. Similar affiliations exist among European musicians. The composers have an elementary business-combine with publishers, which is all right too, but far from completely effective, even in Europe. If they do not demand and secure for themselves complete authority over professional ethics, professional education, and the standards of musical execution, they will shortly find themselves in the position of having these responsibilities assumed for them, formally and legally, by persons not competent to execute them properly, even by persons with non-musical axes to grind.

Already an enormous part of the world's musical activity is administered by a combine of conductors and businessmen. I refer to the international symphony-orchestra industry. Radio and television are even less professional in their standards. The cinema is in the hands of bankers and acting-directors; composers have no voice in the esthetic counsels of that enormous music-producing machine. Musical education is being quietly overpowered by the Appreciation-racket, a money-making scheme of less than doubtful musical value. (Can you imagine a reputable university offering a course in the Appreciation of Surgery, for example, or in How to Listen to Murder Trials?)

Correction of these very grave faults in our civilization must be organized by composers, and such organization must be led by the composers who make their living from composing. Only they have sufficient influence over their colleagues, and the energy necessary to carry the thing through. The others are timid and fatalistic, not daring to move a muscle, lest what they have be taken away. The school-teachers, with their habits of union-organization and their invaluable good manners in discussion, will be able seconds. The kept-boys will applaud from a distance. The journalists and lecturers will try to turn it into a publicity scheme. But only the musical-composition-supported can start it, run it, and carry it anywhere. They are very few in number.

This is the end of my sermon. This is the end of my disquisition on the composer as a political animal.

[The foregoing seems to have stimulated the composers to some action. They are now in pretty complete control of advanced music education, though not yet of primary or secondary. They also collect, even in America, considerable monies from symphonic and radio performances of their works, which they certainly were not doing in 1939. They also judge most of the prizes, awards, and commissions. In Europe they direct almost completely the musical activities of the radio. In America they still have no voice in the music councils of radio or TV or the film industry. Nor are they consulted by symphony orchestras and opera companies, as they are in Europe, though foundations listen to them a little. Composers' power has made some progress in twenty years; much remains to do. A basic-minimum contract with music publishers, for instance, has yet to be established anywhere.]

9

Intellectual Freedom

OR

What can and cannot be censored

W E HAVE SEEN that both the subject-matter and the stylistic orientation of music are economically determined. That is to say that the melodic and rhythmic material, the contrapuntal manner, and the style of its instrumentation are nourishment symbols. Of all the musical elements, only form and, in part, harmony are subject to free choice on the part of the composer.

Harmony itself is partly a stylistic device; and, in so far as it is, it follows the same orientation as the melodic material, its polyphonic and instrumental clothing. This is to say that the ornamental and expressive aspects of harmony, the throwing-in of chromatics and false notes, the degree to which charm, cuteness, and voluntary distortion are employed, are personal characteristics of the composer and are determined by the sources of his personal income. The more fundamental aspect of harmony, its architectural function in music, is less subject to personal variation, because the tonal substructure of musical form is as impersonal a thing as musical form itself.

Let me take an analogy from engineering. The decision to build a bridge at a certain place is dependent on the putative usage a bridge at that place would receive. Also on somebody's ability to pay for the building operations. Everything in the design that has to do with the bridge's putative usage, its structure for function and durability, is determined by the engineer's impersonal, objective knowledge of hydraulics, mathematical mechanics, and the specific strengths of materials. This basic design would be not much different no matter who were paying for the bridge. The decorative covering, however, or the lack of it, the materials and design of the visible surfacing, are symbolic representations of the source of the bridge's financing. Private and municipal constructions have more decorative variety than those financed by railways or by corporate bond-issues. The latter make a great show of their strength lines, of their avoidance of the old-fashioned picturesque. Such surfacing is comparable to the visible material and style of a musical piece. The basic design of the bridge corresponds to what has always been called musical form. Musical form is functional planning, nothing else.

Harmony plays a cardinal rôle in such planning, the whole layout of the tonal syntax being the chief means by which coherence, clarity, and emphasis are achieved in a long piece. This layout is not personal or financial or emotional or charming or grandiose or cute. It is as professional as corset-making or skin-grafting. Real knowledge and a skilled hand are the determinants of success.

In the case of objective music, the content (the subject-matter) is chosen by the person who pays for that music to be written; and it is chosen for its appropriateness to the music's projected usage. Content's little brother, stylistic orientation, is made up (quite unconsciously) by the person who writes the music, as a symbolic representation of his personal attitude toward the income-source. It can even, if the client and the composer are in close accord, represent their mutual attitude toward an income-source. Stylistic orientation is expressed through the melodic material, its contrapuntal clothing, its harmonic and rhythmic ornamentation, and its instrumental coloring.

The form of music is chosen, or rather designed, by the composer to make the piece fulfill a specific function. This function is not invented by anybody usually; it is a social creation. Lest the word "form," which in the visual arts means rather the surface contours of a work than the structural devices for sustaining these, tend to signify stylistic matters in spite of our defining it otherwise, I prefer to speak of music's plan or design. That will avoid also a certain confusion that tends to arise from an unconscious comparison with poetry, whenever specific musical forms are referred to. Because music knows no such fixed forms as poetry does; there is nothing in music comparable to the sonnet, the triolet, the villanelle, the Spenserian stanza, the Alexandrine, *terza rima*. Even music with words rarely follows the metrical mold of its text with much exactitude. The strictest metrical conventions are those observed in music intended for use as accompaniment to social dancing. Music not intended for such usage, though it may call itself waltz, minuet, or pavane, makes no pretense to exact observance. About the only real conventions in music that could legitimately be called forms—and these are conventions of texture, not of meter—are the canon and the round. The much-taught fugue is far more a series of stylistic devices than it is a metrical or tonal formula, only the exposition section having any kind of stable convention about it.

The designing of music is always a practical matter. No composer pays any attention to the metrical conventions of poetic or dance forms unless by following them in songs or in dance pieces he can assure the utility of his music. For music of less specific intent, the possible usages are varied. They may take the form of a concert, of a whistled quotation, a religious ceremony, a sight-reading in the home, an adaptation to spectacular entertainment. Design in music is the planning of it for clarity of communication and for durability under the kind of usage specifically envisaged. Different specific usages of music require different subject-matters and certainly different styles; that is obvious. They also require different design-constructions. The cardinal determinant in music's structural design is length. The limits of this length, what is too short and what is too long, are determined by the social conventions that regulate the occasions of musical usage.

In the case of introspective music, neither the content nor the style is decided by anybody but the composer. These are entirely spontaneous, automatic, "inspired," though in the long run economically determined. They are not directly controllable by the composer or by anybody else. The designing of musical form, however, in all kinds of music, the planning for clarity, for function, and for durability, is not at all spontaneous or unconscious. Like all matters of grammar, syntax, and rhetoric, it is based on social convention and audience-psychology. All knowledge about it is empirical. Success comes from trial and error.

I should like to add here that the same empirical knowledge, the same objective calculation, enters into the procedure of instrumentation, but that that is not a calculation of audience-psychology. It is an adapting of the composer's personal thoughts to instrumental limitations and rule-of-thumb acoustics. In spite of the elaborate nature of its planning, instrumentation is primarily an emotional thing, a translation into sensuous terms of the visceral climate, the subconscious weather conditions in which the composer and his particular material feel most at home. That massive and colorful instrumentation is only incidentally an aid to clarity and emphasis is proved by the frequency with which these last seem to get preserved intact in piano-reductions of orchestral music.

And so to repeat. The composer in front of any subject-matter, whether that is objective or introspective, of any content and its stylistic implications, is passive, masochistic, egocentric. It grabs him by the scruff of the neck and makes him take dictation. The underpinning of all this with structural steel is the problem of musical design. A problem that is objective can only be solved by action, by sadistic experiment. The first process is like child-birth; practically anybody can do it. The second requires judgment, like the bringing-up of offspring. Decisions must be made continually.

I wanted to explain all this, which many people know already (but which many don't), before examining the common musical usages. Because it is quite impossible to discuss esthetics unless it is perfectly clear that there are in music-writing both voluntary and involuntary elements. The current schools of esthetic criticism divide themselves, appropriately enough, along the lines of political philosophy. Let us call their spokesmen the scholastics, the big-business boys, and the Marxians. They all want to know how modern music gets that way. Also what, if anything, can be done about it.

The scholastics are the most informed about the history of stylistic detail. The conservative wing of them talks a great deal about "influences." They tell you who learned what from whom, but say nothing about why Composer A, who knew everybody's music from B to Z, chose to appropriate the formulas of C, H, and J rather than those of E, G, or W. They imply that personal idiosyncrasy determined the composer's ability or wish to accept such and such an influence. The more radical wing among the scholastics leans on *Kulturgeschichte*—finds music, painting, and architecture to be interrelated phenomena, all expressing, at any given period, the same *Zeitgeist*. Both wings are more convincing about the past than about the present, where personal stylistic variations always seem to surprise them.

The big-business boys, the Appreciation-school, are completely hipped on sonata-form. They speak of it as if it were the

key to musical knowledge and mastery of it the test of any composer's value. They even pretend that reading about this highly
controversial subject will lead laymen to accept forcible feeding
on symphonies. (The whole Appreciation-theory supposes an
auditor in chains. It falls quite to pieces if he is physically and
morally free, if he can be allowed, without committing an anti-
social act, to leave the concert hall or radio-side and take up
some diversion for which he has more liking.)

The Marxian school is hipped on the Revolutionary pattern.
They have interesting views (though I think in many cases erroneous views) on how musicians should and do act politically.
They tend to treat musical styles and usages as if they were a
form of political action, which they are not. Musical style, like
political action, is economically determined. The Marxians all
know about that; at least, they ought to. Musical usages, however, are social customs. They transcend political and economic
barriers. And the art of designing music to fit them must of
necessity transcend these barriers too. Also, on questions of
musical subject-matter the Marxians get nervous and moralistic.
[This school of criticism no longer, in the United States, admits
its Marxian bias, though one of its better exponents, Sidney
Finkelstein, is quite open about it.]

Political theories have, in fact, very little more to do with musical creation than electronic theories have. Both merely determine methods of distribution. The exploitation of these methods is subject to political regulation, is quite rigidly regulated
in many countries. The revolutionary parties, both in Russia
and elsewhere, have tried to turn composers on to supposedly
revolutionary subject-matter. The net result for either art or
revolution has not been very important. Neither has official
fascist music accomplished much either for music or for Italy
or for Germany.

Political party–influence on music is mostly just censorship
anyway. Performances can be forbidden and composers disciplined for what they write, but the creative stimulus comes
from elsewhere. Nothing really "inspires" an author but money
or food or love.

That persons or parties subsidizing musical uses should wish
to retain veto power over the works used is not at all surprising. That our political masters (or our representatives) should

exercise a certain negative authority, a censorship, over the exploitation of works whose content they consider dangerous to public welfare is also in no way novel. But that such political executives should think to turn the musical profession into a college of political theorists or a bunch of hired propagandists is naïve of them. Our musical civilization is older than any political party. We can deal on terms of intellectual equality with acoustical engineers, with architects, with poets, painters, and historians, even with the Roman clergy if necessary. We cannot be expected to take very seriously the inspirational dictates of persons or of groups who think they can pay us to get emotional about ideas. They can pay us to get emotional all right. Anybody can. Nothing is so emotion-producing as money. But emotions are factual; they are not generated by ideas. On the contrary, ideas are generated by emotions; and emotions, in turn, are visceral states produced directly by facts like money and food and sexual intercourse. To have any inspirational quality these must be present facts or immediate anticipations, not pie-in-the-sky.

Now pie-in-the-sky has its virtues as a political ideal, I presume. Certainly most men want to work for an eventual common good. I simply want to make it quite clear that ideals about the common good (not to speak of mere political necessity) are not very stimulating subject-matter for music. They don't produce visceral movements the way facts do. It is notorious that musical descriptions of hell, which is something we can all imagine, are more varied and vigorous than the placid banalities that even the best composers have used to describe heaven; and that all composers do better on really present matters than on either, matters like love and hatred and hunting and war and dancing around and around.

The moral of all this is that the vetoing of objective subject-matter is as far as political stimulation or censorship can go in advance. Style is personal and emotional, not political at all. And form or design, which is impersonal, is not subject to any political differences of opinion.

The poets, who, like politicians, use words as their medium, are always disagreeing with politicians about political ideas. Composers don't so much. We are often asked to wonder how the composer, an intellectual, can accept life under an ignominious government. I assure you that that isn't the problem in censorious countries today. The problem is getting the government to accept you. If the composer can eat and work, accepting the government is easy. Besides, all governments are ignoble, at least all I've ever seen or heard of.

Just as the painters are chiefly interested in depicting in two-dimensional paint how three-dimensional surfaces reflect light, the composers are chiefly interested in depicting by sound how their viscera face the facts of life. Hence they rarely get mixed up with government in their musical capacity. The Russian Association of Proletarian Musicians made a beautiful manifesto about musical style, made it three times, in fact. I recommend it to all to read. It was a witty and lifelike description of the immediate past. Its present musical program was of the vaguest, largely educational. Even at that, the Association was dissolved by government decree in 1932. Governments don't like professional states-within-the-state to play with cultural or with social policy.

There is a wave now in leftist circles of pretending that nothing in the world is outside the domain of politics. That is hooey. The ways of holding an audience's attention by musical sounds are not numerous. But they are in no way whatsoever connected with any political theory. The practice and transmission of such knowledge as exists about these is the business of the musical profession and must remain the business of the musical profession under any system of government. Advances in civilization (or even the maintenance of a status quo) depend not upon getting everything absorbed into politics, but on separating wherever possible and keeping separate from political tinkering all the knowledge there is about matters that are not any different no matter what political plans are on the fire.

Again I repeat. Subject-matter may interest politics, or it may not. If it does, the piece containing it may get censored. Works have been known to be censored too for their stylistic orientation, though very seldom. Usage may be ordered or forbidden by the powers that be or the powers that pay. Musical form, which is design for clarity, function, and durability, cannot possibly interest anybody but professionals.

[Since World War II there has been in the Western countries a maneuver on the part of big business and its representatives in government to control the whole distribution of art, literature, and music by calling it mass culture. I suppose the idea came from the impressive domination of these branches that is operated by the Soviet government. The Russian motive, of course, is to direct art's propaganda powers. The Western motive, I am afraid, is largely to make money. Mass culture here involves the toleration of an appeal to mankind's lowest instincts, to its dreams of self-indulgence in acts of anti-social sex and violence. In Russia, at least, mass culture has a higher tone.

The whole concept of mass culture is obscurantist. Does Shakespeare or Beethoven or the Bible lose quality through becoming massively available? No. Are populations elevated by being massively subjected to base literature, obscene photographs, and trivial shows? Again, no. Then, to speak of our enormous facilities, through publication and radio, of distributing art, information, and entertainment as a sociological phenomenon to be worried over under the name of mass culture, but not really to be changed or controlled, is not a culture concept at all but a political one. It is a protective screen against possible professional (hence really cultural) interference with a shameful business.

A great deal of excellent art and harmless entertainment is distributed widely today, along with much that is quite easily recognizable as poison, both moral and intellectual. But nobody is damming up the poison flow. It brings in too much money. Governments do not issue this poison, at least not in the West; but they do not interfere with it much either. This non-interference is a political action, a protection for the distributors. And all proposals to professional artists toward collaboration with massive and heavily commercialized distribution are a political pressure. These are usually baited with money and, if one declines to collaborate, followed by abuse. We are right back in the Appreciation racket, this time more powerful than ever. And only professional solidarity can clear up the obscurantism, take over the musical direction of massive distribution. The medical doctors have done it. So can we.]

10

How to Write a Piece

OR

Functional design in music

I AM NOW going to list the commoner uses of music and describe some of the considerations that composers take account of when designing music for those uses.

THE DANCE-SONG

"Popular" music leaves the composer's hands in most cases as a song consisting of identical stanzas (known as "verses") and a refrain of thirty-two measures (known as the "chorus"). This is the basic "form" for publication and for professional transmission. Rarely does this "form" fail to be altered in auditive usage. Frequently the verse disappears and the chorus becomes the whole tune. It is repeated with varying instrumentation for dancing, cut up and reharmonized for pianistic fun, distorted in stage-shows and movies to accompany acrobatics, emotional scenes, and pageantry. The jazz boys make fanciful variations on it for non-dancing listeners. A dozen completely different versions of the same title are sold as gramophone records or transmitted nightly by orchestras over the air.

The subject-matter in all these transformations is a thirty-two-measure tune. The musical style of its amplification and rendition is personal to every performer or performing group. The "form," usually a series of variations, is determined by each separate usage and fitted to whatever over-all timing is desired. The use of the variation series as a formula of composition comes from no high-brow motivation; it is simply that the variation series is the second simplest way of stretching any short piece of music out to fit a longer piece of time, the first and easiest way being exact repetition. Dance-players, church organists, and the leaders of military bugle corps don't hesitate to use exact repetition. It is not advisable, however, for jazz bands playing to seated auditors to repeat exactly, because both the band and the auditors would get bored.

The whole procedure of musical composition is evident in a

lively way in the small improvisational jazz groups. These employ a free contrapuntal style of playing, because it is easier to improvise counterpoint than harmony (unless you are playing a multiple-voiced instrument, like the piano or banjo or guitar, or an instrument with chord-buttons, like the accordion). The use of the variation series and wherever possible of the "imitative" style of counterpoint saves effort and gives coherence to the whole. The solo cadenza (called in jazz jargon a "chorus") keeps up the interest of the players and produces the profitable rivalries that come from personal success. Each player takes a chorus to make it all seem fair and friendly, takes it when he feels like it, stops when through. All, so far, is unconscious, automatic. Where does reflection come in? What has to be decided on by somebody? Three things only. The tune, the time to start, and the time to stop. The first constitutes the subject of the music. The last two define the proportions of its form— the speed, intensity, and extent at which musical development within the variation series can take place. The variation series is not a form; it is a continuity device. The song-with-verse-and-chorus is a form, but one that exists chiefly on paper. In practice, the small disc, the three-minute jazz number, the song-and-dance come as near being musical forms as so-called "popular" music has to offer, because they are at least bits of continuity within a dimension.

MUSIC AND PHOTOGAPHY

As is well known, the movie was never a silent entertainment. The quiet tick-and-flicker of an unaccompanied film is dangerously soporific, no matter how clear the images or how exciting the narrative continuity. From the earliest days of the movies, the film-exhibitor has called in the aid of musical accompaniment to help him keep the house awake and to lend emotional poignancy to the dangerously frigid spectacle of a series of photographs. To this day the movies are dependent on music to hold the observer's attention and to direct his emotional responses. All of which means that the movie is a true musical form, as truly a musical form as the opera, though without as yet the opera's inseparable marriage of music to words.

Most descriptions of the movies are descriptions of the working methods by which they are made. I do not think these are immutable. Just because it is common practice to take the photographs and then to mount (or "cut") the film and finally to pin on some music, it does not follow that a film made after a musical composition could not be equally effective. The collaboration problem between movie-director and composer is not dissimilar, in fact, to that of the choreographer and the composer who make a ballet. The best result obtains when neither gets very far in time ahead of the other.

The whole esthetic of the movie derives from the fact that it is a photograph. Like all photography, it is naturally low in emotive appeal. We can stand a lot more blood and burst war-babies in a movie than we can in real life or on a stage. It is also low, for the same reasons, in human friendliness. The screen having no human odor at all, the friendliness is all out in the house, never between house and stage. Great actors get carried in triumph by their admirers; but movie stars, unless they are well protected, get torn to pieces by theirs, because these, not recognizing their idol in his human form and with unfamiliar odor, can only achieve a mystic communion with his image by destroying his flesh.

Its naturally low emotive appeal leads the film in three directions:

¶1. The depiction of natural scenery, as in documentaries.

¶2. Exploitation of the pathos of the human face, as in realistic fiction dramas with stars.

¶3. The flight into fantasy, as in comics and animated cartoons.

Conscious compensation by directors and cutters for photography's naturally low emotive appeal has produced a final product with a rather high emotive appeal, higher at least than is commonly obtainable by visual means. The mobility of the camera (plus music) has produced a flexible and powerful art-form.

The same mobility is responsible for the movie's gravest inherent difficulty, the jerkiness of photographic narration. It would be absurd to keep the camera in one place all the time, as long as it can be so easily moved around. This constant shifting of the point of vision over an enormous variety of locales does make, however, for visual discontinuity. This discontinuity in turn is compensated for by an elaborate refinement of cutting. Cutting is the most admired technique in movie-making, the most difficult, and the most indispensable. When each scene's visual time-length is adjusted to a desired emotional impact, and the whole series of scenes bound together by musical continuity, you have a narrative that is not at all low in emotive power, even though the music for the most part at present is not very well adapted to its function.

Documentary subjects are the easiest kind of movie to write music for. The fantasy and the comedy are next. There exist a goodly number of excellent scores of all three kinds. I have never heard a satisfactory musical accompaniment to a spoken film drama. It was all very easy pinning music on to "silent" Westerns. Schubert's *Unfinished Symphony* and Debussy's *En Bateau* were adequate for anything. It is speech that has brought back the film's essential jerkiness, by interrupting the musical continuity.

For comics and documentaries and fantasies there is no grave trouble. All the composer needs to do is to put a continuous accompaniment of appropriate style under each sequence, making just enough timed illustrative "effects" to give everybody a slight shock at the major shifts in the narrative. Even if there is a speaker in the documentary, or some wisecracks to insert in the comic film, all is easy. The music can be stopped for short moments, its volume brought up or down, without its real progress being destroyed.

Before speech came in, the drama film presented the same problem as these others, the chief thing needed being musical continuity interspersed with timed "effects." What has not been satisfactorily solved yet is how to put music to the spoken drama film. How to make music that will be important enough to carry your big moments, and at the same time keep out of the way of the dialogue, is the problem. The future of the drama film depends on its solution. Otherwise, the movies will find themselves more and more limited to the making of documentaries, comedies, fantasies, and something like revues. The film drama cannot live without music, as stage drama can. And it is not getting much use right now out of the music it is living with.

The problem is not insoluble. It is really one of definition. Is the movie a visual art-form, or is it predominantly verbal? It is a visual art-form, of course; don't forget it is a photograph. Its humanly expressive range runs from pantomime to pageantry and back and not much further. But its intensity of expression within that range is greater than any hitherto available. The presentation in a theater of panoramic views of natural scenery and of gigantic enlargements (called "close-ups") of the human face is a possibility absolutely new to art, a possibility that is unique to the moving picture. Fantasy is not unique to the movies. The three-dimensional theater has its fantasy too, which is just as amusing as trick photography. Sleight-of-hand, for instance, is more convincing on a stage than on a screen. And the plastic possibilities of stage scenery, with its variety of stuffs and colors, its enormous range of luminosity, are greater than any plastic beauty the movies (even the colored movies) can touch. Human speech has more variety and power in a theater; music sounds better in a concert hall. Even radio-crooning (that close-up of the human voice) is more poignant without visual interference.

The animated cartoon, charming as it is, is not characteristically cinematographic. It is not even necessarily a photograph. It is a free-hand drawing, photography being merely its commonest projection method. Its relation to naturalistic cinematography is that of marionettes to the real-actor stage. Its whole esthetic, in fact, is that of the marionette theater, even to the use of strained vocalization. Its designers can produce masterpiece after masterpiece because they face no new esthetic problems.

Now any art-medium derives its own esthetic, as well as its power, from what is different about it, not from what is common to it and to other media. And what is specifically different about the movies from all other forms of theatrical entertainment is their ability to move our hearts by true representations of natural scenery and enlargements of the human face. If you will look back in your memory, or into the history books, you will find that at least nine-tenths of all the really famous and unforgettable films are films that were photographed mostly out of doors. And at least one of the most celebrated films in the world, Carl Dreyer's *La Passion de Jeanne d'Arc*, consists in large part of nothing but close-ups taken without make-up on anybody's face. There is no getting around it. The stage can beat the movies at painted scenery, at the plastic disposition of stuffs and colors and lights. The movies are inalienably (even in their most fantastic moments) tied up to some kind of naturalism. The two-dimensional monochrome screen (colored films are very little colored, and at best they derive more of their definition from chiaroscuro than from chromatics), the husky and booming voices, the shortness of scenes and consequent nervousness of even the best "continuity," these technically imposed distortions are as much stylization as anybody can stand. Further distortion of reality is unprofitable.

Plots need not necessarily be naturalistic. They can be as conventional, as romantic, as fantastic as you like; and the high-flown heroic is their oyster. The movies do not have (necessarily) plot trouble, and they are certainly not limited in subject-matter. They don't have necessarily acting trouble any more since a natural style of acting has been adopted. Everybody just acts as natural as he can, and he does that in houses and on grass and in front of landscapes that, if not always quite credible realistically, are invariably naturalistic in intention. What kind of trouble then do they have? They have trouble about words and music.

Words and music are an ancient marriage, the marriage whose eldest offspring are song and the opera. Words go all right with visual spectacles too; that makes the "legitimate" theater. Music and pantomime go fine; that is ballet. Music and photographs of real people or scenery are okay; that is the documentary film. Even music and printed words don't bother anybody; that's what you have at the beginnings of films in a section called Titles and Credits. The combination works one hundred per cent.

The aim and problem of the narrative film is nothing more or less than effective narration. Film narration is photographic narration, and in a photograph people are not convincing unless they look and act natural. If one wishes to look approximately natural, one had better not try to do too much explaining by gestures and facial pantomime, unless the limits of the medium impose that procedure. Before the days of the sound-film, that was the narrative method, that and occasional subtitles. Today it would be ridiculous not to profit by the added naturalism of speech, to pretend that stylized pantomimic explanations are obligatory, when everybody knows they are not. There are no films any more, excepting those of Charlie Chaplin, without some verbal text. That text is inevitably naturalistic too. It is frequently enlivened by wit and wisecrack, just as ordinary conversation is. Seldom is there verbal fantasy or imagery, because these fall outside the naturalistic convention.

There are no films at all without music, which is more necessary even than the spoken word. It ties together the jerky narration (unless the composer of it makes the mistake of changing his music every time there is a change of scene, in which case he exaggerates the jerkiness). It produces quick, strong emotional reactions to reinforce the slow, weak ones that are all you get normally out of photography, out of anything visual, in fact. It also keeps the audience awake.

Photography, words, and music, how may these three elements be welded into an effective narration? You can't cut one out, because the movies cannot do without music, and it would be a little silly today to try to do without speech. Intoning the speech, as in opera, is entirely out of the question in any dramatic medium so completely tied up to naturalism. To put continuous music under the speech ("melodrama" is the technical term in music for this combination), is just as unsuitable to the naturalistic style as operatic *recitativo*. It is always corny and unconvincing unless the music has some naturalistic excuse for being there. To limit the subject-matter of films to stories in which music can be constantly present on naturalistic excuses would be to hamstring the art.

What is done is to open with music under the titles and credits, and then to alternate straight spoken passages with melodrama, with music, and with noises. Noises and music don't go badly together, curiously enough. There is a constant tendency to try to get the music and the words together also, to interpolate songs, because the fact is there isn't enough emotion-producing music in the fictional film today. And there is no musical continuity whatsoever. The documentaries use a continuous symphonic score and a fairly continuous speaker. The procedure works admirably; it does not make "melodrama," because the music is accompanying the film (not the speaker), and the speaker is commenting on the film (not the music). Music and speech exist in such spectacles at the same time; but they have no real connection, hence no serious interference.

There is a tendency in French movie-making to restore the continuous musical accompaniment, only interrupting it for important speeches, and cutting down the total amount of speech in the film to as small a proportion as possible. The system seems to work fairly well and would work even better if the composers who sign the scores could be given time to write their own music, all of it, and if a relatively stable dynamic level for sound-recording could be established. As it is, two hours of interesting music cannot be written and orchestrated in a week; and even if it could, the fading-away and loudening-up practice is musically unsatisfactory, though necessary for the sake of speech-clarity. It contradicts all dynamic variety that takes place at the music's source and makes the orchestra sound as if it were playing steadily fortissimo in a swell-box.

Even this excellent compromise system tends to limit the movies' subject-matter. It works best, really works, only on plots that do not involve music. Because you can't have stage music and pit music both unless you have both a stage and a pit. All movie music comes from the same place, which is a loud-speaker somewhere near the screen. It is musically unclear to jump from commentary or background music to realistic music of any kind, and quite impossible to play the two off against each other antiphonally, unless the sounds come from different places. Using two loudspeakers would be useless, would merely destroy the illusion that any of the music at all comes from the screen. A sharply marked duality of musical style is the only feasible way of marking the transition from background music to realism; and that is a technique not easily applicable, unless one man really writes all the music, or unless two men really write it, casting themselves, as in a play, for their characteristic and personal qualities.

At present, the system of nearly continuous accompaniment, even if the music written for it were stylistically satisfactory, and even if the dynamic level of recording could be adjusted so that clear words and expressive music could cohabit without friction, is still rather insufficient for the narration of themes that involve much musical pageantry. It is over-sufficient and tiresome for any subject that deals familiarly with middle-class life. Music here gets in the way of naturalistic conversation and almost inevitably turns the story into melodrama. The French system is at its best in dramas about life among the dregs and the outcasts or about life in exotic and lonely landscapes, life at sea or in unfrequented mountain-lands, deserts, places where people speak in dialect or with stylized accents and where everything is strange and violent and very very sad indeed. The removal from middle-class life that is inherent in such subjects makes it possible to use such a stylized convention as the nearly continuous musical accompaniment interspersed with picturesque speech.

The tie-up with middle-class naturalism, which seems to be ineluctable, has forced the American films to lean more and more on dialogue (for its naturalistic value) and less and less on music, thus sacrificing a great deal of music's emotional value and practically all of its value as continuity. This choice is not an improper one, but it has created a difficulty. Because the movies cannot live without lots and lots of music, and the insertion of lots and lots of music into naturalistic plays with middle-class dialogue is just now quite out of the question.

There are two ways currently employed of getting music back into the films. One is the interpolation into comic and light sentimental subjects of songs, dances, and night-club scenes, the presence of the latter being a firm convention in French films, where they correspond exactly to the ballet convention of French opera. Less universal, but not uncommon in America, is the insertion of jolly male choruses, military band music, arias from popular grand opera, and bits of such symphonic compositions as are familiar to radio audiences. All these are introduced with a naturalistic excuse of some kind; they are plot music and count as realistic detail, never as commentary or as continuity. They are music, however; and that is always a help. The other way is used for more serious and tragic themes. It demands the insertion, wherever possible, of commentary music. In order that this commentary be not too prominent, an attempt is made to write it in a neutral style. The result is not really neutral; let us call it, for lack of a better term, pseudo-neutral music. There are special composers in all the centers of film-manufacture who specialize in writing this. Do not despise them. They are experts and know exactly what they are doing. They are writing a musical journalese. Their aim is to make music that will be rich in harmonic texture and sumptuous in orchestration, but whose melodic material and expressive content will be so vague that nobody will notice it. Such music fulfills its minimum architectonic function of tying together the continuity at the points where it is absolutely necessary that that be done. It is also useful for underlining a bit of humor or a heart-throb and for creating fortissimo hubbub at the beginning and end of films, the time when people are changing their seats. It gives a general air of luxury by being there at all and by being orchestrated in the "picturesque" style of 1885, the style of Chabrier and of the early Richard Strauss. Its power of self-effacement is its real virtue. Few persons excepting those of predominantly auditive memory (and these rarely go to the movies) can ever remember anything about the music of serious drama films, even whether there was any or not. It is discreet; it is respectable; it comes and goes without being noticed. It carefully avoids ever making any underlining that might engage it subsequently to a close collaboration with the film story. It retires completely before the speaking voice, no matter how banal a remark that voice may be about to utter.

Neither of these ways is very satisfactory. The first turns everything into a musical comedy. The second is both architecturally and emotionally inefficient, because music can't be neutral and sumptuous at the same time. Not in this post-Wagnerian age. A really neutral music would be admirable, if it could be written. It would certainly provide a better contrasting background than the pseudo-neutral does for the insertion of stylized musical numbers. And it would serve as a sonorous foundation on which to erect musical climaxes that could support the big punches of the narrative in a pretty impressive way. It might even provide an approach to the central problem of words and music.

I do not know whether it is possible in this generation to develop a neutral music style. It existed in Europe from the Council of Trent to the middle of the eighteenth century. Its remains are buried in the pedagogical convention known as "strict" counterpoint. The basic rule of such music was the avoidance of any tonal formula that was at all noticeable or that was in any way specifically expressive. The German Romantic rule, our present tradition, is to make the music everywhere as noticeable and as expressive as possible. The international neo-classic style that I spoke about in another chapter was the product, in part, of an attempt to revive non-expressive counterpoint. Its practitioners thought to neutralize the expressive value of unresolved dissonances by making the employment of these obligatory and consistent. It cannot be said that strictly dissonant counterpoint, however useful as a pedagogic device, has provided the world with a stylistic discipline that quite fulfills the functions of the classic one. Rather it is a commentary on the more ancient rules that would make no sense at all to one who was not trained on these. The twelve-tone system of atonality is rather less neutral and more expressive than tonal counterpoint. If either of these modern conventions, or a revival of the classic one, should prove useful in the composition of film accompaniments, nobody would be more delighted than I; but so far I must say they have not done anyone much good. I must make an exception or two, for in French films I have occasionally heard an apt usage of dissonant counterpoint. Not for its expressive value; that is easy and no trouble. I mean as something approaching a really neutral background music, a *senza espressione* style that throws whatever is seen against it into high expressive relief.

It is really too bad the movies got born a century late. They would have served as an ideal dramatic medium for Richard Wagner. He, of course, is every movie-director's dream of a musician. He wouldn't have needed neutral music; he would have taken us all to Valhalla on continuous hubbub with intense expressivity everywhere. And no tommy-rot about pretending that the speaking voice is essential to realism or that middle-class life is in any way interesting. He would have placed the films, once and forever, on that high heroic plane that their colossal powers of visual depiction demand for them. History has willed it otherwise. Wagner did his heroic job, did it on the opera. It is too late now to do the same job on the movies, because the same battle can't ever be fought twice. His goddesses and heroes are fat theatrical screamers who stand around among cardboard rocks and wander through canvas forests. There is nothing naturalistic or credible about them; they are symbols embedded in concert music. But embedded they are;

and Wagner is dead, and stage opera, too, very nearly. The films will have to go now in another direction and invent a new musical stylization. There is nothing to do about being born too late except to become a primitive.

The movie people are all very proud of their art's achievements. They think the movies are in every way just grand. Actors pretend otherwise, but they all think so too; and they are out for movie jobs to a man. Literary authors hate the movies with a violence, whether they work in the films or not. And composers of music, whether they work in films or not, are sad, unhappy, and nervous about them.

Any further progress esthetically in "pictures," as Hollywood so unpretentiously calls them, depends on first restoring the musical continuity. Emotional super-power must start from there. In order to restore musical continuity, either spoken dialogue must be thrown out or a new and practical working solution must be found for the words-and-music problem, a solution that will permit words and music either to let each other alone or to help each other out. At the moment, they are in each other's hair; and the low emotional tension that results is of very little support to the pallid and anesthetic spectacle of narrative photography.

There has been a lot of talk about movie opera. Movie opera is a dead-end. At least it is if by movie opera you mean the screening of well-known stage operas. Original screen opera might be possible if it were called something else. But the word "opera" throws both directors and composers into nervous states that render them unfit for responsible art-work. No art form is so little understood or so stupidly practiced as the opera in this age of its decline. Even over the radio very little has been done except to broadcast repertory stage works, though heaven knows the opera as a musical form is just God's gift to the microphone. Writing contemporary operas for the crooning technique, how has everybody been so dumb as to miss it? I can only explain that miss on the ground that the word "opera" produces such sun-spots on the mental retina that once it is mentioned nobody can see anything but *Tristan* and *Faust* and *Il Trovatore*. I must say that making original screen opera will be no such child's play as making radio opera would be. But the movie banks have money, great big electrical money. There could be no real harm in their making half a dozen screen operas, if only to find out what not to do once the word "opera" shall have been got out of the way and it shall have become thenceforth possible to make serious musical fiction films.

MUSICAL THEATER

Opera is complete musical theater.

Musical theater is a collaboration of the verbal, the visual, and the tonal arts, usually with intention to instruct. The place of music in such a collaboration varies from epoch to epoch. A drum-roll to send up the curtain, accompaniments for dancing and acrobatics, an interpolated song here and there, the eternal off-stage trumpet calls, all these are incidental. It doesn't make much difference whether they are well-made or only fair. The quality of the music makes, however, a great deal of difference when that music is tied up to the dialogue. Such a tie-up is the specific characteristic of serious opera. Because of it, opera has the most ancient heritage of any theatrical form still practiced in the Western hemisphere.

The Greek tragic theater, like most religious ceremonies everywhere, was originally danced and sung. Even as late as Periclean times, when the poets had hogged the show for themselves, and the only religion left in it was a sort of civic morality, the mass recitations were still intoned and the chorus that intoned them pranced on in ceremonial quickstep. The Christians took over most of the Greek theatrical procedures for use in their ceremony of the Mass. This latter is a combination of tragic spectacle (the sacrifice of Our Lord is re-enacted) with practical magic, the elements of bread and wine being transubstantiated into the flesh of God and devoured beneficially by the initiates. Even the word *clericus* (or clergyman) means in late Latin an actor. To this day the Mass is danced and sung, which is to say that the text is intoned and all the movements are regulated. There is even provision for the interpolation of musical set-pieces, of choral entries, and of parades. The reprosodizing of the whole liturgical repertory to fit medieval Latin, which had become quite different in sound from classical Latin, and the composing of set-pieces to ornament this repertory occupied most of Europe's musical world for a thousand years, from the seventh to the seventeenth centuries.

The opera, as we know it, was invented in Florence in 1600, for the purpose of performing non-Christian (specifically, Greek mythological) tragic plays in Italian. The intention was anti-ecclesiastical. But the method employed for carrying out this intention was to take over (to take back rather) and to laicize all the musical procedures of the Church. Nothing could have been more intelligent. Because the formal procedures of music, as we have mentioned before, are not bound up with any ideological content. Also because these procedures were in this case exactly the musical procedures of the Greek tragic mythological theater, the art that it was desired to restore.

If musicians could ever get it through their heads again, after seventy-five years of having forgotten it, that the operatic form is nothing more or less than the form of the Christian Mass, as well as that of the Greek tragic theater, there would be far fewer unsuccessful operas produced in Europe and America every year. One single principle underlies the design, the structure of complete musical theater (whether you call that opera or music-drama). The basic routine of this, as of the Mass and of the ancient poetic stage, is intoned speech. Successive reformers of the opera (every time the opera gets domesticated to a new language it has within a century to be reformed) have varied the proportion of intoned dialogue, set-piece, and instrumental illustration; but they have never thrown out the central procedure, which is intoned dialogue. One might even say that the way to reform opera anywhere is to bring back the attention of composers to the basis of all opera, intoned speech.

You cannot write an opera, as you can a song, by making up a tune and then fitting words to it. You have to start from a text and stick to it. You must scan it correctly and set it to tunes convincingly. In the more vigorous operatic epochs singers even articulate it comprehensibly. Speech so scanned and set, if intoned with clear articulation, is both easier to understand and more expressive than speech that is not intoned; and it can be heard farther.

All the rest of an opera is just the icing on the cake. You can put in all the set-pieces you like and all the symphonic reinforcements. You can have the most beautiful scenery and clothes money can buy, or you can do without. You can regulate the singers' every movement, or you can let them wander around from bench to tree. You can add ballets, earthquakes, trained seals, trapeze acts, and an orchestra of a hundred and fifty musicians with sirens and cowbells. The more the merrier, because the opera is a complete art-form like the Mass, the Elizabethan theater, and the movies. An ideal opera contains one of everything. It is better than a circus because it can include a circus. Also, as at the circus, the audience is part of the show.

The opera has no time limits. It can last ten minutes or seven hours. It has few limits of subject-matter. Religious, moral, or even politically revolutionary themes that would be censored elsewhere so quickly you wouldn't know what had happened are accepted without shock at the opera (and understood). It has no limits about vocal or instrumental style. It is stylistically the freest of all the musical forms and the most varied. It can stand any amount of interpolated numbers, musical, scenic, or acrobatic. Its one limitation is the condition of its amplitude. It must always be a bunch of actors in character singing a play to an audience. Not singing a lullaby or a love song or a lament for virginity betrayed, but singing the remarks and speeches that make up a theatrical narrative. It is not a symphony with voices or an oratorio with scenery or an instrumental accompaniment to a pantomime, though at times it has tended to degenerate to all these.

Let us repeat it over and over. Basic opera is nothing more or less than an intoned play. Start from there, as the opera did and as every reformer of the opera has to, and you will arrive at complete musical theater. Start from anywhere else, and you arrive at incomplete musical forms and at very uninteresting theater.

*   *   *

I shall skip along briefly over the forms of incomplete musical theater such as Protestant church services, plays with incidental music, military ceremonies, and home weddings. The music to these is a sort of yardage that is cut to fit the cue-sheet and the colonel's taste. Putting incidental music to spoken plays does pose a structural problem of acoustic placement, any given bit of music becoming for the play scenery or property or framing, accordingly as the musicians executing it are placed in the wings or on the stage or in a pit. The combination of instrumental accompaniment with non-intoned speech, melodrama, adds tension to very short moments of a play; its abuse is a corny effect. A general rule of use to composers and play-directors is that music for plays works best if it makes some kind of continuity when played without any interruptions.

The most interesting (musically) of the incomplete musico-theatrical forms is the ballet. The great secret about that, the open secret that composers tend to forget, is that ballet music is, believe it or not, dance music. Its first function is muscular, helping the dancers move themselves around. It is a whip, not a musical meditation. Its rhythmic substructure is essentially percussive, because only beat music moves muscles. Music that has a quantitative rhythmic substructure without percussive thumps, the kind of music that comes from pipe organs, merry-go-rounds, player-pianos, harpsichords, and really hot jazz orchestras, is not very good for provoking large muscular movements. The jitterbug twitch is about as far as any of these go.

Ballet music is not limited to percussive music. It is extraordinary the amount of static tone-pattern that can be got into it if you play this off frankly against the muscle-music. Stylistically the ballet is a rich and ample music-form, capable of almost as great variety of expression as the opera itself. I call it incomplete, compared to the latter, because of its lack of human song. Efforts have been made to add singing to the ballet; but these have not been very often successful, because singing is a more powerful medium of expression than bodily movements are. Every time you put vocalism alongside of dancing, the dancing has a way of becoming invisible. And the addition of dancing to a primarily vocal manifestation like opera, though a bit of ballet is pleasant enough as an interlude in a long vocal evening, certainly tends to diminish the intensity of the story-telling at that point. Intoned speech, however, is a strong enough foundation to support any and every kind of ornamental addition that might possibly enrich the whole spectacle, whereas pantomime and bodily prowess, no matter how breathtaking, are not a strong medium of expression. They are always tending (this is history) to lose what expression they have and to become just empty conventions. The reformers of the ballet are invariably preoccupied with trying to make stage dancing mean anything at all.

Like the movies, the ballet is a visual spectacle; and like all things visual, it is emotionally frigid. It needs music for continuity and for emotional intensity. Mixing it with opera is always exciting, though sometimes a little precarious. It is advantageous to the opera to have the movements of the actors regulated by an experienced choreographer. Even naturalistic opera profits by such collaboration. But that does not make a ballet of the opera any more than having a high-class artist design scenery and costumes will turn the visible stage into an oil painting.

Ballet is the expression of human sentiments by means of the muscular members. Its higher schools are opposed to any facial pantomime whatsoever, because facial expressions of any intensity tend to weaken the force of the body's all-over expressiveness, to personalize a highly impersonal art. Ballet is much enhanced, however, by scenery and clothes. The addition to one long-distance visual effect, which is dancing, of another, appropriate decoration, doubles the power of the whole visual spectacle. Just as the addition of music, which is auditory, to declamation, which is also auditory, makes the opera the most powerful auditory expression there is. Putting music under dancing is fine, because dancing needs it. Putting vocalism and dancing together is rarely effective for more than a short moment. Alternating dancing with vocalism, on the other hand, is completely satisfactory and charming, whether that is done with the grandeur of Lully's and of Rameau's sumptuous ballet-operas or with the unpretentious and simple good-humor of that ever-popular number, the song-and-dance.

CONCERT MUSIC

The concert is the purest form of music, though not the most complete. It is not a complete art-form, like the opera, because it is limited to music. It is even a less complete musical form than the opera, because its repertory is limited formally to pieces of a certain length and stylistically to those of a certain respectability. It is music, only music, and (theoretically) high-class music. It tells no story, serves no didactic purpose; and the only spectacle it offers is that of men at work.

It is a very intense little affair. It is the islanders' form of the Communion of Saints, a communication from musicians to the "musical." For outsiders it is either a social ceremony or a place to let the mind wander pleasantly. For the unmusical this mind-wandering consists chiefly of sexual stirrings and memories of natural scenery. The musically sensitive find sometimes that music fecundates all sorts of thought. The meditative possibilities of musical listening are of the highest psychological value; I would not deny them to anyone. Only I insist that persons in a concert hall who are doing their own private business, whether that business is looking impressively social or thinking about love or laying plans for tomorrow, are not necessarily receiving any musical communication, though sometimes they may be doing that too.

In general, the best receivers of musical communications are persons of some active musical experience, persons whose visceral reactions are sensitive to auditory stimuli and who have some acquaintance from practice with the musical conventions by which these reactions are habitually stimulated. Such people are said to "understand" music. You can teach musical analysis to the tone-deaf; but you cannot make them understand music. Because the first condition of musical understanding is some visceral responsiveness to sound, and that you simply have from birth or you haven't. The blood-flow, the liver, the ductless glands, the digestive juices are entirely beyond voluntary control or training. If your reactions to musical sounds are sufficient to make concentration on these a pleasant activity, then of course the conscious mind comes into the process, comes in just as automatically as the viscera do, though a little later in time.

The process of intellection about music that all musical persons go through as they hear music is not a process of describing to oneself verbally the music's meaning. It is a process of being aware sensuously of certain visceral changes and clearly, auditively, separately aware of the sounds that provoke them. This dual process is quite facile when the music is familiar; hence everybody loves old music. With new music everything is much more difficult. Both the visceral reactions and the auditive experience that provokes them must be tasted, very much as one tastes strange foods. One isn't always sure right off whether one is going to "like" them or not. This process of discrimination is an intellectual (though largely unconscious) exercise of personal taste. Taste is knowing what you don't like. It is the knowledge of what you personally cannot take, what you must keep your viscera from getting too intimate with till your mind gets used to the novelty and you can accept the whole thing into your repertory of digestible experiences.

Music that is novel in stylistic orientation, that impinges strangely on the musical ear, provokes violent demonstrations of acceptance and refusal. The broader the musical experience of the listeners present, the more violent the public demonstration. In the great musical centers there is not seldom a physical brawl. The following principles govern taste judgments:

¶1. The degree of any group reaction, favorable or unfavorable, is more significant than its direction. Its strength is roughly proportional, over a certain period of time, to the expressive power of the work. An inexpressive work creates little disturbance.

¶2. The direction of the judgment, for or against, of each separate listener is influenced by his financial interest.

Teachers resist anything which contradicts what they have been telling their students or that threatens to put them in a position of ignorance in front of these. They don't like envisaging a loss of student prestige, because that loss means eventually a money loss.

Composers resist anything that threatens competition. If a work is in similar vein to some piece of theirs, but more expressive, they hate it. Anything in similar vein, but definitely less expressive, they love. About anything quite different from their own work, they are benevolent but fairly silent, because they are already planning a little theft or two of a device.

Persons who have some musical experience but who are not making any money to speak of out of it have a relatively disinterested musical taste; and since the human mind always loves a little bit of change, these persons are eager to understand and to accept. They constitute an advance guard for the absorption of new music.

In places where musical sensitivity is so great and musical experience so general that everybody likes nearly everything, the musical tradition is said to be "decadent." Enormous quantities of music are consumed, but none of it means much. It is elaborate in construction and texture, low in expressive content. In such places and at such times, the consumption of old music (music already absorbed by the profession long ago) reaches a degree of popularity equal to (and in the final stages of decay superior to) that of new music. Nobody cares about either style or design. The music world is like a drunkard who has no digestion. He can't eat. He can only swallow more and more alcohol, any alcohol, till he falls down one day in *delirium tremens*. All the categories get confused and the values falsified. The opera becomes instrumental and unsingable. Ballet, instead of standing on its toes and holding its stomach in, which is where the ballet belongs if it expects to execute any variety of large free movements, stands flat on its feet and sticks its stomach out, waves an arm, and loses its balance. Song-and-dance folklore is imported from foreign climes, and the concert world is taken over by incompetent soloists and by overcompetent orchestral conductors who streamline the already predigested classics to a point of suavity where they go through everybody like a dose of castor oil.

As you see, this description fits quite accurately Germany for the last seventy-five years and not too badly the whole international music world. The concert tradition everywhere is esthetically in a bad way; it can't keep its eyes off the past. The opera too looks pretty sick as contemporary art. None of this is anybody's fault. Civilizations rise and civilizations die, and they usually overlap by several centuries. I am not writing a history of musical civilizations; I am describing the state of music. And the state of art-music everywhere in the West (I don't know Asia or Islam) is unquestionably more than a little bit decadent.

In the Americas popular music is very healthy indeed, though this does not mean that the Great Tradition is about to be taken over by the swing cats. Maybe it is and maybe it isn't; I wouldn't know. It does mean, though, that there is more good music around than ever gets through to the opera houses and to the trusts of concert management. These last, with their one thousand symphony orchestras around the world, however much invested capital they may represent, have about the same relation to today's creative activity in music that the museums (including the so-called "modern" museums) have to contemporary painting. There are musical activities of a popular nature and others of a recondite intellectual nature (far from popular) that enclose the nuclei of the next musical civilization. Without going into the ways and means of forcing that, which would be another book and which could not possibly represent anything but wishful prophecy on my part, it is still easy to see, none the less, that the official, the rich opera-and-concert world of today is the resplendent tail-end of a comet that has already gone around the corner.

The principal "form," design, or pattern involved in concert music is the concert itself, which is a sort of musical meal, proceeding, as meals do, from heavy to light in digestibility. A good deal of ingenuity and taste goes into the designing of this meal, into the fitting of admissible pieces together so that they fall within a given time limit (a quite strict one in most cases) in mutually advantageous juxtaposition. But program-making is not musical composition any more than hanging a show of pictures is oil painting. And the analysis of concert pieces shows that they nearly all have some kind of a plan. If enough pieces have the same kind of plan, that plan gets called a "form."

As I have said before, I am not very fond of the word. I do not think that sonatas and rondos and such are musical forms. I think they are merely rhetorical devices. I except the dance meters, which have a real metrical convention, and the round, the canon, the fugal exposition, which follow a tonal one. In any case, information about them is not lacking. You can read them up in the Appreciation books (mostly misinforming, I admit) or in the professional text-books of musical analysis (which are better). You can learn about them all in half an hour.

Such matters have a practical interest for persons who write music and a lesser but also certain interest for executants. Detailed knowledge about them is just as useful to the layman as a receipt for angel-food cake would be to an unmarried dock-hand. The only real problem involved in musical rhetoric is how to make a piece last some time without getting vague. It must hold the auditor's interest without confusing him. And it must do this, as the movies do it, by continuity.

Music's first dimension is length, a length of time. An important expression of any emotional thing (and music is certainly not much but emotional) requires time. Short expressions can be intense, but only long ones can be ample. Coherence, in any piece of time, requires a continuity plan. Music made to be heard must be very simple indeed, must repeat its chief material over and over. It is not like a book, where the reader can stop and turn back and get the plot straightened out if he forgets. It must have such a simple layout or build-up that nobody can fail to follow it.

If you are still interested in how this gets accomplished, go to the books. The commoner layouts are all listed there and can be learned very quickly. What is important, however, about the structure of a piece is not what layout is used and with or without what traditional observances, but whether an average musician can understand the music. Can he memorize it well enough in a week to communicate it to another average musician? This is where the well-known formal layouts come in. Classifying the layout is the first step in musical analysis. And musical analysis is (usually) the first step in memorizing. That is about its last utility too, I suspect, that it is an aid to memory. Indeed it is a great aid, and the ability to practice it is indispensable to active musicians. I doubt that it is of much value to passive listeners.

Now don't imagine for a moment that I despise musical passivity. No sight is more pleasing to a composer that that of a houseful of completely quiet people listening to some work of his being executed. If any of them are listening analytically, that is perfectly all right by me. The analysis of my music has never lost me a customer yet. But for those who enjoy taking music passively (which is the only way most people not musicians can take it at all), I've an idea the process works better when their minds are really passive. Both to musicians and to laymen I recommend the mastery of non-cerebral receptivity. You can take the piece apart at some other time, at a time when time itself is not of the essence. A run-through performance is for nourishment, not analysis. Let the music quicken your pulse and thicken your blood and turn over your liver and digest your food. Let your mind alone and don't worry about the second theme. Try the music on and see if it fits as is. You'll find yourself remembering it much better than if you tried to analyze it and in doing so missed half of it.

In my student days I used to go to the Boston Symphony

concerts every week. I found that if I arrived with my conscious mind already at a certain degree of musical saturation, as I often did, the only way I could understand anything the orchestra played was by not listening consciously at all. I would read the program. The Boston Symphony program in those days was a whole book, full of historic information and source-quotations. There was enough to last a good two hours; and all very diverting it was too, and cultural, and harmless. The music provided just enough slight-annoyance value (like railway-riding noises) to keep my attention on the reading. And the reading provided a subject for conscious attention to play with that enabled me really to hear the music. Occasionally the music would pull me away from the book and make me listen to it all over me. More often I just read on, paying no attention to the music, and of course never missing a note of it. Later I usually remembered it all, remembered it a great deal better than I should have if I had gone to sleep trying to listen and to analyze.

Musical analysis is a musician's job, just as chemical analysis is a chemist's. A concert is not, after all, even in its most recondite and tendentious examples, a display of musical specimens. A music library is that, if you must; but a concert is a meal. It is a feast, a ham sandwich, a chocolate sundae, nourishment to be absorbed with pleasure and digested by unconscious processes. The body has more use for music than the mind has. Take it or leave it according to the body's taste. Express your pleasure by applause, your displeasure by whistling and stamping, or by not coming again. If you live in a social group that cultivates musical opinions, tell your friends exactly what you thought of a piece afterwards, if you thought about it afterwards at all. If not, say so. And if your responses to the tonal art are low, then why be bothered with concerts anyway? There are always prize fights and tennis matches and matinées and dancing and eating and taking a walk and having a baby and quarreling and reading a book and getting tight. You are wasting good time to submit yourself to music unless you understand it viscerally. If you do understand it that way, then serious musical study and listening will be profitable to you. Otherwise I am afraid they will just confuse the mind with culture. I respect and admire sincerely persons who admit they are not interested in music.

Literally thousands of people go to concerts who are not

responsive to music. Maybe I underestimate the musicality of opera and concert subscribers. I hope so, but I am not convinced. The audiences at cheap popular orchestral concerts are just like audiences everywhere, and I understand their responses without any trouble. The well-to-do (usually female) subscriber, I do not really believe to be musically alert. I am convinced, though I can't prove it, that about one-fourth of the persons who go regularly to high-class concerts have no interest in what they hear and don't remember what they hear, that they are present from quite other than musical motivations, and that they know in advance they are going to be bored. There is, of course, no way of verifying my proportion. It might be much lower or much higher.

In any case, there are plenty of bored ones. Everybody knows that. The more expensive the seats the more boredom there is, as a general rule. These bored ones swell the receipts, of course; but they lower the potential of communication. If they are too numerous, they act as insulators and there is no communication. The receiving potential of audiences runs approximately as follows:

The most sensitive is the hand-picked invited audience, exception being made for invited radio audiences, which consist of company stooges.

Next come the audiences for chamber-music concerts. These contain a high proportion of professional musicians and almost no outsiders.

Audiences at concerts of pianists and solo violinists react rather strongly, on account of the large number of persons present who know from practice the technique and repertory of these instruments.

The same applies in a lesser degree to audiences for vocal soloists and for choral groups. Applause may run high; that means very little. In fact, the lower the culture-level of any audience, the greater that audience's enthusiasm for what it can understand.

The symphony addicts are, it seems to me, not very receptive, though the poor things haven't had much chance to receive, I must say, since world repertory got standardized. The resident orchestras suffer too from the social glamour brought to them by their rich founders and their pseudo-philanthropic trustees. This prestige brings in large numbers of impressive box-holders and subscribers whose active musical experience is low compared to their passive experience. (They have been to everything.) Even among the musical persons present, there are many who have only the vaguest acquaintance with orchestral instruments. Musical communication to these persons is a little incomplete. To the others it is practically nil. I know ladies who have been going to symphony concerts since childhood and who are lucky at sixty if they can recognize eight pieces out of the about fifty that make up the permanent repertory. These women are not stupid; they are just not very musical. They go to symphony concerts for reasons. I don't mean always social reasons, either, although a great many people do go to symphony concerts to be seen, just the way they used to go to the opera. What they like about orchestral concerts mostly, I think, is (a) the conductor and (b) the resemblance of the musical execution's super-finish to that of the other streamlined luxury-products with which their lives are surrounded. They feel at home, as if they were among "nice things," and as if the Revolution (or whatever it is that troubles rich people's minds) were far, far away. I don't think they are entirely bored. But I have always found them musically not very discriminating.

The invited radio audience is sterile. Practically no communication takes place at all; it isn't allowed to. The audience is only there to keep the players from getting bored or from getting mike-fright. It is an unpaid stooge. Applause is only allowed on cue; an adverse reaction of any kind is strictly forbidden, would be cut off the air if it took place.

Don't try to tell me any communication is going on, either, from the broadcasting room to the fireside listener. The listener begins by receiving a communication; but as soon as he learns that his reactions are producing no counter-reaction, he stops reacting. The radio concert is a good occasion to practice at home non-cerebral listening, to hear music while reading a book or washing dishes. Otherwise, the whole effect of radio concerts is dogmatic and scholastic, due to the absence of give-and-take. The best ones are those broadcast from public halls, because there you get a bit of the artist-audience interaction. Even in these broadcasts, there is always a speaker who manages to give you the idea that he is a hired salesman trying to make you sign something about the classics. It is pathetic the way he pleads with us to please believe everything in music is just hunky-dory, when we all know perfectly well that that last piece was a turkey and the house a frigidaire.

The Women's Club concert, the School-and-College-Trade concert and the Modern Music concert are special formulas. Each has its own repertory and its style of rendition, determined by the character of its highly stylized public. This public has in each case a moderately intense but highly stylized receptivity. Its audience reactions to any piece vary little all over the world.

The club formula aims to charm rather than to instruct. It avoids both novelty and brilliance. The school-and-college formula aims to instruct, and to this end seeks the shock value of novel or rare repertories rather than the stylish execution of chestnuts. A too-sophisticated execution is rather frowned on, in fact, and rightly, for it would get in the way of musical communication. A neutral rendition is better for unfamiliar music than a misapplication of some colorful technique to the wrong work or period.

Modern Music programs are made up almost exclusively of first performances in the locality. The audience is restless, picturesquely dressed, intellectually distinguished, and definitely international-minded. At least two-thirds of it is made up of practicing musicians and other artistic professionals. It is a hotbed of musical politics. Critical acrimony runs high.

From 1919 to 1929, these concerts represented the international front-line trench of the newer new music. Since that time new music, at least the music of the younger composers, has appeared more often in the theater, in the films, on the radio, and in private concerts. Because the societies for the promulgation of modern music (those that still exist) have come to represent a vested interest, the right of the previous decade's bright young men to censor this decade's production and to decide on its worthiness for performance beside their own. This decade's bright young men have, in consequence, adapted their music to commercial and private outlets, to the rather considerable advantage of both music and its commerce. The next decade's young (they are turning up in some abundance of late) show signs of inventing a less internationalist form of new-music concert and naturally of running it themselves, as the young people of the 1920's did. They will not do much about concerts of any kind, however, as long as there is any chance of their getting into commerce with applied music.

Just a word about the stylistic conventions of the Modern Music societies. An ideal program for any concert would be made up of pieces that were never intended to be played in concert. Such a program would have a rich variety of subject-matter and of musical style. As soon as a series of concerts, however, becomes a production outlet, composers start producing for that outlet. The concerts of any Modern Music society are primarily an outlet for the group of composers who constitute its program-committee. Any piece is refused that is more spectacular in subject-matter or treatment than the pieces it must appear beside, or sufficiently less spectacular so that somebody's music (you never know whose) might be made to sound a little silly. Let us suppose a young man writes a piece for private reasons, and that some society produces it, and no great harm is done. He is promptly asked to submit another and encouraged to write something especially for the society. That means he must keep in mind, while writing his piece, its relation to the kind of thing that it is likely to have to appear on the program with. If he transgresses that consideration, his piece will not be performed. A piece will be performed by somebody who has kept the unspoken rule and the unannounced pieces in mind.

The esthetic problem thus posed for all composers who do not have a society of their own, but who would like a little outlet all the same, is that of writing music that will not seriously endanger the success of certain other music. Professional advantages are offered as reward for happy solutions. The result of it all, in the 1920's, was the creation of an international school that tended more and more to become neutral in subject-matter, conformist in style. Everybody wonders why the modern symphonies played at endowed symphony concerts sound tame. That is the condition of their being played at all, that they shall not seriously compete with standardized repertory. People wonder too why so much of modern music, though it sounds violent, seems to say nothing comprehensible. That, my children, was the condition of its being played in the concerts of the international Modern Music ring. The dissonant contrapuntal was the only style admitted. It naturally got more and more so and just as naturally less and less expressive. I shall never forget the scandal in the world of modernist music that greeted the appearance in 1927 of Sauguet's ballet *La Chatte* and in 1934 of my own opera *Four Saints in Three Acts*. After twenty years of everybody's trying to make music just a little bit louder and more unmitigated and more complex than anybody else's, naturally everybody's sounded pretty much alike. When we went them one better and made music that was simple, melodic, and harmonious, the fury of the vested interests of modernism flared up like a gas-tank. That fury still burns in academic places. In my own case it is strongest where I was educated. At Harvard and among the Nadia Boulanger coterie in Paris I am considered a graceless whelp, a frivolous mountebank, an unfair competitor, and a dangerous character.

II

Back to the Womb, James

S O FAR I have taken for granted the common assumption of our time that the Arts are a little different from all other skills and from all other branches of knowledge. This assumption is an ancient one, although the definition of what is and what isn't an art has varied greatly from age to age. The modern conception is derived from the Greek mythological metaphor of the Muses, to which has been added, as a divine afflatus informing them all, the Hebraic and Christian concept of a Holy Ghost "who speaks by the prophets."

The three springs that issue from the slopes of Mount Helicon were in Bœotian times supposed to be presided over by three earth deities known as Meditation, Memory, and Song. By Athenian times these three had got subdivided into nine. They were, if I may remind you:

Music, which included the science of acoustics,
Astronomy, which included the science of numerology,
Dancing, both religious and theatrical,
History, whether that was written in verse or not,
Comedy,
Tragedy,
Elegy,
Lyric Poetry, and
Oratory, which included the recital of heroic poetry.

Please notice the enormous preponderance in this list of what we should call Literature and the complete absence of the visual arts.

The medieval schools used a different list. They included under the one word *ars*, which meant craft, the techniques of all the factibilia, of everything that could be made, from cake to sarcophagi. But they recognized seven major branches of learning, namely: Grammar, Logic, Rhetoric, Arithmetic, Geometry, Music, and Astronomy.

The division of all the techniques into Liberal Arts, or those which deal in knowledge rather than skill of hand, Mechanical Arts, which is what we would mean by the *crafts*, and the Beautiful Arts, seven of them in number, is a Renaissance conception. The Beautiful Arts turn out to be our old Greek friends, minus History and Astronomy, and with all the visual or plastic techniques added. That is to say, they are Music, Painting, Sculpture, Architecture, Poetry, Eloquence, and Choreography.

The modern world has a tendency to accept this list, but to group the Seven Arts into three main categories: the visual, commonly called plastic; the verbal, generally denominated as Literature; and the auditive, which means music and all of its collaborative manifestations. There is another modern tendency that wishes to separate all intellectual achievement into the imaginative (laymen call this "creative") and the scholarly branches. This is just another way of saying the Beautiful Arts versus the Liberal and gets us nowhere.

I have often wondered if there were any necessary connection or similarity at all between the visual arts, the verbal, and the auditive, beyond the fact that their practitioners often live in the same neighborhoods when they are young and poor and have to, and consequently are all more or less acquainted. Certainly the ability to consume with discrimination art-products of all three kinds is practically never encountered in any one customer. The paint-lovers are highly indifferent to music, and heaven knows the music-lovers' taste in the plastic arts is elementary. However that may be, the concept of "the Arts" is embedded in our thought and language. About all we can do with it is to relist the techniques, to regroup them along pedagogical, psychological, technical, moralistic, or economic lines. I have myself a little idea that it might be useful to envisage the art techniques according to their working-methods, as solitary versus collective.

I have avoided so far, wherever possible, using the word "collective," because it has been so bound up of late with partisan politics and class warfare that I have preferred to use the word "collaborative," which is much less emotion-producing, to describe art-work that is executed by some person not the designer of it. I find at this point that I need both words, one to describe collaborative design, like the writing of operas, ballets, theatrical works in general, and the planning of architecture, and the other to describe the execution of any design by skilled workmen, whether that design is a one-man effort or a three-man collaboration. So if you don't mind and if you will kindly, before going on, take time out to pacify whatever hopes and fears that word may rouse in your breast, we will hereinafter refer to all art-work as "collective" art which is executed by craftsmen from a design. That design may have been made by solitary or by collaborative methods; if it is executed by other persons than the designer, the work is some kind of a collective product.

It is probably the tendency of all skills to remain collective as long as their techniques are expanding and to become personal, private, solitary, to contract, in short, when no means for further technical expansion are available. Painting and Poetry were collective arts once. Sculpture and Architecture are still, also Choreography and Eloquence (if that means prepared declamation). And so is Music.

I mentioned in the very beginning of this book that there was no such thing, in my opinion, as the Modern Spirit, that there were only some modern techniques. Yet all laymen are convinced that modern poetry, modern painting, and modern music have something in common. What modern painting and modern poetry have in common is the discovery of the mental discipline of dissociation. That is the characteristic thought-device to which we owe both Cubist painting and Miss Gertrude Stein's poetic writings.

For artists the discipline of dissociation is a discipline in spontaneity. For scientists it is a discipline in avoiding spontaneity, which would mean the acceptance of common-sense judgments and axioms. The dissociation of image from design in painting, the simultaneous representation of multiple sight-lines, the juggling of word sounds and the jumbling of word meanings in poetry, are spontaneous, subjective dissociations; the only verification possible of their validity as communication is the equally spontaneous (but collective and hence authoritative) judgment of the whole body of persons who have taste and some training for the reception of beauty visual and linguistic.

This beauty being made all by one man, one would naturally expect criticism to play a large rôle in its reception. Curiously enough, it doesn't. Painting is practically without criticism today and poetry very nearly. Because you cannot criticize without standards, and there are no standards possible for evaluating one-man beauty. There is only voting, yes or no. Criticism of the collective arts is very vigorous, however; and it collaborates in their dissemination and absorption, even in their manufacture.

The discipline of spontaneity has not been very fecund for sculpture, acting, or oratory. It has not worked too badly in architecture. It has not been possible to apply it to music at all in any new way, because music is the one art where it has already been practiced, knowingly and systematically, for centuries. Modernism in music exists all right, or used to; but it has nothing whatsoever to do with modernism in painting or in poetry. Such modernism as exists in musical art (let us be perfectly clear about this) is not so much a matter of any recent vogue for discord, or of any new acoustical discoveries, or of any very great amplification of harmonic resources, as it is a general loosening up, a progressive efflorescence in decay, of the conventions of musical expression. It has been going on since the end of the eighteenth century.

Let me go back a little in history. Every art has its high-brow and its low-brow manifestations, its official canon and its folk-lore. During Byzantine and medieval times painting and sculpture and architecture, all the visuals, were subject on the one hand to a set of esoteric rules called the Principles of Design, largely derived, if I mistake not, from astrology and from mystical numerology; and on the other to the pressure of popular taste, which is always utilitarian, sentimental, and humanistic. From the Italian Renaissance to the French Revolution all three arts became increasingly humanistic, and the esoteric laws of Design fell into progressive disrepute. By the end of the eighteenth century improvisational one-man easel-painting in oil was about all the painting there was. Like that of all one-man jobs, its business was to express private and personal views of

subject-matter, to show how anything looks to one man's Seeing Eye. During the nineteenth century, though certain discoveries were made about light and its depiction by color, design
just didn't interest anybody.

In the early years of the twentieth century, Paris was the
center of an attempt to invigorate all the visual arts by reintroducing design as a major element in pictorial composition. I do
not think this motivation was entirely conscious on anybody's
part. I think the more dominant conscious desire was to bring
painting intellectually up-to-date and thus to please a larger and
less hard-boiled public than the nineteenth-century capitalists, a
public disillusioned about money and politics, that had read all
the socialist and scientific writers and was very nervous about
slum conditions. It is not my purpose to recount in detail how
a proletarian, a populistic movement was turned into the aristocratic and recondite Cubist revolution or to pronounce on the
ultimate success of this last, because the painting-war it started
is far from over. I only want to point out by all this hasty history
that the art of oil-painting had gone so far solitary, private, and
personal by 1900 that it took a revolution within the profession to get it admitted that esoteric matters were involved at all
in the painting of easel-pictures. The painting of these is still
practiced, of course, as a one-man job, subject to no collective
criticism any more valid than market quotations. As a matter
of fact, in Paris today a painter is not even judged by his peers;
he is judged by poets, political philosophers, and dressmakers
(under dressmakers include the periodical organs of women's
wear). Pablo Picasso cannot influence the market price of any
painter's work. Miss Gertrude Stein, André Breton, and *Vogue*
magazine can. The whole profession of painting is anarchy. The
painters, as a group, are as devoid of organization as the visible
world they depict. They are an infinite multiplicity of nice little
men, all got up in trick hair-cuts and coquettish tweeds, parad-
ing their imaginary sex-appeal around with a naïve persistence
only equaled by the naïve persistence with which they produce
by the most advanced methods of automatic workmanship picture after picture almost any one of which might have been
painted by almost any one of them.

The history of poetry is essentially the same, though the timing of the periods is all different. It is a history of progressive

shrinking in both length and subject-matter since the art began to work on a solitary production-system, since it gave up the stage, in fact.

Solitary art-workers, it would seem, tend to produce small-ish works not differing very much from one artist to another in either style or subject-matter. They have the old trouble about solo improvisation, which is practically always conformist and corny. A prepared declamation of poetry can be pretty fine; improvised oratory is mostly silly. Solo improvisation is the triumph of the one-job man on the one-man job. Collective improvisation is a very different thing. Improvisational one-man easel-painting is sold to millionaires as high art. It is mostly today just the folklore of intellectual Paris. Jazz and swing music are sold to everybody as the folklore of dumb-bell America. They have lately, however, through the practice of collective improvisation, come to be among the most varied, elaborate, and expressive of modern art products, and of them all, scarcely excepting the movies, the most widely disseminated.

The question of how modern painting got to be that way, at what point in time it ceased to be designed objective de-piction and became personal depiction, bothers the painters themselves a good deal, though the customers don't seem to care much. They use it as decoration anyway. The question of how Romantic music grew into Modern music bothers every-body but musicians. Because musicians know something that the outsiders, flustered and fascinated by the painting boom and the physical science boom and the psychoanalytic-introspection boom, don't know at all. They know, they still know, how to combine humane expression, a popular, a low-brow thing and always a non-canonical thing, with auditive beauty, which is a set of ancient and esoteric techniques, the employment of which to accomplish sentimental and expressive purposes has been practiced by the musical profession for centuries. And the essential device in that practice is exactly what seems so novel and exciting to painters, the mental disciplines of dissociation and spontaneity.

Let me elucidate. The basic material of Western music, our diatonic scale, is of strictly numerological origin. The only tones admitted in it are those bearing certain simple arithmetical ratios (expressible either by the length of a vibrating body or by the number of air-vibrations produced by whatever means per second) to a basic tone whose frequency of similar vibrations is represented by the number one. The tones so derived constitute our gamut, our whole palette of tonal resource. This gamut is of Greek origin. It has been subject to successive adjustments and amplifications to make it concord with acoustical facts (notably with the whole natural harmonic series), the last of these adjustments being the adoption about two hundred years ago of a falsified, or "tempered," scale for keyed instruments. Other races in other climes use other scales or gamuts. None of them, including ours, concords entirely with the harmonic series or with mathematical acoustics. But for good or ill, ours is ours, and the tonal patterns we write down are written in that alphabet.

When a tonal pattern of any kind is combined with a metrical one, the result is correctly called a musical "composition" whether it expresses anything very definite or not. The pattern of a musical composition may be strictly numerological, esoteric, and magical. Enormous quantities of such music were written during the Middle Ages and still are [notably in the electronics laboratories]. Its first effect on him who executes and on him who listens is none the less a muscular and a viscero-emotional, a personal one. The conscious mind can be made to transfer the muscular and viscero-emotional effects to impersonal verbo-intellectual conceptions by combining music with verbal texts or with social observances of recognizable meaning, such as love-making, story-telling, marching, or dancing.

Among the Greeks, the Chinese, the Hindoos, and the Latin peoples, music was and is predominantly restricted to usages of the latter nature, to matters of which the social significance can be somewhat controlled. The Africans, the Arabs, and the Germanic races are given to the practice of a more directly physical music, which, instead of producing emotional intensifications of socially permissible ideas and actions, produces ecstatic states of a completely physical, nonintellectual, even anti-social character. In the case of the Negroes and Arabs, these ecstasies are expressed muscularly by jerks and catalepsies. Consciousness and attention are as if absent. The usual antidote for over-indulgence in such ecstasies is sexual intercourse. In the case of the Germanic races, the ecstasy takes the form of a muscular relaxation combined with concentration of mental attention on the obscurest of all our sensations, the visceral ones. The antidote for over-indulgence in this practice is eating.

Children who have, by accident or atavism, a facility for remembering and reproducing both tonal and metrical patterns are said to have musical talent. This facility, like all talents, either grows or diminishes. To grow it must be exercised in musical execution. Listening to music will not satisfy musical tendencies or develop musical talent any more than watching sports will satisfy the play-instinct or develop muscles. A person so trained (and training has to include experience) is said to be a musician. Persons whose training and experience are perfectly real, but insufficient to meet the professional competition of the day, are commonly referred to as "musical." Persons who are without experience in musical execution are properly called "not musical." These persons may even show a history of extended lesson-taking. They are unmusical all the same if they cannot separate a musical pattern from its muscular and viscero-emotional effects and remember the musical pattern.

Instrumental training, musical analysis, and the practice of musical composition are based on a complete dissociation of all the elements, not only of the elements of pattern from one another, but of pattern itself from expression. Workers in the verbal and the visual arts do not go, I think, so far in this dissociative breakdown of technique as musicians do. For us melody is one thing. Counterpoint is another. Harmony is still another. In any melodic line the tonal pattern is separable from the rhythmic. In any harmonic progression the chord-series is separable from the voice leading, or melodic structure, of the instrumental parts combining to form that harmony. On the instruments that can play several tones at once, there is not necessarily any melodic structure implied at all (at least not much) in the execution of a harmonic pattern. The instrumentation of a musical piece is also completely separable from the piece's melodic, rhythmic, contrapuntal, and harmonic design. That design is equally separable from the piece's expressive intention, as I mentioned earlier, only the essential themes and the general style of their deployment being really very expressive, and a good eighty or ninety per cent of the musical notes in any long work being what they are, and even being there at all, often, for reasons purely rhetorical. The particular way in which repetition and variation are employed in musical continuity is a matter of free choice by the composer. It is very little imposed by the nature of the music's desired expressive effect. And down to the most insignificant percussive tap or the most neutral harmonic filling, every separate pattern that contributes to the general collective pattern is a consistent musical pattern of some kind. If it isn't you get hubbub.

The proportion of expressive pattern to neutral pattern in any piece varies with local tradition. The Latins love abstraction and the Germanics love collective sentiment. Consequently the Italian tendency is to put all the human expression into one place (the melody) and to frame that element with abstract music like scales, trills, arpeggios, and harmonic plunk-plunk, disposing these in a purely rhetorical, an architectural, way. The Germanics, horrified by this radical dissociation of elements and not really liking abstractions much anyway, accept the advantageous architectonics of the system, and then proceed to conceal these by spreading a rich layer of carefully adjusted expressiveness over all the subsidiary elements.

The Gallic, or French, musical procedure is less radically abstractionist than the Italian and less collectively expressive than the German, though it is predominantly Latin in its frank employment of dissociative methods. Its great contribution to European musical technique is its separation of muscular, or accentual, meter from prosodic, or quantitative, meter. This makes the French the world masters on the one hand of musical prose declamation and on the other, along with their Russian progeny, of ballet music. Also of a kind of musical landscape-painting that it is only possible to do when one can keep the piece static by separating quantitative rhythm from accentual intoxication.

Italian music tends by its abstraction to lack human expressiveness. German music has two besetting sins. One is to get muddy through lack of a sufficiently delicate adjustment among the divers expressive elements; and the other is to go round and round, to get into waltz or march rhythms that put everybody into a narcotic state. The French trouble is overdoing the static, not seeming to get anywhere, because quantitative prose rhythms without much muscular whip-it-up in them are not very interesting to the blood-stream.

The marriage of these three traditions produced in Vienna between the years 1750 and 1850 the highest concentration of humanistic expression into musical form the Western world has ever known. That is history. That flowering is over, at least the best part of it. But the curve of decline is slow, as all historical evolutions are; new things will be under way long before Mozart and Beethoven are forgotten. I want to point out, though, as long as it is still possible to understand a bit the Viennese masters and what they had in their minds, that:

¶1. They practiced all the esoteric musical techniques, the canon, the fugue, prose declamation, imitative vocal counterpoint, and the air with Alberti bass;

¶2. They wrote in all the popular styles of song-and-dance music of all the European ethnic groups;

¶3. Although mostly star performers themselves, they never had improvisational mania or virtuoso disease. (Wagner, not a Viennese, caught the latter in Paris.)

¶4. They fused the popular manner with the esoteric techniques (always the aim of Western art) without ever sacrificing the force of one to the beauty of the other or obscuring the fact that the two are two.

Their technique itself was in the highest degree analytic, every element being completely dissociable from every other, both for instruction purposes and for practice. And texture was equally dissociable from expression. So much so that their greatest triumph was a kind of lengthy instrumental piece of a purely introspective nature which was nevertheless completely comprehensible (on sheer technical grounds) to interpreters and to consumers. They didn't even give these pieces titles or conceive them for any but purely musical usage. The nearest thing I know in any other art-work to the Viennese sonata-and-symphony literature is Cubist painting, and even that is at once less hermetic in construction and less popular in appeal. [I do not consider "abstract expressionism," though it is Cubism's grandchild, as a major tradition, riddled as it is with both improvisation *and* virtuosity.]

This is because painting is a one-man job and doesn't have to be technically competent. Every man who works by himself gets either improvisational mania, which means a sacrifice of hieratic beauty to expression, a thing which is not hermetic at all (and beauty must be hermetic), or virtuoso disease, which means a sacrificing of both humane expression and hieratic beauty to streamlined execution; this, though it may make many a non-stop flight around the world, rarely arrives at being anything more than impressively expensive, rarely penetrates the dumb-bell human heart.

The Viennese musical apogee is long since over, though its tradition still goes on in slow decline. In its early decline it encountered certain foreign popular traditions on the up-grade, namely, those of the Spanish gypsies, the Hungarian gypsies, and the Russian gypsies. The confluence rejuvenated art-music a little, amplified these popular traditions a lot. The slight rejuvenation that took place in art-music between 1890 and 1914 was called Modern Music. Its centers were the ancient centers of esoteric musical knowledge, Vienna and Paris.

Art-music has made no advance since World War I except for the grafting on of a few goat-glands from the Americas. Popular music, however, has made such advances in the United States that the jazz-world today can almost be said to represent an art-tradition, with its academies, its pedagogues, its great men, its written histories, and some highly disinterested criticism. It was in a trade magazine of popular music that I recently found the following recipe for a proper musical performance. Jam, says Henry Dupre of New Orleans, should be played "from the heart, honestly, and for musicians only." Mr. Dupre is here advocating a higher standard of composition, as well as of performance (because jam is not merely execution) than I have ever seen advocated in any publication devoted to modern music of the high-brow schools.

Modern music has been for twenty-five years [make it forty-five] at such a standstill that musicians now practically all understand about it. Laymen, however, are still pretty confused. They are confused because they think it has something to do with modern poetry or with the modern painter's trick of multiple viewpoint. As I explained above, the discipline of mental dissociation is the oldest tradition in music. Also that music, for all the decay of Vienna, is still a collective art in all of its manifestations, high-brow and low-brow. Modern painting and poetry are two other stories. It may be that painting and poetry will hit the bottom of solitude soon and bounce up again into the collective practices. At the moment they are still one-man jobs. Their practitioners are trying to use analytic methods without objectivity and to be spontaneous in an epoch when there are no conventions left through which visual or verbal spontaneity can be made clear. There will be some possibility of comparing music with the visual and the verbal arts when these latter shall have become collective arts again, or when music shall have sunk to being made all alone in a room by one little man, who produces the sounds he wants to hear by electromagnetic means and records the whole on film without recourse to executants. [In 1960 electronic music, on account of engineering necessities, is still produced in collaboration.]

Back to Politics

IT IS frequently proposed that artists and intellectuals should form a solid political front of some kind. I have seen a number of these movements in action, and I do not think musicians make much sense in them. Poets may.

One of the striking things about poets is their passion for collectivist theories of government. They have great disdain, however, for the collectively practiced arts. They are suspicious of architecture and the stage and just barely tolerate music for its possible advantages to poetry whenever some composer sets a few of their verses. Painting they accept if they can command its subject-matter [as the Surrealists did].

They do lots of theorizing about the possible relations between solitary art and collective government. The leftist and revolutionary-minded wings are always getting together (sometimes with a painter or two along to give them the air of not being just a band of unemployed) and issuing manifestos. The sense of these manifestos is mostly something like this: that the chief function of art right now is to aid in bringing about a workers' revolution and that the chief business of the workers' revolutionary government will be to raise the economic and civil status of art-workers. This is a perfectly intelligible demand on their part, if by art and art-workers you understand poetry and poets. It is the natural and proper attitude of any group of persons among whom unemployment runs as high as it does among them. Such a demand would be absurd from members of the musical profession. Mark you that the private adherence of musicians to revolutionary (or anti-revolutionary or counter-revolutionary) political organizations is a legitimate thing and a very frequent thing. That need not bother anybody but our political masters. What is impossible to conceive is that the members of the musical trades and professions should give up a real economic status based on a wide, non-political function

(I mean the supplying of music to its habitual consumers) for a non-paying economic status based at present on a narrow and sectarian function.

It is doubtful if music has any useful service to render to Revolution right now. I have always noticed that workers' concerts, proletarian operas, and demonstrations of mass-singing tend to appease class hatreds and revolutionary fervors rather than to augment them. Also, the trades and professions at which people can (whether they actually do or not) earn a living furnish very few militants to revolutionary movements. What they do furnish to workers' organizations is lots of militant trade-unionists, all out, and very firmly out, for a quick amelioration of their own economic condition. Any musician who feels a need for changing things economically can get co-operation from other musicians and from all the trade-union groups, and he can change lots of things that way. That is a normal formula for effecting social reform and a quite powerful one. I cannot see that it would do the musician (employed or unemployed) any good to join up with the poets, all of whom are unemployed but none of whom have any tie-up (as poets) with the general labor federations.

The only known way for any craft or profession to raise its economic and civil status is by group action through its trade-unions and its professional bodies. Persons and groups who have no trade-union or effective professional body must essay to raise their condition by private means if any. The most common of these means is collaboration with political organizations whose function is to provoke political change. The adherence of musicians to such parties is a private matter and is usually kept so. The influence of such organizations on the policies of trade-unions and professional bodies is operated by interior pressure within those bodies. This is entirely legitimate. The rôle played by militant Marxian organizations in trade-union activity has never been very different from the rôle, for instance, that the Catholic Church and the various inter-denominational religious associations play in organized philanthropy, nor from the dominant rôle played in our institutions of learning by the representatives of banking, commerce, and industry that administer their funds. All that is a matter for trade-unions, social workers' groups, and educational foundations to handle from the inside. They do so handle it for the most part and present, in consequence, a united front to the public.

I have been attacked privately a good deal and once or twice in public gatherings for my unwillingness to announce a political affiliation of any kind, whether of an officially revolutionary or of an anti-revolutionary nature. So, I presume, have many other musicians. I continue to remain outside all that and shall continue to do so for the following reasons:

I believe that trade-unions and professional bodies must function as groups (and as groups of groups) with regard to changes in government and society. Any influence I may be able personally to exert over such transformations is, I think, more effective when operated through worker or professional solidarity. If my union or my professional body disagrees with me about any policy whose adoption I advocate, I can do one of two things. Either I can accept majority rule and shut up, or I can stage a little war. I can call the lay-public to my aid through the press and attempt to produce a change of opinion that way in enough of my colleagues to enable me to alter the previously taken attitude of my professional body. I cannot, however, continue very long manifesting in public my difference of opinion from that of my colleagues without rendering all of us ineffectual. Nothing is more legitimate and proper than that any citizen should have private political or religious affiliations which furnish him guidance in matters of private and even of professional conduct. Nothing is more suicidal, however, than to use one's professional prestige to give weight to public statements of private opinion.

There is no reason for my making a public statement of any kind excepting in my character as a professional musician. In that case I assume responsibility for my statements, and I accept correction of them from other musicians. If I use what professional prestige I have to advertise railways, pharmaceutical specialties, or international sources of ethical guidance, I submit myself to the public in the attitude of any banal celebrity whose interest to the public is just that of any other equally publicized character who may be a has-been tomorrow. I diminish the prestige of my whole profession by using my position in it for non-professional purposes, and I diminish my own influence

within the profession by making public statements on matters
either that do not regard the profession at all or about which
the profession itself contains differences of opinion. Remember
the horse-laugh that went up about all professors and scientists
when forty of them in Germany (I think forty was the number)
signed a manifesto during World War I about who they thought
should be allowed to win it. They had signed, I presume, on
the naïve assumption that their professional distinction was sufficient to convince their colleagues in foreign countries that
the German foreign policy of the moment was nobler than
anybody else's.

Recently I was speaking of these matters with a poet of my
acquaintance who has a certain knowledge of trade-union history and an elaborate knowledge of revolutionary theory. He
explained to me that the musicians were quite right, from a
revolutionary point of view, to maintain strong trade-unions
and to demand every social and economic amelioration; that
such action, when taken by organized trade-groups, did not
constitute an advocacy of social reformism as a complete political program; that, on the contrary, strong unions were the best
possible preparation for a well-working socialism. But when I
told him I had written in this book that professional composers were fools to do anything in public, on the strength of
their professional reputation, that would tend to diminish the
prestige of the whole profession by producing grave discord
within it, and that consequently I recommended to composers
just now to take their political action through their professional
bodies, he accused me of advocating anarcho-syndicalism. It
took me fifteen minutes to get it through his poet's wordy
head that my advocacy of professional solidarity was in no way
connected with any ism or with any messianic ideas about how
a perfect state should function. I do not have any ideas, public
or private, about the perfect state. I do not think professional
people with a professional practice of any kind are likely to go
in much for those ideal static structures. What we are much
more likely to feel about political forms and their administration is that we shall have to defend our professional rights by
eternal vigilance under any kind of government. We are willing
to leave to Cæsar (if we must) everything politic and fiscal,
though we shall grouse no end about that. We must demand,

and, if we demand as a solid professional body, we shall obtain (and keep) from any governing agency of whatever kind in any possible state, both economic security for our members and the musical direction of all enterprises of whatever nature where music is employed.

I fancy that to this end collaboration between composers' professional bodies and the unions of executant musicians, which form, in turn, a part of the general labor federations, will in the long run be a more fruitful collaboration than the present pooling of interests between composers and publishers that is the operating basis of all the performing-rights societies. I think this for three reasons:

¶1. The present mechanism of our collaboration with publishers provides no means for adjudicating disputes between composers and publishers that arise from a disparity in their interests.

¶2. The publishers themselves, mostly small capitalists, are at any moment likely to find themselves owned by large banking and industrial pools. This development has already begun to take place in popular music. When an analogous situation shall have become general in standard music publishing, the only possible way for composers to obtain any recognition by publishers of their legitimate divergencies of interest will be through the aid of some equally powerful combination or organization. The general labor federations are the only non-capitalist organizations in existence that have that kind of power.

¶3. The performing-rights societies are private organizations that collect taxes from public and private musical enterprises. They are at present tolerated by most governments. Their position, however, in both law and equity is far more tenuous than that of the collective-bargaining associations. They are constantly being sued as combinations in restraint of trade and as profit-making organizations whose turn-over should be taxable by municipalities, states, and central governments. So far they seem to have resisted these attacks effectively, most of which are financed by radio companies, movie companies, and similar large tie-ups of electrical patents with banking. The minute the publishers shall have been bought out by these same tie-ups, any association of composers and publishers will be just a company union for the electrical recording-and-transmission combines.

Do not think that I am proposing an industrial union of all music-workers. I don't think that would be a bad idea for executant musicians, copyists, arrangers, musical engravers, teachers, and persons who make musical instruments. Such a development seems to be taking place in America through the American Federation of Musicians (actually a craft-union, but moving toward the absorption of all music-workers). I should approve highly of such a union, but I do not see much place in it for composers, excepting in so far as these may be also pianists or teachers or some other kind of time worker. Because, in spite of all the community of interests and of understanding that exists between the composers and the other musicians, the fact remains that workers who work under somebody else's direction, executing somebody else's plan, and getting paid for it by the hour, have a completely different view of life and a different set of financial interests from persons who work privately, time not being of the essence at all, and who get paid for a piece of work not on a basis of how long that work took to get written but on the basis of how long it takes to play it and how many people listen, who get paid proportionally, that is, to the usage their work receives.

I do not say that it might not be a good idea for governments to guarantee a minimum living to all citizens, composers included. That would be an act of general amelioration which it might be possible to put into effect, though I don't think it ever has been attempted anywhere. It might be equally desirable to limit the profits from professional work to a reasonable figure by slapping super-taxes on composers' incomes. (Don't laugh. Successful authors of all kinds in Soviet Russia make astronomical sums.) Those are extreme but perfectly imaginable social measures. It is difficult to imagine, however, short of a complete socialization of society where nobody got paid for anything, any way of making just compensation to musical authors for the public exploitation of their work (in case any such exploitation takes place and for any reason and by means of no matter what financial backing) on any other basis than that of a fee proportional to the time occupied in performance and to the number of persons listening.

The chief characteristics of professional men are their economic independence and their intellectual authority. That authority and that independence are obtained by never charging the customer for preparation, experiment, or correction but by accepting payment only for professional services rendered. Different kinds of work are measurable for payment in different ways. The time a composer actually takes to write a given piece is not a reasonable or possible way of measuring that work's commercial value. Its value for payment must be measured by its utility, as all professional services are.

Consequently, the composer would be foolish to submit his economic destiny and the protection of his professional interests to any federation of mere musical workmen, at least 99.99 per cent of whose work is measurable for paying purposes by the time they spend doing it. The high-powered soloists and conductors are a little more like us than the anonymous instrumentalists are. They prepare privately, accept in their own name responsibility for public failure, and charge what the market will bear. But even these glamorous characters are not independent and authoritative workmen. They execute somebody else's design, usually on order. Any freedom they have about repertory (even about style) exists only within the narrow limits predetermined by managers. It would not be proper for a composers' professional body to accept any direction whatever from, or any equality in voting with, professional inferiors.

A professional body is not a trade-union. There is every reason for the professional body at certain periods of history to obtain economic privileges from or through the exploiting classes. There is every reason that I know of in this period to obtain and to expect to keep on obtaining what we want through collaboration with our executant workmen, who are better organized than we are and who, if they aren't any stronger than the exploiting classes, are in a little better position to aid us in securing performances and in getting paid for them than the exploiters are. This may seem strange, but it is true none the less. Because the executants have an interest in the continual performance by hand of lots and lots of music, whereas the exploiters' principal interest today lies in the widest possible dissemination of reproductions of the smallest possible amounts of actual musical performance. Whether in the long run the reproduction-systems are beneficial to the musical art remains to be seen. It looks right now as if the executant musicians have, on the whole, more to offer composers than the owners of electrical patents have.

In any case, although I personally favor the collaboration of composers' bodies with musical trade-unions (even to the point of the closed shop, provided the composers' professional body keeps itself open to all composers of every school and reasonable degree of proficiency) rather than with finance-capital, I do maintain that the professional bodies, all professional bodies, doctors, engineers, architects, and the rest, must remain independent bodies, ready at all times to defend their intellectual and economic independence from all organizations of persons not practicing that profession as original designers. This is the only professional policy likely to ensure the survival of the major techniques through changes in government and administration. And I maintain that the preservation, cultivation, and transmission of the autonomous techniques through changes in government and administration are a mark of the great civilizations and a desirable thing for everybody connected with any civilization.

The professional bodies nourish their traditions by the pooling of private knowledge and by the transmission of this knowledge esoterically to persons of (or potentially of) the profession. The consolidation and transmission of professional knowledge is a permanent function. Disseminating the fruits of this knowledge varies with public need and taste. Music is tolerated, regulated, sometimes slightly encouraged by governments, by private capital, and by workmen's protective associations. Sometimes no attention is paid to it at all. On the whole and in the long run, the professional man's working life is indissolubly bound up with his professional colleagues and with the general public, not with governments, not with members of the other professions, not with the social needs of any particular class among his co-citizens. The composer works at his best and society profits from him most not only when he writes music "from the heart, honestly, and for musicians only" but when he takes what political action he takes as the member of an indissoluble professional body.

Everybody nowadays wants to dictate the social usages of art. The authoritarian governments are on the war path to make art serve their foreign policy or their social theories. The revolutionists are doing their best to subject the Beautiful Arts to summary judgment by persons unidentified. A lot of unemployed workers in the solitary arts, chiefly poets, are trying to get a job by turning their talent as dialecticians to the speeding up of political and social change, because they know that a political revolution of collectivist character is more likely to bring them a public again than is any minor amelioration of the status quo.

There is not yet any analogous movement in music, even in the United States, where musicians' unemployment runs high. If the American Federation of Musicians and the American Guild of Musical Artists and the American Composers Alliance are still not entirely the secular arm of international politics or of any pool of bankers, philanthropists, and trustees, that is not because their leadership is superior or their membership dumb. It is because in the Western world Music is still a going concern. In spite of the decay of the Viennese tradition and the growth of the Appreciation-racket, music still gets written, performed, and consumed, lots of it, in all categories. And neither the profession of writing it nor the trade of performing it is quite yet immobilized by friction with the businessmen who organize the dissemination of it.

The island world, for all the physical poverty and mental pretentiousness of its leaders, for all the real suffering that exists among the executants, for all the outrageous designs of finance-capital on consumers' taste and authors' pocketbooks, the island civilization still functions in the world as an integrated civilization, an auditive civilization, the only civilization to which persons whose viscera are audito-sensitive can ever possibly give whole-hearted allegiance.

A 1961 Postlude

MARY GARDEN used to tell young opera singers, "Take care of the dramatic line and the musical line will take care of itself." She did not mean, of course, that good acting can ever justify bad singing. Merely that good singing must find its expression through the shape of that which it was designed to express.

Music is designed to express feelings. These are the sole subject of its communication, the only inner reality it deals with. And the difference between one state of feeling and another, as expressed in music, is largely a matter of shape, shape of melody and shape of larger form. Concentration on anything else gives to a musical action a private and self-indulgent quality that limits communication. It also tends to break down the communal effort essential to the art.

Painting and poetry, one-man jobs, can be self-operative. Music is practiced today only as a collaboration. Even solo improvisation—one of the stricter forms of composition—is nothing but personal fancy within a familiar frame. The whole musical art involves co-operation from the ground up—co-operation, good will, and loyalties. And this co-operation, I maintain, must be used for musical purposes only. I also maintain that musical purposes can be correctly defined only by the profession. If the profession neglects its duty in this matter, groups less responsible to music take over.

That the composing of music is a profession I think I have demonstrated. If I have, then the next step now is for the composers themselves to assume control of everything that regards music—its performance, its distribution, and its explanation. They must exercise an authority comparable to that exercised by the practitioners of law and medicine. Otherwise music will cease to be a liberal art and become a consumer commodity, an article of commerce, an arm of the state.

The history of the liberal professions in the Soviet Union can be a lesson to us all. Literature, painting, and music there have all relinquished their pride. And though they are highly remunerated, their products are virtually without distinction. The legal profession has not done much better, one gathers, largely because Russian law at the beginning of the Revolutionary period already lacked solidly based traditional procedures. Medicine, on the other hand, and scientific research and scholarship—if we except the brief attempt of certain biologists to differ with the rest of the world about the inheritance of acquired characteristics—have maintained reputable international standards.

The submissiveness of the liberal arts in Russia to political (they call it ideological) control has retarded cultural development and will continue to do so for many years in spite of what seems just now to be a slight lifting of the political pressures. The Russian Association of Professional Musicians, which was in no way opposed to the Revolution, and which merely aspired to guide the new music life in a responsible manner, early offered to the state its advice and co-operation. Its manifesto of 1924 is realistic about Russian musical problems and no end penetrating in its criticisms of the West. Its 1926 declaration is far less ambitious, far more subservient to party ideals. In 1932, in spite of an even humbler statement of servitude, the association was abolished.

Whether a less toadying attitude toward the political authority would have preserved the organization one cannot really know. I suspect it might have, knowing governments, all governments, for the bullies they are and how their truculence tends to collapse before a determined group. Perhaps the Russian musicians got organized too late. Ah, but that is exactly my argument. Now, in a time of peace and prosperity, it may be possible to develop a world set-up capable of surviving local changes in power, economics, and ideology. In the midst of political changes, it is not.

There is less probability in the West right now of a Marxist political revolution than there is of a massive reorganization of music's distribution that might be operated by businessmen inspired by the profit motive and abetted by governments avid for cultural advertising. Such a reorganization is indeed in process and indeed in danger of handing over musical standards to irresponsible agents. The German composers, wise in our time, saw to it that in the whole postwar restoration in Germany of music's business—its performance, its publication, its patronage, and naturally its pedagogy—they kept a controlling hand. The authority of a small group of them, about ten, today amounts virtually to a veto power over all musical usages; and they have not wielded their power unworthily. A profession, after all, is ever consecrated and responsible. Responsible to itself, I mean. And not to itself as a power group, but to itself as the sole possible preserver of its knowledge and skills. A profession that is not intellectually autonomous is merely a trade and its product merely a consumer commodity.

When music shall have become just another consumer commodity like chewing gum, its grand epoch will be over. Already a great deal of it is designed, like central heating, to be merely present. Keeping the rot peripheral, preventing it from infecting the heart, is not going to be easy. Too many people make money out of it. But let this book sound a warning, however muted, for musicians to be on their guard lest their sacred rights be handed to outsiders.

I do not like what has happened to music in Russia, and I do not like the whole of what is happening here. There is lots of music around and lots of what passes for its patronage; but there is certainly a tendency parallel to the Russian experiment toward integrating the arts into an industrial-commercial-educational complex, at the expense of their autonomy. Education should serve art, not the contrary.

Autonomy, intellectual and financial, is unquestionably the ideal state for any profession, both for its own well being and for its contributions to culture. And the West, through its long experience of liberal institutions, is better prepared than Russia for developing professional autonomies. It is quite possible that we shall never know here the degrading lack of intellectual freedom that Russia inherited from the Czars and augmented under the Soviet hierarchy. But it is just as possible that we may have to fight a bit toward continuing our own intellectual rights. Believe me, they are under attack.

Such attacks are not always as overt as those of the late Senator McCarthy. They may be masked as encouragement of the arts, with administrators put in control and subsequent threats of withdrawing support; or as documentary studies of the market, which prove that most of the voters prefer corrupt art (as if that fact were either new or significant); or as the protection of a national recording industry, though there is no such thing—there are merely cartels that have made it harder to transport a gramophone record across a frontier than a pint of opium.

The rôle of the arts in contemporary society, Eastern or Western, is more obscure in this century than it has been in some previous ones. That indecision is not due to the aspirations toward autonomy that are common to all the arts. Quite the contrary, as I have tried to show, autonomy makes their functioning more clean, as well as more powerful. If this is so, one must believe in the arts and give them their head. And their head men (in music it is the composers) must not avoid to lead. Lead where? Toward professional autonomy.

Take care of the professional line and the artistic line will take care of itself. That was my message in 1939. It still is.

VIRGIL THOMSON

Acknowledgments

FOR PERMISSION TO QUOTE from letters, poems, and articles, I wish to thank the following: Mrs. Böske Antheil for a letter written me by George Antheil in 1925; Mrs. A. Everett Austin, Jr., for letters written me in 1933 by A. Everett Austin, Jr.; Mrs. Alfred H. Barr, Jr., for letters that she wrote me in 1932 and 1939; Mrs. William Aspenwall Bradley for a letter written me by William Aspenwall Bradley in 1933; Mrs. Bagg and Angus Davidson, administrators, for two poems by Mary Butts (*Pagany*, I:2 [1930]; II:3); Mrs. Theodore Chanler for a letter to Kathleen Hoover written by Theodore Chanler in 1948; Aaron Copland for letters written me in 1931, 1932, 1939, 1943, and 1954; Marian Morehouse (Mrs. Cummings) for a postcard written me by e. e. cummings in 1940; Edwin Denby for letters written me in 1929 and '30; C. Dewitt Eldridge for a letter written to his family in 1938; Roy Harris for a letter written me in 1930; Lou Harrison for a letter written me about 1964; John Houseman for a letter written me in 1939; Georges Hugnet for letters written me in 1930 and '33, for an article entitled "Virgil Thomson" (*Pagany*, I:1 [1930]) as translated by me into English, and for his poem "Enfances" (*Pagany*, II:1); Minna Lederman (Mrs. Mel Daniel) for a letter written me in 1938; Pare Lorentz for a telegram sent me in 1937; Henri Sauguet for a review published in *L'Europe nouvelle*, 1931, and for his musical portrait of me; Mrs. Gertrud Schoenberg for a letter written me in 1944 by Arnold Schoenberg; Daniel C. Joseph, administrator, and Donald Gallup, literary executor, of the Gertrude Stein Estate, for letters written to me and to Georges Hugnet by Gertrude Stein and for her "Poem Pritten on Pfances of Georges Hugnet"; Mrs. J. Sibley Watson for a letter written me in 1930; Yale University Press, New Haven, Connecticut, for a stanza from Gertrude Stein's *Stanzas in Meditation*.

For the loan of pictures used herein as illustrations, I wish to thank Mrs. Böske Antheil, R. Kirk Askew, Jr., Mrs. Ross Lee Finney, Mrs. Roy Thomas Gleason, Johana (Mrs. Roy) Harris, the Harvard University Records Office, Philip Johnson, King's Chapel (Boston), Lincoln Kirstein, Suzanne Peignot (Madame Lauboeuf), the Estate of George Platt Lynes, the New York

Herald Tribune, Lee Miller (Lady Penrose), Miss Dorothy St. Clair, Henri Sauguet, James Soby, the Yale University Library, John Cage, Annette Dieudonné, and Nicolas Nabokov.

For assistance in preparing the manuscript of this book for publication I owe untold gratitude to Briggs W. Buchanan, Professor Richard Burgi, Jason Epstein, Maurice Grosser, Robert Offergeld, Herbert Weinstock, and Gavin Young, all of whom have read it with sharp eyes for both taste and clarity.

New York, 1966   VIRGIL THOMSON

A Note on the Illustrations

PHOTOGRAPHS of René Crevel, Janet Flanner, James Joyce, and Pierre de Massot by Berenice Abbott; photograph of George Antheil by Bain News Service; group photograph of Virgil Thomson, Walter Piston, Herbert Elwell, and Aaron Copland by Thérèse Bonney, also the photograph of Virgil Thomson with Gertrude Stein; of John Cage by Bob Cato; of Kristians Tonny's monoprint portrait of Virgil Thomson by P. Delbo; of Dr. Frederick M. Smith by Straus-Peyton; of Virgil Thomson (frontispiece) by William Gale Gedney; of King's Chapel, Boston, and its graveyard by Haskell; of Virgil Thomson by the *Herald Tribune*; of Geoffrey Parsons by New York *Herald Tribune*–Fein; of Florine Stettheimer's model theater and of Marcel Duchamp's portrait of her by Peter A. Juley & Son; of Frederick Ashton by Ker-Seymer, London; of Pare Lorentz by Dorothea Lange; of Constance Askew, Alfred Barr, and Alexander Calder, also the group photograph of John Houseman, Pavel Tchelitcheff, Aline McMahon, and Orson Welles, by George Platt Lynes; of Maurice Grosser and of John Houseman by Lee Miller; of the quai Voltaire by André Ostier; of Mary Butts, Pablo Picasso, Mary Reynolds, and Virgil Thomson (illustration no. 44) by Man Ray, of Lincoln Kirstein by Leonie Sterner; of Bernard Faÿ and Philip Johnson by Carl Van Vechten; of *Four Saints in Three Acts* by White Studio; cartoon by Charles Strauss from *Saturday Review*; "Peanuts" comic strip, United Feature Syndicate. The author wishes to thank all those who granted permission for the use of these materials.

The photographs are to be found after pages 196 and 516.

Contents

VIRGIL THOMSON

I

Missouri Landscape with Figures

TO ANYONE BROUGHT UP THERE, as I was, "Kansas City" always meant the Missouri one. When you needed to speak of the other you used its full title, Kansas-City-Kansas; and you did not speak of it often, either, or go there unless you had business. Such business was likely to be involved with stockyards or the packing houses, which lay beyond the Kansas line in bottom land. The Union Depot, hotel life, banking, theaters, shopping—all the urbanities—were in Missouri.

So was open vice. One block on State Line Avenue showed on our side nothing but saloons. And just as Memphis and St. Louis had their Blues, we had our *Twelfth Street Rag* proclaiming joyous low life. Indeed, as recently as the 1920s H. L. Mencken boasted for us that within the half mile around Twelfth and Main there were two thousand second-story hotels. We were no less proud of these than of our grand houses, stone churches, and slums, our expensive street railways and parks, and a political machine whose corruption was for nearly half a century an example to the nation.

Kansas, the whole state, was dry. And moralistic about everything. There was even an anticigarette law. Nearly till World War II, one bought "coffin nails" under the counter and paid five cents more per pack than in Missouri. Though Kansas had always been a Free State and supported right in Kansas-City-Kansas a Negro college, most of our colored brethren preferred Missouri, where life was more fun. The truth is that Kansas was Yankee territory, windy and dry, with blue laws on its books; and the women from there wore unbecoming clothes and funny hats.

As for the food, a touring musician described a hotel steak with "I drew my knife across it, and it squeaked." As late as 1948, motoring west with the painter Maurice Grosser, I caused him to drive in one day from Slater, in Saline County, Missouri, to Colorado Springs, 714 miles, by insisting one must not eat or sleep in Kansas. He had yielded, he thought, to mere Missouri prejudice. But when we stopped once for coffee and a hamburger (safe enough), and noticing under a fly screen some darkish meringue-topped pies I asked the waitress what kind they were, she replied, "Peanut butter," he says I turned and simply said, "You see?"

I learned in my grown-up years how beautiful Kansas can be in the middle and west, an ocean of mud in winter and of wheat in summer, with a rolling ground swell underneath and a turbulent sky above, against which every still unbroken windmill turns like a beacon. I came also in those later years to respect her university at Lawrence, especially for music, and to read her free-speaking editors, William Allen White of Emporia, Ed Howe of Atchison. I have wished merely to point out here, in telling what life was like on the Missouri side, that any Southern child from there inevitably grew up making fun of Kansas.

Such fun, of course, was chiefly made in private. Publicly our city was for tolerance. As a multiple railway terminus, it offered welcome equally to old Confederates, to business families from Ohio and New England, to German farmers, brewers from Bavaria, cattlemen from Colorado and the West, to miners, drummers, and all railroaders, to Irish hod carriers, Jewish jewelers, New York investors, and Louisiana lumberjacks, to school teachers, music teachers, horse showers, horse doctors, to every species of doctor and clergyman and to many a young male or female fresh off the farm. In such a cosmopolis mutual acceptance was inevitable. So also was a certain exclusiveness, based on contrasts in manners, morals, and religion.

In my family's case, these conditionings were home-based in "Little Dixie," a central Missouri farming region bounded north, northwest, and northeast by the Missouri River and centered commercially round Boonville, Marshall, and in early days the river town Miami. This district had been settled in the 1820s and '30s by planters from the eastern counties of Virginia and further populated after the Civil War from northern Kentucky. My Virginia great-grandfather Reuben Ellis McDaniel had brought with him in '41 from Caroline County a household of thirteen whites and sixty Negroes. In Missouri he grew hemp and tobacco, traded in staples for his neighbors, raised a family of twelve, took part in the founding of colleges and Baptist churches, sent his sons by river boat to Georgetown College in Kentucky. My Thomson great-grandfather, also a Virginia

Baptist, had preceded him by two decades. My mother's people, settled in Kentucky since the 1790s, did not come till nearly 1880.

Farmers my people were, all of them, with an occasional off-shoot into law, divinity, or medicine, rarely into storekeeping, never into banking. Baptists they were too, and staunch ones. I do not know when it got started in Virginia, this business of their being always Baptists, though family records show persecutions for it in the eighteenth century. And certainly there had long been Baptists in Wales, where many came from. It may be that the Welsh ones (and my mother's people seem virtually all to have borne Welsh names) were Baptist when they landed, a Captain John Graves in 1607, a Gaines shortly after. But the Scottish Thomsons (arriving a century later) and the Scotch-Irish McDaniels may well have been converted in the colonies. In any case, all were Baptists, every forebear of mine known to me, and after the Civil War Southern Baptists.

The third historical fact dominating my childhood—after three centuries of mid-Southern slave-based agriculture and of belief in salvation by faith plus total immersion—was the Civil War. I never heard it called in those days anything *but* the Civil War, either—except for short simply "the war." And I was brought up on it. My grandmother Thomson was a Confederate war widow; all her brothers had fought on that side too, one being killed. My great-uncle Giles McDaniel had at nineteen escaped from the Federal prison in St. Louis, where my grandfather lay dying, returned to his family, made his way from Missouri to Canada and thence to Virginia, where he joined Lee. The Thomson great-uncles, as well, all had war histories. And since Grandma, who was a quietly wonderful storyteller, regularly spent the winter with us in Kansas City, it can be imagined in what detail the war was reviewed as lived through on a Missouri farm by a widow with three small children.

Grandma Thomson, born Flora Elizabeth McDaniel in 1830, was already seventy in my earliest memories of her. These picture her short and slender as to frame, dressed in blacks, grays, or lavender, carrying outdoors or to church a reticule (small handbag with a reticulated metal top that opened like a row of x's), and wearing a bonnet (crescent-shaped small hat, covered with flowers or jet, which sat on her parted hair just forward of

the bun and was held there by ribbons tied beneath the chin).
To others she appeared as a gentlewoman not hesitant of speaking up to anyone, black or white, afraid, indeed, of nothing at all save God's anger and of crossing city streets.

Quincy Adams Thomson, born in 1827, must have owed his pre-names to the presidential incumbent, since he had no family connection to Massachusetts. Like Flora McDaniel he was one of twelve children, and when they were married in 1856 he was twenty-nine. At this point he acquired land from his father and built a house.

Not long afterward, Flora developed an eye condition that required her, for a specialist's care, to travel to Palmyra, near Hannibal. Arrived, she wrote her husband of her pregnancy by saying that on the boat she "would have enjoyed [his] society so much, and besides I had something to tell you about which I will only say it gave me pleasure and leave you to guess."

A month later she is "trying to be patient" till they can be "reunited . . . at no very distant date." Then the next day,

> I received your letter this morning saying you had already started for Kentucky. It was probably better for you to go than Asa [one of his brothers], but if I had been at home I do not know that I would have consented to the arrangement. After all, I should perhaps be thankful you are going to Kentucky instead of Kansas, for though I could never blame you for responding to a call of duty from your parents or country, it would be hard to give you up even for a time.

She adds in postscript, "I wish you had written more about the Kansas excitement. I hear but little said about it here and have no idea what they are doing in Saline [County] and feel anxious to know."

This is all one reads right then, in her letters or his, about the coming troubles; but in October 1857 one of her brothers writes him from College Hill (Columbia, Missouri):

> What has become of Kansas? I can learn nothing from the newspapers. Sometimes I see a piece saying something about it, and very likely before I put the same paper down I see it contradicted. Can learn nothing for certain. Wish you would let me know when the election is to come off, or if it is over, what was the result of

it: I do hope that the Missourians are not so foolish as to let it
be taken from them (though I do really think they deserve it). Is
Gov. Walker for or against the south?

By the end of 1861 the war was on. And Quincy Adams
Thomson, wiry and passionate, looks in photograph like a hot-
head. A letter of September 3, 1861, written to his brother Asa,
who was by that time with the Confederate troops, recounts
the state of the war at home and of the absent brother's farm.

> Your horses look very well considering the work they have
> done. I broke your highlander mare, as you desired, and let a man
> in Col. Price's regiment by the name of Granville Botts have her,
> as you ordered, and I have no doubt but you have seen her before
> this time. . . . I do not intend to let any more of your horses go,
> because you have not any more than you need for your farm. . . .
> There has been much excitement here since you left. I have
> been from my business a great deal. We are still very fearful that
> the Federals will over run this County before you all can get here.
> May the Lord forbid it, though we don't deserve to be treated
> so well. Our trust is in God for the success of our cause, which
> is the cause of religious and political Liberty. Two of my broth-
> ers have been spared to get home from the scene of conflict and
> death safely, and I pray God that my other Brother may not only
> be thus highly blessed, but that he may come home to tell us that
> he has become the soldier of the true and living God.

This last refers, I presume, to Asa's unconverted state.

Eventually eleven of Quincy's brothers and brothers-in-law
served the Confederacy. At this time my grandfather himself was
thirty-four and twice a parent. One year later, when he left for
the war, his wife was carrying her third child. Four months later
still, he was dead. A group of some six hundred Confederate
volunteers, mostly from Saline County and in large part friends,
relatives, and neighbors, mounted on their own horses and in
many cases accompanied by their Negro servants, had organized themselves into a regiment, elected one of their number
temporary colonel, named others as officers and noncoms, and
set out southwest to join General Sterling Price. Within a few
days the regiment was surprised by Federal cavalry, captured,
and shipped in open boxcars to a prison in St. Louis, arriving
there on Christmas Day. Epidemic diseases broke out. Giles

McDaniel escaped by blackening himself with a burnt cork. Most remained, awaiting transfer to the Confederate side in exchange for Federal prisoners. In January my grandfather died, probably of typhoid; and his body, shipped to his wife in Saline County, was buried in the graveyard of their country church. My father, born on January 12, was lifted up for one long look at his male parent. Later, from being so vividly told and retold the event, he almost remembered it. He was a redhead named Quincy Alfred, and he came to look very much like his father.

Flora Thomson had been expected to join her father for the duration. But on that point she was firm. She stayed on her farm, ran it with her own Negroes, not all of them available after Emancipation, and brought up her babies. If marauding troops came by, Blacklegs or Scalawags, she offered them food, which they would have taken anyway, and beddings-down in the hay barn. She never locked her door, esteeming such precaution distrustful of God and futile against armies.

By the mid-1870s she was moving her family winters to Liberty, Missouri, some twenty-five miles north of Kansas City, seat of a Baptist preparatory school and college named William Jewell, of which Reuben McDaniel had been a founder. Here my father studied Latin, English literature, and natural philosophy (as physics was called then); his brother Reuben read law; and his sister Leona (or "Lonie") was got ready for Stephens College, a Baptist female seminary at Columbia. But in those postwar times, with ex-soldiers going all wild and with several of her brothers drinking far more than any gentleman or farmer should, Flora Thomson had added to her canons of Southern Baptist upbringing a clause about total abstinence. No liquor crossed her threshold, nor was it served in her children's houses. I have seen my Aunt Lonie's husband hide blackberry brandy in the carriage house and swallow aromatics after taking it rather than face her on the question.

My father, the youngest, was the first to marry. My mother was eighteen, he twenty-one. His passion was romantic and intense, remained so till his death at eighty-one. Though he had a redhead's temper, I never heard him raise his voice to her. To be her husband was for him as proud a privilege as to be a Baptist or a farmer. For he loved farming too, loved land, loved growing things, loved ingenuities done by hands with

wood and stone, loved everything about life in the country
from Monday's sunrise to Sunday's dinner with guests brought
home from church. His mother, respecting his needs, divided
her land, gave him his share. Young Quincy thereupon built a
frame cottage and moved into it with his bride.

My mother, though born on a farm in Kentucky (in 1865)
and removed to Missouri at fourteen to live on another, had
never known a farm life's loneliness. Her father, Benjamin Watts
Gaines, born in 1832, had lived in a wide Boone County house
full of children and visitors. The Civil War, less passionately
viewed, I gather, in northern Kentucky than in central Missouri,
had passed him by. Along with his brothers, he had offered
himself to the Confederate troops; but he was refused for lacking two fingers. He does not seem to have insisted on showing
them how remarkable a shot he was with the other three. Nor
did he let the Federals draft him. He simply passed up the war,
stayed home, and built a family. After bearing him seven children, his wife Mary Ely Graves died of a "galloping consumption"; and it was chiefly the sadness of her loss that caused his
removal to Missouri in 1879. Here he again married a Kentucky
woman, Elizabeth Hall, who gave him three more children.
When he was not much over fifty, he sold his farm and built
a house in nearby Slater. He never did a stroke of work again
except for gardening. He lived to be a hundred.

As with so many Kentuckians, life at his house was a never-
ending party. My mother, Clara May, from growing up in such
a house and visiting in others like it, had been all her life a
hostess or a guest. Young Quincy from across the road, with his
strict devotion to a widowed mother, his relentless theological
integrities, and his intensely romantic feelings about everything
(indeed, I suspect there were in him, and in his father, possibilities of wildness), was polarized by the complementary characteristics of a young woman who, though she possessed many
graces and all the household arts, knew only one rigor, that of
speaking always with tact.

They were married in the fall of '83; and their first child, Ruby
Richerson, came two years later. All that summer of '85, with
my father constantly out of the house on farm work, Mother
had been much alone for the first time in her life. At twenty,
pregnant and terrified, she acquired an ineradicable distaste

for the country. What tactful softening up of my father's hard passion for the soil went on in the next few years one can only guess. But he did decide eventually on selling the farm. And so they moved to a tiny village called Nelson, where with his newly realized capital he set up a hardware store and tin shop.

The tin shop used his skills in tinkering, repairing, roofing, stove-piping, and the like. Making houses come to life was as good as tilling the ground. But he had no instinct for trade, no skill in collecting monies owed him. And so in about six years he had nothing left. It was probably the depression of 1893, as much as his own inexperience, that brought to an end his adventure in storekeeping. But he never mentioned the famous Panic to me, may not even have been aware of its relation to him; I learned of its existence years later from a history book. But by 1894, and no question about it, he had to move.

The move he made was that of many another farm boy in trouble; he took his family to the city and looked for work. The city was Kansas City (Missouri, of course), and the work he found was as a conductor on the cable cars. For over a year he shared houses on Brooklyn Avenue near Twenty-fourth Street with my Aunt Lula, Mother's sister, and his boyhood friend, my Uncle Charlie Garnett. Then he took a flat of his own at Tenth and Virginia, where on November 25, 1896, his last child was born, a son named Virgil Garnett.

Thirty-five years old, with a wife and two children in his charge and with no money at all save a modest wage, he did not look, to prosperous Saline County, exactly successful. I do not think, however, that my father had ever had much respect for success or any undue aspiration toward it. His mother had prayed for him to hear the "call" and become a preacher. He himself had early become resigned to not hearing it. Always a worker for the Kingdom and early a deacon, he aspired to little earthly reward beyond being a son, husband, and father. Also, if possible, a householder, since life in rented premises (especially in a flat, where there was not even a flowerbed to dig in) seemed to him no proper way. But to buy or build a house he needed credit, and for credit he needed a steady job. The cable cars offered no such security, since their franchise even then was running out. So he took civil service examinations and was appointed to the post office. With a job involving tenure, he could borrow money. His sister Leona was married to a man of substance who had already bought from my grandmother her remaining property, replaced her pre–Civil War small farmhouse with a larger structure, and offered a perpetual home in it to both his wife's mother and his own. He now lent my father, against mortgage, $3,000 for building a house. Thereupon a small lot was purchased on Wabash Avenue, at 2613, and a two-story frame house raised, my father being his own architect and contractor.

From here we moved some ten years later to a slightly larger house in the same block. Surrounding both were yards good for growing flowers and fruit trees and every vegetable. My father arranged his post office working hours so to have daily a half day for gardening. He either rose at five and gardened till noon or went to work at five and gardened all afternoon. He "improved the place" also, building a stone cellar, putting in a furnace, wiring for electricity, painting, paper hanging, roofing, shingling. There was nothing about a house and yard he could not do with joy.

Mother was happy, too, because she could have company. Grandma Thomson came for a long stay every winter, arriving with sacks of chestnuts from my Uncle Will Field's trees and with a telescope valise full of quilt pieces. My cousin Lela Garnett, who would also spend winters with us, brought a piano into the house and gave me lessons on it. It was Lela who taught me, at five, to play from notes. Before that I had only improvised, with flat hands and the full arm, always with the pedal down and always loud, bathing in musical sound at its most intense, naming my creations after "The Chicago Fire" and similar events.

Mother's half sister, Beulah Gaines, would come too, a pretty girl who laughed and danced. She could play anything at sight, delighted the other grown-up young that way, who loved to stand round her at the piano and sing songs. There were sometimes whole house parties of girl cousins and their chums. Where they all slept I do not know, certainly in one another's beds, possibly some on the floor. Cooking went on too, lots of it, and for weeks at a time dressmaking, for Mother could make anything out of cloth, even to tailoring a coat. And there was china painting. From fifteen my sister Ruby had had lessons in that and in water color. From eighteen she received pupils in both and executed orders, firing her china in a gas kiln that stood in the basement. She filled the house with artifacts, earned her own money, and when the Garnett piano went away bought one for me to play and practice on.

A first cousin of my mother's, an amateur violinist, would sometimes play all evening with Lela accompanying; and I remember rolling on the floor in ecstasy at hearing for the first time in real string sound the repeated high F's of the *Cavalleria Rusticana* Intermezzo. By the time I was ten I was playing waltzes and two-steps and schottisches for my sister's friends to dance to. I had learned also by that age to dance the grownups' dances and to play their card games.

Card games and dancing had been brought into our house by my mother's half brother, Cecil, who had come, just out of Slater High School, to work in Kansas City and to live with us. Handsome, full of jollities and jokes and card tricks, playing the banjo, knowing songs and darn-fool ditties, sophisticated about girls and adored by them, he filled the house with a young man's ease and laughter. And not long after Cecil came, his high school chum also arrived from Slater. Being at work, they paid for their board; and every night's dinner now was a company dinner, with steak or chops, hot breads, three vegetables, and dessert. Afterwards the boys got exercise by playing catch or wrestling. In winter there was sometimes reading aloud; the year round, almost always singing.

It was after the boys began to live with us that the larger house was bought. Sometimes their number grew to three or four. Eventually the group withered away, with Cecil going to work in California. Then after my sister's marriage in 1913, she and her husband took two of the upstairs rooms, furnished them with their own things, and lived there for ten years. So that still there was dinner every night and lots of company. My father had for joy his house and garden; my sister had her artisan's life and no housekeeping; I had my music lessons and piano; my mother her Kentucky-style hospitality, so skillfully contrived that she was almost never seen at work and so prettily administered that life seemed to be, as she had always thought it should be, one long party.

Nobody remembers being a baby, but I remember being a

child of two or three and growing from there to school age. Against the backdrop of my father's small but comely house and on a stage peopled by characters of all ages, I took my place quite early as a child performer. I was precocious, good-looking, and bright. My parents loved me for all these things and for being their man-child. My sister, eleven years older, looked on me almost as her own. My relations were pleased at my being able to read and sing songs and remember things. So with all this admiration around (and being, in spite of the praise, not wholly spoiled), I early seized the center of the stage and until six held it successfully.

Beyond our residential neighborhood there were forays into the great world of downtown, of department stores with their smells of dress goods and with their stools that one could whirl around on. I was taken every October to the Carnival parade and carried home by my father sound asleep. But the greatest adventure was going to the depot to meet somebody, usually my grandmother. For this we traveled either on a cable car that went over a cliff and down a steep incline or on an electric one that went through that same cliff in a black tunnel. At the depot itself there were men with megaphones singing lists of railroad lines and towns and numbered tracks. As for the trains, their engines looked so powerful, in motion or at rest, that I did not dare go near them without holding tightly to my father's hand. Even thus, my fear was awful. There was no identity at all between these monstrous machines and their toy images that I cuddled every night in bed.

My mother's sister Aunt Lillie Post could play, with all their pearly runs intact, variations on "Old Black Joe" and "Listen to the Mocking Bird." She did not consent to do this very often, being out of practice; but when she did, she evoked a nostalgia that I could know to have some connection with the prewar South. It was all very polished, poetic, and deeply sad. But saddest of all was a song my mother sometimes sang as prepayment for taking a nap. It was "Darling Nelly Grey," and I could never listen to the end without tears in my throat. All other music, though a joy, was merely sound. But these souvenirs of an earlier Kentucky, rendered by women who remembered, no doubt, its Arcadian landscapes, their father as a young man, and their mother early dead, had over me a power so intense that, as with my terror of the engines at the depot, I could almost not bear for it either to go on or to stop.

When I was only two, which I do not remember, and again when I was five, which I do, my father took me to Saline County for showing me off. I stayed at my Aunt Lonie Field's farm, with pea-fowls on the lawn, visited in Slater my Grandpa Gaines and Grandma Betty, spent nights in other houses, got chummy with a cousin of my own age, Bessie Field, attended my Grandma Thomson's seventy-first-birthday dinner, came home a traveled one.

Since my father's parents had both been born into families of twelve, my father possessed at this time more than fifty first cousins. My mother's extant aunts and uncles and cousin connections would have seemed almost as numerous had not most of them lived in Kentucky, whence they came to visit us less frequently. In my own right I had eight aunts and uncles plus five more by marriage. From my first cousins and the children of my parents' cousins to my grandparents, with their own large numbers of brothers and sisters, my childhood was surrounded by a company that included persons of virtually every age and disposition. It is not to be wondered at that having long appeared successfully before such a vast and varied public, I arrived at my school years self-confident, cocky, and brash.

Some of this expansiveness may have come from living close to Kansas. My cousins from Little Dixie, I must say, had none of it. In any case, in September of 1902, when still five (I would not be six till Thanksgiving), without the prelude of kinder-garten or the benefit of any parental presence (my cousin Lela Garnett went along to enroll me), I entered first grade at the Irving School, on Prospect Avenue at Twenty-fourth Street, wholly unafraid and ready for anything.

2

A Kansas City Childhood

O<small>N MY SECOND DAY AT SCHOOL</small> I got into a fight. That was a surprise to me, and so was the outcome. Physical brawling had not been part of our family life; nor had my father ever shown me, even in play, the stances of pugilism. Neither had I been taught to fear aggression. It simply had not occurred to me ever that I might be attacked, still less that I might be led on (for this may well have been what happened) to attack another boy. In any case, I did find myself, just off schoolyard limits, engaged in fisticuffs. I also found myself losing the match. Then somebody separated us. Neither bore any marks. But my surprise was definitive.

It was definitive because it made clear to me, not yet six, that I was going to have to find other ways toward gaining respect than the head-on physical encounter. A boy named Maurice Baldwin, just as bright as I and just as small, early chose the athletic way. He could always out-wrestle or out-box a boy of his size and out-pitch at baseball many a taller one. But he spent all his out-of-school time keeping up that muscular command. My own choice was simply not to compete. This choice kept me mostly out of fights and always free from broken bones. It also left me time for music and reading. And if it often brought me the taunt of "sissy," it caused me to grow strong in other ways of defense and attack, psychological ways, and in the development of independence.

Nor did it make me an outcast from friendships. My closest associate from nine to thirteen, a half-Canadian boy named Percy Taylor, had attached himself to me in the fourth grade. He was a strong boy and thoroughly adventurous, but formal sports were closed to him because of defective eyesight. The overcompensation of lenses, on the other hand, had made him a facile reader. So together we shared boys' books, historical tales, Dickens, dime novels, fairy tale collections, Webster's Unabridged, and the encyclopedias—all the common reading matter of children except popular science, which interested neither of us. We skated together (in Missouri, that was mostly on rollers), captured moths and butterflies, went fishing (which I found slimy and slow), and took enormous walks.

With Percy's older brother and some more boys we played cave man, raided back porches, stole useless objects at the dime store, and slept in a tent. As we approached pubescence, we pooled our information and shared experiments. Then, after manhood had come firmly to us all, we separated as casually as travelers off a train. No sentiment had been involved; no attachments remained—only a crystal residue, indissoluble in memory's private stream, of the fabulous boyhood years from nine to twelve.

These years had taken place in the first decade of this century, when there were as yet no movies, radio, or television. Our mass-produced entertainment consisted wholly of books and of the Sunday comics. We lived in a middle-class neighborhood in a middle-sized Middle Western city, our whole existence as permeated by rural residues as our residential blocks were checkered with vacant lots; and every car line ended in the country. Downtown there were theaters and big stores and, we had heard, whorehouses. We were proud of all these; they made us feel citified. But in our neighborhoods we lived a small-town life centered on school and church, with lots of play and reading life thrown in. And neither the play life nor the reading, though no doubt watched over, was officiously guided. We thought we were making up our own amusements; and for the most part we probably were, though our games, of course, like all children's games, followed a seasonal calendar as unalterable as the equinoxes.

Our clothing too followed folkways of our time and place, our middle-of-the-world social class. Till the age of twelve we wore knickerbockers, ribbed cotton stockings (black), soft-collar shirts, ties, and coats, in winter always high shoes laced up by means of both eyelets and hooks. On Sundays the collar was stiff and collar-buttoned, the suit of dark blue serge. And since every Sunday suit, unless outgrown, came to be worn for "every day," we were likely to be in blue a good deal of the time. In cold weather we wore overcoats, sweaters being thought a bit roughneck except for athletes; and one winter large fur gauntlets were the fashion. In spring we wore dark blue skullcaps known as "dinks," the tougher types affecting tan felt hats with brim pinned up on one side by a brooch, in Teddy Roosevelt's "rough rider" style.

Since none of us had much spending money, we would walk three miles of a Saturday to the public library, pooling our car-fare nickels for chocolate bars or potato chips. We changed our books, robbed the dime store, ate something sweet or salt, and as often as not walked home again. In the summertime we went on country walks or watched professional baseball through knotholes in a high board fence, though for myself I cared as little for spectator sports as for being a competitor. Those boys whose families permitted, and who could scrape up twenty-five cents plus carfare, would go to a Saturday matinée at the Gillis, a melodrama theater playing *Chinatown Charley*, *No Mother to Guide Her*, and similar classics. Then the following Saturday, in the loft of somebody's carriage house, that same play would be produced in brief, from memory, at ten pins for a place on a plank or one cent for a box seat, literally a wooden box.

Stories of violence and sudden death came later to be exploited by newspapers, during the approach to World War I, as a way of getting people worked up against the Germans. But well through 1910 and beyond, the cowboy world of song and story was still alive; and in the gambling joints of Cripple Creek and Leadville, only a night away by train, gun play was far from extinct. Real violence was easily available to young men who felt the need of it. And country boys, from the age of ten, all carried shotguns for banging away at rabbits and for immobilizing a rattlesnake or skunk. Youth's taste for violence in literature was not starved either; it was merely catered to less massively than now. And my childhood years in Missouri, for all their seeming peacefulness, were contemporaneous both with the Wild West's own Indian summer and with the final flourishing of Victorian blood-and-thunder on the stage.

I was six when I first went to the theater; my sister took me. The play, *Miss Petticoats*, was about a young woman whose father so nicknamed her because her dead mother had called her in French something that sounded like that. I could not follow very well the events of the spectacle; but I loved everything else about it—the dressy clothes, the make-up, the lights and painted scenery, the impersonating of character and simulations of feeling. That night, before going to bed, I put on the show. After that, my sister took me to matinées when she could, though never often enough for me. From the time I first entered a theater—and for all the masses of well-dressed people, the strangeness of the lobby, the chandeliers, the gold, the curtain, the seats that flopped down and up—I never felt anything but completely at home in any theater, backstage or out front.

My own appearances on stage were chiefly musical, playing the piano in student recitals or executing a duet with Helen Walley, the girl next door, at a Grand Army veterans' society to which her grandfather belonged. Once I appeared as William Tell in a scene from Schiller's play, and with an unloaded crossbow shot the apple clean off Ted Sherwood's head. I was not, however, a prodigy performer, merely a willing one.

Actually I had had no lessons in elocution and very poor ones in music. After my cousin Lela Garnett got married, my sister exchanged with certain music teachers china painting for my piano lessons. The first of these was a well-born but ignorant woman who firmly corrected my tendency to play by ear rather than from notes, without giving me any sound training at all in either solfeggio or note playing. The other was a young man whose brother was an actor and who was himself an opera fan. He got me to reading the stories of the operas, put me through the piano score of *Faust*, and taught me to execute quite stylishly, I thought, Leschetizky's arrangement for left hand alone of the Sextet from *Lucia di Lammermoor*. With him I also stumbled my way through bits of Liszt. And diving into any opera score with a splash, I swam with equal delight in the limpidities of *Fra Diavolo* and bathed in the turgid stream of *Parsifal*. I had already played in duet form the chief Italian overtures; and I had begun to frequent summer band concerts for hearing (scored in brass) the great operatic set-pieces and for being ravished on weekly Wagner nights by the most luscious harmonic experience that exists.

By the time I was eleven I had a gluttonous musical appetite and what I took to be vast experience. Actually I had not yet heard a symphony orchestra or a string quartet or an opera, though my acquaintance with opera music, through piano scores and band arrangements, included much of that time's current repertory. And I could play, well or badly, not only Paderewski's Minuet and the pieces by Cécile Chaminade that all students learned, but also some easy Liszt and Mendelssohn and a page or two out of Chopin, as well as a chunky choice of popular songs and lots of ragtime.

These last had come into my repertory through my sister's friends. Whenever they rolled up the rugs, I was requisitioned. It was hard, at nine and ten, to keep a steady beat; but I learned to do it. And because I did it I was allowed to be with the grown-up young. Life among the mating set seemed more romantic to me than the parties that included other ages, for it made me feel almost grown-up. With them, if only for one hour, I could leave off being a brat.

All this time there went on my mother's life of constant cooking and dressmaking and having company, Ruby's life of painting china and firing it in the gas kiln and having pupils, my father's self-contained and happy continuity of working in the garden and of making household additions and of never being absent from church. My school, my piano practice, my play and reading life kept me more occupied than most children. But I also went to church; I had to be ill to get round my father's rule about that. And since I was never ill (rarely missed school a day a year), I went regularly to Sunday school at half-past nine and stayed on for church. In my adolescent years I came to enjoy two of my Sunday school teachers, women only just enough older, say ten years, to make them a civilizing influence. Also, in my adolescent years I played the organ in other churches than Baptist ones and got paid for it. Professional status was at all times a joy, as was indeed, for the most part, church music itself. But I never at any time took to religion. In the Baptist view I am not even a Christian, having never experienced conversion or undergone baptism. I have never felt inferior to the believers, or superior; I simply am not one. Churches are not my home. In the choir room or in the organ loft I earn my fee. But I cannot be a customer; this was always so, is still so. It has nothing to do with the fact that a major part of my music has been either composed for liturgical use or inspired by hymnody.

The loyalties formed in my preadolescent years lie elsewhere than to Bible reading and preachers. They are to music, companionship, and hospitality. The hospitality stems from central Missouri, which was my father's home, and from northern Kentucky, my mother's. Also from a legendary Virginia, as known through my grandmother and her brothers. From this classical mid-South, seemingly so gentle, come my arrogance and my unhesitating disobedience.

Naturally, in a place as Yankee-versus-Rebel conscious as Kansas City, I kept mostly to myself what nostalgias I may have felt for a way of life I had not known anyway and which certainly had never existed in quite the way that anybody still living remembered it. There was nothing left to defend that had not already been defended with lives, and nothing to give up that had not long since been taken away. But slave-owners anywhere, I think, do have, like their slaves, a "tragic sense of life," a fullness in courage and compassion that has made of so many Southerners good soldiers and good judges. Myself, I owe to my Civil War forebears at least my rebelliousness.

However, at twelve I was more bumptious than rebellious. And I had become, moreover, successful at being a schoolboy. My father, as reward for a report card of all A's, though I do not recall it as unique, bought for me a ticket to hear Paderewski's piano recital, my first big-time music event. I went alone, remembered everything, literally every note, including the false ones. And when I was graduated from the Irving School in June of 1909, he gave me his own gold pocket watch.

That same summer there opened near by the first film house to serve our neighborhood. The price was five cents; the show, which repeated itself all evening, an hour long. The program, changed nightly, consisted of an "illustrated song," sung to piano accompaniment and colored slides, and two short films— a drama and a comedy. I must have gone every night. One evening just before opening time, someone came to the house asking if I would substitute for the regular pianist. I went; I played; I earned a dollar, my first receipt from any professional action.

Since the pianist in those days never knew ahead of time what the films were to be, he had to fumble his way through the first show while watching the screen. After that he could with luck hit certain passages on the nose. For comedies one played animated popular music, not disdaining a topical reference such as "I Love My Wife but O, You Kid!" For the dramas one used slower stuff. Being unskilled in improvisation, I simply played pieces I knew while a trap drummer underlined the rhythm and added "effects" such as cowbells, horses' hooves, bass drum thuds, and cymbal crashes. His flyswatter, always at hand in summer, could be useful too for light drum taps. It was soon to become, in fact, under the name of "brush," standard drummers' equipment. My first performance as a film accompanist could not have been brilliant. But I did substitute a few more times that month; and once, appearing in answer to a want ad, I was allowed by a none-too-confident manager to play through an evening at a tent show.

And then, as if these grandeurs were not enough, my Uncle Will Field took me to New York. It had always been his habit in August, when the crops were in, to go somewhere. This year my aunt was not feeling well; and my cousin Bess, inveterately train-sick, hated travel. Determined on getting away from his farm all the same, he telegraphed to invite my company, got it with alacrity. That night I took the Chicago and Alton "Hummer" at six, which picked him up in Slater at nine; and at eight in the morning, having slept in a sleeper and eaten cake there, I was in Chicago.

Since my uncle did not like staying long anywhere, for two weeks we kept on the move. We took a white steamer to Petoskey, Michigan, stopping for a swim at the beach hotel where he had spent his honeymoon, went on to Mackinac Island at the head of the lake and from there through two more lakes to Buffalo, where we drove in a carriage past lovely Victorian houses and admired Niagara Falls. Next we took a train to Albany, where we visited the capitol and its million-dollar staircase of white granite. Then, progressing majestically by day boat down the Hudson, we arrived in New York to stay at a hotel in Times Square.

For a youngster who read regularly *The Green Book* and other theater magazines, this locale was heaven, as all those ladies waiting in lobbies, so beautifully dressed and made up, I knew to be angels, though I did not think them pure. I must have seen lots of New York in three days; but what I remember most clearly is Times Square—its theaters (all closed), its restaurants (very expensive), its hotel lobbies, gloriously lighted and beflowered. The Claridge, the Knickerbocker, the Astor were dazzling to see. We stayed at the less glorious but stylish-enough Cadillac, on the Seventh Avenue corner of Forty-third Street.

The electric signs, more elaborately narrative than today's, were a show in themselves. There were well-dressed spenders, too, and lots of carriages, even motor cars. I had never had so intensely the feel of being at the center of something.

Traveling by ship to Norfolk, Virginia, I entertained a salon full of admirers by playing and singing, was rewarded with a plate of fruit by a Negro in white jacket. I also got my first taste of seasickness.

In Norfolk, the Negro market women in bright bandannas selling highly colored fruits were almost too picturesque to be true. So were the damp ancient churches and colonial graveyards. At Richmond's Jefferson Hotel trout swam in open channels. At Gordonsville bandannaed Negro mammies brought to the train the hugest platters I had ever seen, piled high with fried chicken and with Jeff Davis pie (a confection of sugar and cream and egg yolks), both to be eaten in the hand. At Charlottesville we called on a distant cousin and drove to Monticello. Then we went home, stopping only in St. Louis to change trains. Uncle Will got off at Slater. I arrived in Kansas City just in time for the first day of high school, still only twelve years old, still small for my age, and still in short trousers.

1. My Virginia great-grandfather, Reuben Ellis McDaniel, born in 1799, brought his family and slaves to Missouri in '43.

2. *Above:* Giles McDaniel, Reuben's son, at eighteen, in Confederate army uniform.

3. *Below:* Flora Elizabeth Thomson, his daughter (1830–1919), my grandmother as I knew her.

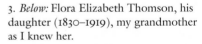

4. Quincy Adams Thomson (1827–1862), my father's father.

5. Flora Thomson and her children—
Reuben Yancy, Leona Townsend,
Quincy Alfred.

6. Quincy Alfred Thomson (1862–1943),
my father, at about the time he moved to
Kansas City.

7. Clara May Gaines Thomson
(1865–1957), my mother, as a young
married woman.

8. Wedding photo, 1883. May is eighteen,
Quincy twenty-one.

9. My cousin Lela Garnett in 1902. She gave me my first piano lessons. I called her Cuz.

10. Ruby, my sister, who was eleven years older than I and a china painter. She bought me a piano and paid for my early lessons.

11. Beulah Gaines, my mother's half sister, who gave piano lessons. She lived in Slater but came to see us often.

12. Cecil Gaines, who came to live with us at seventeen, was a lady-killer, knew card tricks, and played the harmonica.

13. Mother, sixty-two, with Benjamin Watts Gaines, her father, ninety-five. She lived to be ninety-two, he one hundred, both in command of their faculties to the end.

14. The author of this memoir at eleven months.

15. V.T. at twelve, in 1909.

16. V.T. at seventeen.

17. Mrs. Hannah W. Cuthbertson, my sister's art teacher, who later designed Chinese rugs in China.

18. My piano teacher, Geneve Lichtenwalter.

19. Alice Smith, monumental Mormon comrade.

20. Dr. Frederick Madison Smith, psychologist and religious executive, grandson of the Mormon prophet Joseph Smith.

21. As an aviation officer cadet, I studied wireless telephony at Columbia University and weekends went out in society.

22. In Claremont Avenue, where I knew girl piano students from Kansas City.

23. After August 1918 I was a shavetail in the Military Aviation.

24. Dr. Archibald T. ("Doc") Davison, professor of music at Harvard, conductor of the glee club, organist and choirmaster of the chapel, a trainer of choruses and choral directors, my mentor for three years.

25. The composer Edward Burlingame Hill, from whom I learned music's history by helping him (for pay) to give his courses. He also taught me to orchestrate in the French manner. We corresponded until his death in 1960.

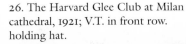

26. The Harvard Glee Club at Milan cathedral, 1921; V.T. in front row. holding hat.

27. King's Chapel, Boston, and its graveyard (*below*).

28. In Paris, 1926, V.T., Walter Piston, Herbert Elwell, and Aaron Copland at Nadia Boulanger's before a concert of works by six young Americans. Absent from this picture, George Antheil and Theodore Chanler.

29. Emmanuel Faÿ, gifted French painter. When he died in New York, 1923, his pictures disappeared and were never found.

30. René Crevel—tubercular novelist, polemicist, surrealist— wrote ten memorable and violent books (one called *La Mort difficile*). He killed himself in 1935.

31. Nadia Boulanger was thirty-four, I twenty-four, when I went to her in 1921.

32. Bernard Faÿ, for circa fifteen years (till the end of World War II) professor of American civilization at the Collège de France.

33. Darius Milhaud and Jean Cocteau, whom I first knew in 1921.

34. Lincoln Kirstein, editor, impresario, and poet, who in the late 1920s painted mechanistic murals in the dining room of the Harvard Liberal Club.

35. Sherry Mangan, earlier a poet, a printer, and the publisher of an advanced magazine, became in the 1930s a revolutionist of the Trotsky line.

36. V.T., ink wash by Christian Bérard, 1930.

37. V.T., a monoprint by Kristians Tonny, 1928, depicting character and attributes. These include dancing, public appearance, love-making, sadness (*"le pessimisme américain"*), piano-playing, a church, church bells, other bells, wine bottles, food, a tomahawk, and several birds or insects. Ideas and remarks are represented as stones. Inspiration comes in waves, lies around in coils.

38. James Joyce as I knew him in 1925.

39. George Antheil arriving in New York, 1927, for the performance of his *Ballet méchanique*.

40. Janet Flanner in 1924, dressed as Uncle Sam for a costume party at Nancy Cunard's and wearing Nancy's father's gray top hat.

41. Pablo Picasso dressed as a matador, somewhere near the time I knew him first, which was 1921.

42. Gertrude Stein and Alice B. Toklas in the middle 1920s.

3

A Musician's Adolescence

THAT FALL THREE DECISIVE THINGS HAPPENED: I acquired a musical mentor; I appeared in print as an author; and I fell in love. The object of my love, with black hair and brown eyes, had been something of a trophy in third grade. There had even been written proof, "Dear Virgil, I love you. I cannot live without you." (It was always the girls, never the boys, who wrote.) But after she had moved away at the end of one school year, no tie remained except for a memory of dark beauty and red hair ribbons.

Then five years later, in high school classes and on the Brooklyn Avenue streetcar, which we both took every morning, the bright sight of her as a young woman of perhaps thirteen (hair ribbons outgrown) made me suddenly to know the bond intact. But who was bound to whom was not the same; this time it was I who could not "live without." She showed no signs of sharing my disturbance, strictly preserved a neutral friendly way. Essays at dates were brushed off too, with tact. I could not by any means provoke an empathy. So my passion fed in secret and on what I took for suffering, nourished itself that way for three long years, till I had turned fifteen, after which time it gave place to youth's euphoria. And soon our geographic separation was to leave only, as before, an image of dark beauty, set permanently this time as my natural magnet.

My debut as an author was no less unhappy. The assignment had been to write a story. And though by this time I had read surely some several hundred works of fiction, I found myself quite sterile for creating one. And so I kidnapped. I copied no lines, but I did retell a tale I had read in a magazine. It was a good tale (a comedy-of-errors type), and I must have told it not badly. Well enough that my English teacher proposed submitting it to the school paper. I could not say no; I did not say no. It was offered with my consent; it was accepted; it was published. And then catastrophe fell. Within the week I was denounced by a fellow student. The facts were undeniable; I did not deny them; and an editors' apology was printed the following month.

No student, no teacher, ever mentioned the incident to me. But in my sophomore year I was not elected to a club. At the end of my fourth year I decided to stay on for another, and that year I did join a society. I also attended an advanced course in composition that I had petitioned into existence. It turned out to be (they were popular then) a course in short-story writing; and a piece I wrote for it was again published in *The Central Luminary*, this time without apology, though the tale itself was plainly, to me, modeled on *Trilby*.

The truth is, and I learned it from these experiences, that I have no gift for imaginative writing. I can describe things and persons, narrate facts. But I do not assemble my pictures and my people into situations where they take on memorability, which is what storytellers do. Nor can I make a language change its sound or words their meaning, which is the faculty of poets. Language, to me, is merely for telling the truth about something; and it was during my high school years that I learned to use it that way.

The teacher most responsible for this training was an old maid cheerful and small with a face like a bulldog. For Miss Ellen Fox grammar was a way of life, and so was promulgating teetotalism after the precepts of Frances Willard. She was a New Englander but not a dour one, a lover of laughter whose own laugh was like a bark. And I never saw her show weakness. One day when from some fault of weather there were no streetcars, she merely got up earlier and walked the five miles to school.

She would mark themes in the left-hand margin with proof-reader's signs such as *p*, *d*, *gr*, *tr*, *lc*, *Cap*, and the like. But the writer had to unmask for himself just where within that line the error lay. And not till every fault had been removed would she accept a piece of writing as work done. No credit was given for unusual excellence, no stigma attached to mediocrity. You did your work or you didn't; when you had done it you got an *A*. At the end of term, if you had done three-fourths, you got a *B*; for one-half, a *C*; one-fourth, a *D*; less than that, an *E* for failure. Her standards of usage were those of any reputable publishing house, her authorities Webster's dictionary and Crabb's *English Synonymes*.

Many found her unreasonably severe. But there is no other way than the hard way (meaning the complete way) to acquire a mastery, as I was already learning from my music teachers; and I am grateful to Ellen Fox for making me prove to myself that it is always possible, if you work at it, to make both sense and grammar. I am inclined, indeed, to credit whatever precedence the sciences have achieved in today's schools over the humanities to the fact that the sciences are still viewed as disciplines, whereas teaching in the artistic branches does tend, I fear, to encourage doodling.

Going back to my freshman status, with its burdens of unrequited love and literary delinquency, scarcely more promising was my first appearance as an actor. This took place in Sheridan's *The Rivals*, in which William Powell, three years my senior, played the male lead, I the drunken butler. Powell's gifts were already commanding—a fine bass voice, clear speech, some grace of movement, and above all, presence. I had no such onstageness, and I was not especially unhappy to find that out. Actually, though I made then no resolve on the matter, I have never since essayed impersonation.

The preceding summer had brought me an encounter that opened the way to eventual decision regarding music as my vocation. This had happened even before my baptism by films and before my grand and glamorous trip to the East. At one of the nightly band concerts in Electric Park I had been spoken to by a musician whom I knew by sight as the tenor soloist from Calvary Baptist Church, where my father was a deacon. With Robert Leigh Murray, a well-washed roly-poly man in his middle thirties, our conversation was all of music. There began at that moment, indeed, a dialogue that was to go on almost without interruption for ten years. This started by his asking my musical accomplishments; and when he learned how superficial they were and how poor was my instruction (for he knew, or knew of, the silly opera buff who had been teaching me), he said right off, as if taking me over, that if I wanted to be a pianist I must have proper lessons.

I do not know how often I saw Mr. Murray that summer, but by fall he was established in my parents' confidence, and in mine, as the mentor of my musical progress. He saw to it that I did have proper lessons and eventually that I earned money to pay for them. He also taught me to play his accompaniments and paid me at commercial rates for doing so. For the next six years we rehearsed at least two evenings a week; and I accompanied always his banquet dates and out-of-town recitals, sometimes playing alone a Beethoven sonata or group of pieces by Schubert, MacDowell, Debussy.

My first proper lessons were from Moses Boguslawski, a pianist of Lisztian brilliance. They ceased when my father could no longer afford them. The next summer, paying for them myself, I went to a friend of Mr. Murray's, Gustav Schoettle, a cultivated Rhineland German, who threw in harmony gratis. The next summer I went to Rudolf King, a Leschetizky pupil, who put me through some tough technical studies and got me to playing solos in public. My heaviest practice took place during the summer. In the winter I went to school, worked for Mr. Murray, played occasionally in public, practiced without guidance.

I also had, at thirteen, organ lessons from Clarence Sears, of Grace Episcopal Church. My original interest in the organ had been monetary, to earn during the summer five dollars a Sunday substituting at Calvary Baptist for Mrs. Jennie Schultz. But the architectural splendors of Grace Church (now the Cathedral of Grace and Holy Trinity) were attractive to an adolescent; and Mr. Sears, to provide experience of the Anglican liturgy, had proposed that I assist him at Sunday services. To this arrangement my father, not willing to see me escape from Baptist influence, had consented only on condition that I attend Sunday school at Calvary beforehand. And Clarence Sears made it worthwhile by giving me more to do than just turn pages. As soon as I had learned my first solo, something by Sir John Stainer with an easy pedal cadenza, Sears, at the end of a Sunday morning service, the exited choir having sung its offstage "Amen," slid off the bench, saying, "Play your piece." I did, and that made me an organist. I continued for about a year to assist him at the instrument and later, when my voice had changed, sang with the choir. He was an excellent teacher and straightforward in his ways, ever treating me as an adult and a colleague. My lessons went on till I left for war in 1917 and for a time in 1919 after my return. But after the first years I no longer helped at services; I was having church jobs of my own.

I think I was fourteen when the awareness of vocation came to me. I do not remember how the subject arose; but somehow, in conversation with my mother, father, and sister—a discussion of my studies and my future—I found myself declaring that there was no use their thinking I was not to be a musician, that I was one already, that music was my life and always would be.

Now the family had never been in the least discouraging about music. I imagine that even then their chief aim was to find out my intuitions of destiny. Well, they found out; and so did I. The vehemence of my statement so surprised me, indeed, that before there was time for any reply I burst out crying and fled upstairs. From that day my musical vocation was never questioned. My father, in fact, though music did not speak to him (he was virtually tone-deaf), seemed ever afterward to accept it for me as related to the ministerial call that his mother had hoped would summon him but that somehow had passed him by.

Five days a week I went to the Central High School at Eleventh and Locust Streets, a turreted red sandstone building from the 1880s just on the edge of the business district. It was hardly a step from the big stores and the theaters; and since classes were over before two, it was easy to linger downtown for looking in shop windows, for reading at the public library, for attending a concert or matinée.

From 1909 to 1917 I saw all the shows. No, not quite all, because burlesque was not my passion, nor vaudeville. But I went to all the full-length plays and musicals, the operas, the concerts, and the ballets. At the Auditorium, seat of our resident stock company, and at Convention Hall, where mammoth attractions played, I could get in by selling candy or by ushering. At weekday matinées elsewhere I paid twenty-five cents for a gallery seat, saving this up out of my weekly lunch-and-carfare allowance of $1.25. For concerts (minimum a dollar) I was dependent on Mr. Murray, who sometimes had free seats in connection with his work as a piano-store executive and who would often take me with him to an evening performance. For several years he also took me to Chicago at the Christmas vacation, where we would stay at a hotel and go to the opera every night, afternoons to the art museum, to recitals, and to plays. He profited as a singer from these excursions and took satisfaction from their benefit to me, for he had assumed the guidance of my musical development, being rewarded only by affection and by my delight in his adult companionship.

It was on the first of these trips that I acquired an admiration for Mary Garden's artistic powers that to this day has not relaxed. Melba and McCormack had voices more classically beautiful; Minnie Maddern Fiske and Sir Johnston Forbes-Robertson could act better to speech. But only Garden (working with certain conductors and fellow singers) has ever in my lifetime produced so homogeneous a blend of words and music. That kind of group workmanship has disappeared from the lyric stage; and French opera, the repertory in which it shows to best advantage, has in consequence lost much of its appeal. As Garden herself said to me in Paris on the verge of World War II, "Opera as you and I knew it is dead."

Opera was anything but dead, however, in my 1914 understanding of it; and it was for wrestling with its most impressive embodiment, the Wagnerian, that I essayed getting a grip on it by means of Wagner's own intellectual instruments. Some of the urgency, of course, with which I began that fall to read German philosophy was due to the war itself. For the next three years, till our country had finally opted for a side, the war put us all under such persistent propaganda pressures that in self-defense one had to try (hopefully) to find out for oneself who these military Germans were. That they were the countrymen of Bach and Beethoven was in their favor. That their present-day music was losing world leadership, forcing them to accept condominium with Russia and France, I strongly suspected. And I was sure that between Beethoven's death in 1827 and that of Brahms in 1897 some radical (and possibly fatal) transformation had taken place in German music that one could hopefully come to understand through following its polemics. My eighteenth birthday, in November, would find me immersed in these. But already, during the summer of 1914, the time had begun for me when thinking about music and reading about it were to be no less an urgency than making it.

This intellectualization of my music life was further aided by my next piano teacher, a woman of somewhat higher cultural attainments than her predecessors. The others, however consecrated, had been just musicians. E. Geneve Lichtenwalter had graduate degrees (an M.A. at least) and read non-fiction books. She also composed, and the texts she chose for her vocal works bore literary distinction.

To pay for my weekly lessons, which cost $2.50, I had taken a $25-a-month job as page at the public library; and it was there that I came upon the absorbing narrative that is Richard Wagner's *My Life*. Although Miss Lichtenwalter, to whom I showed my discovery, knew it for not exactly the whole truth about this amazing genius, she merely remarked, "You must also read his enemy Nietzsche." So I went to the philosophy stacks, found the complete works there in English, began at the beginning. From *The Birth of Tragedy* (a hymn to Richard Wagner) to *Thus Spake Zarathustra* and *Ecce Homo* (self-praise in dithyrambs) by way of all those middle works in which he debunks his former hero, I read, in the order of their composition, the whole set. It took me a year.

Meanwhile I was capturing lions. There was Mrs. Hannah Cuthbertson, my sister's painting teacher, a handsome woman of fifty whose toleration of me initiated a still unended series of friendships with painters that was later to furnish the ambience and norm of my Paris life. There was James Gable, too, an impoverished Englishman and friend of "Cuffbutton" (as eventually I was allowed to call Mrs. Cuthbertson), a generalized man of letters, Eton and Oxford trained but without original talent, who had known as a young man everybody artistic and literary in London or Paris, including Wilde and Douglas and all the painters, and who had been everywhere, read everything. With thus as part of my circle a painter and a writer, in Mr. Murray a vocalist of distinction, and in Geneve Lichtenwalter a pianist-pedagogue of the highest aims, I began to use the hospitable habits of my family for getting all these into conversation. In high school days I had been host to the brighter young at Sunday suppers, and Mother had always encouraged my inviting for dinner anyone I wished. Now I mixed the ages more, hoping, I think, to create and to sustain a symposium of the arts.

In 1915 our local board of education opened a junior college in the newly vacated premises of old Central High School. So I resigned from the library and became a freshman, still living at home, of course. In college, since I found banal the clubs that others organized, I designed my own, got myself elected president, ran it my way. I also started a college magazine and very largely wrote that. It was Midwest-oriented, after the Chicago poets I admired, Masters and Sandburg and Lindsay, but also explosive and polemical, like my other admirations, Shaw and Mencken. I am not impressed today by its college-boy brilliance, but I remember much sport being had at its making.

More significant, or so they seem now, are two less clearly motivated matters. One is the slow progress over the next two years, on the part of myself and of my country, toward getting into the European war. The other is a friendship with a Mormon girl.

Alice Smith, great-granddaughter of the Prophet Joseph Smith, was a fellow student. Her father, Dr. Frederick Smith, president of the Reorganized Church of Jesus Christ of Latter Day Saints, in Independence, Missouri, was a man of learning, also a religious executive both physically and intellectually powerful. His spiritual powers, though sufficient for a modern churchman, rarely went the length of prophecy, albeit on one occasion, when opposed by a majority of his bishops, he did, after prayer, order their retirement with the phrase, "This is the voice of inspiration." As such, his solution was accepted; and as such the gesture served him that first time, in later life perhaps a few times more. He was no habitual prophet anyhow. He was an administrator, a sociologist, and a student in psychology of Morton Prince and G. Stanley Hall. Alice's mother was a gracious lady with tact and wit, inveterately not very well and inveterately my protector.

Not that I needed much protection. Alice, monumentally proportioned and as a consequence lacking a little the experience of boys, was finding out, as I was, that unless one is destined to mate early, intellectual friendships are perfectly possible. She was pretty enough too, indeed not unlike those massive creatures that for a time after World War I Pablo Picasso drew and painted. Having always been a big girl, she was not imprisoned by her flesh; she moved with grace. As for the mind, it was quick like her mother's, tireless like that of her father. For me she was a mirror, also a pupil, someone to educate and to protect a little against being blighted by a virtually indigestible religious inheritance. In any case, we took each other on in good faith, read books together, reviewed each other's manuscripts, made jokes, cooked a little; and I manipulated the Doctor by direct attacks tempered with good manners into relaxing the Mormon conventions about female subservience that were still being held up to his two daughters, out of reaction no doubt to the fact that there was no question of their being applicable to his wife.

Alice wrote in later years a memoir of these times in which she described my criticism of her writing as being "sometimes a little harsh and . . . always delivered with a combination of omniscience and patronage that was hard to take." Also that "he wasn't at all reticent about the fact that he expected to be a great man someday."

At the beginning of World War I, in 1914, Americans had tended in the main, I think, to favor neutrality; few west of the Atlantic seaboard wanted the violence to spread. On the contrary, they wanted it stopped, and not by more violence, but by negotiation. Besides, our fellow citizens of Germanic roots were not, in their instinctive sympathies, anti-German. By 1915, however, "pro-German" had begun to be a dirty word; and by 1916 "neutral" meant pro-Ally. From then on, and with that year's mutinies in Europe put down, our progress toward participation was unstoppable. I am not making any political point in this review of history, merely reciting it as a background against which my own actions took place.

These came to be moved, as I went on growing up, by a desire to get into the fighting. All those millions being killed, the sinkings at sea, the filth and vermin of trench life, the pictures of bayonetted guts and burst Belgian babies, everything about it made it seem, to a boy just going twenty, a lovely war. You wanted to be a part of what so many were experiencing, to try yourself out, prove your endurance. You certainly did not want the war to end without your having been through something. You wanted it to go on till you could get there.

At what moment the civilian officers' training camps were opened, I am not sure; I think in the fall of '16. There was one at Plattsburg, New York, I know, and another at Fort Leavenworth, Kansas. I applied for admission to the latter and was refused. Toward January of 1917, American participation being by then a matter of short delay, I enlisted in a National Guard regiment. There were two of these in the neighborhood, an infantry one in Kansas City and a mounted artillery outfit in nearby Independence. I chose artillery on account of the horses; one could drill with them evenings, go riding Saturdays. I liked being around horses, or thought I did; and joining the Guard made me part of the war. Shortly afterwards, from March 17, when the President and Congress made their declaration, I knew that I should be inducted eventually, along with my regiment, into federal service. So I put my mind back on studies and prepared to pass a pleasant waiting time.

As soon as the college term was over I went with a high school comrade, Ross Rainsburg, to Ann Arbor, Michigan, where he was a student, being also employed nights at a film theater. Once there, I enrolled for courses in gas engines and math and took a job at Ross's movie house. Here I shared with an instructor from the university's Music School both a grand piano and a pipe organ. For comedies we played the usual ragtime and topical songs; for drama we alternated in classical repertory or improvised. Sometimes we improvised together. Neither of us made any use of the cue sheets that were beginning to be furnished with long films.

I also made an attempt to get myself sent overseas with the Ambulance Corps, which turned me down in Allentown, Pennsylvania, on a mistaken diagnosis of flat feet. This enterprise had involved getting myself discharged telegraphically from the Missouri Guard regiment on grounds of having left the state. I also, being that far east, took a trip to New York, where I almost enlisted in the Navy. I was quite ready to take the oath and would have done so had not three sailors at the Brooklyn Navy Yard pleaded with me. I had gone there to be interviewed by the Chief Bandmaster. When the sailors in his office asked my purpose, I replied I had been sent from a recruiting stand on Broadway, where I had seen a poster about bandmaster training. At this, they stared at one another till one said, "He looks a nice kid. Shall we tell him the truth?"

The truth turned out to be, according to them, that there was no assurance at all of a school assignment, that once signed up, I might be shunted off to ship work or to an office, that if I wanted musical advancement I should stay civilian, and that if I wanted real war I should keep out of the Navy. I still rather wanted that course in band conducting, but the sailors' frankness had shocked me back to my original line of quick overseas involvement. So I decided not to wait for the Chief Bandmaster, thanked the boys in white uniform, took my subway to

Manhattan and my train west. In early August, back in Kansas City, I met another high school friend, George Phillips, a pre-medic student. So together we joined the Medical Detachment of my original artillery regiment, now federalized and soon to be heading for camp.

My proto-military maneuvers, going on for a year, had all been known to my family. And the family offered no encouragement, raised no objections. Before my second and final enlistment I had gone to the post office to ask my father's consent. He did not refuse it, simply brought me up to date. "I have been planning to offer you the other house," he said, "if you will sell it. With the money from that you could go away to college." I answered that though going away to college had formerly been what I wanted most of anything, just now I was asking permission to join the army. His reply to that was that on any decision so important to myself he would neither urge me nor stand in my way.

I was to know later that he approved. How could he not? His own father, after all, had been a soldier and so had every other male of his father's generation, as well as of all those earlier ones in earlier wars. Being in a war whenever there was one seemed to him a natural thing. It seemed so to me too. Only in my case, and perhaps it had been that way in other generations, my yearning toward novel experience was a major motive. Neither then nor later did I have much interest in whether any country involved in the war, including my own, was right or wrong. War, I already knew, could not be reasonably viewed as an extension of ethics. After eighteen volumes of Nietzsche and ten of *The Golden Bough* I could only think of it as myth-in-action; and acting out myths was a mystery that I had as much right as any other man to get involved in.

4

My World War I

FOR THE NEXT SIXTEEN MONTHS I lived in uniform. Also in several states—Oklahoma, Texas, New York, Louisiana. But for the immediate next six weeks I lived at home. My regiment, renamed 129th Field Artillery, was not ready for being sent overseas, or even to camp, being short by federal standards in men, officers, and equipment. While waiting for the last to be supplied by Washington and a camp prepared, we stayed in Kansas City, built up the personnel. For the time being, though we all had uniforms, there was no drilling.

Convention Hall had been requisitioned as headquarters, and some of the boys from out of town were bunked there. We took our meals at a restaurant, paid in chits, kept office hours. The Medical Detachment of the 129th—consisting of three officers, called Surgeons, and some fifteen enlisted men, two of whom were graduate pharmacists—received the sick from eight to five (chiefly venereal cases) and vaccinated everybody. George Phillips, whose family had moved to Lee's Summit, a farming suburb, came to stay with my family during the waiting period. We were thus together all the time, remained so later at camp, and never at any moment lacked for things to talk about. At this time, however, we used to like of an evening to wind our woolen puttees very smooth, put on our broad campaign hats at the level, and go adventuring among the downtown young women who had sugar daddies.

Camp Doniphan, near Fort Sill, Oklahoma, to which we were removed about October, was a desert paradise of sun and dust, high winds, and hard ground. So hard was the ground that for setting up the square tents in which, by eights, we were to pass the winter each peg had to be driven into a hole dug out with a pickax and for thirty minutes softened up with water. Also, it was cold that winter, fifteen and twenty below for weeks on end. Even the bread froze, had to be cut with a meat saw. And the dust storms, which penetrated everything—your clothes, your shoes, your gloves, your fur-lined goggles—blew just as hard in cold months as in others.

Fair weather, however, could be beautiful, with the dust that hung high in air creating displays at sunset such as I had not seen before, nor have I since. And the Wichita Mountains to our north, a glory of barren shapes at any time, served on calm afternoons as objective for horseback rides. Our objective almost any evening was the village of Lawton, twenty miles away, a prairie tank-town that we went to simply to be going somewhere, standing in line an hour for a poor meal or a soda, two hours for a good hot bath. The jitneys that took us there were buggy-topped high-riding Fords, which would set a straight course across the billowing land, just as if it were open sea, and which in high winds could easily capsize.

During that fall and winter our division was beaten into right military shape. But no assignment came for overseas. It seemed that all the forces except for a few regulars and Marines, sent as tokens, were having to wait it out in camp till ships and tanks and guns and shells were ready for a great joint moving. Indeed, the American Expeditionary Force that at the end of 1918 turned a stalemated trench war into victory was nowhere seen in Europe before late spring, more than a year after war's declaration. While we waited, draftees were sent in for enlarging our numbers, and some unsatisfactory officers were replaced. One of our most effective officers was Captain Harry Truman of Company D, whom I never met, though I knew well his First Lieutenant George Arrowsmith, a sometime beau of my sister's, who later, as dentist, moved with the President to Washington. Meanwhile bright fall had turned into cold winter and that into spring before at last, in June, the outfit sailed.

But long before that, I had left, having got myself transferred to aviation. There must have been, among the swelling troops, a shortage of flyers, for my application, made at the end of November, when I came of age, was processed so rapidly that within the fortnight I was ordered to Kansas City for tests and an interview. This last was brief; and at its end I was accepted charmingly (yes, that is the word) by an examining officer who asked me just one question—about the compression-and-expansion cycle of a gas-engine cylinder—then, when I seemed to hesitate, gave me the answer. By mid-January I was in Pilots' Ground School at the University of Texas.

I had outsmarted myself by leaving the regiment, which saw

England and France that summer and by fall was fighting in
the Argonne. On the other hand, I had got what I wanted just
then, activity. Though for the next eleven months I was never
to be in danger and rarely in discomfort, I was not ever again
to be bored by the war, because my abilities were being used;
and my life was in consequence brimful of novel experience, of
adventure. I never became fully a pilot, however, because before
that could have occurred the war department found that it had
a glut of pilots and did some foot dragging. Anyhow, though
wings were highly esteemed, I knew now that I wanted, more
than I wanted to fly, to be doing something interesting all the
time. And that is what started happening the day I became a
cadet.

My two-month stay in Austin, Texas, began cold, with frozen
rain on all the trees and all those hilly streets, and ended eight
weeks later with spring full-blown. During that time there had
been no dullness and no leisure. I wrote to Alice Smith March
21:

> We have worked here harder and steadier than I have ever done in
> my life, I think. From 5:30 in the morning till 10 o'clock at night
> we drill and study. The drill is our salvation; if it weren't for the
> two or three hours a day we spend at that we would go mad. The
> rest of the time we take rapid-fire lecture notes. At night we learn
> the day's notes in order to make room in our minds for the next
> day's. . . . The work is entirely a matter of hearing everything and
> remembering it all. . . . Everybody passes a quiz in every subject
> every week or else busts back a week. More than one bust and a
> man leaves the school.

It was at just this time that the Army discovered its excess
of pilots. Francis Poindexter, an athletic top sergeant from my
Kansas City regiment, had in preceding me to Austin by two
weeks gone straight from there to flying school. My class, just
that much too late finishing, was sent to a cadets' concentration
camp in Dallas. After a month there of all-day drill and rifle
practice, I was a fair shot at clay pigeons, but thoroughly restless. So were the others, all the several thousands of us lodged
in frame barracks at the fairgrounds.

At this point a choice was offered. We could either wait for
assignment to a flying school or go immediately, if our academic

record was good, to Columbia University. There we would learn radio telephony, a new method supposedly better than Morse code for controlling artillery fire from the air (the chief use for aviators in World War I). We would not be trained as pilots till after the three-month course; but the chance of an early overseas assignment was at least as good as that of the still untrained ones, maybe better. Naturally I applied, and so did many others. Out of them all, about thirty were selected, mostly men with credits in engineering; and within a day or two we were off to New York.

Here began a third military phase. My time with a regiment of the line had been tolerable for its physical activities, also as a schooling in democracy. The ground school, designed for an elite, had been no less than absorbing by the completeness with which it occupied both mind and body. New York was to offer delights wholly independent of the military experience but come by, in large part, through being a soldier.

Learning the theory of the vacuum tube and the wiring complexities of a "wireless" telephone was no less rigorous under the instruction of Columbia's professorate (including, as I remember, the famous immigrant inventor Pupin) than the engine and airplane work done earlier at Austin. But by this time I was used to stuffing the mind and could do it fast. I could even take time out to teach equations to a buddy. And all the time New York was lying round us, like heaven in our infancy, and awaiting us on week ends.

We were lodged in a semicircular gymnasium behind the library and fed in a cafeteria just above that. We swam in a pool that underlay our sleeping quarters, drilled in the athletic field. An hour and a quarter were allowed for the evening meal before we were due at 7:15 to study under guard in the philosophy library. And since the regular nourishment (something put out by a lunch-counter chain) was the most offensive I had yet encountered, with my buddy of the time, Leland Poole, I used to frequent as often as funds allowed a nearby rotisserie, La Parisienne, where in the window chickens turned on spits.

New York, unlike the other cities I had been to, was in love with the armed forces. And by the spring of 1918 (which I witnessed twice that year, having just come from Texas) New York was organized for showing them a good time. There were dozens of free canteens, dance halls, hostess houses, libraries, reading and writing rooms, bureaus for picking up theater tickets, church parties for meeting girls, and dinner invitations. And the women one met this way—music students, art students, grand ladies, chic debs, working girls—were having the same fun we were. I formed at this time a permanent connection with two households that seemed to have adopted both Leland and me, old New York families that lived in four-story houses, had servants, and dressed for dinner.

I furthermore had friends from Kansas City. Cuffbutton was living with her lawyer son in Elizabeth, New Jersey; and the literate world-traveler James Gable, in warrant officer's uniform, was editing a Navy magazine at Cape May. Also, two girls of my own age, one of whom I had known since second grade, were studying piano with famous teachers and living almost next door, on Claremont Avenue. Through these young artists I came to know others, both young ones and older ones, and to experience from the inside New York's music life. This was no different in kind from Kansas City's, any more than the families I came to know were very different from my own in social attitudes. It was merely that New York seemed to offer, in every domain of excellence, more and better. One did not have to fight one's way to quality. Big Time there—musical, social, intellectual—flourished and passed for natural; beauty and distinction were not alien ideals, but a way of life.

On May 21 I wrote to Alice Smith:

> I have been here a month now and will remain two more, receive a commission as Squadron Radio Officer (probably a 2nd Lt.), fly 5 weeks at Fort Sill, and go across. I am very glad I chose this course, as the fellows I graduated from the ground school with may not be sent over for two years. . . .
>
> Alice, you would love New York in wartime. . . . Saturday was the Red Cross parade. It took from 1:30 till twenty minutes of eight for it to pass; and of course Fifth Avenue was beflagged as only Fifth Avenue can be when it wants to turn itself out. There were nurses and nurses and nurses and ambulance units and boy scouts and home guards and women knitting and more nurses and such a lot of bands. There were bands playing "Onward Christian Soldiers" and bands playing "They Go Wild, Simply Wild over Me," and bugle bands, and a French band that limped and wore blue spiral leggings. . . .

Two months later, also to Alice, I summed up the New York adventure as "a grand lark." In addition,

> my ability to do a couple of parlor tricks on the piano . . . got me places I should most likely never have seen in civilian clothes. . . . I saw a little of the homes of the idle poor and visited in those of the busy rich . . . withal learned many things. As Mr. Gable said when I went to see him in Philadelphia, "One always feels very sophisticated after a sojourn in New York, doesn't one?"

Fort Sill, my next place of residence, had since my earlier stay there lost Camp Doniphan and acquired a flying field. It had also acquired the comforts of a well-run war. It had not lost, however, its outrageous climate. For December's ten below we had now, believe it or not, 120 in the shade without any shade. We got up at half-past four, did desultory flying till half-past one (my pilot's book shows very few hours), ate, spent the afternoon lying on our bunks and cussing, toward sundown bathed and dressed and walked out, usually to the hospitable chintzy bungalow of the American Library Association, where we had tea or supper. After a while we were commissioned and sent away—though not, as promised, to Europe, merely to Louisiana, for playing in the air with wireless telephones.

In this soft aqueous jungle where giant mosquitoes that could bite through any blanket flew in V-shaped squadron formation, our own flying was minimal, mechanics' ranks being decimated by an influenza called in flying circles "hispano-sneeza." We met the Southern girls at dancing parties and were taken by them in motorboats up bayous, where sunset's ever-changing afterglow would last for hours on the waveless waters. We also played bridge at the Officers' Club. And talked about the flying we were not doing.

In less than a month I caught the current flu, which went less hard with us in the South than with those in the North. I wrote Alice that I found being ill

> disgusting . . . well, not entirely, after all, because it got me out of some disagreeable work and gave me a week's mild adventure in the hospital, where I was starved and sweated and purged and rubbed and examined and bathed by a nurse. . . . One day, when I tried to walk, I fainted. That too was interesting, because I had never fainted before.

I returned to barracks ten pounds lighter, all of which I got back by eating a pound of chocolates a day for ten days and not moving from the bridge table. At the end of that time, along with twenty others of my radio-telephony class, I was ordered overseas, with home leave on the way.

Geneve Lichtenwalter gave me a party; Mr. Murray had me photographed in uniform; and I went to church on Sunday with my father. The next seven weeks, spent in New York, were pure play, accompanied, the last five of them, by the frustration of having quite literally missed the boat. I say literally because I had been assigned to a ship, had acquired all the proper equipment (including trench boots from Abercrombie and Fitch and a camel's-hair sleeping bag), and said good-by. Then came the two Armistice Days, the false-news one on November 9, the real one two days later. The false one had been fun, the celebration of it spontaneous. The real one was strictly for civilians. All such were justly joyous at the ending of an awful thing. But for many among the sailors and the military who might have felt romantic, like myself, about adventure, or who were certainly, many many of them, happier to be away from home than back there, or who were not at all eager to leave off being paid—for all sorts of us the riot was a little sad. We had not planned our war that way, but wanted it to go on till we ourselves cried, "Hold, enough!"

And now it had become, through its sudden ending, a dead story. Phillips wrote from France that the boys who had for a year cried, "When are we going over?" were now whining, "When do we go home?" As for myself, in less than five weeks, which is good speed, I had resigned my commission, received my discharge, and gone back to my father's roof.

Here I took up my past and reflected my future. I returned to organ lessons and to the piano. Since the church where I had played just before the war did not choose to give back my job, I got me another. And mid-January, at the second term, I again took up classes at the junior college. Back at my own matters I felt older, more grown-up. I was also thinking hard about getting away, going East again or maybe to Europe for studies.

I had not always of late years been sure whether music should, or properly could, be used as a breadwinner. Perhaps some other form of writing might be my destiny. But with my return to music itself, to piano and organ and choir conducting, I knew where my joy was and would always be—in the sound of music and in making it sound my way. All the same, I was twenty-two and must be getting about the rest of my education. It was already late, but not too late. With money I could manage everything.

Just on the chance, I wrote my uncle for a loan, was refused. It was my friendship with the Smiths that resolved the matter. The good Doctor, a professional himself, knew well my problem; but it was his wife who thought up the solution.

This was to be, simply enough, a loan from the Mormon Church. There was a fund in the church's budget for training teachers. Young Mormons borrowing money from this could either pay it back or teach it out. I protested that I had no intention of teaching in a church college. Mrs. Smith laughed and said she could not imagine me there. Alice urged too; she must have. In any case, Dr. Smith proposed the matter, though not as the "voice of inspiration"; and since the Prophet's mantle still lay over him, no effective objection could be raised. Later, when it seemed I was not likely to repay the $2,000 I had used in my first year at Harvard, Dr. Smith was reproached. As a matter of fact, this debt was one of several matters on which he found himself so strongly attacked by his bishops that he needed inspiration, and got it, to remove them from office.

It was nearly twenty years before I cleared up that debt, and then reluctantly. At the time I had no plan for paying it; all that concerned me was getting East. And Mrs. Smith had said, "I'll make it come out right."

Two other events from that spring remain vivid, my trying out of a drug and my grandmother's death.

The drug had been given me by Dr. Smith. Passing the previous winter, for his wife's health, in the Southwest, he had made inquiries about a hallucinogenic cactus known as peyote. As a student of man's higher powers, notably those of second sight and prophecy, he had read about this plant in Havelock Ellis. In New Mexico he had observed it among the Indians, who eat the dried bud with religious intent, certain Catholic ones taking a tea of it for Communion. He had also tried it out himself at the ceremonies and had experienced its characteristic excitation to feats of endurance and to colored visions. He had informed himself further that the essential drug of it was "neither injurious nor habit-forming." He had described his experience to me and, when I asked if I might try it too, gave me five bumpy little buttons, less than an inch across and hard as wood, saying, "I suggest you take these at night. Just chew them up and go to bed."

I did exactly that, though the taste was so horrid, especially where tough crumbs stuck in my teeth, that eventually I vomited. This clearing of the stomach relieved the nausea without interfering with the drug. The effects, full visions each as complete in color and texture as a stage set, began slowly to appear before my closed or open eyes, then came more rapidly till two hours later they were flashing at least twice every second, with no delay involved in their complete perception. Each one, moreover, had a meaning, could have been published with a title; and their assembled symbolisms or subjects, though not always sequentially related, constituted a view of life not only picturesque and vast, but just as clearly all mine and all true.

I had gone to my room for taking the peyote about eight o'clock, and its full effects were in operation by ten. These continued without letup till around eight the next morning, when I dressed and went about my errands with no fatigue. The last four hours had been a grand prophetic view, always in color, of what my life and future were to be. I saw this in pictures, all symbolic, all quite clear as to meaning, and all arranged in chronological order by decades, even sometimes by exact years of my age.

Though this experience had been in every way splendid, I did not try to reproduce it till somewhat later. I described it to Dr. Smith, of course, an itemized report having been his price. It remained the price when next year I shared the drug and its adventures with Harvard friends. In the next three years I spent a peyote night perhaps ten times. And all were surprising, all visually sumptuous. But in none did the heavens so definitely open as they had done for me that first time, alone in my room.

It was in that same room that my mother woke me one morning with the news of death. My grandmother Flora Thomson, spending the winter with us as usual, had several months earlier taken to her bed. Since there was nothing observably the matter with her, nothing but everything, and since she was in her eighty-ninth year, it seemed clear that she was not to be on earth much longer. She had little to leave behind, having long ago distributed her land and little by little, in the years she had been a widow, spent most of the little money she had had. All the same, she wished to leave a legacy, however small, to me. I was her only male grandchild, and I had been a soldier like her husband. So she sent for her nephew Lex McDaniel, who was a lawyer, changed her will, and bequeathed me one hundred dollars.

Shortly afterward she ceased to be aware. Her speech, however, kept following familiar patterns. She would pray aloud: "Forgive us our sins and come to see us soon." When she died asleep, late in March, we took her to Saline County for burial beside her Confederate soldier, waiting since 1862 in the grave-yard of their country church, called Rehoboth. On the morning of the funeral there arrived by train, for paying her last call on "Miss Flora," a Negro woman of near Miss Flora's age who had in early years belonged to her. This visit was the last to be received by a woman who for the last half of her nearly ninety years had herself been ever a visitor. Indeed, as departing guests are wont to do, she had just made, leaving my father's house, a gift to his youngest child. And it was with that in cash of my own, against some private need, that I left home that August for the promised land of Cambridge, Massachusetts.

5
Harvard, Jumping-Off Place for Europe

HARVARD HAD BEEN CHOSEN for my especial needs, which were three—good keyboard lessons, available in Boston; training in harmony, counterpoint, and composition, said to be excellent at this university; and full access to its arts and letters. My ultimate aim at this time was to become an organist and choirdirector in some well-paying city church and from there to pursue a composer's career.

In Cambridge, on the first day I took a room; on the second I acquired a piano and a piano teacher. The room was in a college-owned house, kept by a Mrs. Brown, at 12 Oxford Street; the piano was a medium-sized grand, bought on time; the teacher was Heinrich Gebhard. I inquired about organ teachers too, but found the best ones all vacationing. And since I still had lots of time to spare (four hours a day at the piano being quite enough), I engaged a teacher for French conversation and in a coaching school brushed up on Cicero, in this way getting ready both to pass the French reading-test and to satisfy a Latin requirement. Of an evening I covered the Boston suburbs and shore drives in the sidecar of a summer school student also re-siding at Mrs. Brown's. And on Labor Day week end I visited wartime New York friends at Sullivan, Maine, in their immense "cottage" overlooking from on high Frenchman's Bay and the island of Mount Desert.

After term began, time stopped; and for the next two years it had no flow. I did my studies, sang in the glee club and in the daily choir (being more often than not engaged on Sun-days elsewhere as organist). For exercise, unless the Charles was frozen, I mostly rowed, sometimes on a lightweight crew, more usually in a single shell. I attended plays in Boston oc-casionally, always the symphony concerts and the many recitals of ancient and modern music offered free to Harvard students at Paine Hall. As often as I could I went to New York, where I still had wartime friends who lived in style and where, invited out, one dressed for dinner. This costume change, along with a tail coat for singing in the glee club, had been acquired from a

Beacon Street tailor for the exact amount of my grandmother's legacy.

The director of the chapel choir and of the glee club was Dr. Archibald T. Davison, known as "Doc," thirty-four, smallish, sandy-haired, and balding. A Scottish disciplinarian of relentless mission, he had already transformed the college glee club from an adjunct of the Mandolin Club into a virtuoso choral society; and he was proceeding in the next few years, through the Graduate School of Education, to transform throughout America music instruction in the schools. It was during my time that he first offered his course (with singing laboratory) in the History of Choral Music. Some years later he was to found today's main model among courses for laymen, known nationally as "Harvard's Music I." A man of great personal reserve (he lived with a widowed mother and did not marry till she died), he had few close friends, just a hand-picked student or two. All the same, he was companionable, much loved, and with younger people quite gregarious. For three years I was his aide and substitute at the Appleton Chapel organ, in conducting the chapel choir and glee club, and for teaching his courses. I was the first, in fact, of a long series of musicians to be marked indelibly by him; and I remained for two decades quite possibly the finest choral conductor of them all.

My faculty advisor was the composer Edward Burlingame Hill, for whose Modern French Music I had signed up in my first term. The next year I assisted him in that course, also in the general History of Music, later in a History of Russian Music. Orchestration I learned only from him. Aloof but not unfriendly, tall, fifty, athletic, well-to-do, and French-trained, he was a Bostonian's ideal of the gentleman-artist. But there were also in him a straightforwardness of statement not unlike my father's and a thoroughness of knowledge certainly related to that of his own father, a chemistry professor and the son of a Harvard president. My friendship with Mr. Hill and with his family long outlasted my attachment to Doc Davison. We wrote each other letters, paid visits, talked of music and musicians forever, until his death, in fact, in 1960.

It was during those first two years that I came to know S. Foster Damon, slender, pale poet with a blond mustache, at that time instructing in English A while preparing privately, since

Harvard would have none of it, the book that was to open up the language of William Blake. Foster was a composer as well as a poet and a scholar—also a close associate of Amy Lowell, whose biographer he became in the 1930s. I do not remember how I first knew him; but I do remember long walks and talks; and I remember his bringing me music and books that he thought I ought to know. Some of these, such as the critical writings of T. S. Eliot and the Irish tales of James Stephens, I found merely informative or charming. Others changed my life. Among these last were the piano works of Erik Satie, a pile of them four inches high, and a thin small volume called *Tender Buttons*, by Gertrude Stein. I returned these favors by introducing him to peyote, which we would take together, sometimes with another poet and English A instructor, Robert Hillyer. Foster has often re-appeared in my life and almost always with gifts in hand, the most remarkable of these being a facsimile collection, with Damon's notes, issued in 1937 at Brown University, of one hundred American popular songs from before the Civil War, a source that has helped me ever since to evoke early times in composing for films and dramatic spectacles. After his wife had lost her mind and the neighborhood urchins of Providence would come to jeer, he built a playroom in his basement, invited them in. For Foster Damon was inveterately an opener of doors.

Among my Harvard musical contemporaries the closest in musical understanding was the organist Melville Smith, brainy and birdlike, a chirruping and twittering companion who could also peck. Melville had a relentless hatred of the bogus and a nose for quality. It was he who in Paris discovered Nadia Boulanger as a teacher ideal for both our needs and led me to her. There was also my almost-homonym Randall Thompson, like myself an acquirer of the choral-writing techniques. And there was Leopold Mannes, who with Leopold Godowski, both of them sons of famous musicians, both of them amateur photographers too, took out in their college days a patent on color photography that led them later to the Eastman laboratories and to perfecting a type of film now known as Kodachrome. A slightly older student from the suburbs, Walter Piston (born Pistone), was by gift the best musician of us all. He had a good mind, too, and firm opinions. But, as for so many of Italian background, both life and art were grim, without free play.

It was the epoch for ankle-length coonskin overcoats, if you could afford one, and for soft brown hats crushed shapeless. Under these we wore for most occasions gray herringbone, its cut the timeless Ivy League three-piece, for formal informality the period's golf togs, which were plus-fours, plaid stockings, and brogues. From late November to March we flapped around a snow-clogged universe in unbuckled galoshes. For Symphony Hall we took a rattling articulated prepayment streetcar known to college boys as "parlor-bedroom-and-bath"; for downtown errands, then as now, the subway. Since Cambridge was a gastronomic desert, on Saturday nights we mostly went to Boston—to the Athens (Greek), to Jake Wirth's (German), to Durgin-Park (steaks), to Hung Far Low (in Chinatown), and to the Boston Oyster House. Speakeasies having not yet appeared, Harvard at the turn of the twenties was almost as dry in practice as in principle. One easy binge was Hostetter's Stomach Bitters. Less effective were the meads and hydromels I brewed with the aid of my massive British landlady from recipes found in a seventeenth-century cookbook, *The Closet of Sir Kenelm Digby, Kt. Opened*. More successfully achieved after same book's formulas were perfumes for pipe tobacco compounded of ambergris and aromatic herbs.

For all the cultural advantages of Boston, plus its lovely sky line made soft and feathery by chimney pots and its sometimes tolerable food, I never really felt at home there or quite at ease. New York, a boastful city, let one swell up. But in Boston, even still, no one expands; the inhabitants seem rather to aim at compressing one another. From my arrival there, I had felt that over all New England, save Maine perhaps, there hung a crowd of enemies to man, of circumvolant Calvinistic warlocks no part of my theology. And I grew to understand the need for placating these every century or so with human flesh and blood. In seventeenth-century Salem those killed off were kin and neighbors; during the Civil War, slave owners resisting reform; right then, though I did not know it, there was coming a need again (first felt in Boston, where in 1919 the police force went on strike) to stop something in its tracks (this time, revolution) through the sacrifice of two Italian immigrants. The sky, so blue on coldest days, the bright white snow, the grass, the lakes, the sea—nature in general seemed not the enemy, though rarely did it bless. But in the wary eyes of everyone and in the necks that never turned around, one could feel the fear that makes them all take exercise, put money by, study forever, and worship ancestors. For me the exercise and study were just fine, though economy as such I scarcely thought a virtue. As for ancestors, I had plenty myself; and I learned early to keep silence on that subject in the drawing rooms, since referring to anything that might have happened before 1620 was almost as if one had blasphemed.

Boston's own silence treatment administered against blasphemy I witnessed at an Appleton Chapel Sunday service. Just at the end of the sermon a young Hindu in blue serge stood suddenly on the first step of the chancel. Rapidly, quietly, distinctly, he said he was Jesus Christ and that he had chosen wisely, he hoped, this place and time for announcing his return, adding that since his identity might be doubted, he would show us in his hands the scars of nails, and in his feet. So far, no one had moved. But as he bent down to untie his shoe, Doc Davison from the organ pealed forth a hymn, which the choir and congregation rose to sing. At the same time the young man was led backstage and from there by outside path to the front steps, whence a professor from the medical school whisked him off in a car. Benediction pronounced, those present exchanged good mornings over the postlude and went off to Sunday dinner. Though for thirty seconds we had been held breathless, neither on this occasion nor afterward did I ever hear this Second Coming mentioned.

Before the end of my first year I had found a quite good organ job at a family-endowed church in a family-owned town south of Boston—North Easton, Massachusetts, seat originally of a shovel factory, now of seven handsome estates all belonging to people named Ames, descendants of the early shovel-maker. There I enjoyed a fair organ, a fair choir, and a fair salary, also a two-month summer vacation. I would go there by train on Saturdays, rehearse, sleep, play one service, eat, come back. On the train I marked papers or did my philosophy reading, finding rail noises good for concentration, just as many of the less music-minded were finding it a help, when studying, to put on radio headphones. I kept this job till I went to France in 1921, and I never got bored with it or quarreled with my minister. In that academic year, my second, I had earned my keep and not done anything unpleasant either, for besides my church job, which paid, I think, $800, I had an assistantship in the music department worth $500, as well as scholarship money.

The summer of 1920 began with the Chapel choir at Commencement exercises singing Josquin des Prés from the top of Sanders Theater to the Belgian war hero Cardinal Mercier. I had stayed on in Cambridge during July, reading and riding, spent August on Frenchman's Bay with my New York friends. I wrote music too, my first inditings, chiefly songs and choral pieces, one of the latter to see print two decades later. In September I went on a wild-goose chase to Missouri. President Lowell had passed me for a Rhodes scholarship at Oxford (though heaven knows why I wanted it); and so had Frank Aydelotte, then a professor at M.I.T. and chairman of the American Committee. When those in charge of the Missouri selection asked for an interview in St. Louis, I decided to risk the fare. It was the president of our state university who received me; and like my examining officer for aviation school he asked one question, "Where are the Virgin Islands?" (just acquired by the United States and in the news). When I replied, "I've no idea," he thanked me and rose, later selecting someone from his own university.

Going on to Kansas City, I found George Phillips, six months back from France, the first of my own contemporaries describable as belonging to a "lost" generation. Not that there was anything personally lost about him. It is simply that Phillips, destined by choice for medicine, had been twice interrupted in his studies, once for a year and a half on the Mexican border as a militiaman, while the regular army invaded Mexico, and later by two years in the Field Artillery. Four years, or nearly, taken out of his medical schooling had lost him for the profession, just as a similar timeout in France had removed many a soldier from the trade in which he would from eighteen to twenty-two have been passing his apprenticeship.

This state of their being lost to a chosen profession is what Gertrude Stein's *hôtelier* Monsieur Pernollet had meant when he said of the returned French soldiers, "*Ils sont tous une génération perdue.*" And that is what Miss Stein told me she had meant when she later applied this remark to American war veterans. As quoted by Ernest Hemingway, who was not at all lost to newspaper reporting, since he had gone right back to it, the term was supposed to mean, I think, that something in the war experience had rendered many permanently rootless. This idea, although obviously true, is nevertheless somebody's mistranslation, for had the Bellay hotel-keeper meant that, he would have said, "*une génération* de *perdus.*"

But George Phillips was really lost to medicine; and though he became a successful journalist, he never got to use, save as an amateur, his instinct for diagnosis by compassion. I have no reason to suppose that he regretted. I merely use his case for pointing out how an observation mainly sociological got turned into a literary slogan.

I have said that for two years time stopped, as indeed it often does in the years just after twenty. Following the showy end of adolescence (for it is easy to cut a figure at nineteen), there are likely to be some vague years spent just working, before one re-appears in the world at twenty-six. My own time underground, unless we count war years, was short of average. I had been late going in, prompt coming out—although for three years after I was twenty-five, so displaced had been youth's order of events, I made no break with my immediate past.

That past can be identified with my plan for being professionally an organist, my future with abandoning in 1925 all intercourse with the instrument. The growing distaste for any such career was to begin in Paris, where I turned twenty-five in 1921. The replacement of a mainly liturgical view of music, begun in Kansas City at Grace Church, by a more secular view, French-oriented—though this too had its roots way back, in my early contacts through Geneve Lichtenwalter with the piano music of Debussy and Ravel and through Mr. Murray with the opera repertory of Mary Garden—had taken place chiefly in Cambridge. Partly through Davison, himself French-trained, but even more through the views and musical ways of E. B. Hill, which were French to the core, I came in my Harvard years to identify with France virtually all of music's recent glorious past, most of its acceptable present, and a large part of its future.

It was consequently no sudden or disconnected event, as

going off to Oxford would have been, for me to move to France in 1921. On the contrary, it appeared to me as natural, though it happened through no planning on my part. It had already been decided in the spring that the glee club would take a trip abroad that summer. It also happened that two traveling fellowships named after music's founder at Harvard, John Knowles Paine, had lately become available. Melville Smith was already using one in Paris. The other I could have if I promised to return after one year and finish my degree. Giving traveling fellowships to undergraduates was not customary; but my good friend Hill was chairman that year, and Davison was warmly disposed. Had the regular chairman, Walter Spalding, not been absent on sabbatical, the vote might not have gone through, since he and I had never quite got on, I disdaining somewhat his courses, he correcting me without cease for my uppishness. But he *was* away, and I *was* appointed, and I *did* stay abroad the next year.

It was in anticipation of this absence that my father and mother came to visit me in Cambridge. That was in late spring, and the weather was fine. Mother enjoyed the rhododendrons in the Yard, my father the feastings on fresh lobster. He was also courtly to a Southern lady, the mother of Oliver Payne, my glee club roommate, who gave parties for them and took them places. One evening, on a ship of the Outside Line, we passed at sunset through Cape Cod Canal and slept aboard. In New York I showed them off to both my bohemian and my stylish friends; nothing went wrong. Nor were they displeased, either, with their first trip East. They went home by way of Kentucky, soon after I had sailed, having shipped ahead my books and music.

6

The First Time I Saw Paris

W E HAD BEEN DETAINED in Le Havre all day on ceremonies and garden parties, so that after an evening train ride through the Frenchest countryside there is, it was going on eleven when at the Gare Saint-Lazare we climbed into horse-drawn buses, especially mobilized, and set out for the rue de Vaugirard. But dark comes late the twenty-first of June; and Paris lamps, some arc-light and some gas, mixed with the dying daylight to produce a luminosity half white, half green. And as from my perch in the upstairs front seat there rolled by like painted scenery the Madeleine, Concorde, Chamber of Deputies, I recognized their every detail. This well-known species of illusion I had experienced exactly once before, on first entering in Kansas City, at the age of ten, the Willis Wood Theatre. It does not happen many times to anyone; but when it does, it stamps upon a color-photographic image the memory of something personally possessed.

The adventures of that two-week stay in Paris—lunching with Maréchal Foch, a tea with Joffre, elegant parties at private establishments and a shocking push at the presidential palace, a masked ball at the Opéra, ballets by Milhaud and Cocteau and all six of Les Six at the Théâtre des Champs-Elysées, singing three packed-house concerts in the Salle Gaveau and conducting at High Mass in Saint-Eustache—all these were to characterize the trip. And after two months of similar occasions in eastern France, Alsace, the Rhineland (still occupied by American troops), Venice, and the Italian east coast (where in Pesaro I conducted a whole concert), I felt very European and almost ready for settling down (with cane and spats) to a Paris winter.

Actually, when the tour disbanded in Geneva, I stayed on in Switzerland for a fortnight and then spent four delicious weeks in England, two of them at Oxford. There in High Street digs right next to Magdalen I wrote some articles promised to *The Boston Transcript* and with an American girl, unoccupied just then by absent Oxford, viewed all the other colleges and gardens. She also taught me to punt. There too I bought a British bicycle with hand brakes and set off alone, shipping my trunk to South-ampton, where, after ten days of sight-seeing cathedrals and landscapes, I took ship for France.

Once more it came over me, though not as a recognition, that sense of owning completely the thing seen, when in a bright September morn at five, having left my bike and luggage at the port, I climbed the cobbled streets of Saint-Malo. I was climbing toward French breakfast with a view. And as I climbed, stepping around tiny women in black beating small laden asses with large sticks and exorting them with cries, I found myself, though just from England, saying, "Thank God to be back where they speak my language." In later years I used to say that I lived in Paris because it reminded me of Kansas City. And Paris can present to anyone, of course, since it contains all possible elements, an image of his origins. In my case, I now learned, not only was Paris to be my new home town, but all France, so little did I feel alien there, was to be like another Missouri—a cosmopolitan crossroads, frank and friendly and actually not far from the same geographic size.

Thus meditating, I progressed possessively through my new-found land (and because of Henry Adams, by way of Mont-Saint-Michel) to Paris, where, although it was to be my home, I still had no house. And this I started looking for while waiting for my lessons to begin. I knew they were to be with Nadia Boulanger, since Melville Smith, who had discovered her that spring, had convinced me she was just right for a Harvard American. But as she would not be in town before October, there was a month during which I could look around. Tempo-rarily staying with a French family, I walked the whole of Paris that lovely fall, pricing rooms and practicing my French, till I finally settled down at 20 rue de Berne in a *maison meublée* chiefly inhabited, like all that street, by daughters of joy.

Nadia's mother, Madame Ernest Boulanger (Princess My-chetsky), delighted in my compromising address. I valued its freedom to make music at night, when my neighbors were out, dining late or dancing, love-time for kept girls being afternoon. And there was a hideous, kindly chambermaid, who washed my socks and all day long on varicosed legs climbed the five flights of circular stairs, bringing me hot water at any time, a tray if I were ill. I was in walking distance both of Boulanger and of a

Swedish church where I could practice the organ. My fifth-floor room (with *cabinet de toilette*) contained, in addition to bed, mirrored wardrobe, and two chairs, a grand piano mounted on blocks and fitted with organ pedals. This I had procured on hire; and at this I worked out fugues by Bach, perfected later in practice at the church. Here too, since the leg-supporting blocks that gave room for the pedal keyboard also raised the height, I used to compose or write counterpoint standing up, using for desk the piano's level top.

Nadia Boulanger, then thirty-four, taught harmony at the Conservatoire, organ-playing and counterpoint at the Ecole Normale de Musique. A tall, soft-haired brunette still luscious to the eye, she had already resigned womanly fulfillment and vowed her life to the memory of her sister (a gifted composer early dead), to the care of her long-widowed mother (who had married her elderly voice teacher at eighteen), and to musically bringing up the young. A certain maternal warmth was part of her charm for all young men; but what endeared her most to Americans was her conviction that American music was about to "take off," just as Russian music had done eighty years before. Here she differed with the other French musicians, who, though friendly enough toward Americans (we were popular then), lacked faith in us as artists. I joined her organ class of three, to which Melville had procured me a scholarship from the Ecole Normale, and also took private lessons in strict counterpoint, showing her, as well, my pieces, which were beginning to pour out. The other organist beside Smith and myself was a gaunt Norwegian lad named Hessenberg. A third American, studying privately, was Aaron Copland, who had discovered her for himself the preceding summer at the just-opened Conservatoire Américain in Fontainebleau.

It was through Bernard Faÿ, a young history professor who had studied at Harvard and who had instigated the glee club's invitation to France, that I made acquaintance with France's newest wave in music and letters. At his family's wide, low-ceilinged flat in the rue Saint-Florentin I met at tea Darius Milhaud, Francis Poulenc, Georges Auric, and Arthur Honegger, all near my age and all well disposed to accept me as a colleague. There came there also my revered Erik Satie, and Marcelle Meyer, pianist, married to the actor Pierre Bertin. And there were musical evenings at the Bertin flat, boulevard du Montparnasse, where Marcelle, athletic like the women on the banknotes, and Poulenc, holding his elbows in and his wrists up like a dancing pig on a postcard, played music by Satie and by Satie's young friends. At the Faÿs' there would be sometimes the poet Jean Cocteau, also Bernard's young painter brother Emmanuel, the very young actor Marcel Herrand, and the very very young novelist Raymond Radiguet, then eighteen (to die at twenty). With Radiguet a certain ease of intercourse developed, with Emmanuel (also just two years ahead of death) exchange of confidence almost without reserve.

In late December, when the public frequentations of Cocteau moved to a bar in the rue Boissy d'Anglas named after a ballet score by Milhaud, *Le Bœuf sur le toit*, a young American painter from Missouri, Eugene McCown, whom I had introduced into the Faÿ circle, was engaged to play jazz on the piano. There was very little jazz in Paris then. The establishment housed two rows of tables, perhaps ten in all, with a piano and a bar at the far end. One drank there champagne for luxury, whiskey for style, or the white wines of Alsace, home base of the host Moyses; but one did not dine there (not yet), although after a theater or concert one could have thin sandwiches or thick *foie gras en croûte*.

Against pale tan cloth side walls hung two large pictures by Francis Picabia, both painted on the finest linen canvas and both of them examples of Dada art. One contained, below its larger-lettered title *L'Œil cacodylate*, the brushed-in signatures of a half-hundred friends. The other bore glued-on incrustations— in an upper corner a Swedish match box (empty) joined by a meandering twine cord to, in a lower corner, a printed invitation (no longer valid) to a party at the house of the once-beauteous opera singer Marthe Chenal. It also bore this legend exactly: *M. . . . pour celui qui le regarde*. Against the pale and very French décor, and to McCown's unquestionably American dance music, Cocteau received on almost any evening. The world that he received was chiefly French, since the English did not discover Le Bœuf till Easter, since the international vice crowd was in Berlin, and since the artistic and literary Americans were crowding the cafés of Montparnasse. Cocteau's group, well-to-do and upper-class, represented a conversation about

Erik Satie (Drawing by Picasso)

Erik SATIE peint par
lui-même, avec une pensée:
« Je suis venu au monde très
jeune dans un temps très vieux. »

the arts among people well-off enough to be making them or rich enough to buy—neither of which, in the still stringent postwar times, could the impoverished very much do.

Raymond Radiguet, 1903–1923
(Drawing by Picasso)

A Dada tone was then the stylish tone for advanced artists and for the art-minded. Even the well-established Pablo Picasso, whom I first encountered at this time, had adopted Dada's debunking attitudes. As explained to me by Emmanuel Faÿ, the Dada principles were simply that all is convention, that all conventions have equal value (or none), and that an artist is therefore free to work in (or invent, if he can) any convention whatsoever that may please him. And Tristan Tzara, the Dada spokesman, had defined all art a "private bell for inexplicable needs."

Such a declaration of independence from commerce, the

academies, and all other entangling alliances was congenial to my natural rebelliousness. I loved the climate of it, its high, thin, anti-establishment air. And though Dada, as a movement, had already been declared dead by its founders (how could so pure an attitude survive?), for me it offered an ethical ideal, as well as an expression of my inmost temper: so relentlessly (in the eyes of many) frivolous, at the same time so resistant to being governed. I think all Americans are a little Dada-minded. What else is our free-wheeling humor, our nonsense, our pop art? And how else can one explain the deep excitement created, well before Dada, by the painting of Marcel Duchamp and the poetry of Gertrude Stein?

If Dada, an aristocratic frame of mind, was a shade right-bankish in its allegiance, music too was a matter of neighborhoods. The ninth and seventeenth *arrondissements*, overflowing to the eighteenth and the eighth, housed virtually all the musical residents. (They still do.) For this reason Montparnasse, though full of convivial Americans, friendly painters, and wild poets, was not my hangout. I knew its cafés and many of their pew-holders; but it was all too much like Greenwich Village to offer me much novel education. So I stuck to my slopes-of-Montmartre music errands and to visiting in friendly houses further west, to operas and concerts for enlightenment, to bicycling in the Bois for exercise. And often, for dining well at almost no cost, I would join up with my own quieter bohemians at the Rendezvous des Mariniers, a tiny bistro on the Ile Saint-Louis.

Before I came abroad, H. T. Parker, reviewer of plays and music for *The Boston Transcript*, had given me a "To Whom It May Concern" letter stating that I was his paper's correspondent. Through entrusting this to Bernard Faÿ, who had connections at the Foreign Office, and through his passing it to Paul Morand, an undersecretary, I early received entry privileges to all spectacles and musical occasions. I had already sent off from Oxford some pieces about the spring season, especially the Ballets Suédois, where I had seen *Les Mariées de la Tour Eiffel*, by Cocteau and Les Six, and Milhaud's *L' Homme et son désir*. I reviewed that fall the Opéra's revival of Berlioz's *Les Troyens*. In the spring I was to cover that of Debussy's *Le Martyre de Saint Sebastien*, with Ida Rubinstein as mime; and I wrote

Les Six by Jean Cocteau (center); clockwise from lower left: Germaine Taillefer, Louis Durey, Georges Auric, Francis Poulenc, Darius Milhaud, Arthur Honegger.

about Schoenberg's *Pierrot Lunaire*, sung by Marya Freund, led by Milhaud; Schubert was on the program, the first music performed in German since 1914. But my piece that changed history was the one about a series of orchestral concerts conducted at the Opéra by Serge Koussevitzky, since this article set in motion a train of events that ended in his appointment as musical director of the Boston Symphony Orchestra.

The train of events was simply this. My article, appearing early in 1922, stimulated interest among the trustees, already considering the replacement of Pierre Monteux, serving since 1919, who, though thoroughly successful in Boston, did not draw full houses in postwar New York, always Germanic and now again turned anti-French. The following season, therefore, they sent their observers to Paris for the Koussevitzky series and, finding his concerts every bit as impressive as I had told, engaged him for the fall of 1924. In July of 1923 H. T. Parker had written, "I owe to you the only available pictures of Koussevitzky, . . . and the trustees of the Boston Orchestra have meditated on your article about him." That Koussevitzky credited me with influence in his appointment was clear from the bosom-pal, run-of-the-house friendship he bestowed upon me in Boston the following year.

In the spring of 1922 I was told again that there was to be no retaining my fellowship, though Doc Davison did send me, from a fund that he administered, more money ($350, I think); and he also caused me to be engaged for the following season as organist at King's Chapel, Boston.

I repaid him by securing, through the enterprise of a choral society president (who mobilized as sponsor Davison's organ teacher, Charles-Marie Widor), a minor decoration, Officer of Public Instruction. (I still have the letters of the lady who managed this. We had tried for the Legion of Honor; but the time for giving him that, when he was appearing with his glee club, had gone by.) For my support next year, in addition to the job at King's Chapel, I was to have the Naumburg Fellowship and my usual assistantship. Meanwhile, planning to stay on well into the summer and to get work done in some healthful countryside, I went off, come June, for a month in Austria.

Austria at that time was not easy to get into; how to do that was taught me by Slater Brown, e. e. cummings's buddy of *The Enormous Room*. You went to Zurich first, where you went to the American Consul, who sent you to the Austrian Consul, who gave you a visa. Then you took a train to Buchs, the frontier, where you could buy an Austrian railway ticket for almost nothing; and you were in Austria. At Brown's suggestion I settled for the Vor-Arlberg village of Imst, where there was a fine view, also a mountain to climb and a hotel providing room and board for fifty cents a day. I went alone, was later joined by Eugene McCown and a vastly companionable fiction writer, John Mosher. Already at the hotel were Matthew Josephson, slender serious American poet, and his ever-laughing wife, chestnut-haired Hannah. Still later, after I left, came Tzara, Jean Arp, Max Ernst—the Dada general staff. Eugene and I wore, for kicks, Tyrolese costume, the kicks taking place in a shelter hut near the top of our mountain, the Müttekopf, where in leather shorts and to the music of zithers we danced the native *Schuhplatteln*.

I did some work too, orchestrating in sketch Schumann's Symphonic Variations. I had to do these all over again in Cambridge, since Mr. Hill did not find them satisfactory. I think myself that they were not, and I know now that orchestration was the branch in which Nadia Boulanger's teaching was less than perfect. Back in Paris, I stayed till mid-August, working at the organ, writing music, and buying books. One was *Ulysses*, by James Joyce, just off the press at Shakespeare and Company. Others were eighteenth-century technic-treatises suggested by Boulanger—de Nardis, for instance, and a two-volume in-folio Choron. Then there were French books, recommended by Emmanuel Faÿ and Radiguet. I still own among these *Le Bon Apôtre* by Philippe Soupault, Cocteau's *Le Potomak*, Gide's *Les Caves du Vatican*. I had read the Proust volumes (there were then only two); and long ago, even before arrival, I had resigned from Anatole France. I had not yet begun on the French classics, nor had I set foot in the Louvre; but I felt at home with France, its music, its food, its people, its reading and writing. And when in late August of 1922 I embarked at last for New York on a ten-day French Line ship in company with two sad returning exiles, Cuthbert Wright, a writing friend, and Helen Winner, estranged wife of another, I knew I should be back.

7

An End to Education

ACTUALLY THREE YEARS WERE PASSED before I returned to
Paris—the first of these in Cambridge, the second in New
York, then another in Cambridge, where from 12 Oxford Street
I also carried on my Boston life. Besides my organ lessons with
Wallace Goodrich, this took place chiefly at King's Chapel. In
that granite Greek temple, pre-Revolutionary, seated in its still
older graveyard on Tremont facing Beacon Street, I enjoyed a
modern four-manual organ and a paid chorus of twenty-four
male voices trained to *a cappella* singing. My predecessor, Dr.
Richard Cabot—a medical man, a philosophy professor, and a
musical amateur devoted to Davison—had induced the congregation to accept Appleton Chapel repertory; and I extended
freedom further by teaching my choir to sing plain chant (in
Latin) and the Holy Thursday Improperia, or Reproaches of
Christ to His Church (which are partly in Greek). And at the
organ, still bearing its crown and miter, I played the full organ
reportory, from Frescobaldi by way of Pachelbel to Roger-
Ducasse and Vierne.

I held three choir rehearsals a week, one of them just before
the Sunday service; and I played a short noon service every day,
as well as an organ recital on Saturdays. At the noon services,
frequented chiefly by lunch-hour strays, I tried out the more
recondite pieces and sometimes improvised, using the most
advanced discord techniques I knew. Regularly there were weddings and funerals, remunerative and no trouble. That is to say,
funerals were no trouble because they could not be planned
very far ahead and because they lasted only twenty minutes.
Since the congregation there tends to be fairly old, I did not
have many weddings; but there were regularly four funerals a
month, except in November and April, the pneumonia months,
when there were nine each.

For both weddings and funerals I found it convenient to
play Bach, avoiding thus both sobs and sentiment, the entrance
and exit pieces that I used most often being the Canzona in D
and the Prelude and Fugue known as "Judgment Day." In that

cultured set-up no one ever asked for Mendelssohn or *Lohen-grin*. About the only observance imposed at all, beyond the eschewing of styles folksy or "common," was avoiding verbal reference to the Trinity. The Virgin Birth, Vicarious Atonement, Adoration of the Holy Sacrament, all of theology's most protested points might be the subject of motet or chant, provided one avoided the mystery of Three in One. There was method, however, behind this liturgical eccentricity.

The land beneath and around King's Chapel had been granted in the 1680s "by K. William and Q. Mary" to be used in perpetuity for services of the Church of England. Nevertheless, at the time of the Revolution, when other Church of England parishes merely broke with the Bishop of London, King's Chapel, the first Episcopal church in New England, became the first Unitarian. But in order to prevent plate and property from being inherited by Trinity parish, it was necessary to keep to Church of England services, or something like them. So the rector of the time slightly rewrote the Prayer Book; and the clergy kept right on wearing its same black gowns with starched lawn collar-tabs. And in that hand-carved white Corinthian interior, blazing with daylight from high windows and cozy with box pews cushioned in rose damask, there still takes place a routine indistinguishable from that of many an English church, save that the Trinity is just not mentioned and that the choice of anthem texts and of their musical setting is so permissive, so culture-conscious, and so catholic that the service, though by its origins Low and Broad, seems to yearn toward sumptuosities virtually Roman. Only a few years ago, on the 275th anniversary of the Church's founding, at a concert given there of music by its former organists, the examples chosen from my work were a Latin Mass (complete with Nicene Creed) and a *Stabat Mater* for soprano solo and string quartet, composed to a text by Max Jacob in French.

For presenting in public my new Paris allegiances, sometime toward spring I gave a concert in Paine Hall at which I offered, out of friendship for my teacher, a choral work by her sister Lili Boulanger, *Pour les funerailles d'un soldat*. Also (and this was the real purpose of the concert, a public program of the Harvard Musical Club) a complete performance, the first in America, of Erik Satie's *Socrate*. This work, still rarely performed, consists of three dialogues out of Plato (cut for length, of course) in the French version of Victor Cousin, set to music for one or more solo voices with orchestral or pianoforte accompaniment. I have subsequently given *Socrate* in other ways; but on this occasion I used a tenor soloist, Joseph Lautner, and played the piano part myself. We prepared the piece for months and gave, I think, a lovely reading. In any case, we liked it; and so did H. T. Parker, who reviewed it. I must say that I have over a forty-year period changed that reading very little, though I have given the work many times—in New York, Paris, and Los Angeles.

Initiated by Foster Damon to the delights of Satie, in Paris I had found him stimulating Milhaud, Poulenc, Auric, Cocteau, Picasso. And I knew his music as the test, almost, of any composer's really inside twentieth centuryness. I did not know yet, though I suspected, that built into it is an attitude of reserve which by avoiding all success-rhetoric has permitted the creation of a musical reality as real as an apple or a child. I did know that its way of speaking, as if nobody were there, was the kind of communication that I liked. I had not in Paris sought companionship with Satie, wishing to get inside his music first, then make my homage later through performance. That way we might find something real to talk about, and a conversation so begun might extend to my own work. Since Satie died before I returned to France, I cannot know what friendship with him might have brought. I only know that during an acquaintance with it of more than forty years his music has never ceased to be rewarding. People take to Satie or they don't, as to Gertrude Stein. And if I have long been associated publicly with the work of both, that is because I was so involved with it in private that the rest was merely announcing my engagement. And if I did not make many converts ever, I at least exposed lots of people to contagion.

The rest of my work that year was academic. With Hill, in solo seminar, I orchestrated piano works by Schumann, Fauré, Debussy, and myself. I also helped him give a brand-new course in Russian music. I gave all Hill's courses, in fact, when he was ill for a month. For the glee club I arranged a mixed-voice work by Lili Boulanger, *Vieille Prière Bouddhique*. I assisted Davison in his Choral Music course, also substituting for him many times at morning chapel. I always sang in chapel weekdays, because that took only a quarter of an hour and because the musical experience was so lovely. While Doc's mother was dying I gave from his notes the choral music course; and after she died I took the glee club on its spring tour, since he did not feel at that moment like conducting publicly or traveling in company.

That year I joined a club. I had earlier been asked to a fraternity but declined. I had never aspired to join the richer groups; but this was my kind of club, a fair eating place (something anyone needed in Cambridge) frequented by a mixed set, artistic and scholarly. Shortly after the war a leftist group had got together under the name of Harvard Liberal Club and leased a house, their *raison d'être* being the discussion of current events. I had not bothered to participate, though asked, because current events, as such, were not my interest. I had found out in high school anyway that liberalism was not liberal, but a doctrinaire position just left of center. (Maurice Grosser put it that "all liberals had had unhappy childhoods.") Many must have shared my lack of interest, since the club remained small and, in spite of aspirations to a world-wide view, parochial. Then suddenly, during my year abroad, it had expanded into a culture group. Two of my Harvard Glee Club buddies, politically conservative types themselves, had made over the membership for diversity of interest. Joining up for eating, I plunged into a world cosmopolitan, cultured, in every way congenial.

Above the main floor of the house, where lay only kitchens and the dining room, there were a sizable parlor and two floors of bedrooms. These last came to be occupied by a group of older members—graduate students and younger instructors—known as "the house party." And this nucleus plus certain associates who, though not residing on the premises, had the run of the upstairs, welded themselves together intellectually and built themselves into one another's lives in a way that years, careers, and matrimony have not undone. This conversation among the arts and sciences became decentralized when the house-and-tutorial system was adopted at Harvard, its chief remaining members becoming Tutors and House Masters. Its recentralization came still later in the Society of Fellows, where the talk is today, I think, the finest anywhere. In 1922, and for the five years following, such talk was available in Cambridge every afternoon at the Liberal Club house party, upstairs over bridge and tea at all the seasons, on long walks up the Charles in spring and fall.

Its leaders were the historians Garrett Mattingly, Allen Evans, and John Coddington; an English major, John Knedler (now Dean of the College at New York University); the physicist (crystalographer) Alan Holden; the painter (naturalistic) Maurice Grosser; the art historian (Sumerian seals) Briggs Buchanan; the historian of achitecture Henry-Russell Hitchcock; and the maker of documentary films Henwar Rodakiewicz. Closely associated were Alexander Mackay-Smith, now a Virginia horse breeder; Oliver Cope, a Boston doctor; Henry Francis, curator of painting in Cleveland; Carleton Sprague Smith, music librarian, and Lincoln Kirstein, editor and poet (later ballet organizer), who was soon to paint the dining room with all-over murals representing steam pipes budding into flowers. Charles Poletti, subsequently lieutenant-governor of New York, used to wait table.

Late in the spring of 1923, Bernard Faÿ came back to Cambridge for lecturing and for launching his first book about Franco-American history, bringing with him his brother Emmanuel, suffering from unrequited love and fed up with France. The Faÿs were a tribe of bankers and solicitors, ultra-bourgeois by financial position and ultra-Catholic through their mother (née Rivière), one of whose brothers was an archbishop (at Aix-en-Provence) and the other (later bishop of Monaco) then pastor of the stylish Saint-Thomas-d'Aquin. Emmanuel was thin-skinned and slender with a nose so high and a head so narrow that he seemed to be all profile. He was strong in mind, weak in body, intense from withheld emotion, in manners sweetly reserved, as if smiling over pain. He loathed the Catholicism of his family.

I showed him Boston and New York. He was alone in New York when I went West. In October he died. Bernard had gone back to France. Though in New York myself, I had neglected him that week; and so had others. It was cold weather. And a lady of means who had commissioned him to paint a room had changed her mind when she learned that paint and canvas alone (the best was all he had thought to use) would cost more than she cared to spend. So one evening in his Stuyvesant Place lodging he took sleeping pills and lay down by an open window.

Found unconscious in the morning, he was removed to a public hospital, where, still unconscious, he died of pneumonia. And in the short time between his being carried away and the sealing of his room, his pictures disappeared. Avery Claflin, his brother's closest friend, and Roy Larson, then a young newspaper man, instigated a police inquiry and carried out on their own some questionings in the house. Not a scrap of actionable information, or of painting either, ever turned up. A small sheaf of drawings is all that remains today from this gifted artist and ever-so-touching young man. Shipped back to France against his written wish, he was given Catholic burial from the Eglise de la Madeleine.

While the same year's spring had been coming to an end, I myself was deep in unrequited love, with all love's classic symptoms of distraction. My passion, like all my intensely conceived ones, came to nothing. The only need for mentioning it here comes from its influence on my academic behavior. When it came to the three-day examinations known as "generals," which one had to pass with distinction in order to be graduated A.B. *magna cum laude*, or even *cum*, I took them casually, did both well and badly, wrote the best exam in orchestration ever seen, according to Hill, and the worst, said Clifford Heilman, in fugue. What proved to Walter Spalding that I should have taken his course in Appreciation was my referring, wrongly of course, to an Introduction in Beethoven's Fifth Symphony. Spalding did not like my counterpoint either, though I was expert at both the Bach kind and the strict kind. He had never quite approved of my having learned the latter at all, especially from a woman. I do not suppose that my exams were better than reported, for certainly both Hill and Davison would have protested any unfairness toward me. But in Spalding's letter informing me of his regret that the department could not recommend me for distinction, I did sense a grain of triumph at the results of my having almost never followed his advice. And no mention was made of the fact, learned by me only later, that a college record containing no mark lower than a B would have entitled me to *cum laude* anyway. My only disappointment, really, was that I was not to have for the following year my $1,400 traveling fellowship. So I left for home without waiting for commencement, receiving my diploma there by mail.

Walter Spalding, evidently regretful of my plight, wrote offering a $1,500 fellowship which had become available through the Juilliard Trust. I could do anything I wished with the money; naturally I would go straight to Paris. But on my passage through New York in late September for a routine interview on the matter, my third-class passage on the *Paris* already engaged, I fell into a tempting opportunity. Chalmers Clifton, pupil and bosom friend of E. B. Hill and a comradely chap (who had been gracious to me in Paris and praised my pieces), had one year earlier accepted to direct the American Orchestral Society, a training orchestra for young players. For the season of 1923/24 he was adding a conductors' class; I could join it if I wished. I did wish and I did join. It was the errands involved with that, in fact, with cancelling my berth and getting settled, that caused me to neglect Emmanuel Faÿ during the mid-October days before his death.

In Clifton's conducting class I learned how to digest an orchestral score; and I conducted several—a Beethoven and a Mozart symphony, I think, a Weber overture, and some French works. And I learned, for participation purposes, to play most of the percussion instruments. Rehearsals took place at the red brick Liederkranz Hall on Fifty-eighth Street. Impatient sometimes with just sitting there, I occupied myself by writing exercises. For I was taking lessons again, this time from an Austrian-trained Italian, Rosario Scalero, who, having no faith in French music-teaching, was putting me through strict counterpoint again. Indeed, so skillful had I become at all the contrapuntal species that I could compose invertible eight-part choruses in one key while the orchestra rehearsed Beethoven in another.

I was not the best conductor in the class, though I had a natural beat. That beat, in fact, schooled to the finical finger-work of choral directing, resisted taking on the looser patterns required for coordinating instruments of differing speech-lag, such as oboe and tuba, kettle drum and flute. It was not till in the 1930s, conducting in an opera house, that I began to be able to relax before an orchestra; and in order to do so I had had to erase the choral beat from my reflexes. I know now that the great orchestral leaders, though they all give choral works, can rarely be trusted to train a choir; and just as certainly, great choral conductors like A. T. Davison or Robert Shaw have seemed never to be quite at ease with instruments.

Since Rosario Scalero disapproved my Harvard-and-Paris approach to composition, I never showed him any of my pieces. I was writing a good deal of music, all the same, including a sizable *a cappella* Mass. And I profited eventually from Scalero's insistence on the "normal" harmonization of a chorale, though I resisted it at the time, Paris having taught me that no such harmonization exists save in the German academic mind. I realize now how right Scalero was whenever I test today's composing students in the colleges. Their counterpoint is fair; they can sometimes orchestrate; but their skill in thoroughbass is virtually nil.

In private Luigi Silva, also studying with Scalero at the Mannes School, would back me up, though not before the Germanized Italian. The cello was Luigi's instrument, and he was already a virtuoso. He gave me cello lessons when I would practice. I liked the ear training of a non-keyboard instrument, but my hands were too small to be stretched effectively. I gave up in the second position. I did acquire in Silva a string-playing mentor, however, the first of several. Two others came into my life that winter, Lillian Fuchs, the viola player, and her violinist brother Joseph. For anything I needed to know about the viola or the violin they were available. They still help me in private with string writing, play me in public.

I began in the spring of 1924 to write about music in magazines. It was H. L. Mencken who got me started. Feeling a little bit the urge to write (and to be paid for it), I had gone to see him and asked for advice, suggestions. "Write me an article," he said, "answering the question, 'What is jazz?' Everybody talks about it; nobody defines it." So I did just that; and he published it in *The American Mercury*, the first attempt, I believe, to describe jazz in technical terms. Primed by two young friends who worked for the Condé Nast publications, I also wrote a piece for *Vanity Fair*. It was quite the thing to write for *Vanity Fair*. Frank Crowninshield, its editor, by publishing photographs of modern art and literary texts by Erik Satie, Jean Cocteau, Gertrude Stein, Colette, and e. e. cummings, had proved that an organ for advertising luxury products is a good place to show far-out culture. He liked my writing and found my up-to-date musical information exactly what his readers needed. For the next year I wrote him a piece about music every month, and only twice was I rapped on the knuckles.

Once was about a title I had proposed, a joke on the magazine's fashion column "What the Well-Dressed Man Will Wear." When I called a piece about the coming season's novelties "What the Well-Dressed Mind Will Hear," it was printed under another title. The second occasion was an article making fun of orchestral conductors. Mr. Crowninshield, in declining to publish it, wrote that the subject was pretty recondite for his magazine, ending his letter, "You must remember that nine tenths of our readers live outside of New York, many of them in the state of Kansas."

I had called orchestral conducting, after *The Seven Lively Arts* by Gilbert Seldes, an "eighth lively art" and remarked that Leopold Stokowski, "panting in a frock coat over the love music from *Tristan* was giving his own show, just as if the director of the Louvre were to exhibit himself, posed and breathing through his nostrils, before a Rubens Venus." When the piece, which I later sold to *The New Republic*, appeared there as "The New Musical Mountebankery," B. H. Haggin wrote in, denouncing me for having turned criticism into "a ninth nonsense art."

The Juilliard Fellowship had lasted one season, that of 1923/24. I had no more money, and I had not returned to France. I was offered at that time by Hill my former assistantship, and by Davison the organ at the Harvard Theological School, a post that carried salary and lodging. Before I arrived in Cambridge, however, Doc had given the post to someone else. He had figured rightly that I was not to be around for long and that he might as well make some other protégé his heir apparent. Wallace Woodworth was the new one, and he stuck. But the director of the Theological School, considering that I had been treated less than fairly, gave me a free room anyway.

I still had my *Vanity Fair* pieces for income, and I went on working for Davison as well as Hill. The job of arranging mixed-voice choral repertory for men only, a chore formerly done by Doc himself, was beginning to be farmed out, often to me. In addition, a Boston music publisher was getting ready to issue these arrangements under the Harvard Glee Club's name. In the course of checking the musical text of a Palestrina motet, "Adoramus Te," I found no printing of it earlier than 1836. When I informed Doc of this and asked him where he had got it in the first place, he admitted that he had taken it from the 1836 volume, showing me at the same time a later book in which it was ascribed to "a contemporary of Palestrina." "But the cadences we sing," I said, "are not the same as those in either book." "I have restored them," he replied, "to what Palestrina must have written." When I suggested that it might be embarrassing to publish the piece as Palestrina's work on no more authority than either of us had been able to find, he pointed out that it would be equally embarrassing to change the attribution. So I said no more. Though in many editions it is still "by Palestrina," musicological studies have now ascribed it, I think, to Agnielli.

Neither did I protest when an arrangement I had made of the *Fête polonaise* out of Chabrier's operetta *Le Roi malgré lui* was published without my being asked, paid, or named. I do not know what other male-voice arrangements by other helpers may be grouped in the same edition under Doc's editorship, but I was amused when he told me some years later, and in all innocence, that he was receiving quite large royalties from the Glee Club collection.

Nadia Boulanger came to America that year for giving organ recitals and some lectures. In New York and in Boston she played the solo organ part in Aaron Copland's First Symphony, a work composed especially for her. When she asked me how I liked it, I replied that I had wept. "But the important thing," she said, "is why you wept." "Because I had not written it myself," I answered. And I meant that. The piece was exactly the Boulanger piece and exactly the American piece that several of us would have given anything to write and that I was overjoyed someone had written. For joy also had been there in my tears.

At the beginning of Koussevitzky's tenure in Boston he had been happy to see me and declared friendship. When I wrote in *The Boston Transcript* an analysis of Prokofiev's *Scythian Suite*, which he was introducing that season, that the work's dazzling final pages were possibly more successful than its earlier movements, he took umbrage. His wife Natalie stopped speaking to me for six weeks, and he himself kept a wooden face during that time. Then he relaxed; he could not hold a grudge. But she never smiled at me again. He got angry at me later many times, usually for my having written something about him that

he did not like; but we always made up. Once I got mad at
him for trying to tell me how not to write a piece. I even, on
account of his discouragement, held back performance of the
piece. Then twelve years later it started being played. That was
my *Symphony on a Hymn Tune.*

By late winter of 1925 I had another church job, again in a
family-owned factory town, Whitinsville, near Worcester. The
chief estates there were all owned, like the factory that made
cotton mill machinery, by families named Whitin or Lasell. Two
members I found I knew already, the son of one Lasell family,
Philip, and the daughter of another, Hildegarde Watson. Hildegarde and her husband, J. Sibley Watson, were close to e. e.
cummings; and Watson was a backer of *The Dial.* Hildegarde's
mother, Mrs. Chester Whitin Lasell, was two years later to become my patron. That spring I made weekly trips to Whitinsville, lunching usually with the Lasells after the service. The
atmosphere was wholly unlike that of the Ameses' town, which
had been ever quiet, smiling, Arcadian. Here one felt hysterias
and tensions. At the frame residence-hotel where unmarried
workers lived, South Europeans mostly, there were flamboyant
waitresses with dyed red hair. And they too were grim; nobody
laughed. At the houses on the hill, where my protectors lived,
there were good wines, pictures, books, every charm and cultural convenience; but there too nobody laughed. After a long
and weary spring I quarreled with my minister, got myself fired,
went off to Paris via Kansas City.

In Missouri I wrote music; played the organ at Alice Smith's
marriage to a Mormon religious executive, an Englishman; gave
orchestration lessons to a Negro composer (teacher at a college
on the Kansas side), holding these on the front porch warm
mornings, just to show off my race relations. For my future
life in Europe I had a ticket, a little money, and a request from
Vanity Fair for articles. This time I sailed with Sherry Mangan,
a comrade from the Liberal Club—poet, classical scholar, and
Irishman of the world who was also by way of becoming a
gargantuan gourmet.

8

Antheil, Joyce, and Pound

IN 1921, EUROPE ITSELF had been my objective. That was where the good teachers lived and all the best composers—Stravinsky, Ravel, Schoenberg, Strauss, Satie, and masses of ingenious other ones, especially among the French, from the aged Fauré, Saint-Saëns, and d'Indy through the middle-aged Florent Schmitt and Paul Dukas down to Darius Milhaud, not thirty, and Francis Poulenc, just eighteen. Already twenty-four myself, I had then been needing to finish learning before I could get on with music writing. In 1925, four years later, only the musical pouring out was urgent; everything else I did got in its way. Organ playing, teaching, and conducting I had practiced successfully; but I did not want to go on doing any of them. They filled up my waking mind with others' music. When I remarked this to E. B. Hill, he declined to press me, like my father on the subject of going to war, pointing out that if I cared about such things I could easily have a professor's career at Harvard, with no doubt a composing and performing life as well, but that if I needed just then to compose only, I had every right to follow my impulse. It had never been my habit to relinquish a thing while learning to do it, but rather to give up only that which I had proved I could do. (A mastered branch could be picked up again.) In quitting at that time teaching and performance, I set for all time my precedent, incorrigibly to be followed in later life, of walking out on success every time it occurred.

My return to Europe in 1925 was therefore both a coming to and a going from. I was coming to the place where music bloomed. I was leaving a career that was beginning to enclose me. I was leaving also an America that was beginning to enclose us all, at least those among us who needed to ripen unpushed. America was impatient with us, trying always to take us in hand and make us a success, or else squeezing us dry for exhibiting in an institution. America loved art but suspected distinction, stripped it off you every day for your own good. In Paris even the police were kind to artists. As Gertrude Stein was to observe, "It was not so much what France gave you as what she did not take away."

But even Eden charges room and board. And in resigning from self-support off two byproducts of my musical education, I had kept a third as ace in hole, that of writing about music. This, I made believe to friends and family, was the least demanding of all and the most remunerative, would therefore be the least inhibiting. I believed this myself for a while; but when I got to France I never wrote again for *Vanity Fair* or for *The New Republic* or for Mencken's *American Mercury*, though all wrote me they awaited pieces, as did also *The Dial* by way of its new editor, Marianne Moore.

The money I had come abroad with in September, exactly $500, was gone by April; but I did not tell my family that, because I did not wish to worry them or put my father to undue sacrifice. Actually, after a bad time in the fall of '26, I did ask him for $100, which he sent without question. That winter and spring I had also small gifts from friends and eventually a commission. In the summer of '27, again destitute, I saved the life of Jessie Lasell, Hildegarde Watson's mother. Out of gratitude she sent me $125 a month for about three years. There were briefer patrons, too, and an occasional fee for performing my music. All in all, I lived for eight years "without turning an honest penny," as I put it. Or a dishonest one, for that matter. For whenever I borrowed money I paid it back. You have to do that when you are poor, to keep your credit.

Living again in the rue de Berne, so far my Paris base, little by little I established outposts across the Seine. The first of these was at 12 rue de l'Odéon, where I already knew Sylvia Beach and was a frequenter of her hospitable bookstore, Shakespeare and Company. And it was there that I made friends with the composer George Antheil, truculent, small boy-genius from Trenton, New Jersey, and the very personal protectorate of Sylvia, James Joyce, and Ezra Pound.

I envied George his freedom from academic involvements, the bravado of his music and its brutal charm. He envied me my elaborate education, encouraged me to sit out patiently the sterile time it seemed to have brought. In a *pneumatique* of November 12, he wrote, "Let me say what I said last night, that I believe in you more than I believe in certainly any other American, and perhaps even a lot more of other nationalities." Antheil's warmth and admiration cheered me through that worried fall, until by January I was deep in a three-movement piece.

George was composing that winter a *Jazz Symphony* for some twenty-two instruments. His *Ballet mécanique* was finished, awaiting its premiere till the piano manufacturer who had had the rolls cut should be able to solve the problem of synchronizing sixteen pianolas, the number George had set his heart on for producing a loudness matching that of the large percussion group. The work eventually achieved public performance but without mechanical synchrony or quite sixteen pianos. Meanwhile he would play the rolls on one piano, pumping hard to keep up enough wind pressure for sounding all the notes at maximum; and in his low-ceilinged one-room flat he managed to make quite a racket.

For composing in tranquillity he had hired a room around the corner and put in it an upright piano not mechanical. Here he composed daytimes, going home for lunch and dinner with his tiny Hungarian wife, Böske, in their room above Sylvia Beach's bookstore. I used to spend the night sometimes in the narrow hotel room, just opposite the barracks of the Garde Républicaine, and be wakened by the sounds of horses' hooves as the troop pranced through the gates to exercise. I slept there because by Christmas I had moved to Saint-Cloud, where Theodore Chanler had lent me an apartment.

Teddy, then eighteen, represented an experiment in upper-class male education, since he had opted, just out of school, for becoming a composer without taking time out for college, but wholly through studying with Nadia Boulanger and living in Europe. From Christmas till April that year he would be visiting his mother in Rome. The two-room flat in Saint-Cloud that he had invited me to occupy was at 66 avenue de Versailles, on the top floor of the topmost house of the topmost hill; and its view was panoramic. This included the distant Sacré-Cœur and the nearer Eiffel Tower, on which at night there was played out in lights, putting Times Square to shame, a repeated drama of being struck by zigzag yellow lightning, then consumed by red flames, after which white stars and comets appeared and finally the name of the sponsor, Citroën.

A friend from the Liberal Club, Maurice Grosser, in France on a Harvard fellowship and practicing to be a painter, came there to stay with me and share expenses. These were minimal, since the wife of the landlord, himself a retired butcher and devoted vegetable gardener, would send up lunch at cost. Then after a morning's work and a tasty meal, we would walk, breathing damp fresh air, in the Saint-Cloud forest on leaf mold and under trees all green moss on their northern sides, full at their tops of gray, ball-shaped mistletoe. Or we would walk along the Seine and round the Longchamp race track in the Bois de Boulogne, sometimes to Paris itself, or to Versailles for cakes and tea, and then walk back.

Sometimes still other friends came out for lunch, the writers Janet Flanner, Sherry Mangan, Victor Seroff (then practicing to be a pianist and living just below at Boulogne-sur-Seine). Every week I went to town by train to show Nadia Boulanger my progress on a piece called Sonata da Chiesa. I also made sketches for my *Symphony on a Hymn Tune*; but these I did not show her, knowing that once the Church Sonata was finished my time of lesson taking would be over. I also went to Paris at other times for seeing people, going places, doing things; and it was when I loitered too late to catch the last train back from Saint-Lazare that I would spend the night in Antheil's room at the Hotel de Tournon.

I often loafed at Sylvia Beach's shop, where I had the privilege of borrowing books free. And I went to parties at her flat, also in the rue de l'Odèon, shared with Adrienne Monnier. If angular Sylvia, in her boxlike suits, was Alice in Wonderland at forty, pink and white, buxom Adrienne in gray-blue uniform, bodiced, with peplum and a long full skirt, was a French milkmaid from the eighteenth century. At her bookstore opposite Sylvia's, La Maison des Amis des Livres, she published a magazine, *Le Navire d'argent*; and under the same imprint a French translation of James Joyce's *Ulysses*, by Valéry Larbaud, was about to be issued. When the book was ready, Adrienne invited Picasso to illustrate it. He demurred, probably out of friendship for Gertrude Stein; but he did consent to read it, a thing he rarely did for any book. After he had returned the manuscript, he comforted Miss Stein, "Yes, now I see what Joyce is, an 'obscure' that all the world will understand" (*"un obscur que tout le monde pourra comprendre"*).

Joyce and Stein, I must explain, were rivals in the sense that, viewed near by, they appeared as planets of equal magnitude. Indeed the very presence of them both, orbiting and surrounded by satellites, gave to Paris in the 1920s and '30s its position of world-center for the writing of English poetry and prose. Hemingway, Fitzgerald, and Ford Madox Ford; Mary Butts, Djuna Barnes, and Kay Boyle; Ezra Pound, e. e. cummings, and Hart Crane worked out of Paris and depended on it for judgment, as often as not for publication too. And all were connected in some way to Stein or Joyce, sometimes to both.

The stars themselves came together just once—briefly and both consenting. That was at the house of the sculptor Jo Davidson. And since Joyce was by that time almost blind, Miss Stein went into another room to meet him, rather than that he should be led to her. But when they had approached, exchanged greetings and good-will phrases, they had nothing to say to each other, nothing at all.

It was through Sylvia Beach that I first met Joyce (at her flat, I think). But it was more in company with Antheil that I used to see him. When during the spring of 1926 Antheil's music and mine began to appear together on programs, Joyce always came to hear us and never failed to tell me that he liked my work. That the compliment was sincere I had no reason to doubt; that it was pleasing to me, coming from so grand a source, no one need doubt. Nevertheless when in the mid-1930s, after my opera *Four Saints in Three Acts*, for which Gertrude Stein had written the libretto, had received some recognition, Joyce offered me his own collaboration, I demurred, as Picasso had done, and for the same reasons. I did not feel like wounding Gertrude Stein, or choose to ride on both ends of a seesaw.

What Joyce proposed was a ballet, to be based on the children's games chapter of *Finnegans Wake*. He gave me a hand-printed edition of that chapter, with an initial designed by his daughter Lucia; and he offered me, for the final spectacle, production at the Paris Opéra with choreography by Leonide Massine. I did not doubt that a ballet could be derived from the subject. My reply, however, after reading the chapter, was that though anyone could put children's games on a stage, only with his text would such a presentation have "Joyce quality." I did not add that in place of the pure dance-spectacle proposed, one could imagine a choreographed cantata using Joyce's words.

It was from a literary source that I had first heard of Antheil, an article in *La Revue de Paris*. And the writer of that had quoted from another work of letters, Ezra Pound's book *Antheil and The Treatise on Harmony*. Antheil was being launched, in fact, by Pound, past master at launching careers (though before this, only for poets). Joyce, Monnier, Beach, the world of Shakespeare and Company, all were fascinated by Antheil's cheerful lack of modesty. He was in fact the literary mind's idea of a musical genius—bold, bumptious, and self-confident; he was also diverting. The resistance to Antheil came from music circles. In spite of the rue de l'Odéon publicity and in spite of a gift for blowing his own horn, George had not broken into the concert programs, even the modernistic ones. His chief glory came from the still unperformed *Ballet mécanique*, composed originally to accompany a film of that name designed by the painter Fernand Léger but early detached from it. Besides this music and an unfinished *Jazz Symphony*, his repertory consisted of a half-dozen songs, a youthful piano piece entitled *Airplane Sonata*, a Symphony for Five Instruments, and a String Quartet. For Ezra Pound's violinist friend Olga Rudge he had written also a Sonata for Violin and Piano, percussive throughout and with bass drum laid on at the end. And he was composing that spring and summer of 1926 a Symphony in F, to be played the next season in a concert organized by himself. I rather think, however, that his first Paris concert performances came through me.

The Société Musicale Independente, founded in 1909 by Gabriel Fauré, was still active, with Ravel, Koechlin, Casella, Falla, Stravinsky, Schoenberg, and Bartók on its board. Boulanger, a member of the program committee (and with Walter Damrosch, her colleague at Fontainebleau, available for bringing in Americans to subsidize it), had conceived the idea of a special concert, outside the regular subscription, devoted to young American composers. On the program were to be my Sonata da Chiesa, for five instruments, piano pieces by Herbert Elwell, a song with flute and clarinet and two pieces for violin and piano by Aaron Copland, a piano sonata by Walter Piston, and a violin-piano sonata by Theodore Chanler. All the works except one of Copland's violin pieces were receiving their first performance anywhere; all were to be played by first-class artists; and all were the work of Boulanger's pupils. Adding the

Antheil String Quartet was my idea; and that too was to be a first public performance.

All these pieces were characteristic of the newest in American talent, as well as of postwar Parisian ways, which is to say that they applied old-master layouts to contemporary melodic inspirations and harmonic concepts. My way of doing this, also Antheil's, was derived from the latest works of Igor Stravinsky; the others had theirs more from Boulanger, who was both an organist conditioned to Bach and a pupil of Gabriel Fauré. A certain unity of musical method, nevertheless, underlay personal variations and gave to the concert a recognizable impact, just as fine executions gave it brilliance. There were lots of people present, lots of laudatory reviews later, along with some shocked ones, the latter mostly with regard to my Church Sonata, which consisted of a chorale, tango, and fugue and made funny noises.

My report on the concert to Briggs Buchanan, my chief confidant, itemizes:

1. The audience was distinguished,

   French music represented by Boulanger, Florent Schmitt, Louis Aubert, Albert Roussel, Inghelbrecht, others.

   Society as mentioned in the program [a long list of patrons and patronesses].

   French criticism by Paul Le Flem, Boris de Schloezer, André Coeuroy, Raymond Petit.

   American music (though their works were not played) by George Foote, Walter Damrosch, Edmund Pendleton, Roger Sessions, Blair Fairchild.

   American critical intelligentsia by Pierre Loving, Gilbert Seldes, Manuel Komroff, Ludwig Lewisohn.

   American diplomacy by the military attaché (in dress uniform), tone-deaf but serious in the performance of his assignment.

   James Joyce also appeared. He never goes out.
2. The performances were uniformly excellent.
3. The program was impressive, though long and tiresome. (Six first auditions are too much.)

   The most impressive work (by number of players engaged, novelty of form, and strangeness of noises produced) was the *Sonate d'Eglise* by V. Thomson. Second in importance on the program (though, in my opinion, not inferior in quality, probably even superior) was the String Quartet of George Antheil. The other works, more modest in pretension, less well realized in style, but all genuinely musical in conception and not bad to listen to, were distinguished by the second movement of Chanler's Violin Sonata, which is a real piece.

And of my own piece:

> In general one may say that leaving out about two ill-advised experiments, the instrumentation is unquestionably a knockout. The chorale has a genuinely new idea. The other movements decently satisfactory. The faults are a dangerous rigidity of rhythmic texture in the chorale, an excessively contrapuntal style in the fugue, and an immature comprehension of the profundities of classical form. The work manifests, however, a mind of great strength and originality. The public awaits (or ought to) with eagerness Mr. Thomson's next work, a symphony in the form of variations on an American hymn tune.

Hardly any time after this concert, I was taken to a chubby and personable young woman who was in the mood to entertain artistically. Alice Woodfin, a musician herself but also a frequenter of society, was the go-between. Mrs. Christian Gross, sugar millionairess and wife of the First Secretary of the American Embassy, had a palatial flat on the Champ-de-Mars at 1 avenue Charles-Floquet—also so much income and so little technique for spending it that when buying Catherine the Great's emerald necklace at Cartier's she had modestly asked if it would be all right to pay at the end of the month. She thought it would be lovely to have concerts of my music at her house; and when I suggested sharing these with Antheil to make the repertory larger (also, his name was better known than mine), she was overjoyed. Four weekly concerts were therefore announced (with tea before and champagne after), Antheil's strong-arm squad, commanded by Ezra Pound, taking care of the guest list and handling finances.

The programs, elegantly performed, contained my Sonata da Chiesa, conducted by Vladimir Golschmann, and *Five Phrases from the Song of Solomon*, accompanied by percussion and sung

by Alice Mock. Antheil's chamber works were also exposed;
and a final gala at the Théâtre des Champs-Elysées presented
for the first time publicly his *Ballet mécanique,* played with lots
of percussion including two airplane propellers, but only one
mechanical piano. I did not attend this concert, since no work
of mine was on the program and since I was a little disturbed
by George's and Ezra's secrecy with regard to material benefits.
Ezra did say to me, on a bench in the Luxembourg Gardens:
"If you stick around with me, you'll be famous." But in view
of how domineering he was, I was not very interested in being
made famous by him, nor in sticking too close; and he must
have felt this. In any case, our brief association soon ended. A
decade later Ford Madox Ford recounted that at one of Mrs.
Gross's musicales Ezra had pointed me out: "You see that little
man there? That's the enemy."

That fall an orchestral concert was held in the Salle Gaveau at
which Antheil's Symphony in F had its *première.* Golschmann
conducted; and everybody was well paid, including, I believe,
the press. As for me, I had received from Mrs. Gross at the end
of our series a check for $500, this to be considered as commis-
sioning a work. I wrote the work but was never able to deliver
it, because by fall she had left her fine flat, her husband, and
her children and eloped with a Mexican. As innocent at musical
patronage as at social climbing, she did not again, to my knowledge, essay either; rumor had it she remained content with love.

Sometime that spring I had written to Briggs Buchanan regarding the winter just past that Antheil had been its "chief
event."

For the first time in history another musician liked my music . . .
said hello. Somebody recognized what I was all about. Or recognized that I was about something worth looking at. Imagine
my gratitude. More particularly since this support and admiration
came from the first composer of our generation (of this there isn't
any doubt) and was supported by deeds. I must admit that the
encouragement has been mutual, that the contact has bucked up
George just as much as me, perhaps more. The point remains,
Antheil is the chief event of my winter. He has admired me, he
has quarreled with me about theories, he has criticized my pieces,
he has consulted me about his, he has defended me to my enemies, to his enemies, to my friends, to his friends. . . . He has

talked, walked, and drunk me by the hour. He has lodged me and fed me and given me money. At this very instant he is trying to persuade a rich lady to give me money instead of to him, although he is perfectly poor himself.

For this effort I had only Antheil's word, for the name of the lady not even that. It is true that he had once given me, at his wife Böske's suggestion, when I was destitute, 500 francs ($20). It is also true that we were companions and believed in each other. My estimate of him as "the first composer of our generation" might have been justified had it not turned out eventually that for all his facility and ambition there was in him no power of growth. The "bad boy of music," as he was later to entitle his autobiography, merely grew up to be a good boy. And the *Ballet mécanique*, written before he was twenty-five, remains his most original piece.

New York heard this work on April 10, 1927, along with the *Jazz Symphony*, at a Carnegie Hall concert vastly publicized and vastly disastrous to Antheil's career. In despair he acquired lung spots; in a long Tunis vacation he cured them. A few years later, after a not wholly successful essay at German-language opera (entitled *Transatlantic* and produced in Frankfurt), he returned to America, where for the rest of his life he earned his living, took care of his health. The living was made not only by writing music, which he did for Hollywood films with some distinction, but also by writing for newspapers on subjects unrelated to music. He conducted a syndicated column of advice to the lovelorn, basing his answers on the probable influence of certain endocrine glands (thymus, thyroid, pituitary, adrenal) over the questioner's destiny. And during World War II he wrote astonishingly accurate military prophecy for a newspaper editor, Manchester Boddy, of the *Los Angeles Daily News*. He also composed one striking ballet (on a Spanish subject out of Hemingway), several English-language operas, and six symphonies.

Earlier that season, in late June of 1926, Ezra Pound's opera had been performed in a stylish execution before a stylish intellectual public at the Salle Pleyel in the rue Rochechouart, where Chopin and Liszt had played. The text was François Villon's *Testament*; and the orchestra contained a *corne*, or animal's horn, five feet long, that could blow two notes only, a bass and the fifth above it, but with a raucous majesty evocative of faraway times. The vocal line, minimally accompanied, was a prosodization of Old French, which Ezra was said to know well. The music was not quite a musician's music, though it may well be the finest poet's music since Thomas Campion. For one deeply involved with getting words inside music, as I was, it bore family resemblances unmistakable to the *Socrate* of Satie; and its sound has remained in my memory.

I had been heart-warmed through a cold and dismal autumn, that year of my return, by the affection of a poet, Sherry Mangan, and sustained in my musical hopes by the faith of a composing contemporary, George Antheil. My music's steady flow had finally begun on the heights of Saint-Cloud through the generosity of the younger composer Theodore Chanler and the companionship of the painter Maurice Grosser. Toward the end of spring, back in Paris, I had experienced for a short time complete poverty. After that had come performances of my work, and these had led to money enough for getting through the summer. With my patron's gift of $500 I went off at the end of July to Thonon-les-Bains, near Évian, where I wrote music and rowed on Lake Geneva. I also met there a Frenchwoman forty years older who became my close companion for thirteen years (not mistress, not pseudomother, but true woman friend ever jealous and ever rewarding) till her death at eighty-three on the eve of World War II.

9
Langlois, Butts, and Stein

LOUISE LANGLOIS (NÉE PHILIBERT) was slender, wore her gray hair short, and smoked constantly. Born in Besançon (Place de la Préfecture), she practiced the historic courage of the Franche-Comté along with the indefatigable letter writing of the French educated classes. Her father, born around 1800, had brought up nine children and at eighty got another on the chambermaid. Louise, the youngest legitimate one, was the darling of her next older brother, a naval officer, later admiral. All their grown lives they wrote each other every day. She married late, he never. Her husband, Dr. Jean-Paul Langlois, had been a professor of physiology. Her friends were chiefly men of learning and general staff officers, powerful people, busy people, all running something. Her closest man friend outside the medical and military clans had been Lucien Herr, librarian and later director of the Ecole Normale, Alsatian exile from 1871, long-time chief of the Socialist party, guide and counselor to Jaurès and Léon Blum. Herr's widow once lent me for a month their farm-house retreat near Montfort-l'Amaury, where I learned from the abundance of Beethoven and of books about Beethoven in his private library the meaning of this composer as a freedom prophet for socialists of the Second International. Madame Langlois's constant traveling companion summers was a woman physician, Russian by birth, who addressed her both ironically and affectionately as "*Princesse*."

Surrounded from childhood by persons of power and brains, she had early become adept, as an academician said of her lately, at attaching to herself men of quality. (*"Elle a toujours eu le don de s'attacher des hommes de valeur."*) She must have suspected me one of those, because after a brief exchange of courtesies between us in a hotel hallway, she set herself out to become my friend; and within three days I was taking regularly my after-lunch coffee with her and her companion. We also took sight-seeing trips together, swapped books, played bridge. By the time we had got back to Paris we were as chummy as a child and its grandmother. Christian Bérard, who came from that kind of people himself, asked in astonishment, after one encounter, "How ever did you *meet* a Frenchwoman of that class?"

Actually that class, the upper-bracket professionals, is the one with which I have always got on best. Even in France, with its secretive family life, I had been received without abrasions in exactly such a clan, the Faÿs, almost as a member of it. There, in an atmosphere at once of friendship and formality, being asked to dinner when there were no other guests and only everyday foods or to tea when we sat down to it in the dining room, twelve strong around a special cake, I had recognized my Missouri grandparents and my Kentucky great-aunts, with their taffeta shirtwaists and diamond earrings, their involvements with religion and church, their sumptuous cooking.

With Madame Langlois (and I never called her anything but that) there was no misunderstanding about important matters. We viewed art, families, friendships, ethics, learning, politics, and patriotism with a closer consanguinity than might have been thought possible, given the distance that lay between us in age, geography, reading, upbringing, and language. Watching her behavior was always a lesson. At her husband's graveside she had refused to shake hands with Alexandre Millerand, President of the Republic, because he had failed to support her husband's research program. The manservant in her boulevard Saint-Germain apartment had shown devotion during her husband's last illness; and on account of her gratitude for this she could not fire him, though he was stealing both money and furniture. So she gave up her apartment, pensioned him off, and went to live for the rest of her life, ten years, in a hotel. Again, crossing the Place Denfert-Rochereau alone on February 7, 1934, when masses of students, fascists, paid hoodlums, and police were involved in a far from spontaneous repeat of the previous day's Place de la Concorde "massacres," she said to the cop who had warned her she must not venture beyond the sidewalk, "I walk where I choose." And she crossed without harm, on her way to play bridge with Mary Reynolds, Marcel Duchamp, and one of her lovely old generals, Filloneau. Just as Roman Catholicism was her faith and France her country, moral elegance and personal bravery were her habit, affection and friendship her daily rite and virtually sole occupation.

Philip Lasell had come from America that fall and taken a

room next to mine in the house at 20 rue de Berne. Gifted for many things but working at none, Hildegarde Watson's cousin was a playboy of wondrous charm. For him I served as guide to the intellectual life, though he also used in this way Jean Cocteau, Mary Butts, and the young French novelist René Crevel. In December, leaving for the South, he dramatized his departure with what I described to Buchanan as

> a sort of ethereal Proustian quarrel (a marvelous quarrel conducted with the greatest dignity and the nearest to an open display of affection that we have ever allowed ourselves, a sort of tearful but indignant graduating exercise, Philip doing his best to be hard toward the institution he was so fond of, and the best he could achieve being to offer me his ten Picassos from which he has never been separated more than three days since he bought them in 1923).

The quarrel being no more than a gesture of temporary farewell, the gift was refused, though the framed gouache prints (five of musicians and five of card players) remained on my mantel for some months. Much later, leaving for America, he offered them again; and this time I accepted a gift but chose, since I could have whichever I preferred, a painted sculpture by Arp made out of wood. René Crevel got the Picassos, which I was happy to abandon. Having lived with them, I knew they were not my magic. The Arp is still with me and gives happiness. The quarrel was so void of significance that I joined Philip in April in the South, and it was through him that I came to know Mary Butts.

Mary was an Englishwoman of gentle birth, a roisterer, and a writer of intensely personal fiction. She was also quite handsome, with her white skin and carrot-gold hair. Her favorite dress was sweater and skirt (the British national costume); and she was fond of wearing, under a tipped-up man's felt hat, a single white jade earring, dollar-size. Like all the well brought up English, she got up in the morning. (Young Americans like to stay up late and sleep till noon.) Every day, too, she wrote with pen in large notebooks. She kept herself and her house very clean and roistered only when the day was done. Then she would have tea, toddle out to a café, meet friends, go on from there. The toddling was due to a knee that if not carefully handled would slip out of joint. It did not interfere with dancing in the walk-around fashion of the time or with a reasonable amount of country walking. What Mary liked most, however, come six of an evening, was a long pub crawl—going with loved ones from bar to bar, dining somewhere, then going on, tumbling in and out of taxis, fanning youth into a flame. Come midnight she would as leave go home and write.

I used to call her "the storm goddess," because she was at her best surrounded by cataclysm. She could stir up others with drink and drugs and magic incantations, and then when the cyclone was at its most intense, sit down at calm center and glow. All her stories are of moments when the persons observed are caught up by something, inner or outer, so irresistible that their highest powers and all their lowest conditionings are exposed. The resulting action therefore is definitive, an ultimate clarification arrived at through ecstasy. This kind of experience, of course, is the very nut and kernel of classic tragedy; and Mary liked using it for leading people on till they shot the works. There was no evil in her; her magic was all tied up to religion and great poetry. But she was strong medicine, calling herself in joke my "unrest cure." And she was sovereign against my juvenile reserves, my middle-class hypochondrias, my "*pessimisme américain*," as Kristians Tonny was to call it. (She used to say that a European young man, waking up in the morning, opens the window, breathes deeply, feels wonderful, while his contemporary from America will close the window, then rush to a mirror and look for signs of decay.)

Accustomed as I had been from my earliest times to strong home remedies, and knowing well the advantages of ecstasy, I still did not like having my emotions manipulated; my resistance to the machinery of Southern Baptist conversion had not made me an easy mark. Nor could Mary's history of men quite recommend her. Marriage to a poet (John Rodker), a daughter by that marriage, escape from it to the continent with a tall Scot who practiced black magic and took drugs, the ensuing death of the Scot, an unforgiving mother, a demanding literary gift quick to bud but slow to ripen—all this had made her a strong woman, as her natural warmth had made her a good one, her classical education and high breeding (granddaughter of William Blake's friend and patron Captain Butts) a sweet and lively one. But none of it had trained her for mating with a musician. Nor could I at thirty take on for long a greedy and determined *femme de lettres* some seven years older. The mental powers were too imposing, the ways inflexible. We had lovely times together, warmths, clarities, and laughter. Then bickering began; and though our separation was not casual, by the time the year was out we were not meeting. That was in 1927. When she died in 1937 I felt almost like a widower.

In one poem Mary had declared her theme:

> From ritual to romance
> Two mediocrities:
> That is to say, without the high-strung moment
> Which in the transition, the passage,
> Undoubtedly occurs.

In another her nostalgia:

> O Lord, call off the curse on great names,
> On the "tall, tight boys,"
> Write off their debt,
> The sea-paced, wave curled,
> Achilles' set.

And back in her own south country, she had pronounced her prayer for abundance:

> Curl horns;
> Straighten trees;
> Multiply lobsters;
> Assemble bees.

It was through Mary that I knew the opium world, at least that part of it which comprised our friends. If I had encountered the drug at twenty I should certainly have tried it. At thirty I was afraid. But I respected its users and did not show disapproval. For the next five years I shared many a pipe vicariously. Once I held a friend's hand through withdrawal. I still enjoy the sweetish smell of the smoke, not unlike that of maple syrup cooking.

My friendship with Gertrude Stein dates from the winter of 1925 and '26. Though addicted from Harvard days to *Tender Buttons* and to *Geography and Plays* (almost no other of her books was yet in print), I still had made no effort toward the writer. I wanted an acquaintance to come about informally, and I was sure it would if I only waited. It did. Having heard in literary circles that George Antheil was that year's genius, she thought she really ought to look him over. So through Sylvia Beach she asked that he come to call. George, always game but wary, took the liberty, since he had been sent for, of bringing me along for intellectual protection, writing to me in Saint-Cloud a *pneumatique* that said, lest I hesitate, "we" had been asked for that evening. Naturally I went. Alice Toklas did not on first view care for me, and neither of the ladies found reason for seeing George again. But Gertrude and I got on like Harvard men. As we left, she said to him only good-by, but to me, "We'll be seeing each other." And still I made no move till late the next summer, when I sent her a postcard from Savoy, to which she replied.

I was thirty that year; and there had been dinner at Josiah Lasell's flat in the Palais Royal. At Christmas, according to my accounting of it to Buchanan, I attended

> two family dinners, great rowdy affairs with punch and champagne and children and movies . . . of Charlie Chaplin and turkeys from Lyon as big as sheep and plum puddings from London and mince pies from a swell Negro restaurant. And an eggnog party in the afternoon. A Xmas Eve tea with Bernard [Faÿ] and Sherwood Anderson. A Xmas Eve party at Gertrude Stein's with carols and a tree and a great Xmas cake with ribbon and candles on it. A dance Xmas night at Nancy Cunard's with Eugene [Mc-Cown] and the hard-drinking artist set.

On New Year's Day I took Miss Stein a musical manuscript, the setting for voice and piano of her *Susie Asado*. Reply was instant:

> . . . I like its looks immensely and want to frame it and Miss Toklas who knows more than looks says the things in it please her a lot and when can I know a little other than its looks but I am completely satisfied with its looks, the sad part was that we were at home but we were denying ourselves to everyone having

been xhausted by the week's activities [actually that was the day she cut off her hair] but you would have been the xception you and the Susie, you or the Susie, do come in soon we will certainly be in Thursday afternoon any other time it is luck but may luck always be with you and a happy New Year to you

always

Gertrude Stein.

My hope in putting Gertrude Stein to music had been to break, crack open, and solve for all time anything still waiting to be solved, which was almost everything, about English musical declamation. My theory was that if a text is set correctly for the sound of it, the meaning will take care of itself. And the Stein texts, for prosodizing in this way, were manna. With meanings already abstracted, or absent, or so multiplied that choice among them was impossible, there was no temptation toward tonal illustration, say, of birdie babbling by the brook or heavy heavy hangs my heart. You could make a setting for sound and syntax only, then add, if needed, an accompaniment equally functional. I had no sooner put to music after this recipe one short Stein text than I knew I had opened a door. I had never had any doubts about Stein's poetry; from then on I had none about my ability to handle it in music. In the next few months I made several Stein settings, the last being a text of some length entitled *Capital Capitals*, composed for four male voices and piano. This is an evocation of Provence—its landscape, weather, and people—imagined as a conversation among its four capital cities, Aix, Arles, Avignon, and Les Baux; and it takes upwards of twenty minutes to perform. But long before that was composed, I had asked Miss Stein to write me an opera libretto, and we had sat together for picking out a subject.

The theme we chose was of my suggesting; it was the working artist's working life, which is to say, the life we both were living. It was also my idea that good things come in pairs. In letters, for instance, there were Joyce and Stein, in painting Picasso and Braque, in religion Protestants and Catholics, or Christians and Jews, in colleges Harvard and Yale, and so on to the bargain basements of Gimbel's and Macy's. This dualistic view made it possible, without going in for sex unduly, to have both male and female leads with second leads and choruses surrounding them, for all the world like Joyce and Stein themselves holding court in the rue de l'Odéon and the rue de Fleurus. I thought we should follow overtly, however, the format of classical Italian opera, which carries on the commerce of the play in dry recitative, extending the emotional moments into arias and set-pieces. And since the eighteenth-century *opera seria*, or basic Italian opera, required a serious mythological subject with a tragic ending, we agreed to follow that convention also, but to consider mythology as including not just Greek or Scandinavian legends, of which there were already a great many in operatic repertory, but also political history and the lives of the saints. Gertrude liked American history, but every theme we tried out seemed to have something wrong with it. So that after I had vetoed George Washington because of eighteenth-century costumes (in which everybody looks alike), we gave up history and chose saints, sharing a certain reserve toward medieval ones and Italian ones on the grounds that both had been overdone in the last century. Eventually our saints turned out to be Baroque and Spanish, a solution that delighted Gertrude, for she loved Spain, and that was far from displeasing me, since, as I pointed out, mass-market Catholic art, the basic living art of Christianity, was still Baroque. And Maurice Grosser was later to remind us that musical instruments of the violin family still present themselves as functional Baroque forms.

Our conversations about writing an opera must have taken place in January or February of 1927, for by March 26 Miss Stein had "begun Beginning of Studies for an opera to be sung." "I think," her note went on, "it should be late eighteenth-century or early nineteenth-century saints. Four saints in three acts. And others. Make it pastoral. In hills and gardens. All four and then additions. We must invent them. But next time you come I will show you a little bit and we will talk some scenes over."

The same day, "The saints are still enjoying themselves." Four days later they had gone firmly Spanish. "I think I have got St. Thérèse onto the stage, it has been an awful struggle and I think I can keep her on and gradually by the second act get St. Ignatius on and then they will be both on together but not at once in the third act. I want you to read it as far as it has gone before you go. . . ."

Going refers to my departure for the South, where a little bit with Philip Lasell but mostly with Mary Butts I stayed till May,

wrote *Capital Capitals*, also some organ variations on Sunday
school hymns. Alice Toklas must have decided by this time not
to dislike me, because Gertrude's letters contain warm messages
from her (referred to now as Alice) and constant declarations of
Alice's admiration for my music. I had in fact become a member
of the household and had begun introducing into it my close
associates.

I began with three poets—the Frenchman Georges Hugnet,
the Belgian Eric de Haulleville, and the American Sherry Mangan, plus the French prose writer Pierre de Massot, who wrote
very beautifully but very little. My painter comrades at this
time were Christian Bérard, Leonid Berman, Eugene Berman,
and Kristians Tonny. I knew also Pavel Tchelitcheff, but so did
Gertrude. Leonid she never took up with. Tchelitcheff, Bérard,
and Eugene Berman (or "Pavlik," "Bébé," and "Genia") were in
full reaction against cubism and striving steadfastly to express,
as Picasso had loved to do two decades earlier, tenderness, mystery, and compassion. Pavlik and Bébé painted only people;
Genia preferred deserted architecture. Leonid's subject even
then was ships, the sea, and fishermen. Tonny, much younger,
was a virtuoso draftsman of Flemish fantasy.

All these young painters, along with the poets, came later to
be termed neo-Romantics; and their movement had influence
not only among the twenty-to-thirty-year-olds but also among
the older artists. Picasso himself, about 1930, essayed to take
over the mystery, humanity, and ink blots of Bérard; but he
could never quite get back for use again the compassion he
had felt when young and poor. So he turned to the harsher and
more calculated spontaneities of surrealism. Gertrude Stein,
affected by us all, began at this time a series of landscape books
that initiated the slow return to emotional content and naturalistic speech that were to give such impressive results at the
end of her life. In mid-April of '27, still writing on *Four Saints*,
she had sent word that "the opera has given me lots of ideas
for a novel I want to write one." And in July, with the opera
barely finished, she wrote of "progressing with my novel," *Lucy
Church Amiably*.

The movement's literary mentor was Max Jacob—poet,
painter, satirical storyteller, Picasso's friend from early youth,
a Jew from Brittany, a penitent, a Catholic, and something of

a saint. Max who had seen Jesus twice—in 1909 on his own Montmartre wall, at Montparnasse in a cinema five years later—was mean and generous, envious and kind, malicious and great-hearted. Most important of all, he could speak straightforwardly, whether ridiculing bourgeois ways or recounting religious experience. Gertrude, who had known him in prewar days, had long since ceased to receive him, on account of his uncleanly person and bohemian ways, which at that time had included sniffing ether. After his martyrdom at German hands in 1944, she spoke of his work with respect and admiration.

The group had no mentor for painting, could have none, because the only artist its members admired wholeheartedly was Picasso; and he was not available to the young. On the contrary—dyspeptic, worried, watchful—he led his life in terror of them, his all-seeing eye and whiplash wit alert to every prey. When Gertrude hung a neo-Romantic landscape by Francis Rose, he asked the painter's name and then the figure. To her reply that she had paid 300 francs ($10) he muttered, half-smiling, "For that price one can get something quite good."

The painters of our group, no father to guide them, developed unsteadily. As draftsmen, all were strong; in painting it is doubtful whether any ever grew to be a master. Three of them, however—Bérard, Tchelitcheff, and Eugene Berman—became world-figures in stage design; and Tonny has decorated many a wall. Leonid Berman alone, remaining strictly an easel-painter, continued to view his seas and their folk, his complex interpenetrations (under a quivering sky) of land and water, with the directness of his early vision.

The poets led less glorious careers. Sherry Mangan was a man of parts, a classical scholar, a lover of women, fine food, and drink. Yet for all his indomitable persistence, he became, as poet, a sterile virtuoso (which can happen with the Irish). So he turned to sex, marriage, book design, journalism, and revolution (as a Trotskyist), in all these domains cutting quite a figure. But in spite of his mastery of the literary forms, he was a failure in them all. He met death in Rome at sixty with an expression of surprise on his handsome face, though he had written me within the week, "There is so little time." Eric de Haulleville died earlier, around forty. He had written well, received awards. The poet in my Paris grouping who failed least toward his art, the one with whom I was most closely associated at this time and who was also most elaborately bound to Gertrude Stein, was Georges Hugnet.

Hugnet was small, truculent, and sentimental, a type at once tough and tender, of which I have known several among the French. (The conductor Roger Désormière was like that; so is today the composer Pierre Boulez.) Self-indulgent early about food and drink, by sixty Hugnet suggested a miniature Hemingway. At all ages his conversation has been outrageous and, if you like outrage, hilarious. Rarely have I heard matched the guttersnipe wit with which he can lay out an enemy. His poetry is liltingly lyrical, pleasingly farfetched as to image, and sweet on the tongue. His most striking contributions to letters, all the same, have been histories of the Dada and surrealist movements and a still unfinished memoir of Paris intellectual life under the German occupation.

I knew Georges in 1926, took him to Gertrude early in '27. He was beginning then, since no one else was doing it, to publish his own poetry and that of his friends, his father (a furniture manufacturer with taste in letters) staking him to the costs. The books came out in limited editions with illustrations by distinguished modern artists. Sold by subscription, they paid their way on condition that nobody receive royalties and the publisher take no salary. Under the imprint Editions de la Montagne, Hugnet brought out that year books by himself, Théophile Briant, and Eric de Haulleville. Others followed by Tristan Tzara, Pierre de Massot, and Gertrude Stein. This last was a collection of ten word-portraits accompanied by drawn likenesses of the subjects, the texts appearing in both English and French, the translations produced by Hugnet and myself. The subjects were:

	drawn by
IF I TOLD HIM:	
A COMPLETED PORTRAIT OF PICASSO	*himself*
GUILLAUME APOLLINAIRE	*Picasso*
ERIK SATIE	*Picasso*
PAVLIK TCHELITCHEFF OR ADRIAN ARTHUR	*himself*
VIRGIL THOMSON	*Bérard*
CHRISTIAN BERARD	*himself*

BERNARD FAY — *Tonny*
KRISTIANS TONNY — *himself*
GEORGES HUGNET — *E. Berman*
MORE GRAMMAR GENIA BERMAN — *himself*

Translating Gertrude Stein had been Madame Langlois's idea, and she had worked out with my aid a piece called *Water Pipe* (*Conduite d'Eau*). The original of this had been printed in the first number, dated February 1927, of *larus the celestial visitor*, Sherry Mangan's magazine, of which, according to the masthead, I was "editor in France." And the translation had been read aloud before a literary gathering at the house of Miss Natalie Barney, salonnière from Ohio, Remy de Gourmont's "*amazone*." This was at an after-tea program devoted to Miss Stein, where I also sang my settings of *Susie Asado* and *Preciosilla*. Madame Langlois attended as well to honor the poet, encountering there an old friend, the historian Seignobos, who was so dumbfounded at meeting her in a salon several ways far-out that he blurted, "What are you doing *here*?" right in front of the hostess-amazon.

Another acquaintance of Miss Barney and of Gertrude Stein, the Duchesse de Clermont-Tonnerre (a member of Miss Barney's feminist literary group that called itself l'Académie des Femmes, also a writer of memoirs under her maiden name, Elisabeth de Gramont), paid honor to us by having performed at her house in the rue Raynouard, during a *Grande Semaine* costume party, our cantata *Capital Capitals*. Getting ready for this occasion, I had holed up in a hotel on the rue Jacob (my definitive move to the left bank), where I made ink copies for the four men to sing from and where I rehearsed them letter-perfect for the event. In the last days my bass took sick; and since replacement was not feasible, I ended by singing his solos from the piano. The party was very handsome, with the garden paths outlined in blue cup-candles and behind bushes a quartet of hunting horns. But the residence, an eighteenth-century gatehouse, was not large; and when the billionaire great beauty Ganna Walska arrived in a *robe de style* six feet wide and surely ten from toe to train, the duchesse, meeting her at the door, exclaimed, "But you know the size of my rooms. Go right out to the garden." And there all evening, in bright white satin, bare-breasted and bejeweled, she paraded like a petulant pea-cock. The Misses Stein and Toklas also came, having delayed their summer exodus by over a month.

All that winter and spring, while I was serving Gertrude Stein as translator, impresario, music setter, and literary agent, she was working for me too, trying to find money for me to live on while our opera got composed. She had done her best with Miss Etta and Dr. Claribel Cone, art collectors from Baltimore; and I had played music for them to no great cash result. Nor had her efforts with a rich friend from Chicago, Mrs. Emily Crane Chadbourne, yet turned to money. She had consulted the sculptor Jo Davidson about other prospects; and he had called up right away Miss Elsa Maxwell, whose life work was showing people how to spend money. Miss Maxwell immediately invited me to lunch at the Ritz, where at a table of twelve I sat between her (Oh, yes, at her right) and a Roman principessa and where, between cocktails and bridge, she outlined for me in detail a custom-made career, which she herself was to take in hand right off.

The first item of this was to be a commission from the Princesse Edmond de Polignac for a work to be performed the next season at one of this lady's regular musical receptions. The last item was to be a production of my opera at Monte Carlo in the spring of 1929, two years thence. And we were both to lunch with the princesse the next Saturday. The Monte Carlo deal appeared to me more credible than the other, because Miss Maxwell was employed at that time by the principality of Monaco as a promoter of its gambling casino, hotels, and beach. It was due to her work and presence, indeed, that the Côte d'Azur, formerly just a wintering place, was beginning its fabulous life as a summer resort. There she might indeed have been able to throw weight, perhaps even to give orders. But the princesse (née Winnaretta Singer) was not only socially stable; she was quite accustomed to making up her own mind and was herself a musician.

I do not know whether Miss Maxwell's plans encountered resistance, or whether she had been bluffing all the time. I do remember that the lunch in the avenue Henri Martin never came off and that within a week after the one at the Ritz, Miss Maxwell made six engagements with me in three days and failed to appear at any of them, leaving word the last time that she had quit Paris. Jean Cocteau, to whom I told the story, offered to write the princesse himself explaining that I was not to be judged from my acquaintances in café society. But I discouraged this, doubting she had ever heard of me.

Cocteau, who had known me since 1921 but who had just lately decided to become acquainted also with my music, now came, at the invitation of Mary Butts, to my narrow room in the Hôtel Jacob, where, accompanying myself at the piano, I sang him *Capital Capitals*, all four voices. The work pleased him, he said, by its solidity, "like a table that stands on its legs, a door one can open and close."

As I reread letters written at that time, I am struck by the intensity with which Miss Stein and I took each other up. From the fall of 1926, in fact, till her death in July of 1946 we were forever loving being together, whether talking and walking, writing to each other, or at work. Once for a four-year period we did not speak, having quarreled for reasons we both knew to be foolish; but for the last two years of even that time we wrote constantly, our pretext being business. I translated into French with Madame Langlois *Water Pipe* and *A Saint in Seven*, with Georges Hugnet *Ten Portraits* and excerpts from *The Making of Americans*. I also produced from among my friends a publisher, Sherry Mangan, who printed her work extensively, or caused it to be printed, including the parallel versions of Hugnet's *Enfances* and her English paraphrase of it, which later appeared as *Before the Flowers of Friendship Faded Friendship Faded*. I set to music *Susie Asado*, *Preciosilla*, *Portrait of F. B.*, *Capital Capitals*, and a film scenario written by her in French and entitled, not quite grammatically, *Deux Soeurs qui sont pas soeurs*. Also two operas, both of which she wrote for me on themes thought up by me. The eventual performance and musical publication of these works was, moreover, bought about by me in every case, though at all times she did her best to further both our interests. She even offered the services of Picasso as stage designer for *Four Saints*, collaboration which I declined, preferring to remain, except for her, within my age group. I did, in fact, right then beseech Bérard to consider designing an eventual production, though at that time he had not touched the theater; and he said yes with joy, began instantly giving off ideas.

First page of *Film: Deux Soeurs qui sont pas soeurs*
by Gertrude Stein, music and ms. by V.T., the instrumental
part being a portrait of Basket I, the poodle whose acquisition
provided the story.

All these maneuvers, I remind myself, had to do with a work not yet in existence, for the opera's libretto, begun in March, was not completed till mid-June; and at that date there was still not any music. There could not have been; I had not seen the text. I was given this almost complete at the end of June, but I did not receive the whole libretto till a month later. When she sent it from the country, I was still at the Hôtel Jacob et d'Angleterre without a penny. By the time it reached me I had embarked on an expedition that was to keep me from composing for several months.

This began as a motor trip through Brittany and Normandy with Hildegarde Watson's mother, Mrs. Chester Whitin Lasell, and a teen-age grandchild, Nancy Clare Verdi. It turned into a two-months' caring-for-the-sick when Mrs. Lasell came down in Rouen with an ear infection. By good luck, and through my friendship with Madame Langlois, I was able to command, in August, out-of-town and out-of-season visits from a first-class otolaryngologist. When eventually the mastoiditis had been cleared up without surgery, Mrs. Lasell was grateful, became for several years my patron. In late September she returned to Whitinsville. In October I ordered clothes and looked for a flat. By November I had taken a studio on the quai Voltaire and begun composing *Four Saints in Three Acts*.

10

17 quai Voltaire

THE QUAI VOLTAIRE is a row of eighteenth-century houses standing between the rue des Saints-Pères and the rue du Bac and looking across the Seine to the Louvre. Just above it sits the seventeenth-century Institut de France, arms open like a miniature Saint Peter's for receiving daily its college of lay cardinals, the forty "immortals" of l'Académie Française. A farther short walk upstream brings the medieval world—the Conciergerie, Sainte-Chapelle, and Notre-Dame. Downstream one passes the 1900 Gare d'Orsay and the eighteenth-century Hôtel de Salm (Palais de la Légion d'Honneur) and looks across to the Tuileries Gardens before arriving at the Chamber of Deputies and Place de la Concorde, both dominating from on high excellent swimming-baths that sit in the Seine without using its water. The situation could not be more central or more historical.

Number 17, where I went to live in 1927 (permanently, as it has now turned out), consists of two houses, each with its courtyard and concierge, plus a three-story pavilion known as *l'atelier d'Ingres*, where the grandmother of our concierge's husband was said to have posed for *La Source*. In the second of the larger houses, dating from 1791 and built over the ruins of the fifteenth-century Abbaye des Théatins, I occupied, five stories up, a furnished studio complete with bath and with a view that included Louvre, Opéra, and Sacré-Cœur. The concierge of the first house, Madame Jeanne, took care of it. She took care of me too, washing my woolens, receiving my messages, ordering anthracite coal for my *salamandre*, and in general looking to my comfort. Her sister, Madame Elise, concierge of the second house, came later to cook for me (and first class she was); but at this time I had no kitchen, only an alcohol stove for making coffee or tea.

The first house was L-shaped; and my landlord, Dr. Ovize, though not its owner, lived there with his wife on the top floor behind a twelve-foot-wide terrace dominating three fourths of the city. The second house, where I lived, was also L-shaped;

and, completed by the Ingres studio, it enclosed three sides of a generous courtyard, turning the back of its principal wing to the Hôtel du Quai Voltaire, at number 19. Madame Elise, my concierge, only slept in this house; she spent her days helping out Madame Jeanne and preparing sumptuous meals for Madame Jeanne's husband, a bonded messenger for the Bank of France. And as if to bind further the two houses, their cousin Berthe (as a live-in servant she could not be called Madame) was maid to my next-door neighbor, the poet Lucie Delarue-Mardrus; and Madame Mardrus herself, ex-wife of an Arabic scholar, Dr. Jesus-Christ Mardrus, was the close friend of Madame Ovize. As a further connection, she shared literary and feministic consanguinities with my friends Miss Natalie Barney and Elisabeth de Gramont, Duchesse de Clermont-Tonnerre.

Berthe, costumed in black, was a schooled servant who addressed one in the third person. When I knocked on her kitchen door one day to ask how to make a mayonnaise, she began, "Monsieur will take a bowl and an egg. Monsieur will break his egg and put into his bowl the yellow only." Though forty or more, she was not afraid of stairs, always running down to find Madame Mardrus a taxi, then climbing back by the steep circular service stairs. Dark men from the Auvergne carried fifty-pound sacks of coal up that stairway too.

Madame Elise was tall, heavy, and beautiful, with blue eyes and white hair. She smiled constantly, unless cooking. Then she would hover, fluttering like a hen and barely breathing, as out of her left hand she would take with three fingers of her right a pinch of something and throw it in, then wait still breathless, as if listening, till she divined the gesture a success. When I began to cook she told me many secret things; and occasionally I taught her an American dish. This she would never put into repertory until her brother-in-law had pronounced it good. And she did not think it right not to eat soup. Thus I discovered that no dinner was too much work if I allowed her to make soup also—which she did well, cooking it always very slowly, while she mended, tending her sister's lodge.

The studio was octagonal and twenty feet tall, with high windows on the north and northeast facets, which were covered at night by rose-colored floor-length curtains, padded to keep the cold out. The walls and carpet were a golden tan; chairs, table,

and dish-cabinet, all from Louis-Philippe times, were of mahogany. A velvet-covered plain couch was my bed. At the top of
some long stairs were a balcony and a very large bath-dressing
room. This had two windows (one with my finest view), its own
heat (gas), and its mechanism (also gas) for heating water, plus
a clothes-closet. I had brought with me some Chinese water
colors and a Persian chess table (gifts of Mary Butts) and the
abstract sculpture by Arp (gift of Philip Lasell). Almost immediately too there was large Bérard, a man's portrait much larger
than life painted in almost-black blues over candlewax modeling
(a gift from Bérard out of his first one-man show). There was
Chinese tea from Boston (via Mrs. Lasell). I acquired a rented
piano from Pleyel. And I had new clothes, the first in several
years, for with the first gift of money from Mrs. Lasell, before
she put me on allowance, I had ordered at Lanvin three suits,
an overcoat, and six poplin shirts with matching underdraw-
ers. I paid for these in cash, made friends, forever after having
credit there.

I said one day to Gertrude, "We are poor as anything and
feeling quite bohemian, and yet we all wear suits and ties and
hats. What did Picasso and Max Jacob wear when they were
young?" But she did not remember, and so she asked Picasso.
"Caps," he replied, "and sweaters, except for Max, who was a
dude," then remembering further, "but we bought our sweaters
at Williams's [British sport shop]."

Madame Jeanne, my caretaker, had black hair and flashing
eyes; and though less monumental than her sister, was more
striking. I have seen her image on the portal of an eleven-century
church (Saint-Lô), along with those of Anatole France and of
an ever remembered old French taxi driver. She was in fact as
basically French as anyone I ever knew; she was France. She
could barely read; she believed America to have been discovered
by Lafayette; and the store called Old England she would write
phonetically in French as Olden Gland. All the same, reciting
the injustices of Madame Ovize toward her sister, she was Sarah
Bernhardt, Réjane, Marie Bell. She was also Corneille and Racine, for what is the language of these at its most lapidary but
the basic French of kings and concierges? "*J'admire ton courage et je plains ta jeunesse,*" says the monarch to the hero of *Le
Cid* ("I admire your bravery and pity your youth"). And the

young Oreste in *Andromaque* confesses, "*Mon innocence enfin commence à me peser*" ("My innocence begins to be a weight").

Of my sculpture by Arp Madame Jeanne had asked, reasonably enough, what it represented. And when I answered that I had no clue, she settled the matter with, "*C'est une idée d'artiste.*" And when to her inquiry about a crystal that looked like pink flowers, I answered that such forms, found in the Sahara, were known as "*roses du désert,*" she observed philosophically, putting it back on the shelf, "*C'est intéressant tout de même la nature.*" For humane understanding she was Madame Langlois's equal; and in her mastery of the tactful remark she could match my mother.

In my first week some composer had been playing me his newest piece, a long, loud, and highly discordant work. The next morning a letter came from my poet-neighbor Lucie Delarue-Mardrus that was a cry of pain. I answered with an invitation to tea, and she accepted. Tall and dark-haired, with soft brown eyes, she was a Norman from Honfleur, poet, painter, even something of a musician. It was around her music making that we made our pact. She liked to practice the violin from twelve to one; and I agreed not to mind music at that hour, since I would surely be shaving, bathing, and dressing to go out. During the earlier morning, when I might be using the piano, she agreed to do her writing in a room from which she could not hear my music. Early afternoons we both were out. Late afternoons she would tolerate whatever she might hear, since she now knew that what came through my walls would always be some dialect of music. I proposed not playing evenings after ten, but she said that music could not be heard from where she slept. So we became friends and began to visit, sometimes at her flat when all six of her tall dark sisters would arrive from Honfleur, sometimes at mine when there were literary people, still oftener at Dr. Ovize's, where there would be lunches lasting for hours, with music afterwards. Here I would play and sing my own, or I would play two-piano Mozart with Madame, a chihuahua-size Jewess from Algiers with deep shadows under green eyes and a mop of bright red hair teased into a headlight.

On November first I had taken possession; on November second I began Act One. Very shortly after, I composed my first song in French, a setting of four poems by Georges Hugnet

that were not related to one another save by their lilting metrics. Henri Sauguet gave it the title of *La Valse grégorienne*, on
account of its chant-like intonings and archaic harmony. The
French found in it no prosodic fault, insisted I sing it for them
all the time. It was so successful, in fact, that I went no farther
just then with setting French. I had my *Four Saints* to be getting on with.

In the early Boulanger days I had trained myself to write
music without instrumental aid, had come indeed to prefer
working that way. For the opera I found myself working differently. With the text on my piano's music rack, I would sing
and play, improvising melody to fit the words and harmony for
underpinning them with shape. I did this every day, wrote down
nothing. When the first act would improvise itself every day in
the same way, I knew it was set. That took all of November.
Then I wrote it out from memory, which took ten days. By
mid-December I had a score consisting of the vocal lines and a
figured bass, a score from which I could perform.

On Christmas night I performed Act One for close friends
only. The party that went along with this performance grew out
of a Christmas box sent at the request of Mrs. Lasell by Rosa
Lewis, King Edward VII's former cook, owner of the Caven-
dish Hotel, clubhouse for London's millionaire bohemia. It
contained three massive objects—a *foie gras en croûte*, a Stilton
cheese, and a plum pudding. By having sent in to go along
with these a salad of apples and peeled walnuts, an aspic of
chicken, and some champagne, I managed to offer a lap supper
to twelve people. What effect my music made I was not sure.
Gertrude Stein was pleased, of course, and Alice too. Everybody, in fact, seemed buoyed up by the opera's vivacity. Tristan
Tzara told Hugnet he had been deeply impressed by a music at
once so "physical" and so gay. I had wondered whether a piece
so drenched in Anglican chant (running from Gilbert and Sullivan to Morning Prayer and back) could rise and sail. But no
one else seemed bothered by its origins. On the contrary, they
had all undergone a musical and poetic experience so unfamiliar
that only their faith in me (for they were chosen friends) had
allowed them to be carried along, which indeed they had been,
as on a magic carpet.

What gave this work so special a vitality? The origin of that lay in its words, of course, the music having been created in their image. Music, however, contains an energy long since lost to language, an excitement created by the contest of two rhythmic patterns, one of lengths and one of stresses. A pattern made up of lengths alone is static, and the stuttering of mere stresses is hypnotic. But together, and contrasted, they create tension and release; and this is the energy that makes music sail, take flight, get off the ground. By applying it to the text of Gertrude Stein, I had produced a pacing that is implied in that text, if you wish, but that could never be produced without measured extensions. Speech alone lacks music's forward thrust.

The theme of *Four Saints* is the religious life—peace between the sexes, community of faith, the production of miracles—its locale being the Spain Gertrude remembered from having traveled there. The music evokes Christian liturgy. Its local references, however, are not to Spain, which I had never seen, but rather to my Southern Baptist upbringing in Missouri. It does not do, this music, or attempt to do, any of the things already done by the words. It merely explodes these into singing and gives them shape. Poetry alone is always a bit amorphous; and poetry as spontaneously structured as Gertrude Stein's had long seemed to me to need musical reinforcement. I do not mean that her writing *lacks* music: I mean that it *likes* music. Much of it, in fact, lies closer to musical timings than to speech timings. The rigamarole ending of *Capital Capitals*, for instance, I have always felt to have small relation to Spenser, Shakespeare, Milton, or Keats; but I do recognize in its peroration-by-repetition the insistences of a Beethoven finale.

If it is the relation of music to words that makes opera in two senses moving, it is the relation of instrumental accompaniment to vocal line that makes an opera resemble its epoch. The singing line from Monteverdi to Alban Berg shows surprisingly little change, because with conscientious composers the words-and-music factor, even through language differences, is a constant. You have only to think of Purcell's *Dido and Aeneas,* Mozart's *Don Giovanni,* Wagner's *Tristan und Isolde,* Bizet's *Carmen,* and Stravinsky's *The Rake's Progress* to realize that the history of the lyric stage is largely the history of its changing instrumental accompaniment.

Now the *Four Saints* accompaniment is as odd as its text,

so odd, indeed, that it has sometimes been taken for childish. In fact, many persons not closely involved with either poetry or music but mildly attached to all contemporary artwork by the conviction that it is thrifty to be stylish have for more than thirty years now been worried by my use of what seems to them a backward-looking music idiom in connection with a forward-looking literary one. That worry can only be argued against by denying the assumption that discord is advanced and harmoniousness old-fashioned. Not even the contrary is true, though the production of complete discord through musical sounds (the only kind of discord that is not just noise) has been practiced since before World War I. The truth is that only artists greedy for quick fame choose musical materials for their modishness. In setting Stein texts to music I had in mind the acoustical support of a trajectory, of a verbal volubility that would brook no braking. My skill was to be employed not for protecting such composers as had invested in the dissonant manner but for avoiding all those interval frictions and contra-puntal viscosities which are built into the dissonant style and which if indulged unduly might trip up my verbal speeds. Not to have skirted standard modernism would have been to fall into a booby trap. On the contrary, I built up my accompani-ments by selecting chords for their tensile strength and by em-ploying in a vast majority of cases only those melodic elements from the liturgical vernacular of Christendom, both Catholic and Protestant, that had for centuries borne the weight of long prayers and praises and of that even longer fastidiously fine-printed and foot-noted contract that we called the Creed.

I set all of Stein's text to music, every word of it, including the stage directions, which were so clearly a part of the poetic continuity that I did not think it proper to excise them. And for distributing all these parts among the singers I assumed a double chorus of participating saints and two Saint Teresas (not alter egos, just identical twins); and I added as nonsaintly com-mentators, or "end men," a *compère* and a *commère*. Though I had Gertrude's permission to repeat things if I wished, I no more took this freedom than I did that of cutting. She was a specialist of repetition; why should I compete? I simply set everything, exactly in the order of its writing down, from be-ginning to end.

Act Two was composed and written out by the end of February; and Acts Three and Four (for *Four Saints in Three Acts* is merely a title; actually there are thirty or more saints and four acts) were finished by summer and written out in July. Generally I worked mornings, sometimes also in the late afternoon. Always I went out for lunch and usually for dinner, unless I had a guest or two, in which case I had *cordon bleu* food sent in from the Hôtel de l'Université. This was a good quarter of a mile from door to door; but a dainty waitress would trip it twice, bearing her platter up five flights with soup and roast, a second time with dessert. When I had grippe a nearer restaurant would send a waiter up four times a day, twice to take the order and twice to deliver it. Otherwise, once out of the house and down my stairs, I usually stayed out till five or so on errands or walks.

Lunch was likely to be at a bistro on the rue Jacob called La Quatrième République, its title an irony left over from immediate postwar idealism. There one encountered almost always the singer Victor Prahl, usually Janet Flanner and her novelist companion Solita Solano, sometimes the reporter Vincent Sheean. The food, excellent and very cheap, was served downstairs by a portly *patron*, upstairs by a domineering waitress who had no fatigue in her as she ran up the circular staircase, or patience in her busy life for Americans who dallied over menus. "*Yvonne la terrible*," Janet would call her. When one young man, mixing his salad, put in a whole teaspoonful of mustard, she teased him harshly, "You must be in love."

My walks that winter were chiefly with Russell Hitchcock, who had come to live near by in the rue de Lille and who was writing his first works on architectural history. Just as earlier and later I walked with Maurice Grosser in the woods outside of Paris from the forests of Rambouillet and Saint-Cloud clean round to the Bois de Vincennes, I walked the city itself, every quarter of it, with Hitchcock. I had done this by myself years earlier, looking for a lodging, but now I saw it from another view, for he could read it like a history book. This is not easy, since French house design has changed little since the seventeenth century. But ornament has changed with almost every decade; and a particular treatment of stone—smooth, rusticated, or vermiculated, with or without indentations—has marked the larger epochs of style. Involved at this time with

Romantic architecture, Russell would love to point out, in contrast to the airy neoclassical design under Louis XVI of the customs barriers at the Porte de la Chapelle, the willful heaviness in the same epoch of Saint-Philippe-du-Roule, almost as massively weighted for romantic expressivity as the Napoleonic Place du Caire, with its trophylike sphinx façade, and the Chapelle Expiatoire, pious Restoration memorial to the executed monarch Louis XVI and his Queen Marie-Antoinette.

Red-bearded and not slender, speaking loudly because he was himself a little deaf, and always dressed with flamboyance, Russell attracted considerable attention; but he pleased the French by his knowledge of their country, by his elegant manners, which were formal without being lugubrious, and by his air, at once *bon enfant* and *gros jouisseur*, of having a wonderful time. He interested very little Gertrude Stein, more Georges Hugnet, who translated his early brochures for publication, a great deal Madame Langlois, who could spot a proper scholar when she saw one. It was through Russell that I first knew the academician Louis Gillet and his wife, who, having young ones themselves, liked other young ones to be about and who had as country house (except Sundays, three to five, when it was on show) the Château de Châallis, near Ermenonville, which belonged to the Académie Française and of which Monsieur Gillet was curator. It was there, in fact, that Louise Gillet was married in the medieval chapel to music of mine. The residence itself had been a moated castle till its eighteenth-century owner, romantically attached to contemplating the Gothic but less so to living in it, had it transformed by dynamite into a ruin and then built himself a modern (Louis XV) house, from which his guests could view in comfort the ivy-clad reminder of times past.

With Henri Sauguet I also walked, but more for poking around slums than for mastering history. We showed each other our music, shared adventures and addresses, bound ourselves together by an unspoken credo (based on Satie) that forbade us to be bogus either in our music or in our lives. In the spring of 1927, coming from Villefranche with Lasell and Mary Butts, I had joined Sauguet at Monte Carlo, where Diaghilev was putting on *La Chatte*, his first ballet. Georges Hugnet too I saw constantly—also Henri Cliquet-Pleyel and his wife Marthe-Marthine. Cliquet was hollow-cheeked and looked Hispanic, save for the large, soft eyes, which could be only French. His wife was plumpish, blond, the classical sou-brette, alert and sex-minded, also a singer of remarkable musi-cianship. With Hugnet and Kristians Tonny—blond, muscular, and Dutch, with the sea at the back of his eyes—we constituted a *petite famille* for dinners and laughter. Cliquet was a pianist of unusual facility, a sight reader of renown, and a composer of willful banality. His music was a tender parody, his life a slavery to pot-boiling jobs. Marthe too was not ever to be prosperous; she had thrown away her singing career for marriage in Ru-mania, and she could not fight her way back. She and Cliquet, though attached relentlessly, did each other no good. He would go into tantrums in which he burned his manuscripts or de-stroyed pictures with razors (*"colères de faiblesse,"* Madame Langlois called them); and she would take to red wine, quarts of it a day. Yet they remained for me gentle companions and colleagues of impeccable solidarity. Around 1928, Hugnet wrote a long poem about the Emperor Commodus, which Cliquet made into a cantata. Cliquet also composed an operetta with book and lyrics by Max Jacob, *Les Impôts*. This was a parody of every operetta in the world, and both verses and music were exquisite. When Cliquet died at seventy, in 1963, he had just completed a work called (actually) *Concerto posthume*. The ear-lier large works such as *Commode* and *Les Impôts*, not yet found, may have been destroyed by him in some frenzied fury.

Hugnet that winter went on publishing, usually poetry books. Tonny continued to draw and to experiment with paint. The three of us together made a gift for Gertrude which was a set of poems by Georges put to music by me and bound up in a cover that Tonny had drawn on silver paper by stylus pressure only. The full title of the offering was *Le Berceau de Gertrude Stein, ou le mystère de la rue de Fleurus, huit poèmes de Georges Hugnet mis en musique par Virgil Thomson sous le titre de Lady Godiva's Waltzes*. Godiva was Gertrude's private name for her Ford, of which the cough and tripping rhythms dominate the piece. Marthe-Marthine first sang it publicly at a concert of my works in May of '28. Georges also made a film that spring in collaboration with a Belgian nobleman, the Comte d'Ursel. It was called *La Perle* and is a Dadalike fantasy that prefigured the surrealist films of Luis Buñuel. For its appearance at the cinema Aux Ursulines I arranged my *Valse grégorienne*, to please d'Ursel, for the five-piece orchestra that accompanied the show.

Lots of people came in and out of my flat that first year, and sometimes there were large parties. For one of these Bernard Faÿ invited a galaxy of literary stars and aged princesses. At another, Scott Fitzgerald stood up on my anthracite-burning *salamandre* with such shaky balance that both he and the stove just missed decline and fall. The novelists Marcel Jouhandeau and André Gide used to appear. Also León Kochnitzky, poet and professional traveler. Not Antheil, who was in America. Nor Ernest Hemingway, whom I never asked. He was part of a Montparnasse hard-liquor set which, though thoroughly fascinated by itself, was less interesting to people not also drinking hard liquor. Robert McAlmon I did find interesting; I also esteemed him as a writer; but just like Hart Crane, who was around for a while and whom I also admired, he was too busy drinking and getting over it to make dates with. Both were better when casually encountered. Mary Reynolds, the queen of American Montparnasse, came often, also Olga Dahlgren, a Philadelphian abroad, and my own painters, of course—Kristians Tonny, Bérard, and Leonid and Eugene Berman. Also a Swiss writer unbelievably impoverished, not always clean, not always sober, his mind ingenious, his talk both learned and funny—Charles-Albert Cingria, who lived in an unheated garret room with a fifteenth-century spinet, a bicycle, and five hundred books and who wrote in the most beautiful French prose small brochures about large historical questions, such as the rights of rhythm in Gregorian chant.

So what with parties and people, with new clothes and stable measurements (for I patronized a Russian gymnast who could keep me at 135 pounds), and with the opera advancing by leaps, time stopped once more. Nothing seemed to be going on, because everything was going right. In April Mrs. Lasell appeared, wholly recovered from her mastoiditis, returning with her brother and sister-in-law from an African trip. She was pleased with my flat and with my general industriousness, as well she might have been. Never before had I worked so fast or so well as I was doing in this comfortable place and with enough money to live more easily than before (just a little more easily, but that made the difference). Anyone could see that I was in phase, that my guardian angel was on the job, and that 17 quai Voltaire was not only the "strange packet ship" that Lucie Mardrus called it; it was for me in every way a magic locale. I did not tell Jessie Lasell that Gertrude's Chicago millionairess Mrs. Emily Crane Chadbourne had at Gertrude's extreme insistence also become temporarily my patron. But that was in part why I was doing so nicely—so nicely indeed that I thought it about time I gave a concert of my works. And I proposed this to Mrs. Lasell; it would cost $500. She thought the idea sound, gave me the money, went home happy. I had also promised to visit her in America at Christmas.

II

Europe after 1925

IT IS EASY TO KNOW that the 1920s were different from the 1930s. What is not so clear in America is that the first decade of the twenty-year World War armistice also had two parts. At the beginning of 1926 I was writing from Paris to Briggs Buchanan, my constant correspondent from college times, that "jazz (highbrow or lowbrow) is a dead art already." I was wrong, of course, since in the 1930s the swing beat was to develop, in the '40s bebop, and in the '50s the "progressive" or "cool" manner, for something happens to jazz in every decade. I was right, all the same, in judging that its basic forms and procedures were not to evolve any further; and they have not done so.

The early twenties, which brought jazz to maturity and to world-wide fame, had also brought fresh subjects into fiction. They gave us, for instance, *Main Street*; the luxury-loving, liquorous world of Scott Fitzgerald; and the chief theme of Ernest Hemingway's high period, which was an American soldier's wartime behavior as reviewed in the peacetime ambience of an Anglo-American bar in Montparnasse (Le Select). The American writers in general, I think, at home or abroad, tended to continue throughout the twenties (and some well into the thirties) their picturing of a world that did not change. For them the early twenties had to go on because they were not finished with writing about them. And journalists kept licking their chops over the "jazz age" long after the Charleston had become a standard feature of American life. This dance coming up in 1925 was quite without relation to the real "jazz age," which since 1912 had practiced a slow, almost motionless dancing in close position. On the contrary, the Charleston's alert tempo and Caribbean beat (of ⅜ – ⅝) led not to petting in public but to the jitterbugging that was to mark the late 1930s, even to disengaged elegance, as in the Lambeth Walk.

For Europeans, the early 1920s offered nothing to cling to. In 1925, when our blockade of central Europe ended (a withholding of food from regions threatened by revolution), the fabulous financial inflation of Germany and the equally fabulous sex-inflation of Berlin began their decline. Ernst Křenek's opera *Jonny spielt auf*, a backward look at Germany's own "jazz age," was finished in 1926. And by that time Alban Berg's *Wozzeck*, forward looking in its compassionate social content, had already been performed (in December of '25). It was at the mid-twenties, or just before, that Arnold Schoenberg codified his way of writing music into the twelve-tone-row technique, also a forward-looking operation, since it encouraged the world-wide composing of nontonal music, offering a rule of thumb virtually foolproof to facilitate a previously recondite practice. This music was to take its place from that time on as part of the new romanticism and eventually, after World War II, to encircle the globe.

In France a new thing had appeared in painting when Bérard, Tchelitcheff, Kristians Tonny, and Leonid Berman, exhibiting as a group in 1926, drew attention by omitting from their work allegiance to cubism. In the same year Jean Arp, at the Galerie Surréaliste, showed nonfigurative sculptures involving curvaceous forms, distinctly a novelty in the abstract discipline. The year 1925, the year of Erik Satie's death, was also the year in which his young protégé Henri Sauguet, in a remarkably engaging short operetta called *Le Plumet du Colonel*, dared the use both of curvilinear melody and of harmony unrelated to Stravinsky's practices, as well as the straightforward expression of sentiment (without irony). That was the year too in which a Paris World's Fair devoted to Les Arts Décoratifs proved how "modern" (and "modern" meant looking back to cubism) the design of textiles, glass, furniture, wrought iron, and the like could be, leaving the painters on whose work these applications were based in the embarrassing position of seeing their dearest innovations, because of their success in industry, rendered useless henceforth for easel-painting. James Joyce, like the American fiction writers who surrounded him (and like the American poet T. S. Eliot, already captured by the admiration of tied-to-the-past young critic-poets), had opted for a career to be built on his own past. His *Work in Progress* (to be entitled *Finnegans Wake*), appearing in *transition* from 1927, was clearly, as to both method and theme, an extension of *Ulysses*. Neither from Eliot,

struggling to survive in London's waste land on what Sherry
Mangan was to call "the lotuses of prose style and Anglican
theology," nor from the great Joyce himself, now nearly blind,
would one know that the epoch had changed.

But it had. From here on out, the tone, whether violent or
suave, was to be romantic. In July 1927 I wrote Buchanan:

> As I began to observe a little while ago, a new generation exists.
> Cocteau says it became possible about the middle of January [al-
> most the date when Stein and I had formed our opera project].
> No one knows why, but it suddenly did. Mary [Butts] says, "The
> good chaps are beginning to get together again." Anyway, six or
> a dozen people have suddenly begun to function. Poor Antheil
> (I am sorry) is not among them.

By the same month's end in 1928 my opera was finished; and
Sauguet's ballet *La Chatte*, a wholly neo-Romantic work, had
been successful in the Diaghilev repertory for over a year. Also
I had given a concert of my works, the first one-man show to
be offered by anyone, I think, of what I firmly believed, as did
Sauguet and the other members of our neo-Romantic group,
to be the newest music that there was.

This concert took place in the refurbished Salle d'Orgue of
the Old Conservatory, the Napoleonic one near the Folies-
Bergère, its organ of that period having recently been made
usable. I had chosen this hall for its novelty value (people like
going to an unfamiliar place) and also for the possibility of
showing off my previously unheard Variations and Fugues on
Sunday School Hymns. Actually almost none of the music on
my program had been performed publicly except the Sonata
da Chiesa, given two years earlier, though *Five Phrases from
the Song of Solomon*, for soprano and percussion, had been
heard privately at Mrs. Gross's musicales and *Capital Capitals*,
for four men's voices with piano, had been offered just a year
before at the Duchesse de Clermont-Tonnerre's costume ball.
The Song of Solomon had been given in New York that spring
at the first of the new Copland-Sessions concerts, and *Capital
Capitals* was to be heard next year in the same series. Absolute novelties included a group of concert-songs in French—
La Valse grégorienne and *Le Berceau de Gertrude Stein*, both
to poetry by Georges Hugnet, and three poems by the late

Duchesse de Rohan, a naïve writer often unconsciously comical whom certain French compared to the naïve painter, Henri (le Douanier) Rousseau.

The French songs had been substituted for a group with texts by Gertrude Stein because my soprano, Alice Mock, though she had sung the Song of Solomon earlier and welcomed an occasion to be heard in it publicly, refused to be associated with the Stein texts. So, rather than let a participating artist censor my program, I engaged another singer. Unable, however, to find an English-speaking one of Miss Mock's quality, I coached Marthe-Marthine phonetically through the Song of Solomon, which finally came off quite well. I did not think it wise, all the same, to expose her to the comedy risks of pronouncing Stein with a foreign accent. So I did for Marthe what I had declined to do for Mock, gave her a batch of songs to sing in French.

Actually my verbally animated French songs were better suited to Marthe's soubrette appearance and rhythmic exactitudes than they would have been to the statuesque beauty and mellifluous vocalism of Miss Mock. André Fleury (now organist of Saint-Germain-des-Prés) played the Sunday school variations; and Roger Désormière conducted the Church Sonata. The *Capitals* were sung by English-speaking males, accompanied by Edmund Pendleton. All the performances were perfect (though the French did not much care for Marthe-Marthine's blonde staginess), and the audience was intellectually select. Cocteau, Marcel Jouhandeau, and Cingria gave literary tone; Roy Harris, Boulanger, and Jennie Tourel the musical. There were painters too (I remember Pierre Roy), the rector of the University, Charlety (mobilized by Madame Langlois), and all sorts of up-to-date young. At the end of the evening Sauguet and Bérard made scandal by quarreling on the sidewalk, not about my music but about Bébé's going off with friends to smoke opium, an indulgence Sauguet could not tolerate. Gertrude Stein was there, of course; but Joyce did not come, since Gertrude was on the program, he not. The press was divided between those who found in my work "exquisite sonorities" as well as "a strong religious feeling boldly expressed" and those who heard in it only "a maximum of cacophony" and judged my whole effort as "no doubt sterile, certainly exaggerated." Gaston Hamelin, one of the players in my Sonata da Chiesa, had taken a fancy two years earlier to the piece and wanted very much to put it on in Boston, where he played first clarinet in the Symphony. Learning that I planned an American trip for the next season, he made a firm engagement to produce the work at a concert of the Boston Flute Players' Club, if I would be there to rehearse it and conduct.

For all the seeming effectiveness of this one-man concert, including a lively press, its afterglow in music circles was not warm. And I could not blame so definite a reserve on Marthe-Marthine's lack of a Franco-funereal singing style. Any in-the-know public could have shrugged that off. It was me they were not taking on. Nobody said so in my presence; but I could feel it, smell it, know it for true that my music, my career, my position in the whole time-and-place setup was something the French power group did not choose to handle. I was not being suppressed, not for the present; that effort was to be made four years later. But certainly I was not being adopted. Nor were any of the power-circle benefits—such as a commission from the Princesse de Polignac or from Serge de Diaghilev—to be coming my way. I was clearly not grist either for the French immortality-mill or for international snob-bohemia.

I am sure that the treatment I began to receive at this time from the talent scouts of both machines, a treatment courteous but reserved, was from their point of view wise and in the long run for me beneficial. It kept me an American composer and removed temptation toward trying to be anything else. A French composer I could never be anyhow; I had always known that. It was all right to be a foreigner working in France, but not a pseudo-Gallic clinger-on. I had not gone to France to save French music, but merely to improve my own. And come to think of it, as I did a great deal in the ensuing weeks during a long grippe-cold (probably acquired for that purpose), I considered the creation of an American music by myself and certain contemporaries to be a far worthier aspiration than any effort to construct a wing, a portico, even a single brick that might be fitted on to Europe's historic edifice.

The matter of living abroad was discussed a good deal in those days, and every so often some New York journalist would throw at you the Latin term expatriate. Other parts of America did not seem to care much where you lived, but Easterners could be jealous of Europe. As Russell Hitchcock put it, none were so upset by our spending all twelve months there as those who went abroad each year for six. It was assumed, moreover, that unless one was in Europe for study or business, one was there for the fleshpots only. Actually, save perhaps in Berlin, those were no more lively there than here. And Paris is not a hard-drinking town, never was. In fact it was the generally hygienic Paris routine—to bed by midnight and up by eight, love-making chiefly in the afternoon, with two tasty meals a day, some calisthenics, lots of walking, a little wine, no hard liquor and no telephone—that was my life. And I flourished on it, did lots of work, free from New York's pressure to conform.

Paris can admire you and let you alone. New York withholds its admiration till assured that you are modeling yourself on central Europe. This is still true; a French musical influence is by definition heretical and only that made in Germany (or to its east) esteemed worthy. As H. L. Mencken put it, "There are two kinds of music, German music and bad music." Right there was my reason for living in France. I believed then, and still do, that German music, after being blessed above all others and having led the world for two hundred years, had failed to keep contact with our century, that it had long since become self-centered, self-regarding, and self-indulgent. If American music was about to take off, as I also believed, any allegiance to contemporary Germany would have to be carried as dead weight. It was not that value had been stripped from the classic masters, but rather that the live tradition in Germany was no longer authoritative, even about performing those masters. And as for German composition at its most advanced—as in the work of the Austrians Schoenberg, Berg, and Webern—this seemed to me to combine the progressive and the retrogressive in a most uncomfortable proportion. The serial technique of-fered a strict counterpoint valuable for channeling a too-facile flow; but it also assumed as normal the textures of nondiffer-entiated counterpoint—a position of retreat from the highly differentiated part-writing of Stravinsky and Debussy, not to mention that of the classical symphonic masters, Mozart and Beethoven and Schubert. For modern harmony the Germans seemed to me tone-deaf, and as for rhythm, children. I did not know just when and how the great tradition had got lost; and the Germans themselves, in spite of Hitler's final stamping it out, have not admitted to this day its disappearance. But I knew the state of music in central Europe for decadent, and I was not having any truck with it.

As an American I had to keep contact with Europe. The new music growing up in my country was being pushed by German-trained musicians and German-culture patronage groups into paths I thought quite wrong for it. By keeping away from these Germanic pressures (and Paris was the only major center where one could do that) I could perhaps through my own music remind my country that it was not obliged to serve another country's power setup.

For the German-Austrian musical complex was still, in spite of a World War lost, in possession of such a structure. The music publishers of Leipzig, Berlin, Mainz, Augsburg, and Vienna were still rich in copyrights and in classical editions. They worked, moreover, in the German way, which is by cartel agreements—price-fixing, dumping, and pressures on the performing agencies. The latter were numerous and powerful, symphony orchestras and opera houses chiefly; and though these enjoyed some autonomy through their sources of subsidy—which were the central government, the separate states, and the cities—they were designed nevertheless for the encouragement of German musicians, for the protection of German publications, and eventually for the world-wide distribution of both. This situation, like the musicopedagogical machinery that had taught us all, had grown up after the nineteenth century had discovered what a gold mine in every sense were the classical masters. And the whole organization of it was central Europe's immortality machine. It was a conservative machine, its main merchandise Beethoven. Later composers like Brahms and Richard Strauss were tails to that kite. And Schoenberg the modernist, though a technical innovator, had kept his expressive content as close as possible to such standard Germanic models as the dreamy waltz, the counterpointed chorale, and the introverted moods of a *Liederabend*.

The French power setup was less massive, less imposing, less intolerant. Its immortality machine was not built for music anyway. France's culture market was for literature, art, and luxury products. And though her music publishers owned sound theatrical properties by Gounod, Bizet, and Massenet, their symphonic and recital repertories, running from Berlioz through Saint-Saëns, Fauré, and Franck to Debussy and Ravel, contained few best sellers; nor were their classical editions a world commerce. Painters flocked to Paris from everywhere because modern art was a going concern there; it made fame and money. Foreign musicians went to France in the 1920s not so much because modern music was prosperous as because it was twentieth-century oriented. There was no pressure for it to be anything else, no weighted emotional ambience. Music was for musicians and for people with brains; it was not for mass consumption. And it was not, as in Germany, big business.

Music in France was organized something like this. The Paris Conservatoire and the two chief opera houses (plus two state-subsidized operetta theaters) were the instruments of a civil service hierarchy. Except for an occasional guest artist at the opera houses and two foreign students a year admitted to the Conservatoire, everybody connected with these institutions was a French citizen. The four subscription orchestras of Paris were less official; but they all received government subsidy, at that time 100,000 francs a year ($4,000) in return for playing one hundred minutes of new French music. The official and semiofficial music world was run by the French for the French, and foreign composers were not much patronized. The idea of encouraging live composers, however, was built into it.

Nonofficial instrumentalities were more open. Among these were three series of modern concerts, the oldest and least radical being the Société Nationale, the moderately radical being the Société Musicale Indépendente, the freshest music being that heard at the Concerts Jean Wiéner. In the thirties another group was to appear, Le Triton, devoted to conserving the dissonant styles. Also a neo-Romantic series, Les Concerts de la Sérénade. All these were run by private groups, and most of their programs were internationally oriented. So also were two privately administered music schools, the Schola Cantorum and the Ecole Normale de Musique, where foreigners were as welcome as in the private studios. For public performance of their music, however, foreigners were limited to the modernist societies, to the graciousness of string quartets and other chamber music groups, and to the kindness of some friendly virtuoso. Special concerts could be organized by anyone; and remarkably fine musicians were available. For such an occasion one needed, of course, not only funds but also enough friends to fill up the hall.

Private musical entertaining was frequent, since music at this time was fashionable. Previously it had not been so, and it is not so now. But during the lifetime of the Diaghilev ballets several stylish French houses and many foreign ones received musicians, dancers, poets, painters, even actors (the less self-centered ones). The chief go-between for artists and hostesses was Jean Cocteau—poet, playwright, and impeccable theater workman. He could launch a fashion, guide a career, organize its social and financial backing. And his main protectorate in music, the group that he had publicized so powerfully after World War I that they came to share condominium with him in the salons, were four composers out of the well-known Group of Six—Milhaud, Honegger, Auric, and Poulenc. I have always imagined that this quartet, though none of them had been at my concert, put thumbs down at this time regarding me. They seemed to remain as friendly as before, and their agent Cocteau could on occasion be quite generously so; but those particular musicians, who would have been the ones indicated by common friendships—literary, artistic, musical—and by our common commitment to Satie for making a hospitable gesture, did not then nor at any time afterwards make one. Neither did any of them speak out against me.

My concert had taken place on May 30. Gathering the grandeurs of it and enjoying the warmths engendered, which were many, took me a month. On July 1 I went to a Basque village called Ascain, six miles upcountry behind Saint-Jean-de-Luz, and started writing out Acts Three and Four. These I put down not with figured bass, as I had done Acts One and Two, but as a complete voice-and-piano score. That took two weeks. I also tempted myself with Spain. I had not wished to view it in reality while still composing music about it. But after nine months of writing an opera on the subject, naturally I was headed that way.

On July 8 I wrote Gertrude Stein, "Every day I walk nearer to Spain," also that it looked "an extremely God's-country sort of country." Another time, "I saw San Iñacio today. By his real

name, just like that. In a chapel on a mountain divide called
the Col de St.-Ignace. And he was handsome and thirty-five
between thirty-five and forty-five and alive [a quotation from
Act Three] and had a black beard and was singing an aria."
Then on the nineteenth, "The opera is finished including the
Intermezzo and Act IV, that is to say . . . the composing is
done. . . . My plan now is to go look and listen to Spain a bit
because I've an idea that Spain makes a special kind of noise
that will bear imitation orchestrally. Her tunes and her rhythms
are too good to be of much use, but I think her *timbre* may
have possibilities." (I had heard Spanish high-squealing laughter
on the beach at Saint-Jean-de-Luz.) On the twenty-fourth, in
company with an American army officer and his wife with whom
I had made friends at the hotel, I set off by car for a week in
the northern parts.

We went first to near-by San Sebastián and from there took
the spectacular hairpin-turn, mountainside road by way of
Zarauz, luxurious and residential, to Castro-Urdiales, a humble
beach resort and humbler fishing town. There we spent the
night; and there, before sleeping, I sketched a whole fourth
movement for my *Symphony on a Hymn Tune*, which had been
awaiting that for two years and a half. We had made a side trip
into the mountains for visiting the Renaissance granite palace
of the Loyola family, birthplace of my operatic hero Saint Ignatius. Every room of the edifice is now a chapel and each more
jeweled than the last—one of them covered with scenes from
the Passion done in silver high relief, another completely lined
with gold-framed foot-square plaques of lapis lazuli. We stayed
a night in Santander, where what seemed the entire Spanish
navy, most of the French, and a large part of the American
were at anchor, beflagged for welcoming the arrivals in a New
York-to-Spain yacht race. We saw the yachts arriving, swam in
the cold Atlantic (out of bathing-machines on wheels), and saw
a bullfight (I loved it). Then via Palencia over high Castile to
Valladolid, where I had my first adventure with a bedbug, and
where I spent absorbed hot midday hours in a museum devoted
entirely to polychrome religious sculpture. To Burgos too we
went, and to Logroño, and to Pamplona, which is spirally approached, and lies at the center of a huge green saucer.

Returned to Ascain, I wrote Hildegarde Watson that the opera was finished and that there were "a ballet and an intermezzo and an appearance . . . of the Holy Ghost and a procession and a great many fine arias for everybody and in general just about one of everything and the whole . . . makes a composition." Also that Spain was "very grand. And very much like Texas. And the Spaniards are all enclosed like Americans and very sad though not about anything in particular and they are sweet and gentle and they like you. They are really very tender. Yes, very tender in their bashful way. I think they love the bull which they kill with such a loving gesture."

Having written earlier to Gertrude's Chicago millionairess, who had given me $1,000 toward completing the opera, that this was finished and the money also, I received a letter from her saying, "I regret that I am not able to help any further, but I was chiefly interested in what you were doing for Miss Stein." Since this seemed final, I wrote her what I termed to Gertrude "a polite and gentle thanks for past assistance." "There remains," I went on, to Gertrude, "Mrs. L's 3,000 francs a month. In the fall I shall give up my flat and either go to a hotel or find a cheaper one. But for the present, status quo and who knows God may provide more luxury to His needy ones."

Then I went to Brittany, to a tiny port called Loctudy, where I visited Madame Langlois and her Russian friend, made fifty pages of orchestral score on my Hymn Tune Symphony. From there to Saint-Malo, joining Georges Hugnet, and with him in a car badly driven over bad roads by Théophile Briant (swimmer, poet, publisher, and art dealer), we went to be with Cliquet-Pleyel and Marthe-Marthine at Bagnoles-de-l'Orne, a Normandy watering place where Cliquet was engaged at the casino. Our hilarious visit eventually got described in a poem by Georges, which I set to music and which Marthe sang in a concert that November. Writing to Gertrude, I said I had

> done a great deal of sleeping and cracked my nose wide open on the bottom of the swimming pool and made a portrait of Marthe for the fiddle. I also played on the piano Acts III and IV because I have worked all summer without a piano and I hadn't heard any of it and wasn't I surprised it is . . . full of inspiration and variety and I can only hope it isn't as bad as my contentment with it would maybe indicate.

When I returned to Paris around the first of September after
a two-month absence, I had been in the Basque lands, in Spain,
in Brittany, in Normandy; and I had brought home a completed
opera, a symphony finally finished and mostly orchestrated, and
two essays in what was for me a new genre, that of the portrait
in music. The first of these had been composed at Ascain, where
a young Spanish woman who played the violin had asked me
to write her something. She had a way of entering the hotel's
dining-arbor with assurance, her equally self-assured mother
one step behind, that pleased me because this granting of priority to youth, in Europe uniquely Spanish, was also our American
way. Otherwise the mother and daughter were not of American
pattern; they were almost like sisters, happy together, discussing but not chattering, alert in repose, occupying themselves
while waiting for the evening, and not surprised that a particular
evening should bring no mating male, though when it did they
would be ready, for Spain is a timeless image of eternity. All this
plus some gesture (Spanish gesture) I endeavored to depict in
music; and although the piece was written to be played without
piano, I called it a *Portrait of Señorita Juanita de Medina Accompanied by Her Mother*. As a matter of fact, the mother later
asked permission to compose an accompaniment for it.

At Bagnoles-de-l'Orne I made another violin portrait, this
time of Marthe-Marthine; and I wrote to Gertrude that "my
portrait trick is developing nicely and seems to be quite new.
That is, for music, since the idea of it comes obviously out of
you." And since with Marthe and Cliquet and Hugnet a concert
was being planned for November, I went on making portraits
that early fall in Paris. I sketched *Miss Gertrude Stein as a Young
Girl, Cliquet-Pleyel in F, Georges Hugnet, Poet and Man of Letters*, and *Mrs. C.W.L.* [Jessie Lasell], all from memory. Then I
did *Sauguet, from Life*, after which I never again made a musical portrait (and I have made upwards of 150) except in the
subject's presence.

Two years before, at Thonon on Lake Geneva, an enlightenment had come to me that made portrait writing possible. This
was the very simple discovery that the classic masters, in terms
of logic and syntax, did not always quite make sense. My sudden awareness of their liberties in this regard so firmly forced
me to take up my own freedom that never again was I to feel

that I must necessarily "know what I was doing." This meant that I could write almost automatically, cultivate the discipline of spontaneity, let it flow.

Now the value of spontaneous work is often zero, especially when it merely follows reflexes, as in pianoforte improvisation. But spontaneity can be original also, if it wells up from a state of self-containment. And it was through practicing my spontaneities, at first in a primitive way, and through questioning Gertrude Stein about this method of work, which was her own, that I grew expert at tapping my resources. Making portraits of people was just beginning to serve me, as it had long served Gertrude, as an exercise not only in objectivity but also in avoiding the premeditated. My associates at this time were many of them fine draftsmen, and I had often watched them finish each drawing in one sitting. Gertrude had long before applied their way to writing. And it was from her success with this (in my view) that I was led to try it in music. My first efforts came out so well, both as likenesses and as compositions, that I was sure I had discovered something. But exploring it could wait. Opera and symphony were my preoccupations right then.

In Paris I took my *Symphony on a Hymn Tune* to a copyist, so that I could have a clean score to show in America; and the pianist John Kirkpatrick (remarkable for his devotion to American composers) made a four-hand transcription of it. I also, while waiting for Gertrude to return, which was late that year, played and sang Acts Three and Four for the closer friends—for Sauguet and Bérard and Tonny and Bravig Imbs (American minor novelist and minor poet) and Georges Maratier (French picture merchant) and Kirkpatrick, of course, and Hitchcock and Madame Langlois and my American composer-colleague Roy Harris (who kept exclaiming over and over, "Living! Living!"). I also wrote a vocal piece entitled *Commentaire sur Saint Jérome* on a text by the Marquis de Sade for a young literary group in Lille, about to publish a magazine called *Les Cahiers Sade*.

On November 14 our concert took place in the ornate ballroom of the Hôtel Majestic. The program included piano music by Cliquet-Pleyel and by myself played by ourselves, poems by Georges Hugnet set to music by Cliquet and myself and sung by Marthe-Marthine, and two extended poems by Hugnet read by the actor Marcel Herrand. There were in addition six of my portraits for solo violin, played by Lucien Schwartz, and *The Death of Socrates*, from Satie, which I played for Marthe to sing. Among the other vocal pieces were my *Commentaire sur Saint Jérome* and *Les Soirées bagnolaises*, to poems of Hugnet that memorialized our hilarious visit to the Cliquets at Bagnoles-de-l'Orne, where

> *une chanteuse blonde*
> *qui chante en ce moment*
> *nous montra du bras*
> *notre nouvelle maison.*

This text, all innocence and camaraderie, shocked more than did the frankly outrageous passage from Sade. Bérard remarked that Georges and I seemed to think we were Goethe and Schiller. Everybody was there, of course. And we had shown our newest work, which is always a pleasure (or used to be) to both shower and shown. Alice Toklas, thinking to please me, said of Cliquet, "He's your Matisse," referring to a time when Matisse and Picasso had shown together at the Salon des Indépendents and where it had seemed, at least to her and Gertrude, that Matisse's facility and brilliance were no match for Picasso's brains. I did not relish the remark, because I was not out to kill off a colleague. My thought was rather that we should stand together while young and still capable of loyalties. At least that is what we had all thought we were doing in this concert of communal admiration.

Two weeks later I took the brand-new *Ile-de-France*, third class; and Madame Langlois accompanied me to Le Havre, where as sister of an admiral she presented me to the captain, who, I wrote to Gertrude,

has since done me all the best honors and invited me to the bridge and showed me all the beautiful electrical devices for steering which never work and had me shown engine-rooms by 1st lieutenant and invited to aperitifs and officers' messes and so I don't really go back much to third class except to dress or sleep or be sick which I was most awfully for 1½ days. . . . There are *primeurs* at table and quails in jelly and *foie gras à volonté*. Raymond Mortimer turned up and we eat together and my Lanvin holds up with the best England can offer. The added swank of my third-class cabin gives me an edge on Britain of which all concerned are conscious and which I try not to accent.

I have a nice cabinmate too, a husky, an aviator in Canada winter postal service between Montreal and Nova Scotia where airplanes wear skis and icicles and he shows me his tattoos and his war wounds and only sleeps four hours and combs his hair over a bald spot and uses Coty's face-powder and eats with officers and dances second-class because he doesn't like dress clothes and really all around a *chic type*.

Regarding a translation into French of excerpts from *The Making of Americans*, which I had begun with Hugnet that fall, then left for him to finish with Gertrude (it was for publication in Georges's Editions de la Montagne), she wrote me on December 3,

> . . . god bless our native land and how are you liking our templed hills, we are peacefully and completely translating[,] it goes, I go alone and then Alice goes over me and then we all do it with Georges and then he goes alone and really it all goes faster than anyone would think. I guess we will get it done on time. Otherwise life is peaceful that is with the usual gentle xplosions. . . .

12

American Interlude

IN FRANCE MY SUBJECT MATTER, my nourishing nostalgia, had been the middle-South farm landscapes of my fore-bears, the half-hick Arcadias of my growing up. Set down now in another America, that of a Massachusetts manufacturing family, there came over me again the sense of displacement which I had experienced earlier in New England, as if that were where I did not belong, did not want to belong, could not bring myself to accept to belong. Paris was both warmhearted and harsh, like Kansas City; Whitinsville was neither of these. It tried to be friendly but could not give itself. I tried to be friendly too, but could not open. It was like being starved and stifled at once—starved for lack of spontaneity, buried alive in a useless luxury.

Jessie Lasell's house, large, wide, and wandering, was a post-Richardsonian manor with wide hallway, a vast dining room, parlors of all sizes, a ballroom, a billiard room, a sun room, a gun room, two pantries, two kitchens, and a great many very large bedrooms with very large baths. None of these bedrooms received furnace heat. There were fireplaces everywhere and Franklin stoves always laid for lighting; but unless one planned to spend the morning alone it seemed not worthwhile to strike the foot-long match. It was simpler to jump from warm bed to warm dressing room to warm bath and preheated towels. This meant that once dressed, one drifted to the downstairs rooms, which being all wide open to one another gave to everything one did a country-club tone, further expressed, if one looked out the windows, by tennis courts, shooting-targets, and stables housing both trotters and saddle horses.

For Chester Whitin Lasell was a sportsman. He had bred, trained, and driven world-champion trotting-racers; at seventy he still rode to hounds, stalked deer, and shot. He had a box in Virginia for quail, a refuge for duck just off Rhode Island, and a place in Maine where the whole family could kill salmon and deer in the fall and from which they brought back pheasant by the brace. He did not pretend to work at business, never had done; he merely practiced the skills of a country squire, and well. So well that his table, from early fall till Christmas, held game in abundance, all of it hung just the right length of time, cooked just the right amount, and served with just the right accompaniments according to classical cuisine, including wines of the best years and vineyards, conserved in a cool cellar since before Prohibition.

Jessie Lasell, from San Francisco, loved forever having company and serving food. A naturally smiling woman midst tight-mouthed New Englanders, I think she found her expansiveness a bit walled in there. In any case, together we laughed and made jokes and gossiped as if breathing a Western air; and we exchanged cooking advice too, for she was wise about ways and knew the right ones, as well as how to engineer a large occasion. She could read aloud too and would oblige, when asked, with Milton's *Lycidas*, Shelley's *Adonais*, or selections from Marianne Moore and e. e. cummings. Everything she read gave pleasure because she spoke in the good San Francisco way, which is to articulate all the consonants and all the vowels.

Others around the house were mostly family—Hildegarde and Sibley Watson (temporarily near by on their farm), divers grandchildren of divers ages, a young architect and his widowed mother, Philip Lasell's parents and brothers and sisters from across the road, Jessie's brother and his Whitin wife, and a small selection of other relations, all named Whitin or Lasell. Family gatherings were inevitable at the approaches to Christmas; but I did miss e. e. cummings, with whom I had so often been there in the earlier time and to whose ironic sallies Sibley Watson, spitting image of Abraham Lincoln, would play straight man. There were large dinners too with guests from Worcester County, Republicans of quiet manners and correct tastes. I remember once Judge Thayer came, who had presided at the trial of Sacco and Vanzetti. He spoke lucidly of the case, showed no feeling.

We dressed for dinner, of course; and the younger ones all day long kept changing their costumes, as if something were about to happen. The monotony of life among these charming people came, I think, from their having been trained to intellectual self-effacement. Their good brains and excellent educations, their experience of the world and basic decency were not to be shown off, or used outside the channels of convention. They read, but not advanced books or unknown ones; they owned pictures and art objects but not distinguished ones, nothing they could not explain to Worcester County; they backed causes, but not dangerous ones; they risked their lives, but only in wars, private airplanes, or polo. Many among them were beautiful; all were gentle, some tending toward the neurotic; not one of them was passionate or mystical or scholarly or aflame. Temperament, among the males, had for generations fled to Europe. I was later to observe, as the girls grew up, a sizable proportion of mating failures, as if, brought up to every privilege, and film-fed, they had imagined that good clothes, good looks, and a trust fund entitled them without further effort to success in love.

An exception was Jessie's son-in-law Sibley Watson, who had always been for sticking his neck out. From a mercantile family in Rochester, New York, aspiring to excellence in medicine, he had teamed up after college days with Scofield Thayer, another with intellectual leanings, to start a literary magazine. The revival of *The Dial* resulted, by far the most distinguished, I should say, among American advanced magazines during the 1920s. The careers of e. e. cummings, Marianne Moore, and T. S. Eliot had been largely launched by it, also that of many another high-quality writer. But Watson believed that an editor should resign at thirty. "Before that he understands everything; after he has chosen his own way he is less open." And Watson had already started on a way of his own, which was to make movies. In his own barn he had completed *The House of Usher* and was preparing *Lot in Sodom*, both of which are now historic films. In the summer of 1930 Hildegarde wrote, "Sibley is putting in by gradual stages, to alleviate expense, a sound-apparatus. We'll have it by fall. Wishes you were here and willing to do a sound-picture of you singing your opera." The new equipment served for making a sound picture out of *Lot* and for adding music to *Usher.* Then he abandoned the experimental cinema, returning to experimental medicine.

During December of 1928 Jessie and I would sometimes be driven to Boston for symphony concerts and for seeing people (she loved the social). On these visits I arranged for concerts that were to take place later and had some music copying done (very expensive, very poor, compared to Paris). The Flute Players' Club, having announced my Sonata da Chiesa for March,

now regretted that there was no money for the musicians. I
had already come across this maneuver that same year, when
the Société Musicale Indépendente in Paris had programed my
Song of Solomon, then let me know I must provide performers. There I had declined to do so. Here, since I thought the
performance important, I paid the $100 required (or rather
Jessie did). I made an engagement near that time in March
for a program of my works at the Harvard Musical Club, and
I promised the Harvard Glee Club a male-voice transcription
of the Procession scene from *Four Saints*. Aaron Copland had
already set a February date for *Capital Capitals* in New York,
and Hildegarde had asked me to give a lecture and musical
program in Rochester whenever I should be coming that way.
It seemed indicated, therefore, to go West in January, running
off my Eastern music dates later. I could then be back in France
by April.

Meanwhile there was Christmas, the last affluent one America
was to see for twenty years. Such a hanging of holly and tying
of ribbons, such a dressing of trees and all that and all that!
Impatient with attaching the shiny balls one by one, I tied them
into bunches and hung them like grapes (much prettier). There
were jewels arriving every day from Tiffany and from Cartier
(on approval), emeralds rejected, a bracelet of square diamonds
chosen. And then it was Christmas, with blue sky and snow, and
the routines all working as they should. (Trust Jessie for that.)
There was dinner Christmas Eve for twelve or sixteen, with—I
can't remember which—wild duck or venison, preceded by Jessie's hot mousse of bay scallops. Afterwards drop-in callers had
the Dickens punch, made by pouring warm beer and mulled
claret over cinnamon sticks and hot baked apples. For breakfast
Christmas day there were quails, strawberries, and champagne.
At eleven the servants came to the ballroom for their presents,
drank something (champagne, I think), and then to recorded
music were danced with by family and friends. Later there must
have been the statutory Christmas feast with turkey or goose or
roast pig, appropriate wines, and ceremonial libations. If so, I
went through it like a man. I was a skillful guest in those days.

After Christmas, my visit over, I went for a few days to Boston, where I showed Koussevitzky my *Symphony on a Hymn
Tune*, which he had asked to see. At his house in Jamaica Plain

I played it to him while he read the score. After one movement he said, "Good!" After two he said, "Very good!" After three he said, "Wonderful!" After the fourth, he threw up his hands and said, "I could never play my audience that." He was not articulate about his troubles with the fourth movement, but he seemed to find it not serious enough for a Boston public. He besought me to salvage the work by writing another last movement. I thanked him for his graciousness and left.

From Kansas City, in January, I wrote the story to Gertrude. She replied with my portrait:

> I am awfully sorry about the symphony but then how could the Russian like it, . . . we believe in you a lot as you can see from the profundity of inclosed portrait, it has a new rhythm with sense . . . I am pleased about the glee club, I hope they will sing it, give it my love I mean the glee club they were so romantic in my youth when in the moon-light they sang Here's a health to King Charles, I like to think of their singing us instead . . . we had a beautiful reunion dinner at the Hugnets in honor of the first outbreak of the edition, it looks as if it were going to be quite alright, we all spoke of you very tenderly, you are as our dear Nellie would say not forgotten by your little friends.

I had expected to stay a month in Kansas City, but when Henwar Rodakiewicz (of the Harvard house party) invited me to Santa Fe (with ticket paid) I did not decline. To see my beloved Southwest again, and in a version far grander than the Oklahoma I had known in wartime, was precious for that replunging into Western things that I was finding so much more tonic than the Northeast. Henwar had married, just out of college, a New England woman thirty years older with brains, heart, high temperament, and wealth. He too made films privately. The ranch near Santa Fe, only one of their several residences (including a yacht), was wide and full of warmth. I stayed a week, maybe two, saw sights and scenery from a Rolls-Royce runabout, observed the social tensions of Taos and Santa Fe. Taos held the richer hostesses and the more conservative painters; Santa Fe, a refuge for tuberculars, was more violent in its drinking, more promiscuous about love, and more experimental in art. Today it is no longer an outpost of bohemia. With four museums, a symphony orchestra, and an opera company it is a culture town, with everybody older and quieter. And lungers don't go West any more. A jolly group they were, as I remember, mostly young, many gifted, all excited (since they ran a temperature), and ready for anything. They gave a lively tone to any place, many of them staying on after their malady was arrested to furnish doctors, writers, intellectual workers, and even statesmen to the Southwest and Colorado, people all the more humane in later years for having faced death when young.

From Kansas City I sent Alice Toklas some Missouri recipes, along with that for Jessie's scallop mousse. As for Missouri weather, "oceans of slush froze last week and everything is now solid ice (motors waltzing)." Of Missouri speech,

> It is curious and interesting. In its provincial condition it is incredibly low. And yet it seems to lose all its horrid quality with only a very little training and to become quite beautiful when properly educated. Unlike Kansas or Illinois, which are difficult to train and almost never lose their harsh intonation. And there are marked differences [in Missouri] between male and female speech.

To Gertrude,

> The portrait is very beautiful and serious and like me too. Yes very serious and with a quite gratuitous beauty an extra beauty *par dessus le marché*. . . . I am on my way to lecture on us at Rochester. I arranged the *Saints' Procession* and wrote a *Conversation for Four Clarinets*. [This at the request of Gaston Hamelin, my Franco-Bostonian admirer]. . . . It was nice visiting my grandfather, who at ninety-seven was full of wise political comment and people comment and questions about French life and agriculture.

And later, "I reread my portrait twice and find it has a very fine texture especially the long middle paragraphs and great variety of sentences and a really concentrated progress . . . which is I suppose what we mean by profundity . . . anyway."

Gertrude in return kept me up on Paris news, about Hugnet's

> beautiful fight Christmas eve at the Select with [Roger] Vitrac purely on the subject of how they that is Hugnet did not like his play and it all ended with their being put out with contusions and [taken to] our *commissariat* around the corner. . . . Poor Gody [Godiva, the car] has lost her stability owing to too many poems and music [a reference to *Le Berceau*] she took to dropping little

pieces of herself and groaning distressfully and once had to be disgracefully rocked in front of the Senate and now I am having a new Ford car and with the unfaithfulness characteristic of us all I am violently . . . devoted to the new. . . . Alice is making tapestry in our leisure moments, I am making sentences in my leisure moments and darn good sentences, otherwise as we were . . . do remember me most kindly to Mrs. Lasell.

Hildegarde and Sibley Watson lived in Rochester, New York, in an Edwardian house on Sibley Place, right next to downtown. On my way East I gave a talk there to invited guests (I remember Howard Hanson, newly director of the Eastman School of Music) in which I explained a little of what our group in Paris thought it was up to. With Philip Lasell, also visiting, I played them Satie's piano duets *Three Pieces in the Shape of a Pear*. I also sang parts of my opera. And as so often happens in some regional center or university, everybody seemed to understand everything and to like it (or almost everybody; I was not sure about Hanson). This can occur only before New York has told them what to think; afterwards they are more reserved. But so far, in Whitinsville, in Kansas City, in Santa Fe my solo performances of *Four Saints in Three Acts* had never failed to please. I gave a similar talk in the Rochester Art Museum. And I watched Sibley's films achieving their form, slowly (as films always do) and with a great rightness (as they almost never do).

Sibley worked at cutting; Hildegarde practiced singing and sometimes painted. The University, the Eastman School of Music, and the Art School provided the bulk of our visitors. There were rich people around and one saw them, but only those who were also workers, aiders, abettors, in some way participants in a world of intellectual exercise. Such an ambience was the only one Sibley Watson would be part of (he never owned a dinner jacket, rarely went even so far as blue serge); and such was the tone of Hildegarde's house in Rochester, bare downstairs of carpets and bric-a-brac, with only some recent paintings and a pianoforte, a large dining room, and an excellent cook whom Hildegarde had never laid eyes on, though she had been in residence for two years.

Her New York house, where I lived for the next two months, was more suited to a woman of elegance, though that too showed interest in contemporary art, what with a bronze nude by Gaston Lachaise in the ground-floor two-story drawing room and expressionist canvases by e. e. cummings all over the staircase walls and upper landings. This luxuriously appointed four-story town house with garden, on Nineteenth Street just south of Gramercy Park, was kept ready for residence, though the Watsons had not lived there for several years, by a caretaker, who made breakfasts for me and for a woman vocal teacher (permanent guest), also for Philip Lasell, who used the house as his hotel. I occasionally had guests of my own in the drawing room, where a full-size grand piano enabled me to make quite an effect demonstrating my music.

My most effective number was the singing of *Four Saints* complete, which by this time I could do from memory. And it was for the purpose of my doing this that Gertrude's friend from olden times Carl Van Vechten gave me an evening party at his flat in Fifty-fifth Street. Twelve people were there, all of them chosen by Carl for their possible usefulness toward producing the opera, toward publishing it or spreading the word about it. The music publisher was Alma Morgenthau Wertheim, who sustained a small press called Cos Cob, publishing chiefly music by Aaron Copland. The other ladies were of literary allegiance—Mabel Dodge Luhan, Emily Clark, Muriel Draper, possibly Blanche Knopf, Fania Marinoff of course (Carl's actress wife), and Ettie Stettheimer. Not one of the men can I recall, though in addition to Carl and myself there must have been four. Men do tend toward self-effacement in a New York drawing room.

After the party we went to a "drag," or travesty ball, in Harlem. At some point an amiable square joined our group (we called them "butter and egg men" in those days); and on our way back downtown in the square's Rolls-Royce Carl recounted what Mabel Dodge had said of *Four Saints*—that this work would do to the Metropolitan Opera "what Picasso did to Kenyon Cox" (an American painter earlier much admired). His reply, no less naïve, was "Then what will I do on Thursday nights?"

The evening had introduced me to several key persons in the New York worlds of opinion-forming and of distributing advanced work, but only one of these acquaintanceships bore fruit directly. Ettie Stettheimer invited me to meet her sisters, and it was with sets and costumes by one of them that the opera came to be produced in 1934. The sisters were three—Ettie, Florine, and Carrie—all of uncertain age; and they lived with their invalid mother in the most ornate apartment house I have ever seen—a florid Gothic structure called Alwyn Court, at Fifty-eighth Street and Seventh Avenue. Their own flat was ornate too but nowhere Gothic, being laid out rather in the marble and gold and red velvet German-royalty style with a fluffy overlay of modern Baroque. There were crystal pendants everywhere and gold fringes and lace and silk curtains so much longer than the windows that they stood out in planned puffs and lay no less than two feet on the waxed floors. Throughout the house were pictures by Florine, a painter of such high wit and bright colorings as to make Matisse and Dufy seem by comparison somber. Ettie, the youngest, a Ph.D. from Heidelberg, had published two novels about intellectualized love; and Carrie, the eldest and usually the hostess, had spent twenty years on a doll's house (now in the Museum of the City of New York). Their associates were all working artists—writers, painters, theater people (plus a film-producing nephew, Walter Wanger)—and these were received at rich teas and sumptuous dinners. One never saw the invalid mother. One felt, however, her presence in the house and knew her appearance (white hair and black lace) from paintings by Florine. The three sisters never went out all at the same time, each in turn staying home so that their mother should never be left alone. This was a discipline of devotion, of course, since the good German servants were always there; and it had gone on since at least 1915, only to end with the mother's death in 1935. Carrie had a small apartment near by for working on her doll's house and Florine a studio at the Beaux Arts Building on Fortieth Street facing Bryant Park. Ettie, short and a little dumpy, tended in the evening to wear red taffeta, puffy as to skirt and tightly closed around each ankle. Carrie, tall, stately, and sad, was for gold and white. Florine liked black velvet. In the daytime they all wore black.

As soon as I had seen Florine's pictures, especially the very large ones now in the Metropolitan Museum, I knew we shared a view about the stage. So I besought her, should there be an American production of *Four Saints*, to consider designing its costumes and scenery; and would she listen to the work, me singing, with that in view? So I did sing it for her one afternoon, and she did accept designing it as a possibility, and she did start finding ideas right away for making it look like the Cathedral façade in Avila executed in crystal and ostrich feathers and red velvet and gold fringe. She actually, one year later (it is dated 1930), painted a picture (with silvered frame) in which an evocation of me is playing and singing midst the attributes of Saint Teresa and Saint Ignatius, along with some imagined ones appropriate to "St. Virgil," "St. Gertrude," and "Florine St."

Copland had found for singing my *Capital Capitals* a group of four men called appropriately the Ionian Quartet, and these I rehearsed daily for the mid-February performance. This came off as very lively indeed, with the audience hilarious, so much so in fact that at one point, to prevent the laughter from getting out of hand, from the piano I held up my right arm, palm out traffic-cop-wise, and stopped the fun from stopping the show. At the end there were bravos. There is no question that the performance constituted a success in terms of pleasure given, press space devoted to it, and intellectual excitement created. And a pattern in that excitement was established at this time which I have come since to expect whenever any work by Gertrude Stein and myself is given in America. The literary consensus is always that the music is lovely but the poetry absurd; whereas the music world, at least nine tenths of it, takes the view that Stein's words are great literature but that my music is infantile. The musical press on this occasion mostly took the latter view, though certain reviewers found it "merry" and "a bright spot on the program." But even the most deeply outraged among them found it less "nondescript," "aimless," and "dreary" than the other pieces, which were a Violin Sonata by Alexander Lipsky, a set of songs by Vladimir Dukelsky, and a Piano Sonata by Roy Harris. As Copland reminded me only recently, "In those days our music always got terrible reviews."

During that same February (we are still in '29) a bright and worldly woman wishing to pay me honor and also to give a stylish party, arranged for the same singers to perform the *Capitals*, with me playing, at the house of her banker, other works of mine filling out the program. I think I played some of my piano pieces; I know Aaron Copland played with me a four-hand work called *Synthetic Waltzes*; there were probably forty-five minutes of music all told. The party took place in a flat newly decorated by the lady who had organized it, with real marble wittily juxtaposed against plaster painted to imitate marble (ever so much more expensive). There was a delicious supper too with vintage champagne (bought at Prohibition prices). The singers received a fee. When I informed our host sometime later that he owed me five dollars for music stands hired, he sent me a check for exactly that amount, saying he did not think I "should be out of pocket at all," adding, "A number of my guests commented very favorably on Sunday evening and since then, so that I think you can feel very well satisfied."

I was still living at Hildegarde's Nineteenth Street house when Emily Clark Balch, a Virginia writer married to a Philadelphian, phoned to ask if she could give me a dinner party of twelve or more, which I accepted. Then she wondered whether perhaps I might consent to play and sing my opera, which she had heard at Van Vechten's. "I haven't lived in New York before, and I don't know how far one can go with musicians." Understanding from this that she did not choose to go as far as an honorarium, and not caring myself to be the season's free party-singer, I replied that I thought the evening at Carl's house should remain unique. She understood my answer, accepted it, produced a fine evening (as to food and drink and people); and we became friends. At table, being asked by an actress how everything had gone off at the banker's party, I said, "Just fine! Everybody was paid but the composer." The actress squealed, "I never heard of paying the composer!" "Not even when he has played the piano," I said, "and conducted and brought in another composer to play too?" This set off an animated discussion that must have lasted all of four minutes and in which everybody agreed I was wrong. Not one among all those prosperous professionals of art would admit my assumption that to provide music for a *soirée* given by a man one hardly knows is a professional service worth at least a gift. (Mozart's father used to say, "My God! Another watch!")

Other essays made in my behalf turned out even less well. The League of Composers, alerted early to my impending presence (probably by Copland), had asked to see scores in view of performance that spring. I sent first instrumental ones and then vocal; none was accepted. And Alma Wertheim, who had a press for publishing music and who had asked for manuscripts, returned them on the grounds that there was "no money for publishing them." Both the Cos Cob Press and the League of Composers were by the carefully neutral tone of their rejections letting me know I was no part of their power-group. And it was always to be that way. When they wanted a favor from me, they asked for it, usually got it. Virtually nothing was ever to be done about my music at any needful moment. Alma Wertheim's press printed four years later, in 1933, one five-minute work. The League of Composers gave me in 1934 and 1949 two of their less remunerative commissions. They performed the five-minute piece (*Stabat Mater*, for soprano and string quartet) after it was already familiar; and at their twenty-fifth anniversary concert, in 1948, they gave my Sonata for Violin and Piano (already in the repertory of the artists playing it, who were available free), a work they had refused in 1931, when it was new, shocking by its use of curvilinear melody and suave harmonic textures, and badly needing the blessing of some establishment.

As to how it came about that for all my musical abilities I was consistently excluded from the musical power-groups, it was plain to me then; I was too terrifyingly frank. Bérard had said of me that "Virgil speaks the truth." And indeed I was forever blurting things out. Among my intellectual equals the habit was stimulating; but in a group of musicians banded together chiefly for capturing patronage, I was bound to be disruptive. Thus it was that in New York 1928 and '29, just as it had come about already in Paris, those who kept me out of their musical politics did so from sound impulse or wise reasoning. I have never been a joiner or much of an operator. And the League of Composers, for all that it worked hard for other composers, was not likely, I judged, to be doing much for me.

New York was a delight, all the same, in nonmusical ways. It was nourishing to be again with Briggs Buchanan and Maurice Grosser, to visit Jere Abbott, at this time a graduate student in Princeton, and "Cuffbutton," my sister's former painting teacher, just home from seven years in China and living in a New Jersey forest. And there was an absorbing new friendship with a dark and handsome tall girl (much too tall). Her name was Dorothy Speare; and she seemed to have sung opera in Italy and to have had lessons there, especially to know well the Milan music world. She had in fact written a novel about Milan studio life that had been published in a women's magazine. Just then it was being made into a play, and Dorothy was convinced that my personality had "just the flair and fillip required" for an important role in it, "that of a young operatic tenor (American student in Milan) who sings and plays." I was reserved about my acting powers but happy to spend hours with her on any subject. So we met often, either at her flat in New York, where she lived with a husband named Christmas, or in Boston, where she visited parents in Newton Center. And sometimes I played for her to sing Italian arias or tried coaching her in Mozart, though she knew more about coloratura style than I did. Nothing ever came of any project beyond our happiness in being together, but we went on meeting whenever we were in the same town. Her novel became eventually a highly successful film, *One Night of Love*, with the opera star Grace Moore in it; and Dorothy, though quite well to do after that, continued to write scripts in Hollywood. The last time I saw her, in 1934, we dined at Twenty-One on caviar and champagne, then went off to the Forty-fourth Street Theatre to see *Four Saints in Three Acts*. Dorothy Speare had beauty, also a certain radiance that must have been the afterglow of her student days. For she was opera-struck, and fatally. She had one story; she had told it; she still could not accept that it was over.

Another whom I saw with pleasure was Van Vechten's friend (and formerly Gertrude's) Mabel Dodge Luhan. I had expected of so legendary a hostess and a muse a personality more inclined toward the showy. To my surprise she was a quiet one; she let you talk. Now a woman who will listen without interrupting is obviously someone to be valued. And when Mabel herself spoke, however briefly, in a voice soft, sweet, and young, you understood her attractiveness to men. I did not see Mabel often that winter, nor ever again later. Nor could I do for her what I think she had hoped, restore to her Gertrude Stein from their estrangement. The causes of that, which went back to Florence before World War I, were unknown to me; and neither Gertrude nor Alice, though they often spoke of her, ever told me the reasons for it.

Less rewarding was a younger hostess, the still handsome and never heartless Muriel Draper, widow of Paul, a singer, mother of another Paul (later to dance), and at this time an author of best-selling memoirs called *Music at Midnight*, all about giving musical parties in London. She was leading now in a Fortieth Street stable a life of resplendent poverty, still party-giving, and receiving the arts and letters every Tuesday for tea. The tea, a gift, was always excellent; the cookies, from Schrafft's, were likely to be twelve for forty people. She had asked me to come half an hour before the others so that we could "really talk." Really talking seemed to mean that I must listen, and that I must accept her opinion as final on everything regarding art. (Later she was to add Marxist politics.)

Actually Muriel was aspiring to dominate through her natural warmth and kindness an artistic and intellectual world of which she was just the playmate. I realized her lack of intellectual continuity when in the middle of an address to me about my music (pronounced with the warmest intimacy and from her gilded stage-throne, as if I were the only courtier that mattered), other callers began to arrive. Instantly she dropped the subject and with it all special treatment; from then on I was just another guest. As a hostess, I must say, she was expert. Her divers domiciles remained for several years among the best New York had to offer as salons of arts and letters, and Muriel could till her death be no less commanding as a guest. Mabel Luhan, who had known her in prewar Florence days, drew a portrait of her in one of the memoir volumes that is both warm and perspicacious.

If New York had received me as a possibly acceptable invader, Boston and Cambridge took me as one of their own. The Sonata da Chiesa, which I conducted at a public concert of the Flute Players' Club, was performed in splendor of sound by first-chair men from the Boston Symphony; and although it shocked some (always has, still does), the society's director expressed in a letter his admiration and that of his colleagues for the work, adding that he would like in the very near future to play me again, "this time without obligation" on my part. I have never taken him up on the offer.

The Harvard Musical Club evening was informal, companionable, and as to repertory comprehensive. My merrier works were received with jollity, selections from *Four Saints* with awe (no reserves), my *Symphony on a Hymn Tune*, played in four-hand piano version, with frankly expressed bewilderment.

(Walter Piston still considers absurd an unaccompanied canon for bass tuba and piccolo.) E. B. Hill, my teacher and good friend, though not bothered by its orchestral textures, was doubtful, as Koussevitzky had been, whether the work would communicate in performance, or as musicians say, "come off." About the opera, on the other hand, he was quite sure. "A good musical idea," he called it. "You've got something there."

Back in New York for leaving, I wrote Gertrude that in Boston everyone was taking my work "very seriously and nobody there thinks any more that I am a bad boy." New York was still dining me and interviewing me and writing Sunday articles about my work. No music publisher, however, no opera house, no conductor was showing interest. Even the League of Composers had given me, through three different representatives, what I took for a planned brush-off. From Paris Gertrude was writing, "Delighted at the success perhaps we will get on the radio and the gramophone yet and have royalties and buy a prize Bedlington terrier and [put in] a telephone and pay for my new Ford car, perhaps, but anyway I am most awfully pleased." And Russell Hitchcock wrote that Madame Langlois would meet me in Le Harve, he in Paris; Cliquet-Pleyel, that the lament he had composed would now be answered:

> Ah, que revienne avril
> et avec lui, Virgil!
> En avril
> ne quitte plus Virgil.

So before March was over, I was back on the *Ile-de-France*, third class as before and with the same special privileges, plus from a dozen demonstrative New York friends baskets of fruit, boxes of candy, tins of caviar, splits of champagne, flowers, books, and from others letters of loving farewell and the ubiquitous telegram. It all made my cabin, shared with some three or five, a trifle crowded.

13
An Epoch Ends

DURING MY FOUR MONTHS' ABSENCE I had sublet the quai Voltaire studio to two American girls. These had turned out, as usual, to be three. And all three had boy friends in and out, actually more in than out, according to Madame Jeanne. The wear on carpets, curtains, and wallpaper had been intense. My amiable landlord, Dr. Ovize, placing no blame on me, agreed that all these must be replaced. The renewals took over a month, during which time the pianist George Copeland, whose acquaintance I had renewed on shipboard, used to like coming there of an evening and sitting among the ladders. Sometimes too he would sit at the piano and play Spanish music or Bach. My favorite was his version of Chabrier's *España*, incredibly busy as to finger and powerful as to volume. Copeland played it as if it were real Spanish music. The Spanish themselves have in my time mostly played Spanish music as if they had learned it in Germany, forgetting its origins in the dance and mooning over it. Copeland also played Debussy well, had begun his career that way; but his Debussy renderings were more subtle for color than tightly structured. It was almost as if he were improvising them. Spontaneity was there, as were also lovely sound, the power of poetic evocation, and a temperament for grandeur, all these qualities showing at their best, probably, in just such an informal circumstance.

On my American tour I had been able, thanks to Christian Bérard, to leave handsome gifts with all the persons who had been especially useful to me or generous with hospitality. Bérard, who was a draftsman of vast fecundity and like many another artist of that time prodigal with his product, had given me twenty or thirty wash drawings before I left, knowing that I would lodge them where they might be loved; and I had done just that. Now he proposed that I sit for my portrait, which he had got interested in doing from having made a series of ink sketches of me for the Ten Portraits by Gertrude Stein that Hugnet was to publish. I posed afternoons at the small private house in the villa Spontini where Bébé lived with his widowed

316

father, an architect. He used the former drawing room for a studio; and this he kept dark, because he as often painted late at night as during the day, using at all hours blue bulbs for light.

Bébé was blond and plump, with a sharply defined small beak of a nose and a carved mouth. The blue eyes, indeed the whole being, radiated intelligence, jollity, and good humor. He was self-indulgent in every way, however, and quite without self-discipline. At this time his grooming, though careless, was not yet willfully negligent. Later he stopped shaving and even washing much; but by that time no one minded, since he had become the playmate of the richest ladies. He was also to smoke opium and drink a great deal. This was after his fashion drawings in *Vogue* were being imitated everywhere and he had become the most admired stage designer in the world. But at twenty-five, Bébé was frequenting his own generation, which considered him their most gifted painter and possibly the one who would lead his art into paths of humane awareness, as Goya had done.

The reasons why Bébé did not do this are all part of his self-indulgence, of his inability to face the travail, the certainties of public refusal and the probabilities of private persecution, the whole painful progress of an artist who wishes to be a great one, who knows he has to be a great one, and who cannot turn back. Bébé did what he could; he was not self-deceived. But he did not, he could not persist as in France Degas had persisted, and Renoir and Monet and Bonnard. So he made stage designs. These were beautiful and appropriate. But all who were touched by his painting, especially his painting of people, came to regret, as he did too, that he had not been able to live up to his genius— for his talent, intelligence, and depth of directly expressed feeling did amount, I think, to that.

At the time he undertook my portrait he had already painted the large dark ones with candlewax under-modeling, and he was not to do these again. Later he was to paint waifs and fashionable women in light bright colorings and some remarkable multifigured murals in private houses, still later a series of self-portraits by the sea. But just then he was more interested in studying me as a model than he was ready for painting a new kind of portrait. I sat exactly twice, I think; and he made a beginning of a head that was like me. I am not sure whether he added a stroke or two later or whether in the course of time the picture may have seemed to him finished enough. In any case, though given to me, it was never delivered. I think Christian Dior had bought it, for it did turn up in a Paris exhibit of Bérard's work held at a gallery where Dior was a partner, still later in a New York gallery, where it was bought by friends of mine who had been touched by its resemblance.

At these same sittings I made a portrait in music which I called *Christian Bérard, prisonnier.* I wrote of both efforts to Gertrude, "Bébé did me again as portrait very good and I did him but very bad." Nevertheless, I later found I liked mine and composed others to go with it. I had already that winter, in Kansas City, written for a quartet of clarinets (at the request of Gaston Hamelin) a piece which I called *Portrait of Ladies.* This was a sound-picture of the way my four Stuyvesant ladies (friends from the New York wartime and from visits in Maine) used to tell a story, all talking at once, in counterpoint rather than in rivalry. Bébé's portrait was for the same four instruments. Later in the summer, at Villefranche, I made two more, one called *Bébé Soldat,* to picture him on his twenty-eight days of reservist's duty, and another called *En personne (chair et os),* evoking the personal presence. Then one day when Maurice Grosser had a cold, I sketched him as *A Young Man in Good Health.* Together these all made up a suite which I called *Five Portraits for Four Clarinets,* and which I sent off to Hamelin, who had them played in Boston. At a music camp in Michigan they were later performed by 150 youngsters. And after World War II Hamelin produced them for the Paris radio. Other performances have been brought to my notice, and I am often asked to lend out score and parts. Until the fall of 1963, when they were run up in my honor at a college in Pennsylvania, I had never heard them.

In June, Aaron Copland arrived, with money from a New York patroness for giving a concert of works by young Americans. There were to be his own *Vitebsk* trio and Two Pieces for String Quartet, also a Sextet by Roy Harris. Of lesser weightiness were a short piano sonata by Carlos Chávez and various vocal works. The latter consisted of three James Joyce songs by Israel Citkowitz (then a pupil of Boulanger) and of five by me (three in French, two by Stein). Marthe-Marthine sang them all, pronouncing phonetically. According to the press, the show was mine, with the Harris piece "also attracting favorable

attention," a result not wholly satisfying, I think, to Nadia Boulanger, who had helped with arranging the program and with
mobilizing an international modern-music audience. At that
time she was viewing my musical development with some reserve.

To Gertrude Stein, in the country, I wrote that

> the concert went off with much success to us you and me, and
> Joyce came & liked us and so did Adrienne [Monnier] who said
> sweet things next day to Mme. Langlois about "*fine et spirituel et
> de l'ironie dedans,*" etc. which I suppose means that Antheil isn't
> "*civilisation française*" any more since he has moved to Germany
> and written an opera in German and so . . . maybe I'm it[,]
> anyway Tonny said it was like an arrived *maître* who loaned his
> *concours* to a concert of aspiring young ones and the Gide faction
> it seems was also there and has passed around the word that I am
> the berries . . . and really it is surprising how much glory seems
> to accrue from a concert that cost nothing in fact was given with
> any intention but that of popularizing me who was supposed I
> guess to be just comic relief.

The last remark was aimed at Boulanger. I knew better than
to ascribe such a motive to Copland, who had always behaved
frankly toward me. Actually he admired my vocal music more
than my instrumental, just as, contrariwise, he held in especial
respect the instrumental works of Chávez and Roy Harris. And
as for my music, vocal or instrumental, attracting more attention than his, Aaron knew how to bide his time. Anyway, he
believed, as I did, that the good ones in our generation must
stick together; and we were each of us sure the other was a good
one. I had written that of him (in *Vanity Fair*) when his First
Symphony was played. And he had written of me just then in
Modern Music:

> Virgil Thomson can teach us all how to set English to music. . . .
> In the opera *Four Saints in Three Acts*, in *Capital Capitals*, in his
> numerous songs he has caught the [amazing variety of] rhythms
> and inflections that make the English language different from any
> other. . . . It would be impossible to translate these compositions
> into any other language.

I was about to receive, nevertheless, from the Hessisches
Landestheater in Darmstadt a request for the score of *Four
Saints*, in prospect of its possible production in German. The

letter was in English, written by the poet Edwin Denby (dancer and assistant *régisseur*) in the name of "Messrs. Rabenalt and Reinking . . . respectively, a young operatic *régisseur* of great promise and reputation in Germany and a young stage designer of genius." They wished to consider my opera for the coming season, and Denby assured me it would receive "a quite exceptionally careful and at the same time brilliant production." Also that "their reputation [and] the great interest in Germany in novel forms of opera would bring the production wide publicity. Besides," he added, "the theater . . . is one of the best in Germany." Denby himself, "almost bilingual," would be of help "in verifying a translation."

My score was in no condition for such a trip. It existed in one pencil copy, and that incomplete as to piano accompaniment and the choral passages. Of orchestral score there was not one page. I did not even have an extra copy of the libretto—about to be printed, however, in *transition*. But even before the Darmstadt group had seen this, it had been suggested that I come there in September to play and sing the opera for them and to offer whatever ideas I might have for "action, stage directions and so on." Once he had read the libretto, Denby expressed himself as "enthusiastic over the possibilities for production which it offers" and "the more eager to see the music." Also, "Mr. Reinking [the designer], who glanced at my copy, was much interested in it." And again he repeated his insistence that as soon as possible I send "at least a piano score."

But I was not to have one available till late September. The Paris concert had kept me in town through June. In July I had gone with Mrs. Lasell to Madrid, where she became ill. Then two weeks in Savoy with Madame Langlois and her Russian companion and Maurice Grosser, who had left New York to be in France again. There it was, I think, that he wrote out his scenario for the opera, a clear plan of action that allowed it to be staged. I did not, till September in Villefranche, have the time to complete a voice-and-piano score in ink. But between Flumet and the south coast I did stop for spending a day or two at Gertrude's newly hired manorial property in the village of Bilignin, near Bellay. There I proposed accepting the invitation to give an audition of my opera in Darmstadt, and since that trip would have been aimed at our mutual advantage, I inquired whether Gertrude would care to share its cost. She declined on the ground that "the libretto had already been accepted." Though this was not quite true, for it had merely been read by an assistant *régisseur* and "glanced at" by a designer, I did not argue the matter. I did not, however, undertake the trip. I went on South, finished the score and mailed it to Darmstadt.

Seven months later, on May 1, 1930, Denby wrote, "The chances are pretty black. The music director can't be prevailed on, and the rest of us interested are the more enthusiastic the better we come to know the opera; still a production is dependent on the [musical] director." Later that year, when I made Denby's acquaintance, he told me the explosion my opera had caused. Darmstadt's bright history in producing left-wing or far-out operas and ballets had been the work of a house-team with progressive ideas, encouraged and protected by the *Generalintendant* Carl Ebert. Ballets by Satie, Milhaud, and Florent Schmitt, operas by Falla, Křenek, and Hindemith had all attracted artistic attention to the city; but these productions had also been costly, losses being only partly recuperated through works of standard repertory needing little rehearsal and no new scenery. Someone in authority, presumably the *Generalmusik-direcktor* Dr. Karl Boehm, had decided to begin tapering off on modernism by taking a firm stand against *Four Saints*.

Had my opera been produced around 1930 in Darmstadt, it would be today a different work from what it became under the conditions of its American première in 1934. Its text would have acquired for twin a German version, and the whole work would have taken on the mood of the German art-theater. I would have scored it, moreover, for a much larger number of musicians; and its future life, in consequence, would have been led in middle-to-large-size repertory houses. Its American production, had there come to be one, would not therefore have been a possibility for the museum director in Hartford who allowed me eventually to give it a Negro cast, an English choreographer, and cellophane scenery designed by an American painter, and where the exiguous theater-pit led me to score it for a very small and special-sounding group. The repertory houses might or might not have taken it on, but its whole Hartford and Broadway adventure and its production as choreographic theater in the Diaghilev tradition would most likely never have taken place. Of the translation project I remember just one line, Saint Teresa's Christmas carol, "There can be no peace on earth with calm with calm," which came out in German not at all unattractively: "*Es kann sein kein Fried' auf Erd' mit Ruh' mit Ruh'.*"

The spring and summer of 1929 had been full of movements and projects. Hugnet's film *La Perle*, which our Belgian friend the Comte d'Ursel had been supervising in a professional studio, got slowly finished. This was a mixture of detective story with amorous episodes and photographic fantasy (such as a friendly cow in a bedroom and a rue de la Paix jewel shop giving directly on to sylvan fields). It was sweetly poetical and lived for a season. Then it became an antique, like all the other films without sound tracks. The Cocteau morality-film *Blood of a Poet* and Luis Buñuel's exercises in horror and shock, *Un Chien andalou* and *L'Age d'or*, were to have more relation, anyway, to the cruelties of the decade that was beginning. *La Perle* remains a charm piece with all the innocence of the 1920s. When d'Ursel's financial resources for making art films had come to an end, the subsidizing of this field was undertaken by a richer patron, the Vicomte de Noailles. This benefactor in turn renounced film making when as a result of an irreligious passage in *L'Age d'or* (the Holy Sacrament being thrown into a gutter) he was threatened with excommunication from the Church and, what to many seemed graver, expulsion from the Jockey Club.

That same spring, the Misses Stein and Toklas, who had been spending their summers at a gastronomic hotel in Bellay, took lease on a seventeenth-century manor house near by, at Bilignin—a move that furnished Gertrude with a geographic center, turned Alice into an ardent cook and gardener. My own landlord, after doing over my studio on my return from America, had begun construction work that was to change my life also. A whole cluster of furnished studios, all with views of historic Paris, came into being at the top of the house; an elevator was added to the main stair well; and my apartment acquired on its upper level a small kitchen. As a result of these additions, various acquaintances came to live in the new studios and I myself started cooking in. For by the next year, when the changes were complete, Mrs. Lasell had discontinued my allowance, so that eating at home became a necessary economy, as well as a possible hospitality formula. Actually I started cooking that fall, using a gas ring that sat on the floor of my bathroom and a single large pot. After the kitchen became available, my concierge Madame Elise made dinners for me at a charge (besides the groceries) of five francs, or twenty-five cents.

But all this was to be part of the 1930s. For the present the 1920s were getting themselves ended without quite knowing they were doing so. The Vicomte and Vicomtesse de Noailles (to the new bohemia "Charles" and "Marie-Laure") gave in June of 1929 their celebrated *bal des matières*, for which everyone was asked to dress in plastics, glass, metal, straw, whatever might suggest only modern times. And the Duchesse de Clermont-Tonnerre, hoping to repeat the success of *Capital Capitals*, had requested for next season a miniature opera, to be written in collaboration with Georges Hugnet.

As I mentioned earlier, there had been laid down in the middle twenties a line of expressivity that was to be all of tenderness, compassion, sweetness of the heart. With the surrealists insisting loudly on a contrasting line of cruelty, subversion, and hysteria, this opposition was to produce in discussions about art a bitterness almost matching that which would accompany the decade's social and political changes. The visible signs of a new time did not, moreover, await the American stock-market collapse in late 1929 but followed hard on the 1928 Franco-German commercial accord. It was in immediate reaction to that event that the long evening dress, floor-length and wide, came into fashion and that for daytime women began to wear the trench coat. For five years or more, in spite of dressmakers' efforts (subsidized by cloth-makers) toward getting women to consume more yardage, their clothing had not changed. Then suddenly they did accept a change—two changes, in fact—the symbolizations, equally urgent it would seem, of military duty in the daytime and of femaleness at night. And these were to remain the dominant themes of women's dressing, at least in Europe, throughout the 1930s, with the constant military actions (in Italy, Spain, and Germany) and the constant threats of paramilitary revolution (in France, in Czechoslovakia) that led up to the five-year militarization of all Europe.

The twenties had been a peaceful and busy time, with lots of parties and dancing and casual sex-lives, and with minor new movements in music, art, and poetry every year. These were essentially a continuation under easy success conditions, of the modernist efforts that before the first World War had blossomed in far tougher weather. The radical art, music, and poetry of before that war were already the classics of our century (indeed still are), and the 1920s had been further enriched by the subsequent produce of the prewar masters, as well as of their pupils and their progeny. And with the formerly subservient ethnic groups no longer just contributors, culturally, to Berlin or Saint Petersburg or Vienna, but national entities with capitals of their own and seats at the League of Nations, a musical league of nations had come into being in which ethnic integrities and international conformities were neatly balanced. Vienna, Berlin, and Paris remained the centers of advance, as well as of musical publication. But one could still have said of Europe that from Bucharest to Lisbon "all God's chillun got modern music." Even the United States, slower to ripen in music than in letters or in visual art, had its modern-music societies and its up-to-date composers. Among these Aaron Copland, Roy Harris, and myself (plus the lone-wolf experimenter Henry Cowell) were the most active and since Antheil's virtual disappearance the most visible internationally.

This in the modern-music sense, of course. George Gershwin, whose *Rhapsody in Blue* was already in the "pop" concerts, none of us ever could compete with for distribution, nor he with us for intellectual prestige. And Brazil, which had already in the nineteenth century produced an international figure, Antonio Gomes (composer of *Il Guarany*), sent to Europe in 1924 Heitor Villa-Lobos, a fountain, a volcano of colorful music, most of it folklorically inspired and all of it as lively as a Carioca carnival. Villa-Lobos told me later of his arrival in Paris and of going to call, with introductions, on all the French composers old and young. Every one of them, he said, after glancing at his music, began to say how charming it was but how much more so it could become if he would compose in their way instead of his. After about the tenth experience he answered, "But I have not come for lessons, only to show you what I have done." Which silenced them. As a result, he became a part of modern music's establishment, with all its intellectual privileges.

Music's evolution in the twenties was still governed by the

prewar masters Stravinsky and Schoenberg. Debussy was dead, Ravel no longer an influence. In France Milhaud, Honegger, Poulenc, and Auric, Hindemith and Křenek in Germany, were minor masters, material for the immortality machines. So were Berg and Webern in Austria; so was Falla in Spain; and so were a few Italians, English, Poles, and Soviet Russians. Music's league of nations, except for Stravinsky and Schoenberg, was a consortium of profit-sharing minorities. And if the epoch seems now to have been a vigorous one, let us say rather that it was active, that lots of music got written and performed, and that modern-music audiences were friendly.

Poetry was similarly geared to the prewar giants—Yeats, Pound, and Stein—with T. S. Eliot as a rising power and with excellent minor masters available in William Carlos Williams, e. e. cummings, Wallace Stevens, Hart Crane (are there more?). French poetry still stemmed from Rimbaud and Mallarmé, coming to contemporary flower in St.-John Perse, Paul Valéry, and Paul Claudel, none of them young. The novel meant Proust (dead in '22) and Joyce; nobody else was doing comparable work. And neither had the minor painters yet become influential. Braque and Picasso reigned; Matisse still functioned. And Picasso himself was wiggling, struggling, twisting to get free of the cubistical trap he had helped to invent. This is not to say that beautiful work was not done in the twenties. It is merely to remind those who look on those years as a golden age that perhaps they were just that, a time when money, caviar, and diamonds; intelligence, amiability, and good looks; talent, imagination, and wit; ambition, success, and charm were available everywhere.

These came together in certain theater spectacles still unmatched. In France and the West the most impressive of these were the Ballets Russes of Serge de Diaghilev. In Germany and central Europe there were the fabulously successful productions of Max Reinhardt, who personally owned over thirty theaters (as well as the historic archiepiscopal palace of Leopoldskron in Salzburg, where he kept his prompt-books in the sacristy safe). Diaghilev and Reinhardt seem to have kept up from the early 1920s an agreement not to invade each other's territory. In any case, we in Paris never saw the Reinhardt shows (though New York did have *The Miracle*); and central Europe remained for the most part ignorant of the Stravinsky ballet scores, the Picasso stage-sets, and all those striking collaborations between advanced composers and advanced painters which gave to the Diaghilev spectacles (already impeccable for dancing) one glory of the time's finest artwork, another, out front, of a mundane firmament, a dynamo-audience generating its own light from the magnetic proximities of talent, vast worldly experience, known sexual prowess, and beauty aflame.

It was not just the presence of Picasso and Joyce and Stravinsky that gave to the Paris twenties an opulent tone, for these were quiet men who worried and worked and for the most part went to bed o' nights. It was the choreographic stage that made the epoch shine. The splendor of this had led other theaters toward high-level collaborative artwork. And it had at the same time opened the doors of the great Paris houses (the London ones too) to artists and writers, to musicians and dancers. Certain patrons were thereby led to furnish money for opera and ballet seasons in a climate of artistic (and sexual) cooperation that caused class barriers for a little time to disappear. After Diaghilev's death these barriers came right up again, save in a very few houses where sex parties or opium had become ingrained. And one can take the date of his death, I think, as significant, because with it the Ballets Russes, which had lit up the West since 1909, overnight went dark. I have suggested that the kinds of painting and music which were to be influential in the thirties (including surrealism and dodecaphony) had all come into being by 1925. I have suggested also that a new temper, not necessarily peaceful, was created in 1928 through the Franco-German commercial accords. And certainly after 1929 grave economic events followed our Wall Street disaster. In a historical change marked by hidden steps as well as headlines, it is not easy to pick out the point, like a continental divide, where the thirties began their downward tragic course. But it might be posible to imagine that the twenties, that lively and legendary time which had preserved all that was ever to be preserved of the even grander epoch in the arts that had come to flower just before World War I, expired on August 19, 1929, with the death in Venice of Serge de Diaghilev.

14

The New Romanticism

IN ALL THE SHOWY LIVING that went on throughout the twenties, the Americans, though not the biggest spenders (leave that to the Indian princes), were certainly in France the most numerous. Wherever there were Ritzes and races, champagne night clubs and gambling casinos, they made up the bulk of the trade, seasoned with a dollop of bejeweled Argentines, a few well-dressed and amorous Brazilians, some impressively casual English and Scots (terrifying gamblers these last), and two or three vastly visible maharajahs. Except for the Greek syndicate that owned the bank at Monte Carlo, all these had come to France because that was where clothes were prettiest, the gambling highest, the really good gems and jewelry cheapest, and the hotels best administered for year-round luxury. Only a few played the game of getting into French society; the best way for that was to be Catholic and do it through marriage. But here and there in the world of hard-driven pleasure one would come on a token Frenchman acting as guide or a French family looking to sell their château. The solvent French went mostly to resorts not internationally fashionable, such as La Baule on the west coast, San Raphael on the south, and beach places on the north that were not Deauville.

Within less than a year after the stock-market tumble began, virtually all the foreign spenders had gone home. The Argentines had turned in their diamonds, the British sold their yachts, the Americans packed up their furs and children, left mistresses behind; only the Oriental potentates remained, and a few foreigners who owned their houses. Mary Garden, ruined by the collapse of the Insull enterprises in Chicago, sold for debts her seaside villa at Beaulieu and shortly afterwards (or so she said) left by accident all her remaining jewelry (uninsurable, since she was a star) in a Monte Carlo taxicab. In the grander hotels of Paris, only half filled in summer, the wintertime became a time of desolation, with tips almost cut off and room clerks, porters, waiters, night men all down to a take-home pay of genuine poverty.

Among the artists and writers too exodus went on, those vowed to preserving the gay twenties being first to leave, since it was clear by the end of 1929 that the postwar time was over. To those of us no longer living in that aftermath no shock came with its demise. We had long since lost taste for its bar-stool discussions of courage, its pride in banal misbehaviors, and had moved into a range of sentiment that seemed to us far fresher. Our new romanticism was no nostalgia for the warmths of World War I or for the gone-forever prewar youth of Stravinsky and Picasso, but an immersion complete in what any day might bring. *Mystère* was our word, tenderness our way, unreasoning compassion our aim.

We did not need to go away, or want to. A small group following a path discovered only a short time earlier (and by Christian Bérard, for certain), we should have found elsewhere few comrades prepared for aiding or abetting us. Our ways of life and art belonged in Europe anyway; they were not ripe for being submitted to home-front pressmen, pedagogical organizers, or price manipulators. And hardly any Americans besides myself were involved.

Our novelty—and I am speaking of less than a dozen poets, painters, and musicians—consisted in the use of our personal sentiments as subject matter. Modern artists of the prewar time had mostly refrained from doing this—Debussy, Ravel, Stravinsky; Matisse, Picasso, Braque; Bernard Shaw and Yeats; Mallarmé and Valéry. For them the theme had always been outside themselves, however secretive or eloquent the statement. And those whose chief careers came after World War I, though their forming had taken place earlier—Pound and Eliot, Joyce and Stein—had scrupulously maintained an objective method. Of all the large-size twentieth-century artists only Proust had pointed up a private feeling; and even with him the search for a particular recall was little more than a pretext for painting a panorama. But in poetry, a century earlier, Wordsworth, Blake, and Byron; in music Chopin and Schumann; in painting, Goya, at least, had all been unafraid to speak their sentiments. In our time the Austrian composers Schoenberg and Berg had spoken of sentiment too, pouring out in their grandly hospitable way the secrets of the soul, of any soul, like May wine for visitors. Perhaps we in Paris, few and young, were only a trickle beside their vast Danubian vats; indeed they seemed to think of us (if at all) as just that, though we believed ourselves of better vintage. It matters not. In an age that kept insistently looking backward—and Vienna most of all—an awareness of the daily present had become our way of life, and in spite of wars and cataclysms was to remain so throughout the 1930s.

I have said we were young; we would have had to be, for constant vibrancy is hard to sustain after thirty-five. But we did have mentors among the older artists. The poets Max Jacob, Jean Cocteau, and Gertrude Stein admired our work. So did the fiction writer Marcel Jouhandeau. The painters among us had no older ones at all to whom they looked for praise. But the composer Charles Koechlin, ever curious about novelty and warm toward youth, followed our music from a distance; and Darius Milhaud was more than tolerant.

Milhaud was in fact the keystone of French music's power structure in so far as it controlled the distribution of contemporary work. And a more devoted chief could scarcely be imagined, self-sacrificing of his time and far-flung as to influence. My own acquaintance with him, a long one, has borne no marks of tension. And if he at no time aided my career, as he did that of so many others, indeed of almost all the others with whom I shared affinity, I have long thought that probably the fault was mine. If I had submitted my music to his judgment, as the others did, and frankly asked for tutelage, I might well have become in those early 1930s as clearly a part of the School of Paris as did Nicolas Nabokov, Vittorio Rieti, and Igor Markevitch, all of them later arrivals than I. But I could no more submit myself to Milhaud, invited or not, than I had been able to submit myself to Ravel when in 1926 he offered friendship. Some unconquerable rebelliousness had made it so. It was for them, discovering me, to make the move; and even then I did not always follow. So it was with all the French to whom I became attached, including Madame Langlois, though there were always to be some nearly-exact contemporaries (Sauguet, for instance, and Cliquet-Pleyel) with whom no such question of protocol arose. With Milhaud, and with Francis Poulenc too, there may have remained a wariness from ten years earlier, when in my Boulanger and fresh-from-Harvard days I had very likely impressed them as a shade uppish.

As for the neo-Romantic upsurge itself, to which Milhaud bore a benevolent and avuncular relation, its identification as a movement was yet to come. Neo-Romanticism in painting was defined twenty years later as "the personality of the painter reflected in the character of the thing seen." This from Maurice Grosser's book *The Painter's Eye*, where he also states that "by reintroducing humanity and personal feelings into an art that had become dehumanized, the Neo-Romantic painters made, I am convinced, the most important contribution to painting since the innovations of the great Moderns, and one which will have much influence in forming the painting of the second half of our century."

Of its musical aspects I wrote in 1933 for *Modern Music* that

> around the personality of Sauguet the present epoch has begun to crystalize. Neo-Romanticism is the journalistic term for it. Spontaneity of sentiment is the thing sought. Internationalism is the temper. Elegance is the real preoccupation. Nobody expects further technical research to supply its own corrective . . . [and] grand passion . . . hasn't recovered from Wagner yet. What about well-bred salon music? That was tried in 1920 and called neo-classicism. (The idea of being well-bred is behind all neo-classicism: Vergil, Racine, and Pope, for example.) It turned out [to need] the same corrective that the late eighteenth century needed [and got from Romanticism], an infusion of warm personal feeling. Sentimental love, spontaneous sympathy, faithful comradeship, playful libertinage, domesticity, tolerant rivalry, and affectionate bickering, these are modes of living still at hand, . . . usable in art. . . . The first twenty years [of our century] occupied themselves with technic. The present age is concerned about feeling. [Only] when these elements [shall] have been . . . coordinated . . . [will there] be a way of living, of contemplating, and of writing grandiose tragedy.

This statement presents a Paris-based view, of course. Music in central Europe had long since adopted an introverted pathos. If our hope in the West was rather to diminish than to augment the anxiety content of art and thus possibly to preserve the whole of modernism from scleroses already developing through success, no such danger existed in the Germanic regions. On the contrary, the danger there after 1933 was total extinction; and even before that time the great migration had begun that was to furnish the United States, Mexico, Brazil, and Argentina with scholars and skilled workers, France's rapidly maturing film art with directors and cameramen. (The French film also benefited from French stage actors, once the sound track had given them their language.)

Except for the noticeable number of departures, the early 1930s in Paris did not seem, right off, to be very different from the twenties. The sun still rose; the Seine still lapped its quays; and prices, most conveniently, fell a little. One did not greatly mind there not being so much money around, so long as one had any at all. And with the departure of the sardonic ones, the heart and its ways became more precious to us. As a result of this new sensibility, most of those who had been free lancing as to love now began to pair off, move into flats, and cook. My first *bœuf à la mode en gelée* came off with beginner's luck simply because Madame Elise, who had told me how to make it, had failed to warn me that it is far from easy. However, along with cooking's delights and mating's conveniences came, of course, mating's frictions. And quarreling, which in the Arcadian twenties had seldom seemed worthwhile, became in the emptiness of the beginning thirties a refuge from boredom, a diversion, the darker side of friendship and of love. Warfare, in fact, though just now chiefly personal, was later to involve class bitterness and national envies and thence to become by 1932 in China, by 1933 in Germany, '34 in France, '35 in America, '36 in Spain, the decade's dominant theme. It was not to be for long a peaceful time, the period that began in 1930; after the financial panic of 1929 the growth was gradual and steady toward the wider holocausts of ten years later.

Nevertheless, with masses of the foreign moving out, the French themselves turned individually sweeter; and those of us who had remained came to be warmly adopted. After 1933 there were refugees from Germany, and from 1936 many Spanish; but as the thirties began we were mostly just Americans alone with the French. And very glad they were to have us too, for a French family feels most secure when it privately owns at least one American. The French need foreigners to admire them. Also, unless there is a peppering of likable outsiders available to whom they can explain France, the French can start explaining it to one another—an urge that throughout their

history has led to civil war. It came almost to that in 1934 and
'35. Then the next year, with thousands of republican Spanish
to take care of, they turned euphoric and stayed so right up to
World War II, even through the first year of that, though their
beloved Americans had thinned out. Americans remain always,
in spite of politics, their favorite foreigners, because though we
are firmly a part of the Judeo-Christian fellowship (a necessity
for brotherly loving and brotherly quarreling), we never bore
them by acting like Europeans.

The English-language literary giants of the 1930s were to be
the same as those already gigantic before—Joyce, Stein, Yeats,
and Pound, with Eliot, though less of an influence in poetry
than these, becoming a power in publication. The magazines
previously devoted to these authors, however, showed a high
mortality. *The Dial* ceased in 1929, *The Little Review* not long
after. Sherry Mangan's *larus the celestial visitor* (hand set in Lu-
tetia type on special paper), which had begun to appear early in
1927, had expired in 1928 after seven issues, largely because he
persisted in paying for manuscripts. His American contributors
had included the largely unknown Hart Crane, Yvor Winters,
R. P. Blackmur, and George Davis. As his "European editor" I
had procured for him poetry and prose from Gertrude Stein,
Mary Butts, Bernard Faÿ, Robert McAlmon, Pierre de Massot,
and Henry de Montherlant. A year later he transferred his un-
expired subscriptions to "a young friend with money"; and the
result was *Pagany*, edited in Boston by Richard Johns[on]. This
quarterly began in January of 1930 and went on, according to
the copies I own, for at least three years. Since Mangan was an
advisory editor, I continued helping him to secure European
contributions, though I never met Johns.

Pagany ran to 150 octavo pages of still good reading, including work by such already famous writers as Ezra Pound, William
Carlos Williams, Erskine Caldwell, Cocteau, e. e. cummings,
and Dos Passos, as well as by others who would be known later,
Paul Bowles, for example, and Harold Rosenberg. It printed a
handful of remarkable poems by Mary Butts and some of her
best stories. The second number contained, by Sherry Mangan,
one of the funniest polemical pieces I have ever read, *A "Note"
on the Somewhat Premature Apotheosis of the Late Lamented
Thomas Stearns Eliot.* (Gertrude, no lover of Eliot, found it
"Jesuit" but not Jesuitical.) And in the winter issue of 1931 there

appeared on facing pages a confrontation of Georges Hugnet's
Enfances, a suite of thirty poems, with Gertrude Stein's English
version of them.

To the opening number Hugnet had contributed (in French)
the first of his regular Paris letters, also a two-page article about
my music. French poets are less hesitant than American poets
to speak up for music; and we know the self-assumed authority with which for fifty years they have backed modern art.
Thus Hugnet could without embarrassment think of himself as
spokesman for the whole intellectual world when he exposed a
point of view that was coming to be a credo. He discerned in
my music, as Bérard had done some time before, two qualities
much admired just then, "simplicity" and "purity," which he
relates in my case to "the singing of Negroes . . . blended with
the rigamarole rhythms of Sunday School songs and children's
games." He finds my music generally "joyous" and "its effect on
the skin beneficial . . . a sort of heliotherapy." He considers my
Sonata da Chiesa to embody "a manner of writing that needs to
be renounced, a 'modern music' of which the high dissonance
content has lost its charm." My *Capital Capitals*, however, is
a "torrent resplendently clear" and my vocal music in general
"a truly novel contribution . . . an Elysian field in which the air
is neighbor to that which one breathes in the garden of Satie."

In Europe the literary twenties had proliferated an armful
of English-language magazines—Harold Loeb's *Broom*, Ford
Madox Ford's *Transatlantic Review*, Ernest Walsh's *This Quarter*, and several less impressive. The transition from that decade
to the next was mirrored after 1926 in a quarterly named exactly
that, *transition*, edited by Eugene Jolas, trilingual poet (French-
Alsatian-American), and sometimes by Eliot Paul. Almost every
number, as I remember, contained a chunk of Joyce's *Work in
Progress*; but every number seemed also to indicate increasing
involvement between Jolas and the surrealists. Early in 1930 I
wrote Gertrude,

> Our friend C[ary] Ross presented translations of poems by our
> equally friend G. Hugnet to our more or less friend E. Jolas latter
> remarking in re same (but not reading poems) that publication
> was impossible because Hugnet belonged to the wrong French
> group. Does this means *transition* gets money from Surrealists?
> (Who in turn ditto from Russia says Bernard.)

The idea that Russian gold could be supporting surrealism, from its beginnings admiring of Trotsky and after 1928 openly anti-Stalinist, was a fantasy that only the Catholic and royalist Bernard Faÿ could have entertained. My correspondence of the time constantly reports wide misses of this sort, also misunderstandings, frustrations, projects initiated only to be abandoned, quarrels threatened, some pacified, some moving in like an Oklahoma twister.

Hugnet kept trying all one summer to make a poem to which I could write a short opera, commissioned by our admirer the Duchesse de Clermont-Tonnerre. He finally produced *L'Invention de la rose*, which he called a *mélo*[*drama*]. Then came another, *Pléthore et pénurie* (surely a 1930s theme). Eventually I renounced the collaboration on grounds that Hugnet was a purely lyric poet without stage instinct. But the duchesse still wanted a piece for her next spring's party; and when I naïvely proposed my just-finished Funeral Oration by Bossuet (for Henriette-Marie de France, widow of England's Charles I), she listened to it with interest but found it (naturally!) not quite right for her costume ball. I also played and sang it for Alfredo Casella, then a conductor of influence in both Italy and France. His comment was, "The best I can say is that it is not a bore." The very idea of turning a Bossuet funeral oration into a solo cantata seemed as outlandish to him as a musical treatment of the Communist Manifesto might to a Russian or that of a sermon by Jonathan Edwards to an American. A few ultra-Catholics were receptive, scenting in it possible propaganda for the faith. Virtually everyone else found it lacking a *raison d'être*. Except, of course, my own courtiers, who admired its declamatory melodies and high-arched Baroque curves, some of them pages long and all built to match Bossuet's long, florid, loose-hung, and as often as not quite illogical Baroque sentences. I mention the Bossuet piece merely to show how detached I was at this time from career calculations and how concentrated on purely musical problems, in spite of my impending loss of income.

Gertrude Stein, at the same time, was trying to move everybody she could for my sake and for the sake of our opera. She ceased communication with the Chicago millionairess who had failed to continue her support of me. She tried to stimulate

English interest in *Four Saints* through writing to a London music critic her sister-in-law was said to know; and I wrote myself, at somebody's insistence, to Charles B. Cochran, London's most enterprising producer of music shows. Gertrude even persuaded me to write to Otto Kahn, Maecenas of the Met, proposing that I play and sing it for him. And she got Muriel Draper and Carl Van Vechten to mention it to Mary Garden, then powerful at the Chicago Opera. Nothing came of these efforts; the time was not for novelty.

Characteristic of the whole new decade, along with wars and massacres, was to be its preoccupation with the price of paintings. The twenties had shown collectors that no major fresh adventure was to be expected from painting itself and that it was consequently time to solidify the values in prewar modernism, that is to say, in the work of the cubists and their predecessors. Following this line, a group of New York collectors had opened in 1929, under the direction of two modern-art scholars, Jere Abbott and Alfred H. Barr, Jr., a Museum of Modern Art that was to become the world model for similar operations. In a decade of declining receipts from stocks and bonds, the buying of Modern Old Masters (Picasso, Braque, Matisse) and of the still inexpensive younger masters (Miró, Ernst, Arp, Dalí) was to be a source of rising wealth for the well advised, and a fascination to the public. In neither New York nor Paris was there to be much movement in art itself, only a great activity in the market. Even the time's most influential movements, the neo-Romantic and the surrealist, were both of them a heritage from the twenties. And if certain ripenings among poets and painters, and the withering away of others, gave drama to inner councils, no basic change took place in either viewpoint. Nor indeed did any change take place in the power structure of contemporary music; those in command were to remain the same.

Surrealism, born out of Dada's demise in the early 1920s, was not concerned with music at all, only with poetry and painting, both of which it essayed to govern through disciplines of spontaneity. In poetry the discipline was that of automatic writing, in painting, the transcribing of dreams, preferably in color and with *léché* (or "tongue-licked") brushwork. "Directed spontaneity" one might call its operation, since no writer or artist was allowed to remain in the group unless his spontaneities conformed to the particular blend of Marx-cum-Freud that constituted the philosophy of its poet-dictator André Breton. As an independent Marxist, Breton favored the intellectual freedoms nurtured by Trotsky; but politically he was nonparticipant, breaking in 1928 with those of his colleagues who accepted the demand of the French Communist party that the surrealists prove their allegiance to Stalin-directed Marxism by joining up and carrying out an anti-Trotsky line. The surrealists from that time on remained (as a group) politically uncommitted, though they still talked about revolution and aspired toward a generalized subversiveness.

They spoke for neither labor nor capital but rather as petit-bourgeois intellectuals. And throughout the 1930s, though politically ineffective, they were to contribute the valuable stubbornness of their class to the dialogue that went on throughout the *bourgeoisie* (both the *petite* and the *grande*) regarding wealth, poverty, civil rights, privilege, class solidarity, private loyalties, and national honor. They were also, like everybody else, to play games, when they could, with art prices. For surrealism, though originally a literary movement, had inherited from Dada the sculptor Arp and the painter Max Ernst and had acquired during the later twenties the painters Joan Miró and Yves Tanguy. Around 1930 Salvador Dalí, an obviously rising value, joined the group; and from then on the names of Pablo Picasso and Marcel Duchamp were also connected with many of their public statements.

The other side of the street, the neo-Romantic—as represented by Bérard, Tchelitcheff, and Leonid and Eugene Berman—was also enjoying prestige and some prosperity. And just as the surrealists for their themes sought out the irrational, the subversive, and the cruel, the subjects of the neo-Romantics were predominantly humane and tender, the feelings you have when you let your mind alone. They spoke, moreover, both to and for the *grande bourgeoisie*, and if their politics were conservative, in some cases even royalist, their avoidance of political action was as strict as that of their surrealist opponents. Their chief defenders also were poets—Jean Cocteau, Max Jacob, and Gertrude Stein. And though their collectors in France were on the whole quite well-to-do (Paris millionaire bohemia), in America their work was bought only by intellectuals, chiefly the friends of Russell Hitchcock, who had been their earliest announcer. Edith Sitwell, who had formed with Tchelitcheff (over portrait sittings) a friendship of iron, managed to make a certain success for him in England. In 1935 he left both France and England for America; in 1938 Eugene Berman moved to New York; during 1939 and '40 Leonid Berman was in the French army, passing the Occupation underground; by 1937 or '38 Bérard, the leader of them all, had wholly given up painting in oil for fashion drawing and stage design. And so their side of the street lost its last contact with the European picture market. Today, with Picasso and his contemporaries having inherited the customers from both sides, the modern-art market, in spite of a prosperous American younger school and a world-wide boom, has remained for basic investment a Modern Old Master market.

It is worthy of note, moreover, that both of the chief contemporary movements, neo-Romanticism and surrealism, were concerned almost exclusively with figurative painting. Abstraction was still a note in sculpture (and in sculpturesque painting, such as that of Tanguy); but the newer painting of the time was generally concentrated on images. In this sense, it was all of it romantic, though surrealism spoke more directly to the mind, neo-Romanticism to the sensibilities. It was only at the end of the decade, after the neo-Romantics (whom the French elegant world had begun to invest in, especially Bérard, who seemed possibly a new classical French painter) had either given up France or given up painting, that the French collectors, as the Americans had done already, settled for the abstract and the nonobjective. The subversive content of surrealism, they had learned in the early 1930s, was of no help to either social or business standing; and the grand return to painting nature and people that the neo-Romantics dreamed of bringing about had failed for lack of a personnel sufficiently tough to face, as artists, a lifetime of persecution from the collectors of pre-World-War-I modern art—in other words, from the Picasso marketeers. Hermetic art became therefore the only safe investment.

In the summer of 1930 I went to Spain again, this time with two painters, Maurice Grosser and the Catalonian Ramón Senabre. The three of us hired on the island of Mallorca a roomy flat in the fishing village of Puerto de Soller, from where we did a great deal of walking and mountain climbing. After a month of that, I moved to a hotel near Palma that had both rocks and a beach. From there I could go by tramcar to the bullfights, or shopping to order shirts and shoes, beautifully made and absurdly inexpensive. I also stayed a great deal in my room, writing music in bed under a mosquito net. Grosser eventually left Soller too, for Senabre's daily distress when the postman failed to bring the check owed to him by his Paris dealer had become too depressing to bear. So the two of us did more mountain climbing; and then he went off to Barcelona, where he took a dismal room near a noisy beach and beside the railway tracks. From this self-punishment I rescued him; and we made our way by third-class trains to Villefranche on the Côte d'Azur, where I wrote more music and he painted still life. I also went back to Ascain on the West coast for some rainy fall days with Madame Langlois.

In 1931 we went to Mallorca again, Grosser and I, both staying in my previous summer's hotel at Calamayor and going out from there on trips. Once we walked from one coast village to another clean round the island. Another time we motored with a young German couple, fraternizing in a wine cellar at Inca with farmers, who gave us all the wines of the island to taste but who would allow no paying. At Valdemosa, we saw Chopin's apartment in the monastery, which seemed to have been moved three times over the last century and to contain no furniture even vaguely authentic, except for an upright piano that might or might not have been the one sent out to him from Paris by Pleyel. Then again to Villefranche by September, relieved to be back in cheerful France. Spain is for me an intense experience always, even when the intensity is that of a deep dissatisfaction not unlike the irretrievable boredom that seems to be endemic among male Spaniards over thirty.

My monthly checks from Mrs. Lasell, which had been announced as stopping, did keep on arriving through 1930 and halfway through the next year. Also, at about that time the United States government essayed to relieve poverty by offering a bonus to the veterans of World War I. My length of service entitled me to $1,094, one half of this to be paid right off. So I decided that rather than merely live it up, I would spend it on a concert of my works. For program I had a String Quartet, the Max Jacob *Stabat Mater*, the Bossuet Funeral Oration (all brand-new), a Violin Sonata, an *Air de Phèdre* out of Racine (which had been given but not yet in a stylish hall), and a set of Inventions for piano that were five years old but that somehow had not yet been played. As locale I engaged for June 15, 1931, the Salle Chopin, recital hall of the new Maison Pleyel. And for performers I engaged the best—the Quatuor Krettly to play my String Quartet; a tenor from the opera, José de Trévi, for the Bossuet; a dramatic soprano from the Opéra-Comique, Madeleine Leymo, to sing the *Phèdre* aria and (with string quartet) the *Stabat*. The American pianist Gertrude Bonime played my Inventions. And an excellent French violinist, Yvonne Giraud (in private life Marquise de Casa Fuerte), who had been ten years absent from the concert stage, took this occasion for returning to it.

Sauguet's review of the concert in *L'Europe nouvelle* mentioned that my music had "singularities capable of disconcerting on first approach. Voluntarily [Thomson] uses a language of extreme purity that could easily be inexpressive, white, and savorless. But he uses it with such intelligence, such tact, and his musical sensitivity is so alert, that this surprising idiom actually gives depth." And far from being shocked, as others were, by my having subverted to musical purposes texts from French literary classics, he drew a parallel between my Bossuet and Racine settings and Erik Satie's of Plato.

This concert also won me the attention of the powerful editor Henri Prunières, who reviewed it both in his own magazine, *La Revue Musicale*, and in *The New York Times*. He complimented my "remarkable feeling for musical declamation," deplored my use of piano tremolo at the end of the Bossuet, opined that I was "destined for the opera." In the same article, reviewing two concerts of American music recently conducted in Paris by Nicolas Slonimsky, he paid honor to *Intégrales* by Edgard Varèse, estimating it as far superior to the works by Cowell, Ruggles, Riegger, Chávez, Weiss, Sanjuan, and Caturla. But he did grant that Charles Ives, composer of *Three Places in New England*, was "manifestly a musician."

There had been other concerts in 1931 involving my music. I still have the program of one given with Cliquet-Pleyel on January 10, in a series called "The Parthenon," where we played my *Synthetic Waltzes* duet, where Marthe-Marthine sang songs of

Gertrude Stein and the *Phèdre* aria, and where I gave a first performance, with Lucien Schwartz, of my Violin Sonata. To this concert came, looking for evidence, the new boy-genius Igor Markevitch. This Russian of barely twenty had been discovered some three years earlier, in 1928, by Diaghilev, then launched by Cocteau, taken up as a cause by Nadia Boulanger, blessed by Henri Prunières, patronized by the Princesse de Polignac, and endowed by the Vicomtesse de Noailles. He needed evidence regarding me because he seemed to be planning for us to become enemies. My not wholly adoring reactions to his music being already known to him (in the Paris of those days everything got to be known), he found my Violin Sonata a work he could easily dismiss as "just César Franck." My reply to this opening of hostilities was made two years later in *Modern Music*, where I remarked that, as with George Antheil, "the career is more interesting than the music." He never forgave me for that, and I am not sure that his career as a composer (he now conducts only) ever really recovered from the wide distribution my article received when reprinted in a New York Sunday paper. It was even believed to have influenced Koussevitzky to postpone playing the new young Russian. I had not meant to hit so hard. But in the 1930s no one pulled his punches. Indeed the whole decade was to be marked by such intensities, by violent loyalties and passionate betrayals, by idyllic loves and out-of-joint ones, by friendships indivisible and by threats relentless, by panoramas of poverty and shocking displays of wealth.

It may have been for feigning prosperity (or was it out of bravado) that the dressmaker Gabrielle Chanel in one of the decade's early years staged in her own sumptuous house, rue du faubourg Saint-Honoré, a show of diamonds. There must have been fifty pieces, all of modernistic design and all involving masses of gems. I remember a flat cigarette case made of square stones held together by almost invisible platinum lines. Another was a limp tiara to be worn in reverse, lying on the forehead like bangs.

Grandeurs like this and miseries walked side by side, as in Louis-Philippe days. And if my own existence illustrated neither, it was no example of rising fortune. At one time I ran clean out of money. Then I learned that my tradesmen would trust me for two and three months. So I began to eat in; and the credit of my butchers, bakers, grocers, and wine merchants, along with the cooking counsels of Madame Elise and my land-lord's tolerance of rent delays, made it possible for me to enjoy in my far-too-expensive quai Voltaire studio an unworried life of working and of having company. Actually, during the years of 1930, '31, and '32 I was happier in France than I had ever been anywhere, felt snugger there and calmer, working away at my music writing and cocooned by friendships, loves, and tasty cooking against the nervous anxieties of America, the de-spairs of England, the disasters that were surely on the march in Germany.

15

A Portrait of Gertrude Stein

GERTRUDE STEIN IN HER YOUNGER DAYS had liked to write all night and sleep all day. She also, it seems, ate copiously, drank wine, and smoked cigars. By the time I knew her, at fifty-two, she ate abstemiously; she neither drank nor smoked; and she was likely to wake, as people do in middle life, by nine. Her volume had been diminished too. Her appearance, nevertheless, on account of low stature (five feet, two), remained monumental, like that of some saint or sybil sculpted three-fourths life size. Her working powers also were intact, remained so, indeed, until her death at seventy-two.

Actually a whole domestic routine had been worked out for encouraging those powers to function daily. In the morning she would read, write letters, play with the dog, eventually bathe, dress, and have her lunch. In the afternoon she drove in the car, walked, window-shopped, spent a little money. She did nothing by arrangement till after four. At some point in her day she always wrote; and since she waited always for the moment when she would be full of readiness to write, what she wrote came out of fullness as an overflowing.

Year round, these routines varied little, except that in the country, if there were house guests, excursions by car might be a little longer, tea or lunch taken out instead of at home. When alone and not at work, Gertrude would walk, read, or meditate. She loved to walk; and she consumed books by the dozen, sent to her when away from home by the American Library in Paris. She read English and American history, memoirs, minor literature from the nineteenth century, and crime fiction, rarely modern art-writing, and never the commercial magazines. When people were around she would talk and listen, ask questions. She talked with anybody and everybody. When exchanging news and views with neighbors, concierges, policemen, shop people, garage men, hotel servants, she was thoroughly interested in them all. Gertrude not only liked people, she needed them. They were grist for her poetry, a relief from the solitudes of a mind essentially introspective.

Alice Toklas neither took life easy nor fraternized casually. She got up at six and cleaned the drawing room herself, because she did not wish things broken. (Porcelain and other fragile objects were her delight, just as pictures were Gertrude's; and she could imagine using violence toward a servant who might break one.) She liked being occupied, anyway, and did not need repose, ever content to serve Gertrude or be near her. She ran the house, ordered the meals, cooked on occasion, and typed out everything that got written into the blue copybooks that Gertrude had adopted from French school children. From 1927 or '28 she also worked petit point, matching in silk the colors and shades of designs made especially for her by Picasso. These tapestries were eventually applied to a pair of Louis XV small armchairs (*chauffeuses*) that Gertrude had bought for her. She was likely, any night, to go to bed by eleven, while Miss Stein would sit up late if there were someone to talk with.

Way back before World War I, in 1910 or so, in Granada Gertrude had experienced the delights of writing directly in the landscape. This does not mean just working out of doors; it means being surrounded by the thing one is writing about at the time one is writing about it. Later, in 1924, staying at Saint-Rémy in Provence, and sitting in fields beside the irrigation ditches, she found the same sound of running water as in Granada to soothe her while she wrote or while she simply sat, imbuing herself with the landscape's sight and sound. In the country around Belley, where she began to summer only a few years later, she wrote *Lucy Church Amiably* wholly to the sound of streams and waterfalls.

Bravig Imbs, an American poet and novelist who knew her in the late twenties, once came upon her doing this. The scene took place in a field, its enactors being Gertrude, Alice, and a cow. Alice, by means of a stick, would drive the cow around the field. Then, at a sign from Gertrude, the cow would be stopped; and Gertrude would write in her copybook. After a bit, she would pick up her folding stool and progress to another spot, whereupon Alice would again start the cow moving around the field till Gertrude signaled she was ready to write again. Though Alice now says that Gertrude drove the cow, she waiting in the car, the incident, whatever its choreography, reveals not only Gertrude's working intimacy with landscape but also the concentration of two friends on an act of composition by one of them that typifies and reveals their daily life for forty years. Alice had decided long before that "Gertrude was always right," that she was to have whatever she wanted when she wanted it, and that the way to keep herself always wanted was to keep Gertrude's writing always and forever unhindered, unopposed.

Gertrude's preoccupation with painting and painters was not shared by Alice except in so far as certain of Gertrude's painter friends touched her heart, and Picasso was almost the only one of these. Juan Gris was another, and Christian Bérard a very little bit. But Matisse I know she had not cared for, nor Braque. If it had not been for Gertrude, I doubt that Alice would ever have had much to do with the world of painting. She loved objects and furniture, practiced cooking and gardening, understood music. Of music, indeed, she had a long experience, having once, as a young girl, played a piano concerto in public. But painting was less absorbing to her than to Gertrude.

Gertrude's life with pictures seems to have begun as a preoccupation shared with her brothers, Michael and Leo. The sculptor Jacques Lipschitz once remarked to me the miraculous gift of perception by which these young Californians, in Paris of the 1900s, had gone straight to the cardinal values. Virtually without technical experience (since only Leo, among them, had painted at all) and without advice (for there were no modern-art scholars then), they bought Cézanne, Matisse, and Picasso. In quantity and, of course, for almost nothing. But also, according to Lipschitz, the Steins' taste was strongest when they bought together. Gertrude and Leo did this as long as they lived together, which was till about 1911. Michael, who had started quite early buying Matisses, kept that up till World War I. After Gertrude and Leo separated, she made fewer purchases and no major ones at all, save some Juan Gris canvases that represented a continuing commitment to Spanish cubism and to friendship. She could no longer buy Picasso or Cézanne after their prices got high, or after she owned a car. But throughout the twenties and thirties she was always looking for new painters, without being able to commit herself to any of them till she discovered about 1929 Sir Francis Rose. From him she quickly acquired nearly a hundred pictures, and she insisted till her death that he was a great painter. No other collector, no museum, no international dealer has yet gone so far.

Looking at painting had been for Gertrude Stein a nourishment throughout the late twenties and thirties of her own life. She never ceased to state her debt to Cézanne, for it was from constantly gazing on a portrait by him that she had found her way into and through the vast maze of motivations and proclivities that make up the patterns of people and types of people in *Three Lives* and in *The Making of Americans.* "The wonderful thing about Cézanne," she would say, "is that he was never tempted." Gertrude Stein's biographers have stated that Picasso also was a source for her and that in *Tender Buttons* she was endeavoring to reproduce with words the characteristic devices of cubist painting. There may even be in existence a quotation from Gertrude herself to this effect. But she certainly did not repeat it in the way she loved to repeat her allegiance to Cézanne. I myself have long doubted the validity, or at any rate the depth, of such a statement. An influence of poetry on painting is quite usual, a literary theme being illustrated by images. But any mechanism by which this procedure might be reversed and painting come to influence literature (beyond serving as subject for a review) is so rare a concept that the mere statement of Gertrude Stein's intent to receive such an influence surely requires fuller explanation. Let us try.

First of all, *Tender Buttons*, subtitled *Objects∴ Food∴ Rooms*, is an essay in description, of which the subjects are those commonly employed by painters of still life. And cubist painting too was concerned with still life. Cubism's characteristic device in representing still life was to eliminate the spatially fixed viewpoint, to see around corners, so to speak, to reduce its subject to essentials of form and profile and then to reassemble these as a summary or digest of its model. Resemblance was not forbidden; on the contrary, clues were offered to help the viewer recognize the image; and cubist painters (from the beginning, according to Gertrude) had been disdainful of viewers who could not "read" their canvases. (Today's "abstract" painters, on the other hand, maintain that in their work resemblances are purely accidental.)

According to Alice Toklas, the author's aim in *Tender Buttons* was "to describe something without mentioning it." Sometimes the name of the object is given in a title, sometimes not; but each description is full of clues, some of them easy to follow up, others put there for throwing you off the scent. All are legitimately there, however, since in Blake's words, "every-thing possible to be believed is an image of truth," and since in Gertrude Stein's method anything that comes to one in a moment of concentrated working is properly a part of the poem. Nevertheless, unveiling the concealed image is somewhat more difficult to a reader of *Tender Buttons* than to the viewer of a cubist still life. For a still life is static; nothing moves in it; time is arrested. In literature, on the other hand, one word comes after another and the whole runs forward. To have produced static pictures in spite of a non-fixed eye-point was cubism's triumph, just as giving the illusion of movement within a framed picture was the excitement of vorticism, as in Marcel Duchamp's "Nude Descending a Staircase." To have described objects, food, and rooms both statically and dynamically, with both a painter's eye and a poet's continuity, gives to *Tender Buttons* its particular brilliance, its way of both standing still and moving forward.

Now the carrier of that motion, make no mistake, is a rolling eloquence in no way connected with cubism. This eloquence, in fact, both carries forward the description and defeats it, just as in cubist painting description was eventually defeated by the freedom of the painter (with perspective making no demands) merely to create a composition. Cubism was always, therefore, in danger of going decorative (hence flat); and the kind of writing I describe here could just as easily turn into mere wit and oratory. That cubism was something of an impasse its short life, from 1909 to 1915, would seem to indicate; and there were never more than two possible exits from it. One was complete concealment of the image, hence in effect its elimination; the other was retreat into naturalism. Both paths have been followed in our time, though not by Picasso, who has avoided abstraction as just another trap leading to the decorative, and who could never bring himself, for mere depiction, to renounce the ironic attitudes involved in voluntary stylization.

Gertrude, faced with two similar paths, chose both. During the years between 1927 and '31, she entered into an involvement with naturalism that produced at the end of her life *Yes Is for a Very Young Man*, *Brewsie and Willie*, and *The Mother of Us All*, each completely clear and in no way mannered. She was also during those same years pushing abstraction farther than it had ever gone before, not only in certain short pieces still completely hermetic (even to Alice Toklas), but in extended studies of both writing and feeling in which virtually everything remains obscure but the mood, works such as *As a Wife Has a Cow, a Love Story*, *Patriarchal Poetry*, and *Stanzas in Meditation*.

Her last operas and plays are in the humane tradition of letters, while her monumental abstractions of the late 1920s and early 1930s are so intensely aware of both structure and emotion that they may well be the origin of a kind of painting that came later to be known as "abstract expressionism." If this be true, then Gertrude Stein, after borrowing from cubism a painting premise, that of the non-fixed viewpoint, returned that premise to its origins, transformed. Whether the transformation could have been operated within painting itself, without the help of a literary example, we shall never know, because the literary example was there. We do know, however, that no single painter either led that transformation or followed it through as a completed progress in his own work.

Gertrude had been worried about painting ever since cubism had ceased to evolve. She did not trust abstraction in art, which she found constricted between flat color schemes and pornography. Surrealism, for her taste, was too arbitrary as to theme and too poor as painting. And she could not give her faith to the neo-Romantics either, though she found Bérard "alive" and "the best" of them. She actually decided in 1928 that "painting [had] become a minor art again," meaning without nourishment for her. Then within the year, she had found Francis Rose. What nourishment she got from him I cannot dream; nor did she ever speak of him save as a gifted one destined to lead his art—an English leader this time, instead of Spanish.

In her own work, during these late twenties, while still developing ideas received from Picasso, she was also moving into new fields opened by her friendship with me. I do not wish to pretend that her ventures into romantic feeling, into naturalism, autobiography, and the opera came wholly through me, though her discovery of the opera as a poetic form certainly did. Georges Hugnet, whom I had brought to her, was at least equally a stimulation, as proved by her "translation" of one of his extended works. She had not previously accepted, since youth, the influence of any professional writer. Her early admiration for Henry James and Mark Twain had long since become a reflex. She still remembered Shakespeare of the sonnets, as *Stanzas in Meditation* will show; and she considered Richardson's *Clarissa Harlowe* (along with *The Making of Americans*) to be "the other great novel in English." But for "movements" and their organizers in contemporary poetry she had the greatest disdain—for Pound, Eliot, Yeats, and their volunteer militiamen. She admitted Joyce to be "a good writer," disclaimed any influence on her from his work, and believed, with some evidence, that she had influenced him.

She knew that in the cases of Sherwood Anderson and Ernest Hemingway her influence had gone to them, not theirs to her. I do not know the real cause of her break with Hemingway, only that after a friendship of several years she did not see him any more and declared forever after that he was "yellow." Anderson remained a friend always, though I do not think she ever took him seriously as a writer. The poet Hart Crane she did take seriously. And there were French young men, René Crevel, for one, whom she felt tender about and whom Alice adored. Cocteau amused her as a wit and as a dandy, less so as an organizer of epochs, a role she had come to hold in little respect from having known in prewar times Guillaume Apollinaire, whom she esteemed low as a poet, even lower as a profiteer of cubism. Pierre de Massot she respected as a prose master; but he was too French, too violent, to touch her deeply. Gide and Jouhandeau, making fiction out of sex, she found as banal as any titillater of chambermaids. Max Jacob she had disliked personally from the time of his early friendship with Picasso. I never heard her express any opinion of him as a writer, though Alice says now that she admired him.

In middle life she had come at last to feel about her own work that it "could be compared to the great poetry of the past." And if she was nearly alone during her lifetime in holding this view (along with Alice Toklas, myself, and perhaps a very few more), she was equally alone in having almost no visible poetic parents or progeny. Her writing seemed to come from nowhere and to influence, at that time, none but reporters and novelists. She herself, considering the painter Cézanne her chief master, believed that under his silent tutelage a major message had jumped like an electric arc from painting to poetry. And she also suspected that its high tension was in process of short-circuiting again, from her through me, this time to music. I do not offer this theory as my own, merely as a thought thrown out by Gertrude Stein to justify, perhaps, by one more case the passing of an artistic truth or method. which she felt strongly to have occurred for her, across one of those distances that lie between sight, sound, and words.

There was nevertheless, in Alice Toklas, literary influence from a nonprofessional source. As early as 1910, in a narrative called *Ada*, later published in *Geography and Plays*, a piece which recounts Miss Toklas's early life, Gertrude imitated Alice's way of telling a story. This sentence is typical: "He had a pleasant life while he was living and after he was dead his wife and children remembered him." Condensation in this degree was not Gertrude's way; expansion through repetition (what she called her "garrulity") was more natural to her. But she could always work from an auditory model, later in *Brewsie and Willie* transcribing almost literally the usage and syntax of World War II American soldiers. And having mastered a new manner by imitating Alice Toklas in *Ada*, she next mixed it with her repetitive manner in a story called *Miss Furr and Miss Skeen*. Then she set aside the new narrative style for nearly thirty years.

In 1933 she took it up again for writing *The Autobiography of Alice B. Toklas*, which is the story of her own life told in Miss Toklas's words. This book is in every way except actual authorship Alice Toklas's book; it reflects her mind, her language, her private view of Gertrude, also her unique narrative powers. Every story in it is told as Alice herself had always told it. And when in 1961 Miss Toklas herself wrote *What Is Remembered*, she told her stories with an even greater brevity. There is nothing comparable to this compactness elsewhere in English, nor to my knowledge in any other literature, save possibly in Julius Caesar's *De Bello Gallico*. Gertrude imitated it three times with striking success. She could not use it often, because its way was not hers.

Her own way with narrative was ever elliptical, going into slow orbit around her theme. Alice's memory and interests were visual; she could recall forever the exact costumes people had worn, where they had stood or sat, the décor of a room, the choreography of an occasion. Gertrude's memory was more for the sound of a voice, for accent, grammar, and vocabulary.

And even these tended to grow vague in one day, because her sustained curiosity about what had happened lay largely in the possibilities of any incident for revealing character.

How often have I heard her begin some tale, a recent one or a far-away one, and then as she went on with it get first repetitive and then uncertain till Alice would look up over the tapestry frame and say, "I'm sorry, Lovey; it wasn't like that at all." "All right, Pussy," Gertrude would say. "You tell it." Every story that ever came into the house eventually got told in Alice's way, and this was its definitive version. The accounts of life in the country between 1942 and 1945 that make up *Wars I Have Seen* seem to me, on the other hand, Gertrude's own; I find little of Alice in them. Then how are they so vivid? Simply from the fact, or at least so I imagine, that she would write in the evening about what she had seen that day, describe events while their memory was still fresh.

Gertrude's artistic output has the quality, rare in our century, of continuous growth. Picasso had evolved rapidly through one discovery after another until the cubist time was over. At that point, in 1915, he was only thirty-three and with a long life to be got through. He has got through it on sheer professionalism—by inventing tricks and using them up (tricks mostly recalling the history of art or evoking historic Spanish art), by watching the market very carefully (collecting his own pictures), and by keeping himself advised about trends in literary content and current-events content. But his major painting was all done early. Igor Stravinsky followed a similar pattern. After giving to the world between 1909 and 1913 three proofs of colossally expanding power—*The Firebird*, *Petrouchka*, and *The Rite of Spring*—he found himself at thirty-one unable to expand farther. And since, like Picasso, he was still to go on living, and since he could not imagine living without making music, he too was faced with an unhappy choice. He could either make music out of his own past (which he disdained to do) or out of music's past (which he is still doing). For both men, when expansion ceased, working methods became their subject.

One could follow this design through many careers in music, painting, and poetry. Pound, I think, continued to develop; Eliot, I should say, did not. Arnold Schoenberg was in constant evolution; his chief pupils, Alban Berg and Anton Webern, were more static. The last two were saved by early death from possible decline of inspiration, just as James Joyce's approaching blindness concentrated and extended his high period for twenty years, till he had finished two major works, *Ulysses* and *Finnegans Wake*. He died fulfilled, exhausted, but lucky in the sense that constant growth had not been expected of him. Indeed, for all that the second of these two works is more complex than the first, both in concept and in language, it does not represent a growth in anything but mastery. Joyce was a virtuoso type, like Picasso, of whom Max Jacob, Picasso's friend from earliest youth, had said, "Always he escapes by acrobatics." And virtuosos do not grow; they merely become more skillful. At least they do not grow like vital organisms, but rather, like crystals, reproduce their characteristic forms.

Gertrude Stein's maturation was more like that of Arnold Schoenberg. She ripened steadily, advanced slowly from each stage to the next. She had started late, after college and medical school. From *Three Lives*, begun in 1904 at thirty, through *The Making of Americans*, finished in 1911, her preoccupation is character analysis. From *Tender Buttons* (1912) to *Patriarchal Poetry* (1927) a quite different kind of writing is presented (not, of course, without having been prefigured). This is hermetic to the last degree, progressing within its fifteen-year duration from picture-words and rolling rhetoric to syntactical complexity and neutral words. From 1927 to 1934 two things go on at once. There are long hermetic works (*Four Saints, Lucy Church Amiably*, and *Stanzas in Meditation*) but also straightforward ones like *The Autobiography of Alice B. Toklas* and the lectures on writing. After her return in 1935 from the American lecture tour, hermetic writing gradually withers and the sound of spoken English becomes her theme, giving in *Yes Is for a Very Young Man*, in *The Mother of Us All*, and in *Brewsie and Willie* vernacular portraits of remarkable veracity.

Her development had not been aided or arrested by public success, of which there had in fact been very little. The publication of *Three Lives* in 1909 she had subsidized herself, as she did in 1922 that of the miscellany *Geography and Plays*. *The Making of Americans*, published by McAlmon's Contact Editions in 1925, was her first book-size book to be issued without her paying for it; and she was over fifty. She had her first bookstore success at fifty-nine with the *Autobiography*. When she died in 1946, at seventy-two, she had been working till only a few months before without any diminution of power. Her study of technical problems never ceased; never had she felt obliged to fabricate an inspiration; and she never lost her ability to speak from the heart.

Gertrude lived by the heart, indeed; and domesticity was her theme. Not for her the matings and rematings that went on among the amazons. An early story from 1903, published after her death, *Things as They Are*, told of one such intrigue in post-Radcliffe days. But after 1907 her love life was serene, and it was Alice Toklas who made it so. Indeed, it was this tranquil life that offered to Gertrude a fertile soil of sentiment-security in which other friendships great and small could come to flower, wither away, be watered, cut off, or preserved in a book. Her life was like that of a child, to whom danger can come only from the outside, never from home, and whose sole urgency is growth. It was also that of an adult who demanded all the rights of a man along with the privileges of a woman.

Just as Gertrude kept up friendships among the amazons, though she did not share their lives, she held certain Jews in attachment for their family-like warmth, though she felt no solidarity with Jewry. Tristan Tzara—French-language poet from Romania, Dada pioneer, early surrealist, and battler for the Communist party—she said was "like a cousin." Miss Etta and Dr. Claribel Cone, picture buyers and friends from Baltimore days, she handled almost as if they were her sisters. The sculptors Jo Davidson and Jacques Lipschitz, the painter Man Ray she accepted as though they had a second cousin's right to be part of her life. About men or goyim, even about her oldest man friend, Picasso, she could feel unsure; but a woman or a Jew she could size up quickly. She accepted without cavil, indeed, all the conditionings of her Jewish background. And if, as she would boast, she was "a bad Jew," she at least did not think of herself as Christian. Of heaven and salvation and all that she would say, "When a Jew dies he's dead." We used to talk a great deal, in fact, about our very different religious conditionings, the subject having come up through my remarking the frequency with which my Jewish friends would break with certain of theirs and then never make up. Gertrude's life had contained many people that she still spoke of (Mabel Dodge, for instance) but from whom she refused all communication. The Stettheimers' conversation was also full of references to people they had known well but did not wish to know any more. And I began to imagine this definitiveness about separations as possibly a Jewish trait. I was especially struck by Gertrude's rupture with her brother Leo, with whom she had lived for many years in intellectual and no doubt affectionate communion, but to whom she never spoke again after they had divided their pictures and furniture, taken up separate domiciles.

The explanation I offered for such independent behavior was that the Jewish religion, though it sets aside a day for private Atonement, offers no mechanics for forgiveness save for offenses against one's own patriarch, and even he is not obliged to pardon. When a Christian, on the other hand, knows he has done wrong to anyone, he is obliged in all honesty to attempt restitution; and the person he has wronged must thereupon forgive. So that if Jews seem readier to quarrel than to make up, that fact seems possibly to be the result of their having no confession-and-forgiveness formula, whereas Christians, who experience none of the embarrassment that Jews find in admitting misdeeds, arrange their lives, in consequence, with greater flexibility, though possibly, to a non-Christian view, with less dignity.

Gertrude liked this explanation, and for nearly twenty years it remained our convention. It was not till after her death that Alice said one day,

> You and Gertrude had it settled between you as to why Jews don't make up their quarrels, and I went along with you. But now I've found a better reason for it. Gertrude was right, of course, to believe that "when a Jew dies he's dead." And that's exactly why Jews don't need to make up. When we've had enough of someone we can get rid of him. You Christians can't, because you've got to spend eternity together.

16

Gertrude and the Young French Poet

NEITHER GERTRUDE NOR I had ever wished to quarrel. Our way was to back off when trouble threatened. For after all we were a sort of team, needing to face the French with a calm front and not be led on to explode at them, for in that case they could win by talking faster. Our partnership involved, moreover, business affairs such as translations, publications, and musical performances. Also, we liked sharing pleasant feelings, our memories of World War I, of Harvard, and of the West. We shared friends too, and that helps to avoid quarreling. She had brought me Carl Van Vechten, Jo Davidson, Natalie Barney, and the Duchesse de Clermont-Tonnerre, more casually the sculptor Janet Scudder and the Sitwells, and ever so practically Mrs. Emily Crane Chadbourne. To her I had brought for inspection Madame Langlois, Mary Butts, Maurice Grosser, Russell Hitchcock, and Pierre de Massot, all of whom she accepted, and two more whom she had adopted with all her heart, the poet Georges Hugnet and the historian Bernard Faÿ. The painter Pavel Tchelitcheff we held no common front about, since my friendship with him was only beginning, while hers was drawing toward its end.

It was in fact over Pavlik, as we called him, that our first unpleasantness occurred. Dropping in one evening in October of '27, I had found Gertrude in a teasing mood; she had that day aborted a cold and was trying to get her mind off her symptoms. "We were just saying," she began, "that you were like the little girl who had a little curl right in the middle of her forehead." Now my proclivity for being either very very good or quite quite horrid was a trait of character long since known, and the quip was all the more apt since my hairline had begun to imitate Napoleon's forelock. Nor was the personal remark in any way offensive, though I should have been warned by it to mind my manners, since Gertrude, who rarely opened with an attack, was surely looking for trouble.

Trouble came with the arrival, also just calling, of Pavlik and Choura, his sister, a well-mannered young woman unquestionably a lady. As the conversation rose and languished, Pavlik seemed consistently reserved toward me, which was not his way unless something was wrong. Thinking to eradicate misunderstanding, should it lie in the only direction I could imagine, I mentioned an American young woman, a singer, who had asked me to coach her through Satie's *Socrate* and then never returned for her appointent. I mentioned her because a member of his household was her regular accompanist; but at her name Pavlik's long face froze, and I realized that his household suspected me of trying to win away a paying customer. This was not true, but I could not argue the matter; I could only, when Pavlik denied knowledge of the incident, drop the subject.

But Gertrude would not let it be dropped. She began to ask irrelevantly and repetitively, "Where did you meet her? How did you come to know her?" Pestered, confused, embarrassed by the whole scene, and feeling set upon, I blurted out, "Through her having slept with one of my friends."

In the silence that followed, Alice observed gently, "One doesn't say that." Whereupon I murmured regret and was allowed to remain quiet. Pavlik and Choura stayed just long enough to make with our hostesses several remarks on several subjects. As they took leave, Choura wished me good-night graciously; but Pavlik, to make clear I had offended, said icily, unsmiling, and without handshake, "*Bon soir, monsieur.*"

As soon as they were gone, both ladies wanted to know details, I furnished them; and they furnished, in return, facts about the financial situation at Pavlik's house which could have made my seeming intrusion, no matter how purely musical, a cause for alarm. We also noted the impropriety of my using before his sister so crude a verb as *coucher avec*. And Gertrude remarked that though I had a perfect right to quarrel with Pavlik, I should not have used her house for doing so.

I was in Coventry for exactly a week. Then I sent her yellow roses, for which she had a liking, with a note that read: "Dear Gertrude/love/Virgil." She replied, "My dear Virgil, thanks for the very beautiful flowers, we may look upon them as a pleasure and a necessity." And that same day, when I met the two ladies on the rue des Saints-Pères, and Gertrude said something about seeing me sometime, Alice added specifically, "Come soon," and nodded as if in complicity.

But though my quarrel was over, Pavlik's had just begun, for from that time he came gradually to be removed from

Gertrude's circle. Bravig Imbs thought Alice responsible for the
severance, that she had already become unfriendly somewhat
earlier, on his having painted a portrait of her that she found
disobliging, and that she had been biding her time till Gertrude,
becoming one day impatient with him, could be maneuvered
into a break. Others—Georges Maratier, for instance—believed
that Alice, as an *éminence grise*, was prone to hasten the excommunication of those she had no taste for (or whose wives bored
her). Myself, I never saw her act toward anyone with open
malice, but she did not conceal her satisfaction at Tchelitcheff's
being no longer received. Gertrude at the same time let me
know by inference that she found it intolerable of Pavlik to
have first suspected me of an intrigue against him and then to
have initiated one against me by asking her, in effect, to choose
between us. And though she did not exactly offer me his head,
it came off in the spring of '28.

Bravig Imbs was to lose his three years later. He had been
devoted for half a decade, serviceable as an extra young man,
good at errands, and pleasing in the home. In the summer of
'28, visiting in Latvia, he had made off with his young host's
fiancée and wired Gertrude, as his mentor, for permission to
marry her. And Gertrude had wired back, says Alice, "Bravig,
you can't do that." He did, however; and Valeska turned out to
be a Russo-Baltic countess in her own right, economical, a good
cook, and far from ugly. When she became pregnant early in '31,
Bravig had to arrange carefully for the coming months, as he
had for source of income only his job at an advertising agency.
And it was natural for him, as a close friend, to announce his
plans to Gertrude. His downfall came from doing this in front
of Valeska.

The plan was for his wife to move in early summer to a country boardinghouse some twenty kilometers from Belley, where
Bravig had often spent vacations himself, and for him to join
her there for two weeks in late summer, just before the baby
was to be born. He did not know that Gertrude, who had in
medical school walked out on obstetrics, had an intense distaste
for the procedures of childbirth. With the prospect of having
a pregnant woman on her hands all summer, for she could not
forego some obligation to Bravig, she went all nervous about
it but could not say no in front of Valeska. It was Alice who

resolved the emergency next day by announcing to Bravig that the friendship was terminated. Their newly installed telephone was the instrument of this one-way communication as she told him at his office, "Gertrude asks me to say that she considers you to have been of a colossal impertinence and that she does not wish to see either of you again." And she did not see Valeska again, as Bravig removed his family to New York in the middle thirties. When he came back with the armies of liberation in 1944, Gertrude's arms and house were open to him, though unfortunately not for long. He became briefly, as "Monsieur Bobby," France's most beloved radio news-announcer. Then he felt that a successful man should learn to drive. Going South in a jeep, he skidded on a rainy curve and died against a tree. My concierge wept as she told me the tragic story. Gertrude, when she heard it, went immediately to his place of residence, which was Francis Rose's flat on the Ile Saint-Louis, taking with her a hardware man and having the locks changed, to discourage theft not only of Bravig's property but also of Sir Francis's.

Georges Hugnet's quarrel with Gertrude came in the fall of 1930 over a matter of publication. His own Editions de la Montagne had already put out two books by her—*Dix Portraits*, in English and French, and *Morceaux Choisis de "La Fabrication des Americains*," in French, with a preface by Pierre de Massot and a portrait by Bérard. She had written me in America the year before, "The french I think are going to like me in translation all thanks to you." For indeed the whole matter of translating her had been initiated through me and mostly done by me, first with Madame Langlois and then with Hugnet. Selections from *The Making of Americans* had been begun by Hugnet with me and finished with Gertrude. They also translated together *Composition as Explanation*. Several years later there was published a longer French edition of *The Making*, translated by Bernard Faÿ and the Baronne Sellière; and Gertrude's autobiographical works, her lectures, and her early stories have been rendered into many languages. I do not know of the more hermetic works appearing in translation anywhere, except for those made with my help into French.

Though she read and spoke French comfortably, Gertrude did not aspire to write in it, beyond the necessities of social correspondence. And she had never used her literary powers for translating works that she admired. For Georges Hugnet, however, who had possibilities, after *La Perle*, for making another film, she wrote a scenario in French that tells how she acquired a poodle. The title of this, *Deux Soeurs qui sont pas soeurs*, contains a grammatical error of which she was perfectly aware but which she declined to correct, as I remember, when her text was published in *La Revue européene*, though it did get changed for *Operas and Plays*. Her other concession to French was to make, in the summer of 1930, a rendering into Stein English of Hugnet's suite of poems entitled *Enfances*. This work was the cause of a quarrel with Hugnet, Alice intervening firmly lest it end. Also of one with me. And since the young Frenchman's poetry had set off Gertrude Stein's in a new direction, it is no wonder that she went all emotional about him.

Hugnet wrote me on learning of the translation, "Really I have friends too strong for me." When Gertrude sent it to him, he had replied from Brittany that it was "more than a translation." To me she wrote of it as her "version" or her "thing," again as "a mirroring of it rather than anything else[,] a reflection of each little poem. . . . I would read each poem and then immediately make its reflection." And as she went on with the paraphrase, she too was overwhelmed by it, needed praise of it from others, which Bernard Faÿ furnished her, along with praise for Hugnet's work.

She wrote:

> My very dear George[s]
>
> *La traduction qui est plutôt reflet, c'set un vrai reflet et de moment à l'autre je suis là-dedans tellement contente de vous et de moi, et quelque fois j'ai un peu peur mais quand même je suis contente de vous et de moi. C'etait pour moi une experience riche et intriguante et les resultat[s] enfin il y a un resultat et nous sommes je suis sûr vraiment pas mecontente de vous et de moi. Mon cher George[s] toute mon amitié et mon confiance et plaisir en vous est toute là-dedans.*

> (The translation is more like a reflection, a true reflection and from each moment to the next I am so pleased with you and with me, and sometimes I am a little afraid but all the same I am pleased with you and with myself. It was for me a rich and fascinating experience and the results after all there is a result and

we are I am sure truly not displeased with you and with me. My dear George all my friendship and my confidence and pleasure in you are all in it.)

Her excitement came from having opened up a new vein of poetry. For in her need to catch an English lilt comparable to that of Hugnet's in French, she had caught the cool temperature and running-water sound of her beloved Shakespeare Sonnets, even to the presence of pentameters, rhymes, and iambs. As a testimonial of involvement with another poet, another language, these versions are unique in Gertrude Stein's work. Three samples will suffice, the first not far from literal.

I

Enfances, aux cent coins de ma mémoire
si ma mémoire est l'oeuvre de la passion,
enfances décimées par les nuits
si les nuits ne sont qu'une maladie du sommeil,
je vous poursuis avant de dormir, sans hâte.
Sans hâte, mais plié sous des tâches ingrates,
tête nue et transpirant de fièvre,
je vous mesure au trajet de la vie
et vos insoumissions, enfances, sont muettes,
enfances si l'enfance est ce silence
où gravement déjà s'installe la mort
et si ma main n'a pas retrouvé sa solitude,
et c'est avouer que je vous laisse libres
hors de mon destin que d'autres voulurent court,
à vos robes d'indienne, à vos plaisirs sanguins.

I

In the one hundred small places of myself my youth,
And myself in if it is the use of passion,
In this in it and in the nights alone
If in the next to night which is indeed not well
I follow you without it having slept and went.
Without the pressure of a place with which to come unfolded
    folds are a pressure and an abusive stain
A head if uncovered can be as hot, as heated,

to please to take a distance to make life,
and if resisting, little, they have no thought,
a little one which was a little which was as all as still,
Or with or without fear or with it all,
And if in feeling all it will be placed alone beside
and it is with with which and not beside not beside may,
Outside with much which is without with me, and not an
    Indian shawl, which could it be but with my blood.

By poem 14 the versions are farther apart.

14

Que me disent amour et ses tourelles?
J'ai perdu la plus belle en ouvrant la main,
en changeant de pas j'ai trompé la silencieuse,
rira l'éternelle en tuant la plus belle,
la morte a su garder son domaine,
en refermant les bras j'ai tué l'éternelle,
l'enfance a renié, renié la souveraine
et c'est ainsi que vont les semaines.

14

It could be seen very nicely
That doves have each a heart.
Each one is always seeing that they could not be apart,
A little lake makes fountains
And fountains have no flow,
And a dove has need of flying
And water can be low,
Let me go.
Any week is what they seek
When they have to halve a beak.
I like a painting on a wall of doves
And what they do.
They have hearts
They are apart
Little doves are winsome
But not when they are little and left.

As the finale approaches they get together again.

26

Embarquons, partons aux Indes,
vanille, vanille,
toutes les nourritures se valent.
Marie, trio de neige,
Eugénie, Irène, l'ordre
a changé son courant d'amour,
l'ordre des mots dans ta bouche,
enfance réveillée par mes désordres.
Sous la pluie sérieuse
quand tournait le vent,
quand remontait le vent
du phare au rocher de la Jument,
en cachant ta tête
tu prenais ce vent
pour ma pensée et sans mal
tu tendais ton bras
vers la croisée où mon absence
a mis le silence au rang de la lumière,
ton absence dans ma solitude,
ce don que la lumière avait fait à ma mémoire.

26

Little by little two go if two go three go if three go four go if four go they go. It is known as does he go he goes if they go they go and they know they know best and most of whether he will go. He is to go. They will not have vanilla and say so. To go Jenny go, Ivy go Gaby go any come and go is go and come and go and leave to go. Who has to hold it while they go who has to who has had it held and have them come to go. He went and came and had to go. No one has had to say he had to go come here to go go there to go go go to come to come to go to go and come and go.

Stanzas in Meditation, begun at this time, take off from the poems written on *Enfances*, preserving their Shakespearian lilt along with Hugnet's suite-of-poems form and his frankness of introspection. Its last number, completed in 1935, reads:

Stanza LXXXIII

Why am I if I am uncertain reasons may inclose.
Remain remain propose repose chose.
I call carelessly that the door is open
Which if they can refuse to open
No one can rush to close.
Let them be mine therefor.
Everybody knows that I chose.
Therefor if therefor before I close.
I will therefor offer therefor I offer this.
Which if I refuse to miss can be miss is mine.
I will be well welcome when I come.
Because I am coming.
Certainly I come having come.

These stanzas are done.

The "two *Enfances*," as Gertrude had begun to call them, were submitted to *Pagany*, which accepted them for publication on facing pages. Hugnet also arranged for their Paris issue as a book to be illustrated by Picasso, Tchelitcheff, Marcoussis, and Kristians Tonny. This was in the fall of 1930. Now let me go back to the spring.

Gertrude had stayed in Paris till the end of April, signed the sheets with Hugnet and myself for the special-paper edition of *Ten Portraits*, then gone off to Bilignin, already late for garden planting. She had also published that spring, at her own expense, her novel *Lucy Church Amiably*, a neo-Romantic landscape piece. In the country she made her English version of *Enfances*, spent much of the summer having company— Bernard Faÿ, the Picassos, Carl Van Vechten.

I spent June and July in Majorca, wrote there the last three movements of my Violin Sonata, the *Phèdre* aria, and a piece in five short movements which I called Sonata No. 3, "for Gertrude Stein to improvise at the pianoforte." She enjoyed the piano she had found in the house at Bilignin, used for her improvising only the white keys. My Sonata was therefore composed for only those.

In late August I spent ten days at Bilignin, and it was near there (waiting in Aix-les-Bains while the ladies did an errand) that I set Gertrude's French film scenario to music, adding to its narrative vocal line a pianoforte accompaniment that is a portrait of the dog Basket (her first of the name), a character in the film. In September I returned briefly to Villefranche, wrote more music, then paid a visit to Madame Langlois in the Basque country, returning to Paris in late September.

All this moving around cost little, as I traveled third-class and either visited friends or stayed in modest lodgings. Also my allowance, which had been announced to end in May, was being inexplicably extended for a few more months. Gertrude, sympathetic as always about my money troubles, wrote,

> Emily C[hadbourne] has opened communications again, via Ellen [La Motte] I said back that I was peeved and thought she had been millionairish the message will probably not be transmitted so there we are, I am happy that supplies have recommenced, I was that sad about it that it was disturbing, I was about to suffer as much as you although as the small boy remarked to an admonishing father not in the same place.

She spent a large part of that fall on my affairs, plotting by mail with Carl Van Vechten about how to attract for our *Four Saints* the attention of Mary Garden and definitely arranging with Hugnet, who came to Bilignin in September, a project for publishing a volume of my music.

His Editions de la Montagne, which were breaking even, had already got into print a half-dozen works of rare prose and modernistic poetry. A musical volume, though more costly to issue, might well recuperate its costs if capital could be found for guaranteeing them. This Gertrude offered to advance in part, and Georges Hugnet's father accepted to furnish 5,000 francs ($200). Gertrude's offer, even more generous, was to provide the remaining needed sums for a project which might run, all told, as high as $800. The book was to be printed by inexpensive methods on very good paper and with illustrations by advanced artists, just as Georges's other books had been issued. And it was to contain vocal works only, since these were the field of my budding reputation and also since the distribution of vocal music could be more easily envisaged under the imprint of a literary publisher than could that of an instrumental volume.

Four Saints in Three Acts was thought of for inclusion but rejected on account of its length. And Carl Van Vechten was proposed for writing a preface, since he enjoyed credit in America as a critic of music. But when he wrote from New York that he might find a publisher there for the opera, we decided to use him for prefacing that, should publication occur, and to combine a selection of other poetico-vocal works with an essay by myself on words and music. A further decision had to be made about including English texts, and the final advisability seemed to be that one language only, French, would be more suitable for selling the book in Paris.

The first plan—a hundred pages that would include *Capital Capitals* (Stein), *La Valse grégorienne* (Hugnet), *Five Phrases from the Song of Solomon*, and the Bossuet *Funeral Oration*—proved cumbersome in every way. So I wrote to Gertrude that

> I had imagined Trois Tableaux de Paris: *La Seine* (Duchesse de Rohan), *Le Berceau de Gertrude Stein* (Hugnet), and *Film* (Stein). But Georges objects to appearing between two ladies and really feels very deeply [opposed] anyway on subject of [the] D[u]chesse de Rohan. And he prefers Racine but that makes a funny mixture and so we settled for the present on four pieces: Fable de La Fontaine (*Le Singe et le léopard*), *Phèdre* of Racine, *Valse grégorienne* of Georges, and *Film* (Stein).

Gertrude replied to this,

> I am being quite thoughtful you see I want this book to do for you something like *Geography and Plays* did for me, make something definite and representative . . . and now this is a feasible idea . . . *Capitals*, Bossuet, and *Gregorian Waltzes* of Georges, that is all on the same more or less idea, and represents three distinct periods and would be saleable, and would show you at your heights, think this over very carefully you see I want you shown at your best and want you saleable to those who are your natural audience, and so far this is the only combination that seems to me to have raison d'être, I don't mind being with two gentlemen, it may of course be too long, that is another matter anyway think about it . . . lots of love my dear, yours, Gtrde.

She kept holding out for *Capital Capitals*, not wishing to be represented by only a French text. But Georges kept insisting that we should not use any English. So that by the time Gertrude came back to Paris in late November I was not certain, in spite of all her sweet-seeming reasonableness, that she would go through with the project.

Georges, moreover, was being difficult. He had had too much success that year. His Editions de la Montagne were gloriously distinguished; in the spring he had won a prize of 20,000 francs ($800) for a short story; he had been put into English by Gertrude Stein and was to be published beside her in both America and France; now he was about to appear with both her and me in a musical volume subsidized largely by her; and besides all that, he had just entered into housekeeping arrangements with a young woman who made him feel continuously successful and happy. Perhaps it was for showing off to her that he began pushing us around. Anyway, before Gertrude was to have her big quarrel with him, I had a small one.

This had to do with a book by Pierre de Massot, *Prolégomènes á une éthique sans métaphysique ou Billy, bull-dog et philosophe.* I had usually subscribed to Georges's publications, and occasionally he had given me an extra copy, copiously inscribed. In the case of Massot—a writer of fine classical reflexes and a friend from earlier days who had fallen into bad times and worse health—I had brought him back into circulation and had even got out of him a much-appreciated preface to *The Making of Americans.* When I did not subscribe for his book, Georges knew I expected one; and when he did not offer one, I angrily demanded one and got it. On December 6 I wrote Gertrude. "I'm afraid I have *a cœur sensible* after all. I thought I had won the little incident with Georges about Pierre's book and was proud of myself but I came home and went to bed of a grippe and so I guess I didn't after all."

Gertrude wrote back,

Sorry about the grippe but look here I am not awfully anxious to mix in but you must not be too schoolgirlish about Georges and also after all he is putting down his 5,000 francs of his father's credit for your book and hell it is a gamble and he could do things with it that would be surer and after all he is doing it and after all nobody else is, its alright but nobody else is so remember the Maine and even if there is a minority report you must not overlook this thing, and besides why the hell should not Pierre give you the book as well as Georges but anyway that is another matter, this is only to cure the grippe, anyway I love you all very

much but I always do a little fail to see that anyone is such a lot
nobler than anyone else we are all reasonably noble and very
sweet love to you . . . Gtrde.

In a very few days, however, she was thoroughly upset herself. The arrangements for publishing in book form the two
Enfances had been left to Georges, so that Gertrude did not see
the subscription blank till it was printed, It read:

GEORGES HUGNET

ENFANCES

SUIVI PAR LA TRADUCTION DE

GERTRUDE STEIN

And in another place it referred to "*Enfances*, by Georges
Hugnet."

Gertrude viewed this layout as disloyal, with her name in
smaller type than his; and neither did she like the word "translation." As she pointed out by letter, he had said himself it was
"not really a translation but something more." Furthermore,
their joint work, she felt, should be presented as a collaboration.
Georges, on the other hand, worried lest subscribers mistake
his poem for a translation by him of an original work by her,
held ferociously to the word "translation" and to a superior type
face for his name, quoting precedents from the French Authors'
League and mobilizing for indignation against the "greedy"
American many writers and painters who already harbored ill
will toward her. So that very quickly sides began to be taken.

Pushed into a defensive position, Gertrude refused to defend
herself in words, simply withheld her text from the publisher,
Jeanne Bucher. Then at Madame Bucher's art gallery she met
Georges; and since they were in a public place, where quarreling is rude to no host, she ceremoniously refused his proffered
hand.

From this moment the break was formal. As Gertrude informed me by letter, "The last act of the drama was played this
aft. you have been very sweet about not saying I told you don't
imagine I don't appreciate it." She also wired *Pagany*, hoping to
forestall their face-to-face publication of *Enfances*. The time was

too late for that, though not for changing a title. So she sent hers as "Poem Pritten on Pfances of Georges Hugnet," and in reply to Boston's telegraphic query Paris confirmed this spelling of the message. Georges, regretting the break, besought me to arrange the matter in any way I could, in order to save the book's publication and to save everybody's face too. Gertrude, being informed of his wish, replied that a solution could no doubt be arrived at and requested that I "act as [her] agent." She considered as fair any layout in which the two names were of equal size and no reference was made to "translation." I actually worked out such a title page, first showing it to her, then negotiating step by step with Georges till he agreed. The authors' names were to be printed at top and bottom (his at top), with the title centered and equidistant from both.

Alice had in the meantime sent me a *pneumatique* asking that I phone her without delay; and when I did so, she specified that whatever proposal was arrived at, it must be "distinctly understood that it comes from Georges." I replied that I would do what I could about that, but could guarantee nothing. Getting Georges's agreement to a layout that I knew to be satisfactory to Gertrude and then persuading him in front of his own Muse (a stubborn Alsatian) that he must not only accept it but submit it as his own, all this was more than anybody's agent could expect to accomplish. So when Georges wrote on the model of the page, "I accept," I was aware, warned by Alice's message, that Gertrude might still refuse it.

It was Alice Toklas who stated the refusal, as she had previously stated the conditions for acceptance. The scene was the big studio drawing room of 27 rue de Fleurus, the time Christmas Eve. I had been asked for dinner, along with Maurice Grosser, toward whom Gertrude had been feeling especially warm, in gratitude for the scenario he had devised for *Four Saints*. ("Maurice understands my work," she would say.) And I knew there would be gifts. So I had prepared one too, a picture for the country house, not an expensive gift but amusing, a Victorian lithograph (in a white frame of the period) representing two ladies in a swing. I was depressed in advance about the evening and exasperated toward the end of one of those dark, wet, winter days; also, on my way to the house, I had dropped the wrapped picture, breaking its glass.

But our hostesses were cheerful; a crèche with small statues from Provence had been set up beside the fireplace; in the tiny dining room, which with its octagonal Florentine table and equally massive Florentine chairs could seat just four, there was venison for dinner; and afterwards, back in the studio, there were neckties and silk scarves from Charvet. When all the ceremonies had been accomplished and well-being established (for nobody had a power like Gertrude's for radiating repose), I brought out the paper. Gertrude looked at it, did not bridle or seem to be suspicious. She merely said in a wholly relaxed manner, like a businessman signing a contract already negotiated, "This seems to be all right." Then she passed it to Alice, saying, "What do you think, Pussy?" And Alice, after seeing the two words written on it, said, "It isn't what was asked for."

I have no further memory of the evening. I know that we all got through it by talking of many things and that we spoke no more of Georges or of *Enfances* and that we wished one another "Merry Christmas" at midnight. Then I went home and by morning had my usual frustration-grippe.

My pocket calendar of 1930 indicates an engagement with Gertrude on the twenty-seventh, and a note from her mailed the day before asks that I bring with me three manuscripts she had lent me. I do not know whether I went or whether, being ill, I sent her the typescripts (one of which was *Enfances*). I do remember that sometime around the New Year Madame Langlois became ill and that though surrounded, as always, by stars of the Medical Faculty, she received attentions from me also, including the regular making and taking to her of strong vegetable broth, a product her hotel could not provide. I was also practicing for a concert in which I was to play my own music. So it must have been two weeks before I made any attempt to continue my visits with Gertrude and Alice. Then one evening, when I rang the bell, Gertrude herself came to the door and said, "Did you want something?" I replied, "Merely to report on my absence," and she replied, "We're very busy now." But I still owed her an announcement of the concert, since certain works with texts by her were on the program. So I sent it with a note saying that both Marthe-Marthine and I hoped she might care to come. Her reply was a largish calling card in matching envelope with, under the engraved name *Miss*

Stein, a handwritten "declines further acquaintance with Mr. Thomson."

If she expected flowers, as after my former moment of offensiveness, she did not receive them, for I was aware of no wrongdoing, unless my failure to discipline Georges for her advantage might be so viewed. In any case, I took her at her word. Two years later, with an American production of *Four Saints* being contracted for, her literary agent, William Aspenwall Bradley, transmitted her suggestion that I write directly regarding certain details. I did so, and she replied at great length warmly. We continued to correspond, on matters regarding our joint enterprises and with increasing warmth. When she came to lecture in America in the fall of 1934, freshly famous for her *Autobiography of Alice B. Toklas*, which had been published the preceding year, and also for *Four Saints*, which had been produced on Broadway just that spring, we embraced at Carl Van Vechten's party for her. There was no point in keeping up in New York a quarrel so purely Parisian and one which for both of us had long since lost its savor. We did not attempt to excuse or to explain; we simply did not mention it.

Gertrude has told this story her way in a narrative called *Left to Right*, written not long after the events and published three years later in *Story*, November 1933. This version does not vary from mine, except that it reveals a certain suspicion on her part that I might have been trying to work for Georges's benefit. She does not mention having asked me to negotiate a settlement "as [her] agent." She might have forgotten that already. And she might have meant by "agent" a personal representative charged with no interests but hers. I am more inclined to think of her as terrified by Georges's rapid mobilization of the French intellectuals and as feeling herself not at all adequate to fighting a war with them and that my failure to fight it for her was a disappointment that she could not bear.

In December of 1963 I read my present account to Alice Toklas, who found no error in it. She said that Gertrude had believed Bravig Imbs to have influenced me in my discussions with Georges, an idea wholly without foundation. And to my question as to how she had come to interfere after Gertrude and Georges were finally in agreement, she answered, "I was only trying to protect Gertrude." Could Gertrude's affection for Georges, almost schoolgirlish in her letters, have seemed to Alice an intensity warranting protection? She added that the friendship with Hugnet was "never a permanent attachment—a youthful thing." On the other hand, she assured me that in my case Gertrude had been "very disturbed by the separation" and "deeply relieved by the reconciliation." I see no reason to doubt her on any of these matters.

17

Neighborhoods and Portraits

O N MY ARRIVAL IN 1921 I had become a Parisian instantaneously, and by 1931 the patina was ingrained. Kansas
City, Cambridge, New York were still my core, my structure;
but Paris was where I felt most at home. Remembering what it
looked like then and earlier, I find little alteration in its forms.
Paris does not change much anyway. Its skyline evolves but
slowly, over centuries; and only surface varies with the time. Its
color, for instance, after World War I, was a thousand shades
of gray from bone to violet. Then gradually, between the wars,
repaintings turned its weathered stone to cream. By the end
of World War II the whole was blanched. Today, all freshly
scrubbed with soap and water, the city has become a golden
blond running in shades from pumpkin to camembert. But she
will turn gray again, no doubt about it, for that is the way with
Paris building stone.

In the Paris of 1921, the inside of hotels and restaurants was
a riot of huge flattened flowers and jumpy stripes inspired by
the painting of Henri Matisse. By 1925 the major source was
cubist painting; and the colorings had turned quite pale. In the
thirties one was to see all-white rooms in private houses, but for
redecorating a public place there was no choice save between
the strictly modern as we know it—a composition of oblongs—
and the convention known in France as "*style auberge*" (called
in America "French provincial"), all chintzes and checks with
copper warming pans and wooden chandeliers. These were
what any decorator had to sell, all that any customer could buy.

The intellectual center for Americans and the English had
remained since World War I Montparnasse. And if its sidewalk
cafés by 1930 seemed less crowded, that was simply because
there were more of them, the original Café du Dôme and
La Rotonde having bred bars, nightclubs, and restaurants of
every variety. There were the all-Dutch "Falstaff," the Swedish
"Stryx," the Anglo-American "Dingo" and "Select," the diversified but Germanically vast "Coupole." During the late thirties
a move took place toward Saint-Germain-des-Prés, where "Les

Deux Magots" and Lipp's had long been frequented by French authors and their left-bank publishers.

The Café de Flore, just opposite Lipp's, was a dreary place till bought by a progressive management and done over to look less nineteenth-century. Offering toast, ham and eggs, and surprisingly good coffee, it came to be frequented by many of the better-off late risers. And as the war approached one saw there of an evening the painters Picasso and Derain, the sculptors Zadkine and Giacometti, the surrealist general staff (headed by poets Breton and Eluard), the loyal-to-Stalin ex-surrealists Tristan Tzara and Louis Aragon, the royalist historians Bernard Faÿ and Pierre Gaxotte, and a dozen dealers in contemporary art, such as Pierre Colle from the faubourg Saint-Honoré and Pierre Loeb of the nearby rue de Seine. Sylvia Beach's bookstore in the 1930s, though still a daytime rendezvous of writers, was less glamorous than before, with Hemingway and Antheil gone, Joyce rarely about.

Montmartre, briefly a painting center before World War I, had from Louis-Philippe times been the neighborhood of musicians. Milhaud and Honegger, Nadia Boulanger, and many another established one lived on its middle and lower slopes. Its top, the former home of Gustave Charpentier and the locale of his *Louise*, was occupied largely by restaurants and by a semi-unemployed bohemia that called itself a Free Commune and elected every year a Communist "mayor." Lower down there were night clubs—the impeccable Zelli's and Brick Top's, the fashionable "Grand Ecart" (a branch of Le Bœuf sur le Toit) all black and crystal, and the Bal Tabarin, where a cancan still ended the floor show. It was to this lower Montmartre that even left-bankers went for a night on the town or for observing French low life in the Place Pigalle and Place Blanche, where pimps and *souteneurs* as stylized as anything out of Jean Genet played cards in cafés while their girls worked the sidewalks. Also, in the boulevards de Clichy and Batignolles ambulant street fairs with rides and rifle ranges seemed to linger on all fall, moving along just a few blocks every week or so, but always turning back when they got to the Plaine Monceau, a rich, gloomy quarter inhabited by vocal teachers and successful singers.

Henri Sauguet had moved in 1929 to the northwestern Batignolles district, where he lived in a small hotel, the Nollet, named after its street. Max Jacob lived there too, and the Italian composer Vittorio Rieti, as did also a laughing young scoutmaster named Gaétan Fouquet, who was to become a professional traveler (he once hitchhiked to India). Also came to live there the violinist Yvonne de Casa Fuerte, and all these made a companionable house full of working and of laughter. Sauguet, a lean and liverish *bordelais* with damp hands, had already composed ballets and chamber music lovely for lyrical spontaneity. And he had begun work on *La Chartreuse de Parme*, which was to occupy him for the next ten years, being produced at last in 1939 by the Paris Opéra. I had felt happy with his music always, and he with mine. And the same people who would find mine light-minded usually mistook his for insufficiently learned. It was not so, however, though wonderfully fresh and pure in heart.

Léon Kochnitzky, who sought from all modern art that which could remind him most intensely of past masters, would reproach me for my devotion to Sauguet and my intolerance toward fabricated masterpieces (toward *"le style chef-d'œuvre"* of Honegger, for example), assuring me that I was inveterately a follower of "false values." I, on the contrary, judged all those who mistook for high quality a mere resemblance to the past to be not gourmets of music but rather its addicts, conditioned to blind pursuit and to repeating patterns. Sauguet and I shared faith in "the emotions you really have" and in their authentic transcript, however thin. And I must say that I still find his music (sometimes frugal, sometimes overflowing) ever a clear source, just as I have ever found his friendship frank, loyal, and without guile.

Max Jacob was another whom Kochnitzky considered a "false value." Eric de Haulleville, following Kochnitzky's malice, would even declare him false clean through—as a poet and as a painter, as a Catholic and as a Jew, as a Frenchman, as a Breton, as a friend. And certainly Max could be hard to take, for meanness and perfidy were as strong in him as generosity of spirit. But even his malice was mercurial. With a volubility uncontrollable he would pour out praise and sarcasm, insults, jokes, apologies, tirades, and rigamaroles at once rhythmical, compassionate, penetrating, poetic, and funny. His verbal virtuosities were not planned nor his harshest words ever less than instantaneously come by. Moreover, he could prophesy, tell fortunes, speak as an oracle. Regarding proletarian demands he announced that there would be no real trouble from the Left in France before 1980, since all that the workers wanted now was the right to live like bourgeois (or as he put it, "*le port ultérieur de la redingote*"). Of Maurice Grosser he said success as a painter would come surely but very late. I was destined, he predicted, to glory, to appearing on great stages, and to friendships with royalty. "But not," he added, "until after forty."

Though his volume of stories in epistolary form called *Le Cabinet Noir* remains a devastating prose picture of French family life, Max was primarily a poet and to my ear a fine one. He made his living during all the time I knew him by painting in gouache and drawing in ink, the results being bought largely by friends and curiosity collectors. His gouaches of French monuments and historic interiors, according to Grosser, were drawn from postcards by ruled enlargement, a method that seemed to make their forms a little flat. Their color, however, had vivacity and depth, a good deal of spit and cigarette ash getting added as the picture progressed. Max's ink drawings were vibrant as to line and invariably religious in theme.

A middle-class youth from Quimper, Max had in Paris sought out intense experiences—through poverty (real), through poetry, and through drugs. At thirty-three there came to him the most intense of all, a vision of Jesus Christ. Overwhelmed, he ran to a parish priest and asked to be baptized, but was refused. When five years later the vision recurred, he knew what to do. This time he consulted the Fathers of Zion, whose specific assignment is to convert the Jews. His godfather at baptism was Picasso. Then for thirty years he wrestled with sin and the devil, as well as with his poetry and painting. "When the sins of the flesh grow fewer," he would say, "those of the spirit increase." In his middle fifties he would pass summers near the monastery at Saint-Benoît-sur-Loire, and after 1936 he lived there always. During the Occupation the monks gave him partial sanctuary under a false name. But toward the end, the Germans, always looking for Jews to persecute, learned of his presence in the town and arrested him. Left outdoors for two days in freezing weather at the railway station of Orléans, he caught pneumonia there and died at the prison of Drancy, his martyrdom preceding by only a short time the Germans' exodus. Today, though twenty years have passed, there is no French edition of all his prose and poetry; nor has any of it at all, so far as I know, appeared in English.

Sauguet and Cliquet-Pleyel set Max to music often. My *Stabat Mater*, to his text, has been performed for over thirty years. On the flyleaf of a gift, *Bourgeois de France et d'ailleurs*, he wrote in 1932 (I translate), "to Virgil Thomson, brilliant and courageous spirit, delightful in friendship, terrible in combat, learned musician and grand innovator, tree of which the root is genius itself, his admirer and his friend Max Jacob."

Was he pulling my leg? Perhaps. Was he caught up in a rodomontade that he could not stop? Everything was possible with Max, including sincerity. Or was he asking pardon for an earlier moment when at my Salle Chopin concert our *Stabat Mater* had been shiningly delivered and where, ever the buffoon, he had remarked, though not to me, that obviously the music was negligible but that his poem, *n'est-ce pas*, was a masterpiece.

I used to tease Roy Harris for writing "masterpieces." Roy had come abroad in 1926, already twenty-eight years old and needing to acquire a technique of composition that could sustain the pouring out that was his urgency. Farmer from Oklahoma and California, he spoke with dry humor and a bonhomie not unlike those of the comedian Will Rogers, then popular as a cowboy commentator. His Western ways were winning; and his musical vocation, only lately clear to him, was serious. He had come to France for help in building mastery, and in order to avoid wasting time had gone to live outside of Paris. After one winter spent on the banks of the Seine at Chatou, he found that neither the dampness nor his wife, a worried reader of intellectual magazines, was good for his work. So he renounced them both and went to live alone on higher ground, near Gargenville, where his teacher, Nadia Boulanger, lived much of the year. There, surrounded by year-round gardening, by wheat fields and ripening fruits, he wrote many of the early chamber works that are still his glory. And my teasing him about his hope of creating masterpieces by remembering the past may well have been unjust, since that was exactly what Brahms had essayed, and also since Roy's own singing line possessed a breadth related to that of the Romantic masters.

Boulanger was impressed by Roy's expressive powers and pleased by his masculine personality. He taught her to drive a car; and she plotted to get him another wife, this time a musician who could help him with his harmony and whose family had some wealth. Roy almost went through with the arrangement and actually did, I think, allow the family to pay for his divorce. But eventually he balked at being "taken over," as he put it, and found for himself a young woman less demanding about marriage but equally amenable to copying music. And so his quiet life of composing and of learning to compose and of being a future great man (for Roy always carried about with him a bit of that) went on for a few more years; and he would come to Paris every week; and almost always we saw each other; and always, just as it had been with Copland and with Sauguet, we showed each other with confidence all our music.

Then one day Roy fell down a staircase and broke his coccyx, which would not heal. And women came from far and close to be with him—his mother and his sister from California, his ex-wife from New York, his copyist-companion from the village. Maurice Grosser said that unlike Saint Teresa, who in my opera was described as "seated and not surrounded," Roy was "surrounded but not seated." Eventually the Guggenheim Foundation and Alma Wertheim, clubbing together, shipped him in plaster to New York, where an operation cleared up the injury.

A letter from the *Mauretania*, mailed in Plymouth, was as breezy as Oklahoma itself. "O thou great Bard of sunny climes and all that," was his address.

> I want to thank you for your last and latest farewell in pure post-Satie vernacular and say that altho all present indications deny that I shall ever walk up your damnably long stairs and eat your good Digestives and drink your good Italian Vermouth and refresh my masterpiece psychology (with its Russian mood flavor) in the gentle breezes of your Dadaistic wisecracks (some damned wise and some somewhat abortive) that altho all present indications deny the above I'm not done writing masterpieces and you've not told me about it for the last time.

Marcel Duchamp's painting career had come to an end through his creation of a real masterpiece, a picture even today little known in Europe but famous in America since 1913. *Nude*

Descending a Staircase had certainly not been planned to remind art lovers of earlier painting, though neither had its perfection been arrived at without study. It is simply that the artist, at twenty-five, was shocked to the depths of his own idealism on learning how successful he had become. By 1912, only three years after cubism's inception, there were already in Paris thirty dealers selling only that; and his *Nude* had been bought on second sale for $30,000. Wishing no truck with any business so inflated or with any success so quickly come by, he renounced painting altogether, created in the next few years at least two sculptural constructions now classical and a half-dozen pieces of perfect "pop" art, then after thirty never worked again. At least he imagined he did not, though he could not tie a string or drive a nail without beauty resulting.

Slender, erect, red-headed, Norman, son of a Rouen *notaire*, brother of a sculptor killed in World War I and of the painter Jacques Villon, he spent his patrimony early, lived virtually without funds, was adored by women. During my Paris years his most adoring woman was an American named Mary Reynolds, a war widow out of Minneapolis (by way of Vassar and Greenwich Village) who received her sustenance from a well-off but grudging father who considered sinful her gracious way of life. Like Marcel, Mary did not pretend to work; but since her friends were mostly artists and poets, and since at various times they had all given her drawings, engravings, and books, she began in the 1930s to learn the art of binding for the preservation of these. Her books and bindings are in a special collection now at the Art Institute of Chicago, given by her brother and itemized in a catalog by Marcel Duchamp, *Surrealism and Its Affinities.*

Straight, well-dressed, and clearly a lady (though she did love roistering and bars), she had formed with Madame Langlois, also straight and proud (though not a barfly), a friendship that involved once every week or two our all three dining together with Marcel or with Maurice Grosser and then playing bridge (the French kind, known as *plafond*, in which you score the extra tricks you take). And at these evenings we would forever discuss, by means of gossip, the ethics of behavior and of art. None could be more approving than they of misbehaviors committed with style, or more intolerant of grubby deportment.

And I would sometimes ask Marcel questions aimed at making it clear to me how he had come to renounce being an artist. On one occasion he answered, "There is never room for more than two at the top; and Picasso and Braque were already there."

From his serene retirement, Duchamp seemed not to be involved any more with schools or styles in art, save as an observer. He was the friend of many artists, from Brancusi to Grosser; but never, saving only once, did I hear him speak of any with disdain. He did observe, that time, that Picasso's large and somewhat indiscriminate production came from the fact that "he gets sexually excited by the smell of turpentine and works every day." Another time, discussing the survival of workmanship over the centuries and the inevitable disappearance of stylistic distinctions, "In seventy-five years nobody will be able to tell a Picasso from a Corot." And of Manhattan as viewed from New York harbor, "Its beauty comes from the fact that nothing you see was built before 1900."

Marcel had been, during the first World War, an intellectual flirt with Ettie Stettheimer and an admiring colleague with Florine. I own Florine's portrait of him, painted in the early twenties, and a large drawing of her, made by him around that time, completely classical as to resemblance and style. After Mary Reynolds's death in 1955 he gave me a realistic leaf made of gold-colored metal, a 1900 piece that had been a present to her from Madame Langlois.

For the late fall of 1931 Aaron Copland had organized a concert of American music to take place in London under the auspices of a British contemporary music society, and he had asked me to participate by rehearsing and accompanying *Capital Capitals*. That same fall he had sent me a young composer, glimpsed the preceding spring at Bernard Faÿ's, his pupil Paul Bowles, who arrived in my studio with a traveling companion on a morning of dazzling sunlight. Was it really the light that dazzled, for I did sometimes receive sun through my northeast window; or was it the radiance that they brought with them, both nineteen, both in camel's hair overcoats, both with yellow hair and yellow cashmere scarfs. They had just taken, or rather Harry Dunham, the wealthy one, had taken, the largest of the new studio apartments at the top of 17 quai Voltaire; and Harry's sister would be coming from Cincinnati to live with them.

They too were going to London for the December concert, since a work of Bowles's was to be played. Meanwhile they were off to Morocco for sight-seeing, had been there already during the summer with Copland. At some point Harry got sent on from Morocco, just as his grandfather had once done, a young Arab servant. This child of twelve turned out to be no helper, but he did have entertainment value from the scrapes he could get into. These continued till Harry's sister Amelia took an occasion of her brother's absence to send the Muslim Tom Sawyer back to Africa, providing money for his travel and a Vuitton suitcase. Since he had no clothes to speak of, he packed up all of Paul's and left with them. The dramas of the irrepressible Abdelkader, of Paul's dainty and devoted sweetheart (a French girl surnamed Miracle), and of the jealous Amelia, intriguing to remove anyone who came close to her brother, provided farce-comedy for a season. Then Harry went back to Princeton, still surrounded by the white light he seemed always to give off; and Paul stayed on to learn to be a composer.

Bowles had thought of himself as first of all a poet, having already during his short stay at the University of Virginia published verse in the advanced magazines, even in *transition*. Neither Gertrude Stein nor Bernard Faÿ nor I nor indeed any of the Parisians to whom he showed his poems could find their quality. His music, on the other hand, Ravel-like piano improvisations, charmed us all, as it had already charmed Copland. And Copland had tried in New York teaching him harmony but had found him a stubborn pupil. In Paris he approached Boulanger for lessons; I had recommended Paul Dukas. He ended by working with neither. Beyond a few meetings with Vittorio Rieti, he actually never succeeded in following any musical instruction, though he tried, persuaded by Aaron and myself that there was no other way to become a composer. Actually he did become a self-taught composer; and later in New York I inducted him into the practice of writing incidental music for plays, which he did (and still does) with imagination. I also, to replace an absent colleague during World War II, caused him to be engaged as a music reviewer on my staff at the New York *Herald Tribune*. This work he did perfectly, because he wrote clearly and because he had the gift of judgment. After the war, returning to Morocco, he practiced both music and letters, gradually renouncing major involvement with the former and becoming instead a novelist and story writer of international repute. He has not gone back to poetry. When I spoke only recently of my wish that he had been asked to take over my critic's post when I resigned it in 1954, he said, "I don't think I could have handled it, any more than I could have followed a career in composition. I lacked the musical training that you and Aaron had."

It was before the London concert that Aaron wrote to ask whether I would write an essay about him for a series of composer's portraits to appear in *Modern Music*. Since 1925 I had declined all requests for writing. But for Copland, who insisted I was not to look upon the essay as a favor and that "if [I] should decide to do it, nothing but [my] honest judgment would please [him]," I did accept. I wrote the article, received $20 for it, and during the next ten years contributed many pieces to that quarterly. Minna Lederman was a first-class editor. She never changed my copy; but she questioned many a time my angle of judgment, made me aware that in so partisan a paper (originally devoted to the entire League of Composers, it had already become by 1931 largely the personal organ of Aaron Copland) I must keep before my mind the differences between New York musical politics and Parisian.

Appearing in print again did me no harm. For just then there seemed to be a chance that something like an American career might be imminent. Since Russell Hitchcock had far and wide been praising my opera, his friend and neighbor A. Everett Austin, Jr. (or "Chick," as he was known), had got interested in doing something about it. Chick was director of the art museum in Hartford, Connecticut, a man of substance, young, my own classmate, an entrepreneur of unrestrained imagination. In that particular moment he was building for himself and family a neoclassical-and-Baroque house that remains to this day bold and beautiful. In fact, from behind all the art activities of Chick Austin peer constantly the learning of Russell Hitchcock and his insatiable taste for grandeur. This influence, plus a restlessness in Chick which amounted to a major drive, caused him to decide, in full time of depression, to build a modern wing to his museum. And because he wanted to produce my opera (for

he loved giving every kind of show), he was planning to build
into the new wing a fully equipped theater.

My English interlude had been a delight, rehearsing and performing with singers of good speech, and walking again after
ten years through Victorian red and earlier black-and-white
London, even though in December the days were dark till noon
and dark again after three—delightful also despite a supercilious
press, for we were all so used in those days to scornful reviews
that we scarcely noticed them. The program itself would today
stand handsomely—a Chávez Sonatina, a Bowles Sonata for
Oboe and Clarinet, Copland's Piano Variations, the Citkowitz
songs from James Joyce, Roger Sessions's Piano Sonata [No. 1],
and my *Capitals* to end with. At Aaron's suggestion I had held
off writing my portrait of his music till I should have heard the
new Piano Variations. I found these grandly expansive, only
regretting that he played them too loud (as composers will do
their own music) and missing in this loudness "the singing of a
certain still, small voice that seems to me . . . clearly implied on
the written page." It was through Aaron also, who was coming
to be a power in New York, that Alma Wertheim's Cos Cob
Press engaged shortly afterwards to publish my *Stabat Mater*.
This was my first musical publication of any kind; and back in
Paris I corrected the proofs with pride, though not with complete accuracy.

But as it began to seem that my American career might be
pointing upward, my French professional relations were lowering. It was in that same December of 1931 that the violinist
Yvonne de Casa Fuerte (with whom I had struck up friendship
playing my Violin Sonata a half-year earlier) began a new series
of contemporary concerts. My music was not programed in this
series, was not ever to be programed there. But I had wanted
it to be, and I am sure Yvonne too had hoped for that. It was
a disappointment to be omitted from the group, because my
chief musical associates were all included—Henri Sauguet, the
Russian Nicolas Nabokov, the Italians Leone Massimo and Vittorio Rieti, and naturally the arrived composers Milhaud and
Poulenc. As I reread now the programs of La Sérénade, I realize
that Igor Markevitch's music was regularly exposed and that two
of his patronesses—the Princesse Edmond de Polignac and the

Vicomtesse de Noailles—were among the backers of the series.
I also know that its organizer, Yvonne de Casa Fuerte, made
efforts throughout 1932 to get my Second String Quartet accepted into her programs. I know too that the group governing
these consisted besides herself of only Milhaud, Poulenc, and
Rieti. She admired the new quartet; Rieti was reserved about it.
Poulenc tried to like it, but after reading it twice still could not.
What Darius Milhaud thought, I do not know. When the work
was decidely not to be played, in spite of Yvonne's support, I
knew I was being refused admittance to neo-Romanticism's
musical Establishment, though I did not fully understand why.
Bérard found the exclusion unfair and told me so. Georges
Maratier, though not involved himself, mentioned some years
later that there had been, to his knowledge, a move to throw
me overboard (*on débarque Virgil*); and Jean Ozenne, who had
had the inside story from Sauguet, tried, also much later, to tell
me why Yvonne had not been able to influence her committee.
I seemed to understand from him, as I had suspected all along,
that Markevitch, though not a member of the committee, had
maneuvered the rejection. I still do not know whether this is
true; the strong opposer may have been Rieti, ever jealous of
my friendship with Yvonne. Today both Yvonne and Sauguet
have conveniently mislaid their memories.

In 1930 I had begun writing string pieces and piano sonatas.
Three of the latter had poured out right off, then a sonata for
violin and piano, divers portraits for the same ensemble, a string
quartet, and the Max Jacob *Stabat Mater*. All these, save the
portraits, had been performed during that year and the following one. I had also composed a Serenade for Flute and Violin,
which I had hoped would be played at the opening concert
of La Sérénade. I had written songs too, their words out of a
poetry cycle by Georges Hugnet called *La Belle en dormant*.
And I had transformed the first and most extensive of my piano
sonatas into a fully orchestrated symphony. My last and most
ambitious effort of this period—which had been one of steady
progress from the mosaiclike structure of *Four Saints* to the
long-line nonrepeating continuity of the Violin Sonata and the
First String Quartet—had been the String Quartet No. 2, in
which all my now considerable experience had been applied
to creating a sonata-structure amply modulatory and cyclically

thematic. I considered this four-movement piece to be authentic as inspiration, solidly built, and for all its classical architecture, a modern work. My surprise had been considerable when the Sérénade group failed to recognize its quality publicly. I was even tempted to think of it as possibly disquieting to the established ones. Whether I was right time has not told, for the piece, though still played, seems neither deeply to offend nor in any other way to attract special notice. My Second Symphony, also of this period, begins now to excite certain hearers; perhaps the Second Quartet will eventually. All I can be sure of now is that it marks a stage in my musical maturing, and I knew in fact in 1932 that I had either broken new ground or brought something to term.

I was so confident of this that I actually paused in my headlong composing and began to look around for other outlets and adventures. An American production of *Four Saints* would offer both; and I was already trying to help that out by organizing, as Chick and Russell and Alfred Barr kept suggesting by letter, a voyage of exploration. They needed me there in order to learn how much financial support some informal auditions of the opera could inspire and how low its costs could be kept down. Marga Barr wrote that she was "dividing acquaintances into two new categories—those who could be useful to Virgil and those who couldn't." I wrote to Harvard, Rochester, and Cleveland, hoping that friends there could help with lecture dates. None could, though Smith College promised one. The Alfred Barrs could offer "a shakedown on arrival," Jere Abbott, lodging for a week. And a kind crippled woman from Wisconsin whom I knew briefly in Juan-les-Pins as a friend of Georges Maratier's American wife asked if she could be allowed to subsidize my trip. So I took this for settled, turned my thoughts to other things.

The thoughts of us all, that spring, had been full of the Ballet Russe de Monte Carlo, where the director, René Blum, brother of Léon, had assembled a whole new generation of ballerinas and turned them over to the young choreographer George Balanchine. New ballets had been ordered too, and new sets, including one by Bérard for a piece called *Cotillon*, with music by Chabrier. Here the neo-Romantic youth-centered view was fully matured and Bébé come full-blown to stage design, his earlier décor for the Comédie Française of Cocteau's *La Voix humaine* having shown him still obsessed by easel-painting. And Lincoln Kirstein, not completely preoccupied any longer with his Cambridge-published magazine *Hound and Horn*, was deeply stirred by it all. He used to stay at the Hôtel du Quai Voltaire and come to my studio every morning for talking about it and to try out, with me as audience, ballet scenarios he had thought up during the night. I could find things wrong with almost all of them, but Lincoln's supply was inexhaustible.

With summer coming on and with no money for going away, I used to walk in the country by the Seine with Eugene Berman, making musical sketches while he filled notebooks with things seen, these to be worked up later into paintings and formal drawings. And I would wonder why he always had to amplify them, when the freshly noted forms were of such beauty. And he would say, "But, Virgil, you must understand that these notebooks are my capital. I do not sell them; I make my pictures out of them."

Then in July the widow of Lucien Herr lent me a country farmhouse for one month. It was at the edge of Grosrouvre, a village near the small city of Montfort-l'Amaury, home of Maurice Ravel, a church town with sixteenth-century stained glass and a pastry shop, just off the Plaine de la Beauce, where wheat is grown, and the Fôret de Rambouillet, where gnomes stack wood in piles. One got to know both these landscapes completely, because one walked. There was money for food but none for bicycles. So every day with Maurice Grosser, who shared the house and the living expenses, and for a time with Marga Barr, who came for a week and whose portrait was painted in a yellow suède jacket, one walked the countryside, explored the forest and its hidden villages—Gambais, with thatched cottages straight out of Hogarth, and Gambasais, where Landru had burned his wives and where, in the garden of his two-story brick-and-rubblestone *villa coquète*, one could have cakes and tea.

It must have been in late summer, when Jeanne Herr's farmhouse was no longer available, that I went to the Côte d'Azur, for it was there I met Rena Frazier, Florence Maratier's Wisconsin friend, who offered to pay for my trip to America saying, "Write me what you will need." I do not know how I got to the South just then, having no money. But I was there; and in Villefranche Lady Rose, Francis's mother, who was clairvoyant, told my fortune prophetically; and at Francis's house in Mougins, above Cannes, I was rude without wishing to be so to Mrs. Patrick Campbell, giant twin to her Pekingese lap dog, both of them drenched in Chanel No. 5. I spoke of having seen her unforgettably in Shaw's *Pygmalion* and asked when she was going to act again. "Never," she answered. "I'm too old and too ugly; nobody would come to see me." "But they advertised Polaire," I said, "as the ugliest woman in the world; and everybody went to see her."

I was also tactless with Rena Frazier when from Paris I wrote her what I thought I should need for the American trip, a sum much larger than just the fare. She replied from Wisconsin that hard times had diminished her resources and asked me to excuse her from the project. It was already October; and I knew no means of getting to America. Then Philip Johnson, on his way home from examining modern architecture in Germany, said not to worry, that he would be glad to lend me $200, price of a round-trip third-class passage, and that in New York I could stay at his flat. So once again I advertised my studio, let it to somebody not now remembered, lent my large black-blue Bérard to Philip Lasell, who had always loved it, and once again took off on the *Ile-de-France*, this time with Mary Reynolds, going home to visit her ailing and ungenerous father, leaving behind on a cold and windy quay Madame Langlois, who had ridden with us to Le Havre, and heading into a December North Atlantic.

18

Adopted by the Modern-Art Distributors

I WAS MET AT THE FRENCH LINE PIER by Jere Abbott and taken to Philip Johnson's flat on Forty-ninth Street, it having been arranged between Philip and the Kirk Askews that I was to be passed back and forth between them. There was also sleeping space at Russell Hitchcock's in Middletown, Connecticut, at Jere Abbott's in Northampton, Massachusetts, and at Chick Austin's in Hartford. At some point I would go to Kansas City, stopping, should I come back by bus, at Cleveland, Ohio, where Harry Francis was a curator of painting, and at Sibley Watson's in Rochester, New York. I should probably not be going to Boston and Cambridge, because my early friend and protector E. B. Hill had written that a lecture-recital was not to be thought of, since "the depression has struck the Harvard Music Department." Nor did I expect performance by the Boston Symphony Orchestra, after the run-in with Serge Koussevitzky four years earlier over my *Symphony on a Hymn Tune*. He and I were still on courteous terms, even affectionate ones viva voce; and I had another symphony all complete that I could have shown him. But it was even sassier than the first, and I saw no reason to embarrass either of us.

Actually, though my errand in America was musical—getting my opera performed—I was not to be moving mainly among musicians, but rather among the avant-garde art distributors. Philip Johnson, originally a classical scholar, had through Russell Hitchcock become interested in contemporary building design; and they had written a book together, *The International Style*, which served as catalog for a photographic show of new architecture that they had assembled for the Museum of Modern Art. Alfred Barr, sole director, since Jere Abbott's retirement to Smith College, of this three-year-old enterprise, was the most powerfully placed among a rising group of modern-art promoters. In modern-art scholarship (a new profession) he was considered impeccable, and his tactful manipulation of trustees with names such as Rockefeller, Ford, Chrysler, Goodyear, Bliss, Crane, Clarke, Whitney, and the like was keeping the museum's rapidly expanding influence on collectors oriented as well toward academic prestige. Russell Hitchcock, as the most knowledgeable historian anywhere of modern building, was being invaluable to the architectural department; and Philip Johnson, Hitchcock's pupil in taste, as he was Barr's in the professional operation, was to become in time the museum's architectural curator. Iris Barry, English and thoroughly intelligent, had invented there for herself a librarian's post and was working in it so well that within another short span, five years, she was to establish at the museum the first Film Library in the world. Both architecture and films, however, were side issues; the museum's major line was painting. For showing that (still strictly on loan) Barr was the guide of policy as well as of selection and of hanging, and the shows that took place under his direction were remarkably successful. Scholarship, showmanship, and the tact of a Presbyterian minister's son were fused in him to produce a leadership of taste that was to influence collectors for thirty years.

Close to Barr and to the museum, but no part of it, were a half-dozen young art historians, some of them already curators, all of them oriented toward the modern. These included, besides Hitchcock at Wesleyan and Abbott at Smith, Agnes Rindge and John McAndrew at Vassar, Agnes Mongan, believed hopefully a modernistic influence at Harvard, and most spectacular of all, Chick Austin, a professor at Trinity College and director of the Wadsworth Atheneum in Hartford, Connecticut. All these had been trained at Harvard's Fogg Museum by Paul Sachs and Edward Forbes; and they all bore allegiance to a common ideal, that of administering collections of art as if these consisted of intellectual capital and of guiding the young, many of them future millionaires, into viewing art collecting as itself an art to be practiced by professional standards. Also they visited one another constantly, constantly, constantly, driving by night and by day up and down the Connecticut Valley, over the hills to Vassar, cross-country to Boston or New York.

In New York their centers of fraternity were the house of Kirk and Constance Askew on Sixty-first Street, the sales-galleries of Kirk Askew on Fifty-seventh (Durlacher Brothers), where Baroque painting was a specialty, and of Julien Levy (importer of neo-Romantic and surrealist painting), and a little bit that of Pierre Matisse (who sold Modern Old Masters, including his father). The back offices of these galleries were open for gossiping every day, and the Askews were at home at six on Sundays. Also every day at five, when one could drop in on the hostess for tea and be given cocktails later by the host.

Kirk Askew was a child of Kansas City, though I had not known him there. Our Harvard ways had crossed through Philip Lasell, whose butterfly brightness, flickering over modern art and music, had brought to my notice the especial flamboyance in both intellect and character of the art history group that centered around Chick Austin. On leaving Harvard, Askew had gone to work in New York and London for a firm of Bond Street art dealers, to whose collector-and-museum trade he was introducing his own generation's faith in the Baroque. His wife was a New England woman of means, of broad cultural experience, and of striking beauty.

Kirk was slight of frame with curvaceous facial forms that gave him a carved-in-mahogany aspect which accorded well with his Victorian house. Constance was curvaceous too, and generous as to bosom. And just as her figure was "advanced" for the decade when breasts were just beginning to emerge, her facial carriage was also of a novel kind. In a time when eyes still were tightly squinted and smiles were grins, Constance Askew's relaxed visage, as calm as that of Garbo, was deeply exciting to the young men of her generation.

The people one saw at the Askews' high brownstone on East Sixty-first Street were a wider world than just the modern-art-distributing in-group. There were story writers (John Mosher and Emily Hahn), musicians (Eva Gauthier, Aaron Copland), stage directors (John Houseman, Joseph Losey), some actors, many literary critics, all the poets (e. e. cummings to Lincoln Kirstein), distinguished Negroes (Taylor Gordon, Edna Thomas), curators from the Metropolitan Museum (Harry Wehle, Preston Remington, Alan Priest), Muriel Draper, of course, and Esther Murphy Strachey (ever literate and talkers both), and as often as not a painter in the flesh (Alexander Brook, Florine Stettheimer), and by 1935 whole bunches of them—Massimo Campigli, Pavel Tchelitcheff, Eugene Berman, Kristians Tonny, Maurice Grosser. Sometimes the novelist Elizabeth Bowen would come from London to stay a month.

I myself for the next three years moved in and out of the guest room almost at will.

The drink, till Prohibition went, was homemade gin. Evenings it was diluted with ginger ale or soda. For cocktails it was shaken up with a nonalcoholic vermouth that produced a flocculation in the glass not unlike that which snows around Eiffel's Tower or New York's *Liberty* when rotated in their filled-with-liquid globes. The furniture was splendidly Victorian, with carpets, seats, and curtains richly colored. In the early thirties all pictures there were modern, but by the decade's end some Italian Old Masters had been inherited. Perhaps the happy years of the Askew salon were ending anyway; I only know we never laughed again there, though the drink had by that time turned to proper Scotch and once in a while, as on Christmas night, champagne.

The Askews' schedule was a firm routine. Both came downstairs for breakfast in street clothes; houseguests, if they preferred, could have a tray. Kirk walked to his office; that was his exercise. Unless a child was in need of watching over, Constance would read in the library till noon. At twelve she drank some sherry while she read. At one she lunched with someone, usually at a speak-easy called Michel's. After lunch she looked at art shows, shopped a little, took a nap. At five came tea, cocktails at six, dinner at seven-thirty, for which one dressed. And every night, except when dining out, the Askews had guests. Then after dinner others came; more drink was served; and talk went on, sharp and hilarious, but more about art than politics or travel. Europe, though a constant theme, could scarcely count as travel, what with Kirk working in London half the year, with me a resident of Paris, and Marga Barr's own mother long a Roman. Besides, all those young and mobile art historians spent their years-off and their summers moving round and round in Europe, just as in winter they circulated constantly up and down the northeastern seaboard.

Often, toward midnight, some would decide for Harlem; but the Askews seldom went along, though Constance might be itching to. Russell, however, and Chick, always in town for just a day or so, loved making a night of it. It was on one of these trips uptown, at a small joint where Jimmy Daniels was just starting out as host and entertainer, that I turned to Russell, realizing the impeccable enunciation of Jimmy's speech-in-song, and said, "I think I'll have my opera sung by Negroes." The idea seemed to me a brilliant one; Russell, less impressed, suggested I sleep on it. But next morning I was sure, remembering how proudly the Negroes enunciate and how the whites just hate to move their lips.

From the time of my arrival in America it had been assumed that *Four Saints in Three Acts* was to be produced. Chick's new museum wing, the Avery Memorial, would be finished the following winter; and he wanted to open it in gala style with a retrospective show of Picasso's work (the first in America), an exhibit of original sketches for Diaghilev's ballets (the Serge Lifar collection, which he was buying for the museum), and a world *première* of the Stein-Thomson opera in sets and costumes by Florine Stettheimer. I had early invited Alexander Smallens to conduct the work. And I had persuaded Florine to go on with her plans for decorating it, though her sisters, fearful of a public failure, were insisting that she give the project up. I had looked around too for a stage director; but none of the old and famous ones was interested, and the young ones seemed to have no prescience about opera. There were no opera workshops then, no ballet companies training choreographers, no ballet companies at all, in fact, only a modern-dance studio here and there, consecrated, sectarian, barefoot. When I went back to Paris in April, I knew my décors and my music were in good hands; but I still had no idea what director or choreographer would add movement.

The intellectual leaders of the group I have described—Barr, Hitchcock, and Austin—were desirous that my opera be produced, because they had as yet no outposts for modernist prestige beyond the visual arts. They dreamed of support through letters and through music, but not much was available in these domains not already tied down to other epochs or occupied by other power groups. Lincoln Kirstein's quarterly magazine *Hound and Horn* had never been, though lively enough, an organ of literary distinction comparable to *The Dial*, now defunct, or to the magazines from Paris, London, Rome that had given off such bright light in the twenties. The thirties, though destined to move radically in the theater, were still, in 1932, holding on to their hats (old hats). And the modern music of the twenties had all been heard.

All except mine, that is; and Stein's poetry was on that shelf too. We both had been much heard about, but our larger works were unknown. Since 1929 there had not been a single performance, to my knowledge, in either New York or Boston of any piece by me until my *Stabat Mater* was given at Yaddo, Saratoga Springs, in May of '32. As late as November of that year, almost as I was sailing for America, the editor of *Modern Music* was warning me by letter not to hope for even a lecture date. My reputation, all the same, was after Yaddo not malodorous; and my opera *Four Saints*, though a product of the twenties, was still new. Actually it had been kept new by the League of Composers' constant refusal of all my suggestions about performing in New York anybody's neo-Romantic music. It was therefore no less apt for exploitation than Stein's still largely unaccepted poetry.

Hitchcock and Barr and Abbott knew my opera from Paris; Chick had accepted it on faith. So had those New York and other friends who were accustomed to respect Hitchcock's insistences, especially when Barr proposed no veto. But their final adoption of it had been brought about by my singing it and playing it on everybody's piano till all could recognize it as something possible for them to admire without intellectual shame. And they could admire it all the more as a property about to be launched by their world rather than by some group mainly musical or literary.

Moreover, it was through their support that Chick knew he could find the money for producing it. Certain friends of mine would gladly contribute (though not one of Gertrude's did); and his art dealers, from the smallest up to Lord Duveen, would feel obliged to. But the Museum of Modern Art trustees could stop many a contribution by turning cold shoulder to Chick's planned gala. It had been my assignment from Abbott to make friends with certain of these and not to offend any. Nor was I offensive to Chick's insurance-magnate trustees, many of whom called Mr. Pierpont Morgan "Cousin Jack." So Chick went ahead with the opera plan in the same way that he accomplished other things, not by seeing his way through from the beginning but merely by finding out, through talking of his plan in front of everyone, whether any person or group would try to stop him. Then once inside a project, he would rely entirely on instinct and improvisation. For he considered, and said so, that a museum's purpose was to entertain its director. And come to think of it, if it does not do that, God help us all!

Production details were left to me. The cast was to be rehearsed in New York, then moved to Hartford for a final week with orchestra, sets, costumes, and lights. Meanwhile, my scoring, luckily not yet begun, could be designed for the size of the theater; and so could Florine Stettheimer's scenery. Decision had been made to produce a work already refused in Germany and not tempting to any professional group in America. Nobody knew yet what it would cost, but I knew something of what it would look like and sound like. And I was not to be stuck with the banalities of professional stage design, the poor enunciation of professional opera singers. I was to have the ultimate in dream fulfillment, a production backed by enlightened amateurs and executed by whatever professional standards I chose to follow.

How I contrived my living for those four months, outside free lodging and free meals, I do not remember. I gave lectures at $100 each in Hartford, in Northampton, possibly in Rochester. One snowy night at Muriel Draper's frame house in East Fifty-third Street I spoke on musical prosody, singing from my own works in English and in French. Russell Hitchcock had provided a grand piano from Steinway's. Admission was charged, $2. I had not done much lecturing except informally. When I asked how I had done, Russell answered tactfully that I seemed to be more at home in writing than in speaking.

In January I went to Missouri for a month, visiting my parents in Kansas City and in Slater my jovial grandfather, just one hundred. I have no other memories of this Western trip beyond attending with George Phillips the weekly meetings of a small and hilarious lunch club of highly intellectual businessmen and professionals. I may have done some writing in Kansas City, words or music; but I am certain I earned no money on the spot.

In New York, especially when staying at Philip Johnson's elegantly bare Turtle Bay apartment, I also wrote articles, though

I think not any music. I tried to renew my connection at *Vanity Fair*, but the new managing editor, Clare Boothe Luce (then Brokaw), did not answer me. Also from Philip's flat I led a social life with friends not of the art world and with certain rich trustees not previously of mine. In January the League of Composers, pressed by Aaron Copland, produced a performance of my *Stabat Mater* duplicate to that of Yaddo. I did not hear it, being in Missouri. I did hear a performance of the work in Philadelphia, given in late March at Smallens's recommendation by The Society for Contemporary Music.

Copland had written me after its Yaddo performance that it was my "first real success in America," meaning by "real success," I think, acceptance without prejudice or *parti pris*. This five-minute work, as a matter of fact, has never failed to communicate, in spite of its French text. It is a perfect work in the sense that I have never felt an urge to tamper with it; it has nothing to ask of me, leads its own life. It must have been the simon-purity of Max Jacob's religious inspiration that held me in line while writing it. I remember starting out to compose music in the twelve-tone convention; then feeling constricted by the method, I let the piece write itself. When it was finished, I went for a walk in the Bois de Vincennes; and there, suddenly, lying on a bluegrass hillside near the empty race track, I had felt all trembly, joyfully tired, and emptied, as by a visitation. But I knew for sure only what I had already known, that visitations did occur to Max.

At some time after I got back from Missouri, Philip Johnson's young sister Theodate arrived to visit him. Was it from Cleveland, their parental place, she came, or from Wellesley, where she had earlier, at college, found a Boston vocal teacher? Anyway, she was getting set to be a singer; and as a brunette with blazing eyes and a jacket of leopard skin, she was looking operatic absolutely. Her soprano voice was warm, her presence commanding, her musicianship carefully acquired. And she was about to move her studies to New York. Wanting to be of help to her, to me as well, Philip proposed a musical evening at his flat to which museum trustees would be asked. And he suggested we give my Second String Quartet, still unheard anywhere.

And so I built a program around that. There was no question of compromising the glorious nudity of his living room with a grand piano. But my *Stabat Mater* with string quartet accompaniment seemed just right. I thereupon engaged a group of young players from the Philharmonic who had been several years together as a quartet. And since a fine Haydn D major was in the repertory, I chose that for leading up to my pieces. ("You set yourself high standards," said Ettie Stettheimer.) Theodate sounded lovely, sang beautiful French, repeated the *Stabat* after the concert was over.

The party, which took place mid-April, accomplished exactly what had been desired. Theodate gave a preview of her singing which was sure to be of advantage later. I heard my quartet and, as I had hoped to do, found it in all ways satisfying, so much so that I overdrank champagne punch and was sick. Philip's friends, too, seemed to find it solid enough to have been paired with Haydn. Philip in fact was vastly content all round. I had been strikingly performed and handsomely received; Theodate had been heard to advantage and admired; and, to the benefit of his own projects, not only had divers influential trustees of the museum climbed his stairs, but Mrs. John D. Rockefeller, Jr., the most important of them, had left still smiling. He proposed that we consider the $200 lent me for my trip as no longer due him, but as a fee paid for my services.

Four days later I sailed at midnight on the *Paris*. The Askews had given a dinner party for twelve, with low-cut dresses, white ties, and champagne. And all eleven took me to the ship, where my fourth of a third-class cabin was found to be crowded with gifts, as on the preceding time, including, from Constance for taking to Paris in the ship's cook's icebox, a cheesecake from Reuben's fourteen inches wide.

19

Orchestrations and Contracts

ALSO TRAVELING THIRD CLASS on the *Paris* were some
seventy-five Americans of the communist faith, pilgrims to
Soviet Russia. I had not previously known the rank and file. Intellectual communists, yes, both Trotskyists and loyalists, even
rich ones who dreamed of a tax-free socialist nirvana, all government "withered away." And in the late twenties one had in
Paris joined working-men's cinema clubs for seeing *The Cruiser
Potemkin* and similar films in halls filled to the last seat, save for
a few art-curious, by laborer families of the Marxist line. But
not since college days in Kansas City, where one boy knew real
"wobblies," had I shared as with these gentle tourists a view
from below of the modern working world.

On their way to spend three weeks in the Soviet Union, in
England they would transfer to a ship for Leningrad. There
they would visit the palace and the museums, travel to Moscow,
see the sacred sites, taste a new world. Some had relations they
hoped to visit; some, knowing that good tools were scarce in
Russia, had brought boxes of these to leave behind. Sweet people they were, soft spoken and believing, many of them Jewish,
though not all, since the Marxist faith has always held appeal for
Protestant Americans dispossessed. For those reduced in social
pride it can supply, as with the Jewish-born, a belief to organize
their lives around, in case religion has somehow got lost. In fact
it was through talking of their Marxist faith with many of the
Jews among them (and speaking to communists in those days
was no crime) that it came to me that for these kindly men and
their gentle wives Lenin was Moses and Russia the Promised
Land. And since belief was stronger in them than any reasoning, I knew I must not hurt them by pointing out the Biblical
origins of their new theology, any more than I would have
teased my Southern Baptist father about his sources of integrity.

I did, though, repay them for their comradeship. The *Paris*,
delayed by loading, was to arrive in England late, which meant
the group would miss their ship for Russia; and the French Line

representative on board proposed to substitute rail transport overland from France. The travelers were resigned to losing one or more precious days but not to the added expense of buying food, and the agent could not agree that his company's responsibility involved more than the railway fares. Nor did he speak English, and not one of them spoke French. So a meeting was held for ironing the matter out, at which I offered to serve my fellow travelers as both interpreter and advocate. As moral backing for our side, I asked Agnes de Mille to be there too. We won; the French Line settled for box lunches. And at Le Havre our partings were fraternal.

In Paris I had errands to perform, such as negotiating with Miss Stein's agent contracts for Chick to sign and some kind of agreement between Gertrude and myself, as parents of a work that was about to leave home. I also had to orchestrate the opera; and to save time in doing that I had a professional copyist write out the words and vocal parts and rule the measure bars for all six hundred pages. Chick was to pay the cost of preparing orchestral score and parts; I was to bring them with me on my return. Florine Stettheimer had promised to work at designing sets and costumes as fast as ideas came, and they were coming fast.

But before I could lay out the score, I had to decide what instruments to use. According to Smallens, I could with careful seating get nineteen men into the theater's pit, fewer if I used up space on kettle drums, pianoforte, or harp. After taking thought, I decided on ten strings, one flute-piccolo player, one oboe–English horn, one bassoon, two saxophones (one doubling on clarinet, the other on bass clarinet), one trumpet, one trombone, one percussion player, and an accordion. This combination was designed to provide for four-part woodwind chords, four-part brass chords (by using the saxophones), complete string chords, and full harmonic support for tutti passages. It turned out to give a strange sound indeed, largely on account of the dominating accordion, but also from the presence of the saxes imbedded among straight symphonic timbres. That strangeness I was not to know until the first rehearsal. When I did hear it I was shocked, then got used to it. In the theater it gave the work a color like that of no other, though this color had been created not through any search for novelty but by trying to achieve with a minimum number of players a maximum number of classical sound combinations.

Paris that spring was busy with ballets; and I went to the new ones, which were many, reviewing them that fall for *Modern Music*. I also gave with Cliquet-Pleyel a concert of works by both of us; but I do not remember playing either alone or with Marthe-Marthine, who sang, anything that had not been heard before. I also posed for an English sculptor, Winifred Molyneux-Seel, who modeled my head. And I recounted to Bérard exactly how Florine was going to decorate *Four Saints* and listened to him describe his new ballet *Mozartiana*; and I admired his picture by Maurice Grosser, which he had already written me was a "*portrait charmant . . . que j'aime*." And again there were daily morning visits from Lincoln Kirstein, deeply excited by the ballets and looking for a way to work with them. He had been urging Chick that they must next year in the museum's new theater stage a "ballet demonstration." And I had taken him to Bérard, who passed him on, I think, to Diaghilev's former secretary, Boris Kochno, though it was actually through Tchelitcheff that he came to speak with Balanchine. Within that year, in consequence, came Balanchine's removal to New York and the founding of The American School of the Ballet.

The year before, ballet in the Diaghilev style had been revived in Monte Carlo and in Paris, with four young Russian ballerinas (all out of the Paris studios), with one young decorator (Bérard), and with the chief heirs of Diaghilev's distinction in command—the choreographer George Balanchine and the scenarist, general taste-director, Boris Kochno. Then Kochno and Monte Carlo had disagreed; and an English poet, Edward James, had staked Kochno to seasons in Paris and London (called Les Ballets '33). Monte Carlo had kept de Basil as organizer, Massine as choreographer, and most of the better dancers. Kochno and Balanchine, using Tamara Toumanova as chief star and Tilly Losch, James's wife, as a modern-dance novelty, produced at the Théâtre des Champs-Elysées seven new works, among them two in the German taste—*Errante* (Schubert's *Wanderer-Fantasie* orchestrated by Koechlin, with décor by Tchelitcheff) and *Les Sept Péchés capitaux*, called in London *Anna-Anna*, a mimed cantata by Bertolt Brecht and Kurt Weill danced by Losch and sung by Lotte Lenya with a male quartet in a set by Caspar Neher. Others were by Milhaud, Sauguet, and Nabokov, plus Tchaikovsky's *Mozartiana* and some Beethoven Waltzes. The Ballet Russe de Monte Carlo repeated at the Théâtre du Chatelet their last year's novelties plus standard Diaghilev repertory, adding to these a new work by Jean Françaix, selections from Boccherini, and Tchaikovsky's Fifth Symphony. At this house were to be found the connoisseurs of fine dancing and the lovers of ballet tradition, at the other all the city's youth and elegance; and both were filled.

Kirstein's capture of Balanchine was later to make dance history in America. Just then, we who had grown up with the Diaghilev tradition were pleased at seeing it so ardently revived. And we were moved by Lenya's singing, at a concert of La Sérénade, in the Weill-Brecht *Rise and Fall of the City of Mahagonny* (a forty-minute version, made for Paris, that seems now to be lost). And diverted by a Markevitch concert containing his finest orchestral work, *La Chute d'Icare*. And impressed by an all-German *Tristan und Isolde* at the Opéra, with Furtwängler conducting and seats at $10 each. What a season! And all the more a joy to me since my own project was simmering nicely.

For keeping down the labor of writing out in score six hundred pages, I had not only had the measures ruled and voice parts written in; I had also made a deal with Maurice Grosser for inking over what I would do in pencil. Through several years of practice, Maurice had become, for helping me out, a music copyist of good calligraphy. And I did not choose to give up pencil scoring, being ineradicably American about that. Europeans more often than not work directly in ink. They write poetry that way; they compose that way. The powers of quick situation-analysis developed from childhood by a pen-and-ink culture may be responsible for Europe's voluminous musical production over the last four centuries; and I am sure that voluminous production is with any art a necessity for excellence. But Americans are slow to make up their minds—in art, in business, in diplomacy; and this propensity toward putting off decision has made us a pencil-and-eraser civilization. Even on the typewriter we are addicted to many drafts. And by telephone, when a European would say yes or no, our characteristic reply is, "Call you back."

In those days, when you had lots of work to do, you went

somewhere, for life away from Paris was a saving, and third-class train fare very cheap. My usual work place was the southern coast; but I did not care to go that far so soon, having been asked, with ticket paid, to spend a week in London with the Askews. So first I went with Grosser to Honfleur, ancient small port town on the Seine opposite Le Havre, where my landlord, Dr. Ovize, knew a country boarding house. This turned out to be a haven of sweet smells and of silence under apple trees, except on Saturday nights and all day Sunday, when youth danced on an outdoor concrete floor to fox trots and javas stentoriously amplified. And after having scored a hundred pages there, I knew the time the whole of the job would take. I had only to average ten pages a day to be through in two months, and this would leave time for a copyist to extract the parts before I left for New York in late October.

In London I stayed longer than was planned, because Captain Peter Eckersley and his wife were giving a ball. Dolly Eckersley, former wife of the conductor Edward Clark, was a tall woman of soft figure and relentless drive. Indeed, she urged her men toward greater zeal than England likes. Clark, as a result, after combing the world for music of the utmost far-outness, had been demoted by the B.B.C. Captain Eckersley was at this time vigorously promoting an invention, a patent for the wired transmission of radio. Such a method would furnish to receiving sets only such programs as were wired into it; the listener could hear no others. Though the device was economical and efficient, the British government had for political reasons declined to adopt it. The German government, on the other hand, was about to settle with Eckersley and his associates for installing it throughout the Reich.

Cooperation between British business firms and Hitler's government was already active; and England had its fascist mood in politics as well, represented by Sir Oswald Mosely's Blue Shirts. And the scientific interests of her husband were leading Dolly toward involvements with Germany that were to become definitive. Being there in 1939 with her fifteen-year-old son by her previous husband, Edward Clark, instead of returning home while she could still have done so or accepting incarceration as an enemy alien, she denied her country, both for herself and in her son's name, and spent the war in Germany. After the war was over she was tried for treason (she had broadcast anti-British matter, as I recall) and did time in prison. The son, a minor, was not held responsible. And Peter Eckersley, honorable, of good family, and well-to-do, managed to keep out of sight by reducing his engineering career to somewhere near zero. When Dolly, finally out of jail, wrote me that she was destitute, I sent her a food package but did not answer otherwise.

It was after my return from London in the summer of '33 that Dolly, writing for herself and for Edward Clark, besought me to be kind to Arnold Schoenberg, then a refugee in Paris. I used to call for him at his hotel and take him walking, since he did not know Paris well or speak much French. Milhaud, it seems, had invited him to the ballets—not a pleasure, since he could not bear the music of Kurt Weill. "Franz Lehar, yes; Weill, no," he said. "His is the only music in the world in which I find no quality at all." He also did not relish, he would say, being a martyr, for he had not previously thought of himself as Jewish. But since this status was now pressed upon him, he went to a synagogue and embraced it formally. Together with his wife and baby daughter, we all three went to New York in late October on the *Ile-de-France*. Years later, when I gave two lectures in Los Angeles, Schoenberg, though weak, came to both and embraced me warmly. At the time of his seventieth birthday he wrote me regarding an article of mine written to honor it, "I wanted already long time ago to write you that I am very pleased with the manner in which you write about my works. It raises hope that one day in the future there will be an understanding of my music. Thank you!"

It was at the Askews' house in Chelsea that I encountered that summer Frederick Ashton, and friendship flourished as I played and sang my opera for him. Freddy had danced in Ida Rubinstein's Paris troupe, but he was not ever going to be a dancing star. With his taste and brains, however, he could move into choreography; and that is what he was beginning to do at the small dance-theater in Sadler's Wells. "Could you imagine staging my opera?" I asked. "O yes, and with delight," was the reply.

The Eckersleys' party had revealed to me the length to which personal quarrels can be carried in English social life. Though cards had been sent out, well over a hundred, everybody asked had also to be telephoned, because anyone who might find himself at the same party with someone he was not speaking to would be certain to create a "situation" by leaving. I also learned how inconsiderate, in those days, English cuisine could be. Gossip had promised that the food and wines at the house of the essayist Cyril Connolly would be unusually fine. Was his menu a practical joke, or merely a summer solution by his American wife? Dinner consisted of three "cold shapes"—mixed vegetables in gelatin, cold meat in gelatin, cut-up canned fruit in gelatin—and the wine was sparkling Burgundy.

While I was still in America, Georges Hugnet had written, "I am disgusted with what is going on everywhere: the politics in France, Hitler, Japan. . . . What a bouillabaisse to make you vomit!" In Paris I had found that others of my acquaintance, especially those who favored royal government (yearning young men, for the most part, who lived by Proust), had joined up with a protofascist group led by a deputy named Doriot; they actually went to drill meetings once a week. In the south, on the island of Porquerolle, where I had gone with Grosser to finish my score, I met a deputy who declared France in a state for civil war and he himself unsure which side to take, the Third Republic's comfortable corruption or the hazardous adventure of armed uprising.

I encountered him again in late September, back in Paris, where the presence of a stubborn proletariat and ready troops had made him hesitate about taking the latter chance. I never knew whether he did, but the civil war then threatening to boil did come to scalding point the following winter. The Comédie Française, directed by the playwright Edouard Bourdet, had produced Shakespeare's *Coriolanus*, accenting all its inferences about a country's need at certain times for dictatorship. This fanning of fires already lit provoked mob protests in front of the Chamber of Deputies till on the sixth of February the mounted Garde Républicaine fired without trumpet's warning, killing several. (A young man I knew, brother of the poet Edouard Roditi, crossing the Place de la Concorde, was crippled by a bullet in the spine.) But the Republic had won. The next day Edouard Bourdet was replaced as director of the Comédie Française by the director of the Sureté Générale, François Thomé (son of the composer of *Simple Aveu*), who remained in office just one day, removing *Coriolanus* from the repertory—an action that only the theater's director could take—and then resigned.

A Paris literary agent, William Aspenwall Bradley, had written as early as January that Miss Stein had "learned indirectly" of the Hartford project regarding our opera and that she "would be happy to have further particulars concerning the production itself, your arrangements with the director Mr. Austin, etc., etc." These particulars being eventually transmitted through him, I proposed that contracts be drawn between Miss Stein and myself, to define our respective rights and obligations, and between Austin and us both, governing the production. I proposed for Miss Stein and myself, since I knew well her pride in authorship, equal sharing in all the opera's benefits. Later I argued that I had been overgenerous. Here is the correspondence about that and about the production plans:

[To Gertrude Stein]

> 17 quai Voltaire
> 30 May [1933]

Dear Gertrude,

Mr. Bradley has communicated to me a passage from one of your letters to him in which you express some reserves about the opera-mounting as I described it. . . .

Before I go on about the mounting, however, I am taking the liberty of mentioning a business matter which I have already spoken of to Mr. Bradley. . . .

At the beginning of my conversations with him I mentioned that although the usual practice was otherwise, I preferred, in view of the closeness of our collaboration and of the importance given to the text in my score, to offer you a 50–50 division of all profits. It has since been called to my attention by the Société des Droit d'Auteurs that such an arrangement defeats its own end and that the contract commonly made in France allowing two-thirds to the composer and one to the author is designed to establish that very equality;

1) because the manual labor involved in musical composition is so much greater than that of writing words that half the proceeds is an insufficient return for the composer, considering him as a joint worker,

2) because a literary work is perfectly saleable separate from the music and thus brings further profit to its author, whereas the music is rarely saleable in any way separated from the text it was designed to accompany. . . .

In view of these considerations would you consider it just on my part to ask that our projected contracts (and any eventual publication of the score) be based on the 2–1 rather than the 1–1 division of profits, a proportion which, as I said above, is the one used in France to secure an equable division of benefits? . . .

About the mounting, we are all in accord that the idea of a parochial entertainment must remain. Miss Stettheimer suggested, however, that since any interior is less joyful than an outdoor scene, and since Sunday-school rooms and chapels have been done in so many religious plays (black and white), perhaps the same entertainment might take place on the steps of a church, in this case the cathedral of Avila itself, although represented in a far from literal imitation. Spring at Avila could thus be expressed doubly. Also the general atmosphere somewhat lightened. The colors and materials she suggests are merely an amplification of the dazzling fairy-tale effect ordinarily aimed at in the construction of religious images out of tin and tinsel and painted plaster and gilding and artificial flowers. Her idea seems to me to be more efficacious than our original one in expressing the same thing, especially in view of the enormous heightening of every effect that is necessary in order to get a dramatic idea across the barrier of foot-lights and music. I must admit I am rather taken by the whole proposal, having seen the extraordinary grandeur and elegance which Miss Stettheimer has produced in her own rooms with exactly those colors and materials. We are all, however, open to persuasion and to suggestions, and no maquettes have been made.

The idea for the May-pole dance in Act II is even less definite than the other. That also is Miss Stettheimer's. The negro bodies, if seen at all, would only be divined vaguely through long dresses. The movements would be sedate and prim, and the transparence is aimed . . . not at titillating the audience with the sight of a leg but at keeping the texture of the stage as light as possible. This end is important to keep in view when there are as many things and people on a stage as this opera requires and all frequently in movement. Naturally, if the transparent clothes turned out in rehearsal to be a stronger effect than we intended, petticoats would be ordered immediately for everybody. I think the idea is worth trying, however. If it can be realized inoffensively, the bodies would merely add to our spectacle the same magnificence they give to classic religious painting and sculpture. One could not easily use this effect with white bodies, but I think one might with brown.

My negro singers, after all, are a purely musical desideratum, because of their rhythm, their style and especially their diction. Any further use of their racial qualities must be incidental and not of a nature to distract attention from the subject-matter. . . .

Very faithfully yours,
Virgil

[To Virgil Thomson]

Belley, Ain, 5 June 1933
[Postmarked Paris, 6 June 1933]

My dear Virgil,

Have just received your letter. I think, in fact, I wish to keep to the original terms of our agreement, half share of profits. It is quite true that upon you falls all the burden of seeing the production through but on the other hand, the commercial value of my name is very considerable and therefore we will keep it 50–50. The only other point in the agreement between [us] is the one referring to the phrase, unreasonably withheld, Bradley will have told you that I think that we should take for granted one another's reasonableness. . . .

I am entirely agreed that the stage setting of out of door scenery would be the best, and I hope there will be the ox-carts, with the donkey, and the river and the landscape. Would it not be possible to have something in the nature of their out of door processions, with daylight and candle light and overhead canvas stretched between the houses. It altogether makes a beautiful light. I supposed one of the reasons for using negroes was the diction, it all sounds very hopeful and about all these things I am quite ready to accept what seems best to those who are doing it. The best of luck to us all.

Always,
Gtrde

[To Gertrude Stein]

17 quai Voltaire
9 June [1933]

Dear Gertrude,

Thank you for your kind and frank letter. If the only reason, however, for holding to a 50–50 division, aside from the natural enough desire to obtain as favorable an arrangement as possible, is the commercial value of your name, I should like to protest that although your name has a very great publicity value as representing the highest quality of artistic achievement, its purely commercial value, especially in connection with a work as hermetic in style as the *Four Saints*, is somewhat less, as I have found in seeking a publisher for our various joint works. . . . Moreover, it is not the value of your name or the devotion of your admirers (I except Mrs. Chadbourne, who began very practically indeed but didn't continue very long) that is getting this opera produced, but my friends and admirers, Mr. Austin . . . and Mr. Smallens and Florine and Maurice, who are all giving their services at considerable expense to themselves, and a dozen other friends who are contributing $100 or more each to Mr. Austin's costly and absolutely disinterested enterprise. The value of your name has never produced any gesture from these people, whereas every one of them has on other occasions manifested his interest in my work by creating commercial engagements for me and by offering me further collaborations with himself. And dear Gertrude, if you knew the resistance I have encountered in connection with that text and overcome, the amount of reading it and singing it and praising it and commenting it I have done, the articles, the lectures, the private propaganda that has been necessary in Hartford and in New York to silence the opposition that thought it wasn't having any Gertrude Stein, you wouldn't talk to me about the commercial advantages of your name. Well, they *are* having it and they are going to *like* it and it isn't your name or your lieutenants that are giving it to them. If you hadn't put your finger on a sensitive spot by mentioning this to me, I should never have done so to you. However, I've got it off my chest now and the fact remains that even were the situation reversed, a 50–50 contract would be, so far as I know, absolutely without precedent. . . .

I am glad you approve of the scenic plans. The second act includes just such a night scene as you have described. I don't know whether a river can be got on the stage too, but I hope so. . . .

Best of greetings.

Always faithfully,
Virgil

[To Virgil Thomson]

Bilignin par Belley, Ain
[Postmarked 11 June 1933]

My dear Virgil,

Yes yes yes, but nous avons changé tout cela [referring to her recent success with *The Autobiography of Alice B. Toklas*], however the important thing is this, the opera was a collaboration, and

the proposition made to me in the agreement was in the spirit
of that collaboration, 50–50, and the proposition that I accepted
was in the spirit of that collaboration 50–50 and the proposition
that I continue to accept is the same. When in the future you
write operas and have texts from various writers it will be as you
and the precedents arrange, but our opera was a collaboration,
we own it together and we divide the proceeds 50–50, and we
hope that the proceeds will be abundant and we wish each other
every possible good luck.

Always,
Gtrde Stein

[To Gertrude Stein]

17 quai Voltaire
22 June [1933]

Dear Gertrude,

Everything is arranged now, at least for the duration of our
present contract and I have signed it and Mr. Bradley is sending it
to you. The copy of score is ready (or will be tomorrow). It is in
the original form plus Maurice's stage directions. I suggest (since
they are neither your nor my invention and though they will be
used in the production are not the only ones that are possible)
that I cross them out of the copyrighted work. . . .

I find on working over the opera and orchestrating it that I
should very much like to make a few simple cuts. You offered me
that privilege at the beginning of our collaboration and I didn't
care to avail myself of it, preferring to set everything and wait for
a later time to make any such cuts in view of actual performance.
I find now that there is a little too much singing and not enough
instrumental relief. I should like to eliminate for example a few
of the stage-directions as sung, especially where they are repeated
frequently. I don't mean systematically to remove them, just a
few repetitions now and then, in every case (or nearly) to replace
them with an instrumental passage of the same length and tune.
This makes a rather amusing effect and is as if an instrument were
saying the words that somebody has just sung. There are also a
few passages that I should like to eliminate for the purposes of
this performance, substituting in one or two cases a short instrumental passage, in others nothing at all. This in view of tightening
the structure musically and making a more simple and effective
musical continuity. The aria in Act III about roses smell very well,
for instance, comes right after another aria for tenor and rather

impedes the advance of the spectacle toward the ballet. I should like to cut it out.

The cuts I propose are only for the purposes of my score for this performance. The copyright score would include everything. I mention the cuts because I don't want to avail myself of a permission offered so long ago without its being renewed. I hope you will allow me to do this. I assure you the theatrical effectiveness of the work will be enhanced.

Many thanks for your gracious acceptance of the consent clause in our agreement. We now have, I think, a simple way of settling any differences that may arise without bitterness. As a matter of fact, we understand each other so well and our interests lie for the most part so close together that I am sure we shall always be mostly reasonable with each other anyway.

Best of greetings.

Always devotedly yours,
Virgil

[To Virgil Thomson]

Bilignin par Belley, Ain
[Postmarked 25 June 1933]

My dear Virgil,

Yes of course you are to make the cuts, the burden of making it a successful performance lies upon you. . . . I am very pleased that everything is arranged, Bradley will be sending me the agreement and I will sign it, and I hope it will all be as successful as possible, we certainly deserve it, do we not. . . . You are quite right about not using Maurice's suggestions in the copy for copyrighting, I am glad he is to be in the show, he certainly helped a lot.

Always,
Gtrde

20

Four Saints in Three Cities

AT PORQUEROLLE I DID MY STINT of ten score-pages a day; and Maurice kept up with me, respacing the notes, inking them in, and erasing the pencil marks. Every day I proofread my work as well as I could with the eye alone (having no piano); and I did this very badly, it turned out, hundreds of faults surviving in the score and consequently in the orchestral parts. And since I had no time for checking these materials before I sailed, my orchestral rehearsals were to cause Smallens untold trouble and me no end of shame. But I did get through my chore, thanks to Maurice, who vowed he would not ever copy music again; and by mid-September I was back to Paris, where I delivered the pages for extraction and for binding, ordered new dress clothes from Lanvin (on credit), and packed up for moving from the quai Voltaire. I could not afford to go on paying rent during an absence I could not calculate; and there were not likely to be subtenants for my studio, since the French had always found it a bit dear, and American money, now gone off gold, had lost two fifths of its worth.

Chick Austin had written in July that a project "about the Russian Ballet in Hartford" had gone through, and that it was "under the auspices of the American Ballet, Inc. that [he hoped] to produce [my] opera, since money is more easily raised for a continuous plan like that." This plan was of Lincoln Kirstein's undertaking, based on founding under Balanchine's direction a school for ballet dancers and a ballet company. The young Edward M. M. Warburg had given money to get this project started; and Chick had offered it a home in his museum. He assured me at the same time that the opera "comes first" and added:

> I think that it will be a winter of fun for all, as I hope that you can spend it mostly in Hartford . . . first with the opera—later orchestrating things for the new American ballets, writing some new scores perhaps and possibly conducting a permanent orchestra which will serve all sorts of purposes. I am hoping to raise

extra money to pay you some sort of salary. Balanchine can do
the ballet for your opera and I don't see why we can't all together
do something of interest if not of importance. . . .

When can you come over and how much money is it going to
take? (Minimum please.)

Please forgive my stinginess—I am not a rich art patron. I'm
just a poor boy trying my damndest to get that opera produced.
Come soon please. We have so much to discuss and plan. . . .
The building seems to be coming along well and the builders
still insist that the theater will be finished on December fifteenth.

By the time I arrived, on October 31, and moved into the
Askews' spare room, it had been decided that only New York
could furnish enough students for a ballet school. So Chick,
lacking the ballet's "continuous plan," transferred the producing of my opera to a concert-giving group he had formed some
five years earlier, called The Friends and Enemies of Modern
Music. He still had no money for the production beyond small
gifts of $100 each that a half-dozen friends had paid toward my
travel and for the copying. And a budget could not be arrived
at till a director had been found. But professional ones showed
little faith in the work; it resembled nothing they knew. And I
was not entrusting it to amateurs.

It was Lewis Galantière who brought me John Houseman,
with whom he had written a play. And Houseman, to my delight, turned out to be a European, a product of French lycées
and an English public school. And when I had played and sung
the opera for him, he said, "This could have been for Etienne de
Beaumont's Soirées de Paris" (the series of spectacles for which
in 1924 Satie and Picasso had produced *Mercure*). Then I told
him of my wish for a Negro cast and about Miss Stettheimer,
who had already built a toy stage and was filling it with dolls,
lace, and feathers, crystal, and cellophane. Did he think the
work would interest him to stage? "It would be fun to try," he
answered. "There is no fee involved," said I, "not for Smallens
nor Florine nor anyone except the cast and orchestra." I knew
that he had not directed previously; neither, for that matter, had
Florine ever worked in show business; nor had I, since my early
movie days in Kansas City. He would have to see his own play
through its opening, of course; and he would always have to be
working at translations from French and German, for that was

how he earned his livelihood. But he would see me through, if I wanted him to. I did. And we began an association that has lasted thirty years—in operas and plays, in radio and films, in television, even in dance and vaudeville numbers, as such moments occur in other dramatic forms.

Houseman took us over, organized us, secured Kate Drain Lawson, working free, to see that sets and costumes got made right, secured also an ace press agent, Nathan Zatkin, and Lee Miller, the most stylish photographer in town, to take our pictures. Houseman drew up a budget right away. And he hired us a rehearsal hall in Harlem, the basement of Saint Philip's Episcopal Church. Aided by a Negro talent scout, I had held soloist auditions in the Askew drawing room; for hearing choristers I moved uptown, engaging there, for access to these, a Negro woman who had the best of them under contract. In return for program-credit as our choral director, she furnished me singers musically literate.

Houseman was more effective in the producer's role than bold in his concepts about *mise en scène*. I felt he would welcome help from a choreographer. There was no possibility of using Balanchine, new to America and busy with his school. So I wished in front of Chick and to the Askews that there were a way of getting Freddy Ashton over. He had never directed opera, but he understood *Four Saints*. We could pay his fare third class, and the Askew household could provide a bed. If he were willing to work free, like the rest, Constance would send a telegram inviting him. So it was sent; and he did accept; and he arrived on December 12, along with Maurice Grosser.

Freddy was a godsend both to Houseman and to me, as well as a joy forever to the cast. Maurice, knowing the opera by heart, helped me to cut it for a smooth trajectory. But for all his inside knowledge of the work, he turned out to be a trouble at rehearsals. He would get nervously excited, which he was prone to do at any time, and communicate impatience to the cast. Deeply upset about the omission of a storm, I think it was, he could not be consoled. Eventually I induced him to stay away from St. Philip's. His excellent observations could not be offered calmly enough to be of use, though he it was, among us all, who really understood the text and who had devised, with Stein's acceptance, a scenario that was bedrock to our production.

That production grew as naturally as a tree. I took the vocal rehearsals; and I kept the tempos firm and the words clear while Ashton choreographed the action, standing, as choreographers like to do, in center-stage and moving the singers round him, at first with their music scripts in hand, so that movements and music and words all came to be learned together. Stein's sentences, set to music, were easy to memorize; to recall them intact one had only to think of their tunes. And Houseman surveyed us all as if unworried, watched over us like some motherly top sergeant, wisely kept the bookkeeping vague, met financial emergencies dead pan.

The Negroes proved in every way rewarding. Not only could they enunciate and sing; they seemed to understand because they sang. They resisted not at all Stein's obscure language, adopted it for theirs, conversed in quotations from it. They moved, sang, spoke with grace and with alacrity, took on roles without self-consciousness, as if they were the saints they said they were. I often marveled at the miracle whereby slavery (and some cross-breeding) had turned them into Christians of an earlier stamp than ours, not analytical or self-pitying or romantic in the nineteenth-century sense, but robust, outgoing, and even in disaster sustained by inner joy, very much as Saint Teresa had been by what she took for true contact with Jesus, Saint Ignatius by dictates from the Holy Ghost. If Beatrice Robinson-Wayne and Edward Matthews, who played these roles, seemed less intensely Spanish and self-tortured than their prototypes, they were, as Baroque saints, in every way as grandly simple and convincing.

The Negroes gave meaning to both words and music by making the Stein text easy to accept. And every day visitors from downtown—playwrights like Maxwell Anderson, reporters like Joseph Alsop, colporteurs of news like Mrs. Ira Gershwin—would come to watch the miracle take place. Eventually a Broadway producer arrived for tasting the show—Harry Moses, a retired manufacturer of underwear, avid of distinction in the theater and not without a nose for it, a flair. The previous year, with *The Warrior's Husband*, he had made a star out of

Katharine Hepburn; and in the following one his production of *The Old Maid*, by Zoë Akins from a tale by Edith Wharton, was to receive a Pulitzer. Moses scented prestige in *Four Saints*, also a bargain, since our production was being made at off-Broadway prices. He realized that the work was not a commercial venture but an art piece, and that if it could be made to pay its way, or nearly, both he and Broadway would gain intellectual credit.

We moved to Hartford the first of February for a week of rehearsals with orchestra, sets, costumes, and lights. The cast stayed in hotels and houses listed by a Negro committee; the staff, for economy, mostly in the guest rooms of Mrs. James Goodwin, Helen Austin's mother. For the last three days of rehearsal Florine Stettheimer and her sister Ettie were at the old-fashioned, still gastronomic Hotel Heublein, as also were Carl Van Vechten, his wife Fania Marinoff, and the art reviewer Henry McBride, who sent almost hourly dispatches to *The New York Sun*. Weather was unbearable out-of-doors (sixteen below), but we scarcely noticed it.

On February seventh and eighth the New Haven Railroad put on extra parlor cars for New York fashionables and for the international museum-and-dealer world arriving to honor the new wing's opening and to see the Picasso show. Serge Koussevitzky had written that regretfully he could not come on any night that week. There did come from Boston, however, the composer George Foote, our only guest, I think, to arrive by air. And there were stylish parties, of course, every night, the finest to my taste being that offered to the cast by the Negro Chamber of Commerce. It was not showy and there was nothing strong to drink, only a pale rum punch in paper cups; but there was Southern-style jazz in a big bare hall. I remember climbing its stairs at midnight and dancing for what seemed about a minute. Then it was five o'clock; the jazz band went home; our week was over.

In a letter of December 6 to Gertrude I had given her a foretaste of its grandeurs.

Hotel Leonori
Madison Avenue at 63rd Street
New York

6th December [1933]

Dear Gertrude,
    . . . The cast of the opera is hired and rehearsals [have] begun.
I have a chorus of 32 and six soloists, very, very fine ones indeed.
Miss Stettheimer's sets are of a beauty incredible, with trees made
out of feathers and a sea-wall at Barcelona made out of shells and
for the procession a baldachino of black chiffon and bunches of
black ostrich plumes just like [for] a Spanish funeral. St. Teresa
comes to the picnic in the 2nd Act in a cart drawn by a real white
donkey [eventually omitted] and brings her tent with her and sets
it up and sits in the doorway of it. It is made of white gauze with
gold fringe and has a most elegant shape. My singers, as I have
wanted, are Negroes, and you can't imagine how beautifully they
sing. Frederick Ashton is arriving from London this week to make
choreography for us. Not only for the dance-numbers, but for the
whole show, so that all the movements will be regulated to the
music, measure by measure, and all our complicated stage-action
made into a controllable spectacle. Houseman is a playwright,
friend and collaborator of Lewis Galantière. He "understands"
the opera too, if you know what I mean by that word. Everything
about the opera is shaping up so beautifully, even the raising of
money (It's going to cost $10,000), that the press is champing
at the bit and the New York ladies already ordering dresses and
engaging hotel rooms. Carl's niece has taken a Hartford house
for the opera-week. . . .

The Stettheimer décors and costumes have been commented
on in many books. The Stein text and my music have also received both praise and blame. The elements that never have
been questioned are the Negro casting and the choreography,
though their examples have been very little followed. Negroes
had not been much used for playing non-Negro roles. Today,
though they are so used, even in opera, they are not used for
their characteristic qualities, but in spite of them rather, as if
one was not supposed to recognize their race. And operas, a
few of them, have been choreographed. But they have been
choreographed for white dancers, who tend always to look arch

in the presence of song, and for white singers, who do not walk well and who stand around like lumps, rather than for Negroes, who can move boldly and who stand with style. It was thanks to the choreography, indeed, and to our cast that the production's major quality shone out—a unity of concept and performance that no one had seen before in opera.

We gave six shows in Hartford, including a preview, charging $10 a seat for that and also for opening night. We then moved to New York and rehearsed for a week, adding more singers to the chorus, a harmonium and strings to the orchestra. We also relit the show to Florine's taste. Since her stage colors were all bright and all clean, never muddy, she had insisted from the start on white light. Now the custom of that time was to produce white light by mixing colored lights; even so skilled a lighting technician as our Abe Feder believed that the only way. But Florine persisted, told him where white bulbs, strong ones, could be bought; and he got her a dazzling effect for the opening scene. She also insisted that Moses buy gloves for all the cast; the ungloved hand she found inelegant. And she made herself, for St. Ignatius in the first act to offer St. Teresa, a multi-colored heart-shaped floral piece, also a large gold sunburst with orange clouds for the last act, both out of cellophane.

Her use of net-backed cellophane has remained unique. On the afternoon of our New York opening the Fire Department required us to spray with waterglass our draped and tufted sky-blue shining backdrop, as well as the pink tarletan palm trees. As soon as the inspectors left, Kate Lawson replaced on these the hopelessly wilted leaves; at eight that night she was ironing out still others so they would stand perky again. It was luck we had been allowed to open at all, for the Fire Department that same week adopted on our account a rule forbidding cellophane ever again to be used on a New York stage. In the 1952 revival of *Four Saints*, in New York and Paris, a woven plastic substitute material was employed; but neither in texture nor in color was it pleasing; and instead of standing out like crystal rock, it drooped in gathers like a window drape.

On our 1934 New York opening night the February cold was still intense, the streets were icy, and there was a taxi strike. But everybody came, from George Gershwin to Toscanini—a showy full house at $6.60 top, though $4.40 was the standard then.

The press was excited and voluminous. *Modern Music*, as if hesitant to take sides, sent two reviewers—Gilbert Seldes, who thought it a lovely show, and Theodore Chanler, who found my music, compared with the rest of the spectacle, "a sow's ear." In 1948 Chanler confessed to my biographer Kathleen Hoover that he had wished to write otherwise but that a composer he deeply respected, encountered that same evening at a reception, had "simply pulverized [him] with scorn and indignation for having *dared* to like it." "I was intimidated," he said.

Copland, as always, spoke frankly, in this case glowingly. "I didn't know one could write an opera," he said. (He was to compose one shortly, *The Second Hurricane*.) And of the orchestral sound, "It's so fresh! When the bassoon plays, it's as if one had never heard a bassoon before." Roger Sessions, on the other hand, told me he thought I had "not made maximum use of [my] orchestral resources."

Whether or not one found the work acceptable, its notoriety was unparalleled since that of Marcel Duchamp's *Nude*. For six months and more the show was named at least once every week in every New York paper and in some paper somewhere in the United States every day. There were constant editorials, cartoons, and jokes about it; all the music and drama critics in the East reviewed it. H. T. Parker came from Boston to hear and see it, caught cold, died with the unfinished article on his desk.

But for all the publicity, Ashton got no offers to do other work in America, none, at least, that he found worthy. Nor did celebrity do me any good, though as Van Vechten had said, I was certainly at that moment "the most famous [meaning "talked-of"] composer in the world." A former English teacher of mine did procure me a lecture date, and for that I paid a short visit to Kansas City. And Lawrence Langner, of the New York Theatre Guild, did propose a possible composing of music for a possible production of a Molière comedy. The project, as I remember it, seemed tentative and not, as planned for staging, a very good idea. Aside from this, there were any number of librettos offered, invariably low-grade comic scripts. No music publisher wished to issue the *Four Saints* in score. No lecture agent cared to take me on. And colleges were as silent as the clubs.

The only paying customer my fame attracted was the

ever-watchful League of Composers. They who had declined my instrumental music seemed to have acquired some confidence in my vocal skills. In any case, a commission was awarded me to compose a choral piece for female voices, the cash value of it their smallest fee, $300.

And Lincoln Kirstein proposed a ballet for which e. e. cummings was to write the scenario. For subject, cummings leaned toward *Uncle Tom's Cabin*; and though I thought the choice a bit Yankee of him, I did not discourage it. When he gave me the text that autumn, called simply *Tom*, I pointed out that it was not a ballet scenario, but a poem about one. I saw no way of getting it on a stage, much less of dancing it; nor has it to this day, I think, been choreographed, though David Diamond did compose a score.

By the time my opera opened at the Forty-fourth Street Theatre, all our staff, excepting Miss Stettheimer and Maurice Grosser, had been put on salary. The $10,000 budgeted for the Hartford production (and overspent) had been obtained through gifts and from the sale of seats. An additional $2,000 (one fourth of this required for an extra rehearsal of the orchestra on account of time-consuming errors in my score and parts) had been lent by Houseman, by Constance Askew, and by Chick himself, all of whom needed to be paid back. The paying of this debt, plus royalties due the author and composer for the Hartford run, was all the compensation Chick expected from Harry Moses in return for his gift of the production. Moses did pay the New York royalties, of course; but those due from Hartford never did get paid. When Gertrude inquired about these, through her agent, I replied we must not pester Chick just now. I also raised the question of paying Grosser, whose royalties, though unforeseen in any contract, were properly a charge against the librettist. But on this matter she was firm, giving no reason, simply saying no—surely, I thought, a case of consent "unreasonably withheld."

We played a month at the Forty-fourth Street Theatre, then moved to the Empire for a fortnight. Smallens, who had not believed the opera would last so long, was obliged to leave at the end of five weeks. So for the final week I took it over, a privilege for the experience it offered, in view of our coming engagement in Chicago. For a concert manager there, Grace

Denton, had offered to subsidize the opera for a week in November at the Auditorium, Louis Sullivan's monumental opera house, still favorable to the sound of music and to voices. And since Smallens would not be available, I was to conduct.

A new backdrop was run up for Chicago, our old one being by then too stiff to fold. By what means Miss Denton cleared cellophane with the Chicago Fire Department I do not know; but it was used. Before I went there to rehearse the orchestra, Smallens had reviewed the score with me, explaining certain ways of beating time and how I must mark my beats into my score, then never change them. The orchestra men, all better than my New York group, contained among the violins three former concertmasters of the Chicago Symphony Orchestra. Only the accordion player, unused to orchestral routines, needed special watching. When he made a false entrance on opening night, I resolved the emergency, which might have led to chaos, by stopping the orchestra, looking at Saint Teresa, then beginning her aria without his interference.

Though the Auditorium stage was twice the width of Hartford's, we did not change at all our set's proportions, kept them the same as for Chick's tiny theater, merely masking the proscenium down to size. And I used my New York number of orchestral players, twenty-six, seating them closely massed for resonance against the pit's back wall. Ashton, long since gone back to England, was not there to rehearse the cast; but one of our singers, Thomas Anderson, who had kept a prompt-book, knew every movement. The performances were as lively as in New York, the press reports just as excited. And there were the usual parties, the last of these being given by a Negro group way out on the tough South Side, where one of our dancers got into an argument and, trying to pull a pistol from his pocket, shot himself in the leg.

My father, now over seventy, retired and motorized, drove from Kansas City with my mother. Jessie Lasell and Hildegarde Watson turned up too. As did also Russell Hitchcock, on a lecture tour, and Joseph Brewer, formerly a New York publisher, just then president of a small college in Olivet, Michigan. Chicago was jolly, hospitable, culture-aware. The Arts Club gave me a luncheon, and the local branch of the American Opera Society bestowed on me its David Bispham Medal. Unused to awards, and feeling a bit ashamed, as if I were being blest by some Establishment, I gave it to my adolescent niece.

Gertrude Stein, newly arrived in America for a lecture tour, had flown from New York with Alice Toklas and Carl Van Vechten. After the first act, still deaf from her first airplane ride and wishing to hear her own words, Gertrude left her seat of honor in Harold McCormick's center box and moved to an orchestra seat down front. After the performance, when photographers backstage were posing her with local potentates, it was McCormick who courteously suggested that I join the group. Otherwise, no one was much aware of me. The party that night was at "Bobsie" (Mrs. Barney) Goodspeed's, a sit-down supper with champagne, twenty at table. Houseman later remarked that Miss Stein's lips showed dark spots such as his father's had when he was ill of Addison's disease. Gertrude, then sixty-two, lived twelve more years. She may, though, have been cancerous already.

When the contracts for Chicago were being drawn, I had told Harry Moses I would not conduct unless Grosser, so far unpaid, was put on royalty for a small percentage. Also that this was not to come from my share. He could either deduct it from Miss Stein's or pay it himself. Grosser was not being insistent; but I was out to win the point from Gertrude. The producer, however, did not wish to pay for Miss Stein's stubbornness; and her agent could do nothing with her. Moses tried simply omitting Grosser from the contracts, then sending them to my hotel by an assistant, who tried to secure my signature through confusion. But I was unconfused, and the assistant gave up. "You make out the contract as you want it," he said at last.

For doing this, I telephoned a Wall Street law firm, which sent me that same night a young man just from Yale, wearing a revolver in a leather holster. "Collecting rent in the slums," he allowed, "is tough these days." He made out a contract from my dictation, Grosser to be paid half of one per cent of the receipts, and charged me $50 for the service.

Next morning Alfred Barr was on the phone. One of his trustees, a woman in the advertising business, needed to make a present to a client who collected autographs. She would love to have something nice by Gertrude Stein. Did I have a letter I would consent to sell?

"Yes," I said quickly, "and the price is $50."

I had, in fact, a fairly recent one about our opera. I had not sold letters before; nor have I since. But selling one of hers to reimburse the cost to me of enforcing payment on a production charge I believed to be owed by her seemed poetic justice. I did not mind that it was Moses who really paid, since he owed me a favor from the New York run, when I had secured Gertrude's consent to a diminution of both our royalties. I did not tell her what I had done; I did not care to risk another quarrel. For Gertrude, about money, did not joke.

21

Communists All Around and High Life Too

BACK IN THE TWENTIES, both Sauguet and I had been regularly under attack for writing simply, as if straightforwardness in music were an outrage. So naturally *Four Saints*, when given in New York, had shocked many by the plainness of its harmony. Nevertheless it seemed to be pointing a way, and for composers the way it pointed was toward the stage. Now for invading the theater, baggage needed to be light. To encumber the social-content stage (for that was where in the 1930s many of us came to be working) with all the impedimenta of modernism was to hinder communication. And communication, after the middle thirties, had become urgent. Noble subjects, moreover, taboo in the twenties, were suddenly available to art. And for treating all such themes—in America sociological, in Russia historical, in Spain patriotic, in France humanitarian—self-consciousness of manner was ineffectual.

It came about therefore that during the 1930s, especially their highly productive last half, music could be contemporary without being hermetic. Obscurity, long the hallmark of modernism, remained a trademark for masters over fifty—for Picasso, Schoenberg, Stravinsky, Joyce—for all but Gertrude Stein. After her return from America in 1935 she more and more transcribed just "outer realities." Likewise, and especially in America, composers moved with the times toward lofty themes and plain speaking about them, as first I, then Copland, Piston, Blitzstein, Antheil, and Douglas Moore began to work for the stage and for documentary films.

My first job in the speaking theater came in 1934 from Joseph Losey, engaged by the Harvard Dramatic Club to direct Denis Johnston's *A Bride for the Unicorn*. To this I added male choruses and percussion, went to Cambridge for fitting them in, stayed through its opening in Brattle Hall on May 2.

My next commission was from John Houseman, planning an off-Broadway season of off-Broadway plays, the first to be Euripides's *Medea* in verse translation by the Negro poet Countee Cullen, using for star the Negro tragedienne Rose

McClendon. Awed in *Four Saints* by the dignity of Negroes' stage presence, Houseman was all for finding out whether this could be used to comparable advantage in poetic tragedy. He wished to mount (in English) not only an ancient Greek play but also a French modern classic, *Le Cocu Magnifique* by the Belgian Fernand Crommelynck, believing its story of violence through jealousy, like that of *Medea*, a natural for Negro inter-pretation. Neither play came to production, though two years later we produced a Negro *Macbeth*. And I did, in Paris that summer of '34, compose the *Medea* choruses.

I also composed there, for my League of Composers com-mission, a Mass for Women's Voices and Percussion, using a severe manner, derived from the medieval, that I esteemed no less appropriate for modern music societies than for nuns. When the work was performed the next April in Town Hall the press gave copious coverage (for after *Four Saints* I was news) but found it no show of force on my part, since I had got through in less than fifteen minutes a text that Bach had made to last out three whole hours.

It was that same summer of 1934 that I declined regretfully James Joyce's invitation to write a ballet for the Paris Opéra after the chapter on children's games from *Finnegans Wake*. I was to reject cummings's *Tom* that fall. A third subject, suggested by Florine Stettheimer and acceptable to Kirstein, was Pocahontas at the court of James the First. Eventually I renounced that too, because I could find no way to give it urgency. For décor it was splendid, but it lacked drama. Even reenacting the John Smith episode would not have saved it, I felt, since plays within plays, unless interrupted, are merely a rite.

In New York, with my last $20, I bought a secondhand piano and in my rooftop hotel room (oh, the crushing September heat that year and the crashing storms!) auditioned replace-ments for Chicago in the *Four Saints* chorus. In October, for Theodate Johnson's Town Hall recital, I accompanied my per-cussive Song of Solomon. My new dinner jacket from Lanvin, double-breasted, as was about to be the style, had an extra pair of buttons that would click most unexpectedly when I damped the cymbals edgewise on my chest.

Back from Chicago in mid-November, I returned to compos-ing portraits of my friends—some for a modest fee, some for

none. In all cases I would give a manuscript. The Friends and
Enemies of Modern Music continued to produce concerts in
Hartford, all of which I organized and in most of which I performed. In December, at Chick's theater in the Wadsworth Atheneum, we offered a new kind of concert—new, at least, for the
twentieth century, though it would have seemed normal to the
eighteenth—namely, one with especially designed stage-sets.

We had already experimented the April before with dramatic
cantatas framed in décors planned out by Chick himself. I remember Theodate in the *Lucrezia* of Handel, melodramatic in
an ominous light-effect, singing dramatic coloratura in black
beside a black piano. This time I was to conduct two scenes
out of Avery Claflin's *Hester Prynne*, an opera based on Hawthorne's *The Scarlet Letter*, with scenery and costumes designed
by the painter Victor White and by Roy Requa, John Houseman directing the stage. Preceding this there were to be played
two string quartets. And Chick, fearing both auditory and visual
imbalance with regard to the opera's massive stage-effects, had
asked Tchelitcheff, just arrived from Europe, to design a décor
for the quartets. He did, and it was ravishing.

The theater's sky-blue cyclorama was its background. A low
black platform large enough to seat four players was backed
by a three-panel screen and framed by a simulated forged-iron
arch draped in white tulle. The arch, made out of rubber hose
suspended by invisible wires, was like a stroke of penmanship.
The screen, painted by Maurice Grosser, bore the first three
pages of my Quartet Number Two, drawn in white on black,
like an engraver's proofs. Maurice also copied out the cello part
in black on twenty yards of pure white tulle. All white and black
against ethereal blue, as insubstantial as the sound of music, the
set gave visual presence to the musicians and picked up the red
brown of their instruments. Maurice, in helping Tchelitcheff,
had broken his vow never again to copy music; but thanks to his
help the screen became musically legible. And thanks to Tchelitcheff the whole effect was in just that spirit of fluffy Baroque
that Chick loved and that was Florine's private kingdom even
more than it was Pavlik's.

At another concert of the Friends and Enemies, this time in
Chick's Venetian drawing room, four composers performed
their own and one another's music. Aaron Copland played

pieces of mine and also his Piano Variations. I played portraits of a half-dozen people present and sang songs by Paul Bowles (one made from a letter of Gertrude Stein) and by Antheil (out of *Alice in Wonderland*). George Antheil played duets with me and by himself a Suite. Bowles offered portraits of the other three composers, plus a Piano Sonatina.

It must have been during that same season that I organized a concert of old music played on old instruments for opening a show of eighteenth-century French art at the Metropolitan Museum, where it turned out that our historic viola bastarda was actually depicted in one of the paintings. The curator was delighted with the whole occasion until he learned that I expected to be paid.

Dates of this kind, some public, some private, kept small sums coming into my bank account. At one time I went to Providence to play and sing for a party given by Charles Brackett, fiction writer and Hollywood film director. At another I went to the Taconic hills for lecturing on my music in a fine house where the hostess, about to take off for Portugal, asked me whether Capri also was "unspoiled." Impertinent as usual, I answered that the word "unspoiled" was scarcely applicable to an island that since Roman times had been a rendezvous for every kind of vice.

It was also in 1935, I think, that efforts began to be made toward organizing the serious composers. Concert and opera soloists had already formed, for collecting fees and strengthening their contracts, The American Guild of Musical Artists (AGMA). And concert managements had been merged into two main trusts. It was the lawyer who had formed one of these, the Columbia Concerts Corporation, itself tied up to recording and broadcasting, who first brought together the composers. The American Society of Composers and Publishers (ASCAP) was not then so hospitable to classical musicians as it is now; and virtually no such composer, consequently, was receiving payment for performances or broadcasts of his music. So that when about a hundred of us were asked to dinner by Milton Diamond and given applications to sign for membership in a projected society, many saw the dawn of a new day.

But I figured that Diamond and his associates were probably moved less by our interests than by theirs and that their proposals had better be examined. So when my colleagues elected me, along with several others, to meet with Mr. Diamond for drawing up bylaws, I went to every meeting, asked embarrassing questions, and confused the lawyer, who knew lots about mergers but very little about authors' rights, into revealing that he was not completely on our side. When these negotiations failed, as I had been determined that they should, the desirability of a composers' society remained. Over the next three years the plans for this were worked out, partly by me, who had in my European years learned something about authors' rights, and partly by Copland, who could mold them into forms acceptable to others. The result of our work was the American Composers Alliance, incorporated in 1939. The eventual outcome of Milton Diamond's project was Broadcast Music, Incorporated, of which the main commerce was selling to the broadcasters, who themselves owned BMI, performing rights controlled by its publisher members.

In the summer of '35 I visited Constance Askew in Stonington, Connecticut, then Grosser in Huntsville, Alabama, then Chick in Castine, Maine. Nothing was accomplished through all this bus travel beyond the delights of friendship and a dozen or so portraits in music. Also, as always when with Chick, lots of planning. This time it was for a festival of the arts, to be held the next February. There would be films, selected by Iris Barry, ballets danced by Balanchine's new troupe, concerts of music selected by me to be performed in stage sets by Alexander Calder and Eugene Berman, and a costume ball designed by Tchelitcheff.

That fall I teamed up with John Houseman for sharing flats; and from October through March we lived in four, some rented, some lent by friends. And Houseman was a joy for living with; he never scolded, and he was away all day. Like a proper Englishman, he got up at eight, bathed, washed in his bath the previous day's wool socks, cooked coffee and eggs, ate, and left. We always breakfasted in French, settling matters that regarded books and plays and actors in that best of all languages for making critical distinctions. In November, when Kurt Weill and his wife, Lotte Lenya, arrived, we thought, with Chick, that it would be good to produce in Hartford Weill's German opera made with Brecht, *Mahagonny*. We took Weill there to see the theater, and I even played through the score with him for setting tempos. But quietly the project was dissolved; and one came to understand that Weill's working association with Bertolt Brecht, as part of a possibly communist-tainted past, was to be buried. And buried it remained until his death. He developed on Broadway a new career which made him fame and money. Lenya, who had been identified with the earlier works, was omitted from the new ones. After Weill's death in 1950 she appeared on the stage again, though still chiefly in Germany, in revivals and subsequent recordings of the operas composed with Brecht.

And just then (we are in November of '35) Broadway began to be aware of a slender, moon-faced actor, Orson Welles, who was playing a small role with Katharine Cornell in *Romeo and Juliet*. My other close director friend, Jo Losey, could not bear him; but Houseman, scenting brains and temperament, brought him to our flat. That Welles could be so overbearing at eighteen was in his favor; that he had already directed plays in Dublin we did not believe. But Houseman was organizing a theatrical production-unit under the Works Progress Administration; and he had faith in Orson, as he had in me. It was around the three of us, with Feder for lighting, that he organized the Negro Theatre in Harlem, which was to be the first of all the federal theaters to open. In fact, with the turn of 1936 both Houseman and I began to have lots of jobs; and all of these we felt sure were important.

Before that time there had been a series of musical performances that were for me important. Copland, ever adept at attracting subsidy, had been put in charge of five one-composer concerts at the New School for Social Research and had chosen as subjects for these the members of American music's most up-and-at-'em commando unit—himself, myself, Roy Harris, Sessions, and Piston. For my program, November 8, I coached my Second String Quartet, *Stabat Mater*, and Violin Sonata, played portraits and a Piano Sonatina, accompanied Ada Mac-Leish singing in French poems by Georges Hugnet.

Eva Goldbeck, Marc Blitzstein's wife, reviewed the concert for *Modern Music*. Less a musician than a polemicist, she wrote almost as if she had been assigned a hatchet job, or in any case permitted the attempt. She spoke of "salon" music with clearly pejorative intent. "Fundamentally sanguine, with a few well-timed sighs," "a slight but graceful voice," "depends on associations[,] as emotional impact is outside Thomson's range or intention," "the relaxed mood of a well-carpeted cocktail hour"—were the phrases with which she must have hoped to kill.

The Federal Music Project, come January of '36, initiated a concert series that still goes on. This invention of Ashley Pettis, called then The Composers' Forum-Laboratory, now The Composers' Forum, has always been a mixture of talk and music, since the public, after the music has been played, is invited to question the composers. I shared the first such program with Roy Harris, Goddard Lieberson, and Isadore Freed; and under the questionings I defended firmly my right to make music after my own aesthetic dictates. I also parried several attempts to invade my political privacy. For the communists, who had turned out in force, were surely hoping that by means of loaded questions they might prove my inveterate trade-unionism and solid colleague relations just a front, as if the *Four Saints* and museum worlds had left me suspect or contaminated. Actually, as that year turned into 1936 I was about to be involved no less with leftist musical politics than with the ultrastylish Hartford Festival.

The latter took place in February of '36, just two years after my opera's opening, The Friends and Enemies of Modern Music still serving as impresario. It comprised five chief events— a showing of historic films, three concerts, and a ball. The films—and this was before such showings were at all common— consisted of the Méliès *A Trip to the Moon*, of 1902; two from 1914, Theda Bara, the original "vamp," in *A Fool There Was* and dance sequences from *The Whirl of Life*, with Vernon and Irene Castle; and René Clair's Dada fantasy from 1924, *Cinéma* (*Entr'acte*), accompanied by the Satie music.

An orchestral concert called "Music of the Connecticut Valley" ran from a Festival Overture of 1896 by John Spencer Camp, through substantial works by Roger Sessions, Frederick Jacobi, Ruth White Smallens, Werner Josten, and Ross Lee Finney, the latter's offering being a set of songs which had won the festival's chamber music prize.

I conducted a program running from the eighteenth-century

French *gambiste* Caix d'Hervelois to modern rarities that included works by Henri Sauguet and Paul Bowles, also a seven-instrument paraphrase by Henri Cliquet-Pleyel of *Swing Low, Sweet Chariot*. I had also inserted my own Sonata da Chiesa. The early music was played on early instruments; the set for the concert was the work of Eugene Berman.

Berman had dreamed of theatrical settings all his grown life. When Chick suggested his actually designing one, almost overnight he made thirty-four water-color sketches, all evocative of seventeenth-century Italian ruins and all showing mud puddles in the foreground. When I questioned the practicality of real mud and water, I was assured that the puddles were there in the sketches only for lifelikeness. And when I asked whether he had calculated the effect on his already complex stage-pictures of musicians, chairs, and instruments, he answered, "They will injure it, of course." The young James Soby, who from having already bought roomfuls of Berman canvases was Chick's diplomatic agent for dealing with him, suggested that passages from several sketches might possibly be combined. But Genia would have none of that. "An artist," he would say "can accept only negative criticism. If the first sketches are not satisfactory, I shall be glad to make others. But I will not be told how to solve a problem." I do not remember how the solution was arrived at, but one of the less busy backdrops came to be used. And Berman was happy; I was happy; everybody was.

The most complex of these concerts was one involving three contrasted works and three stage-sets. Stravinsky's *Les Noces*, conducted by Smallens, was sung in Russian in front of a décor painted after the original design of Natalia Gontcharova, which was in the museum's Diaghilev-Lifar Collection. There was no dancing, however, in this presentation. That appeared only in a ballet called *Magic*, which Balanchine, with Tchelitcheff as designer, had imagined after seeing Chick, as "The Great Ozram," do a sleight-of-hand matinee for friends and children. In this ballet, to music by Mozart, Felia Dubrowska made her last public appearance and America's finest classical male dancer, Lew Christensen, his first.

The piece that I held closest to heart was Erik Satie's *Socrate*. For this performance, America's first complete orchestral one (conducted by Smallens from the pit), I had abandoned the Paris tradition of using just one singer and arranged for two, so as to pass the conversations back and forth. These were Eva Gauthier, soprano, and Colin O'More, tenor; and I did not require the latter always to sing the role of Socrates. For an equal distribution of opportunities, I cast him also as Phaedo, who recounts the death scene.

Alexander Calder's set was an arrangement of geometric forms, all capable of motion. They were supposed to be moved mechanically; but the motors Calder had provided were too weak. So our lighting expert—Feder, as usual—with the help of a stagehand manipulated them by ropes. This mobile sculpture, simple to the eye and restrained in movement, was so sweetly in accord with the meaning of the work that it has long remained in my memory as a stage achievement. Its layout was as follows: The singers stood in evening dress before lyre-shaped black music stands, right and left near the proscenium. Upstage and to the viewer's right, against the sky-blue cyclorama, there hung by invisible wires a scarlet disk. Downstage, also on the viewer's right and also hanging in the sky by invisible wires, was the framework of a globe, drawn in space by aluminum tubing as if to represent meridians of longitude. At center-stage and to the left, also invisibly supported, stood two narrow white rectangles unequally tall.

During Alcibiades's praise of Socrates (from *The Banquet*) nothing moved. During the philosopher's walk with Phaedrus along the banks of the Eleusis, the sphere revolved sedately. For Phaedo's narrative of Socrates's death the sphere stood still while all the other forms moved very slowly. The white stele-like rectangles leaned to right, lay down, became invisible, then stood again, now well to right of center, exposing their other face, which was black. And meanwhile, from the beginning of the death scene, the sunlike disk had been descending diagonally across the sky, so that when the movement of the steles had been completed (from left to right and from white to black) the disk was low and on the viewer's left. Attention to words and music had not been troubled, so majestic was the slowness of the moving, so simple were the forms, so plain their meaning.

The final event of the Hartford Festival, a *Bal des Chiffoniers*, or Ragpickers' Ball, was Tchelitcheff's joke for high society about the Depression. He had papered the covered court's three balconies with newspapers, brushed lines on these in black to simulate draped lace, creating in this way boxes for paying guests, themselves got up in paper or in circus rags. For a *Cirque des Chiffoniers*, with Chick and a fashionable hostess as ringmasters, was theme for the prepared entrances. Of these the program listed seventeen, well more than half of them taking place to music especially composed by George Antheil, Nicolas Nabokov, and Vernon Duke and in costumes designed by Calder, Tchelitcheff, Berman, Alice Halicka. One of Berman's most effective was a walking structure entitled *Hartford in Ruins, A.D. 3095.* Modern art was parodied from Chirico to Brancusi. And there was a ballet, fortunately interrupted by the Fire Department, in which dancers with lighted candelabra on their heads leaped through the paper porticos.

This Hartford Festival, announced as the first, was also the last. And its concerts marked my last service as "musical director" of Chick's Friends and Enemies, for by then I had got involved with plays and films. I was back and forth to Hartford as a visitor; and my ballet *Filling Station* came out there two years later. And Chick went on with his unusual shows of painting and with the producing of rare operas and of classical tragedies such as *'Tis Pity She's a Whore.* He even played the leading role in *Hamlet* to the music I had made for Leslie Howard. But after the war in Europe had begun, and he turned forty, the flame of youth went out of him, though youth's energies were there still when he died in '57. He had not liked not remaining thirty. Also, his team had got dispersed. He had staged an epoch right in his museum, using Baroque art, surrealist art, and the neo-Romantic when all three were exotic to America. He was at home with artists too, loved to admire them, give them comforts and affection, put them to work. One of his finer inspirations, just before his career began to lose momentum, was to commission murals from Kristians Tonny. Completed in 1938, they still light up the side walls of the theater where so many of us worked happily and well.

22
Show Business for Uncle Sam

PARE LORENTZ WAS A FILM REVIEWER beginning to make films. And his first essay, a documentary, had just finished being photographed. Looking for a composer, he invited me to lunch. This was in January of '36. I was not the first one he had interviewed; Copland, I know, and Harris, I think, he had already not got on with. Houseman, whom he had consulted, had suggested me as musically straightforward and theatrically wise; and though Lorentz had yet to hear any of my music, he engaged me on the spot. Our conversation went like this. He first explained his film, asked could I imagine writing music for it. My answer was, "How much money have you got?" Said he, "Beyond the costs of orchestra, conductor, and recording, the most I could possibly have left for the composer is five hundred." "Well," said I, "I can't take from any man more than he's got, though if you did have more I would ask for it." My answer delighted him. "All those high-flyers," he said, "talk nothing but aesthetics. You talk about money; you're a professional."

The film was a documentary about cattle raising, wheat growing, and dust storms on the Western plains. Its sponsor was the United States Resettlement Administration, needing to justify its program of aiding refugee families from devastated areas. Lorentz had begun his film by engaging as story writers a trio of photographers who knew the Southwest—Ralph Steiner, Paul Strand, and Leo Hurwitz; and early he had quarreled with them about their wishing to ascribe the grassland's rape not to just human nature, the Great War, and lack of foresight, but to a more conventional villain of the time, capitalist greed. Next he had fought with Hollywood over the right of our government to purchase, as any U.S. citizen could do, stock shots of World War I, of forty-eight-mule-team reaping, of flood-lit harvesting, and similar subjects not available for him to photograph. With the aid of a former Assistant Attorney General, Mabel Walker Willebrandt, he did secure the release of certain footage. He never secured permission to show his film in houses controlled by the industry, as Hollywood called itself. The industry did not hold with documentaries anyway, still less with films made by the government, above all not with anything well done that was not theirs. And *The Plow That Broke the Plains* was powerful story-telling; documentaries so dramatic had not been made before.

When I was hired, the film was in the cutting stage; and composing music before each sequence has found its true length is rarely advisable. So all that I could do while waiting was to grow familiar with the uncut film through frequent viewings and to look up all the books of cowboy songs and settler folklore, since Lorentz's mind was set (and oh, how rightly!) on rendering landscape through the music of its people. When at last he was through with cutting, he wanted me to write twenty-five minutes of music, symphonically scored, inside a week. I told him I could not do that, because I should be away for four days at the Hartford Festival, but that I would have everything ready for recording within the fortnight. To do this I should need, in addition to the usual copyist for extracting the parts, a musical secretary trained to help with score.

The cost of this he did not mind, since he had foreseen that I might require a paid arranger. It was from Antheil, who had the year before made music for *Once in a Blue Moon*, a Jimmy Savo film, that I got the address of a very young Canadian composer, Henry Brant. Working in pencil, I could sketch-orchestrate everything myself, then check his ink score to be sure it had come out my way, which indeed it had, for the most part. And Brant was such a natural orchestrator that I even asked him once to salt up a passage with percussion. I did not, after one essay, depend on him for string chords or for phrasing, for though he could dispose these admirably, I did not like another's personality to color my sound.

Returned from Hartford with a blasting grippe, I composed at night, scored over Brant's shoulder in the daytime, finished my work as promised. It was recorded in New York by thirty men from the Philharmonic and from the Metropolitan Opera, conducted by Smallens, who was accustomed by then to my music and had a lively understanding of its ways. Nor was he surprised when errors turned up in the parts. Delays caused by correcting these in full recording session ran up the costs, according to Lorentz's stop watch, by something like $500. Teaching a guitarist to play in three-four time against a six-eight beat cost plenty too. But Smallens could work fast; and the Philharmonic boys, used to one another and to achieving balanced sound, produced a symphonic richness not at all common in films.

Then Lorentz disappeared with the sound track into the cutting room, was gone a week. When he emerged, he had recut his film. Some of the recutting had been required by my war music's not being as heavily scored as it should have been. To compensate for phrases of light texture he had rearranged the order of the views, also added cannons and bomb-sounds and tank-noises. All the other adjustments he had made were for illustrating passages in the music. For Pare was musically sensitive to the last degree. He would have preferred, before he cut his film at all, to have a full recording of the music, because details, especially of orchestration, would make him want to match them visually. But since a visual narrative cannot be based on auditory timings, a film must be cut before any score is made. Then after the music track has been recorded, only the sight track can still be manipulated. And it was within this limited flexibility that Pare created, working to the very sound of music, a music-stimulated intensity within each sequence. As a result, photography, words, and music in *The Plow* seem not to be at war with one another but to be telling, all at the same time, the same story.

We were living at this period, Houseman and I, in a furnished apartment on Central Park South; and it was from there that I did all my work for the Negro Theatre. This enterprise, a unit of the Federal Theatre, operated a large Harlem playhouse from prewar times, the Lafayette. Houseman was its director, Orson Welles his assistant, Feder his lighting and technical man, myself in charge of music. I think we were the only whites, save our scene designer, Nat Karson, and a secretary. Ninety percent of all who worked there had to be drawn from the city's relief rolls. And all were paid the same, $23.86 weekly. Establishing such units all over the United States not only for theater workers but also for artists, writers, and musicians was the W.P.A. assignment; and it was urgent because the relief of poverty was urgent. That our unit was the first of all these theaters to open was due to Welles's brilliant planning and to Houseman's administrative tact.

The plan involved, as any repertory project must, preparing two plays at once, the second to be ready in case the first should fail. Our opening spectacle, a play by a Negro on a theme from Negro life, required no written music. Our second, Houseman's dream but Orson's child, was *Macbeth*. And in this Orson showed himself, still just eighteen, as imaginative, foresighted, patient, above all with a knack for making actors act.

The production idea that was to make *Macbeth* seem suitable for Negro performers was that of moving its locale to Haiti, where a Negro usurper could be believable, at least in Napoleonic times, along with his overthrow by revolution. This transfer gave us, instead of Scottish witches, real voodoo, also some most becoming Empire costumes. I say real voodoo because it was provided by a Congolese who had already produced dance spectacles with African instruments constructed by himself and songs remembered from his mission childhood. Asadata Dafora Horton was authentic, all right; we had checked on that. (In the 1960s he was to become Minister of Culture in the Republic of Sierra Leone.) And he could produce with black Americans music and drumming and dance to put the chill up anybody's spine. I once, for the second witches' scene, asked for more chill. "This sounds a little tame," I said. "Is it real voodoo you're giving me?" "Oh, yes, that's voodoo. Yes, that's real all right." "What kind of voodoo is it?" I insisted. "Real voodoo. Yes, real voodoo," was his answer. And it remained his answer till I broke him down. He finally admitted that it was not *evil* voodoo but only charms against the beri-beri. Anything stronger in that black atmosphere, stirred up by rhythm and poetry, might work; indeed it might. I said no more.

Our Lady Macbeth was Edna Thomas, our first Macbeth Jack Carter. When he grew undependable, Maurice Ellis took on the role. Canada Lee was permanently Banquo. There was a sizable pit orchestra, which I conducted at the opening. Also there was a percussion group backstage made up of bass drums, kettledrums, a thunder drum, a thunder sheet, a wind machine—all these not only for simulating storms but also, played by musicians and conducted, for accompanying some of the grander speeches. In this way, on a pretext of rough weather, I could support an actor's voice and even build it to twice life size. This device (really Welles's) requires accurate operation, for with all the percussion rattling, players backstage cannot hear lines but must depend on light-cues; nor can an actor so accompanied change his reading much from one night to another.

The whole production, with its voodoo dancing, its ball scene (for there was waltzing at the banquet), its storms, its battle trumpets, and its marching trees, was melodramatic to the utmost. When late that summer Jean Cocteau turned up, circling the globe in eighty days for a Paris paper, I took him to *Macbeth*. And he savored each ingenious violation of the straightforward, excepting only one: he did not understand the constant lighting changes. His classical theater mind found them distracting till he had seized their function in the spectacle as contributing to the climate of violence. The only element not in this "Wagnerian" key, as Cocteau called it, was the music, which consisted altogether (outside its voodoo realisms, its offstage storms and battles) of familiar suspense-conventions, of pathos passages almost *Hearts and Flowers*, and, in the ball scene, of Lanner waltzes.

From this production I acquired two musical aides—Hugh Davis, player of kettledrums and percussion, and Leonard de Paur, a choral conductor. Davis remained invaluable until he died in the early 1940s. De Paur is a colleague still, though he is famous now and tours with his own choir. But Harlem then was full of lovely people. So was the W.P.A. The times were for sweetness and for joy in work.

My next job, all the same, was bittersweet, the bitter of it being the hemlock taste that permeates all things communist. In such an ambience, someone is always handing you the poisoned cup. And the theater that borrowed me that summer, The Living Newspaper, was up to its ears in commies. My director, also on loan, was Joseph Losey, with whom I had worked before. The script, a montage of scenes from the history of union labor in the United States courts, was called *Injunction Granted*. I used an orchestra of sixteen percussion players, with sixteen bass drums, snare drums, cymbals, sixteen of everything, including bronx cheers. I also had lots of bells and chimes and three electric sirens. I punctuated every exit and entrance, almost every remark, with percussive comment and ironic framing. The complete score came to 496 music cues. The show was less pungent, however, than its predecessor, *Triple-A Ploughed*

Under, which had set the dramatic form. This form was documentary, editorial, frankly hortatory. I regret its passing. Its television heirs, known as spectaculars, are seldom so convincing.

Injunction Granted had been made in summer's heat, high up in a house that received hot winds (and greasy soot) from the East River. There too I helped Paul Bowles through his first theater-piece. The apartment was Alfred Barr's, lent for the summer—a large living room, two bedrooms, and two baths. For several weeks I shared it with the lyricist John Latouche, then impecunious and convalescent; but before I got to working on my next show, he had gone to e. e. cummings in New Hampshire. During the August heat I worked on another show with Welles, who with Houseman and their team—which still included the scene designer Nat Karson—had left the Negro unit, forever playing *Macbeth*, and formed one of their own, called Project 891, at the Maxine Elliott on Thirty-ninth Street. Here I joined them for putting on—at my insistence, as I remember— a nineteenth-century French farce by Eugène Labiche, *Un Chapeau de paille d'Italie*, newly translated by Edwin Denby and Welles together and retitled *Horse Eats Hat*.

Welles directed it, of course; he even played at the opening a character bit and sang a song, though his ear was not for music. The other parts were played by Joseph Cotten, Hiram Sherman, Arlene Francis, Sarah Burton, and Paula Laurence. And if *Macbeth* had in Orson's hands turned Negroid and Wagnerian, this classical French vaudeville became a circus. There was a seven-door set "in one," admirable for hide-and-seek; there was furniture by Bil Baird designed to come apart; there was a ball room with crystal chandelier and a functioning fountain. When at the end of Act One, with guests waltzing and waiters coming in with champagne, our harassed hero, Joe Cotten, jumped to the chandelier, which swung with him, and the fountain below began to spout on him, and then in the pandemonium stagehands began to carry off the scenery and a blank curtain came down as if to end the disaster but itself fell clean to the floor, and the house curtain finally descended, Muriel Draper was overheard to cry, "It's wonderful! They should keep this in the show!"

The music too was like a circus with side shows, for in addition to that in the pit there were on the stage (where all was in the style of 1910, with hobble skirts and hats with ostrich plumes) two dance bands, one for playing turkey trots and one in red coats for playing gypsy waltzes. At intermission, from one stage-box a mechanical piano pumped out period selections; and in another a lady trumpeter in hussar's uniform rendered *The Carnival of Venice*.

The pit contained no less than thirty-five musicians, and both the lower boxes held grand pianos. The music by Paul Bowles, and there was lots of it—overtures, intermezzos, meditations, marches, even a song or two—had been selected mostly out of works already in existence. In that way one can have varieties and richnesses of texture almost never available in music run up rapidly. And for further amplitude, I scored these numbers as a suite for two pianos and orchestra. I made the score myself because Paul had not yet learned to orchestrate. Receiving help of this kind shocked him deeply. Within the year, as a result, he had composed and scored excellent music for Orson Welles's production of Marlowe's *Doctor Faustus*, a ballet for Kirstein and Balanchine's new company (*Yankee Clipper*), and a Negro opera (*Denmark Vesey* by Charles-Henri Ford).

Only in such an enterprise as the W.P.A. Federal Theatre, where maximum employment was the aim, could one have mobilized effectives as numerous as those used in *Macbeth* and in *Horse Eats Hat* or in *Injunction Granted* or in the sumptuous mounting of T. S. Eliot's *Murder in the Cathedral* (with quantities of music by Lehman Engel). And only in a time of general unemployment could one have had directors, artistic collaborators, and technical assistants of such high quality. None of our *Horse Eats Hat* cast was yet famous, though news of Orson had begun to get around. The fact that he could both direct and act was leading him into a career that rose like a rocket, only to begin before he had turned thirty its slow descent. Welles as actor, for all his fine bass speaking voice, never did quite get into a role; his mind was elsewhere. He discovered many an actor's talent; his own he seemed to throw away. And by the time he weighed 300 pounds his presence on stage destroyed the composition. But working with him in his youth was ever a delight, also a lesson that might be called Abundance in the Theater.

Horse Eats Hat played to an intellectual public. It might have broadened its appeal had not our Washington inspectors been bent on combing its language for indelicacies. Every day or two another telegram arrived, ordering that such and such a line be cut. Shortly we knew that someone "down there" did not like it; moreover, audiences were finding the show's satire of itself confusing. So Welles began on Marlowe's *Doctor Faustus*, a spectacle grand enough and far less difficult. And Houseman was getting involved with *Hamlet*; so was I. We remained on the federal payroll, since being paid between productions was the only way we could make our salaries support us. And Houseman is at his best when overworked; he cannot do just one job at a time; he must have two; fatigue excites him.

Our *Hamlet* was for Leslie Howard, a drawing room actor principally, but one who felt that modern plays, for all his great success in them, were not using fully his abilities. I am not sure that Schuyler Watts, an enthusiast just out of Yale, had not convinced him Hamlet was his role. For with Howard in mind, Watts had cut and rearranged the play with great sagacity. And Houseman, engaged to direct it, had gone along with Watts's scheme for placing it in medieval sets, adding a Welles-like richness everywhere and engaging me to furnish lots of music. My novel additive to *Hamlet*, aside from bagpipes in the funeral march, was making a ballet-opera out of *Gonzaga's Murder*. This play within the play, to set it off from the drama going on around it, I treated as if a medieval troupe, accustomed to representing saints and miracles, were intoning it in medieval poses. Agnes de Mille translated this conception into choreography; and visible musicians accompanied it, using tiny drums and cymbals especially made, bamboo recorders, and a rare sort of horn.

This treatment was thoroughly effective save for one mistake. My player of recorders, Youry Bilstin, an expert on old instruments, had found somewhere a handsome serpent made of leather. It would not play, but he proposed to use it as a megaphone, singing into it "hoo" to imitate a hunting horn. The sight of it was so delightful that none of us remarked its shaky sound until on opening night at the Boston Opera House a drunk in the gallery hiccoughed and laughed. That was its end. I tried to quarrel with Houseman on the subject, but he was firm; and anyway I knew I had miscalculated; the chanted play remained without its horn. My music was conducted, on stage and off, by Hugh Davis, my percussionist from Harlem. And for Pamela Stanley, who could sing most sweetly, I set every one of the Ophelia songs. The production, after Boston, played three months on Broadway and something like that time on tour. Never so popular as John Gielgud's *Hamlet*, which was running that same season, through its scenery by Stewart Chaney and its direction by Houseman it was probably more distinguished. And though Howard had not Gielgud's vocal power for the great tirades, in the intimate scenes with Ophelia and with Horatio he was more touching. For the last soliloquy, "How all occasions do inform against me," we placed him on a ship's prow, center-stage high up; and I arranged for offstage instruments, evoking North Sea weather, to build up his voice until it filled the house.

At the middle of November I went to Paris for six weeks, not notifying the Federal Theatre of my absence. I was to start work with Pare Lorentz the first of January on another film. Meanwhile, I wanted to be with Madame Langlois, from whom I had been away two years, and to resume, if only for a time, the flow of friendship's dialogue with Hugnet, Cliquet-Pleyel, Sauguet, Bérard, as well as Gertrude Stein and Max Jacob.

I took with me a film-print of *The Plow That Broke the Plains*, engaged a projection-theater, had friends in to see it. Miss Stein was there, of course; and Cocteau came, bringing the ever so fashionable Daisy (the Hon. Mrs. Reginald) Fellowes; and Hugnet brought the surrealist poets Paul Eluard and André Breton. Breton and Cocteau, though literary enemies, committed no unfriendly act, as English enemies would have felt obliged to do, but in the good French way ignored each other.

I also gave a concert with Cliquet, a small one in his studio apartment. And although Marthe-Marthine sang Satie's *Socrate*, which had not been done in Paris recently, and Paul Poiret, known better as *couturier* than elocutionist, read charmingly from the fables of La Fontaine, there was such a grubbiness about Marthe's interior, with its six-yard window curtains almost in shreds, that Julien Levy, arriving from New York, felt he must reproach me for appearing in an ambience so slummy.

Paris itself had turned political; the leftist Popular Front was a success. The Spanish were embraced by civil war. The King of England had resigned for love. Hitler had caused henchmen to be shot down. Russia was disciplining Shostakovich. In Italy liberals had joined the Fascist party. From America Harry Dunham, my former neighbor of 17 quai Voltaire, arrived just then, traveling via Russia into China. Once there, by unknown means, and carrying a Communist party card, he made his way to the communist provinces, took films that became a news scoop. He also, loving ever an adventure, gave his American passport to a German youth who had none, declaring to our consulate its loss or theft.

Before I took ship I received from Washington, which had discovered I was absent not only from Maxine Elliott's Theatre but also from the country, a pink slip terminating my employment. Arriving in New York on New Year's Eve, I shortly took a flat again with Houseman, this time on Fifty-fifth Street at First Avenue. From there Houseman, still at the Maxine Elliott, produced Marc Blitzstein's *singspiel*, *The Cradle Will Rock*. And at the Neighborhood Playhouse, Orson Welles, with Lehman Engel conducting, produced *The Second Hurricane*, a Copland-Denby high school cantata-opera. As for myself, for the next half year I mostly wrestled with Pare Lorentz.

23

The Theatrical Thirties

LORENTZ AT THIRTY, already getting heavy but still darkly good looking and with an eye that both laughed and calculated, was talkative, ambitious, truculent, ever a battler. He battled with Hollywood and with Washington; he battled with his cameramen and with his cutter. For seven months he battled with me over music, money, aesthetics, every single point of contact that we had. Nor do I think he was not mainly right. I merely note that battling was for Pare a way of life and that even in creating he warred with his teammates. He did not bicker; his tone was gentlemanly; our weekly all-night conferences were warm. But Pare's film was his brainchild not yet born, and he could not be stopped from going on about it. He could not bear that I should have to wait till it was finished to add music. He even seemed to hope that I, by sharing his birthpains, might end by writing music in his person.

At forty I could not write music in anybody's person. Collaborative art, I knew from instinct and experience, can only give a good result when each man offers to the common theme, through his own working methods and at the proper time, his own abundance. An author-director needs to keep all such abundances channelized for nourishing his theme rather than drowning it; of such are his veto rights. But when he suggests textures he is always wrong. These must come out of each man's own technique. An artist cannot be ordered about or hypnotized, but he can be fecundated by another's faith. Here lies the difference between live art and the commercial, that in live work everybody trusts everybody else. But Pare did not trust anybody quite, because from inexperience he did not trust himself.

The music of *The Plow* had poured forth easily. I knew the Great Plains landscape in Kansas, Oklahoma, New Mexico, Texas; and during the War I had lived in a tent with ten-below-zero dust storms. I had come to the theme nostalgic and ready to work; and the film itself, when I first encountered it, was ready to be worked on. The subject, moreover, was highly photogenic—

broad grasslands and cattle, mass harvesting, erosion by wind, deserted farms. *The River* was to be different; its theme was soil erosion by water, not by wind. Its landscape of streams and forests was pastoral, static. Its historical narrative covered a century, its geographical perspective half the continent. And floods, though murderous to land and houses, are not at all dramatic to observe. A film explaining how they come about and how they can be controlled by dams demands a far more complex composition, if one wants to make it powerful, than the blowing away of our dry high-lying West.

Pare's subsidizers in the government, pleased by *The Plow* but aware that *The River*'s theme would be harder to elaborate, were granting him a slightly larger budget for the new film. And Pare, grateful for my underpaid work on the earlier one, was wishing to overpay me a bit on this. So he put me on salary from February first at $25 a day, the wages of a union camera-man. The only trouble with this ingenious solution was that no checks came; I imagine paper work had held them up. Then new floods, grand ones, appeared in the Midwest; and Pare flew out with cameramen to photograph them. But still I had no money, and Pare's office had no news. So I wired him that if he were wishing to fire me by not paying my salary, I should feel free, even obliged, to seek other employment. His answer was telegraphic:

REPLYING TO YOUR LETTER CATEGORICALLY STOP SAID TO YOU COULD NOT PUT YOU ON FULL SALARY UNTIL CAMERA MEN DIS-MISSED STOP AM PAYING YOU EVERY CENT POSSIBLE RIGHT NOW AND MORE THAN BUDGET ALLOWS AND AM STRAINING TO MEET EMERGENCY PAYROLLS STOP DID NOT FORSEE FLOODS OR WOULD HAVE BEEN CUTTING PICTURE LONG AGO STOP YOU WERE EM-PLOYED TO COMPOSE A MUSICAL SCORE STOP THERE IS NO MOVIE FOR YOU TO COMPOSE FOR BECAUSE OF A MEMORANDUM STOP I AM STRAINING TO PAY YOU FOR RESEARCH DURING PERIOD I CARRY CAMERAMEN ON SALARY STOP CAN PAY YOU FULL PERIOD FOR FEBRUARY BUT CONSIDER THAT ONLY UNPROFESSIONAL THING ABOUT DEAL STOP SINCE WHEN DID SHOW HAVE TO BE WRITTEN TO SUIT COMPOSER STOP WITH ARMY WEATHER AND CAMERAS TO WORRY OVER CONSIDER YOUR LETTER UNFAIR AND UNCALLED FOR

LORENTZ

My checks, as promised, did start coming soon. And Pare came back and showed me his new footage. And we went on sitting up nights, drinking together and trying to solve problems by talk that cried out to be solved by work—by visual work on Pare's part, such as cutting his film, on mine by study of regional music sources. This I began to do, actually; and in the course of that, I came upon the gold mine of hymns known as "white spirituals."

The identification of this material as authentic folklore had been made by Dr. George Pullen Jackson, a New Englander from Maine teaching at Vanderbilt University; but only the beginning of his work had yet reached print. When I wrote him for access to the hymnbooks that were his sources, he procured for me the chief ones and on his way to Europe came to see me with recordings of these hymns as actually sung. Maurice Grosser, painting in Tennessee, went out to the hills to look for more such books and found a plowing clergyman willing to lend, since it was "for educational purposes," his precious copy of the century-old *Southern Harmony*. And when Maurice came back to New York, I engaged him on federal payroll, with Pare's complicity, to copy for me all the tunes, their counterpoints and words, that I did not have already in *The Sacred Harp*, the other chief available source for folk hymns.

By this time spring was on; our lease was up; and Houseman had moved out to Rockland County (for sleeping only, since he was in town all day). I had gone to the Chelsea Hotel on West Twenty-third Street, where I was to stay for the next full year. And Pare, who also lived in Rockland County, would come there; and I would sing and play for him my newly-come-upon Americana. He was skeptical, I think, of its value to the film, but he did not battle with me over it. We merely wrestled, testing our defenses. My own absorption in these tunes, though passionate, was not exclusive, since I had just received by gift another gold mine, a collection sent to me by Foster Damon. This was a reprint in facsimile, with learned notes, of one hundred American popular songs running from roughly 1800 to 1850. These filled out my ancient hymn-lore with vaudeville ditties, parlor ballads, and levee hoedowns until, along with what I knew already, I had the Old South richly repertoried. I even went to Washington, spending an afternoon there with old

John Lomax, song hunter extraordinary, and making free with the vast materials, in so far as catalogued, that he had brought back to the Library of Congress.

As Pare, who was a slow worker but persistent, little by little got his film down to thirty-six minutes (four reels) and perfected his accompanying text, a Whitmanesque prose poem about America's rivers, I little by little would sketch music that seemed to me to suit the sequences. But Pare was worried, I think, lest my involvement with white spirituals get out of his control; and he kept on trying to arrest my pregnancy. I quoted to him Eugene Berman's protests against directive criticism. I also pointed out that he did not have a completed film. How could I be guided about what I had not seen? But Pare, though amused by the old commercial ditties, remained unsure about backcountry hymns and worried lest I overuse them in his film. So in June I resigned again, writing him that since he was not finding my work satisfactory, continuing it would do his film no good, and that I was going off to bask with friends in Rensselaerville.

At the end of a week he telephoned to say that he was ready for me now and would I please return. I said, "Pare, I am on strike. If you want me back at all, you must hear my conditions." He waited a moment, then said, "I'll expect you tomorrow." So I went back.

My main condition was that he was not to give me any more musical directions, though he could veto any music I proposed. My second was that I wished, and rather for his sake than mine, to be present in the cutting room, at least a little bit, so that I might possibly be able to discern what his film needs were, which I had so consistently failed to grasp from explanation. He agreed to both, gave me a near-completed timing sheet, and said I was to finish up my score. From then on he liked everything I wrote; and when I played it all in front of the screened picture, he found no alterations needed. So again I called in Henry Brant, and within a week the score was finished. In late July it was recorded in Astoria by Smallens and some forty Philharmonic men, along with Hugh Davis, who played all the percussion and received at the end a standing cheer from his colleagues. Lorentz disappeared then into the cutting room, said he would let me know when I might join him.

For all Pare's constant talk to me about film problems, at no time had I tried to guide his work, though I had offered him full access to mine. I had no wish, God knows, to interfere; nor was I at all experienced in cutting. But since he had submitted many of his problems as if they might be apt for musical solution, I knew the only place to test this was the cutting room. And besides, my fresh eye might just possibly be helpful; in the theater Welles, Losey, Houseman, all had found it so. This is why at the last I came to insist that Lorentz stop lecturing me and let me help him cut the film. He never did. But he did just once invite me to the cutting room during the week he was holed up there with the music track. He summoned me for some time before midnight, and with the union cutter we stayed till morning. Through the movieola I checked their progress as they labored at recutting the whole film to my music. Pare asked for no comment; I uttered none. He made it clear that my being asked there was a courtesy; I made sure to offer no encumbrance. We went home at eight, Pare pleased, I thought, to have outmaneuvered me and infinitely pleased—that I could tell—with the music track.

For composing the last half reel I had had no cue sheets. "Write me a five-minute finale," he had said, "and I'll cut to that." So I used the finale of my *Symphony on a Hymn Tune*, the theme of which, a white spiritual anyway (though I had not known that when I wrote the piece), had been employed earlier in the film. And for this Pare composed his visual peroration to point up every detail of my scoring. I cannot imagine cutting a whole film that way; but the whole film, this time, did not seem to suffer gravely. In fact, when shown, and it was shown widely in spite of Hollywood, audiences would applaud, a thing they almost never do for movies. Despite the film's intractable material and despite Lorentz's constant wars and wrestlings, *The River* seems now, seemed then indeed, to have achieved a higher integration of filmed narrative with spoken poetry and with music than had existed since the sound track's coming into use some eight years earlier. Even when the film was cut by one fourth its length (to twenty-seven minutes, for use in schools) the music remained, through Pare's ingenious clippings and refittings of it, surprisingly apt, and almost as closely integrated to the words and scenes as if it had been composed for the compact version.

I worked also on a full-length film that summer, a documentary called *The Spanish Earth*. This was a view of the Spanish civil war from the republican side and of an irrigation project completed in Castile during the siege of Madrid. The script was by Ernest Hemingway, John Dos Passos, and Archibald MacLeish; and I think Lillian Hellman also did some work on it, though her name does not appear among the credits. The film was photographed under fire by Joris Ivens, with Hemingway overseeing; and the verbal text for it was both written and recorded by Hemingway. When the film was being readied for showing, in August of 1937, the absence of a music track became as noticeable as the fact that there was neither time nor money for composing one. Marc Blitzstein and I, being consulted, offered to assemble a music track out of Spanish recordings available in private collections, chiefly those of Gerald Murphy and Paul Bowles. These contained choral numbers sung by Galician and Basque miners, woodwind *coblas* from Barcelona, and naturally lots of flamenco from Seville. Actually we used flamenco only once, for accompanying a view of the rightists; it did not seem sincere enough for dour Castilian farmers or for republican soldiers. The transfer of these recordings to music track and the matching of this in fragments to the sight track was the work of Helen Van Dongen, remarkably skilled and subtle in film cutting. The result is a film completely documentary, since its views of Spain's patient people and high-lying farmland are accompanied throughout by the real music of that land and people. There may be other filmed narratives as authentic; I do not know them. Certainly there are few of such distinguished authorship.

My other work of 1937, almost wholly for me a year of theater, consisted of a ballet and a Shakespeare play. The dance piece, commissioned by Lincoln Kirstein for his Ballet Caravan, was a slice-of-life called *Filling Station*. George Balanchine, essaying to develop both dancers and dance designers, had found his male wing readier for professional appearance than the female. Dance scores already furnished by Robert McBride (*Show Piece*) and by Paul Bowles (*Yankee Clipper*) had been choreographed by Erick Hawkins and Eugene Loring. That midsummer I had found in Lew Christensen a dancer and director I knew I could deal with, and in the subject offered us by Kirstein a theme I thought I could at least take hold of. Aaron Copland had also been invited to compose for the Caravan's formal opening that winter in Hartford, but he was hesitant. He had in 1934, for Ruth Page in Chicago, composed a ballet, *Hear Ye, Hear Ye!* But it was not till he had heard the scores we three had done and watched the new troupe in action that he undertook the medium again, this time to compose for Loring, who would both choreograph and dance, the remarkable ballet-Western *Billy the Kid*.

For *Filling Station* Christensen and I worked out a suite of "numbers" and "recitatives" to tell the story in appropriate timings. And I wrote a score made up of waltzes, tangos, a fugue, a Big Apple, a holdup, a chase, and a funeral, all aimed to evoke roadside America as pop art. The painter Paul Cadmus designed clothes and a setting for it inspired by comic strips. Christensen, as a filling-station attendant in white translucent coverall, filled the stage with his in-the-air cartwheels and held us breathless with his twelve-turn pirouettes. At the Hartford opening on January 6, 1938, my music was played on a piano by Trude Rittmann, as was also that of the other ballets. Six weeks later the New York W.P.A., with Edgar Schenckman conducting, performed all three with orchestra.

My Shakespeare play was *Antony and Cleopatra*, the star Tallulah Bankhead. The production was a sumptuous one, the cast full of good names, the cost impressive. As I had done for Leslie Howard's *Hamlet*, I engaged Hugh Davis to conduct the music cues; and as always he was perfect. Tallulah too was fine in comedy scenes such as that with the messenger from Rome, but a tragic stance she could not quite assume. She would die outside the pool of light put there for her to fall in; and she could not get the hang of my offstage sound effects, designed to build up her voice. We opened October 13 in Rochester, played Buffalo a week, then Pittsburgh two. In New York the show closed after four performances. Its flaw was a misreading of the play. "What this show needs is female sex," would say Miss Bankhead, using a single word for it, "and that's what I've got." But *Cleopatra* cannot use overt sex appeal; there is not a love scene in it. It is a political tragedy and can only succeed as that. Played for love, it is all build-up and no showdown.

My concert outlets in America had been mainly vocal.

Chamber music groups, modern music groups, and symphony orchestras were all of them resistant to my instrumental music. So firmly so, indeed, that had it not been for the art world of Philip Johnson, Russell Hitchcock, and Chick Austin (plus Alfred Barr's sincere and powerful blessing), my chamber music might have remained as unavailable as my symphonies. Nor had music publication, save for one piece, yet tapped me on the shoulder. Nor recording. For that matter, even the rising and well-protected Copland was not recorded till 1935, though he had won the Victor Company's prize ten years before that. But my opera *Four Saints in Three Acts*, and especially my guidance of its production, had opened the theater to me, including films. The ballet I might have penetrated anyway through Lincoln Kirstein's interest; but my situation in 1938 was that of a vocal composer none too successful save in show business.

In that business I had become a leader, not only for my own generation but also for younger musicians. And this position had been maintained by treating show business as communication, never as glamour, religion, or ideology. Every artist in those days was considered by the communists—who were far more impressive intellectually then than now—as a possible convert. I had learned from the tourists to Russia on the *Paris* that I could without deception be their friend, but also, since all beliefs are tailored to one's needs, that I was not likely to become a convert. I hoped not to be thought their enemy, since socialism is a Christian concept. But I had long since made my peace with Christianity (as heir to it but noncommunicant), and my hopes in socialism were of that same order. I could no more, having avoided Baptist conversion, embrace the Marxists than I could the Catholics. Perhaps less, for the Jewish group within the party, though happy to be making use of me, would never, could never, since my needs were different, allow me even in socialist fellowship to share their Jewishness. Moreover, since their Jewishness, I felt, was half the reason for their membership, I did not need to join a club whose communion, either as Jew or Christian, could not nourish me.

In public matters, especially those involving union membership and fair employment, I took action, signed manifestos, asked for and offered guidance without respect to religion or party membership. In Hartford no such emergencies arose; or if they did, Chick solved them. In film making for my government I followed union practices. In Harlem neither communists nor union men were numerous. When the all-white stagehands' union refused our Negroes, then threatened to picket us if we did not hire their members, Houseman replied, "Go right ahead, if you think you can picket a Negro theater for giving work to Negro unemployed." And at The Living Newspaper, a communist hotbed, I walked the narrow path of modesty. It may be that in such a closed communion the rank and file mistook me for their own.

At Maxine Elliott's Theatre, with Welles and Houseman (all of us indeed) pinwheeling with enthusiasm for a play and presentation that, if not decaying capitalism's flower, was surely no branch of socialist realism, we were all suspect. At one point in the musical rehearsals of *Horse Eats Hat*, of which I was in charge, I got into an argument with the chief of personnel, whose duties were to see that union rulings were observed. But since his resistance to my requests stayed sullen and persistent, I deliberately caused him to explode in anger at me, calling me by the ritual insults, "Rat!" and "Stooge!" For the next day's rehearsal I wore a borrowed button showing hammer and sickle in white on red, above and below them the words, "Vote Communist." That day the rehearsal was frictionless, and at the end my contractor apologized, "I'm sorry for yesterday, Mr. Thomson. If I had only known!" I never let him know he did not know, never had trouble in the house again.

The earlier proposals toward collecting performance fees for classical composers, the plans that I had already helped to scotch, began in 1936 to approach a possibility of reformulation, this time by composers themselves. And I had seen to it that Copland, whatever was done, would be our leader. Neither the League of Composers, which he held in his hand, nor the leftist group, always ready to be organized, had any fear of him. He was then, still is, American music's natural president; nothing could be done without him, with him everything. For this adventure, he called up his commando unit to spearhead it. That unit, throughout the early thirties, had consisted of himself, myself, Roy Harris, Sessions, and Piston. For the meeting he called in New York on December 17, 1937, a meeting well prepared ahead of time by conferences and by my reports on the collection of performing rights in Europe, Copland had replaced Piston, busy in Boston, with the New Yorker Douglas Moore; and he held it in the sacred halls of the Beethoven Association. At that meeting the American Composers Alliance was formed, "to regularize and collect all fees pertaining to the performance of copyrighted music." Its history as a collection group has been spotty, but its influence has nevertheless been large. Of interest both to art and to the economy are the enormous sums now distributed, as a result, by all the societies representing American composers.

Another cooperative enterprise looked toward the publication of American music. Earlier projects of this sort had either ceased to function or were failing. Henry Cowell's periodical, *New Music*, founded in 1927, was limited in circulation; also it seemed in danger of expiring. Alma Wertheim's Cos Cob Press was diminishing its output. The Society for the Publication of American Music had from its inception been in conservative hands. And the standard publishers would not touch anything advanced. Nevertheless, there was good new music around; orchestras played it; the public was receptive. Moreover, there were new ways for reproducing music less costly than engraving it. Still further, our generation and the next were by no means so poorly off as we had been a decade earlier. What with the growth in number of organizations performing and commissioning us, and with the solid salaries of those who taught or conducted, we were all more prosperous than we had been; the depression had been good for us. We would pay for our own publication.

It was in an Automat on Twenty-third Street near my hotel that Aaron Copland, Lehman Engel, Marc Blitzstein, and I drew up the plans for a cooperative music press open to all composers whose music we should find acceptable; it was to be administered by just us four, receiving no salary. The success of this enterprise is historical; and its catalog—containing many works by Copland, Harris, Piston—came to have high value as a property. Its title, The Arrow Music Press, we had hit upon by hazard, after the principle that the less meaning in a name the better. We simply looked out the window and, seeing a lunchroom opposite named Arrow, decided that would do.

The years of 1936 and '37 saw three generations of American

composers, from the elders, Edward B. Hill and Arthur Shepherd, through my own age group to the still-under-thirty Samuel Barber and William Schuman, all in full command of their powers and at work. Ruggles, though no longer working, and Ives were beginning to be played; and Gershwin, who died in '37, was to become a classic. American music was performed across the nation. And in the League of Composers' magazine, *Modern Music*, Edwin Denby was covering the dance; Copland, records and published music; Antheil, from Hollywood, music in films; Goddard Lieberson, radio; Paul Bowles, exotica from Latin America; Colin McPhee and Elliott Carter, the New York premières; myself, the theater, including opera. Also there were sermons by Roger Sessions, whose learning was to the cause of modern music as Alfred Barr's to that of modern art.

The thirties were also memorable for major jazz developments such as the swing beat and the concert band, for blues more powerful than any heard before, for light music that includes the finest of Cole Porter and of Rodgers and Hart, and for an opera that defies dispute, Ira and George Gershwin's world-famous *Porgy and Bess*. The twenties had been a romance because one was young. The thirties were a time of fulfillment for musicians of my age because we were ready for that, and also because our country was ready for us. That readiness was surely in part a result of the depression. During the first half of the 1930s Alfred Barr and Chick Austin had got together wealth not yet immobilized by the depression and scholars not yet captured by fame, developing out of these elements museums that expressed the time. The second half, through federal intervention, saw modern play writing, modern acting and production, and a public ready for noble subject matter all amalgamated. The *Four Saints* audience, part well-to-do, part scholarly and intellectual, all of it lively, experienced, and not easily fooled, was inherited by the ballet. The Federal Theatre audience, poor, part intellectual, part professional, not stylish at all but not easily fooled either, was father to today's off-Broadway public. Together they are the parents of a nation-wide university audience that is no easier to fool than the others and that is our present decade's gift to dramatic art.

By '38 I knew the good time for me was over and that I should be getting back to France. In 1937 Mary Butts had died in England. Her loss was irreparable because it ended the possibility that we might speak again. Another loss was the breakup of a new group, which I called the "Little Friends," all young and a quarter mad. This consisted of Paul Bowles and Harry Dunham, as founding fathers; of John Latouche, an author of light verse; of Marian Chase, who was to marry Harry Dunham, then as his widow to become my closest companion; of Marian's friend Theodora Griffis, whom Latouche was to marry; and of Jane Auer, that very year to become Mrs. Bowles. Also, during 1937, they were abetted in their liveliness by Kristians Tonny, who with his French wife spent that year among us, forever quarreling with Paul about money, and painting Flemish murals in Chick's Hartford theater.

I call these lovely people not quite sane because though not besotted and not corrupted and none of them, God knows, the least bit stupid, all were pursued by fatality, as if the gods would destroy them. Harry, flying a voluntary scouting mission, was shot down in Borneo, 1943. Latouche's wife, divorced, died of an early cancer. Latouche himself, successful, celebrated, died of a massive heart attack at forty. Marian caught bulbar polio in Naples, died coming home. Her mother, friend of them all, was killed in a bus crash. Jane Bowles, after writing one fine novel and one play, suffered a stroke, or a cerebral spasm, that has kept her from writing and may go on doing so. The Tonnys, being European, were not affected by a local curse stemming, as we all knew, from Dunham's white-lighted glamour and his unstated but relentless will to die young. Bowles also has remained immune, but he does not live in America or write much music any more. He writes novels and stories now, chiefly about persons obsessed. Both he and Jane feel safer in Morocco.

The story of the "Little Friends" I insert here because with the Tonnys' departure early in '38, with Dunham's going off to photograph the Spanish civil war, hoping to reproduce his earlier luck in the Chinese one, and with the Bowles-Auer marriage in February '38 and their leaving instantly for Panama and France, the group broke up. I also felt that it was coming to be time to leave; and I looked around for means of doing so. I had received good fees for *The River* and for *Antony and*

Cleopatra, but no more than it took for me to live; and I was
not a spendthrift. For making money to take me back abroad
there were two possibilities: one was doing a show; the other
was writing a book. I chose both. The show was for The Mercury Theatre, Houseman's and Welles's private company that
had grown out of their federal unit. Welles, who had by this
time grown quite fat, felt he should play Falstaff; and for making
this role major, he had boiled down to one all of the Shakespeare plays involving him, calling the result *Five Kings*. It was
to be a grandiose production in the spring of '38; and I was to
furnish lots of music.

Webster's *The Duchess of Malfi* was also being planned, with
sets and costumes to be designed by Tchelitcheff. Welles was
undecided whether I should write the music, or Marc Blitzstein, with whom he had gone all chummy and political since
directing *The Cradle Will Rock* and who had composed him a
neat score for The Mercury Theatre's antifascist, modern-dress
Julius Caesar. I won by taking Orson and his wife to a blowout
at Sardi's, with oysters and champagne, red meat and Burgundy,
dessert and brandy, before he pulled himself into his canvas
corset for playing Brutus. "You win," he said. "The dinner did
it. And it's lucky I'm playing tragedy tonight, which needs no
timing. Comedy would be difficult." Eventually *The Duchess
of Malfi* was renounced; Tchelitcheff went off to Italy and I to
France. But I had learned the play; and Edwin Denby, helped
by Grosser, had made me a cutting. I thought I could write
an opera on the text. In France I spent a summer trying to do
that, only to conclude in the end that its turbulent pentameters
are not for singing and that the whole is irrevocably what it
purports to be, a blank verse melodrama with incidental music.

Up Boston way, Sherry Mangan was getting restless. He had
divorced his English wife, taken up with a trained nurse who
loved him, was living in isolation near Norwood, where he
worked as a book designer. He had also become a follower of
Leon Trotsky, a vocation that was to dry up his springs of poetry
and substitute a faith that he could live by. For Sherry was a Jesuit
at heart, trained to intellection, submissive to authority. He
too was in need of going somewhere again; and Paris seemed
the chosen destination, with prices low and a Trotskyist group

available. So Margarete cashed her life insurance, and I helped out a little; and in the spring they moved their books to France.

Grosser had gone there in January. I stayed behind to compose music for *Five Kings* and to try for an advance from some book publisher. Four of these had been after me, in view of my *Modern Music* articles, to undertake a volume; and I had said, "What about a collection of those articles?" But no; they did not want that; only a through-written book would do. And why should I write a book, laborious enterprise, when I could support myself by writing music? But I could not save up by writing music here enough to keep me writing it in Paris. Besides, I had had enough expansion for the moment. Chick's grandeurs involving music were over; Houseman and Welles, through radio, were rocketing to Mars and Hollywood, no right place then or now for a musician. A period in my life had come to term. Time to go home! And so I called on all four publishers, asking what they could offer as advance. Five hundred dollars, answered three of them. The fourth went to a thousand; I accepted.

Meanwhile, my other home, the Missouri one, needed attention, because my mother had been injured in a car. She did not complain; she merely looked, in bed with her chestnut braids, like a little girl. Like a strong little girl she waited quietly to get well, and like a Kentucky hostess she received. She waited and received for a full year, then aided by a crutch relearned to walk. After three years she left her crutch and for seventeen more, till her death at ninety-two, concealed the signs of stiffness when she moved.

Five Kings had been delayed beyond my contract's deadline, which was April. I had received $200 for waiting. With Pare Lorentz, planning another film, I had no contract; but I offered to come back from France at any time he should be ready for me. Actually, though he once inquired by mail when I planned to be home, he did not go so far as to ask for my return. And when his film *The Fight for Life* was ready, it was Louis Gruenberg who composed the music. *Five Kings*, with its music by Copland, died out of town. Minna Lederman wrote me of the demise. Also that my kind of workmanship was catching on in show business. "Group Theatre," she announced, "is doing incidental music—Bowles's score for a Saroyan piece *My Heart's*

in the Highlands and Aaron's for Irwin Shaw's *Quiet City*."
With ballet, films, and theater all in such felicitous hands, I
knew I could absent myself a while. Besides, if I was going to
turn *The Duchess of Malfi* into an opera, I should need to settle
down where life was quiet. I had been busy (and in America)
long enough.

24

Pastoral

As my story now moves back to France, let us relist for 1938 our cast of characters. Madame Langlois, in my life since 1926, will be living for one more year. Meanwhile, she is lively and elegant, relaxed, distinguished. Sherry Mangan and Maurice Grosser are there, both living in studios on pittances. Theodate Johnson will be with us by the autumn, taking vocal lessons. Georges Hugnet is potent in the councils of surrealism; also, he has a new girl. Henri Sauguet's *La Chartreuse de Parme* is being cast at the Opéra; Germaine Lubin and Raoul Jobin will sing the leads, and Jacques Dupont, Christian Bérard's best follower, will design it. Les Concerts de la Sérénade are dead or dying, the only music series in the world to have expressed the thirties. The thirties have begotten yet another group—all very Catholic, calling themselves at their coming out in 1935 "*la jeune France*." They are Olivier Messiaen (an organist and teacher of harmony), André Jolivet (knowledgeable in Hindu music and a pupil of Edgard Varèse), Daniel-Lesur (out of the Schola Cantorum), and Yves Baudrier (largely self-taught).

In painting, the surrealist clan has been strengthened by survivors of Dada such as Arp and Max Ernst and blessed openly by Picasso and Marcel Duchamp. The neo-Romantics look like a lost cause. Tchelitcheff will do one more work for the Paris stage the next spring, a version of Jean Giraudoux's *Ondine*, laden with ingenuities *à la* Orson Welles and with elaborate dressmaking obtainable only in France. Bérard's last décor before the war will be for Molière's *L'Ecole des femmes*.

A former collector of Bérard canvases, Christian Dior, a bland young man we had all known rich, had lost his affluence, his pictures, and his health. The elder Dior, a manufacturer, had been ruined in 1931. Christian, already partner in a gallery, had sold off his paintings until none remained. In 1934, when he became tubercular, his close friends subscribed each a small sum per month for sending him to be treated in the Pyrenees at Font-Romeu; and in the spring of '35 he came back cured.

In '34, the Dior family house at Granville on the channel coast being unsalable, Leonid Berman had been offered it to live and work in. I collected in March of that year from among our New York friends a similar subscription (each paying $5 a month for half a year, to be repaid eventually in pictures) so that he could work that summer. He bought paints on credit, old canvases for pennies at the flea market, lived alone on $30 a month, painted a whole exhibit for Julien Levy, was reestablished. Christian Dior got reestablished by learning a trade, that of dress design, which Jean Ozenne, a cousin of Bérard, and Max Kenna, an American, taught him in the winter of 1935–36. When I came back to France in '38 he was already working for a *couturier*. After the war, in 1947, he was to have a dressmaking house of his own. He was also to die ten years later, unbelievably successful, but ever a gentle and quiet one, just as he had been when young.

Absent from this cast is Max Jacob, who had gone in '36 to live beside the ancient Benedictine monastery at Saint-Benoît-sur-Loire, where he was to remain, praying, serving at Mass, and writing *Méditations religieuses* until the Germans took him away in '44. Half absent are Cliquet-Pleyel and Marthe-Marthine, he occupied with ill-paid music jobs, she with no jobs, but drinking red wine all day long in a haunted studio shared with four large dogs. Gertrude Stein too is only part-time there, since she likes to spend six months at Bilignin. When I saw her in the fall of '38, she asked me had I left New York for good. I said, "For now, at any rate. I've been successful in the theater, in films, in ballet; I don't like that kind of situation." "Well, here," she replied, "we all go on being nicely unsuccessful."

Gertrude had moved in January of '38 to an eighteenth-century flat in the rue Christine. Picasso had already bought a seventeenth-century house near by. Many of the painters and writers, moving down from Montparnasse and into the low, damp district near the Seine, seemed to be huddling together for protection. This region has been magical since medieval times, propitious to sorcery, curses, and Black Masses. The demarcation line for magic seems always to have run along the Seine and up the rue du Cardinal Lemoine, then from there, including a patch on the north slope of the Mont Sainte-Geneviève (but not the Sorbonne), to go west along the north sidewalk of the boulevard Saint-Germain. Carefully skirting the church of Saint-Germain-des-Prés, I think it rejoins the Seine by the rue Bonaparte, though a stricter survey might find its west limit to be the rue de Seine. In any case, this was the neighborhood of alchemy; and this was the quarter chosen as home in the years just before the new war and during the Occupation by Europe's most remarkable assemblage of talent. Today, with Montparnasse intellectually as dead as Montmarte, and with Saint-Germain-des-Prés become a costume ball, the region I have just outlined, though the artists themselves have mostly moved away, is the largest agglomeration of art dealers and book stores in the world, spilling over clean down to the rue du Bac.

I was to be moving again to 17 quai Voltaire, ever for me a locale of protective magic. A large apartment, the whole third floor, or *bel étage*, was being given up; and my landlord, Dr. Ovize, would cut it into small units to be let furnished. But for me he would leave two rooms unfurnished and lease them to me at a yearly rental of $200. I could have them at the October term and, with a month out for arranging them, be in my new flat by November first. So that was settled. The weather was Arcadian. June with its fresh peas and fragrant strawberries was gone. July was for the country, for writing music, gestating a book. For Grosser too, painting in the country was right, provided he liked the country he was painting in. It always turned out that he worked best in hot regions; but he liked to try others, though rarely happy there.

Since railway fares that summer were cut for foreigners by two fifths, and regional buses were for almost nothing, we set off south without precise intentions beyond wandering eventually into the Jura Mountains. We stopped at Dijon for gastronomy, where after a three-wine lunch, a long walk, and a nap we went through a dinner at Les Trois Faisans which began with a hot mousse of chicken livers. What followed I do not remember, only that next morning Maurice complained he could not go on with any more such meals. So we went to Bourg-en-Bresse, where foods and wines are lighter, sight-seeing the near-by historic church of Brou, and traveled by bus upcountry to Nantua. There we took to its black-forested mountain and bottle-green lake, stayed for a week on the shore, swimming and rowing and climbing, dining on quenelles and crayfish and wild mushrooms, and not getting down to work at all. So we moved by mountain buses into the Jura, at Saint-Claude ate another gastronomic lunch, this one with *morille* mushrooms of the Franche-Comté, and took another diligence to the uplands. There on a high and flowery mountain plain we got off at a village called Lamoura, deeply grassy in the summer time but redolent of winter rains, with its thick stone houses weather-proofed by shingles on the windward side. Grosser found it possible, he thought, to paint there; and in two days I composed two small portraits. But I was restless and proposed a trip. Taking a bus straight south, we came to the Sickle Pass, or Col de la Faucille, where below us lay, at the bottom of a ten-mile slope, the blue half-moon of Lake Geneva and beyond that, fifty miles or more away and dazzling white against blue sky, the grandest mass of mountain in the world, Mont Blanc. I could not turn back; I had to go toward it. But before the long slope above Geneva became Switzerland, we entered a pink French city known as Gex.

We lunched there and went back to Lamoura, Maurice having decided to stay on, I to leave the next day. So I took a bus and steamer to the French side, and was back at the hotel on the cliffs of Thonon, where in 1926 I first knew Madame Langlois and also where I received what had seemed to me then a miraculous enlightenment about music. Absorbed with memories and sculling on the lake, I do not even know whether I worked. Getting back to work after America is never easy, because in Europe one's best work is spontaneous, whereas in America practically all work is done either on order or out of determination. This is a difference not to be quickly brushed aside; in Europe one must always wait till ready—otherwise there is no boldness in the product, nor any ease, nor lightness.

After two weeks Maurice came down to visit me, finding me slim and, so he said, good-tempered. But I felt I should go for a week to Madame Langlois, who had not been well; and she was at Arcachon, on the Atlantic. So Maurice went back to Lamoura, eventually to Villefranche; and I took the Geneva–Bordeaux so-called Express, which pommeled me all night on my sleeping-bench by changing its direction at least twelve times. And at Arcachon, after another bumpy ride, I climbed sand dunes, enormous ones, ate the local oysters out of season, and bathed in a shallow bay so thick with infants that we named its salty taste a "broth of babies."

Not wishing to go to Villefranche by another of those trains which have to back and fill all night for getting round the Central Mountain Range, I traveled via Paris, picked up mail, and stopped at Saint-Tropez to be with the Brazilian singer Elsie Houston, working for shekels just then in a night club. In Villefranche, finally I did get down to work, sketching a whole act of opera and making notes toward a book. My room, which gave on a playground, was filled by piercing childhood shrieks, also by the sound of hunting horns, as boy scouts learning to be *chasseurs alpins* practiced en masse, accompanied by massed drums. Maurice complained from his quieter room that out of a still life carefully arranged and already half painted some chambermaid had eaten a grape, changing the composition.

Describing my summer travels in *Modern Music*, I left out the hunting horns, which are as old as Europe, and tried to indicate what the new France was like. My picture has small resemblance to that of the rich-woman's paradise and poor-man's heaven familiar to us from the 1920s, even less to the motorists' hash house that is France today. I quote from it, abridged:

> The French have become a singing people again after a hundred and fifty years of not being one. It's like this. The law that guarantees two weeks a year of paid vacation to all salaried employees (it is one of the famous Social Laws voted in 1936 by the first Blum government and includes industrial workers) has set the whole population of France to traveling around its own country. Also the forty-hour week (where still applied, which is in most of the nonmilitary industries) makes the two-day week-end quite general. Hence the low week-end railway-fares, which, when combined with low country prices, make leaving town as cheap as staying home, thus keeping a considerable part of the French population constantly moving around even in winter.
>
> That means that about ninety-five per cent of the tourist business is French, but not rich French. So prices have to be reasonable. (Provincial prices are almost exactly the same, in francs, as in 1925.) And French standards about how beds should be made and food should be cooked must be observed. No longer can Americans push up prices just for the fun of it or English ruin the cooking by demanding that everything be boiled in water and served without seasoning. And so we have pre-war standards of eating

and housekeeping plus all the post-war standards of ventilation and sport facilities. There is local fare in peasant pubs. There is *grande cuisine* in court-house towns at twenty-six francs a head. And by *grande cuisine* I mean *la grande cuisine française*, not Swiss hotel-cooking. I mean foie gras and blue trout and Bresse chickens in yellow cream and *morille* mushrooms and crayfish and wild pheasant and venison with chestnut purée and ice cream of wild strawberries or of pistache custard and cakes made only of almond-flour and sweet butter and honey and nothing ever boiled in anything but wine or meat-juice.

Sport-lovers by tens of thousands travel in pairs on tandem bicycles, he in front, she behind, in cycling outfits of identical tweed. Unattached youth goes hob-nailing in bands and sleeps in Youth Hostels. This is the point at which singing comes in. Depression-alcoholism being out of fashion, and the promiscuous love-making of the 1920s even more so, the big family-party that France has become now amuses itself in the old French way by drinking wine, telling stories, and singing songs. They dance too, round dances in peasant styles. The Lambeth Walk, England's first contribution to popular dancing in over three hundred years, is used as a get-together for upper-class occasions. But mostly they just sing the old French nursery rhymes, sea chanties, tragic ballads, ribald medievalries, and always, if the company is anywhere to the left of political center, the great revolutionary songs, the *Crakovienne*, the *Carmagnole* and the *Ça Ira*. On the road they sing, in restaurants, in railway-carriages, in boats, bars, and *bordels*. Always in solo or unison, practically never in harmony. Never either do they vocalize. They sing the French language *as she is spoke*, thin, a little throaty, accurate in vowel and pitch, never muffling a consonant. So far I have not perceived in all this anything that smells of mass-singing-under-a-leader nor any imitation of the choral-society concert-style. It is social music in the same sense that round dancing is social dancing. And a few sprightly vocal teams make up their own topical songs and pay their summer expenses *à la troubadour*.

Mangan, who had arrived with his Margareta toward the end of April, had lived for two months, the two of them, in a thoroughly comfortable Montparnasse flat on $75. When that money was gone, he worried his way through summer by sending off to *Time* reports of art exhibitions, which were paid for with small checks that arrived weeks late. From my various country stations I would advance him cash against these; and

M, as she was now called, would help out by doing odd jobs of nursing acquired through the American Hospital. Meanwhile, Sherry labored to get back his poetic facility and to establish himself in the councils of the French Trotskyists. Though the poverty line he walked was quite precarious, his letters of that summer show elation.

I was elated too, and Maurice, and M, all of us as euphoric about France as we were about not being in America. It was not that America was not in the long run rewarding. It was simply that our country was a trap. Earning enough to live there was not impossible, but earning enough *not* to live there was. Income and costs seemed always to come out even; and the results of money spent lacked surplus value. In France the shabbiest secondhand chair or stool could still be sold again. And living, loving, dining would create an afterglow, whereas at home whatever happened seemed to leave either a bad taste or none at all. Which is what led Grosser to discover that "France is a rich country and America a poor one," and indeed that was so in the days when business figures read the other way. In terms of just plain feeling good, France was in those days, even for the poor, the richest life an artist ever knew.

Maurice, at thirty-five, was selling his pictures for small sums; but he was selling them. He also had a pittance from his family. And he had taken a small but habitable studio on the rue Bonaparte. A single square room five flights up with good light, furniture, and carpet, it lacked only water. When his landlord put in a basin with taps, the house architect, misreading old plans and taking a small air vent for a drain, attached the washbowl to it, flooding the apartment just below. The heat was furnished by a hard-coal Franklin stove of the sort known as a *salamandre*, and for a time this also did not work right. But that fact turned out to be a benefit, for when Dewitt Eldridge, whose father, a doctor, was a friend of Grosser's father, wrote home that Maurice was "having trouble with his salamander," the elder Grosser quickly mailed, without comment, a check for $50.

Grosser was in full expansion as a painter, had been so in fact since 1932. He painted over-life-size fruit and bread and vegetables in high bright colors; he also painted very striking portraits. I have one of Theodate Johnson from that year; and

I remember many sitters climbing his long stairs, a canon from the church of La Madeleine in High Mass regalia and Mary Garden in a tightly flowered small hat. Maurice had by now taken to bicycling and to racing in the woods outside of Paris. A muscular type, he had always needed exercise. Cycling was a winter-and-summer sport that he kept up daily till he came back to America, where he bought a motorcycle, went everywhere on that. In his forties he crossed and recrossed the continent on it before he finally gave it up and bought a car. I was to see quite a bit of landscape and weather myself, riding behind him up and down New Hampshire in 1941, through California in '45.

In the South I had planned out a whole act of *The Duchess of Malfi* before I discovered that singing the text was bound to diminish its impact. Blank verse is in any circumstance no friend to music; and blank verse of the great dramatic masters has never been successfully intoned. Shakespeare in translation, which is to say, without his poetry, has given the opera repertory *Falstaff, Otello, Hamlet* several times, *Romeo and Juliet* even oftener; he has not yet inspired a first-class opera in English. My mistake was to imagine I could help out Webster's text; it did not need me. And without that text the story seemed just gaudy. Nor were my notes toward writing a book worth keeping. Actually, I had accomplished no proper work at all between my June arrival and my September return to Paris.

Nor was I destined to do so till December was over. At the Hôtel Jacob, where I awaited delivery of my flat, I did write quite a bit about matters musical; but my outpourings were inchoate. My preoccupation at this time was only the flat; and for two months, beginning in October, I went to see it every day, traversed the city constantly on errands regarding it.

It was thirteen feet high, with two tall windows catching light all day and sunshine till noon from a wide courtyard; but its gem was a mirrored mantelpiece put there in 1791, when the house was built. The floors were oak parquet, the doors and wainscots painted a Trianon gray. Also, I owned a little furniture, mostly good pieces out of Madame Langlois's flat. I had to put in some lighting fixtures, install hot water (electric) and a washbowl, buy draperies, upholster, paper everywhere. I had a plan about colors too; I wanted lots of them. Bérard had just selected for Jean Ozenne materials for chairs, carpets, walls, and hangings that were highly varied, harmonious by contrast rather than in a key. I wanted a similar variety, but by tints I was to take from Florine Stettheimer, who in Act One of *Four Saints* had displayed against a luminous sky-blue all of the primary and secondary colors. My plan was to do the same against sunlight yellow; and eventually these colors came to be pointed up with added notes of bottle green, of Roman violet, of Bordeaux red, and of a gray rayon satin that when hung as floor-to-ceiling curtains shone like silver. After two months of labor and an expense of just $200, the place was very pretty indeed. And with my pictures by Bérard, Grosser, Tonny, and Leonid, and with a grand piano hired, and a new concierge who was also a first-class cook, I went all snug again, began to have people in. My unframed drawings, however, of which I had quite a number, especially by Bérard and by Tonny, had in five years of being stored against a damp stone wall become so mildewed in their portfolio that they fell to powder as I touched them.

At home again in France, back on the quai Voltaire in my own flat, and once more cocooned by friendships, love, and domestic ritual, I started work with the turn of the year on a book that I knew from the first would be moving forward. I knew also that my earlier stammerings would not be needed; I never even looked at them again. Before the end of May *The State of Music* had been copied in ink, revised again, typed out by Sherry Mangan. My New York publisher had it on June first, as he had hoped. Proofs were to come in August. In July I went off to Italy with Bruce Morrissette, a former classmate of Paul Bowles, a Virginian and a professor of Romance languages.

That winter I had sent musical reports to *Modern Music*, in one of which I described the effects of German refugees, of whom France had harbored many since '33, on French concert life.

> The season's chief controversy so far, believe it or not, is the war between the supporters of two rival German conductors. Furtwängler, the official ambassador of Nazi culture, fills the big Salle Pleyel at a 150-franc top. Scherchen, the unofficial ambassador of émigré German culture, plays a 40-franc top at the smaller Salle Gaveau and doesn't always fill it. Bruno Walter, now a French

citizen, is completely successful and quite outside the controversy. So is Munch, the new Alsatian conductor at the Société des Concerts du Conservatoire.

The Furtwängler audience is rich and fashionable. Lots of chinchilla. He plays sure-fire stuff and stream-lines à la Toscanini. Beethoven, Brahms (yes, I said Brahms), Wagner, Strauss and Debussy are his oysters. His error was an overture by Pfitzner. The Scherchen audience is mostly intellectual and definitely unfashionable, full of German exiles and the international-minded. He plays Bach, Mozart, Purcell, Lully, and some moderns, sure-fire stuff for the liberals. His error was the Beethoven *Grand Fugue*, opus 133, played by full string orchestra. (It sounded terrible.)

A good deal of the side-taking in this war is factitious, worked up for political reasons. A good deal of the enthusiasm at the Scherchen concerts is due to the presence, in a body, of intellectuals who really think they like that sort of concert. Just as the United States is going to have to absorb a goodly number of German composers in these next years, France is having already to absorb and educate a very considerable body of German listeners. This will be a long job, because there are thousands of them. A tedious job too, because they think they are so right about music, are so proud of their bad taste and so ostentatious in expressing it.

A French audience can get violently controversial about a new piece and it can stage a pitched battle about it and have in the police. It is not, however, the habit here either to get hysterical about the classics or to accept orchestral conducting as a major art. The French public is interested principally in music, only incidentally in presentation. It is the only music-listening public in Europe that knows the difference between one good piece and another and that can distinguish design from execution in any given piece. For fifty years Paris has been the accepted world-capital of first performances. Today her concert halls are invaded by Corybantic troupes of classics-worshippers and seekers after soul-states. It is doubtful if she can do or will be asked to do much about the exiled German composer. Technical complexity unjustified by expression, emotional vagueness, most particularly that air of owning all Musical Truth that German composers so naïvely and so impregnably assume, all get short shrift here. Let America handle the composers if she can and she can probably handle quite a lot of them. France has all she can take on, I fancy, with sixty thousand unrestrained music-lovers to digest.

On April 27 Madame Langlois died of pneumonia. I had believed, from her careful deceptions about dates, that she was approaching seventy. Actually she was nearly eighty-four. Not at all the fragile woman she had so long seemed, she was indeed a very strong one for her age. Her surviving older sister, Mathilde Philibert, lived till her middle nineties. And in the French way, on her sister's death she set out, as surrogate, to be my friend, inviting me to lunch, insisting I come and see her every week, inquiring of my health and my career, telling me the progress of the war, when that came on, in a way I could not have known it from the press or even quite from Mangan's Trotskyist prophets, because she knew the generals and their wives.

Learning Madame Langlois's age, and admiring her for having discarded fourteen years of it, kept me from undue grief about her loss. A life so long, a person so fulfilled gives little wish to alter history. Just like my parents, later to depart, she is as much still with me as if she were a book, a gay book and a sweet one, a sourcebook for the conduct of affection and my reference tome for France and all its ways. Her tomb in the Cimetière de Montparnasse, where she lies with the Philiberts, I do not visit. I carry her around with me instead. In that way we can laugh, tell jokes, and bicker, and share an affection that has never dimmed.

In Italy, at Porto Venere, I swam and walked and wrote a little music. And when the proofs arrived I was at Recco, on the Ligurian coast, with Henry Furst, trilingual man of letters out of Brooklyn, who lived in a round stone tower and owned many dictionaries. He was of great help with my galley proofs; and when they had been corrected, we both went to stay with the poet Eugenio Montale at Bocca di Magra. There, with five other men of letters, we sat for days translating into Italian a novel of Henry James, *The Aspern Papers*. And I learned, for all its subtlety in speech, how stiff-necked, academic, and funereal the Italian language can become when written.

Being so near, I thought it wise to take a look at Florence, which I had never seen, traveling by way of Parma to view that city too. I saw no violets there; it seems there are none; but on a plain outside of town is Stendhal's Carthusian monastery, or *chartreuse*; and inside are two of Europe's nobler opera houses—one from Napoleonic times, still used today, and one from the seventeenth century, the Farnese, with its scenery-flats built of stone.

It was in Florence, waiting for my mail and profiting by that week to visit the museums, that I read in the papers of a German pact with Soviet Russia and then of the beginning war itself, confined for that immediate time to Poland. Political events from 1933 on—the Saar plebiscite of '35; the reoccupation of the Rhineland in '36; the Austrian *Anschluss* (spring of '38), the taking of territories that same year in Czechoslovakia—every year some German predatory move had made it clear that one year there would be war. I had known that before I returned to France, and I did not choose to change my life because of it. Current events, of necessity, involve the people caught up in them. But those who play at refugee when under no attack not only are behaving irresponsibly; they also clutter up the roads. And so I waited calmly for my mail, read all the papers, looked at historic pictures, till I could take a train for Paris without feeling I was in somebody's way. My rule for conduct, taken at this time and ever so serviceable in later war emergencies, was very simple: never stand in line.

25

The Quiet War

THE MOST SURPRISING CHANGE IN PARIS was how charming the English had become. All the winter before, they had been intolerable, either under analysis for diminution of income (and psychotherapy adds to no one's charm) or simply sitting in bars and feeling mean. I remember three of them at Le Select simply by withholding a box of matches exasperating the painter Alvaro Guevara until he cried (and Chilean ex-diplomats do not cry easily). But now they were smiling, friendly, and content. Grosser diagnosed right off that the war was to be thanked. "Last year, after Munich," he said, "they were ashamed of their country."

I had written September 6 to Gertrude Stein, still at Bilignin, asking if she was all right and whether I could do anything for her, adding that I was "staying on for a while, at least." She replied, "For the first time in my life I have had a radio in the house and it does discourage one about music, why should there be so much of it, its going on all the time in the air certainly has something to do with the world's troubles." It is one of them, of course; of that I too was sure and am sure still.

Many of France's Americans were undecided about whether to go home; and our Embassy was advising flight, even chartering ships to hasten it, since normal berths were scarce and out of price. Within the first month, most of the nervous ones had been got off, and by November nearly all were gone. Among those who had chosen not to leave were a number who had jobs in France and some with property, also a few habitués attached to living there, like Mary Reynolds and Sherry Mangan and Gertrude Stein.

Sherry and his Margarete would have stayed in any case, I think; but it happened that for the last year he had been importantly employed by *Time*, which had discovered that his trainings as research scholar and as revolutionist were valuable in news analysis. So he ran their Paris office, was prosperous, traveled back and forth to London. At the beginning of the war he moved to Dampierre, in the valley of Chevreuse, and from there commuted daily, bicycling majestically to and from his trains. After a month or so, judging that Paris was not to be bombed, he took the luxurious Harry Dunham studio-flat (with three high balconies to watch the bombings from) and moved into 17 quai Voltaire.

Theodate Johnson had already taken the next-door flat, with two balconies; and the painter William Einstein a studio with one. In January, Leonid came back from painting in the north and moved into one of the still smaller studios. Peter Rose-Pulham, an English poet (I think) and photographer (I know), also moved in. And so the house became almost a club, with nightly dinings in one another's quarters. There was a beauteous American woman, tall and blond, who Sherry and I were convinced was a Stalinist spy. At least her communist acquaintance was extensive and her vocabulary almost a giveaway. The French had arrested all Germans, including the sixty thousand refugees, and she was waiting for her Austrian lover to be released from concentration camp so that she could take him to America. Eventually he was released and taken there. Meanwhile, she seemed to be in amorous dalliance with an American newswriter for purposes political, or so we guessed. In any case, delightful as she was to listen to in tales not wise of her to tell, we thought it safer not to tell her anything.

We knew our telephones were being listened to; we could hear the click. And Theodate, who knew someone somehow from the French counterespionage, had learned from him that I, though earlier suspected of unsafe acquaintances, had by Christmas been graded lily white. Our concierge, as well as Madame Jeanne from the other house, would seem also, according to Theodate's informer, to have given to the police regarding every one of us, including the beauteous blonde, credit for innocence.

At the beginning, I worked for the French radio, as did also Sherry, translating texts for broadcasting in English. All radio stations, during that part of the war, were broadcasting news and comment in many languages. And the receiving set I had inherited from Madame Langlois came to be a pleasure for culturally and politically circling Europe—from Ankara and Moscow to Helsinki, from Rabat and Lisbon to Athlone. The translations were well paid, but I found them time-taking. Sherry, however, became something of a star, it having been discovered that his warm bass voice and perfect enunciation made him an incomparable radio speaker.

Grosser went off to America at the end of October. He had no money for staying on, no chance of earning any, no instinct for adventure—anyway, not in wars. I also think that with his gift for being always right ("his tragedy," as Gertrude liked to put it) he had judged this war to have no ending soon and not likely to bring good to anyone. From its beginning, he had said he was not taking part. He stayed in France just long enough to show he was not afraid and to be assured that his French friends, at home or mobilized, had no need of him. Then he went off to New York via Bordeaux. Yves Tanguy sailed with him. I put them on a night train at the darkened Gare d'Austerlitz, both traveling with all their pictures, both thoroughly relieved at being about to leave at last that foolish Europe.

For the English view, the French view, and that of many Americans was that this war, which they had so long seen coming, was essentially silly. For small countries early invaded—Poland, Finland, Czechoslovakia, Norway, Yugoslavia—the war was a tragedy right off. For fleeing Jews, as for the exiled Spaniards, it offered only further desperation. But to England and France, imperial powers both, it looked as if the Germans were just being naughty, dangerously so in fact, and that a declaration of war might stop that naughtiness. And yet we knew that the Germans meant not to be stopped. There was therefore a mood of general impatience with them, as of solid citizens toward delinquent youth; and the citizens, who were slow getting started, profoundly disliked the need for getting started. So the delinquents went on advancing. The situation seemed so void of reason that when the Germans, after success in Poland, simply sat down in the west behind their fortresses and looked across at the French sitting in theirs, it did for a moment seem as if both sides in the war knew it for foolish and might even back away from confrontation, if that could be done without their losing face. That it could not and that the Germans did not want that became clear very slowly. Meanwhile, we waited, as the French army waited, knowing the whole thing irrational but also realizing that it would not stop.

My cast of characters, by midwinter, had changed a bit. Gertrude Stein was gone for the duration, having early come and

got her pictures, some of them at least, and taken them to
Bilignin. Max Jacob was praying in his monastery. Madame
Langlois was dead. Sauguet and Bérard had been mobilized,
but not Georges Hugnet. Picasso was almost every night at
Saint-Germain-des-Prés. Breton and Eluard were also there, in
uniform. Cliquet-Pleyel did guard duty in mobilization halls
and factories. Jean Ozenne, Christian Dior, Gaétan Fouquet,
Jacques Dupont, almost everybody male not ill was under arms.
Even Leonid Berman, at forty-four, was eventually called up,
having the year before, after twenty years' waiting, received
French citizenship. Paris was empty save for the old, the very
young, and a few, a very few, foreigners.

The rich among these outfitted ambulances. The poor worked
at supporting themselves. Writers wrote; actors acted; painters
painted; dancers danced; musicians did what they could find to
do. The Spanish refugees I rarely saw, save for some Catalan
Trotsky-faithful whom Sherry would allow me now and then
to meet. Without informing me of secret matters, he made no
pretense that he was not involved with revolution. The German
refugees, though wretched in their concentrations camps ("*Es
gibt hier kein' Ordnung*," they would complain), were nevertheless fed there and kept in health. As a matter of fact, the French
medical services, I was told later, had almost used up their drug
supplies in '38 and '39 in preventing epidemics among the Spanish refugees. If none broke out now in the camps for Germans,
and if when invasion finally occurred few of the wounds became
infected, that fact seems to have been to the credit of America,
which sent sulfas and other drugs in quantity.

The State of Music came out in November, bringing me reviews only to be described as raves. Its press, if slightly less
voluminous than that of *Four Saints*, was as praise more nearly
uniform. But the effect of it on sales was just as mild. By March's
end their total was 2,045, about all there was to be. The book,
however, was not ineffective. Composers took to heart its exhortation that they give up political politics and take up musical.
And not for killing one another off but for assuming power, for
directing musical matters instead of being directed. I had given
them two instruments for doing that, a composer's alliance
for collecting fees and a composers' cooperative for publishing
their works. These instruments were in use, both presided over

by Aaron Copland. "It's slow going, I admit," he had written in May, "but I think we are getting to be a force gradually. I wish you were here to help on all this!" The book I wrote in 1939 explaining why and how the designers of music should be administering it became instantly a handbook for that operation which has not yet been replaced. It still circulates, indeed, among the knowing ones, nowadays in paperback.

At the time of its appearance I had more letters from outside the music world than from within. The literary found its wit invigorating, and my friends in art circles and in the theater spread news of it. They also took occasion to write me their delight and at the same time to recount the state of my America.

Both Chick Austin and Russell Hitchcock, it seems, were less active, at least came less often to New York. The Ballet Caravan, Lincoln Kirstein's troupe, had brought out successfully Elliott Carter's *Pocahontas* and Copland's *Billy the Kid*. An organization called the American Lyric Theatre had in May spent $160,000 presenting an opera by Douglas Moore about Daniel Webster, one about Stephen Foster by persons unknown to me, and my ballet *Filling Station*, then had shut up shop for lack of further funds. To quote from divers correspondents, Copland's music for the film *Of Mice and Men* was a "great success"; Marc Blitzstein's *No for an Answer*, auditioned privately at the Askews', had "marvelous music" but apparently libretto trouble; Maurice Grosser was showing at a gallery, with an "impressive public" attending. The Bravig Imbses were receiving in a Washington Square flat that had been murally handpainted by a "little friend." Eugene Berman was as usual "gloomy." Shows of Magnasco and of Poussin at Kirk Askew's gallery were both novel and "important." Barr's Picasso retrospective at the Museum of Modern Art was "the circus of the town" and "probably the best show that Alfred has ever pulled off." Marian Chase and Harry Dunham had been married. An invitation forwarded from Mabel Dodge announced that on January 12, at 1 Fifth Avenue, "Thornton Wilder will elucidate eight pages of *Finnegans Wake*."

None of this picture made me homesick, for it represented little more than a working out of patterns long familiar. The most dramatic of those workings out was told in a letter from John Houseman which announced his break with Orson Welles.

The Mercury's career, from the time you left America, has been one of uninterrupted failure—sometimes honorable, sometimes idiotic and ignominious—but absolutely constant and uninterrupted. Looking back on it now, I can see how inevitably and how cruelly we paid the price of success, of big time, of a publicity-inflated personality (both Orson's and the theatre's). We paid it in every department—in the department of personal relations and loyalties—in the department of public relations, where audience-friendliness was replaced by audience-challenge—in the department of aesthetics, where feelings of grandeur and what-is-expected-of-the-Mercury completely supplanted the simple desire to put on a bang-up show. I allowed Orson—(and the fault is mine as much as his, since by failing to control and influence him I was betraying my one useful function in the Mercury set-up) to use the theatre not only as an instrument of personal aggrandisement but as a tilting-ground for a particular, senseless and idle competition with an uninteresting and essentially unimportant theatrical competitor-actor by the name of Maurice Evans. *Five Kings* was never a pure aesthetic conception—it was conditioned in its conception and in its execution by a desire to go Evans one better in Shakespearian production. Therefore it fell on its face (though it contained notable things and was often wonderful to look at and gave Orson a chance to be a magnificent Falstaff) not through any difficulties of time or technical inadequacies, as Orson likes to tell himself, but because it was a half-baked, impure idea, in which size and "notions" took the place of love and thinking. And it smashed the Mercury Theatre. Not because it was a flop—no flop ever smashed a person or an organization— but because the year which I shall always think of as the *Five Kings* year (since *Five Kings* pre-influenced and pre-distorted, or post-influenced and post-distorted every single thought and action of ours that season) found us fertile, successful, happy . . . foolish perhaps, but in love with ourselves and each other and the theater and the public . . . it left us tired to a point of sickness, loaded with debts and full of hatred and distrust of each other, of our audience, of our theatre—weary and full of fear and loathing for the whole business of producing plays in the theatre. And it left me, personally, without the excitement and, worst of all, without the faith which was, during its brief, brilliant career, the essential quality of the Mercury and before that 891 [the Maxine Elliott Theatre project] and before that *Macbeth*. . . .

Then I suppose you know that during this whole year we had a radio show, for which I did the scripts (and Benny [Bernard] Herrmann the music). At first it was a tremendous amount of fun, playing with a new medium, a medium to which Orson as an actor-producer and myself as a non-radio-writer author were bringing some very exciting new elements. You heard, of course, of the *War of the Worlds–Men from Mars* broadcast. . . . that was about the high point of our radio endeavor. Shortly after that we were bought by a Soup Company—which meant much money, most of which was drained off into *Five Kings*—alas an end of our fun. The thing became a constant squabble with the soup-maker—a compromise between *Saturday Evening Post* material and material not necessarily high-brow but of some human and aesthetic interest. Occasionally a good show gets on—but radio has become (and it still goes as wearily week after week at $5,000 per week) a drudgery and a pain in the neck. It has however been the main contributing element to a very queer and very sinister but also extremely interesting situation . . . the situation of Orson becoming a great national figure (a figure only less frequently and vastly projected into the news and the National Consciousness than Franklin D. Roosevelt, Adolf Hitler, and maybe N. Chamberlain). This has happened (it had begun, I think, before you left) in almost exactly inverse proportion to the success of his artistic and professional endeavors. . . . It is unrelated to his work (it had its origins in *The Cradle Will Rock* [and in] the first brilliant year of the Mercury, and its great growth came out of the Mars broadcast) in fact, it is just about fatal to his work, as it turns out. It is an appetite that grows as it is fed: it is also, in a creative artist, a compensation and a substitute for creation. Since to a theatrical artist the immediate test of his work is public response—if it is found that public response can be stimulated by various forms of monkeyshines (social and mechanical) then the necessity for, even the interest in, creative work inevitably dwindles. . . . That is why, for seven months now, a Picture (under the most magnificent contract ever granted an artist in Hollywood) has been "about to be made," talked of, speculated over, defended, attacked, announced, postponed, reannounced to the tune of millions of words in thousands of publications—without the picture itself either on paper or even in Orson's own mind, having got beyond the most superficially and vaguely conceived first draft. And no effort being made to progress beyond that first draft (partly because of an artist's very natural fears of a new medium but *mainly* because the instant it becomes definite, it has to be made, and the moment it gets made it enters the realm of tangible-work-to-be-appraised instead of potential-work-of-a-genius-which-can-be-talked-about-conjectured-about-written-about. . . .).

And so (and this is really what all this communication is about) I have, not suddenly, but after a great deal of very painful communion with myself, decided to end my theatrical association with Orson. It is not entirely chance, I think, that makes yours the first long and dispassionate letter that I have written to anyone since the break. You are one of the very few—perhaps the only person capable, since you saw it from the very first, of understanding just how much of a decision, how much of an uprooting of a three years' artistic marriage, this means to me. . . . I have not forgotten, after all, that it was you who gave me my first taste of work-in-the-theater-by-those-who-have-faith-in-each-other; I know that you have regarded the direction I have taken with the Mercury and with Orson—if not with disapproval then certainly with doubts. . . . I knew, for some time before you went abroad, that what we were doing or rather the direction in which we were going had already ceased, if not to interest you, at least to give you any personal pleasure. It turns out, of course, that you were right—right from your point of view, that dislikes the notion of work produced on schedule and under compulsion—compulsion of any kind, either of success or of ambition or of desperation or of real-estate obligations or of anything. . . . And ultimately, I suppose you were right, realizing that neither creative work, nor human relationships nor values of any sort can stand up under the kind of pressure to which we submitted them. It is my great virtue that I can impart terrific initial acceleration to any project to which I am a part; it is my great weakness that I am incapable (and not always desirous) of controlling or moderating its speed once it is under way. Instead, there comes a day when I suddenly find myself disliking the direction in which we are moving and sick of that very inertia which I have helped impose upon the object in which I am traveling. At that instant—being an adventurous amateur rather than a creator, and an operator rather than an artist—having made quite sure right along that there is a safety-door open and working, I hurriedly abandon the ship and that is what I did two weeks ago and that is what I am recovering from here in the desert. I am very fond of Orson still and I retain much of my old admiration for his talent: but the partnership is over for good and with it that chapter of my life that is my association with him. It has been many things—very wonderful and very painful and I am very glad that it is over. . . .

For the future my plans are of necessity and of my own volition extremely vague. I have refused already several obvious offers that grew out of the publicity inevitably attendant at this

announcement of our separation. . . . I have agreed to remain a
few weeks to hold Orson's hand while he begins his picture, if
he does begin it. . . . Otherwise I shall go back East in a leisurely
manner. . . . I think I shall do nothing for some months, except
vaguely prepare the ground for next season. [He discharged his
debt to "Orson's picture" by collaborating anonymously with
Herman Mankiewicz on both story and script of *Citizen Kane.*]
I have a very fine play that I own—about President Wilson—but
there is no hurry about that: I have notions for a semi-documen-
tary film: I would like to keep my finger in the radio-pie, partly
because it can be good fun if the game is properly played, and
partly because Television, when it comes, is the Art-Form, which
must of necessity, both for economic and aesthetic reasons, be the
Popular Entertainment of the next generation . . . and Television
is likely to be run, if not by the Government, then at any rate
by the Interests under very rigid control of the Government. I
don't believe the Soup-and-Coffee boys can afford to get into
it—and if they do, there is a fight there that it will be fun to be
in on!

This all sounds very vague and silly, I know, to you in the middle
of your new War. This whole letter is something of a pain in the
neck and I would not send it to you if I didn't somehow feel that,
when you receive it, you will understand just why it is to *you* that
I said it and why, to no one else could I have written just what I
have. . . . I think the truth is that I miss you, more perhaps than
I know even now: not the very pleasant months we lived together
in various apartments in the East-side of New York—though they
were very happy for me—but for more than that. . . . I think for
three years you were the soil of taste and encouragement and
good sense and *esprit* in which the roots to my activities were able
to grow. . . . I know now—and I suspect that you have always
known—just how essential your judgments (not so much on spe-
cifics but on the far more important ground of relative human
and artistic values) were to me in these few years—beginning with
Four Saints—which are the span of my valid theatrical career. I
think if I had had the salutary, intelligent deflating influence of
our evening and breakfast conversations, even for a few days at a
time, I should not today (and Orson would not today) be in the
mess that we are!

What are you doing over there, in your moribund continent,
that is more important than returning here to influence profoundly the cultural life of your time? That is what you did for
three years. . . . (I mean that very seriously) and it is what you

terribly need to do again, for our sakes, (for my sake especially)
if not for yours. . . .

Reviens donc—L'Amérique a besoin de toi! Moi aussi et surtout! Je t'embrasse. John

I answered saying I would be available for work whenever he
needed me, but that I did not think it wise to return "on spec."
Lorentz, moreover, had not summoned me. Copland kept writing he wished "passionately that [I] would come home and
help, instead of sending all that good advice from Paris." His
letter of February 15 ends, "There is a rumor that you are thinking of coming home this spring. Would God 't were true." Only
Marga Barr, a European, seemed to understand that America
was under control and not very interesting, while Europe, being
out of control, was extremely so. "I think you were so right to
stay," she wrote. "Here people are nervous if they think of the
war, but mostly they don't and life goes on perhaps even more
elaborately than usual."

My life was not elaborate at all. I argued politics with Sherry,
practiced the piano, listened to radio broadcasts from all over
Europe, and gave parties. Every Friday night I held an open
house to which friends brought friends. Once in a while the
Mangans came, but mostly the friends and friends of friends
were European—Hugnet, Eluard, Arp, with their ladies, also
Mary Reynolds, Peggy Guggenheim, and whoever among our
soldier acquaintances happened to be on leave. Sometimes there
were more women than men, but not often, since Paris ladies
seemed to find replacements for mobilized husbands and lovers,
then more replacements when the substitutes were called. In
fact, for spending time with their men on leave, there was a protocol. The husband had first right, then the main lover, then his
substitute, and so on through the substitutes for substitutes. So
mostly the ladies with several loves would arrive with one love
or another, as a last resort with someone very young not under
arms. And there would be hot coffee on arrival, for the weather
was cold, and later foie gras sandwiches and little almond cakes
from Poiré-Blanche and a white wine cup containing wild strawberries, available in Paris all year round.

Food was not short that winter, though coal and firewood
were, because the canals that brought them were frozen all of

February. I eventually acquired some *bois de démolition*, oak beams cut up that gave a glowing heat. And then I almost quarreled with M, because she wanted me to share them with her for keeping Sherry's feet warm while he worked, though they had plenty of coal and their own central heat. I economized my logs by wearing sweaters, woolens, and a floor-length dressing gown of camel and vicuña that I had had made for that purpose. Even so, my fingers would get cold as I practiced Bach and Mozart on the piano.

Except for the frying-oils, chiefly peanut from Morocco, nothing was yet missing from the markets; and shot game was more available than usual. War having been declared early in September, the shooting season was not opened at that time. But three months later, wild game had so overrun the fields and forests that at a time when shooting and hunting would ordinarily be over, it was decided instead to let them begin. So from December on, we had partridges and pheasants and larks and blackbirds and quails and wild boar and venison. My concierge, André, who cooked for me, even served one night when I had dinner guests a fillet of fawn, tender, pale pink, and no more than an inch across.

Philip Lasell, also a remaining Parisian, had sent me a case of champagne for my birthday; and there was one bottle left when Nonotte Roederer, a young girl to whom I had become attached, and Nicolas Chatelain, a Russian painter whom I did not know, arrived one afternoon to inform me the first that they had just decided to be married. So we drank it and planned a triple wedding with music. There would have to be a civil one at the Mairie; that was French law. Then after drinks at the neighboring café there would be a Protestant ceremony and reception at Nonotte's mother's flat. And the next day, since Nicolas was Russian, a church affair in the rue Daru Cathedral, with crowns and choruses, and with a Russian party after that. My role was to play Bach on the piano before the Protestant occasion, which I did, having practiced up a fine prelude and fugue. I only got through the prelude, however, because the deaf *pasteur*, seeing me lift my hands, began to speak.

But practicing for this appearance had set me off. From then on I played the piano constantly, recovering my lost finger skills and mastering a whole batch of Mozart sonatas. Mozart was a

major problem in those days; and restudying his works, forging
a new style for playing them which would be convincing to a
music world longing to hear them rendered with a grandeur appropriate to their proportions, had replaced the Bach problem
of thirty years before. Well into June I kept up my investigations, discovering, I think, something like a method for solving
the expressive content of any Mozart piece. At least I made
sure that there *is* an expressive content, and never since have I
been tolerant toward an "abstract" or "absolute" approach to
this composer.

Hugnet had started a magazine in November. Printed on
fine paper and devoted to esoteric poetry, *L'Usage de la parole*
offered as a gift to those who subscribed for copies on even
finer stock a print or etching or handmade lithograph by some
artist of unusual repute. For the first issue this gift was a piece
of music (my *Valse grégorienne*, to poems of Hugnet), a lithograph of my manuscript in a cover by Picasso. It was Georges
who had arranged this with the artist; but knowing Picasso's
way of offering just anything as illustration to no matter what,
and being also somewhat fearful lest his strength, if willfully
deployed, might overpower mine, I asked that the cover bear
only calligraphy, nothing but the title and all our names. To
my relief, he did not seem to mind. Nor have I ever minded
his result. On the contrary, its messy lettering makes me happy
in a way that very little of his handwork does; its magic, for
once, is my magic, hence a blessing; and I have never held its
friendliness in doubt.

Wartime restrictions on lights and subways gave us that
winter the most convenient hours for theatergoing that I have
ever experienced. Plays beginning at half past five and operas at
six produced an audience more alert than after dining. It also
meant one got home before the ten o'clock blackout. With
Mary Garden I often went to the Opéra-Comique, for she had
worked there young and felt attached to it. Also, and most conveniently, she never dined. She liked a good lunch, would often
take me to Larue for that. And I would give her tea with toast
and jam before we went to hear *Louise* or *Carmen* or Xavier
Leroux's *Le Chemineau* (revived that year). She had not sung
in opera since 1931, but she was always in search of those who
could acquire from her something of the dramatic awareness

A music cover by Picasso, 1940

and musical intelligence that had controlled her performances. She did not want pupils; teaching was not her line. But she did want badly to pass on a certain knowledge nowhere else available since Jean de Reszke's death.

We went to hear a girl just out of the Conservatoire sing *Louise*, knowing from word of mouth that she was exceptional. And afterwards, of course, the Louise of all time went backstage to pay her compliments. She would not criticize an artist in the greenroom; she merely asked the girl to come see her. Then at her own flat in the rue du Bac she told her. "Your voice is beautiful," she said, "and so are you. Also you are an actress. Your first act is good, your second better; your third act, with the love scene, is the best. But in the fourth you let the opera down. I suspect you don't quite understand the character. Why do you think Louise left home?"

"Because she was in love with Julien," said the girl.

"But not at all," said Garden. "Louise was a girl who was going to leave home that year."

For other heroines she had solutions too, as guides to understanding their behavior. Of Mélisande she said, "She always lies. Even dying, her answer is ambiguous." Of Carmen the secret is that she is untamable. She does not fear death, only loss of liberty; as she says to her ex-lover with the knife, "Free I live, and free I shall die." And for her dearest operatic memory she chose no role of musical impressiveness, such as Debussy's Mélisande, or of physical display, such as Massenet's Thaïs or Strauss's Salomé, but that of the governess in Alfano's *Resurrezione*, "because it contains everything that can happen to a woman." When her father, eighty-nine, died in December, she brought me duck-billed brandy jugs from Aberdeen. From that time on, she never left her mother, then eighty-three, an image of herself, all slenderness and grooming but of no age. When the invasion came, and German armies were almost at the gates of Paris, Mary Garden decided that her mother really should be got back home. So she mobilized the British Embassy for places, and the two flew to London on the last of the passenger planes. Alone, she would have stayed, she said; she had seen France through a war before. France was her home, as it was mine; and save for the safety of an aged parent, she would have felt disloyal leaving then.

That spring I had started again making portraits; and as the weeks advanced I made one nearly every day. I composed one of Picasso at his house while at the same time he made one of me, one that he did not ever show me. He spoke of Gertrude Stein, regretted passages from *Paris France* that he had heard were over-patriotic. I recognized the judgment of some communist adviser, probably Louis Aragon. But Picasso was displeased with her for writing, as he thought, commercially ("just to have a silver teapot," were his words) and also for not staying in Paris like the rest of us. "Why do you suppose she ran away?" he asked. "Sometimes old ladies are afraid," I answered. "Old men too," he offered, as we slowly climbed the stairs.

That closed the subject. Now he turned to music, remarking that he had only known a few musicians. There was Satie, of course: "He was delicious." And he had been interested in Stravinsky until he found the music "just a bird cage." The idea of musical portraits was new to him; how did I do them? I answered that I drew them just as he would; I took paper, looked at my sitter, then let my pencil move—not doodling, of course, but writing down as fast as possible what came to me. "Ah, yes," he said, "I understand. If you are in the room while I am working, whatever I do is automatically your portrait."

The portrait that I made of the man Picasso, called *Bugles and Birds*, was not at all a portrait of his work, though some suppose that to have been my aim. I do not try evoking visual art; in all my portraits only the sitter's presence is portrayed, not his appearance or his profession. Picasso's presence is also in my portrait of Dora Maar. When she came to pose, he came along, curious, as he said, to see my flat and to watch me at work again. I suspected a bit of Spanish punctilio, as if he felt it not quite right for her to come to my place unaccompanied. But I was honored, of course, and said so. And just as might have been predicted, he came into the portrait; he could not not do so, being in the room. I did not identify the intruder then, but only later came to realize that an assertive bass which makes its entry half way through the piece could only be Picasso, for Dora Maar herself was not like that.

The static war's euphoria that bathed us all continued right on through May 10, when Holland was invaded and France's power of resistance virtually destroyed by bombing, along with most of her airplanes. Some Angel of Mons or Battle of the Marne, it was believed, would surely, miraculously, as in World War I, provide a rescue. Nevertheless, the French authorities did what governments always do when defeat is imminent; they put in charge their most admired commander. General Weygand, who had been in Syria, was recalled and ordered (it could only have been that) to organize the military disaster in such a way that the population would believe it gradual. A surrender at that moment, though the war was already lost, would not have been acceptable in France or in England, perhaps not even to the German government. But only the most inside insiders knew the truth. One of my French Friday-night guests was still insisting as late as June that the invasion was only a trap laid by Weygand. "He is drawing them on," she argued. But Mademoiselle Philibert, who had written to Madame Weygand, felicitating their country on the return of her husband to the chief command, received an answer ending with, "May God preserve France in the trials she is about to undergo!" "Now what do you make of that?" she queried me.

26

Mozart, One Musician's Best Friend

I N LATE APRIL, on the verge of the invasion, I had written to
the editor of *Modern Music*:

My account doesn't make very clear why I have enjoyed my
winter so much. I'm not sure I know exactly. I've tried to tell you
what it's like here musically; for other matters there are plenty of
reports in the weekly press. What I can't describe very well is the
state of calm that permeates our whole intellectual life. Not the
vegetable calm of a back-water country or the relative and quite
electric calm that is supposed to exist at the center of a moving
storm. Rather it is the quietude of those from whom have been
lifted all the burdens and all the pressures, all the white elephants
and all the fears that have sat on us like a nightmare for twenty
years. I am not referring to any imminence of German invasion
or of its contrary. I am talking about that imminence of general
European cultural collapse that has been hanging over us ever
since the last war ended. As long as the tension was mounting
everybody was unhappy. Fascism in Italy, the Jewish persecutions
in Germany, the Civil War in Spain, a hundred other scenes of the
heartbreaking drama have kept us jittery and trembling. It has
been imagined and hoped that possibly some of the brighter boys
might stop the progress of it all by taking thought. Our opinions
were demanded on every imaginable variety of incident in power
politics and in class warfare, whether we had any access or not
to correct information about such incidents (which we usually
didn't) or any degree of political education that would make our
opinions worth a damn, even if we had had access to the facts.
For ten years now all sides have been pressing us to talk; indeed
many have talked, and I should say that in consequence a great
deal less real work got done in those years than was done in the
preceding decade.

That's all over now. We are on the chute. And in spite of the
enormous inroads on a man's time and money that being mobilized represents, and in spite of the strictness of both military
and political censorship over all sorts of intellectual operations,
the intellectual life has picked up distinctly. The lotus-land of
whether surrealism is really gratuitous and whether such and such
a picture by Picasso is really worth the price asked (for, dear

Reader, it was indeed by becoming passionate over such matters that many fled the impossibility of being anything beyond merely passionate over matters like Jewry and Spain, because they knew that mere passion wouldn't get anybody anywhere and that passion was all anybody had to offer on any side, excepting maybe a little quiet opportunism in England and in Russia), anyway, the 1930s, that stormy lotus-land of commercialized high esthetics to which New York's Museum of Modern Art will long remain a monument, have quietly passed away. It is rather surprising and infinitely agreeable to find that poets now are writing poetry again rather than rhymes about current events; that painters paint objects, not ideas; that composers write music to please themselves, there being no longer any Modern Music Concert committees to please. Most surprising and agreeable of all is the fact that the young (with so many of their elders away now and with all their elders' ideas on the shelf) have again become visible as young. They are doing all the things they haven't been allowed to do for some time, such as talking loud in cafés and sleeping with people of their own age. Also, instead of discussing esthetics with intelligence and politics with passion, as their elders did, they are discussing esthetics with passion and politics with intelligence. I find the change a happy one indeed. I also find distinctly agreeable the presence around of young poets and young painters who look us squarely in the eye and say "hooey," who don't even look at us at all if they don't feel like it, who behave toward us, their elders, exactly as we behaved toward ours some twenty-five years ago and as no young people have really been quite able to behave since.

I must admit that young composers are not as visible in the cafés as poets are; they never were. Pianists, however, peep out from every corner. To a man, and at all ages, they are occupied with what seems to be the central esthetic problem in music today, the creation of an acceptable style-convention for performing Mozart. I've spent a good deal of time at that job too this winter, and I have found out some things about Mozart's piano music I shall tell you another time. . . .

I've discovered music all over again. And it turns out to be just as it was when I was seventeen, the daily joy of practicing a beloved instrument and of finding one's whole life filled with order and energy as a result.

But of all that, more another time. Give my best to the fellahs.

Je t'embrasse en camarade.

Virgil

From May 10 till I took a train for the Southwest on June 8, I wrote portraits with accelerating frequency. The Friday nights were kept up too, for, excepting the cafés, my evenings and those at the flat of the poetess Lise Deharme were for our artist kind the only gathering places. My last party took place in the first days of June.

On May 22 I had written my family,

> As you read in the paper, there is more war just now than there was before. Don't believe too much, however, because newspapers do exaggerate. I have not left Paris and I am not expecting to. I could leave on an hour's notice if I thought it advisable, and I shall leave if I think that. It seems to be better just now for everybody to go on quietly and not to be frantic. In Paris the people are calm and confident and good-humored, much more so than last September, and none of the shops have closed. I continue to write music and practice the piano just as before and to have my regular Friday evening parties. I am not nervous or worried or unhappy. I have my music (my own music) packed so that by carrying with me one middle-sized music-trunk I could save one copy of everything. My pictures and household things I am not even packing. I shall leave everything in place if I go away and expect to find them all when I come back. And I am not really expecting to have to go away at all. I am still expecting to make a trip to the U.S. in the fall. I am doing physical culture 3 times a week and I have no stomach or hips any more. I can wear all my ten-year-old clothes. You might send this letter to Ruby.
>
> Love & kisses,
> Virgil

On May 29, the day of the bombardment of the Renault factory on the Seine, I was lunching with the Chatelains in Passy, having just composed a portrait of Nicolas, when the sirens sounded. As usual, we did not interrupt ourselves but went on eating while the food was hot, until a gigantic voice said, "Mesdames et Messieurs, go to your shelters." On top of that came the sound of many airplanes and then of explosions. And so we did go down. Ten minutes later, with the all-clear, we went back to eat our peaches, the first of the season. And after lunch, the portrait of Nicolas being finished, I began one of Nonette.

A few days later I consulted Sherry. The Germans should arrive, he told me, in about a week. He would stay on, of course,

representing *Time*. (The Germans, not liking the way he reported their Occupation, would request him to leave that fall.)
Since our country was not at war with Germany, we were in no
danger save of being bombed, which could happen to one anywhere in France. Theodate also, with whom I had lunch on the
subject one of those fine sunny days, thought she would stay.
She had been working for the Belgian Red Cross, receiving refugees at the Gare du Nord, and would remain at her post until
evacuated. (By waiting for that outcome, she added nothing
to her usefulness, merely lost her voice and a large part of her
luggage.) The Paris doctors, teachers, postal employees, concierges, everyone who had a post would be expected to remain.
However, on reflection, I decided that I should leave simply
because of money. If I should find myself behind the German
lines and be obliged to regain the United States through Switzerland, that might be expensive. That I should be leaving one
day for America was inevitable in view of my thin resources; it
was proper to see your French friends through a war, but not to
impose on them. Nevertheless, I did not wish to clutter up any
of the exits so long as persons really in danger, such as political
dissidents, Jews from all over Europe, Poles, and the English,
were using them. Already all the roads were full of cars. I would
take a train. And I would take it to Oloron, in the Pyrenees,
where Gertrude Newell, a New York lady, had twice invited me
to be a refugee. So I wired her, bought a second-class reserved
seat, and packed.

I called on Mademoiselle Philibert to say good-by, arranged
with my landlord to preserve my books and furniture in case
he found it wise to let my flat, took leave of all friends correctly
and without haste. My hired piano was released and called for.
And Arp, leaving with his wife for Switzerland, brought me as
going-away present on the last of my Fridays a sculpture made
especially for me.

My packing took two days because of a wooden case built for
my pictures. And by agreement made with Leonid, whose canvases were stored in my flat, I had his pictures packed along with
mine. My luggage came, in all, to fourteen pieces. There was
no reason not to take my clothes, for I had bought that winter
suits and overcoats, had even borrowed money for that purpose,
moved by an instinct, I suppose, toward facing disaster, should

it come, well dressed. Arriving in America without funds could be coped with; having to buy clothes there would be inconvenient. Music and books in print I did not dream of taking, only my life's work, my manuscripts, filling up five music trunks. I cushioned the Arp sculpture among the clothes, also the old French silver I had from Madame Langlois.

My trunks and cases being ready, the shipper who had boxed my pictures put them (all but the pictures) on a large flat push-cart and walked them to the Gare d'Austerlitz (the near-by Gare d'Orsay having been abandoned in September). I walked too, as there were by then no taxis, only speeding staff cars in the empty streets. At the station I presented my luggage to a checker, waited seven minutes while the man just come on duty slowly changed to his alpaca coat, put on fresh paper cuffs, and wiped his pen. Then he wrote out a slip for fourteen pieces and assured me they would all be on my train.

The picture case, however, had adventures. I had omitted from it an unfinished sketch by Leonid, then thought I should include it after all. I carried it round the corner to my *emballeur* in the rue de Lille, whose monumental wife, herself the carpenter, said that the case had left, she thought; but she would make a small one for the extra picture. Actually the case had not left, was reopened, then wheeled to the station and also checked. But the delay caused it to miss my train, and that train was the last to leave for Oloron. The case remained throughout the war in storage at the station, and the Germans never were allowed to take it. In 1944, receiving in New York a request that it be called for, I sent the baggage check to Leonid, who reclaimed it and found everything intact.

The trip to Oloron was slow, on account of bomb alerts; the train was dark and crowded. But I slept some, free of luggage worries; and my fellow travelers were considerate. Once, during a long wait in the countryside, when we heard a drilling, trilling noise, a man of middle age said, "*Ça y est!* Machine-guns! I recognize them from the other war." But pretty soon it turned out to be crickets.

Miss Newell, a decorator with literary and theatrical connections, had retired to live in a manor house named Planterrose in a village called Moumour. Her other refugees were a writer, Jamie Campbell; and elderly Venezuelan lady, Madame

Semenario, sister of the composer Reynaldo Hahn; and her daughter Clarita, Comtesse de Forceville, whose husband was under arms. Others came by, some of them soldiers, friends of Campbell or of mine, and were put up for a night or two while on their way to find their families. For with half of France already more than two weeks on the road—women, children, and grandparents fleeing the German troops, or military units disbanded and in disarray—the armistice was followed by still more traveling as families essayed to reunite.

The armistice, asked for on the twelfth of June, was granted six days later. In the meantime, Italy, joining the German side, invaded the South. On the eighteenth, trains and services began to work. And though my picture case did not arrive, mail did, quantities of it, correctly forwarded by my Paris post office. And in the midst of the huge hegira that was France that June, scholastic examinations took place. In every courthouse town, candidates of every age and for every promotion were handed the secret questions. No less than the railway and postal services, the French bureaucracy of education functioned. Wondering how our own would have held up in such a holocaust, I had to remember that we are less used to fighting wars at home and not at all accustomed to invasion.

At Planterrose, among sweet peas and magnolia blossoms, but without gasoline, we fretted; and Marshal Pétain's cracked voice on the radio saying, "Frenchmen, I have sad news for you" was of no comfort. Miss Newell, moreover, needed to get her British butler off to England, along with his eighteen-year-old son. His wife, who was French, and the younger child, a girl, could remain; but grown males must not be captured. A scouting trip I made by autobus revealed, indeed, that every night (this was before the eighteenth, when the Germans arrived) ships left for England from Saint-Jean-de-Luz. So we hired (with driver) the communal bus, which had a right to gasoline; and I took Manlow and his son down to the port. I made at least three trips during those six days before a frontier was drawn between us and the coast. On one of them Miss Newell went along. She had thought we might add Spanish visas to our passports, she and I, just in case we should be leaving in a hurry. But no hurry was then visible, only long queues everywhere.

And we did not choose to stand in line with all those pushing Belgians.

On one of the other trips I met the one-time editor of Chicago's *Little Review*, Margaret Anderson, hoping to procure somehow an American visa for Georgette Leblanc, ex-companion of Maurice Maeterlinck, ex-singer who was old, ill, and French—conditions, all of them, that Washington's representatives viewed unfavorably. I also came upon Eric de Haulleville, who had hitchhiked from Brussels with his wife and with his daughter, aged two. The child, it seems, had by her winning ways induced truck drivers everywhere to give them lifts. Eric, staying upcountry at Dax, was in Bayonne on passport matters; but finding the queues excessive, he decided to come back later. We spent the day together and thanks to his insistent Belgian ways (bluffing a head waiter, for instance, into believing he had reserved a table) actually had lunch at a table. Long suffering from a circulatory ailment, and not bettered by his long walk across France, he was taking the waters before moving south. I did not see him again, for he died in Vence the next year. Georgette Leblanc died also in the South, Margaret Anderson remaining with her to the end.

Eventually Miss Newell's hospitality turned to scolding. Or was it that she merely missed her butler? In any case, come mid-July, I left. On market days communal buses crossed the line in freedom; and the miller, our local mayor, gave me a pass. So with my fourteen suitcases and music trunks I traveled to Bayonne and on to Biarritz. I had enough French money to last perhaps two weeks. Getting to America could no doubt be improvised. So I picked up clothes at Lanvin's local branch, charging them for payment after the war; and the store was pleased that they should be bought by an old customer rather than by German officers. Man Ray was in Biarritz also, knowing he must leave France but worried to have had to abandon his house and car, his pictures, books, and girl friend, not sure either how he was going to secure money for leaving France. A Quaker lady, picked up at the American vice-consulate, solved that problem. She had been administering relief in Marseille until she found her work interfered with by Vichy officials. About to return to Philadelphia with unspent funds, she offered to lend us dollars for traveling to Lisbon, where we could wire for more. So we went to the Germans for exit-permission, the Spanish and Portuguese for visas—all quickly obtained, since there were no crowds any more—using our last French money for train tickets to Hendaye.

Music in manuscript I knew to be a hazard. The Germans might have held me up for months, searching for coded secrets, had not Mozart rescued me. As we left the train a porter had piled our luggage on a pushcart, explaining that after it had passed examination he would walk us across the frontier bridge to Irun. In the empty customs shed he spread our pieces out and told us to unlock them. Man Ray, who had only two, I think, was quickly passed. The examiner, a German peasant soldier, looked hopeless about all mine, then pointed to a small suitcase, as if to say, "Open that." This happened to contain, right on the top, a last-moment thought in packing, a volume of Mozart piano sonatas in which I had marked fingerings, the only piece of print in all my luggage.

As the soldier, suddenly alert with curiosity, opened the volume, I said in German, "*Sonaten von Mozart*." At that he smiled in happy comprehension, said "*Ja! Mozart! Ja!*" and put back the volume, looked at nothing more. In Spain we bought tickets for the Sud-Express to Lisbon, had dinner, observed the civil war's still unrepaired destruction, mounted our sleeping car, and went to bed.

In Lisbon we wired for money, received it, were assigned passage on the *Excalibur* for two weeks thence, August 12. The town was full of refugees, mostly well to do, all seeking visas at the consulates or waiting for ships. Lisbon was not exciting; but the wines were tasty and the *fados*, a species of tavern ballad, mildly pleasing. The city's nature is that of all things Portuguese— easy-going, a little tired, not strong in flavor.

The American ship was rude as to service, frozen as to food. We slept, some sixty males, on the library floor, Man Ray with cameras underneath his pillow. Daytimes we made jokes with expert jokesters, the film maker René Clair and the still-surrealist painter Salvador Dalí. My warmest friend on board was a woman lawyer, Suzanne Blum. She knew that her safety lay in leaving France, being Jewish and also prominent. And yet she worried over where her duty lay, to leave or not to leave her aging mother. Being by now a practiced hand, through long experience of Blitzstein, Kirstein, Grosser, and the Stettheimers, at comforting Jewish emotional indecision, sweetly, firmly I assured her she had done right. So friends we became, and friends we have remained. Along with Madame Langlois, Hugnet, Sauguet, not many more, Suzanne is one of my small handful of French with whom misunderstanding has never occurred.

In New York, as if by occult message, I was telephoned by Kathleen (Mrs. O'Donnell) Hoover, whom I did not know, but who was to become later my biographer. The occultness lay in the fact that my arrival there, like my exit from France, seemed still to be under the sign of Mozart. For what she wanted was that I lecture on his music for the Metropolitan Opera Guild and illustrate my new approach to it, helped out by the singer Frieda Hempel, who possessed from three decades back a quite wonderful older approach.

Then I went to Alexander Smallens's at Stamford for a weekend; and he phoned Geoffrey Parsons, saying, "Virgil is here." Now Parsons, in charge at the New York *Herald Tribune* of all matters cultural, had been in search since March of a replacement for the late Lawrence Gilman as music critic. Knowing my articles in *Modern Music* and admiring *The State of Music*, he would already have made me overtures, according to Alex, had I not been, so Alex assured him, firmly determined on not leaving France. Geoffrey came to Alex's on Sunday. I played him Mozart in a way that pleased him mightily. He offered me the post. But I demurred. I said that if I scotched some sacred cow, as Teddy Chanler had, taking over from Philip Hale on the Boston *Herald*, I also would be fired within six weeks. He simply said, "I think you are not familiar with the ways of a metropolitan newspaper."

Eventually, that is to say by October, I had been looked at by the staff and found companionable. And at lunch Mrs. Ogden Reid had asked me, "How does it seem to you, the idea of becoming our music critic?" I replied that the general standard of music reviewing in New York had sunk so far that almost any change might bring improvement. Also I thought perhaps my presence in a post so prominent might stimulate performance of my works.

On the day I was engaged, October 10, Francis Perkins, my

music editor, though deeply disappointed that he had not himself been named, became forever my firm aide and ally. That night I covered the New York Philharmonic at their season's opening; and the Philharmonic's management and board, one understood, instantly regretted my appointment. Only a few months earlier, Theodate and Sherry, despairing of my seeming quietude and exasperated that I should practice Mozart while Europe burned, had told each other that indeed it looked as if Virgil were finished. Within an even shorter time, when Sherry reappeared, Theo was paying with split vocal cords for having shouted in refugee receiving halls; and he was being sent to Buenos Aires, a city for which he had as little appetite as for New York. Their dear friend, on the other hand, had thanks to Mozart fallen on his feet.

27

The Paper

THE NEW YORK *Herald Tribune* was a gentleman's paper, more like a chancellery than a business. During the fourteen years I worked there I was never told to do or not to do anything. From time to time I would be asked what I thought about some proposal regarding my department; and if I did not think favorably of it, it was dropped.

The city room was an open space filled with flat-top desks, the classical stage-set of a newspaper; but what went on there bore no resemblance to the behavior of city staffs in plays and films. I never saw anyone use more than one telephone at a time, and I never heard anyone raise his voice. Exception was the plaintive call of "Copy!" from someone sending a late review down to the typesetters page by page. Self-control was the rule on that floor, just as the avoidance of any haste that might make for error was the style of the linotypers and proofreaders on the floor below.

But if the *Herald Tribune* was a decorous paper, it was also a hard-drinking one. The Artists and Writers Restaurant next door, in Fortieth Street near Seventh Avenue, a former speakeasy run by a Dutchman named Jack Bleeck, received from noon till morning a steady sampling of our staff, of writers from *The New Yorker*, who seemed in general to like drinking with us, of press agents, play producers, and after-theater parties. After the Late City Edition had been put to bed (in those days around half past midnight), our night staff and the working reviewers would gather there to wait out the next half-hour till freshly printed papers were sent down. Everyone read first his own column and after that those of the others. Then we all complimented one another, as one must before going on to discuss points of judgment or style.

The whole staff was pen-proud, had been so, it would seem, since 1912, when Ogden Reid, inheriting the New York *Tribune* from his father (Ambassador to England Whitelaw Reid), had turned it into a galaxy of stars. And until his death in 1950 it stayed luminous. After that, the care for writing faded and the drinking in Bleeck's bar lacked stamina. I do not insist that drinking and good English go together, though certainly over at the *Times*, in Forty-third Street, the staff seemed neither to roister much nor to write very impressively. In my own case, Geoffrey Parsons had no sooner opened the possibility of my writing for the *Herald Tribune* than a dinner was set up at the Players' Club, with a dozen of the paper's best-drinking old hands to test my sociability. That was in September, and I passed all right.

It was still not known, of course, how I would behave in front of a deadline. And Parsons, naturally worried on my first night, prowled about till I had finished writing, then held his breath in the composing room while I checked my proofs. He suggested in these one change, the omission of a slap at the audience ("undistinguished" had been my word). At Bleeck's, when the papers came down, my piece read clearly as a strong one, though it contained, I knew, any number of faults, including seventeen appearances of the first personal pronoun. I had entitled this review of the concert that opened the Philharmonic's ninety-ninth season *Age Without Honor*; and I had snubbed the orchestra's conductor, John Barbirolli, by publishing with it the photograph of his concertmaster, Michel Piastro. It was unfavorable throughout—"hard-hitting," my admirers at the bar had called it—and it ended with a quote from my companion of the evening (actually Maurice Grosser), "I understand now why the Philharmonic is not a part of New York's intellectual life."

Hired on a Thursday afternoon, I had covered the Philharmonic that night. The next day I reviewed from its home ground the Boston Symphony's opening. The following Tuesday I attended the season's first New York concert of the Philadelphia Orchestra. For the weekend after that, in my first Sunday piece, I compared these groups. And if my first review had been brutal with overstatement, my second set a far more gracious tone ("peaches and cream," Parsons called it).

The quality of this piece was not always to be kept up. Sometimes I would write smoothly, sometimes with a nervous rhythm, darting in short sentences from thought to thought and failing to carry my readers with me. But on the whole I interested them; and almost from the beginning I did observe standards of description and analysis more penetrating and of coverage more comprehensive than those then current in the press. I was aware of this; the music world was aware of it; my colleagues on the paper were immediately aware of the fact that my work had presence. Ettie Stettheimer, neither a musician nor a journalist, compared it to "the take-off of a powerful airplane." My editors, of course, knew the dangers of so showy an ascent. Also that I was heading into a storm.

For from my first review they received, as also did I, reams of protest mail. Mine I answered, every piece of it, and with courtesy. "I thank you for the warmly indignant letter," was one of my beginnings, before going on to some point raised, such as, for instance, that of my own incompetence. Before very long the editors, aware through the secretarial grapevine of how I could win over many an angry one, would send me their own mail for answering, thus making clear no protest could be made behind my back.

But at the beginning they showed me only the favorable letters. It must have been two years before Mrs. Ogden Reid, almost more active at the paper than her husband, admitted that there had been demands for my beheading. What kept the paper firm regarding me, she said, had been the fact that those who wrote to praise me were important novelists like Glenway Wescott, enlightened museum directors like Alfred Barr, art-minded lawyers like Arnold Weissberger, and public-spirited heads of university music departments, such as Douglas Moore—in short, what she called "intellectual leaders"—whereas the protesters were practically all just quarrelsome types without responsibility ("nuts") or, worse, spokesmen for the performing institutions.

The most persistent of these last turned out to be the Metropolitan Opera Association, whose powerful hostesses, bankers, and corporation attorneys seemed to feel that their names on the board of any enterprise should render it immune to criticism. At the slightest *lèse-majesté* they would make truculent embassies to the paper demanding that somebody or other, usually I, be fired. Urged thus to remove my predecessor, Lawrence Gilman, Ogden Reid had twenty years earlier inquired, "Who's running this paper?" Similarly rebuffed regarding me, the ambassadors would remark that with the death of Mr. Gilman music criticism had lost a great prose writer.

The Philharmonic board, though no less disapproving, early gave up direct intervention in favor of a business maneuver. One of them did inquire whether I would accept board membership, but I declined. And several, I believe, "spoke" to Mrs. Reid. But the business threat was early provoked, at the end of my second week, when I diagnosed the soprano Dorothy Maynor as "immature vocally and immature emotionally." From e. e. cummings came, "Congrats on the Maynor review. Eye 2 was there." The Columbia Concerts Corporation, however, of which the Philharmonic's manager, Arthur Judson, was president, held a board meeting over it, and not for determining Miss Maynor's fate, but mine. The decision, one heard, was to withdraw all advertising until my employment at the paper should be ended. This plan might have been troublesome to carry out, since it would have denied our services to all Columbia's artists. But at the time the threat seemed real enough to provoke intervention by another impresario.

Ira Hirschmann, a business executive married to a professional pianist, Hortense Monath, and friend of another, the ever-so-respected Artur Schnabel, had been presenting for several seasons, under the name New Friends of Music, weekly Sunday concerts of the chamber repertory. But weekdays he was advertising manager of Bloomingdale's. So when Hirschmann heard about Columbia's plan, he went to our advertising manager, Bill Robinson, and said, "Mr. Thomson has not yet reviewed my concerts unfavorably, though he well may do so. But whatever happens, I shall match, line for line, any advertising you lose on his account." This incident I also did not know till two years later. But it helps explain the patience of my editors with a reviewer who was plainly a stormy petrel. As a storm bird, I should have preferred to sail above the clouds; but to get there I often had to fly right at them, and bump my beak against their leaden linings.

After twenty years of living inside Europe, I knew well the grandeurs and the flaws of music's past, also that with a big war silencing its present, composition's only rendezvous was with the future. America, for the duration, might keep alive the performing skills. But her strongest composers had shot their bolt in the 1930s and retired, as the phrase goes, into public life, while the younger ones who had not yet done so were getting ready either to be mobilized or to avoid that. The time was not for massive creativity, but rather for taking stock. My program therefore was to look as closely as I could at what was going on, naturally also to describe this to my readers, who constituted, from the first, the whole world of music. The method of my examination and my precepts for progress turned out to be those laid down exactly one year earlier in *The State of Music*.

These principles, as I understood them, engaged me to expose the philanthropic persons in control of our musical institutions for the amateurs they are, to reveal the manipulators of our musical distribution for the culturally retarded profit makers that indeed they are, and to support with all the power of my praise every artist, composer, group, or impresario whose relation to music was straightforward, by which I mean based only on music and the sound it makes. The businessmen and the amateurs, seeing what I was up to, became enemies right off. Those more directly involved with music took me for a friend, though Germans and the German-educated would bristle when I spoke up for French music or French artists. They would even view my taste for these as a somewhat shameful vice acquired in France.

The opposite was true, of course. I had not come to admire the musical workmanship of France from merely living there; I had lived there, at some sacrifice to my career, because I found French musical disciplines favorable to my maturing. Nor did the Germans suspect how deeply I distrusted their arrogance. For French arrogance about music is merely ignorance, like Italian arrogance, or American. But the Germanic kind, based on self-interest, makes an intolerable assumption, namely, its right to judge everything without appeal, as well as to control the traffic—as if past miracles (from Bach through Schubert) were an excuse for greed. And all those lovely refugees—so sweet, so grateful, and so willing to work—they were to be a Trojan horse! For today the Germanics are in control everywhere—in the orchestras, the universities, the critical posts, the publishing houses, wherever music makes money or is a power.

I made war on them in the colleges, in the concert halls, and in their offices. I did not hesitate to use the columns of my paper for exposing their pretensions; and I refused to be put off by sneers from praising the artists of my choice, many of them

"Play! Play as you never played before! Here comes Virgil Thomson."

foreign to the Italo-German axis. My editors found this method not unfair, for they too, through our European Edition, were Paris-oriented. The Germanics would never admit, however, that distributed attention was not mere Francophilia.

My literary method, then as now, was to seek out the precise adjective. Nouns are names and can be libelous; the verbs, though sometimes picturesque, are few in number and tend toward alleging motivations. It is the specific adjectives that really describe and that do so neither in sorrow nor in anger. And to describe what one has heard is the whole art of reviewing. To analyze and compare are stimulating; to admit preferences and prejudices can be helpful; to lead one's reader step by step from the familiar to the surprising is the height of polemical skill. Now certainly musical polemics were my intent, not aiding careers or teaching Appreciation. And why did a daily paper tolerate my polemics for fourteen years? Simply because they were accompanied by musical descriptions more precise than those being used just then by other reviewers. The *Herald Tribune* believed that skill in writing backed up by a talent for judgment made for interesting and trustworthy reviews, also that the recognition of these qualities by New York's journalistic and intellectual elite justified their having engaged me. Moreover, in spite of some protests and many intrigues against me, all of which followed plot-lines long familiar, I caused little trouble. If some business or political combine had caused the paper real embarrassment, either through loss of income or through massive reader protest, I should most likely not have survived, for the Ogden Reids, though enlightened, were not quixotic. As Geoffrey Parsons remarked some two years later, "It is possible to write good music criticism now, because no group is interested in stopping you." Which meant, I presume, that I was not a danger to the war effort.

The *Herald Tribune* represented in politics the liberal right, a position usually favorable to the arts. The know-nothing right and the Catholic right, as well as the Marxist left, are in all such matters, as we know, unduly rigid. And papers of the moderate left tend, in art, to be skimpy of space, the sheets of massive circulation even more so. But papers that are privately owned and individually operated make their address to the educated middle class. The *New York Times* has regularly in its critical columns followed a little belatedly the tastes of this group; the *Herald Tribune* under Ogden Reid aspired to lead them. It did not therefore, as the *Times* has so often done, shy away from novelty or from elegance. So when I took as a principle for my column that "intellectual distinction itself is news," the city desk, though not quite ready to admit so radical a concept, found my results lively, especially my wide-ranging choice of subjects and my indifference to personalities already publicized to saturation, such as Marian Anderson and Arturo Toscanini. In fact, when somewhat later John Crosby, then a staff writer, was asked to start a radio-and-television column, hopefully for syndication, the managing editor warned him against overdoing big-time coverage. "Spread yourself around like Virgil Thomson," he said. "Surprise your readers."

Except for courtesy coverage of opening nights at the Philharmonic and the Metropolitan Opera, I must say that my choice of occasions was by the conventions of the time wildly

capricious. My third review was of a woman conductor, Fré-
dérique Petrides, leading thirty players in a piece by David Diamond. In my second week, reviewing two Brazilian programs
at the Museum of Modern Art, I poked fun at the public image
of that institution, at folklore cults in general, at all music from
Latin America, that of Villa-Lobos in particular, and found an
error in the museum's translation of a title from the Portuguese. I also discovered, for myself at least, a group of young
people called the Nine O'Clock Opera Company, all just out
of the Juilliard School, singing in English at the Town Hall to
a pianoforte accompaniment Mozart's *The Marriage of Figaro*.

My attack on Dorothy Maynor appeared on October 24, a
subsequently much-quoted piece in praise of Artur Rubinstein
on October 26. On the twenty-eighth I reported on a W.P.A.
orchestra led by Otto Klemperer. On the thirty-first appeared
a review of Jascha Heifetz entitled *Silk-Underwear Music*, in
which I called his playing "vulgar." The imprecision of this
adjective and the shocking nature of my whole attack brought
protests on my head from Geoffrey Parsons as well as, through
intermediaries, from Heifetz. Tasteless certainly were my adjectives weighted with scorn; but I could not then, cannot now, regret having told what I thought the truth about an artist whom
I believed to be overestimated. To all such reputations, in fact, I
was sales resistant, like William James, who had boasted, "I am
against greatness and bigness in all their forms."

That winter, along with covering a handful of standard
soloists—Josef Hofmann, Jan Smeterlin, Kirsten Flagstad,
Arturo Toscanini, John Charles Thomas—and with a reasonable attention paid to the orchestras and the opera, I reviewed
Maxine Sullivan (singing in a night club), Paul Bowles's music
for *Twelfth Night* (on Broadway, with Helen Hayes and Maurice Evans), Walt Disney's *Fantasia*, a score of musical books
and magazines, a student orchestra, two youth orchestras, an
opera at the Juilliard School, a Bach oratorio in a church, a
Broadway musical by Kurt Weill, Marc Blitzstein's far-to-the-left
almost-opera *No for an Answer*, Stravinsky's Violin Concerto
turned into a ballet, several other dance performances involving modern music, an economics-and-sociology report from
Columbia University on the "hit" trade in popular songs, the
Harvard Glee Club ("fair but no warmer"), Holy Thursday

at Saint Patrick's Cathedral, a Negro preacher in New Jersey who wore frilled white paper wings over his blue serge suit and played swing music on an electric guitar (he was my Easter Sunday piece), some comical press-agentry received, a W.P.A. orchestra in Newark, three other suburban and regional orchestras, a swing concert at the Museum of Modern Art, an opera at Columbia University, a *Southern Harmony* "sing" in Benton, Kentucky, the Boston "Pops" in Boston, and the Goldman Band in Central Park. By the following season's end I had got round to examining the High School of Music and Art and to considering the radio as a serious source. Recordings I did not touch, because another member of my staff had them in charge.

This staff consisted of myself and three assistants—Francis Perkins, who also served as music editor, Jerome D. Bohm, and Robert Lawrence. Bohm, who had conducted opera in his Berlin student days under Leo Blech, was a German-oriented voice teacher and opera coach. Lawrence, already beginning his career as a conductor, was an enthusiast for French music, especially Berlioz. Perkins, though not professionally a musician, was widely read in music's history and devoted to exactitude. Since 1922 he had kept a catalog, with dates and places, of all the orchestral and operatic works performed in New York City. This was the extension of a somewhat less careful listing begun in 1911 by Edward Krehbiel, and it was unique. He also kept well-indexed clipping books containing all the reviews and news relating to music that appeared in the paper. And he had a shelf of reference books, many of them bought by him, for checking instantly the spelling of a name, the title of a work, the facts about almost anything connected with repertory. And until the department acquired a secretary, it was Perkins who kept the catalog and scrapbooks up to date, as well as sorting out the publicity and announcements, which arrived in vast abundance at the music desk.

For doing this he often worked late into the night "mopping up," as he called it, until three or four or five, then attended early Mass, had breakfast, and went home to sleep. A vintage Bostonian and proudly a Harvard man, he allowed himself no weakness or neglect, nursemaiding and housemaiding us all, lest some misstatement or a skimpy coverage make the paper inglorious. He it was who had in the 1920s and '30s widened the coverage from just the Carnegie-and-Town-Hall beat by slipping out in the course of many an event to visit half of another, something modern usually, that was taking place over at Hunter College or downtown at the New School for Social Research. At this time still a bachelor, he was, as our secretary said, "married to the *Herald Tribune*"; and if he did not sleep on the premises (as he sometimes did at concerts), he very often spent the whole night there.

Replying to my mail, to all those "letters fan and furious" that I sometimes published along with my answers in lieu of a Sunday think-piece, had early earned me stenographic aid. So when the managing editor lent me his own secretary for use on Tuesdays, his day off, this unprecedented precedent caused Perkins too to ask for help, which was granted. And eventually, at her own request, my secretarial abettor, Julia Haines, was allowed to work wholly for the music department, a happy arrangement that long survived my tenure.

Julia was a jolly and sharp-tongued Irishwoman who from having been around some twenty years was on girl-to-girl terms with the secretaries of Ogden Reid, Helen Reid, and Geoffrey Parsons. Her discretion was complete, and so was her devotion to me. She told her colleagues all the favorable news, showing them admiring letters from prominent persons and unusually skillful replies of mine to the opposition. In return they kept her informed of good opinions received in their offices. If they let her know of any trouble about me, she did not pass that on. They could hint, however, at some complaint that Parsons or the Reids would not have wished to make directly. And she would pass back my reply, embarrassing no one.

She also, on the paper's time, typed all my private correspondence—answers to inquiries about publication, to engagements offered, even to personal letters. And thanks to her use of the secretarial back fence, my life was completely exposed. I liked it that way, and so did my employers. Thus no tension that might arise risked becoming exaggerated, a situation especially valuable with regard to Helen Reid. For though we shared mutual admiration, I almost invariably rubbed her the wrong way. My impishness and my arrogance were equally distasteful, and something in my own resistance to her dislike of being rubbed the wrong way led me over and over again to the verge of offense.

Nevertheless, in spite of our tendency to draw sparks from each other, we worked together quite without distrust. After I had once procured music for the Herald Tribune Forum, a three-day feast of famous speakers held every year in the Hotel Waldorf-Astoria ballroom, she offered to pay me for doing this every year; and when I declined payment, my salary was raised. She did not interfere in any way with my department's operations, but eventually she came to ask my advice about pressures and complaints received regarding these operations. And when the general manager of the Metropolitan Opera, Rudolf Bing, surely displeased with my reviewing of his policy statements, sought to cultivate her favor through invitations to his box, she showed him where her confidence lay by inviting me, along with my chief supporter, my discoverer indeed, Geoffrey Parsons, to lunch with him at the paper.

With Parsons there was never misunderstanding. He admired me, forgave me, adopted me into his family. Besides, he was committed to making a success of me, since my appointment had been wholly of his doing. When I misbehaved, as in the Heifetz review, he would correct me kindly, clearly, with reasons, and with always a joke at the end. When during one of my contests with the Metropolitan Opera, he found in my answer to their protest a reference to the "ladies" of the Opera Guild, he reminded me that "lady" is an insulting term because of its irony. "Always attack head-on," he said. "Never make sideswipes and never use innuendo. As long as you observe the amenities of controversy, the very first of which is straightforward language, the paper will stand behind you."

Nevertheless, he would send to my office from time to time a letter pained, impatient, and unclear. These, I came to believe, meant he had been asked by someone, probably Mrs. Reid, to "speak to Virgil." The speakings were not, of course, unjustified, merely out of proportion to the visible fault. And they were not phrased in Geoffrey's normal way, which was ever of wit and sweetness. I would acknowledge them with all delicacy of phrase, almost as if Geoffrey were some irate unknown, and then be more careful for a while. These occasions were not frequent, and no enmity seemed to build up through them. After my first two years they happened rarely, and during the last ten almost not at all. I must eventually have learned smoother ways, for in 1946, on my fiftieth birthday, Carleton Sprague Smith could say, "Six years ago Virgil was one of the most feared men in New York; today he is one of the most loved." Imagine that!

My errors, when they occurred, were of two kinds, those which shocked the prejudices of readers and those which caused inconvenience to management. In the first kind of case I was merely cautioned to watch my language, use no slang, explain everything, be persuasive. For indeed, in expository writing, failure to convince is failure *tout court*. Inconvenience to management arriving through complaint from prominent persons was not necessarily unwelcome, however. The Metropolitan Opera, the Philharmonic, the Museum of Modern Art, the radio establishments that presented Toscanini or owned Columbia Concerts, these were familiar opponents; and battling with them was tonic to us all. For that sport, methods of attack and defense were our subjects of gleeful conference, punctilio and courtesy our strategy; getting the facts right was our point of honor, exposing them to readers our way of being interesting.

The orchestras from out of town, such as Boston and Philadelphia, sent us no embassies. And the standard touring soloists one rarely heard from even indirectly. What seemed most to bother Mrs. Reid and Geoffrey was unfavorable comment on a suburban affair. My questioning the civic value to Stamford, Connecticut, of a quite poor symphony orchestra brought two strong letters from Parsons. Conflict with Manhattan millionaires, I could read between the lines, was permitted, but not with country clubs. Suburbia had long supplied the nut of our liberal Republican readership, and the paper's eventual drama of survival came to be played out against the sociological transformation of those neighborhoods. Discouraging suburbia about anything, I understood, was imprudent. For suburbs, like churches, accept only praise.

Geoffrey was right, of course; he always was. My quality as a reviewer came from my ability to identify with the makers of music; and when I spoke both as an insider to music and warmly, my writing, whether favorable or not, was communicative. But I simply could not identify with organizers and promoters, however noble their motives. Going out of one's way to cover something not usually reviewed is a lark, provided you can get a lively piece out of it. If not, wisdom would leave it to the merciful neutrality of the news columns. But when you are new to reviewing and still reacting passionately, you are not always led by wisdom. And later, when you have more control, you are not so passionate. Neither are you quite so interesting. Because the critical performance needs to be based on passion, even when journalism requires that you persuade. And in the early years of my reviewing, Geoffrey was like a guardian angel, an athletic coach, and a parent all in one, hoping, praying, and probably believing that with constant correction and copious praise I could be kept at top form.

I had entered music reviewing in a spirit of adventure; and though I never treated it as just an adventure, I did not view it as just journalism either. I thought of myself as a species of knight-errant attacking dragons single-handedly and rescuing musical virtue in distress. At the same time I ran a surprisingly efficient department, organized a Music Critics' Circle (still in existence), started a guest-column on radio music to be written by B. H. Haggin and a jazz column with Rudi Blesh as star performer. When the war removed two of my staff members, I took on Paul Bowles to substitute for one of them and later employed the composer Arthur Berger; I also caused the engagement of Edwin Denby for a year and a half as ballet reviewer; and I established a panel of music writers from outside the paper who helped us keep the coverage complete. This pool of "stringers" constituted a training corps that comprised my future music editor, Jay Harrison, and the present *New York Times* staff writers Theodore Strongin and Allen Hughes. At one time or another it included the music historian Herbert Weinstock and the composers Elliott Carter, John Cage, Lou Harrison, William Flanagan, Lester Trimble, and Peggy Glanville-Hicks.

I used no one not trained in music, for my aim was to explain the artist, not to encourage misunderstanding of his work. I discouraged emotional reactions and opinion-mongering on the grounds that they were a waste of space. "Feelings," I would say, "will come through automatically in your choice of words. Description is the valid part of reviewing; spontaneous reactions, if courteously phrased, have some validity; opinions are mostly worthless. If you feel you must express one, put it in the last line, where nothing will be lost if it gets cut for space."

My copy was never cut; neither did it ever make the front page. I wrote in pencil, proofread the manuscript before sending it down, preferring, should errors occur, that they be my own. After the first year I did not go downstairs at all, checking my Sunday proofs at home, sent by messenger. In my first weeks I had asked Francis Perkins how long it would take to get over being unduly elated or depressed at a musical event. "About six years," he had said. And he was right. After that time I could write a review, go off to bed, and wake up in the morning with no memory of where I had been or what I had written. Twice, to my knowledge, I reviewed a contemporary work without remembering I had done so two years earlier. And in both cases my descriptions were virtually identical in thought, though not in words.

I had established my routines very early. During seven months of the year I wrote a Sunday article every week and averaged two reviews. During the summer months I did no reviewing; I also skipped seven or eight Sunday articles. Since these could be sent from anywhere, I toured on musical errands of my own or stayed in some country place writing music. I also wrote music in town, published books, went in and out on lectures and conducting dates. The paper liked all this activity, because it kept my name before the public. Also because I usually came back with a piece about San Francisco or Texas or Pittsburgh (after the war, Europe and Mexico and South America, too), which was good for circulation. To the Herald Tribune Forum I added for musical relief opera singers, Southern hymn singers, Negro choirs, and Robert Shaw's Collegiate Chorale. In all these arrangements, my dealings with Helen Reid were quite without friction or misunderstanding. Indeed, unless I look at my scrapbooks I can hardly remember my last ten years at the paper, so thoroughly satisfactory were they to us all and so little demanding of my time. The dramas had all come in the first four, for those were the years when I was learning my trade while working at it. These were also, of course, the war years, naturally full of emergencies, revelations, excitements, departures, arrivals, surprises, and strange contacts.

28

Europe in America

IF AMERICA IN THE 1920s exiled its artists, the 1940s, especially their first half, saw a meeting of talent here, both foreign and domestic, that made us for the first time an international center for intellectuals. Central Europeans, notably some brilliant musicologists and art scholars, had been coming throughout the 1930s. In 1940 certain English joined us for the duration. And during that winter and all through '41 those who had reasons (and the means) for leaving France arrived in a steady trickle. The painters Eugene Berman, André Masson, and Yves Tanguy were here already; so was Marcel Duchamp. And the surrealist poet André Breton, arriving after the Occupation had begun, came soon to exercise over poets and painters in New York an authority similar to that which for nearly two decades he had practiced in Paris. He did them good, too, freeing poets from censorship by the hatchet men of T. S. Eliot and setting off a movement in painting that has traveled clean round the world. Also, a scholastic group that included the philosopher Jacques Maritain established here an Ecole de Hautes Etudes Libres, which offered French students in exile university credits valid for after the war.

The standard repertory conductors Toscanini and Bruno Walter had established residence before the war. Wanda Landowska, queen of the harpsichord, arrived on Pearl Harbor day. The composers Arnold Schoenberg, Kurt Weill, and Hanns Eisler had been here since the mid-thirties. Stravinsky in the late thirties kept coming in and out till the war in Europe decided him, like Bruno Walter, to renounce his recently gained French citizenship and opt for ours. A short listing of other composers who joined us in the years around 1940 will recall perhaps the brilliancy of the time.

From Hungary had come to New York Béla Bartók, to the West Coast Miklos Rosza; from Poland Jerzy Fitelberg, Karol Rathaus, and Alexandre Tansman; from Czechoslovakia Bohuslav Martinu. Arriving Russians, via western Europe, were Arthur Lourié and Nikolai Lopatnikoff; Nicolai Berezowsky, Vladimir

Dukelsky (Vernon Duke), and Nicolas Nabokov were already here. From Austria came Jacques de Menasce and Ernst Křenek, from Italy Vittorio Rieti and (to Hollywood) Montemezzi, Castelnuovo-Tedesco, and Amfiteatroff; from Germany via London the pianist Artur Schnabel (also a composer) and via Palestine Stefan Wolpe, via Paris the boy-genius Lukas Foss. Directly from France we had not only Nadia Boulanger, the teacher of us all, but the chief then of all the composing French, Darius Milhaud.

Among my own close friends from France, Yvonne de Casa Fuerte was a welcome helper in the music life. To support herself and her son, aged sixteen, she gave French lessons and violin lessons, also playing in pit orchestras such as that of the New York City Opera and, when this was out of season, in musicals by Kurt Weill and for Billy Rose's Aquacade. She also played in concerts. And in the spring of 1943 we organized together a series of Serenades modeled after her Paris originals.

Our patron was the Marquis de Cuevas, who had given us $5,000. Active with us in the planning were the flute player René Le Roy and the pianist Prince George Chavchavadze. Though the printed prospectus names two more, Carl Van Vechten and Aaron Copland, it is not in my memory that either of these ever sat with us for program making. My membership on the music committee of the Museum of Modern Art helped toward use of its auditorium.

There were five of these Serenades, all involving rare music, much of it presented by artists so remarkable and so new (Leonard Bernstein, for instance, and Robert Shaw) that our evenings offered a refreshing and particular splendor. Thomas Beecham conducted a concert, Vladimir Golschmann another. And one that was devoted to the memory of García Lorca produced both a *cuadro flamenco* with Argentinita and a stage-work by Paul Bowles. Entitled *The Wind Remains*, this was a partial setting to music (in the manner of a *zarzuela*) of a part of a play by García Lorca called *Así que pasen cinco años*, partly in prose and partly in verse, partly spoken and partly sung, partly in English and partly (the verse parts) left in Spanish. It was also partly acted and partly danced. The whole thing was quite beautiful but in an artistic sense only partly successful; largely,

I think, because the free form of the *zarzuela* is unacceptable to English-speaking audiences.

Our final concert contained first New York presentations of the Stravinsky *Danses concertantes* and of the Poulenc *Aubade*, the latter with Robert Casadesus as piano soloist. Neither work, however, pleased the press. Olin Downes found the Poulenc "a series of clichés and dull and bad jokes," the Stravinsky "considerably worse." "The pieces were politely received," he said, "and why not? Could a politer set of platitudes be invented? Music guaranteed to upset no one—not even the refugees of the St. Regis." Nevertheless, these concerts were distinguished; and had not my colleague of the *Times* felt moved to crush them, we might have found funds for their continuance. His paper's chronic fear of any take-off toward style came back to mind only the other day, when Howard Taubman, its drama critic, dismissed a play by the poet Robert Lowell as "a pretentious, arty trifle."

Later, just at the end of the war, I helped to organize more concerts, this time benefitting France Forever. I had become associated with this Free French group through the pianist E. Robert Schmitz, ever a patriot as well as a modern-music defender. And I remember particularly fine performances of a new string quartet by Sauguet and of a work composed in German captivity by Olivier Messiaen, called *Quartet for the End of Time*.

It was in the fall of 1940 that I first encountered, through Suzanne Blum, Hervé Alphand, at that time Economic Secretary to the French Embassy. His wife of the time, Claude, who did not much like Washington and who could not bear at all their Vichy associates, was pressing him to resign, which soon he did, going off to join de Gaulle in London and leaving Claude to stay out the war in New York. Sharing a small flat with her mother, she earned money by singing French chansons in New York night clubs, in Montreal, sometimes in Florida, even in Brazil. She was a 1900-style blonde with commanding beauty, a not large voice, and no knowledge of music at all. Her mother, an excellent musician as well as a first-class cook and hostess, taught her everything; she also ran the house. At public appearances, Rudi Révil, a Parisian song composer, would play for her till toward the close she would sit on the grand piano and sing to her own guitar. Though without the relentless intensity of a Piaf, by nature she had star quality.

Loving both her presence and her singing for making me feel that I was back in France, I helped to start off her career by reviewing its debut. Hervé wrote from London to thank me for that. And Claude sent two bottles of claret, left over from their Embassy days, with a note saying, "*Voici le pot de vin habituel dans l'administration.*" Her light touch and her fearless independence reminded me of Madame Langlois. Women at once so courageous and so beautiful are a sort of masterpiece.

The well-to-do refugees who had so shocked Olin Downes included the American-born Lady Ribblesdale (indeed living at the St. Regis, which was a property of her son, Vincent Astor), the Shakespearean scholar Sir Harley Granville-Barker and his American poet wife (at the simpler Mayfair), and the conductor Sir Thomas Beecham, Bart. (installed at the Ritz Carlton with his longtime Egeria, Lady Cunard). With both these last, my friendship was engaged at first sight. It went on too till their respective deaths, though after 1943 their own tie had been cut by Beecham's marriage.

Born Maud Forbes, in California, and inheriting while still young a quite large fortune, she had married around 1890 Sir Bache Cunard and shortly borne him one child, a daughter. After he had welcomed once her return from an extended absence by building a gate marked "Come into the garden, Maud," she changed her name. Sir Bache himself, with fine estates, was a country man; but Emerald, as she now became, loved town. So she mostly lived in London, cutting a figure as hostess, becoming the close friend of George Moore and after World War I of Thomas Beecham.

Earlier concerned with letters and politics, she had moved into music after Sir Thomas became owner and impresario of the Covent Garden Opera House, mobilizing society, the arts, and even government to help him fill its boxes. Later, under Edward VIII, she had abetted the king in his marriage plans. Under his successor she fell into disfavor, but not too gravely, one gathered, since Beecham and his career were an occupation and since, with the war, society was largely dispersed to its jobs and regiments.

Beecham had informed the British government at the beginning of this war that he could not, as he had done during the other, support England's four chief orchestras out of his income. And since opera was to be closed down for the duration, he decided in the spring of 1940 to make a gift to Anglo-Saxon solidarity by going off to conduct in Australia, later in Canada and in the United States. Lady Cunard, at the same time, gave up her house in Grosvenor Square and came to America, accompanied by her lady's maid, to spend the summer visiting in Newport. Come fall, as Beecham's guest, she moved to the Ritz in New York, where till 1943 was played out the drama of his impending marriage to a much younger woman, he denying that nothing of the sort was planned and she well knowing that it was.

As who did not, indeed? There had been a press scandal in Seattle about his sharing a house with the pretty pianist. Then she took residence in Idaho for divorcing *in absentia* her English clergyman. And wherever Beecham appeared as guest conductor, Betty Humby was likely to appear as soloist. There was no concealing their constant proximity, though there was enormous effort on the part of Beecham to save face for Lady Cunard in the destruction of their twenty-year bond, even though the friendship, as he said, had been "for the last ten years only that."

And he himself required a divorce, also procured in Sun Valley. And then he was married in New York, later being divorced and married all over again in England, just to make the whole thing stick. But well before the marrying began, Lady Cunard had gone back to London and taken rooms in the Hotel Dorchester, where she went on giving dinner parties, with wine from the Chilean Embassy and with bills paid out of the sale of jewelry and divers *objets d'art* that had remained after a lifetime of expenditure. She was dead by 1950, having never ceased to be an inflammatory hostess, a tonic wit, an Egeria indefatigable. And to the end she had young poets in attendance, attached almost like lovers.

Small, roundish though less than plump, with china-blue eyes and yellow slightly mussed-up hair, Emerald Cunard had always been pretty and remained so. She also passed for being hard of heart, and certainly she was as relentless as any other career-hostess. After her daughter's communist and Negro frequentations had caused embarrassment, she never spoke to her again, or of her. All the same, she was faithful, with the novelist George Moore and with Beecham, to long friendships deeply engaged. Ever happy with artists, she gave them jolly times, admiration, and money, read their books, hung their pictures, got them posts and publishers, kept them at work, and abetted their love affairs. As an American she could be demanding, even cruel; as a European she was generous and a comrade. For all her preoccupations with grandeur, she was never banal or in friendship dishonest. Nor was she self-indulgent. She merely lived hard every day, reading long into the night; and men of gifts found knowing her a privilege. She once summed up for me a rule, if not of life, of living: "For a good party have beautiful women and intelligent men; for a bad one, intelligent women and beautiful men." Of Beecham she said, "He is deeply sentimental, but also relentless. When he wants a thing, no one can stop him."

Certainly no one stopped him from the marriage he had set his mind on. The young woman, he told Emerald, had awakened in him feelings he "had long thought dead." Betty Humby, on her part, was equally attached and willing to pay with all her strength for the marriage she had long desired. But she wore out that strength in his service. And after she died, fifteen years later, he married again, this time an even younger woman. At eighty, still conducting concerts and recordings and projecting another tour of Germany, he suffered a fatal stroke. For twenty years we had told each other stories, eaten and drunk together, argued and laughed. I know he loved my music, and I think he understood it; I understood, I think, his approach to music making and loved its results. I loved them for resplendent sound and for good sense. He used a shaping hand with Haydn, a warm one with Mozart, a light one for Wagner, and a poetical one (inspired idea!) for Berlioz. And always the sonorities were what musicians call "musical," as if harmoniousness were a virtue, which it is. He once said of his loyal English public, "They have for music little understanding, but they adore the sound it makes."

From our friendship's first beginnings he played my music across the United States, in Canada, in England. No one else has ever made my Second Symphony sound so glowing, though I do not think he was comfortable with the work. *Filling Station* and *The River* he played with more abandon. My operas he professed to adore (*Four Saints* was for him "the finest vocal music in English since Elizabethan times"), but he never conducted them. (The B.B.C. refused him *The Mother of Us All* when he proposed to broadcast it for his seventieth birthday.) My Cello Concerto he played in Edinburgh, paying for an extra rehearsal to get it right. When I began conducting orchestras myself, he at first made fun of me; but he afterwards invited me to Mexico for preparing and conducting under him Mozart's *The Magic Flute*. I did not go, preferring to compose that summer. And by not grasping the precious opportunity, I proved to both of us the innocence of my conducting ambitions. What I chiefly regretted at not being with him was our conversations. For we stimulated each other; and enlivened by Emerald Cunard's bright presence, we were likely to talk far into the night. She would accuse me of being anti-British and I would reply, "No, only anti-English." Then she would scold me for arrogance, praise both of us intensely, and all the time be guiding us toward themes where we could shine. And he would say afterwards, "Virgil is the only man in the world who can keep me up till four."

Others from England spending the war here were the composers Benjamin Britten, Anthony Arnell, Stanley Bate, and the Australian Peggy Glanville-Hicks. Britten I did not encounter often; but I did review his first opera, *Paul Bunyan*, written to a text by W. H. Auden. By finding its music "eclectic though not without savor," its poetry "flaccid and spineless and without energy," I classified myself as no friend of the Empire.

Arnell would call on me every few months with a brand-new symphony; I found his music mostly pretty thin. Then once there was a different kind, grandly funereal and richly sad; and I think I recommended that piece to Beecham. In any case, he played it. He liked, as I did, its tragical and apocalyptic character, and all the more because the run of British composers was continuing to write as cheerfully as if the Empire called for no lament. Lately Britten has composed a *War Requiem* that makes exception to the general British rule, for though their prose literature has had its angry young ones, and though their older novelists and playwrights have faced society's disaster in the language of Oscar Wilde and Shaw, the basic despair of England seems not yet to have touched deeply either music or poetry.

Stanley Bate wrote optimistic music in a British version of the Boulanger style. He could play the piano poetically, too; and Lady Cunard loved piano concertos. So Beecham presented Bate's; and Emerald found him a paying patron, who bought him a Steinway and set him up in an apartment. But Stanley drank too much and quarreled too much and eventually went back to England. Peggy Glanville-Hicks, his wife, stayed here, supporting herself by writing articles and by copying music, achieved distinction as a composer, and became a citizen. Stanley married a Brazilian consul general, Margareda Guedes Nogueira, who backed him up loyally, just as Peggy had done, in his war against the musical Establishment (chiefly controlled by Britten and his publisher, the latter linked by marriage to the throne). So he wrote less and drank more until eventually, after a heart failure or stroke, he drowned in his bath.

Peggy Glanville-Hicks, thin, passionate, tireless, and insistent (for Australian women can indeed insist), might well have been a burden to us all had she not been so willing to turn her hand to musical odd jobs. She wrote for the *Herald Tribune* and for magazines; she copied music; she managed concerts; she ran everybody's errands; she went on lecture tours by bus in the Dakotas; she composed documentary films for UNICEF; she made musicological trips to India for the Rockefeller Foundation; she saw other people's music (particularly that of Paul Bowles, after his return to Morocco) through the perils of recording. She made her own clothes and dressed charmingly. When alone she did not eat much, but she could be a lively dinner guest. She wrote a great deal of music, got it published and recorded, grew as a composer from modest beginnings (as a none-too-remarkable pupil of Ralph Vaughan Williams) into an opera writer of marked originality, setting first *The Transposed Heads* by Thomas Mann, later collaborating with the poet Robert Graves and with the novelist Lawrence Durrell.

She believed, upon some evidence, that the world was out to crush women composers; and she was convinced (from no evidence) that my music editor, Jay Harrison, actually her protector, was for getting her fired. She complained; she stormed;

she telephoned. And with all this she was an indispensable colleague. Even from Greece, where she now lives (still frugally), she continues to fulminate and to be useful. Her generosity is no more to be stopped than her scolding ways. And she remains a memorable composer.

It was also through music that I knew a real French gangster. He had asked for counsel, just at the end of the war, about bringing a French orchestra to America. With perfect discretion, he omitted to mention that his wife, under another name, had sung sizable works of mine in Town Hall. When later I helped her to secure the hall again, he was grateful in the standard gangster way, could never do me favors enough, it seemed.

He lived at the Waldorf-Astoria with his beautiful wife (much younger) and an elderly French maid. Also at the hotel, as his guest throughout the war, was a famous French trial lawyer, to whom he was grateful for having earlier kept him out of prison on charges of white slavery and of trafficking in drugs. He was the eldest of six brothers, Russian Jewish by origin, who had become powerful after World War I in the Marseille underworld. Large assets had been amassed in Alsace and in the Argentine; and he had shipping connections in Jugoslavia. During the Spanish Civil War, with connivance from the French government, I understood, he had run arms into Republican Spain. After World War II he worked directly for his government, he told me, buying coal and steel on the American black market, for these materials were in principle strictly rationed and the French were needing to rebuild their railways quickly.

In addition to his Waldorf-Astoria apartment, he kept one at the Georges V in Paris, and also, to the north, a château for week ends. And if he happened not to be in Paris, through the brother who owned a restaurant I always had access to black-market French francs in any amount. No books were kept; I simply paid later in New York. Then the pretty wife got bored with a singing career, spent more and more time with the Cannes high life; and her devoted husband left off coming to New York. By this time his business was mostly in Europe anyway, "working with the American Army in Germany," he called it. What products he procured I never asked. But he grew richer and richer, and more and more wretched at his wife's long absences. I had grown fond of him; and so had others—Oscar

Levant, for instance, who had taste in gangsters, and Maurice Grosser, who could introduce the French business associates, if need be, to Negro circles. When a work of Nicolas Nabokov was given in Berlin, our friend arrived with cases of the best champagne, brought by air. And when my landlord requested me to bring him from New York a refrigerator, a blender, and a washing machine, these were all bought at wholesale prices and passed through French customs by the President's secretary. Did he eventually perish of despair? For die he did. And did he leave vast fortunes, open or secret? A few years earlier, tried in Morocco for fraud, found guilty, and assessed three billion francs, he had remarked, "Nobody pays a $6 million fine." All the same, he was forever buying rubies and diamonds for his wife. "You never know," he would say. "Someday she may need money."

I hope she has not come to that; I wish her well. For fifteen years this Waldorf gangster family were my friends; and if with their rubies and diamonds hidden away they were less showy as to bosom than Olin Downes's "refugees of the Saint Regis," their hearts were open and their ways were warm. After all, no law says exiles must be poor.

43. Others than I made musical portraits. This sketch of V.T., dated May 4, 1930, is by Henri Sauguet.

44. V.T. in 1927, at thirty-one.

45. Roy Harris came to France in 1926 to study composition with Boulanger, stayed four years.

46. Roger Désormière, a composer from Erik Satie's *groupe d'Arceuil,* become an excellent conductor.

47. Mary Butts was English, an adept of magic, a smoker of opium, a poet, an author of novels and stories.

48. The painter Christian Bérard around 1925, before he had become fat or famous, grown a beard.

49. Georges Hugnet, poet, and Eugene Berman, painter, with Gertrude Stein in 1929 at Bilignin.

50. Sergei Prokofiev and Nicolas Nabokov at Deauville, May–June 1931.

51. V.T. with Gertrude Stein and opera score, circa 1929 or '30.

52. *La Sérénade*, 1932—Vittorio Rieti, Marqués de Casa Fuerte, Milhaud, Prince Leone Massimo, Yvonne de Casa Fuerte, Sauguet, Désormière, and Igor Markevitch.

53. Painters Eugene and Leonid Berman in the south of France, 1937.

54. Pierre de Massot, gifted, poor, frail, violent, addicted through weakness to communism and opium. Even a Scottish wife could not unbind him.

55. The mantel and mirror in my present flat were installed in 1791.

56. Next door to No. 17 is the Hôtel du quai Voltaire, where, according to a plaque, *Charles Baudelaire, Richard Wagner, et Oscar Wilde ont honoré Paris de leur séjour.*

57. *Opposite:* My original studio, above and behind the broad central building (at its right), is visible only from the quai du Louvre.

58. Mary Reynolds in 1931, relentlessly bohemian, relentlessly a lady.

59. Louise (Madame Jean-Paul) Langlois, 1856–1939, my friend for thirteen years.

60. Max Jacob, poet and painter, perhaps a saint, unquestionably a martyr—gouache by Edouard M. Perrot showing the monastery of Saint-Benoît-sur-Loire.

61. Alfred H. Barr, Jr., first director of the first museum of modern art (New York, 1929) and the founder of modern-art scholarship.

62. Philip Johnson, in the 1930s a showman of architecture.

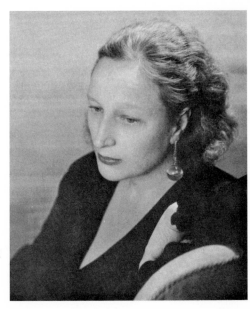

63. Constance Askew, admired by artists and scholars, dealers and curators, poets and people of the theater.

64. *Four Saints in Three Acts*, 1934—St. Teresa photographed as if with Holy Ghost.

65. Florine Stettheimer's miniature theater for designing in real textures.

66. Frederick Ashton (now Sir Frederick), for whom the saints moved gaily with decorum.

67. Florine Stettheimer, drawing by Marcel Duchamp.

68. John Houseman, production director of *Four Saints*.

69. Maurice Grosser, whose scenario was our basis for choreography and action.

70. John Houseman, Pavel Tchelitcheff, Aline McMahon, and Orson Welles—V.T. too—had planned Webster's *The Duchess of Malfi* for Mercury Theatre.

71. Henry-Russell Hitchcock, architecture historian, with "Chick" Austin, museum director, in front of a picture by Balthus.

72. Pare Lorentz, author and director of the documentary films *The Plow That Broke the Plains*, 1936, and *The River*, 1937, for both of which I wrote the music.

73. Alexander Calder, who created for Satie's *Socrate* a mobile stage-set.

74. Theodate Johnson (oil on canvas) by Maurice Grosser, 1938. She had a fine soprano voice, broke it doing war work in France, 1940.

75. Lew Christensen choreographed *Filling Station* for Ballet Caravan and danced the lead, 1938.

Sets by David Hilberman for *The Mother of Us All* at UCLA, 1965.

76. A prologue showing Susan B. at home.

77. Debate, Susan B. Anthony and Daniel Webster.

78. In the last scene Susan's statue is unveiled.

79. John Cage, far-out composer, who wrote with Kathleen O'Donnell Hoover *Virgil Thomson: His Life and Music*.

80. The composer Lou Harrison about 1950.

81. V.T. at the *New York Herald Tribune* in 1940.

82. Geoffrey Parsons, Pulitzer-award–winning chief editorial writer and my mentor at the *Herald Tribune*.

83. Studio playback of *Louisiana Story* music—Helen Van Dongen, editor; Eugene Ormandy, conductor; Robert Flaherty, author and director; Bob Fine, recording engineer; and V.T.

84. Henri Cliquet-Pleyel at seventy, correcting his *Concerto posthume* (sic). He died before its première in '63.

85. V.T. with Igor Stravinsky and birthday cake at Arnold Weissberger's, 1962.

THE *HERALD TRIBUNE* WAS NOT ALONE responsible for my reactivated professional life, for this had put forth buds on my arrival from France. Glenway Wescott had been hopeful that I might compose a ballet with him. Detroit's Pro Musica had offered a lecture and concert. The Metropolitan Opera Guild had engaged me to speak on Mozart, with Frieda Hempel singing arias. And shortly after, Ludwig Bemelmans had sought me out toward collaborating with him on a dance-spectacle about Ecuador. Neither of the ballets came to pass; but after my newspaper debut on October 11, 1940, other proposals started to arrive—for performance and for publication, for lecturing, for composing, for writing articles, and naturally for recommending applicants to the foundations.

It was clear quite early that if I were to lead a practicing musician's life along with that of a reviewer, I should be needing more help than just a secretary. I had to get my music into shape. Also, I needed extra housework. This came to be furnished by one of my Saints, Leonard Franklin, tenor soloist from 1934, a man of impeccable charm and gentle ways. He came to cook and serve, to take care of my clothes, to receive my callers, and to do my errands. And since the Chelsea Hotel did not at that time house colored lodgers, my Saint found a flat near by; and I began to have lots of company.

My musical secretary, Mimi Wallner, a curly-haired athletic blonde just out of Bennington, could copy music, speak French, and play the double bass. She too worked in the apartment, making extra copies of all my unpublished works—which meant virtually all my works—and extracting orchestral parts from my unplayed scores, which meant most of those. With her help my career as a composer could take off.

As long as I had lived abroad, neither conductors nor publishers had shown much interest in my music. Encouraging the composers from near by made better news. And even in the 1930s, when I was a figure in the New York theater, the concert-giving establishments had shown reluctance. My status as an expatriate always going back and forth to France would seem to have dissolved all obligation. They did not even have to read my scores, knowing there would be no pressure here for using them. Then all at once they knew they would be using them. There was no pressure really. But I was in the news; they were aware of me. So they asked which works I wished them to use first and in most cases took them sight unseen. They still, I noted, did not read my scores.

Thus it happened that my works began to travel. And before long I began to travel with them. It was Eugene Ormandy who first found that I could conduct (by letting me show his orchestra how to bounce a rhythm in *Filling Station*). After that, he played a piece almost every year; and I was asked to conduct the Philadelphia Orchestra whenever I liked, in two cases on Columbia recordings. Eventually I conducted almost everywhere, though I was not asked to Boston till after Koussevitzky had retired. I requested no engagement, employed no agent. I merely answered mail and stayed available. Nor did I question any artist's motives. Some may have programed my music to gain good will, though they knew that if they played it in New York, I obviously could not review that concert. Others, taking advice from managements or following private scruples, refrained from seeking favor in this way. Myself, I asked for nothing, held no grudges. But I actually believe that my being alert to a possible conflict of interests kept me more punctilious than most other reviewers about describing each performance truthfully. Certainly my editors found nothing suspect, nor did readers reproach me. When Harl McDonald, manager of the Philadelphia Orchestra, inquired if I thought he should possibly not engage me as guest conductor, I passed his letter on to Geoffrey Parsons; and Geoffrey, after asking at the top, replied that the paper saw no impropriety.

My new works that first winter were theatrical. For a radio program called The Columbia Workshop, John Houseman produced on December 9 *The Trojan Women* of Euripides in a cutting of the Edith Hamilton translation; and I made music after a conception that had not, I think, been ever used before. This was to reverse the usual procedure of putting music between the scenes and sound-effects with them. My scheme of separating the scenes by sound-effect interludes and accompanying

them with music was designed to help the listener distinguish one character from another in a play spoken almost entirely by women.

Cassandra, Andromache, and Hecuba were cast for speaking voices of high, middle, and low timbre—Zita Johann, Joanna Roos, and Mildred Natwick, as I recall. And for pointing up this contrast, as well as for aiding identification, I accompanied them respectively on a flute, a clarinet, and an English horn, giving to each of these solo lines the expressive content of the speech. Then for separating the scenes I composed sound-effect passages depicting weather, marching men, whatever was needed for making events seem real. Actually my woodwind obbligati were a variant of the percussive accompaniments that I had learned to do from Orson Welles in the Negro *Macbeth* and later used to build up Leslie Howard's voice in *Hamlet.* They served in *The Trojan Women* for identifying characters, somewhat less for expressivity, since one could not without more rehearsal time train actresses to read less tearfully and leave emotion to the music's line and shading—as when at Cassandra's mention of her child, it took only a tiny tune in the piccolo's low register to evoke the baby's presence and make us weep. I should like to use again this sensitive approach, but with more time to work it out, possibly notating the reading parts for rhythm and for each voice's rise and fall, obtaining in this way a musical elocution suitable both to Greek tragedy and to the English language.

Later that season I did apply it again, this time to choruses intoned in Greek. The play was the *Oedipus Tyrannus* of Sophocles, the locale the library steps at Fordham University, the producer Father William Lynch, S.J., the choreographer Erick Hawkins, himself something of a Greek scholar. Not being a Greek scholar myself, I had to work phonetically. Father Lynch provided me with a word-by-word translation of the choruses, plus a metrical notation of their quantities, cadences, and stresses; and with this help I composed in Greek a monolinear music, accompanied by drums and wind instruments that underlined the modal melodies. It all came off quite well, as I remember; but the really impressive element was Richard Burgi, a boy of seventeen, who played Jocasta with a grand projection. Encountered some years later, he had followed scholarly proclivities; and as I write he is head of the Russian department at Princeton, a constant customer nevertheless at the Metropolitan Opera, where he identifies himself, I am sure, with the singing actors, especially with powerful projectors like Leontyne Price and Maria Callas. I think this because it seems to be roles rather than musical styles that hold his interest.

There was a production of *Four Saints* in the spring of '41, but without staging. Miss Louise Crane, a young woman of means who wished to serve music, had undertaken a series of Coffee Concerts at the Museum of Modern Art, these to include offerings as offbeat as advanced jazz and Yemenite dancing. She esteemed it a cultural service to revive my opera; and in order to broaden the possible audience (since the museum's auditorium could hold only 480), she proposed two performances, one in the museum, to be conducted by me from a piano, and another at Town Hall, with an orchestra conducted by Alexander Smallens. I reassembled my soloists and chorus with the help of my Harlem helper, Leonard de Paur, and prepared the performances. And since it was possible to consider the one at the museum as a rehearsal for the other, the press was asked to skip that and review from Town Hall. It was here that Sir Thomas Beecham, first making acquaintance with the work and identifying it as a child of the Elizabethan masque, came to accept my music as related to his own Britishness. And he loved to tease me about its idiosyncrasies, such as the double bass that would "first play and then not play." The peculiarity he referred to was actually an equivalent of the organist's device for avoiding monotony by now and then taking his feet off the pedals.

Alfred Wallenstein also conducted *Four Saints* in a beautiful performance on station WOR, a broadcast of 1942 aimed at selling war bonds and paid for by the Treasury Department. The original cast was again got together in 1947 and trained by Leonard de Paur for a Columbia broadcast on the Philharmonic hour; and this time I conducted. I also conducted for RCA Victor, with the same cast and orchestra (renamed for the occasion the Victor Symphony Orchestra), a recording of about half the opera. This was the last time the 1934 cast could be used. When the opera was restaged in 1952 for New York and Paris, only Edward Matthews and his wife were still vocally fresh. So a new cast was assembled. But the old one can still be heard, since the 1947 recording, twice reissued, is still in circulation.

Wallenstein had also urged me to excerpt an orchestral suite from *The River*; and it was he, not Beecham, who first played it. The latter became attached to it, however, because of its Protestant hymn content, which carried him back to Lancashire. And Aaron Copland wrote me it was "a lesson in how to treat Americana." Stokowski also took it up, although much later, and gave to its recording a fine buoyancy. I myself have no attachment to it, probably because its pristine inspiration came from an earlier work, the *Symphony on a Hymn Tune*, a piece for me far more original and more evocative of the South.

Beecham had in 1941 asked for a "major" work that he could play that fall in Philadelphia and elsewhere, and I had proposed my Second Symphony. On his acceptance, I began to reflect as to whether the piece did not require a bit of adjusting, at least orchestrally. A chance for judging that came in the spring, when the Luxembourg conductor Henri Pensis played some of it in Newark. Hearing it for the first time, though it had been in existence for a decade, I concluded that it wanted higher contrasts and a more striking color—in short, that I must reorchestrate. And this I did during the summer months.

Come June, having caught my periodic grippe-cold, I spent a week being cared for at the Askews'. Then I stayed for a fortnight at Woods Hole, Massachusetts, with Mrs. W. Murray Crane, Louise's mother, a friend and patron from my poverty days. In July I joined Mimi Wallner and her parents in Holderness, New Hampshire, where I began to reorchestrate the symphony from sketches I had made while in Woods Hole; and I went on doing this in pencil while Mimi copied out my score in ink. Meanwhile, for my Sunday column, I had read batches of hefty tomes such as Paul Henry Lang's *Music in Western Civilization* and Gustave Reese's *Music in the Middle Ages*, both of which were new that year. Then Maurice Grosser arrived from Alabama on his motorcycle; and on that we toured New Hampshire, visiting at the end the George Footes in stylish Dublin and my beloved teacher Edward Burlingame Hill in Francestown.

Eventually I visited Jessie Lasell too, at her hunting-and-fishing camp in Maine, where I wrote choral music and composed her portrait. Then I joined Grosser again; and we went to Nantucket, this time to be with the Russian-Armenian painter Inna Garsoian. And there I wrote more Sunday articles, covered the island by motorcycle, swam everywhere, and went bluefishing with my colleague Olin Downes. At some point I had been to New York, where I gave the score to Beecham and talked through two full nights with him and Emerald. And with all those changes in air and altitude and with the satisfaction of having done lots of work, I had restored myself from fatigue to vigor after a successful but vastly tiring year.

In 1939 I had received in Paris a letter from John Cage, requesting of me a new work for percussion, to be performed in Seattle. For company on the program there would be a novelty by Henry Cowell, and Lou Harrison's 5th Simfony (*sic*). Being occupied just then writing *The State of Music*, I did not join the concert. Two years later, in New York, Cage phoned to ask if he could play for me the records of a broadcast just made in Chicago of works by Harrison and by himself. He could indeed, I said. And here began a long musical friendship, shortly to be complemented by the arrival East of Lou.

Cage, born in southern California, was half of him Tennessee mountaineer. That is to say that his father had come out of Tennessee and that the lanky and freckled red-haired big-boned son was distilling a clear-as-water musical moonshine without the stamp of any Establishment. At this very moment, having been rebuffed by Aaron Copland, who could not admire a music so abstract, he was organizing a concert of his works to be given at the Museum of Modern Art in collaboration with the League of Composers, Copland's own chief arm of patronage. And Copland did not stop this; few persons, indeed, have ever stopped Cage from anything.

His determination has nothing of Tennessee about it; its relentlessness is of southern California, and only barely hidden by a catlike smile. Already thirty, absolutely confident, and without embarrassment in asking for support, he had become by 1941 the designer of a unique product, its manufacturer, and its sole distributor. And if the abstract character of that product made it easier for him to defend than if it had been a more personal outpouring, the self-assurance with which he would explain it was nonetheless breathtaking. In fact, composers of the hand-work-and-inspiration type have never spoken of their own work so convincingly (for whenever Gluck, Wagner, Schoenberg have done so, we tend to freeze) as have Varèse, Boulez, Messiaen, and Cage, all of whom have practiced an objective method.

With all his rigors, Cage has a wit and breadth of thought

that make him a priceless companion. For hours, days, and months with him one would probe music's philosophy. And after Lou Harrison, with his larger reading and more demanding ear, had arrived from the West, the three of us provided for one another, with Europe and the Orient cut off by war, a musical academy of theory and practice that supplied us with definitions which have served us well and which, through the highly divergent nature of our musical products, have given our methods of analysis wide distribution.

Lou Harrison, child of the Pacific Northwest and of San Francisco, was plump and round-faced; and though he smiled less than Cage, there was joy inside him, both joy and pain. Both of them had been pupils of Henry Cowell and of Schoenberg. Cage's southern California euphoria turned him eventually to Zen Buddhism and to a mushroom-study form of nature cult. A San Francisco sensitivity had first turned Harrison, it seems, toward the not uncommon worship of Mount Shasta, then to Yoga, to nervous breakdown, to the study of Esperanto, to the hospitalization of animals, to the construction of flutes and harpsichords with special tunings, and eventually to a mastery of classical Korean composition methods. In both, the West Coast cultural freedom is dominant, as in Henry Cowell and in Gertrude Stein and in the Northwestern painters Mark Tobey and Morris Graves. And in both, as also in Graves and Tobey, an Asian attraction has balanced the gravitational pull of Europe to keep them solidly anchored over America, though with no limiting local loyalties of the usual kinds, such as to New England, the Midwest, the New or Old South. Spiritually they are not even anchored to the West Coast.

Both, when I first knew them, had produced percussion music. And when Cage, leaving no doorbell unrung in his searches after support, asked for a Guggenheim Fellowship, I wrote unhesitatingly in his favor. He did not receive this aid till 1949, however, when his music had become better known. Moreover, having by that time looked at postwar Europe, I had even greater confidence in his powers. And so I wrote that I considered him "the most original composer in America, if not in the world, . . . also the most 'advanced,' in the professional sense."

For describing Harrison's music the word "original" would be less applicable than the word "personal," for its meaning is intensely his alone. Nor can the concept of "advanced" describe it, since as often as not it embodies a return to some method long since abandoned. Cage's driving ambition and his mono-rail view of art, by which quality depends solely on innovation, have brought him fame and followers. Lou's work, though known and widely loved, is without influence. The fault is one of temperament, I think; he lacks not quality, merely pushing ways. He stayed in New York till 1953, also teaching part-time in North Carolina, at Black Mountain College. Then fearing the strains of a no-money Eastern life, he returned to Cali-fornia, settling near his family at Aptos, in the Carmel Valley, from which retreat he sends out compositions or sallies forth to Rome (where he won a festival prize in 1954), to Tokyo (where his Esperanto opened doors), and to Korea (where he studied classical Chinese composition). His letters now are calligraphed, sometimes on parchment, their contents no less savory than ever. "I made a Phrygian aulos the other day & can well un-derstand why Plato mistrusted it; ascending 12/11, 11/10, 10/9, 9/8, 8/7, 7/6; what an allure! I wait to hear the Dorian now."

My own first view of California came in 1943. John House-man, after more than a year at the Office of War Information, was returning that summer to Hollywood for film producing. He was returning, moreover, by car and with a generous gaso-line ration. Going along offered a lovely trip; and the paper welcomed it, Helen Reid filling my hands with introductions. On our way we stopped to visit in Kentucky, where we helped to put up hay, thinned out the hemp (and not remembering it was marijuana, threw it away), fed sugar to the thorough-breds (when allowed), and drank mint juleps out of silver cups. We also stopped in Kansas City briefly and stayed a week in Colorado Springs. In Los Angeles we took an apartment at the Town House, where I was immobilized all day, there being only one car for the two of us. So I would swim in the pool and write piano études in bed till Houseman would come back and drive me to dinner (with Orson Welles and Rita Hayworth, the Joseph Cottens, Bernard Herrmann) or others would come for me and bring me home (George Antheil, who lived there, Aaron Copland, who was scoring a picture, and the people who ran concerts at the Hollywood Bowl). Also I wrote sometimes a Sunday column.

After a while I went to San Francisco and stayed in the Palace

Hotel, where the food was lovely. And it was there I met, through Mrs. Reid's letter to the owners of the *Chronicle*, their music and art critic Alfred Frankenstein, a reviewer far more sympathetic to my aims (and I to his) than any of my colleagues in New York. Perkins had said of him, "He knows what it's all about." Also there were E. Robert Schmitz, his boisterously entertaining wife, Germaine, and gentle learned daughter, Monique; and from Paris the indefatigable Milhauds, both teaching in Oakland at Mills College. And they would come to Schmitz's house for playing me on two pianos Milhaud's just-completed opera *Bolivar*. I met society people too, was lionized. And of a Sunday afternoon in the social hall of Harry Bridges's Seamen's Union, I heard Bunk Johnson play New Orleans jazz.

Coming back by train, as I must have done, since planes were not proof against priorities, I stopped again in Kansas City, where in the spring my father had died of pneumonia at eighty-one. Mother was still in her house, my Aunt Lillie Post staying with her. This had been the arrangement since April, when I had gone there for the funeral. My father's end had been a gentle one. When he had felt it near, he said, "I think you should get me to a hospital." And once there, he had died after saying, "I'm all right now."

Certain Europeans wrote me letters, most touchingly Nadia Boulanger, whose mother I had known in life and whose own life was one long service to the dead, and Igor Stravinsky, whose own father, remembered, had become for him a cult. My personal regret (for my father and I were warmly attached, though without the possibility of much ease) was that now I could never let him know my shame for harsh things said in adolescent years. But he must have known and long since forgiven me, for he was a Christian and a loving one; and though the former I was surely not, he had always understood me and spared reproach.

Back East, I went to stay with Briggs Buchanan, then living with wife and children in upper New Jersey in a large white house. I wrote more piano études there, and Maurice Grosser joined us. Then in September, borrowing a cousin's car, I went off with Grosser to Somesville, Maine, facing Mount Desert, where Inna Garsoian was painting landscapes. He painted still life, I think, while I turned piano portraits into orchestral scores for conducting that fall in Philadelphia.

The Marquis de Cuevas, founding a dance company at that time, had invited several composers along with myself—Menotti and Bowles, I remember—to compose ballets. He had proposed for me a subject about a lonely fisherman and a sea gull which becomes a ballerina—a theme I found not fresh but not quite faded. It might do if I wrote a lovely sea piece. And already I knew how to make the trumpets caw quite realistically. So I went to Southwest Harbor, a fishing town, to pick up other points of atmosphere. There men in yellow-and-black waterproofs were unloading codfish and throwing them choreographically from ship to dock, all to the sound of radio full blast. Moreover, on inquiry I was told that the whole trip is so accompanied and that even simple setters of the lobster pot no longer go to sea or skirt the coast without for company their beloved box.

"Well, well!" I thought. "Each lonely fisherman is wired for sound! That lets me out, and the ballerina too." So I wrote no ballet. But I later used the trumpet's downward-smeared glissando in an orchestral work called *Sea Piece with Birds.*

I was driven again to California two years later, this time by Chick Austin, who had resigned from his Hartford Museum and was being a playboy. With Houseman I shared a service flat just off The Strip. He was in romance with Joan Fontaine. And once we gave a sumptuous cocktail party, with Lady Mendl and the Stravinskys and naturally the Hollywood social register, for Houseman was important at M-G-M. And we frequented the Cottens and the Herman Mankiewiczes and the Alfred Wallensteins, who lived near, like the Stravinskys. And the surrealist painter Roberto Matta, with an American rich wife, would take us all out to expensive meals.

And we made a two-reel picture for the government, Houseman and I and Nicholas Ray, whom I had worked with in Federal Theatre days. It was an explication for foreign countries (eventually in some forty languages) of how in America we elect our president. Its title was *Tuesday in November;* and though our government's own films, by treaty with the Hollywood government, can almost never be shown publicly in America, it has long been visible to friends and students at the Film Library of the Museum of Modern Art. It is a fine piece of work, though not so dramatic as the Pare Lorentz films that were its model. I used in the score, for expressing a buoyant euphoria, my portrait of Aaron Copland and, for a sidewalks-of-New-York Americanism, my waltz from *Filling Station*. Out of it, I rescued a fugal treatment of *Yankee Doodle*, to make a children's recording, and a Stephen-Foster-like melody that in the two-piano version called *Walking Song* has long served many a duo-team as encore.

It was in San Francisco, again at the Palace, that I received a telegram from the French Embassy awarding me a "mission" to go to France. Since 1944 I had been looking for ways to get there. But the *Herald Tribune*, having only six travel priorities and needing these for its coverage of news, could not afford to waste one just on music. And though I had drunk with friendly colonels through a Washington week end, and they had all promised to "take a crack at it," nobody had yet been able to get me sent abroad. It was Suzanne Blum, back in Paris and knowing I would want to be there too, who had got the invitation out of Emile Laugier, Cultural Secretary at the Foreign Office, for me to spend two weeks in France as guest of the government, for reestablishing contact with French music.

And all the more urgent did going to France seem since Douglas Moore had written me in San Francisco offering to commission an opera for production at Columbia University, and I had wired Gertrude Stein I had an idea for one, and she had written back her delight.

So I called at the French Consulate for my orders, wired Washington for a new passport, asked the paper to pick up a plane passage, and took myself a bedroom on the train called "City of San Francisco" in a car that went through to New York. Nor do I even remember looking any way but East until my plane began to circle round and round over the pale gray stones of Paris, as if to give each passenger a view of the sacred site and to some a glimpse perhaps of house and home.

France in '45

M Y SEAPLANE FROM NEW YORK, after stopping the night
in Botsford Bay, had set down the next afternoon in the
River Shannon. There a small dock, as for motor boats, led to
a path, the path to a cottage surrounded by green fields; and
in the cottage's one long, low room, in which at either end a
peat fire smoked, we were refreshed while waiting for our bus.
This was to carry us for an hour up the estuary, through the
town, and back on the estuary's other arm to a dry-land airport,
whence a British military plane, painted a battleship gray inside
and out, took us to London. There I claimed my room at the
Savoy that the *Herald Tribune* bureau had reserved for me and
telephoned to Emerald Cunard at the Dorchester. I had been
on the way for thirty hours, and it was now nighttime again.
And as I fancied might well be the case, she was giving a dinner
party. Having frequently enough been fed that day, I declined
her "Come right over!" for a half-hour's wash-up and a change
of suit.

The guests in her apartment were eight or ten; and carafes of
Chilean wine, both red and white, were on the table. Among
those present were the usual stylish ones, also an attached
young poet and two members of the new Labour government.
For hostesses, however Tory, must be the seeming friends of
those in power, if only to find out which ones are "corruptible."
And this exactly was the subject, after the cabinet members had
discreetly left. And then we all left, after somehow a moment
had been achieved in another room for Emerald to ask, "Shall
you be seeing Thomas?" and for me to promise news of his
morale. Also to transmit some nylon stockings (then to be had
only in America) without offending the young poet by a gift
so intimate.

And the next day there was breakfast in my room, not with
real coffee, of course, or with rationed bacon, but with delicious
mushrooms on delicious toast. And to the Ritz with Emerald
and some others (for she never lunched in public with one
man), lunch consisting, after the world's best Martinis, of

paper-thin veal cutlets smaller than a playing card. We shopped afterwards, I to see what was in the men's stores, though I could buy nothing without purchase-points, and she to visit a Bond Street jeweler about trading a ruby ring for one less dear. Late afternoon I took a train to Lewes, in Sussex, where at near-by Ringmer Sir Thomas Beecham had bought a house.

I stayed the week end, sleeping away delayed fatigues of travel. And Thomas too seemed to be relaxed in the country air, under the care of his Betty. Naturally he was conducting and recording, though in August not much; and he was planning his next trip to America; and maneuvering financially with the recording companies. Later he was to form a new recording orchestra, the Royal Philharmonic. There is no question that at this time of his life, aged sixty-six, his still vast energies were better nurtured by a young wife-secretary-housekeeper-muse-companion and all-purpose Egeria than they would have been by a driving and driven ex-social leader of his age. For Betty was above all a musician, and save for an only son of twelve (in England not an age that takes much tending) wholly occupied with Beecham and his life. No dinners with cabinet ministers and powerful ladies, no spending of money just for the fun of it. Nothing but work and quietude and gathering his whole career together, as we had so often said he should do, for leaving to posterity a maximum in the form of recordings, books, and edited scores.

Betty's usefulness to Thomas was complete, and Emerald knew that she could never match it. Through a merciful cancer, death came to her five years later. Betty survived in torture nearly fifteen. Till '47 all was bliss unbroken; then began a series of surgical interventions, anemias, and exhaustions. Weighing seventy pounds, she still could not be stopped from traveling everywhere (meaning annually with him clear across America), from attending every long recording session and sitting in at every business conference. Nor could Thomas be stopped from traveling and recording, though increasing attacks of gout would lay him low. He was attentive to Betty and ever patient, but when she died I think he was relieved. The next year he came to New York with just a valet. The following one there was another wife. He was not used to lacking a woman's company; and the new Lady Beecham, surely not yet thirty, was a pretty girl and quietly alert.

In Paris I spent my first night on a day bed in the flat of Suzanne Blum, where with Paul Weill, her husband, they had also their law offices, as is French custom. My own flat I knew to be occupied. And hotels receiving travelers were practically limited to two—the Claridge, on the avenue des Champs-Elysées, and the Ritz. The former gave me a room with carpeting soiled and worn by five years of the military and with one fifteen-watt bulb for light. I stayed there a week, until the Ritz could have me, then moved into a delicious mansard room with balcony on the Place Vendôme. The furniture and carpet were immaculate, the towels and bed linen of the finest. The bath was marble and commodious, the water hot at all the hours permitted. The soap I had brought from New York I kept locked up in my suitcase till I should have time to size up a bit the servants.

Meanwhile, from my window, I used to marvel at the great bronze column that bore on its top Napoleon in Roman toga, while spirally and reading upward were depicted in relief scenes from his glory. At least I fancied this to be their content, though from my distance I could not quite discern. My window, all the same, was on a level with the upper scenes and quite as close as any in the square. I figured therefore that the sculptured story was not intended to be viewed from anywhere; and that even if a closer eye were present, it would need be that of some circling bird, with perhaps a firefly to light up detail.

I stayed at the Ritz till well into November, my expenses paid by our European Edition, rich with French money earned for them during the Occupation by the renting out of offices in their building. And once a week, at least, I sent off an article. These pieces were printed in Europe too and widely read, as was in fact, just then, the whole edition. With paper for printing six or even eight pages, while no other sheet, not even the London *Times*, could manage more than four, our coverage and editorials were more ample. For two years or so they were the best in Europe; and our reader mail, which came from everywhere, was scholarly, punctilious, and thoughtful. Moreover, there was lots to write New York about, with all the state theaters functioning on full repertory, the orchestras revived, and the national radio purged.

Among the radio's musical executives, normally composers, were some I had not known before the war—Henry Barraud, in charge of music, and Manuel Rosenthal, a pupil of Ravel and a conductor of all-embracing curiosity. Roger Désormière was conducting again too, both operas and concerts, also Paul Paray—all those who had been silent for four years. And there were some remarkable performances. I remember a *Pelléas* at the Opéra-Comique with Janine Micheau (Désormière conducting) and a *Phèdre* at the Comédie Française with Marie Bell. I remember these performances, after twenty years, as being grand with a grandeur matching that of the grandest remembered from my early times. And if sentiment a little warms my memory, there are still my reviews, written while the sounds were fresh, to remind me that I was no enchanted adolescent but a man near fifty who had heard everything and was describing for readers, not all of them absent in America, the actual state of music and stage in France.

The orchestral performances, curiously enough, were often better than one had any right to expect, considering the undernourished and irritable state of the personnel, not to mention that many string players were using inferior instruments, having traded their better ones during the Occupation. But Manuel Rosenthal gave a marvelously animated performance of my *Filling Station* suite in a concert of the National Radio Orchestra at the Théâtre des Champs-Elysées; and if Rudolph Dunbar, a Negro war correspondent from Pittsburgh, Pennsylvania, who gave four concerts of American music (all the best of it) in the Salle Pleyel with four different orchestras, did not bring off my Second Symphony anywhere near that perfectly, the fault was surely not that of the orchestra. Nor was it quite mine, who had rehearsed it for him for two hours. Preparing in three rehearsals ninety minutes of foreign music, all of it unknown to the orchestra, is sure to be a hazardous adventure. My work was handsomely applauded and reviewed, all the same. "Paradoxical and poetic" was Sauguet's description of the symphony in *La Bataille*. And *Filling Station* received the honors both of derogatory whistling and of cheers.

The state of French composition I learned from radio colleagues, who had disks, preserved from concerts or rehearsals, covering the whole Occupation. Crude and gritty these were; but they allowed one to hear the pieces, especially when listening with score in hand. Everybody played me everything he had written (Poulenc whole cantatas, also bestowing on me upwards of a hundred newly published songs). And Olivier Messiaen, with Yvonne Loriod, performed a two-hour piece on two pianos.

It was from acetate disks that I reviewed two picturesque works of Manuel Rosenthal with such enthusiasm that cables followed from America asking instantly for scores and parts. Artur Rodzinski, conductor of the New York Philharmonic, wanted the suite about gastronomy called *Musique de table*. And Ormandy desired for Philadelphia the oratorio *Saint François d'Assise*. Both works were played the next season, and Rosenthal himself conducted a bit later at the Philharmonic another picture-piece (his gift was for these), *La Fête du vin*.

The composers brought me all their printed music, and a government office that subsidized recordings bestowed upon me over a hundred disks. These last I gave in New York to the French Culture Office, which had not been able to procure them through French channels. And I acquired all the books, or so it seemed, that had been published since 1940—scholarly books on music, art books, and studies of the cinema. The publisher Gallimard, encountered at a dinner, even sent to my hotel all that had appeared during my absence, at least ten meaty volumes, of crime fiction by my admired Georges Simenon.

Many handsome editions had been brought out since the Germans had left, hand-printed on costly rag. For the French, great lovers of fine paper, had concealed their enormous stocks walled up in cellars, as they had done with wines. So that though newsprint from Norway was rationed and hard to come by, art, literature, and luxury books could now be issued without inconvenience. Thus it was that the most advanced reviews were printing the most advanced authors—Jean Genet, for instance—in editions that made the prewar issues of Georges Hugnet look, except for their art work, almost like pulp.

Revisiting friends was a constant occupation and not at all the easiest of chores. For from the Place Vendôme, which is central, everyone seemed to be living far away. The subways would stop running before midnight, the buses earlier; and taxis were rare. So almost always one walked home from dinner; and if new shoes from America pinched the feet, there was no remedy, since others could not be bought. Or only on the black market and for $200—for $100 if you had black-market francs. This also turned out to be the price of a hat, when in October's cold rain (with no heat in my room, of course) I caught a cold and could not keep my bald head warm or dry. It was also the price of a fair meal for two, with wine, in any of the speak-easy-like black-market restaurants. Unitemized, the total would be jotted on paper scrap, as if it were a telephone number, should police inquire.

At the white-market restaurants, which included all the reputable establishments, prices were regulated; and one gave ration-points as well. The Ritz, where I would have my friends to lunch, served only permitted foods (and in small portions)— poor bread, burned-barley coffee, and saccharine (one tablet offered on a Limoges dinner plate). And with soap a major shortage, there were only paper napkins. The wines, not rationed, still were of the best. And at Larue, where the cellar was historic, one ate, as everywhere, a white fish known as *colin* covered with library paste, while drinking Burgundies of precious years. Once, only once, I caught there a violation, when in the fall oysters became sometimes available, for with these costly delicacies the waiter brought a plate of thin-sliced white bread ever so thinly buttered on the under side.

But when you went to dinner at someone's house, the meal was always copious and rich. For no one would ask a guest to share the vegetable soup and watery boiled potatoes that were standard fare on family nights. But every so often someone would receive from country relations a kilo of butter, a quart of cream, a rabbit, or would simply sell a chair and buy a roast. A feast would then be held and friends invited. Since nobody had an icebox (or any ice), there was no use in keeping meat around.

My urgent matters turned out to be two—recuperating my apartment and getting Gertrude Stein started on the new opera. My gentle landlord, Dr. Ovize, had kept my flat empty for three years, then sometime in 1943, fearing requisition, had sublet it. Later that year he died, leaving the house to his widow and his half brother. The latter, with seeming generosity, offered to liberate the flat in time for my arrival the next year by giving its occupants another in the building. I was not to pay rent on my five-year absence nor expect to be paid for the flat's subletting over the last two. Neither was I to mention the disappearance of minor possessions—a radio and a smallish box of books. The only condition posed by the present occupants was that they take with them the telephone, a sacrifice for me not grave, since the newspaper could get me a priority.

Also, as my landlord explained, I could have it for other reasons. "You are entitled, through your status as a returning Jewish resident, to your apartment and to a priority-B telephone."

"That is all very nice," said I, "but I am not Jewish."

His mouth came open. "But my sister-in-law has always thought that you were like herself." Then, pondering a bit, "Let's leave it that way. I don't have to give you the flat. But I've already spent so much time persuading Madame Ovize of the contrary that I would rather not start all that up again. That is, unless you mind her thinking you a Jew."

"But not the least," said I. "It's a compliment."

And the next year, when I came back in May, I moved into my flat; and with the landlord, who was obliged to go along for my identification, I went to the telephone office and claimed priority. And though I could have done so as a journalist, I chose to do it the other way. So I said yes when the employee asked, "You are an Israelite?" The deception served for nothing, but it amused me.

Gertrude Stein was in love with the GIs. Every day, as she walked her dog, she picked up dozens, asked them questions, took them home, fed them cake and whiskey, observed their language. Its sound and grammar had at this time already been put into a book called *Brewsie and Willie*. And she had also written a play about Occupation life, *Yes Is for a Very Young Man*. When I asked her for an opera about nineteenth-century America, with perhaps the language of the senatorial orators quoted, she hardly thought at all, just started writing. She must have looked into a book or two, just the same, for the political-meeting scene, which she wrote first, has quotes in it (distorted, of course) from the addresses of both Daniel Webster and Susan B. Anthony.

When she chose Susan B. as her protagonist, I could not deny her the feminist approach. When she showed her in a scene of domesticity that might as well have been herself and Alice Toklas conversing about Gertrude's career, I knew that she had got inside the theme and that the work would now be moving rapidly. These two scenes were what she had written by

November of '45. She had also exhausted the American Library in Paris, which then began sending to the New York Public for still more nineteenth-century history. She finished *The Mother of Us All* that winter, sent it to me in March of '46. It was her last completed work; she died in July. By that time we had gone over it together. I did not begin composing till October of that year. I finished all but the final scene within two months. In January I wrote the end and began to orchestrate. It opened on May 9, 1947, at Columbia University.

When I left Paris in November of '45, Gertrude did not seem ill. She was happy with her GIs and with the opera subject. She had met Donald Gallup, a young librarian from Yale who inspired confidence, and she had engaged to give him all her papers. A part of her occupation that winter was to reread all these and to destroy any that might embarrass others. No thought of death was with her, I am sure, for she planned, come spring, to buy a car again. And for the moment everything was happy, even though she must have been harboring for quite some time the cancer that was to destroy her.

France too was happy (all but the "*collabos*"), though working hard and living in discomfort to mend the sickness of its circulation system (its railways and roads and rolling stock and trucks, its lack of power and coal and gasoline). For food and clothing were not gravely lacking, but merely the methods of transporting them. And the transportation center that was Paris, though costly and inconvenient, was a haven.

Unfortunately it was also haven to a half-million or more GIs. One used to see them loafing on the streets, stuffed to the throat with all that GI food, bored with no place to go, and feeling sorry for themselves because the French population did not invite them home. There was food in France, but not enough for that. And there were not families enough to go around. As always, every family owned an American and loved him and spoiled him, in spite of low resources. But the unowned GIs, lonesome and unhappy, would wish that they were back in Germany, where everything, being run by the conquerors, was simpler, the black market easier to manipulate, and love available for merely cigarettes. In France the French were working for themselves and being as hospitable as they could, for the middle classes always like Americans. But the working-class

French and the working-class Americans, probably from differences over communism, were suspicious and did not get along.

How thin the effective contact was I glimpsed in Lyon, where I made a trip as joint guest of the University and of our Embassy's Culture Office. I traveled there by train with perhaps three others, intellectuals from American universities now working for exchange of books and scholars with the French establishments. We had a half car, first class, to ourselves, though every other foot of space was occupied, everyone going somewhere needful, the corridors packed with luggage and babies and old folk. They did not show resentment of our privilege, but I was not happy with it. Had it not been for the sight of all those Frenchmen being helpful to one another and not complaining (a spectacle typically inside-France), I should have at the stops kept to my compartment, to hide my shame at using so much space.

My assignment was lecturing to university teachers of English; I spoke to them in French on "Words and Music." The eagerness of teachers, students, writers, artists, after a four-year cutoff from world access, their eagerness to know what had been done, to talk with other intellectuals, to trade experiences and books, was so alert one scarce could answer all the questions that came pouring out of them. And the attendance at American Libraries of Information was massive, with special interest shown in books on medicine (to bring them up to date) and in our building methods (very strange but fascinating to them because they would be rebuilding very soon). It is hard perhaps to realize nowadays, when French men of learning, business, industry have found their way back to the closed-in life that they prefer, how open and how willing to communicate they were in the first years after liberation. I say this with some reserves regarding business, for there was in those years a strike of capital, which refused to invest in French recuperation till it had become certain that there would be no workers' revolution.

The Communist party at this time was large, its voting power twice the membership. Their admirable organization of the Resistance had enabled them, moreover, to penetrate at the moment of liberation all administrations, including the police. The banking and investing *bourgeoisie* was naturally fearful lest the whole economy and government slip from its hands. And prying out of the civil service all persons possibly disloyal to investors turned out to be a graver operation than merely dismissing a few collaborators. It was like picking powdered glass out of a wound; and it would take years.

Our own industrial workers, detained at home in factories, were little represented in our troops abroad. So that union men capable of entering into communication with Frenchmen of their kind were too few for a people-to-people dialogue. The French workers despised our troops' political naïveté, and these saw a communist in every blouse. When "U.S. go home" began to appear as handwriting on factory walls, our soldiers knew they were not to be loved. And lest fighting break out in the industrial cities, they were shipped home, or back to Germany, or to country compounds where they saw only farmers and off the post would wear civilian clothes.

My coming home took place on a cargo ship packed tightly with GIs, sleeping on the floor and, as the ship tossed, rolling in one another's vomit. There had been no chance of an airplane passage; the best that could be done would be possibly one for Claude Alphand, whom Helen Reid enormously desired to sing at the Herald Tribune Forum. Hervé, then Permanent Secretary for Economic Affairs at the Foreign Office, was better placed than I to lay hands on a priority; but even he had trouble till I proposed that he cable his ambassador in Washington to please request it. So I stayed until this was accomplished, then took my troopship from a floating iron dock in the utterly destroyed port of Le Havre, along with two dozen other males traveling by permission to the United States.

We were twenty-four civilians in one cabin, sleeping on three-decker beds, and with no space outdoors worth trying to stand up in during the wild November storms. Almost all were businessmen of over forty and thoroughly companionable—especially an importer of Swiss watch-movements from New Jersey and a French salesman of Roquefort cheese. Nobody, in those cramped quarters, failed to be considerate; and I made one friend of genuine distinction. This was a physician, a blood specialist, Dr. Camille Dreyfus, who had spent the war in New York and was going back there after an inspection tour at home to close off his researches and move his family to France, a delicate, gentle man with whom one spoke of everything—art, science, politics, religion. One morning, having breakfast at the GI mess, forever loaded down with pork and ham, I realized he had been declining these. And so I said, "Could it be that you eat kosher?" And he replied, "When I can. Not strictly, even then, of course. But as a privilege. Because there are three things I am proud to be—an Alsatian and a Frenchman and a Jew. And I like to wear some badge of them, some sign."

And then eventually we arrived in Brooklyn, where Maurice Grosser met me in a borrowed car. It was a long, slow drive to my hotel. The paper had thought that I was never coming back. But they were pleased to have had all those Sunday articles *not* about politics and wars and armies. No other paper had published anything comparable; they did not mind that my stay had been expensive. Nor did they mind when I told them I was planning to make a wider tour the next year, to go lots of places, and to stay five months.

The year now ending had been full of things accomplished. My *Symphony on a Hymn Tune*, seventeen years unheard, had at last been played. And at the Philharmonic, of all places. For the new conductor there, Artur Rodzinski, had none of his predecessor's cause to shun me. He had already played, in fact, the suite from *Filling Station*. I had reviewed this performance (for a lark), remarking that he had got the tempos wrong. The symphony he asked me to conduct myself; and though I got the tempos right, the orchestra following like lambs, there had been tension at the first rehearsal from their resentment over my early reviews. The press was almost wholly disapproving. My colleague of the *Times* dismissed the symphony as "too trivial and inconsequential, too unoriginal in its material and flimsy in its structure to merit discussion."

On the other hand, a suite from *The Plow That Broke the Plains*, which I had conducted earlier with the Philadelphia Orchestra, was now published and was traveling rapidly through all the other orchestras (Boston excepted) to universal hallelujahs. My first book of Piano Etudes, introduced that spring by E. Robert Schmitz, had received what Broadway calls "mixed notices"; and it was not till a few months later, when Maxim Schapiro began to play this volume everywhere that certain numbers from it became popular. Also a recording, my first, had been brought out, myself conducting the Philadelphia

Orchestra in *Five Portraits*. And a collection of my reviews and Sunday articles, entitled *The Musical Scene*, had received raves unstinted. And the film (by Ray and Houseman) *Tuesday in November* was pleasing to us all. (Today it seems even finer.) Also, I had conducted my Sonata da Chiesa, from 1926, in its first New York hearing. And that summer it had been proposed that I write an opera, also that I go to France for music's purposes. I suppose my cup could be called "running over."

In any case, the pattern was established that was to prevail for about another decade—namely, that I wrote music constantly and brought it through first performance and publication, that I also traveled widely, conducting and lecturing, also that I reported regularly from New York and elsewhere on the music life of Europe and America. I also kept up my wars with institutions; I enjoyed that. Busy, yes; but I had time for dinner guests and to give evening parties. My secretary, Julia Haines, would sum up my life, "Virgil is always fishing or mending his nets."

EARLY IN MAY OF '46 I took the *Ile-de-France*, now returned to civilian service for a season but still with her wartime gray paint and all troopship inconveniences, such as giant
cabins for many males or females. The violinist Zino Frances-
catti would practice in the men's washroom so as not to disturb
his cabinmates. At other times one talked of France with the
Francescattis, Yvonne de Casa Fuerte, and Marcel Duchamp.
In Paris I found Gertrude Stein (quite thin) on the station
platform; and as we kissed she said, "I'm not here for meeting
you. Have you seen Richard Wright?" The Embassy had asked
her to welcome a Negro novelist she was known to admire.

I arrived at my flat with ten trunks of consumer goods—
transparent music paper for composer friends, plain music paper
for students at the Conservatoire, old suits of clothes for everybody, nylon stockings, Turkish towels, quantities of soap, toilet
paper, razor blades, cigarettes, and all kinds of packaged edibles.
The previous year I had found out what was needed; and I had
already sent by freight to the Chatelains a coffin-size box of such
things, most of which had arrived. Chiefly the soaps were missing from it, and ladies' underwear. It seems the customs men
would sometimes take things, thus enlarging distribution, after
all. My own trunks and the electrical appliances for my landlord
had been passed without inspection, thanks to the gangster.

My flat was a little dingy, but complete. And I brought home
my pictures from the Chatelains, where Leonid had stored them
when he rescued his and mine. (How glad I was to see the big
Bérard!) From there came also plates lent and a couch-bed,
both needed after three years' normal breakage. And the violinist Samuel Dushkin, emptying his apartment, lent a piano,
My earlier housecleaner, Madame Jeanne, whose husband was
retiring from the Banque de France, now moved back to La-
Ferté-sous-Jouarre, leaving the conciergerie of the first house
to her sister Elise. There was a new concierge for my house, the
wartime one's husband (such a good cook!) having got into
trouble by his less than perfect care for the possessions of those

absent. And the new concierge, Madame Langlade, brought me a still younger woman named Catherine to clean and cook.

And cook she could, with evident delight. For she loved practicing her art, now that the things to cook well with were beginning to be available. For me almost everything was available through an American commissary recently established for the benefit of journalists and businessmen. So once a week or oftener Sherry Mangan's maid (for the Mangans were back in residence) would go by bus out to Colombes-sur-Seine and bring back for both our kitchens nets heavy with meat and groceries. There would be the usual crackers and spreads and cookies and cornstarch desserts, also tinned vegetables and fruits and dried things, butter and oil, sugar and coffee and tea and chocolate, and grandest of all (O luxury all legal and legitimate!) legs of lamb, fillets of beef, fresh fish, and real live lobsters.

So with Catherine to cook and with nothing to apologize for in possessing all this food, I began to have dinner parties for new friends and old. And Theodate's former lady's maid brought me table linens she had preserved. And Catherine would trot tirelessly the half-mile between my flat and hers to lend me silver when I did not have enough. And make peach tarts with custard filling, or strawberry ones, or greengage plum, because she found catered pastry not yet good enough to serve. Once or twice I gave cocktail parties; and for those she would make thin sandwiches and poundcake. For the first of these receptions she had spread some crackers with peanut butter; and I noticed that the French guests would regard them with curiosity, take one bite, leave the remainder on the mantelpiece. She had warned me they would find its visual aspect unattractive, also that peanut butter was not for grownups.

I invited Gertrude Stein and Alice Toklas to have dinner with the gangster and his wife; they got on famously. Gertrude even invited the wife to come and see her pictures. Just at dinnertime a chauffeur had arrived with a hot dish of jugged hare (out of season), which delighted Alice, who loved strong dark flavors (and things illegal). I had brought out good wine to go with this (Château Lafite, I think), and I teased the gangster for calling it "nice" ("*gentil*"). I also teased Gertrude about something till Alice said, "Don't scold her. She may cry." I had not realized that her strength was low. She went off to the country not long after; I went to Luxembourg and Brussels to conduct. And then I went to Venice and Trieste.

Mr. and Mrs. Ogden Reid, in Paris that summer, invited the *Herald Tribune* staff to dinner at their hotel. And they gasped a bit when told that our postwar European readers were more exigent than New York as to both facts and reasonings; moreover, that New York editorial writers should ask themselves: "What will this read like in Paris?" Helen Reid would have liked to hire my flat for *Tribune* travelers, but luckily I had no right to sublet. Geoffrey Parsons had come to Germany and France, visiting his son, our editor, looking at the conquered, and hoping to drink a little wine in Burgundy. But he became ill in Germany, required surgery, and spent a month at the American Hospital in Neuilly, where I would go with Iris Barry of a summer afternoon to sit with him, swap jokes, and be affectionate.

In August, Lady Cunard came to stay at the British Embassy, where the Duff-Coopers, as she put it, were Ambassadors. So I took her to lunch with some others at the Ritz (much better by then). And I went to a party for her at the Embassy. It was there I saw for the last time Christian Bérard. He wore a dinner jacket and had washed. He was again making fashion drawings for *Vogue* and was designing sets and costumes for the theater— the world's finest of both. When he took me into a corner and said I must not think he had given up being a painter, for he was about to have a show, I assured him I had never doubted him. Actually, that spring in England, he had done large water colors, handsome and original. But back in France he did not persevere. And a little later, after a police clampdown on the trade in opium, he ceased to smoke and drank a good deal more. He suffered a massive stroke in '49 at a stage rehearsal of Molière's *Les Fourberies de Scapin*. He was deciding whether to keep or to eliminate a certain slender spire in the background; and his last words were, "The minaret's all right." ("*Au fond ce minaret est bon*.")

I broadcast that year, as I had done the year before, programs of American music with original commentary. Both these and my musical coverage for the paper seemed, on the whole, less full of discovery than in 1945. I did review, however, at the opera, Méhul's *Joseph*. And seeing at the Cómedie Française another classic just as rarely given, the *Esther* of Racine, I realized that their actuality, their background of news interest, was the fact that the theme of both is Jewish resettlement.

With Nicolas Nabokov and Roger Désormière I heard a Sonata for Flute and Piano by a twelve-tone composer of twenty-one, Pierre Boulez. The piece delighted me because, in spite of its Germanic method, it sounded French, like an only slightly out-of-tune Ravel. Désormière acknowledged the Boulez talent as authentic, but had reserves about the work; he did not really hold with serial music. "You play around with dodecaphony," he said, "and all it does is falsify the ear." Nevertheless, as soon as Boulez wrote orchestral works, he became their chief exponent and interpreter. And Boulez, after Désormière was paralyzed in 1952, would go to see him constantly and sit with him and talk to him, though Déso, as friends called him, could not answer.

My comradeship with Boulez began in 1952, when we spent a whole night walking the streets and talking music. Nor was that the last time, for the eight-hour session was to become our norm. In a Sunday article of 1946 about atonality in France I had spent ten two-column lines on this young man, "the most brilliant, in my opinion, of all the Paris under-twenty-fives." I did not know till some years later that this was the first press notice he had received. After his world-wide success as a conductor in the 1960s, our meetings in Paris, New York, Los Angeles diminished in both frequency and length. I think he was embarrassed lest my prophecy might perhaps be coming true. For I had early warned him of the danger that lay in duplicating, even though not consciously, the career of Marcel Duchamp.

I said to him, "By using carefully thought out and complex ways, you produce by thirty a handful of unforgettable works. But by then you are the prisoner of your method, which is stiff. You cannot handle it with freedom; so you write less and less; at forty you are sterile. This is the trap of all style-bound artists. For without freedom no one is a master."

"*Bien sûr*," he sadly said, and changed the subject.

Now, at forty, he for the most part just conducts; he is careful of his time and energies; he takes forever to complete a work; and when he does, it seems to come out small. Bérard had skirted mastery, settled for success in illustration and in the theater. Duchamp refused to face, after his early remarkable achievements, the hazards of going on being a master. This was exactly what Picasso and Stravinsky, after an even grander youth, had not refused. Boulez, though far from self-indulgent like Bérard and not so self-destructive as Duchamp, may well have failed, all the same, as Europe's finest composing brain and ear, to bring his talent to fulfillment.

In the previous year I had sought permission to look at Germany, but without success. Our Paris editor had asked the military government to invite me, and the request had got as far as the commanding general, Mark Clark. His office, finding no slot for a music critic, suggested I come as a war correspondent. That status, however, would have required a two-or-three-week security check. This year, without any effort on my part, I was asked to several countries, including Germany.

The first of these trips was to Luxembourg and Belgium. In the former I conducted a concert of my orchestral works at the radio station, of which the musical director was Henri Pensis, who had passed the war in America. In that medieval-turreted and modern city I also encountered my first tape recorder, for the radio establishment still owned a prewar German machine, called in French a *magnétophone*, by which my concert was preserved for later broadcasts.

In Brussels I rehearsed for broadcast a concert of my chamber music, staying on the rue Royale in an eighteenth-century townhouse with fine pictures (even a Van Eyck), where my hosts Jacques and Jacqueline Errera were friends from their New York time as refugees. In bombed-out Antwerp I heard Flemish opera. In Malines I was entertained by the carillon, which I described as resembling in sound "a trayful of glasses, its climactic moments not unlike . . . that same tray dropped." And I got fun out of hearing an aria from *Samson et Dalila* on the chattering bells when what they should have been playing, I said, was John Cage. Belgium, far more than France, seemed to have recovered from the war; and being there was like being in a Flemish picture in which everyone is eating and laughing all the time.

Next, barely had I returned when Prince George Chavchavadze proposed that I visit him in Venice, where the princess had just reopened their apartment. Naturally I went; I had not seen Venice since Harvard Glee Club days. I went by a train that got me only to Milan. Then, after a day of waiting, there was another, which took all night to arrive at the watery metropolis. The apartment there was two whole floors in a grape-colored marble palazzo near the Accademia, which had belonged to an American, the late Princesse Edmond de Polignac. It had many rooms, and there were other guests. There would be twelve for lunch or dinner, and George would play the piano. The composer Gian Francesco Malipiero, still director of the musical conservatoire; the Liceo Benedetto Marcello, came to see me and to show me his establishment, with its secret rooms, where precious manuscripts had been hidden from the Germans and where he was now secreting tagless dogs, lest the municipal authorities cart them off for killing.

I was the first musician from outside Venice he had seen since before the war, and he could not have been more companionable. He brought to the house his newest group of string players, called Nuovo Quartetto Italiano, and they used to practice daily in our *sala*, where there was unlimited elbowroom and a cross draft. He showed me his composing pupils Bruno Maderna and Igor Gorini, along with their music. And once, while itemizing relics out of history, he put Richard Wagner's baton in my hand. It was thin, short, octagonal, and of mahogany, not the ebony broomhandle that his contemporaries used to grasp in the fist. And contactually it was impressive because it was his. I felt as if I had touched electricity.

For the holidays of the Holy Redeemer (the *Redentore*) there had been for houseguest a young British officer, the Honorable J. Hamish Saint Claire-Erskine, who asked me, "Could I possibly persuade you to come to Trieste and hear my opera company?" He was culturally in charge there; and Trieste was in the news, because the "Jugs," as we called our Jugoslavian allies, were threatening to take it, though it was technically in Italy. So I drove with him to the troop-filled seaport and reviewed the opera in the moated Castello San Giusto, its summer quarters. The company was indeed first class, with Margherita Grandi and Cloe Elmo for stars. We also visited in the hills above Udine a powerful radio field station captured from the Germans and still run by its German engineers, Nazis all of them, but too proud of their machine to sabotage it.

As I left for Paris, at the railway station I learned from that morning's *Herald Tribune* of the death of Gertrude Stein. In Paris I went straight to call on Alice, found her lonely in the large high rooms, but self-contained. Gertrude had been feeling tired all spring, she said, and they had hired a small house near Le Mans. There Gertrude had felt quite ill, had pain, and seen a local doctor. He had said, "You may need surgery. In any case you should go back to Paris."

At the American Hospital, an operation was recommended; but in view of her weakened state, it was thought best to postpone this till her strength could be rebuilt. Ten days later there was no change in her strength, and she was still in pain. The surgeon, though pressed, refused to operate. So she sent for the director of the hospital and said, "You will send me a younger surgeon, who will do as I ask." And when he came, she said, "I order you to operate. I was not made to suffer."

The words that have been quoted as her last were spoken while she waited for the wheel table that was to carry her to the operating room. As Alice Toklas told me, then and later, Gertrude had asked a little vaguely (for she was already under sedation), "What's the answer?" And Alice, to bring her back from vagueness, said, "What is the question?" It was in reply to this that Gertrude remarked, "I suppose if there is no question, there is no answer." She had earlier remarked, as her nephew's family, eventually to be her heirs, departed, "We don't have to see them again."

She is buried at the cemetery of Père-Lachaise in a double grave under a double stone designed by Sir Francis Rose, the youngest of the painters Gertrude had continued to admire. Half of it awaits to be inscribed for Alice Toklas. Alice herself, though then expecting little out of life beyond seeing through the press Gertrude's unpublished works and taking care of their dog's old age, has turned out to have a busy and thoroughly interesting existence—being visited by innumerable friends, traveling, and writing books herself (two cookbooks and a memoir). Though she believed, as Gertrude did, that "when a Jew dies he's dead," she could not be satisfied of that in Gertrude's case. Gertrude must somewhere exist, like Dante's Vergil. And since she exists, she can perhaps be visited.

It took Alice several years to plan her strategy, and much consulting with Catholic friends and priests. This time there really was a question; so there had to be an answer. The question was how to see Gertrude again; the answer was to become a Catholic. Since Gertrude, she could not doubt, was immortal, Alice had no choice but to take on immortality. But since in her case that could not be done through genius, her only chance was through the Christian faith. She puts it that she "went back to the Church," for she had been baptized, it seems, at twelve; a friend of her mother's, deploring the neglect of her religious life, had been permitted to arrange this. With despair and loneliness thus exchanged for hope, Alice has faced death serenely ever since, though life has clung to her for twenty years. At eighty-eight she had a cataract removed—for reading books and mail, no doubt, but surely too for seeing Gertrude clear.

And then I went to Germany and Austria, the trip arranged by Nicolas Nabokov, who was attached to our military government in a cultural capacity, being in charge of films, theater, and music for the American zone of Germany and for our sector of Berlin. My clearance in Paris took no time at all; and from the day in late August when we left by military plane for Munich till my return in mid-September from Berlin, everything was favorable to us—hotels, planes, trains, and chauffeured cars—because Nicolas, though civilian, held a colonel's rank, and also because he spoke four languages.

We only stayed a single night in Munich, then went by car to Salzburg, where the music festival was going on under American protection, for Salzburg was in the Austrian district administered by our army. The Oesterreichischer Hof, an officers' billet, was our hotel, with the grander Occupation officers, such as generals, installed in the grander country palaces. In every *Schloss* they held their social court, with many dinners, cocktails, picnic trips, the VIPs lodged in the main palace, the younger set staying up late in an adjoining smaller one called the *Kavalierhaus*. And if life among these well-washed captains and their wives, short-haired lieutenants and their girls, was possibly less promiscuous after midnight than the prewar Salzburg festival house parties in those same quarters, it was luxurious in other ways, with the slightest expedition (to the opera, to some scenic spot, to Berchtesgaden and Hitler's ruined eyrie) a cavalcade of Packard limousines.

Charles Munch was conducting the Vienna Philharmonic,

the pianist Nicole Henriot playing concertos with him. She also played Ping-Pong with me and beat me. And we visited Mozart's father's plain but not quite humble residence. Certainly we gaped like yokels at the grandeurs of Max Reinhardt's archiepiscopal Schloss Leopoldskron, with huge bronze animals all around the park. (Taken from Paris by Goering, these had not yet been returned.) I made friends with a young composer, Gottfried von Einem, who played me the first act (all there was then) of his opera *Dantons Tod* (all full of rhumbas). And I urged him on toward getting himself and some other young musicians made members of the festival's committee, which they did, then forced inclusion every year of a modern work. I also made the acquaintance of Herbert von Karajan, not yet conducting publicly again but already having prepared the new *Le Nozze di Figaro*, remarkable for dainty patterlike precision. We went to have tea with him and his wife on their sumptuous mountaintop. And the tea, as I remember it, was real. So also was its accompaniment, no doubt a luxury in that greaseless land, thin black bread laid with paper-thin raw bacon.

In Munich we visited in their bombed-out flat a Nazi's family known to us through Munch; their lack of access to food, heat, clothing was pitiable. And we called on Carl Orff (no Nazi), who played us recordings of his music, including the now popular *Carmina Burana*. Munich had been bombed chiefly with blockbusters; so that it looked worse than it really was, its, redbrick piles only partially collapsed, all pink and whitish like a wedding cake that had been rained on. Frankfurt-am-Main, on the other hand, which had received incendiary bombs, looked actually better than it really was, with every house or public building gutted, its half-walls standing in lush gardens and already covered by luxuriant ivy, for incendiaries stimulate the growth of greenery.

There had been views of our local music officer, the conductor Newell Jenkins, producing opera in Stuttgart whenever he could borrow the half-bombed house from our military, which used it desultorily for movies. Also of a similar setup in Wiesbaden. The duty of culture officers, I should explain, was to aid such Germans as could be denazified in restoring their intellectual institutions. I reported on all this in some detail regarding Salzburg, Berlin, and Dresden. Also on German composers and on the music life in general, for in the Grünewald district of Berlin, where we spent upwards of a fortnight in the house that Nicolas had rented complete with servants, we saw all the musicians there were, traveled freely to the Russian sector of the city, and fraternized with Germans, Russians, everybody—a way of life at that time not discouraged.

Nicolas's eighty-year-old father was staying with him, along with a somewhat younger wife, not his first. They had been living since Revolution times in Poland, a country from which postwar refuge seemed improbable. Then Nicolas learned about a Russian colonel who was in need of penicillin (in an army where venereal disease destroyed careers). So in exchange for the precious remedy, at that time our monopoly, the colonel had got exit permits for the Nabokovs.

My own chief Berlin friendly acquisitions were a German composer, the half-Russian Boris Blacher, and the Russians' music officer, Major Barsky, a great-nephew of Anton Rubinstein. Blacher explained to me why he and not Paul Hindemith should, and most likely would, take over the reconstruction of music teaching. Only a few years later, he had done exactly that; and Hindemith, returned from Yale to Europe with the same hope, was settled not in Germany but in Switzerland. Major Barsky, regretting my small acquaintance with Soviet music, took me to the Soviet music store in Unter den Linden and bought me a pile of scores two feet tall. When I asked him whether, if I went to Russia, I should hear music that was not available outside—in other words, was there an underground— he answered, "No, but you would find colorful folk stuff in the night clubs of Tiflis. And in Siberia, where the new industrial cities all have symphony orchestras, but where the players are just thinly educated Tartars, I think you would be amused by the Beethoven."

Our trip into the Russian zone of Germany came about through a high Russian administrator named Ivanov (just under Zhdanov, as I understood), whom we had met at a cocktail party. He got us the passes in three days (ordinarily it took three weeks) and regretted the delay. Since we ourselves had only three more days, it was proposed that we visit merely Dresden, where the palace of Prince Heinrich of Saxony had been turned into a house for foreign guests. And as our army regulations then required, we went in an army car with a GI driver. Along with us came (as guide, he said) an NKVD major most companionable. That is, he was companionable in Russian. At first he was reserved; then he broke into faint smiles, then guffaws at Nicolas's jokes; and before we were a half-hour out of town they were slapping each other's backs to Russian stories.

In Dresden we were VIPs, no question. The Russian music officer, a Captain Auslander, brought us everyone we asked for—school teachers, composers, publishers, art scholars, the head of the musicians' union. These were brought generally to table, where once we sat clean through the day, and where at every meal, including breakfast, there were red wine, white wine, and champagne. All these in addition to the vodka in your water glass. We went to neighborhood operetta theaters. Also to see the museum pictures, at that time hanging in the Pillnitz, an eighteenth-century palace outside of town. The old museum was completely down, along with the rest of the city's Baroque center—the cathedral, the opera house, the Zwinger palace. The people appeared gravely undernourished, especially all those moon-faced Saxon boys who, with scarcely any girth at all remaining, had shot up at twelve to six feet in height. The Russians sent us off, as we had come, with a basket lunch and bottles of white wine (plus vodka, naturally). Had there been time, they told us, we could have gone to nearby Meissen, where the china factories were. Since these establishments had been taken over by the Russian government, buying from them was not "trading with the enemy."

We chose, instead, one more look at Berlin, the most completely bombed-out great city there ever was. Steel girders from the canopy of a railway station had been wound up by the concussion into giant balls of wire. And the monumental center of the place—Unter den Linden, Schinkel's classic-revival library, the district of the Embassies—looked like the sterile craters of the moon. I had not known Berlin before the war and do not now believe that it could have been compared for grandeur to Rome, Paris, Vienna, London. But in destruction it was beautiful. Twenty years later it is still not much rebuilt, not at all on any monumental scale, though permanently there are shows of city planning held almost on the edge of its eastern sector, where all the city's major monuments await restoring.

On the troopship coming home there were Mary McCarthy and her about-to-be husband, Bowden Broadwater, she writing every day and discussing every sentence with him as if he were a valued editor. Indeed, he may have well been partly that, since her success as a writer seems to have grown to remarkable solidity during the fifteen or more years that they were married.

And there were commies, too, as on the *Paris* back in '33. Only this time, I think, not real ones, just fellow travelers from Harvard returning from a Youth Congress in Prague. They held meetings on board in which they tried to persuade us to take a "unified" (read pro-Russian) view of the cold war. Mary, always entertained by liberals, egged them on. I baited them, and to their leader remarked that his position, once clearly stated, was what was being called just then "appeasement." These yearning lads, I thought, seemed less straightforward, and certainly less confident in their country, than my friendly Russians from Berlin and Dresden, even than the NKVD major, who, when asked the state of his native city, Rostov-on-Don, had cheerfully thrown his arms aloft and cried, "*Kaput!*"

32
The Year I Was Fifty

I BEGAN *The Mother of Us All* on October 10 of 1946. On December 10 the voice-and-piano score was complete up to the last scene. I waited a month before composing that, feeling that I must back off and view the rest. In order to find out what the rest was like, I invited friends to hear me play and sing it. Through performing it for others, as I had done for seven years with *Four Saints*, I could find out how it moved and learn its ways. In January, I composed the final scene; by this time a partial cast was learning roles, with Jack Beeson as *répétiteur*. Otto Luening, who was to conduct, had as yet no orchestral score; but that was not urgent, since we were not opening till May.

The production was for Columbia University's Brander Matthews Theatre, where the house was small but the pit commodious. The cast was part professionals and part students; no one was paid for working in the show. The scenery and costumes were by Paul du Pont; staging was by the choreographer John Taras to a scenario, as before, by Maurice Grosser. I cast all the roles myself, holding auditions in my Hotel Chelsea drawing room. For minor parts we used Columbia students and trained them for understudying the leads. Among the finer singers who took part were Dorothy Dow (later of La Scala) and Teresa Stich-Randall (Mozart specialist and *Kammersängerin*, who now sings everywhere). The names of Belva Kibler, Hazel Gravell, Jean Handzlik, and Alice Howland are remembered by many in the music world, those too of William Horne and Everett Anderson. The stage was beautiful for sight and sound, though not to be compared to my Negroes-and-cellophane *Four Saints*.

The student orchestral players were pretty poor; and Luening, an experienced opera man, was patient, to prevent nervousness on stage. The instrumental textures, therefore, which I had laid out with transparency in mind, were likely to come out on any night with holes in them. Nevertheless, after the fourth or fifth performance, when I felt the players knew their parts as well as they ever would, I asked Luening to speed up the pacing.

"Can you take twenty minutes off the running time?" I said. "Can do," he answered. And with no cuts made, the next performance came out shorter by that much.

Everybody up-to-date came to hear the new opera, and the press was receptive. The Music Critics' Circle, though reluctant to honor a member, even voted it a special award. Koussevitzky, still angry over criticisms, said to his neighbor (textually), "I do not like it to say it, but I like it." And wrote me to offer a commission for another opera. My colleague Samuel Barber, perhaps also smarting, remarked of my plain-as-Dick's-hatband harmony, "I hope you won't mind my stealing a few of your chords."

From its beginning, *The Mother of Us All* has often been produced by colleges, though it was never designed for amateurs and is difficult for young voices. I have not seen all these productions by any means; but in all that I have seen some charm has come through, for there is in both text and music a nostalgia for nineteenth-century rural America which makes any presentation warm and touching. Western Reserve gave it in Cleveland at elegant Severance Hall; and the orchestra, Cleveland's Philharmonia, was first class. Harvard performances in the Civil War memorial Sanders Theater, with only students singing (and not vocal students either), were so perfectly paced by their conductor, Victor Yellin, then a graduate student, that audiences laughed and applauded, wept at the end. Even at the University of Denver, with everything else precarious, an ingenious stage direction gave the spectacle security, enough at least for Stravinsky to comprehend. But it was not till eighteen years after its birth that it got interesting scenery. Then in 1965, at the University of California, Los Angeles, with Jan Popper conducting, an impressive young soprano, Barbara Gordon (my discovery), singing the role of Susan B., and with myself having coached everybody, including the choreographer, a visual investiture was created by David Hilberman which was as original, evocative, and appropriate as what Florine Stettheimer had created in 1934 for *Four Saints*.

The originality of this scenery lay in its representing neither buildings nor landscapes, but, of all things, people. It consisted of a set of giant cutouts painted to illustrate nineteenth-century ladies and gentlemen, for all the world like colored prints from some Victorian magazine. And all these flats could be moved horizontally to closed-in or to open stage-positions. They were dark blue in color, a tone rarely effective in painted scenery but one which, when lightly rubbed with red, can take light in glowing vibrant ways. And to the profiled figures slight additions of flowering branches, brief cases, flags, gave to outdoor scenes, to a departure, to a political meeting complete evocation. Moreover, the gigantic proportions of these pictured people reduced our singing actors to human size, a desideratum in not overlarge Schoenberg Hall, where any smaller scaling of the scenery tends to make giants of the actors and to trivialize them. The *Mother* sets were, in addition, airy. For all their largeness and somber color, they did not weigh on the spirit or box-in the play, but gave it space and lightness, as if great distances lay all about and the stage were just the segment of a continent.

That same spring there took place at Harvard a three-day Symposium on Music Criticism which I had been invited to address. I could not hope to compete for public favor with the English novelist E. M. Forster, planned star of the occasion; but the historians Paul Henry Lang, Otto Kinkeldey, and Edgar Wind, the pianist-pedagogue Olga Samaroff, the learned composer-pedagogue Roger Sessions, caused me no fears. I wanted to be first class, however, if I could. So after I had finished off in March my opera's six-hundred-page orchestral score, I wrote out carefully my assignment, "The Art of Judging Music," and showed it to Helen Reid, who was impressed. My speech was listed for the second of May; so with my opera already in dress rehearsal for opening on the seventh, I decided I could not spare the time for all three Harvard sessions, but would go only for the second, which was mine, also reviewing a concert that would take place that evening. For musical works had been commissioned too—string works by Schoenberg, Martinu, and Piston, choral ones by Malipiero, Copland, Hindemith, and dance works by Martha Graham to scores by William Schuman and Chávez.

Arriving on the night train, I gave my speech at Sanders Theatre in the morning. Next came a lunch in my honor to which Mrs. Kingsley Porter, widow of the Romanesque archeologist, still living at Elmwood, the James Russell Lowell house, had invited 120 people, a sit-down lunch with pasta and steaks and asparagus and an egg dessert, and with wine made on the place by her Italian servants. Back to Sanders Theatre for the questions and the arguments. Then at six-fifteen to the choral concert in chapel with organ and brass. Then to *The Harvard Crimson*, where I wrote my review of the concert and sent it by telegraph, returning to New York by the midnight train and finding in the morning at my door, when I arrived, the Late City Edition containing it. My Harvard speech was published in a volume, along with the other addresses. Also in the *Atlantic*. And I used it as title-essay for my next book of reviews and articles. It is a good piece, probably the best statement now in print of the whole experience involved in hearing music and describing it. But I have rarely used it as a lecture. Partly because any speech, once printed, goes a little dead. And also because the compactions of phrase I put this one through before publication have rendered it unmalleable for elocution. It now reads like a contract. The points are there, but all so close together that the language does not flow quite as it should for being listened to.

Then *The Mother* came on and played its nine performances. Also rehearsals for a broadcast on May 25 of *Four Saints*. I had most of my original cast for this, and I conducted. There was an excellent new tenor replacing Leonard Franklin, who had joined the war and stayed in service. Through all the galling labors and the errands involved in preparing two operas while doing my regular reviews and Sunday articles, it was Theodate Johnson, living in a small house hidden by the store fronts of Third Avenue, who gave me dinner regularly, went to rehearsals with me, provided rest between dates, was my almost constant evening companion. And for publishing *The Mother of Us All*, which she insisted must be done, she assembled subscribers to guarantee the costs.

Four Saints, also to be published, I had rescored a little bit, adding horns in place of saxophones, and two clarinets to relieve the precarious balancing required when woodwinds are only one of each. Ben Weber, a composer who lived off music copying, made me out a handsome new orchestral score. Was this completed also, with new orchestral parts, that busy spring? It must have been, because the broadcast, contracted for an early date in the Philharmonic's empty summer space, was played in the new version and so recorded. I conducted its recording in Town Hall. The RCA-Victor Company was not willing to record all of the opera; forty-five out of ninety minutes, a ten-side album, was their limit. With this in view, and with Maurice Grosser's help, I reduced the score by half through complex cuttings. Ten hours had been reserved for its recording; but three were wasted on a faulty seating plan, one that involved a dozen microphones and left balances to the recording engineer. On arriving at the hall, I had found this arrangement all set up, accepted it on trial against my judgment. After the morning session, we played the records back and found them, as I had known they would be, close-miked and dead. Robert Shaw, a consultant on the job, and Richard Gilbert, the company's classical-music man, agreed. "This afternoon," said I, "we'll do it my way."

I seated the orchestra therefore as for a concert, with chorus upstage, the orchestra and soloists down front. I used one mike, a large one, out by the balcony, and a small one near the choir to pick up diction. Then, with only seven hours to go, but with a layout in which I could control the balances, I began again at the beginning. Largely because of some vocal tones not ideal, the musical performance in this recording is short of perfect. But technically it is a good enough recording to have been reissued twice—as a long-playing disk in 1952 and with some acoustical embellishment again in '64. Its rarest excellence, beyond the charm of Negro voices, is its verbal clarity (up to 98 per cent).

In July I went to lecture in Vermont at Middlebury, stopping at Tanglewood in Massachusetts to address Copland's composition class on writing operas. There Koussevitzky, after tea on his fine terrace, took me by the arm, made over me. He had always had a gift for convincing every person that he was just the one the Maestro had been longing for. He could radiate, he could smile, he could touch you as if he were holding no reserves at all. In my case, of course, I knew that he held many. No farther back that year than February, I had attacked at some length in my column his attempt to suppress through legal action the publication of his biography by Moses Smith.

A Paris lawyer wired me in July that my flat, if left unoccupied, was in danger of being requisitioned against the housing shortage. I also had a cable from Suzanne Blum informing me I was named to the Legion of Honor. "Come over and let's have a ceremony." In Paris I got involved with "*collabos*," the first of these my good friend Bernard Faÿ, who had received just the year before, after a long-delayed trial, a whopping sentence (life imprisonment, seizure of property, and national degradation). Gertrude Stein, to whom I had introduced him, had been wretchedly unhappy at his imprisonment. I shall not try the case in this memoir; suffice it that Suzanne Blum and Paul Weill, who had no reason to love him, but quite the contrary, had found the trial a travesty and Bernard pitiable ("*digne de pitié*"). For Gertrude's sake, and out of friendship too, I essayed what little power I could wield. It was Suzanne who helped the most, for she was legal counsel to a ministry. And it was she, unless I am in error, who procured his removal from the Ile de Ré, an island fortress where his health was being injured, to a prison hospital on the mainland near Le Mans; and it was from this easier situation that a year later he escaped to Spain. In Madrid he taught history at the University, later moving to the University of Freiburg, in Switzerland, where he has remained. Subsequent revision of his case produced a pardon, the restoration of his property and voting rights. He goes now and then to Paris, publishes his books there. He has not been restored, so far as I know, his chair of *Civilization américaine* at the Collège de France.

At one point, discouraged about other help, I had asked the gangster for advice, and he had referred me to the President's secretary. But the secretary, who knew the case, assured me that nothing could be done just then. Several applications for a pardon had come to the President, he said; but all had been refused on account of pressures. Bernard, being intensely Catholic and royalist, and through his eighteenth-century studies a specialist in Freemasonry, had denounced Freemasons by name to the Vichy government; and Masonry, under the Third and Fourth republics, was the cement of the entire electoral structure.

At another time I wished to help a singer, Kirsten Flagstad, who had come back that year from Norway. She had left New York in 1941 to join her husband, had not since sung publicly at any time. Now the husband, though she had had a perfect right to join him, had been a political associate of the traitor Quisling.

When she was announced as intending to sing in America, there were public threats of picketing and of stink-bombs. Looking into the matter to decide my attitude, I learned from the Norwegian Embassy that although this artist had been no patriot, neither was there any juridical hindrance to her traveling in freedom and practicing her profession. I even received from the chief justice of the Norwegian Supreme Court a letter stating this. So I covered in Boston her first concert, incorporating this information in my review. There were minor demonstrations there and a few at her first New York recital. But by the next year she was singing again at the Metropolitan, all the more in voice from her six years' rest.

In Paris it had been requested that I "write something" to help a French opera singer, accused of collaboration and now living under house arrest. This time I replied to my beseecher, an American writer and literary hostess, that when this artist should be free to sing in public I should review her happily, because I had long admired her work, but that I could not try law cases in my column.

In September I went to stay with Suzanne Blum at Cap d'Antibes, along with the handsome Colonel Georges Spillmann. As commander of the First Moroccan Infantry, then in garrison at Villefranche, he suggested giving me my *Légion d'Honneur* with military honors. These consisted of a band, a headquarters platoon, and the regimental mascot, a bearded goat. And in their presence, in a public square in Nice, I was pinned and kissed while bagpipes and drums played *The Star-Spangled Banner* and *La Marseillaise*, both in the florid Moroccan style. Four years later my rank was raised from *chevalier* (or knight) to that of *officier*. That occurred in 1951, when Vincent Auriol, the same President of the French Republic who had signed my diploma, paid a state visit to America. Since it is customary on such visits to award decorations, it came about that Olin Downes, my colleague of the *Times*, was to receive a *chevalier*'s ribbon; but since he had never been especially a friend of France (Germany and Finland his specialties, Russia his passion), the cultural attaché who recommended him must have thought it only right that I be moved up.

I never learned who had obtained me the first decoration. I thought it might have been Suzanne Blum, working through the Foreign Office. When I asked, she said that Hervé Alphand had been my official sponsor ("*a accepté de te patronner*"). Certainly it was Suzanne herself who solved the problem of my flat by suggesting that with my landlord's consent I sublet it to the colonel, about to be made a general and transferred to Paris. This consent involved a little bribe, a little blackmail. For the landlord did not want the place requisitioned (no profit in that); and the colonel, he knew, could requisition it. My proposal, suggested by Suzanne, was that the colonel be allowed to rent it furnished at twice my rent (a low figure) and that the difference be divided with the landlord. This arrangement lasted for twelve years, and the general was a model tenant. He discovered in the neighborhood a perfect *femme de ménage*, whom we shared; and whenever I arrived, he moved out, leaving every picture, ash tray, piece of soap, exactly where it had been when I left. My profit was just enough to keep the walls papered and the curtains fresh. And I had for Paris visits a flat that cost nothing.

I did not go to France, however, till five years later, when in 1952 I took abroad a *Four Saints* troupe. For the present I had one more European errand, showing to Beecham *The Mother of Us All*. Staying in London with him half a week, I sang and played him the opera, which delighted him. "I shall do this at the BBC," he said. But when it came to their considering it for his upcoming seventieth-birthday festivities, the BBC officials turned it down. Meanwhile I watched Thomas recording for His Master's Voice with his new orchestra, the Royal Philharmonic; and I also interviewed the other company, English Decca, deriving from both visits material for a Sunday piece. I also reviewed the Vienna Opera, then playing at Covent Garden. When the *Herald Tribune* bureau had asked for tickets, the reply had been that there were strictly none. However, since my presence would mean coverage, a special arrangement would be made.

I could witness Mozart's *Don Giovanni* from the royal box, under two conditions. The first was that I bring no one with me (presumably to prevent Beecham's coming along for a lark, taking a bow, creating a disturbance). The other was that I keep invisible. To occupy me during the intermissions, the house manager would take me for a walk, buy me champagne, show me the premises. The latter involved a royal ladies' rest room with no washstand or mirror and a royal men's room where a mahogany column, when opened, became a florid and flowing fountain. That was all, save for a flowered china pot embedded in upholstery in a covered box. There was also a downstairs sitting room, with furniture for holding champagne and cigars, where royal gentlemen could sit out whole acts.

The year of 1947 had begun with my making war on the ever-so-powerful Arthur Judson. The Philharmonic's conductor, Artur Rodzinski, had resigned, alleging interference from the manager. And since that manager was also president of Columbia Concerts, a corporation selling soloists to the Philharmonic, I took occasion, in defense of the conductor, to point out the conflict of interest that was involved. My article was a strong one, and the paper backed me up in an editorial. Judson informed me later that he had been angered by my denunciation, that he was now more than ever my enemy, and that he would remain so. This when Eugene Ormandy proposed to the two of us that Judson take on the management of my conducting dates.

My year ended in a small hassle with the Catholic clergy. In November the Pope's encyclical on art and music, *Mediator Dei*, had been printed in the Vatican's news organ, *L'Osservatore Romano*; and our Roman bureau chief, Barrett McGurn, had sent it to me. This encouraged the liturgical use of modern styles in both music and art, unless these are "unseemly in character" or "derived from a vain research for . . . outlandish effects." Naturally I printed it, translating from an Italian text such passages as dealt specifically with music. A flurry of querulous letters from priests editing Catholic papers hinted that the American clergy would have liked to bury the encyclical. And that is what their papers eventually did, publishing it only after many months and then in small sections, a little at a time, with no comment. I remembered that the American bishops had waited twenty years to implement the century's earlier pronouncement about music, Pope Pius X's *Motu Proprio*, of 1903. If now they showed a similar reluctance, that need not surprise. Nor need it stop my cheering. The Pope was news; modern music was my faith; their union was almost too good to believe. It almost made up for the loss of modern music's chief organ of propaganda, the League of Composers' quarterly, *Modern Music*, so brilliantly edited by Minna Lederman, which at the year's beginning had after nearly a quarter-century, in Léon Kochnitzky's phrase, "suspended hostilities."

33

Five Years Go By

IN MY EARLY YEARS AT THE PAPER I did not write much music. I put my symphonies into shape and started them traveling. I orchestrated a dozen portraits for grouping into suites. I extracted other suites from films and from the ballet *Filling Station*. To already available chamber works, choral works, and songs, to organ works and other keyboard pieces, I added in 1943 a book of études for piano, the first of two. In 1945 John Houseman's documentary film *Tuesday in November* gave me a longer breath; after that I composed year after year symphonic works, concertos, chamber music, works in liturgical format, and many for the theater.

The *Mother of Us All*, completed and performed in '47, was followed in 1948 by a film, Robert Flaherty's *Louisiana Story*, for which I wrote an hour of symphonic accompaniment. I was able, moreover, to extract from this music two suites that have been played more, I think, than any other of my orchestral works.

Flaherty had neither Pare Lorentz's self-doubt nor Houseman's compulsion to self-torture. Patient, fearless, and trusting of himself, he could give a guy his head and let him work. And he worked too, went straight ahead, and with Helen Van Dongen, the most sensitive cutter of them all, slowly reduced his footage to the unchangeable timings that a music track must have. In the meantime I had looked up the folk music of the Acadian (or Cajun) people of the bayous. And I had thought too about the landscape music that would be needed for this watery region, which I remembered from my Air Force time in World War I.

But there was no point in going farther without a budget, and for some months there had been no money left. Flaherty had spent all he had on shooting and cutting; and the Standard Oil Company of New Jersey, subsidizers of the project, seemed disinclined to furnish further funds. But Bob went on showing his film (still musicless) to possible backers, until to one of these informal evenings Geoffrey Parsons brought Elmo Roper,

public-opinion expert of the oil company, who was writing a
column at that time in the *Herald Tribune*. And it was Roper,
apparently, who procured the extra money to commission me
and to pay for my music track's recording by Eugene Ormandy
and the Philadelphia Orchestra.

Louisiana Story's music is of three kinds—folk music, scenery music, and noise-music. The Cajun people are represented
by their waltzes and square dances and the tunes of the songs
they sing. Natural scenery is depicted through musical devices
adapted from Mendelssohn, Debussy, and other landscape
composers. The noise-music used is the recorded sound of oil-
well-digging machinery. I call it music because, as compounded
and shaped by Helen Van Dongen into a rich and deafening
accompaniment for a passage of well digging one whole reel
(nine minutes) long, these noises make a composition. Also, I
find this composition more interesting to follow than almost
any of the industrial evocations, including my own, that musicians have composed with tonal materials.

The music track of this film has throughout its length a high
presence, or decibel count. Flaherty saw no reason not to emphasize (up to the point of loudness at which visual attention
would be disturbed) a symphonic accompaniment so little overlaid with dialogue. I know few films—indeed, none other recorded in America—in which orchestral color has been kept so
vivid. Nominated for a Film Academy Award (an "Oscar"), the
music was found unworthy of that honor, I was told, because
the Philadelphia Orchestra's sound track was "unprofessional."
That term meant, I was also told, that our engineers had failed
to "sweeten the line"—a practice long observed in Hollywood
by which the first violin part is recorded as a solo (*molto vibrato,*
naturally) then superposed on the full "take," to add plangency.
A Pulitzer Award I did receive, the only one yet given for a film
score.

I worked on no more films till '57, when I scored *The Goddess,* by Paddy Chayevsky, and a United Nations atomic thriller
by Thorold Dickinson, called *Power Among Men*. These I conducted myself, the latter with forty-five members of The New
York Philharmonic. Chayevsky as a workman, though sincere,
was hard to deal with, because he could give no one, save possibly his analyst, credit for brains. He confessed in full recording

session, all the same, that I had been right and he wrong about a certain musical effect. Then later, with the sound track all complete, he took over the film from its director, John Cromwell, whom he disagreed with on the story's meaning. He thereupon cut out some twenty minutes, I helping him to find the spots where music could be broken. Whether he improved the film I do not know. It has quality and has won European prizes. For my taste, I find the music low in volume; but I liked Kim Stanley as an actress.

In 1964, for the New York World's Fair I worked with Houseman on a one-reel picture called *Journey to America*, to be shown four times an hour in the United States pavilion. Telling the history of immigration almost entirely through prints and still photographs, it is humane, grandiose, and touching. The scoring uses old hymns, folklore, the music of our peoples, much of it nostalgically dissonant. And as always happens when I work with Houseman, we experimented, this time with the timing of commentary. By knowing exactly where it would appear and vanish, I was able to score first softer and then louder and thus to avoid dial-twiddling by engineers. Unfortunately, as also can happen with Houseman, his co-workers did not realize that my scoring was exact, for by slightly misplacing the music track in certain spots they threw some of my results just that much off. My method here, I still think, was a good one; it should be of use in documentaries of which the text is poetry or compact prose. Applying it to jabber would not be worthwhile.

Going back now to the middle 1950s, my experience on a televised production of *King Lear* with Orson Welles and the English director Peter Brook was cartoon comedy. Welles played Lear, of course, but over Brook's head kept revising and cutting the script, directing everybody, and changing everything every day till in the final telecast nobody knew any more which lines were in and which were out. Orson himself, in a fury of improvisation, threw in five from *Richard the Third*. The show, a Ford-Omnibus Spectacular, was for Sunday evening after an all-day dress rehearsal. On Saturday at midnight, as we broke, Brook had said gently, "Virgil, I'm short seven music cues. Do you suppose something could be done?"

"Certainly," I said. "Just show me where." Which he did.

So I went home and wrote them (in bed, as usual). My

copyist came at seven in the morning, took them away, made orchestral parts for my eight (I think) musicians, delivered all to the theater at nine. We then rehearsed the new cues, timed them, and a little later put them in the show. At the telecast, I was in an upstairs studio, where I had a television set for watching the play, headphones for hearing it, a music stand, my score, and my musicians. I was alert in spite of my long night up; but I was also scared, having to bring music in on word-cues when almost nobody was saying the words he was supposed to say. I made no error at that, surprisingly. I was, however, late by half a second on a sight-cue; then right on the nose of my storm-piece came a crash of thunder, thrown in by a watchful engineer, just in case.

Possibly to make up for whatever needed making up for in this production, Orson later played *King Lear* at the New York City Center, this time with electronic weather by Vladimir Ussachevsky and other music by Marc Blitzstein. And this time he fell and broke an arm or leg beforehand, ended up by facing madness from a wheel-chair. I had salvaged from my own *King Lear* a funeral march, later used in Jean Giraudoux's *Ondine*.

The *Ondine* production, with Audrey Hepburn, was directed by Alfred Lunt; and I must say I enjoyed everything about it, even the star's husband, Mel Ferrer, whom Alfred did not care for. Lunt, like Flaherty, was a steady and straightforward worker, knowing infallibly what he did not want. With a director like that, one can use complex cueings and drench the play in music. For *Ondine*, as for *Louisiana Story*, I wrote lots of music cues, fitted them in without misunderstandings; and, helped by sets also of some complexity, we constructed a production at once light in texture and elaborate. Lunt called my incidental music the best he had ever heard; and I certainly found him, among the play directors I had worked with, the most efficient and the best organized.

The Grass Harp, by Truman Capote, was a fragile play sunk by scenery. An interior by Cecil Beaton full of bric-a-brac and china, a tree-house and a tree that filled the stage, were beautiful, all too beautiful. I tried to compensate for their luxuriance by using music sparsely, not too much of it. (My triumph was to fill a sky with falling stars by means of just one chord on a celesta.) Because we were opening in Boston, and the tree was tremendous, we held no dress rehearsal in New York. We gave, however, to an invited group of some two hundred Broadway professionals a last run-through in street clothes on a bare stage with only work lights. The play was touching; everybody wept. After we had got into our scenery in Boston, nobody out front ever wept again. That lovely tree, I thought, if fitted into some romantic opera, might survive for decades at the Metropolitan. Relieved of it, *The Grass Harp* has done well in colleges, little theaters, and clubs.

I worked also, in Stratford, Connecticut, on six more Shakespeare plays; and that was a pleasure because I like to work with Houseman. I like especially his constant worrying about everything. I do not share his penchant for tall women (a six-foot Juliet, for instance) or his fear of stars (assigning an assistant to handle Katharine Hepburn). For she too was a loyal workman who would worry until everything was right. About a music cue that he resisted, I said, "If it doesn't work we can always take it out. What are you afraid of?"

"You must remember," he answered tightly, "that *you* live in an ivory tower." I let that go. But the next day at breakfast, which we took in French, as always, I pointed out that he was the one who had spent twenty years in the limiting landscapes of Broadway and Hollywood, while I was a practical artist, traipsing from Vienna to Buenos Aires, from Mexico to Maine, Rome to Seattle, working in every species of show and concert, rehearsing and conducting orchestras, lecturing in the universities.

That was indeed my life, one third of it. The rest was reviewing music and composing. Among my works composed after 1945, those which touch me most are the Cello Concerto, which was my homage to a long-time friend, Luigi Silva; the Flute Concerto, which is a full-length and resembling portrait of another, the painter Roger Baker; a choral work with orchestra, *Missa Pro Defunctis* (or Requiem Mass), which exploits my skills in choral treatment and liturgical evocation; and *The Feast of Love*, for baritone and orchestra, my own translation from late Latin of the *Pervigilium Veneris*, sex poem of all time. My other works I know will make their way; these also perhaps. But they worry me because I love them.

My reviewing, after 1945, or even earlier, worried no one save those who feared they might get scorched. As I reread these pieces now, I realize that they are written with a skill surprisingly dependable. I am sorry not to find them quite so interesting as the earlier ones. For those are passionate; they sing and curse. It is not strange to me that the collected books of my *Herald Tribune* pieces, appearing in '45, in '48, in '51, sold each a little less well than its predecessor.

At all times I had a vast correspondence, steady readers, and my continuing wars. The correspondence seems mostly out-of-date today. My wars, perennial, were of the David-and-Goliath sort—sling-shooting at the Metropolitan, at the trusts of concert management, at the Catholic hierarchy, at Arthur Judson, at Billy Rose. Between battles I wrote Sunday essays explaining modern music, also arguing that criticism is not just a whirling windmill, but truly an exercise of the mind. These pieces still express one man's experience in the making of music and in the observation of it. My point of view on both was strictly professional, strictly consecrated, and Franco-American. I never believed that geniuses were a special kind of man; I respected only sensitivity and workmanship. And I abhorred the vacuum that modern music had become in Germany, in Italy, and very largely in England, not to mention the emptiness of Soviet Russia.

On a trip made to America, recovering from one of his purgings, Dmitri Shostakovich had heard the New York Philharmonic. Now it happened that on that program, conducted by Stokowski, was a piece of mine called *Wheatfield at Noon*. In his diaries, transcribed for *Sovietskaya Muzyka*, Shostakovich remarked it "a very bad piece," "void of artistic content or meaning," and "most unpleasant to the ear." He had not cared for the Philharmonic either, or for Stokowski. I printed excerpts from his New York diaries in translation, including his opinion of my *Wheatfield*.

From the beginning I had carried on a guerrilla war against the great Toscanini, sniping constantly at his preoccupation with the "wow-technique," at his seeming preference for second-rate singers, at his couldn't-care-less attitude toward modern music, at the blasting sound of his brasses in Radio City's Studio 8-H, at the military-police ways of the ushers there ("the watch dogs of capital," Roy Harris called them), and at the overbearing nature of his publicity. When Stokowski, his associate, jeopardized his usefulness to the National Broadcasting Corporation, presumably by playing too much modern music, a severance was made in Toscanini's name on the pretext that having two conductors was bad for the orchestra. At this point I called attention to the constant presence there of guest conductors, to the fact that for half the week the NBC was a house orchestra anyway, and to the further fact that Leopold Stokowski had never been bad for any orchestra—in effect calling Toscanini a liar. Executives telephoned, of course; but the paper declined apology and stuck with me. There was rumor also that The Old Man would challenge me to a duel. He did not; he merely broke with Eugene Ormandy, whom he knew to be my friend. The latter, though regretful of his loss, made no appeal; nor did he mention to me the estrangement.

I always kept up coverage of the new books on music. Published music I did not review, esteeming its qualities too precarious, unheard. And recordings already had their Sunday column. But after this fell vacant, with new disks piling up, I sometimes would review a few of them. The trouble with record reviewing is the time it takes to listen, all the more tedious from solitary confinement. A concert takes time too; but you can have someone with you, see people there, or even doze. In addition, the recording of a famous work needs to be listened to with score in hand, if only for comparison with other versions. For instance, when in one month alone arrive four recordings of *Die Meistersinger von Nürnberg*, each four hours long, it is only fair to review them comparatively. But record reviews cannot be very long; they become too jubilant, bitter, or personal. And sixteen hours plus writing time for a half column, I could never persuade myself was justified.

My relation to the recording industry became strained after 1953 through my being a plaintiff, along with some thirty others, in a $150 million monopoly-lawsuit against the broadcasters and their affiliates (a lawsuit still unsettled, I may add). Until then my works had been recorded with reasonable frequency. After that time the frequency dwindled. In his pretrial examination another plaintiff, Gian-Carlo Menotti, alleging discrimination against the recording of his operas, replied, when asked whether the neglect could be ascribed to taste, "Impossible! I am the leading composer of operas." In my testimony that a certain work of mine, recorded two years earlier, had not been issued because the company "couldn't think of anything to put on the other side," though there was a work available, recorded by me with the same orchestra (and eventually issued as the verso), I described this quoted reply to my inquiry as "patently disingenuous." At this point the steno-typist and all the lawyers looked up: "What did you say?" "I said 'patently disingenuous.' Make what you can of that." I never knew what they made of it; but it became clear that at Columbia, where I had long been, at least musically, a friend of the house and where my works had caused no loss, I was not again to be recorded much, or soon.

There came also the usual honors—election to the National Institute of Arts and Letters in '48, to the American Academy of Arts and Letters in '59, to the American Academy of Arts and Sciences somewhat earlier. In '49 there were both a Pulitzer Award and my first doctorate (of Fine Arts, Syracuse, and to my surprise not honorary, but a working degree). Grosser had discouraged its acceptance, "You shouldn't get mixed up with that world." But I insisted that as a reputable journalist working for a reputable paper, I could not refuse without discourtesy. And on the platform, also getting hoods, were figures indeed no end respectable—Ralph Bunche, of the United Nations, Lester Pearson, then Canadian Secretary of State for External Affairs, Nathaniel Goldstein, Attorney General of New York, plus other intellectual citizens. There was also a little pale-haired lady named Elizabeth Nightingale Graham, who turned out to be the cosmetics manufacturer Elizabeth Arden. When I told this to Grosser, it was his turn to say, "You see." I got even with him two years later by becoming a Kentucky Colonel, with a commission from the governor of the state. "Now sneer at that," I said. But being a Southerner, he did not try.

I did not accept membership on boards or committees unless I was prepared to do work. I really worked for the Arrow Music Press, of which I was a founder, for the Composers' Forum, and for New York University's Maison Française. I served also on committees at the Institute. And I met throughout its lifetime with the ANTA Music Panel—a group appointed by the American National Theatre and Academy to advise our government in its program of helping musicians to go on tour in foreign countries.

This group was both good tempered and combative; rarely have I been so hugely entertained. The purposes of our existence were two—to select artists for quality, which only professionals can do, and to protect the State Department, through our independent status, against meddlesome congressmen. Very early we demanded veto power and got it; without our approval no musician could travel on the President's Fund or in ANTA's name. In addition, we were not paid, a fact which gave us even greater power. For he who buys advice need not use it. But he who receives it free from professionals has to follow that advice if he wants more.

All decisions were arrived at in our monthly meetings; only in emergencies did we vote by telephone. And the discussions were of a frankness and good will, an untempered hilarity I have never seen elsewhere, either before or since, employed as a committee's operating method. For with musicians like New York's William Schuman, Jay Harrison, Howard Hughes, and Carleton Sprague Smith, with Alfred Frankenstein and Raymond Kendall from California, John Rosenfield from Dallas, Harold Spivacke from the Library of Congress, Howard Hanson from Rochester, Arthur Loesser from Cleveland, and Nicolas Slonimsky from Boston, we were rarely at a loss for the truth about anything, and never for words.

Three panels—music, dance, and theater—had been formed in 1953. When ANTA was relieved by the State Department ten years later, the morale of them all was undermined. We understood that Senator Fulbright's disaffection from one of our musical decisions was causing the intellectual-exports program to be reorganized, and it is quite certain President Kennedy did nothing to stop that. Afterwards the meetings of the music panel were not lively any more and for decision making scarce worth going to. Those of us who have continued to attend do so, I think, in the hope that some day our authority may be restored. Those meetings are an exercise in group criticism, and the program they serve should implement the group decisions.

To be effective, all such decisions must be professional, independent, and without any possibility of being bypassed—a point of view as applicable to art as to shipbuilding.

In the five years when I did not go to Europe at all, between 1947 and '52, I traveled the map of America from Maine to San Antonio, Seattle to Savannah, Duluth to Houston, Denver to Louisville. I got to know my country's orchestras, its colleges, its newspapers, its hotels, its motels, and its restaurants. And I grew attached to Colorado, largely on account of Carol Truax, in those years an educational music executive in Colorado Springs, with whom I cooked, gave parties, organized a festival. One summer, teaching composition there, I discovered (later verifying elsewhere) that American students, even the best of them, though they can write in almost any kind of counterpoint and can sometimes orchestrate effectively, have not been trained at all in harmony.

When young composers went to California, they could call on Stravinsky or Schoenberg, but not both. Schoenberg, I think, was the more tolerant; Stravinsky did not permit divided loyalties. In my case there was no proscription or cause for any. I had no reason to offer Schoenberg overt homage. I did not really like his work that much, though I defended it; and a handful of letters bears witness to his gratitude. On one of my trips to Hollywood, when I addressed the Women's Auxiliary of the Los Angeles Philharmonic Orchestra, Schoenberg came to the lecture, pathetically smaller and thinner than I had known him. At the end I stepped down and went to him. He was happy to see me; we began to talk. But after about a minute his wife tugged at his sleeve, saying, "There is somebody important over here." The next evening he came also, this time to a critics' panel I was part of, sat close to the front, and tried to ask a question. But again she pulled his coat, and he sat down. He went on writing me when there was occasion; and I would send my greetings through the German colony of authors and musicians that had clustered, replacing their lost French Riviera, between the university and the sea.

Stravinsky made no protest at these minor infidelities. For twenty years we saw each other joyfully—in New York, Hollywood, Venice, wherever we were. There was a great deal of party giving too, at his house and mine, of dining and of drinking good French wines. He came often to hear my music, spoke well of it, advised Balanchine about making a dance-piece out of *Louisiana Story*, to be called *Bayou*. The less dramatic of the two orchestral suites, chosen against Stravinsky's preference, failed as a ballet.

At my New York hotel apartment Stravinsky first met Pierre Boulez; and the two of them sat talking on a sofa, in spite of milling guests, for two straight hours. This was after Schoenberg's death, when Stravinsky, guided by Robert Craft, who served as aide and musical adviser, was moving into the power vacuum, as politicians call it, left by the last to die of the twelve-tone triumvirate—Berg, Webern, and Schoenberg. In an earlier time he would not have wished to meet young dodecaphonists (there were plenty of those in southern California), least of all a polemical Parisian who used "neoclassic" as a dirty word.

Some have regretted that Stravinsky in his seventies should adopt Schoenberg's composition method. But even those who still deplore the surrender cannot but be happy that in his eighties he is still composing. As for myself, I find his twelve-tone serial music no less interesting than his neoclassic. Actually I believe it to be a continuation of his neoclassical procedures (using materials from turn-of-the-century Vienna) and neoclassicism itself, in Stravinsky's use, to be an outcome of his impressionist, or landscape, period. In impressionist music, places are evoked; in neoclassical, historic times. In twelve-tone writing it is almost impossible not to call on sentiments characteristic of Vienna between 1890 and 1910. There is, of course, no valid objection to that, nor to any method of composing, nor to any subject.

One can be sales resistant, however, to the publicity that surrounds the twelve-tone serial method, because of that publicity's messianic tone. And hallelujahs for the salvation of *le père Igor* are likely to be absurd from lack of humor. For Stravinsky by nature is himself a jokester, a jokester and a man of simple feelings. There is nothing about him tortured or self-reproachful; he has no overheated Jewishness, no German *Innigkeit* (or introversion). His Russian propensities are for piety, domesticity, and calculated violence. His use of double meaning comes from Paris. And if, like Satie, Picasso, Gertrude Stein, he can multiply his meanings without a smile, in the end (and I should say almost from the beginning) he is, save for the domestic sentiments, a dead-pan comic. For example, exclaiming very seriously in my house, "The oboe is one of the most beautiful instruments God ever created!" he might have been suggesting as a theme for William Blake or Milton *God Creating the Oboe*. It is also purest Stravinskyan *pince-sans-rire*.

For his eightieth birthday, when I cracked a joke myself, he did not like it or understand my malice; but he did not reproach me, and we continued to embrace. His wife, however, began avoiding me and looked the other way when I would pass. The purpose of my move was to test our friendship, to see if under blows it would survive. I did not care much whether it did or not, for I was finding his twelve-tone sanctimoniousness distasteful, and I deplored the celebrity apotheosis he had undergone. So I struck two ways at once. Reviewing *The Flood* for the London *Observer*, I praised the music, pointing out as well its artful irony. Then, in an American magazine, I slapped him hard. Jay Harrison's birthday-piece had been enhanced by four framed testimonials, requested. Shostakovitch bore witness to the master's "great musical genius and endowments." Leonard Bernstein called him "a true immortal," Gian-Carlo Menotti "an indispensable item in a composer's workshop." I found him "a manneristic composer in a manneristic age" and recalled what the eighteenth-century Metastasio had said of himself, "a tolerable poet in an age of mediocrities." My attack's chief interest is its seeming lack of motivation. I had no reason for diminishing a composer I profoundly admired, but we know what men will do to public monuments. And I do not regret it. Or do I? No. I can't. Living monuments are insupportable.

Coming back from trips, I usually stopped in Pittsburgh, Pennsylvania, where my sister lived and where my mother spent the winter. Come spring, she always went back to Missouri, where she had sisters, cousins, nieces, countless friends. When she would visit me, say once or twice a year, Mother was a success, no question, in New York. For she had Missouri forthrightness along with Kentucky tact, and she could stay up late without fatigue. She thought any day a somewhat wasted day unless one went somewhere or had some company. Or in season, of course, did right domestic things such as dressmaking, canning, organizing a sickness, a wedding, a childbirth. So people came to our house, and we went to theirs. We went as well to concerts, the opera, the ballet, the United Nations, the horse show, the dressmakers' openings. And mornings she would mend, shine silver, or simply read, while after lunch, as a Southern lady, she retired. From eighty till her death at ninety-two she was constantly a guest, ever cheerful, easy to have around, never a weight.

The skill of her conversation became proverbial (and how not, for one who viewed life as a party?). When John Latouche asked her did she enjoy Gertrude Stein, she replied, "When I understand, I enjoy her very much. When I don't understand I just don't understand." And of John Cage's music for prepared piano, "It's pretty, but I never would have thought of doing it."

The most successfully explosive of her remarks was made to Betty Isaacs, who when asked, as people are asked in Missouri, what church she went to, replied that though she and the Judge were of the Jewish faith they did not go to temple very often. Mother hardly thought a second before observing, "I don't think it makes any difference whether people go to church or not, so long as they're good christians." She had used the last word as a common noun; the Isaacses loved her forever after.

When she became ill in 1957, I went to see her straightaway in Pittsburgh. "I hadn't planned it this way," was her apology. "I shan't get over this one. But that's all right. I've had a good life." Since I was to conduct shortly in Berlin, at the opening of the Kongresshalle, my sister wondered whether I should go. "Of course I must; Mother would think it foolish of me not to. And surely I can count on her for the tact not to die while I'm away." So I went to Berlin and came back. And then she did die, murmuring, "Open the door." And we took her to Missouri. And I went back to Europe for another engagement. She was a small woman, barely five feet, though plump; and she had been pretty. She never raised her voice. But in her gentle way she was a driver. She saw no reason for accepting in oneself, unless God forced it, any remediable imperfection such as ignorance, poor health, or a lack of manners. As my wartime buddy George Phillips used to say, "Your mother is the one with character, not you."

Nicolas Nabokov returned to Paris in '50 or '51 as world-wide director of The Congress for Cultural Freedom. His first major action there was to organize for 1952 a month-long festival of

twentieth-century music. There were to be variants of this festival in Rome, 1954, still later in Venice, Berlin, and Tokyo, all
of them comprehensive and costly. For the first one—L'Oeuvre
du Vingtième Siècle, in Paris—he wanted passionately to show
my *Four Saints in Three Acts*. The United States government
offered him Gershwin's *Porgy and Bess*. He refused it as sociologically false (a white man's story) and culturally degrading
to Negro actors (because sociologically false). Procuring the
money for *Four Saints* was partly his achievement, partly that of
my lawyer, Arnold Wiessberger. But it was procured; and I took
charge of the production. We showed it first at the Broadway
Theater in New York and then shipped it by plane to Paris—
cast, costumes, and scenery—at the end of May.

34
Traipsing and Trouping

THE JOINT PRODUCERS OF *Four Saints*, the American National Theater and Academy and Ethel Linder Riener, had left all artistic decisions to me. Since most of my original singers had aged vocally in eighteen years, I held auditions and recast the work. Edward Matthews was still impressive as Saint Ignatius and his wife, Altonell Hines, unchanged as the *commère*. Inez Matthews, Edward's sister, though rather a high mezzo than a soprano, sang Saint Teresa I; Betty Allen, Saint Teresa II; Rawn Spearman, the tenor role of Saint Chávez. Among the dancers I find the name of Arthur Mitchell. In my chorus were Leontyne Price, Martha Flowers, Gloria Davey, Olga James, and Billie Daniel. It was a cast of pristine voices, most of them, like Leontyne, straight out of the Juilliard School and proud to be singing opera for pay. The next season, as once before, a new *Porgy and Bess* troupe used the best of them.

The Stettheimer stage-sets were impractical because cellophane, even if it were still available, would not be tolerated by the fire department. Tchelitcheff declined, with love, to do over Florine's opera. Esteban Francés also excused himself, unless there were considerable money to spend on spectacle. Eventually it was decided to reproduce as closely as possible the Stettheimer conception, using in place of cellophane a woven plastic material. I found this material droopy and greasy, its blue-green color dismal. But the costumes, at least, could be correctly copied; and anyway there was no artist available whom I would trust (or who seemed to have the courage) to redesign the opera throughout. It was also decided to reproduce the Frederick Ashton choreography, since this fitted the scenery and since there had remained from 1934 a prompt-book. The choreographer William Dollar, helped by Grosser and the prompt-book, did not do badly by the earlier conception. The musical performance, which I trained and conducted (and which Stravinsky complimented highly) was the presentation's really first-class element. But there was no all-over production brilliance, as in '34.

On my arrival in Paris I had encountered Orson Welles, who said, "Can I be of any help?" "You surely can," said I, "because you know the house; and we may have to adjust our lighting and stage movements." He came to a dress rehearsal at the Théâtre des Champs-Elysées, sat quietly throughout, then at the end showed our singers how to retract their large open patterns at the ends of scenes so as to be off the apron when the curtain fell. Whether he changed the way our lights were hung I am not sure. Grosser says no; my memory says he made certain that at least there were enough projectors in the house to light all those playing in front of the curtain line.

My orchestra was that of the Concerts Colonne, by courtesy of their regular conductor, Paul Paray, thanks to whose firm commitment, during five rehearsals and seven performances (O miracle!) not once did any player send a substitute. Neither the sight reading nor the discipline, however, was comparable to what we are used to in New York. Enthralled for certain by the Negro girls, my men half the time would turn their backs to me. For every entry of a soloist or section, I had to snap my fingers a good two measures in advance. That they could cooperate, however, was revealed at the last performance, when Inez Matthews had a cold. "Don't try to go on," I had said to her. "Leontyne knows the role." But she did go on. So I said to the orchestra, "Please take care with my soprano; don't make her sing loud all the time." Their anti-American resistance to me (three-fourth of them were commies) disappeared at once; and they followed lamb-like, hushing volume at my slightest indication, their eyes on me instead of on the stage.

It had been hoped to tour the new production; there had been nibbles. Venice would have taken it in September, but we were paying American salaries and could not wait. Barcelona could have used us earlier, but our *première* was engaged to the Paris festival. There was talk of our playing a week at Covent Garden; but we were turned down, an executive of that house remarking that "the Royal Opera [was] not quite the place for coons."

The Paris press, conditioned to Josephine Baker and to the Katherine Dunham dancers, feigned some astonishment at our lack of Negro sex display. They also found the scenery, though charming, tinsel-childish. They remarked the voices and performance as first class. The work itself received mixed notices. Some critics found the libretto nonexistent; others saw in it "the old Picasso jokes" ("*Picasso mystificateur*"). Almost all viewed the music's simplicity as "arbitrary." One of them recognized my connection to Satie but wondered regarding us both "whether [we] had renounced richness or merely resigned [ourselves] to poverty." The most perspicacious of them (Marcel Schneider in *Combat*) found in this "Sunday school entertainment," or "camped-up Mass . . . no trace of impiety or sacrilege," merely "a modernistic golden legend." And

> to complete the illusion, Virgil Thomson's music, by perversity, imitates the village sacristan at a harmonium, with his constantly consonant chords, tonic and dominant. Purcell and Couperin are evoked, and other masters of the seventeenth and eighteenth centuries; but Thomson has managed to be different from them while appearing just to copy, with the result that this music, seemingly so facile, so conventional, achieves the utmost of sophistication; perfidious and perverse in its naïveté, it ends up as naïve through perversity.

There were attempts to laugh the whole thing off, as in New York two decades earlier. There were also demonstrations in its favor. Nadia Boulanger gave me a dinner for sixteen. My French banker gave a lunch with rare wines at the Automobile Club for two hundred. And on opening night I had found in my dressing room a basket with fourteen kinds of flowers in it, bearing the wishes of Christian Dior. The most impressive of these gestures was a cocktail party, the hostess both a daughter and a widow of academicians, the guests profoundly dowdy and distinguished, the food and drink not showy, merely perfect, the whole an acknowledgment of my long-held place, both personal and professional, on the inside of intellectual France. (Said Marie-Blanche de Polignac to Nadia Boulanger, "*Il était là comme un coq en pâte.*")

I was also asked to write for musical encyclopedias, to take part in forum discussions and to serve on juries. What I actually did, after ordering shirts and suits, was to go and visit Sauguet near Bordeaux. Of all my French musical associates, he was the one who had matured the most becomingly. In youth a thin man, he was now portly; and his sharp-tongued spleen had given place to warmth, revealing brains, benevolence, and heart. With the painter Jacques Dupont we motored south and east, ending in Aix-en-Provence at the festival. There we joined French music's in-group—Poulenc, Roland-Manuel, the publisher Hervé Dugardin, and more. My opera had not offended them by a too-small or too-large success, and my prestige as a music-journalist gave them every wish to please. There were English present also, but my fatal way with them brought only tensions. The critic of *The Sunday Times* took me to task for my overfrank review of Britten's opera *Billy Budd*, shown also at the festival in Paris. And lunch guests invited by the Dugardins to the garden of a hotel waited an hour for Britten and Lord Harewood to come down. They were delaying, we thought, to see if I would leave. When it turned out that I was of the party, they sent word that one of them was not feeling well.

In the summer of 1953 I conducted in California, Mexico, Newport, and Cambridge (at Harvard). And the following season I conducted in Minneapolis, Cincinnati, Philadelphia, Baltimore, Washington, and New York. There were recordings too, my last for some time to come. And I worked on the *Ondine* with Alfred Lunt. For several years I had been earning more from my music and public appearances than from the paper. In the spring of '53 I decided to resign as of October, thus giving the editors six months to replace me. I was not bored with the job, but I could see boredom far off on the horizon. I had reviewed most of the artists that there were and all the kinds of music. Going on for the sake of a dozen novelties a year, if that, seemed less than urgent. On the contrary, as my mother had said of visiting, one should leave while both you and the others are enjoying it.

But just as I was about to give notice, Arthur Berger, at that time one of my assistants, told me of being offered at Brandeis University a professorship in musical composition with a good salary and four months' vacation. "Do you think I should take it?" was his question. "Of course you should take it," was my answer. But his resignation meant that I must postpone mine; I did not think it right that we leave in the same year. So he told our managing editor, George Cornish, that he would be leaving in the fall; and I told him that I would stay until the next fall.

The idea that I would relinquish a post so little demanding,

so honorific, and so powerful was unbelievable to Cornish, to
Parsons, to Helen Reid, and to young Whitelaw Reid. Unless
perchance I was moving to another paper. But that, not. I had
refused in 1941 *The New Yorker*'s offer to double my *Herald
Tribune* salary. I was simply through with reviewing; I had had
it. But not a one of them believed me. And for a year no plan
was made for my replacement. Then Geoffrey Parsons asked
me for suggestions. I said I did not think I should be allowed
to name my successor. So we left it at that; and in late March
of '54 I went to Europe to take part in another of Nabokov's
music festivals, this time in Rome, and to indulge myself in a
conducting tour.

This began in Barcelona at the gold-and-red-plush Liceo
with a program of American music, all of it unknown to the
orchestra and all of it to be learned in four rehearsals. It was a
long concert with two intermissions, as is the custom there, and
with a soloist, Bernard Greenhouse, to play my Cello Concerto.
I had regretfully renounced Charles Ives's *The Housatonic at
Stockbridge*, knowing that this five-minute work would take
more time to learn than all the rest, time that would be needed
for Copland's *Applachian Spring*, whose assymetric rhythms
would give trouble. In fact, I spent so much time on those that
as my last rehearsal was ending at the oh-so-Spanish hour of
half past midnight, we had still barely read through *Louisiana
Story*. I was announcing that I would take my chance on pulling
that together at the concert when the violinist Casals, brother
of the exiled cellist, made a speech, saying we had worked well
within our given time but that we needed one half-hour more
of practice, and proposing that the orchestra give that time free,
in order to assure the concert's excellence. "We are after all in
Barcelona," was what persuaded them.

In Rome I conducted, as part of the festival, my *Three Pictures for Orchestra*, difficult all of them, but by the radio orchestra well played. This festival, with some fifty composers asked,
was devoted to the music of its guests and to commissioned
works, of which there were twelve. The commissions awarded
to Americans had been two, a Concerto for Violin and Orchestra by Ben Weber, with Joseph Fuchs as soloist, and some solo
scenes from Lou Harrison's opera (after William Morris) *Rapunzel's Daughter*, sung by Leontyne Price. This last piece won

a prize, in fact. Our American representatives made the best effect of any, I think—the composers Copland, Barber, Carter, Lou Harrison, and Ben Weber, the composer and conductor Carlos Surinach, the violinist Joseph Fuchs, the harpsichordist Sylvia Marlowe.

The festival, as if to prophesy the coming time, suffered from a plethora of overcomplex music. At the end of its ten-day term we were exhausted from digesting all those dense and chewy scores and from fighting for them against an indifferent public and a distracted administration. It had been thought appropriate to open the first concert with a fanfarelike work for brass by Giovanni Gabrieli. Three months went by; then just a week beforehand, Paris checking, it was revealed that the music could not be found in Rome. So Paris ordered it to be sent on from Venice. What should Rome know of a Venetian who wrote four centuries ago? Rome has its seven hills and three world powers. And music, as practiced by modern musicians, is not of interest to the Church, the Communist party, or the film industry.

As I left for my tour, Copland, also beginning to conduct, had written me, "Cut a wide swath so we can all go through it." And the next year he made a European tour himself. I conducted concerts of American music in Zurich, Paris, Luxembourg, and Vienna. I also made a trip through Scandinavia for reporting the June festivals. And in July I conducted in New York at the Lewisohn Stadium, giving *Four Saints in Three Acts* in the forty-minute concert version. By this time Edward Matthews was dead (of a motor accident) and Altonell Hines no longer singing well. So I persuaded Inez Matthews, a mezzo anyway, to sing the *commère*, using Leontyne Price and William Warfield for the leads. Leontyne, just two years out, was at her peak. I do not think she has ever sounded or looked more lovely.

I stopped at the office to see Parsons and George Cornish, because at last I had a successor to suggest—Paul Bowles, an excellent composer and a good writer, then living in Tangier. But by that time my successor had been named, the music historian Paul Henry Lang, of Columbia University. So I wished them all well and went back to Europe, where I had still a Paris radio concert to conduct. On a steaming July afternoon with no intermission, nor any time between works more than to put down and to take up scores, the program's ninety minutes, on my feet and sweating, were the most tiring I had ever spent.

It was through this, however, that I made a royal friend. Queen Elisabeth of the Belgians, herself a string player and the close friend of a cellist, heard the broadcast of my Cello Concerto with Maurice Gendron playing. She sent word thereupon by the singer Doda Conrad that she had found this the most interesting music she had heard in many years and that she looked forward to making my acquaintance. I wrote to acknowledge the message, but did not wait on her until the following year. Since that time, I have gone to her regularly, and we have talked of music and of politics. When she asked me hopefully, "You *are* a bit of a revolutionary, are you not?" I answered, "I am always against the government." "So am I," she said, and went off again to Russia. Still later, in the early 1960s, she spent a month in China. Coming back, she said, "Chou En-lai stays with peasants in their houses. He is a great man."

At this I comprehended her opinions. I had never doubted their sincerity, but I had not understood her need for them. As a Wittelsbach princess and a compassionate queen, impatient with parliamentary delays and bourgeois maneuvers, she found it right that a chief of state should visit his people and rejoiced at his care for the humble. Though German, she was no Junker; two wars proved that. On the contrary, she tended to believe that socialism justly administered can save time. I cannot agree with her or disagree; no matter what the government, I'm agin' it. But I did note that her leftist view was royal.

In Kitzbühel I tried to write a piano concerto that Minnie Guggenheimer, of the Lewisohn Stadium concerts, wished to commission. The effort came to nothing, so I studied scores. For I was to conduct at Town Hall in November a Mozart symphony, a suite by Bach, some songs of mine, and the Satie *Socrate*. Examining a manuscript of this, which I had never played with orchestra, I found written in, and signed by the composer Charles Cushing, an English version of the French text. Hooray, thought I, we'll use this. Then, as I went on examining it, I found, as always with translations, slight changes to make. I did not write to Cushing then; but after the *Socrate* had been sung by Phyllis Curtin and Alice Howland, I sent to him in Berkeley, California, a program in which the translation, as altered, was ascribed to both of us. It took him five years to forgive me. But he had still not seen my alterations. After five more years I sent him a vocal score containing my adjusted version. How deeply he resents my interference I may never know. But the work goes beautifully into English; that was his discovery.

Still in search of inspiration for a concerto, and in the rainy Salzkammergut longing for sun, I moved to the shores of Lake Garda at Sirmione, where I received a wire from Zermatt inviting me to hear Pablo Casals give lessons on the cello and to play, with the pianist Mieczyslav Horszowski, Beethoven's five Sonatas and the Variations. I said to Nicole Hirsch, "Let's go in your car." But she said, "I'm not invited." "I can fix that, I think," said I, "by wiring the management that I am bringing the music critic of the Paris *France-Soir*." So we went together by way of Milan and over the Simplon Pass to the cog railway's foot, then up to the high village by the Matterhorn, with its fine Victorian hotels and not one car.

In thirty years I had not heard Casals. Amazed by his musico-technical refinements, I acquired, as evidence, stenographic reports of his public lessons that I still show to players and to teachers. But what struck me most was his ability to play "white," as it is called, to move the bow very steadily, slowly, from point to heel, with no left-hand vibrato to conceal right-arm trembling, and with no such trembling anyway—this at seventy-seven, please remember. Eight years later, in Washington, at the White House, on an occasion when he played there after dinner, at the recital's end I went to look for him. In his greenroom I embraced him and turned to go, found myself nose to nose with President Kennedy. "Hello," he said. "What did you think of the music?" When I told him I had never heard the old man play more beautifully, nor Horszowski either, nor Alexander Schneider, and that their special excellence had been all for him (it could only be that way), he listened intently as if wondering, "Can I use this?" Then with a charming grin and a slight leer of complicity, as if asking for the low-down, he leaned toward me. "Is he really still as good as he ever was?" he wanted to know. For answer I described his bow-arm control. "Say, that will interest my wife. Let's tell her. Jackie, listen to this."

My last date that summer was Venice, where my Flute

Concerto, composed for Elaine Shaffer, Efrem Kurtz's wife, was to have its first performance. The program contained four new works; and the conductor, detained in Milan, would not arrive till the morning of the concert. It was proposed therefore that Bruno Maderna and I, since we were present (Miss Shaffer, too), rehearse our works and get our pieces ready so that Nino Sonzogno, when he arrived, could spend his short time on the other works. This was done, and perfect performances resulted. Also showing in that autumn's festival was a Benjamin Britten opera based on Henry James's *The Turn of the Screw*. I heard this twice, admired it, was able to congratulate Britten sincerely. He even smiled. Since that time, though our paths do not cross much, he has not felt it needful to avoid me.

After my last piece appeared in the *Herald Tribune*, fourteen years from my first, I continued to lead the same life as before. I conducted, gave lectures, wrote music. I missed nothing about the paper but Julia Haines, for secretaries are habit-forming. Minna Lederman is said to have exclaimed, on hearing of my departure, "But how will he get his music played?" Curiously enough, it has gone on being played; my ASCAP reports show almost no decline. And since ASCAP chiefly reports radio performances, and since radio performances tend to follow the number of recordings available, the decline in my recordings would more than explain the slight diminution. And my whole income, cardinal test, has not diminished.

Right off, on my leaving the paper, Pierre Monteux had asked me to dinner. His intake that evening, in his eightieth year, consisted of a pint glass of Pernod with water, six oysters, a fillet steak with *sauce béarnaise* and soufflé potatoes, fresh asparagus with *sauce hollandaise*, ice cream, and for the four of us two bottles of champagne. "I can't drink red wine any more," he apologized. Afterwards, when the other guest had left, Doris, speaking for them both, with Monteux approving, said, "I hope you don't mind our asking about money. But without your *Tribune* salary, will there be difficulties?" I replied that their thought was most considerate, but that I had been independent of the paper for upwards of ten years. "Well, I'm glad," said she. "We were worried about you. And we want you to promise that if you should ever be short of funds you will let us know."

Actually, the only help I needed then was musical. As after

my return to Missouri from World War I, after my return to Paris in 1925, my return to America in 1933 for producing *Four Saints*, my return to New York in the fall of 1940, whenever I have closed off an epoch in my life and opened another, it has taken a little time before the music flows. Relieved from deadline pressures and with nothing I had to do (evenings, at least), I seemed to write less music than before. I wrote songs to old English poetry and to Shakespeare, also songs in Spanish. I did six Shakespeare plays, three films, and a new ballet, *The Harvest According*, by Agnes de Mille (to excerpts she had chosen from existing works, with filling added). I traveled too, to South America, lecturing in Spanish and conducting, to Venice for two festivals, to Berlin for another, eventually to Japan. But I was not content with just moving about, nor with merely composing films, plays, and short recital pieces. It was not till I had completed a forty-five-minute work, the *Missa Pro Defunctis*, and in 1960 brought that through its birth pains in Potsdam, New York (with an orchestra of ninety, a chorus of three hundred), that I knew my reconstruction time was over.

35
A Distaste for Music

WHEN MEN OF LETTERS write about their century, literature inevitably gets star billing. That is the way they present the times they live in, and we have all been brought up to
believe them. It has not been easy, therefore, for a mere musician to review six decades. Nor has he attempted wiring these
for sound. His only effort toward consistency has been to leave
out things not actually seen by him. However, what he did see,
and on some evidence remembers, is not quite the whole of this
recounting, for verity required that he explain just why it was
that he was where he was and how he happened to be looking
at what he saw. Which raised the question: Who was he anyway?

And so it came about that a sketch aimed chiefly at describing
places, times, and persons got turned into a sort of self-portrait.
It had to be shown right off, for instance, that its Midwestern
author was not of the Sinclair Lewis–Sherwood Anderson–
Ernest Hemingway line, all of them worried and preachy, but
rather of the more comic-spirited Booth Tarkington–George
Ade–Mark Twain connection. He had also to be placed in the
pre-World-War-I music life of Kansas City, then in that of postwar Harvard, neither of which was available in books.

Then came the discovery that France was more than just another country, like England or Germany, or even very special,
like Spain or China, but a miracle spot like ancient Greece or
the United States, where more comes out than seems to have
gone in.

Next, joining the European 1920s, of which your observer
instantly became a part, he seems to have learned quite early
that these were not by any means the same 1920s that have
become fixed in American romance as taking place against a
frantic jazz accompaniment and peopled by a generation of
good-looking young expatriates all happily, and some successfully, playing "lost."

The thirties also had to be explored—so different in Europe
from in America but, like the twenties, consisting of two
halves. Unlike the twenties, they are still virgin territory, for

few historians have mapped the trails. Now that they begin to do so, I notice that the American trend is toward dramatizing the Great Depression, even monopolizing it, also toward monopolizing our progress toward workers' rights, as if the Léon Blum government of 1934–6 in France, with its advanced social laws and their enforced acceptance, had not offered a constant working example to our New Deal.

As World War II approached, it was the journalists who warned us. For four years or more they said it would take place. The statesmen of western Europe said it would not; the artists hoped it would not; the European rich from everywhere (manufacturers, bankers, men of business) mostly believed it would not, while both the British and French general staffs acted as if it could not. But when Hitler, bluffing, said it would take place, and nobody stopped him in 1936 from occupying the Rhine, the newsmen knew that nobody intended to stop him.

The intellectual and artistic life of America during that war, though largely still unplotted, is available for study. That of Germany under Hitler and of France during the Occupation still requires uncovering. And it does seem probable that the world's present state, particularly Europe's, will be easier to understand when those dark years shall have been lighted up.

My personal account of America during the 1940s remains that of a musician working on a newspaper. It is amazing what you do not learn there about contemporary history. You see nothing; the cables tell you nothing; the editorials explain nothing. I came to believe after many months fraternizing with them all—with Ogden Reid, Helen Reid, and Geoffrey Parsons, with the managing editor, the city editors, and the specialists—that they were not really on the inside of things. They could package the news, but they were too close to judge it. In prewar Paris times, the foreign correspondents from fifty countries, pooling their thoughts, had come closer to the truth (indeed, they still do) than those same reporters ever can once they are back home, holed up in the plant, and separated from their unofficial sources. The only better prophets, when I still had access to their analysis through Sherry Mangan, were the working Trotskyists. Communists of the Third International, whether Stalinist, Khrushchevian, or other, have never to my knowledge shown any special care for truth, past or present, or any

prescience about things to come. Their conversation is Jesuitical; their acts are as often as not plain treacherous; their political
faith is mythological and religious.

My column, which came to an end in 1954, reported little
of the modern-music war that went on throughout the Eisenhower decade. That war, which was fought between Europe
and America for world control over music's advanced positions,
was won by Europe. Pierre Boulez, Karlheinz Stockhausen, and
their aides now occupy lots of space in the world's press, ride
high, make money, and instruct the young. John Cage and his
associates enjoy honor at home and some in Asia; but they are
virtually without influence in Europe save on those leaders just
mentioned, the ones who early seized there all the paying posts.
These posts are nearly all in Germany, where state-supported
radio establishments are rich and where music publishers are
the world's most prosperous and best organized.

The 1960s in America have seen the financiers of real estate
take over much of music's distribution through building on
slum-clearance property shopping centers for the performing
arts. These developments are subsidized by philanthropic foundations and blessed by government. Recording and radio companies observe them carefully. Indeed, on almost any of their
boards one finds a pair of television executives. These move in
pairs for mutual protection, being not yet trained in art-trustee
diplomacy. So far, these boards are openly conventional in taste
and generally box-office minded. The broadcasting and publishing cartels of Germany, though no less greedy than our business
combines, are at least engaged in furthering the composing art
and do not shy away from modern music. They figure that sound
investment in music's future can lie nowhere but in today's
copyrights.

With music become on both northwestern continents a
power-establishment; with, in Asia, Japan's high music literacy
a stimulus to massive consumption in both the native and the
European styles; and with India, once musically the mother of
us all, rapidly becoming, through the All-India Radio, a pander
to ignorance in every style (not to mention what has been
done by radio toward destroying the Arab tradition through
broadcasts in the Middle East and North Africa of musical artifacts from Cairo's Tin Pan Alley), the standardization of music

everywhere, even when this takes place at a high taste level, is accompanied by a forced consumption repulsive to any but the untrained ear.

Myself, till I was twenty-five or six, I had a glutton's appetite for sound. After that, my need was more for giving out than taking in. So I went to concerts only for a reason—a work of mine, or of a colleague, or of a beloved world-wide living master. Though now and then, for purposes to me mysterious, as in my wartime practicing of Mozart, I would dig into the bedrock below some classic source.

As a result of this almost dietetic intake, my engagement to review for the New York *Herald Tribune* found me at forty-four with my mind unsaturated, my ear quite clean. And thanks to my bosses on the paper, who did not overload me, and to my continued functioning as a practical musician, which refreshed me, I did not go stale. In fact, I was a far more expert listener to music at the end than I had been when I started, fourteen years before.

All the same, I came to realize, once I had given up reviewing it, that I could not bear the stuff in any form. Moreover, observing my composer colleagues, I realized that they too were finding music unattractive. We know, of course, that virtuosos and conductors early dispense with going to one another's concerts. But privately they listen to recordings; they keep up. And in Europe composers can still be seen at musical events. In America, where the very air we breathe is oversaturated with processed auditory stimuli, the composer after forty, of a certainty by fifty, finds the whole musical hoopla unacceptable.

He does not give up composing, for that is his defense against exasperation. And performing can offer comparable absorption, as can shepherding others through rehearsals of his work. But in middle age the music producer is a poor consumer. And staying away from concerts, like fasting for the religious, can be a source of strength and serve good works.

The distaste for music of which I speak is not, however, merely a matter of age. It is a symptom sociologically observable almost everywhere but Buenos Aires and Tokyo, cities where radio still is not abused and where musical appetite runs strong. Elsewhere, more and more at musical occasions one sees only music addicts, unhappily a growing group. For as the music of our time has become progressively intellectualized (thanks to the progeny of Schoenberg), it has alienated more and more the intellectuals.

From Wagner through Stravinsky the musical advance, like that of painting, was applauded, publicized, and financially supported by philosophers, men of letters, intellectual hostesses, disinterested bankers, people of fashion, and far-out royalty. Go to a concert today and look at the faces. Few belong to the intellectual world. Nor do the overheard remarks express ideas, but rather conditionings. For they are a conditioned lot, responding to appreciation propaganda and to market studies; and they all look either vacant or preoccupied. Music can make them applaud or shout; but it never seems to lift them up, give joy.

I must admit too that if the audience for music seems unperceptive, especially as regards the music of our time, the performances of music that we hear (excepting for those that deal strictly with the new kinds) bear little resemblance to their publicity. The orchestras play off pitch, and the singers sing off pitch; no one bothers to blend, to balance, or to get a rhythm right. The effort seems to be toward a driving effect or toward a luscious sound, toward something easily salable in any case. Harmonious musical discourse, as a concept, seems to have disappeared pretty much everywhere.

Were not the performances of my youth still less efficient? Yes and no. The singers were better trained, the violinists and pianists just as communicative. The orchestras were nowhere near so good as they are now, man by man. But no group is any finer than its leader, and our leaders of today are no more sensitive to music than in their time were Mahler, Nikisch, Messager, and (in opera) Toscanini. Our players read faster, learn faster, save time and money; but every concert sounds like a rehearsal. How little the superior training of our symphony men counts for in the long run has been shown up many a time by Leopold Stokowski's lovely work with youth orchestras and Thomas Beecham's with the New York W.P.A. And all symphony men sound crude beside the devoted young who perform the difficult new music so delicately and so precisely for Gunther Schuller or for Pierre Boulez.

With performances overblown, overadvertised, and oversold,

I often think that it would be a good idea for music writers to go underground. But I see no likelihood of their doing so. (And I imagine that if there were a musical underground, I should know it.) The twelve-tone serial composers, after spending nearly half a century outside the Establishment, are now a pressure group achieving power; they will certainly not resign from it now. Nor will the far-outs (percussive or electronic), whose training has ever been twelve-tonal and pressure-groupish. And just as certainly the pranksters, those charming rediscoverers of Dada who make us laugh, will not deny themselves the publicity for which their jolly jokes have been conceived.

Truth is, there is no avant-garde today. Dada has won; all is convention; choose your own. What mostly gets chosen in any time is that which can be packed and shipped. And for everything that can be shipped there is a conditioned public, from the universities, where Cage and Boulez are gods, to those cities, all too common West and South, where Mozart and Brahms are still a rarity and Beethoven's Ninth Symphony has not yet been heard.

Have we entered perhaps an epoch like to that of Louis XV in France, when there were no unsuccessful artists, no persecuted poets, no exiled philosophers (save the rich and vastly publicized Voltaire off in Switzerland), and when the intellectuals of Europe, no matter what their trade or discipline, made up a club that traveled, wrote letters, shared ideas, got one another jobs? This well may be our case. For with all governments except the Vatican and all the rich foundations going in for art, there is plenty of money around for everyone. In Europe, where the channels of art subsidy have been carved out by history, its formulas are not likely to change much. For professionals there—the poets, painters, and composers—are classically not only expenditure's recipients but also its advisers.

America's cultural enterprises—all but the public libraries and the state and Catholic universities—have for three centuries been controlled by amateurs, usually members of the business community. This privilege will not soon be abrogated. Federal government, however, may well be tapped for money. And this will entail some intellectual control such as the Smithsonian Institution exercises over a group of scientific, historical, and artistic enterprises. I have no fear for the ultimate result, given the general excellence of our intellectual establishments. But I do not think it realistic to dream romantically of poverty and persecution for the artist, of an underground, or of a permanent avant-garde.

The acceptance that we worked for from our youth began to take place in the middle thirties with the Works Progress Administration, and every President from Franklin Roosevelt through Lyndon Johnson has put weight behind it. Now we have it, the recognition of art and artists as national wealth. And if we still shall have to insist on our right, as artists, to guide public policies about art, we shall probably achieve influence sooner in the public sector than in that of corporate businesses like radio, television, and recording.

Of what, then, here and now, is music needful? A genius of the lyric stage, I say, a composer who will give stature to the operatic and poetic theater. We also need a music magazine, an organ to keep the intellectuals informed and to win back their lost interest in us. For without their faith and backing, the musical theater, like the concert world, is for its own money-raisers and for addicts.

Philosophical disputes about aesthetics died with Dada. The next steps toward understanding music and toward protecting ourselves from being taste-manipulated lie in two directions, both of them intellectual. The more urgent of these is the establishment of a musical sociology—an investigation of who consumes what and how they come to do it, in other words, a clarification of music's varied roles in our civilization. These studies are cardinal to a consumer industry, especially if federal government and the tax-exempt foundations are to assume a more than superficial involvement.

The other field is comparative musicology. And I don't mean just folkloring in the Orient. I mean the preservation, examination, and confrontation of the civilizing tonal arts of India, of the Indonesian regions, and of the Sino-Korean-Japanese complex. Analyzing their methods in detail and comparing them with our Western history of near two thousand years might answer the questions: What happens when? How does a monolinear music evolve? Does the discovery of the intervallic (or harmonic) phenomenon arrest that evolution? Are rhythm and meter incidental, or are they basic? And what are their possible roles in any music? In which of the great traditions is evolution now complete? In which still active? Hundreds of questions like these merit study, and their answers may indeed bring music back. For merely introspective, or philosophic, aesthetics has ceased to be a valid guide for growth.

There is no reason, I am sure, why music should not grow. Its present overproduction and overdistribution need not lead to eventual neglect and famine, though that may happen if we do not mend our ways, use our heads a little, and stop abusing the market. If the young, for instance, should decide one day to resist the market pressures, first losing interest, then, as they take things over a few years later, neglecting music's educational procedures, they might create a musical moratorium. But eventually music would start up again. And when it did, it might be worse than ever, with all the instrumental skills forgotten.

Seriously, I wish those called to serve the art would pool their brain power to study its operations. Awaiting that far-off moment, many of us, of course, will die. But the present writer, till he does, will fulminate. He will also (God willing) continue to compose. At the moment, a libretto in verse has been completed for him; and putting it to music seems vastly urgent. This book, besides, has gone as far as need be, as far as one man's memory can take it.

From

AMERICAN MUSIC
SINCE 1910

Contents

I

America's Musical Maturity

IN COLONIAL TIMES and during the first century of the republic, music in America grew abundantly and for the most
part unguided. During the latter part of the nineteenth century
a sort of adolescence had taken place, marked by attention to
its educational needs and a preoccupation with its reproductive
forces. In 1867 and '68 the New England Conservatory of
Music, in Boston, and the Chicago Musical College were
founded, their aim being to train performers in the best European tradition, at that time esteemed to be the German. And in
1872 a department of music was founded at Harvard University
to train composers, its model being the English universities,
where the writing of music was taught as a liberal art separable
pedagogically and socially from its performers.

As early as 1842 the Philharmonic Society of New York was
founded for performing symphonic repertory, a precedent to
be followed later in the century by St. Louis (1880) Boston
(1881) Chicago (1891) Cincinnati (1895) Philadelphia (1900)
Minneapolis (1903) San Francisco (1911) and other cities. Opera
companies also came into existence, singing German, French,
and Italian repertory in those languages (though the Metropolitan Opera Company for its first seven years, from 1882 to '89,
gave everything, including Bizet's *Carmen*, in German). And
the organized touring of reputable artists, along with tented
chatauqua seasons in country towns (named after the summer
camps for culture held in Chatauqua, New York) and indoor
"lyceum" courses for the winter, offered high-standard concerts
which served equally to cultivate the layman's taste and to stand
as models for those professionally aspiring. The gramophone
industry too, by 1900, was beginning to distribute passable
performances.

By that time also, composers were appearing whose technique, formed under German masters, was scarcely less competent than that of their similarly trained British colleagues.
George W. Chadwick, Horatio Parker, and Edward MacDowell,
all of whose lives crossed the century line, were the grandfathers

of us all. As educated pioneers, they took title to professional status and passed it to their heirs. That title included right of access to the performing organizations. So that in the decades succeeding the first one of this century, performance of American works by the orchestras of New York, Boston, Chicago, and other cities came to be as acceptable to the public as it was instructive to the composer.

Our early great men, all the same—Chadwick and Parker and MacDowell—are merely ancestors. For all the charm and competence of their music, it is a pale copy of its continental models. Its thin perfume is of another time and place than twentieth-century America; and so, indeed, though more robust by far, is that of its contemporaries in operetta, Victor Herbert and Reginald de Koven. And for all that Chadwick and MacDowell had aspired, like Grieg and Smetana, to depict their country, they did so as European travelers might have done and no whit more convincingly than Dvořák, who during the 1890s spent three years in America, in his "New World" Symphony actually did do.

What separated these men from succeeding generations and even from their pupils was the fact that they had received their higher training and most of their artistic precepts in Germany. Now Germany during the latter part of the nineteenth century, as compared to the vigors arising in France and Russia, was musically a dying swan. It was in France between 1890 and 1914 that the new century, foreseen by Chabrier and Fauré, was being brought to birth in the work of Debussy, Ravel, Stravinsky, and Erik Satie. I realize that during these same decades Richard Strauss and Gustav Mahler were working in Vienna quite successfully and that in Spain Albéniz and in Russia Scriabin were producing original work. But nobody then or now could find in any of the music by these men much to build on. And Arnold Schoenberg, though certainly one of our century's founding fathers, did not become visible as such until around 1910.

As viewed from America, the musical prognosis for Europe was so clearly favorable to France that well before World War I the brighter young Americans had begun to go there for studies. And they came home orchestrating out of Berlioz rather than out of Wagner, adept at modal counterpoint, acquainted with the new harmonic freedoms and metrical subtleties, and habituated to structural and thematic usages other than those that had come to dominate German teaching. German study had unquestionably been of value to the rise of American musicians into a higher level of artistic behavior. Through its help they were leaving off the stiffness characteristic of provincial art and beginning to take on the ease of intercourse, the at-homeness with broader themes, that mark international good usage. It was through their French contacts, however, that they first tasted freedom.

The major problem, after technical mastery, that any maturing music has to face is that of nationalism. Lacking local masters to feed on—the Beethovens, the Mozarts, the J. S. Bachs—is there perchance a folklore than can serve as nourishment? Is the heritage of commercial popular music usable at all? Are you limited to local sources for expressing your time and place? What are your sources anyway? Obviously they must be looked at.

The collecting of Negro spirituals had begun in 1867, just after the Civil War. In 1910 John Lomax published his first volume of cowboy song-poetry and several of the actual tunes. In 1917 the English folklorist Cecil Sharp started publication of the Appalachian ballads. These particular researches, some possibly set off by Béla Bartók's similar work in Hungary and certainly by Sharp's own collecting in England, opened to composers a goldmine of nostalgic feelings and of melodies that would be exploited in the 1930s. By that time a vast library of American-language folklore had been assembled and identified, virtually all of it Anglo-Celtic in origin. Even the Negro spirituals, as we learn from the studies of Dr. George Pullen Jackson, were African only in the manner of their singing, both their words and their tunes having been adopted from Scottish and Scotch-Irish hymnody.

The very popular nineteenth-century songs of Stephen Foster, proclaiming the pathos of Negro life through Celtic melody, though widely sung had failed to generate an idiom. They were beautiful hybrids, but sterile. And their communication was limited, since Negroes, our chief carriers around the country of both melody and rhythm, have never found them appealing. The spirituals themselves, that other Scotch-African crossbreed, seem to have had in them more chromosomes, their contribution to the blues being clearly, I think, a dominant strain. Ragtime, a genre that came up in the late nineties, was weakening by 1914. Its accent was irresistibly American; but it never developed beyond its early congealment as a species of pianoforte virtuosity for the salon (or saloon), poor in musical invention and shallow as expression. Nor did it give birth to jazz; it was merely replaced by it.

The birth of the blues is commonly dated as 1909, the year in which W. C. Handy wrote his now classical "Memphis Blues," though Gunther Schuller allows them a quarter-century of evolution before that. Jazz appeared contemporaneously as a way of playing dance music, an urban folk style that by 1912 to 1915 had become nationally circulated. Though jazz has from its beginnings used commercial pop-tunes for its variations, neither blues nor jazz actually came out of Tin Pan Alley, as we call our popular composers; and they have to this day remained largely independent of the monied distribution channels. There are jazz and blues recordings, of course; but they are often hard to come by and, unlike pop records, are a poor substitute for the real presence. The blues are a true folk art form, with a fixed meter of twelve four-four bars, generally grouped as three-line stanzas, expressing in the first person amorous or economic frustration.* For example:

> Got the Saint Louis Blues, just as blue as I can be;
> That man got a heart like a rock cast in the sea,
> Or else he would not gone so far from me.

Jazz is instrumental, a communal improvisation in four-four time on some popular tune—usually a commercial one which the players have no qualms about turning inside out. Blues and jazz have from their beginnings lived happily together, and both have continued to evolve in subtlety. Both, in fact, are authentic forms with a literature, a history, a tradition of high style in performance, a world public, and no signs of senescence. They have nourished the commercial and stimulated our art music— Darius Milhaud's *La Création du monde* and George Gershwin's *Rhapsody in Blue*, to mention only two celebrated works.

---

*The South distinguishes two main moods, the "po' house blues" and the "who' house blues."

In the intellectual music tradition, the decade between 1910 and 1920 saw the establishment at Harvard in Cambridge, Massachusetts, and at Columbia University in New York of French-trained composers, chief among these Edward Burlingame Hill and Daniel Gregory Mason, teaching younger composers, and particularly teaching them to orchestrate in the French way. In 1916 Ernest Bloch, a Swiss whose earlier career had been led in Paris, came to the United States to compose and to teach (in New York, in Cleveland, in Berkeley, California). On the verge of the same year Edgard Varèse arrived, a pupil of Vincent d'Indy and of Albert Roussel, a friend of Busoni and Debussy, already at thirty-three a leader in the advance-guard.

Henry Cowell, in California, had been performing as early as 1912 piano pieces involving tone-clusters. And Charles Griffes, a French-style impressionist (though he had actually studied in Berlin) in the late 1910s came out of hiding (he had been teaching in a boys' school) with songs, piano pieces, some highly poetic orchestral compositions expertly scored, and a shockingly original piano sonata. Another hidden composer, Charles Ives, who had since 1900 been working mostly in secret, in 1919 actually published one of his larger works, the now famous "Concord" Sonata.

At the end of World War I, Hill in Boston, Mason in New York, John Alden Carpenter in Chicago, and John Powell from Virginia were the major American composers of French formation, Hill and Mason being, along with Bloch, teachers of the brighter young. Percy Goetschius (1853–1943), a German-schooled theorist of great learning, was the chief preceptor for music writing at New York's Institute of Musical Art between 1905 and 1925; but his influence did not survive the 1920s, though till eighty he continued to publish textbooks. Chadwick, MacDowell, and Parker throughout the 1910s and '20s continued to be performed; but their influence was waning. The 1910–20 decade left us strong works by Bloch, by Cowell, by Ives, by Ruggles, by Griffes, perhaps by others. It also left us a French-based pedagogy of composition and, in Ives and Varèse, the example of an ambitious and hard-headed left-wing or experimental school. Both achievements have lasted well beyond midcentury. And it is thanks to them that American music has since 1920 pursued a development parallel to that of

Europe and sometimes leading Europe, as in the case of John Cage during the 1950s.

If the 1910s were characterized not only by changes in the teaching of composition but also by the appearance of radically modernist composers, many of whom did not become known till later, the 1920s, on the other hand, saw a modernist movement organized for the presentation of its own works along with the latest creations from Europe. The International Composers' Guild, beginning in 1922, offered music by its chief promoters Edgard Varèse and Carlos Salzedo; and their concerts, which continued till 1927, included the work of Ruggles and other radical Americans along with foreign novelties by Milhaud, Berg, de Falla, Chavez, Malipiero, Ravel, Stravinsky, Schoenberg, and Webern. Its successor, the League of Composers, founded in 1923, continued a similar policy, included stage works, and after 1933 commissioned composers. The League's remarkably well-edited magazine, *Modern Music*, which covered contemporary music internationally, survived till 1947.

In the very early years of the 1920s, Griffes died and Ives ceased to compose. Cowell, Varèse, and George Antheil continued a modernist line as pioneers in the use of nonclassical sounds and of rhythmic innovation. Carl Ruggles was the author of short works high in dissonance content, achieved through chromatic atonality, that sustained a degree of tension among the interval relations unmatched by any music being written in Europe. To this day it has not lost its excitement; nor has that of Varèse. Cowell's best work, mostly composed after 1940, came to be less radical than its beginnings, evoking with tenderness nineteenth-century rural America and sometimes, as an ethnographer, the traditional musics of Asia.

The 1920s saw also the founding of three remarkable music schools—the Juilliard in New York, the Curtis in Philadelphia, and the Eastman in Rochester, New York. It also saw the rise to fame of Nadia Boulanger in Paris as a teacher of Americans. Beginning in 1921 with Aaron Copland and myself, then Walter Piston, Roy Harris, and Elliott Carter, eventually nearly everybody of my generation studied with her. The American composers who have not passed through her studio mostly belong to a younger generation or to the twelve-tone school. Other exceptions are Samuel Barber, William Schuman, Lou Harrison, and John Cage.

The successful careers of Copland and of Roger Sessions also began in this decade, the end of it leaving American music with a beginning repertory of modernistic orchestral works, many of them recognizably American in feeling. The continuity of this production and the later symphonic contributions of Roy Harris, Randall Thompson, Walter Piston, and William Schuman proved the sound schooling and expressive powers of the American composers who matured in the '20s and '30s. These are in fact, along with Copland and Sessions, today's older masters; and very little of their music has ceased to communicate.

The 1930s witnessed an unprecedented expansion of the symphony orchestra into virtually every small town, every college and high school. According to one study there were by 1937 no fewer than 30,000 of them, all practicing classical and modern repertory and all giving public concerts. And they played American music, because Americans naturally enjoy American music until they have been taught not to. Already, moreover, there was lots of it to play and to enjoy.

So it came about that with the symphonic territory conquered, pacified, and under cultivation, restless spirits undertook a new invasion, that of the stage. Now Americans had been writing operas and getting them produced since back in the other century. Chadwick, Parker, Frederick Converse, de Koven, Victor Herbert, Henry Hadley, Charles Wakefield Cadman, and Deems Taylor had all worked for the lyric stage, but not memorably. Their operas, though history, are today no part of repertory.

The first opera to break new stage ground was my own *Four Saints in Three Acts*, composed to a text by Gertrude Stein in 1928, produced in '34. This was followed in 1935 by George Gershwin's *Porgy and Bess* and in 1937 by Marc Blitzstein's *The Cradle Will Rock*. In the decade's last years Gian-Carlo Menotti, an Italian trained in America, and Douglas Moore, an American schooled in France, began, with *Amelia at the Ball* and with *The Devil and Daniel Webster*, operatic careers that have extended for over thirty years and beyond our frontier. Since that time Roger Sessions, Hugo Weisgall, Gunther Schuller, Samuel

Barber, and Peggy Glanville-Hicks have given us practical works in the operatic format. American opera, though subject to the inherent weakness of most opera today—which lies in its failure to coordinate serious texts with serious music—has since 1934 aspired toward making its story playable on a stage, and keeping the language of it clear to an English-speaking public. Our best works have gone that far.

Around 1930 an invention for combining sound with films had made musical planning urgent for that medium. "The industry," as Hollywood used to call itself, early employed quite competent musicians for this task, mostly German-trained, and then hamstrung them by demanding that the music remain "neutral." This effect was obtained by a casual employment of the Wagnerian *leitmotif*, by drenching the whole in rich orchestral textures, and by avoiding musical characterization, which might have caused a loss of glamour in star rôles. France and Russia were producing a livelier collaboration by using composers more up-to-date musically, such as Darius Milhaud and Arthur Honegger and Serge Prokofiev and the relatively unknown Soviet musician named Y. Stolyar who created such an imaginative musical ending for the first Russian sound-film, Nikolai Ekk's *The Road to Life*. Film "musicals," aspiring little further than to plug commercial songs, were about the same everywhere. And nowhere were real blues or jazz employed, since these styles, through their amazing power to reject impurities, were resistant to standardization.

In the United States it was the "documentary," often government subsidized, that first gave composers a chance to try out their powers. In 1936 and '37 I wrote scores for two films by Pare Lorentz—*The Plow That Broke the Plains* and *The River*—that have become historical (for they are still widely circulated) and that influenced "the industry." Their first influence on the industry was to cause the engagement of Aaron Copland as composer for the film version of John Steinbeck's *Of Mice and Men*. This music, along with Copland's later scores for *The Red Pony* and *The Heiress*, are as close to first-class musicodramatic workmanship as has yet been achieved in America under industry conditions. George Antheil, in those same years, labored manfully to introduce direct expressivity into film music, though without complete success. But Copland and I had proved it could be done, and Leonard Bernstein later wrote picturesque music for *On the Waterfront*. Also Gail Kubik, in *Gerald McBoing-Boing*, a wartime cartoon, had neatly underlined the comedy. In 1949 I received a Pulitzer Award—still today the only one ever given to a film score—for my contribution to Robert Flaherty's *Louisiana Story*.

The 1930s likewise saw American composers take on the ballet. My own *Filling Station*, of 1937, and Copland's *Billy the Kid*, of 1938, are repertory pieces. And these were followed in the next decade by successful dance works from Schuman, Barber, Dello Joio, Bernstein, and Morton Gould. Into all of these theatre domains—the opera, the films, the dance—the break-through into viability must be credited to my work, if only on grounds of priority.

The 1930s, moreover, became our finest period in the creation and the singing of blues. They also invented a variant of jazz called swing and developed a species of partly scored jazz for bands larger than chamber-music size. A vigorous time it was, with every year new operas, films, and ballets, and with the symphony concerts constantly offering not only fresh music by new composers but also some of their finest by already maturing ones like Copland and Roy Harris, whose Third Symphony remains to this day America's most convincing product in that form.

The 1940s brought John Cage from California to New York, where he reinvigorated music's left wing, which had lost its revolutionary fervor. Before the decade was out he had also visited the new radicals in Europe and shown them possibilities they had not known regarding rhythmic structure. Later he taught them the use of random choices in writing music, a method that led them out of the unserviceable complexity that had developed with multiple-row composition, a method of writing in which not only the sequence of pitches is determined, as in classical dodecaphony, by a prechosen order, but all of music's other variables—heights, loudnesses, rests, note-lengths, methods of attack and release—are made to follow also a numerical pattern.

During this same time, the Second World War time, the European masters Hindemith, Křenek, Milhaud, and Schoenberg were teaching in America, as was also Nadia Boulanger. But none of their pupils excepting Cage, who had worked with Schoenberg, proved ready to cope on equality with the new musical energies that burst forth in Europe right after the war under the leadership of Pierre Boulez. The older Americans during this time were writing more symphonies, more ballets, more operas, reproducing their kind through teaching, expanding the repertory, exploring the fuller possibilities of the fields they had opened in the '20s and '30s.

By the end of the 1940s American composers were numerous and fecund, but essentially conservative as viewed from postwar Europe. Around 1950 a new spurt took place, and it took place everywhere. In Europe novelty took the form of electronic composition. In America it produced a new academicism, a modified dodecaphony aimed at producing within a near-atonal texture a maximum of thematic and rhythmic complexity. Elliott Carter and Roger Sessions were the leaders of this new conservatism, and their work has proved more subtle and more sophisticated than that of almost any Europeans working in similar vein. Multiple serialism has been tried very little in America, almost not at all, in fact; and our electronic production, having developed later than the European, is still small in volume, though this situation seems not likely to persist. In Europe, practically all electronic music is created in state-owned radio establishments (chiefly Paris, Cologne, and Milan) where engineers and equipment are furnished free to properly introduced composers. Hence many have tried out the medium and some have produced quite original work. Few, however, have remained long enough in the field to become specialists, excepting only the engineers themselves, several of whom in France have become composing engineers. In America there has been virtually no work done at all at the radio centers and very little private electronic composition, on account of its high costs. In the universities, on the other hand, there have long been calculating-machines; and since 1959 an R.C.A. synthesizer has been available to specially chosen students at Columbia University. It is not available, however, to outsiders; nor is in general the equipment at other universities. As a result, our composers in charge—Vladimir Ussachevsky, Otto Luening, and Milton Babbitt at Columbia, for instance—have by their very persistence, plus their salaried status, become engineer composers. Of late a cheaper instrument, the Moog synthesizer, has put electronic composition at the disposal of almost anyone; and with this new facility we may be about to see thousands of amateurs turning out electronic tapes.

At present virtually every experimental group working in the United States seems to be seated in a university, and possibly a certain scholastic timidity may be causing these composers to shun radical expressive aims. In Europe they are pretty firmly united toward creating a music of the Common Market, an idiom free from nationalistic propaganda and folkloric charm. They also seem to be in their most advanced work preoccupied with bringing to apotheosis the experiments with noise composition that were started by the Italian Futurists around 1910. And I think we may include electronic tape composition in this category.

The consistency of the European effort may well come from a conviction that the Western tonal system had by 1914 ended its evolution. This idea, I may add, is far more commonly accepted in Europe than in the United States, where believing it to be true could make our whole maturity appear as a development that occurred too late in history to be of value. Surely the European effort toward writing atonal music not for noise-making instruments but for those whose design had been perfected over centuries for avoiding tonal obfuscation has been equally a waste of effort, save possibly for proving it could be done. Furthermore, the non-tonal materials such as noise, electronically produced or not, require non-tonal methods for structuring a continuity (scales and intervals will not serve); and for this there is little available beyond an arithmetic of rhythms and durations. Whether chronometrics, calculated or random, can give psychological progress to a series of sounds that are unrelated acoustically, is a matter open to some doubt. Nevertheless, it must be tried, and thoroughly; indeed the effort is well advanced in our universities, always inclined to subsidize art that connects with engineering.

Meanwhile, certain Americans have been experimenting with another possible way out of the impasse created by the exhaustion of tonal resources, which is to learn oriental methods, in hope of producing somehow a fusion of systems that might reenergize both East and West. The Californians Henry Cowell,

John Cage, and Lou Harrison have experimented with Chinese, Japanese, and Korean musical procedures, as the French composers have done with Indonesian and with East Indian. Alan Hovhaness, a Bostonian of Armenian origins, has worked with Middle East materials and a bit with Japanese. And Peggy Glanville-Hicks, Australian by birth, has made for herself out of elements from India, North Africa, and Greece a musical idiom that has proved useful in ballet, and surprisingly so for English-language opera. There is already in America a body of work influenced by Lou Harrison that represents a return to linear composition without the interference of either chords or tempered intervals, and I must say the sound of it is vigorous. It might be ever so welcome that music should turn again toward meaning, and toward the expressive delights possible through scales of different tunings. But the work I know in that direction is still experimental. And certainly no fusion of East and West has yet occurred.

What has occurred is a maturity whereby America is now a music-producing country as well as a music-consuming one. We have rich folk sources and in jazz a major folk art. We have first-class libraries, historians, pedagogues, and performers. We have a population quite expert at listening and terrifyingly addicted to it. And we enjoy the rare advantage of possessing excellent composers of all ages and all schools. No other country in the world, save France, has that. And it does give strength, whether for holding fast against the liquidation of standards or for moving forward, even though all movement may be, as it seems right now, either European-led toward European expressive goals or dominated, as in America, by engineering games.

2

American Musical Traits

EUROPE'S GRANDEST ACCOMPLISHMENT in music, after
those early Christian centuries when it wrenched itself
away from Asia, has been to stage itself as a series of epochs. Its
musical continuity therefore seems a jumpy one, just as its political history does. It is rather as if the late Roman times through
Charlemagne, the Dark Ages, the medieval Renaissance, the
classical Renaissance, the Protestant Reformation with its religious wars, the Baroque age with its high royal prestige, and
Romanticism's revolt against exactly that, producing patriotic
and libertarian revolutions—as if all these intensely highlighted
moments were merely turns in a variety show of which the only
unity is an unchanging geological décor. The tent remains the
same, but each act brings surprise.

The art of rehearsing these changes sub rosa and then mounting them as shows, each in a freshly designed set and with
appropriate music, is Europe's genius for dramatizing history.
That special showmanship, moreover (plus nowadays learned
program-notes about "forerunners" and "influences"), almost
conceals the lack of continuity. The fact remains, nevertheless,
that despite those publicized researches, the entr'actes do not
explain the high moments. Forgetting the jumps, lest ignorance
be alleged, that seem to exist between plainsong, organum, and
Renaissance polyphony, the more recent parts of history, those
we can almost remember, also include great chasms. From Bach
to Haydn, Handel to Mozart, Beethoven (though clearly out of
Haydn) miraculously to Wagner, and from Wagner to Debussy,
nothing is really explained. Each splendid kind acts merely like
itself and appears to us, as it must have done to the contemporaries, profoundly of its time and place.

Now when it was suggested in the preceding chapter that
Europe's major effort in today's musical modernism is to depict
the new Europe, the Common Market, the hope for a Western
solidarity, it was not intended to suggest that the Romantic
afflatus has collapsed. It is still, in fact, the pathos content of
Russian music, of much of German, and of almost all English.

It was the expressive aspiration too of Schoenberg and Alban Berg and for the most part of Anton Webern. Even in America one encounters this, and not only among conservatives but also in many who view themselves as far-outs. Only recently I heard an orchestral work that involved five conductors, random entrances, electronic tapes, piano clusters, and lots of percussion, all of it making a great clatter thoroughly up-to-date. But its expressive model could only have been the symphonies of Mahler, so little of slow-feeling America and so much of tumultuous Vienna was recalled by its risings and fallings.

American music has too short a history to be considered as a series of scenes; there is scarcely enough of it even to make a narrative. I have already sought to identify it as a twentieth-century show beginning about 1910. So let us consider that show as still going on. What story it tells, if any, I do not know, being a part of it. But examined for detail, the music does betray characteristics, family traits, even hemispheric similarities by which our North American music resembles South American and Caribbean almost more than it does that of Europe.

In attempting to describe the characteristics that make American music American, I am not assuming that it is essentially different from European music. Just as North American literature is a branch of English literature, and the South American literatures are branches of Spanish and Portuguese, music in the Americas is the child of Western Europe, indeed of a musically mature Western Europe. The long evolution extending from early Christian psalmody to Handel and Bach had already produced a grammar of style and a vocabulary of feeling well before America began to speak this musical language with any ease.

The sources of American practice in harmony, counterpoint, orchestration methods, and musical structure are therefore European, and indeed chiefly continental European. The tune content of American music, however, has tended more and more in the last fifty years to be derived from the British Isles. There had been earlier on the part of our better educated composers a tendency to imitate the contours of the German masters and of Italian opera. And there has long been some utilization for picturesque purposes of Caribbean songs and dances Franco-Spanish in origin. But since American music became adult and aware, around 1910, say, we have been less and less involved with the expressive urgencies of continental Europe and more and more with our own heritage of feeling.

This heritage has come to us mainly from England, Ireland, Scotland, and Wales. Our non-British settlers have relinquished their native poetry and tunes, preserving these in family or community use only so long as they have continued to speak the languages they spoke when they came here, which is usually just one generation. The melting-pot theory of American life is not, it would seem, a true picture. Because the English-language group has from the beginning absorbed to itself, by means of language, all the others, giving to them its ethics and customs and even going so far as to lend them its racial memories, its folklore, folkways, legends, faiths, and aspirations.

Our immigrants' eagerness for absorption is proved by their constant preoccupation with Shakers and Quakers, with Indians and cowboys, with black men from the swamps and white Protestant mountaineers. Such composers, furthermore, though many of them sons of immigrant parents, show a notable lack of yearning toward their European origins. And our blacks have followed a similar pattern. Brought to our land speaking many African languages and practicing many religions, they renounced all those, adopted us as their own, and became an English-speaking Christian people. They took on, in doing so, our hymns and our poetry. Our blacks had formerly little contact with African music and African art, or till after the 1950s with African political aspirations. They are a part of us; and our Spanish-speaking fellow-citizens in New Mexico refer to them as "Anglos."

Our Anglo-American folklore is vast, varied, and rich. The nourishment it has given to our composers is inestimable, no matter what any composer's geographical or religious origins. At the same time, however, just as some of these have adopted voluntarily the Anglo-Celtic background, almost all of our composers have in one way or another seized upon musical elements from more exotic sources.

From Africa has come to us a subtlety in the use of percussion instruments. For African ways of performing music remain in our South and in the Caribbean, though of the African tunes, not much has survived. Even our well-known tendency toward syncopated rhythm is not African. It is the Scottish snap, straight out of bagpipes by way of hymns. Polyrhythms and multiple metrics, on the other hand, are more highly developed in Africa than here; and these we have adopted from travel and from our studies in musical ethnography.

Out of China and Japan there have come, through the West Coast, the concept of polymodality and the deep satisfactions of non-tempered intervals and non-vibrato execution. On top of our Negro-inspired love of percussion in general, there has come from our Asian contacts a devotion to small, delicate drums and to all sizes of gongs. Africa and Asia meet in America not only on the percussive level, but also in the practice of teasing a tone. The ornamental slide and the blue note, the defining of true intervals by deliberately playing or singing all round them, these are as common to our blues and jazz musicians and to our backcountry hymn-singers as they are characteristic of Korean and Japanese court music, which has so often appealed to composers of West Coast upbringing.

And now I am going to venture out on grounds less charted than those of musical syntax and picturesque additions. I want to find the connection between America's musical composition and her musical performing style. By 1910 the American orchestras, soloists, and schools had, with the help of European teachers, mastered the European performing tradition and been admitted to it. And if their work bore traces of a non-European accent, these were no source of pride. Every effort was made indeed to perform German, French, or Italian music as it was performed in the country of its origin.

On the other hand, young musicians here were passing their childhood in contact with a rich background of hymns and old songs, with the sophisticated art of ragtime piano playing, and with the powerfully burgeoning force of jazz all round them. And to top off this gamey nourishment, there had become available at the same time a method for digesting it.

This method had been found in the new French music, which was exciting to all, and in the just-discovered French pedagogy of composition, then being introduced at Harvard and at Columbia University. German teaching, based on Bach through Brahms and Wagner, had dealt almost wholly with Romantic feelings and with Romantic flexibilities in rhythm. Debussy, his immediate forebears and his French contemporaries, it could neither analyse nor perform convincingly. German teaching still posed as music's universal system; but the American musician, during World War I, punctured that pretense. The classical German composers were not dethroned, of course; but the German pedagogues were. And since French music could now be admired right along with German, and since the French tradition had always encouraged the absorption of exciting influences, it became possible for an educated American musician to incorporate into his musical vocabulary the non-canonical but deeply familiar musical ways of his own grass-roots. At this point, and we are now moving into the 1920s, an American accent in music was no longer a fault of taste; it was beginning to be a source of style.

Let us examine this American accent. The constant presence of dancing (both square dancing and round dancing), the metrical discipline of ragtime piano playing, the tendencies in our folk singing and our hymn singing toward a compulsive rhythm—all these elements have given us the habit of a steady beat and a remarkable ability in performance to sustain such a beat.

From the steady beat comes an appetite, if only to relieve monotony, for irregularly-spaced stress accents. The tension of free stress-patterns heard against a steady meter creates an energy that has been rare in music since Beethoven's death. And although this dynamism reaches its highest point in jazz, I find it also present in most of the American art music composed since 1920, no matter what may be the other stylistic sources of that music. In its last few years, even twelve-tone composition was showing here more interest in solving its rhythmic dilemma (for indeed it always had one) through the laying on of jazzy rhythms than through rhythmic serialization, which was the European way. For jazz can set off energy, and that we like; but a row of rhythms, an ordering of durations, is forever static.

Indeed I think you will find, if you listen carefully to American music as performed by American artists, that a very large part of what has been composed in the last forty years assumes the existence, whether or not this is overtly present at all times in the sound, of a steady continuity of eighth-notes, on top of which other metrical patterns, regular and irregular, lead an independent life.

And there are further extensions of the American way, none of which could exist if a steady beat were not constantly there. One is the large amount of syncopation present. And syncopation, as Bach and Haydn and Beethoven knew, cannot exist unless the beat is steady. Another is the frequence of the non-accelerating crescendo and of its opposite, the non-retarding diminuendo. European musicians have constantly remarked this prevalence in American performance. The phenomenon is virtually unknown in Europe except in pieces that imitate marching armies. But the American, unless some European musical concept interferes, inclines by instinct to keep his rhythm patterns independent of volume patterns.

Elliott Carter has devised a refinement in scoring which he calls "rhythmic modulation." This is a progressive changing of the basic time-beat by easy arithmetical relations in such a consistent way that lengthy accelerations and retards can be operated almost imperceptibly. The result is ever so striking, especially if thematic transformations govern the tempo changes.

The constant presence in American performance of a basic time-unit has created also a new approach to musical declamation. The possibility of executing with precision the varied durations of both vowels and consonants has made setting prose as easy as setting rhymed verse. It has facilitated, moreover, the use of phonetic distortion without loss of clarity. Indeed, distortion of the normal cadence is cardinal both to the creation of comic effects and to reproducing in grand opera the accents of passion. Curiously enough, the most extreme example of this new prosodic declamation is *The Rake's Progress* by Stravinsky, who would not have needed America to arrive at it. For the steady beat is also a Russian habit. And the rhythmically independent vocal line he could have constructed after examples in Debussy's *Pelléas* and in Satie's *Socrate*. But his application of these elements to the setting of English do come out surprisingly comprehensible and almost idiomatic.

The characteristics of American music that I have tried to describe will not invariably be found applicable to the music of Chadwick or Parker or MacDowell, though they do fit the music of Charles Ives. They are present in some degree, I think, in almost everything written after 1925. And they continue to be present, though minimally, in our twelve-tone music, for all its willful subservience to European Romanticism.

Romanticism in its European sense is a period that America never passed through. It is therefore an experience of which Americans bear no group memory. Just possibly the disillusion of today's youth—based in Europe on defeat in World War II, in America on defeats in Asia, and everywhere on fear of the Doomsday Machine—may be producing quite independently of historic Romanticism new patterns of violence and of emotional regression. It may also be that even under seemingly parallel pressures the ways of Europe and America are diverging. In music, I am inclined to suspect that they are. It is not to be imagined that the American characteristics I have described wholly define American music; they merely itemize a few ways in which it differs from the music of Europe. All, of course, are superficial compared to the similarities that inevitably mark the products of a common tradition.

For all their common technical tradition, however, as of right now Europe and America are working at quite separate expressive problems. The European advanced composers are seeking to create an international speech devoid of local, national, or folkloric reference. Today's new music in Europe, whether written by French, Italian, German, or other composers, and whether performed in Paris, Milan, or the Rhineland cities, is an international idiom as abstract as the coal and steel reports from Luxembourg.

That kind of music is practiced here too, though our composers practicing it seem less determined to succeed with it than their European colleagues. Even electronic music, which one might have expected our engineering-minded young to adopt early, has been taken up only in the last ten years, though it has existed in Europe since 1945. Merely to cite names will make my point, I think. Since the death of Edgard Varèse, nobody in America is writing "advanced" music at the level of Stockhausen, Boulez, or Xenakis, not to mention six to a dozen lesser stars on the European team.

What Americans are wrestling with chiefly (and the British too) is opera—trying to make our language serviceable for serious dramatico-musical expression. I cannot predict the success or failure of this enterprise. I merely point out that American music, having become by now a musical speech notably different from European, is testing its maturity on the problem that has ever been the final test of a musical idiom, namely, can you put it on the stage?

That, I think, is what American musicians are mainly set on finding out.

3

The Ives Case

AMERICA's most remarkable native contributors to our century's music, Charles Ives and Carl Ruggles, were born in New England and grew up there. Their remarkableness comes not only from strong personalities but also from the fact that almost alone among New England composers (Henry Gilbert, 1868–1928, was another exception) they never got seriously involved with teaching. Ruggles will be our subject later; for now, let us examine his more popular contemporary.

Charles Ives started life in 1874 at Danbury, Connecticut, an upland rural county seat manufacturing felt hats. He had for father a bandmaster, a Civil War veteran who trained his son's ear and hand and who exposed him at the same time to all the musical pop-art of his day—dance tunes, sentimental songs, darnfool ditties, revival hymns, and patriotic marches. Undergraduate years at Yale, with the expert instruction of Horatio Parker, turned him into a church organist and a well-based general musician. Throughout this time his student works and other youthful pieces passed for wild, and no doubt would today (*vide* the horseplay of his Variations on "America" for organ, composed at eighteen).

Ives's music life quite early went underground, for fighting public sentiment was never his pattern. As a high-school boy he had captained the baseball team; at Yale he played varsity football and was elected to a senior society. He was completely successful at being a conventionally successful American boy. He did everything right, made good marks in school and college, offended no one, though being a musician was certainly no help to his acceptance. Wishing no part of a martyr's life, he worked in a New York insurance firm, later formed his own with a partner named Myrick, married his roommate's sister, wrote a textbook for insurance salesmen, made money, retired (effectively) at fifty-three. For a few years he had played church organs, held in fact an excellent post at New York's Central Presbyterian. But he seems to have learned quite early that reputable musicians in general viewed his compositions with such disapproval that fighting for position would have merely wasted his time. So he renounced all visible connection with music and kept his work a secret occupation known only to his wife and to a few close friends. His open life was that of a businessman, conventional, respected, impregnable to scrutiny. His secret life was that of a Romantic artist—wildly experimental, ambitious, unchanneled, undisciplined, and unafraid.

His years of most abundant outpouring were those from thirty to forty, roughly 1905 to 1915, though the full mature production covers five earlier years and three later, effectively ending at forty-four, when his health broke. After 1924, when he was fifty, he wrote one song (1925) and two accompaniments (1929) to melodies by his daughter; from 1927 he went rarely to his office and in 1930 he retired completely from business. His medical diagnosis has not been published; the weakened heart and incipient diabetes sometimes referred to seem insufficient to explain a life-change so radical and one which was maintained, with progressive deterioration of the nervous system, till the age of eighty. But the fact is clear that his mighty energies and towering determination were gone before his life as a grown man was one-third over. After that he reviewed, when able, the editing of his works, subsidized their publication, blessed younger composers with bits of money, and helped also his contemporary Ruggles, whose work he admired.

Ives never actually heard during his composing years any of his major orchestral works or choral projects. The piano sonatas, violin sonatas, works of chamber music, and songs—all of which he could no doubt hum or strum—may be accepted as more or less finished. I say more or less because quite often there are aleatory passages. But the larger orchestral and choral works—the Fourth Symphony, for example, requiring three instrumental bodies and three conductors—remained at his retirement merely plans. And if they all "come off" today more than handsomely, that is due to the loving editorial hands of Lou Harrison and Henry Cowell, among others, and to the no less loving conductor's hands of Lou Harrison, of Leonard Bernstein, and of Leopold Stokowski.

For Ives's music has attracted the admiration of discerning observers—of Mahler and Webern, of Stravinsky and Schoenberg, of Aaron Copland, John Cage, Elliott Carter, and lately of the English composer-historian Wilfrid Mellers, as well as the devotion of his pianist-editor John Kirkpatrick, who has not only performed and recorded the major piano works, including the massive "Concord" Sonata, but actually catalogued every scrap of the seemingly inexhaustible Ives manuscripts. The publication of this sonata in 1919, followed in 1924 by *114 Songs* (both printed at the author's expense), marked Ives's official emergence from clandestinity and his retirement from composition. His music writing had never, of course, been entirely secret. He had occasionally shown something to a European virtuoso of the piano or violin, who would declare it hopeless; and in 1910 Gustav Mahler, then conductor of the New York Philharmonic, had proposed to play his First Symphony in Germany, a promise cancelled in 1911 by Mahler's death. But for the most part his partisans were to declare their faith far later, since access to his works and a favorable climate for admiring them were not available till after World War I.

Ives has frequently been cited by analysts for his early (so early indeed that in many cases it would seem the very first) consistent use of free dissonant counterpoint, of multiple metrics, of polychordal and polytonal harmonic textures, of percussively conceived tone-clusters and chord-clusters, and of stereophonic orchestral effects requiring several conductors. Practically all these devices, as he employed them, are describable as free, since whatever formal patterning is involved (and very often there is none) has been chosen for each expressive occasion. Ives never explored harmonic, tonal, or rhythmic simultaneities for their intrinsic complexity, as the European composers did who were to follow his example so closely in time (all unaware of him). His temporal precedence has remained therefore a historical curiosity without relation to such systematic investigations of polyharmony, polytonality, and polyrhythm as occurred in the work of Richard Strauss and Debussy, subsequently in that of Igor Stravinsky and Darius Milhaud, of Arnold Schoenberg's pupils, and of Edgard Varèse.

The popularity of Ives's music and its present wide distribution by performance and recording in America, even somewhat in Europe, are actually a response to the direct expressivity of certain works. *The Housatonic at Stockbridge*, for instance, is an impressionistic evocation, an orchestral landscape piece about a river, that even Europeans can enjoy. Longer works such as the Second (or "Concord") Piano Sonata and the Fourth Symphony, though actually structured for holding attention, are seemingly improvisational (even aleatoric) in a way that today's youth finds irresistible for effects of grandeur and chaos. And the jamborees of patriotic marches and evangelical hymns that climax *Putnam's Camp*, the Second Symphony, and many another calling forth of early memories are so deeply nostalgic for Americans that the California critic Peter Yates could sum them up as the only American music that makes him cry.

The present writer too has wept over these. He is less impressed, however, by the "Concord" Sonata, with its constant piling of Pelion on Ossa. It has been his experience that Ives's work in general, though thoroughly interesting to inspect, frequently comes out in sound less well than it looks on the page. Some of this disappointment comes from musical materials which, although intrinsically interesting for appearing to be both highly spontaneous and highly complex, seem to be only casually felt. Their extensive repetition in sequences and other structural layouts would tend to reinforce this suspicion, since real spontaneity does not repeat itself. The opening of the "Concord" Sonata is a case in point. Here is improvisational and, though busy enough, quite easy-going material that simply will not develop; it only "riffs," makes sequences. And if it gets transformed as it goes along, its successive states are as casually conceived as the first; none sticks in memory as an evolving thought.

Another sort of material, Ives's simplest, can be found in certain of the songs. These seem so aptly related to the words both by sentiment and by a naturalistic declamation (for which he had a gift) that one expects almost any of them, embellished as they so often are by an inventive accompaniment, to be a jewel. And yet they do not, will not, as we say, come off. Again there has been dilution, a casual filling-in of measures that would have needed for full intensity an unrelenting tinycraft, thought through and hand-made, such as one finds in Schubert, who was surely his model for song-writing just as Beethoven admittedly was for the larger instrumental statements. Ives's weakness is seldom in the vocal line, which is musically sensitive even when the poetry is poor, but quite regularly in the piano part, which fails to interweave, harmonically or rhythmically, with the voice. As a result it seems to be following the melody rather than providing a structure for it.

Among the rewarding songs is *Two Little Flowers*, composed in 1921 to a poem by his wife, a simple piece in the lieder style of Brahms, say, or Robert Franz. But even here the harmony can seem casual unless carried forward in performance by a rhythmic thrust.

Paracelsus, also for voice and piano, composed in 1921 to excerpts from Browning, begins with an instrumental page of the highest rhythmic and tonal complexity (actually a quotation from Ives's "Browning" Overture). According to the analysis of this work in *Charlie Ives and His Music* by Henry and Sidney Cowell, it is thematically and motivically integrated to ideas expressed in the poem. Nevertheless, the music loses impetus when the poetry begins. Though the voice declaims eloquently, the piano seems to wait for it. The free rhythms in both parts support no clear trajectory, but leave to the singer all responsibility for carrying the music forward.

This unequal and ultimately ineffectual division of labor shows up most clearly in two songs of folkloric appeal—*Charlie Rutledge* of 1914–15 (on a cowboy ballad) and *General William Booth Enters Heaven* of 1914 (out of Vachel Lindsay). The words in both have a tendency to announce the music's illustrative effects rather than to comment on them, a vaudeville routine ill-suited to serious music. To invent examples: "I hear a bird," followed by a piano trill, or "His big bass drum" (boom boom) are comic effects. Only the reverse procedure can properly evoke. *Charlie Rutledge*, moreover, is over-dramatized in the voice. A deadpan cowboy lilt against a dramatic piano-part might have turned the trick. Also, Vachel Lindsay's not entirely ingenuous apotheosis of a Salvation Army leader would surely have benefited by a bit of musical irony. With the bass-drum-like boom-booms and the triumphal hymn so frankly overt, the piece can become an embarrassing game of let's-play-revival-meeting.

Ives in his writings about music made a point of preferring "substance" to "manner." And indeed throughout his work, in spite of references to gospel hymns and village bands, of massive tone-clusters and rhythmic asymmetries, there is virtually no method of writing consistently enough employed to justify a charge of "mannerism." He moves from method to method eclectically, as great composers have always done, to bring out meaning; and his imitations of choiring voices and bands and bugle calls are as literal as he can make them. His ingenuities toward exemplifying ethical principles and transcendental concepts through thematic invention I find less rewarding from the simple fact that they seem self-conscious, lacking in spontaneity. Moreover, they are sometimes not quite first-class; the effect desired is easier to recall than the music itself.

In this sense, though there is no doctrinaire Romanticism of "form determined by content," neither is there any arriving at emotional or other fulfillment through strictly musical means, as in the classical *and* Romantic masters. By "substance" Ives means, I think, sincerity in the conception of musical pictures or ideas. He cannot mean the identity of a musical theme with what he hopes to express by means of it, for if he did the music would be stronger-knit around these ideas, whereas actually it tends to exist beside them like a gloss or commentary. When time shall have dissolved away his nostalgias and ethical aspirations, as they have largely done for Beethoven and for Bach and even for the descriptive leitmotifs of Wagner, what sheer musical reality will remain in Ives's larger works? Where will be the "substance" he wrote so eloquently about and desired so urgently? For all their breadth of concept and their gusto, I have no faith in them. Intentions are no guarantee of quality.

In remaining somewhat unimpressed by the Ives output in general—though there are certainly delicious moments and even perfect whole pieces, usually small, like the orchestral *Housatonic at Stockbridge* and *The Unanswered Question*, possibly also the third of the "Harvest Home" chorales—the present writer has no wish to underesteem the aspiration, the constancy, and the sacrifice that Ives's musical life bears witness to. Nor to undervalue a creative achievement that posterity may prize. Actually, the man presents in music, as he did in life, two faces; on one side a man of noble thoughts, a brave and original genius, on the other a homespun Yankee tinkerer. For both are there; of that one can be sure. How they got to be there need not worry us, for every artist begins in a dichotomy. But how this could remain unresolved to the very end of his creative life might be of interest to speculate about.

Every artist's worklife has its strategy; without that there is no career. And we know from his own words that Ives, in renouncing music as a chief breadwinner, did not walk out on music. When he shortly came to renounce it as even a contributory source (through church jobs) he made that renouncement in order to save his leisure. We also know that busy as he was in business hours, and soundly successful, he still produced between the ages of twenty-four and forty-four a repertory of works larger by catalog than that of most masters. Sometimes these were corrected carefully; sometimes he threw scarcely decipherable pages over his shoulder and never looked into the piles of them. It is certain that parts of works are lost, probable that whole ones also are, and possible that others may have been destroyed by intent.

But for all his haste, he was not really careless. He labored with a fury unrelenting; he also held strongly by certain of his works and cherished prejudices violently sectarian about many other composers past and present, which he stated with wit and profanity. He valued his "Concord" Sonata so highly that after it was finished he wrote a book about it. This book, called *Essays Before a Sonata*, though it was actually written after, is less an explanation of the music than a hymn of praise to the men who were the inspiration of its four movements—Emerson, Hawthorne, Thoreau, and for comic relief the Alcotts. The greatest of these, for him, was Emerson; and there his confidence was so unquestioning that clearly for Ives the Unitarian preacher-essayist had replaced revealed religion. Would that we all could thus say, "I believe!" But the fact that Ives did have this source of faith—along with insurance, of which he also wrote a book in praise—helps us to picture the years of his complete devotion to music and to business, a devotion shared only with the domestic affections—with a wife named Harmony and an adopted daughter, neither of whom caused him any trouble or took much time.

His aspiration to be a great composer would be clear from the *Essays* if it were not equally revealed on every page of his music. And a need for working abundantly to accomplish this is proved by both the voluminousness of his production and the state of his manuscripts. This need must also have led him to a plan. For a man of his ability and known powers of organization to go all self-indulgent and careless during his twenty best years, and regarding music, which was very nearly his whole private life, is not believable. It must be that he simply decided to pour forth his inspiration at all times, finishing off in clean score only such works as demanded that and leaving the rest to be copied out in his retirement years.

Retirement from composition came earlier than he had expected, and the First World War would seem to have hastened his breakdown. His Emersonian confidence in democracy through the "over-soul," and his business-based optimism derived from an idealistic view of insurance, were shaken by Europe's suddenly revealed corruption and her suicidal holocaust, which America had joined. So that when his bodily strength, after years of overstrain, collapsed in 1918, something also happened to the brain. He may have seemed to be just physically ill, but his creative life was arrested.

It is possible to imagine this arrest as an acceptable, though unplanned, consequence of the total strategy. For Ives began immediately to behave with regard to his works as if his retirement from music had been foreseen. He initiated their publication, subsidized their performance, aided young men whose devotion to them and pity for him caused them to spend untold hours on their cataloguing, editing, and promotion. Since it was clear to all, including himself, that he would not write again, his *oeuvre* came to be treated like those of the immortal dead. So confidently, in fact, that by the time of his actual death in 1954 the congress of devoted younger men which was to take care of itemization, description, biography, analysis, and praise had so far done its work that the subject of this might well have been satisfied to wind up his campaign. He had composed voluminously and without fear; later he had witnessed the well-timed issuance of his works, their performance, publication, and recording. Not the present high state of their fame, of course, but enough to show that an apotheosis had begun.

There is no reproach to such a strategy, nor much probability that the sequence of events was accidental. An artist's life is never accidental, least of all its tragic aspects. And the tragic aspect of Ives is neither his long and happy domestic existence nor his short, abundant, and successful-within-his-own-time creative life. It is the fatal scars left on virtually all his music by a divided allegiance. Business may be a less exacting mistress than the Muse, what with staffs and partners to correct your haste. But Ives's music does show the marks of haste, and also of limited reflection. Dividing himself as he did, he had to run that risk. I doubt that he knew, either young or later, how great a risk it was. For if he had, would he have dared to make the ploy for both God *and* Mammon?

I prefer to think he did not, that the transcendental optimist and all-American success boy was simply trying to have everything, and at no cost save the strenuous life. Then the darker aspects of the world, which he had avoided ever and of which his music, all health and exuberance, shows no trace, surfaced with the First World War; and they put the fear of God into him. He stopped composing, became an invalid, retired from business, and abandoned all his earnings beyond what seemed to him a competence. One view of the bottomless pit, plus a decent income justifiably retained for his family, plus care taken for his music's survival, all add up to a New England story complete with personal devil, an angry God, and a maimed production. Less maimed perhaps than that of his pedagogical contemporaries (though among those MacDowell may well survive him), but maimed nevertheless. For it is not teaching that cripples; no master has ever feared that. It is gentility; not giving one's all to art.

4

Ruggles

THERE IS NOTHING notably genteel about Carl Ruggles. He is a bohemian rather, who up to forty earned a living out of music, then found a patron on whose kindness he has lived for over fifty years, supporting also till her death a wife passionately loved and bringing up one son. He has also been for many years a landscape painter. Music he has followed from his youth without qualms about failure, poverty, disapproval, or what-will-people-say. Wiry, salty, disrespectful, and splendidly profane, he recalls the old hero of comic strips Popeye the Sailor, never doubtful of his relation to sea or soil.

A revealing story about him is the familiar one told by Henry Cowell twenty years ago. Having gone to see him in Vermont, Cowell arrived at the former schoolhouse that was Ruggles's studio and found him at the piano, playing the same chordal agglomerate over and over, as if to pound the very life out of it. After a time Cowell shouted, "What on earth are you doing to that chord? You've been playing it for at least an hour." Ruggles shouted back, "I'm giving it the test of time."

As of today, all of Ruggles's music has withstood that test, as has the man. His oldest surviving piece—a song to piano accompaniment composed in 1919—is more than fifty years old; his latest, from 1945, is twenty-five; and he himself, as I write, is ninety-four. His works have traveled in America and in Europe; and though they have not experienced the abrasions of popularity, they have been tested microscopically by the toughest analysts without any examiner finding anywhere a flaw. Excepting perhaps himself, since he has rescored some works several times before settling on their final sound and shape.

Born in 1876 of whaling folk on Cape Cod, he learned to play the violin in Boston and had lessons in the composer's craft at Harvard. Then he got experience of the orchestra in the good way, by conducting one for eleven years. That was in Minnesota. During all this learning time he wrote no music that he cared later to preserve.

There was some work done on an opera, its subject Gerhard Hauptmann's play *The Sunken Bell*; but this was never finished, Ruggles having gained through the effort a conviction that he had no talent for the stage. His earliest work that he has allowed to survive is the song called *Toys*, composed in 1919 at the age of forty-three. Over the next twenty years he produced virtually all his surviving repertory, each piece intensely compact, impeccably inspired, exactly perfect, and exactly like all the others in its method of workmanship.

This method, of which the closest model is the music that Arnold Schoenberg composed before World War I, can be classified among musical textures as non-differentiated secundal counterpoint. By non-differentiated I mean that the voices making up this counterpoint all resemble one another in both character and general shape; they are all saying the same thing and saying it in much the same way. This manner of writing music, whether practiced by Bach or by Palestrina or by Anton Webern, for all of whom it was their usual method, produces a homogeneity highly self-contained, and more picturesque than dramatic.

By secundal counterpoint I mean that the intervals present at the nodal points of the music (say roughly at the down-beats) are predominantly seconds and sevenths. This interval content distinguishes it from the music dominated by fourths and fifths (composed chiefly between the years 1200 and 1500, we call this music quintal) and from the music colored by thirds and sixths (the tertial) that followed the quintal for four centuries. Secundal writing, compared with quintal, which is rock-like, and with tertial, which is bland, produces through continuous dissonance a grainy texture that in most of Ruggles's music is homogenized, or made to blend, by the use of closely similar timbres, such as an all-string or all-brass instrumentation. And as happens in most of Bach, the music comes out polyphonic as to line but homophonic as to sound.

In spite, however, of all its homogeneity (exterior mark of its introspective nature), music like this is never quite without objective depiction. For observing this in Ruggles, the early song *Toys* is most revealing. The words, written by Ruggles himself, are:

Come here, little son, and I will play with you.
See, I have brought you lovely toys.
Painted ships,
And trains of choo-choo cars, and a wondrous balloon,
    that floats, and floats, and floats, way up to the stars.

Let us omit reference, save in passing, to the fact that the father seems to have let go of the balloon before his son could lay hands on it. Also, since stars are mentioned, that the play-hour seems to be taking place out of doors on a moonless night, a most unlikely circumstance. But these are literary quibbles.

Musically the piece, for all its steadily dissonant sound-texture, is illustrative throughout.

It begins with a gesture-like call in the pianoforte accompaniment, stated both before and after the summons, "Come here, little son, and I will play with you."

The phrase "painted ships" is accompanied by a rocking motion that leads to a splash.

The "choo-choo" mention is followed by rhythmic sounds, low in the register and accelerating, that clearly picture a steam-driven locomotive getting up speed.

And the "balloon that floats" not only does so in the piano part, which arpeggiates upward chromatically, but also in the vocal line, which leaps and leaps till on the word "stars" it reaches high B-natural and stays there.

Similarly, the piece for strings called *Lilacs*, though I doubt whether any description quite so specific is intended, is all of short rounded lines at the top and of long gangling tentacular root-like curves in the bass.

And *Portals*, another string piece, has high-jutting points to it that might be either Gothic arches or simply man's aspiration. The quiet moment at the end of an otherwise energetic work could represent man's humility on entering the high portals; but if the earlier part is not the noble gates themselves but merely the soul of man climbing toward them, then the ending must represent him arrived and sitting down to rest. The motto on the score tells us nothing so specific; it merely asks, "What are those of the known but to ascend and enter the unknown?"

Angels, for seven muted trumpets and trombones, is quietly ecstatic from beginning to end, and the angels are not individualized. They are clearly a group, a choir perhaps. I do not even know whether they are singing; they may be merely standing close together and giving off light, as in the engravings of William Blake. Whatever is happening, they are doing it or being it together, for the instruments all pause together, breathe together, start up again together, as in a hymn. Whether this close order depicts a harmony of angels or merely one man singing about them in seven real parts is not important; it could be both. But in any case, the music's sentence structure, always clear in Ruggles, is nowhere more marked than in this work, where ecstasy is communicated through a series of statements about it, each with a beginning, a middle, and a tapered ending, and all separated from one another like formal periods.

The Sun Treader and *Organum*, both scored for large orchestra rather than for a small blended ensemble, achieve homogenization of sound through the constant doubling of strings by wind instruments. And this device, so dangerous in general to the achievement of variety, is here not monotonous, but eloquent rather, as if one speaker were carrying us along on winged oratory. The Ruggles counterpoint is there too, constantly chromatic, flowing, airily spaced but also compact and dissonant, and speaking, for all its rhythmic diversity, as with a single voice. This may be the voice of the sun treader, or it may be a picture of his actions; it matters little. What matters is that the piece go on. It lasts eighteen minutes (long for Ruggles) without any let-up of intensity. *Organum* is longish too, but less choreographic, more songful. Both are full of their message, which is apocalyptic, and yet systematically, intensely self-contained.

The way that Ruggles has of making his music always come out in non-symmetrical prose sentences—a planned spontaneity, one might call it—is not really in opposition to his preoccupation with ecstasy. For that ecstasy in the expression, that unrelenting luminosity of interval and sound, is needful for producing the quality that was his over-all intent and which he calls "the sublime." Now what does he mean, what does anybody mean, by "the sublime"? I should say that this word, when applied to a work of art, can only mean that the work expresses and hence tends to provoke a state of ecstasy so free from both skin sensuality and cerebral excitement, also so uniformly sustained, that the ecstasy can be thought of as sublimated into the kind of experience known as "mystical." Ruggles, in fact, once said as much, that "in all works there should be the quality we call mysticism. All the great composers have it."

The titles of his works and their explanatory mottos mostly tend to evoke, if not a mystical experience, at least the familiar cast and décor of religious visions—*Men and Mountains, Men and Angels, The Sun Treader, Vox Clamans in Deserto, Organum,* or, quite vaguely for once, just *Evocations.* These subjects, save for the presence of angels and for a voice from the wilderness, are not nearly so close to Christian mysticism as they are to pantheism, to a spiritual identification with nature such as can be called forth in almost any New Englander by the presence of lilacs, or of mountains measurable by the size of man.

But it is not the subjects of his ecstasy that create sublimity. Many a witness has gone dizzy looking at beauty. With Ruggles it is with the need for sublimity that dizziness ends and hard work begins. For there is no sublimity without perfection; and for Ruggles there is no perfection until every singing, soaring line, every subtle rhythm and prose period, every interval and every chord has received from his own laborious hands the test of time. There must be no gigantic proportions, no ornamental figurations, no garrulous runnings-on, no dramatization, no jokes, no undue sweetness, no invoking of music's history, no folksy charm, no edifying sentiments, no erotic frictions, no cerebral cadenzas, no brilliance, no show-off, and no modesty. There is nothing in his music but perfectly flexible melodies all perfectly placed so as to sound harmonious together, and along with these a consistently dissonant interval-texture, and a subtly irregular rhythm that avoids lilt.

The auditory beauty of Ruggles's music is unique. It actually sounds better than the early Schoenberg pieces, *Verklärte Nacht* and *Erwartung,* that are perhaps its model, almost I should say its only model. It sounds better because it is more carefully made. Its layout is more airy; no pitch gets in any other's way; the rhythm is more alive; it never treads water, only sun. It is by very hard work and all alone that this perfection has been attained. And it is through perfection, moreover, the intensely functioning refinement of every musical grain and chunk, every element of shape and planning, that a high energy potential has been both produced and held in check, like a dynamo with its complex insulation. And it is this powerful energy, straining to leap a blue-white arc toward any listener, that constitutes, I think, what Ruggles means by sublimity. It is no wonder that out of a ninety-year lifetime there remain fewer than a dozen pieces. Intensities like that cannot be improvised.

Wilfrid Mellers, comparing Ruggles to Arnold Schoenberg, has written in his book of praise to America, *Music in a New Found Land*, that "both were amateur painters who, in their visual work, sought the expressionistic moment of vision. Both, in their music still more than in their painting, found that the disintegrated fragments of the psyche could be reintegrated only by a mystical act. Schoenberg, as a Viennese Jew, had an ancient religion and the spirit of Beethoven to help him; Ruggles had only the American wilderness and the austerities of Puritan New England. For this reason he sought freedom— from tonal bondage, from the harmonic straight-jacket, from conventionalized repetitions, from anything that sullied the immediacy and purity of existence—even more remorselessly than Schoenberg."

Ruggles's dilemma, of course, has been the perpetual dilemma of American composers. On one side lie genius and inspiration, on the other an almost complete lack of usable history. We have access to the European masters, to Bach and Mozart and Beethoven and Debussy, but only through their music; we cannot remember them nor reconstruct what they were thinking about; and what we *can* remember, through our documents and our forebears, is so different from anything Europe knows or ever knew that both to the European listener and to the American, naïf or learned, every inspiration is a scandal. A Frenchman or an Austrian of gifts can be fitted early into his country's immortality machine—nurtured, warmed for ripening, brought to market. An American of talent is from the beginning discouraged (or over-encouraged), bullied by family-life and by school-teachers, overworked, undertrained, sterilized by isolation or, worse, taken over by publicity, by the celebrity machine.

American composers have tried several solutions. One has been to fake a history; that is to say, to adopt some accepted European method of working and to hide behind it so effectively that the ignorant are impressed and the intellectuals immobilized. Horatio Parker, Edward MacDowell, and Walter Piston did this. And their inspiration, discolored by its own shield, lost personality and some of its meaning; but these men did write music of distinction that has not died.

Another way of facing the awful truth is to face it squarely—to discard the concept of distinction, to use any and all materials that come to hand and to use them in any context whatsoever. Walt Whitman did this in poetry, Charles Ives in music, also Henry Cowell in his early years. And though they mostly could not make their art support them, they produced in quantity and their inspirations were not deformed. By sacrificing the ideals of perfection and distinction, as well as all hope of professional encouragement—Ives actually for twenty years hiding away (and wisely, I think) from the danger of professional persecution—they achieved in their work an enormous authenticity.

Ruggles faced the dilemma in still another way, which was to slowly construct for himself a method for testing the strengths of musical materials and a system of building with them so complex, so at every point aware of tensile strengths and weaknesses, that by this seemingly neutral application of psychological and acoustic laws, works were constructed that are not only highly personal in content but that seem capable of resisting wear and time. Poe is a somewhat parallel case in letters. In music Elliott Carter is surely one. And in all three cases—Ruggles, Carter, and Poe—not only has authentic inspiration survived, but beauty and distinction have not been sacrificed. Such artists may wear their integrity like a chip on the shoulder, but it is real. Ambition, "that last infirmity," though it may torment their sleep, has been kept from their work. With Ruggles and Carter the output has been small; but no compromise has taken place, nor has any hindrance occurred to the artist's full ripening.

Good music, reputable and palatable, has been composed in all three of the circumstances I describe—by copying Europe, by working without rule, or by constructing a method—and I fancy that all three ways for getting around the American dilemma will continue to be used. For there is still no "spirit of Beethoven" here, either walking beside you down the street as he does in Vienna, or buried nearby in any of our graveyards. It will be some time before one of our young musicians, feeling the call to speak to man of God, to God of man, or of man to men, will find his feelings channeled by understanding or his consecration accepted. Everything is set here to educate him, to brainwash him, and to reward him with success; nothing is prepared to help him become a great man, to carry out his inspiration, or to fulfill his blessedness.

For inspiration, as we can learn from all great work, comes only out of self-containment. And style, that touchstone of authenticity, comes only from authentic inspiration. What is style? Carrying-power, I say; nothing more. At least, carrying-power is style's direct result. From carrying-power come distinction and fame, recognition while one is still alive. And from them all—from inspiration, style, and distinction, provided the inspiration be authentic, the carrying-power through style very strong, and the distinction of personality visible to all—from all these comes immortality.

Now both Ives and Ruggles have through their music achieved a modicum of that. To Ives has come also, of late, popularity. The music of Ruggles, far more recondite, is also more intensely conceived and more splendidly perfected. Ives belongs (though he is grander, of course) with the homely tinkerers like the eighteenth-century tanner William Billings, and also with the roughneck poets of his own time Carl Sandburg and Vachel Lindsay. But for all of Ives's rude monumentality and his fine careless raptures—welcome indeed in a country vowed to a freedom that its artists have rarely practiced—he falls short, I think, of Whitman's total commitment, as he does also of Emerson's high ethical integrity. Ruggles, judged by any of these criteria, comes out first-class. Europe, where he has been played more than here, has never caviled at such an estimate; nor has his music, under use or after analysis, revealed any major flaw. Standing up as it does to contemporary tests, including public indifference, how can one doubt that it will also stand the test of time?

5
Varèse

FROM 1914 TO 1918 music shone in Europe with a dim light, so low indeed that with most theatres and concert halls shut down, orchestras surviving on a precarious personnel, publication largely arrested, and patronage diverted to war works, young composers with careers to make (once exempt from military duties) looked longingly toward life in the Americas. Thus it came about that in 1916 New York fell heir to the French-trained Swiss Ernest Bloch, to the French harpist-composer Carlos Salzedo (though he had served earlier at the Metropolitan Opera), and to the Italo-Burgundian, schooled in Paris and Berlin, Edgard Varèse. It was shortly too that Carl Ruggles, who in 1917 had lost his Minnesota orchestra through the internment of all his German-citizen players, arrived in the metropolis, teaming up a few years later with Salzedo and Varèse for giving concerts of advanced music. The International Composers' Guild, which they formed in 1921, lasted till 1927, when it was supplanted by a rival group, The League of Composers. Meanwhile in 1922 Varèse had already formed a similar society in Berlin with the aid of his friend and teacher Feruccio Busoni, along with affiliated groups in Moscow through Arthur Lourié, and in Italy through Alfredo Casella.

Born 1883 in Paris, faubourg du Temple, child of a North-Italian engineer and a Burgundian peasant mother, Varèse passed his first two decades at Le Villars in the Maconais with his maternal grandfather, with whom he was happy, and in Turin with his father, who discouraged his musical tastes. Lessons in harmony and counterpoint were nevertheless at last allowed from Giovanni Bolzoni, director of the Turin Conservatoire, and orchestral experience acquired at the opera house there by playing in the percussion section.

By twenty Varèse had scotched all plans for making an engineer of him (though a taste for science was to dominate his life and music) and got himself off to Paris for further training. This took place for two years at the Schola Cantorum (under Vincent d'Indy and Albert Roussel), where he resisted preformulated methods of composing but where he acquired nevertheless a skill in counterpoint and a delight in all the music that had preceded Bach. He supported himself at this time as a musical copyist and librarian's assistant. Moving to the Conservatoire National as a student of Charles-Marie Widor, he attracted also the favorable notice of Jules Massenet; and these strong patrons procured for him two years later a municipal award of money, the *Première Bourse artistique de la ville de Paris*. In the meantime, and very early, he had formed friendships among the avant-garde—with Pablo Picasso, Sar Péladan, Max Jacob, Erik Satie, Amadeo Modigliani, and Guillaume Apollinaire. He knew Lenin too; he had founded a people's chorus; and he was planning an orchestral work of vast scope for one hundred twenty players. At twenty-five, in 1908, he met Debussy. He also moved in that year to Berlin, where he came to know Busoni, Richard Strauss, Gustav Mahler, the conductor Karl Muck, the writers Hugo von Hofmannsthal and Romain Rolland. He also founded a *Symphonischer Chor*, and he collaborated in two productions with Max Reinhardt. To Debussy in Paris he mailed as a gift Schoenberg's *Fünf Orchesterstücke*.

From his beginnings Varèse had enjoyed support from the high placed as well as among the musically advanced. At twenty-seven, in 1910, his orchestral work *Bourgogne* was performed in Berlin through the influence of Richard Strauss by the Blüthner Orchestra under Josef Stransky. Varèse said later of its effect on both press and public: "I became a sort of diabolical Parsifal on a Quest, not for the Holy Grail, but for the bomb that would explode the musical world and allow all sounds to come rushing into it through the resulting breach, sounds which at that time—and sometimes still today—were called noises."

By the time he returned to Paris in 1913 Varèse had formulated clearly his yearning after a music in which pitches would not be bound to the tempered scale nor harmony to any thoroughbass. If Schoenberg had already, as it was said, "freed the dissonance" from harmonic control, Varèse was for the rest of his life to labor at "freeing sound" from any control at all save that of the conscious designer. He did not hold, however, with *The Art of Noise*, celebrated manifesto by the Italian Futurist Luigi Russolo. "Why," he asked, "do you merely reproduce the vibrations of our daily life only in their superficial and distressing aspects?" And he was later to denounce the twelve-tone method of Schoenberg and his pupils as a "doctrinaire" or "establishment-type" modernism.

In 1914 he conducted concerts in Prague that included Debussy's *Le Martyre de Saint Sébastien*. In 1915 he introduced Jean Cocteau to Picasso, was mobilized for war, received a medical discharge, and left for the United States, arriving in New York on the 15th December. All his music had in the meantime disappeared, part of it lost in a Berlin fire, the rest abandoned in Paris. In America he knew only Karl Muck, conductor of the Boston Symphony Orchestra; his fortune amounted to ninety dollars.

As before, he copied music; and as before, he conducted orchestras and choruses. In 1917, with America mobilizing for war, he led a mammoth performance of the Berlioz "Requiem" Mass at New York's Hippodrome. In 1918 he gave concerts in Cincinnati. In that year too he married Louise Norton, poet and translator of French poetry. And he met Carlos Salzedo. The next year he organized the New Symphony Orchestra, of which the first concert received such abuse in the press that his conductorship was dropped in favor of Arthur Bodansky. In 1919 he also began, at thirty-six, a wholly new composer's life. It was as if all Europe, its history and its training and its valued friendships among both classical and modernistic artists, were merely a prelude to America. His first piece composed in the new and now definitive residence he called, in the plural, *Amériques*, meaning, in both the historical and the personal sense, discoveries. Completed in 1921, this work for huge orchestral forces was not heard till 1926, when Leopold Stokowski conducted it in Philadelphia.

Meanwhile, with Salzedo he had organized the International Composers' Guild and begun giving concerts. They played the new Europeans, naturally, but also Ruggles and Ives and Henry Cowell and Dane Rudhyar. And Varèse, with his new-found freedom and his Burgundian's insistence, continued to produce music that for all its authenticity and its novelty in a time which sought out both, never failed to shock. In 1921 he produced *Offrandes*, for voice with orchestra; in 1924 *Octandre*. In 1923 his *Hyperprism* set off New York's first European-sized *scandale*, the next year a similar one in London, where Eugene Goossens gave it for the B.B.C. In 1925 Stokowski conducted *Intégrales* in New York and in 1927 *Arcana*, the second of Varèse's American works for huge orchestra.

Beginning in 1928 Edgard and his wife Louise lived for five years in Paris, where in 1931 he wrote *Ionization*, his first work (and possibly anyone's in the West) composed for an orchestra of percussion instruments. This work, not given till two years later in New York, was the only product of his sojourn in France. Actually, except for a handful of musical friendships revived, his stay there was more remarkable for its literary and visual-arts associations than for musical successes, though most of his earlier works (excepting *Ionization* and *Hyperprism* but including the massive *Arcana* and *Amériques*) were performed in Paris during that time. The American conductor Nicholas Slonimsky was particularly zealous in his favor; and the Paris musician-critics—Florent Schmitt, Paul Le Flem, Emile Vuillermoz, Fred Goldbeck, and Boris de Schloezer—were deeply impressed by his music. But the neoclassical group led by Honegger and Milhaud, backed up by Stravinsky and Jean Cocteau, withheld their support. One composer-pupil, André Jolivet, seems to have been his entire French harvest of direct influence.

Among the visual artists Varèse was always welcome. Sculptors in particular—Giacometti, Zadkine, Calder, Marcel Duchamp—approved his broad aesthetic vistas, as did the painters Paule Thévenin, Amédée Ozenfant, Diego Rivera, and Joan Miró. His metaphysical horizons at this time were dominated by the sixteenth-century alchemist-physician Paracelsus, whose astro-mathematical speculations had also stimulated Charles Ives. As early as 1928 Varèse had presented to the Cuban Alejo Carpentier and to the French poet Robert Desnos, a libretto theme to be entitled *L'Astronome*; and a year later the novelist Jean Giono was at work on *Espace*, another Varèse idea. *L'Astronome*, incomplete, was next offered in 1932 or '33, to Antonin Artaud, who never really worked on it. Nor indeed was it ever to bear music. *Espace* likewise failed of completion, though an *étude* for *Espace* (for choir, two pianos, and percussion) was performed in New York, 1947. *Ecuatorial*, another work of large poetic horizons, did, however, come out of this Paris time, to be completed in New York and presented there in 1934. The text was a Spanish version by the Guatemalan poet Miguel Angel Asturias of a Mayan incantation "vast and noble," according to Varèse's biographer Fernand Ouellette, "which rolls forth in the same accents as David's Psalms." He also compares the work to Satie's *Socrate* for its musical austerity and starkness. The scoring is for a choir of bass voices, with trumpets, trombones, piano, organ, percussion, and two *ondes Martenot* (an electronic instrument).

Though preoccupied by electronics, of which the musical possibilities had been little developed, Varèse wrote one more work for a classical instrument, the flute solo of 1936 *Density 21.5*. This much admired short piece he composed for Georges Barrère's platinum instrument; and its title identifies that metal, though this is now listed in the scientific tables, I believe, as of density 21.45. In 1941 he wrote to Professor Léon Théremine: "I no longer wish to compose for the old instruments played by men, and I am handicapped by a lack of adequate electrical instruments for which I conceive my music." He did not write any music, in fact, between 1936 and 1950, when he began *Déserts* (to be finished in 1954) for orchestra and two tracks of "organized sounds" on magnetic tape, the latter indicated as not indispensable to a performance.

One does not know whether Varèse's long silence was due to his having worked out the precious vein of composition opened in 1919 but by 1934 virtually exhausted, to ill health, which he did suffer somewhat in his middle years, to an emotional depression which throughout the 1930s and the time of World War II had certainly produced in his mind black thoughts and a tragic view of life, or to a need for electronic instruments not yet perfected. A lack of public acceptance for his work may also have contributed. The League of Composers, for example, gave him no support in New York, viewing him perhaps as a rival from the days of the International Composers' Guild. But Varèse was not one to be stopped in his tracks, especially in view of the high regard in which his work was held by musicians of radical stripe. The fact remains, however, that he did cease to compose and even to seek performances, save for bringing out in 1947 the studies for *Espace*. As early as 1932 he had requested from the Bell Telephone Laboratories a niche for sharing acoustical experiments, and financial aid from the Guggenheim Foundation for continuing them. He was not successful.

When *Déserts* was completed in Paris and performed there in 1954 Varèse was already seventy-one. The next year he composed a tape, *The Procession at Vergès*, for inclusion in the Thomas Bouchard film *Around and About Joan Miró*. In 1958 he composed an independent tape work, *Le Poème électronique*, involving two hundred forty small speakers arranged for spacial travelings of sound on the ceiling of Le Corbusier's pavilion at the Brussels International and Universal Exposition, built for the fair by the Philips electrical enterprises and destroyed shortly afterwards. The fact that during the performances cinematic images were projected on the tent-like ceiling does not mean, as many visitors thought, that there was a relation of any kind between the film and the music beyond their beginning and ending together. Actually neither Le Corbusier nor Varèse knew in advance what the other had prepared. Two vocal works engaged his last years—*Nocturnal* (for soprano, choir, and orchestra, 1961) on a text from Anaïs Nin's *The House of Incest*, and the unfinished *Nuit*, also on a text from the same book. He died in 1965 at eighty-two.

Varèse's music leans toward mystico-poetic and mystico-mathematical titles. Never did he explain its relation to these, but certainly they corresponded to some thought or region of thought by which he was inspired. The music itself, moreover, is resistant to analysis, even when there is a verbal text. Such resistance, especially in the early decades of a composition's life, is a mark of quality. Further, Varèse himself was a musician of classical training and he enjoyed many sophisticated friendships, musical and artistic. There is no possibility of taking him for a *naïf* or for a primitive, though there is every reason to recognize in him an extreme romantic spirit, tempestuous, determined, and demonic. That spirit worked for the most part as it had been trained to work, through classical instruments and toward a personalized expressivity. His structural and syntactic freedoms were those of a European who had known both Satie and Debussy, as well as Busoni's acoustical speculations, and who started out in America at thirty-three with the principal works of these masters already behind him.

Debussy's concept of the chord as an acoustical agglomerate expressive in itself but leading nowhere, and of melody as an eclectic choice of pitches bound only to expression, with rhythm, counterpoint, and instrumental investiture serving also the expression, while form, which serves them all, remains nevertheless so free that it can be invented for each piece—all this remains as basic to the music of Varèse as it is to that of Debussy. Where it reaches beyond Debussy is in treating complexes of orchestral sound with the independence that Debussy reserved for the chord. Varèse builds directly with orchestral colors and orchestral agglomerates, diminishing the roles of harmony and melody to a minimum, and developing counterpoint through the super-position and interpenetration of these sound-blocks, rhythm aiding the acoustical clarity by means of a sizable percussion group constantly counterposed, even in chamber-sized ensembles, to the tonal instruments.

The result is very different in sound from the music of Debussy, which is static (like painting or like frieze-sculpture). In Debussy one thing happens at a time, as when an artist draws, until all the needed strokes are there, at which point the piece is finished. With Varèse several things are going on, each moved by its own rhythmic dynamism and all together making a complex of sonorities so rich and so active that one does not dare define it as mere noise; and yet it is not exactly music either. Not at least in the standard sense of pitch-patterns tuned to a common fundamental. Free it is, as French music ever is when at its best, eloquent with the raucous voice of the great Romantics, and wholly thought out, thought through, conceived after no image save its author's sensibility, and entirely indited by hand. It sells no method, cures no ill, refuses truck with all establishments. For sure it is the child of Claude Debussy.

"Music in the pure state," it has been called, and "tornadoes of sonorities." Also "a nightmare dreamed by giants." For even the smallest of his chamber-groupings manages somehow to turn on a great racket, especially when electric sirens become involved. Curiously, no sonic boom, no over-charged loudspeaker is allowed to mar the electronic works. *Le Poème électronique* is for the larger part of its time miraculously delicate, a chamber piece of ravishing quietness, and though played on that most blatant of all sound-sources, an ensemble of loudspeakers (thankfully each one tiny), a work of rare delicacy. One wishes Varèse could have lived to make more like it, for all the opposition of the Philips Company, which Le Corbusier fought off for him, and for all the complexities of almost microscopic wiring that it took two months for the engineers to bring into tune and timing.

Varèse in his later years was the recipient of many honors and awards, including membership in the Swedish Academy, a "Nobel Prize," his friends said, "without the money." On the occasion of his death a tribute by the present writer was pronounced before the American Academy of Arts and Letters, of which he had been also a member. The conclusion of that tribute reads as follows:

From *Amériques* of 1919 to the *Poème électronique* of 1957 he worked with timbre alone, with kinds of sound, great chunks of them, organizing these into a polyphony comparable perhaps to the intersecting polyhedrons that are the shapes of modern architecture. Nevertheless, these pieces are not static like a building, nor even like the music of Debussy; they move forward, airborne. What moves them forward? Rhythms, I think, rhythms counterpointed to create tension and release energy. There are also, in the timbre contrasts and the loudness patterns, designs for producing anxiety and relief, just as there are in tonal music. And these designs create psychological form, though the music is not overtly planned for drama.

It seems to hang together not from themes and their restatements but from tiny cells or motives which agglomerate like crystals. As Varèse himself described this phenomenon, "In spite of their limited variety of internal structure, the external forms of crystals are almost limitless." To have produced with so cool a concept of artistic creation music of such warm sonorous interest and such urgent continuity makes of Varèse, and I think there is no way round this, the most original composer of the last half-century and one of the most powerfully communicative.

6

Aaron Copland

JULIA SMITH'S BOOK on Aaron Copland refers to him on its first page as "this simple and great man in our midst." And indeed from his youth Copland has so appeared. Having known him as friend and colleague for nigh on to fifty years, I too can attest that his demeanor is sober, cheerful, considerate, his approach direct and at the same time tactful. I have never seen him lose his temper or explode. His physical appearance has not radically changed since 1921; nor have the loose-hung suits and unpressed neckties, the abstemious habits and seemly ways which by their very simplicity add up to a princely grace.

Considering the irritability of most musicians, Copland's diplomat-façade might well be thought to conceal a host of plots and poutings, were it not so obviously his nature to be good-humored and an ancient principle with him not to quarrel. When he came home from Paris at twenty-four, his study time with Nadia Boulanger completed, and began to be a successful young composer, it is said that he determined then to make no unnecessary enemies. It is as if he could see already coming into existence an organized body of modernistic American composers with himself at the head of it, taking over the art and leading it by easy stages to higher ground, with himself still at the head of it, long its unquestioned leader, later its president emeritus.

This consecrated professionalism was Copland's first gift to American music; it had not been there before. Varèse and Ruggles, though consecrated artists, showed only a selective solidarity with their colleagues. Ives had been a drop-out from professionalism altogether. And the earlier professionals, the lot of them, had all been individual operators. Copland was the very first, I think, to view his contemporaries as a sort of peace corps whose assignment in history was to pacify the warring tribes and to create in this still primitive wilderness an up-to-date American music.

His first move in that direction in 1924 was to take over de facto the direction of the League of Composers. This gave him a New York power enclave; and his classes at the New School for Social Research, held from 1927 to 1937, were soon to give him a forum. He also wrote in magazines, listing about every three years the available modernistic young and offering them his blessing. Also from the beginning, he had established a Boston beachhead, where the new conductor Serge Koussevitzky, taking over from Walter Damrosch Copland's Symphony for Organ and Orchestra, 1925, thereafter performed a new work by him every year till well into the 1930s.

Copland had in New York from 1928 to 1931, in addition to his access to the League of Composers, his own contemporary series, shared with Roger Sessions and called the Copland-Sessions Concerts. At these he played both American and European new works, attracted attention, distributed patronage, informed the public. His collaboration with Sessions, the first in a series of similar teamings-up, marks a second stage of his organizational work. Having by that time solidified his own position, he could enlarge his American music project by calling on, one after another, personalities comparable to his own for weight and influence.

After the Sessions concerts ended in 1931, Copland shared briefly with Roy Harris, just returned then from his studies with Boulanger, an influence centered chiefly in Boston, where Koussevitzky was launching Harris with the same steadfast persistence he had used for Copland. A close association with Walter Piston began in 1935, when Copland took over for a year the latter's composition class at Harvard. In 1937 with Marc Blitzstein, Lehman Engel, and myself, the four of us founded the Arrow Music Press, a cooperative publishing facility, and with several dozen others the American Composers Alliance, a society for licensing the performance of "serious" music, a need at that time not being met by existing societies.

During the mid-1930s there were five composers—Copland, Sessions, Harris, Piston, and myself—whom Copland viewed as the strongest of his generation both as creators and as allies for combat. And all were to serve under his leadership as a sort of commando unit for penetrating one after another the reactionary strongholds. Their public acknowledgment as co-leaders of American music took place in 1935 at the New School through five concerts, one devoted to each composer's work, all presented as Copland's choice for contemporary excellence in America.

Two foreign composers—Carlos Chavez, during the 1930s conductor of the Orquesta Sinfónica de México and an official of the Fine Arts Ministry, and Benjamin Britten, England's most accomplished composer since Elgar—were to benefit from Copland's friendship, as he from theirs. But his American general staff did not participate in these alliances. Nor have they shared in Copland's influence over our two remarkable composer-conductors Leonard Bernstein and Lukas Foss, though as recognized composers they have all been played by these leaders. In general Copland's foreign affairs and post-war domestic alliances, as well as his worldwide conducting tours of the 1960s, seem more specifically aimed at broadening the distribution of his own music than at sharing the wealth. And this no doubt because his commando comrades had all become successful independently, while the post-war young, having placed their hopes in a newer kind of music (Elliott Carter, Boulez, Cage, the complexity gambit, and the serial-to-noise-to-electronics gambit), have not been able to muster up the personal loyalties needed for calling on his organizational experience.

I have dwelt on Copland as a colleague, a career man, and a mobilizer, because I consider his contribution in those domains to be no less remarkable than that of his music. This music has been analyzed in books by Julia Smith and by Arthur Berger. All its major items are in print and most are recorded. It comprises piano music, chamber works, orchestral works, and ballets, all of high personal flavor and expert workmanship. Less striking, I think, are the vocal works—consisting of two operas, several sets of songs, an oratorio, and a handful of short choral pieces. Among these the choral works are possibly the happiest, because of their animated rhythmic vein. And five Hollywood films made under first-class directors (three, I think, were by Lewis Milestone) on first-class themes (two from John Steinbeck, one from Thornton Wilder, one from Lillian Hellman, one from Henry James) are imaginative and distinguished in their use of music.

Julia Smith has discerned three stylistic periods in Copland's work. His first period, from age twenty-four (in 1924) to age twenty-nine, includes but one non-programmatic, non-local-color work, the Symphony for Organ and Orchestra, composed for Nadia Boulanger to play in America. I found this work at that time deeply moving, even to tears, for its way of saying things profoundly of our generation. The rest of that production time—*Music for the Theatre*, the Concerto for Piano and Orchestra, the necrophiliac ballet *Grogh*, the *Symphonic Ode*, the trio *Vitebsk* (study on a Jewish theme), and divers smaller pieces—is largely preoccupied with evocation, as in *Grogh* and *Vitebsk*, or with superficial Americana, characterized by the rhythmic displacements that many in those days took for "jazz" but that were actually, as in George Gershwin's vastly successful *Rhapsody in Blue*, less a derivate from communal improvising, which real jazz is, than from commercial popular music. No wonder the effort to compose concert jazz came to be abandoned, by Copland and by others.

Its last appearance in Copland's work is in the otherwise nobly rhetorical *Symphonic Ode* of 1929, which led directly into the Piano Variations, high point of his second period, which in turn initiated a series of non-programmatic works that was to continue for the rest of his productive life. The *Vitebsk* trio, in spite of its allusions to Jewish cantilation, can on account of its tight musical structure be listed, I think, among Copland's abstract works. And so can the orchestral *Statements* of 1933–34, so firmly structured are these mood pictures. Of more strictly musical stock are the Short Symphony of 1932–33, later transcribed as a Sextet for Piano, Clarinet, and Strings, the Piano Sonata (1941), the Sonata for Violin and Piano (1943), the Piano Quartet (1950), the Piano Fantasy, and the Nonet for Strings (these last from the 1960s). One could include perhaps the Third Symphony (1946) on grounds of solid form, but I tend to consider it, on account of its incorporation of a resplendent *Fanfare for the Common Man* (from 1942), one of Copland's patriotic works, along with *A Canticle of Freedom* and the popular *A Lincoln Portrait*.

The initiation of a third period, or kind of writing, followed that of the second by less than five years; and it too has continued throughout his life. This embodied his wish to enjoy large audiences not specifically musical, and for that purpose it was necessary to speak simply. Its major triumphs are three ballets—*Billy the Kid* (1938), *Rodeo* (1942), and *Appalachian*

Spring (1944)—all of them solid repertory pieces impeccable in their uses of Americana and vigorous for dancing.

Actually the dance has always been for Copland a major inspiration, largely as an excitement of conflicting rhythms, contrasted with slow incantations virtually motionless. As early as 1925 the unproduced ballet *Grogh* had been transformed into the prize-winning *Dance Symphony*. And his jazz experiments of the later 1920s were closer to dancing than to blues. In 1934 he composed for Ruth Page and the Chicago Grand Opera Company a ballet, or dance drama, entitled *Hear Ye! Hear Ye!*, satirizing a murder trial and based largely on night-club music styles. It was not a success, and with it Copland said good-by to corrupt musical sources, as well as to all attempts at being funny.

Actually his return to ballet and his entry into other forms of show business had been somewhat prepared that same year by the production on Broadway of my opera *Four Saints in Three Acts*. Its willful harmonic simplicities and elaborately-fitted-to-the-text vocal line had excited him; and he had exclaimed then, "I didn't know one could write an opera." He was to write one himself with Edwin Denby three years later, *The Second Hurricane*, designed for high-school use. But my opera had set off trains of powder in both our lives. In 1936 it led me into composing a symphonic background for *The Plow That Broke the Plains*, a documentary film by Pare Lorentz, in which I employed cowboy songs, war ditties, and other folk-style tunes. Again the effect on Copland was electric; as a self-conscious modernist, he had not thought that one could do that either. Shortly after this, Lincoln Kirstein proposed to commission from Copland a work for his Ballet Caravan (the parent troupe of today's New York City Ballet), an offer which Copland declined, no doubt still unsure of himself after the failure of *Hear Ye! Hear Ye!* I, on the other hand, with a brasher bravery, did accept such a commission and produced in 1937 *Filling Station*, another work based on Americana.

At this point Copland reversed his renunciation and returned to his earliest love, the dance, this time by my way of cowboy songs, producing in 1938 for Ballet Caravan *Billy the Kid*, a masterpiece of a dance score and a masterpiece of novel choreographic genre, the ballet "Western." Copland's *Rodeo*, of 1942, made for Agnes de Mille and the Ballet Russe de Monte Carlo, is another "Western." And *Appalachian Spring* (for Martha Graham, 1944) is a pastoral about nineteenth-century Shakers. All make much of Americana, the hymn lore of the latter piece having as its direct source my uses of old Southern material of that same kind in *The River*, of 1937, another documentary film by Pare Lorentz.

If I seem to make needless point of my influence on Copland, it is less from vanity than for explaining his spectacular invasion, at thirty-eight, of ballet and films, and less successfully of the opera. His love for the dance was no doubt inborn, and an acquaintance with the theatre had been developed through long friendship with the stage director Harold Clurman. But his previous ballet experiments had come to naught, and his essays in writing incidental music for plays had not led him toward many discoveries. He yearned, however, for a large public; the social-service ideals of the 1930s and the musical successes of Dmitri Shostakovich having created in him a strong desire to break away from the over-intellectualized and constricting modernism of his Paris training. To do this without loss of intellectual status was of course the problem. Stravinsky's neoclassical turn toward conservatism, initiated in 1918, had offered guidance to the postwar School of Paris and to all those still-young Americans, by the 1930s quite numerous and influential, who through Nadia Boulanger had come under its power.

But they had all preserved a correct façade of dissonance; and this surfacing, applied to every species of contemporary music, was making for monotony and for inflexibility in theatre situations. The time was over when composers—Debussy, for instance, Alban Berg, Richard Strauss—could comb literature for themes suited to their particular powers. On the contrary, themes appropriate to a time of social protest and of trade-union triumphs seemed just then far more urgent, especially to Copland, surrounded as he was by left-wing enthusiasts. He wanted populist themes and populist materials and a music style capable of stating these vividly. My music offered one approach to simplification; and my employment of folk-style tunes was, as Copland was to write me later about *The River*, "a lesson in how to treat Americana."

A simplified harmonic palette was being experimented with

everywhere, of course; and a music "of the people," clearly an ideal of the time, was one that seemed far nobler then than the country-club-oriented so-called "jazz" that many had dallied with in the 1920s. And thus it happened that my vocabulary was, in the main, the language Copland adopted and refined for his ballet *Billy the Kid* and for his first film, *Of Mice and Men*. The German operas of Kurt Weill, which were known to him, performed no such service, though they were all-important to Marc Blitzstein, whose *The Cradle Will Rock* was produced in 1937. Shostakovitch's rising career and some Russian film music may have also been in Copland's mind. But his break-through into successful ballet composition, into expressive film-scoring, and into, for both, the most distinguished populist music style yet created in America did follow in every case very shortly after my experiments in those directions. We were closely associated at the time and discussed these matters at length.

Copland's high-school opera *The Second Hurricane* (to a text by Edwin Denby), produced in 1937, followed Blitzstein's lead into a city-style harmonic simplicity, rather than to my country-style one. It contains delicious verse and a dozen lovely tunes, but it has never traveled far. Nearly twenty years later he wrote another opera, *The Tender Land*, again a pastoral involving Americana-style songs and dances; but that also failed in spite of resonant choruses and vigorous dance passages. When he moved from ballet to films (*Of Mice and Men*, 1939; *Our Town*, 1940) he carried with him no such baggage of vocal ineptitude; nor was he obliged to use the dance for animation. His powers of landscape evocation in pastoral vein and his slow, static, nearly motionless suspense-like moods were useful for psychological spell-casting; and a struggle-type counterpoint, suggestive of medieval organum with rhythmic displacements—taken over from his non-programmatic works—gives dramatic intensity, as in the boy-fights-eagle passage toward the end of *The Red Pony*. For a man so theatre-conscious and so gifted both for lyrical expansion and for objective depiction to be so clearly out of his water on the lyric stage is surprising. The choral passages in his operas are the happiest, for in these he can mobilize four parts or more to produce the same polyrhythmic excitements that are the essence of his dance works, as indeed they often are of his abstract, or "absolute," music. But for vocal solos and

recitatives none of that is appropriate; and his dramatic movement tends in consequence to lose impetus, to stop in its tracks.
There is no grave fault in his prosodic declamation, which is on
the whole clear, though here and there, as in the Emily Dickinson songs, the solo line may be a little jumpy and the vocal
ranges strained. His melody in general, however, his harmony,
and his musical form are those of a master. What is wrong? My
answer is that just as with Stravinsky, also by nature a dance man
muscle-oriented, and even with Beethoven, whose work is so
powerfully rhythmicized, the vocal writing, however interesting
intrinsically, neglects to support the play's dramatic line.

A strange and urgent matter is this line. And its pacing in spoken plays is not identical with the pacing required for a musical
version of the same play. Mozart, with his inborn sense of the
theatre is virtually infallible on a stage; and so is Wagner, even
when in *Das Rheingold* and in *Parsifal* the dramatico-musical
thread may unwind so slowly that it seems almost about to
break. But it never does break, and as a result each act or separate scene develops as one continuous open-ended form. Composers whose music requires rhythmic exactitudes work better
with the dance or in the closed concert forms. Composers conditioned to producing mood units also tend to be ill at ease
about dramatic progress and to treat the story as a series of moments for static contemplation, like Stations of the Cross. On
the other hand, operas constructed as a sequence of "numbers"
(Mozart to Gershwin) do not of necessity lack dramatic animation. Even the musical dramas of Monteverdi, the *opere serie* of
Handel and Rameau and Gluck, can move forward as drama
through their closed-form *arie* da capo and their oratorio-
style choruses. I suspect it is their naturalistic recitatives that
carry them from set-piece to set-piece toward a finale where a
priest in full robes or some deus ex machina, in any case a bass
voice singing *not* in da capo form, releases the dénouement.

The basic need of any ballet or film score is an appropriate
accompaniment for the dance narrative, for the photographed
landscape, or for the mimed action. Opera demands of music
a more controlling rein, for its function there is not to accompany a dramatic action but to *animate* it—to pace it, drive it,
wrestle with it, and in the end to dominate. For that Copland
lacks the continuing dynamism. His schooling in the concert

forms (in the sonata with Rubin Goldmark, in the variation with Boulanger), the rhythmic and percussive nature of his musical thought, its instrumental predominance, the intervalic viscosity of his textures—all of motionless fourths and seconds, as in medieval organum, plus tenths, so beautiful when finally heard but so slow to register—have created a musical vocabulary strong, shining, and unquestionably of our century.

My favorite among the concert works, the most highly personal, the most condensed, and the most clearly indispensable to music, it seems to me, is the *Piano Variations* of 1930. The Short Symphony in its sextet form and the Nonet also remain handsome under usage. The Piano Quartet, though structurally imaginative, suffers from a tone-row in which two whole-tone scales just barely skirt monotony. The Piano Sonata, the Violin Sonata, and the Piano Fantasy have failed on every hearing to hold my mind. And the charming Concerto for Clarinet (1948) with strings, harp, and piano, is essentially "light" music long ago retired to the status of an admirable ballet by Jerome Robbins, *The Pied Piper*.

Suites from the three great repertory ballets, nuggets from films and operas, one overture, divers mood-bits and occasional pieces, and the rollicking *El Salón México*, constitute a high-level contribution to light music that may well be, along with Copland's standardization of the American professional composer, also at high level, his most valued legacy. Certainly these works are among America's most beloved. Nevertheless, the non-programmatic works, though not rivals to twentieth-century European masterworks, have long served American composers as models of procedure and as storehouses of precious device, all of it ready to be picked right off the shelf.

"It's the best we've got, you know," said Leonard Bernstein. And surely this is true of Copland's music as a whole. Ruggles's is more carefully made, but there is not enough of it. Ives's, of which there is probably far too much for quality, has, along with its slapdash euphoria, a grander gusto. Varèse, an intellectually sophisticated European, achieved within a limited production the highest originality flights of any. Among Copland's own contemporaries few can approach him for both volume and diversity. Roy Harris has five early chamber works and one memorable symphony, his Third, but he has written little of equal value since 1940. Piston is the author of neoclassical symphonies and chamber pieces that by their fine workmanship may well arrive at repertory status when revived in a later period; for now, they seem a shade scholastic. Sessions, I should say, has for all his impressive complexity and high seriousness, not one work that is convincing throughout. And I shall probably be remembered, if at all, for my operas.

But the Copland catalog has good stuff under every heading, including that of opera. He has never turned out bad work, nor worked without an idea, an inspiration. His stance is that not only of a professional but also of an artist—responsible, prepared, giving of his best. And if that best is also the best we have, there is every reason to be thankful for its straightforward employment of high gifts. Also, of course, for what is the result of exactly that, "this simple and great man in our midst."

Looking Backward

THE 1930S IN AMERICA had been characterized by an unexpected expansion of the symphony orchestra. In full depression times, with seemingly no money anywhere, the boom
occurred. Schools found ways to buy instruments and scores,
communities hired players and conductors, the Works Progress
Administration organized unemployed musicians into concert-
giving groups often comparable to the dozen or more established orchestras that had long been the glory of our great
cities. And all this, where not strictly amateur, under union
conditions. Till in 1937, according to *America's Symphony Orchestras* by Grant and Hettinger, there were no fewer than thirty
thousand ensembles practicing symphonic repertory and performing it in public.

By the end of the decade, with a war on in Europe and prosperity back, the WPA groups came to be disbanded. But the
popularity of symphonic exercise had become so firmly established in our schools and in our communities that the number
of orchestras went on growing. And in spite of war, and the
enforced absence of many from cultural pursuits, by 1945, according to a report of the National Music League, there were
forty-five thousand orchestras.

Already in the late 1930s, with the orchestral expansion established and successful, it had become known to managers and
educators that another boom was building up, an excitement
about opera. Indeed if the war, with its constant shiftings of
troops and factories and personnel, had not interrupted that
enthusiasm, the founding of opera workshops that characterized the late '40s and '50s might well have got started a decade
earlier.

The Saturday afternoon broadcasts of the Metropolitan
Opera certainly had a great deal to do with spreading this interest, though they could not have started it. For from the early
1930s, when they began, these broadcasts were already popular,
rating in the polls twice as high as the Sunday programs of the

New York Philharmonic and right up in the range of the commercial entertainers.

The orchestra boom had found American composers ready for distribution. Ever since the 1890s they had been writing symphonic works that were structurally coherent, clear in thought, and neatly orchestrated. An American orchestral repertory existed, and there were American composers ready to add to it at a drop of the slightest hint about performance.

The opera boom, even though delayed by a decade, had no such library at hand. Not that there were no American operas. There were many. And a dozen of these had been produced at the Metropolitan and Chicago opera houses—skillfully built works by Parker, Chadwick, Charles Wakefield Cadman, Henry Hadley, Reginald de Koven, Victor Herbert, and Deems Taylor. But nobody wanted to hear them again. The thirst was for new works, along with the European nineteenth-century ones. And the new composers, those whose music sounded like the twentieth century—Copland and Roger Sessions and Roy Harris—were turning out to be either inept at vocal writing or lacking a sense of the stage. Our earlier opera composers had written gracefully enough for voice and sometimes dramatically. But their music, like their librettos, lacked modernity appeal. Reviewing at this point three decades, let us remember that that of 1910 to 1920 had continued the successful career of Horatio Parker—which included two operas, one produced at the Metropolitan—and the unsuccessful career—particularly regarding opera, toward which he had made serious efforts—of George W. Chadwick. The other chief conservatives—Hadley, Converse, Mason, Hill—were pursuing a quiet path. And MacDowell, the most striking of them all, had been dead since 1908.

A modernist trend, barely visible before 1919 regarding Ives, shortly about to become so regarding Ruggles, earlier showy as all get-out with Leo Ornstein, and serio-comic with Henry Cowell in California, this trend had become a movement after the arrival from Europe around 1916 of Ernest Bloch, Carlos Salzedo, and Edgard Varèse. It was in fact this very turning away from an academicized Romanticism, redolent of nineteenth-century Central Europe or of impressionist France, and toward a radically non-academic, even subversive, up-to-dateness that was to give American music a new confidence, backed up by a French turn in the pedagogy of composition (at Harvard and Columbia) and by the invigoration of our low-life ambience through blues and jazz.

Actually it was the gradual fulfilling in America of radical promises already achieved in Europe which gave the "advanced" tone to our music life of the 1920s, with its modern music societies and across-the-Atlantic exchanges of scores and artists. But the modern masters—and everybody knew who they were: Debussy (dead), Ravel, Schoenberg, Stravinsky—were pre-war products. And the young ones—in Europe Milhaud, Honegger, Berg, Webern, Prokofiev; in America Sessions, Copland, Piston, Cowell, along with the Paris-based Virgil Thomson and George Antheil—were not ready to give out a new line. So the old-line Romantics—in Europe Richard Strauss, Rachmaninoff, Dohnanyi; in America the standard academics, plus Deems Taylor and the young Howard Hanson—went right on as if the twentieth century did not exist. At the same time Ruggles and Varèse moved forward from their already advanced positions, and Ives proceeded slowly with the editing and publishing of his works.

The 1920s, with their open power-struggles between modernists and conservatives and even among the modernists themselves, were an active and quarrelsome time. The decade ended with a clear victory for modernism and with the consolidation of a modernist establishment powerful not only in its own concert-giving societies, where it operated to make or break careers, but in the universities as well. Also in the orchestras, where Stokowski, Koussevitzky, and Frederick Stock (following the examples of Karl Muck, Walter Damrosch, Pierre Monteux) backed the leaders of the modernist establishment and even did some testing on their own.

Copland's bare and clangorous Piano Variations, of 1930, closed off the radical decade and initiated a new one, in which young America was to take a new line, at once neo-Romantic and formalistic. The best of Roy Harris's richly meditative chamber music and his eloquent Third Symphony led the way. Sessions and Piston during these years did more teaching than composing; their full maturity was not to arrive till in the 1940s. But the successes of a still younger generation—Samuel Barber

and William Schuman, both born in 1910—enriched the time
with chamber and orchestral works warmly felt and expertly
composed. And if Sessions and Copland themselves represented
a certain retreat from radical modernism, based in both cases
on Stravinsky's neoclassic example, Barber and Schuman and
the slow-ripening Piston were to embody in their works an
even more conservative approach to musical form. They did not
follow the easy-going sequence-routines of Rachmaninoff and
Hanson, directly adopted from Wagner. And they avoided also
free linear expansion as practiced by Harris (though there is a
bit of this in Schuman) as well as the elaborately prepared asymmetries of Copland and Stravinsky (not to speak of Schoenberg's codified language of the heart) for the classical proportions of Haydn, Mozart, Schubert, and Brahms. Old wine in
old bottles seems to have been their aim. And the content varies
from Barber's voice-like rounded contours through the jumpy
themes and jazzy metrics of Schuman (not so far as might be
thought from Stravinsky via Gershwin) to the sophisticated and
hermetic way that Piston expresses private meanings by developing analytically, much as Bartók was doing, materials based
on intervalic contradictions.

In Sessions's work of the period intervalic contradiction was
also explored but rather for the purpose, or so it has long appeared to me, of calling to our attention, by seeming to deny,
a Romantic afflatus that aspired toward nineteenth-century
Vienna. In this sense his music was the least contemporary of
all, unless one counts the wish to reproduce monumental Romanticism in a high dissonance saturation as characteristic of
modern times. Which of course it is. Even Brahms's need for
serving earlier masters—Handel, Mozart, and middle-period
Beethoven—was after all not very different.

In the long run American music has suffered little from the
weightlifters and the muscle-bound. We have no match here for
the heavy strainings of a Reger, a Pfitzner, a Scriabin, a d'Indy;
nor anything that resembles the non-stop outpourings of an
Anton Rubinstein, a Bruckner, a Gustav Mahler, an Albéric
Magnard. There is a bit of all these, of course, in Charles Ives.
And in Sessions, as in Elliott Carter, there is a special kind of
(perhaps American) painful delivery, both of them learned men
who seem determined to use all they know in every piece. In

Ruggles, on the other hand, slow worker though he was, no comparable strain is felt; merely his need for producing, at no matter how much trouble, a homogeneous texture capable of expressing musical thought without digression.

America's problem has from the beginning lain largely in her composers' lack of a plain and unfussy mastery. They are taught so elaborately and mature so late! Moreover, the suspect nature here of anything suggesting distinction is a heavy cross for an artist to bear. Composers of natural gifts we have in plenty, along with a few who once have seemed to be about to establish a firm fecundity comparable to that of Europe's great men. But the hope more often than not has petered out.

Certainly such hope was strong in the 1930s, and not only for concert music but for opera. My own *Four Saints*, produced in 1934; George Gershwin's *Porgy and Bess*, in 1935; Menotti's *Amelia al Ballo*, of 1936; Marc Blitzstein's political-tract *singspiel* of 1937, *The Cradle Will Rock*; Aaron Copland's *The Second Hurricane* of the same year; Douglas Moore's *The Devil and Daniel Webster*, of 1938—all these seemed at the time to be lively, contemporary in feeling, and promising of more to come. Menotti, Moore, and I have indeed composed more operas, and with continuing success, artistically speaking. In the 1950s, Carlisle Floyd composed to his own text a *Susannah* which, though orchestrally inept, was both verbally and vocally first-class. His subsequent works have not been up to the first, though his *Of Mice and Men* may have again, in 1970, hit the jackpot. Samuel Barber's *Vanessa* and *Antony and Cleopatra* impress me as standard Metropolitan operas, and no remarkable improvement on those of Deems Taylor from the 1920s or on Howard Hanson's *Merry Mount*, produced at the Met in 1934. Robert Ward's *The Crucible* (1961), the best so far of the Ford Foundation commissions, is a solid but not quite first-class play by Arthur Miller set to solid but not quite first-class music. Hugo Weisgall's *Six Characters in Search of an Author*, produced in 1959, adds to Pirandello's already complex dramatic fantasy a musical viscosity of doubtful service to the script. Three recent operas also merit mention—*Montezuma* by Roger Sessions, produced in West Berlin 1964, *The Visitation* by Gunther Schuller, produced in Hamburg 1968, and *Mourning Becomes Electra* (on the Eugene O'Neill play) by Marvin David Levy, produced at the

Metropolitan in 1967. I cannot see that any of these mightily Germanic works has added stature to American opera, though all of course are musically professional.

An effort is worth noting here on the part of American musicians to compose short operas of a comedy so broad that one might almost call them comic strips. Menotti's *The Telephone* is surely the most effective of these. But Leonard Bernstein's *Trouble in Tahiti* has also had a merited currency. And I, for one, find Lukas Foss's *The Jumping Frog of Calaveras County* definitely entertaining. Even the usually sentiment-inspired Douglas Moore has written what he calls a "soap opera" entitled *Gallantry*, a charming parody in lyric vein. And George Kleinsinger's *Archie and Mehitabel*, about a cat and a cockroach, though it may be a bit commercial of tone, exploits a humor that is not childish.

This sort of writing, when practiced on a witty book by a composer clearly sophisticated, can be as fluffy as a joke by Ronald Firbank. In heavier hands it tends toward a collegiate coarseness. On the whole I find the tendency possibly useful for propelling the American composer toward light textures and toward an awareness of style, since humor demands stylistic tension far more than tragedy does. Humor can also be a protection against the fragility of sentiments, can even enclose them like a capsule, for easy swallowing. Many more operas than these have been written and produced in the last thirty years. I have tried limiting my mention to works having real distinction and some liveliness. Others too may evince these qualities; I have not heard them all. I have merely wished, after commenting on the 1930s, to review certain outgrowths of that decade's achievement.

These outgrowths have provided in symphonic music virtually no new names, certainly no major ones. In chamber music we have Elliott Carter, a whopping one, and Ross Lee Finney, an authentic one. In opera, apart from one short work by Carlisle Floyd, we have for novelty only the strange case of the Argentinian Alberto Ginastera, whose *Bomarzo* and *Don Rodrigo* productions, heavily subsidized from political sources (largely Rockefeller, I believe), created some stir. Bearing unquestionably some novelty, both musical and aesthetic, these works seem to have achieved also at the New York City Opera an all-time high for musical complexity in the repertory circumstance. That complexity may be illusory, as may well be also their musical quality, though this last I hesitate to believe, considering their composer's known excellence in concert works. An overweening effort to knock out all competitors seems to me the more likely supposition.

In music teaching there has been nothing new of note, since our chief pedagogical establishments training composers all bear the stamp of the older generation. The Eastman School of Music in Rochester, New York, is the creation of Howard Hanson; and today's Juilliard School of Music in New York City bears witness still to the administrative wisdom and the firmness of William Schuman, from 1945 to 1962 its president. Walter Piston at Harvard and Roger Sessions at Princeton and at the University of California in Berkeley gave solid training to composers as different in manner as the stage-oriented Leonard Bernstein, the abstract-and-electronic Milton Babbitt, and the dissonantly introspective Andrew Imbrie. Also Copland and Harris have advised composing students fruitfully; and powerful stimulators they were, both of them, though neither is a drill-master. Actually the only novel addition to America's teaching resources in the last thirty-five years has been Arnold Schoenberg, who, arriving as a refugee in 1934, within two years became an enormous pedagogical presence. Oscar Levant worked under him; Lou Harrison and John Cage were definitely formed by him; also strongly influenced was Leon Kirchner.

Cage and Harrison might be considered heirs of the 1930s, since their work in percussion dates from toward the end of that time. I prefer, however, since both were living then on the West Coast and were still under thirty, to view their subsequent careers, along with those of Carter and Babbitt and the new far-outs, as belonging to a later development. This development, though many of its origins lie on the West Coast, is today far closer in touch with post-war Europe than the now elderly commando unit or the Barber-Menotti-Schuman generation, which had followed so closely, not exactly in our steps, but on our heels.

Succeeding developments will need all they can muster of energy and fresh ways to match those of the 1930s. For that was surely in American music the definitive decade. After 1910 everything led up to it, and after 1940 everything was different. The survival today of Copland's commando and their continued creation of viable works, each in his own style, is evidence both of their individual strength and of that of the time in which they ripened. For their music—along with that of Ives, Ruggles, and Varèse—is what anybody anywhere means by American music. Virtually everything that took place here after 1940, except for the isolated grand achievements of Carter and Cage, is more of same. And if not that, as with electronics and musical "happenings," it has turned to Europe for guidance—to Stockhausen, to Luciano Berio, and to Boulez.

The effort to create both for home consumption and for export a national school of composition has nevertheless succeeded, even though that success has not yet put the United States in a position of leadership in music comparable to that which we enjoy in literature. For if our elderly composers are easily the match for what Europe can offer today in the same age-bracket, our experimental groups are by international standards a shade provincial.

All music today, I fear, is resting on its laurels. And if Europe, both Central and Western, remembers the years from 1890 to 1914 as a Golden Age and the post–World War I as a Silver Epoch, America, even its youth-fringe, looks back nostalgically to the ebullient 1930s, that dramatic and frightening decade which began with economic disaster and ended in a worldwide war.

8

Cage and the Collage of Noises

In 1967 JOHN CAGE, working at the University of Illinois in Urbana with the engineer-composer Lejaren Hiller, began to plan, design, and move toward the final realization in sound (with visual admixtures) of a work lasting four-and-a-half hours and involving a very large number of mechanical devices controlled by engineers, along with seven harpsichords played by hand. Nearly two years later this work, entitled *HPSCHD* (a six-letter version, suited to computer programming, of the word *harpsichord*) was produced on May 16, 1969, in the university's Assembly Hall, seating eighteen thousand people.

By this time the work had come to include as sources of sound not only the keyboard instruments of its title (which Cage pronounces *harpsichord*) but also fifty-two tape machines, fifty-nine power amplifiers, fifty-nine loudspeakers and two hundred eight computer-generated tapes. The visual contributions to this performance employed sixty-four slide-projectors showing sixty-four hundred slides and eight moving-picture projectors using forty cinematographic films, probably silent in view of the general auditory complexities just mentioned.

Richard Kostelanetz, reviewing the event for *The New York Times*, reported further that "flashing on the outside under-walls of the huge double-saucer Assembly Hall . . . were an endless number of slides from 52 projectors" (a part of the sixty-four?). Inside "in the middle of the circular sports arena were suspended several parallel sheets of semi-transparent material, each 100 by 400 feet; and from both sides were projected numerous films and slides whose collaged imagery passed through several sheets. Running around a circular ceiling was a continuous 340-foot screen, and from a hidden point inside were projected slides with imagery as various as outer-space scenes, pages of Mozart music, computer instructions, and non-representational blotches. Beams of light were aimed across the undulated interior roof. In several upper locations mirrored balls were spinning, reflecting dots of light in all directions. . . .

662

The audience," he adds, "milled about the floor while hundreds took seats in the bleachers."

The auditory continuity he describes as "an atonal and structural chaos . . . continually in flux." However, "fading in and out through the mix were snatches of harpsichord music that sounded . . . like Mozart; . . . these came from the seven instrumentalists visible on platforms in the center of the Assembly Hall." The sound appealed to him as in general "rather mellow, except for occasional blasts of ear-piercing feed-back that became more frequent toward the end."

Mr. Kostelanetz identifies the aesthetic species to which this work belongs as "that peculiarly contemporary art, the kinetic environment, or an artistically activated enclosed space." Actually this "artistically activated" space is not very different from the Wagnerian *gesamtkunstwerk*, or music drama (also a mixed-media affair), except for its very modern emphasis on the mechanics of show business. Wagner took these for granted, preferring to use them less as glamour items than for underlining myths and morals. In both cases, I think, the production of ecstasy was the aim; and in both cases surely music (or sound, in any case) was the main merchandise. For Wagner's music is clearly what has survived best out of his whole splendid effort to create a new kind of tragedy. And as for the Cage-Hiller *HPSCHD*, it was already on sale as a musical recording, completely shorn of its visual incidents and compacted down to twenty-one minutes of playing-time, when the great mixed show of it all was put on in Urbana.

In 1937, thirty years before this work was started, Cage had proclaimed his credo regarding the future of music: "I believe that the use of noise to make music will continue and increase until we reach a music produced through the aid of electrical instruments which will make available for musical purposes any and all sounds that can be heard." The composer, in these prophesied times, will not limit himself to instruments or concepts based on the overtone series but "will be faced with the entire field of sound." And new methods for composing with this vast vocabulary, he also stated, were already beginning to be developed, methods which were free and forever to remain free (I quote) "from the concept of a fundamental tone."

The idea of making compositions out of noise, that is to say of sounds not responsible to a common fundamental, had been in the air ever since the Futurist painter Luigi Russolo in 1913 praised as sources for an "art of noises" "booms, thunderclaps, explosions, clashes, splashes, and roars." Busoni too saw music as moving toward the machine. And Varèse was dreaming of electrical help by 1920 certainly. Also George Antheil, Leo Ornstein, and Darius Milhaud had very early composed passages for non-tonal percussion. Cage, however, when he began to compose in 1933, was virtually alone in following out the Futurist noise principle as a career. Others had worked occasionally in that vein, but none other seemed really to believe in it as a destiny or to be able to perfect for its mastery devices for giving it style, structure, and variety. Cage's own music over the last thirty years, though not entirely free of interrelated pitches, has nevertheless followed a straighter line in its evolution toward an art of collage based on non-musical sounds than that of any other artist of his time. He seems to have known by instinct everything to avoid that might turn him aside from his goal and everything that could be of use toward achieving it. Precious little service, naturally, was to be expected out of music's classical models.

The ultimate aim was to produce a homogenized chaos that would carry no program, no plot, no reminders of the history of beauty, and no personal statement. Nowadays, of course, we can recognize in such an ideal the whole effort of pop art. But I do not think that pop art's obvious jokes and facile sentiments were a major motive. I think Cage wanted, had always wanted, to save music from itself by removing its narcotic qualities and its personalized pretentiousness, as well as all identifiable structure and rhetoric. In this regard his aim has been close to that of Erik Satie, whose music he adores. But its consistent pursuit presents a story so utterly American, even West Coast American, that this Frenchman from Normandy with a Scottish mother, though he might well have delighted in Cage's salt-sprayed humor, would have lacked sympathy, I suspect, for his doctrinaire determination.

John Cage is a Californian born in Los Angeles in 1912, whose father had come there from Tennessee. A lanky red-head with white skin that freckles, a constant walker, a woodsman, and a tinkerer, he has all the tough qualities of the traditional mountaineer submissive to no authorities academic or federal. He had good lessons in piano playing and in composition, the latter from Arnold Schoenberg among others. Teaching during the late 1930s at the Cornish School in Seattle, he made friendships in the Northwest that stimulated his take-off as a composer toward East Asian art principles. The painter Morris Graves, the composer Lou Harrison, and the dancer Merce Cunningham all came into his life at this time; and so did the young Russian woman from Alaska whom he married.

He also conducted percussion concerts and composed percussion works. His *Construction in Metal*, of 1939, for bells, thunder-sheets, gongs, anvils, automobile brake-drums and similar metallic objects, is organized rhythmically after the Indian *tala*, in which the whole has as many parts as each section has small parts; and in Cage these parts, large and small, are related to each other in lengths of time as square and square root. In 1938 he also began to "prepare" pianos by inserting coins, bits of rubber or wood, bolts, and other small objects between the strings at nodal points, producing a gamut of delicate twangs, pings, and thuds that constitutes for each piece its vocabulary.

At this time, and for the next decade, Cage's music continued to be organized for phraseology and length after the square-and-square-root principle. Its melodic structure, if one may use this term for music so far removed from modes and scales, is expressive, in the Indian manner, of "permanent" emotions (heroic, erotic, and so forth) though in some cases he does not hesitate, as in *Amores* (1943), to describe things personally experienced, in this case a lovers' triangle. But his melody remains aware of Schoenberg's teaching about tetrachordal structure, and it also observes a serial integrity. Since music without a thoroughbass can seek no structure from harmony, and since Cage's orientalizing proclivities inclined his expression toward "permanent" emotions, as opposed to those which by their progress and change might suggest a beginning, a middle, and an ending, he had available to him no structural method save what he could invent through rhythm.

Now rhythm, being the free, the spontaneous, the uncontrolled element in Schoenberg's music and in that of his Viennese companion-pupils Berg and Webern, appealed strongly to

Cage's inventive mind as a domain offering possibly a chance for innovation. The Schoenberg school had made few serious attempts to solve problems of structure; they had remained hung up, as we say, on their twelve-tone row, which by abolishing the consonance-dissonance antithesis had relieved them of an age-old problem in harmony. The fact that in doing so it had also abolished the scalar hierarchies, previously the source of all harmony-based form, led them to substitute for harmonic structure an interior cohesion achieved through canonic applications of the twelve-tone row, but not to any original efforts at all regarding organic form. Rhythm they never considered for this role, since rhythm, in the European tradition, had long before been judged a contributory element, not a basic one like melody or harmony. And besides, the Germanic practice, in which they had all grown up, had lost its rhythmic vitality after Beethoven's death, and no longer distinguished with any rigor between rhythms of length and rhythms of stress, as Beethoven and his predecessors had done to so remarkable a result.

What the Schoenberg school actually used as a substitute for structure was the evocation of certain kinds of emotional drama familiar to them from the Romantic masters. This is why their music, though radical in its interval relations, is on the inside just good old Vienna. Even Italians like Luigi Dallapiccola and Frenchmen like Pierre Boulez, who took up the twelve-tone method after World War II, being not attached atavistically to Vienna, could not hold their works together without a libretto. Their best ones are operas, oratorios, cantatas. And their only substitute for organic structure was the *sérialisme intégral* actually achieved by Boulez in a few works, a complete organization into rows of all the variables—of tones, lengths, heights, timbres, loudnesses, and methods of instrumental attack. The result was so complex to compose, to play, and above all to follow that little effort was made to continue the practice.

The experiment had its effect on Cage, all the same, almost the only direct musical influence one can find since his early lessons with Cowell and Schoenberg and his percussion-orchestra experiments with Lou Harrison. For Cage, like everybody else, was deeply impressed by Pierre Boulez, both the music and the mentality of the man. Knowing well that twelve-tone music lacked both rhythm and structure, Cage had early aspired in his works for percussion groups and for prepared piano to supply both. Whether he had ever thought to serialize the rhythmic element I do not know; he may have considered his *tala* structure more effective. But he was impressed by the Boulez achievement in total control, and Boulez in return was not without respect for Cage's forcefulness.

At this point—we are now in the late 1940s—Cage sailed off toward the conquest of Europe. But Europe by this time was in the hands of its own youth-centered power group. Boulez in France, Karlheinz Stockhausen in Germany, a henchman or so in Belgium and Italy, were beginning to be a tight little club. They ran a modernist festival at Donaueschingen and a concert series in Paris, dispensed patronage and commissions through the German radio, and influenced publishers. Cage, always pushing, assumed his right to parity in the European councils. He can be overbearing, I know, and maybe was. I do not know what confrontations occurred; but he came back chastened, retired to his backwoods modern cabin up-country from Nyack, became a searcher after mushrooms, found solace in Zen Buddhism.

By 1951 he had come up with another novelty, one that was to sweep through Europe, the Americas, and Japan without bringing him any personal credit. I refer to the aleatory method of composition, in which the variables so strictly controlled by Boulez through serial procedures were subjected, all of them, to games of chance. We may suppose, I think, that between a numerically integrated work of sound and one showing arrangements and orders that reflect only hazard, there is not of necessity much recognizable difference. A similar degree of complexity is bound to be present, provided the variable elements are sufficiently numerous and the game of chance used to control them sufficiently complex to avoid the monotony of a "run." If John Cage was not the first aleatory composer, he may still have been the first to hit upon the aleatory idea. It fits with his modest but perfectly real mathematical understanding, with his addiction to things oriental (in this case to the Chinese *I Ching, Book of Changes*, where he found the dice-game he still uses), with the Zen Buddhist principle that nothing really has to make sense (since opposites can be viewed as identical), and above all with his need at that particular time for a novelty.

According to Gilbert Chase in *America's Music*, Cage first started using chance in connection with thematic invention for getting from one note to the next. Then at each small structural division chance was also used to determine whether the tempo should be changed. This was in a work for prepared piano called *Music of Changes*. But inevitably, with chance involved in the tempo changes, hence in the overall timings, "it was not possible," says Cage, "to know the total time-length until the final chance operation, the last toss of coins affecting the rate of tempo, had been made." And since the work's length could not be decided in advance, the square-and-square-root structural proportions could not be used. Therefore structure, for the first time in Cage's experience of it, became as indeterminate an element in composition as texture, both shape and meaning disappeared, and composition became in Cage's words "an activity characterized by process and essentially purposeless." He has not yet fully explained, however, just how in choosing by chance his musical materials he arrives at the ones to be processed through the dice-game, though there is no question of his "inventing" these materials. He does not; he "finds" them through objective, impersonal procedures.

And so it came about that after Schoenberg had dissolved all harmonic tensions by assuming dissonance and consonance to be the same, and Boulez had through his *sérialisme intégral* removed seemingly all freedom, all elements of choice from composition beyond the original selection of materials themselves and their initial order of appearance, Cage had now made music completely free, or "indeterminate," an achievement he was especially pleased with because it eliminated from any piece both the history of music and the personality of the composer. And such personal elements as were in danger of governing the choice of materials he has endeavored to obviate by treating imperfections in the paper and similar accidents as real notes. His subsequent elaborations of indeterminacy for working with electronic tape, though ingenious, are merely developments of the aleatory or impersonal principle. And thus we arrive with *HPSCHD*, the harpsichord piece of 1969, at an effect of total chaos, completely homogenized save for occasional shrieks of feed-back.

Let me trace again the surprisingly straight line of Cage's

growth in artistry. His father, for whom he had deep respect, was an inventor; not a rich one, for he lacked business sense, but a fecund one. And his inventor's view of novelty as all-important has been John's view of music ever since I first knew him at thirty, in 1943. He prizes innovation above all other qualities—a weighting of the values which gives to all of his judgments an authoritarian, almost a commercial aspect, as of a one-way tunnel leading only to the gadget-fair.

He has, I know, felt warmly toward certain works and composers, especially toward Satie; but he has never really accepted for his own all of music, as the greater masters living and dead have done. Stravinsky's distrust of Wagner, almost anybody's suspicion of Brahms, or Schoenberg's utter impatience about Kurt Weill—aside from such minor irritations, generally composers have considered the history of music as leading up to them. But Cage has no such view. He thinks of himself, on the contrary, as music's corrective, as a prophet denouncing the whole of Renaissance and post-Renaissance Europe, with its incorrigible respect for beauty and distinction, and dissolving all that in an ocean of electronic availabilities. Electronic because those are what is around these days. He knows the sound of any loudspeaker, through which all this must come, to be essentially ugly (he has said so), and he probably knows that the presence of Mozart in *HPSCHD* gives to that work a neoclassical aspect definitely embarrassing. But the enormity of his transgression in both cases humanizes after all the overweening ambition. It is not the first time that an artist has fancied himself as destroying the past, and then found himself using it.

Actually Cage is less a destroyer than a typical California creator. Like many another West Coast artist—Gertrude Stein, for example—he selects his materials casually and then with great care arranges them into patterns of hidden symmetry. The difference between such artists and their European counterparts lies not in occult balances, which have been standard in Europe ever since Japan was revealed to them in the 1850s, but in the casual choice of materials. That Europe will have none of. From Bach and Mozart through Debussy and Stravinsky to Boulez and Berio and Xenakis, just as from Chaucer through Byron to Proust and Joyce, or from Giotto through Picasso, forms themselves, the words, the colors, the sounds, the scales, the melodies are ever precious, the psychic themes adventurous and terrible. Their treatment may be comical or tragic, sometimes both; but the matter must be noble no matter how ingenious the design.

Cage would say of all that, "just more post-Renaissance imitation of nature." He believes, or pretends to believe, that the artist, instead of copying nature's forms, should follow her ways of behavior. As to what these ways are, unless he believes them to be really without pattern, I cannot imagine. A man as well read as he must know that neither biological forms nor crystal shapes are matters of chance, also that animals and plants are as ruthless about seizing food and holding a place in the sun as any European artist ever was.

The truth is that Cage's mind is narrow. Were it broader his remarks might carry less weight. And his music might not exist at all. For with him the original gift, the musical ear, is not a remarkable one. Neither did he ever quite master the classical elements, harmony and counterpoint—a failure that has led him at times into faulty harmonic analysis. His skill at rhythmic analysis and rhythmic construction is very great, one of the finest I have known. And his literary facility is considerable. One book, called *Silence*, contains most of the best among his writings on musical aesthetics. *A Year from Monday* is a joke-book, the clownings of a professional celebrity who has admired Gertrude Stein and played chess with Marcel Duchamp. *Notations* is a collection of reproduced musical manuscripts from 261 composers, some laid out in staves and measures, many in the mechanical-drawing style or the multitudinous chicken tracks that are the individual shorthands, no two alike, of today's musical inventors. The aim of this vastly revealing book, with its gamut of personalities and handwritings, was to raise money through the publication and eventual direct sale of these gift manuscripts for the benefit of a foundation through which Cage aids musicians, dancers, and other artists congenial to his tastes. In *Virgil Thomson: His Life and Music* (the biographical part is by Kathleen O'Donnell Hoover) my works, every scrap of them up to 1959, have all been analyzed with care and described, as often as not, with love. There is some frankly expressed petulance too, and a sincere regret that my career has not followed an undeviating modernism. The catalogue of my music—

complete, detailed, and accurate—is a bibliographic triumph. For Cage is at all times a precision worker.

He is also a major musical force and a leader among us. This leadership is not merely a matter of position and of precept; it is also kept up by mammoth shows like *HPSCHD* and the one produced in 1966 at New York's 69th Regiment Armory and entitled modestly *Variation VII*. Nobody else among the far-outs can lay hands on so much expense-money or has the persistence to carry through such detailed projects in score-planning and in electronic manipulation. Nobody, perhaps, except Iannis Xenakis, who works by a mathematics of probabilities. All this assiduity at the service of music's physical aggrandizement I find more admirable for pains taken than for its ability to hold my attention. Lasting for twenty-one minutes or four and more hours, the Cage works have some intrinsic interest and much charm, but after a few minutes very little urgency. They do not seem to have been designed for holding attention, and generally speaking they do not hold it. Constructed not for having a beginning, a middle, and an ending but for being all middle, all ambience, all media-massage, they turn out easy to taste and quick to satisfy.

A lack of urgency has been characteristic of Cage's music from the beginning. The instrumental sounds, whether altered or normal, are charming at the outset and agreeably varied from one piece to another, even in such delicate gradings of variety as from one piano preparation to another. But whenever I have played his recorded works for students I have found that no matter what their length they exhaust themselves in about two minutes, say four at most. By that time we have all got the sound of it and made some guess at the "permanent" emotion expressed. And there is no need for going on with it, since we know that it will not be going any deeper into an emotion already depicted as static. Nor will it be following nature's way by developing an organic structure. For if the mind that created it, though powerful and sometimes original, is nevertheless a narrow one, the music itself, for all its jollity, liveliness, and good humor, is emotionally shallow.

It is at its best, I think, when accompanying Merce Cunningham's dance spectacles. These could as well, I fancy, do without music at all, so delicious are they to watch. And Cage's music for them is never an intrusion, but just right—cheerful, thin, up-to-the-minute in style. The last of his big machines I have listened to (I avoid those that employ amplification) is the Concert for Piano and Orchestra of 1958. This, heard live, is all of precious materials, since its sounds come from classical instruments, themselves the product of evolution and of careful manufacture. And though the composer has tried hard to remove their dignity—playing trombones without their bells, putting one tuba's bell inside another's, sawing away at a viola placed across the knees for greater purchase—the fact remains that even treated rudely these instruments give a more elegant sound than electric buzzers and automobile brake-bands, or even than tom-toms and temple-blocks. As for the spectacle of David Tudor crawling around among the pedals of his pianoforte in order to knock on the sounding-board from below, that too was diverting to watch, though the knocking was not loud enough to be funny. All in all the visual show added so much to the whole that when, again for students, I played the recording of this piece (made in the hall itself at Cage's twenty-fifth-anniversary concert), we were all disappointed, I think, at its puny and inconsequential sound.

In the long run non-classical sound-sources, especially the synthetic ones, are as great a hazard to music as industrially processed foods can be to gastronomy (not to speak of nutrition). And Cage's compositions, in the days when he used to play or conduct them *live*, were far more agreeable to the ear than the electronically generated ones which dominate his later production. Even those earlier ones conceived for direct audition are less likely nowadays to turn up in the concert hall than they are in the form of recordings. So that the whole of his repertory (saving the famous *4'33"* of silence) tends to be sicklied over with the monochrome of transmitted sound. And this is a misfortune for us all, since much of his work is inspired by the joy of cooking up a piece out of fresh sounds.

The trouble with loudspeakers is as follows. Their transmission of familiar music performed on familiar instruments can be highly resembling, even deceptively so, provided the acoustical size of the original combo is appropriate to that of the room in which it is being heard. This life-likeness diminishes with large amplification or diminution, as with an opera or symphony cut down to bedroom size or a harpsichord solo piped into a theatre. Now any resemblances to an original, as with photography, for example, depend for their vivacity on the receptor's acquaintance with the original or with its kind. Faults of transmission can therefore be forgiven in return for the delights of recognition. But when the source is unfamiliar no comparison is at hand. How can we know what a sound electronically designed would resemble if we heard it pure? We cannot, of course, since it does not exist until transmitted. A flavor of the canned is built into it.

And what is this canned taste? In music it is a diminution of the parasitic noises that condition every instrument's timbre, the scratching of resin on a fiddle string, the thump of a piano-key hitting bottom, the clatter of a flute's finger-mechanism, a slight excess of breath-intake, the buzzing of a reed. I know that these things get picked up too, often in exaggerated form, so exaggerated in fact that they are on the whole better kept out of a recording. But the effort to do this does neutralize a bit the timbre of any instrument or voice. Just as oil painting done by artificial light tends to lose frankness of color and to wear a slight veil, so does any musical sound transmitted by loudspeaker lose some of its delight for the ear. And when that sound is one for which no compensatory acquaintance exists with any original, a whole range of musical creation (that of today's far-outs, for instance) gets drowned in a sea of similarity.

Many of America's far-outs (old masters Foss, Babbitt, and Luening among them) have endeavored to liven up the deadness of speaker-transmission by combining tape-music with that of a live orchestra. Even Varèse, in *Déserts*, tried it once. John Cage, so far, has seemingly abstained from this apologetic stance. For even in *HPSCHD*, with all that went on together in that monster auditorium, I judge there is little likelihood of the seven harpsichords not having also undergone amplification.

The gramophone, as a preserver of standard music, pop or classical, has ever been an instrument of culture, because the record collectors complete their listening experiences through attendance at musical occasions. This was demonstrated in the early 1940s at Columbia University's Institute of Social Research. Radio, it was also determined there, led culturally nowhere, since persons whose musical experience began with that medium rarely proceeded to make acquaintance with the real thing. Considering today's immersion of everybody everywhere in transmitted sound, and especially of the young in high amplification, there seems little chance that any music not transmitted and amplified will long survive outside its present classical habitats—which is to say, opera houses, concert halls, conservatoires, studios, and certain low dives where jazz is played, maybe too in mountaineer heights far from Nashville, and a few churches. Unless, of course, the young, today so hooked on amplification, should suddenly say to rock itself, "Good-by."

But for now the troubled waves are like a sea; and whether the youths and maidens gather three hundred thousand strong in fields near Woodstock, New York, just to be together while rock artists, even amplified, cannot combat the distances; or whether they mill around inside an auditorium built for a mere eighteen thousand souls while a thoroughly prepared electronic happening (accompanied by visuals and swirling lights) is served up, along with allusions to Mozart, under the highest academic auspices and the authorship of two famous masters, is all the same, so far as I can see, though Woodstock, by report, was much more fun.

Both, however, are thoroughly contemporary in feeling. And either or both may mean, like any children's crusade, that we have come to the end of that line. Also that the Viet-Nam war, by ending, might change all sorts of things. Could it send John Cage back to making music, turn him aside from the messianic hope of giving birth to a new age? Destroying the past is a losing game; the past cannot be destroyed; it merely wears out. And moving into a higher age by playing with mechanical toys is a child's game. New ages in art come slowly, silently, unsuspected. And publicity can bring only death to a real messiah. My instinct is to believe that whatever may be valid for the future of music as an art (and *as* an art is the only way I can conceive it) must be taking place underground. Today's prophetic ones, I truly believe, either lie hidden, or else stand around so innocently that none can see them. Otherwise someone would for certain betray them, and the price-controlling powers would shoot them down. I cannot see today's mass-conscious celebrities as anything but a danger to art, whatever in their youthful years they may have left behind for us that is authentic and fine.

Music has its fashion industry and its novelty trade. And John Cage, as a composer, seems today's leader in novelty-fashions, at least for America. From modest musical beginnings, through ambition, perseverance, and brains, he has built up a mastery over modern materials, their choice, their cutting and piecing, their sewing into garments of any length and for many occasions. And he has exploited that mastery, at first as a one-man shop, later as an enterprise employing many helpers, always as a business internationally reputable, and essentially a novelty business. None other on that level, or in America, is so sound. Rivalries, if any, will come from Europe, from that same post-Renaissance Europe he has so long despised and feared. Boulez, for the moment, is not a danger, being chiefly occupied with conducting. But Stockhausen has novelty ideas. And Xenakis, with a higher mathematical training (for that is a requisite now in musical engineering), might well be about to take over the intellectual leadership.

European far-outs are a team and a cartel, as Cage learned more than twenty years ago. No American composer knows any such solidarity. The best substitutes we can mobilize are foundation support, ever capricious; a university position, where everybody is underpaid, over-verbalized, and paralyzed by fear of the students; or a celebrity situation, in which one can have anything, but only so long as the distribution industry permits and the press finds one diverting. In the contrary eventuality artistic death, with burial in an unmarked grave, comes quickly, for unlike Europe, we have no immortality machine.

Perhaps John Cage, with his inventor's ingenuity, should try building us one. And I don't mean the kind that destroys itself, such as the artist Jean Tinguely used to construct. Nor yet the kind that Cage has so often assembled of late years, designed to destroy, with luck, the history of music. I mean something that might relieve today's composers from the awful chore of following "nature's ways" and give them building-blocks again for constructing musical houses that might, by standing up alone, tempt us to walk in and out of them.

But Cage's aim with music, like Samson's in the pagan temple, has long been clearly destructive. Can he really pull the whole thing down around him? You never know. He might just! And in that way himself reach immortality. But his would be no standard immortality of structured works and humane thoughts. It would be more like a current event, "Sorcerer's apprentice sets off H-bomb in Lincoln Center."

It could happen, though. For Cage, like Samson, is a strong one; and he has helpers. They admire what he does and, what is far more dangerous, believe what he says. The young, moreover, seem to be yearning nowadays after a messiah. And a musical one might be the likeliest for them to follow. Indeed, Cage's rigid schedule of beliefs and prophecies, his monorail mind and his turbine-engined, irreversible locomotive of a career all make it easy for the young to view him as a motorized and amplified pied piper calling out, "Get on board-a little children; there's room for a million more."

9

Let Us Now Praise Famous Men

THE FACT that certain European composers methodologically of the left—Stockhausen, Berio, Xenakis—have been engaged to work in America has not made their creations a part of American music any more than the much longer residence here, including citizenship, of Stravinsky, Schoenberg, Hindemith, and Křenek gave to their music a recognizably American cast. A European formation in music is seemingly ineradicable. And so indeed is the lack of one. The cases of Roger Sessions, Roy Harris, Walter Piston, Elliott Carter, Arthur Berger, and Ross Lee Finney, like Edward Burlingame Hill and John Alden Carpenter before them, are significant in this regard. No amount of European overlay, though it may have masked their essential Americanism, has deceived anyone into mistaking them for Europeans.

Similarly, the Cage progeny belong clearly with the American left, whether their work be hand-made or electronically processed. Two early pupils, Morton Feldman and Christian Wolff, have made music of great delicacy and sweetness; others, Gordon Mumma, for instance, and the Japanese Toshi Ichiyanagi, are harder to distinguish from Cage himself. And Earle Brown, in his youth an associate of Cage, has composed music that travels the modernist circuits of Europe, its expressive content being sufficiently American (largely through rhythmic animation) and its workmanship sufficiently European (serial enough) to make it welcome. It is stylish music in any country and most agreeable, being light of texture, steely, and without fragility.

Everywhere, it seems to me, the music of today, for all its internationalist aims and methodology, reflects its origins—French, Germanic, Italian, Spanish—no less than did that of the last century. And in this Tower of Babel the American voice becomes more and more distinct as the volume of our work augments. Naturally also it becomes louder as the university establishments mobilize larger and larger foundation grants, as well as larger and larger locales for its display.

A university rather than a conservatoire background has

characterized American music for nearly a century now. But formerly this university music was related to the humanities. Of late it has taken its tone, and even some of its budget, from the engineering sciences, specifically from electronic studies and from the use of computers. Our musical modernism is no part of any government-sponsored radio and television set-up, as it is in Europe, because America has no such set-up. But we do have rich universities scientifically oriented, and masses of youth handy with a slide-rule.

Also we love free-wheeling. Most of American humor, all of our pop-art, the literary traditions of Walt Whitman, Mark Twain, and Gertrude Stein, whole regions of American life, including the sacred jam-session, derive from the gusto of improvisation. Combine the delights of indeterminacy with the adventure of a dice-game, and you can see how Cage's Americans, complete with foundation funds and university blessings, have come to resemble very little their colleagues of Europe and Asia, in spite of the fact that tapes and loudspeakers sound very much alike all round the world.

So too have the more conventional composers—those who still work with tunings related to a fundamental—come unstuck from their European counterparts. Certainly we have had our quota of Schoenberg followers and of Stravinsky imitators, but so has Europe. The monumental music of Roger Sessions, on the other hand, seems to yearn toward all of Europe, rather than toward just one stylistic sector of it. In the long run I take it to be dominated, like the music of Vincent d'Indy, by an emulation of Beethoven. And if in its pursuit of excellence it occasionally stumbles over its own coils, it is nevertheless work of a high viscosity, a stubborn obscurity, and some grandeur. It is impressive, moreover, not only by weight but by volume, running to eight symphonies and three operas, in addition to concertos and chamber works. It has no parallel in Central Europe, England, or Scandinavia. Even Olivier Messiaen in France and Alberto Ginastera from Argentina are less hermetic. Only Carlos Chavez, in Mexico, writes music of comparable density.

Less weighty than the music of Sessions, that of Ross Lee Finney—dodecaphonic and serial in late years—runs higher in the charm of sheer sound, with no loss of complexity interest, especially his chamber works for strings. Though Germanic in its origins, for translucency it resembles the music of the Frenchman Henri Dutilleux.

The music of Elliott Carter, less abundant than these, and achieving its highest intensity in the chamber combinations, is more complex of texture than either Sessions or Finney and at the same time easier to follow. I am not sure how this miracle comes about; but I fancy some of it is due to the composer's dramatizing instincts and imaginative ear, his ability to couch a complex thought in pleasing sounds. In any case, his Piano Sonata of 1945, his two String Quartets, and his Double Concerto for piano and harpsichord each accompanied by its own chamber group, are works of such striking originality that they have achieved a European success even in these times, when Europe seems to be viewing all our music with severity.

That severity may be due to the fact that our music is not quite like theirs any more. When it was, they could be more tolerant of it. And when it was not, but clearly no rival, as in Gershwin's irresistible *Rhapsody in Blue* or his sweet-singing opera *Porgy and Bess*, they could admire it without stint. When Cage threatened both their modernist assumptions and the hegemony of their rising power-group, he was removed—complimented yes, but firmly excluded from its patronage. Perhaps, like Gershwin, Carter is no danger to Europe from the plain fact that nobody there is even aspiring to write tonal music of that intricacy or of that intrinsic interest. With nobody to feel rivalry, everyone is free to admire. In any case, Carter's chamber works do get round internationally; virtually all find them distinguished and beautiful.

Roy Harris's works, I am sorry to say, do not travel so widely or so well. One can find priceless items among the early chamber works, and there is one remarkable symphony. These alone will preserve his fame. But his later music, though more expert, even in America tends to be less remembered.

Lou Harrison's music resembles nothing written in Europe today. Thirty years ago he wrote symphonies for percussion that could remind one of Java and Siam. Subtly sensuous and never tiring to the ear, they are among our most cherishable properties. In the last decade Harrison's Asian interests have moved to Korea, where he mastered the classical Chinese court music. He has composed in this style for its classical instruments, including the jade gong; and an adaptation of its rhetoric to European textures (not an imitation) has given him vocal works and a film score, *Nuptial*, of surprising and powerful simplicity. Between these two periods of Asian allegiance, he wrote serial pieces (as any pupil of Schoenberg might have done) and a body of work, choral, orchestral, and other, based on historic European tunings *not* tempered (which no other Schoenberg pupil did do).

One such work, a monodic opera entitled *Rapunzel's Daughter* (after William Morris), won a prize in Rome when it was sung there in 1954 by Leontyne Price. The varieties of instrumental tuning for which he has composed include Greek ones and Elizabethan ones, as well as Korean. A work commissioned by the Louisville Orchestra requires for its correct intonation, if I remember rightly, fourteen especially-built flutes. In a work for full orchestra, entitled Symphony on G, just intervals and their commas are employed to rich effect. It is a work of sustained eloquence and high Romantic afflatus, belonging in no way to our university tradition of symphonic writing.

Obviously so accomplished and so varied a production, especially when carried out from so far-off a center as San Francisco, has no resemblance to the stylistically constricted and professionally combative careers that hold attention in the East. But Lou Harrison is a great man (*une grande nature*, the French would say) with a remarkable ear, a composer both authentic and highly original as well as (thank heaven) abundant.

Henry Cowell's music since his death in 1965 has somewhat faded in program frequency. But there is so much of it in all forms and for all occasions that it is bound to remain with us a goodly while. There are more than twenty works in symphonic form alone. He has written for many instruments and under many ethnic influences, including those of the Iranians, the Icelandics, the East Indians, the Japanese, and our own Southern mountaineers. His *New Music* edition, published quarterly from 1927, brought numerous modern composers into print. His book of 1930, *New Musical Resources*, is a classic. *Charles Ives and His Music* (written with his wife Sidney Cowell) is the definitive work on this composer. His analyses of new music published regularly in *The Musical Quarterly* and other professional journals are authoritative and useful. His classes at Columbia University and at the New School for Social Research were ever a source of enlightenment to students. Few musicians indeed have left so deeply their mark on music's life—West Coast, East Coast, Latin America, and Asia—as this modest and indefatigable Californian.

His music is not complex, but it sings. It is not highly polished, but it has structure. It is not strikingly ambitious either, but it has presence. And never is it bogus or vulgar or stupid or falsely inspired. Cowell too was a great man, by his active mind and his ethical behavior, as well as by his high-standard musical abundance.

William Schuman and Samuel Barber are composers of sound repute. The former I cherish for his ballets, especially *Undertow*. The latter has contributed valuably to our vocal repertory in *Knoxville: Summer of 1915* for soprano and orchestra and in his *Hermit Songs*, remarkably to piano literature with a sonata and a concerto that are repertory works. His Adagio for Strings is world-famous. Schuman has no such international status, but his music can be listened to. Both composers are classical as to form, with Schuman regularly, observing a high dissonance texture, Barber following a more Romantic taste in harmony. Schuman has also served as president of the Juilliard School of Music and later of Lincoln Center for the Performing Arts, where administrative efficiency does not seem to have hindered his development as a composer of strongly individual gesture. With all our composers of the establishment—Copland, Sessions, Harris, Carter, Finney, Mennin, even the songful Barber—the rhythmic drive is powerful. They are masters, moreover, of the concert forms—the closed forms—but distinctly uncomfortable in the open-ended continuities of opera, which Douglas Moore and Lou Harrison have handled with greater freedom.

Ned Rorem, after eight years of residence in Paris, has aspired to produce in English a vocal repertory comparable to that of Francis Poulenc. There are also Rorem orchestral works of some brilliance—particularly *Eagles* and *Lions*—and a handful of chamber works—*Lovers*, for instance, and Eleven Pieces for Eleven Players—which, if not quite Carter or Copland, are pleasing to hear. And there are operas, all of them so far unsuccessful. Nor do his choral works, of which there are many, seem to me infallible. Certainly it is in the solo songs, of which there are literally hundreds, that Rorem makes his bid for consideration beside the creators of German and French lieder.

Consideration in this company one can grant him for his taste in the choice of poems and for grace in the melodic line. But no such intensity is present as in the German masters from Schubert through Wolf and Mahler or in the French from Duparc and Fauré through Poulenc. In fact no such intensity exists anywhere in English song (nor does it in Italian, for that matter, nor in Spanish, only a little in the Russian and the Scandinavian). Even the Elizabethans and Purcell, for all their sweetness and their wit, are like the Italians of those same times, more dainty than deep, more decorative for the line of a mood than emotionally penetrating. English-language poetry, sung, has never achieved psychology or drama as we know these qualities through the German and the French.

Consequently Rorem's effort, no less than that of Barber, of Douglas Moore, of Ernst Bacon, David Diamond, William Flanagan, the great Copland himself, and of Ives in concert songs, remains nobler for its persistently setting out on what may well be a hopeless errand than for any world's record achieved. When Poulenc, as a friend, discouraged his vocal efforts and praised the orchestral, Rorem sincerely believed him to be jealous. What can one say of so impregnable a stance? Nothing except that the English art-song is not yet a major form, and that even Benjamin Britten, with all his great gifts, has come nearer to depth in French song—to Rimbaud's *Illuminations*—than he has in English. For devotional texts Britten is ideal; but for cracking the nut of English lyric poetry, he is just another hopeful; and so is Rorem. So are we all indeed. For English opera there may be some precedent—in Britten, in Douglas Moore, in my own work. But for lieder in English I know of no model, excepting the patter songs of Gilbert and Sullivan, which are perfect. And I seriously doubt that Poulenc, Ravel, Debussy, Fauré have any more to offer an American of today than Schubert, Schumann, Brahms, Wolf, Mahler. Or for that matter, the Elizabethans and Purcell. Let us all try very hard to write English songs; by all means let us try. But I have yet to see a break-through in the matter, something as radically alive and different from its predecessors as Schubert's flexible and flowing songs are from the stiff layouts of Mozart and Beethoven. Actually Theodore

Chanler's songs, though few in number, are probably the best we have. And those of William Flanagan have a soaring intensity all unusual to the English language.

Returning to the advanced composers, I have a great devotion to the music of Kenneth Gaburo, which I find utterly delicious for sound, whether vocal or instrumental, directly heard or processed. Like the music of Lou Harrison and of Elliott Carter—though it resembles neither, being more far-out in both methods and materials—I find that it most remarkably comes to life, as if the tired old tempered scale, so hopelessly out of tune when classical harmony is not there to refresh it, had been forgotten and the ear consulted again about making music. Its sentiments, moreover, seem direct and manly, never borrowed. I admire this music for its integrity, and I delight in it.

There are other American composers whose music is precious to me—Ben Weber, Stefan Wolpe, Colin McPhee, Arthur Berger, Leon Kirchner, Irving Fine, Chou Wen-chung, and Henry Brant. The operas of Carlisle Floyd and Peggy Glanville-Hicks, of Jack Beeson, Avery Claflin, and Robert Ward have undeniable quality. And there have been four brilliant composers of Russian birth—Alexander Tcherepnin, Nicolai Berezowsky, Nicolai Lopatnikoff, and Nicolas Nabokov, all of whom have written their finest as Americans.

American is something a musician need not be ashamed to be. Painting was the first humane art to develop here, beginning in the eighteenth century and flourishing in constant touch with England. American letters have a sound nineteenth-century history, and a still stronger one in the twentieth, where they have come to overshadow the parent stem. Music has been the last to ripen, and its story seems to me altogether of this century. That is why I have written these essays. I do not believe any art's history to be one of continuous evolution or steady growth. Music's active epochs are short—from Haydn through Schubert barely fifty years, for instance. And the American maturity I write about may already be over, giving place to a time of noise and its casual arrangement.

I have written elsewhere that I expected the latter half of this century to witness the consolidation of our century's innovations into an amalgamated twentieth-century style. Something like this took place during the last quarter of the eighteenth; and I think it has taken place in our time, since World War II. Everybody successful or establishment-minded writes music now, diatonic or chromatic, with a thickish overlay of dissonance, and since 1950 with a decreasing dependence on serial continuities. Everybody orchestrates brilliantly; everyone has his tune characteristics, his devices harmonic or arithmetical for holding a piece together. Structure and form, nevertheless, remain a problem; organic form does, in any case. With harmony itself become so weak, so little urgent, arithmetical symmetries and the use of librettos have become the main resources.

And exactly as in the late eighteenth century, one composer's work is very much like another's. The chief question now seems: is it music or noise? Both are subject to compositional arrangement, of course, but by different acoustical procedures. Although the performance of the human ear in auditory perception and of the brain in auditory memory are only beginning to be investigated, it is clear already that the future of composition with noise, like that of music itself, will be influenced by the knowledge of how we hear and how certain sounds come to be pleasing or not; hence how arrangements of sound can communicate emotional patterns of anxiety and relief. For these indeed are what give continuity in all the time-arts.

Myself I see no hindrance to the survival of both noise-art and music. Photography did not kill oil painting; on the contrary, it set off in landscape painting a development known as impressionism which invigorated all painting. Similarly, the gramophone and the radio, far from killing off music, have contributed to their distribution, changed their sociology, and corrected their aesthetics.

So I am not worried. Let the boys have fun. Let us all have fun. Let Europe survive. Let America exist. Indeed I am convinced that in music it already does exist. At least that.

A Suggested Reading List

Antheil, George, *Bad Boy of Music*. Garden City, New York, Doubleday, Doran, 1945.

Berger, Arthur, *Aaron Copland*. New York, Oxford University Press, 1953.

Blesh, Rudi, and Janis, Harriet, *They All Played Ragtime*. New York, Knopf, 1950; revised with additions, paperback, New York, Oak Publications, 1966.

Broder, Nathan, *Samuel Barber*. New York, G. Schirmer, 1954.

Cage, John, *Silence: Lectures and Writings*. Middletown, Conn., Wesleyan University Press, 1961; M.I.T. Press, Cambridge, Mass. and London paperback 1966.

———, *A Year from Monday*. Middletown, Conn., Wesleyan University Press, 1969; also in paperback.

Chase, Gilbert, *America's Music: From the Pilgrims to the Present* (2nd edition, revised). New York, McGraw-Hill, 1966.

Cohn, Arthur, *The Collector's Twentieth-Century Music in the Western Hemisphere*. Philadelphia and New York, Lippincott, 1961.

Copland, Aaron, *Our New Music*. New York, Whittlesey House, 1941; revised edition entitled *The New Music*, 1968.

———, *Copland on Music*. New York, W. W. Norton, 1963.

Cowell, Henry, *New Musical Resources*. New York, Knopf, 1930; reissued with preface and notes by Joscelyn Godwin, New York, Something Else Press, 1969.

———, *American Composers on American Music*. Stanford University Press, 1933.

Cowell, Henry and Sidney, *Charles Ives and His Music*. New York, Oxford University Press, 1955.

Harrison, Lou, *About Carl Ruggles* (with a note by Henry Cowell). Yonkers, N.Y., Alicat Book Shop, 1946.

Hitchcock, H. Wiley, *Music in the United States: A Historical Introduction*. Englewood Cliffs, N.J., Prentice-Hall, 1969.

Hoover, Kathleen and Cage, John, *Virgil Thomson: His Life and Music*. New York and London, Thos. Yoseloff, 1959.

Ives, Charles, *Essays Before a Sonata* (edited by Howard Boatwright). New York, W. W. Norton, 1961.

Maisel, Edward M., *Charles T. Griffes: The Life* . . . New York, Knopf, 1943.

Mellers, Wilfrid, *Music in a New Found Land: Themes and Developments in the History of American Music.* London, Barrie and Rockcliff; New York, Knopf, 1964.

Ouellette, Fernand, *Edgard Varèse.* Paris, Seghers, 1966; translated from the French by Derek Coltman, New York, The Orion Press, 1968.

Pound, Ezra, *Antheil and The Treatise on Harmony* (reprint of the 1927 edition with a new introduction by Ned Rorem). New York, Da Capo Press, 1968.

Reis, Claire R., *Composers in America: Biographical Sketches of Contemporary Composers with a Record of Their Works.* New York, Macmillan, 1947.

———, *Composers, Conductors, and Critics.* New York, Oxford University Press, 1955.

Rorem, Ned, *The Paris Diary of Ned Rorem.* New York, Braziller, 1966.

———, *Music and People.* New York, Braziller, 1968.

Rosenfeld, Paul, *Musical Impressions* (selected from Paul Rosenfeld's criticism, edited and with an introduction by Herbert A. Leibowitz). New York, Hill and Wang, 1969.

Schuller, Gunther, *Early Jazz: Its Roots and Musical Development.* New York, Oxford University Press, 1968.

Smith, Julia, *Aaron Copland: His Work and Contribution to American Music.* New York, E. P. Dutton, 1955.

Thomson, Virgil, *The State of Music* (2nd edition, revised). New York, Random House, 1962.

———, *Virgil Thomson.* New York, Knopf, 1966.

———, *Music Reviewed: 1940–1954.* New York, Random House, 1967.

Yates, Peter, *Twentieth Century Music: Its Evolution from the End of the Harmonic Era into the Present Era of Sound.* New York, Random House, 1967.

Gelatt, Roland; Foss, Lukas; Hamilton, David, "The New Music: its Sources, its Sounds, its Creators." *High Fidelity,* September 1968.

Kostelanetz, Richard, "The American Avant-Garde Part I:

Milton Babbitt, Part II: John Cage." *Stereo Review*, April and May, 1969.

Luening, Otto, "The Unfinished History of Electronic Music." *Music Educators Journal*, November 1968.

Peyser, Joan, "The Troubled Time of Marc Blitzstein." *Columbia University Forum*, Winter 1966.

The files of *Modern Music*, Minna Lederman, editor, published quarterly by the League of Composers from the 1920's through 1947, are a gold mine of writing by and about American composers.

Stereo Review, from 1962 to the present, has published extended, scholarly, and informative studies of American composers including Ives, Ruggles, Copland, Hanson, Harris, Barber, Thomson, Gershwin, Gottschalk, virtually everybody major in the field.

From

MUSIC WITH WORDS
A Composer's View

Contents

Preface

THIS IS NOT A TEXTBOOK. It is merely a group of essays about vocal music, as composers face the writing of it, especially to English words.

Most of these pieces are new; the two longest are older. Chapter I is a lecture that I have been giving in clubs and colleges for over fifty years. I have not previously allowed its publication lest distribution in that form injure its earning-power; but I have rewritten it to refresh its language about every ten or twelve years. The next to last piece, a discourse about opera, was published in *Parnassus*, a quarterly devoted to the criticism of poetry.

The chapters do not need to be read consecutively, nor do they make up a syllabus. When I have held classes in vocal composition I have used their materials, but my main procedure there was simply to read over the music that the students had composed and then help them, if I could, to improve it. This method resembles what law schools call "the case system." As a result, the book presents itself less as a program of skills to be progressively acquired than as a body of knowledge which can be browsed in, remembered perhaps, used when needed, and little by little encompassed.

Whether the suggestions here offered are practical can best be learned by trying them out. Whether my opinions about music are in the long run convincing may take some time to learn. I admit right off, however, that my personal views of vocal music are not those commonly held regarding the English-language repertory.

I give far more attention to opera, for example, than would seem to be justified by the meager success that that form has enjoyed in our tongue. And I have not treated extensively our choral music, which has been since the fourteenth century (in Latin) and since the mid-sixteenth century (in English) one of the glories of Europe. Even in America, with our gifted colonials and our inventive folkways—our fuguing-tunes and white spirituals, our blues, show-songs and commercial pops, not to speak of experimental modernisms by Charles Ives and many others—singing in all its forms has been a favored indulgence.

693

These outpourings, especially in the pops and in the folk field, have been so thoroughly written about already as to need no comment from me. Even the concert song, in spite of its constant practice by our best composers, does not seem to have followed in recent times any major creative direction. Nor has it in England either, for that matter.

More and more I tend to find opera, which is the grandest, the most varied, and the richest of all theatrical forms, to be also the most encompassing among vocal possibilities. Getting it into English and making it stick there, to make the writing of English operas seem a worthy way of life, that I think is the preoccupation today of forward-looking composers in both England and America.

Symphonic composition, either there or here, I have little faith in. And chamber music everywhere is chiefly tolerable today as an experiment in methodology. Writing more solo works for the pianoforte, the organ, the violin, or the cello is looking backward to the masters who by creating for these instruments with so comprehensive a palette actually patented, and exhausted, the gamut of feelings that anybody now living can find urgent in the sound of those instruments. There is still fun to be had with woodwinds maybe, just maybe. And the concert song in English is, I fear, a never-never land from which few invaders bring home booty.

But opera composed in English is still unfinished business, worth working at, and possibly, in view of what has happened since 1930 both in the United Kingdom and with us, possibly alive and certainly wiggling. These thoughts may explain the lack of a reasoned balance in my consideration of the field.

They do not justify, of course, the quoting of examples uniquely from my own works. That is a liberty I have taken because they are the repertory I know best. And they actually illustrate most of the situations mentioned in the text. Any student or any instructor can, I am sure, think of others no less apt.

I

A Formal Introduction to the Subject

THE UNION OF POETRY AND MUSIC is older than recorded time. In ancient Greece they were inseparable. All music had words, and all the plays were sung. Nowadays poetry and music live apart. I am speaking of classical music and of poetry for reading, not folk tunes nor the ditties we call "popular." Nearly the whole of our rhymed folklore, as well as the commercial product, still consists of words *and* music.

In popular music, both folk and commercial, a tune may well be older than its verses. Also, many a tunesmith and his lyricist work together. But more commonly, in Tin Pan Alley just as in the backwoods, almost any song begins its life as a melody.

In the world of serious music, on the other hand, it is poems that get music fitted to them. Sometimes, I know, new words are run up for old melodies, and beloved airs from oratorio and opera have been known to be used again, sometimes by their own composers, George Frideric Handel for instance. But nobody, literally nobody ever tries to create an oratorio or opera by first composing an instrumental score, in the hope that someone someday will put a libretto under it.

In performance, things are again reversed. The words of a pop song, though the last element to be added, have first rights toward being understood. Vocalism, in this practice, is less important than enunciation. With art music, on the other hand, beauty of tone may well be the objective. One has to have words to write a concert song, but in performance these are not always easy to distinguish.

All the same, it is pleasanter to understand what music is saying than merely to enjoy the sound that it makes. So if songs really need words (as indeed they mostly do, since the human voice without them is just another wind instrument) then there has to be in the marriage of words and music a basic compatibility in which the text's exact shape and purpose dominate the union, or seem to. I say seem to, because actually a large part of music's contribution lies in the emotional timings, the urgencies about continuity, the whole pacing and moving-forwardness of the composition that only music can provide.

When a composer lays out a text for musical setting, he does something like what an actor would do preparing to read it aloud. He spaces it for its natural word-groups, phrases, sentences, paragraphs, periods. Clarity of meaning is his first objective; second, a reasonable amount of feeling may be laid on. But not overindulgently, we hope, since enunciation must always take precedence. Indeed, we suspect any speaker of insincerity who assumes an undue expressivity, like a radio announcer trying to sell us something.

Actually the composer who simply scans his text may be doing it better service than the one who competes with it to assure us how deeply he feels about it. The basis of communication, in other words, is a plain verbal prosody. Enrichment of this through apt vocal turn, instrumental illustration, even a grandly symphonic structure, all the devices that give music its larger life, are welcome, but only so far as they do not obscure the meaning or misplace an emphasis.

Tennyson boasted that he knew the prosody of every word in English except *scissors*. Myself I do not feel so confident. The word *banana*, for instance, may be easy for a poet. But it can be troublesome for music, as in the once-popular refrain

Yes, we have no bananas.

Later we shall analyze the vowels in this word.

In analyzing any text we must remember that language is not just one word after another. It is printed that way, but not so spoken or sung. In performance it is an arbitrarily ordered string of vocal noises. These may vary in length and loudness; but each is only one kind of sound, represented by a symbol of its own in the International Phonetic Alphabet. And not one of these sounds, heard alone, means anything. When ordered into recognizable rows they are called words, and a list of these, printed out, makes a dictionary. Also, words are attached by common consent to meanings, often to several meanings. But the meaning of a discourse is not the result of their looking in print like a string of words. It is the result of their being organized into word-groups.

These groups sound like words, and they operate like words in the sense that they have accents and durations that cannot, at least in English, be altered or interrupted without changing the meaning. Nor can they be punctuated, though compound words may accept a hyphen.

"How do you do?," for instance, is a word-group admitting no change in the order or accentuation of its sounds. It means consequently not at all what it looks like, a string of words, but what it sounds like, a pattern of phonemes. In this agreed upon pattern lies its meaning. A listing of the phonemes familiar to Europe and the Americas is called the International Phonetic Alphabet. But of that too, more later.

To show how a literary text falls into meaningful word-groups, let me cite the opening lines of Milton's sonnet "On His Blindness":

> When I consider how my light is spent
> E're half my days in this dark world and wide,

What are the word-groups here? "When I consider" is the first; this represents a thought minimally stated. "How my light is spent" is another; it is almost divisible into two thoughts, but not quite. "E're half my days" is clearly the next statement, followed by "in this dark world," and finally "and wide," this last an extension of "dark world," but independent of it.

Nowhere in these lines is any single word meaningful. Only word-groups have that kind of reality. And to maintain its reality each of these must be pronounced without interruption. Moreover, the sonnet itself, read aloud, is not a sequence of its lines or of its words, only of its word-groups. Any string of these can be assembled into a phrase or cut up, if the meaning permits, into short sentences or into exclamations. But they can no more be split up into words than words themselves can be thought of as just letters.

Before being set to music, a text, any text, needs to be mapped into meaningful word-groups, very much as has been done above with the first two lines of Milton's sonnet. After that, they need to be examined in detail, for speaking or for singing, as simply vowels and consonants.

I must explain at this point my aim, which is to establish a method of operation for vocal writing in English or in American. These languages can be considered for singing, I think, as identical. They differ in speech, of course. Winston Churchill and Franklin Roosevelt, for example, did not speak at all alike, though in both cases their diction was clearly upper-class. On the other hand, I defy anyone to find a noticeable difference between Leontyne Price's way of singing English and Kathleen Ferrier's, since both used a singer's approach to the idiom. And it is artists of this class, plus the studios that train them, that exemplify the performance conventions now current.

These conventions, I may add, have not changed much in the last four centuries. A need for constantly explaining them to composers does arise, however, because musicians, with their many differences of education and of racial background, as well as with the heavy preponderance of instrumental music that dominates our modern culture, are often out of touch with vocal traditon.

I may also suggest that the study of linguistics, nowadays a branch of philosophy, is not likely to be of much service to musicians. Phonetics, yes. That is of value for examining word-groups and their regional variations, also for using the International Phonetic Alphabet, should such need arise. A grave trouble with phoneticians is that their inveterate preoccupation with change makes them somewhat indifferent to standard practice. They are fascinated by evolution and decay. Our aim, as music professionals, is more toward the conservation of tested ways.

Returning to the phonemes, individual sounds in any language can vary in length, in loudness, in timbre (or vocal color), and in pitch. Variations of pitch, the up-and-downness of a phrase or word-grouping, we may call cadence. European languages do not consider cadence a fixed pattern. Chinese does. A classmate of this writer, living in China, boasted of having undergone a nose-and-throat operation merely to facilitate pronunciation of the highest (is it the fourth or fifth?) of the Chinese nasals.

Cadences in English, though they may tend toward the conventional in local usage, are not fixed by custom. On the contrary, they are free and often quite fanciful. In German they can be even more so. One remembers a waiter offering a second serving, "Wünchen Sie auch Fisch?," as if it were fresh water to the dying. Also note the exaggerated, indeed almost comical risings and fallings of the voice of Arnold Schönberg's German cantata *Pierrot Lunaire.*

English and American, of course, show many differences of cadence, as in the familiar "I say," and "Are you there?"

In Continental European music generally, cadence, being a free element, becomes for melody a source of illustration, as well as of emotional intensities.

To remind us of how vivid the sound-pictures can be let us recall Brahms's song about a blacksmith, "Der Schmied," in which the subject is evoked by both the vocal line and its piano accompaniment.

Brahms, "Der Schmied," op. 19, no. 4

Also Richard Wagner's exultant cry of the Valkyries as they gallop through the air on horseback, carrying to Valhalla some slain hero.

Wagner, Die Walküre, *act 3*

Henry Purcell's Englishman is even more specific about attempting "from love's sickness to fly-y-y."

Purcell, The Indian Queen

And similarly for Franz Schubert's jumping trout.

Schubert, "Die Forelle"

But the most elaborate of all such descriptions is the tenor solo which opens Handel's *Messiah*, where the most expert (by far) of England's vocal composers (a foreigner too he was, north German by way of Italy) offers a musical idea so bold as to be almost a caricature of its text. Coloratura for the male voice seems neither to have fazed him nor shocked the faithful, when he depicted Isaiah's promise to flatten out the earth in order to "make straight in the desert a highway for our God."

Handel, Messiah

Stresses, in English, are not free at all; they are fixed for both speech and singing. You cannot with impunity change the tonic accents of English words or word-groups, because if you do you change the meaning.

When Macbeth, about to commit a regicide, seems to hesitate, his wife cries, "Give me the knife!" Now every actress must have decided in advance which word in that exclamation to emphasize, *give* or *me* or *knife*, because in her choice lies the possibility of three distinct meanings.

On the other hand, if you pronounce Pepsi-Cola as Pepsicola, you make it meaningless in English, though it can sound convincing, if still meaningless, as possibly an Italian word.

In English the length of sounds, especially for singing, is more variable than their stressings. Their length can vary from very short to very long. Church chanting shows this variability in its simplest form:

"O come, let us sing unto the Lord; let us heartily rejoice in the strength of our salvation."

This is a series of word-groups, none of them extensible in the context. The whole last line (to "salvation") goes best in patter.

Latin lends itself to melisma (or florid vocalizing), English to patter, French to syllabic individualization.*

A - dieu   no-tre pe - ti - te ta - ble

Massenet, Manon

As a reminder that the art of putting English to music is largely a matter of not disturbing the fixed elements, let me repeat that the attributes of speech-sound are: stress, or accentuation, which in English is unvariable; cadence, which is extremely variable—but only within the limits of the third attribute, quantity, since certain sounds are considered extensible and others not. Accents in English cannot be changed without changing the meaning. Cadence can be widely varied to illustrate meanings or to intensify them, but only where the phonemes, or units of speech-sound, are in themselves extensible.

O - vos_   a - ni - mae_ be - a - tae, ex - sul - ta - te,_ ju - bi - ta - te

al - le - lu - ja, al - le - lu - ja,_

Mozart, Exultate jubilate

* The standard practice in setting French is one note per syllable. This makes a whole syllable out of every mute *e*. Omitting a mute *e* makes the style colloquial (as in *Madam'* or *M'sieur*). Also, a florid musical style can use slurred vowels. But the standard practice of one-note-per-syllable is what gives to French vocal music the air of being all recitative.

Let us examine these extensibilities a little, beginning with the consonants. For indeed consonants do vary in length, from the instantaneous *p* and *t* to the infinitely extensible *l* and *m*, which can last till breath gives out. Undue prolongation of these is not, let me remind you, good style in art singing, though the popular canon encourages it.

Vowels are much simpler, because none is instantaneous. They are commonly classed for timbre as open, closed, or nasal; for duration as long or short. Their lengths give little trouble so long as one allows a bit of time for the long ones and does not expect the short ones to be held. *Home* is a long word; one can make it quite long but not really short, because both its vowel and its final consonant invite holding. *Pit* is a completely short word; it cannot be extended at all and understood. Two short consonants here cut off at both ends a vowel already short.

All vowels, even the shortest, are variable for length, because the consonants that surround them control their extensibility. Let us observe what the longer consonants can do to short vowel sounds, and vice versa.

There are lengthened short vowels, for instance, in *rest* and *love*. These are extended by the consonants that frame them. But the same vowels as those in *rest* and *love* are radically shortened by their consonants in *pet* and *putt*.

Then there are shortened long vowels, as in *pope* and *gate*. These same vowels *o* and *a* need more time in *home* and *lane*. The long consonants *h*, *m*, *l*, and *n* stretch them out.

Along with our vowels we must include the diphthongs and the mutes. A diphthong is two or more vowels heard in succession, such as *eye* and *you*. Mutes are decayed vowels, such as the *a* in *sofa*, and they all sound alike.

Diphthongs in English are numerous, though less so, I think, than in Russian or Portuguese. They include the so-called vowels *i* and *u*, but not the merely apparent diphthongs spelled *aw* or *ou*, whenever these are pronounced as simple vowels, as in *thaw* and *through*. Certain consonants also have a vowel behavior. The written letter *r*, for instance, except when it occurs at the beginning of a word, as in *rapid*, or between two vowels, as in *arrange*, or in combination with a short consonant, as in *betray*, is very likely to behave as if it were a vowel. It combines, for instance, with all the vowels, as in *ar*, *er*, *ir*, *or*, *ur*. In *York*, it almost makes a diphthong of the *aw* sound; in *Jersey*, it becomes the French vowel *eu*. The exact extensibility for singing of these *r* vowels is uncertain, but in general they seem to have the same minimum length as the long vowels. At the end of a word, however, they approach the brevity of a mute like the *a* in *sofa*—as in *builder, contractor, driver, passenger, motor*, and *river*. They are not true mutes, however, because for singing some can be extended, as in *S'wanee River*.

Way   down up - on   de   Swan - ee   rib - ber,

Foster, Old Folks at Home (S'wanee River)

Singing will always show up vowel decay. The *e* sounds in *angels* and *roses*, for instance, cannot be treated as *eh*, nor yet as *uh*. A bit of the French *eu* will serve well here. The first syllable of *Jerusalem*, on the other hand, is customarily sung in the best English choirs as *Juh*, lengthened by a fairly open mouth. In all three cases it helps to push the lips forward just a bit. None of them is a pure vowel any longer, but neither are they quite yet fully decayed into mutes.

A mute is the shortest vowel sound possible. It has no color—and no extension. No matter how you spell it, it sounds like *uh*. French is full of mutes, as in the first syllable of *besoin* or the last one of *père*. So is German.* The mutes in English are troublesome to unmask, since many of them, though spoken, are rarely sung, for example *heav'n, sev'n, elev'n*. The final syllable here, unlike the final *a* of *sofa* or of *banana*, should not be extended at all in singing. This last word seems to have one

---

*In German the mute is called a *Schwa*, and it is pronounced, since classical German observes no elisions. Nor liaisons either, even in compound words, where only a slight hesitation separates the elements—two consonants in the case of *Konzertstück* (or concerto), a vowel requiring a stroke of the glottis in *Liederabend* (or song recital), and especially in compounds where the vowel itself is double, as in *Goetheabend* (or Goethe evening). Omission of the schwa can occur occasionally, but only on a very short note or in pop songs, never in speech. The very common term *heute Abend* (this evening), and there are many like it, is not a compound at all but a word-group which behaves like a compound.

elision, one mute, and only one proper vowel, that being of medium length, not indefinitely extensible. It could be written *b'nanuh*. The English poets, as Edgar Allan Poe pointed out, have all treated *sev'n* as one syllable.

Scissors resembles *river*. The vowels are the same, one short, with accent, and one long. Three sibilant consonants do, however, tend to tighten the rhythm of *scissors* and to speed it up.

And so, to repeat about English quantities, or durations, before returning to the stresses. All phonemes have some duration, and consonants are as variable in this respect as vowels. The only reason I do not treat them in detail is simply that though certain of these are indefinitely extensible, say *l* and *m*, the present conventions governing art music and its rendering do not admit their undue prolongation, even for expressive purposes. The vowel sounds in such music are, on the other hand, on account of their extensibility, the carriers of the free (or expressive) element in song, the up-and-downness of a melody, which I call cadence. The mutes and the short vowels, which are mostly not extensible, contribute more vigorously to the rhythmic design of a tune than to its shape. The long vowels and the diphthongs are all extensible, though not equally so, because the surrounding consonants have an effect on vowel lengths, as do also the conventional stresses in words and in word-groups-that-operate-as-words.

The word-group "How do you do?" contains two diphthongs and two long vowels. Though all of its sounds are theoretically extensible, only the final syllable *oo* can be held, and that not much. In fact, under heavy usage the other vowels tend to disappear, leaving only one true vowel and one mute, as in *H'do*.

Let us turn now to the stresses. Tonic accents in English are fixed. There are a few exceptions, such as gladiolus versus (in American) gladiolus and our library versus the English library. But such variants only call attention to the fact that English words normally admit no uncertainty about stress. Our language has many worrisome quantities (as in *scissors* and *banana*) but its stresses are firm.

French is just the other way. Its quantities are exact, but its tonic stresses are almost completely displaceable. It is the freedom of the stresses in French, in fact, that has encouraged an erroneous belief that French has no tonic accents. Unusual variations of stress in French simply mark the foreigner, or the social out-sider. Changing the stress does not make a passage hard to recognize, and it does not alter the meaning of a French phrase. Only a change in word order can do that, such as "Donnez-le-moi le couteau" or "Le couteau, donnez-le-moi."

In single English words or in word-groups any change in the conventional stress makes for either comedy or nonsense.

In longer word-groups, or in sentences, shifting the stress will radically alter the meaning, as in "Give me the knife!"

In brief, stresses are the firmest element in our language. That is why it is the stresses and not the quantities that we mark in scanning verse. And the composing of these for expressive purpose is an author's job, not a composer's, who can do little more, in setting a text, than to avoid the violation of an already fixed pattern. It is, in fact, the conflict between our fixed stresses and the fixed duration of the short vowels that produces in vocal music our characteristic syncopation, as in the word *river*. Note that *er*, actually the French *eu*, here acts as a long vowel.

The whole story of English prosody in music is contained in the first line of Stephen Foster's *Old Folks at Home* (*S'wanee River*). Let us pretend to compose this, and see what happens.

If we plot only the stresses, they come out exactly as in the tune.

Now let us plot the quantities. They come out almost exact, with a syncopation on *river* inevitable. The spondee (or equalization of both stress and quantity) of *S'wanee* is merely voluntary, not inevitable, since the river's real name is *Sewanee*, in three syllables. (America tends to invent spondees, in fact, as in *Jap-Ann*.)

Now we are free to arrange the cadence, its rise and fall, for expressivity. Treating *Sewanee* as a two-syllable spondee makes for folksy diction. The octave skip gives distance, farawayness, hence nostalgia. The rising third permits a long last syllable, which adds more nostalgia. And so we have a melodic line that consists of words *and* music, a song phrase. It is a good one too, because its elements are mated, not just living together.

Instrumental accompaniment, where that seems needed, is another problem, because it has its own laws, exactly as the building of a melody does. But also, as in the vocal part of the composition, there is a range of activity where the imagination is free to illustrate a scene or to provoke a sentiment. But there are also passages where the composer can do little more than to underline (or to contradict) a melody's harmonic implications, or to punctuate the natural breathing points of the voice-line. What I must point out about both the voice-line and whatever instrumental accompaniment the composer may add is that their composing is not wholly a matter of improvisation.

Prosodic declamation, let me insist, is a constant in mature languages, from Schütz to Schubert, say; from Rameau to Poulenc; from Byrd to Britten; from the *Prayer-Book of Edward the Sixth* to *Four Saints in Three Acts.* Accompaniments change with fashions in emotional refinement and in dissonance content, but prosodic declamation, even in the florid style, changes very little, because the language itself, once mature, changes hardly at all.

Many devices for aiding melodic invention are historic and available—the visual, the sentimental, the comic, and of course the accents of passion. Out of any of these sources a perfect song or operatic recitative may spring full-blown from the subconscious. But sometimes a composer needs to balance rival urgencies—say, the structural and the expressive. In such a case, and all art work is full of them, he may have to accept a compromise. But compromises are not what makes art beautiful. Beauty is not a product of opposing forces, which neutralize each other, but of vector forces, which combine. And the combining of words with music is a technique no less frozen and no less free than the combining of instrumental parts with one another into a harmonious or a nonharmonious counterpoint. Some of the procedure is rigid, and that makes it a technique. Some of it leaves free play to the fancy, and that makes vocal writing an art. Observing only the rigidities will not make art a communication, because there is no communication without some expressive intent. And neither will expressive intent make either art *or* communication. These can only be made by an expressive intent, conscious or unconscious, working within a framework of accepted customs.

The deliberate violation of these traffic rules is any artist's privilege, in many cases his glory. Ignorance of them, however, is no excuse for messes. There are lots of English-speaking composers on the road these days, many of them hoping to arrive at Parnassus by way of the opera, the oratorio, the vehicles of choral setting and of song. And it is terrifying to watch them break up their means of transport every time they come to a textual passage that presents anything beyond average complexity of word-groupings or of enunciation. This essay is not offered as a course in how to avoid such mishaps. There is, to my knowledge, no such course available in the English-speaking world. What *is* available is a body of surviving folk song and a repertory of vocal composition in English covering more than four centuries, in which the composer can find for himself solutions for many of the emergencies.

None of the problems is new, and a composer with an ear for his own language can solve many of them without consulting precedents. The only fatal procedure is to forget that English is one of the most varied and expressive of all languages. Attempts to write music in it, or to sing it, as if it were Italian or German or French or Russian or Yiddish (and I've heard every one of these tried) are bound to failure.

Admitting that English really exists, however, that its nature is its nature, and that its behavior under stress is no less individual than that of any other language is to put oneself in a position from which its musical employment can be seriously, even hopefully perhaps, envisaged.

2

Word-Groups

I F THE SINGING OF WORDS is to be thought of as intoned speech, which it is, then for any singer the main question is: "Who's talking?"

It is also the first decision to be made by the composer before setting a text. The assumption to be avoided in every case is that music, certainly the vocal part of it, speaks only for the composer. It is not the voice of the composer, any more than the characters in a play represent the author of it.

Impersonation is the whole of almost any dramatic situation; and it is as unavoidable in liturgical uses as it is in theaters or on the concert stage. A sacred text may offer us the voice of a Prophet, or that of worshipers met together for praises and prayers, or of a biblical narrator, or of the Holy Comforter, even of God Himself. The composer is merely a transmitter of such a message. In liturgical situations this is rarely chosen by him, though for recital songs the choice may indeed have been his own. On secular occasions the vocal line is usually the voice of a poet, even when impersonating someone else's rejoicings or laments; or he too may also be just a storyteller.

After we, the listeners, have learned who is talking, we have some right as well to know what he is talking about. And the closest we can get to that is through hearing his words. An obscure verbal text—and believe me both poets and prophets love to hide their meanings, or themselves to hide behind a mass of meanings—an obscure text is best transmitted by its own words clearly projected. Certainly any willful obscurity on the literary side is not helped by faulty enunciation. Vowels insufficiently differentiated, consonant finals omitted, and tonic accents misplaced produce a confusion that renders even the most straightforward writing inept as communication.

At this point we must remember that the cardinal difference between language sung or spoken and language written down is that the latter presents itself to the eye as a string of words separated by spaces and arranged in lines. These words are spelled out in letters that give us only their sound. The letters themselves have no meaning; they are merely signs for sound.

Words, translated into sounds, do have meanings, often several quite different meanings; but the transmission of thoughts or of feelings requires that the words be pronounced (or read) as word-groups. Word-groups and groups of word-groups, which are where communication begins, are not indicated in the usual layouts of written or printed language, though shorthand systems do include abbreviations for some of the commoner word-groups. Groupings must therefore be determined by the speaker or, if they are to be sung, by the composer, before they can be presented to a listener. They are the minimal transmission units of either speech or song.

Let me give a few examples. "How do you do?" is a word-group. Its constituent words, though frequently used in other groupings, here have to be said together. All word-groups behave like words, this particular group as if it were a four-syllable word with a tonic accent on the last. Any attempt to separate the syllables or to misplace the accent will produce confusion. Also, though punctuated as a question, it is never so pronounced, being simply a salutation, nothing more.

Its commonest answer, "Very well, I thank you," does tend, curiously enough, toward the rising voice. This is a two-part word-group with possible accents on *well* and *thank*. If sung as an answering recitative for two persons, it allows the accent on *thank* to be weakened just a trifle, in order to bring out the rhyme of *do* and *you*. Metrical verse, rhyming, and patter all allow distortion in word-groups, and especially in groups of word-groups.

They actually invite the imposition of rhythmic patterns on to natural speech-cadences. In English, however, the displacement of a tonic accent will almost invariably either change the meaning of anything or produce nonsense. I suggest therefore to composers preparing to set words that they line out the verbal text into word-groups and their relevant further groupings.

My first example is Milton's sonnet "On His Blindness," a poem so little oratorical and so deeply reflective that it seems scarcely suitable at all for musical setting. It could, however, be set for singing, just as it can be marked for recitation. And in either case the word-groupings would be the same.

In my analysis ⌐⎯⎯⎯⌐ indicates a single word-group. For double or larger groupings I use ⌐⌐⌐⌐.

I include here also William Blake's "Tiger! Tiger!" and a song from Shakespeare's *Measure for Measure*. The latter lines, actually written to be sung, are so exigent musically that their grouping comes out in at least one of them, quite surprisingly, to compress the words *lips* and *away* into a unit every bit as strong as "How do you do?"

Take, O, take those lips away

Here are all three poems broken down into their constituent word-groups and groups of word-groups:

John Milton, "*On His Blindness*"

When I consider how my light is spent

E're half my days in this dark world and wide,

And that one Talent which is death to hide,

Lodg'd with me useless, though my Soul more bent

To serve therewith my Maker, and present

My true account lest he returning chide,

Doth God exact day-labour, light deny'd,

I fondly ask; But patience to prevent

That murmur, soon replies, God doth not need

Either man's work or his own gifts, who best

Bear his mild yoke, they serve him best, his State

Is Kingly. Thousands at his bidding speed

And post o'er Land and Ocean without rest:

They also serve who only stand and wait.

William Blake, "*The Tiger*"

Tiger! Tiger! burning bright

In the forests of the night,

What immortal hand or eye

Could frame thy fearful symmetry?

In what distant deeps or skies

Burnt the fire of thine eyes?

On what wings dare he aspire?

What the hand dare seize the fire?

And what shoulder, and what art,

Could twist the sinews of thy heart?

And when the heart began to beat,

What dread hand? and what dread feet?

What the hammer? what the chain?

In what furnace was thy brain?

What the anvil? what dread grasp

Dare its deadly terrors clasp?

When the stars threw down their spears,

And water'd heav'n with their tears,

Did he smile his work to see?

Did he who made the Lamb make thee?

Tiger! Tiger! burning bright

In the forests of the night,

What immortal hand or eye,

Dare frame thy fearful symmetry?

William Shakespeare, "*Take, O, Take Those Lips Away*"
(a song from *Measure for Measure*)

Take, O, Take those lips away

That so sweetly were forsworn;

And those eyes, the break of day,

Lights that do mislead the morn.

But my kisses bring again, bring again,

Seals of love, but seal'd in vain, Seal'd in vain.

Please note that no single word or word-group has here any meaning save in the context. It is merely a unit for pronunciation. It cannot be interrupted, nor can its conventional accent be changed. Double or triple word-groups do allow, if the speaker or composer so chooses, a slight hesitation between the groups, though not a real pause. The natural word and word-group accents remain firm. And a meaning related to that of the sentence that encloses them has begun to appear. This cannot be complete, of course, until a verb turns up.

I suggest that beginning composers, and those whose native language is not ours, practice this analysis of texts into meaningful word-groupings as an exercise in the idomatic enunciation of English. It cannot guide their melodic invention, but it will surely help toward giving to any text its maximum of plain speaking.

Regarding common phrases as word-groups. "In a minute" is a group, just like "How do you do?" In any context it behaves like a single word and is indivisible.

"Just a minute" is not so straightforward. It can be broken apart into two elements, and accented in several different ways. Like Lady Macbeth's "Give me the knife," it can change its meaning with different stresses. It is therefore a dual group, not a single one, and must be represented as just a minute.

Single word-groups, even in nonsense poetry, remain intact unless they are subjected to distortions that result from a rigorously applied rhythmic sequence. This can produce a highly comic effect without disturbing the real identity of the words.

Gertrude Stein, "*Susie Asado*"

Sweet sweet sweet sweet sweet tea.

Susie Asado.

Sweet sweet sweet sweet sweet tea.

Susie Asado.

Susie Asado which is a told tray sure.

A lean on the shoe this means slips slips hers.

When the ancient light grey is clean it is yellow, it is a silver seller.

This is a please this is a please these are the saids to jelly.
These are the wets these say the sets to leave a crown to Incy.
Incy is short for incubus.

A pot. A pot is a beginning of a rare bit of trees. Trees tremble, the old vats are in bobbles, bobbles which shade and shove and render clean, render clean must.

Drink pups.

Drink pups drink pups lease a sash hold, see it shine and a bobolink has pins. It shows a nail.

What is a nail. A nail is unison.

Sweet sweet sweet sweet sweet tea.

The poems here marked for their constituent word-groups are all relatively familiar—one each by Milton, William Blake, and Shakespeare, and one by Gertrude Stein. I do not insist that my analysis of their multiple groupings is the only one possible, though I do think my single groups are correct. Those involving more than one do tend, in their contexts, to cohere. And there is in Blake's "Tiger!" a whole line that seems to allow no interruption when it says, ". . . and when the heart began to beat."

These layouts are not for the composer to follow literally, though no single group will permit any change of accentuation; nor can its run-through be interrupted. Also, they have little to do with expression; they are merely phonetic units that when strung out in a given order do produce a verbal discourse, and inevitably some kind of meaning.

3
Occasions for Singing

As for the kinds of music available to word setters, the choice is large and generally determined by occasions—liturgical, theatrical, social, or casual.

The following are among the most common:

1. *Melodrama*—familiar with films, television, and stage plays—is instrumental music played along with speaking, sometimes called "voice-over." Here the musical continuity must dominate, but without obscuring the words or competing with them for loudness. A flowing musical texture is likely to work best, with a minimum of counterpoint.

2. *Church chanting* is a repeating music-pattern for reciting a lengthy text. It uses a plain harmonic accompaniment, or none. Clarity has no urgency here, since the texts—psalms, prayers, and canticles—are familiar. If they are not, then a clean enunciation is needed in which crescendo, diminuendo, and rhythmic emphasis are to be avoided.

3. *Patter* is a rapid articulation of verses, usually comic and rhymed, which invites in the accompaniment both rhythmic support and comical additions.

4. *Recitative*, rhymed or unrhymed, mimics the patterns of speech. Verbal clarity is important here, and some expression may be of value. Only one person sings at a time. Accompaniments to recitative must be harmonically straightforward and as simple as possible. Rhythm, if overt, must not interfere, nor should contrapuntal interest ask for attention. A verbal text and its easy reception are the essentials.

5. *Arioso* is informal as to structure and expressive in its purpose. Less static than an aria, it is valuable for advancing the drama.

6. The *aria*, either classical or modern, is a set-piece. It explains with intensity, is an emotional outpouring or, at the least, a sustained account. Paired with a free-form recitative, it can easily last twenty minutes. It is of great value to opera or oratorio, where it can offer detailed characterization and invite extended audience enjoyment of both the story and its musical

setting. It does not advance the drama; it merely intensifies by musical means its emotional content. It can be declamatory in mood, or quiet.

7. The *duet* is an aria for two persons that can also be either declamatory (argumentative) or jointly declarative, as in love scenes. The accompaniment may be illustrative, as in the love-making passages from Wagner's *Tristan und Isolde*, or merely supportive, as so often with the Italian masters, even in love scenes.

8. *Concerted pieces* are static like arias. They usually mark a confrontation, as in the celebrated quartets from Verdi's *Rigoletto* and from Mozart's *Don Giovanni*. They are sustained by their musical continuities, but they also involve strong contrasts of character. Their vocal counterpoint is therefore differentiated, nonhomogeneous; also, it is generated largely by characterization. Choral additions, once identified, can enrich the literary background.

9. The *madrigal* is a vocal work for individual voices, commonly four to six, in which the counterpoint, no matter how elaborate, is homogeneous, that is to say, nondifferentiated by characterization. It is not a dramatic form, but a lyric poem or ballad set for joint performance by a small number of singers, often without accompaniment. Its relation to the verbal text is the same as that of a recital song; verbal clarity is important. Its liturgical equivalents are the choral motet (unaccompanied) and the anthem (with keyboard support).

10. Ballets can also involve some vocal presence, spoken or sung. In these works, though dancing takes first place, hearing the words is helpful.

11. In the *scena*, any opera may have a moment of pantomime along with the singing. This must, however, advance the dramatic action.

12. The most elaborate of all vocal usages is the scene- or act-finale. This summarizes the story before a pause, or terminates it. Musically and dramatically finales are free in form. They can include recitatives, solos, concerted numbers, choral comments, as well as confrontations, quarrels, surprises, discoveries, happy endings, insoluble dilemmas, and tragic outcomes. The second act finale of Mozart's *Marriage of Figaro* and the whole of Wagner's *Götterdämmerung*, which finishes off all four operas

of "The Nibelung's Ring," are triumphs of musical invention without sacrifice of dramatic credibility.

Modern choral music, I may add, as we encounter it today in church services or in oratorios on sacred texts, is rarely convincing. Musically ingenious it often is, but somehow many find it hard to believe that the composer himself really trusts, deeply trusts the truth of the text he has been setting. It is rather as if all the texts, sacred as well as secular, had been approached wholly as dramatic pretexts for choral experiment.

It has long seemed strange to me that nobody has yet made an oratorio out of the Communist Manifesto of 1848 by Marx and Engels. It is a text of remarkable eloquence, and for many an article of faith proudly held.

Choral contributions to symphonic works, with or without vocal solos, are not primarily vocal music. The voice-parts in these are less important as musico-literary collaborations than as adjuncts to the orchestral writing, even when the words are by famous poets.

The concert song is a special form. In the seventeenth century it appeared in Italy and in England with high musical distinction, though the poetry used was not always of the highest quality. Then it became inactive till Schubert revived it in the early years of the nineteenth century. The experiments of Haydn, Mozart, and Beethoven toward invigorating it are negligible. Arias they could write handsomely, and did; but their simple songs, save for some ingenious accompaniments, are on the whole stiff and not very responsive to interpretation. Religion (Protestant) had brought out devotional moods and continued to do so, but secular poetry remained in all the languages of Europe far superior to its musical treatments.

With Schubert a miracle occurs. The music becomes not only of equal quality with the very best German verse but also its mate. It gets inside a poem and stays there, intertwined unforgettably, never to be thought of henceforth as not a part of the whole idea. This miracle continued to reproduce itself for the better part of a century in the songs of Schumann, Brahms, Hugo Wolf, and Mahler, before German inspiration started running thin.

Meanwhile, its musico-poetical intensity had moved into French with Fauré, Duparc, Debussy, Ravel, and Francis Poulenc.

That expansion also lasted about a century, but since the death of Poulenc in 1963 it has lost vigor. Nor has anything comparable appeared elsewhere. Isolated songs of good quality have been composed in the Scandinavian countries, in Russia, occasionally in the United States and England, certainly in Brazil. But in spite of a huge production in the last three regions, there has been nothing anywhere comparable to the great lieder of Germany and France that came to life in those countries, and only those, between, say, 1810 and 1960. Is it over, this miraculous mating of lyric poetry with music? Quite possibly.

Choral writing goes on busily everywhere with great expertness, with the best intentions, and with enough good musical ideas to keep the choirs a part of the modern-music establishment. Opera writing too goes on apace, though with little sympathy, I must say, from the great houses anywhere except in France, and occasionally in England. But opera is all the same the musical domain where music's life is least nearly extinct. Symphonic composition? Dead as a doornail. Important piano works? Yes, there are many. Chamber music has still some life in it too, though not much liberty. Musical fun and games, let's face it, are today in the musical theater. And I don't mean the theater of dancing, where audiences avid for bodies pay little attention to sound. I mean the singing stage, both popular and classical. In both these domains activity is constant. Should miracles begin to happen there none need be surprised. And not just one miracle but a chain of them, a going-on phenomenon of the kind that happens somewhere in music about every half-century with seemingly no preparation, no reason for it, and no promise in it save for the fact that it does keep going on.

That I should like to see; and indeed I may see it, since it is almost the only door in classical music still ajar.

4
Making Everything Clear

An OPERA may be just a string of numbers, all complete as musical forms. And the seams that hold them together can be so smooth that transitions are not perceived. Also, as in French opéras comiques or in Viennese operettas and American musicals, the songs may be interspersed with spoken dialogue and with dancing. In every case, however, the story line is dependent on music for its pacing. A verbal text needs to be heard without effort, but the continuity that controls our attention is the musical one.

Music's intrinsic devices for holding attention are harmony, counterpoint, rhythm, and melody. The first two are largely a pleasure in hearing chords and in differentiating the expressivity of intervals as they occur in melody. These constitute specifically the musical experience. Rhythm, in the harmonic context, merely marks harmonic changes. It can also help to speed up the pacing or to hold it back. Counterpoint is by its nature multiple in both melody and rhythm. Harmonically it may assume as consonant any set of intervals, and from the twelfth century to our own this assumption has changed several times. Varieties of harmonic usage, also of rhythms both plain and multiple, actually constitute a string of musical customs that we may call the history of style.

Melody changes less noticeably than the other elements, being so frequently attached to words and to what they declare. Imitations of birdsong, cries of joy and pain, descriptions of nature in all its chaos, triplets addressed to the Holy Trinity, arbitrary orderings of the chromatic scale, all these are the constants of instrumental practice.

As for the observance in vocal music of correct, or naturalistic, speech cadences, they are the very substance of vocal writing. Once established by composers for the musical handling of any language, these cadences change very slowly. As I have remarked elsewhere, from Monteverdi to Verdi, from Rameau to Ravel and Poulenc, from Schütz to Schönberg, and from

Byrd to Britten, it is the instrumental textures, the accompaniments, so to speak, that constantly change fashion, actually about every fifty years.

But the relation of words to music in all of Europe's chief languages barely changes at all. Vocally Stravinsky composed for the most part in classical Russian, and Schönberg, even in the yodeling *Sprechstimme* of *Pierrot Lunaire*, changed neither the phonemes nor the stresses of High German.

Composing for the voice does follow, of course, certain practical customs. Songs for the pop trade, just like recital songs, seldom employ a wider vocal range than the eleventh, say C to F. And the spreads possible for choral singers, whether children or college students, are known to publishers. Operatic roles for large theaters have long ago assumed for vocal soloists a two-octave range and a certain amount of voice-power, enough certainly to cut through an orchestra. Operatic vocalism also tolerates the distortion of many normal procedures.

Liturgical chant in the Anglican church, a sixteenth-century replacement for Latin chanting, is clearly the model from which English theatrical recitative has developed, insofar as this exists at all, both the English theater and the American being highly resistant to it. Its comical derivative, on the other hand, known as patter, has long flourished in English, and far more becomingly than in any other European language save possibly Spanish. Italian tolerates it occasionally, German and French almost never. Patter also suits Brazilian Portuguese, as in the hundreds of songs by Heitor Villa-Lobos. It can also accommodate itself to rhythmic overlays and melodic rigamaroles. These can be either comical in effect, or so seemingly inept that they actually give a fresh dimension to more serious music.

For very serious music, like sacred oratorios and tragic operas, the commoner forms of distortion we call "the accents of passion." These serve to depict or to bring about moments of emotional intensity so extreme that they require very high notes, or very low ones, many of these to be held, or viciously spit out. Actually, distortion consists of whatever changes from the usual are needed to make vowels carry in the highest and lowest registers and also for giving the music enough time to shake up the listener, to astonish him. It does not permit, however, any displacement of the conventional accents of English speech. A verbal text may easily be repeated for clarity, but obscuring it is not good style.

Actually, good style in speech or singing is designed to minimize the variations that inevitably creep into use. Phonetic experts, the professors of linguistic history, seek out such variations, classify them regionally and sociologically, define their unstable vowels, and derive from them "laws" of linguistic evolution. Public speakers, actors, and vocalists are standardizers, seeking ever to establish a method for projecting speech and for teaching it to others, for communicating in this way to a very large number of listeners. "Good" English is no affectation; it is the most practical way there is to carry meaning to multitudes.

I therefore recommend to composers that they leave the professors of phonetics out of their calculation, because these scholars are more interested in variations from standard practice than in supporting it. Their most useful tool for us is an invention known as the International Phonetic Alphabet, which consists of easy-to-read signs for all the phonemes, or single sounds, that exist in most languages. This, combined with lessons from a good voice teacher, will serve as guides to vocal setting. And listening to fine actors and orators will provide a schooling in the use of word-groups and of their combining into meaningful phrases that are indispensable for projecting a text.

It is customary nowadays for public speakers, particularly those reading from a prepared text, to underline in their script all significant words, which is to say, those that *must* be understood, those from which the whole meaning of a sentence could in fact be comprehended, even if many a minor word should fail to reach the listener. I recommend the practice of strongly projecting all such words, and I suggest that composers place them in any vocal line well up in the middle register. In a low register they may get lost, while at the top of the voice vowels may come to be altered and consonants omitted. The upper half of the middle register is where sung words can be enunciated best. Adjusting any vocal line to this acoustical fact is not difficult, and it is bound to be rewarding to all concerned.

5
Helping the Performers

FOR COMPOSERS COACHING SINGERS I do not advise that they essay to give them voice lessons. "Placing" a young voice and keeping an older one "placed," not to speak of placing it all over again, so often needful after the menopause, are chores with which technicians alone are to be trusted. The following hints may be useful, however, toward helping vocalists to project an English text without injury either to that text or to the singing mechanism.

In any language consonants need time to be heard. They are heard most clearly when they anticipate slightly the musical beat or follow it. A skillful accompanist can be of great help by seeming to keep the time-count while actually accommodating its pace to the soloist's need.

Consonants need always a clean ending, a slight *uh*, to avoid their making, at that point, no sound at all. This *uh* may be weak, in the lieder style, or strong, as is required for opera houses; but it must be there. Only when a consonant, or any string of them, occurs between two vowels can that tiny grunt be omitted.

English vowels, as spoken, so often tend to become diphthongs that for singing them some correction of casual speech-ways may be needed. The Spanish, ever addicted to phonetic spelling, write *baseball* as *beisbol*. The word *meeting*, also for Spanish an adopted one, is changed to *mitin*, since that language admits neither the short *i* nor the sound of our *ng*.

English vowel distortions for singing are chiefly a matter of using the nearest equivalent in the Italian-that-vocalists-learn for any part of a syllable requiring to be held.

Short vowels, of course, cannot be held for long, nor can mute vowels like the third *a* in *banana*. No, nor the final short *i* in *country*, *sympathy*, *melody* and the like, in spite of its constant misuse in folkways and indeed by live composers too.

I read some years ago a book by a well-known songwriter in which the examples were from the composer's own works.*

*Bainbridge Crist, *The Art of Setting Words to Music* (New York: Carl Fischer, 1944).

And I remember well a passage in which the word *kiss*, hard enough to sustain at any time, was supposed to be held on an F-sharp (G-clef top line), an effort which at the tempo indicated, and with a hold added, would require at least twelve seconds. This cannot be done, of course, without using a different vowel. Such violations are not merely ineptitudes of student work; they appear constantly in the music of professional composers.

A legitimate distortion is to substitute for a final *ar*, *er*, *ir*, *or*, *ur* the French vowel *eu*, as in "S'wanee Riv*er*." This is a true vowel sound, can be held, and is not really very different from good English usage anyway. It is also more suitable for the first syllable of *Jerusalem* than *ay* or *ee*, which tend toward the comic. *Angels* and *roses* too can benefit from a bit of the *eu* coloration, produced by merely pushing the lips forward.

Two prohibitions that I find it very important to suggest are any alteration of the customary stresses in English words and word-groups, or any change in volume that might be used to produce these accents. Accents produced by a throat push, or by any semblance of *fp*, are anathema in singing. They injure the voice and are ugly anyway. A musical phrase correctly prosodized by the composer will need no gratuitous accenting by the singer. And rhythmic stressings in the music are far best left to the accompanist. My own rule is never to misplace a tonic accent and never to allow my singers to furnish one.

To articulate a highly expressive melody with rhythmic freedom, but without duplicating this freedom in the accompaniment, was recommended by Mozart. Also by Chopin, who called it *tempo rubato* (stolen time). In popular music, particularly blues and jazz, it is called "hot." Actually it is an ancient practice. The medieval precept *Psallemus metrice vel rhytmice* leaves no doubt that the difference between measure and beat was accepted as early as the tenth century. And certainly the further duality of vocal versus instrumental—*cantus atque musica*—makes clear some freedom of operation. Moreover, just listen to the recordings of all those famous vocal artists of before and after World War I. They sang legato or staccato, portamento or detached, but nary an accentual stress will you hear. That kind of thing is for the orchestra.

Among the available kinds of vocal sound, only standard European-style studio production is acceptable today in concert and in opera. Falsetto, or use of the male head-register, though occasionally still heard in France, is not generally admired elsewhere either in the theater or in concert performance.

Crooning, a sort of humming-with-the-mouth-open, is effective chiefly in radio and recordings. It can be ineffably sweet.

The "female baritone," heavily colored by "chest" as opposed to "head" or "mixed" resonance, though common in commercial entertainment, has no place in classical vocalism.

A common error of singers today is the constant use of crescendo-diminuendo ($<>$) on single notes. This seems to be due to shallow breathing; but since it is injurious to clear enunciation, I think a composer is wise to discourage it. It can sometimes be corrected courteously by asking for a more sustained melodic line, smoothing out to be achieved by singing the lower notes louder and the higher ones less loud.

In concert songs, one can ask for, and hope to hear sung, any vowel in any range and in any volume from p to f. For this accomplishment the highest and lowest notes of the vocal ranges cannot be used. They require too much vowel distortion, as do pp and ff in those same outlying regions. The concert song is a piece of poetry as well as of music, and no tampering with that equilibrium is of any help to the work.

Opera, on the other hand, and large-hall oratorio ask for extremities of range and volume, and demand in consequence greater distortions of "natural" speech and heavier emphases on "the accents of passion" than the lieder style, which is all for intimacies.

6

The Longs and Shorts in Singing

ANYTHING can be set to music. A text may be in prose or in verse or in some style in between. It can be as informal as a conversation or as strictly set up as a creed or contract. It can also be as clear as a love-call, as obscure as the transcript of a mystical state, as abstract as an exercise for vocal practice.

If it is in any known language, it is a string of words or word-groups; and these consist of recognizable consonants and vowels. Such strings have their controls. All vowels, for instance, even those called short, are capable of some extension in singing. So indeed are certain consonants, though this extension is not often called for, excepting that of the *m* sound, as in humming. Vowel extension is strictly framed, though not limited, by the consonants which precede and end the vowel sound. Exceptions occur in words or groups that begin with a vowel or end with one. In the first case the vowel requires a glottis-stroke to get it started, as in *apple*;* in the second case it can simply be dropped half-said, as in *banana*.

In spoken English, syllabic stresses are as firmly a part of any word-group as are its vowels and consonants, and these stresses cannot be altered, as was remarked earlier, without changing the meaning of the phrase in which they occur. And the same is true for singing, though certain instrumental helps may be necessary in order to avoid making stress-accents with the voice, which are always unpleasant and possibly injurious.

Conventional patterns of versification are of three kinds—lengths, stresses, and rhymes. A pattern of lengths—or quantities, as they are called in the classrooms—deals with syllables, and the vowel lengths in these are mostly controlled by consonants. English poetry actually follows quantitative patterns more often than is generally recognized, the fault being one of nomenclature, since the so-called long vowels frequently occur in short syllables, and vice versa.

*Bizet wrote to the librettist of *Carmen* regarding a song-lyric for that opera, "I call to your attention that in this poem of thirteen lines nine begin with a vowel."

Any pattern of stresses, though more sharply observed in speech than in singing, is in music largely an illusion, enforced against the very nature of our language by compositional and vocal device. Even in speaking, stress patterns can sometimes be attentuated. Take the familiar lines that open Chaucer's *Canterbury Tales*:

> Whan that Aprille with his shoures soote
> The droghte of Marche hath percèd to the roote,
> And bathèd ev'ry veyne in swich licour
> Of which vertu engendred is the flour

This passage seems to demand no stresses anywhere, but to be merely an alternation (not quite exact) of long syllables with short ones. And as such, it invites singing, as Chaucer's verse in fact so often does.

Consistently accentual verse is rare in English, though an occasional strong accent can be valuable for literary emphasis. For example, in Shakespeare's *Measure for Measure*,

> Take, O, take those lips away

somehow makes the word *lips* both strong and important. And in William Blake's "Tiger! Tiger!" just listen to this:

> What immortal hand or eye
> Dare frame thy fearful symmetry?

For either recitation or singing, the *l* sound of *fearful* requires, in order not to disappear altogether before the *s*, a certain extension plus maybe even a short holding back to prepare for the *symmetry* idea. And these delays, followed by the false rhyme of *symmetry* with *eye*, creates a poetic effect quite tremendous.

Compared to the complexities of patterning caused by both quantitative meters and accentual, rhymes present no great problem to a composer. All the same, he should know the kinds of them and recognize them when they occur in poetry.

End-of-the-line rhyming is not hard to observe in music, nor to avoid observing. Following it strictly, of course, can generate monotony. Interior rhymes and assonances, which rarely occur as a pattern, can often be pointed up to advantage. False rhymes, in English a very strong effect, can usually be given lots of emphasis. The rhyming of words ending in a short *y*, such as *melody*, *sweetly*, and the like, is troublesome for a poet, but even more so for a composer. Under no circumstance, I think, can treating the *y* sound as a double *e* be condoned, though you may find an occasional precedent for it in folk music. Rhyming penultimate or antepenultimate syllables can be entertaining in comic poetry, say *bunny* with *honey*, or *funny* with *money*.

Rhymes, neither the patterned ones that appear at line-endings nor the informal ones that can turn up anywhere, need not be emphasized by the singer. Indeed, just as in recited poetry, they may well be softened a bit to avoid monotony and to carry the sentence forward. A good false rhyme, however, is likely to need some space around it to make it clear, as when in the Purcell and Dryden *King Arthur*, for instance, a hymn to the glories of England boasts of her export trade:

> Foreign lands, thy fishes tasting,
> Learn from thee luxurious fasting.

And when the pagan river-nymphs essay to tempt the good king from his chastity, it is with a false rhyme naturally.

> Come play with us an hour or two;
> What danger from a naked foe?

In patter songs, however, rhyme will be all the more welcome if you give it speed, as in Gilbert and Sullivan's *Pinafore*:

> And so do his sisters and his cousins and his aunts,
> His sisters and his cousins whom he reckons up by dozens,
> His sisters and his cousins and his aunts.

There is, as we know, a long musical history of suggesting stress-accents without using stresses. Before the invention of the orchestra, when music was still dominated by instruments incapable of stress-accents, namely the pipe organ and the harpsichord, there was simply no easy way of signaling to the listener what the meter of any piece was supposed to be. It might be duple meter or triple or even some additive string of these, such as occurs in liturgical chant or in recitative.

Before Bach one cannot be sure of exactly what happened in rendering meter, but by his time certainly a method had been established for making the measure clear on instruments which could not play downbeats. This was a technique of composing themes, and of starting off almost any piece, with a note longer than those that follow.

Bach, Das Wohltemperierte Klavier, *book 1, fugue in c#*

Bach, Fugue in e for organ, "The Wedge"

Bach, Trio Sonata for Organ no. 1

Bach, Die Kunst der Fuge, *principal theme and its inversion*

Bach himself, in the forty-eight fugues of *Das Wohltemperierte Klavier*, did not always follow this recipe. He was very likely to hold our attention by beginning a fugal subject in the middle of a measure, preferably on the second count of say six, and continuing in regular eighth-notes or sixteenths until the counter-subject, by appearing clearly on a downbeat, gets us straightened out.

Nevertheless, a long first-count has remained characteristic of practically all the music of the great masters even as late as Claude Debussy and Igor Stravinsky.

A further device, still used by organists and harpsichord players, for making a long note sound like a strong note is either to hold back an imperceptible moment before sounding it or to hold on to it a similar small amount of time before continuing.

Singing, when practiced in the manner now considered classical for recitals, oratorios, and opera, no more invites the strong accents characteristic of English speech than orchestral string playing will tolerate unneeded up-bow crescendos and down-bow diminuendos, or carelessly easygoing heel-of-the-bow attacks. A sustained line at any volume in any range is the norm of musical utterance today, even for instruments of percussion. Any alteration of this for expressive purposes must be clearly intentional; otherwise it creates a misunderstanding.

Similarly, singing holds our attention best when the sound of it is a steady sound. This should be so whether the pitches are high or low, the volume loud or soft. Anything beyond this kind of vocal discipline, including the proper enunciation of words and word-groups, must be planned, laid on, an added grace, a gift to the listener. And for this the listener will surely be grateful; not as grateful perhaps as the voice lovers will be for a beautiful sound, but as grateful as any lover of fine music can be for a musicianly performance. Actually, for an artist of native powers less than those of a Flagstad or a Pavarotti, musicianship is the only way to get by.

So please, my singers, make your accents by other means than plain vocal stress. Use your consonants to delay the vowel sounds or to anticipate them. Also to close them off cleanly. Let me think you are stressing the syllables that seem to require that; but at the same time keep on pouring out sound with the steadiness of a pipe organ. That is the way Caruso worked, and Chaliapin, and Rosa Ponselle, and Schumann-Heink, and Nellie Melba, and John McCormack, and all the rest of those wonderful artists now dead but still remembered and also preserved for us in their recordings. The great ones in opera, in oratorio, in lieder, all sang like that. They enunciated too, and a few could even act. But whatever they did besides to vocalize, they did under musical controls—whether moving or miming or just standing still. And certainly, when singing both words and music, they were making music speak.

7
Instrumental Helps and Hindrances

IN THE MATTER of accompaniment, especially for concert songs, the same question arises as for the voice line: "Who is speaking?"

The simplest accompaniment, and by far the most effective for songs of modest pretension, is a literal doubling of the voice-line supported by plain harmonies. This gives the song a musical shape while helping to carry the tune. It is practically universal in the popular styles and by no means without value to the classical. It speaks, along with the melody itself, for the author of the words. And a bit of countermelody can sometimes add warmth.

More common among skilled composers is a contrasted accompaniment, which gives harmonic support as needed, but which at the same time depicts something. Schubert's jumping trout, anybody's running water, imitations of the Spanish guitar, of a church organ, of a marching band, of trumpet calls, all these can provide a further embellishment to the voice of the poet. By adding an almost visual evocation they add richness to the music and help to dramatize a situation.

Here are a few suggestions about the various kinds of music that can be used as contrasting accompaniments.

1. With triadic harmonies I advise keeping the accompaniment harmonically complete; don't expect the singer to help you define a chord. Seventh-chord harmonies must also be fully expressed. With harmonies still more complex a great deal of hidden note-cueing will be needed for safety.

2. If a countermelody is used, be sure the listener can recognize its identity and purpose. Who is it that is singing along with our soloist and what is he saying?

Also, the voice, though it may seem independent of the countermelody, is pretty sure to need some helping out from discreetly placed cue-tones.

3. Do not change the identity of the contrasting music without making clear what is taking place. Background music can represent people (crowds and choruses), or machines (industrial noises), or animals (say birds). Or it may be a voice of nature,

like running water or rustling leaves. It can give us explosions too, with maybe some fire. Rain and wind are easy, storms quite common. Cats are easier than dogs. Horses in motion are no trouble at all. Rocks, mountains, things that neither move nor make a noise are very hard to evoke. In general it is unwise to try evoking more than one kind of thing at a time, or even in the same piece.

4. In opera, themes that characterize people are a heritage often credited to Wagner. Mozart used dance-meters to define social class—minuets for the upper, country dances for peasants. All such signals can be counterpointed for dramatic complexity and they can be just as distinctive as *Leitmotive* in a concerted number or an act-finale.

Bach regularly illustrated the about-to-be-sung words in his chorale preludes for organ, sometimes with almost comic effect, as when angels trip down from heaven, or when Adam's fall from grace is pictured by a descending major seventh on the pedals.

The most entertaining of all these antics are Handel's detailed uses in the *Messiah* of the vocal line itself to picture valleys being "exalted" and "rough places plain," as well as "people that wander" chromatically "in darkness" all round the minor mode, until suddenly, in steadier pitches, they "have seen a great light."

5. Musical illustration has long used earlier musical styles to evoke periods of history. The medieval and baroque are easy to characterize, classical Greece and Rome much harder. Places such as Spain, Scotland, India, and Japan can be situated through instrumental textures such as guitars, bagpipes, and stringed instruments plucked, or through their vocal folklore. Even in the United States musical styles are used to suggest class—jazz or gospel for blacks, commercial pop for the middle classes or for youth, show-tunes by Cole Porter, Gershwin, and the like for a country-club world.

6. A very old convention is to use against a free melodic line an accompaniment made wholly of abstractions. The most familiar of these is the oom-pah, of which there is, I must say, a surprising amount in Beethoven's *Fidelio*. But no less abstract are scales, arpeggios, and repeating rhythms. These can be compared in our own time to the squares, circles, and discs found regularly in the paintings of Joan Miró and the sculptures of Alexander Calder. They are as modern as anything could be and also as ancient as the egg-and-dart pattern or the Greek key. I

recommend them highly, and suggest further that they can be employed very effectively with off-key harmonies and contradictory rhythms. Dissonant intervals, after all, are not the only form of modernism. Multiplicities, contradictions, contrasts, and distortions are no less valuable.

May I add that polymetrics and polyharmony, delightful as they are, need special handling. Rhythmic independence in the accompaniment is also welcome if the voice-line is simple. If not, it may interfere with projecting the words.

Multiple harmonies may interfere with the voice-line unless the latter can be recognized as belonging to one of the harmonic lines. For these latter I recommend using only common chords—major and minor triads, the diminished seventh, dominant seventh, or any grouping of tones from the six-tone scale. Such chords must be heard in close position, and contrasted to one another in timbre, in height, and, when practical, in volume. Harmonic lines may be counterpointed against one another, but not within a chord, as by suspensions. By keeping all harmonic identities recognizable and separate, you will be rewarded will a "musical" effect, an on-pitch blend of instrumental sound that sets off most surprisingly the vocal. Be careful in all this to keep the volume down. And remember the accompaniment's identity, who or what it purports to represent by being the way it is.

Beethoven, Fidelio

Vocally a showpiece for dramatic soprano with a full two-octave range (B–B).

The accompaniment doubles, or almost, the voice-line, a wise procedure when the singer is on stage and the orchestra half buried in a pit.

The orchestra also gives us, often right along with the melody itself, richly harmonized, almost every accompaniment formula known to music. These include broken chords, arpeggios, bits of oom-pah, repeated notes, ejaculated chords, syncopated chords, tremolando sostenuto, martellato, or agitato, and scales both smooth and jerky. The purpose of all this variation seems to be holding the listener in a state of anxiety while building for the singer a series of climaxes.

The aria, though structured by a master musician, contains far more excitement than drama, a situation that tends to characterize the whole opera.

Falla, Siete canciones populares españolas, *no. 2,*
Seguidilla murciana

Here we have Spanish so rapid that it approaches patter and a characteristic Spanish cantilena rhythmically controlled. The control is a guitar initiation that supports the dance-pattern, a seguidilla.

The poem is a version of the proverb which advises those who live in glass houses not to throw stones.

8

The "Musical Idea"

S UPPOSE WE ARE about to write a piece for singing. Suppose also that we know the kind of public usage that piece will have—in church, say, or recital, concert, light theatricals, as incidental music in a play or film, an aria in some work for choir and orchestra, or a major position in an opera. Next we need to know what the verbal text is. Now how do we get started on the music?

Some composers first look toward finding for the words a suitable rhythm. This approach to melody is, I think, largely American. Europeans are more likely to think in tones and to lay on metrics afterward. Their shaping of the tune can follow any number of patterns remembered from music's history.

The oldest of these is essentially vocal, derived from the plainchant and constructed out of the tetrachords that define the church modes. Writers as modern as Debussy, Stravinsky, and Arnold Schönberg have often used these modes for a source. And practically every composer since Mozart has used arpeggios.

Many composers find a harmony first, then let the melody cover its constituent tones. This is ancient practice, being derived from the imitation of trumpets and hunting-horns, for which an arpeggio is actually the scale of the instrument. French folk songs, many very old indeed, are virtually all of them either horn-calls, or else they are modal tetrachords fitted to language. In modern times too, both soldiers and sailors have tended to set their bugle-calls to words.

Horn-call melody, old French

739

Beethoven, Symphony no. 3, horn-call theme

This is almost a horn melody. Only the A's are not quite in tune.
Mozart, Don Giovanni

Imitating a vocal style for performing instrumental music, "making it sing," is constantly being recommended to us. But the evocation of instruments by the singing voice is no less familiar. Sopranos pretending to be flutes, mezzos as clarinet or English horn, are thoroughly effective. And writing in the florid bassoon style for a bass soloist was for Handel ever a jolly game. So also, for many another composer of the eighteenth century, was asking his chorus to work in disjointed syllables, for all the world as if they were an orchestra of bowed strings.

And there is a shivering chorus in Purcell's *King Arthur* that I find strange. I am not at all sure how these repeated notes should be sung.

We may assume, I suppose, that a choir can do whatever any singer can, though the extremes of operatic range may be ill

Purcell, King Arthur

advised, as indeed they are too for many a soloist. There is little difference between solo writing and the choral possibilities, though individual characterization of persons is not common in group work. A chorus can easily sing like an assembly of soldiers, of course, or angels, or union members, or simply friends and neighbors. And in Russian operas they quite regularly, since Mussorgsky, represent the soul of the Russian people.

In every case, of course, vocal music, whether for soloists, concerted groups, madrigalists, or massed forces, has to have some kind of a tune; and the tune must fit the words. The tune can come from anywhere—from church chant, folk song, or instrumental imitation. It can make like marching armies, crowds in chaos, or women at their household chores, but only rarely like single characters declaring their feelings or their future intentions. *I* and *me* are a bit more convincing in the madrigal style, particularly when individual voices are contrasted.

How does a tune, or melody, come about? How is it made? My analysis of its elements, its materials, goes rather like this. Its smallest fragment, like a word-group in spoken language, is generally called a motif. This has tones chosen from a modal tetrachord, a scale, or an arpeggio. Let me cite the motif that starts off Beethoven's Fifth Symphony, which has both a tonal shape (two descending thirds, one major and one minor, make up the tetrachord) and a meter (da-da-da-daaah twice).

Beethoven, Symphony no. 5

The first line of the *Dies Irae*, on the other hand, though clearly a modal tetrachord, is rhythmically indeterminate.

Thomas of Celano, Dies Irae

When you enlarge a motif and vary it, say you lengthen it to present an antecedent and a consequent, you have a musical phrase, but still not a melody. Just running on is not melody either. We call that melopoeia.

A formal melody may be short, but it is likely to include at least three full phrases, which can be heard as a beginning phrase, a middle one, and some kind of a final one, an ending. When Saint-Saëns gave pupils his famous assignment, "Bring me eight measures that I can play without accompaniment," he was asking for a complete musical statement, long enough to have three recognizable sections and plain enough to need no booster from chordal harmony.

I know that adding harmony to everything can be a temptation, because chords are music's chief intoxicant. They are what sends chills up your spine, not melody nor counterpoint nor rhythm. But chords, whether in sequence or casual, are only one of music's materials, and omitting them is one of the disciplines in learning to compose.

Now I come to the really indispensable chip in creating music, which I am calling here the "musical idea." And a musical idea, just like any other kind of idea, can be either fresh or stale, but it must be about something; it is an object with two aspects, like a coin.

A melody joined to a harmony, or contrasted with one, can constitute a musical idea; and so can a song with accompaniment. The song itself in that case, its own words and melody, are also a musical idea, perhaps even a full statement of one.

Any duality, of course, any mixture of musical elements, is no better than the materials that went into it. A simple oom-pah bass with a country fiddle can work beautifully when both are straightforward, authentic. A slightly more uncommon contrast, say a rhythm of three-against-four, can excite the attention of musical sophisticates, though since Brahms it is no great novelty. A bigger surprise comes in Rimsky-Korsakov's *Spanish Caprice* where he accompanies a violin cadenza with snare-drum rolls. Any suddenly encountered strangeness in the contrast can delight a musical mind. It can also deeply shock one less open to the unfamiliar. Actually the introduction of surprise rhythms, along with strident orchestral sonorities and less-than-suave harmony, are the circumstance that has produced the unmistakably "antimodern" musical reaction now common for well over a century. All musical ideas, I know, are not necessarily good ones. But you cannot write music without a musical idea. The best of these do involve, have always involved, even the oldest ones around, some still refreshing surprise. And the quality of authenticity, of a no-nonsense approach to music, is often the biggest surprise of all.

To repeat. You cannot write music without a musical idea, but a musical idea is not a composition. An extension of the idea into a three-part statement is composition. And the further extension of this statement through repetition, variation, and contrast can make a composition of some amplitude. The amplitude may tend toward an emotional pattern of anxiety-and-relief. It can also make, through auditory imitations and rhythmic recalls (especially of motion), suggestions of the visual or the kinetic, as well as reminders of other musical sounds, many kinds of them. In every case the overall patterning and the timing of its reception by the human body are musical. Even a piece with words to it, a vocal work composed for singing, makes its continuity and its climax, if there is to be one, through devices specifically musical.

The words are always there, of course; and they do create a metrical pattern of phonemes. This is a vocal work's only intrinsic continuity. Emotionally and factually they may seem to be telling their own story, but in reality they are doing very little more than to explain the music. By the very nature of musical reception, its unbelievable speed and intensity as compared to language, a piece of vocal music is primarily music. The words are received much more slowly, and they may even be in a foreign language. No wonder they must be set with precision, articulated with love, and projected with a constant care. They are related to the musical idea that frames and explains them, but they are themselves no part of it. Giving to the listener an illusion that they are really needed for full enjoyment is a triumph of certain great musical artists. Others get by, especially singing high and loud, with little effort toward anything more; and these are as often as not the artists whom voice lovers reward.

9

Both Words and Emotions Are Important

W HEN I BEGAN in the early 1920s to compose music for
texts by Gertrude Stein, my main purpose was musical.
Or let us say musical and linguistic. For the tonal art is forever bound up with language, even though a brief separation
does sometimes take place in the higher civilizations, rather in
the way that the visual arts will occasionally abandon, or pretend to abandon, illustration. The musical art, moreover, in its
more ambitious efforts toward linguistic union, has regularly
entwined itself with liturgical texts and dramatic continuities.

Now the liturgical connection has been operating successfully ever since medieval times and even earlier; but in Western
Europe it regularly had bypassed the local dialects and the budding languages, remaining attached for administrative reasons
to the formalistic, the far less vivid Latin. The first modern
tongues to take on music liturgically (the first gesture after their
doctrinal breakaways from Rome) were English and German,
both in the sixteenth century. The Latin-based local idioms
had made no great effort toward entering the Catholic liturgy
until today's ecumenical trend got them involved. But toward
the end of that same sixteenth century, which was producing
liturgically such remarkable results for English and for German,
Italian musicians in Florence had begun to perfect for secular
purposes (for the stage) a blending of music with language so
miraculously homogenized that a new word had to be found
for it. They called it *opera*, or "work"; and work was actually
what it did, invigorating the theater internationally in a manner most remarkable. For the English poetic theater, after the
times of Elizabeth I and James I, began to lose vigor at home
and never seemed able to travel much abroad. But the Italian
lyric theater in less than a century had begun to implant itself
in one country after another and in one language after another.
Born around 1580 as tragedy to be sung throughout (which is
its profound originality and from birth its unshakable integrity),
opera took on French with Lully in the middle seventeenth

century, German in the late eighteenth with Mozart, Russian in the nineteenth, beginning in the 1840s with Glinka.*

Serious opera seems never to have felt quite comfortable, however, in English or in Spanish, languages of which the poetic style, highly florid, made music for the tragic theater almost unnecessary. Comedies with added song and dance numbers existed of course everywhere; but music rarely served in them for much more than sentiment, being too slow, hence too clumsy a medium for putting over either sight gags or verbal jokes, except in patter songs.

Nevertheless, English-language composers have never stopped making passes at the opera. It is as if we bore it, all of us, an unrequited love. My own hope toward its capture was to bypass wherever possible the congealments of Italian, French, German, and Russian acting styles, all those ways and gestures so brilliantly based on the very prosody and sound of their poetry. For an American to aspire toward avoiding these may have seemed overambitious. But for one living in Europe, as I did for several decades, it may have been an advantage being able finally to recognize the foreignness of all such conventions and to reject them as too hopelessly, too indissolubly Italian or French or German or Russian, or even English, should some inopportune British mannerism make them seem laughable to us.

Curiously enough, British and American ways in both speech and movement differ far less on the stage, especially when set to music, than they do in civil life. Nevertheless, there is every difference imaginable between the cadences and contradictions of Gertrude Stein, her subtle syntaxes and maybe stammerings, and those of practically any other author, American or English. More than that, the wit, her seemingly endless runnings-on, can add up to a quite impressive obscurity. And this, moreover, is made out of real English words, each of them having a weight, a history, a meaning, and a place in the dictionary.

The whole setup of her writing, from the time I first en-

---

*The Florentine group (or Camerata) had begun with Greek music studies by Vincenzo Galilei. Giulio Caccini's *Euridice* dates from 1600. Monteverdi's *Orfeo* was produced in Mantua, 1607; but his later works were mostly performed in Venice.

The latter city is said to have supported at one time in the eighteenth century seventy-five neighborhood theaters all giving opera.

countered it back in 1919, in a book called *Tender Buttons*, was to me both exciting and disturbing. Also, as it turned out, valuable. For with meanings jumbled and syntax violated, but with the words themselves all the more shockingly present, I could put those texts to music with a minimum of temptation toward the emotional conventions, spend my whole effort on the rhythm of the language, and its specific Anglo-American sound, adding shape, where that seemed to be needed, and it usually was, from music's own devices.

I had begun doing this in 1923, before I ever met Miss Stein; and I ended it all by setting our second opera, *The Mother of Us All*, in the year of her death, 1946. This was actually her last completed piece of writing, and like our earlier operatic collaboration *Four Saints in Three Acts*, from 1927, had been handmade for me.

Four Saints is a text of great obscurity. Even so, when mated to music, it works. Our next opera, separated from the other by nineteen years and by a gradual return on her part to telling a story straight, was for the most part clear.

Both *Four Saints* and *The Mother* offer protagonists not young, not old, but domineeringly female—Saint Teresa of Avila and Susan B. Anthony. In both cases, too, the scene is historical; and the literary form is closer to that of an Elizabethan masque than to a continuous dramatic narrative. But there the resemblance ends. The background of the first is Catholic, Counter-Reformational, baroque, ecstatic. The other deals with nineteenth-century America—which is populist, idealist, Protestant, neighborly (in spite of the Civil War), and optimistic. The saints are dominated by inspirations from on high, by chants and miracles, by orders and commands, and by the disciplines of choral singing. The Americans of *The Mother*, group-controlled not by command but by their own spontaneity, are addicted to gospel hymns, darn-fool ditties, inspirational oratory, and parades. Nevertheless the music of the work, or so Carl Van Vechten found, is an apotheosis of the military march.

I do not know that this is true. All I know is that having previously set a text of great obscurity, I took on with no less joy the setting of one so intensely full of meanings, at least for any American, that it has never failed at the end to draw tears.

For this result, my having earlier worked on texts without

much overt meaning had been of value. It had forced me to hear the sounds that the American language really makes when sung, and to eliminate all those recourses to European emotions that are automatically brought forth when European musicians get involved with dramatic poetry, with the stage. European historic models, music's old masters, are not easy to escape from. And if any such evasion, however minor, takes place in *The Mother*, that is due, I think, to both Miss Stein and myself having for so long, in our work, avoided customary ways and attitudes that when we got round to embracing them we could do so with a certain freshness.

Opera in the Vernacular

O PERA AND ORATORIO are made up of two kinds of writing. One is used for set-pieces, which communicate emotion; the other for conversations, which communicate facts.
And though many composers, notably Richard Wagner, have
aimed to make the two styles seem one, the fact remains that no
matter how carefully the seams are concealed the two are not
of the same stuff. And both are necessary to a musico-dramatic
narrative.

A set-piece can sometimes get by with incorrect (that is, unclear) communication of words. But explanations have to be
understood. Recitative must therefore either be spoken, which
is not always appropriate if the subject is a noble one, or set to
music by a skilled workman. The mark indeed of a dramatic
master is far less his ingenuity in writing set-pieces than the way
he handles his recitatives. As high points of accurate and expressive writing in this style I should like to recall here the German
recitatives in Bach's *Saint Matthew Passion*, the Italian ones in
Mozart's *Don Giovanni* and in Rossini's *Barber of Seville*. Musical conversation of high quality in a more modern manner exists
in the first act of Wagner's *Walküre*, also in Debussy's *Pelléas et
Mélisande* and in Erik Satie's *Socrate*.

No translation of vocal music, particularly of recitative, is ever
quite first-class. Making the quantities, the stresses, *and* the
expressive design of a good words-and-music marriage all come
out convincing in a foreign language is virtually impossible.
That is why translated opera is occasionally so shocking. And yet
the kind of understanding in the theater that is only possible in
one's own language is desirable. Germany, France, and Italy sing
practically all foreign operas in their own languages.* England,

---

*Information from Craig Rutenberg, répétiteur at New York's Metropolitan
Opera, states that the principal houses of Berlin, Hamburg, Munich, and usually Düsseldorf now use the original languages, while the regional houses,
even Stuttgart, tend to sing only in German. In France, he adds, the provincial
houses still use translations, with only Paris and Lyon singing operas consistently in their original languages. (Before the last war such a procedure was far
from consistent.)

the United States, Spain, Portugal, and the Latin American countries tend to use, where possible, the original languages. Formerly opera in Russia was polyglot, just as here. The Soviets now use mostly Russian.

It is exactly the countries that have long produced original operas in their own language—Italy, France, Germany, Russia, the countries where opera has taken root—that are the least bothered by translation's inefficiencies. I think this is due to the existence there of a large body of work well written for the local tongue. When the basic repertory has something that gives everyone pleasure (and there is no greater pleasure in music than hearing one's own language vocalized), it becomes unthinkable to deny anyone that pleasure, even though the degree of the pleasure, in foreign works, is far from complete.

But even where there is no such basic local repertory, audiences do not always feel happy about translations. They want to feel that somewhere in the opera deal they are getting something authentic, even though this may involve the sacrifice of comprehensibility. Germany had Italian opera always, until first Mozart wrote two and Beethoven one and then Weber about eleven operas in correctly prosodized German. After 1815, there was a real German repertory, and all the foreign operas were translated into German, and it never again occurred to anybody in Germany or Austria that German was not the most appropriate language in the world for singing, including the performance of foreign operas.

Here in the United States we are not quite ready for such a transition, though supertitles flashed on a screen are beginning to help. There are already a few operas well written in the English language—Gershwin's *Porgy and Bess*, perhaps; Hall Johnson's dramatic oratorio *Green Pastures*; Marc Blitzstein's *Cradle Will Rock*; Gian Carlo Menotti's *Medium* and *Consul*; my own *Four Saints in Three Acts* and *Mother of Us All*, just possibly my *Lord Byron*, not to mention the whole rich catalogue of Benjamin Britten. But all these operas still do not make up a repertory. When there are a dozen more, opera in English will cease to be a cause; it will be a fact. And reformers will then be agitating to keep foreign works in their original languages, instead of to get them out of these. What we need now is simply more operas written in English that sounds like English, put to music in such a way that there is no mistaking what language is being sung and what the words being sung are. In other words, we shall find foreign opera satisfactory in English when we shall have a repertory of a dozen or more successful operas composed in English. At that time we shall also train our singing actors primarily to work in their own language, because that will be the language that our basic opera repertory will have been composed in.

II

The Nature of Opera

LET ME BEGIN MY FINALE by talking about anyone, particularly a composer, feeling at home in theaters, having stage-sense. In France they call it *le sens du théâtre*. In any language it means an awareness of the fact that in show business—any kind of it—there is a show and there is an audience. It takes two to play theater.

Historically speaking, not all the great poets have been gifted for the stage. Shakespeare, Ben Jonson, Marlowe, Ford, and Dryden all were. Milton was not. Nor were the Romantics—Byron, Shelley, Keats, and Coleridge. Any more than were all those novelists and storytellers, from Sterne through Dickens and on to Henry James, Proust, and Joyce.

George Frideric Handel was thoroughly a stage man. Johann Sebastian Bach was not, though his *Saint Matthew Passion*, with its moving recitatives for Jesus, its terrifying crowd scenes, and its audience-participation hymns, approaches the dramatic oratorio. Mozart had an enormous stage gift; Haydn a very small one, in spite of his fifteen operas; Beethoven almost none, though he aspired to it. But Weber was wise in the theater, and Wagner virtually infallible.

What is this mysterious talent that seems to have skipped half the population? It shows up in children as impersonation, or as simply showing off, in the manipulating of family and friends through charm, later as a form of adolescent sex appeal in mimicking movie actors. And wherever the stage-sense is true, it is accompanied by an instinct for timing. In playing comedy, as in telling a joke, timing is almost the whole trick. Tragedy, sob stories, and soap opera require a less wary trajectory. Just keep them going; eventually tears will flow.

Composers of our own century have often worked well for the stage. Richard Strauss wrote upwards of ten successful operas; Debussy with *Pelléas et Mélisande* wrote only one, though there are also two fine ballets, *Khamma* and *Jeux*, as well as a pair of dramatic oratorios, *The Prodigal Son* and *The Martyrdom of Saint Sebastian*. Stravinsky's *Fire Bird*, *Petrouchka*, and *Rite of Spring*, to mention only his early ballets, are tops in their field, while *Les Noces* (in Russian), *Perséphone* (in French), and *Oedipus Rex* (in Latin) are first-class ballet-cantatas. There are also two far-from-negligible Stravinsky operas, relatively early *The Nightingale* (in Russian) and quite late *The Rake's Progress* (in English). Alban Berg's *Wozzeck* and his uncompleted *Lulu* are modernistic adaptations of German literary classics. Ravel, in France, wrote two successful operas, *L'Heure espagnole* ("On Spanish Time") and *L'Enfant et les sortilèges* ("The Spellbound Child"), as well as one world-famous ballet score, *Daphnis et Chloé*. The French composers of our time have in fact, like their predecessors, virtually all composed for both the singing and the dancing stage. Hence the abundant theatrical production of Milhaud, Honegger, Sauguet, and Poulenc. While in England Benjamin Britten, and in Russia Shostakovich, Prokofiev, and others have produced both operas and ballets with stage-quality.

If modern poets—Rimbaud, Valéry, Yeats, Rilke, Pound, and the surrealists—have written more often for readers than for actors, T. S. Eliot did compose four thoroughly practical plays and Gertrude Stein, in addition to quite a lot of texts that she called plays (and which have indeed been staged), was the author, along with the ballet-with-words *A Wedding Bouquet*, of two genuinely effective opera librettos—*Four Saints in Three Acts* and *The Mother of Us All*, plus just possibly *Doctor Faustus Lights the Lights*.

In Germany, Russia, Norway, France, Italy, Spain, and England, playwriting is still literature, with Chekhov and Ibsen and Shaw and Pirandello among the classics. American authors have on the whole worked less well for the stage than at storytelling, reporting, history, and polemics. Or to compare them with the novelists alone, no American playwright, not Tennessee Williams nor Thornton Wilder nor Edward Albee nor even Eugene O'Neill, has produced anything comparable in power to Herman Melville's *Moby-Dick* or to the novels of Hawthorne, Henry James, Theodore Dreiser, John Dos Passos, and William Faulkner. It is *not* that Americans lack stage-sense. Our light musicals are today's world model, and we have produced both fiction films and documentaries of the highest prestige. Also our designs for dancing are original and often first-class. It is only on the speaking stage that show business has in America tended to be low business.

A good deal of this has been pointed out before; much of it

is covered in a lecture I sometimes give called "America's Un-requited Love for Opera." Just now I am taking that love for granted, though you may not esteem it unrequited. And since so many of our composers are now writing operas, or planning to do so, I am going to take the liberty of suggesting certain things about the nature of opera which may be helpful.

Opera, let us understand this right off, is not light enter-tainment. It is drama at its most serious and most complete. It is also the most complex operation in music and the most complex in stage production. Even a circus is easier to mount.

Its complexity, moreover, involving the collaboration of po-etry, visual design, and often dancing—along with music both vocal and instrumental—creates necessities that are more de-manding than those of the concert. An opera is not a concert in costume. Neither is it just a play with music laid on. It is a dra-matic action viewed through poetry and music, animated and controlled by its music, which is continuous. It owes to poetry much of its grandeur, to music all of its pacing. But since opera involves both intoned speech and mimed action, its pacing must permit both verbal clarity and convincing impersonation.

Now the opera is no such ancient form as verse tragedy, miracle plays, or even the light comedy with songs. It has a his-tory of only four centuries and has never created a repertory in Spanish, Portuguese, Greek, Dutch, Polish, or the Scandinavian tongues, though it has enjoyed a certain popularity through translation in English and in Flemish. The twentieth century has witnessed sustained efforts, not yet wholly successful, toward making opera seem to grow naturally in the English and Ameri-can languages. Whether these experiments can be stabilized remains undetermined, but the problems they raise are being labored at on both sides of the Atlantic.

For a successful outcome, certain preliminaries are essential. The composing fraternity must master the musical prosody of its language. This is in general better handled in the United Kingdom than in the United States. Over there the history of it all goes quite far back, to Henry VIII at least, and is preserved in libraries, remembered in the schools. Here the matter is ne-glected in schools and largely ignored in the homes where so many of our finest musical creators have grown up without ever hearing English spoken idiomatically.

For experimental opera productions, there needs to be available also a galaxy of young voices naturally well placed and with access to lessons. This situation is better on our side, Britain's colloquial speech, save for the Welsh and the Irish, being notably lacking in the nasal content necessary for differentiating vowels and for enabling them to cut through an orchestra. Canadian speech and South African are similarly soft, but Australian is very good for singing. That continent has long produced great voices; it may one day write operas for them.

In the matter of production Britain and the United States are both active, though they approach their opportunities differently. England lends its best facilities (Covent Garden, the English National Opera, and the big festivals) to its best composers. The works of Benjamin Britten, William Walton, Michael Tippett, and Peter Maxwell Davies have been effectively launched from these. Thea Musgrave, being a woman and Scottish, seems to get better treatment in America.

The opera houses of New York, Chicago, and San Francisco, on the other hand, though they have mounted works by composers as famous as Victor Herbert, Reginald De Koven, Deems Taylor, and Samuel Barber, seem not yet to have set a trend or created a school. Nor, for all its assiduities toward the contemporary, has Houston, Texas. Our most lively new operas have, with few exceptions, come out of the opera workshops in our colleges and universities. Among the exceptions are George Gershwin's *Porgy and Bess* and Marc Blitzstein's *Regina*, both of which originated in commercial theaters, and my own *Four Saints in Three Acts*, which began its playing life in an art museum, the Wadsworth Atheneum of Hartford, Connecticut. The University of Indiana, where John Eaton's *Cry of Clytemnestra* was first heard, has the finest facilities of any college for producing operas, also a remarkable voice faculty and nine theaters on campus. Columbia University's now-defunct Opera Workshop is deeply regretted. It is there that Menotti's *Medium* and my own *Mother Of Us All* were born. Unhappily, Columbia for a long time had no home for opera.* It once had, in the Brander Matthews Theatre, borrowed from the Drama Department, an

---

*On 15 September 1988 The Kathryn Bache Miller Theatre, at 116th Street and Broadway, was formally opened by Columbia University.

ideal casting situation whereby professionals from the New York pool, all unpaid, could give time to students playing small roles and understudying large ones. Singing on a stage with even one artist of experience is like playing in an orchestra at the same desk with a professional. That sort of apprenticeship, though hard to come by, is unutterably valuable. And so, of course, is hearing one's own composition conducted, staged, and sung by people who know what *cannot* be done in opera.

One of those things, believe me, is to "act," to simulate emotion by any means whatsoever except through the singing voice. Impersonation yes. That is created by costume and aided by a minimum of controlled movement (call it choreography if you like). But the emotions of high tragedy, insofar as these make up the substance of opera, are projected by the singing voice alone, not by any contributing circumstance. The popularity of opera recordings, which bear no visual aids to comprehension, has long been witness to this. Comic moments, let us admit, do permit a modicum of acting.

Regarding the advantages of British versus American production of operas in English, let us not underestimate the power of Great Britain's promotion machinery, which operates through its embassies and consulates. Henry Barraud, formerly music director of the French Radio and Television, told me not long after World War II that foreign pressures toward performance did not tend to come, as was commonly supposed, from the Soviet Union. "I don't hear twice a year from the Russians," he said, "but not a week goes by without my receiving a demand from the British Culture Office to perform some work by Benjamin Britten."

American artists' careers, on the contrary, practically all suffer from official neglect. The chief American composer to profit abroad from the State Department's blessing was George Gershwin, whose opera *Porgy and Bess* toured internationally with partial government support, for two years. An opera of mine, *Four Saints in Three Acts*, got from the State Department a small contribution toward its Paris trip of 1952, and Douglas Moore's *Ballad of Baby Doe*, similarly blessed, went to Berlin and Yugoslavia. Otherwise, official encouragement for trips abroad has been generous to performing groups without specifying at all that U.S. music be played. And lecture tours have been awarded occasionally to composers. Unfortunately the countries where performance might help a composer professionally are likely to be omitted from the State Department's plan. England, France, Germany, Italy, and Scandinavia are not judged to be "sensitive areas" meriting the support that has regularly promoted good will toward our country in Turkey, Burma, India, the South American republics, and black Africa.

In any case, operas are being written all over the United States and the United Kingdom and many are produced, listened to, and internationally reviewed. Americans do tend, however, to go off half-cocked. They are without any serious mastery of the words-and-music techniques (and I mean orchestral accompaniment as well as word-setting). The British are limited in their productions by a lack of critical support from the universities and also by their music publishers, who, like most other British businesses, are monopoly-oriented. Literary publishers there, responsible to a longer and a grander history, still enjoy a somewhat competitive setup. English composers, however, unless they are pushed by the establishment, very frequently get squeezed out of distribution. The late Stanley Bate, a fecund and charming composer rarely heard today, is a case in point. Lord Berners is another.

Both countries have libretto trouble. The British tend to emulate their own literary classics—Sir Arthur Sullivan in *Ivanhoe*, Vaughan Williams in a version of Shakespeare's *Merry Wives of Windsor* called *Sir John in Love*, and in *Riders to the Sea* by John Millington Synge. Benjamin Britten, by using minor poets, major novelists, and slightly scabrous themes, was more successful. It is to foreign-language opera, however, not English, that Shakespeare, and once or twice Sir Walter Scott, have made their most valid contributions through (in Italian) *Lucia di Lammermoor, Hamlet, Falstaff, Macbeth*, and *Otello*; (in French) *Hamlet* and *Roméo et Juliette*. Let us not forget either how charmingly Britten has handled *A Midsummer Night's Dream*.

English masterpiece poetry in the original can throw almost any composer. The British suffer too from the lack of a solid history in composing for the stage, their musical strength lying mainly in the comic vein and the liturgical. Nor is there a history of serious libretto writing; both Nahum Tate's *Dido and Aeneas* and Dryden's multimedia *King Arthur*, though among the best, do skirt dangerously the tempting shallows of light verse. In general the British composer has neither found good serious librettos nor, with the exception of Britten's *Peter Grimes* (based on a poem of George Crabbe), shown marked ability for handling a dramatic theme.

The current American trend is to use for librettos cut-down versions of successful plays. The playwriting techniques of Eugène Scribe and Victorien Sardou applied to stories by Dumas *jeune*, Victor Hugo, and similar sources have produced in Europe such unshakable repertory works as *La Traviata*, *Rigoletto*, and *Tosca*. These same techniques applied to materials nondramatic in origin have caused the creation of *Faust* and *Carmen* and *Louise* (all faultless librettos). By pursuing this course of facile story-interest and by including lots of historical subject matter, libretto writing achieved in nineteenth-century France, Italy, and Germany an acceptable standard which replaced for a post-Revolutionary public the earlier models of Metastasio and da Ponte. Actually, libretto writing on the Continent has by now well over three centuries of history as a literary form that can be entrusted by those administering public funds to poets, or even to prose writers with a tolerance for music and some sense of the stage.

The American libretto, whether poetic or in prose, has suffered from the banality of American playwriting. Even music cannot bring to life its commonplace emotional occasions nor sustain its garrulous dialogue. I realize that dialogue is in general the American playwright's first gift, but even this at its compact best cannot hold up a tragedy of which the emotional content provokes no terror.

Invigorating the opera repertory by modernizing its musical textures and by introducing up-to-date story-themes are classical ways of keeping contemporary opera a part of the intellectual life. Any holding back in such matters by poets and composers is bound to discourage the endowed production agencies, which prefer a bold approach. Commercial producers—in films, television, or theater—are more timid. They like the excitements of novel sex, psychology, politics, mating manners, and religion; but they fear box-office failure for modern music.

Opera is rarely commercial; it is almost entirely endowed.

Virtually none of it is self-supporting, not even the popular works of Richard Wagner and of Puccini. The whole operatic establishment, whether its funds be of capitalist origin, as with us, or Marxist-Leninist bureaucratic, as in Russia, is endowed, subsidized, tax-exempt. And its operators are subject to criticism for the way they spend public monies both by the press and by the head people of our universities, conservatories, and libraries, all of whom are also spending public monies. The results, for all the squabbling that goes on about "advanced" versus "conservative" repertory, is a higher degree of both freedom and responsibility in operatic production than is dreamed of in commercial show-biz.

There is actually lots of courage around, as well as money, for opera production. So much indeed that I wonder whether the timidities of opera composition in America and Britain may not be due more to underdeveloped musical skills than to hesitancies about subject matter. Certainly there is a dearth of strong librettos in the English-speaking countries.

Now let me go back to the beginnings of opera in the years just preceding 1600. We can do this because the basic format has since changed very little. The variations of this can be infinite, and the story-line is always a bit colored by local needs whenever the format moves into a new language. But that format must be preserved, or opera will fail to take root. In my view of it, the basic recipe reads somewhat as follows.

What, you may ask, is an opera anyway? It is a dramatic action involving impersonation, words, and music. Without impersonation it is a cantata. Without music, but with impersonation, it is a play. Without words, but with impersonation and music, it is a dance spectacle. With only impersonation it is a pantomime. Any of these can be comical, serious, or mixed.

A comic opera mainly impersonates without dignity, makes fun of us all, alternates jokes with musical numbers, lays charm on with a trowel.

A serious opera tells a mythological story which leads, unless interrupted by some superhuman agent, to a tragic outcome. The mixed comedy, or tragicomedy, is always, like Mozart's *Don Giovanni*, more tragic than comic.

Now what is a dramatic action? It is what happens inevitably to persons opposed to one another by character, circumstance, or desire. The energy leading to this outcome is latent in their differences of desire and in the unalterable nature of character.

It is not a drama unless events are described or mimed by actors impersonating the characters involved.

It is not an opera unless both words and action are expressed through music and carried forward by it.

It is not a satisfactory opera unless the words, the action, and the circumstance are made more vivid through music than they could ever be without. Because words sung carry farther than words spoken (or even shouted); because instrumental music can intensify suspense or calm, explosions of energy or its complete arrest; and because landscapes, weather, history and its monuments, all sorts of contributory detail can be evoked by musical device.

This is not to say that musical tragedy is grander than poetic tragedy. The fact is simply that after opera came into existence in any language, poetic tragedy became a thing of the past, however glorious, with opera taking over the contemporary effort toward complete theater.

Moreover, your spectacle will not hold the stage, unless the story of it, the dramatic action, moves forward. Otherwise you may be left with a static spectacle on your hands—something like an oratorio in costume, Stations of the Cross, or a song-cycle.

Music, please remember, is the great animator. Without it dancing goes dead and so do liturgies. Only spoken plays can survive without it. Even films and television spectacles tend to freeze up, just as dancing does, without musical help. Music is warming, emotional, acoustically surrounding, a bath. The visual always keeps a certain distance, hence is cooler than the musical experience. Lincoln Kirstein says, "The life of a ballet is the life of its musical score," meaning that when the dancers are no longer moved (literally) by the music, the work drops out of repertory.

Let's look at this musical element, the slippery substance that can so firmly change the specific gravity of anything. Seriously employed, it is a "noble" material, and for any serious subject needs to be carefully composed and carefully executed. The slapdash may go down in nightclubs or drinking joints. Similarly for casually selected materials and for their arrangement in some accidentally determined order. Such elements are too frail to sustain a serious mythological subject or to prepare us for a tragic ending.

While we are discussing mythology, let us stipulate that history, fairy tales, lives of the saints, anything anybody can almost believe can be subsumed under that head. From *Samson et Dalila* through *Cenerentola, Tannhäuser,* and *Boris Godunov* to *Madama Butterfly, Giovanna d'Arco,* and *Billy the Kid,* all are believable stories about believable people. And music makes these people seem bigger, blows them up to mythological size. It even overblows them toward collapse in the case of Cinderella (who is hence better for dancing than for song). Also for the super-monumental and political (say George Washington, Napoleon, Abraham Lincoln). Singing could only diminish them.

But let us say you have a sizable heroine or hero in mind. How do you go about procuring a libretto? My own way is to address myself to a poet. This is dangerous because English-language poets have over the last century and a half been most of them quite clumsy at handling a dramatic action. They can't avoid talking in their own person, seem unable to write dialogue objectively. But I think there is no way around that. The poets must simply reeducate themselves if they are at all stagestruck.

How they can do this I do not know. But I am sure that the poets who have no innate stage-instinct (that well-known *sens du théâtre*) cannot be taught it, though a latent stage-sense can perhaps be brought to life. The matter is a difficult one. If the composer himself has a feeling for the stage, that fact solves only half the problem. But it may help him in choosing a poet. If he does not have it he should leave opera alone, and if he cannot pick a poet who also has a bit of it, their collaboration is not likely to produce a viable stage work. There is no final test of that, of course, short of full-scale production. The history of every opera establishment is strewn with costly failures.

It is just possible that further research into the history of libretto writing may reveal standards by which the English-language libretto can be adjudged a legitimate poetic form. If so, then the poets may come to face it without thinking of themselves as betraying their art. Actually poets are less fearful of music (they all love being set) than of the stage itself.

Opera, to be worth looking up to, has to be poetic theater.

And librettos, I think, are best when custom-built. Readymades, even in the form of a well-structured prose play cut down to libretto size, are rarely satisfactory in English. They are not even literature, chopped up like that, pinched here and let out there to accommodate musico-emotional timings, which are quite different from the verbo-emotional.

By musical versus verbal timings I do not mean that communicating emotion to an audience by words alone takes any more time, or less, than by music or by words and music. On the contrary, a strong emotion can be extended in any medium to last, say, twenty minutes, if sufficient variety of texture is available. But twenty minutes of speech will pour out more words than twenty minutes of music can handle. A love scene from *Romeo and Juliet* set to music as recitative would be jabber; and if set uncut as cantilena, with all the vocal extensions needed to make singing eloquent, could seem interminable. Too many words can get in music's way. So also, I may add, can too many notes obscure the text.

A libretto needs to be, in general, much shorter than a play. Otherwise it may lack flexibility for being fitted into musical continuities. It also needs poetic language. Not pompous language, nor florid, nor overloaded with imagery. But nobly plain, if possible compact, and somehow appropriate to myth-size characters.

An opera libretto must be animated by its music, and the emotional progress of the drama must conform to musico-emotional timings, not speech-play timings. To sustain and extend to its acceptable limit any musico-emotional situation, the use of structural devices specific to music is the available method, the only method. This is what is meant by the earliest Italian name for opera, *dramma per musica*, well as by Richard Wagner's demand that his own theater works be referred to as *Musikdrama*.

For the best musical result, poetic textures and all characterizations need to be a little plainer than for spoken tragedy, and an excess of visual imagery is to be avoided.

In my opinion, plots, intrigues, and planned suspense, however exciting they may be on the comic stage or in melodrama, tend to make a tragic outcome seem not inevitable. Operas based on legend, myth, fairy tale, biography, or national history tend therefore to be both poetically and musically richer than those corseted by a tight play-structure.

Complex musico-dramatic structures dealing with humor and sentiment or with satire are not an uncommon variant of "serious" opera. Mozart's *Marriage of Figaro* and its companion-piece Rossini's *Barber of Seville*, Wagner's *Meistersinger von Nürnberg*, Strauss's *Rosenkavalier*, Verdi's *Falstaff*, and Puccini's *Gianni Schicchi* are notorious cases in which the domination of a whole work by its musical continuity has turned comedy into a serious enterprise. Actually these works, which survive almost exclusively in the larger houses, are far more monumental than funny.

The comic speaking-stage shows no history of growth, development, or decline since the earliest antiquity, in the West since Greece and Rome. The tragic stage in poetry, on the other hand, has a history. It matures in any language once, then dies, leaving behind monuments of literature that live forever.

The tragic opera, a late invention, has not yet died out in any language. It has left us moreover three legacies previously unknown—the proscenium stage, the pit orchestra (a curtain of instrumental sound through which all is filtered), and the monumental singing voice.

The comic musical stage, liturgical ceremonies, and song recitals do not, in general, require great vocal range or power. The tragic musical stage, the opera, or *dramma per musica*, had perfected by the middle 1630s a training for loudness and flexibility in all the vocal ranges (as well as a name for it, *bel canto*) that has survived to this day as the training system for operatic voices, those with a minimum range of two octaves at all levels of loudness. Operas are still written to be sung by such voices, and pit orchestras in our opera houses are also of monumental proportions, rarely fewer than fifty players.

Such is the equipment available today in the professional houses, the conservatories, and the colleges. It also includes usually some kind of built or painted scenery, artificial lighting, appropriate costuming, and a modicum of controlled stage-action.

I say a modicum because with any musical production being completely rehearsed and always conducted, and with today's other popular serious stage medium, the dance, equally controlled and regulated, it is not wise to allow singers to improvise their "acting." Still less is it wise to allow stage directors the kind of freedom toward distortions and even contradictions of the stated dramatic action that have lately been current.

On the other hand, singers are neither dancers nor acrobats. Excessive pantomime is not suitable to vocalists or to their bodies, which need to save breath for singing. The best solution of the "acting" problem is to use choreographers with a sense of music and some taste, for moving the singers around (with grace if possible, and minimally) so that at major musical moments they can stand still in a good acoustical spot and proceed to act with the voice, which is after all what the art of singing is.

Enabling singers to make words clear and meaningful is part of the composer's art. Another is to reveal character and feelings by musical device. This may be operated within the vocal line, as with Mozart and the Italians, or by orchestral means, as with Wagner and many French composers.* In any case, specific expressivity is more easily achieved through line, vocal or instrumental, than through harmony, the latter being highly valuable for structure, for holding our attention on the expressive line. Orchestration too may be useful in pointing things up. Extreme variety in the orchestra, however, though delicious in concert music, can seem finicky in opera, as it so often does with Berlioz and Rimsky-Korsakov. Wagner, Debussy, Mozart, Verdi, even Stravinsky, have offered more dependable support to the expressive element by keeping orchestral color steady and clearly related at all times to the voice. Never forget that no matter how interesting orchestral sound may seem, singing is what opera is about. And this is as true of Wagner's stage works as of Bellini's. Actually Wagner's music-dramas are today opera's chief vehicles for power vocalism. In every house they receive the most careful musical treatment and offer us the grandest voices.

So let us restate the situation in reverse order.

---

*An example of characterization by vocal line is the coloratura of the flighty young page Oscar in Verdi's *Ballo in maschera*. On the other hand, it is orchestral chord-sequences that identify with such massive weight Wotan's Valhalla in Wagner's "Ring," and with evasiveness Debussy's Mélisande.

Wagner, Das Rheingold, *Scene 2*

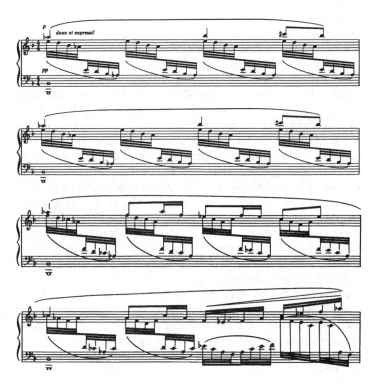

Debussy, Pelléas et Mélisande

Opera is singing. This singing is both monumental and flexible—loud, soft, high, low, fast, slow.

Opera exposes through impersonation and poetic dialogue a serious dramatic action. This is a serious action because it faces at all times the possibility of a tragic outcome. And it is moved forward toward whatever outcome may be its destiny by instrumental music and by singing. A dramatic action is opera's thread and purpose. Poetry is its explanatory method. Singing is its sine qua non, its language.

As regards the words-and-music factor, that is a constant in any mature language, established early on by composers, and is not likely to alter much after that. So that the vocal line of Italian music, or French or English or German or Russian, tends to remain closely tied to the classical pronunciation of those languages.

Other musical textures, however, such as harmonic and contrapuntal styles, rhythmic devices and orchestral coloration, insofar as these are expressed instrumentally, vary with history and fashion. From Monteverdi to Nono, from Rameau to Poulenc, from Purcell to Britten, from Schütz to Schönberg, and Glinka to Stravinsky, the voice-parts of operas and oratorios in any language are almost interchangeable, though their instrumental accompaniments can vary from Baroque, Rococo, and Romantic to polytonal, nontonal, even twelve-tone serial. Excellent opera music has indeed been composed in all these manners.

A similar history seems to obtain for librettos. Opera stories certainly have varied far less in the last four centuries than has good poetic diction. Dryden, Molière, Metastasio, Racine, Goethe, Maeterlinck, von Hofmannsthal, Claudel, T. S. Eliot, W. H. Auden, and Gertrude Stein have all, in consequence, served effectively the lyric stage.

My recipe for the structure of serious opera, as stated above, is the classical one and not likely to be radically altered. In the domain of stylistic orientation, however, poetic as well as musical, anything goes, provided the voice parts are correctly prosodized, and can be heard clearly through the other kinds of sound.

Now let us suppose you have an opera, well written for the words and for the voices that are to sing them, embodying a story line, or myth, that the authors consider worthy and touching, the whole supported throughout by appropriate instrumental music. Let us suppose also that you have an offer of production under reputable circumstances. How do you go about protecting your conception?

If you cannot procure for the occasion a producing director whom you trust to understand your dramatic concept, you are out of luck. Stage directors, designers, costumers, and choreographers, all working along different stylistic lines (and with no deep knowledge of the script, plus none at all of the music), will turn your work into a variety show. Musical direction and casting are less of a hazard, since the conductor will surely have read the score. But miming and movements, as improvised by the stage director, and the clumsy efforts of singers to act while singing, will be very hard to correct unless your producer is friendly.

Singers, let me say it firmly, must not be allowed to stagger, lurch, weave about, or make faces. Musical expression comes from singing the words and the music, not from mugging. Nor from doing anything else while singing. Any movement required should be done at other times, between phrases, never on the phrase, except in comedy.

Neither should singing ever be done in profile. Maximum beauty of sound and maximum verbal clarity come from facing the audience. With a quarter-turn, half the sound and sense are lost. With a half-turn, you lose three-fourths of the words. Singing at full turn, back to the audience, can be used occasionally for dramatic effect, but only on clear vowels sung *ff*. No consonants will carry. Conversations in opera can be very effective with all faces turned out, hands and arms being used to identify the person addressed. To look at people when they sing, that offers them attention. Let them also look at you when you sing. But everybody, while singing, must look straight out, even in love-duets. There is no other way to assure a musical balance or to hear the words.

The acoustical necessities of opera, different from those of the spoken stage, require therefore, instead of the improvised bits of "business" that so often light up spoken dialogue, a form of regulated movement not far from what the dance world calls choreography. In opera the music is completely planned; in ballet so is the dancing. In serious opera all stage movements should be agreed upon and directed. When this is done, the singing improves, characterization clears up, and emotion communicates.

The planning of such movement, with all attention to acoustical needs and to full visibility between singers and conductor, can be done quite early in the rehearsal time. A *Sitzprobe*, or seated rehearsal, though valuable for musical cueing and for choral balances, need not involve intense expression. (Some singers will always be "saving their voices" anyway.) It is in the later rehearsals and the early run-throughs, after movements and positions have been set, that individual expression and an interplay of feeling can be encouraged. These will for the most part come about automatically, once they have been facilitated by appropriate gestures and positions. In my recommendations for operatic staging, expressive intensity is never demanded until the moves and positions are right. Then it comes without asking and can be further refined in coaching sessions with the répétiteur.

Moves and positions are a matter of stylistic authenticity, hence of choreographic taste. Every opera needs a stage-director aware of acoustical needs and of singers' limitations, but for the best musical results he needs a co-director skilled in dance expression and in regional ways. English characters, for example, do not move like Italians. Neither do French or Germans.

Regarding the cuts that many conductors make, all I can suggest is that they be tried out in rehearsal. Then, if both the composer and the librettist are consenting (but only then) leave them in during the early performances. After all, nothing, during the first years of an opera's life, is to be thought of as permanent. This remark applies strongly to interventions of the stage-director. With the conductor matters are different; by the fifth performance all tempos and volume levels should be firm, the pacings too, even the overall timing of the show. And his markings can then pretty safely be considered as part of the score.

As a last word, let me preach a little to the poets. It is a good two hundred years now since a sense of the stage was expected of you. Some, nevertheless, have still a certain yearning for the boards, and all of you, I think, like to hear your lovely verses sung. The opera libretto may be a secondary form, but it is a worthy one, honored by many of poetry's best names, just as incidental music to poetic plays has been composed by practically all of music's great ones. And don't be afraid of asking help from someone instinctively wise in stage matters. W. H. Auden, by himself theatrically weak, with the help of Chester Kallman made his work stick on the stage, even the singing stage, the most demanding of them all.

And don't get mixed up with composers who have no respect for poetry, who think they can pick up a plot just anywhere and treat their librettist like a hired man. The subject of serious opera has to be something that touches both you and the composer deeply enough to inspire you both through long labor. Opera writing, in my view, is a two-man job. It takes a poet and a composer, working at the same theme, to pull it off. It also helps if they can bear each other's company for the length of time they may be working together. But if they share a liking for the opera's theme, that should be fairly easy. That and keeping other poets' and other composers' noses out of the enterprise.

12

After All

NOW LET US SUM UP.
     How to write music for English words is the problem.
It cannot be solved by imposing a procedure. Every work is
different, and so is each composer's mind. Nevertheless, there
are choices to make, and whether these are better made step
by step or in unplanned jumps is moot. For now I shall merely
enumerate things to be done.

1. A text in prose or in verse, whether chosen or imposed,
must be there for working on; and the composer must have
accepted it. Some texts will turn out to be hopeless for music,
others unsuitable for present use. Instinct and experience must
be the guide.

2. Laying the text out in word-groups will at some point help
toward clarifying both the plain meaning (if there is one) and
its expression, its rhetoric.

3. Selecting a vocal range to suit the text and the occasion
will save time. Many concert songs can later be transposed, of
course, quite satisfactorily. Arias have too wide a range to allow
much shifting.

4. By now you will be looking for what I call a "musical
idea," a way of turning the text into a tune. This may or may
not involve vertical intervallic relations, a harmony, whether
expressed in full or merely present by moments. In either case
you can now start composing a vocal line. This, if it fits the
words for both sound and sentiment, will be itself your "musical
idea," which subsequent additions and corrections will merely
amplify. And let us remember that developments can proceed
as effectively by contrast as by similarities.

5. An instrumental accompaniment, at its simplest, should:
    (a) help the listeners to follow the tune
    (b) help the singers to carry the tune; keep them on pitch
    (c) not obscure the verbal text by attracting undue
        attention.

6. It can also do these things in a more sophisticated manner, reinforcing expression at the same time by illustrating the

text. Illustration can be either visual (linear), visceral (kinetic), or emotional (with spinal chills).

    7. It can situate a scene:

        (a) by geographic, ethnographic, or sociological references

        (b) by evoking historic musical styles

        (c) by depicting weather, animated or calm

        (d) by suggesting water, foliage in motion, clouds, crowds, animals, or birds.

    8. It can set off a florid vocal line by contrasted monotonies of:

        (a) rhythm, in an identical meter or in a quite different one

        (b) abstractions such as the "Alberti bass" (oom-pah), scales, arpeggios, even chords not clearly related to the vocal line but rhythmically distributed.

    9. If there is to be no tonal accompaniment at all, then the singer or singers must be able to stay on pitch without it, which is rare. There are, of course, clandestine ways of helping them out, such as concealing woodwinds among the choral singers, or a small pianoforte behind them. And the prompter, from his box, can usually, by singing along, lead wandering soloists back to the pitch.

    10. In all cases, especially those in which the accompaniment itself is part of the "musical idea," the instrumental contribution must take the lead, give tempos and pacings, create a musical structure and sustain it. Only a skilled accompanist or an experienced orchestral conductor can do this. No vocalist can handle with freedom a vocal line or a dramatic one without a sustained music line for support.

    11. When any song, or longer work, seems finished, read it through quickly for wrong notes, many of which will correct themselves in rehearsal anyway.

    12. Read it through again, this time for continuity, line, trajectory. If at any point it fails to hold your attention, it is sure to lose interest right there for listeners. Correct these points carefully, maybe cutting, which is always easier to do than to add or to rework.

A long-line trajectory is as important for short works as it is for long ones and for sections of long ones. To achieve this, some quite ruthless cutting may be necessary; you will not regret it. You can restore the cuts later if you find a better solution.

Also, I suggest aiming for continuity in all the contributing elements. I mean by this that the vocal line itself should make a composition. The accompaniment too, even when it is as simple as an oom-pah, and harmony must also make a pattern, a chorale, as the French call it. So too the sequence of orchestral colorations. Every element of the work needs to have a way of beginning, of going on, and of ending. Pay attention to matters like these, and you will be paid back in rapt attention from your listeners. Also in the freedom and ease of expression you will be providing to your interpreters.

13. Do not attempt to have an opinion about your work, to review it, so to speak. If you like to write for some imaginary audience, then that audience must consist only of yourself and strangers.

14. Your collaborators on any enterprise are always, of course, to be taken seriously. They are your team. Musicians working together, hearing together, feeling together, and projecting together, that is the miracle, the experience we prize above all others. And its parallel delight, which is working together with respected colleagues in a theater, or on a film set, can be no less rewarding when through a similar miracle you turn out, all of you, to be "working on the same show," rather than on five highly different versions of it. This kind of thing does not happen every day, but when it does it gets remembered on both sides of the curtain.

Appendix

THE INTERNATIONAL PHONETIC ALPHABET, created in the 1880s by the International Phonetic Association, is a system for writing all the sounds currently used in spoken languages, at least in those known as Indo-European.

Each of these sounds is represented by a sign which represents that sound and no other. Combining these sounds into the strings we recognize as words or word-groups constitutes an act of performance called pronunciation. This varies with respect to both sound and meaning in French, German, and the other subgroupings we call languages. It also varies within each language, both by region and by social class.

To illustrate some of the regional variations, as these can be heard today among educated persons, I have had transcribed phonetically a familiar prose passage, the opening sentences of Abraham Lincoln's Gettysburg Address.

I am not suggesting that composers need to use this phonetic alphabet in setting verbal texts. But I do think that some acquaintance with it is likely to facilitate their work, if only in checking current standards for articulating clearly their own language.

KEY TO PHONETIC SYMBOLS

Unless otherwise indicated, all key words illustrate standard American pronunciation (Chicago).

a	b<u>a</u>ck (northern England), p<u>o</u>p	f	<u>f</u>at
ɑ	c<u>o</u>d (New England)	g	<u>g</u>et
ɒ	h<u>o</u>t (southern England)	h	<u>h</u>en
æ	c<u>a</u>t (southern England)	i	h<u>ee</u>d
ʌ	c<u>u</u>p (southern England)	ɪ	h<u>i</u>t
b	<u>b</u>et	j	<u>y</u>et
d	<u>d</u>ebt	k	<u>k</u>in
ð	<u>th</u>y	l	<u>l</u>et
e	b<u>e</u>t	m	<u>m</u>et
ə	sof<u>a</u>	n	<u>n</u>et
ɛ	h<u>ea</u>d	ŋ	ha<u>ng</u>

o	b<u>eau</u> (French)	z	<u>z</u>oo
ɔ	c<u>augh</u>t (southern England, New England)	ʒ	A<u>s</u>ia
		eɪ	h<u>a</u>te
p	<u>p</u>et	ou	h<u>oe</u>d

o   b<u>eau</u> (French)

ɔ   c<u>augh</u>t (southern England, New England)

p   <u>p</u>et

r   <u>r</u>am

ɾ   pe<u>r</u>o (Spanish)

s   <u>s</u>ue

ʃ   a<u>ss</u>ure

t   <u>t</u>en

θ   <u>th</u>igh

u   <u>ou</u> (French), wh<u>o</u>'d

ʊ   h<u>oo</u>d

v   <u>v</u>at

w   <u>w</u>et

z   <u>z</u>oo

ʒ   A<u>s</u>ia

eɪ   h<u>a</u>te

ou   h<u>oe</u>d

:[as in i:] indicates long vowel

~[as in ñ] indicates nasalized vowel

ˌ[as in ņ] marks a consonant that becomes syllabic because the vowel next to it is deleted in rapid speech

'[as in 'sevņ] placed before syllable bearing main (word) stress

Fourscore and seven years ago our fathers brought forth on this continent a new nation conceived in liberty and dedicated to the proposition that all men are created equal. Now we are engaged in a great civil war, testing whether that nation, or any nation so conceived and so dedicated, can long endure. We are met on a great battlefield of that war.

CHICAGO

for skor ən 'sɛvņ jɪrz ə'gou ɑr 'faðərz brat forθ an ðɪs 'kãņent ʌ nu: 'neiʃņ kən'si:vd ɪn 'lɪbərri æn 'dɛdɪkeirəd tə ðə prapə'zɪʃņ ðæt ɑl mɛn ɑr kri'eirəd 'i:kwļ. nau wi: ɑr ən'geidʒd ɪn ʌ greit 'sɪvļ wor 'tɛstɪŋ wɛðər ðæt 'neiʃņ or ɛni: 'neiʃņ sou kən'si:vd ən sou 'dɛdɪkeirəd kæn laŋ ɛn'dur. wi: ɑr mɛt an ʌ greit 'bærˌfi:ld ʌv ðæt wor.

BOSTON

fɔə skor ən 'sɛvn̩ jɪəz ə'gou ɑuə 'fɔðəz brɔt fɔθ ɔn ðɪs 'kɔ̃ņɛnt ʌ nu: 'nɛlʃn̩ kən'si:vd ɪn Illbərri æn 'dɛdɪkeirəd tə ðə prɔpə'zɪʃn̩ ðæt ɔl mɛn a kri'eirəd 'i:kwl̩. nau wi: ar ən'geidʒd ɪn ʌ greit 'sɪvl̩ wa: 'tɛstlŋ wɛðə ðæt 'neiʃn̩ or ɛni: 'neiʃn̩ sou kən'si:vd ən sou 'dɛdɪkeirəd kæn lɔŋ ɛn'djuə. wi: a mɛt ɔn ʌ greit 'bærl̩fi:ld ʌv ðæt wa:.

DALLAS

for skor ən 'sɛvn̩ jɪrz ə'gɛu auə 'faðəz brɔət forθ ɔn ðɪs 'kantənənt ʌ nɪu 'nʌiʃn̩ kən'si:vd ɪn 'lɪəbəti æn 'dɛdɪkeirəd tə ðə prapə'zɪʃn̩ ðæt ɔəl meən ɔr kri'eirəd 'i:kwl̩. nau wi: ɔr ən'gʌidʒd ɪn ʌ grʌit 'sɪvl̩ wor 'tɛstɪn hwɛðə ðæt 'nʌiʃn̩ or ɛni: 'nʌiʃn̩ sou kən'si:vd ən sou 'dɛdɪkeirəd kæn lɔuŋ ɛn'djuə. wi: ɔr meət ɔn ʌ grʌit 'bærl̩fi:ld ʌv ðæt wor.

NEW ORLEANS

fɔə skɔə ən 'sɛvn̩ jɪəz ə'gʌou aə 'fɔðəz brɔt fɔəθ ɔn ðɪs 'kantənən ʌ nju: 'neiʃn̩ kən'si:vd ɪn 'lɪbəti æn 'dɛdɪkeirəd tə ðə prapə'ziʃn̩ ðæt ɔl mɪn ɔ kri'eirəd 'i:kwl̩. nau wi: ɔr ən'geidʒd ɪn ʌ greit 'sɪvl̩ wɔ: 'tɛstɪn hwɛðə ðæt 'neiʃn̩ or ɛni: 'neiʃn̩ sou kən'si:vd ən sou 'dɛdɪkeirəd kæn lɔŋ ɛn'djuə. wi: ɔ mɛt ɔn ʌ greit 'bærl̩fi:ld ʌv ðæt wɔ:.

RICHMOND

foə skoə ən 'sɛvn̩ jɪəz zei ə'gʌu auə 'faðəz brɔət foəθ ɔən ðɪs 'kantənənt ʌ nu: 'neiʃn̩ kən'si:vd ɪn 'lɪbəri æn 'dɛdɪkeirəd tə ðə prapə'zɪʃn̩ ðæt ɔəl mɪn a kri'eirəd 'i:kwl̩. nau wi: ar ən'geidʒd ɪn ʌ grʌit 'sɪvl̩ wɔ: 'tɛstɪn hwɛðə ðæt 'neiʃn̩ or ɛni: 'neiʃn̩ sou kən'si:vd ən sou 'dɛdɪkeirəd kæn lɔuŋ ɛn'djuə. wi: a mɛt ɔən ʌ grʌit 'bærl̩fi:ld ʌv ðæt wɔ:.

SAN FRANCISCO

for skor ən 'sɛvn̩ jɪrz ə'gɛu ar 'faðərz brɔt forθ ɔn ðɪs 'kɔ̃ņɛnt ʌ nu: 'neiʃn̩ kən'si:vd ɪn 'lɪbərri æn 'dɛdɪkeirəd tə ðə prɔpə'zlʃn̩ ðæt ɔl mɛn ar kri'eirəd 'i:kwl̩. nau wi: ar ən'geidʒd ɪn ʌ greit 'sɪvl̩ wor 'tɛstɪŋ wɛðər ðæt 'neiʃn̩ or ɛni: 'neiʃn̩. sou kən'si:vd ən sou 'dɛdɪkeirəd kæn laŋ ɛn'dur. wi: ar mɛt ɔn ʌ greit 'bærl̩fi:ld ʌv ðæt wor.

RECEIVED PRONUNCIATION (ENGLAND)

'fɔː skɔːr ən 'sɛvn̩ 'jɪəz ə'gəʊ ɑː 'faːðəz 'brɔːt 'fɔːθ ɒn ðɪs 'kɒntɪnənt
ə 'njuː 'neɪʃn̩ kən'siːvd ɪn 'lɪbətɪ ən 'dɛdɪkeɪtɪd tə ðə 'prɒpə'zɪʃn̩
ðət 'ɔːl men ə krɪ'eɪtɪd 'iːkwəl. 'naʊ wɪ ər ɪn'geɪdʒd ɪn ə 'greɪt 'sɪvl̩
'wɔː 'testɪŋ wɛðə 'ðæt 'neɪʃn̩ ɔːr 'ɛnɪ 'neɪʃn̩ 'səʊ kən'siːvd ən 'səʊ
'dɛdɪkeɪtɪd kən 'lɒŋ ɪn'djuə. wiː ə 'mɛt ɒn ə 'greɪt 'bætl̩fiːld əv ðæt
'wɔː.

SCOTLAND

'foːr skoːr ən 'sɛvn̩ 'jiːrz ə'goː ʌur 'faðərz 'brɔt 'forθ ɔn ðɪs
'kɔntinənt ə 'njuː 'neʃn̩ kən'siːvd ɪn 'lɪbərte ən 'dɛdɪketəd tə ðə
'prɔpə'zɪʃn̩ ðət 'ɔl men ər kri'etəd 'ikwəl. 'nʌu wi ər ən'gedʒd ɪn ə
'gret 'sivl̩ 'wɔːr 'testɪŋ hwɛðər 'ðat 'neʃn̩ ɔr 'ɛne 'neʃn̩ 'soː kən'siːvd
ən 'soː 'dɛdɪketəd kən 'lɔŋ ən'dʒuːr. wi ər 'mɛt ɔn ə 'gret 'batl̩fild
əv ðat 'wɔːr.

A Short Reading-List

As was remarked earlier, this is not a textbook; it is a how-to book by a workman with experience in both writing and performing vocal music. Its aim is to share some of that experience with other workmen, viewing the subject from a composer's point of view. Any composer's extra time, I think, is best spent with music itself, both classical and modern, and with reading what other composers have written about their working methods.

There is not as much of this last as one might wish; but it is precious, all of it, as it turns up in Mozart's letters, for instance, and in Richard Wagner's autobiography *Mein Leben* (Munich, 1911; trans. in E. Newman, *Fact and Fiction about Wagner* [London, 1931]). In the memoirs of Hector Berlioz (Paris, 1870; ed. and trans. D. Cairns, London, 1969) there is less of it than of attention to his literary sources. But the published correspondence between Strauss and his librettist, *Richard Strauss und Hugo von Hofmannsthal: Briefwechsel: Gesamtausgabe* (Zurich, 1952; trans. Hanns Hammelmann and Ewald Osers as *A Working Friendship: The Correspondence between Richard Strauss and Hugo von Hoffmannsthal* [New York, 1961]) is full of revelations. So is Wilfrid Mellers's *Harmonious Meeting: A Study of the Relationship between English Music, Poetry and Theatre, ca. 1600–1900* (London, 1965).

On the purely musical side, but still by composers, I suggest the treatise on composing with twelve tones *Introduction à la musique de douze sons* by René Leibowitz (Paris, 1949). Also the *Thesaurus of Scales and Melodic Patterns* by Nicolas Slonimsky (New York, 1947); and *Technique de mon langage musical* by Olivier Messiaen (Paris, 1944; trans. John Satterfield, 1957).

The most useful orchestration books are practically all by composers, from the *Grand traité d'instrumentation et d'orchestration modernes* of Berlioz (Paris, 1844) and its modernization by Richard Strauss in *Treatise on Instrumentation* (published together in a trans. by Theodore Front, New York, 1948); to *Principes d'orchestration* (Paris, 1921), a two-volume work by Nikolay Rimsky-Korsakov illustrated by his own music; to the handbook *Technique de l'orchestre moderne* by

Charles-Marie Widor (Paris, 1904), indispensable for its listing of all the intervals and chords that are practical for stringed instruments. The general compendia *Orchestration* by Cecil Forsyth (London, 1914), *Orchestration* by Walter Piston (New York, 1955), and *Thesaurus of Orchestral Devices* by Gardner Read (New York, 1953) are also handy to have around.

Certain works of sheer scholarship, but written from the composers' point of view, are also valuable. Among these I recommend *J. S. Bach* by Albert Schweitzer (trans. from the German by Ernest Newman, New York, 1958) and *Rhythmic Gesture in Mozart: "Le Nozze di Figaro" and "Don Giovanni"* by Wye Jamison Allanbrook (Chicago, 1983). *Rhythm and Tempo: A Study in Music History* by Curt Sachs (New York, 1953) is also very much worth reading, and so are *Le lied romantique allemand* (Paris, 1956) and *Wagner et le wagnérisme* (Paris, 1946), both by Marcel Beaufils.

Additional titles are *The Pronunciation of English* by Daniel Jones (Cambridge, England, 1958); *The Singing Voice* by Robert Rushmore (New York, 1984); *The Singer's Manual of English Diction* by Madeleine Marshall (New York, 1946); and *French Grand Opera: An Art and a Business* by William L. Crosten (New York, 1948), which exposes the power structure clear down to the *chef de claque* at the Paris Opéra, which seems to have become by 1830 the first of the great modern houses.

Composing in Latin for the Catholic liturgy is scarcely worth the trouble nowadays, since the ecumenical council known as Vatican II abolished its use in 1963. This turn toward services in the vernacular has proved generally acceptable almost everywhere but in France, where the language itself resists being chanted, and is not musically comfortable in liturgical set-pieces either.

A similar abolition of Latin in the Anglican liturgy had taken place much earlier, under Henry VIII. When this monarch broke with Rome, he took over Church properties, thus making it possible to go on holding services, albeit in English, and to keep the great choirs functioning.

A huge job was here set out for translators, as well as for composers; but they seem to have taken it up with energy and dispatch. The prayer book of the 1650s named for Edward VI provided a handsome English text. A new translation of the whole Bible was also begun at about this time. And a method for singing in English the psalms and canticles—the ever-so-ingenious Anglican chant—had been created, and the composition of motets and anthems got well under way within less than half a century. Services in the vernacular were in England a popular success, though most of Ireland had stayed Catholic; and Scotland, stubborn as usual, turned Calvinist. The composers of England even found time (and a busy market) for madrigals and glees, theatrical songs, and all sorts of music for masques.

The English masters from the sixteenth century till the death of Purcell at the end of the seventeenth, in 1695, produced vocal music of remarkable variety and flavor. And within another fifty years, George Frideric Handel, a German composer trained in Italy, had pulled it all together, including the setting of English, into a style of vocal composition, still using the big choirs, that has survived to this day. Styles in instrumental accompaniment have changed constantly, as they always do. But the English vocal line in Benjamin Britten's twentieth-century operas, and, for all its debt to American rock-pop, that of the Beatles, would still, I am sure, be found acceptable by Handel himself.

Vocal music in America has followed for the most part a different model. Our early psalm books, our "white spirituals" and fuguing-tunes, gospel ditties, blues, torch-songs, and show-tunes (the mating-music of our musical comedies, which tends ever to follow the rhythmic patterns of social dancing)—all this is different here, except for the mating-music. And for sedate hymns, which follow a British model perfected in the eighteenth century, with Handelian harmonies and Handelian verbal prosody.

Opera composition in the United States has tended toward historical subjects like Salem witchcraft, as in Robert Ward's *Crucible*, and Douglas Moore's regionally picturesque *Ballad of Baby Doe* (about early Colorado) and *Carrie Nation* (which deals with the temperance movement in Kansas). Marc Blitzstein's *Cradle Will Rock* and his cantata *No for an Answer* are political tracts. Such, too, is my own (with Gertrude Stein) *Mother of Us All*, while George Gershwin's *Porgy and Bess* and my *Four Saints in Three Acts* (the latter also with Gertrude Stein) are saturated with homage to the Negro voice.

As regards texts written *for* music, I strongly recommend

Words for Music by V. C. Clinton-Baddeley (Cambridge, England, 1941) and *The Tenth Muse* by Patrick J. Smith (New York, 1970), a history of opera librettos.

All these books and many others can make good reading, but I still insist that composers avoid overindulgence in mere information, and that they save their eyes (and ears) for music itself.

OTHER WRITINGS

MUSIC AND CULTURE

Music's Tradition of Constant Change

"TRADITION" AND "CHANGE," as words, are so heavily weighted with hopes and fears that it is impossible to describe with them convincingly any moment of time in music's history. Nevertheless, there have been periods so tranquil that one is tempted to believe no major change was taking place, while during others the evolutionary process was so rapid that, to the casual-minded, change rather than tradition might well seem to have been in the saddle.

Take the European nineteenth century, for instance, after the death of Beethoven. The transformation of musical techniques and expression through Weber, Mendelssohn, Chopin, Schumann, Berlioz, Wagner, Verdi, Moussorgsky, Franck, and Debussy was constant and continuous. At the same time, tradition—the Beethoven tradition—was the basis of musical pedagogy. And none of these composers, not even Debussy, though he complained a little about Beethoven, dreamed of dethroning him as the sun king. On the contrary, they all aspired to contribute to the tradition that had arrived through Beethoven at so splendid a maturity.

Naturally there were both radical and conservative temperaments around; there always are. Wagner publicized his own music as "the music of the future," implying by this slogan that everybody else's was of the past. And Brahms, with his own consent, was announced by Hanslick as the defender of the classical tradition against Wagner's irresponsible practices. But both Wagner and Brahms were clearly out for inheriting Beethoven's prestige.

A century later, it looks as if both were wrong about themselves too. Wagner's music had its biggest "future" between 1890 and 1910. Since the latter date his popularity has declined steadily and by 75 per cent. His orchestration procedures,

Based on a talk delivered in Venice at the International Festival of Contemporary Music, an event of the twenty-ninth Biennale di Venezia, in the summer of 1958.

however, his chromatic harmony, his German declamation, and his symphonico-dramatic textures are still studied in conservatories. Brahms, on the other hand, has enjoyed ever since his death in 1897 a rising incidence of performance, so that today he ranks at the box office second only to Beethoven himself.

There is really no equating the radical with the progressive and the conservative with the reactionary. Saint-Saëns, a conservative type himself, strengthened French music by introducing from Germany the use of sonata form, whereas Richard Strauss, for all his apparent radicalism of style and subject, added very little that is usable today either to the German tradition or to modernism in general. All that one can be sure of, between 1827 and 1914, is that change was rapid and that tradition—the classical tradition of Haydn and Mozart and Beethoven—was firmly respected everywhere. Both tradition and change, indeed, were so strongly entrenched that their representatives could not afford *not* to cooperate. And this is how our century came to assume that the musical tradition creates by its own nature a climate of constant variation in no way destructive to the noble mountains of the past or erosive to the fertile valleys of the present. The truth of this belief is not demonstrable. But its widespread acceptance in our time has assured modern music a hearing and has tended, moreover, to associate the sacred concept "progressive" with any music that bears any aspect of technical novelty.

The fifty years that ended with Beethoven's death were probably the first period in Western music's whole history that produced a body of work clearly visible to the immediate heirs of it as a classical repertory. Music, for the first time ever, had become a major art. And if in the century succeeding, German music followed a normal pattern of decay through giganticism, loss of muscular tone, and general decalcification, Italy nevertheless enjoyed from Rossini through Puccini a rejuvenation of the opera, in Russia secular music was born and came to a striking maturity, and France, from Berlioz through Debussy, experienced a miracle. Germany herself, in her luxuriant decline, gave us Strauss and Schönberg. At the same time, Brazil, Spain, Bohemia, Scandinavia, Hungary, and North America began sending up shoots. It was a brilliant century, full of change and excitement, and everywhere solidly nourished on the masters. Creation has rarely been more active, pedagogy more powerful.

The speed of evolution accelerated, and the excitement of it all mounted till about 1914. Debussy, who had already given his major piano works, as well as his opera *Pelléas et Mélisande* and his symphonic poem *La Mer*, composed in 1913 his ballet *Jeux* and shortly thereafter his three sonatas. Indeed, the five years preceding World War I brought with them, like a last wave breaking on the Western beach, Stravinsky's *Firebird*, *Petrouchka*, and *The Rite of Spring*; Schönberg's completed *Gurrelieder*, *Five Orchestral Pieces*, and *Pierrot Lunaire*; Ravel's *Shéhérazade*, *Valses Nobles et Sentimentales*, and *Daphnis et Chloë*. Every one of these works was striking, original, and powerful in expression. Every one of them, moreover, brought to maturity some composing technique predictable from the classical syntax.

Debussy's novel achievements were full freedom of form; verbal-musical amalgams more electric than those of Bach, Rameau, Mozart, Rossini, or even Schubert; and (shared with Schönberg and Stravinsky) a consistent 100 per cent dissonance saturation to delight the ears of Bach, who had so often provoked that experience mechanically through the use of organ mixture stops. Further achievements of the time included Stravinsky's raising of rhythm to the rank of a major component in composition, Schönberg's heightening of chromaticism to the confounding of all tonality, outlandish and wonderful loudnesses, and a pulverization of musical sound to the ultimate of delicacy.

All these achievements completed and crowned the classical repertory without in any way invalidating it. Indeed, it looks now as if Western music, that vast development which began with early Christian psalmody and which invented and perfected, one by one, the Gregorian chant, counterpoint, multiple metrics, harmony, a dozen wind and string instruments, the simultaneous, differentiated employment of all these in the lyric drama, the oratorio, the choreographico-musical narrative, and the extended instrumental forms, had come to an end. With the classical symphonists, the Western musical language was mature; in the work of the classical modernists it became free. And this last result, like all the others, was produced by classically trained musicians working within the framework of the classical tradition.

That tradition remains unshaken. Indeed it has lately been

further buttressed by musicological studies. Nor have the contributions of modernism been discarded; they have become a part of our classical tradition. Nevertheless, music's rate of evolution has slowed down noticeably since World War I. Of really powerful works produced in the last forty years I can name you only five: Igor Stravinsky's *L'Histoire du Soldat*, Erik Satie's *Socrate*, Honegger's *Pacific 231*, Darius Milhaud's *La Création du Monde*, and Alban Berg's *Wozzeck*; and these were all written before 1926. I know nothing of comparable originality composed since then, except possibly some very short pieces by Anton Webern. The music of Sibelius and Bartók, though powerful on the expressive plane, does not seem, technically speaking, to have changed anything.

Today there is little active change going on. There is only tradition, and that tradition includes all the modernisms of yesteryear. The modernist branch of our tradition, now wholly official and more than a little pompous, possesses, as our tradition has always done, a diatonic and a chromatic style. Our century's diatonic style, commonly referred to as neoclassicism, is an eclectic mixture of pre-World-War-I liberties with earlier, tighter syntaxes. Its practitioners dominate pedagogy, publishing, and performance. Twentieth-century chromaticism, as simplified about 1926 by Schönberg into a rule of thumb known as serial dodecaphony (or the twelve-tone row technique), marks the music of a smaller group that essays through a publicity at once pious and pugnacious to seize the positions of power now held by the neoclassic representatives. In neither camp is there much novelty of either expression or method; in both, rather, there is a sectarian adherence to certain parts of the Great Tradition, as if all of it were too much for anybody to live with.

There are those who maintain that the Western musical language, because it is now complete, must be scrapped. This is to argue that the English language, once it came to maturity in the plays of Shakespeare and in the King James version of the Bible, was thenceforth useless to literature. The contrary, of course, is true. And though any of civilization's instruments may slowly decline in vigor after its first maturity, that decline is likely to be accompanied by a wider and wider utilization over many centuries.

Music as a language, though long may it live, will not, I fear, be evolving much more. There will not be another Beethoven, nor a Bach nor a Mozart nor even a Debussy, because our musical language is complete and its gamut explored. We can only codify it now. We can export it to Asia and Africa. We can also finish off some jobs worth doing at home and long put off. A conquest of the English language by opera is possibly, at this moment, imminent. The vast and fertile field of Spanish declamation has barely been touched. The continental opera itself awaits for its revival the perfection of a new recitative, viable for films and television. In general, for the West, constructive advance seems more urgent on the vocal than on the instrumental front. But there is still room for movement in every direction.

The directions most encouraged today in Europe are rhythmic research and integral serialism. The former stems from American sources (Henry Cowell, Edgard Varèse, John Cage) and from the pre-1914 Stravinsky. Its purest form (also mostly from America) is that of music for nontonal percussion instruments. The combination of rhythmic research with twelve-tone chromaticism has produced in Europe a twelve-tone music in which not only the tones themselves but also durations, pauses, loudnesses, instrumental colors, high and low pitches, methods of attack and release—every variable in music, in fact—are subjected to a systematic organization into ordered series. Complete organization of this kind is known as integral serialism, and its more celebrated practitioners are Pierre Boulez in France, Karlheinz Stockhausen in Germany, and Luigi Nono in Italy.

I find this music utterly charming in sound and refreshingly innocent in expression. There is nothing wrong with it except the publicity advanced in its favor that it is another "music of the future." This pretension is absurd, because the idiom is not that novel; it is still a dialect of Bach and completely comprehensible to any classical musician. It is a game played with classical elements.

I doubt seriously whether there are unexploited devices available for starting a radically new musical tradition. I do believe, however, that success will not wholly pass by the rhythmic experimenters and the 100 per cent serialists. I can imagine them making lovely scores for all the better films about space travel, where their invigorating metrical asymmetries and their generally antiseptic and up-to-date sounds will give an effect much more appropriate than pathos. If this happens, they will have contributed to the still living tradition of musical impressionism—that is to say, of atmospheric evocation. And we shall all be very happy. For they are loyal workmen, and their music unquestionably has charm. My only dispute with these excellent friends and colleagues is that I simply cannot see them as subversive. I can just barely see them as late contributors to traditional modernism.

Now, modernism in music, to begin retracing my argument, is a concept from the late nineteenth century that urges an attitude of receptivity toward anything that may seem progressive either in syntax or in subject matter. It is an open-door policy regarding change, and the official representatives of tradition itself have not always been unfriendly toward it. In any case, modernism long ago won so many of its battles with reaction and won them so decisively that by the end of World War I they were sharing condominium in the conservatories.

Little by little, however, as the supply of musical novelty diminished, the encouragement of novelty was transformed from an open-door policy into a doctrinaire position. This position, as upheld in the magazines of musical modernism and in the programs of the contemporary music concerts, maintained that there could be no authentic or valuable composition that did not embody some technical novelty, the corollary being, of course, that any work which did embody a technical novelty was more valuable than one which did not.

To realize the absurdity of this position one has only to remember that music's master builders, Bach and Mozart and Beethoven and even Wagner, were none of them research men. Awareness of this fact, as well as the increasing scarcity of novel devices, turned the young musicians of the post-World-War-I generation toward an exploitation of established modernism through the mass media—radio, films, and dance spectacles—and through oratoriolike *grandes machines* designed to divert a mass public by the mobilization of orchestras, soloists, choruses, and that most antimusical of all instruments, the speaking voice. These efforts have not produced masterpieces. But they have popularized, officialized, and standardized the modern vocabulary so effectively that it is very hard today to distinguish by the ear alone the work of one contemporary composer from that of another.

I do not wish to imply that no musical research today is valid and no expression authentic. But I do consider that both technical advance and expressivity have shown, since World War I, or at least since 1925, a decline in vigor. A parallel situation exists in both painting and poetry. We are living in a time of cultural recession. Politics, economic organization, and the arts of war appear to be on the move. The fine and applied arts, in this epoch of wide cultural distribution, are definitely conservative. This conservatism, at least in music and in painting, is based on a tradition of modernism once radical, now completely academic and official.

The modernist musical tradition has never denied its derivation from Beethoven and Bach. The classics of yesteryear are no less classical today. It is also clear, however, that musical evolution, which has been extremely active for two centuries, has for the time being lost its dynamism. The situation is no doubt temporary. All the arts are in a low part of their curve, because the world is up to something else. And one of the things it is up to is distributing its cultural produce to a world-wide market. It is enlarging and standardizing that market with a remarkable energy. And it has been possible to undertake such a standardization because we, the musicians, had already standardized, brought to completion, and officialized our whole tradition, classical and modern.

So what do we composers do now? There is only one thing possible: change the assumptions on which we operate. We shall have to forget for a time about novelty and change and tradition and all such great big wordy ideas. I propose to you that every composer has plenty of small ideas, technical and expressive ones, and that these ideas are all valid if sincerely and competently acted upon. It is better to work with the ideas one really has, however minor they may seem, than to try to follow an outworn line like modernism-at-any-price. Especially in a time when there are so few "modernistic" ideas available at any price. In other words, the tradition of constant change must be thrown overboard and freshness found through other preoccupations.

The standardization of compositional procedures is a fact;

we cannot fight that. Anyway, we have produced it ourselves both knowingly and inevitably, through the intense and highly intellectual organization, over centuries, of our whole musical tradition, creative and executional. The standardization of audiences is also a fact; and though composers have contributed toward bringing it about, we are not wholly happy with the result. It is better for business than for creative advance. Our dilemma is that we believe in creative advance but are unable to make very much of it right now through technical innovation. Moreover, we are suspicious, as a source of inspiration, of mere expressivity; in our unconscious it lies uncomfortably close to commercial motivations and the relaxing of standards. So also for the tricky concept of sincerity.

We may well be reduced, all the same, to seeking innovation through expressivity, instead of expressivity through innovation, and to finding expressivity through sincerity, though sincerity at its purest leads straight to anarchy and through anarchy to the destruction of both tradition and progress. It is my belief, regarding musical composition, that today only sincerity and anarchy are valid. There is no good line or bad line, no clearly progressive and no reactionary. We are not fighting from positions any longer, or among ourselves. We are fighting individually against the distributors and the standardizers. We are fighting for our lives and for music's life, because all this vast distribution by phonograph and radio, this amplified inundation of the world with sure-fire classics and banal modernities, can kill the art of music. But till the sad day comes when nobody educated would be caught dead listening to music, it may just be possible to follow for a while the best lesson in the whole classical tradition, which is that individual freedom is honorable, and to succeed by private pushes and private tinkerings in keeping the giant musical machine in some kind of motion. It will require the efforts of many people all over the world to counteract music's present incipient sclerosis. And the time may be short. But I for one should hate to see the day when there will be music, music everywhere—and no surprise or spontaneity in any of it.

The Atlantic Monthly, February 1959

Music in the 1950s

Examining the state of music *now*, in 1960, as compared with its state ten years ago, I shall not be able always to judge changes by the criterion of progress. One is a little close in time for that. And anyway, I am not sure what progress means. It can mean improvement; but it can also mean decline, as when we speak of the progress of a disease. Also, music's state today could present so great a variety of changes—like the political map of Africa, say—that the mere enumeration of these might be more information than one man's estimate of their worth. Actually, I should like to essay just that: a description of the music world now, as compared in divers aspects and details, with that of 1950. Fitting its changes into any pattern at all, whether of amelioration or of decay, or even estimating whether, beneath them all, music may possibly be just plain standing still, like the Rock of Gibraltar, neither of these tempting exercises can promise profit save when wrought with facts.

First, from the viewpoint of performance, no change at all is visible. The standard Western instruments and the standard ways of playing them are the same. The piano, the strings, the wind instruments sound exactly as before. A dearth of string players, though frequently announced, is not yet an orchestral emergency. Nor have string teachers, in spite of much thought taken, yet made any major breakthrough in matters of method that might simplify learning to play the instruments.

The art of singing, which seems never fully to have recovered from World War I, was not further injured by World War II. But it has never regained the popularity it held before 1920 both in public performance and in gramophone recordings. Indeed, the earlier recordings bear witness to a beauty of tone and a sophistication of style rarely matched since. Singing, moreover, has not even essayed what today's chromatic and twelve-tone music cries out for, namely, the production of a clean white tone without vibrato.

Musical composition has been livelier. Integrated serialism, or multiple-row composition, as announced in the 1940s, has

Based on a talk delivered in Berlin at the tenth-anniversary conference of the Congress for Cultural Freedom, on June 20, 1960.

been developed during the 1950s with unquestioned artistic integrity, though in small quantity. The first extended works composed in this technique were, I believe, by Pierre Boulez. The use of hazard in composition has also been exploited in the last decade. Painters had begun exploring a similar vein some forty years earlier; but chance as an element in music writing, save for those primitive composing-machines that Mozart found briefly diverting, is surely a novelty of our time. Its first user was, I think, John Cage.

Music composed directly on electronic tape, generally known as *musique concrète*, is another effort begun in the late 1940s that has continued throughout the 1950s. Its repertory is still small and its artistic value a matter of dispute; but it too is a novelty of our time, the product of serious effort on the part of perfectly serious composers and engineers.

The acoustical engineers have been collaborating with architects in the designing of new concert halls. Many of these are quite handsome structures. Almost none, however, except for some small ones, is acoustically satisfactory. As a matter of fact, there has not been built anywhere in Europe or America since 1900 an acoustically successful hall or music theatre seating more than 2,600 persons. Nineteenth-century construction methods permitted better results, as witness notably the Auditorium Theatre in Chicago, not now in use, and the Academy of Music in Philadelphia.

Related to acoustics are certain new studies of the nature of auditory perception. It is not for me to explain these here. They are available in the scientific journals.* These investigations are very important to music: they could not *not* be. One of the conclusions already reached—though whether overhastily one cannot yet know—is that serial music, if correctly pitched in twelve equal divisions of the octave, is not perceived by the ear as musical sound. Its arithmetical beauty exists on paper and in the mind, but it is rarely a musical experience in the strict auditory sense. Certainly this music is easier to write than to listen to. According to the latest investigations of the ear, serial music is largely *Augenmusik*.

---

*See the article and bibliography in *Gravesaner Blätter*, IV 13 (1959). published in English and German by Ars Viva Verlag, Mainz, Germany.

Why the performance of a Schoenberg piano piece is less acceptable to the ear than that of a Bach organ fugue, which is no less shockingly out of tune, I leave for others to explain. All we need note here is that the scientists have the serial composers a little worried. Pure heterophony, however—such as is produced by noise-making groups and percussion orchestras—gets a clean bill of health from them. The ear can dissociate noises exactly in the proportion that musical tones are not present.

By a musical tone I mean a sound containing one fundamental pitch and possibly some of its natural overtones but with a minimal proportion of parasitic noises and of overtones from other fundamentals. The simultaneous hearing of musical tones whose fundamentals are related to one overtone series constitutes the harmonic phenomenon, or the experience known as intervals. This experience owes its very existence, its perception by the brain, to the fact that the ear itself contains a musical instrument, or vibrating chamber. This instrument cannot be bypassed by music. Willy-nilly it will produce a harmonic perception if the constituent elements for this are present in the auditory stimulus. On the other hand, if they are not predominant in the stimulus, the harmonic phenomenon will not take place.

The fact that Western music has for eight centuries differed from all other existing traditions through its exploiting of the harmonic phenomenon may have little bearing on contemporary aesthetics in the West. For East Asia, of course, that aspect of our music is its chief attraction. I cannot promise you that the new studies in auditory perception will constitute firm evidence in the long-standing dispute about twelve-tone music. Nor whether any other evidence will be brought forward to settle the case. It seems unlikely, however, that it can be decided without scientific testimony. Short of that, it will just have to wear itself out, like the eighteenth-century *querelle des bouffons*.

Meanwhile some division of spoils has been going on. By division of the spoils I mean that the neo-classical and other diatonic writers who have for twenty and more years now held all the chief posts in pedagogy, radio, publication, criticism, public instruction, and musical philanthropy, have in the last decade relinquished under pressure a few of these to twelve-tone writers. They have also, almost to a man, all written twelve-tone or other chromatic pieces.

Chromatic complexity and rhythmic or metrical complexity are surely the mark of practically all the ambitious works of music composed in the 1950s. This is not wholly true of the opera; but it does apply to most of the symphonic and chamber music of our younger musical leaders such as Henze and Hartmann in Germany, Carter and Kirchner in the United States. Even certain older writers, such as Stravinsky, Dallapiccola, Copland, and Chavez, have further neutralized and elaborated their textures. The 1950s seem to have stabilized an international style void of obvious folkloric content. A maximum of dissonance saturation—characteristic in general of our century's art music—and a minimum of historical allusion or stylistic reference, such as abounded in the music of the neo-classical school, make this music appropriate for manufacture anywhere and for distribution everywhere—excepting the Soviet Union, of course.

For all that luridness of expression, for all those representations of emotional introspection, abnormal psychology, and eerie weather that chromatic textures invite and rhythmic elaborations underline, the music of today, written by no matter whom, is surprisingly non-committal. No shadow of willful charm lies over it; no plain or urgent communication peers through its complex surface. It is as if the whole world of musical creativity had caught the same disease and were hiding behind identical symptoms its terrifying and terrified divergencies of heart.

Can it be that this century, as so many other centuries have done, is approaching stylistic maturity in its last half, that all the mannerisms and devices exploited individually over the last sixty years are coming to be amalgamated now into a common language? This consummation, though devoutly to be wished, has been hindered up to now by the war about dodecaphony—the twelve-tone technique. Today's international idiom certainly gives larger rights to the chromatic manner than that of the 1930s did. Actually, right now the accepted way to write music is probably over-chromatic, because any epoch's chromatic style—and indeed every epoch has one—is not likely to suffice for more than about 10 per cent of its expressive needs. Chromaticism is too slippery and too monotonous to cover the full gamut of our feelings. It has been useful in a decade of self-pity and of conformity. And arithmetical symmetries in rhythm have

offered some refuge in a time of cold wars and urgent concealments. (As William Blake said, "In a time of dearth bring out
measure and number.") But I doubt that the present fad for
gratuitous complexity allows for quite the breadth of expression
that the coming decades will, must, require of a classical idiom.

In the domain of musical aesthetics, or usages, a notable fact
of the 1950s has been the very great preoccupation of Western composers with the opera. Save for Stravinsky's *Agon*, few
major musical scores for ballet have been produced. Symphonic
composition has run thin of substance too, though by volume
there has been a good deal of it. But everybody, almost, has
written an opera or is writing one.

From the Soviet Union, just after the war, came Prokofiev's
War and Peace, later his *Angel of Fire*. France gave us Milhaud's
David, Sauguet's *Les Caprices de Marianne*, Poulenc's *Mamelles
de Tirésias*, *Dialogues des Carmélites*, and *Voix Humaine*. From
England came Britten's *The Turn of the Screw* and operas by
Lennox Berkeley, Tippett, Arnell, and Walton. In Germany,
Liebermann, von Einem, Orff, Egk, Henze, and Fortner have
produced striking operatic works. In the Western hemisphere
Stravinsky, Menotti, Barber, Blitzstein, Douglas Moore, Peggy
Glanville-Hicks, Hugo Weisgall, Carlisle Floyd, Aaron Copland,
Nicolas Nabokov, Carlos Chavez, and Juan José Castro have
composed operas of far more than minor merit. Spain, Brazil,
and the Low Countries have not yet joined the opera club.
Scandinavia has produced one entry, the Iron Curtain countries
none. Italy, opera's motherland, though she still bears her child
a faithful love, bears one that today goes largely unrequited.

As for radio, films, and television, I do not know a single
recent item of major quality as music, any musical novelty, departure, or innovation of distinction. Though Italy, Holland,
Germany, England, and the United States have made efforts
toward television opera, none of these, it seems to me, has been
quite successful artistically. And film opera is even farther away
from a solution of this knotty problem. It is knotty because the
camera is naturalistic, whereas the opera is poetic theatre, hence
stylized theatre. Getting contemporary dialogue into musical
recitative would probably be the big breakthrough, but nobody
has achieved that convincingly yet.

Jazz, curiously enough, has been quiet too. A style known
as "progressive," or "cool," has been the main vogue. It hardly

makes any noise at all. Just last winter, however, a saxophone player named Ornette Coleman has revived in New York the "hot" style in a manner hotter than ever before; and that was a pleasure to those of us who cherish jazz for its majestic sound as well as for refinement of improvisation. A species known as Rock 'n' Roll, if you are interested, is on the decline. It never was a branch of jazz anyway; it was commercialized hillbilly aimed at selling gramophone records to persons between nine and fourteen.

Now let us move into the business office. Grants for composers and commissions abound in Europe now, as in the Americas. Foundations, orchestras, opera houses, festivals, and rich publishing firms order works by the half-dozen. Publication and performance are available to composers on a massive scale. The recording of contemporary music, however, which was so active ten years ago, has been slowed down by the introduction of stereophonic discs. These are so expensive to make that small enterprises cannot produce them. And the large companies are so involved with remaking the standard repertory that their attention to new music has fallen off.

The recording of serious music, in fact, is an enterprise gravely in need of subsidy. In a world where every symphony orchestra and opera house, every ballet troupe and puppet show, is sustained by subsidies, public or private, it is improper that the preservation of musical performances should be left wholly in commercial hands. The support of a contemporary and classical recording program should be a matter of concern to governments and to cultural foundations. Supporting music through endowed performing organizations such as symphony orchestras is not enough. Everything reputable should be recorded and made available both for cultural propaganda purposes and for history. Such an invasion into the record business, especially if operated by governments or foundations, might even cut through the barrier to international distribution now represented by cartels and protective customs charges. Few products are as hard to transport from one country to another as a gramophone record.

Except for the recording industry (which does work internationally, though under self-imposed restrictions abusive to cultural distribution), the whole music world these days seems to be hedgehopping frontiers as if Europe, Asia, Africa, and the

Americas were the terrain of one vast steeplechase. Cold War on the cultural front has found music ever so useful as a means of seducing the affection of peoples. This may be a good thing. Whether it is good for politics one cannot know yet. But it gives trips to musicians, gets performers and composers round the globe, provokes paying engagements and performing-rights fees. Every government in the world and every international business organization, occasionally even the Roman Papacy, now uses modern music and art for propaganda purposes. And all this too is part of our musical distribution.

That distribution includes films, radio, television, the touring of opera, ballet, and theatre troupes, the massive displacement of symphony orchestras, the sale of gramophone recordings, and the forcible hearing of music in bars, restaurants, barber-shops, art museums, steamships, railway stations, even in airplanes. Music has invaded every home and every public edifice, every royal reserve and every aboriginal isle. The world is now an auditory landscape so vast that, save for a few figures of natural publicity charm (like Stravinsky, say, or Maria Callas), individual music makers pass virtually unnoticed. Perhaps this is why the composers more and more sound all alike, why they seem to have adopted, in spite of their twelve-tone war, a uniform way of writing music. Chromatic, complex, and massively dissonant, they move in phalanx and regiment like armored tanks. What have they got on their minds? Asserting their rights to a share perhaps in the profits of global distribution. In any case, the composers of the world seem to have united, as if some tribal instinct, or burgeoning of class solidarity, had made them all aware that there is little place today for individualized achievement. Considering the powerful organization of our distribution mechanisms, they may be right.

It is the size of any cultural distribution that determines whether the thing distributed is to be considered as a mass medium of communication. I am suggesting to you that music in all its forms tends today toward the massive operation. In the United States, for instance, there are hundreds of symphony orchestra groups, professional and amateur. Germany alone has 120 opera houses. And radio listeners are counted by the millions everywhere. Even the universities (of which there are thousands) constitute no elite nowadays but simply a mass public like any other.

Really there is not much elite anywhere any more, and no *avant-garde* at all. There is very little music written today, even the most complex, that is genuinely recondite. The most advanced atonalists are already box-office. Nor does their music long resist analysis; indeed, it explains far too easily for comfort. It seems made for mass distribution and will, I am sure, attain it.

What worries everybody, or should, is how to preserve, in mass-media distribution, the qualities of beauty and distinction that were formerly music's glory. Actually the operators of the mass media themselves are not wholly inimical to quality. A good deal of style can be present in films. Commercial radio is opposed to it, however. Educational organizations are not. Neither are Western governments, on the whole. The Soviet Union and the Arab League, if one can judge from Moscow and Cairo broadcasts, do not approve of distinction. They want to make common men out of everybody. So also, it would seem, do the Christian churches.

In any case, I do think that an increasingly mass-media and mass-distribution view of music, even in its most seemingly occult laboratories, has been a mark of the last decade. This trend is not necessarily permanent, but it is present now. And it may account for a certain standardized and ready-to-wear quality (as opposed to the hand-made elegance of earlier masters) that is depressingly characteristic of so much music written in this time.

Harper's Magazine, November 1960

Music Now

A REPORT on the state of music today will have to begin with some recall of its state in other modern times.

Back in 1914, on the verge of World War I, musical modernism was already mature and successful. The works of Debussy, Ravel, Schoenberg, and Stravinsky had thrown sharp profiles

The thirty-ninth annual Blashfield Address, delivered in New York City at the joint ceremonial of the American Academy of Arts and Letters and the National Institute of Arts and Letters on May 25, 1960.

against the sky; and these were clearly not nineteenth-century profiles. Nor was the sky a nineteenth-century sky. The Wagnerian storms were over and the rainbows of Valhalla washed white. It was clear and ready for anything, with just enough windiness around to carry forward the fires of revolution.

For the advanced composers of the time did appear in those days, both to the radical-minded younger musicians and to the conservative older ones, as leading a revolution. And the revolution they were leading, as most revolutions do, had provoked a war. If today the war about modern music is no longer a cause, that is because, like all wars between generations, it has been won through the mere survival of the younger side. We all take the twentieth century for natural, simply because most of the people now active either as creators or as consumers were born and brought up in it.

After World War I it had already come about that the musical climate was one of successful, or achieved, revolution. The bases of a new musical expression and of a slightly fresh way of dealing with musical sound, had all been laid down by our great leaders. The next generation were merely sons of the revolution. And though innovation was still being admired, as a matter of modernistic principle, the main musical activity between the two World Wars was what Gertrude Stein, in her 1926 Oxford lecture, called "equilibration and distribution." Distribution we shall be speaking more about later, because after World War II it becomes really massive.

Contemporary music between the two World Wars did not, however, in spite of its faithfulness to a revolutionary past, obey any unified command. Modernism in one form or another was the order of the day; but its practice was sectarian and the members of different schools did not fraternize easily. Igor Stravinsky and Arnold Schoenberg, for instance, though both resident in Los Angeles during the late 1930's, never met, even in battle, and never felt the need, for all the world-wide leadership they both exercised, of anything resembling a summit conference. The Russian impresario Diaghilev and the Austrian Reinhardt did, it now appears, have a cartel agreement by which Reinhardt's productions were not shown in western Europe and the Russian Ballet refrained from invading the central regions.

On the verge of World War II, in 1939, let us say, there were about five separate kinds of contemporary music available, all of them reputable, all skillfully practiced, and most of them with a history of at least two decades of public acceptance. Composers representing the five kinds could be viewed as occupying a fan-shaped enclosure rather like the French Chamber of Deputies, where those who favor change sit on the left and the defenders of privilege on the right.

On music's right, twenty years ago, sat the survivors of Late Romanticism. These included Richard Strauss, Sergei Rachmaninoff, and Ernst von Dohnányi, all still writing music, and Jan Sibelius, still an impressive figure, though he had ceased to compose about 1926.

Next to them on the left, though still to right of center, sat the eclectical modernists, composers like Hans Pfitzner in Germany and certain young Americans of the time whose work was animated by some delight in dissonance and some brash sound, but of which the nineteenth-century allegiance was betrayed by its basic structure, all built of sequences and working toward climaxes.

The central section, and by far the largest, was occupied by composers whom one may call either neoclassical writers or Impressionists, since they worked both veins. This large and powerful group still exists; and it still operates, as it did then, under the intellectual hegemony of Igor Stravinsky, Darius Milhaud and Paul Hindemith. They occupied, and still occupy, virtually all the seats of power; and they distribute the patronage. For several decades now they have headed just about every conservatory in the world, every college music department, every musical magazine of distinction. They have conducted the symphony orchestras, run the publishing houses, written the musical criticism, distributed the prizes, the travelling fellowships, the commissions and the cash awards. In Europe they administer the radio too. In America they advise the foundations.

The reason why our century's neoclassic composers are the same men as the musical landscapists is that they do not essay to emulate history, like Brahms (who was called a neoclassic in his time), but rather to evoke it, as if history itself were a series of picturesque landscapes, like Scotland or Ceylon. Their relation to music's past, even among our most academical types, is a product of modern historical awareness and the modern style-sense. They adapt to present-day service details from older times very much as our parents turned square pianos into writing desks or—as I once saw back in the 1920's—used a mediaeval chalice for an ash tray.

A smallish branch of the neoclassical and Impressionist group is sometimes called, or used to be, neo-Romantic, though the term is embarrassing because of its earlier association with such heirs of real Romanticism as Sibelius and Rachmaninoff. I mention this group because I am one of its founding fathers, along with Henri Sauguet. We seem to have started it in Paris about 1926. The idea for it, like many of our ideas, probably came out of Erik Satie. Our parallel workers in painting (and our close companions) were Pavel Tchelitcheff, Christian Bérard, Eugene and Leonid Berman. What we had in common was a respect for the integrity of our own and of one another's personal sentiments.

Now most of the century's earlier artists—Debussy and Ravel, for instance—had viewed with disfavor the use of poetry, music, or painting to express personal sentiments. Even today Picasso, Stravinsky, Hindemith, and T. S. Eliot are not likely to allow themselves any such indulgence. Nevertheless, a century before, personal sentiments had furnished some of poetry's and of music's best material—as in Schubert and Schumann and Chopin, for instance, or in Blake and Byron. It was our scandal, in an objective time, to have reopened the old Romantic vein and to have restored, in so far as our work was successful at all, private feelings to their former place among the legitimate themes of art.

This curious move on our part, which many observers mistook for reactionary, actually brought us over to the very leftmost position possible within the middle party of contemporary music. That was a position contiguous through its choice of subject-matter to that of the chromatic and atonal world, which occupied the terrain just to the left of our central grouping.

The chief subject-matter of these last composers had long been abnormal psychology and their method of treatment something one might call emotional micro-analysis. Schoenberg's cantata *Pierrot Lunaire* and Alban Berg's opera *Wozzeck* are characteristic and fine examples of chromatico-atonal music from our century's first quarter. The one contact between their studied luridness and our spontaneous lyricism was the fact that both described interior rather than exterior realities. Our methods of composition and our climate of feeling were as different as Paris can be from Vienna. Nevertheless, we did together open up the hard flank of Impressionist and neoclassical objectivity and thus rendered possible, I think, the transfusions and the graftings that have made blood-brothers today out of all composers.

My fifth and farthest-left grouping of pre-War days we might call the rhythmic research fellows. Henry Cowell and Edgard Varèse were its leaders. The movement was small but outspoken. Nowadays this group is quite large and includes within its wide arms not only the percussion writers and the specialists of pure noise-composition but the tape-tamperers too, those who construct music directly on magnetic ribbon without the intervention of hand-played instruments. Also, their use of arithmetical structures, which are about the only structures available to non-tonal music, has been picked up by the chromatic composers, especially by those accustomed to employing tone-rows in fixed numerical series.

Today the fences between our five stylistic groupings are all broken down, and desegregation is general. The Late Romantics have all died. The eclectical Romantics, with no conservative support left them, have moved into the neoclassical and neo-Romantic neighborhoods. And these neighborhoods are in constant flirtation with both the chromatic composers of the former middle-left and with the arithmetical constructors from music's engineering or factory suburbs. The result is a melting pot, where everybody practices at least a little bit all the techniques and where everybody's music begins to sound more and more alike.

Such a consolidation seems on the whole desirable both for music and for its business. For its business it provides a standard product to meet the demands of massive international distribution. With thousands of symphony orchestras in the world, millions of radio listeners, millions of gramophone recordings sold, and every government exporting music to every other as a form of political propaganda, some standardization both of the product and of the consumer has been inevitable. From an artistic point of view the standardization has some virtue too.

It may well be that our century's styles and devices are coming to be amalgamated into a classical style, or universal idiom, that will serve the masters of our century's last decades for the creation of master works.

Such a consummation, I hope, is not far off; but I do not think it is complete just yet. Most of the music written since World War II has been, on the whole, over-chromatic tonally and over-elaborate rhythmically. As a result, it has tended toward obscurity, toward poverty of expression rather than toward wealth and variety. In a time of fears and conformities, of cold wars and urgent concealments, the composers of Europe and America who consider themselves leaders seem to have ambushed themselves against all possible interrogation, and behind a thick wall of complexity to be hopefully hiding their hearts from the common view.

We all speak a common idiom nowadays, but one not perfected yet for full communication. It may be that the stabilization of our vocabulary will come through opera. Certainly the Western composers are making a massive assault on this ever-so-resistant fortress. The fortress is resistant because nineteenth-century opera, which is still our basic repertory, had got its stories and its music so admirably fitted together that they cannot now be torn apart. A nineteenth-century type of play just will not work with twentieth-century music, and a really twentieth-century play, if there is such a thing, seems to need less musical complexity than any opera house is accustomed to furnish to its patrons; or at least it requires a different kind of sensitivity from that for which the standard repertory-house routines have been designed.

In general, most modern operas have too many notes in them; their music tends to crush both words and meaning. Nevertheless, the opera is the place where modern music will have to be made to work. Complexities and other games played for their own sake can be entertaining in the concert hall, even quite impressive. But in the theatre everything must serve. Today our century's own proud and raucous musical idiom may be preparing itself to serve, and thus to conquer, the opera. But I do not know a composer living, not an old one or a young one, who has yet made more than just a tiny dent on the masonry of that moated monument.

Our composers are a united front for action, and the distribution of their works is global business. But I wish they were better prepared for global distribution. Maybe in ten years they will be speaking more clearly, saying more things. Just now I cannot help feeling that they are being at once garrulous and secretive. Also that there is far too much music in the world.

I do not feel this because I get tired of musical sound itself. Musical sounds are always a pleasure. It is unmusical sounds masquerading as musical ones that wear you down, and the commercializing of musical distribution has given us a great many of these as a cross to bear. It has also given such currency to our classics that even these the mind grows weary of. Because though musical sound is ever a delight, musical meaning, like any other meaning, grows stale from being repeated. Perhaps that is why so many of our contemporary composers feel safer hiding it.

After all, most of the arts today, save possibly history and reporting, reflect a manneristic epoch. Music is merely the latest to assume the mask. When one remembers the high and hilarious hermetisms that both poetry and painting have enjoyed in our century, one need not be surprised that music, in its own slow time and for its own quite private reasons, should at last have got into the game.

Proceedings of the American Academy of Arts and Letters
and the National Institute of Arts and Letters, 1961

Music Does Not Flow

COMPARING HISTORY to a stream, no doubt an urgent idea when new, seems nowadays less vigorous, especially regarding the arts. So also does belief in their continuing progress, as if any series of related events involved necessarily a destination.

Myself, I prefer to think of the arts as a museum or as a wine cellar. These comparisons would leave room for paying honor to great soils, great years, great workmen, also for preserving ancient methods. Museums and libraries are mainly devoted

The James Lecture of the New York Institute for the Humanities, delivered at New York University on April 27, 1978.

anyway to conserving works and ways that it is no longer practical to imitate.

Gertrude Stein used to say that nothing changes from generation to generation except what people are looking at. Actually, what people have thought they were looking at, arranged in chronological order, makes up whatever consistent fairy tale that history can be imagined to illustrate. And though repeating patterns do seem to recur in any such narrative, organic development is notoriously difficult to identify. In the arts, certainly, the creating, elaborating, and transmitting of techniques are basic procedures, but among these there are few long-term growths. They are more like inventions—say the fish net, the wheelbarrow, or pie crust—which once they have come miraculously into being stay on. And as for the game of "influences," which reviewers, and sometimes even historians, like to play, it is in my view about as profitable a study as who caught cold from whom when they were all sitting in the same draft.

Nevertheless, since what people are looking at changes constantly, everything can seem to be changing. Also, the things that don't change, like wheelbarrows and fish nets and pie crust, are always there. Playing games and eating and childbirth and death, for example, change almost not at all; they merely get arranged into stories about people doing them, into literature. And in this literature people move around and talk; sometimes they even sing. This makes for plays and films and operas. And in all these kinds of entertainment the element that affects people most intensely, that makes chills to run up and down the spine, the digestive apparatus to work faster, and the breath to hold or catch, is music. This element has no precise meaning and no dictionary. But it does provoke intensities; and it provokes these so rapidly and so powerfully that all the other elements—the verbal ones and the visual ones for sure—more often than not call on music's transports for reinforcing their own cooler communications. Music's lack of specific meaning, moreover, allows it to be attached to other continuities without contradicting them. The way that singing can give acoustical reinforcement to speech—can shape it, help it to run along and to carry—this is music's gift to liturgical observances, to prayers, hymns, and magical incantations, as well as to mating ceremonials like social dancing.

The composition of music not intended for provoking movement or for singing, and involving no spectacle other than that of men at work, is a quite recent invention, dating as a public show from, at the earliest, about 1600. But its elaboration during the last four centuries has made of music in Europe and in the West generally an art independent of liturgical circumstances, of dancing, of poetry, even of the singing voice.

Now how can an activity without meaning hold the attention of people who are not doing anything but just sitting there? Well, it would seem that over recent centuries there has developed for instrumental music, if not a vocabulary of meanings, a way of suggesting things that is capable, shall we say, of halfway evoking them and thus of attaching its own intensities to quite a variety of thoughts.

These evocations are of three kinds. There is that of the human voice singing metrical verse or intoning unmetered prose. Everything verbal, from lullabies to oratory to rigmaroles, is receptive to this kind of treatment. Instrumental music of this kind is in Europe called strophic.

A second kind, though perhaps it should have come first—it is so ancient and so easy to do—known as choric; and it can remind us, through a one-two, one-two beat, of marching, or through more fanciful countings-out, of dancing, either ritual and religious, or social.

There can also be attractions for the mind through the following of some tonal texture, as in Sebastian Bach's fugal patterns. I do not know a Greek-origin word for this kind of music; but when it is enlivened by unexpected waits and irregular stresses, this exploiting of the surprise factor, as both Bach and Beethoven practiced it so masterfully or as we encounter it nowadays in a jam session, could be called, I suppose, spastic.

In any case, it is one of the things that instrumental music does, music that is made only for being listened to. And the assemblage of all these kinds of musical gesture—the poetico-oratorical, the movement-provoking, the intellectually complex and surprising—into a composition involving many kinds of variety is the very special achievement of our Viennese masters—Mozart, Haydn, Beethoven, and Schubert. And what do all their grand sonatas and symphonies communicate? Anxiety-and-relief patterns, I should say, experiences cerebral from their ability to hold attention, but surely emotive and visceral in their immediate effect.

The continuity devices that purely instrumental music has employed toward these ends are the only discoveries I know of in music's history that even remotely resemble new species. And they were certainly not arrived at by organic evolution. Even today they are so far from having a clear morphology that there is no textbook anywhere for teaching them, no *Formenlehre*, old or new.

Now let us look a little into the permanent materials of music, which are tones, intervals, and their ordering in time. By time I mean measured time. The recitation of prose and poetry also exists in time, but that time is not a chain of fixed durations. Movies also are a time art; and their small bits joined together into a continuity, though this final cutting can be measured, every second of it, these bits really make up only a psychological pattern not meant to be perceived independently.

Music's time patterns, on the other hand, are there to be noticed. Their rhythmic and metrical structure controls the tonal one so powerfully that it actually gives to music most of whatever clear meaning it may seem to have. Rhythm is therefore both a stable and a stabilizing element and can be viewed as a constant, something of which neither the nature nor the function changes, though its designs may be infinitely various. And these designs, for all their constantly recurring elaborations in different times and places, are limited by the inability of the human mind to perceive as a unit any count larger than two, three, or just possibly a fast five. Rhythm, therefore, is hopelessly tied up to footwork and to language, to meaning, to expression. It can copy, but it cannot grow or evolve. Speeds and loudnesses, moreover, being subject to choice by performers, are no firm part of any pattern. The so-called "harmonic series"—all the intervals that can be generated from one fundamental bass tone—are another constant in musical organization. The pitch of the fundamental on which a composition is based can vary from piece to piece, or even from one performance to another. But the relation of that fundamental to its overtones remains the same whatever its exact pitch may be. These intervals are fixed by nature, and our awareness of them is very ancient.

Actually the Greeks knew much of what we know regarding

the first dozen or more of these, the Hindus and the ancient Chinese possibly more than the Greeks. Their number, though theoretically infinite, is for practical performance limited to about half a hundred, or fewer. Mixing them gives great variety to sound color. Transposing them into a single octave for use as modes or scales is a convenience. Falsifying them to facilitate pattern-making has long been common practice, the European "tempered scale" of twelve equidistant semitones being already more than two centuries old. A somewhat less acceptable tuning practice is to mix the overtones of slightly different fundamentals. This produces an acoustical interference known as vibrato. Mixing those from distant fundamentals is likely to cause more complex interferences and to erase clear pitch. We call these mixtures noise.

Sound patterns made from scale tones, commonly called "music," have long been thought to be good for the spirits and to give pleasure. Noise has no such reputation; indeed it is known to produce exasperation and bad temper. And though it is easy to compose noises into a pattern, it has been a fancy of only recent times to call such arrangements music. Modern art-workers, I must say, do like joining contradictions into a single concept. Nevertheless, the contradictory terms embodied in the idea of noise-music are not by any means terms of equal semantic weight. In fact the sounds of noise, being governed by no single harmonic series, are only weakly interrelated and thus cannot lend themselves nearly so well to acoustical structuring as the sounds of music do. Entertaining they can be, as we know from our percussion orchestras. And at places in Africa, notably Nigeria and the Cameroon, persons at some distance are said to communicate words without the help of any pronouncing voice. All this is both lively and useful. It makes a valued addition, in fact, to our repertory of ear experiences, and is capable, by isolating the rhythmic element, of encouraging rhythm's growth in complexity. There is nothing wrong with it so long as it is not offered as a substitute for music's ancient and visceral tone ecstasies.

Moreover, the harmonic series and its intervals are not only a delight, they are another of music's constant elements. They exist in nature, and though refinements in their perception may (just may) show a history of progress, the way these are perceived is built into the human body. I am not a specialist in this matter, but I can tell you a few things I have read. One is about an experiment carried out some years ago in Switzerland that tends to demonstrate that musical intervals are received by the brain not as a mixture of tones but as a resultant of their overlay.

The experiment goes as follows. You channel into one ear a pure pitch electronically produced and low enough in volume so that there will be no convection by the skull. Into the other ear you feed a similar sound pitched higher by the interval of a fifth. According to the account published in *Gravesaner Blätter*, July 1955, the brain does not hear these two pitches as an interval but only as a noise. On the other hand, if you feed both tones into one ear, either ear, the brain will instantly recognize the fifth.*

More extended speculation about music's relation to acoustical perception is to be found at the beginning of a very long book by a famous Swiss conductor, the late Ernest Ansermet. This is entitled *Les Fondements de la musique dans la conscience humaine* (or "The Basis of Music in Human Consciousness"). Its reasonings are derived from further evidence regarding the human ear's attachment to the harmonic series, even perhaps of its evolution therefrom. This evidence, according to Ansermet, is that the semicircular canals of the middle ear have a shape, definable by natural logarithms, which compels the air within them to vibrate in response to the harmonic series, also governed by natural logarithms.

Our learned conductor argues further that twelve-tone-row music, which uses only twelve intervals, all tempered and all uncorrectable on keyboard instruments, is a road leading to no musically pleasurable destination. Arnold Schönberg, its inventor, has been said to boast that this method of composition would assure for at least two more centuries the predominance of German music. Myself, I find that in the music of the chief twelve-tone masters—Schönberg, Berg, and Webern—though it bears many marks of individual genius, the actual sound of its built-in off-pitchness tends to be sensuously not very satisfying. Also, I see no reason why music today should seek to perpetuate

---

*An attempt to reproduce this experiment made several years ago in Princeton, New Jersey, gave indecisive results. The operating engineers from RCA found it successful, but the musicians present all maintained that they could identify as separate tones the pitches independently produced.

a German domination. Neither can I do more about the new researches on musical hearing than to hope they are right. And I cherish this hope because I like music to be in tune and to sound well. I also think that the intervals when sounded in tune have a great variety of expressive power, whereas twelve-tone-row music has always tended rather toward monotony of expression.

What I do hope for sincerely is proof that not only do intervals exist as an experience built into the brain but that chords as well may turn out to have a real existence. From my own experience I would willingly award this to six of them, which any musical child can recognize. They include the major and minor triads, the diminished seventh, the dominant seventh, the augmented triad, and any three or four notes out of a whole-tone scale. All mixtures outside of these I tend to identify as either real chords with added notes, as tone clusters, or as agglomerates. Real chords sounded simultaneously can, of course, create a polychordal complex, and the acoustic principles that govern the use of these in composition, as well as the psychological ones involved in their perception, merit investigation by composers as well as by psychologists. Polyharmony is after all a natural extension of the contrapuntal principle.

Moreover, in spite of Arnold Schönberg's practice of treating all the intervals as having equal rights, whether they are scored in stack-up to look like chords or laid out in a row like melodies, we all know, I think, that they differ in strength, by which I mean their power to build a loudness. Also, they may well differ in expressive intensity, in their relation to our built-in awareness of them, and thus to some kind of pleasure-pain gamut. In Berlin at the Institute for Comparative Musical Research there is an instrument that produces electronically (that is to say, in a pure state) the first fifty or more of them; and among these there is a major seventh so sharp, as related to our experience of this interval in its more common varieties, so sharp that I found hearing it actually painful. The belief of Alain Daniélou, the institute's former director, is that the whole interval gamut is allied to our repertory of feelings. And though it is far from certain that any such relation is codifiable verbally, we may well be able to experience fifty shades of emotion.

Certainly we have no such number of names for identifying

them. And they unquestionably vary in their *affect* through associations, proximities, colorations, stresses, and durations—their rhetoric, in short. Actually I see no reason to deny that the constants of music, which begin with rhythm and meter and go on to cover all the possible combinations of tones within any harmonic series, are not only structural elements for aiding memory but expressive vocabularies as well. Not dictionaries of emotion, not at all, but repertories of device for provoking feelings without defining them.

Now the defining of our sentiments has long been a preoccupation of religions and of governments. And the most powerful of these tie-ups has always been music's marriage to poetry. Music has no connection at all with touch, taste, or smell; and Muzak piped into art galleries has never taken on. Films and dancing do require music, but they don't want it overcomplex. Actually Igor Stravinsky's most elaborate ballet scores—*Petrouchka*, say, and *The Rite of Spring*, even *The Firebird*—have tended to shed their choreographies and to survive purely as concert pieces.

More durable matings have long taken place between music and words, and the music in any such union is likely to prove stronger than the words. How often has a fine melody worn out its verse and taken on another! Or crossed a frontier and changed its language! Tunes move as easily from the secular to the sacred as from the Ganges to the Mississippi. And all that is part of the way things change in what people are looking at.

What does not change, or hardly at all, is the way words and music fit when they do fit. That too seems to be a constant. Instrumental styles vary with fashion, but the singing of prose and poetry changes little throughout the life of a language. During the Middle Ages, so long as Latin was for Western Christians the language of worship, the musical settings of liturgical texts, being monolinear, could be melodically quite elaborate. For much of this time, of course, Latin was a dying language, immobilized by its plethora of long vowels and by the progressive erosion of its quantities. Nor was understanding it essential. No wonder Church music tended toward the flowery and the complex.

With the Protestant reform, a German syllabification came into use. With the English prayerbook of Edward VI, 1549, patter was discovered, for that is basically the character of Anglican chant, as it is a propensity of spoken English. In Italy and France, where Church Latin still survived, the seventeenth-century invention of musical tragedy in the vernacular, or opera, forced the local languages to find each its own musical characteristics.

My point is that when any language becomes a mature language, with a dictionary and a grammar, almost immediately the musical wing establishes a prosodic declamation for singing it. And this prosody remains. Instrumental style in music shifts constantly, vocal style very little. Here is therefore another constant element. Just think of Italian opera from Claudio Monteverdi to Luigi Nono. The handling of words in recitative, aria, or arioso has hardly changed at all, even when the vocal treatment was at its most florid. The stories of Italian opera have changed a little, and the music illustrating them quite a lot. But the words-into-music factor has hardly moved at all. The same is true in French opera from Lully and Rameau to Debussy and Poulenc. And if *Pelléas* contains little in the form of aria or setpiece, its vocal line is nonetheless French recitative that Rameau himself might have written.

The German cantatas of Schütz and the oratorios of Sebastian Bach are vocally of the same family. And the songs of Franz Schubert were so clearly the model for all who came after, including Hugo Wolf and Mahler, even for Arnold Schönberg, that Richard Wagner himself, the master of them all for theatrical German, could so nearly copy Schubert's practice while enlarging it for the stage that one might almost call the singing parts of any Wagner opera just lieder louder.

A special treatment of the vocal line needs to be mentioned here, which is that of Arnold Schönberg's *Pierrot Lunaire* and which he called *Sprechstimme*. This is a stretching out of normal German speech cadences to their farthest limits, with no precise pitch controls observed save by five accompanying instrumentalists. It is not quite melodrama (or speech-to-music); rather is it a sort of yelping-to-music all the more effective for its exaggerated naturalism. And the vocalist's role in these twenty-one tiny pieces is actually easier to perform than would be any on-pitch musical line jumping about like that. Moreover, since the German language often does jump about and feels right doing so, the voice part of *Pierrot* is not unrelated to the recitatives of Jesus in Bach's *St. Matthew Passion* or to the upward full-octave swoops of Brunhilde's battle cry in Wagner's *Die Walküre*.

As for Igor Stravinsky's cantata in French, *Perséphone*, and his English opera *The Rake's Progress*, though they contain what seem to be faults of prosody, they do come over as language quite clearly. And their resemblance to classical French or English declamation is much closer than any parallel that might be drawn between their instrumental textures and those of historic composers English or French. English musical declamation from Tallis through Purcell, Handel, Sullivan, and Britten is virtually unchanging, especially if you recognize Anglican chant as one of its sources. And the extremely high ranges in certain songs of William Flanagan, or of the Italian Silvano Bussetto, are merely flights of musical fancy. They do not alter very much the vowels or at all the stresses of spoken language.

In enumerating the musical elements that are not subject to change, no matter how much the ways of using them may vary, I must not omit to point out that the invention, elaboration, and eventual abandonment of technical devices do tend to follow a repeating pattern. That pattern is especially clear with regard to the historic periods of music's successive expansions. I speak of the West, of course, of Europe, of the music we know as ours. In Asia, Africa, and Indonesia, music may not behave the same way. From this distance the musics of India and of China-Korea-Japan seem relatively permanent, at any rate subject to changes in method that come about far more slowly than with us.

Our musical energy-booms, if I may call them that, have averaged over the last twelve hundred years an active life of about three centuries each. I refer to the monolinear music of early medieval times, which after its codification in the time of Pope Gregory VII created a large and fully written-down repertory, came to the end of its creative strength in the twelfth century. At that time a contrapuntal music very different in methods and procedures, as well as in expressive content, had been invented. Originally called *organum novum* (or a new tool), this music was no longer monolinear but composed as two and three tunes made for being heard together in pitch relations governed by intervals of the harmonic series. These were primarily fifths, fourths, and octaves, with secondary permissions accorded to major seconds and minor sevenths; also, to allow for fluidity of movement, to passing thirds and sixths.* Superposing on all such elaborations metrical observance no less elaborate came to produce in the fourteenth century liturgical music of a high complexity.

Whether the sound of it was ever as complex to the ear as it appears in score would depend on the technical sophistication of those who heard it. In any case, toward the beginning of the fifteenth century these particular complexities were quite rapidly abandoned. Their replacement for the Renaissance centuries, roughly the fifteenth and sixteenth, was a polyphony far easier to follow, being dominated by the more sentimentally appealing thirds and sixths and even by common chords. But eventually that music too went the way of all repertories.

For it is not humanity's habit with music to incorporate its predecessors' high skills into those used by succeeding generations. It is rather that these skills, along with the kind of expressivity that they deal in, tend to be abandoned whenever a new kind of expression, embodied in a new technique, comes into favor. And if the high practices are not altogether lost, that fact is due to their preservation in manuscript and occasionally, in some privileged liturgical corner, of a permitted archaic practice. Such survivals also tend to disappear eventually, so that even the notation of yesteryear's music now needs scholarship for its deciphering.

In cases where older music survives along with the new, the older tends to assume an antiquarian rigidity. Establishments may go on performing earlier music, but nobody writes new music in the old way. These simultaneous existences are visible today in Japan and Korea, where an ancient court music is still preserved and taught, still played as a homage to history, while the new musics—Eastern, Western, and pop—carry on virtually the whole of music's creative life.

It is visible too in Roman Catholic churches, where every modernism, after repeated papal denunciation, finally gets admitted to the service. A researched version of Early Medieval

---

*This may sound strange because it is contrary to later practice. It is true nevertheless for the thirteenth and fourteenth centuries.

repertory was decreed in 1903 to be the authorized music for Catholic worship. And twentieth-century styles of composition have still more recently been blessed in an encyclical of 1946. But the ancient Gregorian plainchant, however devoutly performed, is not a method by which anybody today is likely to compose. And to make survivals further precarious, the ecumenical rules, ordering services to be held no longer in Latin but in any convenient vernacular, will inevitably put our still enjoyed modernisms, along with the revived plainchant and restorations of Late Medieval *Organum* and Renaissance polyphony, all of them right back into the library.

Today's music may also be approaching the end of a major expansion. Everything we can still feel as ours dates from, at the earliest, around 1600. From then, or a bit earlier, come the Anglican chant, the Lutheran hymns, the opera, the ballet, the oratorio. Also the fully developed keyboard instruments such as the pipe organ and the harpsichord with their terraced dynamics, all those blessed violins which made possible the orchestra, and the pianoforte with its facile crescendo.

In the late eighteenth century the stiff continuity-textures of canon and fugue came to be somewhat abandoned in favor of the freer, almost organic expansions of symphonic and chamber music. We call the noblest of these layouts—as used by Haydn, Mozart, Beethoven, and Schubert—sonata-form, though that term was unknown to any of these masters. The historian Paul Henry Lang once told me that he had found the word only as far back as 1838, when Schubert, the youngest of them all, had been dead for ten years.

It is these masters, rather than Bach and Handel, who occupy the central position in today's repertory. And it is the codification of their practices in harmony, free structure, freely differentiated counterpoint and rhythm, and eventually, by Berlioz, in orchestral scoring, that define current music. So also, of course, do the operatic procedures of Mozart, of the Italian and French theater composers, and of Richard Wagner.

Also, with the impoverishment of noble patrons through the French Revolution, and with the building of public halls for the orchestra's growing possibilities of loudness, a paying public had come into existence. And along with this came publishers, managers, copyright laws, and a vast reorganization of pedagogy.

All these still exist. They are today's musical establishment, enlarged of course by the recording industry, which preserves
(though for how long we do not yet know) performances of
the central repertory and also of music's outlying regions. These
last include every kind of music available in every part of the
world. And music of all kinds is also distributed by radio and
by recordings to every part of the world, indeed to every hut
and palace in it.

All this has created not only a codification of the Baroque
and Romantic repertories but also a sales empire so large and
so powerful that its eventual collapse, if earlier empires are a
model, can be easily envisaged. The date of such a collapse is
not available to me, nor do I see it as imminent. Empires take
a long time to fall. I must say that many composers in our time
have seemed to be working toward a speedup of such destruction. And along with these intellectual efforts there has taken
place through radio and the jukebox such a massive distribution of music's mere presence that inattention has long been
quasi-universal. And inattention, as we know, can kill anything.

Now the ideas that evolution is a constant and that perpetual
enrichment of the musical art is inevitable are ideas I have been
endeavoring to disprove here, or at least to discourage. And
the thought that music, for all the present hypertrophy of its
distribution, may be in one of its historic declines regarding
creative energy is one that has been pressing itself upon me for
some time. Nor do I perceive any prospect of a major renewal.

The practical methods of Baroque and Romantic music,
their exploitation, expansion, and codification, as well as their
embodiment in a repertory of concert and theater pieces that
both professionals and straight music lovers can accept, all that
seems to have come to term about 1914. The constants of music
have not altered, but their utilization within the assumptions of
our recent centuries would seem to have reached some kind
of a terminus. Their high point of interior organization and of
expressive intensity had already come with the work of the
Viennese symphonic masters roughly between 1775 and 1825.
Some amplification of volume, extension of length, and inten-
sification of sensuous appeal have taken place since, but these
achievements too had all been pretty well finished off, I think,
by World War I.

One may point out also that the United States came to participate in this European history at only about that time, too late to have taken a major part in music's major branchings out or in any decline of its flowering. Our musical needs therefore and our contributions, if any, are likely to lie outside of Europe's narrative. Our folklore and our jazz, now studied in many European academies, are phenomenal creations. Indeed, they may lead us elsewhere than toward joining Europe. If jazz could replace classical counterpoint, it might justify our abandoning the classical line. I find such an eventuality quite improbable. But I have observed that the commercial establishment, by fighting jazz relentlessly, has strengthened it. Also, that in its fight for life, black music, jazz, has developed a remarkable ability to reject impurities. Actually it is a persecuted chamber music with nearly three-fourths of a century's history of survival.

Among our century's incompleted efforts, music for electronic tape has not lived up to what many thought was its early promise. Neither has noise-composition. As for the arithmetical overlays that some had put faith in for renewing music, the twelve-tone-row method has now, in spite of a vigorous burst after World War II, virtually faded away. The aleatoric, or accidental, ways of composing have probably, except for John Cage, now approaching seventy, lost much of their attraction for the young. Stochastics, or the calculation of probabilities, has one brilliant adherent, Yannis Xenakis. And the electronic big machines, though valuable for calculation, have actually invented nothing. Processed sound effects are what their taped products most strongly resemble.

The philosophers of modernism show, along with some hope toward music's renewal, a notable willingness to abandon most of its past except for teaching purposes. But there is also among educated people (today a mass public in itself) a distaste for being manipulated by managers and marketers. The composer Milton Babbitt has even proposed that musicians go underground. To a laboratory, I presume, in which tape composers would work alone or in small groups.

This idea is a tempting one for circumventing the addicts who make up most of music's public, including the opera fans, the electronics wing, the rock-music youth, and the more intellectually oriented but no less maneuverable school-and-college trade, the complexity-lovers. Obviously the only way to escape from them would be to turn toward something fresh. But there is very little available in music today, or in any contradictory non-music, nothing existing anywhere to my knowledge that was not in existence thirty years ago.

The question often asked, "Where is music going?" is to my mind unanswerable because I cannot see it going anywhere. Nor is anyone standing on its bank. Music, to my view, is not a stream in which a composer drops his line and with luck pulls up a fine fish. Nor is it a mysterious wave-force traveling from past to future which may, also with luck, carry us to higher ground. It is not like that at all. It is merely everything that has been done or ever can be done with music's permanent materials. These are rhythm, pitch, and singing. The first, being mainly imitation, is highly communicative. The second, let us call it harmony, is calculative in the handling, intensely passional in the result. The third, the words-and-music operation, appeals to everybody and is the avenue, almost the only avenue, to lasting fame. But it is also a discipline, never forget, and a game, like chess or contract bridge, to be played for high stakes against religions, governments, and music's whole secular establishment. That play, which will decide your life or death as an artist, cannot be avoided.

The purpose of this essay is to warn young composers away from a relaxed attitude toward their art. Look out, I say, lest its permanent pitfalls trip you. Music itself is not in motion. But you are. So do be watchful. Please. Unless, of course, you are a "natural" and can write music without remembering its past. But that involves the discipline of spontaneity, the toughest of all disciplines. Just try it sometime.

The New York Review of Books, December 17, 1981

MUSIC FOR THE THEATER

Opera Librettos

THE TENTH MUSE: *A Historical Study of the Opera Libretto*, by
Patrick J. Smith. 417 pp. Knopf, 1970.

HISTORICALLY opera is a branch of the poetic theater. That
is what it started out to be, and that is still its most permanent
identity. Indeed, the constant correction of its besetting faults,
such as commercialism of management, artistic irresponsibility
of singers, and the perpetual weakness of its public, of any
public, for mechanized scenery, has been aimed less toward
eliminating humanity's low motives than at restoring to favor
its highest ones. So that all those famous operatic "reforms,"
which since the seventeenth century have taken place about
every fifty years, have used as their source of energy a faith in
worthy (or "noble") themes, in dramatic integrity, and in poetic
diction.

In other words, opera's dramatic and verbal basis has over
and over again gone back to school, regularly sent there by
powerful musicians like Gluck and Wagner, occasionally by professional poet-or-playwright librettists like Metastasio in the
seventeenth century, Calzabigi and da Ponte in the eighteenth,
Eugène Scribe and Arrigo Boito in the nineteenth, Hugo von
Hofmannsthal and Bertolt Brecht in the twentieth. As a matter
of fact many of these historic returns, as well as certain works
of individual perfection, like Mozart's *Le Nozze di Figaro* and
Bizet's *Carmen*, have owed their successful outcome to team-
work between a composer and a librettist.

This was not the case with Metastasio, who was more influential than any composer of his time, and whose librettos were
actually published and read, though the music to his operas was
not. Metastasio, out of sheer artistic need, produced the first
Italian Reform by daring to eliminate sentimental subplots and
distracting scenic displays and by taking the trouble to couch his
dramatic actions in clear mellifluous verse, thus circumventing
with *opera seria* vulgar show biz and establishing it for the next
century and a half as a noble form. Actually he created *opera*

seria by firmly imposing on a loose Italian practice the formalities of the French classical theater.

Eugène Scribe too, though less careful in his verse, accustomed the composers of French *grand opéra*—Meyerbeer, Auber, and Halévy—to the structural advantages of a well-made play, a tradition that has survived in opera through Bizet, Puccini, and Richard Strauss, exactly as it was developed on the spoken stage through Sardou, Dumas *fils*, Ibsen, and Shaw.

Gian Francesco Busenello had worked closely enough with Monteverdi to produce in *L'Incoronazione di Poppea* both a perfect play and a perfect libretto. Lully had established in France serious opera, or *tragédie lyrique*, working through his librettist Philippe Quinault. And Raniero da Calzabigi had operated the second Italian Reform largely working for Gluck.

Berlioz and Wagner wrote their own librettos. And if the former's *Les Troyens* is a bit loosely organized, covering as it does most of Virgil's *Aeneid*, it also contains, according to Patrick J. Smith, "some of the most beautiful stage poetry in the language"—strong words about a dramatic literature that includes Corneille, Racine, and Molière.

Calling Richard Wagner "a librettist who also wrote music" may similarly shock some. It is probably intended to. But it is not intended to diminish his musical credits, merely to emphasize his extreme expertness as a dramatic author. And if Mr. Smith considers Metastasio's "astonishing achievement" as "the zenith of librettistic art," he states also, early in the book, that "not until Richard Wagner would there be a librettist who could handle complexity with such assurance and dexterity."

Smith's own amazing achievement is to have produced a word's-eye view of the musical stage covering nigh on to four centuries. And if he considers the actual verse of librettos (or the prose in which they sometimes now appear) as not needing to be quite first class, and complexities of characterization as also a luxury, he is firm in his history-based conviction that a libretto's strength is its dramatic organization.

For that there is no substitute, not even good music. And if the nineteenth-century Italian melodrama, as exemplified in Verdi, leans less on the well-made play than on excitement produced by a series of highly emotional moments, that too can serve for structure if the excitement is kept up, even though certain plots from Spanish sources, such as *Il Trovatore* and *La*

Forza del Destino, may seem loose-hung without their musical showpieces and their tense timing trajectory.

In discussing these matters from full historic reading and with copious quotations from Italian, French, and German librettos, all elegantly here translated, Mr. Smith has given us a work not only of unusual learning but also of many distinguished judgments and surprising insights.

Classical-tragedy opera and mythology opera, which filled the houses for more than two centuries and which came to an end with Richard Wagner and his running mates of the French *grand opéra* and with Verdian melodrama, contain an astonishing number of happy endings. The *lieto fine* was in fact their norm. Modern operas that end with some personal disaster unmitigated by any theory of dramatic justice, but exemplifying rather the fatalistic view that nobody can win, not even the bad guys—this kind of opera, from *Carmen, Cav* and *Pag*, all the Puccini works, *Salomé, Pelléas*, and *Wozzeck* to Menotti's *The Consul*, the operas of Benjamin Britten and Carlisle Floyd and Alberto Ginastera—all are *opéras-comiques* in their descent from the amorous pastoral, the comic skit, the cruel joke. Also in their occasional use of the spoken word for cutting through music to reveal some raw reality.

But from the beginning, opera's best authors, either librettists themselves or musicians working through librettists and stage designers (a department ever important in French theater), have aimed for, and occasionally achieved, total organization and (for performance) total control. Lully got it; so did Gluck, Wagner, the masters of French *grand opéra*, Boito (though he was unable to "bring off," or even to complete, his ambitious *Nerone*), Richard Strauss, and, in one opera each, Claude Debussy and Alban Berg. And every time it has occurred there has been a vast reverberation down the corridors of history.

Whether it is soon to reoccur Mr. Smith does not opine. Certainly no signs of it are visible here, in Europe, or in Europe's Eastern marches. But any writer of music or of poetry itching to flex his muscles in a stage work could not do better than to begin his exercises with *The Tenth Muse* as sparring partner. By taking libretto writing for a serious art it restores one's faith in opera, which for all its past and present ailments is approaching a four-hundredth birthday.

It will go on too, for sure. Because any composer with stage sense can write an opera. Indeed they mostly do, and often quite pretty ones. But for libretto writing there ought to be a textbook. Just possibly this is it.

Tidbits:

It cannot be emphasized too often that any considerations of the libretto which ignore its dramaturgic elements ignore the life-pulse of the work. Music can develop and strengthen that pulse, and in some cases even supply it when it is missing in the libretto, but the basic drive must be found in the libretto.

Wagner's stage grasp of the proscenium esthetic is as comprehensive as Shakespeare's of the Globe Theater thrust stage with balconies.

[Wagner's *Ring* cycle offers] a macrocosmic overview of the cosmos of which *Das Rheingold* is a microcosm— the whole standing as a staggering tour de force, by far the greatest structural achievement ever carried to fruition by a librettist.

[Emile Zola, who wrote six librettos for Alfred Bruneau,] is the most underrated of the French libretto writers. [If] his librettos are a classic example of the libretto overshadowing the music—another example are the operas of Ferruccio Busoni.

[Boito's life was haunted by] the duality of the creative vs. the critical and adaptive mind. Because opera is a combination of libretto and music, and because the question of creativity is secondary to the value of the whole, Boito will live for his Verdi adaptations [of plays by other men].

The W. H. Auden–Chester Kallman librettos achieve less than their intentions, partly because their verse is inferior to Auden's other poetry but largely because they show too clearly their philosophical and structural seams. [They are] patchworks of half-assimilated ideas.

The librettos to the operas of Benjamin Britten and Gian-Carlo Menotti can be instanced as demonstrating the continuing power of nineteenth-century ideas on the shaping and content of the libretto.

Gertrude Stein must be considered as the librettist who created a positive approach to a redefining of language and [of] play structure . . . In this sense she stands in relation to Erik Satie in music.

The New York Times Book Review, October 4, 1970

Music for Much Ado

ADDING MUSIC to Shakespeare's plays is for the composer a discipline of modesty. Some music is invariably required; but this has been so carefully limited by the poet, boxed in to the play's bare needs that one comes out of the experience convinced that the Bard was wary of all music's disruptive dangers and ever so careful lest musicians, a powerful and privileged group in Shakespeare's England, steal the show from poetry.

The tragedies sometimes ask for just one song, rarely more. Occasionally it is possible to add at the end, as in *Hamlet*, a funeral march. The rest of the music can be done with trumpets and drummers, two of each. They announce royal exits and entrances, indicate from off stage the advance and retreat of soldiers, even evoke (by an antiphony of pitches and motifs) armies in combat, triumphs, and defeats. The drummers can also, on cymbal, bass drum, thunder drum, tam-tam, bells of all sizes, wind machines, and other sound effects, produce the storms, fogs, and other species of foul weather that play so important a part in the tragedies.

It is usually better to produce these effects through musicians rather than through stagehands, to score them and conduct them, to control them in timing and volume through a series of electric light cues coming directly from the stage manager. (No one can hear word cues while playing percussion.) Only in this way, and after much rehearsal, can they be used to build an actor's vocal resonance acoustically, like a good musical accompaniment, rather than compete with it, fight against him, destroy his finest flights.

The comedies require few battles and no bad weather, allow for a bit more music. There may be an extra song, sometimes a moment of dancing, the evocation of a balmy night, a brief wedding, and, instead of the funeral march, with luck a gracious musical ending not unlike our modern waltz finales. In general, however, the music cues are brief and, as in the tragedies, limited to the minimum needed for defining an atmosphere. Nowhere in Shakespeare, save in *Henry VIII*, which is not wholly from his hand, will the composer be allowed to create the massive ecclesiastical ceremonies, grand marches, ballets, balls, and dream sequences that abound in Marlowe and Webster. Everywhere the music must be straightforward, speak quickly, take no time at all out of the play's dramatic pacing.

Under modern union rules and heavy costs, the musicians may be as low as four in number. The choice of instrumentalists for meeting the play's musical requirements with a minimum of monotony is a matter for much care. Gone are the days when Mendelssohn could use a full orchestra for *A Midsummer Night's Dream*, filling the theater with symphonic sound and holding up the play for the musical working out of themes, the injection of intermezzos and of expansive "numbers." Today's stage music must offer economy in every domain.

Stylistically, music for a spoken play must always be subservient to the visual element and to the verbal as well. A production, first conceived by the director, must be sketched for the sets and costumes before the composer of incidental music can effectively plan his contribution. A sumptuous visual style needs richness in the auditory too, and a meager, or bare-stage, production invites music of minimal luxuriance. In every case, music is an extension of the decorative scheme.

There is also the matter of time and place. Many a director and his stage designer find it helpful to take a script out of its period. Sometimes the script itself gives such a choice. *Hamlet*, for instance, can with equal ease be put into a medieval Denmark, into a Renaissance Denmark (contemporary with Shakespeare), or into modern dress. Music should accentuate, underline the chosen background. Consequently it should not, for the best result, be even thought about by the composer, before the period references of the production have been determined. Suggesting through the musical style of Richard Wagner or of Tchaikovsky the plush comforts of Queen Victoria's time (which was theirs), or using neat Mozartean turns and balances, however appropriate these might be in a setting of eighteenth-century court life, is not likely to be of much help in *King John* or in *The Merchant of Venice*. Stage music need not be historically authentic, but it should help to evoke, like the settings and the costumes, whatever time and place the director has chosen to evoke in his production.

The performances of *Much Ado About Nothing* that were first produced at the American Shakespeare Festival Theatre in Stratford, Connecticut, during the summer of 1957 represented in their visual and musical design exactly the sort of director's choice that I am describing. That choice has seemed arbitrary to many. Taken originally by the co-directors, John Houseman and Jack Landau, accepted with delight by Katharine Hepburn and Alfred Drake, the Beatrice and Benedick, as well as by Rouben Ter-Arutunian, who designed the sets and clothes, and by the present writer, who wrote music for the production, it seemed to us all, and still does, I think, imaginative and wise, a contribution even, to the play and to its comprehensibility in our time.

The decision, a radical one, was to set the play somewhere in northern Mexico, in what is now Texas or southern California, in the middle of the nineteenth century. Shakespeare had put it in a Sicily of his own time, or a little earlier, under the Spanish occupation. Now, this locale is not a vague one like "the seacoast of Bohemia" in *The Winter's Tale* or the Illyria of *Twelfth Night* or the even vaguer Vienna of *Measure for Measure*, slight masks, all of them, for English country life, or for London. The people in *Much Ado* are as characteristically Spanish as those in *Othello* and *The Merchant* are Venetian. They are proud, simple, sincere, energetic, and deeply sentimental. Even the villain is proud of his villainy and quite frank about it. None of them has the malice or the snobbery or the vainglory or the need of being two-faced about things, the divided mind or the indirection that abound in Shakespeare's other plays. Everybody is child-like, surely Catholic, and deeply, tenderly, permanently oriented toward affection. Also there is no war between the generations.

Since Shakespeare says these people are Spanish colonials, and since their characteristics are in fact recognizable today as those of Spanish colonials, changing their nationality would be a mistake. Surely the young Claudio who, believing he has caused the death of his beloved by doubting her virtue, accepts as a penance for his sin to marry sight unseen a cousin (nonexistent) invented by his fiancée's father is none of Shakespeare's English young men. Only as a Spaniard, believing in sin and its consequences, fatalistic, loyal to the results of his own actions, can he be believed and sympathized with. No matter how the setting of it may be altered, the play must remain a picture of life among well-to-do Spanish landed gentry.

The Sicilian background is less demanding—not demanding at all, in fact. The monuments of that isle, its history, and its geography, save for some casual mention of Messina, play no part. Using Sicilian landscape or architecture, Hispano-Sicilian clothes, especially from three or more centuries back, would tend to confuse rather than to clarify the play's understanding today. And transporting it to Shakespeare's England, always a possible choice, would not be a happy one, so thoroughly un-English is the love story.

And so, as a result of meditations and of searches after other alternatives, the idea was conceived that a rich ranch house in Spanish North America would be just the place for Hero and her father, for Claudio and his young friends just back from brilliant conduct in some military action. Beatrice and Benedick, of course, fit into any time or place that offers a background of mating and matchmaking. The whole play, it was agreed, could be brought to life in such a setting with a maximum of recognition on the part of twentieth-century Americans and a minimum of violation to the poet's meaning.

Now, the music cues in such a setting are no different in placement or in length from what they would have been had the play been left in Sicily. But their character, their whole style and texture, were of necessity determined by the adopted time and place. Like the scenery and the costumes, the easy movements and the formal dances, they had to evoke nineteenth-century Spanish America.

With that in mind I went to the New York Public Library and examined all the collections of folklore and old popular tunes from northern Mexico and the American Southwest. I copied out everything that I thought might possibly be useful. Then I consulted with my directors to determine the spots where music might be needed, desired, possible to introduce, and about the number of musicians the production budget would allow.

As it turned out, I got nine instrumentalists; and I chose a flute (doubling on piccolo), a clarinet, one percussion player (who could also play bells, or glockenspiel), two trumpeters, one viola, one cello, and a man who could play both guitar and double bass. In addition, the management provided, just for singing the songs, the famous countertenor Russell Oberlin (dressed as a peon of the ranch). There was also a conductor, not really necessary; but since he was attached to the theater that season, and could also play the piano, he was a useful luxury. I arranged placement for my musicians in a covered pit where they could be heard but not seen; and the electrician placed microphones and loud-speakers so as to amplify my string section without that amplification being detectable.

I shall not give here the list of music cues, because we did not follow exactly the script of the play. Nowadays virtually any director does make cuts for brevity and for modern pacing. He transposes the order of scenes. He allows only one or two intermissions. He may add moments of pantomime and dancing, if the story invites them. He may even interpolate an extra song from some other Shakespeare play, if he has a charming singer, or omit those already there, if he does not. In short, he cuts and reshapes the play to a modern audience's taste for a clean trajectory. He does not, of course, rewrite the prose or poetry. What he does is comparable to the cuttings, transpositions, instrumental substitutions, and adjustments of orchestral balance that any conductor makes for the performance today of an oratorio by Bach or Handel. Such changes are every bit as legitimate as using women instead of the boys that Shakespeare's time required in the female roles. But they do make every director's production a "version," and they do determine for that version the placement of the music cues.

In the Houseman-Landau version of *Much Ado* the soldiers returned from war by marching down a main aisle, led by a fife and drum playing quickstep. For this I used the most commonplace tune possible, the familiar Jarabe Tapatío, generally known as *Mexican Scarf Dance*, and speeded it up for excitement. I later used *La Golondrina* too, this timed as a habanera. These tunes, plus another almost equally familiar, reappeared in different instrumentations, as if they were familiar banalities of the time and place (which, indeed, they were). They helped to establish a folksy and easygoing Spanish-American ambiance. They also served to set off by contrast the more refined musical background of the ball.

For these latter I found authentic bits from the old Southwest, took two dance tunes from Spain, and composed a waltz. I needed a waltz for romantic feeling. But our Spanish Americans had no waltzes of their own. They used (bought copies of it by the thousands) a German waltz called *Over the Waves* (to them, *Sobre las Olas*). This did not seem right to me to use; it is too familiar to be effective save in ironic or caricatured version. And I needed a waltz with some lift in it. So I wrote one that might have come from anywhere, that evoked the romantic feeling that upper-class people everywhere in the nineteenth century associated with three-four time.

The famous song beginning "Sigh no more, Ladies" I composed in two versions and used in two places. One version was in espagnoloid Scottish style, with syncopations derived naturally from the word accents, and a vocal flourish at the end. The other was a fandango in which the words clicked like castanets. This latter so deeply offended the taste of my singer, an expert in Elizabethan songs and madrigals, that eventually it was removed from the production, just to please him.

It so happened in this production that almost every cue was "source" music, a situation ever to be wished. "Source" music means, in show business, music that can be supposed to come from some source, on or off stage, that is part of the play. It includes the trumpets that announce a king, the drums of the military, anybody singing a song, music that might be part of a household, such as dance music, dinner music, anything present or overheard that offers a realistic excuse for being present or overheard. This kind of music is truly "incidental," though it may be as necessary as any property sword or goblet. And it is the most expressive of all play music, because, its presence being dramatically explained, it can underline moments of tenderness, produce suspense, emphasize climaxes, aid the play through music's great power of producing emotion, without the audience experiencing the shock that comes from a breaking of the dramatic illusion.

More dangerous, but sometimes indispensable for creating a mood, is music that is purely atmospheric, an auditory addition to the scenery. Forests, moonlit gardens, shooting stars (I once produced this last effect through one chord on a celesta), all those states of nature that need to be felt as palpable but that cannot be rendered delicately enough by scenic or lighting effects—these can be, must be, essayed through music. Here the music has a poetic, not a realistic source. It is the voice of Nature.

Music can also speak with the voice of Memory. Soliloquies, confessions of yearning, recalls of innocence and childhood can without embarrassment to the listener be accompanied by soft music of specifically evocative character. Shakespeare, we are told, used for this purpose recorders, a species of flute. Intermezzos and introductions, when not truly "source" music, can also recall, announce, or anticipate without stepping out of the play. Overtures, of course, can only announce, and consequently are best when justifiable as "source" music. Anything else becomes the voice of the manager, the barker at a side show, and is ill suited to the poetic theater. An overture that is like a preview of the scenery can be very effective, however.

Beyond those conventions I know no musical usages that are appropriate to the poetic stage. "Source" music is always the best, but the voices of Nature and Memory need not be excluded. They must only be handled with tact. Occasionally a brief sound effect can be good too, if introduced and ended before the audience has time to realize its instrumental source. This is like physical pain made audible. A tam-tam roll *ppp poco crescendo* as Othello's epilepsy comes on him, a disembodied electronic whine as Banquo's ghost appears to Macbeth, such effects are in the best Elizabethan tradition. If they come off, they are very powerful. But if anyone in the audience laughs, they must be abandoned.

Among the voices I do not consider it proper to represent through stage music are those of the author, who has chosen language as his idiom and should not step out of that convention; the voice of the producer, who is no part of the play; and those of the director, designer, costumer, and composer. These collaborators are speaking, we may presume, for the author by helping the play to speak for him. Their self-exploitation is as offensive as that of an actor who insists on playing some publicized or imaginary image of himself instead of the role we have come to see him do. Stage music, to serve well in performance, must be objective, modest, and as loyal a collaborator of the director's and the designer's plan as of the author's play. That way lie all the possibilities of boldness and of daring. And that way too, so far as Shakespeare's plays allow music at all, lies the only possibility there is for a composer to serve, as a worker, the great Shakespearean texts.

In our Spanish-American *Much Ado*, there was a short overture, a habanera, to set the locale. Its "source" in the play's reality might be considered to be a café or dance hall outside the gates of the ranch, where our first scene was placed. There was reception music, Hispanic, for the opening of our second scene. From time to time a sentimental Spanish melody, one of those heard elsewhere in the play as café or dance music, was overheard on a guitar beneath some love scene or soliloquy. And there was formal dancing to music during the masquerade. Also, waltz music for the grand march out to supper. Balthasar sang his song to guitar accompaniment. And we ended our Act I on Beatrice's soliloquy with waltz music under it, like a memory, crescendo.

Act II began with café music, and the Dogberry scenes of municipal justice were framed in similar material. Dressing the bride was preceded and in part accompanied by an *alborada*, a salute to the marriage morn. Later there were wedding bells and wedding music. Then more café music, dance tunes on a tinny piano, to mark the police action as taking place among persons of banal taste, whose lives were drenched (literally) in hand-played bar ballads, as ours are in mechanized musical banalities.

Exactly such a tune opened our Act III, and comic drums accompanied a change of guard at the police station. Benedick's song, brief, amateurish, and absurd, was not accompanied. Then came funeral music for the tomb scene and for the song *Pardon, Goddess of the Night*, followed by wedding music again, by dance music, and at the end by a fanfare and general waltzing.

Transitions from one scene to another were usually covered by music, either in continuation of the preceding mood or in anticipation of what was to follow. We put as much music into the play as we could, endeavoring thus to keep the comic and the sentimental tones constantly present and warm. We hoped also that the abundant presence of music on two levels of taste—the vulgar and the genteel—would help us to underline the basic premise of the production, which was that the story takes place on a vast estate with many sorts of people around and many kinds of life going on. It is all a shade provincial; but there are great hospitality, many arrivals and departures, injustice administered casually, military forays, cooks, chambermaids, peons, and musicians constantly available for producing a ball, a wedding, a funeral, anything needed in the life of this rich, easygoing, isolated Spanish family.

My music cues would not be applicable stylistically to a production differently conceived. I have described them here for what they were, an auditory extension of the scenery and costumes. These latter illustrated visually the directors' conception of the play. That conception was based on what the directors and their collaborating artists considered to be the nature of the play's people and message. Theirs is not the only legitimate view of these. But once decided on and accepted as a basis for production, it determined the character of the scenery and of the music. As for the amounts of music used and its exact placement, we were obliged, in spite of all our efforts toward abundance, to limit our largesse. The controls that Shakespeare once and for all built into this script, as he did into every other, cannot be broken through without doing violence to the script. To make an opera (or even an operetta) out of a Shakespeare play requires abandoning most of the Shakespeare in it.

Theatre Arts, June 1959

The Rocky Road of American Opera

TWENTIETH-CENTURY COMPOSITION, except for a small and wholly distinguished chamber-music repertoire, has been predominantly of the theater. It is for the stage—the singing stage as well as the choreographic—that our time's finest composers most striking works have been conceived.

The choreographic stage, since long before the death of Sergei Diaghileff over thirty years ago, has been widely popular. Good dancing and good dance designing have toured the world and have even made their way into the commercial theater. But since 1940 neither scenic and costume design for ballet spectacles nor the composition of original scores for dancing has quite kept up with earlier standards of imagination. Second-rate scenery, or none at all, and ready-made music have apparently seemed to our best impresarios and choreographers safer investments, on the whole, than novelty. At least that is the way it looks to a musician. Or perhaps, with the opera in full boom, there have not been enough musical ideas to go round.

Actually the opera, the oratorio, the cantata, the lied, everything that has to do with singing, have from the earliest years of the century continued to inspire composers. From Claude Debussy's *Pelléas et Mélisande*, of 1902, through Arnold Schoenberg's *Erwartung*, *Pierrot Lunaire*, *Die Glückliche Hand*, and *Moses und Aron*; from Igor Stravinsky's *Les Noces*, *Oedipus Rex*, *Symphony of Psalms*, and *The Rake's Progress* through Darius Milhaud's *Orestes* trilogy and some dozen operas; from Arthur Honegger's *King David*, *Antigone*, and *Judith*, Paul Hindemith's *Mathis der Maler*, and Alban Berg's *Wozzeck* and *Lulu* through Francis Poulenc's amazing and ingenuously charming song repertoire and his operas, along with those of Benjamin Britten, Serge Prokofieff, Henri Sauguet, Luigi Dallapiccola, and the Germans who have won notice since the Second World War—Boris Blacher, Gottfried von Einem, Rolf Liebermann, Wolfgang Fortner, and Hans Werner Henze—the history of song in our century is a continuingly rich one if viewed in terms of musical creativity.

It does not seem quite so bountiful today if you look at it from the viewpoint of singing, which is more often than not poorly schooled and careless. Our choruses are fair, but they are nowhere nearly so expert as our orchestras. As for operatic production, it suffers from everything. The great houses have fine organizations and, in spite of their complaints, plenty of money. All the same, my own experience in reviewing operas all over Europe and America has been that about one performance in fifty has coherence and style.

Fifty years ago the opera-house orchestras were less good,

and the visual productions, for the most part, were less ambitious artistically, although certain stars had their own spectacular costumes. But singing, as everybody knows, was practiced to perfection by the Italians, by the French, and by the Germans. Even English-language artists like Nellie Melba and John McCormack, not to mention Lillian Nordica, Emma Eames, and Louise Homer, were vocalists incomparable by any standards we know now.

As for repertoire in the great houses, it was no larger than now, I think; but it did contain a higher proportion of contemporary works. The major companies all produced one or two new operas a year, and some of these stayed on for a time. Today the great twentieth-century lyric works are not nearly so available to listeners in our opera houses as are the same epoch's instrumental masterpieces to concert-hall listeners.

There is no reason to believe that the paucity of contemporary pieces during an opera season is entirely the fault either of the impresarios or of the public. And certainly it cannot be blamed on the composers. One has only to review the list indicated earlier to realize that there are dozens of first-class modern operas. Myself, I do not know where the block lies. But the fact remains that in every city where there is an opera season—and in the two Germanies alone there are more than a hundred and twenty—a twentieth-century public is being presented with a nineteenth-century repertoire. Indeed, the situation has come to be so taken for normal that many of our mid-century composers are trying to write nineteenth-century operas.

I insist on characterizing the centuries because I think there is something curious about the theater in our time that makes it not wholly of our time—as the films, for instance, are. There is twentieth-century painting; and everybody can recognize it, whether its manner passes for conservative or radical. Twentieth-century music is equally characteristic; it exists; it is of the world we live in. Twentieth-century theatrical production, of course, is everywhere; and it is vastly different from anything our grandparents saw. But twentieth-century dramatic literature is not that distinctive, or that abundant. Actually the theater of today is top-heavy with production devices and very thin of literary or human content. And it is not twentieth-century content itself that is thin. It is the lack of it in the theater that makes the theater thin.

This circumstance affects the composition of opera in that so long as it exists it is not easy for a composer to lay his hand on a poet or playwright whose dramatic ideas are worth putting to music. Librettos have a way of turning out to be either just a nineteenth-century type of intrigue plot, wholly uncomfortable in a twentieth-century suit, or a film-like, disjointed continuity that avoids its dramatic responsibilities, hoping that musical form will hold it together. This is something that musical form cannot do. Musical form can only hold music together; dramatic narrative must also be self-sustaining.

Actually, operas in our time have mostly come off best when their texts have least resembled *La Traviata* or *Die Walküre* or *Faust* or *Der Freischütz* or *Boris Godounoff*. An exception is George Gershwin's *Porgy and Bess*, which bears a strong resemblance to *Carmen* both in its story and in its musical treatment. Other likenesses aside, it is an opéra-comique, like *Carmen*, consisting of musical numbers separated by spoken dialogue. Likewise, the operas of Gian-Carlo Menotti, through their propinquity to veristic turn-of-the-century melodrama, bear a strong perfume of Leoncavallo and Mascagni. This smell of the past has not prevented their world-wide success, but it has tended to remove them from serious musical consideration.

Could a more distinguished musical texture, as in *Madama Butterfly*, or a more passionate melodic line, as in *Cavalleria Rusticana*, have saved these works for the repertoire? Yes, certainly. But verismo, even at its best, is a treacherous manner for opera today, since it tends, by overweighting the drama with violence, to emasculate the musical element. Also dangerous is the comic-strip opera—the sort of thing represented by Menotti's *The Old Maid and the Thief*. Farce in music is rarely very funny, as witness Verdi's *Falstaff* and Ravel's *L'Heure Espagnole*. Only the richest musical fancy can keep it from boring the listener, once he knows the joke.

Europeans have done well with the dramatic oratorio, a static type of work that permits stage presentation but that leans heavily on choral masses and classic musical forms for sustaining interest. Most of Milhaud's operas are of this type; and so, I presume, is my own *Four Saints in Three Acts*. This kind of piece also invites choreographic direction, the spectacle, when danced, stiffening into a frieze, and the music, with its large choral presence, tending more towards the ceremonial than towards the truly dramatic.

Boris Blacher has made radio operas that please by their concentration and brevity, but they do not seem to work well on a stage. Neither do Milhaud's *Opéras-minute*, although their musical content is exquisite. Television has produced in Europe a few contemporary operas composed for that medium; they seem mostly to be involved with electronically-produced weather music. Menotti's *Amahl and the Night Visitors*, an American production, is better suited to the television medium than anything I have encountered in Europe. On the whole, I should say, European opera librettists have been more adventurous than have the Americans, with the single exception of Gertrude Stein. And American composers of opera have found themselves limited, for the most part, by texts of mediocre literary quality.

Hugo Weisgall's *Six Characters in Search of an Author*, after Luigi Pirandello's play, has no such limitation, nor has Roger Sessions's *The Trial of Lucullus*, after Bertolt Brecht. Although neither of these works quite flows musically, they are both serious operas in the European sense. So is Nicolas Nabokov's *The Holy Devil*, which has a text by Stephen Spender.

Carlisle Floyd's *Susannah* is a brilliant example of the folk-opera—both the text, which is his own, and the music, although its viability may well be limited by orchestral ineptitude. Kurt Weill's folk-opera *Down in the Valley* and his veristic *Street Scene* do not seem to me sincere or artistically durable in the way that his German operas composed to texts by Bertolt Brecht do, particularly *The Rise and Fall of the City of Mahagonny*. A flavor of the commercial permeates the whole this composer's American work.

Indeed, a certain flavor of commercialism is present in a great deal of American opera. Douglas Moore's *The Ballad of Baby Doe*, although it is surely melodically sweet and spontaneous, is nevertheless a case in point. The impression it gives is that the composer was hoping to appeal to a mass public through a relaxing of standards literary and musical. I believe such a compromise to be ill-advised. It would certainly not widen the distribution of a concert work; quite the contrary. Nor can it be maintained the the opera public is reactionary. It is well known that a clear dramatic expression will often explain the presence of some recondite musical device or novel usage, causing it to be accepted far more easily in the theater than in the concert hall. The history of opera is full of such examples, the latest being perhaps that of Berg's *Wozzeck*, which enjoyed a wide European success in the 1920's and 1930's, a time when atonal music was rarely found acceptable in concert form.

Nor do I share the idea, commonly expressed in this country, that our sophisticated Broadway musicals are evolving towards American opera. They are not extending composition or choreography; they are diluting them for easy sale. Opera has sometimes diluted itself, as with the attenuation of Wagner by Humperdinck, although it more commonly conceals its poverties under complication, as with the involution of Wagner by Strauss, for instance. But always in works that deserve to last there must be something that can survive the thinning process; there must be something strong, original, and completely of its own time.

There are such works in our century. One could even admit to the group the Strauss operas. Charpentier's *Louise*, the operas of Puccini, and maybe those of Janáček. But towering above are Debussy's *Pelléas et Mélisande*, Berg's *Wozzeck* and *Lulu*, and Stravinsky's *Le Rossignol* and *The Rake's Progress*. And clustering around these are the operas of Britten and Poulenc, of Francesco Malipiero and Ildebrando Pizzetti, of Prokofieff and Dallapiccola, of the new Germans, who began really with Ferruccio Busoni and who survive in Blacher and Carl Orff and Henze, of the great Debussy progeny Paul Dukas and Albert Roussel, of the monumental Milhaud and the tender Sauguet, plus Paul Hindemith and Honegger and Schoenberg.

All this makes high company, clearly not any part of show business. If opera in America does not attain the intellectual status of European work, as our symphonic and chamber music has done, then we shall have failed to participate in one of our century's noblest achievements, the lyrico-dramatic. This would indeed be a disappointment, and crash programs supported by foundations have been organized to deal with the emergency. Even our opera houses are now showing good will, for money. In the long run, of course, everything is up to the composer—if he has a libretto.

Setting just anything to music will not do. Nor will taking some famous play of another time and setting it no matter how. Nor can you grow librettists in a college workshop, although you can teach young people, as Professor George Pierce Baker did at Harvard, that dramatic composition is not altogether a casual exercise.

Still, suppose that a good composer, one with imagination, skill, and some cultural content, does find a reputable writer he can work with, and suppose that in due time a work for the lyric stage is born. What happens next? Normally such a work will be refused by the Metropolitan Opera; and that will be a favorable outcome, I think, since the Metropolitan has, to my knowledge, not in twenty years done anything but injury to contemporary opera. The New York City Opera does less real harm to a piece, although everything comes out of that mill a little roughed-up and tawdry. The college workshops are a last resort full of a mighty good will and little else, with immature singing and amateur acting—sometimes, however, with a quite good orchestra. The alternative, if you are Gershwin or Menotti, is Broadway. There you can get a pretty good acting and singing performance, if you bellow for it, and a fair orchestra. But any production at all is hard to come by.

I don't know any easy cure for these troubles. A decent literary text for theater music is very rare. So is a loyal and delicate performance, on the stage, of anything. With or without crash programs, all the same, America, to regain her artistic self-respect, is going to have to produce both literature for her opera composers and honestly representative performances of their work. Otherwise we shall find ourselves barefoot in Bayreuth.

HiFi/Stereo Review, February 1962

The State of Opera

WHAT IS the state of opera in America? Something like this, I think.

Standard repertory is performed by our Metropolitan Opera on a level rarely matched by that of any other great house, and the annual losses here are less than those of almost any of the other great houses. These losses, however, are met here by private gifts, not, as in Europe, by Government subsidy—a situation far from reassuring in today's tax-ridden world. The Met could not possibly run for eleven months a year, as the chief companies of Europe do. Nor can it afford to re-stage more than three of its older works a year. New works are at present no part of its program at all, save maybe once in five years, or when paid for by gift.

The public in America is, all the same, avid for opera. Every manager knows that. This thirst has made possible the re-creation of opera seasons in Chicago and New Orleans, as well as the survival at high quality of the troupe serving San Francisco and Los Angeles. Companies and short seasons of less ambitious tone, notably those of Dallas, Santa Fe, and Central City, Colorado, as well as of many other cities, notably Boston and Philadelphia, have fed this hunger. And opera workshops in the colleges have nourished the intellectual appetite for rare and contemporary works. But the fact remains that the American public's turn after 1940 from symphony to opera (which was not really a switch of taste but an addition to taste) has not been rewarded by opportunities for operatic attendance in the way that a similar turn from chiefly recital fare toward the symphony had been rewarded in the 1930s by the establishment of many orchestras.

The reason for this failure was not, I think, the high cost of opera. The symphony orchestra boom had cost money too, plenty of it; and the founding of all those new orchestras, over 200 of them fully professional, had taken place in a decade of financial depression. No poverty had stopped any city from paying union wages to its new group, nor any school or college from buying bassoons. On the contrary, during the war, after the war, and all through the 1950s money was plentiful. It cannot have been budgets that held up the opera boom. Nor is our country timid when it desires a thing. What has retarded here the development of opera? A lack of know-how.

In the past, when we lacked artistic or technical know-how, we imported it from Europe. That is what we did for orchestral players, opera singers, and conductors, before we learned to grow our own. And we still use, for the most, imported repertory. More in the opera houses, I must say, than in the concert halls, but everywhere a majority of works written in Europe. And this for the simple reason that the classical masterpieces of music were all composed there, and long before we were in any effective way composing at all.

Why can we not import now the personnel we need for putting a sound operatic establishment into every city? The answer is that no such personnel exists. Good European singers are neither as numerous nor as efficient as American singers. Actually we are furnishing singers to most of the European houses, better ones than Europe can provide in the numbers required. And the European conductors and opera managers, what few are available, are amazingly limited in their scope. The Italians only know Italian ways, the French French ways. The Germans and Austrians are a little broader (and far less corrupt); but they still view America as a province of Europe, which at this date, in music, it is not.

America aspires to domesticate the opera, to transform it to its own purposes, to make it speak our language, verbal and musical. Opera cannot fully satisfy our public as merely the external repetition of an ever-narrowing repertory, and one that grows every year less meaningful to our young people as an image of the lives they are leading. Certainly the classics alone do not make a full life, for living people. Living people like some Aaron Copland and Samuel Barber with their Beethoven, some George Gershwin and Gian-Carlo Menotti along with their Bizet. We know that the older kinds of opera can be depended on to work for us; but we would like to feel that it is all right, too, that our boys should work for the opera.

And here we come up against another problem of know-how. Our composers are quite without preparation for meeting the public's interest in opera with viable works. They are unprepared because not one of our music schools, college departments, or conservatories has trained them to familiarity with the musico-dramatic circumstance.

They know the closed forms required by concert usage; they know concert pacings and concert unities of style; and they can orchestrate. But they feel out of place in the open forms of the lyric stage; and they have never been taught the placement and quantities of the English consonants (or vowels either), the phraseology of English declamation, or how to throw into relief the meaningful syllables of any sentence. They know the registers of the clarinet and which are good for warmth, which for projection. But they have never been told (or shown) what happens to a soprano on fourth-space E or to a tenor on the neighboring F. Their ineptitude at handling both the English language and the human voice is shocking.

Generally, also, today's young American composers show poor literary judgment in their choice of texts for dramatic treatment, nor have they had much help from their literary associates, since our best poets and playwrights have not been able to solve for the musical stage any of the problems that govern musical stage timing. (How could they, not being musical workmen?) And they have not always been willing, either, to entrust this work to musical hands. Second-class writers have collaborated aplenty, but with small sense of the verbal values that go to create a distinguished text. On the whole, the American libretto is shoddy work.

As a result of both musical and literary confusion, American operas that have aspired to communicate with the public have far more often than not gone off half-cocked. The day when a great composer could set twaddle and get away with it has long since gone by, if it ever existed. The operas that have stayed in repertory have strong librettos, all of them. Some of these librettos, of *Pelléas et Mélisande* and of *Louise*, for instance, are literature. Others, like those of *La Traviata* and *Madama Butterfly*, are condensed from perfect plays. But to take a text that is not quite literature and then to add music that is not quite good music solves no problem at all, creates nothing, not even show-business. It merely falls into the same morass as contemporary European opera.

For European opera is bogged down, too. It has gone all gummy in sound and mostly meaningless as drama. There is no help for us there. Nor any here either, except to lift ourselves by our own bootstraps, which is exactly what the workshops are trying to do.

It is also what the Ford Foundation is trying to help us do. Theirs is a crash program of twenty-four operas, six each for New York's City Opera and Metropolitan and six each for Chicago and San Francisco, all to be paid for on handsome terms and all carrying production costs for the house that commissions them through the Foundation. Our city troupe and San Francisco's have already mounted some of these works.

Quality, so far, has been middling. One work received a Pulitzer Award, but we know the Pulitzer committee's long-proved poor judgement in opera. In another instance, the Metropolitan seems to have accepted "on principle" a work about Sacco and Vanzetti, under the impression that these names were merely fiction, like those of archie and mehitabel, or Romeo and Juliet. The reaction of both the Metropolitan's and the Ford Foundation's politically conservative trustees to the announcement of this choice makes eventual production of the work at that house seem a bit improbable, though its composer is an opera writer of experience.

Actually, in our city houses, as in the colleges, the opera movement advances voluminously but at a snail's pace. Every-body wants well-sung and stylish performances of the old works. These are not hard to achieve with money. But everybody wants modern works too, things up-to-date and of our time that will make us all feel as if we were hearing a serious and not at all commercialized "musical," a kind of *West Side Story*, perhaps, without the hokum, something, say, with a minimum of quality comparable to that of *Porgy and Bess*. Works less valid than these will never make repertory.

And works as good as these, with or without subsidy, are not seeing the light every year. That is why the development of good American opera is bound to be slow. The European operatic sources from which we formerly drank *Pelléas* and *Rosenkavalier* and *Wozzeck*, yes and *La Bohème*, too, and *Madama Butterfly* and *Louise*, have all run dry. We have no mother to guide us any more. And our colleges, where opera is concerned, are as lost in the woods as our big-city establishments. We can only move blindly, all of us; and none knows whether he is moving forward, backward, or in a circle.

The chief hope is that with every composer in the country writing operas and every house, for pay or not, producing them, the mere volume of this effort will give birth to a "school." If this happens, quality will develop automatically; it always does. But it does not seem likely that any Center for the Performing

Arts can do more than show good will toward a movement so massive and so sluggish as that represented by America's operatic aspirations.

This is not to discourage foundation support. On the contrary, financial pump-priming will need to be continued, in all probability, much longer than is at present envisaged. And our classical houses must not be impoverished either. There is nothing wrong with the Metropolitan that money could not cure. A twenty million dollar invested endowment, earning a million a year toward fresh productions of old works (along with a few novelties), would do wonders. Our New York City Opera could become a great People's Opera for half that sum. And a People's Opera for prosperous and culturally ambitious proletarian New York could easily dominate the world scene for musical advance, as our New York City Ballet, working before that same public, dominates its field for musical imagination and choreographic advance.

Opera is not established in America as solidly as the symphony orchestra and the ballet are. These have schools for training personnel, great directors, a repertory, a vast and genuinely knowledgeable public. The opera, though of longer history, has proved slower for implantation. The roots are there, but they do not easily take nourishment. We shall simply have to keep on trying till they do. And be patient, as well.

Lincoln Center for the Performing Arts is deeply involved with the Metropolitan Opera. It may do wonders for the Old Lady of Thirty-ninth Street. Or it may kill her, because removal to the new premises is irreversible, whereas both costs and acoustics there are still uncertain.

The movement toward creating an American opera as contemporary and as efficient as our concert music, our painting, our dancing, our novels, and our films stands in less danger of a fatal move, from the mere fact that no move of any kind involving the creative opera movement is just now being envisaged at the Lincoln Center.

The strength of our opera movement lies in its widespread distribution. It is everywhere in America, like good hamburgers, good paperbacks, and churches. In Santa Fe, garage mechanics and their wives have taken to their hearts, believe it or not, Stravinsky's *The Rake's Progress*. The summer season just recently closed there has been its third in the repertory in five years, a world-record for that work. Central City and New York have loved Douglas Moore's *The Ballad of Baby Doe*. The whole world has heard happily George Gershwin's *Porgy and Bess*. Menotti's operas have traveled almost as widely. And every college is encouraging some local composer toward writing for the lyric stage.

There is surely some justification for hope, in view of the sound operas we have already produced, few though they be. It would probably be over-optimistic, however, to expect a real repertory of American operas (and at least fifteen first-class ones will be needed for that) to be created within five years, or even in fifteen. Nor need we imagine that the products of our growing pains will have much to offer as grist to the highly professional mills of Lincoln Center. Nor can those pains expect much solace early from that, or any other, real-estate-and-performing-arts power complex. American operas must be created before they can be distributed.

The New York Times, September 23, 1962

OPERA REVIEWED

Blitzstein on Record: From Regina *to* Juno

Marc Blitstein, a major contributor to the English-singing stage (American branch), is both composer and word-author of two recent Columbia releases. These consist of the musical numbers that framed and ornamented a play-with-music version of Sean O'Casey's *Juno and the Paycock*, recently visible on Broadway under the title of *Juno*, and *Regina*, Mr. Blitzstein's full operatic setting of Lillian Hellman's *The Little Foxes*, available for several seasons now at the New York City Opera Company.

Also on view still in the fifth year of its run at a small downtown theater, is *The Threepenny Opera*, Blitzstein's powerful translation of *Die Dreigroschenoper* by Bert Brecht and Kurt Weill. If performances or recordings were still available of *The Cradle Will Rock* and *No for an Answer*, the Blitzstein musical theater would be virtually complete for inspection. And such an inspection would show, I think, that the cardinal inspiration behind it all is the Brecht-Weill *Dreigroschenoper*. This is not to allege improper influence, merely to point out a source. And that source does seem to account for both the moralistic sociological tone of the stories invented or chosen by this composer and the commercial-toward-colloquial flavor of the musical treatments.

Of the two recordings just released, *Juno* is the less commanding musically. The tunes are picturesque enough (more so than their lyrics) and thoroughly (quite relentlessly, indeed) Irish of cast. But for all their stylistic adherence to the play's background they sound to this listener more earth-bound than earthy. Their performance, moreover, both by the actors who do not really sing, like Shirley Booth and Melvyn Douglas, and by those who do (though not in the Irish manner) like Jack MacGowran, Monte Amundsen, and Loren Driscoll, is nowhere air-borne by any Hibernian afflatus. The whole seems, indeed, a bit word heavy for taking flight. Orchestrally, thanks to Blitzstein and his aides (Robert Russell Bennett and Hershy Kay), this music has a variety and an evocative power far superior to the deafening ways of the routine Broadway "musical." Like all Blitzstein's music, *Juno* has "hit" quality only time will tell.

Time has already told us that *Regina*, which was first presented in 1949, is a repertory piece. Its story line is strong; its
characters have reality; its music animates and enlarges them all,
as good opera music must. Here is a work that fills an operatic
stage and fulfills the listener. Not a perfect piece, perhaps, but
a machine that runs—that runs, moreover, as an opera must,
on music, not on words or on situational drama.

Regina is not a necklace of "numbers," like *Carmen* or *Porgy
and Bess*. Neither is it a symphonic structure supporting vocal
yelps, like *Wozzeck* or *Electra*. Still less is it a conversation in
music, like Debussy's *Pelléas* or Poulenc's *Carmélites*. Its model,
I think, lies somewhere in Italy, as well as in the Weimar Republic.
The latter gives it its hatred-of-the-rich tone, its impersonal and
class-angled view of villainy. Also, through the Kurt Weill–Bert
Brecht operas, its preoccupation with verbal values. Nevertheless Puccini is around, and Montemezzi and Alfano and Wolf-
Ferrari too, as indeed they also are in the Weill-Brecht operas.

They show up here in the wide ranges of the vocal lines and
in their way of constantly working all over those ranges. There is
little of the metrical cantilena in arias and still less of the psalm-
like patter in recitative that English texts invite. There is indeed
almost no recitative or aria writing in the classical sense. There is
chiefly a treatment of the text's rhymed prose through a special
species of arioso, a declamatory setting of words and phrases
that moves, in this work, between actual singing and actual
speaking with utter lack of embarrassment. Now this casual relation to the operatic convention and the use of wider vocal skips
than are normal to English both betray German allegiances.
It is the loose structure of the orchestral accompaniment, its
busy but subservient role in the opera, its way of underlining
an emotional point *after* the exact event that causes it, rather
than *before* or *during*, that lead one, in seeking the sources of
its method, toward Italy.

Certainly its musico-verbal line, though ever clear, save when
it goes too high for enunciating, has little indigenous American flavor. Without its words, in fact, little of it would suggest
having been composed for English. Similarly, the orchestral
composition of the opera is tonally so restless and expressively
so eager at every moment to serve the verbal phrase that it does
not offer to the scenes much structural continuity or hardly

anything (save for Negro spirituals that begin and end the play) of local atmosphere.

Nevertheless *Regina* tells its story. And it is the vocal line that tells it, not the orchestral. It tells it not only by letting the words come out clearly but also by generating through tonal restlessness and rhythmic surprise a state of excitement that never ceases. This vocal line is chiefly loud. Eighty-five per cent of it, I should say, is sung *forte* or *fortissimo*. And it repeats its phrases well beyond the needs of clarity. This repetitive quality tends to make the whole opera seem wordy and the "numbers" (of which there are some) interminable. But in spite of everything, the work moves along; and in moving it holds the attention. It holds the attention, moreover, by a musical means, even though the interest created by music is used consistently for throwing the weight of attention toward the moral understanding of the play away from emotional identification with anybody in it.

An exception, in this opera, to Blitzstein's objective treatment of roles is that of Birdie, a broken woman and something of a dipso. Elisabeth Carron's reading of this compassionate part is wholly touching. Also, it is vocally the best performance present. Carol Brice, as the Negro servant Addie, sounds more beautiful; but the role offers little occasion for expressive variety. Brenda Lewis, as Regina herself, is coarsely powerful in the middle and low ranges, shockingly harsh at the top. And Helen Strine, as Alexandra, sings with a trembling voice and uncertain pitch, though she speaks beautifully.

Joshua Hecht sings in the bass role of Regina's cardiac husband some impressive low notes, and the Hubbard brothers, Ben and Oscar, are well intoned by George Irving and Emile Renan. Loren Driscoll is wholly effective as Leo.

Vocally, in general, this recording shows the New York City Opera in average-to-better form, which is quite good form, as opera singing runs nowadays. The orchestra and chorus, under Samuel Krachmalnik, are excellent; and the pacing of the whole seems effective. If any fault were to be found on the engineering side, it might lie in a certain microphone proximity. This is good for enunciation, but it tends to place the listener right in the Hubbard house rather than in a theater, so that though we gain in closeness of association with the characters of the story, we lose both dramatic and musical perspective.

The present listener, in any case, was convinced at the end that he had known every character in the story and that he had heard a good opera about them.

Saturday Review, May 16, 1959

The Crucible *and* The Wings of the Dove

HENRY JAMES'S NOVEL *The Wings of the Dove* is the story of a young Englishwoman who persuades her lover to court, with a view to marriage, a rich American girl about to die. When the scheme is revealed and the girl, dying, leaves her fortune to the young man anyway, he, thoroughly ashamed, refuses the legacy and resigns from the love affair.

Arthur Miller's play *The Crucible*, a study of the Salem witchcraft trials as group hysteria, shows how an honest man loses his life through being denounced by a bacchante in revenge for his unwillingness to continue adulterous dalliance with her.

Both these excellent tales have recently been made into operas—*The Wings of the Dove* by Douglas Moore (libretto by Ethan Ayer), and *The Crucible* by Robert Ward (libretto by Bernard Stambler). And both have been produced in the fall season of the New York City Opera at the expense of the Ford Foundation, which had also commissioned their writing. Both of the works, as well as their performances, have done credit to their sponsors. They may not represent the highest artistic achievement; they represent in every way, however, solid workmanship and worthy effort.

Both operas have prose texts, though in *The Crucible* rhymed hymns occur, and *The Wings of the Dove* offers, in the London drawing-room scene, one formal song, and in the Venice garden, a ballet accompanied by madrigals. Aside from these moments, the music follows a plan of continuous composition within each act or scene. It does not consist of "numbers" strung on a recitative—like *Carmen, Faust, The Marriage of Figaro*, or *Porgy and Bess*. Both *The Dove* and *The Crucible* are therefore "lyric dramas," like *Louise, Madame Butterfly, Pelléas and Mélisande*, and *I Pagliacci*. Neither composer has essayed to write a "music drama" like *Tristan and Isolde* or *Elektra* or *Lulu*; but both have accepted the convention of naturalism, or of *verismo*, as this has come to be known in opera, in consequence, both *The Dove* and *The Crucible* are cousins-german to the major stage works of Montemezzi and Alfano, of Leoncavallo, Wolf-Ferrari, and Menotti. Their great-uncle is Puccini, and an older stepbrother is Deems Taylor. Indeed, Samuel Barber's *Vanessa*, for all its vocal elegance, is not unrelated to these more direct emotional outcries.

It is, in fact, their constant emotional insistence that gives to *The Dove* and *The Crucible* their major limitations. In *The Dove* it removes the upper-classness that Henry James had so carefully built into his characters in order to explain their behavior about money. Feeling strongly about money, of course, is universal. But when anybody wears his feelings right on his vocal cords, he inevitably comes to seem a little common.

The people in *The Crucible* were conceived as having upper-classness too, but of another kind—that of a white, colonial, theocratic society. Their constant displays of passion and harassment, though clearly a part of the story, are so little contrasted with any New England reticence that what might have been thoroughly terrifying, if shown as a strict community turned violent, comes out somehow less mythological than it should and, consequently, less tragic and less grand.

In Robert Ward's *The Crucible*, the musical structure—based on sequences, ostinatos, and pedal points—is plain and strong, moving the drama smoothly forward. The orchestral sound of all this is pleasing, too, and transparent enough to let the words come through. The music's weakness lies in its adherence to the tradition that musical materials should be both neutral as expression and rich in sound. This convention, which, though it comes from Hollywood, has never worked to the artistic benefit of any movie, is even more unsuited to the stage, where music needs, for its maximum effectiveness, to be strongly characterized thematically and highly varied in sound. *The Crucible*, though orchestrally most agreeable, suffers from an excess of neutral thematic materials, from insufficiently characterized vocal lines, from overrich chords, and everywhere from a lack of strong tunes. It lacks also the atmosphere and progress of tragedy. For all its clean sound and excellent structure, this music would be better suited to describing an overstuffed society than one pushed to hysteria by harsh food, harsh climate, and harsh laws.

Douglas Moore's *The Wings of the Dove*, like *The Crucible*, lacks contrapuntal interests and is harmonically note-heavy. Though its orchestra has less charm than Ward's, its vocal lines are perhaps a shade more song-like. It is a little short of the energy needed to move it forward, depending more on the play itself than on musical device. As a result, the music has an improvised-at-the-piano sound, such improvisation having used as vocabulary short musical motifs that identity persons and places.

For all that Moore's vocal line lets itself be sung—makes singing a pleasure to hear, indeed—the voice parts are not very meaningful. As imitations of good English speech, they jump around too much to be believed, and, as dramatic expression, their having jumped around from the beginning (even the butler's replies are declamatory) makes their subsequent activities unemphatic because they are uniformly overemphatic. We have, then, a score which asks for constant emotional intensities (no matter what social occasion is going on) without achieving such intensities through varieties of melody or counterpoint. They are merely signaled by orchestral emphases and percussive accents, rising scales, chromatic slides, and trills. These sound more like sound effects than like music. And the singing they accompany is a kind of sound effect, too. It reminds one of opera, but it is neither recitative, aria, arioso, nor good clean patter.

And so, with both the accompaniment and the declamatory line built for emotional emphasis and for very little else, the cast of *The Dove* has gone in for acting out these emphases while also singing them, ever a dangerous practice in opera. We have long known as operatic actors the staggerers and the lurchers. This cast has added a species scarce seen in these parts since the turn of the century, namely, the wincers. Every unwelcome remark— and the script has many, being a society drama based on mental cruelty—every one of these unpleasant revelations is received like a blow, like some sudden knife-in-the-guts, judo twist, or pinch. I do not blame entirely the singers or their director, because these wincings are as often as not built into the music. But I do think that the authors of this opera, by conceiving *The Wings of the Dove* as a conflict of expressed emotions rather than of concealed character traits, have given us a high life closer to Victorien Sardou than to Henry James, and a quite unmoving spectacle, for all its melodrama.

Neither Moore nor Ward, I think, has tried to avoid the

musical responsibilities involved in wrestling a story-plot into a musical composition; but I do think they have both somewhat underestimated the difficulties. For the naturalistic play in prose is among all dramatic forms the most resistant to musical trans-formation. Taking a script that is not quite literature and adding to it a score that is not quite music may satisfy commercial show business, but the Ford Foundation and New York City Opera are not in the business of mounting shows. They are in the profession of encouraging art. Both Ward's opera and Moore's fall short, I think, of full achievement as either show business or art. In Ward's, the art workmanship is more expert. Both, indeed, uphold a reputable standard in that regard, but neither solves any of opera's major problems.

Myself, I do not believe that those problems, which are largely due to the prevalence in public favor today of plot operas over music operas, are to be solved by composing more plot operas. Neither do I think, in spite of Gian-Carlo Menotti's dra-matically striking stage works, that there is any musical future in plot operas. They are a debased musical form that grows weaker every decade.

Now, opera based on history, poetry, legend, religion, or politics and involving music that adds nobility and beauty to its theme is the grandest thing in entertainment. But unless the music of such a work ennobles everything else in it and also is thoroughly absorbing as music, it does more harm than good by being there. Even the acting operas of Strauss and Puccini and Massenet offer some intrinsic musical interest. *The Crucible* and *The Wings of the Dove*, though loyal efforts surely, do not impress me deeply as music. Of the two, I find *The Crucible* musically the more pleasing; but I am sure both stories could be told as well in words. Such is ever the hazard in musical realism.

Show, January 1962

Stravinsky's Flood: *A Spectacle for Television*

THE STORY of Noah's Ark, lately come into sudden favour, is not one to inspire much mystical meditation or fresh theology, but it does have innocence appeal and can offer entertainment to the light-hearted.

It is a little surprising, all the same, that Igor Stravinsky, who has never, but never, played the musical child, should have accepted for the celebration of his eightieth birthday to collaborate with a commercially sponsored television enterprise so patently disingenuous as the one broadcast last Thursday night from New York City over the networks of the Columbia Broadcasting System.

Stravinsky's music is a cantata entitled *The Flood*, and the television spectacle that illustrates it is called "Noah and the Flood," with a cast including Elsa Lanchester and Laurence Harvey. The musical score involves an orchestra, a chorus, three vocal soloists, and several speaking voices. The spectacle comprises modern classical dancing in tights, choreographed by Balanchine, pantomime in heavy masks, camera effects of clouds and of water, and illustrative stage-props photographed from toyshop models. The whole is a hash from any visual point of view. Musically, it is a slender but perfectly real piece by Stravinsky.

It is slender because it has a story to tell rather than a musical idea to carry out. That story is told through compact quotations from the Book of Genesis and from the Chester Miracle Play that inspired Benjamin Britten's cantata on the same subject. Seraphic comments in Latin (from the Roman Liturgy) constitute the brief choral entries. The orchestral interludes that represent the building of the Ark and the Deluge are expeditious, spare of notes. Twenty-three minutes of playing-time dispose of the whole work, and neither sustained musical development nor any climactic loudness is ever mobilized. *The Flood* is like a master's thumbnail sketch for some grander monument.

It is also the work of a master who has listened carefully to the music of his youngest pupils and who is inclined toward courting their favour, following their mode. There is just enough use of twelve-tone rows to reassure the older faithful and little enough to make happy the restless ones who themselves nowadays are seeking exit from the labyrinth. The music has, moreover, a seemingly casual quality that is ever so up to date. Its musical materials are many of them small note-groups, motif-like aggregates such as are now referred to by those who compose with them as musical "events" or "happenings." And Stravinsky, composing with them, has set them out one by one with plenty of air between them, for all the world as if their incidence and proximity were a product of hazard.

"The Building of the Ark" has clearly in it, nevertheless, an evocation of carpentry. And the "Deluge," which begins and ends with a lightning flash on the piccolo, has for musical substance variations on a twelve-tone row that itself depicts wave-motion and that gets repeated over and over with a certain freedom but also with the relentless thrust of a mounting inundation. These two orchestral interludes, the chief musical chunks of the cantata, are brilliantly self-sufficient.

The classical dancing that accompanies the first, though pleasingly executed, illustrated nothing, added nothing. And the struggles with a large cloth (all too reminiscent of the Loie Fuller Ballets) that went on certainly with illustrative intent, during the flood could not match with visual interest the music of that scene.

The cantata's choral passages are wilfully stiff and hieratic, even more so than the view of Byzantine cherubim, framed and in rows, that was their visual accompaniment. "The catalogue of the animals" that went into the Ark was recited to so thin a musical background and illustrated by so banal a parade of small wooden toys that no dramatic intensity was created at all. Lucifer's tenor solos, however, gave us perfectly the vanity and boastful temper of the overweening archangel. Also the voice of God, scored as a duet for two basses, gave a surprisingly effective result. One alone would have risked being over-pompous. Two kept the expressivity down, made their singing impersonal. And, come to think of it, God really was two in Noah's time, since the Son had not yet suffered incarnation.

The visual background of this seemingly modest but ever so tough and charming little cantata was for the most part undistinguished and everywhere of questionable appropriateness. The whole could so easily have been put together out of Byzantine mosaics, or out of modern glittering backdrops and dancers in jewelled clothes, like a number from some religious festival opera. It could even have been staged as a rehearsal, with studio décor and street clothes.

Any kind of consistency would have been an advantage to it. From being subjected to so great a variety of visual treatments, in the end only the music of it spoke.

Observer Weekend Review (London), June 17, 1962

CRITICS AND CRITICISM

On Good Terms with All Muses

JAMES GIBBONS HUNEKER: *Critic of the Seven Arts*, by Arnold T. Schwab. 384 pp. Stanford University Press, 1963.

JAMES HUNEKER was the perfect reviewer. And he rarely wrote in ignorance. He had almost a painter's eye for pictures; his memory of a play or a book was alert; and his musical ear was first-class. And if he was often most convincing about works of art, literature, and music that were unknown to his readers, his essays were from that fact all the more informative.

From 1887, when he began to write for *The Musical Courier*, till his death in 1921 as music critic of *The World*, he was America's chief announcer of European novelty—literary, dramatic, pictorial, and musical. He loved novelty, and loved explaining it; he would fight to the death for any sort of artistic distinction (of which Europe was producing a good deal in those years); and by doing so he achieved a certain distinction himself. Beerbohm Tree said of him, "He has a splendid thrust."

Remy de Gourmont said he had "a real talent for explaining music to the layman." And well he might have, music being the branch, after letters, in which his capacities were most highly developed. After twenty years of piano study, much of it done under the best teachers, he was still not a concert pianist or a master pedagogue. But his most durable work remains a product of that study and of the consecration to music that had made study of it urgent. That is *Chopin: The Man and His Music*, published in 1900 at the age of forty-two, a book in which neither the information nor the judgments have been gravely eroded by time.

But curiously enough, it was in music that his roving reporter's mind found least to feed on. He was announcing early the dramatic works of Ibsen, Maeterlinck, Strindberg, Yeats, Laforgue, Hervieu, and Wedekind. He followed in belles-lettres hard on the discoveries of Huysmans about diabolism, of Havelock Ellis about sex, in spicy literature of Arthur Symons, and in contemporary esthetics of Georg Brandes. He wrote about the painting of Cézanne and Matisse a good ten years before the

New York Armory Show of 1913. He attacked Kipling, defended George Moore and Henry James. He propagandized even for artists in America, if their work showed advance tendencies. In fiction William Dean Howells received his accolade; in painting he proclaimed the authenticity of John Sloan, Robert Henri, Childe Hassam, George Luks, John Marin; in music he had good words for Edward MacDowell, George Chadwick, Horatio Parker.

His real musical admirations, all the same, were Brahms and Richard Strauss. In the thirty-five years that he spent publicizing contemporary art work in all the media (on the assumption that "living artists were more interesting to study than dead ones"), he omitted to turn his sharp powers of attention and exploration on the music of Debussy, Schönberg, or Stravinsky. Tchaikovsky and Dvořák, when they were here in the Nineties, he recognized as not wholly first-class; and he maintained sound reservations early and late about Puccini. But for all his love both of music and of "advance," he never came to grips with the really advanced music of his time.

George Bernard Shaw once wrote him "you are an incontinent naïve sort of big baby." And on another occasion, "Your work is very good as far as it is a record of your first-hand impressions from works of art. All the rest of it is execrable." And the insult is not far from true. Huneker's reviews of art and artists, though lively in their time, are today expendable, since they respect neither literature, learning, nor original thought. They are frequently sound; he had the gift of judgment. And they are often vivid as to phraseology. But there is very little in them not available elsewhere. For all his historic place in American journalism as the preceptor of H. L. Mencken, George Jean Nathan, Benjamin DeCasseres, and Carl Van Vechten, Huneker survives in the paperbacks through one book only, *Painted Veils*, a fictional report on sex among the opera stars. How wise was he when he doubted whether criticism ever would do much to improve art or public taste!

The present life of him—detailed, informative, documented, indexed—does everything possible toward answering questions. It will be a nice volume to have around.

New York Herald Tribune Books, September 8, 1963

A Free Critical Spirit

OLIN DOWNES ON MUSIC: *A Selection of His Writings During the Half Century 1906–1955*, edited by Irene Downes. Preface by Howard Taubman. 473 pp. Simon and Schuster, 1957.

OLIN DOWNES was the last of the music reviewers to enjoy music. He consumed it with delight and described it with gusto. The music that nourished him most, moreover, was contemporary music. Lip service he paid to the classics, but the nineteenth century and the eighteenth were just history to him unless they could throw light on the twentieth. He never took sides in that phony war between the present and the past that used to fill so much press space and that still provides a dream life for musical managements. Olin Downes lived and breathed in his own time, wrestled with living angels, took on big bouts, indeed, with virtually every one of them.

All this comes out clearly, and quite surprisingly, in the volume entitled *Olin Downes on Music*, edited by his widow, Irene Downes, and issued on his seventy-first birthday. The book consists of reviews and Sunday articles from *The Boston Post*, where he worked from 1906, and from *The New York Times*, where he was music critic from 1924 till his death in the summer of 1955. The selection is catholic enough to include many reviews of recitals (Menuhin's first, Paderewski's last) and of the stars of stage and symphony, from Emma Calvé and Mary Garden through Marian Anderson's entry last year into the Metropolitan Opera, and from Karl Muck through Koussevitzky, Toscanini and Beecham to Leonard Bernstein and Jean Morel. But the weight of the contents is heavy on the side of composition. Whenever a new piece was played that piece got Downes's attention and most of his space.

In 1906 he knew very little repertory. By 1907 he could swim joyfully in Debussy's *La Mer*. In 1908 he had no fear left of Strauss's *Heldenleben*. In 1909 he found "inexhaustible inspiration" in *Pelléas et Mélisande* and gave his heart to Sibelius, whose symphonies he found "disconcertingly vital," "towering," "sublime." This devotion to Sibelius, later shared by a love for the music of Ernest Bloch, remained throughout his life a touchstone for all that music could mean to him of sincerity, boldness and vigor.

The stylists he was always a bit suspicious of, though he loved in Debussy the side that was "glamorous" and "passionate," and he admired Stravinsky early. *The Firebird* he estimated "a well-nigh perfect masterpiece of its kind," the *Petrouchka* scoring "a marvel of genius" and *The Rite of Spring* a work of "unprecedented energy, definiteness and power." But he considered Stravinsky in all his subsequent works to be "a case of arrested development." Ravel he could enjoy too for fine craftsmanship, "firm traditions and conscience." But to him Schoenberg's music, "however original and masterly in workmanship," was "very ugly" and in its artistic conceptions "decadent."

Among the Americans he perceived some freedom, some warmth, some boldness (always his ideals) in Gilbert, Mac-Dowell, Griffes, Ives, Gershwin and Gruenberg. He took off his hat to a ballet by Deems Taylor, to operas by Virgil Thomson, Marc Blitzstein and Menotti, to a symphony by William Schuman. Though respectful of Piston, Harris and Copland, he does not seem to have been much moved by their music. Always he sought the deep breath, the warm heart, the monumental structure, the free spirit unconfined by consistencies of style. And he deplored that so many of the country's great ones—Strauss, Debussy, Puccini and Stravinsky—had in their forties, if not before, lost their inspiration, their ability to communicate authentic feeling urgently. He was no doubt equally sad that his beloved Sibelius, now ninety, has done no work at all since he was sixty.

Olin Downes was not a scholar nor, save incidentally, a newsman. Neither was he a creator nor in any major sense a performer. Still less was he a capricious or highly personal reactor. He was simply, like all good critics, a participant observer. He swam in the full musical current of a great epoch, kept his head up, breathed deeply, clung to rocks, waved at the fishes, had a wonderful time.

The epoch he swam in is over, was over before he died. Nowhere in music today is there anything that could be called a current or a movement. World-wide distribution has for the time being stopped all progress in musical creation. Naturally reviewers everywhere, lacking a dynamic situation, have turned querulous and insecure. Olin Downes himself in his last decade wrote more and more obits to the departing great. He was even reduced, for lack of novelty available, to writing raves about

Mozart and Moussorgsky and to discovering Tchaikovsky's *Pathétique*, subjects he had not previously found it worth his while to treat.

Any reviewer who finds quickly the compact phrase, as Downes did, has clearly a talent for letters. If he has also a talent for judgment and no fear of using it, as also Downes had, then he is a good reviewer. A good reviewer does not have to be right; he has only to have a good mind and to speak it. And if his judgments are both informed and sincere, they will, like the best of the music he reviews, both carry some conviction and bear, at least for a while, the test of time.

Downes's reviews today make delightful reading, in many cases more so than when they were hot off the press. They seem sounder in judgment, infinitely more brilliant as to phrase and more sustained in their enlightenment. It is clear now that by thirty he had breadth, because by then he had heard everything. But from his beginnings, at twenty, he had had warmth and honesty. And in 1912, at twenty-six, he had already written, "Criticism, of course, has value only in ratio to the strength and distinction of its subjective element." The man who wrote that sentence knew the whole function of reviewing. It also happens, for our joy, that he wrote passionately, from the heart and with no mean gift of understanding.

New York Herald Tribune Books, January 27, 1957

B. H. Haggin's Toscanini

CONVERSATIONS WITH TOSCANINI, by B. H. Haggin. 261 pp. Doubleday, 1959.

B. H. HAGGIN, like many another reviewer, has repeatedly essayed analysis of the Toscanini power without, it has always seemed to me, any unusual success. The glamour of the maestro's executions and the impeccable sincerity that controlled them were never in dispute. Some of his working methods, moreover, were quickly adopted by other conductors. Particularly his habit of following the printed score rather more closely than had been the previous custom. Certain of his interpretations too, chiefly matters of tempo and trajectory, have gone into tradition. But the essence of the Toscanini temperament, the nature of his contribution to music's rendering, has not yet been described. The present volume is less an effort at further analysis than an attempt to preserve for posterity divers facts in evidence, including the author's known opinions. Previously unpublished, I believe, is the record of his personal acquaintance with Toscanini.

The subject matter of their encounters was strictly music. Toscanini denounced the faults of other conductors and just as often his own. His angers in private and explosions in rehearsal, the outrageous and cruel ironies he addressed to his co-workers, were part of the man's real presence. His exasperations, expressed harshly but without malice, gave him a musical common humanity. So did his constant worrying about tempos and balances, about getting everything "right." In all these ways he was a typical musician. Indeed, the whole view of Toscanini here presented, fresh and warm, is a series of candid shots taken off and on stage.

The author has not feared, moreover, to show either himself or his subject in weak postures. Nor has he suppressed a deadly comment made about him in a dressing room "filled with visitors." "When Walter introduced me to him Toscanini again smiled and extended his hand and said nothing. There was an exchange in Italian between Walter and his father; then, as Toscanini was drawn away by someone else, Walter said to me: 'Father said about your new book: "He writes like God: he knows what is good music and what is bad music. I do not know what is good music and what is bad music: but *he* knows."'"

Less ironical was his later admission to the critic, "You have better ear," which means in context, that Toscanini knew he was not able to judge recorded sound dispassionately. Recording engineers seem to have agreed on this point.

It is too bad that Mr. Haggin, who has ear, some perspicacity about music, and an alert attention, cannot verbalize more precisely his passionately remembered musical experiences. For example, in protesting against the word "streamlining," as applied by the present writer to a Toscanini rendering, he offers as substitute, "the plastic coherence imparted to the form in sound by Toscanini's sense for continuity and proportion in the continuum of sound moving in time." This is gobbledygook.

There is no question, however, that the Toscanini secret, the essence and grandeur of him, lay somewhere in his way of imagining and producing a continuity. So exciting indeed was this forward movement, with no sacrifice of the written-in detail, that Mr. Haggin, even at his best, can only describe it in excited words. "Hair-raising," "breath-taking," "incandescent," and "apotheosized" occur repeatedly, along with "revelation" and "dazzling sublimity."

But in spite of all these evidences of ecstasy, our author measures every move of his hero with a relentless assumption of his own "rightness" about music. Only twice in the book, by my count, does he suspend sentence to say "I think." And just once does he alter an earlier estimate (about the quality of a kettledrum sound).

Otherwise, he assumes his judgment of works, tempos, balances, blends, and meanings—everything that reviewing deals with—to be definitive and all opposing estimates vain. In describing a Haydn symphony as recorded by Toscanini, he pronounces ex cathedra that "the articulation and sense" of the Minuet "require a slower tempo than his," that "the Andante pace . . . is too fast for the music," and that "the Allegro molto of the finale is not only too fast but is too rigidly maintained." And he even goes so far as to allege that "a personal antipathy . . . impelled Toscanini's ear to hear incorrectly the objective facts of Schnabel's performances."

Opinions like these, stated as if they were "objective facts," make up the final eighty-five-page discography that lists, or purports to, all of Toscanini's recordings that have ever been issued for sale.

In expressing personal estimates as if they were fiery truths, Mr. Haggin behaves, of course, like many another reviewer of records. The shut-in listener, with no audience around him to move with or against and no performer before him to shout at, for or against, tends ever to explode his pent-up reactions. Passionately presented likes and dislikes are surely more characteristic of the record reviewer generally than are tolerance, wisdom, and modesty. Though Mr. Haggin seems to imagine himself a tower of objectivity and everybody else as irresponsible, actually his performance is not very different from that of his colleagues.

The present writer tends to view Haggin's whole critical work, including the present book, as pretentious out of all proportion to its musical value, though the latter is considerable. He has had pleasure, all the same, in reading *Conversations with Toscanini* for its story content. That part of it, however brief, is the tenderly detailed account of a cherished acquaintance with one of our century's most commanding musical figures.

New York Herald Tribune Books, April 12, 1959

Instruments of Criticism

THE CRITICISM of anything, it seems to me, needs to begin by describing and identifying, by answering the question, What Is It Like?

It may well end there too and still be informative. But for getting inside something, whether by intuition or by bits of brain work, there is a second question, What Is It About? And that's the hard one.

The third, How Does It Go?, is much easier, since to answer involves little more than remembering the whole and quoting selections, though both the remembering and the selecting will depend from whatever describings and analyzings of both text and subject matter may have preceded.

In all three operations the result is determined more by the intellectual instruments used than by empathy on the part of the user. The analysis of poetry, for instance, is at least in part an objective technique, defensively so indeed today since the fear has grown up that some still more external approach—structural, phonetic, or abstract, or abstract linguistic—might permanently rob meaning of its primacy. As for the visual arts, though neither technical nor aesthetic analysis has yet been outlawed, any criticism of these comes dangerously close to an Appreciation Racket of which the aim is to enforce identity among historical values, aesthetic values, and market values.

So let me stick to music, the art I know best, and testify that thematic analysis still works for pieces thematically constructed. Also that rhythmic analysis can be fairly sophisticated in America and in France, though beyond the Rhine, Alps, Pyrenees, or Channel virtually nothing of the kind takes place. Also that traditional methods of harmonic analysis, outmoded but not replaced, are not yet gravely missed, since little of today's music shows awareness of the common chords as acoustical facts, beyond the care that skilled composers take to conceal them. Further, orchestration has been described well by orchestrators, and instrumental virtuosities by instrumentalists. Conducting, since Richard Wagner wrote a small book about it, has been analyzed by few, although experienced conductors often know more than they can formulate. And the human voice remains hard to talk sense about, for lack of an agreed-upon vocabulary in any European language to explain the acoustics of phonation or to identify varieties of vocal timbre.

All the same, music does get described more or less convincingly in a few books and in some reviews. A rough identification of consanguinities—such as school of Schoenberg or follower of Stravinsky—is not too hard. And almost anyone can spot national characteristics, even in a time like now, when national characteristics are out of fashion. For in every country that has national characteristics the different ways thought up for hiding them are themselves a national characteristic.

The subject matter of a piece, what it is really about, or mainly about, is harder to unmask. One may need clues, come upon by accident or intuition and then followed up either by recondite analytical techniques or by a dogged tailing of the culprit's mind through work after work and noting its compulsive behavior. His basic temperament too may be significant, but for identifying that we lack new words. The older ones—sanguine, choleric, and the like—no longer mean much. Neither do psychoanalytic terms, as applied by laymen. The once familiar contrast of classic versus romantic, moreover, today convinces hardly anybody, beset as we all are by dozens of such two-dimensional, either-or choices.

And yet there is still validity in the concept of romanticism, whether or not the grander classical ideal may have been temporarily abandoned. For romanticism is our most vigorously present past, especially in music; and surely it is a guide to how masses of our young nowadays behave.

Several years ago Sidney Finkelstein offered another pair of opposites. While denying "classic" as a mentality, he granted the word applicability to work that has survived its origins long enough to become familiar in the classroom. And those origins, all of art's possible origins indeed, he divided into "romantic" and "neoclassic." I must say these make a neatly balanced pair, with romanticism including whatever is weighted on the side of spontaneity, and neoclassicism representing an awareness of the past and the use, however modernized, of formulas recalling an art's history. So fair a deal between the courageously contemporary and the no less brave conservationists grants to all the work of today full legitimacy. It also allows us to accept as classics both Shakespeare and Milton, one wildly romantic and the other, with his devotion to Greek and Latin models, about as neoclassical a type as you could find anywhere.

And yet Finkelstein's idea, though helpful in a traffic jam where everybody was crowding to join history as a "classic" ("mainstream" was the word), did not of itself make history. It gave equal parking rights to moderns till their time should come to be classics, but it left them after that as just items in a pedagogical car pool.

Donald Sutherland, in a vastly diverting book called *On, Romanticism* (New York University Press, 1971), has proposed a three-way division of styles—classic, romantic, and baroque; and his examples are neither limited to, nor necessarily included within, the periods of art history commonly so named. He identifies Aeschylus, Pindar, and the Etruscans with a baroque view of life, finds well-developed romantic attitudes in Pompeian painting and in Virgil, views Gertrude Stein and Picasso as predominantly classical artists.

Nevertheless, the three temperaments appear to have reached their fullest expansion during the epochs now named for them. The baroque, for example, was never so complete as in sixteenth-century Spain, with Saint Teresa of Ávila, Saint Ignatius Loyola, the plays of Calderón de la Barca, the expulsion of infidel Jews and Moors, the burning of Christian heretics. Nor were letters, art, and architecture ever quite so serenely classical as in fifth-century Greece, say from 480 to 415 B.C., to use Sutherland's dating. As for romanticism, the Romantic Era surely did itself proud, especially in England, with Turner in painting, with Wordsworth and Byron and Shelley in poetry (not Keats, whose taint of mannerism is akin to the baroque), and in French music from Berlioz through Debussy, with Victor

Hugo France's prime number in poetry, with romantic painting full-fledged in Watteau, Géricault, and Delacroix, then turning all calm and objective and classical with the impressionists and Cézanne, only to go baroque and violent again with Van Gogh and Toulouse-Lautrec. The natural violence of these painters became in surrealism a planned violence, especially with Dalí, though as a movement in poetry surrealism had early and late proclaimed itself super-romantic.

Germany produced romantic composers of the very first water in Schumann and in Richard Wagner, but according to Sutherland no properly romantic poet except Hölderlin. After Luther, he says, German life and art were mainly baroque, with a relaxing of baroque stiffness into the rococo toward the end of the eighteenth century. And the French Revolution, which might have brought the Germanics to romanticism, seems to have frightened them with all that liberty—unprepared for it as they were by religion, art, philosophy, or political history—and turned them to baroque ideas of conquest. Thus were produced over two more centuries wave after wave of military adventurism, culminating at Auschwitz with *autos-da-fé* for racial heretics, and all planned for proving the viability of one-man government, that most baroque of all political forms.

The fifty years in Vienna from 1775 to 1825, which brought to ripening Haydn, Mozart, Beethoven, and Schubert, were the richest that music has ever known. So rich that musicians have long ago named that time and place music's High Classical Period, in spite of the fact that it had no contemporary parallel or near precedent in poetry, in politics, or in the visual arts. In those all was romantic improvisation, wild melodrama, revolutionary enthusiasms, wars of robbery and liberation, and of course romanticism's cagey little brother, the prestigious employment of models out of "classical" Greece and Rome. This last took place everywhere but was most notable in the United States and France, especially regarding architecture and politics.

Josef Haydn's musical mind was classic for its self-containment and its objectivity; but his inspiration, more lyrical than dramatic and more apt for landscape than for characterization, was by its spontaneity romantic. Mozart's ease with formal proportion was a classical trait which rococo grace of detail could not obscure. And his fine hand for character, for dramatic organization, for the theatre, in short, gave him enormous freedom in both the open lay-outs of stage music and the closed ones habitual to concerts. He was a classical type, no question, but full of romantic liberties, capable of strong passions, and sometimes in a finale, as of the "Jupiter" Symphony, so moved by fury that only a controlled speed in performance will reveal it for what it is, an isotope of the baroque ordered violence.

Now Schubert, to skirt for a moment Beethoven's Promethean rock, was quite without violence, a natural romantic, a fountain of melodies all purling with surprise key-changes and seemingly capable of going on forever, even inside the confines of closed form. He perfected, moreover, that most romantic of all musical creations, the German *lied*, or concert song, utterly married to its poem and utterly free at the same time from any feeling of constraint. Efforts in similar vein by Mozart and Beethoven and by the ever-melodious Haydn had been by comparison stiff, unyielding. And the florid *da capo* arias of Handel and Bach, though they constantly vary and contort, do not move forward. They are as static psychologically as any baroque sculpture of some suffering saint permanently fainting among stone clouds and lit up by a gilded sunburst.

It would seem that Richard Wagner, according to Marcel Beaufils in *Le Lied romantique allemand* (Gallimard, 1956), took off from Schubert's word-setting to create his grand-scale music dramas. These he structured for stentorian singers as a blow-up in volume and a stretch-out in time of Schubert's more naturalistic way with German poetry. So that it is not unfair, vocally speaking, to call *Tristan und Isolde* just *lieder* louder.

Instrumentally, Wagner took off from the development sections of Beethoven, which are romantic in their constant mood changes and their restless moving forward, but baroque in their preoccupation with struggle and with contrasts of storm and serenity, with worry and joy. But there was in Beethoven's early work a care for shapeliness which persisted throughout his middle period, in spite of certain experiments toward opening up the finales through transformation of the thematic material, tentative in the "Waldstein" Sonata, bolder in the "Appassionata." As for his last period, marked by even grander struggle formulas, more extended contrasts, and looser continuities designed for dramatizing his materials rather than for building structures with them, all here is romantic, pantheistic, freedom-seeking, mankind-centered, yet at the same time, as also peers out in Mozart, baroque in its propulsive fury, its taste for violence, its thirst for grandeur, its relentless insistences.

What is of classic import about all four of the great ones is that their structures stand up and that they invite habitation. Though regularly monumental by proportion, they are rarely oppressive or inconvenient. Such works serve mankind; and save for occasional moments in Beethoven of a bad-boy rambunctiousness or of an overweaning aspiration (the Missa Solemnis, I think, has a bit of this), they rarely bore. They can fail to interest, but they cannot offend. In all, the straightforwardness, humanity, and sound workmanship, their frankness, reasonableness, availability, and utter absence of camp make them classical artists. They may be squares; classics often are. But they are neither out to convert you, as the baroque so regularly are, nor swimming around in states of cerebral anesthesia and high sensual euphoria, as is the romantic way.

Now let us go back to *On, Romanticism* and to Donald Sutherland's metaphysical analysis of style. Classical art he defines as concerned with Being, romantic art with Becoming, and baroque art with a polarity between the two, as if both could perhaps be had at once. The classic mentality likes unity, self-containment, and stability, and leaves space around its creations. In action it is purposive, direct, and neither malicious nor sentimental. It does not come at you, nor drip over you.

The romantic mentality values change, multiplicity, fluidity, potentiality, on-goingness; is emotionally unstable; has visions aplenty, but little sense of time. Nor is it in general tied down to any reality, though "realism" is one of its transformations (not "socialist realism," however, which is preachy, dogmatic, and thoroughly baroque). It loves trips, transports, and drugs. Second sight, the gift of prophecy, though anyone can have it, is a proclivity of the romantics. Miracles, on the other hand, though many can do them too, are a specialty of the baroque.

The baroque temperament is defined by Sutherland as "a fixation on the contradictions and tensions between Classic and Romantic, Being and Becoming, Space and Time, Permanence and Change." No wonder that when it moves it goes straight up, it levitates, for that indeed is where the baroque tends, while the classic sits, stands, or walks, the romantic swims and flies.

Or to change the figure, God the Father, less prone to anger now than in His early days, presents a classical visage. The Holy Ghost, all disembodied breeze and spirit, is the romantic member of the Trinity. While Jesus, with His sermons, eloquence, miracles, compassion, and crushing wit, His organizational propensities, His God-and-man duality, and His shocking death (plus Resurrection) is a triumph of the baroque.

So too, in letters, is Gerard Manley Hopkins, as was in painting and sculpture Michelangelo, a founding father indeed of the Baroque Age. And the modern spokesmen for poetry Ezra Pound and T. S. Eliot, though they preached classicism, were as baroque as the next man when they came to write. The *Cantos* and *The Waste Land* are in fact so loosely structured, so instressed, and so bejeweled with quotations (these less for reinforcing their author's thought than hung there as trophies from his reading) that all the familiar patterns of the baroque mind show through like silver under a gilding once the cultural references have been buffed away.

Criticism too can be viewed in triplicate, with the classical mind preoccupied by criteria, definitions, and estimates—always controlled by reason, of course, and often by plain common sense. Classical too are the How-To-Do-It treatises like Horace's *Ars Poetica*. In general, classical criticism is knowledgeable and, in its point of view, professional; but it need not be exhaustive or over-scholarly.

The latter kind of "take-out," as the press would call it, and as it is practiced in the quarterly reviews, is baroque, tendentious, and reactionary, with the exercising of authority always on its mind. In Sutherland's view it can also be a menace, especially when motivations are ascribed, for then it smells of "questioning," of the Inquisition, of the stake.

Romantic criticism, on the other hand, though often eloquent, is both casual and loose. It is not designed, like classical criticism, to communicate a recipe or an estimate, and still less, like the baroque, as propaganda for its own author or for threatening those who resist conversion. Its purpose actually is to spread a contagion. And its main substance, whether in polemics or in praise, is the writer's need to be sharing what he feels.

In that sense, the present essay is a romantic piece, since my desire is to pass on the news that Donald Sutherland, who did something of the kind twenty years ago in a book called

Gertrude Stein: A Biography of Her Work (Yale University Press, 1951), may have netted another tiger. This one, though larger, might possibly too, if whipped and brought under discipline, prove useful to critics.

Short of that, its future in the circus seems assured. For as you can see from my citings, its chances as intellectual entertainment are promising. To figure out who among us is baroque (and how far), who looks and acts romantic but isn't really, or to point the finger of classicism at some artist whom everybody knows but nobody can use in this romantico-baroque age—all that can make for endless diversion in the parlor and be no end showy in the book sections. If I were still writing music reviews, I might be tempted to try it out myself. Maybe that is what I'm doing here. In any case, I have found Sutherland's idea novel and his book *On, Romanticism*, which expounds it, the most exciting intellectual adventure of my last several years.

But there I go! With excitement a thoroughly baroque taste and adventure a romantic one, I too am catching tigers by the tail. Not to mention the shockingly classical statement with which this article started out.

P.S. The clock, an invention of Baroque time, led composers to demand strict tempos for the fugue, itself a baroque texture. Proof lies in the fugue's constantly syncopated rhythms, which can come out clean only in measured time. (How different from romanticism's *rubato* and its subjecting of every speed to the demands of *crescendo*, also a romantic invention!) The Baroque period, however, loving twoness in everything, was likely to precede almost any fugue with a fantasia virtually unmetered.

There were many baroque contributions to science and mathematics, notably Newton's gravitation and his differential calculus, though his ether is romantically fluid. Romantic science gave us evolution, progress, electricity, laws governing the expansion of gases (whence the steam engine and the automobile), also relativity, the inside of the atom, and the adventure of its fission, of which the planned explosion, apocalyptically baroque, has given us a transcendent instrument of war and a preview of the Doomsday Machine.

Back to music. Erik Satie's was a classical mind and his *Socrate* a musical work as serene as its verbal text out of Plato. Debussy was a romantic not unlike Shelley. Stravinsky, whether violent or neoclassical, was all baroque. So too, though for a different reason, was Schoenberg of the double allegiances, who at the same time that he was romantically "liberating" the dissonance wrote a textbook of classical harmony.

Schoenberg's perpetual dividedness is best revealed in his book *Style and Idea* where Germanic love for struggle and for either-or choices led him to grant equal significance to the expressive content of a work and to the technique in which it is composed. This attitude, common in our century, has led all in the arts toward a straining to equate composition methods with subject matter. These methods are thereupon referred to as "styles" and their observance classed as a virtue, their neglect as theological error. And a work's theme, its inspiration, its real presence, its miracle, has lost credit, since only manner now has market value.

At the risk of displeasing the modernism-in-art Inquisition I should like to propose putting the concept of style on a higher shelf than method. I find that its presence in a work, no matter what the manner, gives added value, even though it may at the same time render that work opaque to analysis. Surely the idea in any work, its specific matter and content, is a reality not to be confused with presentation. Different manners of presentation can be for some themes equally becoming. But what a work must have for long-life communication is style itself, style in the singular. In my view, style is not something an artist does; it is something he has. And everybody knows he has it; there is no mystery about that. So why should such a gifted spirit as Arnold Schoenberg, or Pierre Boulez in a recent article praising Stravinsky for adopting in old age the twelve-tone method (*Saturday Review*, May 19, 1971), find "style" and "idea" to be rivals, when common sense knows them for teammates? But the baroque mind, for all its polemical brilliance and dazzling dichotomies, was never strong, we know, on common sense.

Prose, Spring 1972

The State of Music Criticism

TODAY'S OUTPOURING of classical music through professional concerts, not to speak of college and community orchestras, as well as by records and radio, plus 124 subsidized opera houses in the two Germanies alone, is a phenomenon strictly of our time. The Appreciation industry in America and *Les Jeunesses Musicales*, spreading out from Europe, have also worked to increase distribution, by offering, along with the music itself, technical explanations designed for laymen. In no earlier epoch ever has the ear been so helpfully drenched. And yet the criticism of it all, the reporting of music events by knowing and skeptical minds, has not, as an art itself, grown by what it feeds on.

Actually, reviewing music in the daily press of Europe and South America or across the United States has altered very little during our century. Altered in kind, I mean. The attitudes adopted for reacting to music or used in observing it, the styles considered acceptable for writing about it, even the types of reviewer appointed to major papers—none of these has gone through notable change.

It is merely that the amount of everything is smaller. In no American city is there the number of papers there were in, say, 1910 or 1920. And among those still surviving, none can offer its former spaces or the late deadlines appropriate for filling them. Musical coverage is further obliged to brevity by a reader interest in the dance, of late become sizable and demanding.

Time was when the dailies of New York, Chicago, Boston glowed with happy hatreds and partisan preachments. Today there are too few in any city to sustain a controversy or to reflect a consensus. Consequently the tone just now is blander and less urgent. Occasionally one finds a Sunday article animated by perspicacity, a columnful of red-hot controversy among correspondents, or a brilliant review of some novel item, though rarely, it must be admitted, very rarely in the daily papers.

The musicological quarterlies still take on old music, though seldom its performance. Depth analysis of written notes is their method, and one which keeps them inevitably a bit late about picking up the contemporary.

The monthly magazines fail with live music for other reasons.

Their delay in production, sixty to ninety days, tends to produce in both reader and writer an inattentive attitude toward events so long gone by. They cover recorded music admirably, but for anything else the retard is killing. Actually it limits them mainly to discussing trends and careers.

It is the weekly magazines that still produce, as they have always done, our most readable reports on music, whether as studies of composers' works and temperaments or as straight concert coverage. B. H. Haggin (formerly) in *The New Republic*, Leighton Kerner in *The Village Voice*, Herbert Kupferberg in *The National Observer*, Robert Craft in *The New York Review of Books* (a fortnightly), Irving Kolodin (however brief) in *The Saturday Review*, and *New York* magazine's Alan Rich (now and then outrageous for inaccuracies but the only muckraker we have), these are the writers that I tend to keep up with, if only in the hardcover reprints that keep so many of their best reviews an actuality.

Andrew Porter, formerly of *The Financial Times* (London), is, after a year's absence as a Fellow of All Souls (Oxford) now working again at *The New Yorker*. His previous year's articles written here have already been republished and reviewed. *A Musical Season* is their title (Viking, 1974). Opera is their chief subject. Opera is also Porter's liveliest activity—as translator, editor, historian. Like many another English reviewer, he writes in sentences; his thought seems to come out that way. I don't mean oratorical or poetical sentences, just plain declarative ones, straightforward and grammatical. Their lack of splash does not mean they don't dive deep.

As for operatic knowledge, just now that field is pretty vacant. Nobody reviewing in America has anything like Porter's command of it. Nor has *The New Yorker* ever before had access through music to so distinguished a mind. And if Porter seems once in a while to be plugging his English friends, I am sure that if I were working on a London paper (the Anglo-American musical blockage being what it is) I should look for occasions to mention American composers.

Not that Porter is immune to faults of judgment, or even of style. He can get so tied up in detail that decision fails him. Explaining the past has small value unless it leads to conclusions and to fair statements of them. Similarly for his reviewing style, the itemized report card can be a let ball; it has no bounce.

Reviewing, unless it is an interplay between facts correctly stated and ideas about them fairly arrived at, makes no point. And Porter, I must say, whether writing of old music or of new, on most days keeps within the rules. So comfortingly, indeed, that when I do not see his magazine, I miss him. It is not his well-informed stance that especially holds me, or his "inside opera" serve. What I find absorbing is the spectacle of a good mind playing with good equipment on a good court.

Robert Craft, once his master's voice for Igor Stravinsky, has become since the latter's death the no less official biographer, with access to books and documents concerning the composer's early life, all translated, presumably, with help from the widow. Publication of these proceeds irregularly in *The New York Review of Books*, by Craft impeccably edited and by him quite frankly thrown into question when suspect of inaccuracy.

Other Craft reviews from that paper and elsewhere have been gathered along with these into a volume called *Prejudices in Disguise* (Knopf, 1974) notable for its musical penetration and journalistic punch. Craft takes a joy in polishing his sword that reminds one of his mentor's deadly way. The Leonard Bernstein *Mass*, for instance, is given a sustained high kidding, along with bits of sharpshooting at Harold Schonberg. And the philosopher Theodor Adorno's politicized twelve-tone commitment seems almost to be riding toward an equal pratfall. What saves it here is Craft's own no less shocking commitment to the Stravinsky interests. In a text of 200 pages, less than half of which is about Stravinsky, that master's name appears 360 times.

But Craft is fun to read, hilarious, explosive, wild with puns and pornographies. He is also, as a conductor, thoroughly knowledgeable about scores and precise in citing passages from them by their measure numbers. And if he is a shade overzealous as salesman for one composer, he is no less active regarding another. Indeed, I have suspected that for all his twenty-five-year service to Stravinsky's person, career, and family life and his obviously real attachment to these, his musical preferences actually lean toward the works of Arnold Schönberg, Alban Berg, and Anton Webern. Certainly such an allegiance preceded his joining Stravinsky; and it seems to have influenced, after Schönberg's death, Stravinsky's own turn toward twelve-tone composition.

Ned Rorem's reprint of formal pieces from *The New Republic*, along with bits of more improvisatory material, is frankly titled *Pure Contraption* (Holt, Rinehart and Winston, 1974). The essays themselves, less penetrating musically than Craft's and less learned than Porter's, are nonetheless better made for easy reading. They are more gracefully written, for one thing; their English is meaningful, picturesque, idiomatic, in every way alive. And their malice is far less seriously intended. He pays off a few scores—against Copland and myself, for example—without bothering to make any musical point at all. And he pokes equally harmless fun at Elliott Carter's tendency toward "the big statement," a sort of music-writing that we used to mock in French as "*le style chef-d'oeuvre.*"

Actually Rorem is not a dependable critic, in spite of a good mind and a pretty good ear; his egocentricity gets in the way. It prevents his seriously liking or hating anything. He is scarcely involved anymore even with his private life which for some years furnished him literary materials as well as a devoted public. In a recent interview published jointly in San Francisco by *Fag Rag* and *Gay Sunshine*, his burden is how little he cares about his prose and how devotedly he indites his music. Actually it is his lack of literary ambition, I think, that gives to his writing so much charm, along with the eight years' residence in France that firmed up his mind and his manners. His music has no such ease. But the writing reads, as our black friends say, right on.

Henry Pleasants has been publishing polemical criticism for many years, much of which may have come out first in periodicals. I know that before the last war he worked on a Philadelphia paper and that he now reviews music from London for the *New York Herald Tribune*, Paris edition. Some years ago he defended in a book the theory that serious American music is inferior to pop and jazz. Marc Blitzstein remarked of it, "That's sixty percent true, but we're not taking it from him."

His apparent eagerness to get on some winning side showed up in a book of panegyrics, *The Great American Popular Singers* (Simon and Schuster, 1974). Mixing up blues, gospel, and straight commercial is not uncommon in discussions of the singer's art, though it is not an ideal approach. Confusing the term *bel canto* with the florid, or coloratura, style is even farther from sound practice. Treating only highly paid artists, as he does here, tends to remove any book from serious consideration, notwithstanding that Pleasants himself is an informative journalist and a straightforward writer.

Rolling Stone, a thick weekly tabloid devoted to pop and rock, is charmingly written for the most part and sometimes distinguished. I recommend it. It does not read like paid advertising; it reads like criticism, though I am no judge of the materials it purports to cover. Nor do I know what interests own it. I merely enjoy its vigor.

If the reviewing of pop music and rock is largely blurb, the reviewing of jazz, both performance and recordings, tends toward wild statement, intolerable eloquence, billingsgate, denunciation, and patriarchal poetry. Since much of this is written both about and by blacks, it is full of protest too, about white monopoly of management and of the recording industry, about hopes for liberation and its possible achievement through a black revolution. Not since 1920s Marxist dithyrambs from Russia have I read such passionate statements of hope-in-spite-of-a-sewed-up-situation. Hope defines our blacks' attitude toward society. Toward music they show pure faith, complete confidence, and pride in a communion. Naturally any expression of this reads a bit like the psalms of David.

Some remarkable reviews of jazz recordings of rock groups from Ann Arbor and Detroit, originally published in the magazine *Jazz and Pop*, are reprinted as *Music and Politics* (World Publishing, 1971). These are by John Sinclair and Robert Levin, white men both, though you might not suspect this from the writing, only from their high tolerance of rock music, a syndrome rare among blacks. Sinclair, the more ecstatic, was actually chairman, when he wrote, of the White Panther Party; and he composed these essays in Marquette Prison while serving a nine-and-a-half-to-ten-year sentence, presumably for his political views, though his indictment had been for "possession of two marijuana cigarettes."

In any case, he was allowed a record player, received discs, wrote about them, and sent the reviews out. The longest and finest of these, entitled "Self-Determination Music" contrasts the freedom expressed in good pop music, as by the Rolling Stones, for instance, or by an impecunious Detroit group, with the enslavement of the musicians themselves, whether to publicitary lives and conspicuous consumption or to economic repression and virtually no consumption. In either case his faith lies with the music and his hope is in its power, if not to redeem the social economy, at least to transcend its horrors.

Robert Levin's lead article is a story told him by the black drummer Sunny Murray of how repeated efforts were made both in New York and in Europe to assassinate him because of his addiction to the New Jazz and to playing it with Cecil Taylor. His tale is a gaudy one and quite impressive. Ornette Coleman, when told of an attempt made right on Seventh Avenue to run down Murray with a Thunderbird, is said to have answered, "Listen, those people paid me *not to play* for a whole year." The story goes through poison efforts in Denmark, drugged drinks, and eventually a ship bound for America being evacuated by helicopters because of a provoked epidemic aimed at killing off Murray. All this was part of a war among blacks over (believe it or not) a way of playing jazz, a "new system" he calls it (actually polymetric and non-tonal) for improvising. Then one day the attacks on him "suddenly, strangely, just stopped . . . Since around that time," adds Murray, "I've been cool."

Cuba has a musical magazine called *Música*, which treats generally of Latin folk styles and reports programs from that country's major cities. Havana maintains a symphony orchestra, a classical ballet troupe, and some chamber music. Since the revolution, except for lots of Czech guest conductors, Cuba has lost outside contacts so radically that even Afro-Cuban popular styles, including the famous steel bands, have been very little exported. As a result, Havana's position as the leading Tin Pan Alley for Hispanic pop tunes has been taken over by Rio and Mexico City. Since Hispanic constitutes roughly fifty percent of the world's pop consumption (the rest is made in the U.S.A.) Cuba's losses in both money and prestige have been considerable.

Música now proposes that Cuba lead all of Latin America toward a prestige apotheosis in which modernistic far-out techniques will be put to ideological uses, thus relieving a popular music stalemate that is not merely Latin but worldwide. My dear children, ideologies, Marxist or other, have never done much for music. Nor is anybody in Latin America, I think, disposed right now to let Cubans, exiled or native, run anything. Moreover, I for one believe strongly that today's far-out music techniques, however novel they may seem when dimly heard about behind a blockade, are in general tired, run down, and overadvertised.

Which brings me back to the state of music criticism. Essentially, this practice seems not to have evolved or declined within my lifetime, although music itself, the material of reviewing, has experienced during that time an enormous rise and fall.

I mean music as composition, of course. Performance may or may not have improved since 1900; that is disputable. There is more of it, in any case. But composition, contemporary composition, is where reviewing comes to life. Complaining about interpreters or rooting for them, however legitimate, is just fidgeting. Criticism joins the history of its art only when it joins battle with the music of its time. But music right now, after more than a century of a modernism grand and powerful, has taken to playing with mechanical toys and to improvisational tinycraft or, at best perhaps, gone underground.

It may be that hiding from the distribution mafias is music's last hope for sweetness and freedom, not to mention for protecting what remains of any composer's musical ear. But such an event would even further constrict the press by leaving it very little new to write about.

The New York Times, October 27, 1974

MEMORIES AND MILESTONES

A. Everett "Chick" Austin, Jr., 1900–1957

THE IDEA of a cultural institution designed to spread enlightenment along the whole cultural front is dear both to our century and to the one that preceded ours. Atheneum is the nineteenth-century name for such an enterprise. Most of the establishments bearing that name have long since turned into just libraries with a lecture hall, but the ideal has never been abandoned.

Universities have essayed to embody it too, and their efforts have led to a broadening of art experience for the young. Unfortunately the immaturity of their student public tends to stabilize many of the cultural branches as practiced there, especially the spoken stage, the dance, the opera, at an amateur level. The penetration of many such efforts into the adult life of a community has remained, in consequence, somewhat superficial.

The art museum today, at least in the United States, also strives for a full cultural expression. It does not try to replace the library and the university altogether, but it does endeavor to supplement their activities. Music and the stage, pageantry and dancing, have indeed in most of our newer museum structures a built-in home where delights for the ear are offered in happy proximity to enjoyments for the eye.

Chick Austin (and for all who knew him well the formal "A. Everett Austin, Jr." was never more than a baptismal pseudonym) was a pioneer in converting an atheneum and an art collection into a museum in the modern meaning. Toward this end he caused a theater to be built into the Avery Memorial wing of the Wadsworth Atheneum, which was erected during his tenure as its director. And in that theater he produced plays, operas, ballets, all sorts of stage spectacles, old and new.

Most of these were new, so new indeed and so distinguished that their listing contains an extraordinary number of first appearances of works and artists whose names are now classical.

Tribute written for the catalogue of a memorial exhibition at the Wadsworth Atheneum, Hartford, Connecticut, on view from April 23 to June 1, 1958.

Eugene Berman's first theater set was made for a concert which I conducted there in 1936. Here Pavel Tchelitchew produced in 1934, also for a concert, his first stage set to be seen in America. Frederick Ashton had made his American debut as choreographer earlier that year with the opera *Four Saints in Three Acts.* That same production embodied the first stage direction of John Houseman and the unique sets and costumes of Florine Stettheimer. Unique also is the mobile set designed by Alexander Calder for the *Socrate* of Erik Satie, given in 1936. Operas by Avery Claflin, George Kleinsinger and Ernst Křenek also came out on those boards. Eva Gauthier, Ada MacLeish, Elsie Houston and Maxine Sullivan all sang there their most distinguished programs. And Ballet Caravan (direct progenitor of the New York City Ballet) danced there in 1937 three original American works, including a world première. Among my own works that were first performed publicly in that theater are the opera *Four Saints in Three Acts* (libretto by Gertrude Stein), the ballet *Filling Station* (choreography by Lew Christensen) and a String Quartet (No. 2).

Long before the Avery Memorial was built Chick had started bringing Hartford up to date on music through concerts held in private houses. He had organized for the purpose a subscription society, which he called "The Friends and Enemies of Modern Music." They gave, as I remember, some six concerts a year; and the works played were almost all contemporary. I remember one concert held at Chick's own house, where five American composers—Roy Harris, Aaron Copland, George Antheil, Paul Bowles, and myself—all played and sang works by one another.

When the Avery Memorial was opened in February 1934, the Friends and Enemies moved their concerts into that theater and enlarged their scope. It was at this time that operas and ballets came into the series. We also began (I say "we" because from 1934 through 1936 I was listed as their "musical director") to give concerts in specially designed stage sets. Tchelitchew, Berman, and Calder contributed memorable ones. Chick himself designed others. All were ingenious, imaginative, and beautifully executed.

These sets involved two lines of experiment that have not, so far, been pursued further in the theater. One is the designing of stage sets for particular concerts. The other is the use of a sculptor's awareness about space and solidity as a help to theatrical mounting.

Building sets for single concerts was current in Europe till the end of the eighteenth century, and many famous artists designed them. But our present musical tradition has tended to consider these a frivolous effort and possibly distracting. Certainly their design is a special problem, to make them appropriate but not illustrative, interesting but not over-busy. And certainly they are not cheap, not in time nor thought nor money. But when they are imaginative and tasteful they can add glory to an occasion and a glamour all unforeseen appropriate to music performed in an establishment devoted mainly to the visual arts.

As for sculpture on the stage, that too is not without precedent. Serge de Diaghilev, of course, used easel painters to great advantage; Picasso, Matisse, Braque, Gris, Derain, and many others brought modernist excitement to his repertory. In Russia and in Germany before World War I, a movement in art known as Constructivism had already brought to the speaking stage an exploitation of vertical space through the use of ladders, steps, and runways, that the classical ballet, which works from a floor, could not much use. But this kind of construction became very early a form of functional building, useful for adding dynamism to stage direction, if not always emphasizing through beauty the poetic expression of the play. Diaghilev also, as late as 1927, had put on the stage for Henri Sauguet's ballet *La Chatte* constructivist statuary by Gabo and Pevsner. However, in that whole rejuvenation of staging that our century has witnessed and to which the painters, like the choreographers, have contributed so abundantly, the sculptor and the architect have not been used as they should have been.

Calder's set for Erik Satie's *Socrate*, three dialogues out of Plato set for voice and orchestra, is so plain to look at and yet so delicately complex in its movements (for it does move and without injury to musical effect), so intensely in accord with the meaning of the musical work and yet so rigidly aloof from any over-obvious illustrating of it, that it remains in my memory as one of our century's major achievements in stage investiture.

Its layout is like this. The orchestra is in the pit. Two singers, a man and a woman, stand very far downstage and at the two sides, dressed in evening clothes and singing from black music stands. Upstage is a sky-blue backdrop or cyclorama against which hangs high at house right (by invisible wires) an enormous disk of bright red. Downstage to house right hangs (also by invisible wires and high) a large sphere made of fine aluminum tubing to represent meridians of longitude. It is hollow and transparent, a mechanical drawing in the round. Centerstage and to the left stand two tall flats of different heights, also invisibly supported, painted white.

During the first section of the work, which recounts Alcibiades' speech in praise of Socrates from "The Banquet," no scenery moves. During the second, the walk with Phaedrus along the river Eleusis, the sphere revolves on its invisible axis at a moderate speed, neither fast nor slow. During the third movement of the work, which recounts the death of Socrates, the sphere is still, but all the other hanging objects move. The white flats tilt to the right and very slowly lie down, first on their edge and then flat, becoming visible. Then they turn over, come up black, the color of their other side, and slowly stand erect again, this time at stage right. Meanwhile, from the beginning of this section, the red disk has been moving diagonally (and very slowly) across the blue backdrop till at the end, when the movement of the flats from left to right (and from white to black) has been completed, the disk is low and on the viewer's left. Both the composition of the stage picture and the balance of its color have been changed. So has its meaning. But the music has not been interfered with, so simple are the pictorial elements and so sedately magical their movements.

Others surely will analyse Chick's sources of intellectual orientation and enumerate his many contributions to private collecting, to museum administration, and to public enlightenment. And in those achievements he will be A. Everett Austin, Jr. For me he remains Chick and a sheer delight for wholeness as a man. He had talent, taste, energy, good looks and pride in them. Passion, too, and affection and warmth and loyalty. He liked food and clothes and driving cars and buying things and putting on a show. He was never afraid to do what he wanted to do, and what he wanted to do was to make art live and to enrich everybody's life with it. He was no snob. He was simply a man of taste with a vast love for all that has beauty and distinction and with a missionary's vocation.

The man of taste in our time is so often devitalized and a prig, and the man of talent so often an ignoramus, or else all pushing and political, that Chick, in our memories as well as in his achievements, still burns with a special flame. He not only bought works of art, exposed and conserved them, he caused them to be brought into existence, to attain the fulfillment of performance. He was nobly an amateur in everything he did, but there was nothing amateurish about anything he did. He worked hard and played hard, as indeed did everybody around him. He would not tolerate us otherwise. Wherever he passed, he changed the world. Those who did not wish their world changed did better to avoid him. Trying to fight him, as trustees sometimes did, meant certain defeat, perhaps for both sides, because Chick was a whole cultural movement in one man and, in the full sense of the word, irresistible.

He used to like to say that the main purpose of a museum was to keep its director entertained. And certainly, if it doesn't do that, God help us all. Certainly, also, one wishes there were more men like him to take both culture and fun as straightforward activities and not mutually exclusive. In my view, these are the only ones safely to be trusted with the spending of public monies and the administering of our cultural properties.

A. Everett Austin, Jr.: A Director's Taste and Achievement,
Wadsworth Atheneum, 1958

Nadia Boulanger at Seventy-five

NADIA BOULANGER, who will conduct the New York Philharmonic in four concerts beginning February 15, and who will later this year celebrate her seventy-fifth birthday, has for more than forty years been, for musical Americans, a one-woman graduate school so powerful and so permeating that legend credits every U.S. town with two things—a five-and-dime and a Boulanger pupil.

Her discovery by America occurred back in 1921 when three American students, all new to Paris, came upon her independently. The first of these, Melville Smith, is now director of the Longy School of Music in Cambridge, Massachusetts. The others were Aaron Copland and this writer. All three found her so perfect a purveyor to their musical needs that they quickly spread the news of her throughout America.

She was thirty-four years old at that time and a stately brunette. She held professorships at the French National Conservatoire, at the Ecole Normale de Musique, and at the newly founded American Conservatory in Fontainebleau. She was also second organist at the church of the Madeleine and a member of score-reading committees for the Concerts Colonne (second oldest orchestra in Paris) and the Société Musicale Indépendante (the most advanced of the modern-music groups).

She had already suffered bereavement, including that of her sister Lili, a composer of unquestioned gifts for whom she still wears mourning. Already too, she had renounced all worldly desire for personal fulfillment as a woman or as a composer, devoting herself solely to her remaining parent and to nurturing the musical young. And she was already enmeshed in that schedule of seeming overwork that she has maintained without fatigue to this day, quite commonly receiving students as early as seven in the morning and as late as midnight.

In her fourth-floor apartment at 36, rue Ballu she gave, still gives, private lessons in all the chief musical branches—piano-playing, sight-reading, harmony, counterpoint, fugue, orchestration, analysis, and composition. There too, among the 1900 furniture and the mortuary mementos of her father, who had also been a professor at the Conservatoire, and of her beloved sister, first woman ever to win the *Prix de Rome*, she held her organ classes at a built-into-the-parlor instrument of two manuals and full pedal keyboard.

And there, of a Wednesday afternoon, took place weekly gatherings of pupils (strictly by invitation) at which the most modern scores of the time (by Stravinsky and Schönberg and Mahler) were analyzed and played on the piano, and the rarest madrigals of the Renaissance (by Monteverdi, Luca Marenzio, and Gesualdo di Venosa) were sung in class. At the end of each session copious cakes were served and tea poured with frightening accuracy by the trembling hand of Mademoiselle Boulanger's aged, roly-poly, and jolly Russian mother, the Princess Mychetsky.

Within the first decade of Boulanger's discovery by America, there came as students to this consecrated circle of pedagogy and high musical thought Walter Piston, Herbert Elwell, Roy Harris, Roger Sessions, Douglas Moore, Theodore Chanler, and Elliott Carter. There also passed through her masterful teacher's hands during the 1920s and '30s Robert Russell Bennett, Arthur Berger, Marc Blitzstein, Paul Bowles, Israel Citkowitz, David Diamond, Irving Fine, Ross Lee Finney, Peggy Glanville-Hicks, Alexei Haieff, John Lessard, Harold Shapero, Elie Siegmeister, Howard Swanson, Louise Talma, and John Vincent. George Gershwin she refused to teach lest rigorous musicianship, acquired at thirty, might impede his natural flow of melody.

For she could not conceive, still does not admit, that musical training without rigor can be of value. Herself a product, on the French side of musician-ancestors of the highest professional standing who go back into the eighteenth century, she favors a no-nonsense approach to the musical skills and a no-fooling-around treatment of anyone's talent or vocation. As a Russian woman, on her mother's side, she is furiously loyal to her students, deeply affectionate, and relentlessly maternal. By both national standards she insists that every composer must be a musician and every musician, at least by training, a composer.

For all her authority and high recognition in the French musical establishment, her greatest influence has been on foreigners. Jean Françaix is almost her only French composer-pupil of international standing. The other French composers of our century have been taught by Fauré, by André Gédalge, by Charles Koechlin, and, during the last two decades, prodigiously by Olivier Messiaen. But it was Boulanger who formed, in addition to literally hundreds of Americans, the Russian Igor Markevich, the English Stanley Bate and Lennox Berkeley. And she powerfully influenced by her teaching the great Rumanian pianists Dinu Lipatti and Clara Haskil.

If today there are fewer Americans than formerly in her immediate entourage, they have been replaced by fantastically gifted Turks, Iranians, Lebanese, Indians, and Egyptians. Being midwife to developing musical nations would seem to be her basic role.

She told the first Americans who came to her that they would find no model in Western Europe for their growing pains, and very little sympathy. On the other hand, she maintained, America in the 1920s was very much like Russia in the 1840s, bursting with inspiration but poorly trained. Strict training and real musicianship needed to be inculcated without injury to the music-writing urgencies. These it was important to establish early in daily habit, like the bodily functions, so that difficulties of unaccustomed musical exercise would not be uselessly added to the labor of creation.

Her teaching of the musical techniques is therefore full of rigor, while her toleration of expressive and stylistic variety in composition is virtually infinite. She does not, however, encourage her students in twelve-tone-row composition, which she considers to be a form of musical "speculation," in the philosophical sense of the word, rather than a road to expression. She has found that Stravinsky, whose "genius" has already protected him through many another perilous adventure, experimenting with it in his seventies is not reproachable. Nor can she find it in her heart to blame the young Pierre Boulez for far-outness, considering the phenomenal brilliancy of his mind and the impeccable nature of his musical ear. She does believe, however, that serial dodecaphony is in general a musical heresy and that its influence risks creating as permanent a division among musicians in the West as the Protestant Reformation did among Christians.

All this, the musical Left might easily answer, is also "speculation." And if the young need lessons in traditional music-making, as Boulez himself admits, then these can be accepted from any competent musician, even from Nadia Boulanger. But competence at teaching the musical disciplines and a conservative-to-tolerant attitude toward students' compositions do not fully explain the vast musical influence she has exercised over the last forty years.

The real utility of this remarkable woman would seem to be not in her mastery of musicianship or in her devotion to high standards, virtues that are not hers alone. What she does possess to a degree rarely matched is critical acumen. She can understand at sight almost any piece of music, its meaning, its nature, its motivation, its unique existence; and she can reflect this back to the student like a mirror.

Suddenly he sees that which has caused him pain, struggle, and much uncertainty unveiled before him, without malice or invidious comparisons, as a being to which he has given birth.

Naturally he is grateful. His work has been taken seriously, has received the supreme compliment of having its existence admitted.

Viewed in this warmly objective way, his piece may seem to him worth correcting, or it may not. If its faults appear to be minor, eliminating them can be a joy. If his child seems born to be permanently a cripple, he may cherish it but not let it out into the world. Or he may let it die in a drawer and try to avoid the next time whatever has caused the hopeless deformity. All such decisions are up to him.

The lessons take place with the teacher at the piano, the student in a chair at her right. She reads the score before her silently at first, then little by little begins to comment, spontaneously admiring here and there a detail of musical syntax or sound, expressing temporary reservations about another. Suddenly she will start playing (and perfectly, for she is a fabulous sight-reader) some passage that she needs to hear out loud or that she wishes the student to hear as illustration to her remarks.

She may eventually ask if the author does not perhaps find the whole work underdeveloped or overextended. She may point out the stylistic sources of its material and how these have been not at all considered, may even have been gravely contradicted, by their harmonic treatment.

Throughout the session she will have perceived music avidly and with pleasure, described it quickly, diagnosed its needs with humility.

About these needs the student can always argue, either right then with her or later with himself. Anyone who allows her in any piece to tell him what to do next will see that piece ruined before his eyes by the application of routine recipes and of bromides from standard repertory. The student who seeks his remedies at home, alone, will grow in stature. And she will wrestle with him in talk week after week, building up his strength for him as he himself wrestles his musical ideas into clarity and coherence.

Writing music, as Boulanger understands it, is exactly like writing a letter. It can come painfully or with ease; but it must come from the heart, and it must communicate. Speaking "from the heart," let us add, means speaking only for oneself. Nobody can write your music for you.

In the long run, learning to write music under Boulanger's care is a matter of training the hand and ear, and of establishing the custom, the habit, of giving birth to musical works. It is as simple as that and as utterly valuable, particularly so in countries where giving birth to musical works has become intensely urgent but is not yet a schooled procedure.

Preconceiving the kind of works her pupils are to write was never the Boulanger method. Nor does she encourage it in her students either. Strictness and premeditation, in her book, are only for training circumstances, like a dancer's exercises at the bar. The creative act should be free, a gratuitous communication or, as Tristan Tzara put it once, "a private bell for inexplicable needs."

That way, she believes, lie all the possibilities there are of originality, of individuation, of truth, and of humane expressivity. Any other approach to the creative act in music, according to Nadia Boulanger, is timid, conformist, and artistically dishonorable.

Certainly the intensity of her belief and the speed of her musical understanding have filled the non-French world with musicians grateful to France on account of her. The honors being offered her here are not her first. She has led the Philharmonic before; and she has conducted too the Boston Symphony, the Philadelphia Orchestra, the Royal Philharmonic of London, the best Parisian orchestras, and many others. She has taught at Harvard, at Santa Barbara, and in Baltimore.

Nowadays she travels constantly, especially behind the Iron Curtain to Poland, Rumania, and Hungary, though she is by no means a Communist, being by conviction both Catholic and Royalist. What she likes to observe there is the way music survives under political change.

Countries large and small, new and old, are grateful to her, though perhaps the newer countries use her powers best. And America, it would seem, must be considered musically a new country. At least it is not a long-ago-matured one like France or Germany, Italy or England, though it ripened musically before any other country in this hemisphere except Brazil.

All this is part of the Boulanger world-picture. She is a one-woman Musical UN, encouraging growth and obliterating ignorance. She does not fear the largest, like America, nor neglect the smallest, like Monaco, where she bears the title of Maître de Chapelle to His Highness the Prince. At the drop of a hat she would probably move in on Russia. She speaks the language, knows the problems, could certainly give advice on how to exploit more fully than is being done the talent resources there and the possibilities of creating on a vast scale music of beauty and distinction.

America does not greatly need her now, though she remains our alma mater. Her pupils are teaching in our every conservatory and college, carrying on her traditions of high skill, expressive freedom, and no nonsense. She loves us for old times' sake, as we love her: and she adores revisiting us. But her real work today is with students from the just-now-developing musical regions. That way lies her ability to go on being the greatest music teacher in the world so long as her physical powers shall remain. As of now, they seem to be limitless.

The New York Times Sunday Magazine, February 4, 1962

William Flanagan, 1923–1969

WILLIAM FLANAGAN'S sudden death last summer has left us our memories of him, of course, and his music. Both are precious. But it does seem a shame to have lost him so early (he was only forty-three) and so tragically (since he was in full evolution as an artist, not gravely threatened by poverty, and in the midst of composing a work that he set store by).

Rereading his music recently and re-hearing the recordings, it occurred to me that in Flanagan we have a striking parallel to the poet Hart Crane, who died at thirty-three, leaving behind him a small production but a major one.

Personally they were not too different either. Both physically strong, self-destructive, given to wrestling with angels as well as with the demon rum, they were pursued by violence only in the flesh. It seemed to leave their art alone, which remained serene, ecstatic, richly textured, standing outside of time.

Tribute read by Virgil Thomson at the Flanagan Memorial Concert, Whitney Museum of Art, New York, on April 14, 1970.

Also like Crane, Flanagan was largely self-taught. Aaron Copland showed faith in him and David Diamond gave advice about form, but mostly Flanagan ripened as an artist by choosing his influences. He knew what he could grow on, and he grew rapidly.

His first major choice for the nourishment of his vocal works was Copland's songs to poems of Emily Dickinson. These inspired him early, and their examples of the disjunct vocal line and of concentration on the emotional content of poetry rather than on the verbal recitation of it not only marked the early Herman Melville songs but actually developed into a method that in his late works was deliberately anti-prosodic.

He would choose poems of quality and then seemingly throw them away by setting them to a vocal line which by its indifference to the meaningful syllables and by its love for extreme vocal ranges made clear enunciation of the text virtually impossible. This willful distortion of the prosodic values gave him at the end a certain connection with far-out Europeans like Berio, Boulez, Bussotti, and even more extreme vocal manipulators. Flanagan did not despise verbal clarity in music, but he grew more and more impatient with it. After all, we can read the poetry, and in many cases we know it already.

His A. E. Housman songs do get into a lilt whenever the verses do, which is quite often. And Flanagan's writing for male singers is a model of prosodic propriety. But in his very best work, such as *Another August*, he threw overboard the whole consideration of correct declamation, at least where it interfered with flexibility and with the musical exploitation of those very high soprano ranges for which he had a great love.

Another August, like all of Flanagan's music, is notable for the extreme beauty of its musical materials. Also for its imaginative and constant transformation. The sound of it, vocally and instrumentally, is to me an utter delight, as the richness of its musical thought and statement are beyond compare.

If the parallel between Flanagan and Hart Crane holds at all, this work will be in Flanagan's production what *The Bridge* was in Crane's.

For the beauty of its materials, its distinguished harmony, its far-darting melodic line, the freedom and grandeur of its structure, the vastness of the concept and simplicity of the

proportions produce in this work a wholeness at once volup-
tuous and pure. We shall not soon hear its like, I think. For
there is nothing like it. It is a monument which, though it has
traceable origins, stands alone, as all great music does, giving
off its own secret, powerful essence to performers and to listeners alike.

I knew it was fine and told him so. But I regret that I did not
tell him oftener. And besides, though it was beautiful to start
with, it has become, I think, even more so since his death, as is
the way with all things genuinely original.

A Virgil Thomson Reader, Houghton Mifflin, 1980

Elisabeth Lutyens, 1906–1983

ELISABETH was an enchanting companion and, in spite of lank
hair and a nose like a razor blade, something of a beauty. That
shows up in the photographs. She was also full of warmth, wit,
and a lively animation. Her musical powers were indefatigable
and prodigious.

England has over the last century produced several fine
women composers. So have the United States and France. Italy,
Germany, Russia, Spain, and Scandinavia have produced none.
Also, like the United States and France, England has tended
to neglect hers. Not willfully, of course, but just enough to
make them struggle. They have not been denied training or
performances or publicity; but they do have trouble getting
published, and they are seldom handed out the best teaching
posts. And they seem to have had no access at all to that plugging of British artists that takes place regularly through the
embassies and consulates. This is average treatment for women
in the countries where any treatment at all can be said to exist.

Elisabeth Lutyens might have got on a bit faster had she been
French or American, though I must say that for an English girl
family distinction and high birth are not quite the hindrance
professionally they can be in America. What chiefly slowed her
professional progress seems to have been her strong intellect
and a fierce ambition. These plus an independence both professional and personal which refused even to consider compromise
or second-rateness.

Music in England over the last two centuries has, unlike the poetic tradition and the novel, generally settled for middle-brow status. There have been no radical invention of ways and means nor any eclosions of such clear-to-all genius as have marked music's progress in continental Europe. England has had to look for its high models abroad. And unless those models have come to live in England, as Handel did, their discovery has often come a bit late. The music of Anton Webern, for instance, which Lutyens did not encounter till she was past thirty, along with that of Arnold Schönberg, she could recognize instantly as for her a good road; but there was no one to show her how it happened to be there or where it led, till in 1938 she met the conductor Edward Clark, who had been a friend of both and actually, from 1910 to 1914, a pupil of Schönberg. She was already thirty-two.

So she set herself to learn their ways of writing, including the famous twelve-tone method, and within half a decade had mastered them, war and babies notwithstanding. She had married Clark in 1942 and adopted him permanently as her guide, philosopher, and true love. Actually this remarkable musician, who knew everybody in musical Europe and who had in the previous two decades opened doors to most of them at the BBC, did virtually no other useful work from the time of his encounter with Liz till his death in 1962 than to advise and counsel and console her.

Indeed, consolation was about the best he could offer, once she had become a master of music-writing and mature as an artist. For neither of them knew how to maneuver a career in so unpopular a style of composition and without any help just then from the BBC, where Edward had earlier been a power. Actually it was not till William Glock became controller of music there in 1958 that Lutyens began to receive commissions, performances, and honors from the Establishment.

But she went on composing stubbornly, not only twelve-tone music but all sorts of other kinds, whatever kinds and occasions she could get toleration for, including incidental bits for the theater and over a hundred film scores. It is notable and surprising proof of her musical integrity and her consecration that this pot-boiling seemed in no way to vulgarize her production, which remained ever distinguished, beautiful, wide in its choices of theme and subject, and technically advanced. Her music is to my knowledge the most distinguished produced in England during her main functioning years, from 1940 to 1980. And certainly it is the finest written during that time by any woman whose work I know, save possibly the Franco-American Betsy Jolas.

Others had more popular appeal, and some, particularly Britten, worked with a more spontaneous sense of the stage. But none enjoyed the ease that she did among the high altitudes of both poetry and musical ideas. Truly, amazingly, and in spite of all precedents, Elisabeth Lutyens has left music that can with profit, I am sure, be more closely examined than it has been. It can also, if not just yet then eventually, be listened to with delight by large numbers of people.

I am not prepared to write a treatise on the whole Lutyens catalogue nor to list the many pleasures to be found there. But I do wish, in view of her so recent death, to state here, for her friends and to my colleagues, the admiration that I cherish for her work and the deep respect in which I hold the artist who composed it.

Grand Street, Summer 1983

Edwin Denby, 1903–1983

EDWIN AND I were friends for well over fifty years. I first knew him in 1929. He was working in one of the German opera houses, the Hessian State Theater in Darmstadt, which was quite famous for its modernistic productions—not merely modernistic but by young and contemporary writers who were famous, far-out ones, like Darius Milhaud and Satie and so forth. Edwin wrote me knowing that I had written an opera on a text of Gertrude Stein (*Four Saints in Three Acts*), saying that his colleagues might very well like to produce it there, and what did I think of the idea that he, being bilingual in German and English, would be responsible for the translation. He was spending the summer in Collioure in the southeastern part of France; and on my way either to or from (I forget which) the island of Majorca, I stopped for a day or so there, and we had a fine visit and made friends. I had not seen him before.

After that I sent to the opera house, or sent to him for the opera house, a copy of the libretto so that they would know how far out that was. And they still wanted to see the score, so I managed to make a copy of the score and sent it along. It produced a kind of explosion. It was refused. They'd been doing perhaps too many modern or modernistic works and not enough *Trovatore*s.

Anyway, the musical wing revolted at that point in regard to my opera. And the whole troupe, a rather famous director, and decorators, and the ballet people, including Edwin, all moved up to Berlin. This included Rudolf Bing, no less.* A couple of years after that, the thing broke up with the German political conditions, and the main part of the troupe moved off to England to Glyndebourne.

Edwin resigned from the ballet in Berlin and came to live in New York, and shortly after, many of his nice German friends turned up. He was surrounded by very nice artistic German friends, who didn't feel that there was much for them in Germany at that particular time.

I remember his giving a party for his New York friends and his nice German friends—he was already living in the loft on Twenty-first Street—and the party was going just fine. It was a very distinguished assemblage of people, and Edwin had bought and distributed large monuments of cheese and about a dozen bottles of extremely expensive Scotch whisky. One of the German composers arrived at the top of that long staircase—and, coming in there, seeing this highly simplified décor, so to speak, but with all of his nice friends there, both German and American, couldn't quite make it all out. And he wondered if this weren't—if he'd got into some kind of slum

*In 1929 at Darmstadt's Hessisches Landes theater (actually two theaters, the larger for opera, the smaller for plays and operettas, operating for a ten-month season), Denby was working as a dancer and assistant régisseur. His colleagues included Generalintendant and stage director Carl Ebert; Ebert's assistant artistic administrator, Rudolf Bing; Generalmusikdirektor and principal conductor Karl Böhm; the conductors Max Rudolf and Carl Bamburger; stage director Carl Maria Rabenalt; and designer Wilhelm Reinking. In 1931 Bing, Ebert, and others assumed artistic management of one of Berlin's three opera companies the Städtische Oper (City Opera) in Charlottenburg, and Denby joined as a dancer. His associates here included the conductors Fritz Stiedry and Fritz Busch, designer Caspar Neher, composer Kurt Weill, and his wife, Lotte Lenya.

where he didn't belong. But there were friends, and it—ah! all of a sudden he understood—it was some kind of a charade. And he said, "Ach! Ich verstehe. Künstler ohne Gelt" ("Artists with no money!"). That was the number, apparently, that he thought was being done.

In 1936 Edwin and I actually worked on a show together for the Federal Theater. He made the translation of that from French. It was a farce by Labiche known in French as *Un Chapeau de paille d'Italie*, and which we called *Horse Eats Hat*. It was a brilliant production. Oh, very brilliant. And if the names were printed today, of course, it would make an all-star cast. Nobody in it was really particularly well known then except Orson Welles. But Orson was in the cast, and Joe Cotten and Hiram Sherman, Orson's wife, Virginia, Arlene Francis, Paula Laurence. The music was by Paul Bowles, who had never done music to a show before. There was a great deal of it, and he didn't feel quite as if he could get through making an orchestra score, so I did that more or less for him. And it was all, as I say, all very brilliant indeed, and we had lots of fun. Paul was so shocked at having to have his music orchestrated by somebody else that he hastily learned how to orchestrate and he did a great many theater productions after that, all distinguished and everything nice; and he never permitted anybody to orchestrate his music.

In '37—that was the next year—Edwin was the librettist for a high-school opera, *The Second Hurricane*, by Aaron Copland, which was produced at the Henry Street or the Grand Street Theater, again under the best of circumstances, with Lehman Engel conducting and Orson Welles directing the stage.

After that I was mostly in Europe, and I didn't see Edwin until in the early forties, when I came to New York to work on the *Herald Tribune*. And after we got into the war, our dance reviewer, Walter Terry, went to the war and the post was empty. So I suggested to the management that Edwin—who had been writing for Minna Lederman's magazine, *Modern Music*, quite fine dance articles—be engaged as a replacement. He was; and he was a great success. Everybody adored him. Everybody adored his writing. But in slightly less than two years, the war was over and Walter Terry came back and was legally entitled to his job, and there was no way of keeping Edwin on, much as everybody wanted to. So he worked for other papers or magazines. But his dance reviews, of course, were always collected. They became famous instantly and they still are. He's probably the most famous dance critic, or the most admired, that anybody knows about now.

But you see, all this time Edwin was writing poetry. And the ease and grace of the dance criticism sort of obscured the qualities of the poetry. Only recently, after his death, Lincoln Kirstein published a piece, sort of a tribute, in *The New York Review of Books*, in which he gave Edwin full credit for the excellence of that poetry. I'd always adored it, but it was hard for other people to take. The admirers of his poetry found it a great deal harder to swallow than the dance criticism, which went down so easy. Because the poetry was complex, compact, and gritty of texture. It didn't run on like Shelley, nothing like that. It stuck in your teeth, much more like the Shakespeare sonnets.

Still later, at Frank O'Hara's funeral, Edwin Denby referred to O'Hara as the greatest living poet. I rather like to think of Edwin in that way myself.

Ballet Review, Spring 1984

Lou Harrison at Seventy

It was Mozart's boast that he could master any composer's musical style within a week and by the end of that time compose in it adeptly enough to deceive experts.

Lou Harrison has something of that virtuosity himself. The singer Eva Gauthier, who had spent some years in Java, told me that a symphony of Lou's for percussion orchestra was the only Western music she had ever heard that both felt and sounded like Indonesia. There is also a Mass that not only looks Elizabethan on the page but that when performed with Elizabethan tunings takes on a harmoniousness both surprising and convincing. And there are twelve-tone orchestral works which might well be taken for the music of some hitherto unknown contemporary of Arnold Schönberg.

As for the original side of him—early and late his dominant devotion—his work with gamelans and also with instruments of the Korean court tradition (including a jade gong, no less) are not only evocative but, as a result of serious studies undertaken over the last twenty years, authentic.

And he mixes things with infallible imagination. I think of a concerto for pipe-organ and percussion, delicious for the very sound of it, and a work for ten specially-tuned flutes (and they really blend).

As for more deliberate mannerisms, no one could better evoke the bubbly French "pop" style of 1920 than Lou has done in his *Eiffel Tower Wedding Party*. And his restoration of a missing page from Charles Ives's *They Are There!* is famous for its almost note-for-note exactitude when matched against the original, which turned up later.

There is nothing labored about all this. Lou Harrison is not making plastic roses for funeral parlors. He is simply speaking in many personae and many languages. The message itself is pure Harrison. And that message is of joy, dazzling and serene and even at its most intensely serious not without laughter.

I remember several years ago that for a gigantic San Francisco "be-in" regarding the yearned-for ending of war in Viet Nam, when Lou was asked to write a large work involving chorus, orchestra, and soloists, he did exactly that, in three movements. And he called it ever-so-happily *Peace Piece*.

A Lou Harrison Reader, edited by Peter Garland,
Soundings Press, 1987

BOOK REVIEWS

Sincere Appreciation

THE JOY OF MUSIC, by Leonard Bernstein. 303 pp. Simon and Schuster, 1959.

THE JOY OF MUSIC, by Leonard Bernstein, is a completely sensible book. Let not its title put you off. This is no set of do-it-yourself recipes for writing successful Broadway musicals or for making the New York Philharmonic eat out of your hand. It is about as realistic a book of music appreciation as this hardened assessor has yet encountered.

The main meat of it consists of seven television scripts written and delivered by Mr. Bernstein in recent sessions on the famous *Omnibus* programs. These hour-long telecasts with musical illustrations by orchestras, choruses, and soloists, further clarified by screen-size views of musical notation, made history not only as television but also as education. In the course of explaining to laymen the art and technique of orchestral conducting, the nature of jazz, the climate and conditioning of contemporary music, the grandeur of grand opera, the Americanness of American musical comedy, the laborious revisions that Beethoven went through before arriving at the final form of his Fifth Symphony, and exactly why Sebastian Bach is Western music's high point of both form and content, there is virtually not one superficial judgment or hollow phrase.

Bernstein is readable because he is literate and sincere. His expositions have clarity because he has mastered his material. And his judgments are sound and not sectarian because they are based on a full acquaintance with up-to-date musical analysis. He admits to seeking in his lectures "a happy medium somewhere between the music-appreciation racket and purely technical discussion." But their quality for this reviewer comes from their showing at the same time no connection whatever with the ignorant or racketeering aspects of music appreciation and no temptation to do anything about music at all except to understand it right as structure and as communication and to make it come out right, as structure and as communication, in performance.

It is as if all the most important questions about music were being answered by a man of brains, knowledge, talent, experience, and consecration. All of which Bernstein has, of course. And if at forty-one he is a showman of impeccable marksmanship and a personality of infallible charm, the fact remains that he is a real intellectual, trained at Harvard as well as at the Curtis Institute, by Fritz Reiner as well as by Serge Koussevitzky, speaking languages, reading books, equally stimulated by general ideas and by specific problems.

His power to argue with a poet-philosopher gives the book its opening excitement. This is a conversation between himself and Stephen Spender about the literary approach to music. His modesty as a composer is expressed in two skits called "Whatever Happened to That Great American Symphony?" and "Why Don't You Run Upstairs and Write a Nice Gershwin Tune?"

At all points the book speaks from personal experience, hence from real knowledge. At no point does Bernstein mouth the platitudes about sonata form, for instance, that mar every academic book of music appreciation that I have ever seen. And if in the course of communicating real experience and real knowledge, hence real enthusiasm, Bernstein leaves us free to infer that his favorite pieces are Bach's *St. Matthew Passion* and Puccini's *La Bohème*, he leaves us just fully assured that even a professional has a right to have favorites and that it is better to confess a true love than boast of a false one.

Bernstein's loves in music do not seem false, even though they seem to fall mostly within a good box-office range. There are just enough of them that do not—Erik Satie and Darius Milhaud, for instance—to make the list convincing. Bernstein functions chiefly in the good box-office range anyway, though not out of low motives. He is neither a charlatan nor an egghead. He is a middle-brow intellectual. And if the symphony orchestra itself appeals chiefly to middle-brows, it is often capable of interesting them intellectually as well as sensually.

When Sir Thomas Beecham announced last year that British audiences had no particular understanding of music, that "they merely enjoy the sound of it," he described a situation all too current in the United States, the situation of a city's symphony orchestra failing to be a part of that city's intellectual life. It is encouraged generally by conductors of inferior cultural attainments and by almost all managers. It does not develop when Bernstein is around.

Bernstein's is not an original mind, but it is a sound mind and an active one. *The Joy of Music* does not contain a single idea, I think, that is not available elsewhere. But neither does it contain a single one not passionately apprehended and assiduously tested by the author.

You do not have to read the book if you are an experienced professional like Mr. Bernstein. In any musical condition short of that you will surely find it rewarding. And no matter what your conditioning about music you will be amazed at the large amounts of correct technical information he has been able to package for mass consumption through TV. That is an intellectual achievement.

New York Herald Tribune Books, November 29, 1959

Wanda Landowska

LANDOWSKA ON MUSIC, by Wanda Landowska. Collected, edited, and translated from the Polish by Denise Restout assisted by Robert Hawkins. 434 pp. Stein and Day, 1964.

BORN IN 1879 in Poland, Wanda Landowska was characteristically a product both of the nineteenth century and of Eastern Europe. In Warsaw she studied piano with teachers who specialized in Chopin. At sixteen she went to Berlin to learn to compose; and it was there that she formed the musical attachment that was to guide her life, an unquenchable passion for the works of J. S. Bach.

At twenty-one she "eloped" to Paris with a compatriot, Henry Lew, who, though he had adventured in journalism and in acting, was primarily an ethnologist. It was largely under his guidance, in fact, and certainly with his help, that she shortly began the historical studies that led her to publish in 1909 a pioneering book about the harpsichord and its repertory, *Musique Ancienne*, titled in its American edition of 1924 *Music of the Past*. She had formed friendships almost instantly, moreover, with the French performing musicologists of the Renaissance,

Charles Bordes and Henri Expert, with the medievalist Maurice Emmanuel, and with the Bach scholars André Pirro and Albert Schweitzer.

Presented to Paris in 1901 as a rising composer and as a piano virtuoso of some renown, by 1903 she was beginning to play Bach on the harpsichord—to the vigorous disapproval of Charles Bordes, though not of Schweitzer. In the latter's famous *Jean Sebastien Bach, le Musicien-Poète*, of 1905, he praised her performance of the *Italian Concerto* on a Pleyel harpsichord, though this instrument has usually been thought of as having come into existence later, since the public debut of the large Pleyel with octave bass did not occur until 1912.

In the meantime, however, Landowska toured Europe unceasingly from Russia to Portugal, always with some sort of harpsichord, at first playing on it only one piece per concert, so disturbing was its sound in Bach to piano-conditioned ears; and everywhere by mouth and by print she preached its virtues. Everywhere too Henry Lew was her personal representative and impresario. Indeed, she became so used to his care that she took it for nonexistent and refused to believe, touring America alone in 1923 with four very large Pleyels, that she needed either a concert manager or anyone in charge of logistics.

During her touring years she amassed a notable collection of keyboard instruments, old and new, acquired valuable books and manuscripts, bought eventually at Saint-Leu-la-Forêt, just north of Paris, a comfortable house to lodge them all, adding to its garden a hall for playing concerts of a Sunday to paying pilgrims and establishing there her *Ecole de Musique Ancienne*.

Save for one unhappy essay at teaching in Berlin, where she moved with Lew in 1913 and where, being caught by the 1914 War, they were prisoners on parole until its end, France was her home from 1900 till the end of 1941. When on Pearl Harbor day she arrived in America as a Jewish refugee, she was interned at Ellis Island because the name on her passport was Lew and not Landowska, as on the ship's list. Letters from known musicians, however, procured by the singer Doda Conrad, got her released overnight, along with her cased-in-lead harpsichord. This going-away gift from a Swiss pupil she had awaited some eighteen months in Marseilles, her own instruments and library having all been left behind in her hasty departure from

Saint-Leu of June 1940. Henceforth she lived only in New York and in Lakeville, Connecticut, where till near her death at eighty, in 1959, she continued to play, teach, and record her repertory.

Denise Restout, her pupil, musical assistant, and constant companion for twenty-six years, has preserved the notes, diaries, and manuscripts that were not lost in the systematic sacking of her house in France; and a selection of these, translated, forms the main part of the present book.

These vary in seriousness from the highly documented emendation of a Bach fugue—subject to the casual remark that this same fugue (the first of the forty-eight) always makes her "think involuntarily of the overture to *Die Meistersinger*." They are in fact a monologue at once learned and lively, penetrating, and to any musician communicative, yet as often as not improvisatory, dithyrambic, and embarrassing.

The book's beginning part is a condensed version of *Musique Ancienne* incorporating six earlier articles and one later one. The second section, mostly new, details the observations of a knowledgeable and passionate interpreter about the keyboard works of J. S. Bach, W. F. Bach, C. P. E. Bach, of Handel, of all three Couperins, of Rameau, Chambonnières, Scarlatti, Purcell, and the Elizabethans—in other words the harpsichord repertory as established by Landowska. Also, on the Haydn Concerto, which she brought to light, and on certain piano concertos and sonatas by Mozart. Biographical items are being kept back for another volume and those considered overtechnical for mere reading reserved for direct pedagogy. A third part, which might well have been entitled *Rhapsodic Remarks*, is salted up here and there by a neat malice toward contemporary composition. For of recent times she really liked only Gershwin and jazz.

Wanda Landowska was an interpreter of high temperament, a technician of phenomenal finger discipline (one wholly invented by her for the harpsichord), and a scholar whose learning was used only to facilitate familiarity with times past and identifications with composers long dead. Her origins as an East European still remembering Romanticism, her subsequent submission in France to the disciplines of musicology, and her constant covering of the entire continent on scholarly errands and concert tours all made of her an exemplary European and an embodiment of what used to be called "*la grande sensibilité européene.*" Her view of Europe as a diversified breeding ground of individuals rather than as a stud farm for producing characteristically French or German genius types, enabled her to see differences and similarities in European history with a fresh eye. And her special position in the great musical centers as both a foreigner and a woman made it urgent to permit herself no weaknesses regarding mastery.

A certain Easternizing of the West (in Vienna absorbed by "pop" music, in France this went straight to the top) was clear in the 1830s with Liszt and Chopin being adopted by Paris. Later the Russian virtuosos also came to stay, and in our time the whole entourage of Diaghilev, including Stravinsky. Only eight years younger than Landowska, the half-Russian Nadia Boulanger gave also to the teaching of music in France a dimension just newly available. And this novel dimension, the same indeed as Landowska's—for in its origins it was both an outsider's view and a woman's—was an ability to recognize in any music its uniqueness and particularity, in other words, to spot by instinct what makes one piece of it different from another, surprising resemblances, of course, helping out this identification.

Wilhelm Friedman Bach, for example, "makes [Landowska] think of Brahms, while Karl Phillip Emanuel strongly evokes Schumann. His [C.P.E.'s] excessively sorrowful and morbid character indicates degeneracy . . . Whereas Johann Sebastian's music, carved out of granite, powerful and inexorable, is sensuousness itself, that of . . . Karl Phillip Emanuel, the king of the gallant style, is emotive, but devoid of sensuousness."

And as one argument for the influence on Chopin of Chambonnières, Couperin, and Rameau (indirect, for Chopin surely did not know their music) she remarks that "the fundamental trait of the harmony in Couperin as well as in Chopin is the consubstantiality of this harmony with the melody . . . This is why it is impossible to suppress the slightest retard and to change the placement of an imperceptible passing note without altering the logic of the harmony or the expressive truth of the phrase."

"Rameau's Sarabande in A-major, [though] only twenty-eight bars long, . . . is the queen among [his] works for the harpsichord. Its unrestrained surrender, its ardor, the rustling of its immense arpeggios, the irresistible sweetness of its melody, and its regal deportment give a most shattering denial to those who see Rameau only as a calculator and maker of treatises."

"Scarlatti," on the other hand, "depicts neither the sumptuousness of palaces nor the ostentatious magnificence of princes. It is the people whom he loves . . . the motley and swarming crowd."

And in her description of individual pieces by Bach, Handel, Purcell, and the rest she is always alert to identify a dance rhythm. None so quick as she, indeed, to unmask an allemande, or to observe (though not in the present book) that a certain middle movement in Mozart is a love scene between two persons who are at the same time dancing a minuet.

This kind of detective work is always intuitive and as often as not unconvincing. A dance meter once revealed remains revealed, but a feeling identified bears little evidence. In fact, another speed than the accustomed one can radically change any assumption about a passage's meaning. But that is of no matter. Because for choosing a speed, every performer is obliged to assume a meaning. And this meaning must take into account not only the author's notation but all that can be learned from interior and exterior evidence about what the piece might originally have been intended to mean. For all music has meanings, often multiple meanings. And the music of a past time cannot be restored as communication without a great deal of study, a great deal of worrying about it, and a great deal of trying it on for fit with respect to known models. It is not that in the long run any one solution is the right one; it is rather that many solutions are demonstrably wrong. And certainly Landowska in her playing and in her recording came far more often than not to articulate a piece in a way that all musicians, both the knowing and the merely instinctive, could be happy about. This was her gift, an early facility for rightness perfected through study.

An awareness of the dance was always present in her playing wherever the music gave excuse for that, along with a certain relentlessness in the rhythm that was neighbor and kin to that of Boulanger—a feminine, all too feminine relentlessness, but nonetheless commanding. And though her way with an expressive line could lean toward a Chopin-playing manner of the 1890s, of personal display there was never any trace; she worked wholly within the framework of the music, clarifying it with knowledge, warming it with all her resources of training and temperament. Consistently hot in the blood but cool of head, she was as incomparable a pedagogue, moreover, as she was a performer. She could animate any student to his potential. Indeed, there are in all today's welter of harpsichordists virtually none who are not her pupils or the pupils of her pupils.

Yet not one plays with her especial grandeur. Some have her share of learning, a few of them more than that. But there is something a bit parochial about them all. For no one is nourished today by the whole of Europe. Its partition has made that impossible, its partition plus sterilization in the virile parts, all of which lie in the East. "*La grande sensibilité européene*," which came out of the East, will not exist again in our century. Nor will anyone collect out of the present book pearls comparable to those that are everywhere in Landowska's recordings. Students may get a hint or two helpful toward the rendering of Landowska's repertory. But her rhapsodic style may well put other readers off. ("Oh, the burning delights, the mortal anguish I experience in playing!") For indeed she was a gusher, in every use of the term.

The truth is that performing artists rarely write well about music. Though they may communicate wisdom, they tend rather to overstate everything, simply because language for them refuses to sing. To verbalize the emotional content of music is impossible anyway. Nevertheless, it has to be tried. Because the history and analysis of a work without reference to its content are futile, and musicology's only proper end is musical performance. The rest is fringe benefits. Nor is there value in any scholastic hope of "merely playing the notes." Notation is too vague for that; its translation into sound depends on too many unwritten conventions, most of them lost. Where these cannot be retrieved they must be imagined. Not to have the courage for this is to bury a resurrected past all over again.

The aging Wanda knew how personal were many of her readings, and she confesses it. At the same time she claims her right, on grounds of experience, much learning, and an impeccable sincerity, to restore to our hearing as best she can the sound and sense of Bach. That is where the young Wanda had started out; she wanted to see him truly. At the end she was far from sure about the objective truth of what she saw; but she knew she had seen many, many wonders and that she had put some on view. And if she was not exactly modest, never that, humble she remained before music's miracles.

But not before big modern reputations. Of Tchaikovsky she wrote, "He cries louder than any suffering could justify." She found Prokofiev's *Suggestions Diaboliques* "ridiculously silly." "The sumptuousness of Stravinsky dazzles me," she writes, "but rarely gives me happiness." "An air-conditioned room," she finds him, "compared to the normal temperature of the street." She speaks with consideration of Poulenc and of de Falla, both of whom wrote harpsichord concertos for her; but her disappointment with the de Falla work, often expressed privately, does not appear in this volume. Actually she played it seldom, considering the composer to have made errors of balance that should have been corrected when she pointed them out. She even warned one pupil that "it injures the hands." Toward the end of the book she begins to wonder "what modern music can bring me." She had never doubted the music of earlier centuries.

Though this book gives us close-up views of the long-since-ended harpsichord war and of its winning general, it is finally tedious because we know beforehand how that war came out. Landowska's sketchy notes, moreover, though sharply penetrating about composers and their pieces, are too deeply overlaid with self-advertisement to constitute a worthy or becoming self-portrait. There is charm, however, in the persistent gallicisms of their translation—*genial*, for instance, where informed by genius is meant; *wonderment* for, I presume, *émerveillement*; *appeasement* for the calming of a fever; the use as English words of *chatoyant* and *melisms*, not to mention the innocent confusions that result from calling Chopin "the Cantor of Poland" and from constantly referring to music of the seventeenth and eighteenth centuries as "ancient."

A life-and-times objectively reconstructed could have had major interest. A fingered and phrased edition of the Landowska repertory would certainly have value for professionals. The present grab bag of casual observations and incomplete analyses, for all its air of being the harpsichord's inside story, is woefully short of hard-core material. Though the volume is handsomely designed and has glowing photographs, as a ten-dollar book it is strictly for the fans.

How Dead Is Arnold Schönberg?

ARNOLD SCHOENBERG LETTERS, selected and edited by Erwin Stein. Translated from the German by Eithne Wilkins and Ernst Kaiser. 309 pp. St. Martin's, 1965.

IN 1910 Arnold Schönberg, then thirty-five, began to keep copies of all the letters he wrote. Many of these were about business—teaching jobs, the publication of his works, specifications for performance. He would seem around that time to have arrived at a decision to organize his career on a long-line view involving the dual prospect of his continuing evolution as a composer—for he was clearly not one to have shot his bolt by thirty—and of his counting on pedagogy, for which he had a true vocation, as his chief support.

His plan was to become a private teacher (*privatdozent*) at the Academy of Music and Fine Arts in Vienna, avoiding by the modesty of such a post both the anti-Semitic attacks and the anti-modernist attacks that he felt would make it impossible for him to be offered a staff appointment. Actually he was offered a staff appointment two years later; but by that time he had got what he could out of Vienna and removed to the more lively center that was Berlin.

The plan of 1910 had been calculated to play down his own music and call attention to his qualities as a teacher by bringing to the notice of the academic authorities the work of two pupils, Alban Berg and Erwin Stein.

> Perhaps after all the two men in whose hands the Conservatoire's destiny lies, can be brought to realize who I am, what a teacher the Conservatoire would deprive itself of, and how ungifted it would be to take on someone else when I am to be had for the asking. And alas I am to be had!!!

But no sooner was he had than he found a way, always his preoccupation, of leaving Vienna. For though he loved his native city, he suffered from its perfidy toward music. And indeed Vienna is a bitch. Her treatment of Mozart and Schubert proved that. And even those who led her on a leash—Beethoven, say, and Brahms—got little profit out of their dominance, save in Brahms's case a certain satisfaction from administering through a henchman on the press local defeats to Wagner and to Bruckner.

Schönberg at twenty-six, in 1901, had moved to Berlin, but two years later he was back home. The 1910 displacement lasted five years, till 1915, when he was obliged to return for mobilization. He was then forty. At fifty he left Vienna again, this time for good, to accept a teaching post in Berlin at the Prussian Academy of Arts. By then he was world famous, but he was still poor. And he had come to insist in the hearing of all not only on his skill as a teacher but on his absolute authenticity as a composer. He left no slighting remark of foe or friend unprotested.

"I am much too important," he wrote in 1923 to Paul Stefan, "for others to need to compare themselves to me." Further, "I thoroughly detest criticism and have only contempt for anyone who finds the slightest fault with anything I publish." These are the words of one who has long since lost youth's bravado, who has been critically flayed and left with no skin at all to cover his nerve ends.

Except for his usual reaction to critical attacks, mostly foreign by this time, the years from 1926 to '33 seem to have been his least painful. He was an honored artist well paid; and he worked for only six months a year, these of his choosing. This freedom allowed him to spend winters south, eventually in Catalonia, where he found relief from a growing respiratory weakness.

The letters from this time are those of almost any successful musician. To conductors and impresarios he itemizes everything, exactly how his works are to be played and exactly what circumstances he will not tolerate. To enemies and to friends he draws an indictment for every rumored slight, then offers full forgiveness if they will admit him right. In fact, he is right; he has had to be. After all the persecutions and misunderstandings he has suffered, he cannot bother to blame himself for anything. He protests, though, against all who refuse him understanding and honor and against all anti-Semitism, especially the anti-Semitism of Jews who descend to that level by refusing his music. For in success he still must fight; fighting has become a conditioned reflex. And he cannot quite relax enough, even with time and money, for going on with the two great opera-oratorios, *Moses and Aaron* and *Jacob's Ladder*. Indeed, he did not ever finish them. For he was tired; his health was under-mined; and soon he was to be a refugee.

From the summer of 1933, when he left Germany for good, till his death in 1951, he wrote a great deal of music and did untold amounts of teaching in the Los Angeles region, where he had gone for his health in the fall of '34 and where UCLA picked him up cheap at sixty, then at seventy threw him on the scrap heap with a pension of thirty-eight dollars a month for feeding a family of five. America, no less than Austria, be it said, behaved like a bitch. And though he found here through Ger-manic connections publishers for his work, money dispensers such as the Guggenheim Foundation could not see their way to helping him.

The sweetness and the bitterness of Schönberg's American letters are ever so touching. The European correspondence rings like a knell, for he never ceases to sing out that save for himself and his pupils music is dead. In America he fancies for a moment that his teaching can bring it to life. Then come the disillusionments, first that the basic teaching is too poor for him to build on (he can thus teach only the simplest elements) and second that American music has detached itself from the Germanic stem. He despises equally the reactionary concert programs of Toscanini and the heretical modernisms of Kous-sevitzky, neither of whom plays his works. And in his mouth the word *Russian* has become an injury.

He writes in 1949 to his brother-in-law Rudolf Kolisch:

Fundamentally, I agree with your analysis of musical life here. It really is a fact that the public lets its leaders drive it unresistingly into their commercial racket and doesn't do a thing to take the leadership out of their hands and force them to do their job on other principles. But over against this apathy there is a great activity on the part of American composers, la Boulanger's pu-pils, the imitators of Stravinsky, Hindemith, and now Bartók as well. These people regard musical life as a market they mean to conquer [in contrast to his own Germanic view of it as a religion] and they are all sure they will do it with ease in the colony that Europe amounts to for them. They have taken over American life lock, stock and barrel, at least in the schools of music. The only person who can get an appointment in a university music department is one who has taken his degree at one of them, and even the pupils are recruited and scholarships awarded to them in order to have the next generation in the bag. The tendency is to suppress European influences and encourage nationalistic methods of composition constructed on the pattern adopted in Russia and other such places.

He is quite right, of course; and the shoe pinches. The only advantage he can see is that

the public is at the moment more inclined to accept my music, and actually I did foresee that these people, so chaotically writing dissonances and that rough, illiterate stuff of theirs, would actually open the public's eyes, or rather ears, to the fact that there happen to be more organized ways of writing a piece, and that the public would come to feel that what is in my music is after all a different sort of thing.

The basis of Schönberg's claim had not before been that he was doing "a different sort of thing," but rather that he was doing the same thing Bach and Brahms had done, and even Mozart, and that any novelty involved was merely a technical device for continuing classical music-writing into modern times. He did not consider himself different from the earlier German masters (for him the only ones one need take seriously) or from living ones either, but merely, as regards the latter, a better workman. But in America's wider musical horizon, which included (along with Germany) France, Italy, Russia, and the Orient, he felt obliged to assert his distinction as a difference in kind. His neighbor in Hollywood, Igor Stravinsky, was doing in fact just that, had been doing so ever since he had observed it being done in Paris by Pablo Picasso. In Picasso's assumption geniuses were a species, with only a few available, and with consequently the right to a very high price. Poor Schönberg, who for all his artist's pride was humble before talent, even student talent, may not have been considered eligible for the big money simply because he naively believed that professional skill and an artist's integrity were enough. In any case, never in his published letters or other writing did he lay claim to special inspiration, to divine guidance, to a genius's birthright, or to any form of charismatic leadership.

But in America he felt impotent and outraged that music should be taking off without his consent, that pregnancy should not await the doctor. Indeed he tended to consider all such independences as irresponsible and as probably a plot against his music. Another plot, indeed, where there already had been so many! And so he came to view our movement as the work of men differing from him not only in degree but also in kind. And the integrity represented by himself and his pupils he ended by denying to almost everybody else.

Yet he remained a fine companion; there was no deception in him. And he went on writing letters to everyone in praise of the artists he had loved—in painting Wassily Kandinsky and Oskar Kokoschka, in architecture Adolf Loos, in music Gustav Mahler, Anton Webern, and Alban Berg. For himself he demanded honor and begged money. He despised the State of Israel for trying to create a music "that disavows my achievements"; then later he aspired to citizenship and offered to revise the whole of music education there.

The self-portrait that is distilled from these letters is that of a consecrated artist, cunning, companionable, loyal, indefatigable, generous, persistent, affectionate, comical, easily wounded, and demanding, but not the least bit greedy. That artist we know from his music to have been a Romantic one; but he was not romantic about himself; he was too sagacious for that, too realistic. And he was too preoccupied with the straightforward in life ever to have become aware, even, of the great dream-doctor Sigmund Freud, though they were contemporaneous in Vienna, with neither of them exactly ignorant about contemporary thought.

We know him for a Germanic artist too, for whom every major decision was a square antithesis, an either-or, for whom a certain degree of introversion was esteemed man's highest expressive state (*inwardness* is the translation word for what must have been *Innigkeit*), and for whom our century's outbreak of musical energies represented only a series of colonial revolutions to be suppressed, floods to be dammed, drained off, and channelized, naturally by himself acting alone. The dream is unbelievable, but in today's world not far from having come true, like Dr. Freud's sexual revolution.

Schönberg's music and teaching are at present a world influence of incomparable magnitude. Nor have the vigor and charm of his personality ever been in doubt. Nevertheless his work is still not popular. Like the music of Bruckner and of Mahler and, until in recent decades only, that of Brahms, it has the savor rather of a cause than of plain nourishment. Mozart, Beethoven, and Schubert in the past, Debussy and Stravinsky in our time, have been as clear to us as Santa Claus. Not so Arnold Schönberg, at least not yet. But the man has long been precious to those who knew him; and now the letters, with their punctilious indignation and casual buffoonery, their passionate friendships and irascible complaints, their detailed accountings and their Olympian self-regard, their undying optimism under the most humiliating poverty and disregard, have given us a man that many will come to love and laugh at and get angry at and cherish, just as if he were still with us.

And perhaps he is. In Vienna, certainly, Mozart still walks beside one, Beethoven is at his window, and Schubert is drinking and writing songs in any tavern. The whole career of Arnold Schönberg resists historical pinning down. Not in the Vienna of 1874, where he was born, nor in that of 1900, where he was virtually unnoticed, nor in Berlin of the early teens and late twenties, where he was a power, nor in the Hollywood of '34 to '51, where he was merely beloved, in none of these places did he sum up a time. He slipped into and out of them all, just being Arnold Schönberg, and everywhere except in Berlin being roundly persecuted for that. Even today I would not be too sure he is not writing music over many a student's shoulder and putting in many a violation of his own famous method just to plague its more pompous practitioners.

Certainly he is being a plague to Igor Stravinsky, whose adoption of that method after the master's death has left him in a situation almost as skinless as that of Schönberg in life. Certain known attacks on Stravinsky's music, therefore, some of them published here, have obliged him, as a confessed Schönbergian, to take cognizance of these with what grace he can muster, which is considerable. Reviewing the *Letters* last October in the

London *Observer*, he accepted their strictures with a gallant mea culpa and paid higher praise to their author than he has ever paid, I think, to any other musician.

"The lenses of Schönberg's conscience," he said, "were the most powerful of the musicians of the era, and not only in music." Also, "the *Letters* are an autobiography . . . the most consistently honest in existence by a great composer." Actually Stravinsky's exit from a seeming impasse has been ever so skillful and handsome. And its warmth of phrase is such as to make one forget almost that the gesture was imposed. Imposed by what? Simply by the fact that a great and living master had been resoundingly slapped by a dead one.

As for how dead Arnold Schönberg really is, let us not hazard a guess. The Viennese composers have never rested easy.

The New York Review of Books, April 22, 1965

On Being Discovered

MUSIC IN A NEW FOUND LAND: *Themes and Developments in the History of American Music*, by Wilfrid Mellers. 543 pp. Knopf, 1964.

AMERICA'S ART MUSIC has not heretofore aroused much enthusiasm among Europeans. Our ragtime was parodied lovingly, if not enviously, by Debussy, Satie, and Stravinsky. And jazz, though harder to make grow, did flower in the fugal finale of Milhaud's *La Création du Monde* of 1924. It also stimulated, beginning in the 1920s, serious historical studies by Robert Goffin and Hugues Panassié, more recently by André Hodeir. The examination of our Appalachian folklore had been started around 1915 by Cecil Sharp, an Englishman. And our commercial popular music had already, after World War I, replaced the Viennese for worldwide export. George Gershwin had even been successful in both kinds of production, since his *Rhapsody in Blue* for piano and orchestra and his opera *Porgy and Bess* had become, by the mid-1950s, as familiar to everybody everywhere as his songs.

But the Gershwin experience remains unique and not clearly a witness for America's art-music tradition. Everywhere our jazz and pop are respected, but not so our symphonic and opera creations, our chamber music and our lieder. How comes it, then, that a European musicologist devotes a whole book to them? The answer is simple; he has fallen in love with us. Not with all of America, perhaps, but certainly, as is clear on every page, with our music. He has felt the energy and the violence behind it and come to penetrate its surfaces, whether these be rough or glassy, arriving through a composer's understanding—for Wilfrid Mellers is also a creative artist—at acceptance (and with joy) of the fact that American music is at its best when least entangled with Europe.

Though his title, *Music in a New Found Land*, suggests that Professor Mellers (now of York University) has only recently discovered us (perhaps through his two years' tenure as Mellon Professor at the University of Pittsburgh), this is not exactly the case. As early as 1950, in his book *Music and Society*, he was treating the transatlantic theme as "American Music and an Industrial Community." This essay seems to be the fruit of his wartime friendship in England with the late Marc Blitzstein, through whom he had got to know not only the latter's social-consciousness operas but also the music of Aaron Copland and Charles Ives. In fact, it is almost exclusively out of these three composers that a viewpoint, or *aussicht*, was erected, somewhat after the Marxian plan, for interpreting the "good" strain in American music as ethical, objective, didactic, and mainly of the theater.

The present book, dedicated to Aaron Copland and to the memory of Marc Blitzstein, enlarges that view to include almost everybody, naturally reducing somewhat the salience of these two, but not removing from the central position Charles Ives, whom he considers "the first authentic American composer and . . . still the closest America has come to a great composer, parallel to her nineteenth-century literary giants." Blitzstein has even been demoted from this high intellectual company to a place in "sincere" show business, somewhere between Gershwin and Leonard Bernstein. And Copland has been flanked, in Edgard Varèse, Elliott Carter, and John Cage, with figures seemingly of his size, and hieratically extended, through Roy Harris, Roger Sessions, Samuel Barber, and myself, by secondary figures occupying, at least in this book, comparable space.

All such rearrangements of official history are easy for a foreigner to do. And Mellers has long been adept, as in *François Couperin and the French Classical Tradition* and in his earlier studies of Erik Satie, at seeing around corners. For his mind is fast and sure-footed like a squirrel, storing up nuts for a long feast in the hollow of any tree. But the tree has to be there.

His tree, though another might have done as well, is a set of ideas about American literary history that have been standing available for some years now, ideas about the influence on American art of the Puritan Tradition and of the Genteel Tradition, about how Americans are dominated by dreams of purity (hence of childhood) and a yearning for the absolute (hence utter tranquillity, outer space, or death), and about how every artist is at heart either a country boy or a city boy. All these ideas, once serviceable, are a little tired by now, better for hanging out journalistic light wash than for housing nourishment. Which is not to call them wholly valueless, though through overuse they have indeed lost meaning. And none of them is specific to America, anyway. The Puritan Tradition is stronger in Spain, the Genteel more terrifying in Soviet Russia, the preoccupation with death more prevalent in Germany; and as for identification with childhood, it is a solid literary tradition in both England and France.

It would be a pleasure to credit the patent excellence of Mellers's judgments to some intellectual method better suited to either deriving them or defending them, but I can find no such reasoning. I see rather an intuitive recognition of quality, good guesses, and a brilliantly improvisatory literary style. In whatever he says Mellers tends to carry you with him. And the amazing rightness of his estimates, which may well remain for a decade or two ninety percent definitive, are all the more impressive from the fact that they are not very different from the estimates confidentially circulated now among the members of music's in-group. Their surprisingness comes partly from their being so suddenly gathered together in one package, and partly from the blinding brightness of their expression. Mellers, as a scholar, could easily be convicted on points, for his book contains many errors and omissions. But no writer on the subject has before described our music so faithfully or handled it with so much love.

Ives's integrity, we read, "is synonymous with his experimental audacity"; and this in turn springs from, first, "the pioneer's courage: his desire to hack a way through the forest since he has, indeed, no alternative," and second, "the radical innocence of spirit without which—as we have seen in the literary figures—the pioneer could hardly embark on so perilous an adventure." The core of Ives's work is "acceptance of life-as-it-is in all its apparent chaos and contradiction," every kind of musical material and technique being usable "as experience dictates, and often simultaneously, since all experience is related and indivisible." The search for unity within such a chaos is, moreover, "a transcendental act" and his view of the sonata "an attempt to impose the unity of the Will on the chaos of experience," as he believed Beethoven to have done. But having behind him only "the American wilderness, not Viennese civilization and a long musical history," he cannot travel so far and consequently merely "glimpses, but does not enter, his paradise."

In Carl Ruggles's music "the surging spring of the lines, the persistent tension of the dissonance, is like the pain of birth; nothing is preordained, all is a growing." And comparing him to Arnold Schönberg, he says:

> both were amateur painters who, in their visual work, sought the expressionistic moment of vision. Both . . . found that the disintegrated fragments of the psyche could be reintegrated only by a mystical act. Schoenberg, as a Viennese Jew, had an ancient religion and the spirit of Beethoven to help him; Ruggles had only the American wilderness and the austerities of Puritan New England. For this reason he sought freedom—from tonal bondage, from the harmonic straight-jacket, from conventionalized repetitions, from anything that sullied the immediacy and purity of experience—even more remorselessly than Schoenberg.

But "his dedication to the sublime also means that he has to be inspired to carry it off." Hence the very small production.

Roy Harris is for Mellers a "primitive" and his music "fundamentally a religious affirmation," where often, toward the end of any work, "the religious lyricism has been metamorphosed into the American violence."

In Aaron Copland's case, complete artistic realization has been achieved, but only by a "severe limitation of [expressive] range," for the "quintessential Copland" is "a wistful urban loneliness." The Piano Variations of 1930, his "first masterpiece," is "bare and hard," "almost skeletal," differing from European music and from most of that by Ives, Ruggles, or Harris in its "lack of lyrical growth." As a construction it is "steely and monumental, yet at the same time a profoundly human expression of courage." The Piano Fantasy of twenty-five years later—"the third of Copland's major piano works—is also the greatest: for it fuses the stark energy of the Variations with the still serenity of the Sonata's last movement." He considers Copland "not a 'great' composer" but "a very important composer in twentieth-century history, for he is the first artist to define precisely, in sound, an aspect of our urban experience."

In Elliott Carter, "the values represented by Ives and Copland come to terms," which is to say that the polymorphous spontaneity of Ives has been transformed through Copland's constructivist influence, into controlled composition, with no loss to expressivity. Ives's realistic depiction, however (of country fairs and such), has been abandoned by Carter, as in Beethoven's last quartets, for transcendental unity-in-multiplicity and for seeking at the end a breakthrough into the beatific.

A similar dream of salvation through the procedures of monumentality Mr. Mellers posits as the drama of Roger Sessions. In fact, it seems to him the essential drama of all the New England composers. And he identifies it with the soul struggle of Beethoven, in one chapter praising such an aspiration to power and integrity, in another finding it profitless to seek repetition of Beethoven's experience.

Certainly the more novel and "progressive" of our composers —from Griffes and Varèse to Harry Partch and John Cage— have "taken off" not from Beethoven's achievement but from Debussy's, from his isolation of individual sounds as sensuous experience and the recomposing of these into contiguities of continuous delight with no care for either monumentality or personal salvation. Cage himself has indeed, rather more effectively, I suspect, than today's painters and poets, carried the post-Impressionist, post-cubist Dada tradition into our time and become, through a willed Will-lessness that prays to, and moves toward, silence, "a beatnik saint whose disciples proliferate."

Whether Samuel Barber's music is mainly an evocation of

adolescence, like Tchaikovsky's and Rachmaninoff's, anyone can argue. Certainly, for all its sweetness and fine workmanship, it is no part just now of our intellectual life. And I should be the last know whether there is justice in the oft-drawn parallel between Satie and myself. Mellers says that "both the technical methods and the cultivated naivety are the same." But when he essays to identify the disciplines of spontaneity as "inconsequential" and "childish" regressions (in both my case and Gertrude Stein's) he misses the fact that simplifications, abstractions, radical compactions, and restored-to-beauty commonplaces, no less than Debussy's and Cage's "liberation of the individual sound," are inherent to all our century's radical art, and especially to that Paris-centered modernism which from Picasso in painting to Robbe-Grillet in writing has served as norm and mainstream for artists working west of the Rhine. Even music's Vienna School, though it tampered little with Romanticism's meaning-clichés, early strove to neutralize and to pulverize music's materials.

With Copland, the author's city-dweller premise still allows Mellers to admire the landscape music, provided it is from a lonesome landscape. With Carter, his determination to find everywhere a search for transcendental experience leads him to suspect in the Double Concerto, where he finds no lyric line, a denial of "man's humanity," which is "his first offering to God." And with me he has a hard time making his "adult child" hypothesis fit the *Mass for the Dead*, while before *A Solemn Music* he simply gives up and admits "unexpected emotional depth." The Violin Sonata and the string quartets he wisely avoids to review.

One of the great joys of Mellers as a musical analyst is the ease with which he throws away his instruments of meaning-detection for an instantaneous, instinctive, on-the-spot, straight-to-the-heart-of-the-matter interpretation of anything and everything. And if this practical spontaneity leads him to understand, through his composer's empathy, virtually everything but schooled spontaneity, it gives his musical heart permission to love whatever sounds in a fresh way, or speaks from another heart. So that one scarcely feels a need to argue with him. It may be just as well, all the same, to remark that an increasing number of persons are writing about twentieth-century modernism who were never connected with it. Also that England, even more than America, occupies in that movement a provincial situation. So that when an English musical mind (one, moreover, quite free of ties to the British Establishment and also one remarkably informed regarding France) turns its illuminating scrutiny on to the American musical mind, there is the possibility, as happened when Ernest Newman discovered Sibelius in Finland, of undue gratitude being shown for survivals from the gamut of feeling of another century.

But since Mellers is the only European so far to look us over with any completeness, and since his view, however hasty, is wildly favorable, it is perhaps ungracious to cavil. Just the same, for all its pellucid penetration and warmth of love, his examination of American art music does seem a bit casual, when compared to the best European studies of jazz.

His treatment of popular music in the book's second half, though many of its descriptions of disc performances may be as spontaneous in thought as in phrase, profits from the existence of a dozen other histories. Its justification is that pop and jazz are needed to make a whole picture of America. For jazz is the most astounding spontaneous musical event to take place anywhere since the Reformation. And pop music here has come so near giving birth to top music—in Gershwin, Blitzstein, and, just maybe, Bernstein—that a Marxian philosopher could not resist opening the question of its relation to musical authenticity.

The three cases are not identical, obviously. Gershwin came from Tin Pan Alley, by way of the Lisztian rhapsody, to giving a Broadway play operatic status. And although the theme of that is a white man's view of Negro life (hence phony throughout), its translation into melody is a lovely one because Gershwin was a pure heart.

Blitzstein was an intellectual musician, a pupil of Schönberg and Boulanger, also a Marxist, who found in the operas of Kurt Weill out of Brecht a populist formula capable of being used for passionate propaganda. In so using it, he revealed himself as a natural theater composer and a master of characterization through the parody of musical styles. Copland, in films or ballet, never went so far.

Leonard Bernstein is an even more elaborately trained classical musician—by Harvard, the Curtis Institute, Fritz Reiner, and Koussevitzky. But he also spent certain youthful years in Tin Pan Alley working for Warner Brothers. His symphonic works are coated with Broadway, and his Broadway shows are braided throughout with Tanglewood. Successfully to court a mass audience in the language of Stravinsky and Milhaud proves the musical sophistication of that audience to be far greater than that of any mass audience in Europe. But it does not make Bernstein an operetta composer like his earlier French counterpart, André Messager, who was a no-less-fine classical conductor.

"Blitzstein, in 'purifying the dialect of the tribe,'" to quote again, "creates works which are related to musical comedy but could not be mistaken for it; Bernstein, in writing a musical comedy, cannot entirely avoid capitulation to commercial values." In other words, Gershwin and Blitzstein have in different ways fulfilled their talents. Bernstein, perhaps because of their stultifying abundance, has not yet fulfilled his.

Here endeth the second lesson from Wilfrid Mellers, the first having been a 1950 sketch for this, now extended and improved. Further extension and improvement may come or not; but American music will be better off for what he has told us already about ourselves. Professor Mellers has other preoccupations too, notably, I believe, a history of English words-and-music from medieval times. Everything he writes is full of enlightenment; I should not care to limit him, or to miss one essay. But seeing ourselves as others see us is as good as having your fortune told. And Mellers has given us not only the joy of being looked at, but the satisfaction of being voted for as well.

The New York Review of Books, June 3, 1965

The Tradition of Sensibility

DEBUSSY: *His Life and Mind. Volume II: 1902–1918*, by Edward Lockspeiser. 337 pp. Macmillan, 1965.

GEORGES BIZET: *His Life and Work*, by Winton Dean. 304 pp. J. M. Dent (London), 1965.

ALBAN BERG, by Willi Reich. Translated from the German by Cornelius Cardew. 239 pp. Harcourt, Brace & World, 1965.

THE PATH TO THE NEW MUSIC, by Anton Webern, edited by Willi Reich. Translated from the German by Leo Black. 67 pp. Theodore Presser Co. with Universal Edition, 1963.

CLAUDE DEBUSSY, our century's most original composer, was ill-born, ill-bred, and virtually uneducated save in music. In that he had the best (Paris Conservatoire) and earned his *Prix de Rome*. Though an autodidact in the non-musical branches, he was alive to painting and to poetry, including the most advanced. Already in youth he had made friends with the difficult and demanding Mallarmé; and he himself had literary gifts. He wrote about music as *Monsieur Croche, antidilettante* (a personage fabricated after the Monsieur Teste of his friend Paul Valéry); he indited "*proses lyriques*" and set them; and he carried on with all those close to him a correspondence phrased in racy language. Those close to him included the poet Pierre Louÿs, the romancers Marcel Proust and André Gide, the composers Ernest Chausson and Erik Satie, later Maurice Ravel, Igor Stravinsky, and Edgard Varèse. And if eventually he broke with virtually all of these but Satie, or they with him, Debussy was for all his bearishness, bad temper, and constant money dramas, a delicious friend and tender companion, even to his wives and mistresses, two of whom tried suicide when he moved out.

Abstention from personal discipline, organization, and plan was part of his working method, for sensibility cannot be maintained by rule. It needs to be coddled, teased, caressed, enraged. The eye that can see through fog, the ear that can penetrate a din, the instinct for pain that can lead one to touch his own nerve knots—these faculties were sought out in Debussy's time. One need only remember Whistler's London landscapes, the *Elektra* of Hoffmannsthal and Richard Strauss, the *Salomé* of Oscar Wilde, to realize that on a still grander level Proust, Monet, and Dr. Sigmund Freud were also dealing with the dark, and using more highly sensitized antennae.

The disciplines of sensitivity are in every way exasperating. And the highly sensitized Debussy was not an easy one to bear with, for he lived at both the geographical center and the time center of a movement in all the arts that required the artist to vibrate constantly. The epoch was for dredging the unconscious, for catching a moment of truth on the wing through awareness of some fleeting impression, through keeping one's senses sharp and clear, one's emotions undefined. To live by intuition and to create through a sensuality intensely imagined is not easy for youth, still overpowered by childhood's traumas and by bourgeois prestige. And after thirty-five, vibrancy cannot always be depended on; it may need the help of drugs or drink or of elaborately varied sexual fun and games.

From Baudelaire through Rimbaud, the best poets have not in general made good husbands. Not in France. Nor yet the composers there—Fauré, Chabrier, Debussy, Satie, Ravel. And painters everywhere are the very prototypes of bohemia. But simple roistering is not enough. I am talking of an art seemingly fluid and unseizable but which yet remains in memory because it comes out of unnamed feelings intensely experienced. And this was the art that centered in France between roughly 1850 and World War I. This was the art, moreover, that in all its forms—Impressionism and the *Fauve* in painting, diabolism and psychological acuities in literature, helped out by the philosophico-sensual music-dramas of Richard Wagner—shaped the life and mind of Claude Debussy, the time's only musical mentality capable of carrying on the Wagnerian ecstasy.

"His life and mind" is the subtitle of Edward Lockspeiser's two-volume account, the second volume's debut being today's occasion. Lockspeiser has been about his Debussy research for more years than I could certify. His *Debussy* in the Master Musicians series bears a Preface date of 1936; and since that time he has issued amplified editions and other books, Volume I of the present study having come out in 1962.

The work completes, corrects, and binds into a bouquet all previous studies of this composer, of which there are many in French and English, only a few in German. It is footnoted entertainingly, copiously illustrated, and elaborately appendixed. Among the rare materials included are (in French) Mallarmé's article on Maeterlinck's *Pelléas et Mélisande*, a stenographically reported conversation about German music between Debussy and his former teacher, the composer Ernest Guiraud, a ten-page account of Debussy's project for making something operatic out of Shakespeare's *As You Like It* (a plan that occupied him from early youth till death without any of the music ever getting written), and an article by Manuel de Falla on Debussy's uncanny ability to evoke Spain. The only error I noted anywhere is the statement that André Caplet was musical director of the Boston Symphony Orchestra from 1910 to 1915, instead of the Boston Opera Company.

It is not my desire to reduce Lockspeiser's rich volumes to a digest. But mention may be made of his perspicacious treatment of the painting influences on Debussy, since a parallel with Impressionism has long been current. Nor is this wholly without meaning, especially when applied to the piano music. Lockspeiser, however, assures us that Debussy's attitude toward painting as a style-source was no mere fixation on the Impressionists, but rather an awareness that evolved with modern art itself. Throughout his youth, for instance, he was attached to the composition-style of Hokusai and to the Japanese-inspired layouts of Degas, both of which got into his songs and piano pieces. Of the three great tryptichs for orchestra—*Nocturnes*, *La Mer*, and *Images*—the first, composed in the early and late 1890s, bears surely an imprint of the painter Monet; while the second, though through its fragmented continuity still (1905) an Impressionist work, is suffused by luminosities out of Turner. *Images*, from 1911—consisting of *Ibéria*, *Rondes de Printemps*, and *Gigues*—reflects the sharper colorings of *Fauve* painting, though in all three of its sections literary origins dominate, especially in the tragic *Gigues*, probably inspired by a poem of Verlaine.

Though Debussy himself was reticent about strict parallels in his work, he actually said, or wrote, as I remember, regarding the early *Nocturnes*, which have always seemed to us so "coloristic," that his intention had been to create with orchestral timbres the equivalent in music of an all-gray painting method known as *grisaille*. This surprising remark can only mean that he was using timbre contrasts as the Impressionists used colors, for their ability, by seeming to come forward or to retreat, to give an illusion of foregrounds and distances. In this sense the work is only incidentally coloristic, like Monet's early landscapes of the Normandy coast, brightness being merely a by-product of color's functional use for creating luminosity and perspective.

The opera *Pelléas et Mélisande* breathes quite another air. The Merovingian family of Maeterlinck's play can be imagined as seated somewhere north of Rouen, perhaps in the sunny and fertile country around the Abbey of Jumièges, which is after all not far from Saint-Wandrille, where Maeterlinck himself had an establishment. Debussy's characters and score, on the other hand, are hardly Romanesque at all, but rather out of *art nouveau*. This form of decoration (known in French as *le modern-style*), coming from the pre-Raphaelites by way of Barcelona and Holland, had found in France its ultimate sinuosity of line, its coloristic pallor, its devitalized females and giant floral forms.

And the people of Debussy's opera, just like those in 1900-manner art, are ineluctably enmeshed and intertwined with their décor. Not with outdoor scenes of sheep and meadows, as in the play, but with wells and parapets and slippery stone stairs and tidal caves and tower bedrooms from which long blond hair let down till it enwraps brings on the only climax in the score. This opera is not landscape music but passion music about people who feel intensely all the time. And their watery medieval residence is neither Metrostyle nor Romanesque nor Gothic. It is actually, it would appear, Poe's House of Usher, a theme the composer had cherished from his youth.

One should not go too far with the visual-arts approach to Debussy's music. It is useful as a stylistic reference, but his main source was literature. Even when inspired by sea views, landscapes, weather, perfumes, architecture, night, or fireworks, his music is no direct transcript of experience. It is more likely to be an auditory evocation of a verbal evocation of some sensuous delight, and that delight itself a dream of art. Debussy's evocations, whether visual or not, are immobile, the emotion that holds them in suspense being a response to style itself, *une émotion d'art*. And his most vibrant pages are those in which a literary transcript of some visual or other sensuous experience has released in him a need to inundate the whole with music.

This music, though wrought from a vast vocabulary of existing idiom, is profoundly independent and original. This is as true of the piano music as of the orchestral pictures. None of it really sounds like anything else. It had its musical origins, of course; but it never got stuck with them; it took off.

The most remarkable of these flights is that of the opera *Pelléas*, which for the first time in over a century (or maybe ever) a composer gave full rights to subtleties below the surface of a play, not merely to action and to verbal discourse. The result is a union of music and poetry inspired in general by Wagner's ideal (itself straight out of Schubert) and specifically by the sound of the orchestra in *Parsifal*, of which Debussy declared that it glowed "as if lighted from behind." And the sensitivity with which the whole is knit, also an ideal that dominated European art for upwards of a century, never again produced so fine a fabric.

Richard Strauss, taken to *Pelléas* by Romain Rolland, remarked that if he had been setting that play he would have used a different kind of music. I'm sure he would have, and no doubt much louder. But *Pelléas* is part of music's high canon in a way no Strauss opera is. And if opera today is to be saved from itself (and Strauss)—for its present enslavements to "theatrical" values and mere plot are suicidal—there is no other model so propitious as this work, which is at the same time, and intensely, both poetry and music.

The last time it was in repertory at the Metropolitan, quite several years ago, a well-meaning person is said to have asked the conductor Pierre Monteux, "Do you suppose *Pelléas* will ever be really a success?" He answered, "It was never intended to be."

The composer of *Carmen*, France's other impeccable opera (this one thoroughly successful), is the subject of biographical treatment in *Georges Bizet: His Life and Work*, by Winton Dean. Bizet had been little studied before 1948, when Dean published his excellent 250-page biography, with musical examples, in the Master Musicians series (J. M. Dent & Sons, London). Then ten years later came *Bizet and His World*, by Mina Curtiss (Knopf, 1958), twice as long and twice as well-informed. Mrs. Curtiss had through the last heir of Bizet's widow come upon basketfuls of musical manuscripts, letters, and diaries; and though not a musician herself, she found their panorama of Roman and French artistic life between 1855 and '75 tempting to write about.

She had hoped that Marc Blitzstein might work with her by analyzing scores, but he was writing an opera of his own and did not care to take on a job of scholarship. So Mrs. Curtiss, omitting judgment on matters musical, simply wrote a Life and Times. A fine book, too, it turned out to be, as all books about the French nineteenth century are that are prepared with love and carefully.

Winton Dean, working from the Curtiss book, as well as from some supplemental sources, has put together a biography that includes textual examination of the scores, a book for musicians that is not gigantic (300 pages), but that is sound and sensible. Mrs. Curtiss's volume, longer and more detailed, gives a grander panorama. Hers is the one for Comp. Lit. students. And what is Comp. Lit. anyway but nineteenth-century France?

Across the Rhine and down the Danube, we encounter again the sensibility tradition, this time out of Vienna and restated in our century. To Willi Reich, a pupil of Alban Berg, now author of his musical biography, this sensibility is only in the music. For his hero seems to have led a proper family life, spent summers in the mountains, frequented no dangerous companions. He depended rather on the German classic masters to guide him through the dark forests of abnormal psychology. And indeed they got him handsomely through two operas suffused with it—*Wozzeck* (after Büchner) and *Lulu* (after Wedekind)— actually our century's only runners-up to *Pelléas.*

The fact is that Berg's master, Arnold Schoenberg, did with the sensibility tradition what Central Europe always does with anything regarding art, which is to organize it for pedagogy. In that state it can be packaged and sold. Debussy, even at the height of Debussyism, had refused all truck with reproducing his musical kind, also with propositions for freezing his own sensibility at yesterday's level. When a jacket blurb begins, "Alban Berg is one of [Oh, those weasel-words "one of"!] the most important composers of the twentieth century," then later ties together his humanity, his "high spirituality" (not my quotes), and his artistic sense of responsibility, it tempts one to put the whole thing down as advertising.

Nevertheless, out of my own perverse fascination with the

Germanic view of music as something strictly for scholastic temperaments, I read the book, found it informative and no doubt useful for reference. Willi Reich, I may add, is a reputable Swiss critic and almost a founder-member of the Schoenberg-Berg-Webern conspiracy to make the past and future read their way.

Alban Berg, I am sure, was less dogmatic than this book depicts him, though with Germanic types, with all of them, there is a tendency to think in simplified alternatives—black or white, right or wrong, our team against all the others in the world. And this is what leads them to present any art work as a case to be argued, usually with emotionally weighted words.

Willi Reich's book shows Berg doing just that in three articles from the early twenties—"Why Is Schoenberg's Music So Difficult to Understand?" "The Musical Impotence of Hans Pfitzer's 'New Aesthetic'," and "Two Feuilletons," an attack on Schoenberg's critics. These are polemical writing involving musical illustrations, music analysis, and German puns. And though I do not really believe that art can be effectively defended by vilifying those who do not understand it, these pieces are admirable for the aptness of the musical quotations analyzed and entertaining for their sheer pugnacity.

Anton Webern's tiny book of lectures given privately in 1932 and '33 and here transcribed from shorthand notes seem to me without value as musical theory and quite irresponsible in their use of terms, at least as these are translated (though I find the charming word *Zusammenhang* quite neatly rendered as "unity"). Their interest lies in the stammering state of mind with which matters of musical usage are discussed, as if all the composer's predecessors were right there egging him on and at the same time holding him back at the slightly sinful game of let's-invent-something. Actually something had been invented, though not by Webern, by Schoenberg; and Webern's self-conscious astonishment about it is hard to believe.

Debussy had said forty years earlier that tonality should be got rid of (*"il faut noyer le ton"*). And Webern had learned from Schoenberg how to do exactly that. He was a dainty composer and a modest man who should never have got mixed up with the steam-roller aspects of twelve-tone-serial propaganda. But with Schoenberg and Berg for chums, how could he not?

The New York Review of Books, December 9, 1965

"Craft-Igor" and the Whole Stravinsky

STRAVINSKY: *The Composer and His Works*, by Eric Walter White. 608 pp. University of California Press, 1966.

THEMES AND EPISODES, by Igor Stravinsky and Robert Craft. 352 pp. Knopf, 1966.

Reviewing Igor Stravinsky's life, works, career, polemical statements, or any books regarding these, one can stipulate that he has been since 1910 a major modern force, that he is now the most admired living composer, and that in the present decade he has revealed himself as a remarkably sharp musical observer. The latter personality let us call Craft-Igor, since it is a double one, in which the voice is the voice of Robert Craft, but the head is of Igor Fyodorovitch.

In *Themes and Episodes*, fifth volume of this perfect impersonation, though the voice takes formal leave of personal diary-keeping, surely Craft has not for the last time served as chief of English language protocol for the master's many verbalizing needs. Also, the composer's wife, Vera de Bosset, becomes a speaking member of the trinity. And most welcome she is, since with her painter's prodigious visual memory she gives us Stravinsky in domestic close-up while watching over him as one might a patient or a child, and writes about his life, his house, his habits with unfailing warmth, good humor, and good sense. This in two long letters written to a cousin in Russia and translated anonymously with infinite grace. One does hope that in future chats she will be present, if only to give us the logistics of a life so far flung geographically and at the same time so tightly tied into a three-person package by the great man's urgencies regarding daily work, liquor, bodily symptoms, and the highest fees.

Craft has served Stravinsky during fifteen years as assistant conductor and during ten as interviewer for eliciting from him printable statements of musical opinion. Also, as traveling companion and cultural guide the young-man-who-reads-many-books has been a door opener. It was not till Craft became a close associate that Stravinsky showed any notable interest in either Arnold Schönberg or in twelve-tone serial music, both of which he now follows piously, at least within the limits of his eighty-five-year-old's power of self-transformation, which is considerable. And in the domain of Renaissance vocal music, which he has taken in late years almost for his own discovery, he must have been guided toward many an odd practitioner—Heinrich Isaac, for instance, or Gesualdo di Venosa—by the reading of the younger musician. If not to these, then at least to the minor Elizabethan poets and to Dylan Thomas; for Craft, right along with his alertness to music, is a *fin lettré* aware of trends in literary prestige.

As a writer he is less straightforward than either of the Stravinskys. Vera, in this regard, is the perfect one. Igor, as a Russian experienced in at least four other languages, is fascinated by words of Latin origin. And as an artist, moreover, he is prone to lay out any contemporary composer or rival performer who displeases him, which most of them do, as well as to rewrite the history of music for his own benefit, as every other composer throughout music's history has done who has written at all.

Is it Stravinsky's love of verbal legerdemain that has led Craft on, or his own propensity for giggles that makes him so fond of "hard" words? In his latest travel diary one comes upon: nictitating, clerihew, mystagogical, anastomosis, antitragus, geminate (a noun), pendunculates, pargeting, testudinarious, stercoral, scorbiculated, examinate, strigil, castrametation, cyclothymic, paranomasia, enchaféd, eldritch (adjective), coffle, and deturpation, as well as "the marvering and crizzling of the parison, which is glass in its bubble-gum state."

In turning Stravinsky's own pages, do not miss the interview on Anton Webern and the present state of "Anton-olatry" (p. 115 *et seq.* of *Themes and Episodes*). Here are a major musician's work described, current trends observed, esthetics compared, an estimate proposed, and the interviewer gently teased—all with a knifelike critical penetration, a compacted irony, and a wealth of sideswipes, even at himself, that are a lesson in how to deflate a cult without injury to the revered composer inside.

And for plain answers to far from simple questions, let me paraphrase a reporter's interview that does not appear in these books, published in 1957 by *Buenos Aires Musical.*

Q. Is musical form "mathematical"?
A. It is neither exactly arithmetical nor an affair of equations; but it is related to a mathematical way of thinking.

Q. What of electronic music?

A. I find its sounds boring. What interests me is the notation.

Q. What does sincerity mean to you?

A. It is a *sine qua non*, but guarantees nothing.

Q. Is your duration-universe the same as formerly?

A. No. Nowadays my music is more compact. Certain parts of *Agon*, for instance, contain three times as much music, by the clock, as many of my earlier works.

Q. Isn't there something oriental about the duration-universe of serial music?

A. Not specifically. Moreover, I have no contact with the orient nor any understanding of it.

Q. Are there any new developments today in rhythm?

A. In *Le Marteau Sans Maître* by Pierre Boulez and in *Zeitmasse* by Karlheinz Stockhausen *accelerando* and *ritardando* are regulated from point to point by metronomic indications. Thus speed control eliminates fixed *tempo* and gives to music a wholly new agility. Beyond this interesting device, there has been nothing new in rhythm for fifty years, not since my own *The Rite of Spring*.

Q. Is there any danger in today's search for mere novelty?

A. No. But it does make life hard for critics, especially in Germany, where they are supposed to act as a brake on impetuosity.

One could cite, I am sure, the whole of Stravinsky's contribution to the Craft-Igor books without noting one deviation from clarity, though of malice (as against a fellow-Russian composer, Vladimir Dukelsky, whom he addresses as V. D.), venom (attacking with vitriol a puny reviewer who had not admired his work), and self-praise (the constant insistence on his own importance to the history of music) there are aplenty.

Musicians, we know, tend toward extreme irritability; and exasperation, of course, is the right of any artist. We like it when a life-giving spillover breaks through the proprieties. But when a great man takes to quibbling about the obvious, one could wish he would pick on someone near his size. And that he would remember too the importance of the place, as great as can ever be estimated with certainty during an artist's life, that has long been stipulated in this one's favor.

However, though a sizable niche is certain, the placement of it is far from settled. The present study of his life and works by Eric Walter White, which aims to clarify the matter, is a compendium of virtually all that is known about both the man and his music. It is one of those terminal biographies, like Lock-speiser's of Debussy or Ernest Newman's of Richard Wagner, that are the glory of England's music-and-letters tradition. After publishing a book called *Stravinsky's Sacrifice to Apollo* at the exact point, 1930, where Paul Collaer's illuminating *Stravinsky* left off, White has gone forward with a will to make his study complete, and backward with a determination to get everything right, attesting on every page his devotion to both truth and music.

Collaer's book, long out of print in French and never, I think, available in English, contains a more lively analysis of the early works, white-lighted as it is by a near-contemporary's under-standing. The Swiss conductor Ernest Ansermet, writing of the same early works in various volumes, has a comparable way of carrying us back to a time when the Russianness of all musical Russians, with their so-fresh tunes and so-fresh harmonies, was heady nourishment, and when the shocking, immense presence of Stravinsky's music, from *The Firebird* and *Petrushka* through *The Rite of Spring*, was making clear that the century was on.

Stravinsky's work has received the homage of analysis and explication in book form by composers as impressive as Alfredo Casella, Gian Francesco Malipiero, Nicolas Nabokov, Alexandre Tansman, and Roman Vlad, not to mention critical examina-tions by the hundreds, among which those of Boris de Schloezer and of the conductor Robert Siohan are in my judgment the most meaty. Heretofore, Italians and the France-centered have done best by him. The Germans, though voluminous, have not been notable; nor have the Americans nor previously the English, save for White's earlier (1948) *Stravinsky: A Critical Survey*, itself to come out in German two years later.

From now on, any serious study of the composer must begin with White's *Stravinsky: The Composer and His Works* if only because of its completeness—completeness of biographical mat-ter, of documentary aids, of contemporary opinion quoted, of works described and musical examples analyzed. Besides all this there are reprints, in their original French or English, of divers articles and lectures by Stravinsky and a selection of letters to Stravinsky from Debussy, Delius, Ravel, and the novelist Jules Romains. The analyses and their musical quotations, especially if one fills them out from Collaer's book, are prodigiously abundant and revealing. Nothing is lacking but the Craft-Igor conversations.

It is doubtful whether any composer, saving only Richard Wagner, has ever been so expansive in print. Nor were any, save Wagner, Rossini, and possibly Satie, one half so entertaining personally. And among all those whom we know from their writings, only Wagner and Stravinsky seem to have felt the need for reasserting constantly their demand for a particular place in history.

One regrets this insistence, while realizing its probable source. Both composers, of course, through coming late to music, retained the insecurity of the autodidact. Both achieved success early through a remarkable gift for orchestration and through the soundness of their instinct for the stage. Both, moreover, lavished on their stage works the richest symphonic textures. Wagner, however, as a German, had to explain away not writing symphonies. He knew that theater music alone, no matter what its excellence, would not admit him to Valhalla. And so, all perfectly true and tiresome and repetitive, he explained over and over what he had done, and gave it a new name, *Musikdrama*.

Stravinsky, being Russian, had no qualms about writing for the stage; but as a Russian with affinities toward the West, he knew he must become a Western master. He could not be a primitive like Moussorgsky, since no one can be a stay-at-home and a traveler. In his three most famous ballets, all composed before he was thirty, he had so firmly proved himself a master of impressionism that he scared the daylights out of Claude Debussy. That French road he never explored extensively again. For the rest of his life he yearned toward Italy, through the opera, both *seria* and *buffa*, and toward Germany, through oratorio and the symphony.

Opera he never quite mastered, terrified lest the human voice escape his strict control. But he did, in *Oedipus Rex*, produce an oratorio about a Greek tragedy that is closer to the original aims of opera than anything else written in the whole time of opera. Craft considers it Stravinsky's masterpiece, though others choose *Petrushka*, and there are supporters for *The Rite*, even for *Les Noces* and *L'Histoire d'un Soldat*. In any case, *Oedipus* is a mighty work composed at forty-five by the century's "most lucid creative genius," to quote Henri Sauguet. What it lacks of directness, as in *Petrushka*, it replaces with irony and with a stiff-necked, almost doctrinaire, absorption in the history of music. I doubt that its formal perfections completely save it. Anyway, *Petrushka* is no less perfect; and its form is less self-conscious, more organic.

Organic form is an invention of the German classic masters. Possibly derived as a concept from the German literary sentence, of which the outcome remains in suspense till the very end, when verbs appear, it was developed for fugal writing by Bach and Handel. In Haydn, Mozart, Beethoven, and Schubert it became sonata form, though not one of these knew the term. For them it grew like people or like trees, no two alike but all with a morphological identity.

On Schubert's death, through Brahms and Bruckner and Mahler, it ran to giganticism and finally fell apart. French efforts by César Franck and his pupils to reconstitute scholastically the species brought no life infusion. Vienna wisely neglected these and relaxed in happy decay, later to tie itself in tight chromatic knots.

The only composer after Schubert to achieve lifelike organic forms, self-sustained and self-contained, of which the inner complexities, as in Mozart, reflect no outward strain, was Debussy. In this sense, *La Mer* is a true and proper symphony, held together not by passion or by pathos or by storytelling, but simply by its own well-functioning muscular and nervous systems.

Organic form is the ideal Stravinsky has struggled toward in all three of his mature symphonies, including the choral one, and beginning even earlier, is my guess, in the Symphonies for Wind Instruments in Memory of Claude Debussy. The Symphony of Psalms is a lovely oratorio with a theme-song ending. The Symphony in Three Movements is a touching selection, or olio, of remembered patriotic and Russian feelings. Edward T. Cone's analysis of the Symphony in C, first published five years ago in *The Musical Quarterly*, reveals this extraordinarily interesting work (a "masterpiece," in Mr. Cone's opinion) to be a wrestling match with the ghost of Josef Haydn in which Stravinsky changes all the rules.

Formerly, one might have taken Stravinsky's past-oriented

sonatas, concertos, duos, and the like for witty evocations of some epoch or personality, a cubistico-impressionist reassembling of characteristic detail with everything delightfully in the wrong place. Both Collaer and Ansermet knew, all the same, that below the fashionably equalized surface tensions were diversified interval tensions and harmonic distortions, and rhythmic controls too, of the highest musical interest. In the Symphony in C, as in the Symphonies for Wind Instruments, these almost produce life. That they do not quite, perhaps, succeed in doing so is due in large part, I am sure, to the composer's unwillingness to sacrifice one jot or tittle of his modernity, of his unbreakable surface tensions and high-viscosity dissonance content. The rest of the failure (still relative, for it was a more-than-noble effort) is probably due to the fact that all other attempts to revive organic form, excepting only that of Debussy, have run afoul of the modernist esthetic. How Debussy succeeded no one knows; but I am sure that he did succeed and that Stravinsky has continued to try. Also that in the short works of his old age he seems to be maybe approaching success. That he has not quite produced the miracle is proved, I think, by the fact that believing him to have done so remains a sectarian view. Had he succeeded, the works in question would have become popular without delay, as his early impressionist ballets did.

He failed to master the opera, *if* he did, for a comparable reason. He could not let go of his dissonance controls and his rhythmic corsetings. Gravest of all, he tried to incorporate ballet stylizations. When he finally abandoned these, and also his high-dissonance saturation (though he kept the rhythmic corset), he produced *The Rake's Progress*, a popular piece that travels. It is not a success, however, in any meaning of the term that musical consensus would sustain. The poetry of W. H. Auden, though pretty, is too eighteenth-century-mannered for strong impact. The musical setting of this, for all its fragmentation into static syllables—a way with Stravinsky ever since his earliest Russian-language works—is surprisingly comprehensible verbally and melodically diverting. Even within its metrical straightjacket, put there to prevent interpretational freedom, it could still communicate the story, were not that story—an incredible mélange of *Little Red Riding Hood*, *Dr. Faustus*, and an inversion of *Oedipus Rex* in which the hero murders not his father but the woman in his motherly sweetheart and marries, in the form of a bearded lady, his father-image—were not all this, I fear, so utterly silly as to preclude any emotional involvement that the music might provoke.

Stravinsky has known these problems and faced them manfully. He has, in fact, talked and written about little else in the last forty years. They are the fulfillment theme of his dearest aspiration and the burden of his critical denouncements. He may win through yet on the symphonic level. Meanwhile, thanks to his insistent self-exposure in the matter—as well as of all his daily pains and vigorous quarrels, his joyous hospitality, and his happy home—his friends and readers would pardon an occasional failure. His glory as the last master of impressionism, could he be satisfied with that, would do ever so nicely for posterity. Moreover, no one is a universal genius. Neither Bach nor Beethoven, for example, was at home in opera; and Mozart, in either choral works or lieder, was nowhere so tightly packed with meanings as in his chamber works, his symphonies, his still unmatched, incomparable operas.

Could it be that the masters of modernism, in aiming to make everything as different as possible from what came before and at the same time aspiring to resemble preceding masters both in freedom of composition and in the organizing of that freedom into a humane discourse universally meaningful, have all stubbed their toe on the same rock? In other words, can a modernist become a classic? The answer is certainly yes. Because Debussy did it. And so did Stravinsky, barely thirty. After that? Well, he has worked and traveled and talked and traveled and worked. He has worked well and talked well and, as one says of wine, traveled well. He has perhaps not yet solved all of music's problems, but he has through his brilliantly arbitrary and essentially happy music and through his lively talk become an indispensable part of our lives.

What is it Macaulay said of Samuel Johnson? That "our intimate acquaintance with what he would himself have called the anfractuosities of his intellect and of his temper serves only to strengthen our conviction that he was both a great and a good man."

The New York Review of Books, December 15, 1966

The Genius Type

NOTES OF AN APPRENTICESHIP, by Pierre Boulez, collected and edited by Paule Thévenin. Translated from the French by Herbert Weinstock. 398 pp. Knopf, 1968.

PENSER LA MUSIQUE AUJOURD'HUI, by Pierre Boulez. 170 pp. Editions Gonthier (Paris), 1963.

SÉMANTIQUE MUSICALE: *Essai de psychophysiologie auditive*, by Alain Daniélou. 118 pp. Editions Hermann (Paris), 1967.

THAT THE CONCEPT represented in popular esthetics by *avant-garde* is applicable to music today, or in our century for that matter, would be hard to demonstrate. The idea that art has a continuous history which moves forward in both time and exploration is no less a trouble for dealing with the real artifacts, though a bit of it is required for explaining short-term developments like the classical symphony—Haydn through Schubert is only fifty years—or the growth of non-tonal music from its germinal state of 1899 in Arnold Schönberg's *Verklärte Nacht* to the completed formulation of the twelve-tone method around 1923.

The trouble with *avant-garde*, originally a term in military tactics, is that it assumes the adventures of individual and small-group experimenters to be justifiable only as they may open up a terrain through which some larger army will then be able to pass. But it fails to explain who constitutes this army and what is its objective, since a military advance, however massive, is not a migration. It cannot be the world public of concert subscribers and record buyers, since many important achievements, both unique and influential, arrive at such distribution far too meagerly and too late to serve culture consumption efficiently. The music of Erik Satie and of Schönberg's group are cases in point. It is all published now and largely recorded but still not much played; the armies of musical exploitation, industrial and academic, have not carried it along with them in their world conquest.

The idea that original work of this quality nourishes the younger composer is no less hard to justify. It becomes a part of his education, naturally; but his uses of it are inevitably dilutions, since innovations in art are generally brought to full term by their inventors (and a few close comrades) long before distribution gets hold of them. Actually, distributors tend to adopt only that which seems complete, presenting it as a novelty, which it may be for them, or as "experimental," which by this time it is not, save as a sales line. Short-term developments certainly represent a true evolution. But incorporating them through the professional conservatories into the living tradition of music is a hit-or-miss affair, any occupation rights in these centers of power being reserved for successful modernists, themselves mostly diluters of their sources. American universities have a way of taking up the more successful moderns, subjecting them to institutionally certified examination, and then sinking their remains in a mud puddle ironically called "mainstream."

Europeans tend to think of history less as a river and more as a library or museum, where any citizen can seek to be culturally entertained, informed, or inspired by high example. (The designers of women's fashions are forever adapting to their use models from the libraries of historic costume; working as fast as they do, they are less bound than prouder artists to the fads of merely yesterday.) Western Europe, in fact, tends to view itself altogether as a museum and the creators of its major artifacts as a special type of workman, the "genius." This kind of artist cannot be imagined without the background of a long cultural history and a pedagogical tradition based on the achievements of that history. The German composer, the French painter, the English poet—Beethoven, Schubert, Cézanne, Degas, Shakespeare, Keats—can often create remarkably with only minimal preparation, since the tradition of sound workmanship and a full history of it have been as close to his childhood as sports and cars and soda fountains to ours. In the American language genius merely means a high I.Q.; in Europe it means that you can speak for your time in language of precision and freedom.

Now the very idea that artists of genius have existed and still appear and that their works are entitled to preservation tends to destroy confidence in progress and also in history as a stream. Nevertheless, it is not possible today for the artist in any metropolitan center to conceive his talents as functioning otherwise than in some kind of continuous career. And it is equally impossible for him to carry on such a career without a belief in some version of his art's recent history. It may even become necessary for him to retell polemically that history, in order that it may appear to others a preparation for him. The European composer's view of himself as not only an heir of music's past— a member of the family—but also an end-of-the-line genius terminating an important short-term development has turned him into an inveterate explainer of music. No major composer of our century, I think, possibly excepting Ravel, has failed to write at least one book. The painters have written too, and brilliantly; but criticism, scholarship, and the price conspiracy have all denied them authority. The writings of Schönberg, Webern, Berg, Debussy, Satie, Stravinsky, Bartók, Milhaud, Messiaen, and Pierre Boulez are living witnesses to musical thought in our time; and they constitute, right along with historical studies, a valid part of music's verbal script.

Boulez, now forty-three, is unquestionably a genius figure and typically a French one, though the Germans captured him some fifteen years ago through a publication contract (with Universal of Vienna), later taking physical possession through a well-paid composer-in-residence post in Baden-Baden at the Southwest Radio. Meanwhile he had toured the world constantly as music director for the theatrical troupe of Madeleine Renaud and Jean-Louis Barrault. From 1954 they offered hospitality in the Théâtre Marigny, later in the Odéon-Théâtre de France, for his Concerts du Domaine Musical, the only musical series in the world, to my knowledge, which attracts a broad intellectual public of not only musicians but also painters, poets, scholars, and others professionally distinguished. Along with Boulez's own works these programs contain whatever is most far-out in Germany, France, Italy, and Belgium, and quite regularly homage-performances of works by the founding fathers of dodecaphony and occasionally of Bartók, Varèse, Stravinsky, Elliott Carter, Earle Brown, Iannis Xenakis.

Boulez himself is responsible for rehearsing these concerts and for most of the conducting. Passionate, painstaking, and aurally exact, as well as long used to exercising musical responsibility, Boulez is today a conductor of such remarkable powers that although he still works chiefly in the modern repertory, he has been led (or captured) to undertake lengthy tours in Germany,

England, and the United States, as well as gramophone recordings, that have in the last decade placed him among the world's most-in-demand directors and at the same time diminished radically his output as a composer.

That output, before 1960, was in spite of its textural complexity both large and, in the view of all who follow post–World War II music, of the very first importance. Actually today's modern movement, though it contains at least a dozen composers of high quality, is dominated by the three over-forty masters who genuinely excite the young—Pierre Boulez, Karlheinz Stockhausen, and John Cage. All three, moreover, have proved effective teachers of their own composing methods. And two of them, the Frenchman and the American, have long been engaged in criticism and musical polemics. As to whether the former's conducting career will remove him from critical writing, as it seems already to have done from composing, my guess is that it will, though the Boulez tongue, sharp and fearless, will not easily be kept quiet.

More than a decade back, Boulez's writing of music already showed a tendency to taper off, though without any remarked lowering of quality. On the contrary, his last contribution, of 1960, to a long-labored work in progress for divers instrumental and vocal combinations, entitled *Pli selon pli* (a "portrait of Mallarmé" in nine movements of which the last, "Tombeau," impressed me deeply) was notable for its technical maturity, sonorous vibrancy, and full freedom of expression. Should his composition cease altogether, nobody would be more regretful than I, because I like this music, find it full of energy, fine thought, and beauty to the ear. For anybody's orchestral conducting, on the other hand, I lack the ultimate in admiration. There has been so much of it around, all absolutely first class; our century has been rich that way, richer than in first-class composition. I would trade in a Toscanini any time for a Debussy.

Is Boulez another Debussy? He seems to have all the qualities. Excepting the one that only shows up in retrospect, the power of growth. Without that, or lacking confidence in that, he may be, as I have written elsewhere, another Marcel Duchamp. This case is rare, but not unknown in France. (Rimbaud is another.) The strategy is to create before thirty through talent, brains, determination, and hard labor a handful of unforgettable works, then to retire into private or public life and wait for an immortality which, when all can see production is complete, arrives on schedule. What does not arrive is technical freedom and the expressive maturing that enables a genius type to speak at forty still boldly but now with ease, with freedom, and with whatever of sheer humane grandeur may be in him.

The heartless mature artist does of course exist, even in the upper levels. Richard Wagner, though financially a crook and sentimentally a cheat, was not one. Just possibly Mallarmé was. Max Jacob said of him, "a great poet, were he not obscure and stilted" (*guindé* was the word). And Boulez, who loves the deeply calculated, expressed in a very early essay (from *Polyphonie*, 1948) his private hope for a music that would be "collective hysteria and spells, violently of the present time"; and he admits to "following the lead of Antonin Artaud" in this regard. At twenty-three (he was born in 1925) some can produce hysterical effects at will. But for professional use, dependably, a method is needed; and the methodical stimulation of collective hysterias (in class warfare, in politics, in religion) has been plenty frequent in our time. I doubt that Boulez today aspires in music just to be a Beatle. Actually Boulez today is as impressive in his musico-intellectual celebrity as the Beatles are in their more modest operation. How he got that way will no doubt be told us, in some version, by recorded music's press agents. What they will not tell us is what he thought about on the way up. And that is exactly the subject of his book from 1966 called *Relevés d'Apprenti*, translated as *Notes of an Apprenticeship*.

This is an anthology of reflections on music published between 1948 and 1962, written, as he speaks, with brio and with a vast repertory of allusions. In French it is not easy to make out, because the vocabulary is overreplete with technical terms from mathematics (which Boulez seems fairly familiar with), from philosophy (less confidently used), from musical analysis (where he is both precise and inventive), and from the slang of intellectual Paris (also the source of his syntax when in polemical vein). The translation, though obviously made with care, is in the long run no less labored than the composer's own prose and often just as hard to follow.

The pieces of high technical interest are among the earliest, from the years of his twenties, when he was building a method and formulating principles. Here we find electronic music and its possibilities (which he does not overestimate) studied from experience and thoughtfully, its Paris Establishment radically debunked. We also find dodecaphonic theory taken apart by an expert. He recognizes that there is nothing about the tempered scale of twelve equal semitones (a tuning adopted by J. S. Bach to facilitate modulation) that renders it indispensable to modern music. True intervals, of which there are at least fifty-two, could as well be employed. Audible octave-spacings are limited to seven. Loudness-levels, though theoretically infinite in number, are surely not practical to distinguish by ear beyond five or six. The shapes of a tone's duration—wedge, pear, teardrop, and their mirror images, including the double wedge—are not many more. And the extent of durations—the raw material of rhythm—is not governed, save for ease of performance, by any numerical necessity at all, though lengths of time, unlike music's other variables, are measurable, hence describable, by numbers. Timbres also are practically infinite; and though they are possible to serialize, few composers have bothered to try.

With all this variability inherent in music's materials, and the number twelve not essential to any of them, it is not surprising that Boulez considers the twelve-tone music of Schönberg to be "a failure," though the idea of serialism itself a boon to music. His admiration for Anton Webern's music, however, is not diminished by the dodecaphonic nonsense; rather he considers it saved by the tension of its intervalic layout and by its creation of forms out of musical materials rather than out of pathos from Old Vienna, which Berg and Schönberg were likely to use. Boulez, like Cage, for all his disillusioned view of dodecaphony, remains convinced that in serialization of some kind lies music's only hope. I must say that virtually all the composers who deny a hierarchy among intervals come sooner or later to substitute for this hierarchy an order of tones arbitrarily chosen for each work and called a row, or series.

At one time or another everything that regards today's music is discussed, always with a furious intensity and generally with penetration. For hazard and its planned use he has only disdain, unless it comes about that his own cerebration (should we read the unconscious?) leads a writer toward unexpected revelation, toward organic form, or toward some vastly valid experiment. In favor of all these he quotes from Mallarmé, "Every thought occasions a cast of the dice."

How to choose a row that will lend itself to development, expression, and intrinsic musical interest is treated in another book by Boulez, published in Germany, 1963, and entitled *Penser la Musique Aujourd'hui*. Here his love of Webern and his own penchant for arithmetic lead him into much eloquence about the hidden symmetries available through subdivisions of the number twelve. Also into a lumpiness of style ever so hard to keep the mind on.

From recent years there are in the present book ten articles written for the *Encyclopédie Fasquelle*. Here the tone is not polemical at all but informative, and the judgments are fair and generally warm, though without conventional compliments. They are entitled "Chord," "Chromaticism," "Concrete (Music)," "Counterpoint, Series," "Béla Bartók," "Alban Berg," "Claude Debussy," "Arnold Schoenberg," and "Anton Webern," with an extra one on Schönberg's piano works, written for the jacket of a complete recording of these by Paul Jacobs. The article on Debussy is considered by Jean Roy in *Musique Française* (of the *Présences Contemporaines* series), Debresse, 1962, to be "the most penetrating and complete study [of this composer] ever published." In passing, I should like also to recommend from the same brilliant but erratic musical encyclopedia the understanding article on Richard Wagner by a Boulez pupil, Gilbert Amy.

Here, and indeed throughout the book, the Boulez skill in musical analysis and his preoccupation with rhythmic discovery dominate the investigations. He cannot forgive Schönberg and his group for their rhythmic conventionality, as he cannot forgive Stravinsky, who was rhythmically radical, for not really knowing how to write music. He recognizes that a certain impotence in that regard led toward rhythmic construction of the most original kind. All the same, Stravinsky's lack of aptitude for writing in the Western conventional way, with Conservatory solutions always at hand to use or to avoid, he finds deplorable and probably responsible for the neoclassic "decline" into which Stravinsky fell after World War I, when he could not carry forward his rhythmic researches because of poor "writing." By "writing" (*écriture*) Boulez means harmony and counterpoint and the procedures of development (not orchestration, of course, at which Stravinsky was a master).

Beyond the intercourse with a major musical mind which this

book offers as a delight throughout, for all the linguistic jambs, its major contribution to musical understanding is a long and detailed examination of Stravinsky's *Rite of Spring*. Every piece of this is given some attention and the two most original ones (hence most resistant to analysis), the Prelude and the Sacrificial Dance, receive depth study such as is rare today and has been since Donald Tovey's now fifty-year-old writings on Beethoven. The fact is mentioned that much of this material, especially the rhythmic analysis of the Sacrificial Dance, is the work of Olivier Messiaen. So be it. The full treatment is there, replete with musical quotations; and its availability now in English makes it an item for every college and music library to own.

The Sacrificial Dance, as examined in 1951, turns out to be exactly the sort of calculation toward collective hysteria that Boulez had declared his faith in three years earlier. The piece represents, as we know, a dancing to death by exhaustion on the part of a young girl chosen for sacrifice. And the collective hysteria that sustains her in the ordeal is not at all a product of rhythmic monotony, so commonly the provoker of group excitement. The rhythms that accompany this event are designed rather to stimulate hysteria in the theater, in the hope that this may induce an illusion of meaning shared, of presence at an ancient savage rite. These rhythms induce hysteria, if they do, by simulating it. The simulation consists of insistence on asymmetrical thumps, tonally and percussively huge. Their hugeness is standard orchestration. Their asymmetry, though novel, is also achieved by method, by a rhythmic calculation seemingly so secret that no amount of rehearsing will reveal to the merely spontaneous ear an identifiable pulse. (Robert Craft, who has heard and conducted the work possibly too often, now finds that "in the last section of the Sacrificial Dance, . . . where the basic meter is three and twos are the exceptions, the effect can sound precariously like a waltz with jumped record grooves.")

What is revealed by Messiaen and Boulez, as rhythmic analysts, is the fact that the continuity is constructed out of small rhythmic cells arranged with a certain symmetry, as structures always are, but with non-symmetrical interruptions by other cells. All are composed of twos and threes, naturally, since the mind breaks down all number groupings into these (plus fast fives, just occasionally possible to hear as units). The whole is a hidden pattern not altogether different from those found in folklore by linguistic students and anthropologists. Not that the Dance was composed by instinct only, though Stravinsky never confessed that it was not; but its asymmetry is so strongly organized that the exposure of a plan behind it is almost as exciting a discovery as that of the symmetries governing marriage customs among Australian aborigines.

Boulez indeed reminds one of the French anthropologist Claude Lévi-Strauss. His language is confusing, but his mind is not confused; it is merely active. Active and very powerful. So powerful that no music resists for long its ability to dismantle a whole engine and put it together again. It is moreover a loyal mind that puts things back right. Darius Milhaud said of him, "He despises my music, but conducts it better than anyone." As an analyst, a critic, and an organizer of musical thought I do not know his equal. As a composer I know none other half so interesting. The personality—in the best French way both tough and tender—has been proved in every musical circumstance and every careerlike stance irresistible. Its toughness is half the charm, its tenderness the source of critical acumen and, in his music, an emotional dynamo wired for power transmission and shielded by mental rigor.

That a European genius type of such clear-to-all authority should give up creative work is unbelievable. That he should be tempted by the Klingsor gardens of orchestral celebrity is not strange at all; but if his heart is pure, as it heretofore has seemed to be, he will possibly make his way through to the Grail. That would mean complete artistic fulfillment—which can only be what he aims toward, and what we hope for. There is precedent for a major artist's resting in his forties. Richard Wagner, Arnold Schönberg, and William Blake are noted examples, seven years the usual period for lying fallow. But Boulez has already been silent, as composer and as critic, for most of eight years; and his orchestral adventure is still on an up-curve. No signs of let-up there. On the contrary, I note a temptation even more dangerous than mere conducting. So far, Boulez has made his career almost entirely out of modern music, a phenomenon not witnessed in big-time since Mary Garden. And that way, for a conductor, lies missionary madness.

So I am worried. Strauss, Mahler, and Leonard Bernstein are another case. They had always conducted; they needed money; and they wrote music like windmills, at the turn of a leaf. Wagner and Schönberg are better parallels. And they finally came through; that's the best I can say.

Meanwhile, another pungent book has come from France, this one directly—*Sémantique Musicale* by Alain Daniélou (Paris, Hermann, 1967). Subtitled *Essai de Psychophysiologie Auditive*, it examines the musical experience through communications theory, the physical structure of the ear, and the known, or supposed, facts about auditory memory. In 118 pages, including diagrams, it opens a major matter and offers believable information about it.

Ernest Ansermet's *Les Fondements de la Musique dans la Conscience Humaine* (Neuchâtel, Editions de la Baconnière, 1961) purports to do the same (without information theory but with lots of mathematics and phenomenology) in two large volumes. I shall not discuss the latter work since brevity would be unfair. I merely mention it as another example of Europe's interest in certain musical facts-of-life which before long we shall all be turning our minds to. Musicology is all right, when useful. Analysis and professional judgments are cardinal to the act. But polemical esthetics, commonly referred to as "criticism," are for any purpose but salesmanship, so far as I am concerned, pure lotus-eating. As practiced by Boulez in his twenties, however, they seem a mere incrustation to analysis and judgment and, before the authority with which he already exercised those prerogatives, appear not deeply ingrained, but more like colored lichens on a rock.

P.S. Regarding the difficulties of translation presented by the Boulez supercolloquial style, let me cite a passage from the chapter "Alea," first published in 1957 in the *Nouvelle Revue Française*. Comparing a facile use of chance (the "aleatory") in music-making to the "never very miraculous" dreams described by hashish fanciers, the French text reads: "*Paix à l'âme de ces angéliques! on est assuré qu'ils n'iront point dérober quelque fulguration, puisqu'ils n'en ont que faire.*"

Herbert Weinstock renders this: "Peace to the souls of these angelic beings! One is sure they will never steal any lightning, that not being what they are up to."

In *Perspectives of New Music*, Fall-Winter 1964, this same passage translated by David Noakes and Paul Jacobs reads: "Peace to these angelic creatures; we can be sure they run absolutely no risk of stealing any thunder, since they wouldn't know what to do with it."

Now using *thunder* instead of *lightning* for *fulguration* is not important. Less exact literally, it is perhaps more apt as image. What arrests me about the sentence is its ending. And here I find the Noakes and Jacobs rendering superior.

I have not counted up or noted down all the suspect items, but here are just a few examples of how tricky this kind of French can be.

[*Debussy*] *est un fameux, un excellent ancêtre.* Now the basic meaning here of *fameux* must be *whopping*, or something like that, for that is the common slangy use of it and far more emphatic in this connection than the literal, the one-dimensional *famous*, used on page 34.

The American localism *tacky* is used on page 331 for *pâteuse* to characterize the parody music in Berg's *Lulu*. *Thick* or *muddy* would have been closer to the French and more descriptive.

Again of Berg, his propensity for allusions to other music is several times referred to as *citation*, though this word in French means less often that than simply *quotation*.

The year of the *Wozzeck* première is given on page 315 as 1923 (impossible since it was the result of fragments having been heard by Erich Kleiber at a concert conducted by Hermann Scherchen in 1924). The French text gives 1925, which is correct.

For using the word *conduct* to signify the medieval form *conductus* I find among my household dictionaries no precedent. The French word is *conduit*, a past participle like the Latin word, which is standard usage among English-language musicologists. If *conduct* had not been paired on page 294 with *motet*, and both words italicized, I doubt if I should have been able to identify it.

Of Schönberg, "*la suite de ses créations qui commence avec la Sérénade*," would have been perfectly clear as "the works that followed the Serenade," or better, "the series of works that began with the Serenade." Its rendering on page 271 as "the sequences of Schoenberg's creations that began with the Serenade" is confusing, since sequences, in the plural, are a compositional device and one practically never employed by Schönberg.

Just flyspecks, one may say, on a fine book; and I agree. But there are far too many for easy reading. Time after time one is obliged to consult the original, and that is not easy to read either. But it means what the author wishes it to mean; and with such tightly reasoned trains of thought, his language could not have been simplified much farther. Again a reminder of Lévi-Strauss and of all that exuberant intellection spouting nowadays in France like springs and geysers.

The New York Review of Books, September 26, 1968

Berlioz, Boulez, and Piaf

THE MEMOIRS OF HECTOR BERLIOZ, MEMBER OF THE FRENCH INSTITUTE: *Including His Travels in Italy, Germany, Russia, and England, 1803–1865,* edited and translated from the French by David Cairns. 636 pp. Knopf, 1969.

BAUDELAIRE–BERLIOZ, edited by Miron Grindea. *ADAM International Review,* Nos. 331–333. 124 pp. Curwen Press (London)/ University of Rochester, 1969.

BERLIOZ AND THE ROMANTIC CENTURY, by Jacques Barzun. Third Edition. Volume 1: 573 pp.; Volume 2: 515 pp. Columbia University Press, 1969.

BERLIOZ AND THE ROMANTIC IMAGINATION, edited by Elizabeth Davison. Catalogue of an exhibition organized by the Arts Council and the Victoria and Albert Museum on behalf of the Berlioz Centenary Committee in cooperation with the French government, on view from October 17 to December 14, 1969. 146 pp. The Arts Council (London), 1969.

PIAF, by Simone Berteaut. 459 pp. Editions Robert Laffont (Paris), 1969.

THE MEMOIRS OF HECTOR BERLIOZ, in a new translation by David Cairns, I had got involved with as a book for possible review. Good reading it was too, all about music in Romantic times, written by a man who could really write and who was also a real composer. Nothing phony there, no self-deception, no bluffing, no self-pity, just the tale of a French musician who was successful in England, Austria, Hungary, Germany, Russia—everywhere but in France. Invited everywhere to remain, also to visit the United States for a very large fee, he could not keep away from Paris long, where the cabals, intrigues, and dirty deals (in all of which he knew exactly who his enemy was and why and usually said so) gave to his career the aspect of an intermittent volcano as dangerous to the establishment as only a clear mind with a sharp tongue can be.

Nevertheless, in spite of all the hindrances, his career grew, his works got written, performed (most of them), and even published, he became a member of the Institute, he received important commissions. It may have been the sparks and rosy glow sent up by his local explosions which brought invitations from afar. But all the same, honors received, return visits ever more profitable, were not merely the benefits of celebrity. There were solid musical satisfactions too, due to the superior musical facilities available in Germany, in Austria, in England, and even in Russia—the competent players, the good halls, the musically educated listeners, the warmth and generosity of foreign colleagues. And all these availabilities seem to have been the direct result (or so Berlioz believed) of, in England, managerial monopoly, elsewhere of absolute monarchy, as a circumstance favorable to art.

His inability to speak well or to write a letter in any language other than his own may also have been a help on tour since nowhere could he provoke the quarrels, take the liberties, indulge the ironies that his fatal facility with French and his experience as a journalist rendered so tempting to him on home ground.

The picture of Paris between 1821, when young Hector (from near Grenoble) arrived at eighteen to study medicine, and 1869, when he died there, is highly detailed in Jacques Barzun's two-volume biography *Berlioz and the Romantic Century*, originally published in 1950, now out in a new edition. And a quarterly "international review" called *ADAM* (anagram for Arts, Drama, Architecture, Music), published simultaneously in London and at the University of Rochester, New York, devotes a sizable issue (Nos. 331–333) to making a duet out of Berlioz and Baudelaire, stormy petrels both.

Particularly charming among the publications celebrating the centenary of Berlioz's death is the catalogue of a show entitled *Berlioz and the Romantic Imagination*, which took place from October 17 to December 14 in London at the Victoria and Albert

Museum. Here some 419 items are listed, almost a third of them reproduced—letters, documents, musical manuscripts, photographs, drawings, engravings, and paintings of all sizes from the miniature up to very large ones by Delacroix, Ingres, Turner, and many more. There was music by Berlioz discreetly audible in the rooms, and a miniature theater where one could gaze down as from a dark top gallery to a lighted stage whereon a tiny photograph of Harriet Smithson (whom Berlioz both loved and unsuccessfully married) seemed to be heard reading the lines of Ophelia.

The Paris Opéra, we read, has revived (to generally unfavorable opinion) Berlioz's five-hour opera *The Trojans* (on his own poem, after Virgil); but Covent Garden had got ahead of Paris by giving this work (complete for the first time ever) in 1967. The English press has been dithyrambic in the matter, though whether because of the work itself, which is not only long but theatrically static, or because of Colin Davis (England's newest good conductor, heard last session at the Metropolitan in Berg's *Wozzeck* and Britten's *Peter Grimes*) I cannot testify.

I have heard cut versions of *The Trojans* several times, first in Paris, 1921, most recently in Los Angeles last year. It has always struck me as being full of remarkable music, almost none of which I recognize. There must be a great deal of variety in the degree to which different conductors infuse it with animation. For animation, save in certain spots like the Storm and Royal Hunt, and the military march to which Dido mounts her funeral pyre, is not built into the work, though the music is often busy.

That busy-ness is special to Berlioz. In Mozart, Weber, Rossini, Verdi, the florid writers in general, when the vocal parts are active the accompaniment is not. In Wagner the orchestra tends generally to be very active indeed against a vocal line moving only by long notes, a most effective contrast. In *The Trojans* vocal and orchestral activity seem to run parallel, producing no contrast at all, whether there are lots of notes on stage and in the pit or whether the animation drops out of both, leaving us with a slow solo and a virtually motionless accompaniment.

An alternation of static pictures and oratoriolike choruses with numbers that run like a house afire is characteristic of Berlioz. The ball scene and the "Queen Mab" scherzo from

Romeo and Juliet, the Rakoczy March and "Song of the Flea" from *The Damnation of Faust* are famous examples of the latter. The static first three movements of the *Symphonie Fantastique*, followed by the fiery last two, exemplify the jerky pacing that permeates this composer's work. The result is, for all his music's high originality and much grandeur in the literary content, a certain embarrassment whenever the stage is evoked. I have not heard the operas *Benvenuto Cellini* or *Beatrice and Benedict*, but I tend to view *The Trojans* as less an opera than an oratorio *about* an opera.

Certainly this composer's dramatic works have over a century and more rebuffed the best intentions of producers and conductors, whereas his concert music and certain excerpts from his stage works, if presented in concert form, have long proved rewarding to both performers and public. The truth is, I think, that while the Berlioz music, like Beethoven's, is full of an abstract "drama," as his life and emotions seem also constantly "theatrical," he did not really possess, any more than Beethoven did, the stage sense. Only in the concert forms, the closed ones, did his highest powers come to life.

Accounts of Berlioz can be a delight, even though a good part of that pleasure comes from the picture of Romantic times that goes along with the account. He himself, though artists' portraits and eyewitness stories are numerous, his life and career documented almost to a fault, remains largely unknowable beneath all the detail. He tells you about his music, his family affections, his passions, his finances; but the why of them all is slippery. And the same is true of his esthetics and his professional attitudes. Nothing leads to anything else; the violent intentions are never carried out; the passions are never assuaged; the lonesomeness is never relieved. His life and art do not lead parallel courses; how could they, being each so jumpy? For a man of his brains, breeding, gifts, and positive genius to have failed so signally at projecting a clear image of himself, either as a private man or as a public figure, has left posterity with plenty of anecdotes and lots of quite wonderful music, but little human reality to remember, as with Beethoven or with Wagner, or as with Mozart and Schubert, to love.

His statue, meditating, is in the small Paris square named Vintimille, near which he lived. Max Jacob used to tell a story that illustrates his way of appearing to be always present and yet not quite. It seems that in his later years he used to come there after lunch and meditate. And two music students would come there too, to watch the great man meditate. Then on the day when they had read in the paper of his death, they said, "Let's go just the same and pay our respects." So they did. And the man they had watched so lovingly for so long was seated there, meditating, just as before.

After all the exasperations and delights of dealing with Berlioz, it was a pleasure to move from the V. and A. over to Covent Garden, where Pierre Boulez was conducting Debussy's *Pelléas et Mélisande*. Here is a work all vaporous, if you like, but nowhere presenting the esthetic obscurities of Berlioz and at no point refusing itself the stage.

For the record, let us set down that the orchestral reading was of a perfection previously not encountered by this reporter, who has heard virtually all of them, including that of André Messager, its first conductor. The textures were everywhere transparent but never misty, the emotions frank, warm, and never dissociated from the stage. It is the special quality of this work that though the orchestra comments constantly, and even individual instruments comment on the progress of the play, the pit never becomes a Greek chorus speaking for the author; it remains an extension of the stage. And in scenes of conflict it speaks for the stronger character, for him who dominates. Even the interludes, added originally to fill up time during changes of set but preserved nowadays for their intrinsic beauty, are extensions of the drama. They are not scenery, not warning of events to come, but quite simply the way some character, the one we are following at that instant, feels.

The composer has in fact so completely identified himself from moment to moment with his characters' sensibilities that he has largely omitted, save possibly in the death scene, any structuring of the music that might support the dramatic structure. Heard in concert the work has continuity but little shape; and even its continuity is constantly broken into by stage emotions so intense that the singers are likely to be left suddenly all alone with the words, unaccompanied. They are alone with the play too, for at all those moments when the orchestra seems to hesitate, the dramatic line, the impetus, is largely a responsibility of the stage.

It is this particular relation between stage and pit that makes *Pelléas* unique. Every other opera in the world, even those with spoken dialogue, is carried forward by musical forms. In classical opera these forms are arranged, in spite of their individual ABA and similar layouts, to move forward as expression, like a cycle of songs. Since Wagner, each act or scene has tended to be an open-ended musical form thematically inspired by the dramatic action but controlled by musico-emotional timings. Even the series of concert forms—sonata, variation, and the like—that underpins Berg's *Wozzeck*, in the end adds up to an open form governed by the needs of expression; and for a certainty that expression is paced at a musical rate of audience absorption rather than at a verbal one, as in a play, or at a visual one, as in a film.

Now *Pelléas* is really an opera, or *drame lyrique*, as Debussy called it. It is a play recounted through music, not a language-play with incidental music. And the timing of that music is under the control of one musician, the conductor. Nevertheless, the music's expressivity does move back and forth from the pit to the stage. And every time the orchestra, by pausing, hands this expressivity to the stage, it becomes necessary that the singers sing their words so urgently and move in a pantomime so convincing that the lack of an instrumental continuity is never felt.

That is why the work requires in its major role not just any singer, but a singing actress. And this leader of the team, whose presence must be felt always, even when she is absent, needs to be surrounded, as in chamber music, by cooperative soloists. The stage director, moreover, should guide them all toward creating a pantomime as tense as the musical score that describes it. Debussy himself, in a 1908 testimonial to the services rendered by Mary Garden in the 1902 premiere, remarked that the role of Mélisande had from the beginning seemed to him virtually impossible to project ("*difficilement réalizable*") on account of all those "long silences that one false move can render meaningless."

Mélisande, so eager to be loved but so skittish about being touched, is rarely shown in the opera as in contact with even her husband. When he is ill she gives him her hand for a moment, only to have him discover she has lost her wedding ring. Later he takes hold of her twice, once by the hair in a jealous fury, again to plead on her deathbed for some fact that might justify his jealousy. Only with Pelléas is she not averse to the laying on of hands; and when standing just below the tower window he winds her hair about him in orgasmic ecstasy, she is probably, though no party to it, aware of what has happened. In any case, from that time on, a magnetic field of force moves them closer and closer till love is declared and the harsh castle gates, by locking them out, precipitate embrace.

The tension of animal magnetism is the basic drama of this opera, its tragedy, and in the long run its theme. For Mélisande, beneath her reticence, is a flame that consumes. That is why she is a star in the play and must be played by a star. The others resist destruction; she resists nothing but physical contact, a resistance that makes it in each case inevitable. And in the emergency that she has brought about, in every emergency indeed, even dying, she lies. She wants to be loved. She will do anything to be loved. Except tell the truth. Or show gratitude. Utterly self-centered and reckless, she wreaks havoc without thinking or recognizing. And the play of her unbridled libido against the fixities of a well-bred French family (Merovingian minor royalty) reveals character in each instance. It turns Golaud, her husband, repeatedly to violence. It lights the fires of passion in his half-brother Pelléas, a young man easily enough inflamed. It brings forward the essential indifference and all the sententiousness of Arkel, their grandfather (according to Pierre Boulez, "Pelléas grown old"). The other two, Geneviève their mother and Golaud's young son Yniold, horrified by all the violence unleashed, can only view any of it as disaster.

There is somewhere a theory that Mélisande is really Bluebeard's eighth wife. This might explain her having brought along in her flight the golden crown which she has just dropped into a forest pool when Golaud discovers her; "*C'est la couronne qu'il m'a donnée*," she explains. She has clearly been through a traumatic experience which has left her terrified of bodily contact. Whether it is the experience that has turned her psychopathic or whether she just grew up that way we shall never know. But dangerous she is for sure, behind that sweet façade;

and never are we to divine what she thinks about. All we shall know are her refusals and her compulsions.

And never does Debussy's orchestra give us her feelings. Her leitmotif is a shifty one, harmonically and rhythmically undecided. The others are all straightforward; and through them the play of passions, fears, joys, and resignations can be expressed. Though her physical presence is a powerful one, we are never allowed to view the story from her point of feeling; she seems to have none. She is the source of everyone else's feelings and consequently of their actions. But she herself sits at the dead center of a storm; everything takes place around her, nothing inside her. Nothing, at least, that we can see or hear.

Now the Covent Garden production, for all its orchestral warmth and musical perfection, gave us little of the Maeterlinck play as I have described it and as Debussy set it into music. It is not that the singers did not work well; they did everything the conductor had asked of them in the coaching rehearsals. They even sang a highly reputable French, though for not one of them was the language native. It was rather that the stage director, Vaclav Kaslik, did not seem to feel the same tensions in the play that Debussy did. His characters moved around the stage like items out of a libretto, who did not need to worry because the music would take care of everything. The fact remains, however, that it does not. There are spots in that opera, many of them, where the poetry is so heightened by a vocal line half sung, half spoken but yet on pitch, and the accompaniment so thinly washed in, or so absent, that only an acting line intensely controlled by a choreographic line naturalistically conceived (and concealed, as was the custom of its time) can sustain the spectacle at the level of its orchestral presence.

These excellent singers will no doubt be able in the recording just now completed to give more character and more conviction by "acting with the voice," as they had done occasionally in the seated piano rehearsals. But publicly both stage and staging seem to have got in their way, and certainly some bulky costumes did. The set, a unit structure with changing backdrops and forestage elements added, was the work of Josef Svoboda, the costumes by the third member of a team from Czechoslovakia, Jan Skalicky. Among all these elements I found only the scenery helpful, and that I fancy Debussy might have approved,

for its use in outdoor scenes of hanging gauze strips to produce different kinds of hazy weather and different times of day.
Quite effectively and often charmingly did these strips, aided
by shifting lights and heights and by the imaginative backdrops,
produce the dank tarn, house of Usher atmosphere that we
know to have been desired by both Maeterlinck and Debussy.
The only scenery that squarely failed was that of the final bed-
chamber, which resists an open stage, since the high small window and shaft of sunlight required by the text, not to speak of
Mélisande's hushed fading away and tranquil death, virtually
demand enclosure.

Unit sets, whether firmly constructed or assembled out of
modules that get regrouped, are ever a disappointment for portraying the difference between indoors and outdoors. And there
is nearly always one scene at least in which they fail entirely.
The elements that are constantly being reassembled, moreover,
are rarely of sufficient intrinsic beauty to permit being looked
at for a whole evening. Their lack of visual novelty, by halfway
through the show, becomes oppressive. The story advances and
the music moves forward, while the scenery just plays a game.
I sometimes think the unchanging set, whether built for the
purpose or independently monumental like the steps of a library, injures a dramatic spectacle less than the most ingenious
selection of movable elements. These can save time at scene
changes, though there are other ways of doing that; but nothing can make them suit all parts of a play equally, and nothing
can relieve their aggravating monotony.

The conductor, who had hoped for Wieland Wagner to direct
the stage, eventually chose the Czech team, though there is
little precedent for a well-organized and well-organizing Eastern European mind effectively coming to grips with this seemingly unorganized and ever-so-French triumph of sensibility
over organization. For *Pelléas* is not only unique as an opera
(recitative throughout and a highly emotional, willfully form-
less accompaniment); it is also an anti-opera. It avoids all the
devices that make Verdi and Wagner, Mozart and Monteverdi
easy to listen to—sustained song, rhythmic patterns, structural
harmony, orchestral emphases, solos, ensemble pieces, built-in
climaxes.

Even its naturalistic vocal line is not always so natural

regarding the words as one might think. Much of it is closer to psalmody than to speech. Then at times it actually does imitate speech, using small intervals only, as Jean-Jacques Rousseau had recommended for French recitative. At others it employs, as Paul Landormy describes, an evocation of language such as we hear it silently inside ourselves—"a manner of speech quite strange," he says, "but striking, and very hard for singers to achieve, tending as they do to stiffen the vocal line through an over-strict observance of note-values, instead of making it supple, as they should."

I am afraid the Covent Garden cast, also chosen by Boulez and carefully prepared, sinned in exactly this respect. Being foreigners to French and with little residence in France to loosen their tongues, they gave us the written notes as exactly as any English horn or flute player in the orchestra. They performed indeed as if they were a part of the orchestra rather than as real persons who might be the subjects of the orchestra's comment. Except for the small boy singing Yniold, who really got into his role—the French of it, the music of it, the impersonation of fear—the stage artists in large part simply stood or moved without much meaning, while following in excellent voice the conductor's beat.

I am also afraid that Pierre Boulez, like Toscanini before him, does not really enjoy accompanying star performers. He has chosen before—in the Paris *Wozzeck* of several years back—a cast of just-under-first-class singing actors, exactly as Toscanini was wont to do for his NBC broadcasts. And they have seemed in both cases a bit awed by the honor. Also thoroughly preoccupied with making no mistakes. His casting of the singing voice has long seemed to me less a loving one than that of an executive seeking a sensible secretary. He can love words, I know, especially those of Mallarmé, which have inspired him, and of René Char, whom he has so often set. But the sound of the singing voice, the personality of a singer acting out his role, seem rather to bring out the carefulness in him than to invite the incandescence of joint effort. This he achieves with the orchestra, and it could not be more ravishing to hear. But I do miss, as I so often did with Toscanini, a catering to the stage, a feeling that singing and the acting out of a role could be allowed to give us pleasure without our being held to a one hundred percent concentration on him and his sacred instrumental score.

After all, singers are not oboes or horns. They are voices with personalities, and the opera is a musical exercise that cannot long exist without exploiting voices and personalities. *Pelléas et Mélisande*, in particular, is an opera, or *drame lyrique*, that depends far more than many another on an equality between pit and stage. An intimacy of musical with dramatic communication is its essence, its need, its sine qua non. It is the hardest opera in the world to perform satisfactorily, because it is the model, the dream that all French opera since Gluck has sought to realize, an exact balance of music with dramatic poetry. And wherever this opera has approached equilibration, its needle of balance has become so quivery that many like Toscanini, like Boulez, have seemed to hope that a wholly disciplined rendering would dissolve that nervousness. Which it does, of course, but at the cost of radically unbalancing the spectacle and forcing it to depend not on the vibrancy and miracle of a poetry-and-music duet, as in the best lieder, but on a musical run-through controlled by one man.

And so in Boulez's *Pelléas* we have no opera at all but rather the rehearsal of one, a concert in costume destined to end up as a recording. I will spare its excellent singers publication of their names in this connection. On discs they will surely make a better effect. There a complete subjection to the musical score may seem more suitable than in an opera house. I am sorry about the Covent Garden production, musically so sumptuous, orchestrally so stunningly alive, stage-wise so casual in spite of pretty sets. Musical accuracy is of course always welcome, and far from universal. But for the rest of opera, I have never been convinced that Boulez had much liking for fine voices or for striking personalities. And as for visual investitures, very few musicians have taste in that domain.

From Berlioz, with his perpetual frustrations, amorous and professional, by way of Mélisande, so timid and so destructive, to the life of Edith Piaf may seem a far jump. And yet in London I made it. Somehow, just that far enough from France but not too far, these three sad stories became suddenly for me illustrative of the French tragic sense of life, with all the rigidity, the sweetness, and the violence that things French can have. For those who knew her living, the memories of her joviality and her wild intransigence have scarcely at all begun to fade; and for those who knew her only through her art the discs are there preserving that enormous voice and all that vast authority of singing style.

And now there is a book called *Piaf*, by her half-sister Simone Berteaut, long-time confidante and beloved chum. This runs in large octavo to 459 pages of French. The French of a child who grew up without schooling, French of the streets, of the *parigots*, of Ménilmontant the toughest neighborhood, the most picturesque language in the world. If only for its imaginative vocabulary the book is a gem. (By comparison Raymond Queneau's *Zazie dans le Métro* reads like the scherzo of a professional grammarian, which it is.) And the life of "La Môme Piaf" therein told with such impeccable compassion and high spirits is so grand, so moving, and so tragic that one is inclined to salute the volume as a great book. Certainly, for anyone who can mobilize an understanding of its dialect, it is great reading.

Born of a mediocre pop-style singer and a street acrobat, Edith Gassion was passing the hat for papa at six and singing alone for pennies by nine. Meantime, during papa's military service, she had been brought up quite nicely in a whorehouse, and by an operation cured of blindness. The name Edith had been given her at birth in 1915 because of the heroic English spy Edith Cavell, whom the Germans had just shot in Belgium. "Piaf," which means sparrow, came with her first indoor singing engagement, along with its preface La Môme, or Babychild, since she was right off the streets and so tiny. After the murder of her boss had closed the nightclub, "La Môme Piaf" was abandoned for "Edith" as she fought her way back to jobs and to public favor. The recounting of all this and of her eventual worldwide fame, her primacy indeed, in that most demanding of musical genres, the French *chanson*, is the framework of the narrative, studded too with the listing of her chief lovers, who included the heavyweight champion Marcel Cerdan, of her chief pupils (Yves Montand and Charles Aznavour among many), and of her faithful friends (especially Marlene Dietrich and Jean Cocteau).

As a star she bought fur coats, dresses, and jewelry, lived in a fine house, gave costly presents. And yet she remained a slave to the slum ways of her childhood. She believed bathing danger-ous to the health, drinking-water to be full of microbes, and alcohol (along with wine, of course) beneficial for preventing "worms." During the later years of her life she became addicted to morphine. And she was constantly being broken up in car crashes. With all these disasters knocking her out, she constantly sang in public, constantly took on new lovers. She even married one of them, a Greek hairdresser, leaving him at her death 45 million francs of debt ($90,000), which he paid off. To a doctor who warned her late in 1960 not to fulfill an engagement at the Olympia with, "Madame, to go out on a stage now would be suicide," she answered, "I like that suicide. It's my kind."

And she did appear, stumbling, weaving about, screaming her songs, including a brand-new one, *Les Blouses Blanches*, about madness, at the end of which she cried out triumphantly to her almost-not-breathing public, "I am not mad." And after singing every night for something like fifteen weeks, she went on tour for six, finishing up in a hospital, as she so often did toward the end.

Between 1951 and 1963 her sister lists:

4 motor accidents
1 attempt to kill herself
4 morphine cures
1 drug-induced sleeping cure
3 comas from liver disease
1 attack of raving madness
2 of delirium tremens
7 operations
2 bronchial pneumonias
and a pulmonary oedema.

In addition she had an inoperable cancer.

When she died in early October of 1963, on the same day as her good friend Jean Cocteau, who died preparing a broad-cast in her praise, an ambulance brought her secretly from the South, where she had been resting, to her apartment in the boulevard Lannes. It seemed more suitable that she should be thought to have died in Paris, that she lie there in *chapelle ardente* for her friends, and that there be a proper Paris funeral. Actually no Mass was sung, the archbishopric having forbidden any service for one who had "lived publicly in a state of sin." Some forty thousand fans, however, broke through the barriers at Père-Lachaise; and there was a detachment from the Foreign Legion in full uniform, with regimental flag unfurled, standing at attention for the prayers.

Like Mélisande, she had been ever destructive to herself and to others. One of her lovers died in an air crash hurrying to meet her on demand. Another crashed too, but not by fault of hers. The car crashes seem mostly to have been drenched in alcohol, as was her life in fact. Marcel Cerdan's defeat in New York as world's champion boxer was clearly a result of her insistence that he go places with her, stay up nights with her, and break training. She lived for love and art, consuming her lovers and creating artists—song-poets and composers as well as singers. She was relentless, ruthless, inexhaustible, courageous, and self-indulgent to the ultimate degree, without self-pity. If my pairing her with Hector Berlioz and with Debussy's heroine may seem due to a merely fortuitous encounter of them in a foreign land, let us remember that Piaf's art, that of the French *chanson*, is the one that most nearly parallels the higher musical endeavors, not only in style, power, and guts but also in the dedication of its masters.

In this respect Edith Piaf was no Mélisande at all, nor yet a creator like Berlioz or Debussy. But she was, in the discipline of her preparations and performances, a not unworthy colleague of Pierre Boulez. This discipline she could inculcate too in forming other artists; it was that logical and her mind was that clear, her musical ear, her sense of the stage, equally faultless. It is even possible that had she put her mind to it (and for twenty-five years she did read books, knew poetry) she might have arrived at a woman's comprehension (though the role itself was surely not for her) of Mélisande. It takes a special kind of ruthlessness, like Piaf's or Mary Garden's, to see through another ruthless one, to respect her for not whimpering, and to avoid in consequence betraying her to men.

The New York Review of Books, January 29, 1970

Scenes from Show Biz

RUN-THROUGH: *A Memoir*, by John Houseman. 507 pp. Simon and Schuster, 1972.

JOHN HOUSEMAN (*né* Jacques Haussmann of Anglo-French parentage) was born, 1902, into a world of international speculation (chiefly wheat futures), brought up in its life style of palace-hotels, chic spas, plushy motor cars, and Swiss scenery, trained to its practice in Buenos Aires and London, glorified by success as an operator moving through Kansas City, Detroit, and Seattle and then bankrupted in New York in 1929, this also quite successfully, since the sum of his liabilities was for that year modest, a meager $300,000.

Having long cherished literary hopes from his schoolboy and youthful successes in England, and having married the beautiful actress Zita Johann, he retired into letters cushioned by her earning capacity, her loyalties, and the hospitality of a Welsh aunt who owned a small house in Rockland County. Eventually, however, in spite of a few early stories published and a couple of plays produced, the literary career faded, as did also the marriage. Engaged in 1934 by the Friends and Enemies of Modern Music to direct and produce at the Wadsworth Atheneum in Hartford, Connecticut, an opera entitled *Four Saints in Three Acts* (by Gertrude Stein and yr. serv. V.T.), which he co-directed with Sir Frederick Ashton, he knew from this his first backstage involvement that the theater was to be from then on his mistress.

Houseman's memoir takes it for granted that his readers understand the producer's role in mounting any spectacle, but for those to whom the function is unfamiliar it may be suggested that it resembles in many ways that of a magazine editor. And though in an established situation editors and producers rarely use their own money (since its loss can be quick, huge, and therefore definitive), in an earlier or experimental stage they may find backing among friends and even risk their own slight resources. In all cases they use their own taste, which in the theater is likely to be centered at the beginning of any producer's career on one playwright, one stage director, or one actor. Guthrie McClintic with Katharine Cornell and Richard

Barr with Edward Albee, John Houseman with Orson Welles are examples.

The choice of collaborating artists—actors, scenery and costume designers, lighting specialists, a composer if needed—is only administratively the producer's right. For the best result a joint decision with the playwright, the director, or the acting star is mandatory. Actually any dominant artist is likely to originate such choices and pass them on to the producer. The producer cannot be bypassed; nor can he in general be depended on for deep originality. Therefore one with brains, taste, and courage is the ideal—exactly the Houseman case.

The *Four Saints* experience had given Houseman affection and respect for black actors and confidence in his knack for summoning their qualities. And along with this his British rather wonderfully cool warmth, his considerate good manners, also British, and his elaborate cultural background in foreign letters and languages all went to make up a hand that he knew he could bid on. There was also his experience through wheat gambling in taking risks, the essence of any career in show business.

His trump card was an ace in the form of Orson Welles, aged nineteen. This association brought to both of them a phenomenal success in theater, radio, recording, and films, of which the details are history, many of these put down for the first time in Houseman's book. They opened in the spring of 1936 at the Lafayette Theater in Harlem for the Works Progress Administration their famous black *Macbeth* and later that year Marlowe's *Doctor Faustus* at Maxine Elliott's on Thirty-ninth Street, also preparing for production Marc Blitzstein's labor movement opera, *The Cradle Will Rock*.

The latter, when forbidden by Washington to open at all, they transported to another theater. And thus began the Mercury Theatre, a repertory operation chiefly known for Welles's stagings of classical plays. The Mercury made money on Blitzstein's *Cradle*, on a modern-dress *Julius Caesar*, and on the Elizabethan Thomas Dekker's *The Shoemaker's Holiday*. They lost on *Danton's Death* by Büchner and on Shaw's *Heartbreak House*, ruined themselves on *Five Kings*, and closed.

The Mercury's first season had for capital $10,500 contributed by friends and by an unknown who without solicitation had sent $4,500. The second season used $17,000, most of it from habitual Broadway investors. The losses on *Five Kings*, quite large, were shared with the Theatre Guild. Neither Houseman nor Welles had a personal fortune, though Welles was anticipating at twenty-five a bit of inheritance. This he at one point in the Mercury's life tried unsuccessfully to sell. Sizable fees, however, from broadcasts and recordings did help out. For the team was employed by CBS as Mercury Theatre of the Air and later as the Campbell [Soup] Playhouse. It was in fact under the latter sponsorship that an over-realistic broadcast based on H. G. Wells's *War of the Worlds* created a twenty-four-hour national emergency. In spite of this blunder, these weekly broadcasts went on for another year or more, with Houseman writing the scripts and Welles commuting by sleeper-plane from Hollywood. For by that time, 1939, he was engaged in a cinematic apotheosis that was to culminate in *Citizen Kane.*

Their cooperation had been from the beginning one of constant good will and of minimal frictions, though Welles did occasionally stage a tantrum, in one case accusing Houseman of trying to poison him. But that was late in the association and so obviously designed to avoid rehearsing something Welles was not sure about that neither mentioned it next day. Welles was full of striking production ideas, designed the layout of his own stage sets, discovered many an unknown actor and made him famous—Joseph Cotten, for instance, and Hiram Sherman— directed all the plays, and often acted in them. Houseman ran the office, paid the help when there was money, and negotiated every script and every production idea with the Communist Party's culture commissar, a man named Jerome (for Orson under Marc Blitzstein's guidance had become a fellow traveler).

Houseman also worked on scripts, especially for the broadcasts, matching Welles's almost nonexistent fatigue threshold, while Augusta Weissberger, a secretary who could neither type nor take dictation, but who, like their lighting girl Jean Rosenthal, could rustle up practically anything at any time, catered to Welles's every whim about food and drink at impossible hours. And they were impossible, for Welles loved rehearsing all night. He was often in fact obliged to, the theaters he worked in being generally in use at other times, evenings and matinees by his own performances, during the day by crews of carpenters building things backstage for the next play.

Houseman during this time lived in casual lodgings or in furnished flats shared with yr. serv., where I rarely encountered him save at breakfast, which we regularly took in French. Welles also moved frequently, married for the first time, took a house at Sneden's Landing, had a baby, rode to work in an aged Rolls-Royce, moved to the St. Regis, where an air-conditioned room (they were few in those days) mollified his hay fever. He managed, even early, to spend money like a star. Later, with record royalties coming in and with huge radio fees, his profligacy impressed even Hollywood. Much later, in the middle and late 1940s, with earnings very large and unpaid federal taxes no less so (by 1950 easily $200,000 and growing at compound interest) he went to live and work abroad, where he still resides.

But all that makes a third period, not covered in Houseman's volume. His first was in New York theater and New York radio. His second began in Hollywood with *Citizen Kane*. And before this film was completed in 1940 Houseman had resigned from the team. A restless man who cannot bear not working, he became furiously impatient with Welles's having loafed in Hollywood for upwards of a year, under a contract phenomenal for its generosity about both money and working conditions. Welles himself, engaged to write, direct, produce, and act in an original film on any subject he might choose, had very slowly come to the idea of using as his theme the life and career of William Randolph Hearst. Pressed for help on the script, Houseman rendered a final service to the film career by taking Herman Mankiewicz up to a mountain top and squeezing it out of him. Then he wrote to me, back in Paris, a historic letter about the break. This has been printed in my own memoirs, but is included in *Run-Through* for its remarkably straightforward analysis of a professional partnership worn through and a friendship no longer tenable. Returned to New York, Houseman worked with Welles once more, presenting on Broadway in 1941 Richard Wright's *Native Son*.

The over-all time covered by the Welles-Houseman collaboration, begun in 1935 with Archibald MacLeish's verse play *Panic*, was therefore six years. But their intense production period, which included Federal Theatre shows beginning in the spring of 1936, the Mercury Theatre of 1938 (along with records issued, mainly of readings by Welles), and the CBS broadcasts, for which Houseman wrote scripts till the fall of 1939, their continuous association before the public lasted for just three and a half years. The Mercury Theatre itself actually existed in New York for only fourteen months, another four being occupied by *Five Kings*, a montage of Shakespeare's Falstaff plays, which closed out of town.

Welles created after *Citizen Kane*, his film about William Randolph Hearst, one other film approaching the excellence of that, *The Magnificent Ambersons*, after the novel by Booth Tarkington. His career, both here and in Europe, has remained big-time; but it has given to the world no such electricity as he furnished in America between the ages of twenty and twenty-six when teamed up with Houseman's practical intelligence and ready-for-anything executive abilities. Nor has Houseman since their separation ever found another genius needing that badly his incomparable services or able to call on them so urgently.

Houseman himself has served as producer for many films of distinction—*Julius Caesar*, for instance, *Executive Suite*, *Lust for Life*—but he has never actually directed one. He has, however, directed stage shows as memorable as *Lute Song*, a musical, and the Leslie Howard *Hamlet*. There have also been TV programs (the CBS Lively Arts series), several sound-and-light spectacles, two documentary films, and from 1960 to 1965 forty remarkably well-acted plays produced at UCLA, in most cases directed by him. (Through those years Hollywood had maintained a pool of actors.)

His most brilliant recent operation has been the organization, aided by the late Michel Saint-Denis, of a drama division at the Juilliard School, planned after the model of similar schools set up by the French director in Strasbourg and London. Houseman's long experience in films and theater, in handling actors and other artists, in every sort of dramatic enterprise (and one must not forget the Office of War Information with its multilingual overseas radio broadcasts, which he directed in 1942 and 1943), and his passion for high quality theater (rather than for theories of direction and methods of acting) have in three years turned his Juilliard classes into an acting instrument approaching that excellent instrument of music the Juilliard Orchestra. He has also established at Juilliard, through directing a half-dozen works of musical theater for their American Opera Project, a standard of operatic stage direction that has brought him the respect of all stage people and the unalloyed gratitude of musicians. For the staging of opera (using singers, not actors, and these normally chosen for musical reasons only) has become in recent years a matter of general concern. Not every director succeeds with it as Houseman seems to have done.

The present memoir ends with him shouting orders (he is not shown quite that literally in the book, but vividly so I do remember him) to a polyglot vast floorful of desk workers at the wartime propaganda center on West Fifty-seventh Street (now the offices of *The New York Review*). An English publisher might have brought out more, say two volumes. Perhaps another may yet appear. It will be needed for the full story of Houseman's career in show biz, top show biz indeed from the start, and for the extended report that only he can offer on the school for acting at Juilliard. This is important, since America has not previously had so serious a conservatory for that, both Yale and Carnegie-Mellon being chiefly known for training directors and electricians, Harvard in Professor Baker's day for its playwrights.

In writing about this memoir, therefore, I simply cannot accept its convention that Houseman's meaningful life ended in the middle of World War II. What ended with that war was the partnership with Orson Welles. But since Welles was only one of his two formative theater associates (the other, according to the text, being yr. serv. V.T.) and since that earlier association has never ceased, is indeed operative at this moment regarding another opera by V.T. (*Lord Byron* with libretto by Jack Larson), there may be expected eventually a report on the V.T. approach to opera (his choice of themes, his choice of poets, all texts to be clearly enunciated, a completely choreographed stage, and NO ACTING).

I never liked Welles much, nor he me, though we respected each other's abilities and we collaborated loyally on two productions, the black *Macbeth* and a French farce for which music by Paul Bowles was used, orchestrated by me (*Un Chapeau de paille d'Italie* by Labiche, renamed for the occasion *Horse Eats Hat*), which we both were proud of; also on a 1956 TV spectacular of *King Lear* directed nominally by Peter Brook. And I was instrumental in persuading him to direct in 1937 Aaron Copland's *The Second Hurricane* and to undertake with Houseman that same year Blitzstein's *The Cradle Will Rock*. He later came to my aid in Paris in 1952 when the American troupe of my *Four Saints* needed help in adapting their stage movements to the recessed curtain line of the Théâtre des Champs-Elysées.

But Houseman needed him as a wet nurse needs a baby. Both were naturals of the speaking stage, not the operatic or the choreographic; and with the speaking stage I include TV and films, where both men are well known to have done quality work. Both were tall men, too, and on the portly side (Welles at twenty very thin, at twenty-one a bit of a monster, at thirty growing toward 300 pounds). Both were sons too of glamorously spendthrift fathers. Both were sexually excitable by overwork, and both needed overwork. Houseman to this day when doing one job at a time can lose interest, when doing two at once (or even three) is a dynamo of relentless care for everything.

Both as well were classically educated and traveled, also intruders on the New York scene, where the rich private producers, the solidly subscribed Theatre Guild and even the young Group Theatre resented them, for Welles was too gifted and Houseman too able to be easily taken over. If it had not been for the newly created Federal Theatre and its torrents-of-energy head Hallie Flanagan, a professor from Vassar, their partnership might have died with its first effort, MacLeish's *Panic*. Houseman with his sturdy qualities would have got on eventually. But Orson, with so full a temperament and (no question) a genius for directing, as well as the finest bass speaking voice ever heard, restless too, and with a real presence, for sure he would have had his breakthrough early.

But the duumvir, having assembled a team of invincible technicians and inspired actors (for Orson they would surpass themselves), went forward in so short a time to light up America (press and professionals, quoted in the book, attest to this) that it is hard to imagine them separately, or as putting out separately anything comparable to the effulgence with which their joint work shone during the years from 1936 to 1940. Welles has heretofore accepted full credit for that radiance. Houseman's documented story hogs no stage, but it does tell how the Welles career began. He tells it modestly enough and not without wit and humor but henceforth the fact is clear that in his great first half-decade Orson was a team of two—front man with genius and an office man with brains. Every star actor or director has had such a one making his career possible, even in some cases guiding it toward compromise and commercial exploitation.

Welles's was luckier than most. And if it amounts to little more today than mere distinction, his own self-destructive propensity was the cause.

The partnership with Houseman was an enterprise that worked through a shared faith in Welles's genius, hence mutual trust, with all their powers in full operation. No wonder they inspired loyalties. And no wonder John Houseman in his memoir has a story to tell. This is a story of artistic satisfactions. Families can die or divorce, marry, move away, or end by boring the very guts out of you. But an artistic result achieved through common effort and publicly attested does not fade. It does not fade because there never could have been, never was any doubt about it. And so the telling of how it came to be becomes an act of history. Not a theory about history or a meditation on its meaning, but an act regarding it, like your grandmother, who lived through the Civil War, telling you exactly what it was like.

Houseman wouldn't kid you; for him the Orson years are glorious enough told right. And that they *are* told right I can bear witness, because I was there, in many moments a participant, in virtually all the rest John Houseman's confidant as well as daily housemate in five New York residences shared.

What might be Welles's version we cannot guess, although the facts as known could scarce be different. Those regarding *Citizen Kane* are in a book by Pauline Kael,* which Houseman has no quarrel with. And the disastrous "invasion from Mars" has been similarly reported.† What would be interesting to know from Welles is how he remembers feeling about those years as they went by. Maybe nothing at all, he was so busy. But surely with his lively mind, his gift for sizing up people, and his direct way of speech, surely he would remember most of it right and tell some of it straight, though he still gets credit on the screen for the story and script of *Citizen Kane*, which, though Houseman also worked on it, Herman Mankiewicz actually wrote. His trouble would no doubt be, as it always was, such an abundance of ideas and of ingenious solutions that right up to opening night curtain his shows were never really set or finished, still being created, still alive.

---

* *The Citizen Kane Book* (Little Brown, 1971).
† Hadley Cantril, *The Invasion from Mars: A Study in the Psychology of Panic* (Harper and Row, 1966).

As an actor Welles's qualities were voice (deep, beautiful, controllable, and strong) and presence (when he was on stage you never saw anyone else). These plus brains, breeding, and a not inconsiderable learning (in dramatic literature, stage history, and languages) were to his advantage. His negative qualities were mostly the product of his monstrous person—over-tall, loose-hung, white-fleshed, flat-footed, moon-faced, later a gigantic blowup of itself. Energy he did not lack nor, according to him, great sexual abundance. But his physique would not do for glamour heroes. No Romeo he, nor Cleopatra's Antony, nor Hamlet. Only the monstrous and the monumental lay in his reach—King Lear, Othello, Citizen Kane, just barely Jane Eyre's Mr. Rochester.

This limitation in one so young, a hatred too, I am quite sure, of exhibiting his ungainly proportions, turned him toward directing plays instead of always having to show himself. And the satisfactions of not appearing gave such delight that his work as a director was always marked by joy. And so the legend grew that he was better off directing than acting. Happier he was, for sure. Who could be happy on a stage, looking like that? But in radio, with the body concealed and full vocal variety unleashed, he was in my memory also a miraculous actor.

A further limitation to his powers lay in the fact that like many another artist of the virtuoso type, he had shot his bolt early, astonishingly early in fact, since by the age of twenty-six, when normally an artist first begins to walk alone, Orson Welles had done practically all the work for which he is today remembered. Since that time a sound professionalism has stayed with him, but there is little depth or surprise in the work accomplished.

It was exactly this precocity that attracted Houseman, his mastery at nineteen of the whole professional gambit. No wonder the man of thirty-two became pupil to the boy genius and of his exploding career the servant. No wonder, as well, that by the time Welles's full expansion was complete the pupil had already left that phantom ship, henceforth condemned to sail the foreign seas with no more cargo than its own flying Dutchman, tragically doomed, never quite a wreck, nor ever quite redeemed.

The New York Review of Books, May 4, 1972

Untold Tales

WITHOUT STOPPING: *An Autobiography*, by Paul Bowles. 379 pp. Putnam's, 1972.

THE THICKET OF SPRING: *Poems 1926–1969*, by Paul Bowles. 56 pp. Black Sparrow Press, 1972.

PAUL BOWLES was in the Orson Welles–John Houseman orbit, which was discussed in the last issue, for two shows—*Horse Eats Hat* and *Doctor Faustus*—and for one play never produced, William C. Gillette's farce *Too Much Johnson*—though some filmmaking for certain parts of that play did go on, intended for interpolation with music by Bowles. He was almost exclusively a composer during the 1930s. Earlier, in the late twenties, he had written poetry and published in *blues, transition*, and other spots of the literary outfield. In the Forties he took up fiction and travel writing, through both of which he has earned money and an international public.

His autobiography is called *Without Stopping*. Why *do* they choose such shallow titles? (John Houseman's is called *Run-Through*, though as a life's run-through it is short by thirty years.) Bowles's title too I suspect of being casually selected, since his life as I know it and as it is told by him has shown no such continuity. Rather is its characteristic that of having several times changed directions.

For Bowles, though he began his life-in-art as a poet, spent a good fifteen years (more too) as a practicing composer, a critic, and a collector of folk music. The turn to travel writing was preceded by a long history of moving about in semitropical countries and of picking up languages. French, Spanish, and Arabic are those in which he is most accomplished. And in the course of his travels he picked up stories too, also acquired a knack for shaping them and for assembling others out of "found" elements, which is what most storytellers do anyway, since inventing a human character is inconceivable.

Eventually Bowles got to taping the stories told him by an Arab friend and translating these, a procedure which relates to his habitual folklore collecting. And now we see him telling his own story, as a gentleman of fifty-nine residing in Morocco, though still moving around the globe along the warmer parallels of latitude, an accomplished writer who has known everybody and been lots of places and remembers lots of stories about all those people and places.

Unfortunately these stories do not get told. Not that the experienced storyteller fails; he simply declines to tell them. He hints at their existence; that is all. So that except for an utterly charming account of his forebears and his childhood upstate near the Finger Lakes, his autobiography is a geographical *décor* peopled by celebrities from Krishnamurti to Gore Vidal, none of whom we ever see in close-up. And his reticence covers also himself. No friendship is declared, no love admitted. Which after all is the way Bowles has always led his life. He has been intensely loved by friends both men and women. And he has accepted their love with its attendant perquisites. Whether he ever returned it none of us has much known from services rendered, though his attentions to his wife Jane during the last decade, when mental illness has progressively alienated her, have been constant. If Paul was displeased with you he told you so, and firmly. If he was happy in your presence he laughed with joy. But nothing to him, possibly even his marriage, was ever an engagement.

And so his life, as told, unrolls like a travelogue. I would not have expected out of him either "confessions" or true-story gossip, anything indiscreet or scabrous. But Paul has always been so delicious in talk, games, laughter, and companionship, so unfailingly gifted for both music and letters, so assiduous in meeting his deadlines with good work, so relentless in his pursuit of authenticity among his own ethnic associates (and all others) that it is a bit surprising to find oneself in the same flat pattern of casual acquaintance that includes everybody else he ever knew (excepting perhaps his father, whom he seems to have pretty actively disliked, though he never broke away).

His book is a pleasure to read for its felicities of phrase, and its celebrity-column distinction is not unlike an album of photographs by Cecil Beaton. But neither its brain-work nor the emotions hinted at go deep. Lots of facts are there, all checked and verified I am sure. But their assemblage and their viewing, their choice and staging are deadpan. In this sense it is a characteristic work of twentieth-century art, which in its heroic early decades, those in which Paul Bowles grew up, gave to everything, as stylistic priority, an equalized surface tension.

This quality exists as well in Bowles's music, for which I have admiration and which I accept. I accept it in fact with fewer reserves than I have about his fiction, which can at times appear made-up, rather than spontaneously created out of depths. But avoiding depths while searching for authenticity is harder to do in letters than in music, where feelings cannot be hidden or their absence glossed over. Bowles as a man of letters I admire, but I cannot in that role fully accept him.

A certain diabolism in his nature, a constant preoccupation with destructive magic, gives to the presentations of evil, which dominate his novels and other myth creations, an aspect of being either all too true, or, if not that, just a shade phony. This danger has long been clear. After a country visit at eighteen with Gertrude Stein, she summed him up as follows:

> I was the most spoiled, insensitive, and self-indulgent young man she had ever seen, and my colossal complacency in rejecting all values appalled her. But she said it beaming with pleasure, so that I did not take it as adverse criticism. "If you were typical, it would be the end of our civilization," she told me. "You're a manufactured savage."

She also considered him a manufactured poet, as did several others of us, Bernard Faÿ, for instance. We could not take the poetry at all. Having not seen any of it in forty years, I looked at it again in a volume recently arrived, *The Thicket of Spring: Poems 1926–1969*. These include twenty-one items from 1926 to 1930 (the year he was eighteen), five from the mid-1930s (two in French), nine from 1938 and 1940, two from 1969. The early ones are chiefly about landscape and cruelty, along with references to black magic as a current practice. I do not wholly reject the later poems, as I did the teen-age efforts I knew in 1931. But neither am I convinced that they are more than shallow pools. Their nature is that of "satirical verses," as the Romantics used that term, or of what the French call *vers de société*, slightly shocking thoughts wittily phrased. For Bowles, though revolted by the standard violence of our time, is still in love with personal tortures and evil spells, as well as the God-created malice of snakes and tigers.

Poetry cannot be his true vocation, or he would have kept on. But not giving it up altogether and letting it be issued now can only mean that he still accepts his adolescent work. This from a man punctilious about his literary behavior, his image, could mean that having come to the end first of his musical vein and then (I am supposing) of his fictional and mythological propensities, and having faced this turning point in his life by reviewing all of it, especially the bedrock of his forebears and early years, he is moving carefully, tentatively, hopefully toward, for his sixties and beyond, seriously mining the poetic vein.

What the main theme of that might be I do not divine, since the preoccupation with evil that his novels and stories are full of is no longer fresh. He could, of course, apply it to a new theme. And the autobiography does hint, ever so gently, at such a theme, which I take to be a feeling of emptiness, indeed despair, at the final closing off of dependable communication with his wife. That he loves her deeply I cannot doubt after thirty-five years of friendship with them both. But he could not easily say it, even to her. The despair of her approaching loss, however, does come up in his book almost to the surface. The rest, except for the family matters, is one long in-color newsreel.

May that interminable newsreel wear him down, the very thought of it, till he starts making sense again! I think he did make sense in music. I have never thought his literature was for real, least of all the meager poetry. But if that vein, however thin, but mined assiduously, as he does any vein, should produce eventually even one small nugget, the whole history of Paul Bowles's literary skills and talent would be different from what has thus far taken place.

The New York Review of Books, May 18, 1972

Elliott Carter

FLAWED WORDS AND STUBBORN SOUNDS: *A Conversation with Elliott Carter*, by Allen Edwards. 128 pp. Norton, 1972.

SINCE WORLD WAR II Elliott Carter has been our most admired composer of learned music and the one most solidly esteemed internationally. His chamber music in particular (which includes the Double Concerto for Piano and Harpsichord, each accompanied by a separate instrumental group) is respected by composers and viewed by instrumentalists as a challenge to their virtuosity. Extremely well written for exhibiting virtuosity, Carter's music is always hard to play, but seldom hard to listen to; though complex for eye and hand, it ever delights the ear. In this sense, though in no other, Carter is a parallel to Franz Liszt. For high seriousness and monumental form, however, his aspiration, like that of so many other Americans—Ives, Harris, and Sessions, for example—emulates Beethoven. (This is not a European habit; the monumentally inclined over there seem content with Tchaikovsky and Mahler.)

Elliott Carter, moreover, is a man of culture. He knows languages, reads Greek, has traveled. His musical history includes not only the Harvard and Nadia Boulanger orbit, long standard for American composers, but also a close friendship with Charles Ives. He learned the choral routines under Archibald T. ("Doc") Davison, show biz under Lincoln Kirstein and George Balanchine, for whose early dance companies he served as musical adviser and composed two ballets. For a short time too he taught at St. John's College in Annapolis, which is probably where a good deal of his classical reading took place, such as Plato and Lucretius. For some years I have noticed that the Great Books method of instruction, however quickly it may run off of the undergraduates, will occasionally go deeper with the young instructors, especially those for whom it is a second plunge.

In any case Elliott Carter has read everything and been everywhere, and he has reflected about music as well as written it. He has also written *about* it under that impeccable trainer Minna Lederman, editor of the regretted quarterly *Modern Music*. So that whatever he has to say about music is not only penetrating as thought but gracefully expressed. And if a certain pessimism permeates his view of whatever or whomever has not contributed to the blazing of his own fine complex trail, he is courteous for the most part toward those who have.

It is surprising that at sixty-three, with so solid a career laid out and so splendid a repertory to exploit, Carter has not been the subject of a biographical brochure, nor has there yet appeared regarding his work any sustained attempt at analysis. The recently issued *Flawed Words and Stubborn Sounds: A Conversation with Elliott Carter*, by Allen Edwards, aspires to give us the composer along with his views on music. But the questioner is so full of his own views that the composer has to spend time blowing away fog which might have been employed to greater advantage in direct observation. All the same, a great deal of Carter's remarkable intelligence and good sense does come through. And if these offer less enlightenment regarding his own work than about the musical situation in general, that is only natural, to his credit even, since no artist, especially a successful one, is ever much good at explaining himself.

His account of his youth and educational background, however, is very good indeed, involving as it does practically everybody, practically everybody's music, and the adventures of a very bright young man in sizing them all up and picking out everything that he might eventually, in his full maturity, be using. The thoroughness of his investigations and the decisiveness of his rejections, especially his acquisitiveness in stockpiling musical, literary, all sorts of humane and other cultural experiences, is virtually without parallel among American musicians.

Actually Carter, in spite of economic and cultural advantages, was slow to ripen. The process was long and painful, also complicated (perhaps cushioned) by psychosomatic maladies. He was thirty-seven when his first breakthrough occurred, his first work wholly free and original, the Piano Sonata of 1945. Since then his production has been steady, its quality stable, its individuality unquestioned. His excellence in general renders academic much of the technical talk in the latter half of the present book. When he mentions, for instance, music's having moved into a "post-tonal" epoch, the word has little meaning. So has the assumption that music has "moved," has in fact ever "moved," though it changes constantly, if not in syntax, surely in meaning.

Carter also refers to his use in certain later "works" of four-note chords containing all the intervals. One such would be C–C#–E–F#. Whether this is in any acoustical sense a chord, rather than merely an agglomerate, I question. It is certainly a combination of intervals numerically arrived at, hence easy to manipulate in today's vernacular. It is also bound irretrievably to the conventions of tempered tuning, so tightly bound indeed as to render it acoustically void of identity in any music that might aspire to be considered "post-tonal."

But Carter is not far-out in either theory or practice. His music's textural basis is the invertible counterpoint characteristic of fugue. His game is instrumental virtuosity, and it is in this field that his most ingenious discoveries have been made. His expressive sources are likely to be literary though not narrative (philosophical meditations on infinity, rather) and its forms asymmetrical. It is therefore both Romantic (by inspiration) and neo-Romantic (through its dependence on planned spontaneity). His neoclassical allegiance to invertible counterpoint is also a Romantic element tending toward sequence structure, though its preoccupation with virtuosity is hard-edged baroque. All in all, it is a past-oriented music, not one that dreams of transforming the art, and Carter is a conservative composer, in the sense that his aim is to say modern things to the classically educated.

His youthful taste for quality and flair for finding it, along with his nowadays wisdom in defining it, are all a part of the man and of his music. And the spectacle of him, as Carter's unusual mind and forthright tongue bring out, is that of an artist very little fooled by anyone, or self-deceived. As a man of culture and skills he believes in an elite. As a man of means he disdains to make the adjustments that would be required for seeking popularity. He writes therefore as an elite composer for an elite public, for consumers with education, some leisure, and a consecration to cultural experience.

As we know, who can remember when plays, ballets, concerts, and museum shows were frequently aimed at such a public, its being educated and well-to-do was never enough. The only consumer we respect today is one whose life is consecrated to a skill, in other words a professional. Beyond these lie the limbo of nonresponsibility, of mass publics addicted to mere consumption.

The view is not a popular one. And Elliott Carter is not a popular composer, not in any sense now possible to conceive. But he is an interesting man and his music is interesting. Interesting intrinsically, I mean, not just fun and games or a jolly noise, but appealing to the mind and to the heart as well as to the musical ear. A great deal of the man is in this book, not any of the music; but the man is seen wrestling, if not quite with music, with the formulation of ideas provoked by the wrestlings that unquestionably went on during the gestation of his music.

That is certainly the meaning of its title, which is a quotation from the poet Wallace Stevens. And if maybe some of this is shadow play (inevitably), some of it is also real (it has to be). That too is interesting. Intrinsically.

The New York Review of Books, August 31, 1972

Wickedly Wonderful Widow

STAYING ON ALONE: *Letters of Alice B. Toklas*, edited by Edward Burns. Introduction by Gilbert A. Harrison. 426 pp. Liveright, 1973.

No BOUQUET OF LETTERS by Alice Toklas could fail the reader; she was such a vivid character, vivid and voluble. So voluble indeed that after thirty-eight years with Gertrude Stein, for Toklas a time of relative reticence, during the next twenty she fulfilled herself in words, both spoken words and epistolary, to a degree hardly less than Stein herself had done.

She gave out published articles and three books, two on cooking and one a memoir. But what she wrote for print she wrote for money; naturally it does not vibrate like her letters. These, virtually identical with talk, could fill volumes and no doubt will. Especially if some active scholar should one day trace down all the stories, plots, and intrigues that with their dramatis personae make up the content.

The present assemblage begins on the day of Miss Stein's death, July 27, 1946. The loss, voluntary destruction, and general nonavailability of Miss Toklas's earlier correspondence with California family and friends, as well as the meagerness, during their years together, of her communications with Gertrude's particular associates, seem to have made those last years alone the best field for a first coverage. During that time she poured out her voice to friends, enemies, tradesmen, lawyers, agents, and publishers with virtually no withholding of facts and no more distortion of them than might be expected from a lady whose private life had become a matter of public interest.

The theme of that later life was responsible widowhood. Though never reconciled to Gertrude's death, she accepted the fact of it and undertook at once its sacred duties. These comprised the getting into print of Gertrude's unpublished writings (eventually eight volumes), the advancement of her literary fame, and the preservation of her picture collection.

The publication, aided at the Yale University Press by Thornton Wilder and Donald Gallup, editorially by Carl Van Vechten, was subsidized through the sale of all her Picasso drawings, pornographic and other. The posthumous fame was encouraged by Alice's praise or discouragement of authors wishing to write about Miss Stein. Her usual tactic was to be difficult of access, then less difficult, then to broadcast through visitors and correspondents her blessing on the essay or her distaste for it. Donald Sutherland's *Gertrude Stein: A Biography of Her Work* (Yale, 1951) received and continued to receive her highest hymning. *When This You See Remember Me: Gertrude Stein in Person* by W. G. Rogers (Rinehart, 1948), though it brought minor scoldings, was warmly welcomed. John Malcolm Brinnin's *The Third Rose: Gertrude Stein and Her World* (Little, Brown, 1959) she tended to disapprove, though she was aware of its favorable influence. On the other hand, Elizabeth Sprigge's *Gertrude Stein, Her Life and Work* (Harper and Brothers, 1957) she never forgave. She did not specify her objections, but her scorn was intense. And she continued for years to speak of its author in a tone of invective generally reserved for Ernest Hemingway, whom she hated as one can only hate people to whom one has been unjust.

Alice's love and dislikes, as a matter of fact, she did not deign to argue; she would declare them in a ukase, backing this up, if at all, by stories of kind attentions or by denigrating remarks. And I do not imagine that either her highly emotional attacks on people or her gushing approval of them actually influenced Gertrude's fame as a writer. This was rising when she died, and it continued to rise, Alice serving chiefly as rooter for the home team, out for victory every day or, if that failed, to fire a manager, kill an umpire.

With Leon Katz, a scholar who had achieved access at Yale to the early fiction (scandalous for its time, every piece of it) and to the diary-like notebooks which Gertrude had kept from 1902 to 1911, she was in the end cooperative, so eager was she to get a look at the notebooks whose very existence she had not known. When she also expressed hope that they not be published right away Katz reassured her. Actually her examination by him and of them took place more than twenty years ago, and still their annotated version has not appeared. The deal struck was simple and fair. Alice was to answer all questions in return for being shown the transcript (the books themselves being still at Yale). Her only demurrer was that she need not volunteer information not directly asked for. In this way Alice learned what Gertrude had been doing and thinking for the five years preceding her own arrival (1907) and for the four that followed. And Katz became the world expert on Gertrude's life and work, at least through 1911, the year she wrote *Tender Buttons*.

Alice's dream of keeping the picture collection intact produced the poverty which dominated her last years and to which, had not friends formed a small committee for keeping her alive and for struggling with three batteries of lawyers—American, French-American, and French—our heroine might well have succumbed—old, bed-ridden, and blind—to despair if not outright starvation.

Alice had been left for her lifetime Gertrude's income from all sources, plus the right to dispose of properties as she saw fit, including the pictures. But her reluctance to grant the eventual heirs (Gertrude's brother Michael's three grandchildren) any control over her possible dissipation of their fortune produced some lack of confidence. And on her side, distrust of the guardians grew into such bad will that war became inevitable and continuous; no peace-making effort on either side provoked any act of generosity. Or of justice either, since Alice, when several million dollars in picture-capital had been sequestered, could not even pay her char; and the heirs themselves, with Alice surviving, had to wait more than twenty years before touching any part of that capital. Alice, about the pictures, had been tactless, probably illegal; but neither was I aware at any time, following the affair closely, of a single one of the estate lawyers being anything but dilatory, secretive, and obstructionist.

Had Alice, after selling off drawings to pay the Yale Press, continued to raid the collection, even for her own comfort (which had certainly been Gertrude's wish), then, should the heirs have come to protest, bargained with them toward anticipating a settlement, it is possible all parties might have benefited. And certainly Alice's treatment of the heirs' parents, Allan Stein and his wife Roubina, though in the early years of her usufruct this had been courteous enough, left open later very few possibilities of arrangement. In no circumstance would she countenance any sale from the collection for their benefit, though at least once she secretly disposed of a minor Picasso for her own.

All that is part of a story which eventually, I presume, will be fairly told. In these letters we hear it only through Alice's plaints. Nor do we sense it even then with amplitude. In fact, it has not been the practice of the present editor to annotate the sorrows or the accusations in a way to make them convincing, beyond the basic facts of the bereavement and of the survivor's faith in her loved one's genius. These come through; everything else is suspect, on account of Alice's penchant for excessive statement, whether of thanks, praise, or distrust.

Did Alice really "like" Thornton Wilder, for instance? I doubt it. She was grateful to him; he had been useful to Gertrude in Chicago and regarding Yale. But he kept putting off writing a preface for *Four in America*; it had to be insisted on and wangled for. She confessed to Mildred Rogers that he "has such a seeing eye and then what he doesn't see he has felt and the combination has always made me a little afraid of him." But how she butters Wilder's sister! With unctuous compliments for the two of them and constantly little recipes, homefolks recipes involving short cuts, substitutes, and easy ways out. These are not, as cuisine, serious; nor are in general those she sent to Mildred Rogers and some others. To a publisher's wife she did tell how to make hollow fried potatoes (the round ones, not the flat *pommes soufflées*), but unless I am quite wrong about those deep-butter delights she forgot to say that they require clarified butter.

When agitating for another sacred assignment, which was the liberation of a French friend convicted of wartime collaboration, she could be devoted without letup. But I have no evidence, in the letters or elsewhere, that she was of help, even though the final solution of his plight was favorable. Since I was involved myself in certain efforts toward improving the situation of this friend (for a longer time mine than Gertrude's) it may be of interest to show here through my own correspondence a fuller picture.

In an undated letter from the fall of 1946, written the day after his condemnation, she wonders, "Is it the moment for the intervention of . . . ?" and suggests another possible course of action.

Twice during December she wrote me again about the case. On December 28, 1946, "There has been no news of your friend—but it is neither surprising nor discouraging. There is—it would appear—more danger in appealing the case than the lawyer is ready to risk—but there are several other things to do and any one is possible to succeed if it can be pushed far enough."

After a devoted friend of the victim had consulted Washington concerning possible pressures from there, I wrote to Alice that the American government seemed at that moment not inclined to ask of France favors for "a minor collaborator." This tactless phrase drew anger; on January 25, 1947, she wrote:

> I was aghast at your attitude to [——] and the verdict. You haven't lived in France lately or you couldn't feel as you do— only [——'s] personal enemies believe him capable of such crime as you believe he committed. And we know with what positive pleasure he collected enemies. No—you have some Frenchmen on your side but they were always his personal enemies—or the French who passed the Occupation in New York possibly. Please do not ever let us speak of it again. My memory is not as good as it was so all this won't trouble me as long as it would have in the old days. Didn't you once quote Madame Langlois—"How astonishing that such a corrupt person ['*un garçon aussi corrompu*' had been her phrase] should write such pure music." I'm sure the music for *The Mother of Us All* [at that moment about to be completed for a spring premiere] is pure if you want it to be pure and that it is intriguing, vital, and beautiful. For your music I will make any confession of faith you want—but for what it is surrounded by—*Dieu m'en garde*. What do you nourish it on? You may well answer that you are not a pelican of course. I don't agree with Madame Langlois' *mot*. It's not the corruption that puts me off—it's the being mistaken. You see so clearly in your music. Perhaps the rest of us see any thing clearly because we haven't your gift. Let it go at that.
>
> Would you for Gertrude's sake not mention [——'s] name to a living soul until his situation has changed. I could under that condition easily be
>
> as ever
> Alice

To this invigorating explosion I replied that she might as well keep her shirt on; I was not quarreling with her, nor resigning from a situation that might possibly still be helped out.

Following that, she wrote warmly on April 20 and May 9. On July 2, "About your not coming over I'm more disappointed than I can say." Then, as a postscript, "Should you hear any rumors that Gertrude and I were Christian Scientists please deny them."

I did not answer the request, knowing full well that the fact was true of Alice, though not of Gertrude. I did not, however, either spread such a rumor or have occasion to deny it; and I never spoke to Alice about the matter, even when we discussed later her having become a Catholic.

Neither did we ever again have sharp words. Her outburst and my reply seem to have relieved a hidden tension that had been there between us since first we met, in 1926. And some-time in the 1950s (I cannot find the letter at this time) she wrote me a declaration of faith and friendship, *amende honorable* complete.

Actually our correspondence went on year in year out, as did our meetings; and it is full of references to her friends, to my friends, to all the people she liked and disliked most. These letters are plenty indiscreet, sometimes malicious or outlandishly overstated. Printing them out of context, with no framework of notes to make them seem less cruel, makes Alice appear as even more irresponsible of tongue than she was and the book's editor as perhaps willfully disobliging toward her victims.

For instance, the wife of a certain painter is dismissed as "poisonous"; in a later mention she is "admirable, competent, devoted." Was the slap worth printing? Alice was in fact not at all a poor judge of character, but her pen was hasty.

She could also misstate facts when Gertrude's interests or her own were involved. In the latter case she could be treacher-ous, lay plans, eliminate from Gertrude's life intimates whose closeness had reached a danger point. This procedure had been operated, I am sure, regarding Gertrude's brother Leo and also Mabel Dodge Luhan. I know that it explains the break with Ernest Hemingway, and I actually saw it used on the young French poet Georges Hugnet.

In all these cases, while ostensibly moving "to protect Gertrude," Alice was also protecting her own monopoly of

Gertrude's sentimental life. Whether Gertrude saw through the maneuvers, actually knew when plotting was afoot, I seriously doubt. Alice could so easily make it appear that some good friend's loyalty was being withdrawn; and Gertrude would then feel rejected, hopeless about going on, henceforth reliant only on Alice's affection. Later she might have regretted the lost friend had not Alice covered every mention with character smears and with scorn. In no case was any reason for the break or for its permanence ever stated; even Gertrude came to pretend that with Leo and with Hemingway the intimacy had just "withered away." Hemingway at least knew better, and that Alice, not Gertrude, was the enemy.

There were also minor excommunications, but for any of these there was usually an admissible reason. The four major ones, however, follow a pattern—an amorous attachment on Gertrude's part (yes, even possibly to her brother), a separation without stated reasons, then, largely on Alice's part, a campaign of frightfulness, of scurrility, and a blank wall against all attempts to research the relationship. Probably Mabel Dodge and for certain Hemingway (he said so) found Gertrude desirable. Hugnet, who did not, was amazed, in an intellectual friendship, at the quasi-love letters she would write him. Leo's thoughts I know not.

It would be interesting to learn regarding Alice's *autos-da-fé* how the victims felt. Hemingway told all in a well-known letter to William G. Rogers. Hugnet's adventure I knew as it occurred. For him there was nothing traumatic; he took it for a plain quarrel between *gens de lettres* about prestige. And along with real disappointment he got sizable rewards—a Stein-language version of his long poem *Enfances*, published in 1930 on parallel pages in *Pagany*, later independently as *Before the Flowers of Friendship Faded Friendship Faded*, and a hundred or more letters in Gertrude's warmly spontaneous French, which he sold not long ago quite profitably "to an American university."

I know only too well how harshly Alice spoke of the heirs, the disdain she felt for their parents and for their legal guardian. She tells in a letter of the present collection how she refused their mother's request for financial aid through sale of a picture by pointing out that she didn't have to "keep a car." Their lack of regard for her was evident when Alice, in spite of her lawyers' efforts and of the friendly succor organized by Doda Conrad, became increasingly in need of ready cash to pay indispensable helpers. One of these was owed at Alice's death wages covering several years. But while Alice complained of her opponents constantly, they kept a civil silence. And waited.

Their waiting was rewarded, as was Alice's determination to keep intact the collection, since the final price paid by a group of American investors, trustees of New York's Museum of Modern Art, was said to be, for the main items, $6,500,000; and the pictures finally were shown together, along with some that had belonged to Gertrude's brothers, at that museum. Indeed, they seem not yet to have come on the open market.

Aside from this partial victory, due as much to the stubbornness of the heirs in trust and to her own estate lawyers as to any effort of hers, Alice Toklas's more than twenty years of "staying on alone" chalked up no major success, merely gratifications. Publication of the remaining works, ordered in Gertrude's will, could scarcely have been omitted. Likewise, Gertrude's literary fame would have grown, as it has in fact gone on growing, even with Alice no longer tending it. Her efforts at procuring the liberation of the alleged collaborator were quite without effect. His own poor health in prison, compassionate transfer to a hospital, escape from there at his own risk and expense, a belated presidential pardon brought about through his brother's persistence and tolerated by his political enemies (themselves too grown compassionate after a shamefully skimpy trial and an admittedly improper sentence), these saved his life and brought him liberty. As a scholar he has taught successfully since in Spain and Switzerland, written new books and published them in France. His rehabilitation and return, I may add, gratified not only Alice.

She was happy also with the success of Gertrude's posthumous opera *The Mother of Us All* and the revival of *Four Saints in Three Acts*, which she saw in Paris. And she never failed to express delight with books by people she approved, though I must say her tastes were peculiar. She considered Mercedes de Acosta's memoir *Here Lies the Heart* a "tremendous accomplishment," a "new volume" of James Joyce's letters "incredibly woefully ignorant uneducated and blastingly uncultivated."

Alice Toklas herself was none of those. For good or ill, she was a lady. She knew the household arts, was adept at hospitality, could in a most accomplished manner both read and write. Her expertness in all such ways, plus volubility and wit, made her a delicious companion. And her utter devotion to Gertrude Stein gave her detachment in other relationships, justifying any walk-out, any lie or treachery or plotting. I am not sure she did not practice on occasion unfriendly magic, just as she burned candles to Sainte Geneviève for bringing about beneficial events, long before Roman Catholicism had become her faith.

What that conversion really amounted to is hard to judge. She had been born and reared in a well-to-do skeptical family, Jewish but not Orthodox, and at twelve, to please a friend of her mother's, was baptized a Catholic. No record of the baptism has been found, but it may have got destroyed in the Fire. Later she became a Christian Scientist, how much later I do not know; but she wrote Donald Sutherland at seventy, on October 8, 1947, "for the first time in fifty-three years I'd to see the doctor," in other words, not since she was seventeen. Conversion from Moses to Mrs. Eddy is common, from Science to Holy Church very rare. In 1957 the need felt must have been very great for Alice Toklas, at eighty, to make her First Communion. (An American priest had credited her California baptism.)

Admittedly the transfer of faith had been motivated by a desire (self-centered of course) for reunion with her great and beloved Gertrude, whom God, she believed, could not possibly have failed to receive. She writes after this of praying for people, and surely she made some gifts of money to her priest. But no lessening of her propensities to scorn, malice, anger, even gluttony, appeared. By nature a spendthrift and a showy one, she entertained at only the most expensive restaurants, giving hundred-dollar tips plus the fifteen percent already charged. One wonders whether some of this throwing-away was not perhaps a getting even with the heirs, and whether they were not perhaps quite wise in withholding her access to unlimited cash. Also whether, had they not done this, she might eventually have made substantial church gifts out of money they considered rightfully theirs.

With even urgent expenditures prevented, Alice's friends saw to it that to the end she had a roof, a maid, medical care, and for food a few necessary luxuries. Also to the end, impotent, incontinent, and almost blind, she thanked them, as a lady should, in warmest terms, restating in every letter her affection, offering her prayers, adding dirty cracks about the young Steins and about Ernest Hemingway, still unforgiven, though dead.

What curses she might have launched against the present volume I can only guess, considering its casual tone, and also how she had always fought with editors, even the best. I must say I am shocked myself at the absence throughout the book of the three dots that acknowledge an omission, though several of the recipients have assured me that their letters have been generously cut. Such punctilio might have made perusal more difficult; but it *is* the custom, and neglecting it is unfair to both writer and reader. So is an incomplete index. Actually the letters as printed tell no consistent story, however close a portrait they may give of the Toklas daily life, her tempers, her temperament, her sorrows and happy times. What access there had been to a fuller and fairer story I cannot judge. My own two hundred or more communications were not seen, since my initial reluctance toward entrusting these led to no further inquiries. Other sources may have been similarly hesitant. But Alice's tirades and massive indiscretions do invite some reserve.

Among the book's unimportant errata that I have noted, here are a baker's dozen:

1. To Picasso's "*bateau lavoir*" studio, where he painted Gertrude Stein's portrait, there is no "nearby Seine," the rue Ravignan, near the top of Montmartre, being at least two miles away. (p. 16)

2. Picasso arrived in Paris in 1900, not 1903. (p. 16)

3. Elliot Paul, though often a contributor to *The Chicago Tribune* and occasionally to *The New York Herald* (their Paris editions), was never the editor of either. (p. 51)

4. Toklas's miscalling the *office des changes* an *office d'echange* needs correcting. (p. 73)

5. Georges Maratier's American friend was Ed Livengood (not Livergood). (p. 76)

6. The statement that at a reading of Picasso's play "Georges Hugnet supplied the music" needs further explanation, since this excellent poet was no musician at all. (p. 115)

7. Le Colombier (not Columbier) was the name of the house near Culoz. (p. 136)

8. Angel Regus (for Reyes) is no doubt an unchecked misreading of Alice's penmanship, as Aaron Copeland (for Copland) might be anyone's mistake, surprising though it is. (p. 172)

9. Paul Bowles knew Stein and Toklas from 1931, not 1935. (p. 189)

10. Opaline bowls, surely, not opalier. (p. 190)

11. Lunch at Le Bossu, yes, not Le Bosse. (p. 205)

12. The Mallorcan twisted coffee-cake is an *ensaimada* (not *ensimada*). (p. 214)

13. Former head of the Vassar Art Department was Agnes Rindge (not Range). (p. 238)

None of these slips is grave, though they all indicate negligence about checking dates, proper names, and foreign-language references. In general the book, though handsomely printed on good stock with surfaces hard enough for reproducing photographs, is editorially not quite first-class, in spite of prefatorial credits to Donald Gallup (in charge of Yale's Gertrude Stein Collection) and Leon Katz (editor of Stein's notebooks). Nevertheless the book is a joy because Toklas the woman was for real—gushy, gossipy, grudge-holding, and unforgiving, but also generous, warm, lively, perspicacious, vastly sociable, and civilized in the Victorian, the Edwardian, the pre–World War I way, which is the good way or, as she would have put it, the San Francisco way.

I do hope she has made it to Heaven and is no longer alone but finally with Gertrude forever, though in spite of all her social charms, she might become a nuisance there if she went in for "protecting" her friend. And dear Gertrude would be happy to have her there, certainly for the housekeeping, but most of all for help in analyzing character and in remembering exactly who everybody is and how to put them into stories that can be repeated throughout eternity in exactly the way that they will have finally come to be told by them to each other.

The New York Review of Books, March 7, 1974

Making Black Music

BIRD LIVES! *The High Life and Hard Times of Charlie (Yardbird) Parker*, by Ross Russell. 404 pp. Charterhouse, 1973.

BLACK MUSIC: *Four Lives*, by A. B. Spellman. 241 pp. Schocken, 1970.

BLACK MUSIC, by LeRoi Jones. 221 pp. Morrow, 1967.

BLACK NATIONALISM AND THE REVOLUTION IN MUSIC, by Frank Kofsky. 280 pp. Pathfinder Press, 1970.

REFLECTIONS ON AFRO-AMERICAN MUSIC, edited by Dominique-René de Lerma. 271 pp. Kent State University Press, 1973.

BLACK TALK, by Ben Sidran. 201 pp. Holt, Rinehart and Winston, 1971.

URBAN BLACK MUSIC (more often called "jazz") was formerly written about, say back in the 1930s, as if it were an objectively describable modern phenomenon like French impressionism, with a clear history of derivations, influences, and individual achievements.

Any armful of such studies would have to include, among the very best, those in French by Hugues Panassié, Robert Goffin, and André Hodeir, in American by Winthrop Sargeant, Wilder Hobson, Rudi Blesh, Gunther Schuller. And there are more, excellent compendia, fully respectful of the miraculous. For jazz and blues were recognized early, especially by Europeans, as a domain of musical creation quite different from any "classical" or "light" music then existing. And the practice of communal improvisation, the essential jazz miracle, was indeed the most remarkable explosion of musical energies since Lutheran times, when whole populations took to the road in song.

Jazz music had been quite skillfully imitated in the early 1920s by a white group called Dixieland. To describe it and to catalogue it was a further step toward encompassing it. Another had been the incorporation of certain rhythmic, melodic, and verbal devices into the reigning "light" style of show songs and social dance, a surface transformation that gave to America —in the work of Jerome Kern, George Gershwin, and their colleagues—a commercial product that rivaled for worldwide favor the Viennese. This music too was sometimes called jazz, at least by whites; and its distribution involved the better night-clubs, the recording industry, show business, radio, and after 1929 musical films.

Black urban music, the real thing, led a separate existence, continuing to evolve, for the most part, in the gangster-controlled slums of Chicago and Kansas City, where its lovers kept one another in touch and recordings got put out on modest labels. It never got into the movies or noticeably on chain radio. Its complete intolerance of anything not itself, its innate strength for rejecting impurities, made it virtually useless to big commerce. The rapidity of its evolution, moreover, especially after 1940, and the internal dissensions among blacks themselves regarding this have kept everyone busy. There has been no time of late for neat packaging or for massive distribution, even were such deemed desirable. And anyway, ever since the middle 1950s rock-for-ages-nine-to-fourteen has so thoroughly occupied the seekers after mindlessness that radical changes in both the style and the expressive content of jazz have taken place with very little interference from outside.

The essentially black content of real jazz was signaled as early as 1948 in *Jazz: A People's Music* by Sidney Finkelstein (Citadel Press). Fifteen years later, 1963, LeRoi Jones, in *Blues People: Negro Music in White America* (William Morrow), essayed a sociological view of the art, replacing the earlier musicological approach with one based on direct knowledge of black life. This kind of study, a parallel to the discovery of black English, has revealed black life as a subculture strongly concentrated on music. Religion, ethics, sexual mores, and family life are also highly developed there, and characteristic. There is a gift for cooking too, though as yet no cuisine. The visual arts are hardly visible at all; but literature, I fancy, may be approaching a takeoff through the stage, where the eloquent, poetic, and vividly ironic black language might one day come to make white diction sound as vapid as most white music.

Certainly music is for now the chief Negro art, and black life is sewn through with it. At every instant it is the understood reference, the universal binder. European classical composition, Anglo-Saxon folklore, Hispanic dance meters, hymns, jungle drums, the German lied, ragtime, Italian opera, all are foods for the insatiable black hunger and grist to its grind. As if inside all U.S. blacks there were, and just maybe there really is, some ancient and African enzyme, voracious for digesting whatever it encounters in the way of sound.

The technical and stylistic developments in black urban music that have taken place since the late 1930s are recounted in a whole shelf of books; but even when musicology still comes to the fore in these, sociological and political backgrounds tend nowadays to dominate the picture. Charlie Parker, according to his biographer Ross Russell, was "the first of the angry black men." Born in Kansas City, Kansas, 1920, brought up musically in a Missouri-side ghetto, dying world famous at thirty-five in, of all places, the Stanhope Hotel on upper Fifth Avenue, he was, again to quote, "the last of a breed of jazzmen apprenticed at an early age, styled in emulation of great master players, tempered in the rough-and-tumble school of the jam session, a master of his craft by the end of his teens, disciplined to the exacting requirements of the big swing bands, and, eventually, the maverick who turned his back on the big bands to create, almost singlehandedly, the musical revolution of the Forties." This sentence tells mostly all, except that the tenor sax was his instrument, and that before his early death in 1955 he had planned to study formal composition with Stefan Wolpe and Edgard Varèse.

Black Music: Four Lives, by A. B. Spellman, examines the achievements and hard times of pianist Cecil Taylor (classically educated in music), saxophonist (chiefly on soprano) Ornette Coleman, pianist Herbie Nichols, and Jackie McLean (alto sax player and college dropout). This generation, still under fifty, frequently well educated, and in private life approaching the bourgeois, believes in jazz as the important serious music of our time. And if most of their professional dates, or "gigs," still take place in white-owned, exploitative, small nightclubs (dismal dumps backstage every one of them and grim saloons out front), this still unbroken bondage is the economic straight-jacket of all jazz musicians' lives and a constant burden of their complaints.

Education has developed their artistic thought, however, or at least their verbalizations of it. A great deal of discussion seems to go on among them now about inside matters like "form" and "meaning." And if the form employed for improvising is still that of variations on a chosen melody, the bass beat under these has become so free and the harmony surrounding them so far-out (read non-tonal) that the melodic transformations they undergo on trumpet and sax are rarely recognizable anymore as related to the original theme.

Nevertheless, these far-out jazzmen work closer than most of our far-out intellectual composers do to classical principles of rhythm and harmony. They do not throw traditions overboard; they reinterpret them, aiming rather toward creating a music based decreasingly on the monotonies of dance accompaniment and more on the songfulness of blues, the common-ground nobility of gospel hymns. There is even a tendency, derived probably from the example of Ornette Coleman, to do without piano, guitar, or whatever else might enforce tempered tunings, and to work both in and around true intervals and their expressive variants. But improvisation is still insisted on as a musical method (no arrangements, no big bands). And a special attitude toward knowledge and culture is recommended, namely, "learn everything but keep it in the subconscious." While at work never analyze, merely improvise—that, after all, is the true discipline of spontaneity.

Black Music, LeRoi Jones's second book on the subject, is sociology, criticism, a preachment, and just possibly literature, so clearly is it thought, so straightforwardly expressed. It treats all the main artists in New Jazz, explains their work musically, the expression in it humanely in terms of black life. And since black life takes to religious experience as naturally as to music, the sermonizing comes through quite void of self-consciousness.

His thesis is summed up in a quotation from tenor sax player Archie Shepp: "The Negro musician is a reflection of the Negro people as a social and cultural phenomenon. His purpose ought to be to liberate America aesthetically and socially from its inhumanity. The inhumanity of the white American to the black American as well as the inhumanity of the white American to the white American is not basic to America and can be exorcised, gotten out. I think the Negro people through the force of their struggles are the only hope of saving . . . the political or the cultural America."

Fine by me; let them save us if they can. And their best chance is through music. Besides, should God himself turn out to be a Negro mammy ("She's black," they do say) nobody would feel more secure than this unreconstructed Confederate. But the trouble is that in spite of TV and radio, possibly because of them, many whites hate music; too few have any ear for it at all.

Black Nationalism and the Revolution in Music, by Frank Kofsky, takes off from an assumption that "hard bop reflected and gave musical expression to . . . the first stirrings of the contemporary black liberation movement." Further parallels between music and life are noted in the ways the more advanced players strive to simulate the sounds of human speech, and not just speech in general but "the voice of the urban Negro ghetto, . . . to distill for your ears the quintessence of Negro vocal patterns [e.g., Archie Shepp's "growly, raspy tenor saxophone locutions"] as they can be heard in the streets of Chicago, Detroit, Philadelphia, Harlem." Also in the persisting practice of group improvisation, which symbolizes a "recognition among musicians that their art is not an affair of individual 'geniuses,' but the musical expression of an entire people, . . . the subordination of the individual to the group."

Bebop is here defined as "harmonic improvisation[,] with the metrical unit an eighth-note [replacing] melodic improvisation with the metrical unit a quarter-note." The latter was characteristic of pre-1940s jazz. In my judgment, adoption of the eighth-note unit, long prevalent in Caribbean dance music, was the radical change that set off all the others. By eliminating a thumped-out quarter-note bass, it invited metrical complexities in all the parts, including bass and drums. And this new freedom virtually imposed harmonic elaboration, which in turn weakened the tyranny of the tune and led, at least with Ornette Coleman, to a fantastic development of the florid bel canto style. All three of these developments seem, both in Coleman and in John Coltrane, to have caused their abandoning the customary piano, thus dispensing with "the framework of tempered pitch."

The marketing of so sophisticated an art in "dingy rooms before half-drunk audiences" is the burden of a litany that appears and reappears in all these books.

The summing up of previous examinations plus testimony

from virtually all hands comes in a remarkably readable book edited, prefaced, and concluded by Dominique-René de Lerma. This covers in essay form and in dialogues black music in college and in pre-college curricula, soul music, gospel music, field work in Africa, the black composer himself in relation to dance, journalism, white history, white society, Negro society, information sources, and every known kind of establishment. How to teach black kids classical music without turning them off, how to cure academic prejudice against playing by ear, against the fact that blues are "about sex," against teaching anything at all not chronologically, against admitting black music to the history books, against an ingrown pedagogy that assumes "white is right." All these things and more are in this richly charged volume. And black control of Black Studies is declared a sine qua non.

But the main text of my sermon today is *Black Talk*, by Ben Sidran, white American jazz performer with a Ph.D. in American Studies from the University of Sussex in England. Its basic assumption is "that black music is not only conspicuous within, but *crucial to*, black culture." This culture is, moreover, an *oral culture* and thus radically opposed to our *literate culture*, which was once an oral tradition, of course, but which is now congealed by its literacy into verbal, hence largely visual, methods of transmission. Orality, therefore, though "a common denominator for all cultures, is, after extended generations, the basis for an alternative breed of culture." And the relation of black music to other oral traditions of Afro-American life is still a question which has been far more ignored than explored.

Now the literate world, dependent on print plus pictures, is a visual world, existing only in space, which is essentially static. Whereas the things that we hear exist in time, which runs on; they relate to an oral continuum. There has come about, it would seem, from these radically different ways of receiving communication an "utter misunderstanding" of each other by blacks and whites which, through the consequent rejection of oral-mindedness by the essentially literate, has by reaction "contributed to the cohesiveness and coherence of the black culture." Moreover, since the orals are more given to moving around than to sitting still (reading), they tend to be restless. And here rises a "unique problem of leadership within the oral community, how to impose leadership, in the Western sense," on a group that values nothing so much as spontaneous improvisation. Therefore, since music, which, "in terms of social sanctions, is one of the more legitimate outlets for black actionality—indeed, during various periods of black history, it has been the only outlet—it follows that black musicians have traditionally been in 'the vanguard group' of black culture."

Now "orality" leads not only to music but to many other forms of group action, and all groups easily adopt rhythmic communication. Also, "tension released through rhythm is strongly associated with the sexual act." And since in sexual as well as other rhythmic acts, time (measured clock-time) tends to get lost, "rhythm can be used to manipulate the greater environment, inasmuch as alterations in time concept can affect the general 'structure of feeling.'" As for losing one's sense of time, anybody knows that with our black friends punctuality is not to be counted on. What one may not have noticed, certainly not much read about, is that "the development of rhythmic freedom has generally preceded social freedom for black Americans." Interesting if true; at any rate, cases are cited.

Now we all know educated and uneducated blacks—professionals, people of business, performing artists, even hired help—who *work* by the clock, though they may not *live* by it. They *read* too, are scholars, handle money, write books. Probably their great psychic skill is moving in and out of orality, to drop at will one way of living and take up another. The Japanese have this faculty, especially those who work in Western clothes, then at six go home to put on kimonos and toe-socks, sit on the floor, and feel normal. We understand an actor moving in and out of a role. Why not anyone out of a verbal situation into music?

How long can black oral culture survive in our verbal civilization? As long, I suppose, as there is black music. The National Advisory Commission on Civil Disorders (the "riot commission" appointed by Lyndon Johnson in 1967) reported, to the president's extreme embarrassment: "Our nation is moving toward two societies, one white, one black—separate and unequal." Just why they are so separate and so unequal is the question raised in *Black Talk*. It seems certain that there is a fundamental opposition of oral vs. literate, auditory vs. visual between the two societies and that this has so far resisted all efforts—cultural, sexual, legal, criminal, and humane—to bridge the chasm.

To live within a nonverbal, if somewhat dizzy, continuum has certainly been the aim of many rock addicts. But the politically radical movements of the 1960s among white college students were not nourished on rock but on the very best black avant-garde jazz. Ben Sidran has information about that. And the black underground itself has been joined aplenty by whites without losing any of its blackness.

Whether there is to be a black political revolution remains doubtful indeed, though if such a thing were to come about, black music and black musicians would likely control its "structure of feeling." As to black music redeeming us all, including the tone deaf, Ben Sidran surely knows better than that, though he does believe music (any music?) to be "a great force for unity and peace today." I find him most convincing when in a final paragraph he esteems it "not altogether irrelevant to suggest that a subculture emotionally and culturally entrenched is not one that can be coerced by violence—or even blatant injustice— nor one that is willing to retreat very far."

Musically there has been no retreat. Since jazz, its best music, and perhaps eventually ours, does seem to be going onward and upward.

The New York Review of Books, October 17, 1974

A Good Writer

JANET FLANNER'S WORLD: *Uncollected Writings 1932–1975*, edited by Irving Drutman. Introduction by William Shawn. 368 pp. Harcourt Brace Jovanovich, 1979.

LONDON WAS YESTERDAY, *1934–1939*, by Janet Flanner, edited by Irving Drutman. 160 pp. Viking, 1975.

THE CUBICAL CITY (1926), by Janet Flanner, with a new afterword by the author. 433 pp. Southern Illinois University Press, 1974.

PARIS WAS YESTERDAY, *1925–1939*, by Janet Flanner, edited by Irving Drutman. 232 pp. Viking, 1972.

PARIS JOURNAL, *1965–1971*, by Janet Flanner, edited by William Shawn. 438 pp. Harcourt Brace Jovanovich, 1972.

PARIS JOURNAL, *1944–1965*, by Janet Flanner, edited by William Shawn. 615 pp. Atheneum, 1965.

MEN AND MONUMENTS. 297 pp. Harper and Brothers, 1957.

PÉTAIN: *The Old Man of France*, by Janet Flanner. 53 pp. Simon and Schuster, 1944.

CITIZEN GENÊT came to the United States in 1793 as minister from France's First Republic. Though on account of political indiscretions a recall was asked for by President Washington in that same year, he actually stayed on as a resident and married here. During his short diplomatic tenure he had sent home letters loaded with information. In 1925 the late Janet Flanner, already resident in France's Third Republic, adopted the revolutionary Citizen's name for signing a fortnightly letter from Paris to *The New Yorker*. Why she took on a pseudonym for reporting is not clear, save possibly to distinguish a journalistic function from a literary, since she was already author of a novel, to be published the next year.

Some years later, easily thirty, when the present witness referred to Miss Flanner as an "ace journalist," she took umbrage at the term. "I am not an 'ace journalist,'" she said, "I am a writer, a good writer." Well, by that time a good writer she was, a very good one; and a fine reporter too, imaginative in her coverage and alert in phraseology. If the snippets of early work quoted from *The New Yorker* in *Paris Was Yesterday* are typical, she had started off as a journalistic writer of concision with a bright carrying power, whereas her literary style in *The Cubical City*, though still perhaps readable, is weighed down by descriptive overwriting.

Actually, if one reads the books in something like reverse order beginning with the most recently published, *Janet Flanner's World* (or better still, the two volumes of *Paris Journal*, which cover the years 1944 to 1971), it becomes clear that their reporting, though vivid, became substantial only in the early 1930s. An exception would be the short profile of Isadora Duncan from 1927. Then in 1933 the Flanner account of how two housemaids of Le Mans, the Papin sisters, murdered their lady and threw her remains about before going at last upstairs to bed together—the original events on which Jean Genet later based his play *Les Bonnes*—is crime reporting unquestionably brilliant. And so were her extensive 1934 reports of the Alexander Stavisky case, a swindling affair which led to his assassination (almost certainly by the police) and to the bloody firings on February 6 into a mass of citizens on the Place de la Concorde (also by the police and with no warning by trumpet-call).

Another complex swindling story, that of the famous Madame Hanau, was written up in 1935. In the meantime Flanner had told about French crimes (not always in *The New Yorker*) with such liveliness that a publisher asked her for a whole book of them. She declined on the ground that Americans might have trouble believing that "in France nobody ever murders anybody he doesn't know."

With the 1935 full-length portrait from London of H.R.H. Queen Mary and the 1936 profile from Berlin of Reichskanzler Adolf Hitler, Janet Flanner became visible as an almost political observer—well informed, picturesque as to language, and responsive to the sympathies of middle-class, educated Americans.

It is certain that Flanner, though thirty when she took up journalism, matured along with the magazine she was to be so fitting a part of for over half a century. And it is also certain that *The New Yorker* itself went through quite a bit of maturing in its early days, for all that it is not easy now to imagine so sedate a publication having ever experienced insecurities.

Some years back, going through old stacks of it in a garret, I was amused to discover (actually it was Julien Levy pointed it out) that for its first years *The New Yorker* was a magazine of humor specializing in sex. Then in 1927 someone cleaned it up. It had started out with a fresh device, the one-line joke, originally an invention of the novelist Ronald Firbank. It also profited from a novel advertising policy, which was to write up shops and restaurants even before they advertised. Its third major experiment was a scholarly treatment of the news (to check everything), along with an aspiration (intact today) toward perfect proofreading.

Scholarship techniques for collecting the news had already been set up by *The New Yorker*'s predecessor, *Time*. And *The New Yorker* has preserved these, notably in its full-length articles. *Time* did less well with them, because its regional source reports, first rewritten in collecting centers like London, Rome, Buenos Aires, and Tokyo, then being recast at home into a lingo known as "*Time* style," ended up as often as not quite different from what the original had said. (I remember a piece about myself from around 1939, I think it was, that contained according to my count at least one error per sentence.) World coverage, with a world war to cover, saved the magazine, "*Time* style" came to be abandoned, and an excellent newsweekly was preserved.

But *The New Yorker* just seemed to go on as it was, while changing imperceptibly from an originally "smart" publication into the slightly left of center political organ it has been for two decades now, its fine fiction, its huge reportages, and its luxury-trade advertisements making dependable reading matter for airplane trips and even for keeping around the house.

Janet's manner changed gradually too, along with the tone of the magazine, which, as the European war approached, was becoming less heavily addicted to the light touch and more unashamedly straightforward, as war reporting augmented and eventually became a necessity. When the European war was over, with plenty of serious soldiering still active in Asia, the Middle East, and Africa, neither Janet nor her paper went back to their earlier attitude of gently kidding the rich. If a time should come when there are, for however briefly, no wars or other holocausts to keep us sober-minded, perhaps we shall all go back to promoting luxuries and making fun of the buyers. But Janet will not be with us, though surely we shall again and again reread her deliciously serious stories of French life, art, and politics as she told them every other week for thirty years.

Journalism that can be collected into books is already of tested quality; and a further accolade comes when such books can be read still again. For myself all Janet Flanner's reporting books are a delight to swim around in, also to follow as a stream. But I am an addict, as she was, of French living, and I too take French politics seriously. Garrett Mattingly used to tell his students that "the history of Europe is the history of France," and that may well be true today, for all of Russia's power and Germany's new wealth.

In any case Janet's continued story of French politics since World War II is to me a convincing performance, and not so much because her sympathies were the "right" ones to have as because she knew better than most observers what the French political parties were up to. That, for an outsider, is no small chore.

Americans writing about France tend to make French people seem very small and to underestimate their sincerity. Not Janet. For her Léon Blum was ever a great man and Mendès-France the hope of one, in spite of their frequent failures. As for de Gaulle, either active or just waiting, she grants him always his full stature, which even physically was enormous, and she recognizes in him the chief author of today's France, though from his return in 1944 till his death in 1970 his very presence, no less than his deeds, never ceased to terrify her, as they did also his most loyal countrymen.

She had attained already by the early 1930s a fairly detailed understanding of the French political system, the result of a friendship with the French novelist Germaine Beaumont, who also helped toward improving her French. Later she came to know the French Communist Party with its almost independent status and its appeal for workingmen and their housewives, as well as for French intellectuals of the revolutionary tradition. I take it that the poet, novelist, and chief party theoretician Louis Aragon, a long-time friend, may well have been Janet's main source of clarity regarding party maneuvers. Trotskyist reasonings she seems less familiar with. But her inside view of French politics was ultimately enriched hugely by her acquaintance with André Malraux, whose portrait is the chief novelty in *Men and Monuments.*

Another art-and-politics excursion in the same book is called "The Beautiful Spoils," which deals with Hitler's personal acquisitions in France, Italy, and Holland; the vast plunderings of Göring (the more knowledgeable of the two and the greedier); and the eventual "liberation" by a handful of American specialists of practically everything not actually destroyed. For this information she probably had access to someone French (my guess is Georges Salles, then Directeur des Musées de France) and certainly to sources in the American army.

Living in New York from the summer of 1939 till 1944, when she returned to France and Germany as a war correspondent in uniform, she composed from official and unofficial sources, from arriving Europeans, and from her own files thoroughly credible pictures of life in occupied France and a four-part

profile, *Pétain: The Old Man of France*. Here also she first published her story of the escape from France during the winter of
1942 and 1943 of Mary Reynolds (called in the narrative Mrs.
Jeffries), a woman in her late forties who had traveled clandes-
tinely for six months by trains, trams, and buses, also by walking
over the Pyrenees, before she arrived finally in New York and
collapsed into bed at the Waldorf. This last weakness, which
Miss Flanner omits, followed a forced vaccination for small-pox
by American medical authorities, an apparently unclean needle
having produced a festered leg which kept the patient supine
for six weeks.

Flanner's *Paris Journals* (1944 to 1965 and 1965 to 1971) give
us for those years a two-volume report on life and politics in
France which I find an enchanting continued story. *London Was
Yesterday*, which contains the Queen Mary profile, has other
pieces from the 1930s and is ornamented by photographs of
London's handsomest actors and noblest ladies; but it does not
come to life as the Paris pictures do. English life and politics
are harder to open up anyway, and the English newspapers tell
you nothing. (Even the lordly *Times*, silent for nearly a year,
was scarcely missed.)

Of Flanner's other postwar reportings, those from Italy are
the most picturesque, those from Germany quite gripping. She
could and did read the Italian press, and was somewhat con-
versant in that language; everywhere I am sure she neglected
neither press contacts nor private occasions to inform herself.
But Americans' fascination with Rome after World War II lasted
maybe a decade at most. As seat of three world powers—the
Catholic Church, the Communist Party, and the film industry,
all impenetrable—and of a brand new republic incapable of
governing, it was certainly no place to write home about with
confidence.

Germany after the last war was far more comprehensible,
especially to those who spoke and read German (which Janet
could do). Her letters about the Nuremberg trials in *Janet
Flanner's World* are a grand performance for their attention
to enlightening detail, for their missing very little of who out-
classed whom in the courtroom fracases, and for an almost
compassionate view of the losers, in spite of their obvious guilt
and their haughty pretense that the whole thing was a frame-up.

But German is heady stuff even today and hard to take in large doses. Back in Paris, with side trips, Janet was happily at home in a hotel room (nowhere did she cook or keep house, ever), lunching out always and dining with friends (she was faithful to them all), reading the whole press every day, going to concerts and to art shows (as an amateur with high toleration), and even keeping up with the new writers, especially the French ones. Steadily she did all of this day after day plus weekends in the country, still reading and talking and listening, for she was a good listener. She was a steady character too, neither an angry one nor jealous nor passionate nor prone to excitements. Level-headed and laborious she always was, and lovely to be with. One wonders how she got through all that writing and the preparations for it.

Was that writing literature? She hoped and rather thought it might be. If literature is something you can read several times and still keep your mind on, then for me Janet Flanner is exactly that. So I keep her books around me. But if they *are* literature, what is their species? Poetry they are not, nor fiction nor formal history nor, after the war freed her from wisecracks, was she a professional humorist, though her Midwestern ways with common sense and with debunking the proud made her cousin to Mark Twain and to George Ade. No busybody she, no reformer, do-gooder, brave bullyboy, or buttinsky. That would be another kind of Midwesterner, including the great Hemingway himself, whom as a writer she adored.

The format of her own writing is closer, I think, to an English model. Let us call her a diarist. Columnist won't do; she was personally too reticent for that. Let us think of her perhaps with Samuel Pepys, who could go on and on about London, and still make us wish for more.

The New York Review of Books, January 24, 1980

The New Grove

THE NEW GROVE DICTIONARY OF MUSIC AND MUSICIANS, edited by Stanley Sadie. Twenty volumes. Macmillan (London), 1980.

WHEN A WIDE-COVERAGE REPORT is issued by a business or a government, the issuing agency can be held responsible for every statement in it. When a work of scholarship is issued by a publishing house, only the author is responsible for his remarks, unless libel, obscenity, or blasphemy is involved. When the work has been written by many different people, however carefully selected by committees and controlled by an editor, nobody can reproach directly either the publisher or his editor, let alone the writers, with individual misstatements, outlandish opinions, or careless language. A reasonable proportion of such accidents is to be expected; what portion is tolerable depends on the price of the work. In *The New Grove Dictionary of Music and Musicians*, there are surprisingly few stumbling blocks and many occasions for gratitude, so huge is its gamut of information, so peaceable its continuing attitudes, so generally easy to read its English writing.

All the same, one looks for an editorial attitude regarding, say, contemporary composers. Everybody, or nearly everybody, is there. Serious efforts have been made to describe their work and to identify it. Also, in considering it, in estimating what one might call its specific gravity, care seems to have been used toward distinguishing small achievers from real minor masters, and both of these from careers which, no matter how limited their world public may be (as with Arnold Schoenberg, for instance), are unquestionably Big Time. Not that any of these terms is applied. But I do note the prevalence of judicious attitudes and a civil tongue, to such a generalized extent indeed that some briefing from the editor must be assumed. Either this, or simply that a choice of writers predominantly from among those professionally occupied with writing about music rather than with performing it or composing it (predominantly British too, I may add) has assured throughout the work a tone of informed common sense that is both easy-going and easy to follow.

This kind of bland civility makes the dictionary a delight to cruise in. And an infinitude of unexpected refreshment tables makes it actually more fun for chance encounters than any other work of its kind I know, even the jolly and somewhat irresponsibly French *Encyclopédie Fasquelle*.

Its novel approaches to musical lexicography comprise—in addition to usual subjects like harmony, modes, scales, notations, and the like and of course composers, theorists, and performers—a truly vast array of locales and geographic situations. Music is covered by cities (including Canada's Halifax), states (including the Vatican), countries (including all the United Nations), regions (Anatolia, East Asia, Micronesia), and all the continents with their subdivisions.

It is these extra parts of the world that provide such rich reading in ethnomusicology. And with this come lots of photographs of inhabitants playing instruments. Indeed the volumes reflect abundantly our century's musicological adventures, and its lively illustration department has made of it a picture book showing sculpture, painting, pottery and portraits, architecture, landscape, and show business from innumerable times and places.

Going back to composers, the living and the near living, there does seem to have been editorial control over the length of the entries that discuss them. To each a given number of words was assigned, this to be accompanied by lists of compositions, of books and articles *by* the subject, and of references *about* him. The writers of the articles have in most cases made out these lists. Whether *their* length was assigned I do not know, but that of the prose treatment was. And this measurement in advance, though needed for controlling the dictionary's volume, does constitute an editorial comment, one sometimes quite surprising, in fact.

For the following list of examples, I have measured entries by the number of pages covered, including photographs, music quotations, catalogues, and bibliographies. They are selected cases, but typical I hope of main threads in the tissue of Western music.

From Germany and Austria, Richard Wagner has 41 pages, his father-in-law Franz Liszt (actually not German save for his music) has 45, Brahms comes next with 34, then Hugo Wolf with 28, and Mahler with 26½. Close to that stand Arnold

Schoenberg (24), Richard Strauss (22), and Bruckner (19). Hindemith comes next with 15, then Alban Berg (13), Anton Webern (11½), Stockhausen (8), Henze (7), Max Reger (6). Distinctly minor, according to editorial apportionment, are Hanns Eisler (just under 5), Busoni (3½), Boris Blacher (3), and Mauricio Kagel (3). Not German at all but cousins to the German line are Bartók with 28 pages, Janáček with 15½, and Grieg with 13.

Among the Russian masters, Glinka has 13 pages; then there are Moussorgsky (13), Rimsky-Korsakov (14), Balakirev (9), Borodin (8), and Prokofiev (15). Topping all these are Tchaikovsky's 27 and Igor Stravinsky's 25 (these last two topping also, but just, Richard Strauss and Schoenberg). Szymanowski, a Pole and closer musically to France, gets 5.

In Italy Verdi takes the sweepstakes with 30 pages, Puccini placing far behind with only 10. Among the stragglers one finds Gian-Francesco Malipiero (6½), Luigi Dallapiccola (5), Luciano Berio (5), Luigi Nono (4), Alfredo Casella (3), Sylvano Bussotti (3), and Ottorino Respighi (less than 2).

In the French group, Berlioz rides strong with 30 pages, Debussy following with 22. Bizet gets 14, Fauré 12, Ravel also 12, Gounod 11, Boulez 8, and César Franck 7. Darius Milhaud and Olivier Messiaen also chalk 7 each. Among slow runners we find Erik Satie (5), Vincent d'Indy (4½), Charles Koechlin and Emmanuel Chabrier (4 each). The nineteenth-century pianist-composer Valentin Alkan comes in next with 3½, Gilbert Amy also with 3½, and Arthur Honegger a bit short of 3. André Jolivet scores just over 2 pages, Georges Auric, Henry Barraud, and Henri Sauguet slightly under that. Lili Boulanger and her sister Nadia are each awarded half a page.

Benjamin Britten leads the British lineup with 15½ pages. Ralph Vaughan Williams rates 12, Michael Tippett 11, Sir Arthur Sullivan 9, and Frederick Delius 6. Sloping down from there, William Walton and Peter Maxwell Davies measure 4½, Lennox Berkeley 3½. At 2½ and 2 we find Arthur Bliss, Frank Bridge, Elisabeth Lutyens, Thea Musgrave, Peter Warlock, and Sir Hubert Parry. Lutyens and Musgrave, unless I have read hastily, are the only female composers from anywhere to receive two pages of attention. Even the French-American Betsy Jolas, though warmly praised, is confined to a bit over one column.

American composers receive in general brief treatment,

except for Charles Ives's 14½ pages, of which 8½ are lists, and Kurt Weill's 10½. Aaron Copland's entry runs to 6 pages, John Cage's to 5½, Edgard Varèse's and Elliott Carter's to 5 each. Four-page entries honor Louis Moreau Gottschalk, Edward MacDowell, Henry Cowell, and Roger Sessions. Three-page treatments go to Gian-Carlo Menotti and Virgil Thomson.

Most of the following have received just two pages, a few 2½: Louis Armstrong, Milton Babbitt, Samuel Barber, Marc Blitzstein, Duke Ellington, George Gershwin, Charles T. Griffes, Roy Harris, Lowell Mason, Walter Piston, Wallingford Riegger, William Schuman, Harry Somers (Canadian), and Carl Ruggles.

Those limited to one page or a bit over include Arthur Berger, Leonard Bernstein, William Billings, Henry Brant (born Canadian), Earle Brown, Henry F. Gilbert, Lou Harrison, Andrew Imbrie, Leon Kirchner, Otto Luening, Daniel Gregory Mason, Nicolas Nabokov, Dika Newlin, Ned Rorem, Gunther Schuller, Carlos Surinach, Randall Thompson, Vladimir Ussachevsky, Hugo Weisgall, Cole Porter, Quincy Porter, and John Philip Sousa.

Of those receiving less than one page one notes Ernst Bacon, Theodore Chanler, Ruth Crawford, Edward Burlingame Hill, Howard Hanson, Frank Loesser, Dane Rudhyar, and David Tudor. From the other Americas Heitor Villa-Lobos rates 3½, Carlos Chávez and Alberto Ginastera each a little over 3.

Please note that these ratings represent in no direct way popularity, fame, genius, or distinction. They are an editor's judgment, after consultations, of course, of each composer's probable Importance in a historical panorama that might be visible on a clear day from England. And any composer, at no matter what length, can receive high praise or summary judgment.

Let me cite a few examples. Charles Hamm writes, "John Cage [5½] has had a greater impact on world-wide music than any other American composer of the twentieth century." Bayan Northcott says that Elliott Carter (also 5½) "at his best sustains an energy of invention that is unrivalled in contemporary composition." He also shows "a grasp of dynamic structure comparable, among twentieth-century composers, only with Berg." Aaron Copland's (6) constant use of material from folk sources is admired by William A. Austin as "the individual quality he [has] given so many borrowed melodies." This individual quality in his own music is further diagnosed as what "listeners all over the world continue[d] to respond to . . . and to recognize."

In the entry on Benjamin Britten I have not been able to isolate any statement quite so comprehensive as these, but I did notice that the genuinely informative essay about him, if not entirely drenched in honey, is certainly spread with the very best butter. More abrasive is the brief article on Byron the poet. Here his lordship is jostled by the word "outsider"—upper-class epithet for the socially unacceptable—and his love-life with Augusta, the half-sister by whom he had a child, is dismissed as an "affair."

Two cases of an apologetic use of "perhaps" occur in otherwise straightforward sentences. One of these picks out Hugo Weisgall as "perhaps America's most important composer of operas" (Bruce Saylor). The other remarks of Arnold Schoenberg that "perhaps no other composer of the time has so much to offer" (O. W. Neighbour).

For a real "rave," as such writing is known journalistically, I offer the following on Karlheinz Stockhausen by G. W. Hopkins:

> He has gathered in a great synthesis all the means available to the composer of the twentieth century, not excluding his heritage from the past, and he has drawn from thought the techniques—indeed, the new language—which can present them in a fashion at once ordered and elemental. It is this elementality which explains the 'drama' of Stockhausen's music, and in the breadth of the synthesis it achieves lies all the justification for its grandeur.

So you see, this dictionary has every kind of writing in it. There are pictures too and lots of them. It approaches the multiple aspects of music from many angles and makes a good show out of the whole. If a few slip-ups occur, I must say I ran across only a very few, and no real howlers. Among the slips let me note (without reproach, only surprise) the absence from individual consideration of two poets whom many composers have set—the English mystic William Blake and the French visionary Max Jacob, as well as the German playwright Georg Büchner, source for *Dantons Tod* by Gottfried von Einem and Alban Berg's *Wozzeck*. Also, for whatever the fact may mean, the Eastman School of Music at Rochester, New York, which Americans hold in high esteem, is summed up in one line and a half.

Actually the coverage of anything, twentieth-century music for instance, is so dispersed that reading it up means jumping about in all twenty volumes. For American music alone there is excellent information under United States Music, also under thirty or more U.S. cities, under Orchestra, Orchestration, Oratorio, Opera, Symphony, Film Music, Theatre Music, Folk Music, Dance, Jazz, Rock, Chamber Music, Stage Design and stage designers, Librettos and librettists, as well as under names of individual composers.

In many cases it is the larger subjects that have been the most wisely written about since these have been mostly assigned to highly knowledgeable writers, or even to groups of them. Single composers tend to get more casual treatment on account of the limited space allowed them, and certainly in some cases from the acceptance of such assignments by writers of lesser preparation.

Famous modern composers, on the other hand, are more likely to be covered by specialists capable of treating them in depth—Stravinsky by Eric Walter White, Debussy by Edward Lockspeiser, and Ives by John Kirkpatrick. Schoenberg and Boulez have, I think, been treated with less authority. The account of "serious," or classical composition, in the article on United States Music, benefits from the knowing hand of Gilbert Chase, as do many references to Latin America and Spain from that of Robert Stevenson. A very brief piece called Libretti (1½ pages only) is signed by two specialists of that subject, Edward Dent and Patrick J. Smith. And there is a remarkably fine essay on Music Criticism from the historian Winton Dean.

One is happy with *The New Grove* for much good reading. Americans may feel impatience with it for certain strangenesses in the proportions, as if its values were not quite either those of an enlightened Europe nor yet of informed America. All the same no German, French, or other encyclopedia of its kind has so far granted to America anything like the amount of space that *Grove* has. This generosity was inevitable, I suppose, since there were bound to be hopes over there for selling sets here. Nevertheless, there it is.

After all, what comparable compendia have American scholars or their publishers ever produced? We have not rivaled so far the *Encyclopaedia Britannica*, nor so far Oxford's *New English Dictionary*. Till we do even half as well regarding music, let us all be grateful to *Grove*.

Notes: Quarterly Journal of the Music Library Association, September 1981

Copland on Copland

COPLAND: *1900 through 1942*, by Aaron Copland and Vivian Perlis. 404 pp. St Martin's/Marek, 1984.

AARON COPLAND, ex-president of American music, retired some twenty years ago from prolific composition but was still practicing recently as a distributor of American work and an authority on its appreciation. He enjoys lifetime protection by historians and is regularly consulted by whoever may be contemplating any changes in the official view of things.

That view remembers him as the head of a commando unit which won for America fifty years ago a vote on the international councils controlling performance, pedagogy, and patronage. That unit consisted of himself, Roger Sessions, Walter Piston, Roy Harris, and this writer, all born between 1894 and 1900. Their pioneering made life easier for their heirs such as Marc Blitzstein, Samuel Barber, William Schuman, Norman Dello Joio, and Leonard Bernstein. These, aided by the Californians Henry Cowell, John Cage, and Lou Harrison, built on the movement a fortress.

This bulwark of progress has now assured to all Americans access to our symphony orchestras, opera and ballet companies, and also to the concert-and-chamber-music consortium. Earlier workers had never had it quite so good so young. Now those around fifty—Glass, Riley, Reich, and their computer chums—have begun to be taken up abroad, even in European premises supported by taxpayers. There is no stopping the movement now—not, at least, till the whole great musical machine bursts apart and collapses into the electronic sea around us.

It is surely proper that the man who got this movement

under way, or who was chosen by consensus to front it, should be celebrated in a festschrift, for that is what the present book chiefly is—a galaxy of praise and gratitude from his co-workers.

Copland, by Aaron Copland and Vivian Perlis, actually the first half of a two-volume work, covers the years 1900–1942. In addition to enlightening tributes by helpers and colleagues, it also contains excerpts from Copland's own letters and diaries. A few passages written in the third person are presumably by Perlis; the rest of the book is in the first person, appearing thus to come from Copland himself.

However, the undistinguished quality of their writing, so different from the compact straightforwardness of language in the direct quotations, is not what this reviewer would expect from Copland. Nor is the content exactly what an artist of his experience would be expected to include. There is virtually no portraying of character here regarding people continuously present in his career—say, Nadia Boulanger, Serge Koussevitzky, Minna Lederman. Even the members of his family and his lifetime friend Harold Clurman come out shadowy. Likewise, all those helpful colleagues, stubborn conductors, hesitant patrons, gushing friends, and pupils overgrateful for benefits received come to life only when writing in their own person. And there is far too much about the public success or failure of each successive piece, too much quoting of reviews, and almost no analysis of significant passages.

On the other hand, since any artist young and poor is more attractive than the same artist old and prosperous, early sources of Copland's upkeep through family, friends, appreciation lectures, cheap commissions, and borrowed apartments, all realistically exposed here, are highly entertaining to read about. And the frank admission of some fellow-traveling in the Depression decade, adventures that almost every American artist had in those years, is most welcome after so many cover-ups from so many certainly more guilty.

The liveliness, the intellectual vigor, the sustained animation that made the 1920s and '30s remembered as a glamorous time manage surprisingly to shine through this patchwork continuity. So, too—and clearly—do the energy, the sustained trajectory that characterized America's breakthrough into the musical big time.

One might also note, though the book does not, that America's admission to the councils of classical music was simultaneous with our virtual takeover of popular music, and with an explosion in black music, or jazz, that was heard round the world.

Vanity Fair, September 1984

CHRONOLOGY

NOTE ON THE TEXTS

NOTES

INDEXES

Chronology

Born Virgil Garnett Gaines Thomson, November 25, in an apartment at East Tenth Street and Virginia Avenue, Kansas City, Missouri, the third child and only son of Quincy Alfred Thomson and Clara May (Gaines) Thomson. (Father, the son of a Confederate soldier who had died during the Civil War, was born in 1862 in rural Saline County, Missouri, and had struggled there as a farmer, and then as the owner of a hardware store. He had recently moved to Kansas City with the financial help of his brother-in-law, Virgil's namesake Charlie Garnett, and found work operating a cable car. Mother, born in 1865 in Boone County, Kentucky, was the city-loving, socially ambitious daughter of a retired land investor. The couple, whose families were neighbors in Slater, Missouri, met in 1879 and were married in 1883. Their first child, Ruby Elizabeth Richerson Thomson, was born in 1885. Their second, Hazel Louise Thomson, was born in 1890 and died of diphtheria at the age of two.) Thomson's family is Lowland Scottish on his father's side and mostly English and Welsh on his mother's. His parents are staunchly Southern Baptist, and, from infancy, Thomson is exposed to Sunday hymns at Calvary Baptist Church, where his father is a deacon.

1899
Father passes civil service exams and finds better-paying work as a post office administrator. With backing from Charlie Garnett, secures a loan to purchase a lot at 2629 Wabash Avenue, where contractors build a two-story frame house of his own design.

1901
When Charlie Garnett moves his family to Colorado, his daughter, Lela—who, like Thomson's sister, Ruby, is fifteen years old—stays behind to continue her education at Kansas City's Central High School. She moves into the Thomson house, bringing with her an upright piano. Young Thomson is fascinated by the instrument and, he will later recall, begins to improvise on it "with flat hands and the full arm, always with the pedal down and always loud, bathing in musical sound at its most intense. . . . It was Lela who taught me, at five, how to play from notes."

1902 Enters first grade at the Irving School (grades 1–6), on Prospect Avenue at Twenty-fourth Street, and is immediately designated by fellow schoolboys as a victim. "On my second day at school I got into a fight," Thomson later recalled, "and found myself losing the match. . . . My surprise was definitive." His strategy for avoiding future beatings is to refuse to fight. "If [this] often brought me the taunt of 'sissy,' it caused me to grow strong in other ways of defense and attack, psychological ways, and in the development of independence."

1906 When Lela marries and moves out of the house, taking the piano with her, sister Ruby, a talented potter who earns her own money by selling her work, buys Virgil a used upright of his own. She also pays for lessons from local teachers, and shows him off at her evening parties, at which he plays waltzes, two-steps, and German polkas.

1908 Graduates from sixth grade with class's highest marks and, as a reward, father buys him a ticket to a piano recital by Ignace Jan Paderewski. A lover of Sousa marches, attends the many free summer band concerts in Kansas City's public parks. In fall enrolls at Central High School (grades 7–12). Father buys new, bigger house at 2613 Wabash Avenue, on the same block as the previous residence.

1909 Meets Robert Leigh Murray, a thirty-eight-year-old tenor soloist at Calvary Baptist Church, who for the next ten years will be his musical mentor. A talented singer who had once toured nationally with various male quartets, Murray is employed as a salesman for the Olney Company, distributor of Knabe pianos in the Kansas City area. Thomson is Murray's frequent guest at Knabe-sponsored recitals by singers such as John McCormack, Johanna Gadski, and Mary Garden, and pianists such as Vladimir de Pachmann and Ferruccio Busoni.

1910–11 Through Murray's connections, family hires piano teachers appropriate to Virgil's talents, Moses Boguslawski (a Russian interpreter of Liszt) and, later, Gustav Schoettle (a German exponent of Bach), both affiliated with the newly founded Kansas City Conservatory of Music. Learns how to accompany a singer, and earns professional wages as Murray's recital pianist.

1912   Works with Rudolf King, a former student of Polish pianist Theodor Leschetizky, on technique and solo performance. Practices two hours a day during the school year, four hours a day in the summer. Also pursues organ studies with Clarence D. Sears of Grace Episcopal Church, and plays organ at Grace every Sunday morning at eleven, immediately following his nine o'clock Bible class at Calvary Baptist.

1914   Graduates from Central High School with honors in English literature and composition, shorthand, and public speaking. In summer becomes a student of E. Geneve Lichtenwalter, whom he will always consider his most important teacher. A midwestern native who had lived in New York, France, and Germany, a reader of history and philosophy, and a lover of poetry that she set to her own music, she is more than a pedagogue to Thomson; she is an intellectual role model and a window into the "good life." Under her auspices, he makes his recital debut in downtown Kansas City, performing works by Franz Schubert and Edward MacDowell. "The boy is not quite 18 years old," reports the *Kansas City Star*, "but in last night's exacting programme showed a broad musical understanding. His execution . . . is smooth, rhythmic, and interesting." Takes postgraduate classes at Central High School and works as a page at the Kansas City Public Library.

1915   In September enters the two-year program at the newly opened Kansas City Polytechnic Institute, a junior college where he will study English composition, French, Spanish, math, and science. Forms an all-male arts club he calls the "Pansophists" and edits its little magazine, *Pans*.

1916   Nearly expelled from the Polytechnic for reading aloud to a mixed audience of Pansophists and coeds from Edgar Lee Masters's *Spoon River Anthology*, a book the school's administration considers deeply shocking. His reputation is saved by classmate Alice Smith, who testifies before an investigative committee that Thomson had advised all young women who might be offended to avoid the reading. Alice, the Stanford-educated great-granddaughter of Joseph Smith, founder of the Mormon Church, becomes Thomson's lifelong friend and correspondent.

1917   On March 5, as the United States prepares to enter World War I, Thomson—five foot five and 130 pounds—enlists in the National Guard field artillery. Upon completing the spring semester at the Polytechnic, joins his unit in Independence, Missouri, for basic training. In August transfers to the Kansas City headquarters of the Medical Corps Detachment of the 129th Artillery, where he administers vaccinations and does paperwork. Spends fall at Camp Doniphan, in Fort Sill, Oklahoma, where he is "shaped up, drilled, and disciplined" with the rest of the 129th.

1918   In January accepted by the Aviation Section, Signal Corps, and studies radio technology at the School of Military Aeronautics, in Austin, Texas. In April sent to the Signal Corps's technical school for radio officers at Columbia University, New York City, and in July is made second lieutenant. Transferred first to Fort Sill, and then to Gerstner Field, in Lake Charles, Louisiana, for flight training. In September is ordered overseas, but before he can be deployed, the war ends, on November 11. Thomson, almost twenty-two, returns to his parents' house in Kansas City.

1919   Takes further classes at the Polytechnic, applies to various eastern colleges, and in the spring, with the help of a $2,000 loan secured by Alice Smith's father, enrolls at Harvard College. "Harvard had been chosen," Thomson will later recall, "for my especial needs, which were three—good keyboard lessons, available in Boston; training in harmony, counterpoint, and composition, said to be excellent at this university; and full access to its arts and letters. My ultimate aim at this time was to become an organist and choir-director in some well-paying city church." Upon arriving in Cambridge in August, purchases a brand-new Stieff mahogany grand ($875) and, to the delight of his landlady, installs it in her boardinghouse just north of Harvard Yard. Studies privately in Boston with German-born pianist Heinrich Gebhard, another former student of Leschetizky. Takes lessons from American organist Wallace Goodrich, dean of the New England Conservatory, and rents organ time (25¢ an hour) at Harvard's Appleton Chapel. At Harvard his faculty advisor (and advocate) is the American composer Edward Burlingame Hill, who urges him to take his class on modern French music and to write music criticism. His harmony teacher (and antagonist) is department chairman Walter R. Spalding, who forces him to take Music I in an effort to cure him of his "uppishness." But it is Archibald T. Davison, a pioneer of early music studies and the director of the Harvard Glee Club, who has the greatest influence on his musical development. Davison, by teaching undergraduates to sing seldom performed early church music rather than pep songs, has for seven years been making the Glee Club a force in Boston's musical life while also expanding America's concert choir repertoire. Thomson joins the sixty-member Glee Club as a tenor, and reports to sister Ruby that "the choir is wonderful. We sing medieval things in Latin without accompaniment, and sing them beautifully."

1920   In spring takes paid position as part-time organist and choir director at a Unitarian church in North Easton, Massachusetts, twenty-five miles south of Boston. Meets Harvard English instructor S. Foster Damon, a proponent of the avant-garde who introduces him to the works of Erik Satie and Gertrude Stein, both of whom will become shaping artistic influences. At end of term is named teaching assistant to Professors Hill and Davison. In Kansas City for the summer, composes his first pieces, two songs set to texts by Amy Lowell and William Blake (favorites of Damon) and a choral setting of Psalm 130 ("De profundis"). In fall becomes assistant director of the Glee Club, for which Davison plans an eight-week concert tour of Europe the following summer.

1921   Meets H. T. Parker, music editor of the *Boston Evening Transcript*, who while reporting an article on the Glee Club is impressed with Thomson's quick wit and knowledge of music history. In spring, Hill and Davison arrange to award Thomson the music department's John Knowles Paine Traveling Fellowship for 1921–22. Their plan is for Thomson to tour Europe with the Glee Club and then stay on in Paris for a paid year of study at the newly founded American Conservatory in Fontainebleau. On June 11, the Glee Club leaves New York for Le Havre on the French steamer *La Touraine*, and en route rehearses its program: the French and American national anthems; Palestrina, Praetorius, Hassler; Gregorian chants; English part-songs; folk songs arranged by Brahms and Dvořák; and recent works by Borodin and Sibelius. The concert itinerary includes Paris, Dijon, Nancy, and Strasbourg; Koblenz and Wiesbaden; Milan, Rome, Naples, Venice, and Ravenna. After the tour, Thomson spends two weeks in Switzerland and four in England before beginning his studies in Paris.

His principal teacher at the American Conservatory is the French organist and composer Nadia Boulanger, whose other students include the twenty-one-year-old Aaron Copland. Thomson's acquaintance with the Glee Club's French liaison, the Harvard-educated Bernard Faÿ, leads to encounters with Jean Cocteau, Picasso, Darius Milhaud, Francis Poulenc, and, most important to Thomson, Erik Satie.

1922   At the invitation of H. T. Parker, writes pieces about Paris musical events for the *Boston Evening Transcript*, including an article on a conductor as yet unheard-of in America, the Russian phenomenon Serge Koussevitzky. (Thomson always maintained that this article "set in motion a train of events" that culminated in Koussevitzky's appointment as music director of the Boston Symphony Orchestra in 1924.) Continues his studies with Boulanger, spends hours every day at the piano and the organ, and composes a few more short pieces. In late August he reluctantly leaves Paris, promising himself to return soon. Again takes up residence in the boardinghouse near Harvard Yard, resumes organ lessons with Wallace Goodrich, and takes a demanding but prestigious one-year job as the choir director and noon-service organist at Boston's historic King's Chapel (Episcopal). Joins the Liberal Club, an undergraduate dining club whose members include the poet and polymath Lincoln Kirstein, the aspiring painter Maurice Grosser, and a handsome, pensive junior named Briggs Buchanan.

1923   Overcommitted at King's Chapel, nostalgic for Paris, and troubled by his strong attraction to Briggs Buchanan, Thomson struggles through his final semester at Harvard. Passes the music department's general examinations, but is denied a "degree with distinction" for what Professor Spalding terms his "mediocrity" in harmony, counterpoint, and fugue. ("We wish you to know," Spalding writes on behalf of the faculty, "that we have a high opinion of your general musical ability . . . but we regret that your grammatical knowledge of the subject is so deficient that this distinct deficiency is apparent in your writing of music.") Nevertheless, when the Juilliard Trust gives Spalding $1,500 to award to a deserving senior, he gives the prize to Thomson. Uses the money to move not to Paris but to New York City, where he takes an apartment at 55 East Thirty-fourth Street. Joins the American Orchestral Society, a training

orchestra recommended by Professor Hill, and there studies conducting with Chalmers Clifton, director of the Society, and composition with Rosario Scalero, a teacher of
music theory at the Mannes School of Music. Begins an
intense correspondence with Briggs Buchanan, in which he
explores, explicitly, his artistic interests and ambitions, and,
allusively, his sexual longings.

1924   In September returns to Harvard as a salaried teaching assistant to Hill and Davison just as Buchanan, to Thomson's
surprise and distress, leaves Cambridge for a job on Wall
Street. Accepts post as Sunday organist at Village Congre-
gational Church, in Whitinsville (near Worcester), Massachusetts, and becomes the regular weekend guest of the
Lasell family, the wealthy patrons of Worcester's musical
life. Writes concert reviews for the *Boston Evening Transcript* and, at the suggestion of H. L. Mencken, a musical
analysis of jazz for *The American Mercury*, his first article
for a national magazine. Realizing that his feelings for Buchanan are keeping him in the States and hindering his
professional progress, resolves to go to Paris. Sets sail in
September, having found a traveling companion in John
Joseph Sherry Mangan, a friend from the Liberal Club who
will help him fight loneliness during his first months in
France. Rents a student flat on the rue de Berne and frequents Shakespeare and Company, Sylvia Beach's Left Bank
bookstore, where he meets James Joyce, Ernest Hemingway, Ford Madox Ford, Ezra Pound, and the young American composer George Antheil, who will become a friend.
Resumes studies with Nadia Boulanger and brings Antheil
into her American Conservatory circle, which now includes
Copland, Walter Piston, and Theodore Chanler. In September is surprised to encounter his Liberal Club acquaintance
Maurice Grosser, just arrived in Paris on a Harvard painting
fellowship. When, at Christmastime, Thomson is offered
use of a two-room flat in the Paris suburb of Saint-Cloud,
he asks Grosser, seven years his junior, to move in and share
expenses. Their friendship will soon deepen into the most
enduring attachment of both their lives. Although after
1934 they do not always live together, they will remain devoted to each other until Grosser's death in 1986.

1925   Writes a series of what Thomson calls "sassy and classy"
pieces on musical topics for the American monthly *Vanity Fair*, a bible of the Jazz Age. In July is shocked by the

sudden death of Erik Satie, age fifty-nine. Introduced by George Antheil to Gertrude Stein, whom Thomson impresses with informed and sincere enthusiasm for her work. In Thomson's phrase, he and Stein "get on like Harvard men."

1926   Under the tutelage of Boulanger, completes his first major concert work, a three-movement *Sonata da Chiesa* (Church Sonata) for five instruments. In May the piece receives its premiere at a well-attended concert of new American music sponsored by the Fontainebleau conservatory. Secretly experiments with setting texts by Stein, hoping, as he later writes, "to break, crack open, and solve anything still waiting to be solved, which was almost everything, about English musical declamation. My theory was that if a text is set correctly for the sound of it, the meaning will take care of itself. And the Stein texts, for prosodizing in this way, were manna." The first text he sets is "Susie Asado," a prose poem from 1913, collected in Stein's *Geography and Plays* (1922).

1927   On New Year's Day, presents the music for "Susie Asado" to Stein, who is deeply moved and impressed. Immediately follows up with settings of her prose poems "Capital Capitals" and "Preciosilla," with results so satisfactory to Stein that she proposes she and Thomson write an opera together. After toying with subjects drawn from *Bulfinch's Mythology* and Parson Weems's *Life of Washington*, they agree to treat the lives of the saints, especially Teresa of Ávila and Ignatius Loyola. By June, Stein has finished the libretto, which she calls *Four Saints in Three Acts*. Thomson will devote most of the next thirteen months to writing the music. In the fall, with the benefit of patronage from the Lasell family, Thomson secures an eighteenth-century studio at 17 quai Voltaire, his Paris residence for the next fifty years.

1928   By New Year's Day he is fully engaged with the text of *Four Saints*. Seated at his piano, he reads the words aloud, repeatedly, until musical rhythms, contours, and shapes suggest themselves. Taking no liberties with Stein's libretto, he sets every word—including the stage directions—to melodies born of American hymn tunes, Negro spirituals, and band music, and of the cadences of plain midwestern speech. Finishes the piano-vocal version in July, and then begins scoring the work, which, he tells the Lasells, "will be the longest task of all, certainly the dirtiest, and there is a ballet and an intermezzo and a personal appearance by the Holy Ghost. . . ." Also returns to work and completes a symphony on the Baptist hymn "Jesus Loves Me" and four sets of organ pieces called *Variations on Sunday School Tunes.* After receiving from Stein the gift of an abstract verbal portrait—the short prose work "Virgil Thomson," later collected in her book *Portraits and Prayers* (1934)—Thomson becomes fascinated with the idea of making abstract "musical portraits" of persons of his acquaintance. Begins to write short "sketches from life"—musical ideas jotted on staff paper while his subject sits five or six feet before him—with the aim of evoking some aspect of the sitter's character. Stein's methods encourage him to "try to write automatically, cultivate the discipline of spontaneity, let it flow." The portraits are sketched in silence, usually in about an hour. Thomson does not pause to try out what he has written on the piano, "to hear, correct, or criticize"—such adjustments are left for later. "My effort while at work is to write down whatever comes to me in the sitter's presence, hoping as I transcribe my experience that it will, as the painters say, 'make a composition.'" He will make seven such portraits in 1928, and about 130 more over the next five decades, most of them short works for solo piano.

1929 Spends winter in America, trying to find a producer for *Four Saints* and to arrange performances of his recent concert pieces. In Boston plays his *Symphony on a Hymn Tune* for Koussevitzky, who happily follows the score until, in the middle of the final movement, he throws up his hands and says: "I could never play my audience *that!*" (The symphony will not have its premiere until 1945.) In February, plays and sings a one-man piano version of *Four Saints* to an invited audience at the New York apartment of critic Carl Van Vechten, an advocate of Stein's work. Returns to Paris and writes several chamber works, including a piano sonata that will become the basis for his second symphony.

1930 Friendship with Stein becomes strained by petty misunderstandings within their shared social and professional circles. From Stein's perspective, Thomson is guilty of repeatedly siding with her rivals, detractors, and "glory-grabbing" French translators, especially the poet-publisher Georges Hugnet, which leads to fewer invitations to her home.

1931   In January, "Miss Gertrude Stein," in a one-sentence letter, "declines further acquaintance with Mr. Virgil Thomson." Thomson, hurt and angry, continues to search for a producer for *Four Saints*. Writes his second symphony, which will not be performed until ten years later, and his first string quartet.

1932   Becomes a regular contributor of articles to *Modern Music*, the journal of the League of Composers, a New York–based organization dedicated to nurturing the American audience for twentieth-century music. For the next fourteen years, until the journal's folding in 1946, he will write on topics ranging from Copland and Gershwin to swing band syncopation and Charlie Chaplin's film scores. Completes String Quartet No. 2 and a *Stabat Mater*, with French text by Max Jacob, for soprano and string quartet.

1933   In the spring, visits America to help lay foundation for the first production of *Four Saints*. Through the efforts of Van Vechten and his friends—including architect Philip Johnson and art dealer Kirk Askew—a group of backers has formed. A. Everett "Chick" Austin Jr., director of the Wadsworth Atheneum, in Hartford, Connecticut, schedules the premiere for the following winter in the Atheneum's new Avery Memorial Theater. Thomson energetically handles all artistic aspects of the production, hiring a conductor, Alexander Smallens, and a designer, the faux-naïf modernist Florine Stettheimer. Retires to the French countryside to finish the score, and gingerly renews contact with Stein to discuss contractual matters. In October, returns to New York, where he hires a young, untried John Houseman as director and Frederick Ashton as choreographer. Through Van Vechten's contacts in the Harlem music world, hires choral director Eva Jessye and an all-black cast—six soloists and thirty-two choristers. Rehearsals start in early December.

1934   *Four Saints* receives its premiere at the Wadsworth Atheneum on February 8. Described by *The New York Times* as a combination "opera, stage cantata, farce, [and] Hasty Pudding show" whose text "is a superb vehicle for [Thomson's] melodic virtuosity [and] cunning," it is an immediate *succès de scandale*, selling out its weeklong Hartford run before moving to Broadway for forty-eight further performances.

Stein, at home in Paris, receives a vivid firsthand report from her collaborator: "In every way it was very, very beautiful and of course there were some who didn't like the music and some who didn't like the words . . . but there wasn't anybody who didn't see that the ensemble was a new kind of collaboration and that it was unique and powerful." Upon his return to Paris, Thomson is asked by James Joyce to set to music the guessing game episode of his "Work-in-Progress" (*Finnegans Wake*), but Thomson declines, in part because Stein considers Joyce a "rival." In October, Thomson travels to Chicago to oversee a one-week run of *Four Saints.* There he reunites with Stein, then on the first leg of a six-month American publicity tour. On opening night, Thomson later recalls, the estranged collaborators "kiss but do not quite make up."

1935   Temporarily based in New York City, Thomson organizes a series of concerts for the Wadsworth Atheneum. In the fall, at the invitation of producer John Houseman, composes incidental music and creates sound effects for the Orson Welles/Federal Theater Project's all-black production of *Macbeth*, to be mounted the following spring.

1936   In January, introduced by Houseman to Pare Lorentz, filmmaker for the U.S. Resettlement Administration, a New Deal agency tasked with relocating Oklahoma farm families displaced by drought, wind, and soil erosion. Lorentz, editing a twenty-six-minute documentary on the man-made causes of the Dust Bowl, is facing a tight government deadline and needs music for the film immediately. Thomson delivers the score—a fluid stream of cowboy tunes and mood music—in less than a month. *The Plow That Broke the Plains* is released in May to excellent reviews.

1937   Writes the score for *The River* (1938), a second documentary short by Pare Lorentz, on the man-made causes of floods and the need for dams in the Mississippi delta. (In 1942 Thomson will make concert suites from his scores to *The River* and *The Plow That Broke the Plains.* For his admirer Aaron Copland "they are a lesson in how to treat Americana.") Lincoln Kirstein, Thomson's friend from the Harvard Liberal Club, now the founder-director of the Ballet Caravan dance company, commissions music for *Filling Station* (1938), a comic dance designed "to evoke roadside America as pop art." Thomson's score, a cartoon soundtrack for the antics of a mock-heroic gas station attendant, is the first ballet written by an American composer on an indigenous American theme.

1938 *Filling Station*, choreographed by Lew Christensen, receives its premiere at the Wadsworth Atheneum on January 6. In the spring, Thomson accepts a thousand-dollar advance from Thayer Hobson, the publisher of William Morrow & Co., for a book of linked essays on music and contemporary culture. In June moves back to Paris, and begins work on a second opera—a musical setting of John Webster's *Duchess of Malfi*—but abandons the project by the end of the summer. Renews acquaintance with his friend Sherry Mangan, who, in a series of late-night conversations, asks Thomson basic questions about music, musicianship, and economics that sharpen his thoughts about the book he has promised Hobson. In October he begins to write and, forgoing his piano and his social life, completes the book within six months.

1939 Thomson's book *The State of Music* is published by Morrow in November. In it he describes the modern musician's lot in relation to those of his fellow artists and to the workings of American society. He writes about how musicians are and should be educated, how and why modern music gets made, and, in matters of employment, commissions, awards, and patronage, "who does what to whom, and who gets paid." He argues that music is a profession and that its makers, especially its composers, must take control of its creation, performance, and distribution lest it become "a mere consumer commodity." Reviews are widespread but sales are dismal—only two thousand copies in the first year. Still, the book is a sensation within the world of criticism— and a scandal within the world of philanthropy—and makes Thomson's reputation as a wit, a critic, and American music's strongest advocate.

1940 In June Germany invades France, and Thomson leaves Paris only a few days before the city is occupied. Sails from Lisbon to the United States on August 12, and takes a furnished apartment on the second floor of New York's Hotel Chelsea, at 222 West Twenty-third Street. (Thomson will move into a ninth-floor suite in 1943, and he will keep the

Chelsea as his American residence for the rest of his life.) In mid-September spends a weekend at the Connecticut home of conductor Alexander Smallens, and there is introduced to Geoffrey Parsons, lead editorial writer and the man in charge of cultural coverage at the *New York Herald Tribune*. Impressed by *The State of Music*, Parsons invites Thomson to succeed the late Lawrence Gilman as the paper's chief music critic and head of the music department. Later, in an interview with the paper's publisher, Thomson will be candid about his reasons for accepting Parsons's offer: "The general standard of music reviewing in New York had sunk so far that almost any change might bring improvement. Also I thought perhaps my presence in a post so prominent might stimulate performance of my works." He joins the staff on October 10, and his first review, a withering appraisal of that evening's concert by the New York Philharmonic, runs the following morning.

1941   Settles into his *Herald Tribune* assignment, and quickly establishes a routine. "During seven months of the year I wrote a Sunday article every week and averaged two reviews," he will later recall. "During the summer months I did no reviewing; I also skipped seven or eight Sunday articles. Since these could be sent from anywhere, I toured on musical errands of my own or stayed in some country place writing music. I also wrote music in town [and] went in and out on lectures and conducting dates. The paper liked all this activity, because it kept my name before the public." Builds a department that within four years includes columnists Rudi Blesh (jazz), Edwin Denby (dance), and B. H. Haggin (radio and recordings). Solicits pieces from such critic-composers as Arthur Berger, Paul Bowles, John Cage, Elliott Carter, Peggy Glanville-Hicks, and Lou Harrison. ("I used no one not trained in music," he wrote, "for my aim was to explain the artist, not to encourage misunderstanding of his work.") His mission, as writer and editor, is "to expose the philanthropic persons in control of our institutions for the amateurs they mostly are, to reveal the manipulators of our musical distribution for the culturally retarded profit-makers that indeed they are, and to support with all the power of my praise every artist, composer, group, or impresario whose relation to music is straightforward, by which I mean based only on music and the sound it makes." On November 17, Thomson's Symphony No. 2 (1931) is given its premiere by the Seattle Symphony, Sir Thomas Beecham, conductor.

1942   On March 14, arrested in an F.B.I. raid on a gay bordello near the Brooklyn Naval Yard. He is bailed out by Geoffrey Parsons, who successfully keeps the incident out of the papers. The arrest report remains on the record, but no charges are ever filed. (All his life, Thomson—haunted since youth by a sense of shame, and by the public humiliation and imprisonment of Oscar Wilde—strove to keep his homosexuality an entirely private matter. He never mentioned his sexual orientation in print, and vocally disapproved of those who did. In the last year of his life he told his biographer, "I didn't want to be queer. No! No! No! That was another hurdle I didn't want to have to jump over. . . . Nowadays it's much easier [but in my youth] you didn't mention it . . . you didn't tell anything.")

1943   Father dies, age eighty-one, on April 6. "My personal regret," Thomson later writes, "was that now I could not let him know my shame for the harsh things said in adolescent years. But he must have known and forgiven me long ago, for he was a Christian . . . and had always understood me and spared reproach."

1944   At the invitation of conductor Eugene Ormandy, orchestrates eight of his musical portraits, which, on November 17, are given their premiere in Philadelphia. Meets Ned Rorem, a twenty-year-old composition student at the Curtis Institute of Music, who leaves school to become his copyist. Thomson pays him twenty dollars a week, and gives him free lessons in orchestration. ("In the eighteen months I worked with Virgil," Rorem will later write, "I was to learn more than during the long years, before and after, spent in the world's major conservatories.") In the fall receives a letter from Gertrude Stein suggesting that they collaborate on a second opera. He tells her that, musically, he would like to treat a theme from nineteenth-century America, "but, please, let's not have any foolishness about Abraham Lincoln. That can't be done!"

1945   On February 22, at Carnegie Hall, Thomson's *Symphony on a Hymn Tune* (Symphony No. 1, 1928) is given its premiere by the New York Philharmonic, in a performance conducted by the composer. In March *The Musical Scene*, a collection of Thomson's articles and reviews from the *Herald Tribune*, is published by Alfred A. Knopf. ("As a literary craftsman, the author is probably unsurpassed in his field," says *The New York Times Book Review*. "His unfavorable opinions are disarmingly sincere—and utterly venomous. His praises are sung with the joy of a child about to receive a second helping of ice cream.") In April, Eugene Ormandy produces a Columbia Masterworks recording of Thomson conducting the Philadelphia Orchestra in a performance of five of the orchestrated musical portraits. (*Five Portraits*, released as a set of two 78-rpm discs, is the first commercial recording of Thomson's work.) In early summer, representatives of Columbia University's Theater Associates inform Thomson that the late Alice M. Ditson, a wealthy opera-lover with ties to the university, has left them a sum of money with which to commission and mount new works. In August, just weeks after the end of World War II, Thomson visits Paris to meet with Gertrude Stein and discuss the opportunity that Columbia has laid before them: a Broadway budget production of a new Stein-Thomson opera for the spring of 1947. After a week of brainstorming, they agree to write a pageant on the life of the early feminist Susan B. Anthony.

1946   On March 16, Stein sends Thomson the text of her libretto, *The Mother of Us All*. Thomson, writing from New York on April 15, tells her that "it is sensationally handsome and Susan B. is a fine role." The libretto will be the last major work that Stein completes; that spring her health deteriorates suddenly, and she dies of stomach cancer, age seventy-two, on July 27. After a trip to Paris to consult with Stein's companion and literary executor, Alice B. Toklas, Thomson clears his schedule and begins work on the music for the opera. He has a piano-vocal version by December 10, which he auditions for his closest composer friends and his receptive Columbia patrons.

1947   Thomson scores the opera throughout the spring, and *The Mother of Us All* receives its premiere at Brander Matthews Theater on May 7. Otto Luening, professor of music at Columbia and Barnard, conducts an orchestra of student and faculty musicians, and American soprano Dorothy Dow sings the title role. Reviews are mostly favorable:

Olin Downes of *The New York Times* calls it "adroit, entertaining, expressive" and "a piece of admirable métier and
integrated style. . . . It is to be seen." A truncated version
of *Four Saints*, abridged and conducted by Thomson, is
released on disc by RCA Victor to good reviews and strong
sales. "I am sorry now that I did not write an opera with
[Stein] every year," Thomson remarks in his liner notes. "It
had not occurred to me that both of us would not always
be living." Receives order of merit from the French Légion
d'honneur.

1948   In March *The Art of Judging Music*, a second collection of
Thomson's articles and reviews from the *Herald Tribune*, is
published by Alfred A. Knopf. ("Paste-up collections of old
reviews usually make for very dreary reading," says *The New
Yorker*. "Mr. Thomson's book is an exception, because he
can discuss even the most ephemeral musical event in relation to the whole art. He is also, of course, a very witty and
astringent writer.") In May elected a member of the National Institute of Arts and Letters. Completes the score to
Louisiana Story, a feature-length documentary by Robert J.
Flaherty. For this film—a nearly wordless study in the effect
of the oil industry on the environment and the folkways of
Cajun Louisiana, told from the point of view of a twelve-
year-old boy—Thomson writes over sixty minutes of music,
his longest composition outside his operas. When it opens
in New York on September 18, the film and its score receive
uniformly excellent reviews.

1949   On May 2 the music for *Louisiana Story* is awarded a Pulitzer Prize—a first for a motion-picture score. Thomson will
fashion two suites from the soundtrack, *Suite from "Louisiana Story*," conducted by Eugene Ormandy in New York
and Philadelphia that fall, and *Acadian Songs and Dances*,
used by George Balanchine as music for his ballet *Bayou*
(1952). Composes two works for band, *At the Beach* and *A
Solemn Music*, the latter in memory of Gertrude Stein.

1950   Concerto for Cello and Orchestra (1949), a great favorite
of Thomson's among his compositions, is given its premiere by Ormandy and the Philadelphia Orchestra, with
Paul Olefsky, soloist.

1951   In March *Music Right and Left*, a third collection of
Thomson's articles and reviews from the *Herald Tribune*,
is published by Henry Holt & Co. ("Together with the

two previous collections," writes Roger Sessions in *The New York Times Book Review*, "it reflects in a striking way the seriousness, the directness, and the basic simplicity of Thomson's critical approach," which is built on "principles difficult to improve on.") Composes incidental music for the Broadway adaptation of Truman Capote's novella *The Grass Harp*, which will run for thirty-six performances in the spring of 1952.

1952 In April a revival of *Four Saints*, with an all-black cast including Leontyne Price and Inez Matthews, mounted at New York's Broadway Theater by the American National Theater and Academy. Thomson is artistic director, publicity consultant, and conductor of the pickup orchestra. After a two-week run, the production travels to Paris where it is presented at the Théâtre des Champs-Elysées. In October completes *Three Pictures for Orchestra*, comprising the "musical landscapes" *The Seine at Night* (1947), *Wheatfield at Noon* (1948), and a new work, *Sea Piece with Birds*. Writes music for Agnes de Mille's ballet *The Harvest According*, which receives its premiere at the Opera House, Chicago, on December 29.

1953 As music consultant to the Rockefeller Foundation, is crucial to the development of the "Louisville project," through which the Louisville Orchestra, under the direction of conductor Robert Whitney, makes the commissioning, performance, and recording of new works for orchestra a centerpiece of its mission for the next quarter-century. Also helps develop Louisville's First Edition Records, the first orchestra-owned record label and a vital producer of recordings of twentieth-century music. Writes incidental music for the Orson Welles–Peter Brook production of *King Lear*, broadcast live on October 18 as part of CBS television's *Omnibus* series. Begins a four-year romance with Roger Baker, an American painter twenty-nine years his junior.

1954 Increasingly in demand as a guest conductor and lecturer, eager to write more books and better music, and convinced that, after fourteen years, he has little left to learn about writing music journalism, resigns from his position at the *New York Herald Tribune*, effective October 1.

1955–58 Various attempts to begin a third opera—on *The Bacchae* of Euripides, on Robert Lowell's *The Old Glory*, on Truman

Capote's "A Christmas Memory"—all come to nothing. "Relieved from deadline pressures and with nothing I had to do, I seemed to write less music than before," Thomson later remarked of this difficult period, which he termed his "reconstruction time." "I wrote songs to old English poetry [Thomas Campion, John Donne, John Woodcock Graves, William Blake] and to Shakespeare, also songs in Spanish [Reyna Rives]. I did [incidental music for] six Shakespeare plays [and] three films . . . I traveled too, to South America, lecturing in Spanish and conducting, to Venice for two festivals, to Berlin for another, eventually to Japan. But I was not content with just moving about, nor with merely composing films, plays, and short recital pieces . . ." Mother dies, age ninety-two, on October 27, 1957.

1959   Begins what will be a two-year collaboration with thirty-four-year-old poet Kenneth Koch, who brings him into a circle of young acquaintances including Frank O'Hara, John Ashbery, and James Schuyler. Sets two groups of Koch's previously published poems (*Collected Poems* and *Mostly about Love*) and urges the poet to write an original libretto on a subject of shared interest: Haussmann, Napoleon III, and the rebuilding of Paris. Meets frequently with Koch, commenting incisively on his libretto as it develops. In May, elected to membership in the American Academy of Arts and Letters. In June the critical-biographical book *Virgil Thomson: His Life and Music* is published by Thomas Yoseloff, New York. Ostensibly the disinterested work of two writers, Kathleen Hoover (the "Life") and John Cage (the "Music"), it was in fact commissioned, edited, and—to the authors' abiding dismay—extensively rewritten by Thomson himself.

1960   Completes a major commission from the State College of Education at Potsdam, New York: *Missa pro defunctis,* a Requiem Mass for double chorus and orchestra. It receives its premiere in Potsdam on May 12, with Thomson conducting. With this creative success, Thomson will recall, "I knew my 'reconstruction time' was over." In December, after more than a year of intense collaboration, Thomson abruptly abandons work on Koch's libretto, cryptically declaring it "a soft egg." (Koch is hurt but resilient. "How could you stay mad at Virgil?" he later said. "I had a good ride even though I wound up back in the garage.")

1961　At the suggestion of Jason Epstein, publisher of Vintage Books, revises the text of *The State of Music* for a new generation of readers. Writes new introduction and afterword to the book, and, in footnotes to the 1939 text, adds comments on the current music scene. ("Autonomy, intellectual and financial, is unquestionably the ideal state for any profession, both for its own well being and for its contributions to culture," he writes. "[Music must] take care of the professional line, and the artistic line will take care of itself. That was my message in 1939. It still is.") Blanche Knopf, who with her husband, Alfred, had published him in the 1940s, invites Thomson to write his memoirs. He signs a contract in August that promises delivery in 1964.

1962　In April, *The State of Music* (second edition) is published in Vintage paperback. Visits Los Angeles and is introduced by Ned Rorem to the poet and actor Jack Larson. Reads Larson's poems, some of which had been set to song by Rorem, and is much taken with "The Candied House," a verse play on the theme of Hansel and Gretel—not what he expected from the young man who, for six years in the 1950s, had played Jimmy Olsen in the Superman television series.

1963　Thomson proposes that Larson try his hand at a libretto. He suggests a subject that he had once proposed to Gertrude Stein, and, more recently, to Gore Vidal: scenes from the life of Lord Byron. Byron was "a genius, a millionaire, a hero, a lover, and a beauty," Thomson explained—the very epitome of the artist as self-made man. "He simply would not be told how to behave, or how not to behave," and would make a wonderful hero for "a poetic drama with music."

1964　Composes the score for *Journey to America*, a ten-minute documentary about immigration written and produced by John Houseman for the United States Pavilion at the New York World's Fair. (Thomson's concert suite adapted from the score is titled *Pilgrims and Pioneers*.) Delivers his memoirs to Knopf, and, under editor Herbert Weinsock, spends much of the next year revising and enlarging them, transforming a sometimes technical account of his life in music into a warm and gossipy personal history of his Kansas City boyhood, Paris youth, and New York maturity. Larson completes a draft of his *Lord Byron*, which he has conceived as a modest work in two acts. (One admirer characterizes it as "a literate, conversational piece ideally suited to productions in smaller companies"—and, more important, to Thomson's methods of prosody.) Presents the libretto to Thomson and, with the composer's permission, to their friend in common John Houseman. Houseman is enthusiastic about it as a work for the stage, and Thomson says, "It sings."

1965   In January writes a long article on the life and works of Wanda Landowska for the recently founded *New York Review of Books*, a journal that will welcome his essays and criticism for the rest of his creative life. (Subjects he will treat include Boulez, Stravinsky, Janet Flanner, Paul Bowles, Alice B. Toklas, and jazz.) In May is presented the Gold Medal for Music from the American Academy of Arts and Letters. On November 28, Allen Hughes, a cultural reporter for *The New York Times*, publishes an interview-cum-press-release by Thomson and Larson announcing their collaboration.

1966   In the wake of the *Times* piece, Thomson receives inquiries about *Lord Byron* from several opera companies. In the spring accepts a generous preemptive commission from the Metropolitan Opera, made possible by emergency grants to the Met by the Ford and Koussevitzky foundations. The production, according to general manager Rudolf Bing, will be sumptuous—a "grand opera" appropriate to the Met's brand-new hall at Lincoln Center. Larson is distressed by having to reconceive his modest "conversational piece" as a work that will satisfy the Met: "Their audience needed two intermissions, so Virgil needed a three-act libretto. The huge stage would require larger scenes with a bigger cast . . . and a large chorus . . . and a ballet." Larson, in consultation with John Houseman, expands the work accordingly, and delivers a new libretto in July. Thomson, delighted, spends much of the summer at the MacDowell Colony, in Peterborough, New Hampshire, working on the vocal lines. In October his memoirs, *Virgil Thomson*, are published by Knopf to strong sales and favorable reviews. (Alfred Frankenstein, in *The New York Times Book Review*, calls the book "an invaluable contribution to the history of music, theater, film, literature, and painting in the twentieth century . . . crammed with short, brilliant character sketches of Thomson's friends . . . a cast of characters which is unbelievably immense.") In the fall is Visiting Professor of Music at Carnegie Institute of Technology, in Philadelphia.

1967   To capitalize on the success of the memoirs, as well as on nostalgia for the recently shuttered *New York Herald Tribune*, Thomson edits a selection of his music journalism from the 1940s and '50s. Published in June by Vintage Books, *Music Reviewed* contains the author's choice of pieces from his three previous collections and fifty-five uncollected items from the last five years of his *Herald Tribune* tenure.

1968   As the Met becomes more involved in the creation of *Lord Byron*, work on the opera is, in Thomson's words, "beset by disputes, misunderstandings, deceptions, concealments, delays, wrong decisions, and plain stupidities." Bing is determined that the opera be a highlight of the Met's 1971–72 season, his last as general manager. Larson continually rewrites the libretto to meet Thomson's and the Met's ever-changing demands for something "grand."

1969   On April 9, a tryout of key scenes from *Lord Byron* is presented by Thomson in a rehearsal room at the Metropolitan Opera, with two soloists and a chorus of nine, accompanied by a staff pianist. Though the performers are well prepared and take a sincere delight in the music, by the end of the audition Rudolf Bing turns markedly cold toward the composer. Five days later, in a letter to Thomson, Bing confesses that he has "grave doubts whether this is a piece suitable for a 4000-seat house." He declines to put *Lord Byron* on the Met's schedule, and suggests it might "first be done somewhere else"—perhaps Dallas—"to see what effect the work has in a large opera house." Thomson is not entirely surprised—Bing's conservatism was legendary—but he is devastated.

1970   At the invitation of WNCN-FM, hosts *Virgil Thomson at the Chelsea*, a partly scripted radio program recorded in his hotel apartment and broadcast Monday nights at 10. This limited series, which runs all year through September 28, features Thomson playing and discussing recordings of his work, interviewing friends and fellow-composers, and commenting on the music world past and present. Writes

American Music Since 1910, the inaugural volume in Nicolas Nabokov's "Twentieth-Century Composers" series. This brief study—Thomson's text runs to ninety pages—recounts "American music's discovery of its own distinct national idiom" through chapters on Ives, Ruggles, Varèse, Copland, and Cage, with glances toward dozens of other composers. The book concludes with an appendix, "The Operas of Virgil Thomson," commissioned by the author from critic Victor Fell Yellin, and a set of biographical notes on 106 American composers, each of which concludes with a tart summing-up by Thomson. (Milton Babbitt: "[His] music has the clarity of distilled water and just possibly the sterility." Christian Wolff: "A Cage disciple so devoted to musical purity that throughout his educative years he avoided all musical education." Eric Salzman: "The best critic in America for contemporary and far-out music, his own work, as can happen with critics, is in danger of neglect.")

1971   In January, *American Music Since 1910* published by Holt, Rinehart & Winston. Receives the Handel Medallion of the City of New York, the city's highest prize for achievement in the arts. In the spring Peter Mennin, president of the Juilliard School, proposes that the Juilliard American Opera Center produce the premiere of *Lord Byron*. Mennin suggests, for director, John Houseman, since 1966 the head of Juilliard's drama department, and, for conductor, Gerhard Samuel, associate conductor of the Los Angeles Philharmonic. Thomson then enlists Alvin Ailey as choreographer and David Mitchell as production designer. In August completes the score and begins to audition Juilliard singers for the twenty-eight-member cast. Rehearsals, preparations, and adjustments by Thomson and Larson will continue throughout Juilliard's 1971–72 academic year.

1972   On April 20, *Lord Byron* receives its premiere at the Juilliard American Opera Center. The reviews are mixed: Harold C. Schonberg of *The New York Times* judges the score "very bland," "distressingly banal," and "frequently gaggingly cutesy," but Patrick J. Smith of *High Fidelity/Musical America* calls it "a masterpiece . . . a genuine musical entity of great beauty. Whatever its final standing in relation to the Stein operas, *Lord Byron* is a credit to our premier opera composer." (When, in January 1977, WNYC-TV broadcasts a video recording of the Juilliard production, the work again divides the critics, but Andrew Porter, in *The New Yorker*, writes that it is "an elegant and cultivated piece," "[its] simplicity that of a master," and it "does not deserve neglect." In a personal letter, Thomson thanks Porter sincerely: "To be treated as a serious composer of operas, just imagine! And not as the operator of some shell game, or some talented amateur who had once met Gertrude Stein in Paris.")

1973   Writes *Cantata on Poems of Edward Lear*. Problems with hearing, which had begun during the writing of *Lord Byron*, make it difficult for Thomson to compose further works: "My own pitches are so completely falsified by now," he tells an old friend, "that I cannot listen to music . . . and get a reliable report of it from my ears." Prepares two series of talks, one on the function of music criticism, the other on prosody, that will earn him several short-term academic residencies, first at the University of Bridgeport and Trinity College, Connecticut, then at Dominican College and Otterbein College (1974), California State University at Fullerton (1975), and UCLA (1976).

1974   Hires Victor Cardell, his former student at Trinity College, as the first of many personal assistants who will answer his phone, type his letters, buy his groceries, and help him face the challenges of growing older. Cardell also helps him catalogue his personal and professional papers—including twenty-five thousand letters—for eventual sale to an academic library, an enormous and painstaking five-year task.

1975   Accepts final large-scale commission, the music and scenario for a comic ballet for the Erick Hawkins Dance Company. *Parson Weems and the Cherry Tree*, based on songs from the Federal period and written for seven instruments, animates episodes from the life of George Washington, a theme long dear to Thomson. After it is given its premiere at the University of Massachusetts, Amherst, on November 1, the piece is toured extensively by the Hawkins troupe throughout America's bicentennial year.

1976   In the spring Thomson teaches a class in music journalism at the Yale School of Music, and there renews acquaintance with Donald Gallup, a soldier friend of Stein's during the war years, now curator of the Yale Collection of American Literature. In celebration of both the U.S. bicentennial and

Thomson's eightieth birthday, *The Mother of Us All* is revived by the Santa Fe Opera, Raymond Leppard, conductor, in a lavish production starring Mignon Dunn as Susan B. Anthony and with sets and costumes by painter Robert Indiana.

1977 Receives the Edward MacDowell Medal, a lifetime-achievement award presented annually by the MacDowell Colony. Sells his flat at 17 quai Voltaire. Interviewed at length by John Rockwell, music critic for *The New York Times*, for a Virgil Thomson tribute number of *Parnassus: Poetry in Review* (Spring/Summer 1977).

1979 Sister Ruby, age ninety-three, dies June 5. Through Donald Gallup's initiative, the Yale School of Music Library agrees to purchase most of Thomson's personal and professional papers for $100,000. As a condition of the sale, Yale librarians make photocopies of all of Thomson's correspondence, which are delivered to the Chelsea in 154 archival boxes.

1980 As a present to himself for his forthcoming eighty-fifth birthday, instigates the publication of *A Virgil Thomson Reader*, a six-hundred-page omnibus collecting excerpts from his seven published books, most of them long out of print, and some twenty previously uncollected pieces, early and late. Enlists John Rockwell to help make the selection and to write an introduction. Makes a gift of his book manuscripts to the Rare Books and Manuscripts Library of Columbia University.

1981 *A Virgil Thomson Reader*, published in November by Houghton Mifflin Company, receives the year's National Book Critics Circle Award for Criticism. Is flattered when Anthony Tommasini, an acquaintance pursuing his doctorate in music at Boston University, chooses Thomson's musical portraits as his dissertation topic. ("How nice to be a subject, not a source!") Grants Tommasini many personal interviews and full access to his scores, and provides introductions to dozens of his "sitters."

1982 In May receives honorary doctorate in music from Harvard.

1983 In December is a recipient of the Kennedy Center Honors, a lifetime-achievement award presented annually by the John F. Kennedy Center for the Performing Arts, Washington, D.C.

1984   Bitterly disappointed when the fiftieth anniversary of *Four Saints* passes without a revival by a major opera company. A production by the Stuttgart Opera, designed and directed by the American theater artist Robert Wilson, is delayed and then postponed indefinitely.

1985   On December 7, a semistaged production of *Lord Byron*, scaled back to two acts by composer and librettist, is presented at Alice Tully Hall, Lincoln Center, by the short-lived New York Opera Repertory Theatre, Nancy Rhodes, director. Thomson is frustrated by both the stiffness of the performance and the mixed reviews. (The critic and pianist Samuel Lipman, writing in *Grand Street*, finds little fault with the Thomson-Larson opera as a work of art, and argues that its "perceived failure" stems mainly from the fact that "the courage to produce a work such as *Lord Byron* is not to be found anywhere in the land.")

1986   Impressed by the substance and style of Tommasini's dissertation and with the quality of his music reviews for the *Boston Globe*, Thomson invites him to be his authorized biographer. (*Virgil Thomson: Composer on the Aisle*, will be published by W. W. Norton eleven years later, in 1997.) Thomson grants Tommasini unlimited access to his papers and sits for countless hours of recorded interviews. When Ileene Smith of Summit Books, an imprint of Simon & Schuster, asks Thomson for a volume of selected letters, he enlists the music critic Tim Page to make the selection and do the annotation. Though Page and his wife, Vanessa Weeks Page, are credited as editors of the volume, it is very much Thomson's book: he insists on full approval over the volume's contents. Over the Pages' objections, he rewrites their annotations; he also revises the texts of his letters, sometimes altering their meaning. In November, PBS broadcasts *Virgil Thomson at 90*, a one-hour documentary by John Huszar. Maurice Grosser dies, age eighty-three, on December 22.

1987   Invited by John G. Ryden, director of Yale University Press, to write a handbook on prosody. Spends the year working on this brief book, which codifies, in twelve straightforward chapters, all that he knows about setting words to music.

1988   In June *Selected Letters of Virgil Thomson* is published by Summit Books. ("In his long life, Mr. Thomson has waged a subtle yet merciless campaign against pomposity," writes Bernard Holland in *The New York Times*. "His main virtue [as composer, critic, and correspondent] is simplicity without simplemindedness. . . . Good Americans refresh us not with profundity but with directness. Virgil Thomson is one of them.") On August 9, at a ceremony in the White House, is presented the National Medal of Arts by President Ronald Reagan. In November, upon finishing his book on prosody, his body suddenly begins to fail him.

1989   Receives constant care and attention from his personal assistant, three aides, and a night nurse. Takes up residence on his couch, and there corrects proofs of his final book, tape-records memories for Tommasini's biography, and puts his affairs in order. On September 10, *Music with Words: A Composer's View* is published by Yale University Press. Shortly thereafter Thomson retires to his bed and, calmly but firmly, begins refusing food. On the morning of September 30, dies at home, in Suite 920 of the Hotel Chelsea, at the age of ninety-two. On November 25, a memorial service partly planned by Thomson is held at the Cathedral of St. John the Divine in New York City. At his request, no eulogies are delivered; instead, his musical intimates and champions perform a program of his compositions for an audience of nearly two thousand admirers. "In between the performances," reports the *Times*, "came pithy bits of Mr. Thomson's recorded voice from documentaries made in recent years—touching, yet proudly free of the slightest hint of sentimentality." Thomson's ashes are buried in the family plot, near the bodies of his parents, in Rehoboth Cemetery, Slater, Missouri.

Note on the Texts

This volume presents a selection from the writings that Virgil Thomson published after October 1, 1954, when, at the age of fifty-seven, he ended his fourteen-year tenure as chief music critic of the *New York Herald Tribune*. (A selection from Thomson's writings for the *Herald Tribune* has been published in a companion volume, *Virgil Thomson: Music Chronicles 1940–1954*.) It contains the complete texts of two books: the second, revised edition of *The State of Music* (1962), a work first published in 1939, and *Virgil Thomson* (1966), a volume of memoirs. It also contains the nine chapters Thomson contributed to *American Music Since 1910* (1971), a volume of essays on twentieth-century composers that also included an introduction and supplementary chapters by other contributors, and the complete literary text of Thomson's last book, *Music with Words: A Composer's View* (1989), a handbook on prosody with musical illustrations. (The section of *Music with Words* titled "Musical Illustrations from the Works of Virgil Thomson"—comprising annotated excerpts from opera scores and art songs, none of them keyed to the literary text—has been omitted from the present volume.) The final section collects, under the heading "Other Writings," thirty-eight items that Thomson published in books and periodicals between 1958 and 1984.

The first edition of *The State of Music* was published, in hardcover, by William Morrow and Company, New York, in November 1939. (Thomson wrote this, his first book, in his studio at 17 quai Voltaire, Paris, from December 1938 to May 1939. His account of its composition can be found on page 463 of the present volume, and his account of its critical reception on pages 470–71.) In early 1961, Thomson was invited by Jason Epstein, an editor at Random House, to revise the book for publication as a Vintage paperback. For this second edition— "annotated and updated" for readers and musicians of the sixties generation—Thomson wrote a new preface and "postlude," corrected errors and infelicities, cut certain irrelevant passages, and inserted a good deal of new material, some of it relegated to footnotes but most of it, as he writes in the preface, "placed in brackets and printed along with the [1939] text to permit cursive reading." The second edition of *The State of Music* was published, in paperback, by Vintage Books, New York, in April 1962. The text of the first Vintage printing is used here.

Virgil Thomson was commissioned by Blanche Knopf, the wife of Alfred A. Knopf and president of the Knopf publishing house. (Knopf had published Thomson's music chronicles *The Musical Scene* and *The Art of Judging Music* in the 1940s.) Thomson signed a contract for a volume of memoirs in August 1961, which stipulated delivery of a manuscript three years later, in August 1964. His first draft, an account of his musical life from his Kansas City boyhood through the eve of World War II, satisfied neither Mrs. Knopf nor Herbert Weinstock, the music historian and Knopf manuscript editor assigned to the book. Together they urged Thomson to expand his memoirs to include a chapter on his years at the *New York Herald Tribune*, an account of the creation of *The Mother of Us All*, and a concluding essay on the state of music in the 1960s. In close consultation with Weinstock, Thomson reworked the manuscript through the fall of 1965, and *Virgil Thomson* was published, in hardcover, by Alfred A. Knopf, New York, in October 1966. (Chapter 15 had appeared, as "A Portrait of Gertrude Stein," in *The New York Review of Books*, July 7, 1966; Chapter 27 had appeared, as "The Paper: A Critic's Tale," in *HiFi/Stereo Review*, November 1966; and an excerpt from Chapter 35 had appeared, as "A Distaste for Music," in *Vogue*, September 1, 1966.) A British issue, printed as part of Knopf's initial press run, was published, in hardcover, by Weidenfeld and Nicolson, London, in February 1967. A paperback reprint, incorporating several factual corrections by the author, was published by Da Capo Press, New York, in May 1977. The text of the 1977 Da Capo paperback is used here.

American Music Since 1910 was commissioned by Anna Kallin and Nicolas Nabokov as the first of five projected volumes in their Twentieth-Century Composers series. (This series, published simultaneously in the U.S. by Holt, Rinehart, and Winston and in the U.K. by Weidenfeld and Nicolson, also included *Twentieth-Century Composers: Germany and Central Europe*, by Hans Heinz Stuckenschmidt, 1970; *Twentieth-Century Composers: Britain, Scandinavia, and the Netherlands*, by Humphrey Searle and Robert Layton, 1972; and *Twentieth-Century Composers: France, Italy, and Spain*, by Frederik Goldbeck, 1974. A concluding volume, on Russian and Eastern European composers, was never realized.) The core of the volume consisted of the nine chapters by Virgil Thomson reprinted here. (The contents also included an introduction by Nicolas Nabokov and two supplementary chapters by other contributors—"The Operas of Virgil Thomson," by Victor Fell Yellin, and "Music in Latin America," by Gilbert Chase—all of which are omitted from the present volume. Also omitted are twenty-four pages of black-and-white photographs with captions by Thomson, and a now out-of-date biographical dictionary of 106 American composers.) *American Music Since 1910* was assembled by Thomson and the editors of the Twentieth-Century Composers series from the winter of 1968–69 to the spring of 1970. It was published, in hardcover, by Holt, Rinehart, and Winston, New York, and by Weidenfeld and Nicolson, London, in January 1971. (Chapter 1 had appeared, in somewhat different form, as "America's Musical Maturity: A Twentieth-Century Story," in *The Yale Review*, October 1961; Chapter 3 had appeared, as "The Ives Case," in *The New York Review of Books*, May 21, 1970; and Chapter 8 had appeared, as "Cage and the Collage of Noises," in *The New York Review of Books*, April 23, 1970.) The text of the first Holt, Rinehart, and Winston printing is used here.

Music with Words was commissioned by John G. Ryden, director of Yale University Press, at the suggestion of Thomson's friend Harold Samuel, an adjunct professor of music at Yale University and a manuscript librarian at the Yale Music Library. Thomson assembled the book from the winter of 1996–97 to the fall of 1998 in consultation with his former assistant Charles Fussell, who suggested most of the musical illustrations in the text. *Music with Words* was published, in hardcover, by Yale University Press, New Haven and London, in September 1989. (Chapter 3 had appeared, as "Occasions for Singing," in *Grand Street*, Spring 1989; Chapter 9 had appeared, as "Words and Music," in *The New York Review of Books*, April 13, 1989; and Chapter 11 had appeared, in somewhat different form, as "On Writing Operas and Staging Them," in *Parnassus: Poetry in Review*, Fall/Winter 1982.) The text of the first Yale University Press printing is used here. (As noted above, the section titled "Musical Illustrations from the Works of Virgil Thomson" has been omitted from the present volume. In the Yale edition, it followed Chapter 12.)

The section titled "Other Writings" presents thirty-eight items that Thomson published in books and periodicals between 1958 and 1984. These items have been organized under six headings, "Music and Culture," "Music for the Theater," "Opera Reviewed," "Critics and Criticism," "Memories and Milestones," and "Book Reviews."

Under the heading "Music and Culture" are printed four general essays that are based on lectures.

"Music's Tradition of Constant Change" appeared in *The Atlantic Monthly*, February 1959. (It also appeared, as "Music—Ending the Great Tradition," in *Encounter* [London], January 1959.) It was based on a talk delivered in Venice at the International Festival of Contemporary Music, an event of the twenty-ninth Biennale di Venezia, in the summer of 1958. The text from *The Atlantic Monthly* is used here.

"Music in the 1950s" appeared in *Harper's Magazine*, November 1960. (It also appeared, as "Looking Back on a Decade," in *Encounter* [London], November 1960.) It was based on a talk delivered in Berlin at the tenth-anniversary conference of the Congress for Cultural Freedom, on June 20, 1960. The text from *Harper's Magazine* is used here.

"Music Now" appeared in *Proceedings of the American Academy of Arts and Letters and the National Institute of Arts and Letters*, 1961. (It also appeared in *The London Magazine*, March 1962.) It was based on the thirty-ninth annual Blashfield Address, delivered in New York City at the joint ceremonial of the American Academy of Arts and Letters and the National Institute of Arts and Letters on May 25, 1960. The text from *Proceedings* is used here.

"Music Does Not Flow" appeared in *The New York Review of Books*, December 17, 1981. (It also appeared, in slightly different form, as "Music Does Not Flow: Constant and Variable Elements in Music's Patterning," in *Humanities in Review* I, 1982.) It was based on a James Lecture of the New York Institute for the Humanities delivered at New York University on April 27, 1978. The text from *The New York Review of Books* is used here.

Under the heading "Music for the Theater" are printed four pieces concerning opera and incidental music for the stage.

"Opera Librettos" appeared, as "The Tenth Muse: A Word's-Eye View of Opera," in *The New York Times Book Review*, October 4, 1970. Thomson collected it, under the present title, in *A Virgil Thomson Reader* (Boston: Houghton Mifflin, 1981), the source of the text used here.

"Music for *Much Ado*" was commissioned by Francis Fergusson, general editor of the Laurel Shakespeare series, as part of the critical commentary for a mass-market paperback edition of *Much Ado About Nothing*, edited and annotated by Charles Jasper Sisson (New York: Dell, 1960). It also appeared, as "Music for *Much Ado About Nothing*," in *Theatre Arts*, June 1959. Thomson collected it, under the present title, in *A Virgil Thomson Reader* (Boston: Houghton Mifflin, 1981), the source of the text used here.

"The Rocky Road of American Opera" appeared in *HiFi/Stereo Review*, February 1962, the source of the text used here.

"The State of Opera" appeared, as "Opera: It Is Everywhere in America," in *The New York Times*, September 23, 1962. The text from *The New York Times* is used here, under a title supplied by the editor.

Under the heading "Opera Reviewed" are printed three reviews of opera performances, recordings, and broadcasts.

"Blitzstein on Record: From *Regina* to *Juno*," appeared, as "Mid-Month Recordings: From 'Regina' to 'Juno,'" in *Saturday Review*, May 16, 1959. The text from *Saturday Review* is used here, under a title supplied by the editor.

"*The Crucible* and *The Wings of the Dove*," appeared, as "Opera: 'The Crucible' and 'The Dove,'" in *Show: The Magazine of the Arts*, January 1962. The text from *Show* is used here, under a title supplied by the editor.

"Stravinsky's *Flood*: A Spectacle for Television" appeared, as "Stravinsky—'The Flood': An Opera for Television," in *Observer Weekend Review* (London), June 17, 1962. The text from the *Observer* is used here, under a title supplied by the editor.

Under the heading "Critics and Criticism" are printed five pieces concerning music criticism and those who write, publish, and read it.

"On Good Terms with All Muses" appeared in *New York Herald Tribune Books*, September 8, 1963, the source of the text used here.

"A Free Critical Spirit" appeared, as "Olin Downes: A Free Critical Spirit," in *New York Herald Tribune Books*, January 27, 1959. The text from *Books* is used here, under a title supplied by the editor.

"B. H. Haggin's Toscanini" appeared, as "Arturo Toscanini's 'Rightness' Versus That of B. H. Haggin," in *New York Herald Tribune Books*, April 12, 1959. The text from *Books* is used here, under a title supplied by the editor.

"Instruments of Criticism" appeared in *Prose*, Spring 1972, the source of the text used here.

"The State of Music Criticism" appeared, as "A Drenching of Criticism, but a Drought of Critics," in *The New York Times*, October 27, 1974. Thomson collected it, under the present title, in *A Virgil Thomson Reader* (Boston: Houghton Mifflin, 1981), the source of the text used here.

Under the heading "Memories and Milestones" are printed tributes to six of Thomson's mentors, colleagues, and contemporaries.

"A. Everett 'Chick' Austin, Jr.," appeared, as "The Friends and Enemies of Modern Music," in *A. Everett Austin, Jr.: A Director's Taste and Achievement* (Hartford: Wadsworth Atheneum, 1958), the catalogue of a memorial exhibition on view at the Wadsworth Atheneum from April 23 to June 1, 1958. In 1980 Thomson revised the text for inclusion in *A Virgil Thomson Reader* but, in the end, omitted it from the final manuscript. This revised text, from The Virgil Thomson Papers in Butler Library, Columbia University (MS 1240, Box 17), is used here, under a title supplied by the editor.

"Nadia Boulanger at Seventy-five" appeared, as "'Greatest Music Teacher'—at 75," in *The New York Times Magazine*, February 4, 1962. (It also appeared in *Piano Quarterly*, Spring 1962, and *Music Educators Journal*, September/October 1962.) Thomson collected it, under the present title, in *A Virgil Thomson Reader* (Boston: Houghton Mifflin, 1981), the source of the text used here.

The text of "William Flanagan" was read by Thomson at the memorial concert for William Flanagan presented in the Composers' Showcase series at the Whitney Museum of American Art, New York, on April 14, 1970. Thomson published it, under the present title, in *A Virgil Thomson Reader* (Boston: Houghton Mifflin, 1981), the source of the text used here.

"Elisabeth Lutyens" appeared in *Grand Street*, Summer 1983, the source of the text used here.

"Edwin Denby" appeared as Thomson's untitled contribution to "Edwin Denby Remembered—Part I," a collection of thirteen tributes solicited and edited by the choreographer and dancer William Dunas, in *Ballet Review*, Spring 1984. (Further tributes collected by Dunas appeared in the Summer and Fall issues.) The text from *Ballet Review* is used here, under a title supplied by the editor.

"Lou Harrison at Seventy" appeared, as "A Note Regarding Lou Harrison," in *A Lou Harrison Reader*, a festschrift compiled, edited, and privately printed by the composer and writer Peter Garland (Santa Fe: Soundings Press, 1967). The text from *A Lou Harrison Reader* is used here, under a title supplied by the editor.

Under the heading "Book Reviews" are printed sixteen miscellaneous book reviews and review-essays.

"Sincere Appreciation" appeared, as "Leonard Bernstein Conducts a Stimulating Medley of Essays in Appreciation," in *New York Herald Tribune Books*, November 29, 1959. The text from *Books* is used here, under a title supplied by the editor.

"Wanda Landowska" appeared in *The New York Review of Books*, January 28, 1965. Thomson collected it in *A Virgil Thomson Reader* (Boston: Houghton Mifflin, 1981), the source of the text used here.

"How Dead Is Arnold Schoenberg?" appeared in *The New York Review of Books*, April 22, 1965. Thomson collected it in *A Virgil Thomson Reader* (Boston: Houghton Mifflin, 1981), the source of the text used here.

"On Being Discovered" appeared in *The New York Review of Books*, June 3, 1965. Thomson collected it in *A Virgil Thomson Reader* (Boston: Houghton Mifflin, 1981), the source of the text used here.

"The Tradition of Sensibility" appeared in *The New York Review of Books*, December 9, 1965, the source of the text used here.

"'Craft-Igor' and the Whole Stravinsky" appeared in *The New York Review of Books*, December 15, 1966. Thomson collected it in *A Virgil Thomson Reader* (Boston: Houghton Mifflin, 1981), the source of the text used here.

"The Genius Type" appeared in *The New York Review of Books*, September 26, 1968. Thomson collected it in *A Virgil Thomson Reader* (Boston: Houghton Mifflin, 1981), the source of the text used here.

"Berlioz, Boulez, and Piaf" appeared in *The New York Review of Books*, January 29, 1970. Thomson collected it in *A Virgil Thomson Reader* (Boston: Houghton Mifflin, 1981), the source of the text used here.

"Scenes from Show Biz" appeared in *The New York Review of Books*, May 4, 1972, the source of the text used here.

"Untold Tales" appeared in *The New York Review of Books*, May 18, 1972, the source of the text used here.

"Elliott Carter" appeared, as a discrete part of the omnibus review "Varèse, Xenakis, Carter," in *The New York Review of Books*, August

31, 1972. Thomson collected "Varèse, Xenakis, Carter" in *A Virgil Thomson Reader* (Boston: Houghton Mifflin, 1981), the source of the text excerpted here.

"Wickedly Wonderful Widow" appeared in *The New York Review of Books*, March 7, 1974, the source of the text used here.

"Making Black Music" appeared in *The New York Review of Books*, October 17, 1974. Thomson collected it in *A Virgil Thomson Reader* (Boston: Houghton Mifflin, 1981), the source of the text used here.

"A Good Writer" appeared in *The New York Review of Books*, January 24, 1980, the source of the text used here.

"The New Grove" appeared, as one of four untitled reviews of *The New Grove Dictionary of Music and Musicians*, in *Notes: Quarterly Journal of the Music Library Association*, September 1981. (The four reviews, a special feature of *Notes* edited and with an introduction by Susan T. Sommer, music librarian of the New York Public Library, were published under the journal's recurring section heading "Book Reviews.") The text from *Notes* is used here, under a title supplied by the editor.

"Copland on Copland" appeared in *Vanity Fair*, September 1984, the source of the text used here.

This volume presents the texts of the original printings chosen for inclusion but does not attempt to reproduce nontextual features of their typographical design. Headnotes to the book reviews printed in "Other Writings" have been standardized by the editor. Otherwise, the texts are presented without change, save for the correction of typographical errors. Spelling, punctuation, and capitalization are often expressive features and are not altered, even when inconsistent or irregular. The following is a list of typographical errors corrected, cited by page and line number: 24.14, folk-lore; 26.37, world,; 54.34, a rich; 63.4, syntatic; 70.40, stricly; 110.21–22, Sydney Finklestein,; 113.36, The doctors; 114.18, pagaentry.; 118.39, Karl; 120.39, commenting the; 152.36, publicatiom; 162.17 (and *passim*), Composers'; 171.25, Henri Charles Strauss; 185.18, shingling, There; 221.14, (German) to; 229.22, *fois*; 234.30, Widor) a; 240.39, Stuyvestant; 242.10, Orchestral Association,; 250.30, La Société; 252.4 (and *passim*), *the*; 254.7, piece."; 259.26, thought; 260.13, Picasso's; 270.11 (and *passim*), Chadbourne Crane; 278.24, *fois*; 282.22, Challis; 301.15, wandering was; 304.3, programmed; 333.1 (and *passim*), George; 334,18, France widow; 338.37, $1,094 one; 347.26, Francise; 357.24, me to; 363.13, Lamotte; 364.13, Boussuet; 380.28, known) had; 382.31, *La Sérénade*; 383.34, Russes; 398.3, Les Ballets Russes; 399.7, Doctor; 401.15, Proust) had; 402.25, practise; 412.23–24 (and *passim*), Koussevitsky; 417.18, beginnig; 424.13, 1938; 425.14, Katherine; 425.23, Harlem which; 433.16, Asadota; 435.16, Forty-first Street; 438.25, Fellows; 446.8–9, Western

Billy, 446.20, Trudi; 449.14, 1922; 468. 13, blonde; 480.23, liberty,; 481.5, *Paris, France*; 485.38, Nonotte.; 514.20, insist) might; 538.37, Doctor; 539.37, Maxime; 552.2, Bowdoin; 576.3, L'Art du; 585.1, Shafer; 603.3, Massachusetts and; 611.20, "influences") almost; 614.40, forbears; 621.7, expense) marked; 629.36, nature) music; 630.15, son and; 633.8–9, *New-Found*; 683.34, Rudyar; 639.25, Ozenfants; 639.28, horizons did,; 650.6, film *Of*; 658.2, producing at; 658.40, Martin; 660.10, York is; 662.11, 1969 in; 663.11, this this; 670.23, *A Week*; 673.33, harpsichords'; 674.13, New York just; 697.25, extention; 699.6, *lunaire.*; 716.7, televison; 724.30, *Psalemus*; 727.8, droughte; 727.22, they; 728.27, reckons by the dozens,; 729.10, Wohtemperirte; 742.24, indispensible; 747.21, Theresa; 753.21, *A Birthday*; 755.37, Mathews; 777.24, 1960; 778.1, indispensible; 787.15, Edgar; 795.22 (and *passim*), Carlyle; 815.1, 1906; 815.24, thought; 827.40, Jarobe; 835.20 (and *passim*), Berthold; 842.11. novelties) would; 846.19, Elizabeth; 918.25, Edgar; 923.37, spirtuality; 922.33, *Bizet*,; 922.38, wellinformed.; 923.37, spirtuality"; 945,33, Music) published; 950.35, her,; 959.28, Forty-first Street; 961.5, Sneeden's; 961.33, Houseman,; 967.8, *Dr.*; 999.21–22, everybody is; 1001.35, Elizabeth; 1004.2, esteem. is; 1004.31, music; 1005.3, *Encyclopedia.*

Notes

In the notes below, the reference numbers denote page and line of this volume (line counts include headings). No note is made for material included in standard desk-reference books, including *The Concise Baker's Biographical Dictionary of Musicians*, eighth edition, revised by Nicolas Slonimsky (New York: Schirmer, 1993), *The Grove Book of Opera*, by Stanley Sadie (New York: Oxford University Press, 1996), and the *Oxford Dictionary of Music*, sixth edition, edited by Michael and Joyce Kennedy with Tim Rutherford-Hayes (New York: Oxford University Press, 2012). Quotations from Shakespeare are keyed to G. Blakemore Evans, editor, *The Riverside Shakespeare* (Boston: Houghton Mifflin, 1974). For further biographical detail than is contained in the chronology and in Thomson's memoirs, see Kathleen Hoover and John Cage, *Virgil Thomson: His Life and Music* (New York: Thomas Yoseloff, 1959), Anthony Tommasini, *Virgil Thomson: Composer on the Aisle* (New York: Norton, 1997), and Virgil Thomson, *A Virgil Thomson Reader* (Boston: Houghton Mifflin, 1981). For complete texts and dates of most of the letters by Virgil Thomson, Gertrude Stein, and Alice B. Toklas excerpted here, see Tim Page and Vanessa Weeks Page, editors, *Selected Letters of Virgil Thomson* (New York: Summit Books, 1988), and Thomas Dilworth and Susan Holbrook, editors, *The Letters of Gertrude Stein and Virgil Thomson: Composition as Conversation* (New York: Oxford University Press, 2010). Many episodes in American cultural history discussed in chapters 12 to 29 of *Virgil Thomson*, including the original production of *Four Saints in Three Acts*, are recounted in detail by John Houseman in *Run-Through: A Memoir* (New York: Simon & Schuster, 1972), by Nicholas Fox Weber in *Patron Saints: Five Rebels Who Opened America to a New Art, 1928–1943* (New York: Knopf, 1993), by Steven Watson in *Prepare for Saints: Gertrude Stein, Virgil Thomson, and the Mainstreaming of American Modernism* (New York: Random House, 1999), and by Eugene R. Gaddis in *Magician of the Modern: Chick Austin and the Transformation of the Arts in America* (New York: Knopf, 2000). The festschrift "A Tribute to Virgil Thomson on His Eighty-first Birthday," edited by Herbert Leibowitz (*Parnassus: Poetry in Review*, Spring/Summer 1977), collects memoirs by Thomson's musical friends and acquaintance. Most of the writings that Thomson published during his tenure at the *New York Herald Tribune*, including the complete texts of *The Musical Scene* (1945), *The Art of Judging Music* (1948), and *Music Right and Left* (1951), are collected in *Virgil Thomson: Music Chronicles 1940–1954*, edited by Tim Page (New York: Library of America, 2014). For an annotated bibliography of Thomson's writings, as well as a list of his musical works and a discography, see Michael Meckna, *Virgil Thomson: A Bio-Bibliography* (Westport, Conn.: Greenwood Press, 1986).

THE STATE OF MUSIC

8.37–39   the W.P.A. . . . played a vigorous role in American music] The Federal Music Project (FMP), founded in July 1935, was one of the first arts programs created under President Franklin D. Roosevelt's "New Deal" poverty-relief program. In 1939 the FMP was subsumed into the Works Progress Administration as the WPA Music Project, which continued through June 1943. During its eight years of existence, the FMP/WPA Music Project created and funded thirty-four city and regional orchestras, sponsored dozens of concert series, and put music teachers in the schools and ethnomusicologists in the field. It promoted American composers by underwriting the Composers' Forum–Laboratory series of concerts and symposiums, and by commissioning incidental music, musical theater, and ballet music for Federal Theater and Federal Dance projects. The FMP/WPA did not have a dedicated opera program.

9.3   BMI] Broadcast Music, Inc., founded in 1939, administers performance rights, broadcast and recording rights, and licensing fees for some 8.5 million musical works. ASCAP, founded in 1914, does much the same for another 10 million.

11.9   three books] *The Musical Scene* (New York: Knopf, 1945), *The Art of Judging Music* (New York: Knopf, 1948), and *Music Right and Left* (New York: Holt, 1951).

15.26–27   "artists don't need criticism . . . praise,"] This well-known remark by Gertrude Stein was first recorded in the 1939 edition of Thomson's *State of Music*.

17.2   deadly-upas-tree] The sap of the upas tree (*Antiaris toxicaria*) yields a deadly poison used by Indonesian aborigines on blow darts and arrow tips. In medieval travelers' tales, the upas—especially one ancient specimen on the island of Java—was said to exert a baleful influence on all who dared come near it.

22.25   American Artists' Equity] Artists' Equity Association, established in New York City in 1947, promotes economic opportunities for, and defends the intellectual property rights of, America's visual artists.

22.36–23.1   Dynamic Symmetry] Theory of composition in visual art employing geometric shapes, ratios, and proportions found in nature, popularized by the American art teacher Jay Hambidge (1867–1924) in his book *Dynamic Symmetry: The Greek Vase* (1920).

28.13   "aspire to the condition of music,"] See Walter Pater (1839–1894), "The School of Giorgione" (*Fortnightly Review*, October 1877), reprinted as Appendix A of his book *The Renaissance: Studies in Art and Poetry* (third edition, revised, 1888).

29.36   Joinville] From 1910 to the late 1980s, Joinville-le-Pont, a suburb northeast of Paris, was the center of the French film industry.

39.2 *Mighty Lak' a Rose*] Popular song (1901) by American composer Ethelbert Nevin (1862–1901), with lyrics, in an ersatz African American dialect, by Frank Lebby Stanton (1857–1927).

40.27 Bossuet . . . "the most famous island in the world."] Jacques-Bénigne Bossuet (1627–1704), Roman Catholic minister to the court of Louis XIV, used this phrase in his 1670 funeral oration for Henrietta, daughter of France and queen of England, consort to Charles I. (In 1930, Thomson composed a musical setting for this text, *Oraison Funèbre de Queen Henriette-Marie de France, Reine de la Grande-Bretagne.*)

41.17 Veronese] The Renaissance painter known as Veronese (Paolo Calliari, 1528–1588) headed a workshop of artists and artisans, including his sons and brothers, that decorated significant buildings—sacred and secular, public and private—in and around Venice.

42.25–27 Conducting . . . he wrote the first treatise on the subject.] See Hector Berlioz, "Le Chef d'orchestre—théorie de son art" ("The Conductor—Theory of His Art"), appendix to the second edition of his *Grand Traité d'Instrumentation et d'Orchestrations Moderne* (1855).

50.14 American Guild of Musical Artists] AGMA, founded in 1936, is the labor union representing performers of choral music, recital music, opera, and dance. It is closely allied with the Actors' Equity Association (stage actors, directors, and crew), founded in 1913, and the American Guild of Variety Artists (circus acts, magicians, cabaret singers, stand-up comics), founded 1939. Together with the Screen Actors Guild and the American Federation of Television and Radio Artists (SAG-AFTRA), these unions constitute the American Actors and Artistes of America (the "Four A's"), the performing artists' organization of the AFL-CIO.

50.15 American Federation of Musicians] AFM, founded in 1896, is the trade union representing musicians in the United States and Canada. It is a member organization of the AFL-CIO and the CLC (Canadian Labour Congress).

62.31 *De Motu Proprio*] A "motu proprio" is a statement issued by the pope "on his own impulse" and addressing a topic of pressing concern to the church. In November 1903, Pope Pius X issued a *motu proprio* regarding church music, which Thomson, commenting on it in 1948, called a revolutionary document. "Its pronouncements were three," wrote Thomson: "(1) Gregorian chant was declared the official and true music of the Catholic liturgy; (2) the sixteenth-century 'Roman school' of polyphony (or Palestrina style), ordained as appropriate for the grander ceremonies of the church [. . .], was so nominated for its derivation from Gregorian chant [. . .]; and (3) musical styles associated with the opera"—that is, all musical styles developed since 1600—"were condemned as non-liturgical, irrespective of their musical merits." For more by Thomson on this subject, see "The Catholic Church Accepts Modern Music," collected in *Music Right and Left* (1951).

64.32 "private bell for inexplicable needs."] "Sonnerie privée pour besoins inexplicables": Tristan Tzara (1896–1963), "Dada Manifesto [March 23] 1918," in *Dada* 3 (Zurich: Mouvement Dada, December 1918).

69.36 Schola Cantorum] Private music school (Schola Cantorum de Paris) founded in 1894 by the French composer and pedagogue Vincent d'Indy (1851–1931). Conceived as an alternative to the Conservatoire de Paris, it offers to this day a curriculum emphasizing mastery of Gregorian chant, sixteenth-century polyphony, and Baroque and early Classical works.

69.37 The sonata-form was invented . . . by K. P. E. Bach] By 1765 Carl Philipp Emanuel Bach (1714–1788) had perfected (if not actually invented) the classical sonata form.

70.1 introduced into France by Reyer] Pianist Ernest Reyer (1823–1909) was trained by his aunt, Louise Farrenc (1804–1875), one of France's leading exponents of the German piano tradition. But it is not Reyer but rather Farrenc's daughter and pupil, Victorine Farrenc (1826–1859), who is thought to have introduced the sonata into France. According to David Dubal's *The Art of the Piano* (1989), "In 1845 at the age of nineteen at Erard's recital hall, Victorine played Beethoven's . . . Sonata Op. 106, the *Hammerklavier* [1818], a rare event in Paris or anywhere at the time."

70.18–19 first reference to it in print . . . in 1828.] "Sonata form" was first described, as the "grande coupe binaire," by Antonin Reicha (1770–1836) in the second volume of his *Traité de haute composition musicale* (1826). The term "sonata form" was popularized and perhaps coined by Adolph Bernhard Marx (1795–1866) in the fourth volume of his *Lehre von der musikalischen Komposition* (1845). The music historian Paul Henry Lang (1901–1991), professor of musicology at Columbia University and Thomson's successor as chief music critic of the *New York Herald Tribune* (1954–65), appears never to have published his research into the first use of "sonata form." On page 815 of the present volume, Thomson, writing in 1978, says that Lang once told him he had traced the term to 1838, not to 1828.

73.5–7 1932, the year the Philadelphia Symphony . . . lay off modern music.] Among Stokowski's offending programs was the U.S. premiere, on April 8, 1932, of Arnold Schönberg's *Gurre-Lieder* (1911).

73.34–74.9 The W.P.A. . . . paid its way.] See note 8.37–39.

77.21–22 "the way to become a classic . . . any way."] Juan Gris, "Des possibilités de la peinture" ("On the Possibilities of Painting"), lecture at the Sorbonne, Paris, on May 15, 1924, printed, in French, in *The Transatlantic Review* (June–July 1924).

89.5 Walter Damrosch] German-born conductor and composer (1862–1950) who from 1928 to 1942 was also the host of NBC's *Music Appreciation Hour*, a weekly radio program broadcast during school hours and designed for use in the classroom.

89.7–9 Appreciation studies . . . later in book form.] The journal *Studies in Philosophy and Social Science* (1926–41), founded at Goethe University, Frankfurt, by Leo Lowenthal, was published by the Institute of Social Research at Columbia University, New York, during the final two years of its existence. In those years it published, among much else, research conducted by Princeton's Radio Research Project into the effect of broadcast radio on American culture. The "Appreciation studies" alluded to by Thomson ("The Radio Symphony: An Experiment in Theory," by Theodor Adorno, and "Invitation to Music: A Study of the Creation of New Music Listeners by the Radio," by E. A. Suchman) appeared first in the journal and were then reprinted in *Radio Research 1941*, edited by Paul F. Lazarsfeld and Frank N. Stanton (New York: Duell, Sloan & Pearce, 1941).

89.9–12 orchestral repertory . . . in book form] John H. Mueller and Kate Hevner, *Trends in Musical Taste* (Indiana University Humanities Series, pamphlet no. 8. Bloomington: Indiana University, 1942), and John Henry Mueller, *The American Symphony Orchestra: A Social History of Musical Taste* (Bloomington: Indiana University Press, 1951).

90.6 Ethelbert Nevin] See note 39.2.

99.15–23 The Home Relief dole . . . revolt.] The Federal Art Project/WPA Art Project, which employed visual artists, designers, and craftsmen, ran concurrently with the Federal Music Project/WPA Music Project (see note 8.37–39).

99.24–38 none of the music for which Soviet composers have been disciplined . . . personal unhappiness.] For more by Thomson on Soviet composers and their censorship by the state, see the three Sunday *Herald Tribune* articles of 1948–49 collected as "From the U.S.S.R." in *Music Right and Left* (1951).

110.21–22 Sidney Finkelstein] Finkelstein (1909–1974), a Brooklyn-born critic of music, literature, and the arts, was a member of Thomson's music staff at the *New York Herald Tribune*. A member of the Communist Party USA, he also wrote for *New Masses, Masses & Mainstream,* and other Marxist publications and was the author of, among other books, *Jazz: A People's Music* (1948).

118.39 *La Passion de Jeanne d'Arc*] French-made silent film (*The Passion of Joan of Arc*, 1928) produced, directed, and co-written by Danish filmmaker Carl Theodor Dreyer (1889–1966).

127.1 opera . . . was invented in Florence in 1600] The Italian composer Jacopo Peri (1561–1633) is widely considered the "inventor" of opera—that is, of the music-drama incorporating vocal arias, recitative, and choral and instrumental music. His work was the culmination of the many and various innovations of the so-called Florentine Group (or *Camerata*), a salon of late-Renaissance humanists and musicians founded in 1573 to revive classical Greek drama and create a new style of musical theater. Peri's *Euridice* (1600), with a libretto by Ottavio Rinucinni (1562–1621) and additional music by Giulio

Caccini (1551–1618), is the first extant opera. (It was preceded only by Peri and Rinucinni's lost work *Dafne,* of 1597.) Based on Ovid's telling of the myth of Orpheus and Eurydice, *Euridice* was created as a wedding entertainment for Henry IV of France and Maria de Medici. It received its premiere at the Palazzo Pitti, Florence, on October 6, 1600. (Caccini, using the same Rinuncinni libretto, wrote a rival version of *Euridice*, which was performed at the Palazzo Pitti on December 5, 1602.)

141.3   Sauguet's ballet *La Chatte*] The scenario of *La Chatte* ("The Cat," 1927), a comic ballet by French composer Henri Sauguet, concerns a young man whose kitten is magically transformed by Aphrodite into a beautiful young woman—who chases mice. Commissioned by Diaghilev, it was choreographed by George Balanchine for the Ballets Russes. See also note 282.32.

141.12   Nadia Boulanger coterie] Students and faculty of the American Conservatory in Fontainebleau, where the charismatic Franco-Russian pedagogue Nadia Boulanger (1887–1979) was a leading teacher, first as an instructor in harmony (1921–35) and then as the school's director (1953–78). For Thomson's biographical tribute to Boulanger, see pages 880–86 of the present volume.

151.14   Alberti bass] Homophonic arpeggiated accompaniment, popularized by harpsichordist Domenico Alberti (1710–1740), that states the notes of a harmonic triad one at a time in the following pattern: low/high/middle/high.

152.32   Henry Dupre] Radio personality and jazz enthusiast "Uncle Henry" Dupre (1906–1980) was music director of station WWL, New Orleans, from 1932 to 1957.

162.17   American Composers Alliance] ACA, co-founded in 1937 by Thomson, Copland, Blitzstein, and others, is a membership organization of American composers dedicated to the publishing, performance, and licensing of American concert music. Since 1944 it has been closely affiliated with BMI (see note 9.3).

163.2–4   "Take care of the dramatic line . . . itself."] This well known remark by the Scottish-American soprano Mary Garden (see note 202.2) was popularized by Thomson in "Advice to Opera Singers" (1942), a *Herald Tribune* article collected in *The Musical Scene* (1945).

163.34–164.19   The history of the liberal professions in the Soviet Union . . . was abolished.] For more of Thomson on Soviet music manifestos, see "Composers in Trouble" (1948), a *Herald Tribune* article collected in *Music Right and Left* (1951).

165.34–35   late Senator McCarthy] Joseph R. McCarthy (1908–1957) was a Republican senator from Wisconsin (1947–57) who, after 1952, used his position as chairman of the U.S. Senate Committee on Government Operations to launch inquiries into the activities of supposed communists in the U.S. government. The resulting widespread public suspicion of those academics, intellectuals, artists, and public servants holding supposedly "un-American" views was popularly known as "McCarthyism." After December 2, 1954, when the Senate censured McCarthy for behavior "contrary to senatorial traditions," McCarthyism began to fade.

VIRGIL THOMSON

177.13 *Twelfth Street Rag*] Ragtime melody (1914) by Kansas City–based pianist and composer Euday L. Bowman (1887–1914).

177.15 H. L. Mencken boasted for us] See "Journal of an Expedition into the Midlands XII: Kansas City, Mo.," by Chicago-based journalist De Lysle Ferrée Cass, in Mencken's magazine *The Smart Set* (August 1923).

177.26 Negro college] Western University, founded in 1865 as Quindaro Freedman's School, was a historically black college in northwestern Kansas City, Kansas. It closed its doors in 1943.

177.33 Maurice Grosser] Grosser (1903–1986), was an American painter, writer, world traveler, and longtime companion of Virgil Thomson. He was the author of four books—*Painting in Public* (1948), *The Painter's Eye* (1951), *The Critic's Eye* (1962), and *Painter's Progress* (1971)—and an occasional art critic for *The Nation* (1956–67). He also devised scenarios for both of the Stein-Thomson operas. His paintings, mostly naturalistic portraits, still lifes, and landscapes in oils, are in the collections of the Museum of Modern Art, the Brooklyn Museum, and the Museum of Fine Arts, Boston, among other institutions.

178.11–12 William Allen White . . . Ed Howe] White (1868–1944) was, after 1895, the owner-editor of the daily *Emporia Gazette* and, after 1922, a Pulitzer Prize–winning syndicated columnist; Edgar Watson ("Ed") Howe (1853–1937) was the idiosyncratic editor of the *Atchison Daily Globe* (1877–1911) and of *E. W. Howe's Monthly* (1911–33), a little magazine of "Indignation and Information."

178.20 drummers] Slang for traveling salesmen, "drummers-up" of business.

180.5 Quincy Adams Thomson, born in 1827] Thomson's grandfather was actually born on February 1, 1828. He died on January 30, 1862, two days before his thirty-fourth birthday.

181.3 Gov. Walker] Robert J. Walker (1801–1869), a Democrat from Pennsylvania, was appointed fourth Governor of the Kansas Territory by President Buchanan in May 1857. Walker, though he was personally pro-slavery, resigned in December 1857 rather than support the unpopular, Buchanan-backed Lecompton Constitution, which, had it been adopted, would have admitted Kansas into the Union as a slave state against the wishes of most of Walker's constituency.

181.11 Col. Price] Sterling "Old Pap" Price (1809–1867), former Governor of Missouri (1853–57), was in September 1861 a colonel in the Missouri State Guard. He was commissioned a major general in the Confederate States Army in March 1862.

182.14 Blacklegs . . . Scalawags] Civil War–era slang for, respectively, swindlers and Southerners sympathetic to the Union and to Reconstruction.

185.6–11 Thereupon . . . same block.] The address of Alfred Quincy Thomson's first house, built in 1899, was actually 2629 Wabash Avenue. The family moved into the larger house at number 2613 in 1908.

187.15 Carnival parade] Every October from 1887 to 1912 Kansas City hosted the Priests of Pallas Parade, a Mardi Gras–style celebration with horse-drawn floats, costumed performers, street food, and music.

187.29–30 "Old Black Joe" and "Listen to the Mockingbird"] Minstrel show tunes by, respectively, Stephen C. Foster (1853) and Richard Milburn and Septimus Winner (1855).

187.35 "Darling Nelly Gray."] Song (1858) by Benjamin Hanby, the college-aged son of a United Brethren minister active in the Underground Railroad. The singer is a grieving Kentucky slave whose sweetheart has been suddenly sold by her master to a plantation owner in Georgia.

191.12–13 *Chinatown Charley, No Mother to Guide Her*] American melodramas, the one Owen Davis's 1906 cautionary tale of poolrooms and opium dens, the other Lillian Mortimer's 1905 play of innocence, deception, shame, and redemption.

191.33 *Miss Petticoats*] Play (1903) by "Dwight Tilton," pen name of American writers George Tilton Richardson and W. Dwight Quint, adapted from their best-selling novel of 1902. "Miss Petticoats," raised as the only child of an American widower, is a young New Englander woman with many local suitors who belatedly discovers that she was born a European princess.

192.24–25 Leschetizky's arrangement . . . *Lucia di Lammermoor*] *Andante finale* (Op. 13), by the Polish pianist Theodor Leschetizky (1830–1915).

194.38 "I Love My Wife but O, You Kid!"] Popular song (1902) written and recorded by the vaudeville duo of Harry Armstrong and Billy Clark.

195.16–17 Chicago and Alton "Hummer"] Express train on the Chicago & Alton line connecting Chicago, Kansas City, and St. Louis.

195.31 *The Green Book*] Monthly magazine (1909–21) that in its original editorial format (1909–14) featured "Pictures and Stories of the Theater."

196.15 Jeff Davis pie] Chess pie with cinnamon, raisins, dates, and almonds, named for Jefferson Davis (1808–1889), president of the Confederate States of America (1862–65).

198.9 *Trilby*] Episodic novel of Bohemian Paris (1894) by the French-born British writer and *Punch* cartoonist George du Maurier (1834–1896). Its heroine, Trilby O'Ferrall, is a tone-deaf Irish artists' model. She comes under the spell of Svengali, a hypnotist and singing coach, who transforms her into an opera diva.

198.22 Frances Willard] American educator and reformer (1839–1898) who founded, in 1883, the World Woman's Christian Temperance Movement.

198.28 *p, d, gr, tr, lc, Cap*] Pronoun, diction, grammar, transpose, lower-case, capital.

198.37–38 Crabb's *English Synonymes*] English writer George Crabb (1778–1851) published his *Dictionary of English Synonymes* in 1816. It was the model for *Roget's Thesaurus* (1852).

199.12 William Powell] American actor (1892–1984) best remembered as the suave detective Nick Charles in the six *Thin Man* movies (1934–47).

199.26 Robert Leigh Murray] Murray (1871–1936), a lifelong bachelor, was twenty-five years older than Thomson. On Thomson's seventeenth birthday, Murray presented his protégé with a copy of Oscar Wilde's *De Profundis* inscribed "To a lad whose friendship is a very pleasant thing to me."

200.5 Moses Bugoslawski] Born in Chicago of Russian immigrants, Bugoslawski (1888–1944) was for twenty years (1908–28) the head of piano instruction at the Kansas City Conservatory of Music. After 1916 he enjoyed a national career as a recitalist and soloist.

200.8 Gustav Schoettle] Born and trained in Stuttgart, Germany, Schoettle (1873–1923?) immigrated at age twenty to Missouri, where he was a teacher, recitalist, and accompanist long associated with Carl Busch and the Oratorio Society of Kansas City. He was later head of the music school at the University of Iowa (1910–16) and founding director of the first Des Moines Orchestra (1914–16).

200.10 Rudolf King] King, who had studied piano in Vienna, taught privately in Kansas City circa 1895–1925.

200.15 Clarence Sears] American organist (1882–1956) who in 1909 left New York for Kansas City to accept the job of music director at Grace Episcopal Church. In 1913 he began a forty-five-year tenure as organist and choir director at the city's St. Paul's Episcopal Church.

200.28 Sir John Stainer] Stainer (1840–1901), a prolific composer of Anglican church music, was organist at Magdalen College, Oxford (1860–71), and St. Paul's Cathedral, London (1872–88).

201.25 Auditorium] Kansas City's Auditorium Theater (1887–1960), on the corner of Ninth and Holmes streets, was from 1890 to about 1915 under the management of one William Blande, artistic director of the Blande Stock Company, sometimes billed as the Auditorium Company. By 1920 the Auditorium building had been repurposed as a movie house.

201.26 Convention Hall] Kansas City's first convention center, at the corner of Central and Twelfth streets, was opened in 1899. In 1936 it was leveled to make way for its successor, Municipal Auditorium, at Central and Thirteenth.

202.2   Mary Garden] Scottish-American singer Mary Garden (1874–1967) was Thomson's ideal of the operatic soprano and a valued friend. She rose to prominence at the Opéra-Comique, Paris, where she created the role of Mélisande in Debussy's *Pelléas et Mélisande.* Her American career was spent mostly in Chicago (1910–32) with the Chicago Grand Opera, the Chicago Opera Association, and the Chicago Civic Opera.

202.37   Lichtenwalter] A graduate of the University of Kansas, Eva Geneve Lichtenwalter (1867–1951) earned an M.A. under pianist E. Robert Schmitz (see note 509.21) at Columbia University. She continued her music studies in Germany, France, Chicago, and New York before settling, in 1906, in Kansas City. In 1909, at the age of forty-two, she opened the Lichtenwalter School of Piano Playing in the Studio Building at Ninth and Locust.

204.9   Alice Smith] Alice Myrmida Smith (1899–1973) was a friend and correspondent of Thomson's until the end of her life. In 1924 she married her father's protégé F. Henry Edwards (1897–1991), of Independence, Missouri, a British-born minister of the Reorganized Church of Latter Day Saints (1920–70).

204.10   Dr. Frederick Smith] Frederick Madison Smith (1874–1946), grandson of the Prophet Joseph Smith Jr. and son of Joseph Smith III, was the third prophet-president of the Reorganized Church of Latter Day Saints (1915–46).

204.22   Morton Prince and G. Stanley Hall] Prince (1854–1929), a Boston-based neurologist, was a founder of the study of abnormal psychology; Hall (1846–1924), a specialist in childhood development and educational theory, was the first president both of the American Psychological Association and of Clark University, in Worcester, Massachusetts.

205.4   Alice wrote in later years a memoir] In 1949 Alice Smith Edwards was asked by Kathleen Hoover (see note 491.9), who was then beginning research for her book (with John Cage) *Virgil Thomson: His Life and Music* (1959), to write down her recollections of Thomson. Her brief memoir (1949–50), used by Hoover as a biographical source, remains unpublished except in excerpts.

211.21   Pupin] Michael (Mihajlo) Pupin (1858–1935), Serbian-born physicist and physical chemist, held many lucrative patents, notably one for loading-coils (inductors) that increased the efficiency of transatlantic communications cables.

212.39–40   "They Go Wild, Simply Wild over Me."] Popular song (1917) by Fred Fisher, with lyrics by Joseph McCarthy.

215.35–36   Havelock Ellis] English physician and psychologist Ellis (1859–1939) published the autobiographical "Note on the Phenomena of Mescal Intoxication" in the British medical journal *The Lancet* (June 5, 1897). He later published popular articles on his peyote experiences in *Contemporary Review, Popular Science,* and other mass-market magazines.

218.34   Paine Hall] Paine Hall (1914), a four-hundred-seat concert hall located on the second floor of the Fanny Peabody Mason Music Building in Harvard's

North Yard, was named for the American composer John Knowles Paine (1839–1906), who, in 1872, was appointed Harvard's first professor of music.

219.4 Archibald T. Davison] A. T. "Doc" Davison (1883–1961) was an American composer, conductor, musicologist, and pedagogue. Educated at Harvard, he worked for the university all his adult life, as organist and choirmaster (1910–40), director of the Harvard Glee Club (1912–33) and the Radcliffe Choral Society (1913–28), and professor of music and musicology (1917–60). A collector and champion of early music, he was coeditor of the two-volume *Historical Anthology of Music* (1946, 1950) and, from 1922, general editor of Schirmer's Concord Series of teaching scores.

219.19 Appleton Chapel organ] Appleton Chapel stood in Harvard Yard from 1858 to 1930, when it was incorporated into the present Memorial Church, opened in 1932. Thomson played the four-manual organ built for the chapel in 1912 by the Ernest M. Skinner Company of Boston (Opus 197). This organ, modified in 1932 (Opus 197-A) to accommodate the remodeled chapel, was replaced in 1967 by a new organ built by C. B. Fisk of Gloucester (Opus 46).

219.24–25 Edward Burlingame Hill] A native of Cambridge, Massachusetts, E. B. "Ned" Hill (1872–1960) received his B.A. in music from Harvard College in 1894. After studies in New York and Paris, he taught music history and composition at Harvard from 1908 until his retirement in 1940, and was chair of the music department from 1927 to 1935. He wrote instrumental music for orchestra, including four symphonies, four symphonic poems, and several suites. He was also the author of *Modern French Music* (Boston: Houghton Mifflin, 1924), based on his Harvard lecture notes of 1910–22. In 1971 Thomson remembered him as "a sound impressionist composer, a master of orchestration, and a valued pedagogue."

219.38–39 S. Foster Damon] A native of Massachusetts, Samuel Foster Damon (1893–1971) graduated from Harvard in 1914 with a B.A. in music. He was one of the Harvard Aesthetes, a group that also included Malcolm Cowley, e. e. cummings, John Dos Passos, and Robert Hillyer, all of whom appeared in the influential anthology *Eight Harvard Poets* (1917). After serving in World War I he returned to Harvard as an instructor of English. In 1926 he joined the faculty of Brown University, where he taught until 1968. His books include pioneering studies in the art and poetry of William Blake, a life of Amy Lowell, and two anthologies of Danish poetry in English translation.

220.1–2 book that was to open up the language of William Blake.] S. Foster Damon, *William Blake: His Philosophy and Symbols* (Boston: Houghton Mifflin, 1924).

220.16–19 facsimile collection . . . before the Civil War] S. Foster Damon, editor, *Series of Old American Songs, Reproduced in Facsimile from Original or Early Editions in the Harris Collection of American Poetry and Plays, Brown University* (Providence: Brown University Library, 1936).

221.16   Boston Oyster House] Thomson means the Union Oyster House (est. 1826), at 41 Union Street, Boston.

221.21–22   *The Closet of Sir Kenelm Digby*] *The Closet of the Eminently Learned Sir Kenelme Digbie, Kt., Opened: Whereby is Discovered Several Ways for Making of Metheglin, Sider, Cherry-Wine, &c. together with Excellent Directions for Cookery: As also for Preserving, Conserving, Candying, &c* (London, 1669).

222.1   the sacrifice of two Italian immigrants.] Nicola Sacco and Bartolomeo Vanzetti, avowed anarchists who, in July 1921, were found guilty, after a controversial trial, of murdering two persons during an armed robbery the previous year. Despite widespread public protests, all appeals were denied by trial judge Webster Thayer (1857–1933) and the Massachusetts Supreme Court. Sacco and Vanzetti were sentenced in April 1927, and died in the electric chair the following August.

222.32–33   family-owned town south of Boston] North Easton is located twenty-five miles south of Boston, in Bristol County, Massachusetts. In 1803 Oliver Ames moved his father's shovel-making shop there from a neighboring town, and when, fifty years later, both the U.S. government and the Union Pacific Railroad signed exclusive contracts for Ames Shovels, the community prospered as "Shoveltown U.S.A." In 1875 the Ames family built the Unity Church of North Easton, architecturally significant for its stained-glass windows by John La Farge and its pulpit by Henry Handel Richardson.

223.14   one of the latter to see print two decades later.] Thomson's first completed choral work, *De Profundis* (a setting of Psalm 130), was composed in July 1920. This piece for mixed chorus was revised three decades later, in 1951, and published by Weintraub Music Co., New York.

223.40–224.1   "*Ils sont tous une génération perdue.*"] "You are all a lost generation," remark attributed to "Gertrude Stein in conversation" on the epigraph page of Hemingway's novel *The Sun Also Rises* (1926). For more on Hemingway's interpretation of this remark, see "*Une Génération Perdue,*" Chapter 3 of his posthumous memoirs, *A Moveable Feast* (1964).

225.12   Walter Spalding] Spalding (1865–1962), Harvard '87, taught music at Harvard from 1895 to 1932 and was chair of the music department from 1905 to 1927. His books include *Music: An Art and a Language* (1920), *Music at Harvard* (1935), and textbooks on harmony and counterpoint. In a tribute upon his retirement, his colleague E. B. Hill said that Spalding "realized the extent to which 'musical appreciation' might enter the lives of the general student. . . . [After Spalding] a college music department could henceforth not remain merely a school for technical study, but must extend its benefits to the whole student body."

227.31   *maison meublée*] Furnished rooming house.

228.32   Bernard Faÿ] Bernard Marie Louis Faÿ (1893–1978) was a Paris-born historian of Franco-American relations. In 1919–20, while enrolled as a student at the Sorbonne, he was a visiting fellow at Harvard, the experience that fostered his lifelong association with the university. He later held a number of academic posts both in France and in America. In Paris during the 1920s he became a close friend of Gertrude Stein and Alice B. Toklas, and made French versions of Stein's *Making of Americans* (*Américains d'Amérique,* abridged and translated with Baron J. Seillière, 1933) and *The Autobiography of Alice B. Toklas* (*Autobiographie d'Alice Toklas,* 1934). He was also Stein's agent for her American tour of 1934–35. His books available in English translation include *Benjamin Franklin: The Apostle of Modern Times* (1929) and *George Washington: Republican Aristocrat* (1931). For a summary on his notorious career in Vichy France, see note 558.3–7.

229.6   Bernard's young painter brother] Emmanuel Faÿ (1898–1923), an untried artist who would die of pneumonia in New York City at the age of twenty-five.

229.22–23   *foie gras en croûte*] Chicken liver pâté in a pastry crust.

229.27   *L'Œil cacodylate*] *The Cacodylic Eye.*

229.33   *M. . . . pour celui qui le regarde.*] *M. . . . for the Eye of the Beholder.*

231.14–15   "private bell for inexplicable needs."] See note 64.32.

232.28   H. T. Parker] Henry Taylor Parker (1867–1934), who signed his work "H.T.P.," was chief music, dance, and drama critic of the *Boston Evening Transcript* from 1905 until his death.

234.3–4   My piece that changed history] "Kusevitsky, Conductor," *Boston Evening Transcript* (February 8, 1922).

234.27   King's Chapel, Boston] At Tremont and School streets, opposite the Parker House hotel. In 1731, King's Chapel (est. 1686) became the first church in New England to house an organ. Thomson played the chapel's seventh organ, a four-manual instrument built in 1909 by the Ernest M. Skinner Company of Boston (Opus 170). It was replaced in 1964 by C. B. Fisk Opus 44.

237.40   *Socrate*] *Socrate,* which Satie called "a symphonic drama in three parts," was composed, for piano and voice, in 1917–18 and orchestrated in 1920. Satie, who used texts of Plato's dialogues in French translations by Victor Cousin (1792–1867), employed sopranos for all four parts (Alcibiades, Socrates, Phaedrus, and Phaedo).

239.17   "all liberals had had unhappy childhoods."] Quip by Maurice Grosser, quoted by Gertrude Stein in her book *Everybody's Autobiography* (1937).

240.7   Briggs Buchanan] Buchanan (1904–1976), the son of a Wall Street financier, was Thomson's first homosexual crush, the "chief confidant" of his early adulthood, and a lifelong correspondent. After Harvard he became a Yale-based art historian specializing in Sumerian seals and artifacts.

240.8 Henry-Russell Hitchcock] American historian of architecture (1903–1987) whose more than twenty books include *The International Style*, with Philip Johnson (1932), and *In the Nature of Materials: The Buildings of Frank Lloyd Wright* (1942).

240.9 Henwar Rodakiewicz] American filmmaker (1902–1976) whose works include several documentaries and the experimental silent film *Portrait of a Young Man in Three Movements* (1931).

240.13 Lincoln Kirstein] Poet and polymath Kirstein (1907–1996), the son of the president of Filene's department store, co-founded the literary quarterly *Hound & Horn* (1927–34) while an undergraduate at Harvard, then moved it to New York City. In 1934 he brought George Balanchine to America and, with Edward M. M. Warburg (see note 408.28), founded the School of American Ballet and, two years later, the Ballet Caravan dance company. The Caravan was succeeded by several other Kirstein-Balanchine dance companies, culminating in the New York City Ballet, founded in 1948.

240.19–20 first book about Franco-American history] Bernard Faÿ, *L'Esprit révolutionnaire en France et aux États-Unis à la fin du XVIIIe siècle* (1925), based on his doctoral thesis at the Sorbonne.

241.14 unrequited love] See note 240.7.

241.21 Clifford Heilman] American composer William Clifford Heilman (1877–1946), Harvard '99, was assistant professor in music at the university in 1915–25.

242.7 Chalmers Clifton] Clifton (1889–1966), Harvard '12, was chosen by Mrs. E. H. Harriman, the philanthropist-founder of the American Orchestral Society (1920–30), to lead the society's orchestra from September 1922 until its disbanding eight seasons later. In 1935–45 Clifton directed the New York City FMP/WPA orchestra (see note 8.37–39).

242.25 Rosario Scalero] Italian composer and violinist (1870–1954) who, during seven years in Vienna (1900–1907), studied composition with Eusebius Mandyczewski. Scalero was an instructor in music theory at the Mannes School of Music, New York, from 1919 to 1927.

242.40 Robert Shaw] American conductor Shaw (1916–1999) founded, in 1941, the Collegiate Chorale, a choir notable for its vocal excellence, its racial integration, and its frequent use by Toscanini as the unofficial chorus of the NBC Symphony Orchestra. In 1948 he founded a second choir, the Robert Shaw Chorale, which he led through 1953.

243.27 "Write me an article."] "Jazz," *The American Mercury* (August 1924), collected in *A Virgil Thomson Reader* (1981).

243.34 Frank Crowninshield] Paris-born American journalist Crowninshield (1872–1947) was an art and theater critic until asked by Condé Nast to create the monthly *Vanity Fair*. He oversaw the magazine for its entire first series, from January 1914 to February 1936. (The magazine was revived by Condé Nast Publications in March 1983.)

244.5   another title] "The Future of American Music," *Vanity Fair* (September 1925).

244.5–6   article making fun of orchestral conductors.] Published, as "The New Musical Mountebankery," in *The New Republic* (October 25, 1925).

244.11–12   *Seven Lively Arts*] Pioneering collection of essays on American popular culture (1924) by Gilbert Seldes (1893–1970), a critic and editor at the *Dial* magazine.

244.18   B. H. Haggin] Juilliard-trained pianist Bernard H. Haggin (1900–1987) early abandoned performance for music journalism. After a three-year stint at the Brooklyn *Eagle* he was music critic of *The Nation*, from 1936 to 1957. Thomson hired him as the radio-music critic for the *New York Herald Tribune* (1946–49). He was the author of several popular books on music, including *Conversations with Toscanini* (see pages 857–60 of the present volume).

244.29   Wallace Woodworth] G. Wallace Woodworth (1903–1966), Harvard '24, taught music at the university all of his adult life and eventually succeeded A. T. Davison (see note 219.4) in all his teaching duties.

245.14   *Fête polonaise*] At the invitation of A. T. Davison, Thomson arranged the *Fête polonaise* (for men's chorus and two pianos) for the Harvard Glee Club in 1924. When published in *The Harvard University Glee Club Collection*, Concord Series no. 93 (Boston: E. C. Schirmer Co., 1926), Davison, the Concord series editor, credited the *Fête polonaise* to "Emmanuel Chabrier; arr. by V.G.G.T." (Virgil Garnett Gaines Thomson).

246.11   Philip] Philip Bradford Lasell (1905–1987), Harvard '26, was the "playboy" son of Mary Frances Krum and Josiah Manning Lasell, the latter the co-heir, with his brother Chester Whitin Lasell, to the Whitin Machine Works (1831–1966), a large textile factory in Whitinsville, Massachusetts.

246.11–12   Hildegarde Watson . . . J. Sibley Watson] Hildegarde Lasell (1888–1987), an accomplished concert soprano, was the daughter of Jessie Maud Keeler and Chester Whitin Lasell. In 1914 she married James Sibley Watson Jr. (1894–1982), an heir to the Western Union telegraph fortune and, successively, a medical doctor, a pioneering independent filmmaker, and, in partnership with his wife, a philanthropist. He was also publisher of the modernist literary monthly *The Dial* (see note 303.16–18).

246.14   Mrs. Chester Whitin Lasell] Jessie Maud Keeler (1863–1950) married Chester Whitin Lasell in 1886.

246.27–28   Alice Smith's marriage] see note 204.9.

246.29–30   college on the Kansas side] Western University (see note 177.26).

246.33   Sherry Mangan] Poet and journalist John Joseph Sherry Mangan (1904–1961) was the editor of *Larus the Celestial Visitor* (1927–28) and a contributing editor of *Pagany* (1930–33). After 1934 he was a foreign correspondent for Time Inc. magazines in Paris and Buenos Aires, a freelance literary translator, and a devoted Trotskyite.

247.37–38   "It was not so much . . . what she did not take away."] Gertrude Stein, in "An American and France" (1936), published in *What Are Masterpieces* (Los Angeles: Conference Press, 1940).

248.17–18   I saved the life of Jessie Lasell] Thomson diagnosed, and then found treatment for, Mrs. Chester Whitin Lasell's severe middle-ear infection. See page 273 of the present volume.

248.27   Sylvia Beach] American bookseller and private printer (1887–1962) who from 1919 to 1940 owned Shakespeare and Company, the premier English-language bookshop in Paris.

248.30   George Antheil] In 1971 Thomson wrote that the career of American composer George Antheil (1900–1959) "suffered from overweening ambition, [though] his music has many qualities of excellence. Almost any work has delicious moments along with pompous ones. As a result, his music, though not strongly current in repertoire, does not die. Pieces of it are constantly being revived."

248.36   *pneumatique*] The pneumatic postal service of Paris (1866–1984) moved express mail through a network of suction tubes connecting most of the city's post offices. Standard correspondence could not be sent by pneumatic post, only lightweight letter-sheets that, when folded and sealed at their gummed edges, formed their own envelopes. These postcard-sized letter-sheets, printed on light blue stock, were known as *pneumatiques*.

249.23–24   Theodore Chanler] In 1971 Thomson summed up the achievements of his friend and fellow-American composer (1902–1961) as follows: "Chanler's chamber music, inspired by Fauré, expresses with distinction feelings really felt. His songs, among the finest of our time in English, are impeccable for prosodic declamation and imaginative in their use of accompanimental polyharmonies."

250.12   Janet Flanner] American writer (1892–1978) who, after 1925, was the Paris correspondent for the *New Yorker* magazine, publishing there under the penname "Genêt." See also pages 992–98 of the present volume.

250.12   Victor Seroff] Georgian writer on music and dance (1902–1979) known for his lives of Isadora Duncan, Franz Liszt, Sergei Prokofiev, and Dmitri Shostakovich.

250.25   Adrienne Monnier] Paris bookseller and private printer (1892–1955) whose store, La Maison des Amis des Livres ("House of the Friends of Books"), opened in 1915 and, like Shakespeare and Company, closed in 1940 due to the German Occupation.

250.31 *Le Navire d'argent*] Paris literary monthly (*The Silver Ship*), edited by Jean Prévost, that featured not only French writers but also Hemingway, Eliot, and other contemporary Americans in translation. There were twelve issues, dated June 1925 to May 1926.

251.30–31 children's game chapter of *Finnegans Wake.*] "The Mime of Mick, Nick, and the Maggies" (Book II, Chapter 1 of *Finnegans Wake*, 1939), first published (as "Continuation of a Work in Progress") in *transition* 22 (1933) and then as a pamphlet by Servire Press (The Hague, 1934).

252.3–4 *Antheil and The Treatise of Harmony*] Four hundred copies of this pamphlet, containing two essays by Ezra Pound ("Antheil" and "The Treatise on Harmony"), were printed in Paris by Three Mountains Press in 1924.

254.22–23 Mrs. Christian Gross] Born Virginia Randolph Harrison (1901–?), Mrs. Gross was the daughter of Francis Burton Harrison, first governor-general of the Philippines, and Mary Crocker, heir to a California railroad fortune. She married Christian Gross, a Chicago-born hero of World War I, in 1922, but soon left him for Marius de Zayas, a Mexican artist and gallery owner based in New York City.

255.1 Alice Mock] California-born soprano (1896–1972) who, in the 1940s, was also a supporting actress in several Hollywood features.

256.32 one striking ballet] *The Capital of the World* (1955), inspired by Hemingway's short story of the same title (1936).

256.35 Ezra Pound's opera] Pound's music for *Le Testament de Villon* was composed in collaboration with English pianist Agnes Bedford (1892–1968) in 1921–22, and then edited by George Antheil in 1923. His libretto was an adaptation of the Old French poem *Le Testament* (1461), by François Villon (1431–1463). Pound revised the opera's score and libretto in 1933.

256.37 Salle Pleyel] The original Salle Pleyel (1839–1927), at 22 rue de Rouchechouart, seated three hundred concertgoers. The current Salle Pleyel, opened in 1927 at 252 rue de Faubourg Saint-Honoré, seats more than twenty-four hundred. Both were originally owned by the Paris piano makers Pleyel et Cie, founded 1807.

258.3 LOUISE LANGLOIS] Madame Langlois (1856–1939) was the widow of Dr. Jean-Paul Langlois (1862–1923), a celebrated physiologist specializing in public hygiene and workplace safety and efficiency.

258.16 Lucien Herr] At the turn of the twentieth century, Herr (1864–1926) and his young wife, Jeanne Cuénod Herr (1885–1980), hosted a socialist salon in Paris whose members included Charles Péguy, Léon Blum, and Jean Juarès.

259.36–37 Mary Reynolds, Marcel Duchamp] American war widow Mary Louis Hubachek Reynolds (1891–1950) arrived in Paris in 1921, and there became an accomplished professional bookbinder. After 1923 she was the companion of the French artist Marcel Duchamp (1887–1968). For Thomson's extended biographical sketch of the couple, see pages 376–78 of the present volume.

260.21–22   painted sculpture by Arp made out of wood.] This sculpture, *Étoile* (1926), by Jean Arp (1887–1966), is 13½ inches tall. For decades it resided on the mantelpiece in Thomson's front room at the Hotel Chelsea. It is now in a private collection.

260.27   Mary Butts] English fiction-writer and poet (1890–1937). Her books of the 1920s included *Speed the Plough and Other Stories* (1923); her first two novels, *Ashe of Rings* (1925) and *Armed with Madness* (1928); and the epistolary fiction *Imaginary Letters* (1928), illustrated by Jean Cocteau.

261.33   John Rodker] English poet and publisher (1894–1955) whose short-lived Ovid Press (1919–21) brought out books by T. S. Eliot, Ezra Pound, and Wyndham Lewis.

261.34–35   a tall Scot who practiced black magic] Cecil Maitland (d. 1922), a protégé of occultist Alaister Crowley (1875–1947). Butts collaborated with Crowley on his arcane volume *Magick: Liber ABA*, Book 4 (completed 1936).

262.10–14   From ritual . . . occurs.] From Mary Butts, "Rites de Passage," *Pagany* (Summer 1930).

262.16–20   O Lord . . . Achilles' set.] From Mary Butts, "Heartbreak House," *Pagany* (Summer 1931).

262.23–26   Curl horns . . . Assemble bees.] From Mary Butts, "Corfe," in Louis Zukofsky, editor, *An 'Objectivists' Anthology* (Le Beausset, France: To Publishers, 1932).

263.20–21   Josiah Lasell] Philip Lasell's father. See note 246.11.

263.33   *Susie Asado*] Poem by Gertrude Stein (1912), collected in *Geography and Plays* (Boston: Four Seas Company, 1922). For the complete text of the poem, see pages 714–15 of the present volume.

264.24   *Capital Capitals*] Play by Gertrude Stein (1923), published in the Paris-based little magazine *This Quarter* (Spring 1925) and collected by Stein in *Operas and Plays* (Paris: Plain Edition, 1932). Thomson's setting, for four male voices and piano, was completed in April 1927.

266.8   three poets] Paris-born Georges Hugnet (1906–1974) began as a poet and small-press printer but in later life was a versatile man of letters—critic, editor, publisher, translator, book designer, and rare book dealer. Baron Eric de Haulleville (1900–1941), of Brussels, wrote a handful of poems and tales that appeared mainly in *transition*. For a sketch of Sherry Mangan, see note 246.33.

266.10   Pierre de Massot] French poet, writer, and socialist (1900–1969) closely associated with André Breton, Tristan Tzara, and the Dada movement.

266.11　My painter comrades] Paris native Christian ("Bébe") Bérard (1902–1949) was a figurative painter, a fashion illustrator for Chanel and Schiaparelli, and a designer for the Ballets Russes and Jean Cocteau. Russian-born Leonid Berman (1896–1976) was a painter of maritime life and the author of a memoir, *The Three Worlds of Leonid* (1978), for which Thomson wrote the preface. Berman's younger brother Eugene ("Genia," 1899–1972) was a painter of landscapes and, after World War II, a designer of sets for the Metropolitan Opera. Dutch-born artist Kristians Tonny (1907–1977) was a painter, draftsman, and book illustrator.

266.13　Pavel Tchelitcheff] Russian-born surrealist painter Pavel ("Pavlik") Tchelitchew (1898–1957) was a designer of sets and costumes for Dialghilev in Paris and, after World War II, for Balanchine in New York.

266.38　Max Jacob] French poet, writer, critic, and painter (1876–1944). For Thomson's extended biographical sketch of Jacob, see pages 373–75 of the present volume.

267.16–17　Francis Rose] English painter (1909–1979) who began his career as a set designer for Diaghilev's Ballets Russes. His pen drawings decorate *The Alice B. Toklas Cook Book* (1954) and the second edition of Stein's story for children, *The World Is Round* (1965).

268.26　Théophile Briant] Breton poet (1891–1956) and publisher-editor of the occasional literary journal *Le Goéland* (*The Gull*, 1934–56).

268.28　a collection of ten word-portraits] Gertrude Stein, *Dix Portraits* (*Ten Portraits*), with texts in English opposite French translations by Georges Hugnet and Virgil Thomson; preface by Pierre de Massot (Paris: Éditions de la Montagne, 1930).

269.12–13　Natalie Barney . . . "*amazone.*"] Natalie Clifford Barney (1876–1972), an American expatriate poet and feminist who wrote mainly in French, was the dedicatee of *Lettres à l'Amazone* ("Letters to the Amazon," 1910), a record of her platonic friendship with the book's author, French Symbolist poet Remy de Gourmont (1858–1915).

269.14–15　*Preciosilla*] Stein's poem "Preciosilla" (1913) was collected in *Geography and Plays* (Boston: Four Seas Company, 1922). Thomson's setting of the text, for piano and voice, was done in 1927.

269.16　Seignobos] Charles Seignobos (1854–1942), historian of the French Republic and professor at the Sorbonne.

269.24　Elisabeth de Gramont] Aristocratic French memoirist (1875–1954) and lifelong companion of Natalie Barney.

269.36　Ganna Walska] Polish-born operatic soprano and, from 1922 to 1931, the wife of Chicago industrialist Harold McCormick (see note 418.7). McCormick's lavish promotion of her mediocre career as a singer was the source of a storyline for the film *Citizen Kane* (1941).

270.8   Miss Etta and Dr. Claribel Cone] The Cone sisters, Etta (1870–1949) and Claribel (1864–1929), were among the first American collectors of Matisse, Picasso, Van Gogh, Gauguin, and other modern French artists. The Cone Collection, comprising more than three thousand items, is the cornerstone of the modern collection of the Baltimore Museum of Art.

270.10–11   Emily Crane Chadbourne] Arts patron Emily Rockwell Crane (1871–1964), an heir to the Crane plumbing-fixtures fortune, married the lawyer Thomas Chadbourne in 1896. She built a significant collection of modern French and American folk art, much of it now in the Art Institute of Chicago.

270.13   Elsa Maxwell] American radio personality, syndicated gossip columnist, and society hostess (1883–1963).

270.20–21   Princesse Edmond de Polignac] Yonkers native Winnaretta Singer (1865–1943), an heir to the Singer sewing-machine fortune, married the French composer Prince Edmond de Polignac in 1893. The couple established a salon at their Paris mansion and became patrons to the city's musical avant-garde.

271.21   *A Saint in Seven*] Play (1922) by Gertrude Stein, published in *What Are Masterpieces* (Los Angeles: Conference Press, 1940). Thomson and Langlois's translation, "Un Saint en Sept," appeared in *Orbes* 2 (Spring 1929) with an introduction, "La Vie de Gertrude Stein," by Georges Hugnet.

271.22–23   excerpts from *Making of Americans.*] Thomson and Hugnet's translation, *Morceaux choisis de la Fabrication des Américains*, was published by Hugnet's Éditions de la Montagne in 1929.

271.28   *Portrait of F.B.*] "Portrait of F. B." (1908), short prose work by Gertrude Stein, in *Geography and Plays* (Boston: Four Seas Company, 1922). Thomson's song *Portrait of F.B. (Frances Blood)* (1929) is for medium voice and piano. The subject of Stein's portrait is actually one Florence Blood, a onetime close companion of Stein's brother, Leo.

271.30   *Deux Soeurs qui sont pas soeurs.*] Film *Deux Soeurs qui [ne] sont pas soeurs* ("Two Sisters Who Are [Not] Sisters," 1929), scenario by Gertrude Stein, written in French, published in *Portraits and Prayers* (New York: Random House, 1934). Thomson's song based on the text (1930) is for medium voice and piano.

274.22   *La Source*] Ingres's oil of a female nude emptying an ewer, begun in 1820, was finished and exhibited in 1856. It hangs in the Musée d'Orsay.

274.29   *salamandre*] Small French-made Franklin-style heating stove, usually fitted into a working fireplace. It burns hard, inexpensive, smokeless anthracite coal.

275.9   Lucie Delarue-Mardrus] Prolific French journalist, historian, and sculptor (1874–1945) whose many lesbian lovers included Natalie Clifford Barney (see note 269.12).

276.1   Louise-Philippe times] Circa 1830–48.

276.9 a large Bérard] Christian Bérard, *Portrait of Walter Shaw* (1927). Oil and beeswax on board, 39¼ x 23¾". The painting is now in a private collection.

276.13 Pleyel] See note 256.37.

276.39–40 *Le Cid*] Verse tragicomedy in five acts (1637) by Pierre Corneille (1606–1684).

277.1 *Andromaque*] Verse tragedy in five acts (1667) by Jean Racine (1639–1699).

277.9–10 "*C'est intéressant tout de même la nature.*"] "Nature is interesting in all its forms."

281.18 Victor Prahl] American concert pianist and recital singer (1893–1953) who, after World War II, was a professor of music at Smith College.

281.19 Solita Solano] Penname of American journalist Sarah Wilkerson (1888–1975), a *National Geographic* reporter and longtime literary assistant to G. I. Gurdjieff.

281.19 Vincent Sheean] American journalist (1899–1975) whose bestselling memoir, *Personal History* (1935), was source material for the Hitchcock film *Foreign Correspondent* (1940).

282.14 *bon enfant* and *gros jouisser*] Good child and great sensualist.

282.19 Louis Gillet] French art historian and literary critic (1876–1943) elected to the Académie Française in 1935.

282.24 Louise Gillet] Louise-Dominique Gillet (1905–1984) was the daughter of Louis Gillet. At M. Gillet's request, Thomson composed his Church Organ Wedding Music for her wedding in 1940.

282.32 Henri Sauguet] A protégé of Satie, Sauguet (1901–1989) remained close to Thomson all his life. Thomson thought his music's most powerful qualities were "warmth and sincerity." "Sauguet does not purge the emotions," he wrote in 1953, "he feeds them, makes them flower, give off perfume. The drama in his stage works is as intimate as in his chamber music, just as his chamber music is capable of evoking vast scenes and lofty laments worthy of the opera."

282.39 *La Chatte*] See note 141.3.

282.40–283.1 Henri Cliquet-Pleyel . . . Marthe-Marthine.] French composer Cliquet-Pleyel (1884–1963) and French soprano Marthe Boutte ("Marthe-Marthine," 1891–1948) were companions throughout the 1920s.

283.15 "*colères de faiblesse,*"] Angry acts of weakness.

283.32–35 *Le Berceau . . . Waltzes.*] "The cradle of Gertrude Stein, or the mystery of the rue de Fleurus: Eight poems by Georges Hugnet, set to music [medium voice and piano] by Virgil Thomson under the title *Lady Godiva's Waltzes*" (Paris: Éditions de la Montagne, 1928).

283.39   Comte d'Ursel] Henri d'Ursel (Henri, Eighth Duke of Ursel, 1900–1974), working under the pseudonym Henri d'Arche, produced, directed, and wrote the scenario for the half-hour film *La Perle* ("The Pearl," 1929), based on the story by Georges Hugnet. For a synopsis of the movie's action, see page 322.

284.9–10   Jouhandeau . . . Gide . . . Kochnitzky] Marcel Jouhandeau (1888–1979), French Catholic mystic and pioneer of homosexual fiction; André Gide (1869–1951), French Nobel laureate in literature (1947); Léon Kochnitzky (1892–1965), Belgian neoclassical writer and musicologist and political associate of Gabriele D'Annunzio.

284.15   Robert McAlmon] American publisher (1895–1956) of William Carlos Williams's *Contact* magazine (1920–23) and of Contact Editions, which brought out Hemingway's *Three Stories and Ten Poems* (1923) and Gertrude Stein's *The Making of Americans* (1925).

284.20   Olga Dahlgren] American painter and collector of fine glass paperweights (1892–1968).

284.25   Charles-Albert Cingria] French Swiss polymath, writer, and musician (1883–1954).

286.16   *Main Street*] Satirical novel (1920) by American writer Sinclair Lewis (1885–1951).

287.38   *transition*] Influential Paris-based literary journal (1926–38) edited by American Eugene Jolas (1894–1952). See also page 333 of the present volume.

288.2–3   "lotuses of prose style and Anglican theology,"] Sherry Mangan, "'A Note': On the Somewhat Premature Apotheosis of Thomas Stearns Eliot," *Pagany* (Spring 1930).

288.35   Copland-Sessions concerts] Concert series (1928–31), formally the Copland-Sessions Concerts of Contemporary Music, comprising ten events—eight in New York and one each in London and Paris. Organized by Aaron Copland and Roger Sessions, the concerts presented new music by North American composers.

289.1   Duchesse de Rohan] Marie de Rohan (1600–1679), known as Madame de Chevreuse, was a favorite of the court of Louis XIII. Thomson's *Trois Poèmes de la Duchesse de Rohan* (1928), for voice and piano, consists of "A son Altesse la Princesse Antoinette Murat," "Jour de chaleur aux bains de Mer" (translated, by Sherry Mangan, as "Hot Day at the Seashore"), and "La Seine."

289.23   Edmund Pendleton] American pianist and composer (1899–1987) who was the longtime organist and choir director at the American Church in Paris (1935–75).

289.40   Gaston Hamelin] Innovative French woodwind player (1884–1951) who from 1926 to 1932 was first clarinet in the Boston Symphony Orchestra.

291.17–18   "There are two kinds . . . bad music."] H. L. Mencken, in a letter to Isaac Goldberg, May 26, 1925, printed in Goldberg's *The Man Mencken: A Biographical and Critical Survey* (New York: Simon and Schuster, 1926).

296.31–32   described in a poem by Georges, which I set to music] *Les Soirées bagnolaises* (1928), for middle voice and piano.

298.27   Bravig Imbs] American poet, novelist, art critic, and radio news reader (1904–1946), co-author of books with André Breton, Bernard Faÿ, and Georges Hugnet, and, throughout the 1920s, a close friend of Gertrude Stein and Alice B. Toklas.

298.28   Georges Maratier] French painter, art dealer, editor at Hugnet's Editions de la Montagne, and lover of Kristians Tonny.

298.32–33   *Commentaire sur Saint Jérome*] Sade's text, from the "Minski the Cannibal" episode of his novel *Juliette* (1797), states that Jerome, while traveling in the British isles, witnessed Scots eating the buttocks of young shepherds and the breasts of young women. Sade offers that he, the narrator of the novel, would much prefer the former of these meals, as the flesh of a man is, all cannibals agree, superior to that of a woman.

299.2   Lucien Schwartz] Longtime concertmaster of Paris's Orchestre des Concerts Pasdeloup.

299.8–11   *une chanteuse blonde / . . . / notre nouvelle maison.*] "The blond singer / who sings at this moment / showed us on her arm / our new house."

299.37   *primeurs . . . à volonté.*] "New wines" and "all you can eat."

302.31   Judge Thayer . . . Sacco and Vanzetti.] See note 222.1.

303.16–18   Scofield Thayer . . . *The Dial*] Thayer (1889–1982) was an American poet, art collector, philanthropist, independent filmmaker, scientist, and, from 1920 to 1926, editor of the modernist literary monthly *The Dial* (1920–29).

305.10   with my portrait] Gertrude Stein, "Virgil Thomson" (1928), short prose work published in *Portraits and Prayers* (New York: Random House, 1934).

305.20–21   our dear Nellie] Eleanor Joseph ("Nellie") Jacott (1874–1938), a good friend of Stein from her California childhood.

306.22–23   *par dessus le marché*] Into the bargain.

306.34   [Roger] Vitrac] French surrealist poet and playwright (1899–1952).

306.37   *commissariat*] Police station.

308.14   Carl Van Vechten] American photographer, novelist, dance and music critic, and impresario of the modernist and Harlem Renaissance movements (1880–1964). He met Gertrude Stein in 1913, became her first American champion, and, with Alice B. Toklas, handled most of her posthumous literary affairs.

308.18–19   Alma Morgenthau Wertheim . . . Cos Cob] American patron of
the arts Alma Morganthau (1887–1953) married investment banker Maurice
Wertheim in 1909. In 1929 she founded Cos Cob Press to publish music scores
by contemporary composers including Copland, Harris, Ives, Piston, Sessions,
and Thomson.

308.21–23   Luhan . . . Clark . . . Draper . . . Knopf . . . Marinoff . . . Stettheimer]
Mabel Dodge Luhan (1879–1962), of New York and Taos, society hostess and
patron of the arts; Emily Tapscott Clark (1890–1953), of Philadelphia and
Richmond, publisher-editor of the critical monthly *The Reviewer* (1921–25);
Muriel Draper (1886–1952), of New York and London, journalist, tastemaker,
and social activist; Blanche Knopf (1894–1966), president of Alfred A. Knopf,
Publisher, Inc.; Fania Marinoff (1890–1971), Russian-born actress of stage and
screen and wife of Carl Van Vechten; Henrietta Walter ("Ettie") Stettheimer
(1875–1955), author, under the penname "Henrie Waste," of the feminist novels
Philosophy (1917) and *Love Days* (1923).

308.32–33   Kenyon Cox] Paris-trained American artist and educator (1856–
1919) whose draftsmanship, canvases, lectures, and journalism were a reactionary argument against modern art.

309.1–2   Ettie, Florine, and Carrie] The Stettheimer sisters, Henrietta (see
note 308.21–23), Florine (1871–1944), and Carrie (1869–1944), lived in Alwyn
Court, a French Renaissance apartment building at 180 West Fifty-eighth
Street, with their wealthy German-born mother, Rosetta (Walter) Stettheimer
(1841–1935). Florine, a painter and poet, was trained by Kenyon Cox and Robert
Henri at the Art Students' League. Among her most well known works is the
five-by-four foot "Cathedrals of New York" series (1929–42), four canvases now
in the collection of the Metropolitan Museum of Art.

309.19   Walter Wanger] Prolific Hollywood producer (1894–1968) whose films
spanned *The Sheik* (1921), with Rudolph Valentino, to *Cleopatra* (1963), with
Richard Burton and Elizabeth Taylor.

310.5–6   picture . . . in which an evocation of me is playing and singing] Florine
Stettheimer, *Portrait of Virgil Thomson* (1930). Oil on canvas, 38½ x 20⅛". Art
Institute of Chicago (Gift of Virgil Thomson, 1975).

311.12   Emily Clark Balch] Emily Tapscott Clark (see note 308.21–23) was married to Philadelphia banker Edwin Balch from 1924 to 1927.

311.36   League of Composers] American composers' organization founded in
1923, in New York City, with a mission "to produce the highest quality performances of new music, to champion American composers in the United States
and abroad, and to introduce American audiences to the best new music from
around the world." In 1954 it became the U.S. chapter of the International
Society of Contemporary Music.

312.33   Jere Abbott] Art historian (1897–1982) who became, in 1929, associate
director of the Museum of Modern Art, reporting to the founding director,
Alfred A. Barr Jr. (1902–1981).

312.40 novel about Milan] "Prelude," an autobiographical story by Dorothy Speare (1898–1951), appeared in *Pictorial Review*, August 1927. In 1929–31 it was adapted for the stage, under the title "Don't Fall in Love," by Speare and the Broadway script doctor Charles Beahan. This play, never produced, provided the story for the Columbia Pictures musical *One Night of Love* (1934), directed by Victor Schertzinger.

313.39–40 widow of Paul . . . mother of another Paul] Muriel Sanders, heir to an investment fortune, married Paul Draper (1887–1925), a notable singer of German lieder, in 1908. Their firstborn child was Paul Draper Jr. (1909–1996), a tap dancer and choreographer trained at the School of American Ballet.

315.23–26 *Ah, que revienne avril / . . . / ne quitte plus Virgil.*] Ah, April returns / and with it, Virgil! / In April / don't leave, Virgil.

316.10–11 George Copeland] American pianist (1882–1971) who was a protégé and champion of Debussy, giving several U.S. premieres of his works. He was also a favorite accompanist of dancer Isadora Duncan and a specialist in Spanish music.

317.31 he undertook my portrait] Christian Bérard's portrait-sketch of Virgil Thomson (May 1929) is now in a private collection.

318.33–34 concert of works by young Americans] The concert was given, in the Salle Chopin on rue Daru, on June 17, 1929. The songs by Thomson, sung by Marthe-Marthine, were *La Valse Grégorienne* (Hugnet), *La Seine* (Duchesse de Rohan), *Le Berceau de Gertrude Stein* (Hugnet), *Susie Asado* (Stein), and *Preciosilla* (Stein).

318.37–38 three James Joyce songs by Israel Citkowitz] American composer Citkowitz (1909–1974), a protégé of Aaron Copland in New York and Paris, published his *Five Songs from "Chamber Music"* in 1930.

319.9–10 *"fine et spirituel . . . dedans,"*] Fine and spiritual and with irony inside.

319.29 I had written that of him] In "The Cult of Jazz," *Vanity Fair* (June 1925).

319.31 *Modern Music*] Journal of the League of Composers (1924–46), edited by Minna Lederman (see note 380.17).

319.32–37 Virgil Thomson can teach us . . . any other language.] Aaron Copland, "From a Composer's Notebook," *Modern Music* (May–June 1929).

320.1 Edwin Denby] American poet and dance critic (1903–1983). For Thomson's biographical sketch of Denby, see pages 890–93 of the present volume.

320.2 *régisseur*] One who stages (rather than choreographs) a ballet.

320.16–17 libretto—about to be printed] Gertrude Stein, "Four Saints in Three Acts: An Opera to Be Sung," *transition* (June 1929).

322.21 Vicomte de Noailles] Arthur Anne Marie Charles (1891–1981), who, with his wife, Marie-Laure Bischoffsheim (1902–1970), were adventurous patrons of French composers, surrealist painters, and independent filmmakers.

325.40 *The Miracle*] Spectacle-pantomime (1911) by German playwright Karl Vollmöller (1878–1948). The Broadway production by Max Reinhardt (1873–1943), creator of the Salzburg Festival, opened at the Century Theater on January 16, 1924, and ran 175 performances.

327.30 Insull enterprises] Midwestern holding-company and power-grid empire controlled by American business magnate Samuel Insull (1859–1938), whose philanthropic interests included Chicago's opera companies.

330.14–32 around the personality . . . grandiose tragedy.] Virgil Thomson, "Now in Paris," *Modern Music* (March–April 1933).

331.15 *bœuf à la mode en gelée*] Braised beef with carrot and onion, in aspic.

332.15 *The Little Review*] Roughly monthly review of the international avant-garde (1914–29), edited and published in Chicago and New York by Margaret Anderson (1886–1973). It published Eliot, Pound, Yeats, and the first thirteen chapters of James Joyce's *Ulysses.*

332.26 *Pagany*] Boston-based literary quarterly, edited by Richard Johns (1904–1970), that published eleven issues between 1930 and 1933.

332.38–40 A "*Note*" . . . *Eliot.*] See note 288.2–3.

333.5–6 two-page article about my music.] Georges Hugnet, "Virgil Thomson," translated from the French by Basil Klingstone, in *Pagany* (Winter 1930).

334.17 Funeral Oration by Bossuet] See note 40.27.

334.39 Chicago millionairess] Emily Crane Chadbourne (see note 270.10–11).

335.3 Charles B. Cochran] English theater impresario (1872–1951) who brought Diaghilev's Ballets Russes to London and championed the career of Noël Coward.

335.5 Otto Kahn] Investment banker and philanthropist Otto Hermann Kahn (1867–1934) was chairman of the board (1907–31) and president (1918–31) of the Metropolitan Opera, owning 84 percent of the company's stock at the time of his death.

335.17–18 Jere Abbott and Alfred A. Barr, Jr.] See note 312.33.

337.2 Edith Sitwell] English poet and critic Sitwell (1887–1964), who never married, nurtured a complicated passion for the homosexual painter Pavel Tchelitchew from 1927 until his death in 1957.

337.37–38 Ramón Senabre] Like Grosser, Ramón Jao Senabre (1893–1978) was a figurative painter of portraits, still lifes, and landscapes.

339.15 Sauguet's review of the concert] "Oeuvres de Virgil Thomson," in the weekly *L'Europe Nouvelle* (Thursday, June 18, 1931). The translation from the French here is Thomson's own.

339.26 Prunières . . . reviewed it] See Henry Prunieres (Henri Prunières), "American Compositions in Paris," *The New York Times* (Sunday, July 12,

1931). Prunières (1861–1942), who founded the monthly *Revue Musicale* in 1920 and edited it through 1939, was a Paris correspondent for *The New York Times* from 1924 to 1935. He actually wrote that Thomson "seems made for the opera."

340.14 two years later in *Modern Music*] Virgil Thomson, "Igor Markevitch, Little Rollo in Big Time," *Modern Music* (November–December 1932). Excerpted in *The New York Times* for December 25, 1932.

346.1–2 "everything possible . . . image of truth,"] William Blake, in one of the "Proverbs of Hell," from *The Marriage of Heaven and Hell* (1790).

347.24–25 "painting [had] become a minor art again,"] Stein wrote, in "Saving the Sentence," Chapter 1 of *How to Write* (1929), "Painting now after its great moment must come back to be a minor art."

352.10 *Things as They Are*] *Things as They Are*, an eighty-seven-page work subtitled "A Novel in Three Parts," was printed posthumously, in 1950, by Banyan Press, of Pawlet, Vermont, in an edition limited to 516 copies. It was reprinted, as "Q.E.D.," in *Q.E.D., Fernhurst, and Other Early Writings*, edited by Donald Gallup (New York: Liveright, 1970).

357.30–31 They also translated . . . *Composition as Explanation.*] *Composition comme explication* (1929), Hugnet and Langlois's French version of Stein's Cambridge Lecture of 1926, was commissioned but not used by the Paris-based Franco-American review *Échanges*. It remains unpublished.

358.5 grammatical error] See note 271.30.

362.17 *Pagany*, which accepted them] *Enfances*, by Georges Hugnet, with Stein's facing-page English version titled "Poem Pritten on Pfances by Georges Hugnet," appeared in *Pagany* (Winter 1931). Stein's poem was later printed alone as *Before the Flowers of Friendship Faded Friendship Faded: Written on a Poem by Georges Hugnet* (Paris: Plain Edition, 1931).

362.19 Marcoussis] Polish-born painter, cartoonist, and engraver Louis Marcoussis (1878?–1941) lived most of his adult life in Paris.

363.12–13 Ellen [La Motte]] American nurse (1873–1961) who wrote books about her experiences in Europe during World War I and in Asia treating opium addicts. She was a close companion of Emily Crane Chadbourne (see note 270.10–11).

364.21 *Le Singe et le léopard*] Thomson's song based on La Fontaine's fable "The Monkey and the Leopard" (Book 9, Fable 3) was composed in 1930.

365.15–16 Prolégomènes . . . philosophe.] Pierre de Massot's book ("Prolegomena to an Ethics without Metaphysics, or Billy, Bulldog and Philosopher") was printed for Hugnet's Éditions de la Montagne in 1930.

365.26 *cœur sensible*] Tender heart.

366.28 Jeanne Bucher] After 1926, Paris bookseller and gallery owner Marie-Jeanne Bucher (1872–1946) printed several artist's books and volumes of poetry under the imprint Éditions Jeanne Bucher.

369.8–9 William Aspenwall Bradley] American literary agent (1878–1939) whose Paris-based firm, the William A. Bradley Agency (1923–83), numbered Gertrude Stein, James Joyce, Ford Madox Ford, and Richard Wright among its clients.

369.21–23 *Left to Right . . . Story,* November 1933.] Stein's story actually first appeared, as "Left to Right: A Study in the New Manners," in the U.K. edition of *Harper's Bazaar* (September 1931). It was collected posthumously in *Reflection on the Atomic Bomb: Volume I of the Previously Uncollected Writings of Gertrude Stein,* edited by Robert Bartlett Haas (Los Angeles: Black Sparrow Press, 1973).

372.32 *souteneurs*] Pimps.

373.3 Gaétan Fouquet] French photographer and author of travel guides who found commercial success, with his partner Camille Kiesgen, as the impresario of Connaissance du Monde (founded 1945), a series of popular film documentaries and multimedia stage shows featuring explorers and world travelers.

373.5 Yvonne de Casa Fuerte] Violinist and advocate for modern music (1895–1984) who taught at the Paris Conservatory and, after World War II, in New York City. She also founded and directed La Sérénade (1931–38), a Paris concert series devoted to new French music.

373.7 *bordelais*] Native of France's Bordeaux region.

373.9 *La Chartreuse de Parme*] Sauguet's four-act opera ("The Charterhouse of Parma"), with a libretto by Armand Lunel after Stendhal's novel, was given its premiere at the Paris Opéra on March 16, 1939.

374.5–6 "*le port ultérieur de la redingote*"] "Back pocket of a frock coat."

375.7 *Bourgeois de France et d'ailleurs*] Jacobs's affectionately satirical "field guide" to the "Bourgeois of France and elsewhere" was published in 1932.

375.19 Roy Harris] In 1971 Thomson wrote of the American composer Roy Harris (1898–1979) that his "best works have a deeply meditative quality combined with exuberance. Even without citation of folklore they breathe an American air. His music reflects high artistic aims and a sophistication of thematic, harmonic, and instrumental usage . . . with frequently great beauty in the texture." Thomson especially admired Harris's early chamber works and the third of his thirteen symphonies.

376.39–377.1 *Nude Descending a Staircase*] Duchamp's oil on canvas *Nu descendant un escalier, No. 2* (1912) was the notorious centerpiece of the so-called Armory Show, the international exhibition of modern art at New York City's 69th Regiment Armory in the winter of 1913.

377.16–17   brother of a sculptor . . . and of the painter Jacques Villon] Duchamp's elder brothers were Raymond Duchamp-Villon (1876–1918), a cubist sculptor, and Emile Gaston Duchamp (a.k.a. Jacques Villon, 1875–1963), a cubist painter and printmaker.

377.29–30   *Surrealism and Its Affinities*] The catalog and bibliography of the Mary Reynolds Collection, compiled by Hugh Edwards and Reynolds's brother, Frank Brooks Hubachek, was published by the Art Institute of Chicago in 1956. It features essays by Marcel Duchamp, Jacques Villon, Jean Cocteau, Djuna Barnes, and others.

378.20–22   I own Florine's portrait . . . resemblance and style.] Both Florine Stettheimer's "double portrait" of a seated Marcel Duchamp and his female alter ego Rose Sélavy (1923) and Duchamp's pencil drawing of Stettheimer's head and neck (1926) are now in private collections.

378.31–32   Paul Bowles] American composer and writer (1910–1999). In 1971 Thomson wrote that "Bowles's fiction has a worldwide readership, deserved. His songs and chamber music, though less known, are expressive, distinguished, and picturesque, often with an ethnic background (Mexico, Spain, Morocco). His stage music benefits from a strong theater sense. His songs can be quite delicious." For more of Thomson on the life and work of Bowles, see pages 967–70 of the present volume.

378.38   Harry Dunham] American cinematographer, documentary filmmaker, and broadcaster (1910–1943) who worked for Pathé News in Paris and New York. When Dunham, an Air Force lieutenant during World War II, was shot down over Borneo, Copland dedicated his Sonata for Violin and Piano to his memory.

380.15   I wrote the article] Virgil Thomson, "Aaron Copland," *Modern Music* (January–February 1932).

380.17   Minna Lederman] American music critic (1896–1995) who, in 1923, became the founding editor of the quarterly *League of Composers' Review* (1924–46), renamed in 1925 *Modern Music*. For more on Lederman and *Modern Music*, see Thomson's article "A War's End" (1947) in *The Art of Judging Music* (1948).

380.27–28   A. Everett Austin, Jr.] After three years as assistant curator at Harvard's Fogg Museum, Chick Austin (1900–1957), at the age of twenty-six, became director of the Wadsworth Atheneum, in Hartford, Connecticut. Thomson's biographical essay on Austin (1958) is printed on pages 876–80 of the present volume.

381.11–12   Citkowitz songs from James Joyce] See note 318.37–38.

381.22   my first musical publication] Virgil Thomson, *Stabat Mater*, for soprano and string quartet, with text, in French, by Max Jacob (New York: Cos Cob Press, 1933).

381.38 La Sérénade] See note 373.5.

382.15 Jean Ozenne] French comic actor of stage and screen (1898–1969) who, in his youth, was also a fashion designer and fashion illustrator.

383.28–30 a kind crippled woman . . . Georges Maratier's American wife] Rena Frazier was a close friend of fellow-Midwesterner Florence Tanner, who in 1929 married Georges Maratier.

383.34–35 René Blum, brother of Léon] Frenchman René Blum (1878–1942), an opera and ballet director based in Monte Carlo, had been an associate of Diaghilev's Ballets Russes for more than a decade when, in 1929, Diaghilev suddenly died of diabetes. In 1931, in order to continue ballet in the Diaghilev tradition, he co-founded, with the Russian impresario Colonel Wassily de Basil (1888–1951), the Ballet Russe de Monte Carlo, which employed most but not all of Diaghilev's former company. In 1934, Blum and de Basil dissolved their partnership, scattering the performers. De Basil, debarking to Paris, created a new company, the Original Ballet Russe (1934–47), and Blum, after a couple of years regrouping, founded the Ballet de l'Opera de Monte Carlo (1937–present). (René Blum's brother Léon Blum, 1872–1950, was three times the prime minister of France between 1938 and 1947.)

384.19 widow of Lucien Herr] See note 258.16.

385.5 Mrs. Patrick Campbell . . . Polaire] "Mrs. Pat" (1865–1940), born Beatrice Stella Tanner, was the celebrated English stage actress for whom Shaw created the role of Eliza Doolittle. Polaire (1874–1939), born Émilie Marie Bouchard, was a French chanteuse and silent-screen actress.

385.17 Philip Johnson] American architect and architectural historian (1906–2005) who in 1930, at the age of twenty-four, founded the department of architecture and design at the Museum of Modern Art.

386.5 the Kirk Askews] R. Kirk Askew (1903–1974) was an American dealer in modern art who began his career in 1927 at the New York branch of Durlacher Brothers, London. In 1938 he bought the firm, running both branches through 1969. In the 1930s he and his wife, Constance Atwood Askew (1895–1984), ran an influential Sunday-night salon at their home at 166 East Sixty-first Street.

387.7 Iris Barry] British movie critic and curator (1895–1969) who founded the London Film Society in 1925 and the film department of the Museum of Modern Art in 1932.

387.20 young art historians] Agnes Rindge (1900–1997), later Agnes Rindge Claflin, longtime director of the Vassar Art Gallery and a specialist in baroque and modern sculpture; John McAndrew (1904–1978), architectural historian at Vassar, New York University, and the Museum of Modern Art; Agnes Mongan (1905–1996), curator of drawings, and later director, of Harvard's Fogg Art Museum.

387.27–28 Paul Sachs and Edward Forbes] Sachs (1878–1965) was an heir to the Goldman Sachs fortune and designer of Harvard's museum-studies curriculum; Forbes (1873–1969) was director of the Fogg Art Museum from 1909 to 1944.

387.39 Julien Levy] Art dealer (1906–1981) and proprietor of New York's Julien Levy Gallery (1931–49).

388.1 Pierre Matisse] Art dealer (1900–1989) and proprietor of New York's Pierre Matisse Gallery (1931–89). He was the youngest child of Henri Matisse.

389.39 Jimmy Daniels] Nightclub host and singer (1908–1984) whose Harlem establishments included Jimmy Daniels' (1939–42) and, later, Bon Soir and the Little Casino.

390.9 Avery Memorial] The Avery Memorial Building at the Wadsworth Atheneum was the first International Style museum building in America. Designed in 1932–33 by the New York firm of Morris & O'Connor, it was built with money from the estate of Samuel Putnam Avery Jr. (1847–1920), an art dealer, collector, and Atheneum patron. The Avery Memorial opened its galleries in January 1934, and the spare, intimate, state-of-the-art Avery Theater, with its 299 blue-velour seats, in February.

390.12–13 Serge Lifar] French-Russian dancer, choreographer, and memoirist (1905–1986) who, after a long association with Diaghilev, was ballet master of the Paris Opera in 1930–44 and 1947–58.

390.15–16 Alexander Smallens] Russian-born conductor (1889–1972) who, when Thomson met him in the early 1930s, was assistant conductor of the Philadelphia Orchestra and a guest conductor of New York's Stadium Symphony (the New York Philharmonic's summer-concert orchestra).

391.31 Lord Duveen] London art dealer Joseph Duveen (1869–1939) specialized in selling European masterpieces to wealthy American buyers.

393.2 Clare Boothe Luce] Clare Boothe Brokaw (1903–1987), later the wife of *Time*'s Henry Luce, joined the staff of *Vanity Fair* in 1929. She was managing editor from December 1932 to February 1934.

393.28 Theodate] Soprano recitalist Theodate Johnson (1907–2002) made her debut at Town Hall in 1934 and performed through the end of World War II. In 1949 she joined the staff of *Musical America*, and was the magazine's owner-publisher from 1959 to 1964.

394.29 Reuben's] Midtown New York delicatessen, run by Arnold Reuben and family from 1908 to 1966.

395.9–10 *The Cruiser Potemkin*] Cinematically innovative silent film (1925), better known as *Battleship Potemkin*, by Soviet director Sergei Eisenstein (1898–1948).

395.13   "wobblies,"] Members of the Industrial Workers of the World (IWW), an international trade union, founded in Chicago in 1905, with roots in Marxism and socialism.

396.9   Agnes de Mille] American modern dancer and choreographer (1905–1993) who, in 1933, was a member of Anthony Tudor's London Ballet.

397.8–9   Winifred Molyneux-Seel] English avant-garde sculptor (fl. 1930s) and entrepreneur-designer of the SeelSlym brand of women's undergarments.

397.13   "*portrait charmant . . . que j'aime*."] "Charming portrait . . . I love it."

397.23–24   ballet in the Diaghilev style had been revived] See note 383.34–35.

397.31   Les Ballets '33] Les Ballets 1933 was the first ballet company led by Russian choreographer and dancer George Balanchine (1904–1983), who, with Diaghilev's right hand, librettist Boris Kochno (1904–1990), had quit de Basil and Blum's Ballet Russe de Monte Carlo at the end of its first season (see note 383.34–35). With the backing of poet and London stage impresario Edward James (1907–1984), Les Ballets 1933 created seven new ballets and booked four weeks of repertory at Paris's Théâtre des Champs Elyseées and London's Savoy Theater. It was after a London performance of Les Ballets 1933 that Lincoln Kirstein (see note 240.13) first met Balanchine, an occasion that led to the founding of New York's School of American Ballet (1934) and the Ballet Caravan dance company (1936).

397.40   Lotte Lenya] Austrian actress and singer (1898–1981) who met the composer Kurt Weill in 1924, married him in 1926, and was his muse and greatest interpreter, in German and English, until his death in 1950.

399.17   Peter Eckersley and his wife] Captain Eckersley (1892–1963), a pioneer of British radio, was a broadcast personality, the first chief engineer at the BBC, and the holder of several radio-related patents. His wife, the singer Dorothy "Dolly" Stephen, whom he married in 1930, was a Nazi sympathizer who had met Hitler through her friend Unity Mitford.

399.18   Edward Clark] Conductor Edward Clark (1888–1962), a fierce advocate of modern music, was music director of the BBC from 1924 to 1936. He was married to Dolly Stephen (see note above) from 1921 to 1930.

399.33–34   Mosley's Blue Shirts] British MP Sir Oswald Mosley (1896–1980) left the Labour Party in 1930 to found the New Party, which was dedicated to labor reform on the national socialist model. Mosley soon merged his party with the larger British Union of Fascists, which cast an admiring eye to Mussolini, Hitler, and Franco. Thomson here seems to confuse the Irish fascists of the 1930s (known as Blueshirts) with Mosley's British fascists (known as Blackshirts).

400.10   Arnold Schoenberg] Austrian-born Schoenberg (or Schönberg, 1874–1951) found popularity as a Late Romantic composer and then notoriety as a leading figure of the musical avant-garde, known for his atonal works (1908–22) and, later, his experiments with the twelve-tone system. He settled in California in 1933, became a U.S. citizen in 1941, and taught at the University of Southern California and UCLA. For more of Thomson on Schönberg, see pages 904–10 of the present volume.

400.14   Franz Lehar] Austro-Hungarian composer (1870–1948) of *The Merry Widow* (1905) and other light operas.

400.24   an article of mine] For Thomson's seventieth-birthday tribute to Schönberg, see "Schönberg's Music" (1944), in *The Art of Judging Music* (1948).

400.30   Frederick Ashton] English dancer and choreographer (1904–1988) associated with Britain's Royal Ballet after 1933 and was the company's director from 1963 to 1970. His repertory creations include *Cinderella* (1948), *Daphnis and Chloe* (1951), *Sylvia* (1952), and the ballets for the film *Tales of Beatrix Potter* (1970).

400.31–32   Ida Rubinstein's Paris troupe] Ballet company (1911–35) led by Ida Rubinstein (1885–1960), Russian-born actress, dancer, and patron of the arts. (Ashton danced in the company from 1928 to 1931.)

401.5   Cyril Connolly] When Thomson met him in the 1930s, Connolly (1903–1974) was a book critic for *The New Statesman*. He was later the founder and editor of *Horizon* magazine (1940–49) and then chief book critic of the London *Times*. His first wife was the Pittsburgh-born socialite Jean Bakewell.

401.16   Doriot] Paris-based Jacques Doriot (1898–1945) was, in the 1930s, a nationalist-socialist political leader on the model of Britain's Oswald Mosley (see note 399.33–34).

401.38–39   the composer of *Simple Aveu*] The *Simple Aveu* ("Simple Confession," c. 1878) of French pianist-composer François (Francis) Thomé (1850–1909) was once an internationally popular parlor piece.

405.40   nous avons changé tout cela] "But we have changed all that." Catchphrase from Molière's 1666 farce *Le Médicin malgré lui* (*The Doctor in Spite of Himself*).

408.28   Edward M. M. Warburg] Warburg (1908–1992), the wealthy son of a New England investment banker, was a Harvard friend of Lincoln Kirstein. Besides being a cofounder of the School of American Ballet and the Ballet Caravan (see note 240.12), he endowed Iris Barry's film department at the Museum of Modern Art (see note 387.7) and was a trustee of the Metropolitan Museum of Art.

409.23   Lewis Galantière] American translator of French literature (1895–1977), especially for the theater. In 1933 he and John Houseman co-wrote the Broadway comedy *Three and One*, adapted from the French of Denys Amiel.

409.23 John Houseman] Romanian-born English actor and stage director (1902–1988). For Thomson's review of Houseman's memoir *Run-Through* (1972), see pages 958–66 of the present volume.

410.7–9 Lawson . . . Zatkin . . . Miller] Kate Drain Lawson (1894–1977), American actress and costume designer for Broadway and television; Nathan Zatkin (1903–1998), Broadway publicist and sometimes producer; Elizabeth "Lee" Miller (1907–1977), American fashion model turned fashion photographer and, during World War II, a London-based war correspondent for *Vogue*.

410.15 Negro woman] Eva Jessye (1895–1992), whose Harlem-based Eva Jessye Choir (originally the Dixie Jubilee Singers) was a leading black choir in New York City from the late 1920s to the early 1970s.

411.26–27 Beatrice Robinson-Wayne and Edward Matthews] Robinson-Wayne (1904–1998?), the original St. Teresa I, was lead soprano of Harlem's Donald Haywood Choir, and Matthews (1907–1954), the original St. Ignatius, was a baritone recitalist in Boston, later a teacher of vocal music at Howard University.

411.36–39 Harry Moses . . . *Warrior's Husband*] Moses (1873–1937), who produced seven Broadway plays between 1932 and his death five years later, had his biggest success with a 1932 revival of Julian F. Thompson's Amazonian farce *The Warrior's Husband* (1924).

412.13 Helen Austin's mother] Helen Goodwin (1897–1988) married Chick Austin (see note 380.27–28) in 1929.

412.26 George Foote] Foote (1866–1956), a French-born Harvard-trained composer, was known for his art songs and chamber music.

414.7 We gave six shows in Hartford] After a preview on February 6, *Four Saints in Three Acts* was given its world premiere at the Wadsworth Atheneum on the evening of Wednesday, February 7, 1934, and ran through Saturday, February 10.

414.15 Abe Feder] Innovative lighting designer (1910–1997) whose company, Lighting by Feder, worked not only in New York theater but also in architecture.

414.37 New York opening night] *Four Saints* opened at the Forty-fourth Street Theater on February 20, 1934, and ran through March 17. It then moved to Broadway's Empire Theater on April 2, and ran through April 14. There were forty-eight New York performances.

415.18 Duchamp's *Nude*] See note 376.39–377.1.

415.23 H. T. Parker] See note 232.28.

416.40–417.2 Grace Denton . . . at the Auditorium] Grace Denton Esser, Chicago's "Madame Impresario," booked *Four Saints* at the Auditorium Theater from Wednesday, November 7, through Saturday, November 10, 1934. There were five Chicago performances.

417.26　Thomas Anderson] Anderson sang the part of St. Giuseppe.

417.36　Joseph Brewer] Brewer (1898–1991), former publisher of Dial Press and patron of Ford Madox Ford, was president of Olivet College from 1934 to 1944.

417.40　David Bispham Medal] From 1921 to 1934 the American Opera Society of Chicago conferred its Bispham Memorial Medal Award (named after American operatic baritone David Bispham, 1857–1921) on the year's best opera written in English.

418.7　Harold McCormick] Chicago businessman (1872–1941), Chairman of International Harvester, president of the Chicago Opera Association (1915–21), and a financial backer of the city's several subsequent opera companies.

418.12　"Bobsie" . . . Goodspeed's] Elizabeth Fuller Goodspeed (1893–1979), the Francophilic wife of a Chicago financier, was a socialite, arts patron, and president of the Arts Club of Chicago from 1932 to 1940.

420.29　My first job in the speaking theater] *A Bride for the Unicorn* (1933), a comedy by the Irish playwright Denis Johnston (1901–1984), received its American premiere on May 2, 1934. American director Joseph Losey (1909–1984) directed the undergraduate production by the Harvard Dramatic Club.

420.36–37　*Medea* . . . Countee Cullen] Houseman's production of the *Medea* of Euripides, translated into English verse by the Harlem Renaissance poet Countee Cullen (1903–1946), was abandoned due to the long, final illness of its leading lady, Rose McClendon (1883–1936). Cullen published his text as the centerpiece of his collection *The Medea and Some Poems* (1935). Thomson's incidental music—later published as *Seven Choruses from "The Medea,"* for women's chorus and percussion—was completed in August 1934 and first performed in 1942.

421.5　*Le Cocu Magnifique*] Farce ("The Magnificent Cuckold," 1921), in French, by Belgian playwright Fernand Crommelynck (1886–1970).

422.13　Avery Claflin's *Hester Prynne*] In December 1934, when two scenes from it were staged at the Wadsworth Atheneum, *Hester Prynne* (1932), by American composer Avery Claflin (1898–1979), was otherwise unproduced. Claflin also wrote operas based on "The Fall of the House of Usher" and *Uncle Tom's Cabin*. In 1971 Thomson wrote that Clafin's operas, "broadly conceived both as drama and as musical style, have not yet come to please strongly today's somewhat finicky taste in stage music."

423.16–17　Charles Brackett] American screenwriter and producer (1892–1969) notable for his enduring collaborations with director Billy Wilder, including *The Lost Weekend* (1945) and *Sunset Boulevard* (1950).

423.28　(AGMA)] See note 50.14.

423.36–37　Milton Diamond] Diamond (1859–1955), longtime chief attorney for the American Federation of Musicians (see note 50.15), was the founder, in 1939, of BMI (see note 9.3).

424.12–13   American Composers Alliance] See note 162.17.

424.40   *Mahagonny] Rise and Fall of the City of Mahagonny (Aufstieg und Fall der Stadt Mahagonny*, 1930), songspiel by Kurt Weill with libretto by Bertolt Brecht.

425.13   Orson Welles] Later a director, writer, and producer of stage, film, and radio, the actor Orson Welles (1915–1985), at age nineteen, made his Broadway debut (on December 20, 1934) as Tybalt in the Katharine Cornell–Guthrie McClintick production of *Romeo and Juliet*. For Thomson's biographical sketch of Welles, see pages 959–66 of the present volume.

425.22–23   Negro Theatre in Harlem] The Negro Theater Unit of New York (1935–39), headquartered at Harlem's Lafayette Theater (at 132nd Street and Seventh Avenue), was the most active and longest-lived of the thirteen American Negro companies created by the Federal Theater Project. Under the initial direction of John Houseman (1935–36) it employed some two hundred black performers and stagehands and produced some thirty plays from 1936 to 1939. (Upon its founding, the only white employees were Houseman, Orson Welles, Virgil Thomson, the Swiss costume and scene designer Nat Karson [1908–1954], and Houseman's secretary, all of whom left at the end of the first season.) The New York Unit's success led directly to the founding of the American Negro Theater (1940–49), with headquarters at the Schomberg Center for Research in Black Culture.

425.35–36   Ada MacLeish] American soprano Ada Hitchcock (1892–1984) was married, in 1916, to the poet and playwright Archibald MacLeish (1892–1984).

425.37   Eva Goldbeck . . . reviewed the concert] Eva Goldbeck (1901–1936), "A Thomson Soirée," *Modern Music* (November–December 1935). Goldbeck's review, remembered by Thomson as a pan, argued that his music, while often seemingly "pretentious and frivolous . . . is intrinsically honest and serious" and marked by a "severe and fluent technique."

426.7–15   The Federal Music Project . . . aesthetic dictates.] See note 8.37–39. The second Composers' Forum–Laboratory concert—the first in its regular concert-and-interview format—was presented on January 8, 1936, at the Federal Music Theater, 110 West Forty-eighth Street, New York City.

426.8   Ashley Pettis] Pettis (1892–1978), director of music education for the F.M.P./WPA Music Project, conceived the Composers' Forum-Laboratory as a means of cultivating a larger audience for American concert music.

426.22–23   Hartford Festival] The First (and only) Hartford Festival was held February 9–16, 1936, at the Wadsworth Atheneum. The *Bal de Chiffoniers*, better known as The Paper Ball, was given the evening of Saturday, February 15. The concert organized by Thomson, titled "Matinée Musicale: Chamber Music Ancient and Modern," was given on the final afternoon of the festival.

427.16   James Soby] Hartford native James Thrall Soby (1906–1979), a critic and collector of modern art, was a curator at the Wadsworth Atheneum

(1928–38) and the Museum of Modern Art (1940–57). Soby also organized and wrote the catalogue essay for *Eugene Berman: A Retrospective Exhibition* (Boston: Institute of Contemporary Art, 1941).

427.38 *Socrate*] See note 237.40.

428.2–3 Eva Gauthier . . . Colin O'More] American mezzo-soprano Gauthier (1885–1958), whom Thomson called "the high priestess of modern song," and American tenor O'More (1888–1945?), who sang light opera under the name James Herrod.

429.22 *'Tis Pity She's a Whore*] Jacobean tragedy (c. 1629) by English playwright John Ford (1586–1639).

430.3 PARE LORENTZ] American documentary filmmaker, critic, and journalist (1905–1992), born Leonard MacTaggart Lorentz, in Clarksburg, West Virginia. When Thomson met him, in 1936, he was known as a movie reviewer for *Scribner's, Vanity Fair*, and other magazines, and as the author, with Morris L. Ernst, of *Censored: The Private Life of the Movie* (1930).

430.22 United States Resettlement Administration] New Deal agency (April 1935–December 1936) that built poverty-relief camps for Dust Bowl–era landowners, sharecroppers, and migrant workers. It was superseded, on January 1, 1937, by the Farm Security Administration.

431.3 *The Plow That Broke the Plains*] American documentary featurette (1936), produced, written, and directed by Pare Lorentz for the United States Resettlement Administration. Narrated by Thomas Chalmers. Music by Virgil Thomson (orchestrated by Henry Brant and conducted by Alexander Smallens). Running time: 26 minutes.

431.21 *Once in a Blue Moon*] Paramount comedy (1935), written and directed by Charles MacArthur and Ben Hecht, starring Jimmy Savo (1892–1960), a small, bowler-hatted Italian-American circus mime and juggler who, in the 1930s, became a vaudeville headliner and, briefly, a Hollywood star.

431.23 Henry Brant] Canadian composer, orchestrator, and multi-instrumentalist (1913–2008) who wrote for radio and films throughout the 1930s and '40s. In 2002 he won a Pulitzer Prize in Music for his organ concerto *Ice Field*.

432.27–38 Negro Theatre . . . relief of poverty was urgent.] See notes 8.37–39 and 425.22–23.

432.32 Nat Karson] See note 425.22–23

433.3 a play by a Negro] *Walk Together Chillun!*, written and directed by Frank Wilson (1886–1956), opened on February 2, 1936, and closed on February 29. There were twenty-nine performances.

433.5 *Macbeth*] The "Voodoo Macbeth," produced by John Houseman and directed by Orson Welles, opened on April 14, 1936, and closed on June 20. There were sixty-four Harlem performances. Then, on July 6, 1936, it moved to Broadway—the Adelphi Theater, on West Fifty-fourth Street—where, after eleven performances, it closed on July 17. The production then played the country at other African American theater venues (Bridgeport, Dallas, Indianapolis, Chicago, etc.) through the end of the year.

433.16–17   Asadata Dafora Horton] Pioneering musician and theater impresario (1890–1965) who, after moving from Sierra Leone to Harlem in 1929, brought African drumming and African dance to Western audiences as a performer and a producer.

433.30–32   Thomas . . . Carter . . . Ellis . . . Lee] Edna Thomas (1885–1974) was an actress, singer, and vice president of the Negro Actors Guild; Jack Carter (1902–1967) later played Mephistopheles in Houseman and Welles's *Doctor Faustus* (1937); Maurice Ellis (1905–2003) played the Narrator in Brecht and Auden's *Duchess of Malfi* (1946); Canada Lee (1907–1952), a former prizefighter, had the longest career of these four, playing Bigger Thomas in the Houseman-Welles *Native Son* (1941) and supporting roles in many Hollywood features.

434.17   *Hearts and Flowers*] Lachrymose American melody (1893) by German immigrant Theodore Moses-Tobani (1855–1933) that, during the silent era, was used reflexively by theater pianists to accompany "sad" or "tender" sequences.

434.19–21   Hugh Davis . . . Leonard de Paur] Two African American musicians: Davis (fl. 1930s) was the music director of *Macbeth* and, later, the Leslie Howard *Hamlet* and the Tallulah Bankhead *Antony and Cleopatra*, all with incidental music by Thomson; De Paur (1914–1998) was a choral director, conductor, and arranger and, for seventeen years during the 1960s and '70s, the director of community relations for Lincoln Center.

434.30   The Living Newspaper] The Living Newspaper Unit of the Federal Theater Project was founded in 1936 by playwright Elmer Rice (1892–1967) and FTP director Hallie Flanagan (1890–1969). Each production was shaped as a series of skits around a common theme—affordable power, fair and safe housing, sexually transmitted diseases, etc.—with capitalism usually cast in the role of villain. *Triple-A Ploughed Under* dealt with the plight of the American farmer, and *Injunction Granted* the problems of workers and consumers in a world run by monopolies. Conservative newspapers and Roosevelt Administration censors were highly critical of the Living Newspaper.

435.9   John Latouche] American lyricist and librettist (1914–1956) whose stage name was "John La Touche." He wrote lyrics for Broadway musicals, ribald songs for the cabaret singer Madame Spivy, and, most significantly, the libretto for Douglas Moore's opera *The Ballad of Baby Doe* (1956).

435.16   Project 891] Houseman and Welles's project for the WPA Federal Theater after the Negro Theater Unit in Harlem was, according to the official government paperwork, WPA Project No. 891. "Project 891" (1936–37), also known as "The Classical Theater," was a repertory company resident at Maxine

Elliott's Theater (1908–60), at 109 West Thirty-ninth Street. During its single season, Project 891 produced three significant plays: *Horse Eats Hat* (Labiche via Denby and Welles), *Doctor Faustus* (Marlowe), and *The Cradle Will Rock* (Blitzstein).

435.20   *Horse Eats Hat*] The play, adapted by Edwin Denby (see note 320.1) and Orson Welles from a French farce (1851) by Eugène Labiche (1815–1888), opened at Maxine Elliot's Theater on September 26, 1936, and closed on December 5. There were sixty-one performances.

436.19   Kirstein and Balanchine's new company] Ballet Caravan (see note 240.13).

437.12   Our *Hamlet*] William Shakespeare's *Hamlet*, produced by and starring Leslie Howard (1893–1943), directed by Mr. Howard with John Houseman from a text adapted by Schuyler Watts (1912–1997), opened at the Imperial Theater, New York, on November 10, 1936, and closed on December 13. There were thirty-nine Broadway performances. Cast: Mary Servoss (Gertrude), Wilfred Walter (Claudius), Pamela Stanley (Ophelia), Joseph Holland (Horatio), et al. Agnes DeMille choreographed the Players' Mime. Production and costume design by Stewart Chaney. Incidental music by Virgil Thomson, conducted by Hugh Davis.

438.5   John Gielgud's *Hamlet*] Gielgud's *Hamlet*, produced and directed by Guthrie McClintic and co-starring Lillian Gish as Ophelia, opened on Broadway on October 8, 1936, and ran for 132 performances.

438.25   Daisy . . . Fellowes] Paris-born socialite of American heritage (1890–1962) and Paris editor of *Harper's Bazaar*. She was the niece of Princesse Edmond de Polignac (see note 270.20–21).

438.32   Paul Poiret] French designer (1879–1944) whose innovations in women's fashion included the tailored suit coat with matching skirt.

441.2   *The River*] American documentary featurette (1938) produced by Pare Lorentz for the United States Farm Security Administration. Written and directed by Pare Lorentz. Narrated by Thomas Chalmers. Music by Virgil Thomson (orchestrated by Henry Brant and conducted by Alexander Smallens). Running time: 36 minutes.

442.10   Dr. George Pullen Jackson] American musicologist (1874–1953) whose pioneering work *White Spirituals in the Southern Uplands* was published by the University of North Carolina Press in 1933. For Thomson's consideration of Jackson's lifework see "America's Musical Autonomy" (1944) in *A Virgil Thomson Reader* (1981).

442.19   *Southern Harmony*] *The Southern Harmony, and Musical Companion: Containing a Choice Collection of Tunes, Hymns, Songs, Odes, and Anthems, Selected from the Most Eminent Authors in the United States*, by William Walker (1809–1875), was privately printed in New Haven, Connecticut, in 1835. The fifth edition (1854), "Thoroughly Revised and Greatly Improved [by the Author]," was reprinted in 1939 (New York: Hastings House/WPA's Writers' Project of Kentucky) and has since become the standard.

442.22   *The Sacred Harp*] *The Sacred Harp: A Collection of Hymn Tunes, Odes, and Anthems, Selected from the Most Eminent Authors*, by Benjamin Franklin White (1800–1879) and Elisha J. King (1821?–1844), was privately printed for the authors in Philadelphia in 1844. The book went through three further editions during B. F. White's lifetime and has since gone through several more under various editors.

442.35–36   reprint in facsimile . . . of one hundred American songs] See note 220.16–19.

443.1   John Lomax] American musicologist (1867–1948) who, as curator of the Library of Congress's Archive of American Folk Song, documented cowboy ballads, Cajun music, and songs in the blues tradition.

443.10–11   Berman's protests against directive criticism] See page 427.

445.2   *The Spanish Earth*] Independently made American documentary silently financed by Broadway producer Herman Shumlin (1898–1971) and directed by the Dutch-born French photographer Joris Ivens (1898–1989). The music was selected and arranged by Virgil Thomson and Marc Blitzstein in collaboration with sound director Irving Reis (1906–1953). Running time: 52 minutes.

445.33   *Filling Station*] One-act ballet (1937) by Virgil Thomson, with scenario by Lincoln Kirstein. It received its world premiere at the Avery Memorial Theater, Wadsworth Atheneum, Hartford, Connecticut, on January 6, 1938. The original Ballet Caravan production, directed by Kirstein and Lew Chistensen (1908–1984), featured choreography by Christensen with set and costume design by Paul Cadmus (1904–1999). The dancers included the three principals of the Ballet Caravan: Lew Christensen, as Mac, the filling-station attendant, and Erick Hawkins (1909–1984) and Eugene Loring (1911–1982) as truck drivers Ray and Roy. The pianist was the Ballet Caravan's music director, Gjertrud "Trude" Rittmann (1908–2005).

446.23   *Antony and Cleopatra*] William Shakespeare's *Antony and Cleopatra*, produced by Laurence Rivers and directed by Reginald Bach from a text adapted by William Strunk Jr., opened at the Mansfield Theater, New York, on November 10, 1937, and closed on November 30, 1937. There were five Broadway performances. Godfrey Tearle was Antony to Tallulah Bankhead's Cleopatra.

449.14   *New Music*] *New Music: A Quarterly of Music Compositions*, edited by Henry Cowell for the New Music Society of California, published, in the words of its prospectus, "not music criticism, but music itself." The first issue was dated Fall 1927, the last Winter 1957. The magazine, which published significant scores by Ives, Varèse, Ruggles, and others, seldom enjoyed more than six hundred paid subscribers.

449.36 Arrow Music Press] Arrow Music Press, incorporating Cos Cob Press (see note 308.18–19), opened for business in 1938. Its sole employee was publisher and business manager Harrison Kerr, who energetically ran the press from 1939 through 1946. In 1956 the four founders sold the Arrow catalog, dormant for most of the preceding decade, to Boosey & Hawkes, Inc., New York.

451.7 Marian Chase] Chase (1915–1951), the daughter of a U.S. Army colonel from Louisiana, met Harry Dunham (see note 378.38) when he worked for Pathé news in New York City. They married in 1940.

451.9 Theodora Griffis] Connecticut socialite "Teddy" Griffis (1915–1956), the daughter of an executive at Paramount Pictures, was married, briefly, to John La Touche (in 1940–42).

451.10 Jane Auer] Jane Auer (1917–1973) married Paul Bowles in 1938. As Jane Bowles she published a novel, *Two Serious Ladies* (1943), a play, *In the Summer House* (1958), and a handful of short stories.

451.12 his French wife] Kristians Tonny's common-law wife was Françoise Henry (1902–1982), a leading historian of Celtic art.

452.4–5 Mercury Theatre] Houseman and Welles's Mercury Theater Company, a commercial venture continuing the work of Project 891 (see note 435.16), produced six Broadway plays (1937–41), the abortive *Five Kings* (see note below), and a radio series, *The Mercury Theatre on the Air* (1938, continued from Hollywood as *The Campbell Playhouse*, 1938–40). With Hollywood's RKO studio it also produced two motion pictures, *Citizen Kane* (1941) and, without Houseman's participation, *The Magnificent Ambersons* (1942).

452.9 *Five Kings*] Welles's Falstaff play, *Five Kings* (1938–39), never made it to Broadway. Overlong, over-budget, and under-rehearsed, it died in previews in Boston and Philadelphia. The project, cherished by Welles, was later realized as the film *Chimes at Midnight* (1965).

453.18 I accepted.] In the spring of 1938, Thomson signed a contract with Thayer Hobson (1897–1967), president of William Morrow & Co., New York, for what would become his first book, *The State of Music* (1939).

455.11 Lubin . . . Jobin] Germaine Lubin (1890–1979), Wagnerian soprano long associated with the Paris Opéra; Raoul Jobin (1906–1964), French Canadian tenor who would sing for the Metropolitan Opera throughout the 1940s.

455.12 Jacques Dupont] After learning his craft with Diaghilev's Ballets Russes, Dupont (1906–1976) designed operas for all the major French houses as well as for the Metropolitan Opera. He was also a favorite of Frederick Ashton at the Royal Ballet (see note 400.30).

455.17 *"la jeune France."*] "Young France," a group founded by André Jolivet and including Messiaen, Daniel-Lesur and Baudrier.

456.8–10 Dior . . . Ozenne . . . Kenna] In 1935–36 Christian Dior (1905–1957), then a failed young art dealer recovering from tuberculosis, learned the rudiments of fashion design from his roommate Jean Ozenne (see note 382.15) and Ozenne's companion, the American designer and painter Max Kenna (1902–1970).

457.15 *bel étage*] In Renaissance architecture, the main floor (or *piano nobile*) of a large house, which is usually, but not always, the first floor.

457.40 quenelles] fish cakes; croquettes.

459.6–7 Elsie Houston] Brazilian soprano (1902–1943) who specialized both in recitals of classic songs in Spanish and in Portuguese and in nightclub performances of Afro-Brazilian "Voodoo" chants. She took her life at age forty.

459.12 *chasseurs alpins*] Mountain infantry; an elite corp of the French army.

459.22–460.35 The French have become . . . à la troubadour.] Virgil Thomson, "French Landscape with Figures," *Modern Music* (November–December 1938).

460.36 Margareta] Sherry Mangan would marry Margareta Landin (1906–1953), his second wife, in 1940.

462.35 Trianon gray] Copyrighted background "brown-gray" color of a Louis Vuitton bag.

463.28 Bruce Morrissette] Morrissette (1911–2000), a professor of Romance languages at the University of Chicago, was later the chief American translator and explicator of Alain Robbe-Grillet.

463.34–464.42 The season's chief controversy . . . to digest.] Virgil Thomson, "More from Paris," *Modern Music* (January–February 1939).

465.26 Henry Furst] Furst (1893–1967), working closely with his Italian wife Orsola Nemi, translated Benedetto Croce into English and Melville, Poe, Henry James, and Henry Miller into Italian.

467.9 Alvaro Guevara] London-based Chilean painter (1894–1951), chiefly a portraitist, who was associated with Roger Fry, Duncan Grant, and the Bloomsbury set.

468.7 William Einstein] American abstract painter (1907–1972) who was part of the O'Keefe–Stieglitz circle.

470.20–21 "*Es gibt hier kein' Ordnung*,"] "There is no order."

471.39–40 letter from John Houseman] Written, according to Houseman's memoir *Run-Through* (1972), during the week before Christmas in 1939.

472.18 Maurice Evans] British actor of stage and screen (1901–1989) noted for his work in productions of plays by Shakespeare and Shaw.

472.43–44 Benny [Bernard] Herrmann] American composer of film scores (1911–1975) remembered for his collaborations with such director-producers as Orson Welles, Alfred Hitchcock, and Ray Harryhausen.

473.4   *War of the Worlds–Men from Mars* broadcast] The Mercury Theater's *Campbell Playhouse* episode for October 30, 1938, featured Orson Welles's headline-making adaptation of H. G. Wells's science-fantasy novel *The War of the Worlds*. Welles's script was written in the form of fictional "news bulletins" that led some listeners, especially those tuning in to the show in progress, to believe that America was indeed being invaded by beings from outer space.

473.6   Soup Company] Campbell's, sponsor of CBS Radio's *Campbell Playhouse* series.

475.5–7   He discharged his debt . . . *Citizen Kane.*]] Herman J. Mankiewicz (1897–1953) was a Hollywood screenwriter and script doctor whose work, most of it uncredited, included contributions to such films as *The Wizard of Oz*, *Dinner at Eight*, and many of the Marx Brothers' vehicles. He and Welles shared the Academy Award for Best Original Screenplay for *Citizen Kane*.

475.8   a very fine play . . . about President Wilson] *In Time to Come*, by Walter Huston and Howard Koch, with Richard Gaines as Woodrow Wilson, was a Broadway flop of 1941–42.

476.3–4   Reviens donc—L'Amérique a besoin de toi! Moi aussi et surtout! Je t'embrasse.] Therefore come back—America needs you. Me too and all of us! A kiss to you . . .

476.36   Poiré-Blanche] Pâtisserie at 196 boulevard Saint-Germaine, Paris.

477.1   *bois de démolition*] Wood salvaged from a building site.

477.25   Nicolas Chatelain] Painter and writer (1913–1976) who, after World War II, was a longtime White House correspondent for *Le Figaro*.

478.12   *L'Usage de la parole*] Hugnet published three numbers of his journal ("The Use of the Word") between December 1939 and the summer of 1940.

480.4   Jean de Reszke's death] Polish tenor Jean de Reszke, a pillar of the Paris Opéra, died in 1925 at the age of seventy-five.

481.5   *Paris France*] Memoir and meditation on the "Frenchness" of France, published as brief book by Scribner's in 1940.

483.5–484.43   My account . . . Virgil] Thomson's letter to Minna Lederman, dated April 18, 1940, was published in full, under the heading "Paris, April 1940," in *Modern Music* (May–June 1940).

485.4   Lise Deharme] French surrealist poet and salon hostess (1898–1980) who was a muse to André Breton.

486.24   Gertrude Newell] Broadway producer, set designer, and interior decorator whom Thomson first met through Gertrude Stein in the 1920s.

489.5   Georgette Leblanc] French operatic soprano, stage actress, and writer (1869–1941) who was the companion of the Belgian playwright Maurice Maeterlinck from 1895 to 1915. Her subsequent lovers were many, including Margaret Anderson (see note 332.15).

489.8   Eric de Haulleville] See note 266.8.

490.38   Suzanne Blum] French lawyer (1898–1994) whose clients included the Duchess of Windsor, Charlie Chaplin, Rita Hayworth, and, pro bono, Thomson and Stein's good friend Bernard Faÿ (see note 558.3–7). In 1932 she married her business partner, Paul Weill, who died in 1965.

491.9   Kathleen (Mrs. O'Donnell) Hoover] Kathleen O'Donnell Hoover was chair of the Memorabilia Committee of the Metropolitan Opera Guild and author of *Makers of Opera* (1949). She also wrote "The Life," in *Virgil Thomson: His Life and Music* (1959), a monograph coauthored by John Cage (see note 523.7).

491.15   Frieda Hempel] German soprano (1885–1955) who sang with the Metropolitan Opera from 1912 to 1919.

491.18   Geoffrey Parsons] Parsons (1879–1956) was chief editorial writer for *The New York Herald Tribune* (1924–52; Pulitzer Prize, 1942) and the man in charge of the paper's cultural coverage. Though not Thomson's editor, he was his boss and journalistic mentor. See note 503.25.

491.21   Lawrence Gilman] American composer, editor, and cultural journalist (1878–1939) who was music critic of *The New York Herald Tribune* from 1925 until his death.

491.28–29   Teddy Chanler . . . Philip Hale . . . Boston *Herald*] Philip Hale (1854–1934) was music critic of the Boston *Herald* from 1903 until his death more than thirty years later. His immediate successor, thirty-two-year-old Theodore Chanler (see note 249.23–24), was rejected by the paper's readership for seeming too young and lighthearted for the post. His tenure lasted only a few weeks in November–December 1934.

491.33–34   Mrs. Ogden Reid] Helen Miles Rogers (1882–1970) was the longtime social secretary to the wife of Whitelaw Reid, founder of the *New-York Tribune*. In 1911 she married the Reids' son, Ogden Mills Reid (1883–1947), who inherited the paper in 1912 and merged it with the rival *New York Herald* in 1922. As Ogden Reid's alcoholism deepened during the 1920s, Mrs. Reid emerged as the de facto head of the family business. She was vice president of the *Herald Tribune* from 1922 to 1947, and president from 1947 to 1955.

491.40   Francis Perkins] American music journalist and editor (1898–1970) who was a member of the staff of the *New-York Tribune* and *Herald Tribune* from 1919 to 1962.

496.9–10   Columbia Concerts Corporation . . . Arthur Judson] Columbia Concerts, Inc., an artists' management service, was founded in 1930 as an offshoot of William Paley's Columbia Broadcast System (CBS Radio). By 1940 it handled bookings for the majority of America's classical music talent. Arthur Judson (1881–1975), the co-founder and president of Columbia Concerts, Inc., was also business manager of both the New York Philharmonic and the Philadelphia Orchestra.

496.18   Ira Hirschmann] Hirschmann (1901–1989), an American businessman and music impresario, was vice president of marketing for Bloomingdale's during the 1940s and '50s. He was later founder of New York's pioneering classical music station WBAF-FM (1946–53).

498.1–2   "*Play! . . . Here comes Virgil Thomson!*"] Cartoon by Charles Strauss (1911–2000), *The Saturday Review of Literature* (January 30, 1943).

500.24–25   "I am against greatness and bigness in all their forms."] William James, in a letter to Mrs. Henry Whitman, June 7, 1899, collected in Henry James's *Letters of William James*, Volume 2 (Boston: Little, Brown, 1926).

501.7   *Southern Harmony* sing] See note 442.19.

501.24   Edward Krehbiel] Krehbiel (1854–1923) was music critic of the *New-York Tribune* from 1884 until his death thirty-eight years later.

503.25   "Always attack head-on,"] For a sampling of Parsons's editorial memos to Thomson from 1940 to 1943, see "The Art of Gentlemanly Discourse," in John Vinton, *Essays After a Dictionary: Music and Culture at the Close of Western Civilization* (Lewisburg, Pa.: Bucknell University Press, 1977).

503.41   Carleton Sprague Smith] Smith (1905–1994) was an independent musicologist, chief music librarian for the New York Public Library system, scholar and impresario of Hispanic music and culture, and an accomplished flutist.

505.17   Rudi Blesh] American jazz critic and impresario (1899–1995) who wrote *They All Played Ragtime* (1950) and the authorized life of Buster Keaton (1966). As cofounder of Circle Records (1946–52) he rediscovered, recorded, and managed the career of ragtime pianist Eubie Blake.

505.20   Arthur Berger] American composer and critic (1912–2003) who wrote the first book on Aaron Copland (1953). Thomson admired his chamber works, and thought his Woodwind Quartet of 1961 "one of the most satisfactory pieces for winds in the entire modern repertoire."

507.17–18   hatchet men of T. S. Eliot] Critics and poets such as those published in *The Criterion* (1922–39), the literary quarterly edited by T. S. Eliot, which championed the classical and traditional in arts and culture.

508.35   *Así que pasen cinco años*] *Once Five Years Pass* (1931), play in three acts by the Spanish poet and dramatist Federico García Lorca (1898–1936).

509.6   Olin Downes] Downes (1866–1955) was music reviewer for the *Boston Post* (1906–24) before becoming chief music critic for *The New York Times* (1924–55). His books include two critical studies of Sibelius, whose work he championed, and the posthumous omnibus *Olin Downes on Music* (see pages 855–57 of the present volume).

509.6–11   "a series of clichés . . . St. Regis."] See Olin Downes, "Stravinsky Hears Own New Work," *The New York Times* (April 28, 1943).

509.15–17 Howard Taubman . . . trifle."] See Howard Taubman, "Lowell, Poet as Playwright," a review of Jonathan Miller's production of Robert Lowell's "My Kinsman, Major Molineux," based on the story by Nathaniel Hawthorne, at the American Place Theater, New York (*The New York Times*, November 2, 1964). Taubman (1907–1996) was drama critic of the *Times* from 1960 to 1965.

509.21 E. Robert Schmitz] Paris-born pianist and pedagogue (1889–1949) whose specialty, as performer and scholar, was the work of Debussy.

509.27–28 Hervé Alphand . . . Claude] Hervé Alphand (1907–1994) was a career diplomat who, in 1956–65, would be the French Ambassador to the United States. His wife, Claude (b. 1918), was a chanteuse and guitarist who performed on the French and American nightclub circuits.

510.8–9 "*Voici le pot de vin habituel dans l'administration.*"] "Here is the usual bribe [pot-de-vin] of the administration."

510.17–18 Sir Thomas Beecham . . . Lady Cunard] Sir Thomas (1879–1961; knighted 1916), Britain's first great international conductor, had a long association with Covent Garden and the London Philharmonic and Royal Philharmonic orchestras. During World War II he worked in America, first in Seattle, where he directed the symphony orchestra (1941–43), then in New York, where he was a guest conductor at the Philharmonic and the Metropolitan Opera. His consort, the former Lady Cunard, known as Emerald, was born Maud Alice Burke (1872–1948), in San Francisco. (Her marriage to Sir Bache Cunard, founder of the Cunard shipping line, lasted from 1895 to 1911.) At her London salon (1906–40) she made an especially close friend of the Irish novelist George Moore (1852–1933), and it was she who introduced Edward, Prince of Wales, to Wallis Simpson. It was shortly after her divorce that she began her liaison with Beecham, which, despite his very public marriage to Lady Utica Wells, lasted until 1943.

510.18 Egeria] Legendary nymph who was lover and advisor to the second king of Rome, hence any beautiful, intelligent, female counselor and companion to a man of influence.

510.26–27 "Come into the garden, Maud,"] See Alfred, Lord Tennyson, *Maud*, Part I, poem 22 (1855).

511.19 Betty Humby] Humby (1908–1958), an English concert pianist twenty-nine years Beecham's junior, won a scholarship to the Royal Academy of Music at age ten. She was married to an Anglican vicar, the Rev. Cashel Thomas, when, on tour in the States in 1941, she became Beecham's lover. After she divorced her husband *in absentia*, and Beecham divorced Lady Utica, his wife of forty years, the couple married on January 19, 1943. Humby died of a heart attack at the age of forty-nine.

513.25–26 Benjamin Britten, Anthony Arnell, Stanley Bate . . . Peggy Glanville-Hicks] Britten (1913–1976), English composer, conductor, and pianist, renowned for his operas; Richard Anthony "Tony" Arnell (1917–2009), English composer, mainly of orchestral works; Bate (1911–1959), English composer and pianist, greatly influenced by Ralph Vaughan Williams and Paul Hindemith. Glanville-Hicks (1912–1990), Bate's wife from 1938 to 1949, was an Australian composer, pianist, and critic. She was a member of the *New York Herald Tribune*'s music staff from 1949 to 1958.

513.27 I did review his first opera] See Virgil Thomson, "Musico-Theatrical Flop," *New York Herald Tribune* (May 6, 1941).

517.20 Leonard Franklin] St. Ferdinand (and, after Embry Bonner left the show, St. Chávez) in the original production of *Four Saints*.

517.26 Mimi Wallner] Wallner (1920–2007), Thomson's copyist and secretary from 1940 to about 1945, married the oboist Robert Bloom and had a long career as a music teacher.

519.1 *Peanuts*] *Peanuts*, by Charles M. Schulz (1922–2000), syndicated comic strip for Sunday, July 18, 1954.

521.7 Louise Crane] Miss Crane (1913–1997), of Dalton, Massachusetts, was the daughter of Winthrop Murray Crane (1853–1920), a former governor of Massachusetts (1900–1903) and heir to the Crane & Co. papermaking fortune, and his second wife Josephine Porter (Boardman) Crane (1873–1972), a cofounder of both the Museum of Modern Art and the Dalton School. Mrs. Crane was a backer of the original production of *Four Saints in Three Acts*. Louise Crane was a devotee of modern music, the literary executor of her friend Marianne Moore, and a close friend of Elizabeth Bishop.

521.33–34 I also conducted, for RCA Victor] Virgil Thomson/Gertrude Stein: *Four Saints in Three Acts: Abridged by the Composer*. Virgil Thomson, conductor of orchestra and chorus. RCA Victor 12-0451-55 (five 78-rpm discs). With Beatrice Robinson-Wayne (St. Teresa I), Ruby Greene (St. Teresa II), Inez Matthews (St. Settlement), Edward Matthews (St. Ignatius), Charles Holland (St. Chávez), David Bathea (St. Stephen), Randolph Robinson (St. Plan), Altonell Hines (Commère), and Abner Dorsey (Compère). Total time: 46:29. Recorded June 1947; released 1948. (For an account of the recording session, at New York's Town Hall, see page 557 of the present volume.)

521.38 Edward Matthews and his wife] Matthews (see note 411.26–27), the original St. Ignatius, and mezzo-soprano Altonell Hines (1905–1977), the original Commère.

522.22–23 Woods Hole . . . Mrs. W. Murray Crane] The Crane family (see note 521.7) had a summer home at Penzance Point, in Woods Hole, Massachusetts.

522.39–40 Inna Garsoian] Garsoian (1896–1984), a former set and costume designer for the Ballet Russe de Monte Carlo, specialized in deserted urban landscapes. She summered on Nantucket from 1935 to 1945.

523.7 John Cage] Cage (1912–1992) was an American pianist, composer, writer, artist, and iconoclast. In all of his work his chief pursuit was to break down distinctions between "music" and "noise," "composition" and "accident," "prescription" and "indeterminacy" in service of an argument that all sound, whether composed and performed or not, is of aesthetic interest. Among his critical writings is "The Music," in *Virgil Thomson: His Life and Music* (1959), a monograph coauthored by Kathleen Hoover (see note 491.9). For Thomson's extended biographical-critical essay on Cage, see pages 662 to 676 of the present volume.

524.3 Lou Harrison] Harrison (1917–2003), a composer, dancer, playwright, critic, editor, and maker of musical instruments, created a list of works that is, in Thomson's description, "long and highly varied as to instrumentation and musical format." For Thomson's tribute to Harrison at seventy, see pages 893–94 of the present volume.

525.35 Rita Hayworth] American actress (1918–1987) who was married to Orson Welles from 1943 to 1947.

526.3 Alfred Frankenstein] Frankenstein (1906–1981), a critic for the *San Francisco Chronicle* from 1934 to 1979, was also a writer of art history and a freelance museum curator.

526.13 I heard Bunk Johnson] Willie "Bunk" Johnson (1870?–1949), American jazz trumpeter of the early New Orleans style.

527.35 *Tuesday in November*] American documentary short (1945) produced by United Films and John Houseman for the U.S. Office of War Information, Overseas Branch. Directed by John Berry with Nicholas Ray, with animated sequences by John Hubley. Written by John Houseman. Music by Virgil Thomson. Running time: 17 minutes.

528.21–22 Douglas Moore . . . offering to commission an opera] American composer Moore (1893–1969) joined the faculty of Columbia University in 1926, and with the success of his opera *The Devil and Daniel Webster* (1938) became chairman of the music department. In 1940, with money from Columbia's Alice M. Ditson Fund, he spearheaded the creation of the opera program of Columbia Theater Associates, which, from 1940 to 1957, annually commissioned a new work to be performed by the university's Opera Workshop, a mix of student, faculty, and professional musicians. The first commissioned opera, *Paul Bunyan*, by W. H. Auden and Benjamin Britten, was performed in 1941 (see page 513). Others in the series included *The Medium*, by Gian Carlo Menotti (1946); *The Mother of Us All*, by Gertrude Stein and Virgil Thomson (1947); and Moore's own *Giants in the Earth* (1951), winner of a Pulitzer Prize for Music. All of the operas were performed at Columbia's short-lived Brander Matthews Theater (1940–58), a 280-seat facility at 117th Street and Amsterdam Avenue.

530.39 another wife] In 1959, Beecham married his former secretary, Shirley Hudson, whom he had known since 1950.

531.28 Once a week . . . I sent off an article.] Thomson's pieces from postwar Paris are collected, in the section "From Overseas," in *The Art of Judging Music* (1948).

535.28–29 When I asked her for an opera . . . America] When *The Mother of Us All* (1947) was revived off-Broadway in 1956, Thomson wrote a memoir, "How *The Mother of Us All* Was Created," for the April 15 issue of *The New York Times*. The part of the essay that is devoted to Stein's libretto follows:

The Mother of Us All is an opera about American public and private life in the nineteenth century. That was a time, rare in history, when great issues were debated in great language. As in the Greece of Pericles and Demosthenes, in the Rome of Caesar and Cicero, in the England of Pitt and Burke, historical changes of the utmost gravity were argued in noble prose by Webster, Clay, and Calhoun in the Senate, by Beecher and Emerson in the pulpit, by Douglas and Lincoln on the partisan political platform.

These changes, which became burning issues after the Missouri Compromise of 1820, dealt with political, economic, racial, and sexual equality. And the advocated reforms—excepting woman suffrage—were all embodied in the Constitution by 1870. In fifty glorious and tragic years the United States grew up. We ceased to be an eighteenth-century country and became a twentieth-century one. Surely, it had long seemed to me, surely somewhere in this noble history and in its oratory there must be the theme, and perhaps even the words, of a musico-dramatic spectacle that would be a pleasure to compose.

So it came about that in 1945, when Douglas Moore, for the Alice M. Ditson Fund of Columbia University, asked me to write an opera, I turned with this theme to my old friend and former operatic collaborator Gertrude Stein. She liked it and began at once to read and reread the words of the period. She exhausted the American Library in Paris and the librarian obtained more books for her from the New York Public Library. She asked me if I minded her making feminism the central theme and Susan B. Anthony the heroine. I did not. And so she began to write.

She showed me the first two scenes in October 1945. In March 1946 she sent me the whole libretto. It was her last completed work. In May and June we talked about it, agreed on some transpositions in order of the scenes and on the possibility of certain cuts, these to be left eventually to my discretion. She obtained also the promise of the painter Maurice Grosser, who had added to our earlier opera, *Four Saints in Three Acts*, a workable scenario for staging, that he would do the same for *The Mother of Us All*. In July she died. I had not yet composed any of the music. . . .

The libretto deals with real persons and invented persons, with historical celebrities and with their friends and neighbors. The celebrities speak in the style of their historic utterances, sometimes even in quotations from them. The others speak straight American.

There is little in the libretto that is not directly comprehensible. All the same, its dialogue is far more an expression of the characters themselves than a vehicle for advancing the plot. As in real life, the people of the play, especially when more than two are present, rarely answer one another or even listen. They tend rather to say what is urgently on their own minds.

In Shakespeare and Shaw the characters talk mostly about what they have done or are going to do, defending their past and future actions with argument, poetry, and wit. In Gertrude Stein's plays they rarely defend their actions. They merely give you their own emotional and character background. The language of Stein's later plays is the essence of American English, but their story line is that of Corneille and Racine and the court ballets of Molière. They are French classical theater in the American dialect.

Stein's libretto for *The Mother of Us All* was excerpted in *Harper's Bazaar* and *Town & Country* magazines at the time of the opera's premiere (in May 1947) and then published, in full, in Stein's posthumous *Last Operas and Plays*, edited by Carl Van Vechten (New York & Toronto: Rinehart & Co., 1949), 52–88.

536.12   Donald Gallup] Gallup (1913–2000) met Stein and Toklas when, as an American GI, he took part in the liberation of Paris. Later, as a curator at the Beinecke Library, he arranged for them to donate their papers to Yale. After Toklas's death, Gallup became the literary executor of the Estate of Gertrude Stein and Alice B. Toklas.

536.20   "*collabos*"] Those French citizens who, during the Germany occupation, collaborated with the Nazis.

537.24   American Libraries of Information] Temporary libraries established throughout postwar Europe and Asia by the U.S. Information Service to promote a better understanding of America overseas.

539.18–30   My *Symphony on a Hymn Tune* . . . to merit discussion."] Thomson led the Philharmonic in a performance of his first symphony (1926) on Thursday, February 22, 1945. Olin Downes's review appeared in *The New York Times* on the following morning.

539.35   My first book of Piano Etudes] Virgil Thomson, *Ten Études for Piano*, with an introduction, technical notes, and fingerings by Robert E. Schmitz (New York: C. Fischer, Inc., 1946).

539.37–38   Maxim Schapiro] Russian pianist (1885–1958) who, in 1953, recorded Thomson's *Ten Études* (Decca DL 4083).

539.39   a recording, my first] Virgil Thomson, *Five Portraits: Virgil Thomson Conducting the Philadelphia Orchestra*. Columbia Masterworks X-255 (two 78-rpm discs), 1945. The portraits, orchestrated by Thomson for this recording, are *Bugles and Birds* (Pablo Picasso); *Percussion Piece* (Mrs. Chester Whitin Lasell); *Cantabile for Strings* (Nicolas de Chaterlain); *Tango Lullaby* (Flavie Alvarez de Toledo), and *Fugue* (Alexander Smallens).

543.17   Duff-Coopers] Alfred Duff Cooper (1890–1954), British Ambassador to France (1944–48), and his socialite wife, Lady Diana Cooper (the former Diana Manners, 1892–1986).

544.5 Pierre Boulez] French composer, conductor, pianist, and writer (1925–2016). For Thomson's profile of Boulez at age forty-three, see pages 933–44 of the present volume.

544.19 a Sunday article of 1946] "Atonality in France" (October 27, 1946), collected in *The Art of Judging Music* (1948).

544.35 "*Bien sur,*"] Of course.

545.29 which I described . . . dropped."] See "Musical Belgium" (September 1, 1946), collected in *The Art of Judging Music* (1948).

548.15–16 Nicolas Nabokov . . . cultural capacity] In 1945–47 the Russian-exile composer Nicolas Nabokov (1903–1978) acted as civilian cultural advisor to the U.S. military in occupied Germany.

552.1–2 Mary McCarthy . . . Bowden Broadwater] Mary McCarthy (1912–1989) was, in 1947, known as the author of the novel *The Company She Keeps* (1942) and as a prolific writer of magazine pieces. She married her third husband, Bowden Broadwater (1920–2005), an art editor at *The New Yorker*, in 1946. They divorced in 1960.

553.3–10 I began *The Mother of Us All* . . . the final scene] In his 1956 memoir "How *The Mother of Us All* Was Created" (see note 535.28–29), Thomson makes the following comments about the music of the opera:

The composing was begun October 12, 1946, and seven of the eight scenes that make up the opera were finished by December 10. Then I played and sang them to my friends—tried them out, so to speak. And in January 1947, I composed the epilogue, in which Susan B. Anthony, dead and turned to marble, sings as a statue from her pedestal her own (and Gertrude Stein's own) funeral oration. The opera was orchestrated during February and March, and it was produced, beginning May 9, at the Brander Matthews Theater at Columbia . . .

The music of *The Mother of Us All* is an evocation of nineteenth-century America, with its gospel hymns and cocky marches, its sentimental ballads, waltzes, darn-fool ditties, and intoned sermons. Only in descriptions of weather, which has no period, does it engage the dissonant elements. Like the libretto, which deals with the attitudes and speeches, the play-games and the passions of our Victorian forebears, it is a memory book. It is a souvenir of all those sounds and kinds of tunes that were once the music of rural America and that are still the basic idiom of our country because they are the oldest vernacular still remembered here and used.

553.11 Jack Beeson . . . *répétiteur.*] American composer (1921–2010) who was a professor of music at Columbia University from 1945 to 1988. A *répétiteur* is the pianist and vocal coach for an opera company.

553.11–12 Otto Luening] American conductor and composer (1900–1996) with a specialty in opera. He taught at Columbia University from 1944 to 1970.

553.13 we were not opening till May] *The Mother of Us All,* an opera in two acts, received its world premiere at the Brander Matthews Theater, Columbia University, New York, on May 7, 1947. There were nine performances. (See also note 528.21–22.)

553.18 Paul du Pont] Costume designer for Broadway and television (1906–1957) long associated with the Eaves Costume Company.

553.18–19 John Taras] American choreographer and balletmaster (1919–2004) long associated with George Balanchine and the New York City Ballet.

553.24–25 Dorothy Dow . . . Teresa Stich-Randall] Dow (1920–2005) was the original Susan B. Anthony, and Stich-Randall (1927–2007), the original Henrietta M.

553.25–28 The names of Belva Kibler . . . and Everett Anderson.] The original cast of *The Mother of Us All* included Belva Kibler (Anne), Hazel Gravell (Gertrude S.), Jean Handzlik (Isabel Wentworth), Alice Howland (Constance Fletcher), William Horne (Jo the Loiterer), and Everett Anderson (General Grant). It also included Bertram Rowe (Daniel Webster) and Robert Grooters (Virgil T.).

554.29–33 Then in 1965 . . . my having coached everybody] The UCLA Opera Workshop revival of *The Mother of Us All,* directed by the Czech-born conductor and pianist Jan Popper (1907–1987), opened at Schoenberg Hall, UCLA, on May 13, 1965, and closed on May 23. There were seven Los Angeles performances.

554.34 David Hilberman] Ohio-born artist Hilberman (1911–2007) had a distinguished career as an animator for Disney, UPA, and Hanna-Barbera before deciding, in the early 1960s, to become a theatrical set designer. He was a student in UCLA's Master of Theater Arts program when he designed the sets for the 1965 revival of *The Mother of Us All.*

556.8 My Harvard speech was published] "The Art of Judging Music," delivered at Sanders Theater, Cambridge, Massachusetts, on May 2, 1947, was published in *The Atlantic Monthly* (December 1947) and in Richard M. French, editor, *Music and Criticism: A Symposium* (Harvard University Press, 1948) before appearing as the title essay of Thomson's *The Art of Judging Music* (1948).

556.30 for publishing *The Mother of Us All*] *The Mother of Us All: An Opera,* by Gertrude Stein and Virgil Thomson, scenario by Maurice Grosser, with three photogravure plates by Carl Van Vechten, was printed, in stiff wrappers, in an edition of a thousand copies, by Music Press, Inc., New York, in 1947. An additional fifty-five numbered copies, signed by the composer, were printed on special paper and bound in hard covers.

556.33 *Four Saints,* also to be published] *Four Saints in Three Acts: An Opera,* by Gertrude Stein and Virgil Thomson, scenario by Maurice Grosser, with six photogravure plates, was printed, in stiff wrappers, in an edition of eight hundred copies, by Music Press, Inc., New York, and Arrow Music Press, New York, in 1948. An additional thirty numbered copies, signed by the composer, were printed on special paper and bound in hard covers.

557.1–2 I conducted its recording in Town Hall] See note 521.33–34.

557.38 his biography by Moses Smith.] *Koussevitzky*, by Moses Smith (New York: Allen, Towne, and Heath, 1947). For an account of Koussevitzky's unsuccessful attempt to suppress the biography, see Virgil Thomson, "The Koussevitzky Case" (February 25, 1947), in *The Art of Judging Music* (1948).

558.3–7 In Paris I got involved with "*collabos*," . . . Bernard Faÿ . . . national degradation).] During the early years of World War II, Bernard Faÿ (see note 228.32), a professor of American civilization at the Collège de France, was a well-known critic of American and French Freemasonry. During the Occupation (1940–44) he was enlisted by the Vichy government as part of its anti-Masonic project, for which his duties included editing the propaganda monthly *Les Documents Maçonniques* ("Masonic Documents"), helping compile a list of some sixty thousand French freemasons, and producing the 1943 documentary *Forces Occultes*, an "exposé" of the worldwide Jewish-Masonic conspiracy. During these years he was also the personal protector of several Jewish friends still resident in France, including Gertrude Stein and Alice B. Toklas. Immediately following the liberation of Paris, in August 1944, Faÿ was arrested and accused of collaboration with the Germans. Stein wrote a letter asking the court for leniency, and Thomson's friend the Paris lawyer Suzanne Blum, herself a Jew, defended his case pro-bono. After an eight-day trial in November–December 1946, Fay, at the age of fifty-four, was stripped of his political rights, his professional status, and his personal property, and sentenced to hard labor for life. In 1951, while convalescing in a prison hospital, he managed to escape to Switzerland with the help of a sympathizer. Eight years later, in 1959, he was pardoned by French president René Coty. Faÿ, however, elected to remain in Switzerland, where he continued to teach and write books until his death in 1978. For more on Stein, Toklas, and Faÿ during the German Occupation, see pages 977–79 of the present volume.

558.36–559.9 Kirsten Flagstad . . . in my review.] See "Flagstad in Boston," *New York Herald Tribune*, April 7, 1947.

559.14 a French opera singer] Germaine Lubin (see note 455.11), who, because she performed for Nazi occupiers in 1942, was placed under house arrest as a suspected collaborator in 1944.

561.36 *Motu Proprio*] See note 62.31.

563.15 *Louisiana Story*] American feature film (1948), part fiction, part documentary, produced by Robert Flaherty Productions Inc. in association with the Standard Oil Company. Directed by Robert J. Flaherty. Written by Robert J. Flaherty and Frances H. Flaherty. Cast: Joseph Boudreaux (The Boy), Lionel Le

Blanc (His Father), E. Bienvenu (His Mother), et al. Music by Virgil Thomson (orchestrated by Henry Brant and conducted by Eugene Ormandy). Running time: 78 minutes. Thomson's score was awarded the Pulitzer Prize in Music for 1949.

564.34–35 *The Goddess.*] American feature film (1958) produced by Milton Perlman for Columbia Pictures. Directed by John Cromwell. Written by Paddy Chayefsky. Cast: Kim Stanley (Emily Franklin), Lloyd Bridges (Dutch Seymour), Steven Hill (John Tower), et al. Music by Virgil Thomson. Running time: 108 minutes.

565.36 *Power Among Men*] British-American documentary feature (1959) produced by Thorold Dickinson for the United Nations Department of Public Information Services. Directed by Alexander Hammid. Written by Thorold Dickinson and J. C. Sheers. Narrated by Laurence Harvey. Music by Virgil Thomson. Running time: 90 minutes.

564.11 *Journey to America*] American documentary short (a.k.a. "Voyage to America," 1964) produced by Graphic Films Corporation and John Houseman for the United States Pavilion of the New York World's Fair. Directed by Benjamin Jackson. Written by John Houseman. Narrated by Alexander Scourby. Music by Virgil Thomson. Running time: 10 minutes.

565.28 *King Lear*] Television drama (broadcast live on Sunday, October 18, 1953) produced by Paul Feigay and Fred Rickey of the Ford Foundation TV-Radio Workshop for CBS's *Omnibus* series, Andrew McCullough, series director, Alastair Cooke, host. Adapted (from the play by William Shakespeare) and directed by Peter Brook. Cast: Orson Welles (Lear), Natasha Perry (Cordelia), et al. Music by Virgil Thomson. Running time: 90 minutes.

566.21 The *Ondine* production] The Playwrights' Company production of Giraudoux's 1938 play *Ondine*, in an English adaptation by Maurice Valency, opened at the Forty-sixth Street Theater, New York, on February 18, 1954, and ran 157 performances. Directed by Alfred Lunt. Cast: Audrey Hepburn (Ondine), Mel Ferrer (Ritter Hans), et al. Music by Virgil Thomson.

566.34 *The Grass Harp*] Play in two acts (1952) by Truman Capote, adapted from his novel of 1951. Produced by Saint Sibber with Rita Allen, it opened at the Martin Beck Theater, New York, on March 27, 1952, and ran thirty-six performances. Directed by Robert Lewis. Cast: Johnny Stewart (Collin Fenwick), Mildred Natwick (Dolly), Ruth Nelson (Verena), Georgia Burke (Catherine), et al. Music by Virgil Thomson, conducted by Claude Monteaux.

568.5–6 books of my *Herald Tribune* pieces] See note 11.9.

571.1 ANTA] The American National Theater and Academy was founded by the Federal Theater Project in 1935 to fund and foster noncommercial alternatives to Broadway theater. After World War II it evolved, through the efforts of the U.S. State Department, the CIA, and other interested entities into a vehicle for exporting American theater to foreign countries as part of democracy's war of ideas with communism. This new, postwar ANTA developed many of its early projects at the ANTA Playhouse (1950–53), on West Fifty-second Street, New York. The International Exchange Service of ANTA, created by Congress in 1953, set up advisory panels on music, dance, and drama and charged them with evaluating performing-arts groups to tour abroad through ANTA's international Cultural Exchange Programs. Thomson was a member of ANTA's Music Advisory Panel for all ten years of its existence, 1953 to 1963.

575.38–39 Nicolas Nabokov . . . Freedom] From 1951 to 1967, Nicolas Nabokov (see note 548.15–16) was General Secretary of the Congress for Cultural Freedom (CCF), a Paris-based international arts organization (1950–67) dedicated to "free intellectual exchange, free intellectual inquiry, and free creative expression in the arts and letters." The cultural activities of the CCF, conceived to counter Soviet influence on the intellectual elite of Western Europe, were covertly funded by, among other entities, the Central Intelligence Agency. One of Nabokov's first projects for the CCF was overseeing the international arts festival "L'Oeuvre du XXe Siècle" ("Masterpieces of the Twentieth Century," Paris, April 30–May 30, 1952), which featured concerts, lectures, and art exhibitions showcasing twentieth-century masterpieces from the United States and Western Europe. It was Nabokov's desire to conclude his festival with a new production of *Four Saints in Three Acts* that led to the U.S. government-sponsored Broadway revival of 1942.

576.10–11 I took charge of the production.] The Broadway revival of *Four Saints in Three Acts*, produced by ANTA (see note 571.1) in association with Ethel Linder Reiner, opened at the Broadway Theater (Broadway and West Fifty-third Street) on April 16, 1952, and closed on April 25. There were fifteen New York performances. The show then traveled to Paris (Théâtre des Champs-Élysées, May 30–June 4, 1952) for seven more performances (see note above). Credits: Virgil Thomson, musical and artistic director; William Jonson, associate conductor and choral director; Paul Morrison, stage design and costumes (after Florine Stettheimer); William Dollar, choreography (after Frederick Ashton); Maurice Grosser, stage direction.

577.8–11 Inez Matthews . . . Allen . . . Spearman] Inez Matthews (b. 1917) was St. Settlement in the original cast of *Four Saints in Three Acts*; Betty Lou Allen (1927–2009) was later the Commère in the first complete recording of *Four Saints* (1973); Rawn Spearman (1920–2009) was a writer and educator in Harlem as well as a tenor soloist.

577.12 Arthur Mitchell] American dancer and choreographer (b. 1934) who was eighteen years old in 1952. Four years later he would become the first black principal dancer in the New York City Ballet, and in 1969 the founder and guiding spirit of the Dance Theater of Harlem.

577.12–14 In my chorus were . . . Daniel] Leontyne Price (b. 1927), making her Broadway debut, was St. Cecilia, and Martha Flowers, one of two Besses in the original *Porgy and Bess*, was St. Settlement. Gloria Davey, Olga James, and Billie Daniel were among the female chorus.

578.12–13   Concerts Colonne . . . Paul Paray] French conductor Paray (1886–1979) was music director of the Concerts Colonne, a Paris-based orchestra (founded, in 1897, by violinist-conductor Édouard Colonne) dedicated to contemporary music, from 1932 to 1956.

578.37–38   Josephine Baker . . . Katherine Dunham dancers] African American dancers Baker (1906–1975) and Dunham (1909–2006) entertained Paris between the wars with shows steeped in American-jazz, Afro-Caribbean, and Creole influences.

579.8   (Marcel Schneider in *Combat*)] "L'Oeuvre du XXe siècle: Four Saints aux Champs-Élysées," *Combat* (June 3, 1952). The English translation here is Thomson's own.

579.32–33   "*Il était là comme un coq en pâte.*"] French idiom, meaning roughly "Thomson's place inside French culture is like the chicken's place inside the pie."

580.5   Hervé Dugardin] Dugardin (1910–1969) was founder-publisher of Éditions Amphion, one of Paris's most prestigious music presses.

580.9   critic of *The Sunday Times*] Ernest Newman (1868–1959) was music critic of the London *Sunday Times* from 1920 until his death thirty-nine years later.

580.9–10   my overfrank review of . . . *Billy Budd*] "The Trouble with *Billy Budd*," *New York Herald Tribune* (June 22, 1952). Thomson thought the opera all pathos and no drama, and so "essentially sentimental": "It mostly just feels very sorry about the sad fate of its hero."

580.20   *Ondine*] See note 566.21.

580.31   Arthur Berger] See note 505.20.

581.2   young Whitelaw Reid] Reid (1913–2009), the son of Odgen and Helen Reid, succeeded his mother as chairman of the Herald Tribune Company in 1955.

581.10–11   another of Nabokov's music festivals] "La Musica nel XX Secolo" ("Music in the Twentieth Century"), April 4–15, Rome, Italy.

582.24–25   In July I conducted . . . *Four Saints*] Thomson conducted the Stadium Symphony Orchestra (New York Philharmonic) in excerpts from *Four Saints in Four Acts* at Lewisohn Stadium, New York, on July 26, 1954. Leonard de Paur (see note 434.19–21) conducted the chorus. Soloists included Leontyne Price (St. Teresa I) and William Warfield (St. Ignatius), with Inez Matthews, Elwood Smith, Rawn Spearman, Betty Lou Allen, Calvin Dash, and others.

582.36   Paul Henry Lang] Lang (see note 70.18–19) was chief music critic of the *Herald Tribune* from 1954 to 1965.

583.36   Charles Cushing] California-based American composer (1905–1982) and brass band conductor.

583.39   Phyllis Curtin and Alice Howland] Sopranos Curtin (b. 1921, the muse of Carlisle Floyd) and Howland (who had sung in Thomson's *Mother of Us All*).

584.8–10   I moved to the shores of Lake Garda . . . to hear Pablo Casals] See "Casals and the Matterhorn," Thomson's final Sunday essay for the *New York Herald Tribune* (September 14, 1954), collected in *Music Reviewed: 1940–1954* (New York: Vintage, 1967).

585.1   Elaine Shaffer, Efrem Kurtz's wife] Shaffer (1925–1973) was principal flutist of the Houston Symphony Orchestra from 1948 to 1953. Her husband, Russian conductor Efrem Kurtz (1900–1995), was music director of the Houston Symphony during the same period.

594.20–21   a libretto in verse has been completed for him] *Lord Byron*, by Jack Larson (1928–2015), written in 1962–63. The libretto would be revised many times before the opera's premiere, in 1972.

AMERICAN MUSIC SINCE 1910

595.2–3   AMERICAN MUSIC SINCE 1910] In 1987 Thomson proposed that Da Capo Press, New York, bring out a reprint edition of *American Music Since 1910*, which had been published in hardcover in 1971 and was then out of print. The following preface to that unrealized reprint, dated September 10, 1987, was found in fair-copy typescript among the Virgil Thomson Papers at the Irving S. Gilmore Music Library, Yale University (MSS 29A, Box 73, Folder 150). It is printed here, only slightly abridged, for the first time. Copyright © 2016 by Virgil Thomson Foundation, Ltd.

My life as a professional musician covers the same span of time as this book.

By the end of 1910 I was fourteen years old, a sophomore in high school, a performing piano soloist, vocal accompanist, and church organist already beginning to quarrel with my Music Committee.

That was in Kansas City, a highly reputable music center in those days, and not too far from Chicago for spending Christmas vacations there and going every night to the opera. During the Great War, being twice posted to New York, where soldiers could get in free to practically everything, I continued my musical experiences. Still later, during college days, these went on also in Boston, then for many years in Paris. And after 1940, when I began reviewing music for the *New York Herald Tribune*, an even broader gamut was available.

Actually I can still remember today the kinds of sound made by Paderewski and Busoni, by Mary Garden and Nellie Melba, the legato singing of John McCormack and Alessandro Bonci, the slightly buzzy voices of Sarah Bernhardt and Minnie Maddern Fiske, and the light-as-a-feather high leaps of Vaslav Nijinsky.

I have heard and seen them all, known most of them, and worked with some of the best in theaters, in films, in opera houses and in concerts. So that what I am reciting here is both ear-witness testimony and something of an inside story. [. . .]

But let us go back to 1910. Ragtime, an American style of piano-playing and of composing for it, had come into existence about 1896, according to Rudi Blesh, and by 1910 was being replaced by black music from New Orleans. Blues and jazz, perfected there in earlier decades, had traveled up to Memphis and to St. Louis and were settling in Chicago. Digging in not much later in Kansas City and still flourishing there, they have now taken over another Midwestern black center, Detroit.

Classical music styles, at the same time, were beginning to be indistinguishable from their European sources, so clearly, in fact, that Nadia Boulanger, a Franco-Russian music teacher in Paris, already attracting by 1921 certain restless Americans, had become convinced that U.S. music was about to "take off," just as the native product had done around 1850 in Russia.

She was right, of course, because Gershwin's *Rhapsody in Blue*, of 1924, Aaron Copland's First Symphony (with organ), of the same year, Roy Harris's early chamber music, and my opera *Four Saints in Three Acts*, of 1928, were like nothing ever heard in Europe. Even Edgard Varèse, a French import of 1916, and two clandestine New Englanders, Ives and Ruggles, were already working here in quite new ways.

Naturally also, everybody here but Gershwin was getting bad reviews. The anti-modern mafia, matched of course by the vested interests of modernism itself, was giving everything that smelled even a little bit fresh lots of free advertising. This sort of thing had been going on in Europe ever since Mozart's time, but the full treatment was a novelty for Americans. Fry, Paine, MacDowell, and their associates had been tolerated in more genteel fashion.

Newly composed American music has always, I think, been more encouraged than hindered by its negative public reception. Our popular songs and dances, long successful, now heavily capitalized, seem to have taken over the world market as much through sheer vitality as through plugging. Jazz is still a persecuted chamber music, forbidden on chain-radio and by the major recording agencies. Nevertheless, it is the music miracle of our century.

Concert music of the classical tradition, modernistic or not, has everywhere encountered, I think, far less opposition than is commonly supposed. There has been some, of course, both here and in Europe, but most of this has been, still is, *interesée*.

Before World War I our chief symphonic conductors, mostly German, were less afraid of modernism itself than of French music. Unprepared for the school of Paris, which included after 1910 Stravinsky of course, they thought to crush it by neglect. But the 1930s changed that here, when it turned out that all those lovely orchestras of the Works Progress Administration and the newly aspiring college and high-school groups (by 1937 said to number more than thirty thousand) were playing American-made music to American audiences, and nobody was minding at all.

Actually, the organized opposition to modern music-styles, as to local efforts both here and in Europe, seems to have been inspired by an international cartel of recording companies. It still is, in fact, though they occasionally let through a prestige piece by someone already famous or something fully subsidized. In Europe they cannot prevent the performance on state-supported radio or television of works of their own citizens. Actually such performances are the price of their subsidies, that and the state control of news broadcasts. But in the U.S., where chain radio is governed by the same owners as the recording companies, the control is pretty complete. Even more indeed because the recording companies can control the rehearsal time of the major symphony orchestras, at least of those they record.

You see, nothing is ever programed by any symphony orchestra that cannot be rehearsed on that orchestra's full tax-exempt budget. And since our chief orchestras all put out every few years a new set of Beethoven's symphonies or of Brahms's, or nowadays of Mahler's, the rehearsals and performances that must precede any recording are an obligation of the orchestra's music director to the recording agency. Compliments to local composers and to the lovers of novelty (and very insistent they can be) fill up the rest of the time. But standard repertory is what the recording companies are selling over and over, and that is what the orchestras must be playing over and over if the profits from record sales are to relieve the board members from perpetually having to raise money. This procedure may or may not be an abuse of the tax laws. But it is how the better symphony orchestras work.

Also the buying public is induced to keep on buying new versions of standard repertory by school and public courses in Music Appreciation, themselves a device for plugging standard repertory. The better appreciation courses can also be a source of enlightenment to laymen. Others stand in the way. But the result of all this preoccupation with music is that America has today the most devoted and sophisticated public for classical music that exists anywhere and surely the largest. And that public, by one means and another, gets hold of practically all the music there is, both old and new.

We are beginning, moreover, to export our music. The Germanic regions and England, long centers of resistance to foreign imports, are now staging festivals to honor the American product. The Latin countries have been slower on the up-take. But Scandinavian and Dutch audiences are pushovers. Russia, both anti-modern and xenophobic by government policy, has not yet let open the floodgates. Poland, Czechoslovakia and Hungary know us well. So do South America and Japan, though these last, while intensely music-minded, seem at present to seeking from us chiefly novelties. [. . .]

In 1910 we were a rich country importing as needed European

musicians and European works. Now we are an exporting country, sending out world-wide both our black music and our pops, but also even bassoon players and their like, conductors, classical soloists, and whole schools of composers, John Cage's group for instance, and that of Phillip Glass.

I am ever so happy to have been a functioning part of this remarkable expansion. As a musician, I am proud of my country.

V.T.
New York 1987

599.36   Chadwick . . . Parker . . . MacDowell] Thomson described George W. Chadwick (1854–1931) as a "stage-oriented composer [of] vigorous gesture" whose operas (*Judith*, 1901; *The Padrone*, 1912) "never achieved the success they probably deserved." Horatio Parker (1863–1919) was "a sound teacher"—at Yale his students included Charles Ives—"but very little of his once impressive production is alive today. *Hora Novissima* [an oratorio of 1898] survives in the choral societies of England, also a few anthems." Edward MacDowell (1861–1908), the first chair of the music department at Columbia University, was "our nearest to a great master before Ives. His short works for piano still speak to us."

600.13–14   Herbert and . . . de Koven] German-educated Victor Herbert (1859–1924), the founder of ASCAP (see note 9.3), was a composer of popular musical entertainments, including the operettas *Babes in Toyland* (1903) and *Naughty Marietta* (1913). The operettas of composer-critic Reginald de Koven (1861–1920) included *Robin Hood* (1890) and *Rob Roy* (1894). These two, said Thomson, were "the revered masters of the Vienna-style American operetta," and de Koven was "the most melodious of them all."

601.17   collecting of Negro spirituals had begun] The first such collection was *Slave Songs of the United States*, by William Francis Allen, Charles Pickard Ware, and Lucy McKim Garrison (New York: Simpson & Co., 1867).

601.18–19   first volume of cowboy song-poetry] *Cowboy Songs and Other Frontier Ballads*, collected by John A. Lomax, M.A., with an introduction by Barrett Wendell (New York: Sturgis & Walton, 1910).

601.20–21   Cecil Sharp . . . Appalachian ballads.] *English Folk Songs from the Southern Appalachians, Comprising 122 Songs and Ballads, and 323 Tunes*, collected by Olive Dame Campbell and Cecil J. Sharp (New York: Putnam, 1917).

601.28   studies of Dr. George Pullen Jackson] See note 442.10.

602.8   W. C. Handy] Alabama-born bluesman and songwriter (1873–1958) whose song "Memphis Blues," written in 1909, was published in 1912.

602.9   Gunther Schuller] See Gunther Schuller (American composer and music historian, 1925–2015), *Early Jazz: Its Roots and Musical Development* (New York: Oxford University Press, 1968).

602.23–25 *Got the Saint Louis Blues . . . so far from me.*] From "St. Louis Blues," song by W. C. Handy (1914).

603.4–5 Hill . . . and Mason] E. B. Hill (see note 219.24–25) and Daniel Gregory Mason (1873–1953), MacDowell Professor of Music at Columbia University (1929–40). Mason wrote three symphonies and other orchestral music but was better known as a writer of books about music.

603.7 Ernest Bloch] Swiss-born composer (1880–1959) who, according to Thomson, "as a pedagogue rendered important service to American composers. His own music, sincerely felt and of high technical quality, had a worldwide public. *Schelomo* [for cello and orchestra, 1917], which offers Jewish pathos with cello virtuosity, is a repertory work justifiably popular."

603.10 Edgard Varèse] Varèse (1883–1965) is the subject of chapter 5 of *American Music Since 1910* (pages 636–43).

603.13 Henry Cowell] Thomson said that Cowell (1897–1965) used "in a convincing manner" the music of "Ireland, Japan, India, Iran, Iceland, and other ethnic sources, including the Appalachian mountains and the Southern farm regions of the United States. The variety of his sources and composing methods is probably the broadest of our time. And if his work, for all its grace, wit, and imagination, occasionally lacks intensity, it is never . . . lacking in sincerity." See also pages 680–81 of the present volume.

603.14 Charles Griffes] Thomson wrote that Griffes's music, mostly French-inspired impressionist works for piano, "is first class all through and can be played anywhere." Griffes's dates are 1884 to 1920: "His death at age thirty-five seems somehow unfair."

603.19 Charles Ives] Ives (1874–1954) is the subject of chapter 3 of *American Music Since 1910* (pages 619–27).

603.24 Carpenter . . . Powell] Thomson wrote that John Alden Carpenter (1876–1951) "was an impressionist composer of superficial but perfectly real charm. His works embodying whimsy, gentle sentiments, and the picturesque"—including *Adventures in a Perambulator* (orchestral suite, 1914) and *Krazy Kat* (ballet, 1922)—"are more striking than his monumental ones." John Powell (1882–1963) was "a vigorous pianist and composer, quite a figure in the [twentieth] century's early decades."

603.35 Ruggles] Carl Ruggles (1876–1971) is the subject of chapter 4 of *American Music Since 1910* (pages 628–35).

604.1–2 John Cage] Cage (1912–1992) is the subject of chapter 8 of *American Music Since 1910* (pages 662–76).

604.10 Carlos Salzedo] French harpist, pianist, composer, and conductor (1885–1961) who, in 1909, was hired by Toscanini as harpist for the orchestra of the Metropolitan Opera. He later worked as a soloist, founded several New York chamber ensembles, and taught harp at Juilliard, the Curtis Institute of Music, and his own Salzedo Harp Colony, in Camden, Maine.

604.14–15   League of Composers] See note 311.36.

604.17   *Modern Music*] Edited by Minna Lederman (see note 380.17).

604.20   George Antheil] See note 248.30.

604.34   Nadia Boulanger] For Thomson's biographical tribute to Boulanger (1887–1979), see pages 880–86 of the present volume.

604.35–36   Copland . . . Piston . . . Harris . . . Carter] Aaron Copland (1900–1990) is the subject of chapter 6 of *American Music Since 1910* (pages 644–53). Walter Piston (1894–1976) was, in Thomson's words, "a neoclassical composer of Parisian cast, skilled technician of the orchestra . . . and author of today's best book on counterpoint." For Thomson's comments on Roy Harris, see note 375.19 and page 679 of the present volume. Elliott Carter (1908–2012) wrote "music of unusual complexity and refinement, at its most striking in chamber works, including the Double Concerto [for harpsichord and piano, 1956]. . . . His genius is to have combined intellectual elaboration with auditory delight with no loss of intensity to either." For more of Thomson on Carter, see pages 679 and 970–74 of the present volume.

605.1   Barber . . . Schuman . . . Harrison] Samuel Barber (1910–1981) wrote "romantic music, predominantly emotional, embodying sophisticated workmanship and complete care. Barber's aesthetic position may be reactionary, but his melodic line sings and the harmony supports it." For more of Thomson on Barber and on William Schuman (1910–1992), see page 681 of the present volume. For Thomson on Lou Harrison (1917–2003), see note 524.3, pages 679–80, and pages 893–94.

605.3   Roger Sessions] For Thomson's comments on Sessions (1896–1985), see page 678 of the present volume.

605.8   Randall Thompson] Thompson (1899–1984) is widely known for his choral works, especially his *Alleluia* (1940), which has sold upward of a million copies. "He is also the author of a most effective symphony," wrote Thomson of his No. 2 (1931), "and one of our most indigenous-sounding string quartets" (1941).

605.15   According to one study] John Henry Mueller, *The American Symphony Orchestra: A Social History of Musical Taste* (Bloomington: Indiana University Press, 1951).

605.25–27   Converse . . . Hadley . . . Cadman . . . Taylor] Harvard-trained Frederick Converse (1871–1940) wrote three symphonies, many symphonic and chamber works, but, as Thomson noted, "of a great career, in its time, little remains." The same can be said of Converse's equally prolific classmate Henry Hadley (1871–1937), whose most enduring legacy is the Berkshire (Tanglewood)

Music Festival, founded 1934. Charles Wakefield Cadman (1881–1946) was a Pittsburgh-born composer and ethnomusicologist who lived among the Omaha and Winnebago, collecting their songs on wax cylinders and drawing on their melodies for chamber works and art songs. Composer, critic, and broadcaster Deems Taylor (1885–1966) wrote three operas and a good deal of incidental music. "All show stage sense," wrote Thomson, "but they lack memorable melody."

605.36–37 *Amelia at the Ball . . . The Devil and Daniel Webster*] *Amelia al Ballo* (1936), a one-act comedy, was the first opera written by the Italian-born Gian Carlo Menotti (1911–2007). It was performed, in English, as *Amelia Goes to the Ball*, in 1937. *The Devil and Daniel Webster: A Folk Opera in One Act* (1938), by Douglas Moore (see note 528.21–22), with a libretto by Stephen Vincent Benét, was a Broadway success in 1939.

605.38–606.2 Since that time . . . operatic format] See pages 658–59 of the present volume.

607.3 *Gerald McBoing-Boing*] Seven-minute cartoon, adapted from Dr. Seuss by UPA Studios (1950), that won the 1951 Academy Award for Best Animated Short. Its score was by Oklahoma-born Gail Kubik (1914–1984), a composer, violinist, and radio music director whose 1952 Symphony Concertante was awarded a Pulitzer Prize.

607.10–11 Dello Joio . . . Gould] The ballet scores of Norman Dello Joio (1913–2008) include *On Stage* (1945) and *Diversion of Angels* (1949). Thomson considered him a "composer of warm lyrical outpouring [whose] music moves forward, speaks with authority." The ballet scores of "pop-concert-oriented" composer Morton Gould (1913–1996) include *Interplay* (1945) and *Fall River Legend* (1947), both of which, Thomson noted, are "repertory dance works."

608.34–40 since 1959 . . . engineer composers.] The Computer Music Center at Columbia University (originally the Columbia-Princeton Electronic Music Center) was founded in 1958 by two Columbia music professors, Russian composer Vladimir Ussachevsky (1911–1990) and the German-born Otto Luening (see note 553.11–12), together with Princeton's Milton Babbitt (1916–2011). The Center's room-sized RCA Mark II Synthesizer (a.k.a. "Victor," 1957–59), commissioned by Columbia with a grant from the Rockefeller Foundation, is still in use.

610.3–4 Alan Hovhaness] Composer (1911–2000) whose music, said Thomson, "interests through sheer continuity and lovely sound. . . . Its variety from piece to piece is infinite."

610.5–6 Peggy Glanville-Hicks] See note 513.25–26.

612.5 an orchestral work that involved five conductors] *Antiphony I* (1953), by Henry Brant (see note 431.23).

616.14 "rhythmic modulation."] Also known as "metric modulation" or, in Carter's favored phrase, "tempo modulation."

617.34–35 Stockhausen . . . Boulez . . . Xenakis] The European avant-garde of the 1950s and '60s: Karlheinz Stockhausen (1928–2007), German pioneer of electronic music, aleatory music, and serialism; Pierre Boulez (1925–2016), French composer, conductor, pianist, and writer who, early in his career, shared Stockhausen's experimental interests (see pages 933–42 of the present volume); and Iannis Xanakis (1922–2001), Greek-French composer, architect, and engineer who brought set theory and game theory into musical composition. Others on this "European team," as Thomson calls them, were the French composer Luciano Berio (1925–2003) and the Italian Luigi Nono (1924–1990).

619.7 Henry Gilbert] Boston-based American composer and ethnomusicologist who collected African American and Creole melodies, often adapting them to his own ends.

619.13 father] George Edward Ives (1845–1894), a former Union Army bandmaster, was a pianist, cornet player, music teacher, director of a theater orchestra, and choir director in Fairfield County, Connecticut.

619.32 Myrick] Julian Myrick (1880–1969), who had worked with Ives at Mutual Life Insurance Co. (1898–1906), was a partner in Ives & Myrick, at Nassau and Liberty streets, New York, from 1906 to 1930.

619.32 married his roommate's sister] Ives married Harmony Twitchell (1876–1969), the sister of his Yale roommate David Twitchell, in 1908. The couple adopted an infant daughter, Edith Osborne Ives, in 1914.

621.1 Wilfred Mellers] English music historian, musicologist, and composer (1914–2008) who, after 1964, was head of the music department at the University of York. He wrote about Ives in *Music in a New Found Land* (see pages 910–17 of the present volume.)

621.2 John Kirkpatrick] American pianist and music scholar (1905–1991) who gave the first public performance of Ives's "Concord" Sonata on January 20, 1939, at New York's Town Hall. He later became a professor of music at Yale University and the curator of Yale's Charles Ives archives. He was also a champion of Ruggles, Copland, and Harris.

621.5–6 publication of this sonata . . . *114 Songs*] Charles E. Ives, *Second Pianoforte Sonata: "Concord, Mass., 1840–60"* (Redding, Conn.: Privately printed by G. Schirmer, New York, for the composer, n.d. [December 1920]); Charles E. Ives, *114 Songs* (Redding, Conn.: Privately printed by G. Schirmer, New York, for the composer, n.d. [August 1924]).

622.9–10 Yates . . . the only American music that makes him cry.] See "Ivesiana," by Peter Yates (1909–1976), in *The New York Review of Books* (September 3, 1970): "It is the transcendent *sound* of Ives's music," writes Yates, "which produces in me this embarrassing effect. . . . If it's the nostalgia and not the sound which has brought Mr. Thomson, too, to weeping, we share a sympathetic response but not the cause."

623.13–14   *Charles Ives and His Music*] Henry and Sidney Cowell, *Charles Ives and His Music* (New York: Oxford University Press, 1955).

625.19–20   He valued his "Concord" Sonata so highly . . . he wrote a book about it.] Charles E. Ives, *Essays Before a Sonata* (New York: Knickerbocker Press, 1920), 124 pages.

628.5–7   patron . . . wife . . . son.] Ruggles's patron was sculptor Harriet G. Miller (1892–1971). His wife (m. 1908) was contralto Charlotte Harriet Snell (1880–1997). The Ruggleses' son, Micah Haskell Ruggles, was born in 1916.

628.13–20   A revealing story . . . test of time."] See Henry Cowell, "Carl Ruggles: A Note," preface to *About Carl Ruggles*, by Lou Harrison (Yonkers: Oscar Baradinsky at the Alicat Book Shop, 1946).

628.22–23   song . . . composed in 1919] *Toys*, for soprano and piano.

630.36–37   "What are those . . . Unknown?"] From Walt Whitman's "Portals," a two-line poem first printed in the fifth edition of *Leaves of Grass* (1871): "What are those of the known but to ascend and enter the Unknown? / And what are those of life but for Death?"

632.8   *Vox Clamans in Deserto*] "A Voice Crying in the Wilderness."

633.7–9   Mellers . . . *Music in a New Found Land*] See pages 910–17 of the present volume.

634.30   "that last infirmity,"] Cf. John Milton, "Lycidas" (1638): "Fame is the spur that the clear spirit doth rise / (That last infirmity of noble mind) / To scorn delights and live laborious days . . ."

635.24   William Billings] Boston-based composer (1746–1800) who made his living as a tanner. He wrote hymns, anthems, and many of America's earliest choral pieces.

636.19   League of Composers] See note 311.36.

636.36   Schola Cantorum] See note 69.36.

637.26–30   "I became a sort . . . called noises."] From "Autobiographical Remarks (dedicated to the memory of Ferruccio Busoni)," talk delivered, in English, at Princeton University on September 4, 1959. Published, in French, as "Le Destin de la musique est de conquérir la liberté," in the Montreal music journal *Liberté: Musique de Notre Temps* 1.5 (Varèse number: September–October 1959).

637.38   *The Art of Noise*] Luigi Russolo (1885–1937), *L'Arte dei rumori* (Milan: Edizioni Futuriste di "Poesia," 1916). Russolo's manifesto was written, in 1913, as an exhortation addressed to the Futurist composer Balilla Pratella. (Thomson quotes the English version provided by Derek Coltman in his translation, from the French, of *Edgard Varèse*, by Fernand Ouellette [New York: Orion Press/Grossman, 1968]. See note 640.2)

638.34   Dane Rudhyar] French-American composer (1895–1985) whose brief orchestral pieces, most of them dating from the 1920s, were admired by Ruggles, Cowell, Ruth Crawford, and others.

640.2   Fernand Ouellette] French-Canadian poet and novelist (b. 1930) and author of *Edgard Varèse* (Paris: Seghers, 1966). See note 637.38.

641.4   *Around and About Joan Miró.*] Sixty-minute television film (1955) produced and directed by Jerusalem-born Thomas Bouchard (1895–1984), who specialized in documentaries about artists at work. Varèse's tape was created to accompany a three-minute sequence of the film.

641.5   *Le Poème électronique*] Varèse's three-track, eight-minute tape played continuously inside the Philips Pavilion of the Brussels World Fair, April 17–October 19, 1958. The Pavilion was designed by Le Corbusier and Iannis Xenakis (see note 617.34–35), who also collaborated on the film that Thomson describes here.

642.29–30   "Music in the pure state . . . tornadoes of sonorities . . . nightmare dreamed by giants."] The three quotations, samples from the Paris music world's reaction to Varèse's percussion piece *Ionisation* (1929–31), are from avant-garde publisher Henri René Julliard (1900–1962), in *Le Cahier* (March 1932); Breton composer Paul Le Flem (1881–1984), in *Comoedia* (February 29, 1932); and French composer Florent Schmitt (1870–1958), in *Le Feuilleton du Temps* (November 26, 1932). The English translations are by Derek Coltman (see note 637.38).

643.11–30   From *Amériques* of 1919 . . . powerfully communicative.] From Virgil Thomson, "Edgard Varèse, 1883–1965," a commemorative tribute read by the author at the annual dinner meeting of the American Academy of Arts and Letters on December 10, 1965, and published in *Proceedings of the American Academy of Arts and Letters and the National Institute of Arts and Letters* for 1966.

644.3   JULIA SMITH'S book] *Aaron Copland: His Work and Contribution to American Music* (New York: Dutton, 1955).

645.12–13   Copland-Sessions Concerts.] See note 288.35.

645.29   Arrow Music Press] See note 449.36.

645.30   American Composers Alliance] See note 162.17.

646.25   Arthur Berger] Author of *Aaron Copland* (New York: Oxford University Press, 1953). See note 505.20.

648.20   "I didn't know one could write an opera."] See page 415.11 of the present volume.

648.29–30   Lincoln Kirstein . . . Ballet Caravan] See note 240.13.

649.13   Harold Clurman] Clurman (1901–1980), a theater director and drama critic, was Copland's Paris roommate for nine months in 1921–22. The two were close friends ever after.

652.1   Rubin Goldmark] American composer and educator (1872–1936) who, first as a private instructor and then, after 1924, as Head of Composition at Juilliard, helped to shape many American composers, including Copland and George Gershwin.

654.12–13   *America's Symphony Orchestras*] Margaret Grant and Herman S. Hettinger, *America's Symphony Orchestras—And How They Are Supported* (New York: Norton, 1940).

655.33   Leo Ornstein] American composer and performer (1893–2002) who, from 1910 to 1925, was a foremost exponent of percussive pianistic modernism. "His *Danse Sauvage* of 1915," said Thomson, "can still be listened to."

658.22–23   Carlisle Floyd] Floyd (b. 1926), like Menotti, wrote both libretto and music for his many operas. "In *Susannah* (1955)," wrote Thomson, "Floyd has composed an opera of repertory status." Thomson also thought well of his *Of Mice and Men* (1970).

658.27–30   Barber's *Vanessa* . . . produced at the Met in 1934.] The Metropolitan Opera commissioned only a few American operas during Thomson's lifetime, among them Samuel Barber's *Vanessa* (1958) and *Antony and Cleopatra* (1966), Deems Taylor's *The King's Henchman* (1927) and *Peter Ibbetson* (1929), and Marvin David Levy's *Mourning Becomes Electra* (1967). *Merry Mount* (1934), based on Hawthorne's "May-Pole of Merry Mount," was the sole opera by Howard Hanson (1896–1981), whom Thomson judged "a Romantic composer of warm heart."

658.31–32   *The Crucible* . . . Ford Foundation commissions] For Thomson's review of the premiere of *The Crucible* (1962), see pages 847–50 of the present volume. Ward's opera was one of some two dozen whose composition and production were underwritten by the Ford Foundation in the late 1950s through the 1960s. Others included *Six Characters in Search of an Author* (1959), by Hugo Weisgall (1912–1996); *The Harvest* (1961), by Vittorio Giannini (1903–1966); *The Passion of Jonathan Wade* (1962), by Carlisle Floyd; and *The Wings of the Dove* (1962), by Douglas Moore (see pages 847–50).

659.5   short operas of a comedy so broad] *The Telephone* (1947), one-act opera by Menotti; *Trouble in Tahiti* (1952), one-act opera with music and libretto by Bernstein; *The Jumping Frog of Calavaras County* (1951), "after-dinner opera" in two scenes by Lukas Foss (1922–2009); *Gallantry* (1958), one-act "soap opera" by Douglas Moore, complete with parody commercials; *Archie and Mehitabel* (1954), an opera conceived as a phonograph record, by George Kleinsinger (1914–1982), Thomson's fellow-resident at the Chelsea Hotel.

659.33   Ross Lee Finney] American composer (1906–1997) noted for his art songs and for his chamber works, including eight string quartets. For Thomson's comments on Finney, see pages 678–79 of the present volume.

659.36   Alberto Ginastera] Argentinian composer (1916–1983) whose sexually frank opera *Bomarzo* (1967) was banned by Argentina's President Onganía.

662.4 Lejaren Hiller] Princeton-trained research chemist and tinkerer (1924–1994) who, as an undergraduate, studied music with Milton Babbitt and Roger Sessions. By the mid-1950s he was writing computer-assisted music for string quartets and making electronic music tapes in the University of Illinois' "Illiac" computer lab.

662.22–23 Richard Kostelanetz . . . *New York Times*] Richard Kostelanetz, "They All Came to Cage's 'Circus,'" *The New York Times* (May 25, 1969).

663.29–38 "I believe . . . fundamental tone."] John Cage, "The Future of Music—Credo" (1937), in *Silence: Lectures and Writings* (Middletown, Conn.: Wesleyan University Press, 1961).

664.3–5 Luigi Russolo . . . roars."] See note 637.38.

665.10 young Russian woman from Alaska] Cage was married to the artist and musician Xenia Andreyevna Kashevaroff (1913–1995) from 1935 to 1945.

667.37 *I Ching*] In the 1950s Cage composed certain works in which sounds, durations, tempos, etc., are determined by the performer in consultation with the *I Ching, or Book of Changes*, as translated from the Chinese by Richard Wilhelm and Cary F. Baynes (Bollingen Series XIX; Princeton, N.J.: Princeton University Press, 1950).

668.1 Gilbert Chase . . . *America's Music*] See "Innovation and Experiment," chapter 27 of Gilbert Chase's *America's Music: From the Pilgrims to the Present*, second edition (New York: McGraw Hill, 1966). Chase's quotations come from John Cage, "Composition as Process" (1958), a lecture-essay on his prepared-piano piece *Music of Changes* (1951), collected in *Silence: Lectures and Writings* (Middletown, Conn.: Wesleyan University Press, 1961).

670.22–26 *Silence* . . . *A Year* . . . *Notations*] Three books by John Cage: *Silence* (see note above); *A Year from Monday: New Lectures and Writings* (Middletown, Conn.: Wesleyan University Press, 1967); and *Notations*, with Alison Knowles (New York: Something Else Press, 1969), conceived as a fund-raiser for the Foundation for Contemporary Arts (New York), which supports the work of individual visual and performing artists.

671.38–39 Merce Cunningham's dance spectacles.] Cunningham (1919–2006), a modern dancer and choreographer, was, after 1938, Cage's closest artistic collaborator and, from 1945, his life companion. Cage was music director of the Merce Cunningham Dance Company from its founding, in 1953, until his death in 1992.

672.14 David Tudor] American composer and pianist (1926–1996) who interpreted the works of John Cage, and sometimes collaborated in their writing and execution. Many of his works were written for the Merce Cunningham Dance Company, of which he was music director from 1992 until his death four years later.

675.30 Jean Tinguely] Swiss artist (1925–1991), certain of whose kinetic sculptures, which he called Metamechanics, were engineered to explode or otherwise self-destruct in a kind of Dada performance art.

676.12–13 "Get on board-a . . . a million more."] Cf. the chorus of "The Gospel Train," African American spiritual first collected in the Fisk Singers' *Jubilee Songs* anthology (1872): "Get on board, children, there's room for many a more."

677.17–28 Cage progeny . . . fragility.] New Yorker Morton Feldman (1926–1987), whose music, said Thomson, "is notable for its delicacy of sound and transparent textures"; self-taught, French-born Christian Wolff (b. 1934), whose pieces are "quiet, short, and very beautiful"; Massachusetts native Gordon Mumma (b. 1935), a horn player who also builds his own electronic instruments; Japanese composer Toshi Ichiyanagi (b. 1933), who was married to and collaborated with Yoko Ono from 1956 to 1962; and Earle Brown (1926–2002), whose "far-outness [was] manicured and groomed, always clear in sound, generally sparse in texture." All were students of or collaborators with Cage, and most wrote music for Merce Cunningham and David Tudor.

680.33 His *New Music* edition] See note 449.14.

681.32 Ned Rorem] American composer and writer (b. 1923) whose art songs have won him musical distinction and whose diaries, beginning with *The Paris Diary* (1966), have won him literary celebrity.

682.17–18 William Flanagan] For Thomson's memorial tribute to Flanagan (1923–1969), see pages 886–88 of the present volume.

682.40–683.1 Theodore Chanler's songs] See note 249.23–24.

683.5 Kenneth Gaburo] American composer (1926–1993) whose work includes orchestral, chamber, choral, and electronic music. Thomson said that "Gaburo is at once far-out and 'musical,' imaginative and advanced, a strong composer in no way casual. Pierre Boulez has remarked the originality of his vocal writing."

683.38 I have written elsewhere] See "Music Now," pages 798–804 of the present volume.

686.35–37 Gelatt, Roland . . . September 1968.] The cover story of the September 1968 number of *High Fidelity* was a forty-page feature called "The New Music—Its Sources, Its Sounds, Its Creators." It consisted of a general introduction by Roland Gelatt, associate publisher of the magazine; "Composition in the 1960s," an essay by Lukas Foss; and "A Synoptic View of the New Music," an article by David Hamilton, music editor of W. W. Norton, Inc., publishers.

MUSIC WITH WORDS

698.10–11 Leontyne Price's way . . . and Kathleen Ferrier's] African American soprano Leontyne Price (b. 1927), from Laurel, Mississippi, was educated at Juilliard, and English contralto Kathleen Ferrier (1912–1953), from Higher Walton, Lancashire, was educated at the Royal Academy of Music.

699.3 "Wünchen Sie auch Fisch?,"] "Would you like more fish?"

703.5 "O come, . . . the strength of our salvation."] *Venite, exultamus Domino* (Psalm 95).

707.4–5   "Donnez-le-moi le couteau" or "Le couteau, donnez-le-moi."] "Give me the knife" or "The knife, give it to me."

724.30   *Psallemus metrice vel rhytmice*] Latin: Give praise in rhyme or in rhythm.

724.33–34   *cantus atque musica*] Latin: Song and music.

726.35   the librettist of *Carmen*] Ludovic Halévy (1834–1908) collaborated with Bizet on the lyrical passages of *Carmen* (1875) while Henri Meilhac (1830–1897) focused on the narrative.

742.13   Saint-Saëns . . . famous assignment] Camille Saint-Saëns' sole teaching appointment was as head of piano studies at the École Niedermeyer, Paris, from 1861 to 1865. His composition students included Gabriel Fauré and André Messager.

745.24–29   Italian musicians in Florence . . . most remarkable.] See note 127.1 for more on the Florentine Group and the birth of opera.

746.36   Vincenzo Galilei] Galilei (c. 1520–1591), a lutenist, composer, and music theorist, was the father of the astronomer Galileo Galilei. He was also a moving force of the Florentine Group (see note 127.1), for which he developed "monody," in which a solo voice sings over a rhythmically independent bass line (*basso continuo*). This innovation led directly to *secco recitativo*, or the style of "dry recitative" used in the operas of Peri, Caccini, and Monteverdi.

753.21–24   *Wedding Bouquet . . . Doctor Faustus Lights the Lights.*] In 1936, in the wake of the success of *Four Saints in Three Acts*, the British composer-artist-polymath Lord Berners (1883–1950) conceived a choral concert-piece based on "They Must. Be Wedded. To Their Wives," a text from 1931 by Gertrude Stein. Stein collaborated with Berners on the choral text, which became the ballet-with-words *A Wedding Bouquet*. The ballet, with a scenario by Constance Lambert, choreography by Frederick Ashton, and production design by Lord Berners, was given its premiere at Sadler's Wells Theater, London, on April 27, 1937. Berners then commissioned an opera libretto from Stein, *Doctor Faustus Lights the Lights* (1938), but in the end did not set it to music. In 1949 Thomson toyed with the idea of completing the opera, but was discouraged from doing so by Stein's literary executor, Alice B. Toklas.

754.1–2   "America's Unrequited Love for Opera."] This lecture, on American opera and of the institutions that have (and have not) supported it, was never published.

755.33–756.3   Columbia University's now defunct Opera Workshop . . . large ones.] See note 528.21–22.

760.31   Lincoln Kirstein] See note 240.13.

771.11   "Alberti bass"] See note 151.14

OTHER WRITINGS

784.26   The fifty years that ended with Beethoven's death] That is, the period 1777 to 1827.

792.37   *Augenmusik*] "Eye-music," or music that is more beautiful on paper, as a visual or intellectual experience, than it is perhaps in performance.

793.32   *querelle des bouffons.*] "Quarrel of the Comic Actors" (1752–54), common name for a heated and prolonged aesthetic debate among French critics and operagoers over the respective virtues of the French and Italian operatic styles.

795.2–3   "In a time of dearth bring out measure and number."] Cf. William Blake, from "Proverbs of Hell," in *The Marriage of Heaven and Hell* (c. 1790): "Bring out number, weight & measure in a year of dearth."

797.1–9   Cold War . . . propaganda purposes.] See notes 571.1 and 575.38–39.

799.24   1926 Oxford lecture] Gertrude Stein, *Composition as Explanation* (London: Hogarth Press, 1926), an essay on modern artistic expression and the forms it takes, and on the modern artist's "using everything" and "beginning again," collected in *What Are Masterpieces* (Los Angeles: Conference Press, 1940).

805.3–4   Gertrude Stein used to say . . . looking at.] See *Composition as Explanation* (note above): "The only thing that is different from one time to another is what is seen and what is seen depends upon how everybody is doing everything. This makes the thing we are looking at very different and this makes what those who describe it make of it, it makes a composition, it confuses, it shows, it is, it looks, it likes it as it is, and this makes what is seen as it is seen. Nothing changes from generation to generation except the thing seen and that makes a composition."

807.8   *Formenlehre*] German: Theory of musical form.

809.15–16   a very long book by . . . Ernest Ansermet.] Ansermet's two-volume work, published in Switzerland in 1961, has yet to be translated into English. An English-language lecture summarizing its content, which he delivered throughout the 1960s, was titled "What Everyone Should Know About Music."

810.31   an instrument] This instrument is called the Semantic Daniélou, after its inventor, the French ethnomusicologist Alain Daniélou (1907–1994). Daniélou is also the author of a book on the perception and emotional experience of musical intervals, *La Sémantique Musicale* (see page 942 of the present volume).

814.37–815.2   A researched version . . . Catholic worship.] See note 62.31.

815.24–28   sonata-form . . . dead for ten years.] See note 70.18–19.

820.17–18   Patrick J. Smith] American music critic (b. 1932) and former editor of *Opera News* (1988–98).

825.11 *The performances of Much Ado*] The American Shakespeare Festival production of *Much Ado About Nothing* opened on August 3, 1957, at the American Shakespeare Festival Theater, Stratford, Connecticut. After completing its summer run, the production enjoyed an eight-week tour throughout New England and the Mid-Atlantic states. The cast included, in addition to Hepburn and Drake, Lois Nettleson (Hero), Richard Easton (Claudio), Stanley Bell (Don Pedro), John Colicos (Leonato), Morris Carnovsky (Antonio), Sada Thompson (Margaret), and Larry Gates (Dogberry).

825.12 *American Shakespeare Festival*] The nonprofit American Shakespeare Festival (1950–82) was founded by playwright and patent lawyer Lawrence Langner (1890–1962) with the support of, among others, Lincoln Kirstein (see note 240.13). The Festival Theater, in Stratford, Connecticut, was built in 1954–55, and opened in July of 1955 with a production of *Julius Caesar* directed by Denis Carey. By the end of the ASF's first summer, John Houseman (see note 409.22) was engaged as artistic director, a title he held for four seasons (1956–59). Thomson wrote incidental music for five of Houseman's ASF productions: *King John* and *Measure for Measure*, in 1956; *Much Ado About Nothing* and *Othello*, in 1957; and *The Merchant of Venice*, in 1958. Also, Thomson's music for *Hamlet* (see note 437.12), written for Houseman in 1936, was adapted by the composer for the ASF production of 1958.

827.11 *Russell Oberlin*] American countertenor (b. 1928) who was a cofounder of the New York Pro Musica (1952–74), an ensemble devoted to medieval and Renaissance music. He played the role of Balthasar in the ASF *Much Ado*.

827.40 *Jarabe Tapatío*] Traditional mariachi tune, better known as the "Mexican Hat Dance" than (as Thomson has it) the "Mexican Scarf Dance."

828.2 *La Golondrina*] "The Swallow," song (1862) by Narciso Serradell Sevilla (1843–1910). The country-and-western lyric "She Wears My Ring" (1960), by Felice and Boudleux Bryant, is written to the melody of *La Golondrina*.

828.14 *Sobre las Olas*] Waltz (1888), by Mexican composer Juventino Rosas (1868–1894), strongly associated in the United States with trapeze acts and fairground pipe organs.

828.20 "Sigh no more, Ladies"] *Much Ado About Nothing*, II.iii.62–74.

830.34–35 *Benedick's song*] *Much Ado*, V.ii.26–29: "The god of love, / That sits above, / And knows me, and knows me, / How pitiful I deserve—"

830.36–37 *Pardon, Goddess of the Night*] *Much Ado*, V.iii.12–21.

837.4 *George Pierce Baker*] Baker (1866–1935), a professor of drama at Harvard University (1887–1925), ran Workshop 47, the first undergraduate playwriting workshop in America, which encouraged the young Eugene O'Neill, George Abbott, Philip Barry, and Sidney Howard.

840.36 *what the Ford Foundation is trying*] See note 658.31–32.

841.4–5   One work received a Pulitzer] *The Crucible*, by Robert Ward (see pages 847–50 of the present volume), was awarded the Pulitzer Prize for Music in 1962.

841.7–8   a work about Sacco and Vanzetti] Marc Blitzstein was at work on a three-act opera, provisionally titled "S/V" or "Sacco and Vanzetti" (see note 222.1), at the time of his death, at the age of fifty-eight, in 1964.

841.9   archie and mehitabel] Archy the cockroach and Mehitabel the cat, characters created in 1916 by newspaper humorist Don Marquis (1878–1937) for his New York *Sun* column, provided the inspiration for an opera by George Kleinsinger (see note 659.5).

842.25–27   Lincoln Center . . . Old Lady of Thirty-ninth Street.] The original Metropolitan Opera House (1883–1967), sometimes called the "Old Met" or the "Old Lady of Thirty-ninth Street," stood at 1411 Broadway, between Thirty-ninth and Fortieth streets. Today's opera house, at 30 Lincoln Center Plaza, opened on September 16, 1966.

844.8   *Juno . . . Regina*] The Playwrights' Company production of *Juno*, a play-with-music in two acts, with music and lyrics by Marc Blitzstein, book by Joseph Stein (based on the play *Juno and the Paycock* [1924] by Sean O'Casey), opened at the Winter Garden Theater, New York, on March 9, 1959, and closed on March 21. There were sixteen Broadway performances. It was staged by José Ferrer and choreographed by Agnes De Mille; Robert Emmett Dolan was music director, and the music was orchestrated by Robert Russell Bennett and Hershy Kay. Cast: Shirley Booth (Juno Boyle), Tommy Rall (Johnny Boyle), Melvyn Douglas (Captain Boyle), Jack MacGowran (Joxer Daly), Monte Amundsen (Mary Boyle), and Loren Driscoll (Jerry Devine). The original-cast recording (released April 1959) bears Columbia Records catalogue numbers OL-5380 (mono) and OS-2013 (stereo).

   The original production of *Regina*, an opera in three acts by Marc Blitzstein (based on the play *The Little Foxes* [1939] by Lillian Hellman), opened at the Forty-sixth Street Theater, New York, on October 31, 1949, and closed on December 16. There were fifty-six Broadway performances. The New York City Opera revived *Regina* in 1953, and again in 1958. The 1958 version was staged by Robert Lewis and choreographed by John Butler; Samuel Krachmalnik was music director. Cast: Brenda Lewis (Regina), Helen Strine (Alexandra), Elisabeth Carron (Birdie), Carol Brice (Addie), Joshua Hecht (Horace), George Irving (Benjamin), Emile Renan (Oscar), and Loren Driscoll (Leo). The three-disc recording by this cast (released December 1958) bears Columbia Records catalogue numbers 03L-260 (mono) and 03S-202 (stereo).

847.5   The Crucible *and* The Wings of the Dove] *The Crucible*, an opera in four acts by Robert Ward, libretto by Bernard Stambler (from the play [1953] by Arthur Miller), received its world premiere at the New York City Opera on October 26, 1961. It was staged by Allen Fletcher; Emerson Buckley was music director. Cast: Joyce Ebert (Betty Parris), Norman Kelley (Reverend Parris), Debria Brown (Tituba), Patricia Brooks (Abigail Williams), et al.

The Wings of the Dove, an opera in three acts by Douglas Moore, libretto by Ethan Ayer (from the novel [1902] by Henry James), received its world premiere at the New York City Opera on October 12, 1961. It was staged by Christopher West and choreographed by Robert Joffrey; Julius Redel was music director. Cast: Regina Sarfaty (Kate Croy), John Reardon (Miles Dunster [Merton Densher]), Dorothy Coulter (Milly Theale), et al.

850.33   *Stravinsky's* Flood] "Noah and the Flood," a one-hour special presentation in the occasional *Breck Golden Showcase* series, was broadcast by CBS Television at 9:00 P.M. EST on the evening of Thursday, June 14, 1962. Produced by Robert D. Graff, directed by Kirk Browning, and written by Jack Richardson, the presentation, part live performance and part arts documentary, was hosted by Laurence Harvey. Robert Craft conducted the CBS Symphony Orchestra and Chorus in the world premiere of *The Flood: A Musical Play* (1962), by Igor Stravinsky, with a text by Mr. Craft. Cast: Sebastian Cabot (Noah), Elsa Lancaster (Mrs. Noah), and Paul Tripp (Caller of Animals). Vocal soloists included John Reardon and Robert Oliver (together, the Voice of God) and Richard Robinson (Satan). The dances, by George Balanchine, were performed by Jacques d'Amboise (Adam/Lucifer), Jillana (Eve), Edward Villella (Satan), and other members of the New York City Ballet. Costume and set design by Rouben Ter-Arutunian.

853.5   JAMES HUNEKER] Huneker was born, in Philadelphia, in 1857. His novel *Painted Veils* came out in 1920. He published some sixteen other books, most of them collections of magazine and newspaper criticism. (His biographer, Arnold T. Schwab [1922–2014], was a longtime professor of English at the University of California–Long Beach.)

853.18   "He has a splendid thrust."] Herbert Beerbohm Tree (1852–1917), English drama critic and theater manager, to the London actor-writer Francis Neilson, in 1901, as quoted by Neilson in "Miscellany," his column for *The Freeman* (March 2, 1921).

853.19–20   "a real talent . . . layman."] Remy de Gourmont (1858–1915), French poet and literary critic, in a postcard to Huneker, May 26, 1900.

854.20–23   "you are an incontinent . . . execrable."] George Bernard Shaw, from letters to Huneker dated August 13, 1905, and September 16, 1905, both in response to Huneker's essay "The Quintessence of Shaw" (1903) as revised and expanded for his collection *Iconoclasts* (1905).

855.2   Olin Downes] See note 509.6.

857.28   B. H. Haggin] See note 244.18.

857.29   Toscanini] Arturo Toscanini (1867–1957) was an Italian-born conductor. As music director of La Scala (1898–1908, 1920–26), the Metropolitan Opera (1908–14), and, especially, the New York Philharmonic (1926–36), he enjoyed an international reputation as "The Maestro," the most famous conductor of opera and orchestral music of his time. After 1930 he became a national institution when CBS began its weekly broadcasts of Philharmonic concerts, the most listened-to classical radio series in the country. In 1936 David Sarnoff, director of CBS's chief rival, NBC, invited the sixty-nine-year-old Toscanini to create and direct his own orchestra. Sarnoff built the maestro a twelve-hundred-seat concert hall and broadcast facility—"Studio 8H" at NBC headquarters, Radio City, in Rockefeller Center—and, in close consultation with him and his appointed deputies, hired the members of the NBC Symphony Orchestra. Toscanini made his debut with the orchestra on Christmas Day, 1937, and his final appearance on April 4, 1954.

861.7   Wagner wrote a small book about it] *Über das Dirigieren* (1869), by Richard Wagner; translated, as *On Conducting*, by William Reeves (London, 1887).

861.38   Sidney Finkelstein offered] In his book *Art and Society* (New York: International Publishers, 1947). See note 110.21–22.

862.19   Donald Sutherland] American librettist and arts critic (1915–1978) who was a professor of comparative literature at the University of Colorado–Boulder from 1940 to 1965. In a memorial tribute published in *Denver Quarterly* (Fall 1978) Thomson wrote that Sutherland's magnum opus, *On, Romanticism*, "offers a three-way choice of artistic temperaments and their operating methods—classic, romantic, and baroque—a proposal so radical of a problem long unsolved by the dualistic approach that it threatens the whole layout of literary and artistic history. Actually the shock of the book seems to have stunned the scholastic world. Everybody serious about culture and its study has read the book or heard of it. Don't be deceived about that. But practically nobody has taken up its offer . . . For now, it [Sutherland's "three-way choice"] is an 'underground' idea. In a generation or two it will no doubt surface somewhere . . . in some fresher view of art and culture that might straddle the visual, the verbal, and the auditory. This outcome none of us living will ever see. But I am convinced that something of the kind will come about. And when it does, *On, Romanticism* will be, if not its Bible, the voice of a major prophet."

864.22   according to Marcel Beaufils] See *Le Lied romantique allemand* ("The Romantic German Lieder," 1956), by Marcel Beaufils (1895–1985), a longtime professor of musical aesthetics at the Conservatoire de Paris.

868.7   *Style and Idea*] In 1948 Schoenberg collected fifteen of his essays on music under the title *Stil und Gedanke*. An English-language edition, *Style and Idea*, translated and with an introduction by his American student Dika Newlin (1923–2006), was published by Philosophical Library, New York, in 1950.

868.29   Boulez in a recent article] "Stravinsky and the Century: Style or Idea?," a memorial tribute to Igor Stravinsky (1882–1971), translated from the French by David Noakes.

869.6–7 *Les Jeunesses Musicales*] Founded in Brussels in 1945, Jeunesses Musicales International ("Musical Youth International"), a global nonprofit organization loosely affiliated with the United Nations, nurtures young musicians and young audiences through a vast array of international educational offerings.

870.9–13 Haggin . . . Kerner . . . Kupferberg . . . Craft . . . Kolodin . . . Rich] B. H. Haggin (see note 244.18); Leighton Kerner (1927–2006) was music critic of *The Village Voice* from 1957 to 1998; Herbert Kupferberg (1918–2001) was on the music staff at the *Herald Tribune* before becoming music critic for *The National Observer* (1962–77); Robert Craft (1923–2015), conductor, composer, and amanuensis to Igor Stravinsky, wrote occasionally on music for *The New York Review of Books* from 1969 through 2002; Irving Kolodin (1908–1988), historian of the Metropolitan Opera, was music critic of *Saturday Review* from 1947 to 1982; Alan Rich (1924–2010), cofounder (1968) and music critic (1968–81) of *New York* magazine, later chronicled the music scene in Los Angeles.

870.18 Andrew Porter] South African–born, Oxford-educated music critic (1928–2015) whose column "Musical Events" appeared regularly in *The New Yorker* from 1972 to 1992.

871.22 Harold Schonberg] American music journalist (1915–2003) who was chief music critic of *The New York Times* from 1960 to 1980.

871.41 Ned Rorem] American composer Rorem (see note 681.32) has been writing essays on music for *The New Republic* and other opinion magazines since the mid-1960s.

872.25–32 Henry Pleasants . . . we're not taking it from him."] Pleasants (1910–2000), educated as a pianist at the Curtis Institute, was an American music journalist who, after 1945, was based in London. He wrote for *Stereo Review* and *Opera Quarterly*, and from 1967 to 1997 was London music correspondent for the *International Herald Tribune*. Thomson here alludes to his book *The Agony of Modern Music* (New York: Simon and Schuster, 1955).

873.24 *Jazz and Pop . . . Music and Politics*] Jazz Press, of New York City, was founded in 1961 by publisher and record producer Bob Thiele. Its chief work was a monthly magazine, conceived as a rival to *DownBeat*, that was launched as *Jazz* in 1962, broadened its focus as *Jazz & Pop* in 1967, and ceased publication in 1972. It also published three books, under the Jazz & Pop Books imprint, with World Publishing Company, the last of which was *Music and Politics* (1971), a collection of pieces by two of the magazine's jazz writers, John Sinclair (b. 1941) and Robert Levin (b. 1939). Sinclair, based in Michigan, was the manager of the Detroit rock band MC5 and a founding member of the far-left anti-racist White Panther Party. In 1969 he was arrested for marijuana possession and served two years of a ten-year sentence. Levin contributed to *DownBeat*, *The Village Voice*, *Rolling Stone*, and other publications, and wrote liner notes for more than a hundred jazz LPs.

874.5–9 Murray . . . Taylor . . . Coleman] Sunny Murray (b. 1936), Cecil Taylor (b. 1929), and Ornette Coleman (1930–2015) are three pioneers of the New Jazz of the late 1950s and early 1960s (now commonly referred to as Free Jazz).

874.20 *Música*] Founded in Havana in 1970, *Música* (now the *Boletín Música*) is the classical music quarterly of Casa de las Américas, the Cuban cultural ministry.

881.12 Lili] Lili Boulanger (1893–1918), a composer mainly of vocal works, was the first woman to win the Prix de Rome (in 1913, for her cantata *Faust et Hélène*). Never in robust health, she died at the age of twenty-four.

885.12–13 "a private bell for inexplicable needs."] See note 64.32.

886.18 *William Flanagan*] Flanagan was born in Detroit, Michigan, in 1923. In 1971 Thomson wrote that "a soaring vocal afflatus and an extreme beauty in the melodic materials give to Flanagan's music a distinction and an authenticity quite unusual." *Time's Long Ago!* (1951) is a song cycle to texts by Herman Melville. His cycle to poems by A. E. Housman is called *The Weeping Pleiades* (1953). *Another August* (1968), for soprano, piano obbligato, and orchestra, has for text a poem (1966) by James Merrill (1926–1995). Flanagan also wrote incidental music for many plays by Edward Albee, and at the time of his suicide, in 1969, he and Albee were collaborating on an unfinished opera, "The Ice Age."

888.13 *Elisabeth Lutyens*] Lutyens, the daughter of the architect Sir Edward Lutyens, received her musical education in Paris and London. She wrote chamber music, vocal and choral music, orchestral pieces, and six operas. She also wrote a great deal of film music, most of it for the BBC and for London's Hammer studios. Her autobiographical memoir, *A Goldfish Bowl*, was published in 1972.

889.13 Edward Clark] See note 399.18. Clark was married to Elisabeth Lutyens from 1942 until his death, in 1962.

890.4–5 Betsy Jolas] French avant-garde composer (b. 1926) who specializes in vocal works.

891.11 Rudolf Bing] American opera impresario (1902–1997) who was general manager of the Metropolitan Opera from 1950 to 1972.

892.32 Walter Terry] Pioneering American dance critic (1913–1992) who, after his long stint at the *New York Herald Tribune* (1939–42, 1945–66), wrote for *Saturday Review.*

893.7–8 Lincoln Kirstein published a piece] "On Edwin Denby," by Lincoln Kirstein, *The New York Review of Books* (September 29, 1983).

895.13 *Omnibus* programs] *Omnibus* (1952–61) was a weekly "arts magazine" produced for network television by the Ford Foundation TV-Radio workshop. In its earlier seasons the show was eclectic, mixing one-act plays and live music recitals with documentary shorts, but by the third it usually featured a sixty- or ninety-minute presentation on a single subject. In the fall of 1954 Leonard Bernstein (1918–1990) presented the first of his seven hour-long *Omnibus* lectures on musical topics, "Beethoven's Fifth Symphony." This was followed by "The World of Jazz" (1955), "The Art of Conducting" (1955), "American Musical

Comedy" (1956), "Introduction to Modern Music" (1957), "The Music of Bach" (1957), and "What Makes Opera Grand?" (1958). Edited scripts of these seven lectures, illustrated with stills from the television broadcasts, make up most of *The Joy of Music*.

896.37 "they merely enjoy the sound of it."] Beecham told a reporter for the *New York Herald Tribune* in 1958 that "the British may not like music, but they absolutely love the noise it makes."

898.18 Henry Lew] Polish authority on Jewish folklore (1874–1919) who married Wanda Landowska in 1900.

898.36 Doda Conrad] Polish-German concert bass (1905–1997) who became a U.S. citizen during World War II. He was one of the Army's so-called Monuments Men in Berlin, and made his musical career in New York and Paris.

899.5 Denise Restout] French keyboard player (1915–2004) who became Landowska's pupil in 1933, when she was eighteen and Landowska fifty-four. She soon became Landowska's teaching assistant and, eventually, her life companion and heir to estate. The house they shared after 1947, Oak Knoll, in Lakeville, Connecticut, became, after Landowska's death in 1959, the Landowska Center, a teaching studio and museum for Landowska's papers and instruments. In 1964 Restout published *Landowska on Music*, edited and translated with Robert Hawkins, a teacher of English and French at Lakeville's Hotchkiss School.

903.12–13 Poulenc and de Falla . . . wrote harpsichord concertos for her] Poulenc's *Concert Champêtre* (1927–28), for harpsichord and orchestra, and Falla's Harpsichord Concerto (1926), for harpsichord and chamber ensemble (flute, oboe, clarinet, violin, and cello).

904.29 Erwin Stein] Austrian pianist, conductor, teacher, and music publisher (1885–1958) who was Schönberg's pupil from 1906 to 1910. His edition of Schönberg's letters, the subject of this review, was first published in Germany as *Arnold Schönberg: Ausgewählte Briefe* (Mainz: B. Schott's Söhne, 1958).

905.19 Paul Stefan] Austrian music critic, historian, and biographer (1879–1943) who was briefly a private student of Schönberg.

909.40 Reviewing the *Letters*] Igor Stravinsky (with Robert Craft), "Schoenberg Speaks His Mind," *The Observer* (UK), October 18, 1964. This review, revised and expanded, was collected, as "Schoenberg's Letters," in Stravinsky and Craft's *Themes and Episodes* (see pages 925–27 of the present volume).

910.25 Goffin . . . Panassié . . . Hodeir.] See Robert Goffin (1898–1984), *Aux Frontières du Jazz* (1932); Hugues Panassié (1912–1974), *Le Jazz Hot* (1934); André Hodeir (1921–2011), *Le Jazz, Cet Inconnu* (1945).

910.27 Cecil Sharp] See note 601.20–21.

911.9 Wilfrid Mellers] See note 621.1.

911.17–18 "American Music and an Industrial Community"] This essay, used by Mellers as the concluding chapter of his *Music and Society*, originally appeared in the magazine *Our Time* (UK) for March 1946.

912.2–4 *François Couperin* . . . Erik Satie] Mellers's book on Couperin appeared in 1950. His essay "Erik Satie and the 'Problem' of Contemporary Music" appeared in his book *Studies in Contemporary Music* (1947), a collection of his articles from *Scrutiny* and other publications.

919.31–32 Edward Lockspeiser's two-volume account] Lockspeiser (1905–1963), an English composer, conductor, and musicologist, published the first volume, *Debussy: His Life and Mind, Volume I: 1862–1902*, in 1962.

919.34–35 Master Musicians series] Series of short, scholarly biographies of composers conceived by book editor Frederick Crowest, for J. M. Dent, London, in 1901. The series, which has published more than a hundred titles, is currently edited by R. Larry Todd for Oxford University Press.

922.33 Winton Dean] English musicologist (1916–2013) who wrote extensively on both Handel and Bizet. *Georges Bizet: His Life and Work*, the book reviewed here, is a revised edition of his *Bizet* of 1948. Dean would revise the book again in 1975 and in 1984.

922.37 Mina Curtiss] Mrs. Henry Tomlinson Curtiss (1896–1985) was the sister of Lincoln Kirstein (see note 240.13). Thomson, who first knew Curtiss as the personal secretary of John Houseman (see note 409.23) during the 1930s and '40s, was her musical and literary advisor on the book *Bizet and His World*.

923.19 Willi Reich] Austrian musicologist and critic (1898–1980) who, in his books and journal articles, was a critical champion of the Second Viennese School.

924.22 Anton Webern's tiny book] *The Path to the New Music*, two lectures on the twelve-tone system, edited by Willi Reich, was originally published, as *Der Weg zur Neuen Musik*, by Universal Edition A.G., Vienna, in 1960. The book's English translator, Leo Black (b. 1932), worked for Universal Edition before becoming a music producer at the BBC (1960–88).

925.18 Vera de Bosset] Russian dancer and painter (1888–1982) who, in 1940, became the second wife of Igor Stravinsky (1882–1971). She was the co-author, with Robert Craft, of *Stravinsky in Pictures and Documents* (1979).

927.27 Vladimir Dukelsky] Russian composer and popular songwriter (1903–1969) better known by his American stage name Vernon Duke.

927.41 Eric Walter White] British composer, musicologist, biographer, and arts administrator (1905–1985) whose first of several books on Stravinsky, *Stravinsky's Sacrifice to Apollo*, appeared in 1930. A second, expanded edition of *Stravinsky: The Composer and His Works* was published by the University of California Press in 1979.

928.6 Collaer's . . . *Stravinsky*] *Strawinsky* (Brussels: Éditions Equilibres, 1930), a brief biography by the Belgian ethnomusicologist Paul Collaer (1891–1989), has never been translated from the original French.

930.34–35 Edward T. Cone's analysis] "The Uses of Convention: Stravinsky and His Models," by American composer and pianist Edward T. Cone (1917–2004), *The Musical Quarterly* (July 1962). This issue of the quarterly was a festschrift for the composer at age eighty.

932.34–38 "our intimate acquaintance . . . good man."] See Thomas Babington Macaulay's biographical article on Samuel Johnson in the *Encyclopaedia Britannica* of 1856, often reprinted separately as *Macaulay's Life of Johnson*.

935.14 Pierre Boulez] French composer, conductor, pianist, and writer (1925–2016). As a composer (trained by Olivier Messiaen and René Leibowitz) he was a pioneer of serialism and electronic music. As a conductor he specialized in interpretations of twentieth-century classics—Debussy (see pages 948–54), Berg, Schoenberg, Stravinsky—but surprised his critics with faithful readings of Beethoven, Berlioz, Schumann, and Wagner. His American career included tenures as guest conductor with the Cleveland Orchestra (1970–72), music director of the New York Philharmonic (1971–77), and principal guest conductor of the Chicago Symphony Orchestra (1995–2015).

935.23 theatrical troupe] The Compagnie Renaud-Barrault (1946–59), founded by the French husband-wife team of Jean-Louis Barrault (1910–1994), an actor, mime, and director, and Madeleine Renaud (1900–1994), an actress, was resident at the Théâtre Marigny, Paris, until 1954. Boulez was their music director from 1946 to 1954, when he left to start the subscription series Concerts du Domaine Musical (1954–73).

936.23 *Pli selon Pli*] "Fold by Fold."

938.40–41 "Every thought occasions a cast of the dice."] From Mallarmé's poem "Un coup de dés" (1897).

939.4 *Penser la Musique Aujourd'hui.*] An English version of this collection, *Boulez on Music Today*, translated by Susan Bradshaw and Rodney Bennett, was published by Harvard University Press in 1971.

939.10 *Encyclopédie Fasquelle*] That is, the three-volume *Encyclopédie de la Musique*, edited by Michel François (1916–2004) et al., published by Éditions Fasquelle, Paris, in 1958–61.

940.31–33 "in the last section . . . record grooves.")] See Robert Craft, "*The Rite of Spring*: Genesis of a Masterpiece," *Perspectives of New Music* (Autumn–Winter 1966).

942.11–12 Ernest Ansermet, *Les Fondements de la Musique dans la Conscience Humaine*] See note 809.15–16.

944.27 THE MEMOIRS OF HECTOR BERLIOZ . . . David Cairns] Chapters of *Mémoires de Hector Berlioz, comprenant ses voyages en Italie, en Allemagne, en*

Russie et en Angleterre, 1803–1865 were serialized in French publications throughout the early 1860s. The *Mémoires* were privately printed by Berlioz in 1865, and posthumously published in Paris in 1870. British musician, journalist, and biographer David Cairns (b. 1926) followed his translation of the *Mémoires* with a two-volume biography, *Berlioz: The Making of an Artist, 1803–1832* (1989) and *Berlioz: Servitude and Greatness, 1832–1869.*

945.30   *Berlioz and the Romantic Century*] French-born American cultural historian Jacques Barzun (1907–2012) also published an abridged one-volume edition of this biography, titled *Berlioz and His Century: An Introduction to Romanticism*, in 1960. It went through several editions, the latest released in 1982.

946.17   Colin Davis] English conductor (1927–2013) notable for his championship of Berlioz.

948.11–12   Boulez . . . *Pelléas et Mélisande.*] The Václav Kašlík production of *Pelléas et Mélisande* (1902), an opera (*drame lyrique*) in five acts by Claude Debussy, libretto by Maurice Maeterlinck, opened at the Royal Opera House, Covent Garden, London, on December 1, 1969. There were seven London performances. Pierre Boulez conducted the orchestra and chorus of the Royal Opera House (Douglas Robinson, choirmaster). Sets by Josef Svoboda, costumes by Jan Skalicky. Cast: Elisabeth Söderström (Mélisande), George Shirley (Pelléas), Donald McIntyre (Golaud), David Ward (Arkel), Yvonne Minton (Geneviève), and Anthony Britten (Yniold).

954.36   Edith Piaf] French chanteuse (1915–1963) born Edith Gassion but known as "La Môme Piaf" ("The Little Sparrow"). From the 1940s on she was an international celebrity, a best-selling recording artist who wrote the lyrics to many of her signature songs, including "La vie en rose" (1945) and "Non, je ne regrette rien" (1961).

955.7–8   Simone Berteaut] Singer and writer (1916–1975) who, from the age of fifteen, was the constant companion of Edith Piaf, who called her her half-sister "Momone." Berteaut's *Piaf* was translated into English, by Gislaine Boulanger, as *Piaf: A Biography* (London: W. H. Allen, 1970; New York: Harper & Row, 1972). She followed this book with an autobiographical memoir, *Momone* (Paris: Laffont, 1972), which has yet to be translated into English.

955.26   Edith Cavell] British field nurse (1865–1915) who, after helping some two hundred Allied soldiers escape from occupied Belgium into the Netherlands, was arrested and, after a court-martial, executed by a German firing squad.

955.36   Marcel Cerdan] French-Algerian boxer (1916–1949) who was world middleweight champion in 1948–49. He died, in a plane crash in the Azores, four months after losing his title to Jake La Motta.

956.15   *Les Blouses Blanches*] "The White Coats," meaning "The Doctors."

959.38   *Five Kings*] See note 452.9.

960.11 *War of the Worlds*] See note 473.4.

961.29–30 historic letter . . . printed in my own memoirs] See pages 472–76 of the present volume.

961.37 *Panic*] Verse play (1935), by Archibald MacLeish (see note 425.35–36), concerning the stock-market crash of 1929, told in the manner of a Greek tragedy with chorus. Produced by John Houseman and Nathan Zarkin for the Phoenix Theater Company, it opened at the Imperial Theater, New York, on March 14, 1935, and ran two performances. The director was Jack Light, the choreographer Agnes De Mille. Orson Welles, in his first lead role on Broadway, played, at age nineteen, a sixty-year-old American financier named McGafferty.

962.21 CBS Lively Arts series] Eleven hour-long episodes of *The Seven Lively Arts*, an Emmy-winning Sunday-afternoon "arts magazine" series modeled on the Ford Foundation's *Omnibus* (see note 895.13), were broadcast by CBS Television from November 1957 to February 1958.

962.27–28 drama division at the Juilliard School] In 1968 Houseman and the French theater artist Michel St. Denis (1897–1971) established the Drama Division of the Juilliard School, a four-year degree program in acting, directing, and theater studies. Houseman was the program's director through the spring of 1976, and during his tenure also helped develop Juilliard Opera (a degree program in voice and opera studies), the American Opera Project (Juilliard's opera production company, now an independent entity), and The Acting Company (an independent touring company made up largely of Drama Division graduates).

963.10–11 Perhaps another may yet appear.] After *Run-Through* (1972) Houseman published three further memoirs, *Front and Center* (1979), concerning the years 1942 through 1955, *Final Dress* (1983), concerning 1955 through 1974, and the wide-ranging *Unfinished Business* (1988).

963.17–18 Harvard in Professor Baker's day] See note 837.4.

967.35 Arab friend] Mohammed Mrabet (b. 1936), a Moroccan visual artist and storyteller.

968.16 Jane] See note 451.10.

968.35 Cecil Beaton] English fashion and portrait photographer (1904–1980) whose work for *Vogue* and *Vanity Fair* chronicled the "smart set" of the 1920s through the 1960s.

969.22 Bernard Faÿ] See note 228.32.

971.15–16 Archibald T. ("Doc") Davison] See note 219.4.

971.18 two ballets.] Between 1935 and 1947, as music director and later friend of the Ballet Caravan troupe (see note 240.13), Carter wrote two ballets, *Pocahontas* (1939) and *The Minotaur* (1947).

971.28–29   Minna Lederman . . . *Modern Music*] See note 380.17.

974.1–2   its title . . . Wallace Stevens.] The phrase "Flawed words and stubborn sounds" is from the last line of "The Poems of Our Climate" (1938), a poem collected in *Parts of a World* (1942), by Wallace Stevens (1879–1955).

974.15   three books] The works of Alice B. Toklas (1877–1967) are *The Alice B. Toklas Cook Book* (1954), *Aromas and Flavors of Past and Present* (1958), and *What Is Remembered* (1963).

975.35   Leon Katz] Katz (b. 1919) is a playwright, dramaturge, and professor emeritus of drama at Yale University.

977.15–18   Wilder . . . *Four in America*] Thornton Wilder wrote an introduction to *Four in America*, by Gertrude Stein (New Haven: Yale University Press, 1947), a suite of fantastic alternate biographies of George Washington, Ulysses S. Grant, Henry James, and Wilbur Wright.

977.32   liberation of a French friend convicted of wartime collaboration] Bernard Faÿ. See notes 228.32 and 558.3–7.

978.25   Madame Langlois] See note 258.3.

978.32   *Dieu m'en garde.*] God forbid.

979.18–19   *amende honorable*] Act of penitence, usually public.

979.38–39   I actually saw it used on . . . Georges Hugnet.] See "Gertrude and the Young French Poet," chapter 16 of *Virgil Thomson* (pages 354–70 of the present volume).

980.25–26   Hemingway told all . . . William G. Rogers.] W. G. Rogers (1896–1978), one of Gertrude Stein's "doughboy" friends, was the author of the memoir *When This You See Remember Me: Gertrude Stein in Person* (New York: Rinehart & Co., 1948). Writing on July 29, 1948, from Finca Vigia, Hemingway congratulated Rogers on his book, gave a personal account of the Hemingway–Stein–Toklas relationship, and noted Toklas's need "to break off friendships" and to fling Stein's closest male friends, including Hemingway himself, "into the outer darkness." This letter, first printed in an edition of one hundred copies by the Gotham Book Mart (1972), was collected by Carlos Baker in *Ernest Hemingway: Selected Letters, 1917–1961* (New York: Scribners, 1981).

980.28–34   And along with real disappointment . . . American university."] In 1973 Georges Hugnet sold his Gertrude Stein papers to the Humanities Research Center (now the Harry Ransom Center) at the University of Texas.

981.1   Doda Conrad] See note 898.36.

981.36–37   Mercedes de Acosta's memoir] *Here Lies the Heart* (New York: Reynal, 1960), by American poet, playwright, and lesbian style icon Mercedes de Acosta (1893–1963).

982.8 Sainte Geneviève] The patron saint of Paris in the Roman Catholic and Eastern Orthodox traditions.

982.19 Mrs. Eddy] Mary Baker Eddy (1821–1920), founder of the First Church of Christ, Scientist (Christian Science).

985.19–20 Panassié . . . Goffin . . . Hodeir] See note 910.25.

985.20–21 Sargeant . . . Hobson . . . Blesh . . . Schuller.] Winthrop Sargeant (1903–1986), American violinist who left the New York Philharmonic to become a music critic, first for Time–Life and then for *The New Yorker* (1949–72), and the author of *Jazz: Hot and Hybrid* (1938) and *Jazz: A History* (1964); Wilder Hobson (1906–1964), American trombone player and music critic, mainly for *Saturday Review*, and author of *American Jazz Music* (1939); Rudi Blesh (see note 505.17); and Gunther Schuller (see note 602.9).

986.22 *Jazz: A People's Music*] See note 110.21–22. In a 1949 review, Thomson described the book as a not always successful "class-angle" attempt to explain "the nature of this music, its development and its vigor under persecution, in terms of Marxist sociology."

986.23 LeRoi Jones] Jones (1924–2014), later known as Amiri Baraka, was an American poet, playwright, and critic of black music, culture, and society.

987.10 Ross Russell] Russell (1909–2002), who recorded Charlie Parker as the founder-producer of the Dial label (1946–55), also wrote *Jazz Style in Kansas City and the Southwest* (Berkeley: University of California Press, 1971).

987.25 A. B. Spellman] Spellman (b. 1935) is an American poet, jazz critic, and longtime arts administrator at the National Endowment for the Arts.

987.26–28 Taylor . . . Coleman . . . Nichols . . . MacLean] Cecil Taylor (see note 874.5–9); Ornette Coleman (see note 874.5–9); Herbie Nichols (1919–1963), and Jackie MacLean (1931–2006) were, when Spellman chronicled them, pioneers of the free jazz movement of the late 1950s and early 1960s.

988.32 Archie Shepp] American tenor saxophonist Shepp (b. 1937) is also a poet, playwright, and professor of black studies.

989.7–8 Frank Kofsky] Kofsky (1935–1997) was a musician and a professor of history at California State University–Sacramento. His *Black Nationalism and the Revolution in Music* was revised and expanded as *John Coltrane and the Jazz Revolution of the 1960s* (New York: Pathfinder Press, 1988).

990.2 Dominique-René de Lerma.] American musicologist (1936–2015) who published more than a thousand papers on African American music and was chief consultant of Columbia Records' nine-disc Black Composers Series (1974–79).

990.16–17 Ben Sidran] Sidran (b. 1943) is a jazz and rock singer, keyboard player, and record producer as well as a critic, oral historian, and broadcaster. Besides *Black Talk* his books include *Talking Jazz: An Oral History* (1991) and *Ben Sidran: A Life in the Music* (2003).

991.34–35   National Advisory Commission on Civil Disorders] In July 1967, President Johnson appointed an eleven-person commission (1) to examine the causes and consequences of race riots that since the summer of 1965 had erupted in several American cities, and (2) to recommend a national course of action to prevent further race riots. The National Advisory Commission on Civil Disorders, led by Illinois governor Otto Kerner, reported its findings in February 1968. The report concluded that the nation was "moving toward two societies, one black, one white—separate and unequal," and warned that unless conditions were remedied, the country faced a "system of 'apartheid'" in most of its major cities.

993.8   CITIZEN GENÊT] Edmond Charles Genêt (1763–1834) was France's minister to the United States in 1793–94. His protests against U.S. neutrality in the war between France and Great Britain angered President Washington, who demanded his recall by France.

995.34   Garrett Mattingly] Pulitzer Prize–winning historian (1900–1962) who was a professor of European history at Columbia University from 1947 until his death.

996.15   Germaine Beaumont] French novelist and political journalist (1890–1983) who translated Virginia Woolf from the English and brought something of Woolf's style into her own writing.

999.17–18   *The New Grove Dictionary of Music and Musicians*] The original "Grove Dictionary" was a reference work, *A Dictionary of Music and Musicians*, edited by Sir George Grove (1820–1900) and published, in four separately released volumes, in 1879–89. *The New Grove* (1980) was the sixth edition of the work, reimagined for the late twentieth century and retaining less that 3 percent of the material published in previous editions.

1000.4   *Encyclopédie Fasquelle*] See note 939.10.

1002.31–39   Hamm . . . Northcott . . . Austin] American musicologist Charles Hamm (1925–2011), a chronicler of the postwar avant-garde and historian of popular music; English composer and critic-reviewer Bayan Northcott (b. 1940); American musicologist William A. Austin (1920–2000), longtime professor at Cornell University and author of *Music in the Twentieth Century* (1966).

1003.4   entry on Benjamin Britten] By English musicologist Peter Evans (b. 1929), author of three books on Britten, including *The Music of Benjamin Britten* (1979), now in its third edition.

1003.8   brief article on Byron] By English music critic John Warrack (b. 1928), author of several studies in opera history.

1003.16–21   Saylor . . . Neighbour . . . Hopkins] American composer Bruce Saylor (b. 1946), a former pupil of Weisgall; O. W. Neighbour (1923–2015), music librarian at the British Library and a specialist in Schoenberg; British composer-pianist G. W. "Bill" Hopkins (1928–2011), translator and editor of writings by and about Stockhausen.

1004.28 Robert Stevenson] American ethnomusicologist (1916–2012) who, based at UCLA, studied Latin American and Spanish music and edited *The Inter-American Music Review* (1979–2000). He contributed nearly three hundred articles to *The New Grove Dictionary*.

1004.30 Dent . . . Smith] Cambridge don Edward J. Dent (1876–1957) wrote frequently on opera and was a prolific translator of librettos. His essay on librettos in the fifth edition of the *Grove Dictionary* (1954) was revised and updated for *The New Grove* by Patrick J. Smith (see note 820.17–18).

1006.5 first half of a two-volume work] Copland and Vivian Perlis (b. 1928), a music historian at Yale University, published the other half, *Copland: Since 1943*, in 1989.

1006.19 Harold Clurman] See note 649.13.

Index

Abbott, Jere, 312, 335, 383, 386–87, 391
Absolute versus program music, 30, 63
Abstract expressionism, 7–8, 23, 152, 347
Abstraction in music, 9–10, 150, 650, 733
Abstraction versus representation, 7–8, 25–26, 30, 337, 346–47
Académie des Beaux-Arts, 53
Accents of passion, 721–22, 725
Accompaniment, instrumental, 732–38, 779
Acosta, Mercedes de, 981
Acoustics, 148, 767–68, 792–93, 809, 861
Adams, Henry, 227
Ade, George, 587, 998
Adorno, Theodor, 871
Aeschylus, 862
Africa, music in, 148, 601, 613–14, 808, 813, 987, 990
African-American music, 67, 601, 614, 733, 817, 874, 985–92, 1007
African Americans, 67, 388, 512, 541, 873; culture of, 986–92; in *Four Saints*, 321, 390, 403–4, 409–14, 417, 578, 582, 779; in Missouri, 177–79, 181–82, 196, 217, 246; as musicians, 501, 532, 874, 987; in opera, 436, 499, 916; as singers, 333, 506, 557, 779; in theater, 420–21, 425, 432–35, 448, 520, 846, 959, 963
Afro-Cuban music, 874
Agnelli, Salvatore, 245
Akins, Zoë, 412
Albee, Edward, 753, 959
Albéniz, Isaac, 600
Alberti, Domenico, 151, 771
Alcott, Bronson, 625
Alfano, Franco, 845, 848; *Resurrezione*, 480
Allanbrook, Wye Johnson, 778
Allen, Betty, 577
Alphand, Claude and Hervé, 509–10, 538, 560
Alsop, Joseph, 411

American Academy of Arts and Letters, 570, 643, 798
American Artists' Equity, 22
American ballet, 256, 408–11, 413, 416, 424, 427, 429, 436–37, 445–47, 471, 517, 527, 573, 586, 607, 610, 646–52, 681, 877, 971
American cinema, 122, 125, 424, 430–32, 440–45, 451, 453–54, 527, 563–66, 586, 606–7, 646, 648–52, 680, 960–62, 965
American Composers' Alliance, 162, 424, 449, 645
American English, 698–99, 706, 747–48, 754
American Federation of Musicians, 50, 159, 162
American Guild of Musical Artists, 50, 162, 423
American librettos, 758
American Lyric Theater, 471
American Mercury, 243, 248
American music, 8–9, 50–53, 58–59, 65, 69, 73–76, 93, 97–99, 102, 105, 110, 122, 125, 133, 152, 159, 162, 228–29, 248–57, 264, 266, 271–72, 281–86, 288–91, 297–99, 303–4, 306, 308, 310–12, 314–15, 318–19, 323–24, 331, 333–34, 338–40, 362–64, 375–76, 378–83, 386, 391, 393–94, 416, 420–39, 447–50, 462, 485, 500, 505, 513, 515, 518, 522–28, 532, 539–40, 543, 563, 567–69, 581–83, 586, 599–687, 719, 733, 779, 784, 787, 794, 797, 800, 817, 856, 870, 877, 881–82, 893–94, 906–7, 910–17, 967, 969–74, 985–92, 1001–3, 1005–7. *See also individual composers*
American National Theater and Academy (ANTA), 571, 577
American opera, 141, 251, 256–57, 265–73, 277–81, 288–89, 294–98, 304, 306–11, 313–15, 319–22, 334–35, 363–64, 367, 369, 376, 382–83, 386, 390–92, 396–97, 402–22, 426, 429, 437, 439, 447, 450, 454, 463, 471,

1131

Index of Compositions by Virgil Thomson

*This book is set in 10 point ITC Galliard, a
face designed for digital composition by Matthew Carter
and based on the sixteenth-century face Granjon. The paper
is acid-free lightweight opaque and meets the requirements for
permanence of the American National Standards Institute.
The binding material is Brillianta, a woven rayon cloth
made by Van Heek-Scholco Textielfabrieken, Holland.
Composition by David Bullen Design. Printing and
binding by Edwards Brothers Malloy, Ann Arbor.
Designed by Bruce Campbell.*